Clause 8 Publishing

Intellectual Property in the New Technological Age: 2020

Volume II: Copyrights, Trademarks & State IP Protections

Peter S. Menell
UC Berkeley School of Law

Mark A. Lemley
Stanford Law School

Robert P. Merges
UC Berkeley School of Law

Shyamkrishna Balganesh
Univ. of Penn. Law School

ISBN-13: 978-1-945555169 (Clause 8 Publishing)

For Claire, Dylan, and Noah

P.S.M.

For Rose, as always

M.A.L.

For my brothers, Bruce, Paul, and Matt

R.P.M.

For Irene and Marky

S.B.

PREFACE

When we embarked on this project more than two decades ago, we envisioned many things, but not that it would lead to self-publishing a casebook.

A lot has changed since we began collaborating. At the time that we launched this project, most intellectual property courses were taught along particular mode of protection lines: patent law, copyright law, trademark law, and trade secret law. From our research and real world experience, we recognized that digital technology blurred the traditional doctrinal lines. We set out to design a book for the emerging technological age. We built the book around core philosophical frameworks, broad integrated coverage, and a pedagogical model that emphasizes problem-solving.

Over the ensuing years, our insight and framing proved enduring. Nearly all manner of enterprise and organization—from high technology start-ups to traditional manufacturing and media companies, government agencies, and even educational institutions—came to confront a broad range of intellectual property issues spanning the full spectrum of protection modes. The survey intellectual property course became a core subject at our law schools and many others across the United States and around the world. That much we had at least dreamed of.

But we did not foresee entering the publishing business. During the formative stage of our careers, we were thrilled to gain the interest of established publishers. Our book hit the market just as the Internet was gaining traction. The IP field expanded rapidly and we found ourselves churning out new editions every two or three years to keep pace with the increasing velocity of IP law. Little, Brown's law book division was acquired by Aspen, which was then acquired by Wolters Kluwer. The market for our book continued to grow.

Yet as advances in digital technology reshaped the world around us—from Internet search to online publishing—we, and our adopters and students, saw relatively little change in our publishing market. Prices continued to rise each year. Publishing schedules remained rigid. The publishing of our book seemed suspended in time. Most frustratingly, our students were paying $250 for a book that generated just $15 in total author royalties. This pattern conflicted with the thrust of our book and scholarship. Advances in digital technology and competition should have been driving prices down, not up. Our frustration grew.

These issues came to a head in September 2014. When our publisher indicated that we missed the deadline for getting our book into the summer 2015 catalog, we dusted off our original publishing contract from December 1993. In checking the revision clause, we recognized that we held the copyright in the work *and* retained the right to prepare derivative works.

Once we realized that we had the right to shift to self-publishing, we faced a choice: stay with a leading publisher or take on the start-up costs and day-to-day operations of self-publishing. Peter had been writing about disintermediation in the media industries and strongly believed the time was ripe to branch out on our own. He posed a simple question: how would we view this choice ten years down the road? A quick review of self-publishing options indicated that we could substantially reduce the cost of our book while providing students with more convenient access—both digital versions and print-on-demand. We could also move to annual editions and take control over the production pipeline. This would ensure that our book was always current. Although striking out on our own involved some risk and additional tasks, failing to take this path would perpetuate an obsolete and unjustifiably costly burden on students at a time when they can ill afford it. We decided to take the plunge.

After reviewing options, we decided to begin our self-publishing experiment with Amazon. (We retain copyright ownership and hence flexibility to try other platforms as the marketplace evolves, an important lesson from various media markets.) Amazon's publishing platform imposes size limits that required us to divide our book into two volumes: Volume I covering Philosophical Perspectives, Trade Secrets, and Patent Law (we also included the patent preemption cases from Chapter VI for those interested in studying those materials in conjunction with the trade secret and patent law chapters); Volume II covering Copyright Law, Trademark Law, and State Law IP Protections (including the preemption materials). The volumes are available as eBooks and through Amazon's on-demand publishing platform. This has the virtues of reducing the weight of what students need to carry around on a daily basis and creating more modular teaching options. We also distribute Chapters I and II on SSRN so that students can sample the book before committing to the class.

Which brings us to what we hope is a New Publishing Age for all manner of academic publishing. In addition to releasing IPNTA2--- (we plan to designate new editions by publication year rather than volume number), we launched Clause 8 Publishing, a new publishing venture to "promote Progress" in intellectual property education (and possibly more). We plan to introduce a series of complementary products, enhancements, supplementary texts, multimedia, and other resources for adopters and students—at low cost and with easy accessibility. You will be able to learn about these resources at IPNTA.com and Clause8Publishing.com.

Peter has managed the transition of our book to a self-publishing model and has taken the lead on establishing this platform. Those interested in adopting our book (or anything else about the project) should contact him at pmenell@law.berkeley.edu. (Please include "IPNTA" or "Clause 8" in the subject line.) IPNTA2016, the first self-published edition of "Intellectual Property in the New Technological Age," more than exceeded our hopes. Sales for IPNTA increased above the highest sales of prior editions, resulting in savings to students of over $1 million in the first year. IPNTA2017, IPNTA2018, and IPNTA2019 continued on this path. IPNTA2020 updates the text to reflect the most recent developments in this rapidly evolving field of law.

We are pleased to add Shyamkrishna Balganesh to this project. He has established himself as a leading intellectual property scholar with particular expertise on copyright and the common law.

In retrospect, the subject matter covered by our original edition—philosophical perspectives on intangible resources, promoting progress in technology and creative expression, and competition policy—set us on the path to DIY/New Age publishing. Copyright law seeks to harness market forces to encourage creative expression and widespread dissemination. It builds bridges between creators and those who value their work. Digital technology and the Internet enhance these powerful forces by lowering the costs of creation and providing the virtual dissemination bridges. We feel fortunate to have liberated our book and very much look forward to working with law professors and students in building a more productive marketplace and community for IP teaching materials.

Peter S. Menell   Mark A. Lemley   Robert P. Merges

July 2020

♀ NEW FEATURES

Rapid advances in digital and life sciences technology continue to spur the evolution of intellectual property law. As professors and practitioners in this field know all too well, Congress and the courts continue to develop intellectual property law and jurisprudence at a rapid pace. For that reason, we have significantly augmented and revised our text.

The 2020 Edition reflects the following principal developments:

• **Trade Secrets**: Congress passed the Defend Trade Secrets Act of 2016, one of the most momentous changes in the history of trade secret protection. The new law opens up the federal courts to trade secret cases, provides for ex parte seizures of misappropriated trade secrets in "extraordinary circumstances," and establishes immunity for whistleblowers.

• **Patent Law**: The past several years have witnessed some of the most significant developments in U.S. patent history—from the establishment of the new administrative review proceedings at the Patent Office to important shifts in patent-eligibility, claim indefiniteness, enhanced damages, and equitable remedies at the Supreme Court and means-plus-function claim interpretation and infringement doctrine at the Federal Circuit. We have also significantly expanded coverage of design patents.

• **Copyright Law**: Congress passed the Music Modernization Act. We have added an important new case on moral rights. The past few years also witnessed important developments in the Online Service Provider safe harbor, fair use.

• **Trademark Law**: We have integrated important cases on genericide, federal registrability of disparaging marks, merchandising rights, likelihood of confusion on the Internet, and remedies.

• **Other State IP Protections**: We have updated material on the right of publicity, an active and growing area. We have also reorganized the chapter and focused it on IP regimes.

ABOUT Clause 8 Publishing

Clause 8 Publishing is a digital publishing venture founded and managed by Peter Menell. Mark Lemley, Robert Merges, and Shyamkrishna Balganesh serve on the Editorial Board. Inspired by Article I, Section 8, Clause 8 of the U.S. CONSTITUTION, Clause 8 Publishing seeks to promote production and dissemination of the highest quality and most up-to-date educational resources at fair prices and in a way that ensures that much of the revenue flows to authors. It aims to streamline the publishing process, take full advantage of evolving digital platforms and print-on-demand functionality, and develop innovative educational resources.

Clause 8 Publishing plans to produce annual editions of INTELLECTUAL PROPERTY IN THE NEW TECHNOLOGICAL AGE.

Over the coming years, Clause 8 Publishing aims to support a series of complementary products (statutory supplement, primers, problem sets, multi-media presentations) and resources for intellectual property professors, students, judges, and policy makers. It aspires to lead the academy toward more productive and just publishing models. More information will be available at Clause8Publishing.com and IPNTA.com.

ACKNOWLEDGMENTS

We are indebted to a great many people who have helped us since this project began in 1991. We would like to thank our many colleagues who reviewed earlier drafts of the book and provided helpful guidance. While many of these reviews were anonymous, we have also benefited from the advice of Lynn Baker, Paul Heald, Tom Jorde, and Pam Samuelson, each of whom read several different drafts of the book as it made its way through the editorial process. We gratefully acknowledge the research assistance of Evelyn Findeis, Edwin Flores, Ryan Garcia, Shari Heino, Toni Moore Knudson, Christopher Leslie, and Barbara Parvis. We would also like to thank Michele Co for exceptional secretarial and administrative assistance in completing the original text.

We are grateful to many colleagues for providing suggestions for improving this book over the years. In particular, we would like to thank Fred Abbott, Amit Agarwal, John Allison, BJ Ard, Ann Bartow, Andrew Chin, Julie Cohen, Ken Dam, Robin Feldman, Terry Fisher, Michael Jacobs, Patricia Judd, Dmitry Karshtedt, Marshall Leaffer, Jake Linford, Glynn Lunney, Ron Mann, David McGowan, Chuck McManis, Roberta Morris, David Nimmer, Tyler Ochoa, Ruth Okediji, Lucas Osborn, Lisa Ouellette, Malla Pollack, Peggy Radin, Lisa Ramsey, Jerry Reichmann, Sharon Sandeen, Paul Schwartz, Jacob Sherkow, Lon Sobel, Allan Sternstein, Mark Thurmon, Ty Trejo, and several anonymous reviewers for their comments and suggestions in preparing the second, third, fourth, fifth, and sixth editions. We have also benefitted greatly from the research assistance and proofreading of Alex Barata, Adam Blankenheimer, Will Buckingham, Amber Burroff, Brian Carver, Concord Cheung, Colleen Chien, Sarah Craven, Louise Decoppet, Will Devries, Amit Elazari, Tom Fletcher, Ryan Garcia, Ines Gonzalez, David Grady, Andrea Hall, Jade Jurdi, Robert Damion Jurrens, Victoria H. Kane, Jeffrey Kuhn, Michelle A. Marzahn, Megan McKnelly, Selena R. Medlen, David Moore, Roberta Morris, Pilar Ossorio, Ryan Owens, Stephanie N.-P. Pham-Quang, Laura Quilter, John Sasson, Michael Sawyer, Helaine Schweitzer, Shannon Scott, Michael Liu Su, Laurence Trask, Allison Watkins, Joel Wallace, Reid Whitaker, Emily Wohl, and Tarra Zynda.

We thank Amit Elazari for production assistance and Israel Vela for design and website development assistance.

SUMMARY OF CONTENTS

I. INTRODUCTION

II. TRADE SECRET LAW

III. PATENT LAW

IV. COPYRIGHT LAW

V. TRADEMARK LAW

VI. STATE IP PROTECTIONS

TABLE OF CONTENTS

Chapter I: Introduction   **1**
- A.   Philosophical Perspectives   2
  - 1.   The Natural Rights Perspective   3
    - JOHN LOCKE, TWO TREATISES ON GOVERNMENT (1698)   3
  - 2.   The Personhood Perspective   7
    - Margaret Jane Radin, *Property and Personhood*, 34 STAN. L. REV. 957 (1982)   7
  - 3.   Distributive and Social Justice   12
  - 4.   The Utilitarian/Economic Incentive Perspective   16
    - i.   Promoting Innovation and Creativity   16
      - a.   Economic Incentive Benefit   19
      - b.   Costs of Limiting Diffusion   20
    - ii.   Ensuring Integrity of the Marketplace   26
- B.   Overview of Intellectual Property   30
  - 1.   Trade Secret   34
  - 2.   Utility Patent   34
  - 3.   Design Patent   35
  - 4.   Copyright   35
  - 5.   Trademark/Trade Dress   36

Chapter II: Trade Secret Law   **41**
- A.   Introduction   42
  - 1.   Historical Background   42
  - 2.   Theoretical Justifications for Trade Secrets   43
    - i.   Property Rights   44
    - ii.   Tort Law   44
    - iii.   IP: A Third Way?   46
  - 3.   Overview of Modern Trade Secret Protection   47
- B.   Subject Matter   50
  - 1.   Defining Trade Secrets   50
    - *Metallurgical Industries Inc. v. Fourtek, Inc.*, 790 F.2d 1195 (5th Cir. 1986)   50
  - 2.   Reasonable Efforts to Maintain Secrecy   61
    - *Rockwell Graphic Systems, Inc. v. DEV Industries, Inc.*, 925 F.2d 174 (7th Cir. 1991)   61
  - 3.   Disclosure of Trade Secrets   70
    - i.   Voluntary Disclosure by the Trade Secret Owner   70

ii.	Distributing a Product that Embodies the Trade Secret to the Public	71
iii.	Public Disclosure by a Third Party	73
iv.	Inadvertent Disclosure	74
v.	Government Disclosure	75

C. Misappropriation of Trade Secrets — 77
   1. Improper Means — 77
      E. I. du Pont deNemours & Co. v. Christopher,
      431 F.2d 1012 (5th Cir. 1970) — 77
   2. Confidential Relationship — 83
      Smith v. Dravo Corp., 203 F.2d 369 (7th Cir. 1953) — 83

D. Proper Means and Immunity — 89
   1. Independent Discovery and Reverse Engineering — 89
      Kadant, Inc. v. Seeley Machine, Inc.,
      244 F. Supp. 2d 19 (N.D.N.Y. 2003) — 90
   2. Public Policy Limitation — 97

E. Agreements to Keep Secrets — 101
      Warner-Lambert Pharmaceutical Co. v.
      John J. Reynolds, Inc., 178 F. Supp. 655 (S.D.N.Y. 1959) — 102

F. The Case of Departing Employees — 106
   1. Confidentiality and Use of Trade Secrets — 107
   2. Ownership of Employee Inventions — 108
     i. The Common Law Obligation to Assign Inventions — 108
     ii. Assignment Agreements — 110
     iii. Trailer Clauses — 111
   3. Nonsolicitation Agreements — 112
   4. Noncompetition Agreements — 115
      Edwards v. Arthur Andersen LLP,
      81 Cal. Rptr. 3d 282 (Cal. 2008) — 115
      PepsiCo, Inc. v. Redmond, 54 F.3d 1262 (7th Cir. 1995) — 126

G. Remedies — 133
   1. Injunctions — 134
      Winston Research Corp. v. 3M Corp., 350 F.2d 134 (9th Cir. 1965) — 135
   2. Damages and Disgorgement — 140
   3. Criminal Trade Secret Statutes — 141
   4. Federal Criminal Trade Secret Liability — 143

H. Federal Preemption — 146
      Kewanee Oil Co. v. Bicron Corp.,
      416 U.S. 470 (1974) — 146

Chapter III: Patent Law   **153**
- A.   Introduction   156
  - 1.   Historical Background   156
  - 2.   An Overview of the Patent System   161
    - i.   Requirements for Patentability   162
    - ii.   Rights Conferred by a Patent   163
    - iii.   Patent Prosecution   164
  - 3.   Theories of Patent Law   168
- B.   The Elements of Patentability   169
  - 1.   Novelty   169
    - i.   The 1952 Regime   170
    - ii.   The Nature of Novelty   172
      - *Rosaire v. National Lead Co.*, 218 F.2d 72 (5th Cir. 1955) 172
    - iii.   Statutory Bars   179
      - *In re Hall*, 781 F.2d 897 (Fed. Cir. 1986)   179
    - iv.   Statutory Bars: Public Use and On Sale   183
      - *Egbert v. Lippmann*, 104 U.S. 333 (1881)   183
    - v.   Statutory Bars: The Experimental Use Exception   189
      - *City of Elizabeth v. Pavement Company*,
        97 U.S. 126 (1877)   189
    - vi.   Priority Rules and First-to-Invent   194
      - *Griffith v. Kanamaru*, 816 F.2d 624 (Fed. Cir. 1987)   197
    - vii.   The America Invents Act Regime   202
      - a.   The AIA: A Simpler Structure   202
      - b.   No Geographic Restrictions on Prior Art   204
      - c.   Novelty vs. Priority   204
      - d.   The AIA Grace Period   204
      - e.   Scope of Prior Art: On Sale or in Public Use   205
  - 2.   Nonobviousness   207
    - *Graham v. John Deere Co.*, 383 U.S. 1 (1966)   207
    - i.   Combining References   218
      - *KSR International Co. v. Teleflex Inc.*,
        550 U.S. 398 (2007)   218
    - ii.   "Secondary" Considerations   231
    - iii.   The AIA   233
  - 3.   Utility   234
    - *Brenner v. Manson*, 383 U.S. 519 (1966)   234
    - *In re Fisher*, 421 F.3d 1365 (2005)   240
  - 4.   Disclosure   247
    - *O'Reilly v. Morse*, 56 U.S. 62 (1853)   248
    - **i.**   Enablement   257
      - The Incandescent Lamp Patent, 159 U.S. 465 (1895)   258
    - ii.   The Written Description Requirement   268

The Gentry Gallery, Inc. v. The Berkline Corp., 134 F.3d
    1473 (Fed. Cir. 1998)   269
    iii. Best Mode   275
  5. Patentable Subject Matter   276
    i. The Evolution of Patentable Subject Matter Limitations   277
      a. Early Development of Patent Eligibility Limitations   277
      b. Funk Brothers: The Emergence of Eligibility Skepticism   279
      c. The New Technological Age   280
      d. The Rise of the Federal Circuit and Dismantling of Patentable
        Subject Matter Limitations   283
    ii. The Supreme Court's Revival of Subject Matter Limitations   285
      Mayo Collaborative Services v. Prometheus Laboratories,
        Inc., 566 U.S. 66 (2012)   286
    iii. Patenting of Molecular Biology/Biotechnology   304
      Association for Molecular Pathology v. Myriad Genetics,
        Inc., 569 U.S. 576 (2013)   307
    iv. Reassessing Patent Eligibility   316
      Berkheimer v. HP Inc., 890 F.3d 1369 (2018)   316
C. Administrative Patent Review   320
  1. Post-Grant Review   322
    i. Timing and Sequencing   323
    ii. Coordination with Other Proceedings   324
  2. Inter Partes Review: Successor to Inter Partes Reexaminations   324
    i. Timing and Sequencing   325
    ii. Coordination with Other Proceedings   325
  3. Covered Business Method Review (CBMR)   326
  4. Derivation Proceeding   327
D. Claims and Claim Construction   328
  1. Patent Claiming and Claim Formats   329
    i. The Evolution of Patent Claiming: From Central Claims to
      Peripheral Claims   329
    ii. Claim Formats   331
  2. Judicial Claim Construction   332
    Phillips v. AWH Corporation,
      415 F.3d 1303 (Fed. Cir. 2005) (en banc)   334
  3. Canons of Claim Construction   350
    i. Ordinary vs. Contextual or "Particular" Meaning   350
    ii. "Lexicographer" Rule   351
    iii. Disclaimer of Subject Matter   351
    iv. "Claim Differentiation": Contextual Meaning from Other Claims
      353
    v. Purpose or Goal of the Invention   353
    vi. Construing Claims to Preserve Their Validity   354

vii. Narrow Construction Preferred 355
4. The Special Case (and Problems) of Functional Claims – § 112(f) 359
5. Claim Indefiniteness 363
Nautilus, Inc. v. Biosig Instruments, Inc.,
134 S. Ct. 2120 (2014) 363
E. Infringement 371
1. Direct Infringement 371
i. Literal Infringement 371
Larami Corp. v. Amron,
27 U.S.P.Q.2d 1280 (E.D. Pa. 1993) 371
ii. Infringement Under the Doctrine of Equivalents 375
Graver Tank & Mfg. Co. v. Linde Air Products Co.,
339 U.S. 605 (1950) 376
2. Indirect Infringement 387
i. Inducement 387
Global-Tech Appliances, Inc. v. SEB S.A., 563 U.S. 754
(2011) 388
ii. Contributory Infringement 395
C.R. Bard, Inc. v. Advanced Cardiovascular Systems, Inc.,
911 F.2d 670 (Fed. Cir. 1990) 395
iii. Joint Infringement 398
Akamai Technologies, Inc. v. Limelight Networks, Inc., 797
F.3d 1020 (Fed. Cir. 2015) (en banc) 400
F. Defenses 406
1. Invalidity and the Presumption of Validity 406
2. "With Authority" 408
i. Express or Implied License 408
ii. The Exhaustion Principle/First Sale Doctrine 408
3. The "Experimental Use" Defense 411
Madey v. Duke University, 307 F.3d 1351 (Fed. Cir. 2002) 411
4. Prior User Rights 416
5. Inequitable Conduct 417
Therasense, Inc. v. Becton-Dickinson, Inc., 649 F.3d 1276
(Fed. Cir. 2011) (en banc) 417
6. Prosecution Laches 426
7. Laches, Statute of Limitations, and Equitable Estoppel 426
8. Patent Misuse 427
*Motion Picture Patents Co. v. Universal Film Manufacturing
Co. et al.,* 243 U.S. 502 (1917) 427
G. Remedies 435
1. Injunctions 435
eBay, Inc. v. MercExchange, LLC, 547 U.S. 388 (2006) 437
2. Damages 441

		i.	Lost Profits	442
		ii.	Reasonable Royalty	444
			a. The Basic Inquiry	444
			b. The Georgia-Pacific Factors	446
			c. Royalty Base and Apportionment	448
			d. FRAND Licenses	451
	3.	Enhanced Damages		452
		Halo Electronics, Inc. v. Pulse Electronics, Inc.		
		Stryker Corp. v. Zimmer, Inc., 136 S.Ct. 1923 (2016)		452
	4.	Attorney Fees		460
H.	Design Patents			460
	1.	Requirements for Patentability		463
		i.	Claim Requirements	463
		ii.	Novelty	465
		iii.	Nonobviousness	465
	2.	Ornamentality/Non-functionality		466
		L.A. Gear, Inc. v. Thom McAn Shoe Co.,		
		988 F.2d 1117 (Fed. Cir. 2008)		469
	3.	Infringement		472
		Egyptian Goddess, Inc. v. Swisa, Inc.,		
		543 F.3d 665 (Fed. Cir. 2008) (en banc)		472
		Richardson v. Stanley Works, Inc.,		
		597 F.3d 1288 (Fed. Cir. 2010)		482
	4.	Remedies		487
		i.	Injunctive Relief	487
		ii.	Damages	487
I.	International Patent Law			492
	1.	Procedural Rules		492
		i.	Coordinating International Prosecution	492
		ii.	The Paris Convention	493
		iii.	The Patent Cooperation Treaty (PCT)	494
	2.	Substantive Harmonization and GATT-TRIPs		495
J.	Federal Preemption			497
		Bonito Boats, Inc. v. Thunder Craft Boats, Inc.,		
		489 U.S. 141 (1989)		497

Chapter IV: Copyright Law — **503**
A.	Introduction			506
	1.	Brief History of Copyright Protection		506
		i.	1909 Act	509
		ii.	1976 Act and Related Reforms	509
		iii.	Berne Convention Accession	510

iv.	The Digital Age	510
2.	An Overview of the Copyright Regime	510
3.	Philosophical Perspectives on Copyright Protection	512
B.	Requirements	515
1.	Original Works of Authorship	515
	Feist Publications v. Rural Telephone Service,	
	499 U.S. 340 (1991)	517
2.	Fixation in a Tangible Medium of Expression	530
	H.R. REP. NO. 94-1476 94th Cong., 2d Sess. 52–53 (1976)	
		530
3.	Formalities	535
i.	Notice	536
ii.	Publication	536
	a. 1909 Act	536
	b. 1976 Act/Pre-Ratification of Berne Convention	538
	c. Post-Ratification of the Berne Convention	538
iii.	Registration	539
	a. 1909 Act	539
	b. 1976 Act/Pre-Ratification of Berne Convention	540
	c. Post-Ratification of the Berne Convention	540
	d. Registration Must Be Made Prior to Filing Suit	540
iv.	Deposit	541
4.	Restoration of Foreign Copyrighted Works	541
C.	Copyrightable Subject Matter	543
1.	The Domain and Scope of Copyright Protection	543
	H.R. REP. NO. 94-1476 94th Cong., 2d Sess. (1976)	543
i.	Literary Works	544
ii.	Pictorial, Graphic, and Sculptural Works	545
iii.	Architectural Works	545
iv.	Musical Works and Sound Recordings	547
v.	Dramatic, Pantomime, and Choreographic Works	548
vi.	Motion Pictures and Other Audiovisual Works	549
vii.	Semiconductor Chips Designs (Mask Works)	549
viii.	Vessel Hull Designs	550
ix.	Derivative Works and Compilations	550
2.	Limitations on Copyrightability: Distinguishing Function and	
	Expression	553
i.	The Idea-Expression Dichotomy	553
	Baker v. Selden, 101 U.S. 99 (1879)	553
	Lotus Development Corp. v. Borland International,	
	49 F.3d 807 (1st Cir. 1995), 526 U.S. 233 (1996)	561
	Morrissey v. Procter & Gamble,	
	379 F.2d 675 (1st Cir. 1967)	574

ii. The Useful Article Doctrine   578
        H.R. Rep. No. 94-1476 94th Cong., 2d Sess., 47, 54–55
        (1976)   579
        Star Athletica v. Varsity Brands, 137 S.Ct. 1002 (2017)   580
iii. Government Works and Edicts   599
D. Ownership and Duration   604
    1. Initial Ownership of Copyrights   604
        i.   Works Made for Hire   604
                Community for Creative Non-Violence et al. v. Reid,
                490 U.S. 730 (1989)   605
        ii. Joint Works   616
                Aalmuhammed v. Lee, 202 F.3d 1227 (9th Cir. 2000)   617
        iii. Collective Works   626
        iv. The Rights of Authors and Publishers in Electronic Compilations
                                                                                    626
    2. Duration and Renewal   630
        i.   1909 Act   630
        ii. 1976 Act   630
        iii. Sonny Bono Copyright Term Extension Act of 1998   630
    3. Division, Transfer, and Reclaiming of Copyrights   638
        i.   Division and Transfer of Copyright Interests Under the 1909 Act
                                                                                    638
        ii. Division and Transfer of Copyright Interests Under the 1976 Act
                                                                                    639
        iii. Reclaiming Copyrights   639
E. Rights and Infringement   643
    1. Direct Infringement   643
        i.   Traditional Copyright Rights   644
                a.   The Right to Make Copies   644
                        Arnstein v. Porter, 154 F.2d 464 (2d Cir. 1946)   646
                        Nichols v. Universal Pictures Corporation, 45 F.2d 119 (2d
                        Cir. 1930)   653
                        Computer Associates International v. Altai, Inc., 982 F.2d
                        693 (2d Cir. 1992)   668
                b.   The Right to Prepare Derivative Works   688
                        Anderson v. Stallone, 11 U.S.P.Q.2d 1161 (C.D. Cal. 1989)
                                                                                    689
                c.   The Distribution Right   700
                        Kirtsaeng v. John Wiley & Sons, Inc., 568 S.Ct. 519 (2013)
                                                                                    703
                d.   Public Performance Right   715
                        American Broadcasting Companies, Inc. v. Aereo, Inc.,
                        134 S. Ct. 2498 (2014)   716

		e.	Public Display Right	732
	ii.		Moral Rights	732
			Castillo v. G&M Realty L.P., 950 F.3d 155 (2d Cir. 2020)	734
	iii.		State and Common Law Copyrights	742
	iv.		Digital Rights	744
		a.	Audio Home Recording Act	744
		b.	Anti-Circumvention Provisions	745
2.			Indirect Infringement	750
	i.		The Analog Age	750
		a.	Respondeat Superior	750
		b.	Vicarious Liability	751
		c.	Contributory Liability	752
			Sony Corporation of America v. Universal City Studios, Inc., 464 U.S. 417 (1984)	753
	ii.		The Digital Age	761
			MGM Studios Inc. v. Grokster, Ltd., 545 U.S. 913 (2005)	761

F. Defenses   779

1.			Fair Use	779
	i.		The Formative Era	779
	ii.		Codification and Early Post-Codification Interpretation	780
		a.	*Sony Corp. of America v. Universal City Studios, Inc.*, 464 U.S. 417 (1984)	781
		b.	*Harper & Row, Publishers, Inc. v. Nation Enterprises*, 471 U.S. 539 (1985)	783
		c.	The "Transformative" Turn	787
			Pierre N. Leval, *Toward a Fair Use Standard*, 103 HARV. L. REV. 1105 (1990)	787
			Campbell v. Acuff-Rose Music, Inc., 510 U.S. 569 (1994)	789
	iii.		The Modern Fair Use Landscape	801
		a.	Conventional	801
			American Geophysical Union v. Texaco Inc., 60 F.3d 913 (2d Cir. 1994)	802
		b.	Contextual/Different Purpose	815
			Blanch v. Koons, 467 F.3d 244 (2d Cir. 2006)	817
		c.	Functional/Technological Purpose	833
			Authors Guild v. Google, Inc., 804 F.3d 202 (2015)	834
2.			Online Service Provider Safe Harbors	839
			Viacom Int'l, Inc. v. YouTube, 676 F.3d 19 (2d Cir. 2012)	840
3.			Other Defenses	859
	i.		Independent Creation	859
	ii.		Consent/License	859
	iii.		Inequitable Conduct	859
	iv.		Copyright Misuse	859

v. Immoral/Illegal/Obscene Works 860
vi. Statute of Limitations 860
G. Remedies 861
1. Injunctions 861
2. Damages 864
i. Actual Damages and Profits 865
Sheldon v. Metro-Goldwyn Pictures Corp., 309 U.S. 390
(1940) 865
ii. Statutory Damages 869
3. Attorney's Fees and Costs 871
4. Criminal Enforcement 872
H. International Copyright Law 876
1. Evolution of the International Copyright System and U.S. Participation
876
2. International Copyright Treaties 879
i. Berne Convention for the Protection of Literary and Artistic
Works 879
ii. Agreement on Trade-Related Aspects of Intellectual Property
Rights (TRIPs) 880
iii. Other Copyright Treaties 882
3. Protection of U.S. Works Against Infringement Abroad 882
4. Protection of Foreign Works Against Infringement in the United States
886

Chapter V: Trademark Law **889**
A. Introduction 891
1. Historical Background 891
2. Trademark Theory 892
3. The Basic Economics of Trademarks and Advertising 894
B. What can be protected as a trademark? 900
1. Trademarks, Trade Names, and Service Marks 901
2. Certification and Collective Marks 902
3. Trade Dress and Product Configurations 904
C. Establishment of Trademark Rights 905
1. Distinctiveness 905
i. Classification of Terms and Requirements for Protection 905
Zatarain's, Inc. v. Oak Grove Smokehouse, Inc., 698 F.2d 786
(5th Cir. 1983) 906
ii. Genericness 919
Elliott v. Google Inc., 860 F.3d 1151 (9th Cir. 2017) 920
iii. Distinctiveness of Trade Dress and Product Configuration 933
Two Pesos, Inc. v. Taco Cabana, Inc., 505 U.S. 763 (1992)
933

iv. Product Configuration   940
      Qualitex Co. v. Jacobson Products Co., Inc.,
      514 U.S. 159 (1995)   940
      Wal-Mart Stores, Inc. v. Samara Brothers, Inc.,
      529 U.S. 205 (2000)   947
v.   Functionality   955
      TrafFix Devices, Inc. v. Marketing Displays, Inc.,
      532 U.S. 23 (2001)   955
2. Priority   967
i.   Actual Use in Commerce   967
      Zazu Designs v. L'Oreal, S.A., 979 F.2d 499 (7th Cir. 1992)
                                                                    967
ii. Intent-to-Use Application Process   975
iii. Geographic Limitations on Trademark Use   977
iv. Secondary Meaning and Priority   979
      Laureyssens v. Idea Group, Inc., 964 F.2d 131 (2d Cir. 1992)
                                                                    979
v.   Priority and Trademark Theory   983
a.   Reducing Search Costs   983
      b.   Incentives to Create Trademarks   983
      c.   Priority and the Prevention of Trademark Races   985
3. Trademark Office Procedures   988
i.   Principal vs. Supplemental Register   988
ii. Grounds for Refusing Registration   989
      a.   Immoral, Scandalous, or Disparaging Marks   991
      b.   Geographic Marks   993
      In re Nantucket, Inc., 677 F.2d 95 (C.C.P.A. 1982)   993
iii. Marks Which Are "Primarily Merely a Surname"   997
iv. Opposition   1001
v.   Cancellation   1001
vi. Concurrent Registration   1002
4. Incontestability   1003
      Park 'N Fly, Inc. v. Dollar Park and Fly, Inc.,
      469 U.S. 189 (1985)   1003
D. Trademark Liability Analysis   1008
1. Threshold Issue: Trademark Use   1008
      Rescuecom Corp. v. Google, Inc., 562 F.3d 123 (2d Cir.
      2009)   1009
2. Trademark Infringement and Related Doctrines   1017
i.   Confusion-Based Infringement   1017
      a.   General Multi-Factor "Likelihood of Confusion" Test   1018
      AMF Inc. v. Sleekcraft Boats,
      599 F.2d 341 (9th Cir. 1979)   1018

3.		Types of Confusion	1026
	i.	Confusion as to Source	1026
	ii.	Confusion as to Sponsorship	1027
		a. Trademarks and Organizational Forms: The Growth of Franchising	1029
		b. Merchandising	1030
		Board of Supervisors for Louisiana State University v. Smack Apparel Co., 550 F.3d 465 (5th Cir. 2008)	1031
	iii.	Reverse Confusion	1042
	iv.	Timing of Confusion	1043
		a. Initial Interest Confusion	1043
		Multi Time Machine, Inc. v. Amazon.com, Inc., 804 F.3d 930 (9th Cir. 2015)	1044
		b. Post-Sale Confusion	1054
	v.	Dilution	1057
		Louis Vuitton Malletier S.A. v. Haute Diggity Dog, LLC, 507 F.3d 252 (4th Cir. 2007)	1060
4.		Cybersquatting	1075
5.		Indirect Infringement	1077
		Tiffany Inc. v. eBay Inc., 600 F.3d 93 (2d Cir. 2010)	1077
6.		False Advertising	1089
		MillerCoors, LLC v. Anheuser-Busch Companies, LLC, 2019 WL 2250644 (2019)	1089
E.	Defenses		1108
	1.	Abandonment	1108
		i. Cessation of Use	1108
		Major League Baseball Properties, Inc. v. Sed Non Olet Denarius, Ltd., 817 F. Supp. 1103 (S.D.N.Y. 1993)	1108
		ii. Unsupervised Licenses	1116
		Dawn Donut Company, Inc. v. Hart's Food Stores, Inc., 67 F.2d 358 (2d Cir. 1959)	1116
		iii. Assignments in Gross	1121
	2.	Exhaustion/First Sale	1123
		i. Resale Without Requisite Quality Control	1123
		ii. Repackaged Goods	1124
		iii. Repaired and Reconditioned Goods	1124
	3.	Fair Use	1125
		i. Descriptive/"Classic" Fair Use	1125
		KP Permanent Make-up, Inc. v. Lasting Impression I, Inc., 543 U.S. 111 (2004)	1125
		ii. Nontrademark (or Nominative) Use, Parody, and the First Amendment	1130

Mattel, Inc. v. MCA Records, 296 F.3d 894 (9th Cir. 2002)
1130
4. Other Defenses   1144
   i.   Laches   1144
   ii. Unclean Hands   1145
        a. Fraud in Obtaining Trademark Registration   1146
        b. Trademark Misuse   1146
F. Remedies   1147
   1. Injunctions   1147
        *Herb Reed Enterprises, LLC v. Florida Entertainment
        Management, Inc.*, 763 F.3d 1239 (9th Cir. 2013)   1147
   2. Damages   1152
        i.   Infringer's Gain and Mark Owner's Loss   1152
        ii. Corrective Advertising   1158
        *Big O Tire Dealers, Inc. v. The Goodyear Tire &
        Rubber Company*, 561 F.2d 1365 (10th Cir. 1977)   1158
        a. Note on the Trademark Counterfeiting Act of 1984   1165
G. International Issues   1166
   1. U.S. Trademarks Abroad: The New Internationalization   1167
   2. Foreign Trademarks in the United States:
      Limited Internationalization   1168
   3. Note on the "Gray Market"   1169
   4. Worldwide Famous Marks   1171

Chapter VI: State IP Protections   **1173**
A. Federal Preemption   1174
   1. Patent Preemption   1174
        Kewanee Oil Co. v. Bicron Corp.,
        416 U.S. 470 (1974)   1174
        Bonito Boats, Inc. v. Thunder Craft Boats, Inc.,
        489 U.S. 141 (1989)   1179
   2. Copyright Preemption   1184
        i.   Express Preemption (and Limitations)   1184
        COPYRIGHT LAW REVISION Report No. 94-1476 (1976)   1186
        ii. Contract   1190
        ProCD, Inc. v. Zeidenberg, 86 F.3d 1447 (7th Cir. 1996) 1190
   3. Trademark Preemption   1201
B. Misappropriation   1204
        International News Service v. Associated Press,
        248 U.S. 215 (1918)   1204
C. Idea Submissions   1220
        Nadel v. Play-by-Play Toys & Novelties, Inc.,
        208 F.3d 368 (2d Cir. 2000)   1220

Desny v. Wilder, 46 Cal. 2d 715, 299 P.2d 257,
110 U.S.P.Q. 433 (Cal. Sup. Ct. 1956)   1232
D.   Right of Publicity   1241
Midler v. Ford Motor Co., 849 F.2d 460 (9th Cir. 1988)   1244
White v. Samsung Electronics America, Inc.,
989 F.2d 1512 (9th Cir. 1993)   1249
Comedy III Productions, Inc. v. Gary Saderup, Inc.,
25 Cal. 4th 387 (2001)   1258

EDITORIAL NOTE

We have selectively omitted citations and footnotes from cases without the uses of ellipses or other indications. All footnotes are numbered consecutively within each chapter, except that footnotes in cases and other excerpts correspond to the actual footnote numbers in the published reports. Many of the problems in this text are taken from actual cases. In many instances, we have altered the facts and the names of the parties for pedagogical purposes. In a few cases, however, particularly in the trademark chapter, we felt that it was important to the problem to use the name of a product or company with which the reader would be familiar. Readers should understand that the problems are hypothetical in nature and that we do not intend them to represent the actual facts of any case or situation.

CHAPTER IV:
COPYRIGHT LAW

A.	Introduction	506
	1. Brief History of Copyright Protection	506
	i. 1909 Act	509
	ii. 1976 Act and Related Reforms	509
	iii. Berne Convention Accession	510
	iv. The Digital Age	510
	2. An Overview of the Copyright Regime	510
	3. Philosophical Perspectives on Copyright Protection	512
B.	Requirements	515
	1. Original Works of Authorship	515
	2. Fixation in a Tangible Medium of Expression	530
	3. Formalities	535
	i. Notice	536
	ii. Publication	536
	a. 1909 Act	536
	b. 1976 Act/Pre-Ratification of Berne Convention	538
	c. Post-Ratification of the Berne Convention	538
	iii. Registration	539
	a. 1909 Act	539
	b. 1976 Act/Pre-Ratification of Berne Convention	540
	c. Post-Ratification of the Berne Convention	540
	d. Registration Must Be Made Prior to Filing Suit	540
	iv. Deposit	541
	4. Restoration of Foreign Copyrighted Works	541
C.	Copyrightable Subject Matter	543
	1. The Domain and Scope of Copyright Protection	543
	i. Literary Works	544
	ii. Pictorial, Graphic, and Sculptural Works	545
	iii. Architectural Works	545
	iv. Musical Works and Sound Recordings	547
	v. Dramatic, Pantomime, and Choreographic Works	548
	vi. Motion Pictures and Other Audiovisual Works	549
	vii. Semiconductor Chips Designs (Mask Works)	549
	viii. Vessel Hull Designs	550
	ix. Derivative Works and Compilations	550
	2. Limitations on Copyrightability: Distinguishing Function and Expression	553
	i. The Idea-Expression Dichotomy	553
	ii. The Useful Article Doctrine	578

		iii.	Government Works and Edicts	599
D.	Ownership and Duration			604
	1.	Initial Ownership of Copyrights		604
		i.	Works Made for Hire	604
		ii.	Joint Works	616
		iii.	Collective Works	626
		iv.	The Rights of Authors and Publishers in Electronic Compilations	626
	2.	Duration and Renewal		630
		i.	1909 Act	630
		ii.	1976 Act	630
		iii.	Sonny Bono Copyright Term Extension Act of 1998	630
	3.	Division, Transfer, and Reclaiming of Copyrights		638
		i.	Division and Transfer of Copyright Interests Under the 1909 Act	638
		ii.	Division and Transfer of Copyright Interests Under the 1976 Act	639
		iii.	Reclaiming Copyrights	639
E.	Rights and Infringement			643
	1.	Direct Infringement		643
		i.	Traditional Copyright Rights	644
			a. The Right to Make Copies	644
			1. Copying	646
			2. Improper Appropriation	653
			3. The Special Case of Computer Software	667
			4. Limitations on the Exclusive Right to Copy	683
			5. Compulsory Licensing of Musical Compositions	684
			i. Mechanical Compulsory License I: Cover License	684
			ii. Mechanical Compulsory License II: Digital Phonorecord Delivery (DPD)	686
			b. The Right to Prepare Derivative Works	688
			c. The Distribution Right	700
			1. The Scope of the Distribution Right: Does It Encompass Making a Work Available?	700
			2. Limitations on the Distribution Right: The First Sale Doctrine	702
			d. Public Performance Right	715
			1. What Constitutes a "Public Performance"?	715
			2. Blanket Public Performance Licenses and Collecting Societies	727
			3. Treatment of Sound Recordings	728
			4. Statutory Limits on Performance and Display Rights	729
			i. Public Interest Exemptions	729
			ii. Compulsory Licenses	730
			e. Public Display Right	732
		ii.	Moral Rights	732

	iii.	State and Common Law Copyrights	742
	iv.	Digital Rights	744
		a. Audio Home Recording Act	744
		b. Anti-Circumvention Provisions	745
2.	Indirect Infringement		750
	i.	The Analog Age	750
		a. Respondeat Superior	750
		b. Vicarious Liability	751
		c. Contributory Liability	752
	ii.	The Digital Age	761

F. Defenses — 779
  1. Fair Use — 779
    i. The Formative Era — 779
    ii. Codification and Early Post-Codification Interpretation — 780
      a. Sony Corp. of America v. Universal City Studios, Inc. (1984) — 781
      b. Harper & Row, Publishers, Inc. v. Nation Enterprises (1985) — 783
      c. The "Transformative" Turn — 787
    iii. The Modern Fair Use Landscape — 801
      a. Conventional — 801
      b. Contextual/Different Purpose — 815
      c. Functional/Technological Purpose — 833
  2. Online Service Provider Safe Harbors — 839
  3. Other Defenses — 859
    i. Independent Creation — 859
    ii. Consent/License — 859
    iii. Inequitable Conduct — 859
    iv. Copyright Misuse — 859
    v. Immoral/Illegal/Obscene Works — 860
    vi. Statute of Limitations — 860

G. Remedies — 861
  1. Injunctions — 861
  2. Damages — 864
    i. Actual Damages and Profits — 865
    ii. Statutory Damages — 869
  3. Attorney's Fees and Costs — 871
  4. Criminal Enforcement — 872

H. International Copyright Law — 876
  1. Evolution of the International Copyright System and U.S. Participation — 876
  2. International Copyright Treaties — 879
    i. Berne Convention for the Protection of Literary and Artistic Works — 879
    ii. Agreement on Trade-Related Aspects of Intellectual Property Rights (TRIPs) — 880
    iii. Other Copyright Treaties — 882

3.   Protection of U.S. Works Against Infringement Abroad   882
4.   Protection of Foreign Works Against Infringement in the United States   886

A.   INTRODUCTION

This chapter explores the broad and expanding domain of copyright law, a principal means for protecting works of authorship. Although focused upon expressive (and non-functional) works, copyright has since its inception responded to advances in technologies for reproducing, disseminating, and storing information. Copyright laws emerged in the wake of the printing press and have evolved to encompass other methods of creating, instantiating, and reproducing works of authorship, such as photography, motion pictures, and sound recordings. The development of broadcasting technology—enabling the performance of works at distant points—triggered a second wave of expansions and adjustments to copyright. The digital revolution represents a third distinct wave of technological innovation reshaping copyright law. By bringing about new modes of expression (such as computer programming, synthesized music, video games, and interactive multimedia works) and empowering anyone with a computer and an Internet connection to flawlessly, inexpensively, and instantaneously reproduce and distribute works of authorship, digital technology represents possibly the greatest set of challenges to copyright law. This latest wave is just cresting—as the Internet and digital technology have become widely diffused—and hence the future of copyright law is very much in flux.

We begin with a brief survey of the origins of copyright law, its philosophical underpinnings, and of its vast provisions. Building upon this introduction, we examine copyright subject matter, ownership structure, rights (including infringement analysis), defenses, and remedies. We integrate the new and rapidly developing frontier of digital copyright law. The chapter concludes by surveying international dimensions of copyright law.

1.   Brief History of Copyright Protection

The invention of the printing press in the West provided the impetus for the establishment of copyright protection.[1] Working from wine press technology from his native Rhine Valley, Johannes Gutenberg, a German goldsmith, developed a printing press with wood and metal movable type by the year 1440. Gutenberg experimented with this technology for the next decade with funding from a German businessman. An infusion of new funding around 1450 enabled Gutenberg to build a larger press, ultimately leading to the first printed version of the Bible in 1452. This extraordinary technological achievement encountered some resistance from nobles, who refused to tarnish their libraries of hand copied manuscripts with printed books; the Catholic

---

[1] Printing technology developed in the Far East much earlier, resulting in the earliest dated printed book ("Diamond Sutra," a Buddhist scripture) using a block printing technology in China at least as early as the year 868. A printing device using movable clay type was invented in China in 1041 by Bi Sheng.

Church, which sought to control technology of mass communication; and the Islamic world, with its calligraphic traditions. Nonetheless, the printing press spread rapidly across Europe. With its highly developed guild system and fertile technological culture, Venice emerged as the "capital of printing" in the late fifteenth century.

Not surprisingly given Venice's progressive, humanist tradition, patent protection presaged the development of copyright. The Venetian Republic granted Johann Speyer, a German goldsmith and the first printer in the city, a patent in 1469 for the printing press, affording Speyer an exclusive right to print books in all Venetian territories for the next five years. *See* JOHN FEATHER, PUBLISHING, PIRACY AND POLITICS: AN HISTORICAL STUDY OF COPYRIGHT IN BRITAIN 10–11 (1994). Within a few decades, the Venetian Cabinet recognized for the first time exclusive rights in the printing of particular books (as distinguished from the technology of reproduction), awarding Daniele Barbaro a ten-year exclusive grant to publish his late brother's book on Aristotelian ethics. *See* Christopher May, *The Venetian Moment: New Technologies, Legal Innovation and the Institutional Origins of Intellectual Property*, 20 PROMETHEUS 159, 172 (2002). Ease of entry into printing and an oversupply of books ultimately led the Venetian Senate to restrict the printing privilege to "new and previously unprinted works." By the middle of the sixteenth century, a new decree organized all of Venice's printers and booksellers into a guild and provided a means for allowing the Church to suppress heretical works.

With the growth of international commerce and the emergence of London as a leading center of trade, England became a focal point for the development of copyright law. The first "copyright" was granted in England by royal decree in 1512, not long after the introduction of the printing press in England.[2] *See* ELIZABETH L. EISENSTEIN, THE PRINTING REVOLUTION IN EARLY MODERN EUROPE (1993). For political reasons, the Crown consolidated the new printing business in the hands of the Stationers' Company. It granted printers of this company—not authors—the exclusive right to control the printing and sale of books, forever. Not incidentally, the government conferred these copyrights upon loyal publishers who would not publish books that the Crown considered politically or religiously objectionable, and indeed it subjected the printing business to the oversight of the Star Chamber. *See* David Lange, *At Play in the Fields of the Word: Copyright and the Construction of Authorship in the Post-Literate Millennium*, 55 LAW & CONTEMP. PROBLEMS 139 (1992).

After the exclusive right of the Stationers' Company ended in 1695, members of the company faced substantial competition in the printing of books for the first time. They promptly sought assistance from Parliament. In 1710, Parliament responded by passing the Statute of Anne. The Statute of Anne vested in *authors* of books a monopoly over their works. Unlike the perpetual rights granted to publishers by decree, the statutory right was limited to only 14 years, with an additional 14 years if the author

---

[2] Prior to royal decrees, an author had the property right to physical possession of his manuscript as well as copyright protection at common law. *See* H. Tomás Gómez-Arostegui, *Copyright at Common Law in 1774*, 47 CONN. L. REV. 1 (2014).

survived expiration of statutory copyright. The statute required registration to obtain the penalties and forfeitures of the statute.

In Europe, copyright protection came to be seen as a natural right of authors. Jean Le Chapelier, a member of the French National Convention and the reporter of the French Copyright Law of 1793, proclaimed "fruit of a writer's thoughts" to be "the most sacred, the most legitimate, the most unassailable, and . . . the most personal of all forms of all properties." *See* Jane C. Ginsburg, *A Tale of Two Copyrights: Literary Property in Revolutionary France and America*, 64 TULANE L. REV. 991, 1007 (1990). Yet even this tradition recognizes that ideas, as opposed to their expression, must not be private property.

Most of the United States passed state copyright laws modeled on the Statute of Anne shortly after gaining their independence. The Massachusetts Constitution stressed the importance of education, access to knowledge, and encouragement of literature and science as cornerstones for a democratic society and social harmony. Problems with applying conflicting state laws across state borders led to a general consensus that a national law was necessary, and thus the Constitution expressly granted power to the federal government to create both patents and copyrights. In advocating enactment of the nation's first intellectual property laws during the very first State of the Union Address, President Washington presciently declared that

> there is nothing which can better deserve your patronage than the promotion of science and literature. Knowledge is, in every country, the surest basis of public happiness. In one in which the measures of government receive their impression so immediately from the sense of the community as in ours, it is proportionably essential.

One of the first acts of the new Congress was to pass the Copyright Act of 1790. That Act, like the Statute of Anne, granted authors protection for books, maps, and charts for 14 years, with an additional 14-year term if the author survived expiration of the first copyright term. The 1790 Act required copyrights to be registered with the local district court and notice to be published in local newspapers. As technology for making and reproducing works of authorship expanded and the arts flourished, Congress amended the Copyright Act to extend to new media and means of exploitation. By the end of the nineteenth century, copyright protection extended to prints, musical compositions, dramatic works, photographs, graphic works, and sculpture. Since the advent of the printing press, advances in the technologies for creating and distributing works of authorship have played a critical role in shaping copyright law. *See generally* Peter S. Menell, *Envisioning Copyright Law's Digital Future*, 46 N.Y.L. SCH. L. REV. 63 (2003); PAUL GOLDSTEIN, COPYRIGHT'S HIGHWAY: FROM GUTENBERG TO THE CELESTIAL JUKEBOX (2d ed. 2003).

The Copyright Act has undergone numerous changes during its history. Although these changes are embodied en masse within Title 17 of the U.S. Code, it will be helpful to put this immensely complex statute into historical perspective. Here is a brief sketch of the principal milestones and motivating forces behind the evolution of U.S. copyright law over the past century:

i.   1909 Act

The most significant overhaul of the Copyright Act since its founding occurred in 1909. Like the piece-meal amendments of the nineteenth century, the 1909 Act further expanded protection to include "all writings," reaching works in progress and speeches, among other new matter. Copyright protection lasted for an initial term of 28 years, with an additional 28 years available upon renewal. Failure to provide proper notice upon publication of a work forfeited protection.

The requirements of registration and notice of copyright put the U.S. at odds with an emerging European consensus prohibiting any formality to copyright protection. Establishing compliance with formalities proved difficult in this relatively primitive technological era. Authors prevailed upon signatories of the Berne Convention for the Protection of Literary and Artistic Works (initially promulgated in 1886), as revised in 1908 in Berlin, to prohibit any formal prerequisites to copyright enforcement in foreign tribunals. As a result of its registration, notice upon publication, and domestic manufacturing requirements, the U.S. was not eligible for Berne membership.

ii.   1976 Act and Related Reforms

Advances in technology for creating and distributing works of authorship—most notably, sound recording and broadcasting—as well as anachronisms of the 1909 Act (such as the dual term of protection) periodically aroused interest in reforming the Copyright Act through the middle of the twentieth century, but no significant legislation resulted. In 1955, Congress requested that the Copyright Office undertake a series of studies aimed at assessing the copyright system and set in motion an effort aimed at comprehensive reform of the statute through negotiation among the principal interest groups affected by copyright policy. The complex process bogged down over the treatment of cable television and jukeboxes. With the rise of record piracy in the late 1960s, Congress passed, as interim measure, a law providing federal copyright protection for sound recordings in 1971. Congress finally approved the omnibus reform in 1976. This law continues to serve as the principal framework for copyright protection in the United States.

The 1976 Act expanded both the scope and duration of protection. All written works became protected upon being "fixed in a tangible medium of expression," even if they were unpublished. The duration of copyright was expanded to the life of the author plus 50 years, or 75 years in the case of anonymous works, pseudonymous works, and works made for hire. Furthermore, the formal notice and registration requirements were loosened, although not discarded. In other respects, the 1976 Act weakened intellectual property protection by establishing several new compulsory licensing regimes, approving numerous exemptions from liability, codifying the fair use doctrine that had been developing through the courts, and preempting most state and common law protections that impinge upon federal copyright protection. In 1980, Congress expressly incorporated protection for computer programs into the Copyright Act. At the urging of the major copyright industries, Congress added an additional 20 years to the duration of copyright protection in 1998.

iii. Berne Convention Accession

As the global content marketplace expanded to unprecedented levels in the 1980s and piracy of copyrighted works in many corners of the world increased, the United States joined the Berne Convention in 1989 as a means for expanding protection for U.S. works throughout the world and enhancing U.S. influence on the direction of global copyright protection. As a result, Congress approved several amendments between 1988 and 1994 scaling back formalities, extending protection for moral rights and architectural works, and restoring copyright for foreign works under protection in the source country but in the public domain in the United States so as to bring U.S. copyright law into compliance with the minimum standards set forth in the Berne Convention.

iv. The Digital Age

By the early 1990s, advances in digital technology were beginning to be felt in the major content marketplaces. The traditional content industries feared that widespread availability of technology for making low-cost, perfect copies of digital media could undermine their ability to enforce their rights. In response, Congress has passed several detailed amendments to the Copyright Act during the 1990s aimed at reforming copyright law for the digital age. The Audio Home Recording Act of 1992 regulated the design of digital audio tape technology and imposes a levy on the sale of devices and blank media intended to compensate copyright owners for losses from home copying. The Digital Performance Right in Sound Recordings Act of 1995 afforded creators and owners of sound recordings a basis for earning income on digital streams (webcasts) of their works. The No Electronic Theft (NET) Act of 1996 expanded criminal enforcement for piracy over digital networks. The Digital Millennium Copyright Act (DMCA) of 1998 afforded copyright owners rights against those who circumvent copy protection technologies and insulated online service providers from liability for infringing acts of their subscribers subject to various limitations. The Music Modernization Act (MMA), passed in 2018, substantially overhauled digital music licensing and extended federal copyright protection to pre-1972 sound recordings.

2. An Overview of the Copyright Regime

Although the copyright and patent laws flow from the same constitutional basis and share the same general approach—statutorily created exclusive rights to foster progress—they feature different elements and rights, reflecting the very different fields of creativity that they seek to encourage. We sketch below the basic elements and rights of copyright law. As you review these features, contrast them to the analogous provisions of the patent law. How do you explain the differences?

A protectable copyright has the following elements:

- *Copyrightable Subject Matter.* The subject matter protectable by copyright spans the broad range of literary and artistic expression—including literature, song, dance, sculpture, graphics, painting, photography, sound, movies, and computer programming. Ideas themselves are not copyrightable, but the author's particular expression of an idea is protectable.
- *Threshold for Protection.* A work need only exhibit a modicum of originality and be fixed in a "tangible medium of expression."
- *Formalities.* Notice of copyright is required on all works published prior to 1989. Registration of a copyright is not strictly required for its validity, but is required of U.S. authors prior to instituting an infringement suit. Deposit of copies of the work is required to obtain registration of copyright.
- *Authorship and Ownership.* The work must have been created by the party bringing suit, or rights in the work must have been transferred by the author to the party bringing suit. In the case of "works made for hire," the employer and not the original creator are considered the author and the owner of the work.
- *Duration of Copyright.* A copyright lasts for the life of the author plus 70 years, or 95 years from first publication in the case of anonymous works, pseudonymous works, works made for hire (or 120 years from the year of creation, whichever occurs first).

Although the United States Copyright Office registers works, unlike the Patent and Trademark Office, it does not conduct a search of the prior art or make any assessment of validity (other than to ensure a modicum of creativity). The Copyright Office functions more like a title registry office. A copyright is protectable at the moment the work is created.

In relation to patents, the ease with which copyrights may be obtained and the duration for which they last are counterbalanced by the more limited rights accorded and the numerous and substantial exceptions and limitations to protection. Ownership of a valid copyright confers the following rights:

- *Reproduction.* The owner has the exclusive right to make copies. She may sue a copier for infringement if the copying is "material" and "substantial," even if the copy is in a different form or is of only part of the whole.
- *Derivative Works.* The owner has the exclusive right to prepare derivative works, which are works based on the original but in different forms or otherwise altered (such as translations, movies based on books, etc.). These derivative works are themselves copyrightable to the extent that they contain original expression. Note that the right to create derivative works is closely related to the right to reproduce and employs essentially the same standard for infringement.
- *Distribution.* The owner has the right to control the sale and distribution of the original and all copies or derivative works, including licensed copies. However, this right extends only to the first sale of such works. The owner does not have the right to limit resale by purchasers of her works (except in certain limited circumstances).

- *Performance and Display.* The owner has the right to control public (but not private) performance and display of her works, including both literary and performance-oriented works. This right extends to computer programs and other audiovisual works. The owner generally does not, however, have the right to prevent the display of a particular original or copy of a work of art in a public place.
- *Anticircumvention.* The Copyright Act prohibits the circumvention of technological protection measures (such as encryption) designed to safeguard digitally encoded works, subject to several exceptions and limitations.
- *Moral Rights.* Visual artists possess an attribution right in their works as well as rights to prevent intentional distortion, mutilation, or other modification of their work, and to block destruction of works of "recognized stature," subject to several limitations.

Like patents, copyrights are protected against both direct and indirect (contributory, vicarious, or inducement) infringement.

These rights are limited in several ways. The fair use doctrine, intended to create leeway for criticism, comment, news reporting, teaching, scholarship, and research, applies a balancing test to determine whether a use of copyrighted material should be permitted without the owner's authorization. In addition, the Copyright Act establishes compulsory licensing for musical compositions, cable television, and webcasts, among others, and exempts some uses from liability. The Act also establishes a safe harbor that partially immunizes online service providers from monetary liability for infringing acts of their subscribers.

There is a more fundamental difference between patent and copyright law. Copyrights do not give their owner the exclusive right to prevent others from making, using, or selling their creations. Rather, they give the author only the right to prevent *unauthorized copying* of their works, as well as the right to prevent some limited types of uses of those works (such as public performances) when derived from the copyright owner. The independent development of a similar or even identical work is perfectly legal. This means that copyright law must have some mechanism for determining when a work has been copied illegally. While in some cases direct proof of copying may be available, in most cases courts determine whether copying has occurred on the basis of the defendant's access to the plaintiff's work and the extent which the two works are similar. If copying is proven—whether directly or by inference—then infringement will be found if the defendant's work is substantially similar to protected expression—in whole or substantial part—in the plaintiff's work.

3. Philosophical Perspectives on Copyright Protection

In the vast body of court decisions, legislation, and commentaries on copyright law, one can find references to a great many philosophical justifications for copyright protection. Lord Justice Mansfield, writing in the mid-eighteenth century, stated: "From what source, then is the common law drawn, which is admitted to be so clear, in respect of the copy before publication? From this argument—because it is just, that an author should reap the pecuniary profits of his own ingenuity and labor." *Millar v. Taylor*, 4 Burr. 230, 238 (1769). This ruling was overturned by the House of Lords five years later, in *Donaldson v. Becket*, 98 ENG. REP. 257 (H.L. 1774).

Scholars have long debated the philosophical foundations of copyright law. *See generally* ROBERT P. MERGES, JUSTIFYING INTELLECTUAL PROPERTY ch. 8 (2011); Alfred Yen, *Restoring the Natural Law: Copyright as Labor and Possession*, 51 OHIO ST. L.J. 517 (1990) (tracing roots of natural law in American copyright law); Justin Hughes, *The Philosophy of Intellectual Property*, 77 GEO. L.J. 287, 350–53 (1988) (suggesting various strains of the personhood justification in American copyright law). The German philosopher Immanuel Kant offered a justification for copyright rooted in the ideal of individual autonomy. *See* Immanuel Kant, *On the Wrongfulness of Unauthorized Publication of Books*, *in* IMMANUEL KANT: PRACTICAL PHILOSOPHY 29-35 (Mary J. Gregor trans. 1998) (1785). And, as we have seen, the "natural right" of the author to control the use of his work and to be rewarded for it is one of the significant underpinnings of at least some American copyright jurisprudence. *See* BENJAMIN KAPLAN, AN UNHURRIED VIEW OF COPYRIGHT 79 (1967).

The predominant philosophical framework undergirding American copyright law, however, is utilitarian. The Constitution grants Congress the power to enact copyright laws in order to "promote the Progress of Science and useful Arts." Art. I, § 8, cl. 8. In the early decision of *Wheaton v. Peters*, 33 U.S. (8 Pet.) 591 (1834), the Court treated copyright as a statutory creation designed primarily to enhance the public interest and only secondarily to confer a reward upon authors. *Id.* at 661. Justice Stewart described the basic purpose of the Copyright Act as follows:

> The limited scope of the copyright holder's statutory monopoly, like the limited duration required by the Constitution, reflects a balance of competing claims upon the public interest: Creative work is to be encouraged and rewarded, but private motivation must ultimately serve the cause of promoting broad public availability of literature, music, and the other arts.[8] The immediate effect of our copyright law is to secure a fair return to an "author's" creative labor. But the ultimate aim is, by this incentive, to stimulate artistic creativity for the general public good. "The sole interest of the United States and the primary object in conferring the monopoly," this Court has said, "lie in the general benefits derived by the public from the labors of authors."

Twentieth Century Music Corp. v. Aiken, 422 U.S. 151, 156 (1975). *See also Mazer v. Stein*, 347 U.S. 201, 219 (1954). And Justice Stevens has commented that:

---

[8] Lord Mansfield's statement of the problem more than two centuries ago in *Sayre v. Moore*, quoted in a footnote to *Cary v. Longman*, 1 East *358, 362 n.(b), 102 Eng. Rep. 138, 150 n.(b) (1801), bears repeating:

> [W]e must take care to guard against two extremes equally prejudicial; the one, that men of ability, who have employed their time for the service of the community, may not be deprived of their just merits, and the reward of their ingenuity and labour; the other, that the world may not be deprived of improvements, nor the progress of the arts be retarded.

> The monopoly privileges that Congress may authorize are neither unlimited nor primarily designed to provide a special private benefit. Rather, the limited grant is a means by which an important public purpose may be achieved. It is intended to motivate the creative activity of authors and inventors by the provision of a special reward, and to allow the public access to the products of this genius after the limited period of exclusive control has expired.

Sony Corp. of America v. Universal City Studios, Inc., 464 U.S. 417, 429 (1984).

American copyright law can thus be seen as primarily striving to achieve an optimal balance between fostering incentives for the creation of literary and artistic works and the optimal use and dissemination of such works. Nonetheless, copyright law reflects other philosophical perspectives as well. Society grants copyrights both because it wants to encourage creation and because it wants to reward authors for their work. Copyright also reflects the Lockean principle that authors deserve to own the works they have created. The law limits the duration and scope of copyrights because it wants to make sure that copyright protection does not unduly burden other creators or free expression, that works are widely disseminated, and that the next generation of authors can make use of ideas in creating still more works. As we will see later in this chapter, international pressure and appeals by artists have brought increased recognition of the moral rights of artists. These policies interact in complex ways. In many cases, there is still great controversy over which policy should predominate.

COMMENTS AND QUESTIONS

1. How can we strike the proper balance between fostering incentives for the creation of literary and artistic works and the optimal use and dissemination of such works? Does the same duration of protection for all copyrightable works—whether books, computer programs, songs, paintings, or choreographic works—make sense? Do other justifications beyond the utilitarian balance better explain copyright's structure and provisions?

2. Contrast the way in which copyright law, trade secret law, and patent law vary along the following dimensions:

- threshold for protection
- duration of protection
- rights conferred
- treatment of independent creation
- defenses to infringing use

To what extent can the differences among these legal regimes be explained by differences in the subject of coverage (and the nature of the creative process in these areas)? Differences in the philosophical justifications for these modes of protection? Other factors?

3. The term "copyright" reflects the underlying philosophy of the Anglo-American regime for protecting literary and artistic works—regulation of the right to make *copies* for the purpose of promoting progress in the arts and literature. The emphasis is on the

benefit to the public, not the benefits or rights of authors. By contrast, the civil law analog to copyright has a different name and orientation. In France, the comparable body of law is *droit d'auteur,* which translates to "author's rights." The laws in Germany and Spain are similar—*Urheberrecht* and *derecho de autor.* This civil law tradition derives more from a Kantian (natural rights) or Hegelian (personhood) justification for legal entitlements, and thus focuses on the rights of *authors.* Thus, the civil law countries have long expressly protected the moral rights of authors—e.g., the right of an author to prevent the mutilation of his or her work after it is sold. *See generally* Jane C. Ginsburg, *A Tale of Two Copyrights: Literary Property in Revolutionary France and America*, 64 TUL. L. REV. 991 (1990).

Of what significance is the underlying philosophical perspective—whether utilitarian, natural rights, or personhood—for the structure and content of copyright law? Which perspective is more appropriate as a matter of social justice? Public policy? Can these perspectives be effectively harmonized without losing their coherence?

4. To what extent does the open source model of collaborative creativity dispel the principles underlying traditional copyright law? Does the Internet's essentially free distribution system call for radical changes in the structure of copyright law? Should copyright law be strengthened or weakened in the digital age? What considerations guide your analysis? *See* Peter S. Menell, *This American Copyright Life, Reflections on Re-Equilibrating Copyright for the Internet Age*, 61 J. COPYRIGHT SOCIETY OF THE U.S.A. 235 (2014); ROBERT LEVINE, FREE RIDE: HOW DIGITAL PARASITES ARE DESTROYING THE CULTURE BUSINESS, AND HOW THE CULTURE BUSINESS CAN FIGHT BACK (2011); YOCHAI BENKLER, THE WEALTH OF NETWORKS: HOW SOCIAL PRODUCTION TRANSFORMS MARKETS AND FREEDOM (2006); ERIC VON HIPPEL, DEMOCRATIZING INNOVATION (2005); LAWRENCE LESSIG, FREE CULTURE: HOW BIG MEDIA USES TECHNOLOGY AND THE LAW TO LOCK DOWN CULTURE AND CONTROL (2004); PAUL GOLDSTEIN, COPYRIGHT'S HIGHWAY: FROM GUTENBERG TO THE CELESTIAL JUKEBOX (2d ed. 2003).

B.   REQUIREMENTS

1.   Original Works of Authorship

17 U.S.C. § 102. Subject Matter of Copyright: In General

(a) Copyright protection subsists, in accordance with this title, in original works of authorship fixed in any tangible medium of expression, now known or later developed, from which they can be perceived, reproduced, or otherwise communicated, either directly or with the aid of a machine or device. . . .

The legislative history to the 1976 Copyright Act provides:

The two fundamental criteria of copyright protection—originality and fixation in a tangible form—are restated in the first sentence of this cornerstone provision. The phrase "original works of authorship," which is purposively left undefined, is intended to incorporate without change the standard of originality established by the courts under the present copyright statute. This standard does not include requirements of novelty, ingenuity, or esthetic merit, and there is no intention to enlarge the standard of copyright protection to require them. . . .

As developed by the courts, originality entails *independent creation* of a work reflecting a *modicum of creativity*. Independent creation requires only that the author not have copied the work from some other source. As the eminent copyright jurist Learned Hand observed,

> If by some magic a man who had never known it were to compose anew Keats's *Ode on a Grecian Urn*, he would be an "author" and, if he copyrighted it, others might not copy that poem, though they might of course copy Keats's.

Sheldon v. Metro-Goldwyn Pictures Corp., 81 F.2d 49, 54 (2d Cir. 1936). This highlights an important distinction between patent and copyright law.

> The alleged inventor is chargeable with full knowledge of all the prior art, although in fact he may be utterly ignorant of it. The "author" is entitled to a copyright if he independently contrived a work completely identical with what went before; similarly, although he obtains a valid copyright, he has no right to prevent another from publishing a work identical with his, if not copied from his.

Alfred Bell & Co. v. Catalda Fine Arts, Inc., 191 F.2d 99, 103 (2d Cir. 1951).

> Courts have set the threshold of creativity necessary to satisfy the originality requirement quite low. Copyright law does not require that a work be strikingly unique or novel. . . . All that is needed to satisfy both the Constitution and the statute is that the "author" contributed something more than a "merely trivial" variation, something recognizably "his own." Originality in this context "means little more than a prohibition of actual copying." No matter how poor artistically the "author's" addition, it is enough if it be his own.

Id. at 102–03. Courts say they will not judge the artistic merit of a work:

> It would be a dangerous undertaking for persons trained only to the law to constitute themselves final judges of the worth of pictorial illustrations, outside of the narrowest and most obvious limits. At one extreme some works of genius would be sure to miss appreciation. Their very novelty would make them repulsive until the public had learned the new language in which their author spoke. It may be more than doubted, for instance, whether the etchings of Goya or the paintings of Manet would have been sure of protection when seen for the first time. At the other end, copyright would be denied to pictures which appealed to a public less educated than the judge.

Bleistein v. Donaldson Lithographing Co., 188 U.S. 239, 251–52 (1903) (finding a circus advertisement to be sufficiently original). Courts have rarely found literary or artistic works to fall below the *de minimis* originality threshold of copyright law. The few exceptions generally relate to slogans and exceedingly modest variations on another work. *See* 37 C.F.R. § 202.1 Material Not Subject to Copyright ("(a) Words and short phrases such as names, titles, and slogans; familiar symbols or designs; mere variations of typographical ornamentation, letter or coloring; mere listing of ingredients or contents . . . (e) Typeface as typeface."); H.R. REP. NO. 1476, 94th Cong., 2d Sess. at 55 (noting that Judiciary Committee "does not regard the design of typeface . . . to be a copyrightable "pictorial, graphic, or sculptural work" due to their "intrinsic utilitarian function . . . in composing text or other cognizable combinations of characters."); *but see* Hall v. Swift, 786 F. Appx. 711 (9th Cir. 2019) (holding in suit against Taylor Swift that the six-word phrase "players gonna play, haters gonna hate" was sufficiently original to be copyrightable).

A more difficult problem arises when an author creates a work in a mechanical or functional manner. Such assemblage of information can be costly and time consuming (entailing significant "sweat of the brow"), but may lack creativity. Should copyright law protect such works? Proponents of copyright protection for so-called "sweatworks" draw upon Lockean (labor theory), economic (without protection, there would be inadequate incentives to compile data), and fairness (unjust enrichment) rationales. *See* Robert Denicola, *Copyright in Collections of Facts: A Theory for the Protection of Nonfiction Literary Works*, 81 COLUM. L. REV. 516 (1981). Opponents of copyright protection for "sweatworks" see these works as in conflict with the rationale of protecting creativity. Furthermore, they point to the dangers of monopoly and wasted resources if several competing companies do the same fact-intensive work to produce the same product. The Supreme Court examined this set of issues through a constitutional lens in the following case.

Feist Publications v. Rural Telephone Service
Supreme Court of the United States
499 U.S. 340 (1991)

Justice O'CONNOR delivered the opinion of the Court.

This case requires us to clarify the extent of copyright protection available to telephone directory white pages.

I

Rural Telephone Service Company is a certified public utility that provides telephone service to several communities in northwest Kansas. It is subject to a state regulation that requires all telephone companies operating in Kansas to issue annually an updated telephone directory. Accordingly, as a condition of its monopoly franchise, Rural publishes a typical telephone directory, consisting of white pages and yellow pages. The white pages list in alphabetical order the names of Rural's subscribers, together with their towns and telephone numbers. The yellow pages list Rural's business subscribers alphabetically by category and feature classified advertisements of various sizes. Rural distributes its directory free of charge to its subscribers, but earns revenue by selling yellow pages advertisements.

Feist Publications, Inc., is a publishing company that specializes in area-wide telephone directories. Unlike a typical directory, which covers only a particular calling area, Feist's area-wide directories cover a much larger geographical range, reducing the need to call directory assistance or consult multiple directories. The Feist directory that is the subject of this litigation covers 11 different telephone service areas in 15 counties and contains 46,878 white pages listings—compared to Rural's approximately 7,700 listings. Like Rural's directory, Feist's is distributed free of charge and includes both white pages and yellow pages. Feist and Rural compete vigorously for yellow pages advertising.

As the sole provider of telephone service in its service area, Rural obtains subscriber information quite easily. Persons desiring telephone service must apply to Rural and provide their names and addresses; Rural then assigns them a telephone number. Feist is not a telephone company, let alone one with monopoly status, and therefore lacks independent access to any subscriber information. To obtain white pages listings for its area-wide directory, Feist approached each of the 11 telephone companies operating in northwest Kansas and offered to pay for the right to use its white pages listings.

Of the 11 telephone companies, only Rural refused to license its listings to Feist. Rural's refusal created a problem for Feist, as omitting these listings would have left a gaping hole in its area-wide directory, rendering it less attractive to potential yellow pages advertisers. . . .

Unable to license Rural's white pages listings, Feist used them without Rural's consent. Feist began by removing several thousand listings that fell outside the geographic range of its area-wide directory, then hired personnel to investigate the 4,935 that remained. These employees verified the data reported by Rural and sought to obtain additional information. As a result, a typical Feist listing includes the individual's street address; most of Rural's listings do not. Notwithstanding these additions, however, 1,309 of the 46,878 listings in Feist's 1983 directory were identical to listings in Rural's 1982–1983 white pages. Four of these were fictitious listings that Rural had inserted into its directory to detect copying.

Rural sued for copyright infringement. . . .

II

A

This case concerns the interaction of two well-established propositions. The first is that facts are not copyrightable; the other, that compilations of facts generally are. Each of these propositions possesses an impeccable pedigree. That there can be no valid copyright in facts is universally understood. The most fundamental axiom of copyright law is that "no author may copyright his ideas or the facts he narrates." *Harper & Row, Publishers, Inc. v. Nation Enterprises*, 471 U.S. 539, 556 (1985). Rural wisely concedes this point, noting in its brief that "facts and discoveries, of course, are not themselves subject to copyright protection." At the same time, however, it is beyond dispute that compilations of facts are within the subject matter of copyright. Compilations were expressly mentioned in the Copyright Act of 1909, and again in the Copyright Act of 1976.

There is an undeniable tension between these two propositions. Many compilations consist of nothing but raw data—i.e., wholly factual information not accompanied by any original written expression. On what basis may one claim a copyright in such a work? Common sense tells us that 100 uncopyrightable facts do not magically change their status when gathered together in one place. Yet copyright law seems to contemplate that compilations that consist exclusively of facts are potentially within its scope.

The key to resolving the tension lies in understanding why facts are not copyrightable. The *sine qua non* of copyright is originality. To qualify for copyright protection, a work must be original to the author. *See Harper & Row, supra*, at 547– 549. Original, as the term is used in copyright, means only that the work was independently created by the author (as opposed to copied from other works), and that it possesses at least some minimal degree of creativity. 1 M. NIMMER & D. NIMMER, COPYRIGHT §§ 2.01[A], [B] (1990) (hereinafter Nimmer). To be sure, the requisite level of creativity is extremely low; even a slight amount will suffice. The vast majority of works make the grade quite easily, as they possess some creative spark, "no matter how crude, humble or obvious" it might be. *Id.*, § 1.08[C][1]. Originality does not signify novelty; a work may be original even though it closely resembles other works so long as the similarity is fortuitous, not the result of copying. . . .

Originality is a constitutional requirement. The source of Congress' power to enact copyright laws is Article I, § 8, cl. 8, of the Constitution, which authorizes Congress to "secur[e] for limited Times to Authors . . . the exclusive Right to their respective Writings." In two decisions from the late 19th century—*The Trade-Mark Cases*, 100 U.S. 82 (1879); and *Burrow-Giles Lithographic Co. v. Sarony*, 111 U.S. 53 (1884)— this Court defined the crucial terms "authors" and "writings." In so doing, the Court made it unmistakably clear that these terms presuppose a degree of originality.

In *The Trade-Mark Cases*, the Court addressed the constitutional scope of "writings." For a particular work to be classified "under the head of writings of authors," the Court determined, "originality is required." 100 U.S., at 94. The Court explained that originality requires independent creation plus a modicum of creativity: "[W]hile the word *writings* may be liberally construed, as it has been, to include original designs for engraving, prints, &c., it is only such as are *original*, and are founded in the creative powers of the mind. The writings which are to be protected are *the fruits of intellectual labor*, embodied in the form of books, prints, engravings, and the like." *Ibid.* (emphasis in original).

In *Burrow-Giles*, the Court distilled the same requirement from the Constitution's use of the word "authors." The Court defined "author," in a constitutional sense, to mean "he to whom anything owes its origin; originator; maker." 111 U.S., at 58 (internal quotation marks omitted). As in *The Trade-Mark Cases*, the Court emphasized the creative component of originality. It described copyright as being limited to "original intellectual conceptions of the author," 111 U.S., at 58, and stressed the importance of requiring an author who accuses another of infringement to prove "the existence of those facts of originality, of intellectual production, of thought, and conception." *Id.*, at 59–60.

The originality requirement articulated in *The Trade-Mark Cases* and *Burrow-Giles* remains the touchstone of copyright protection today. *See Goldstein v. California*, 412 U.S. 546, 561–562 (1973). It is the very "premise of copyright law." *Miller v. Universal City Studios, Inc.*, 650 F.2d 1365, 1368 (CA5 1981). Leading scholars agree on this point. As one pair of commentators succinctly puts it: "The originality requirement is *constitutionally mandated* for all works." Patterson & Joyce, *Monopolizing the Law: The Scope of Copyright Protection for Law Reports and Statutory Compilations*, 36 UCLA L. REV. 719, 763, n.155 (1989) (emphasis in original) (hereinafter Patterson & Joyce). *Accord, id.*, at 759–760, and n.140; NIMMER § 1.06[A] ("[O]riginality is a statutory as well as a constitutional requirement"); *id.*, § 1.08[C][1] ("[A] modicum of intellectual labor . . . clearly constitutes an essential constitutional element").

It is this bedrock principle of copyright that mandates the law's seemingly disparate treatment of facts and factual compilations. "No one may claim originality as to facts." *Id.*, § 2.11[A], p. 2-157. This is because facts do not owe their origin to an act of authorship. The distinction is one between creation and discovery: the first person to find and report a particular fact has not created the fact; he or she has merely discovered its existence. . . .

Factual compilations, on the other hand, may possess the requisite originality. The compilation author typically chooses which facts to include, in what order to place them, and how to arrange the collected data so that they may be used effectively by readers. These choices as to selection and arrangement, so long as they are made independently by the compiler and entail a minimal degree of creativity, are sufficiently original that Congress may protect such compilations through the copyright laws. NIMMER §§ 2.11[D], 3.03; Denicola 523, n.38. Thus, even a directory that contains absolutely no protectable written expression, only facts, meets the constitutional minimum for copyright protection if it features an original selection or arrangement. *See Harper & Row*, 471 U.S., at 547. Accord NIMMER § 3.03.

This protection is subject to an important limitation. The mere fact that a work is copyrighted does not mean that every element of the work may be protected. Originality remains the *sine qua non* of copyright; accordingly, copyright protection may extend only to those components of a work that are original to the author. . . .

This inevitably means that the copyright in a factual compilation is thin. Notwithstanding a valid copyright, a subsequent compiler remains free to use the facts contained in another's publication to aid in preparing a competing work, so long as the competing work does not feature the same selection and arrangement. As one commentator explains it: "[N]o matter how much original authorship the work displays, the facts and ideas it exposes are free for the taking. . . . [T]he very same facts and ideas may be divorced from the context imposed by the author, and restated or reshuffled by second comers, even if the author was the first to discover the facts or to propose the ideas." Ginsburg 186-8.

It may seem unfair that much of the fruit of the compiler's labor may be used by others without compensation. As Justice Brennan has correctly observed, however, this is not "some unforeseen byproduct of a statutory scheme." *Harper & Row*, 471 U.S., at 589 (dissenting opinion). It is, rather, "the essence of copyright," *ibid.*, and a constitutional requirement. The primary objective of copyright is not to reward the labor of authors, but "to promote the Progress of Science and useful Arts." Art. I, § 8, cl. 8. *Accord Twentieth Century Music Corp. v. Aiken*, 422 U.S. 151, 156 (1975). . . .

III

There is no doubt that Feist took from the white pages of Rural's directory a substantial amount of factual information. At a minimum, Feist copied the names, towns, and telephone numbers of 1,309 of Rural's subscribers. Not all copying, however, is copyright infringement. To establish infringement, two elements must be proven: (1) ownership of a valid copyright, and (2) copying of constituent elements of the work that are original. *See Harper & Row*, 471 U.S., at 548. The first element is not at issue here; Feist appears to concede that Rural's directory, considered as a whole, is subject to a valid copyright because it contains some foreword text, as well as original material in its yellow pages advertisements.

The question is whether Rural has proved the second element. In other words, did Feist, by taking 1,309 names, towns, and telephone numbers from Rural's white pages, copy anything that was "original" to Rural? Certainly, the raw data does not satisfy the originality requirement. Rural may have been the first to discover and report the names, towns, and telephone numbers of its subscribers, but this data does not "'owe its origin'" to Rural. *Burrow-Giles*, 111 U.S., at 58. Rather, these bits of information are uncopyrightable facts; they existed before Rural reported them and would have continued to exist if Rural had never published a telephone directory. The originality requirement "rules out protecting . . . names, addresses, and telephone numbers of which the plaintiff by no stretch of the imagination could be called the author." Patterson & Joyce 776. . . .

The question that remains is whether Rural selected, coordinated, or arranged these uncopyrightable facts in an original way. As mentioned, originality is not a stringent standard; it does not require that facts be presented in an innovative or surprising way. It is equally true, however, that the selection and arrangement of facts cannot be so mechanical or routine as to require no creativity whatsoever. The standard of originality is low, but it does exist. *See* Patterson & Joyce 760, n.144 ("While this requirement is sometimes characterized as modest, or a low threshold, it is not without effect"). As this Court has explained, the Constitution mandates some minimal degree of creativity, *see The Trade-Mark Cases*, 100 U.S., at 94; and an author who claims infringement must prove "the existence of . . . intellectual production, of thought, and conception." *Burrow-Giles, supra*, at 59–60.

The selection, coordination, and arrangement of Rural's white pages do not satisfy the minimum constitutional standards for copyright protection. As mentioned at the outset, Rural's white pages are entirely typical. Persons desiring telephone service in

Rural's service area fill out an application and Rural issues them a telephone number. In preparing its white pages, Rural simply takes the data provided by its subscribers and lists it alphabetically by surname. The end product is a garden-variety white pages directory, devoid of even the slightest trace of creativity.

Rural's selection of listings could not be more obvious: it publishes the most basic information—name, town, and telephone number—about each person who applies to it for telephone service. This is "selection" of a sort, but it lacks the modicum of creativity necessary to transform mere selection into copyrightable expression. Rural expended sufficient effort to make the white pages directory useful, but insufficient creativity to make it original.

We note in passing that the selection featured in Rural's white pages may also fail the originality requirement for another reason. Feist points out that Rural did not truly "select" to publish the names and telephone numbers of its subscribers; rather, it was required to do so by the Kansas Corporation Commission as part of its monopoly franchise. *See* 737 F. Supp., at 612. Accordingly, one could plausibly conclude that this selection was dictated by state law, not by Rural.

Nor can Rural claim originality in its coordination and arrangement of facts. The white pages do nothing more than list Rural's subscribers in alphabetical order. This arrangement may, technically speaking, owe its origin to Rural; no one disputes that Rural undertook the task of alphabetizing the names itself. But there is nothing remotely creative about arranging names alphabetically in a white pages directory. It is an age-old practice, firmly rooted in tradition and so commonplace that it has come to be expected as a matter of course. *See* Brief for Information Industry Association et al. as *Amici Curiae* 10 (alphabetical arrangement "is universally observed in directories published by local exchange telephone companies"). It is not only unoriginal, it is practically inevitable. This time-honored tradition does not possess the minimal creative spark required by the Copyright Act and the Constitution.

We conclude that the names, towns, and telephone numbers copied by Feist were not original to Rural and therefore were not protected by the copyright in Rural's combined white and yellow pages directory. . . .

COMMENTS AND QUESTIONS

1. *Originality Intent?* The Court's conclusion turns critically upon the premise that the framers of the Constitution—through their use of the word "authors" and "writings"—intended originality as the touchstone and the bedrock for copyright protection. Does this square with the scope of protection for the 1790 Act—books, *maps*, and *charts*—approved by many of the framers during the first Congress? *Cf. Burrow-Giles Lithographic Co. v. Sarony*, 111 U.S. 53, 56 (1884) (expressing doubt that the constitutional language makes creativity or artistic accomplishment a prerequisite to copyright protection); Jane Ginsburg, *Creation and Commercial Value: Copyright Protection of Works of Information*, 90 COLUM. L. REV. 1865, 1873–93 (1990). Are maps and charts valued for their accuracy (factual content), their creativity

(expressive content), or both? Why would the first Congress of a new nation bordering vast and largely unexplored territory seek to promote only "creative" rather than *accurate* maps and charts? Is the premise of the *Feist* decision—an originalist form of constitutional analysis—factually credible? Or is this a case of questionable history masquerading as post-hoc rationalization? On the other hand, if accuracy and not creativity is valued, is copyright the right vehicle?

2. *Is Anything Truly Original?* Drawing upon postmodern literary theory, some scholars question the very concept of originality as a romantic myth. *See* JAMES BOYLE, SHAMANS, SOFTWARE, AND SPLEENS: LAW AND THE CONSTRUCTION OF THE INFORMATION SOCIETY (1996); Peter Jaszi, *Toward a Theory of Copyright: The Metamorphoses of "Authorship,"* 41 DUKE L.J. 455 (1991); David Lange, *At Play in the Fields of the Word: Copyright and the Construction of Authorship in the Post-Literate Millennium*, 55 LAW & CONTEMP. PROBLEMS 139 (1992). From this perspective, nothing is truly original; all authorship derives from the work of those who came before. Do you consider this argument persuasive? Does this approach suggest that the goal of identifying and rewarding "originality" is misguided? If so, what sorts of works *should* we protect?

3. *Protectability of "Created" Facts.* Who is Fred Flintstone's spouse? Most people readily answer "Wilma." Wikipedia concurs:

> Wilma is the red-headed wife of caveman Fred Flintstone, daughter of Pearl Slaghoople, and mother of Pebbles Flintstone. Her best friend is her next door neighbor, Betty.

Wilma Flintstone, WIKIPEDIA, https://en.wikipedia.org/wiki/Wilma_Flintstone.

But is that a "fact"? It would seem to be, but according the *Feist* decision it is not: "facts do not owe their origin to an act of authorship." 499 U.S. at 347. Professor Justin Hughes questions this logic:

> *Feist* is wrong because many facts clearly owe their origin to discrete acts of human originality. These human-created facts function in the social discourse no differently than the temperature in downtown Chicago on a particular date or the frequency with which "Old Faithful" erupts in Yellowstone Park. Indeed, the facts most unimpeachably discovered—ice core depths in Antarctica, planets orbiting distant stars, new species of animals—are often less important to your daily life than many facts that are human-created—such as the credit rating that Equifax gives you or the valuation your insurer gives your car after an accident.

See Justin Hughes, *Created Facts and the Flawed Ontology of Copyright Law*, 83 NOTRE DAME L. REV. 43 (2007). What are the ramifications of this observation for copyright protection for the following categories of "created" facts?

- Physicians' Current Procedural Termination (CPT)—the American Medical Association's coding system for medication procedures. *See Practice Mgmt. Info. Corp. v. Am. Med. Ass'n*, 121 F.3d 516, 517 (9th Cir. 1997), *amended by* 133 F.3d 1140 (9th Cir. 1998) (holding federal agency's adoption of work as standard in preparation of Medicare and Medicaid claims did not render copyright invalid, but that the Association engaged in copyright misuse by licensing work to agency, which regulated submission of Medicare and Medicaid claims, in exchange for the agency's agreement not to use competing coding system).

- Jerry Seinfeld and Larry David created a complex and fickle ensemble of characters—Jerry, George, Elaine, Kramer, Newman, the Soup Nazi—based in part on real people, their relationships, and their experiences. To what extent are they and the incidents that the *Seinfeld* television series portrays protectable. *See Castle Rock Entertainment Inc. v. Carol Publishing Group*, 150 F.3d 132 (2d Cir. 1998) (holding "facts" about Seinfeld episodes copyrightable).

- Southco's nine-digit part numbering system for its line of mechanical fastener parts in which different digits denote functional characteristics of each product—e.g., installation type, thread size, recess type (Phillips or slotted), grip length, type of material, and knob finish. *See Southco, Inc. v. Kanebridge Corp.*, 390 F.3d 276 (3d Cir. 2004) (Alito, J.) (en banc) (holding part numbers used to identify and distinguish among types of screw fasteners not protectable).

- The Red Book, a well-known listing of regional car valuations reflecting the publisher's editors' projections of the values for the next six weeks of average versions of most of the used cars (up to seven years old) sold in that region. *See CCC Info. Servs., Inc. v. Maclean Hunter Mkt. Reports, Inc.*, 44 F.3d 61, 63 (2d Cir. 1994) (reversing district court decision finding the valuations to be unprotectable facts and holding that the Red Book numbers as well as the selection and arrangement of the Red Book to be protectable expression).

- A comprehensive weekly report of wholesale prices for collectible United States coins, used extensively by coin dealers. *See CDN Inc. v. Kapes*, 197 F.3d 1256 (9th Cir. 1999) (holding that a list of wholesale prices for rare coins listed by publisher contained sufficient originality to attract copyright protection).

Does the *Feist* definition of facts—as things that are "discovered" but not "created"—illuminate or complicate the analysis of these contexts? Are phone numbers discovered or created?

4. *Fictitious "Facts" and Copyright Estoppel.* Suppose that an author writes a manuscript that she holds out to the world as fact, even though the work is fictional. Should that author be able to prevent another from appropriating these fictitious "facts" in another work, such as a movie, on the basis of copyright infringement? The courts have developed a defense of copyright estoppel to bar such lawsuits: "equity and good morals will not permit one who asserts something as a fact which he insists his readers believe as the real foundation for its appeal to those who may buy and read the work, to change that position for profit in a law suit." *Oliver v. Saint Germain Foundation*, 41 F. Supp. 296 (S.D. Cal. 1941) (dismissing lawsuit by alleged copyright owner who averred that his manuscript had been dictated by a spirit from another planet); *Urantia Found. v. Maaherra*, 114 F.3d 955 (9th Cir. 1997) (concluding that copyright did not extend to words allegedly dictated by a deity, but human selection and arrangement of the

scripture could be copyrightable); *see also Hoehling v. Universal City Studios, Inc.*, 618 F.2d 972 (2d Cir. 1980).

5. *Historical Facts and Research.* It is clear that copyright law does not protect historical facts on the ground that such information is not original. Some courts have extended this doctrine to deny copyright protection for historical research. In *Miller v. Universal Studios*, 650 F.2d 1365 (5th Cir. 1981), an investigative reporter spent more than 2,500 hours researching a bizarre kidnapping and rescue in which the victim had been buried alive in an underground coffin for five days. The researcher and the victim published a book describing the events. After efforts to obtain movie rights for the book failed, Universal Studios proceeded to produce a film based largely upon the book. The Fifth Circuit held "the valuable distinction in copyright between facts and the expression of facts cannot be maintained if research is held to be copyrightable." 650 F.2d at 1365.

Should copyright deny protection for the discoveries of historians? Is this consistent with the incentive basis for copyright protection? What arguments can be made in defense of the doctrine? To what extent is the selection and arrangement of facts protectable under copyright? What about an original theory interpreting historical research? *See* Jane C. Ginsburg, *Sabotaging and Reconstructing History: A Comment on the Scope of Copyright Protection in Works of History After* Hoehling v. Universal Studios, 29 J. COPYRIGHT SOC'Y 647 (1982).

6. *Policy Analysis of Database Protection.* Putting aside the debatable historical analysis underlying the *Feist* decision, is the Court's determination sound from a larger policy perspective? *See* Jerome H. Reichman & Pamela Samuelson, *Intellectual Property Rights in Data?*, 50 VAND. L. REV. 51 (1997). Is there any room for protection of factual compilations after *Feist*? *See Experian Info. Solutions v. Nationwide Mktg. Servs.*, 893 F.3d 1176 (9th Cir. 2018) (holding that Experian could protect its database matching 250 million names to addresses, but only against "bodily appropriation" of the database; the defendant's database was only 80% of the size of plaintiff's database).

In the wake of *Feist*, owners of databases and other factual compilations have turned increasingly to contract law to protect their "sweat of the brow" investment. *See ProCD, Inc. v. Zeidenberg*, 86 F.3d 1447 (7th Cir. 1996). These cases allow database vendors to protect by contract what they cannot protect by copyright, so that someone who copies a database may be liable for breach of contract even if the database is composed entirely of unprotectable facts. (On this point, compare the discussion of protecting trade secrets by contract in Chapter II(F)(1)(ii).) As we will discuss in Chapter VI, these cases pose difficult questions relating to federal Copyright Act preemption of state contract law and the enforceability of shrinkwrap and click-wrap licensing agreements.

An alternative to contract protection is the development of a new intellectual property regime designed specifically to protect "sweatworks." Several scholars favor a separate statute to protect some "sweatworks." *See* Jane C. Ginsburg, *"No Sweat?" Copyright and Other Protection of Works of Information After* Feist v. Rural Telephone, 92 COLUM. L. REV. 338 (1992); Wendy J. Gordon, *On Owning Information: Intellectual Property and the Restitutionary Impulse*, 78 VA. L. REV. 149 (1992) (corrective justice approach justifies giving authors a right—albeit conditional and defeasible—to a reward for their efforts).

The European Community has adopted this approach. *See* Directive 96/9/EC of the European Parliament and of the Council of 11 March 1996 on the Legal Protection of Databases, 1996 O.J. (L77) 20. The EC *sui generis* regime does not protect data directly, but rather the efforts of those who make a "substantial investment" in compiling "collections of independent data . . . arranged in a systematic . . . and individually accessible" manner. Others are free to collect the same data themselves. Such protection expires after 15 years, although substantial changes to the database (such as updating) restart the clock. Some scholars worry that such protection will hinder the progress of science by causing unnecessary duplication of effort, raising the transaction and direct costs of scientific research, constraining fact checking, and complicating efforts to reformat and otherwise improve data collections. *See* Stephen M. Maurer, P. Bernt Hugenholtz & Harlan J. Onsrud, *Europe's Database Experiment*, 294 SCIENCE 789 (2001).

The Directive has been interpreted fairly narrowly, so that its impact may well be less significant than first feared. *See, e.g.*, *Fixtures Marketing*, Case C-46/02, [2004] ECR I-10365 (European Court of Justice, 2004) (investment in creation of soccer league schedule was irrelevant to issue of substantial investment in the database; all that matters is investment in presentation of data itself, which was minimal; so soccer league schedule not protected under the 1996 Database Directive); *Football Dataco v. Yahoo*, Case C-604/10 (European Court of Justice, 2012) (no protection for soccer league schedule under separate, independent copyright theory [as opposed to database protection]; not enough original authorship to make league schedule copyrightable). But evidence also suggests it did not spur new investment in databases in Europe. European Commission, *First evaluation of Directive 96/9/EC on the legal protection of databases* 5 (DG Internal Market and Services Working Paper, Brussels, 12 December 2005) ("Introduced to stimulate the production of databases in Europe, the new instrument has had no proven impact on the production of databases.").

Should Congress amend the Copyright Act to protect such "sweat of the brow" works? Is Congress constitutionally empowered to protect such works under the Intellectual Property Clause? Could such legislation be grounded on the Commerce Clause? Is it necessary, given the success of a number of database companies without direct protection in the decades following *Feist*?

7. *Photography.* During the early development of photography, great skill was required to capture even a basic portrait. The photographer paid special attention to lighting, composition, exposure, and printing. Today, even a monkey can take a selfie, although it does not qualify as an author under the Copyright Act and lacks standing to assert infringement. *See Naruto v. Slater*, 888 F.3d 418 (9th Cir. 2018). Yet Ansel Adams and Galen Rowell have captured some of the most beautiful images of nature. Do photographs clear the originality threshold? Why? *See* Rebecca Tushnet, *Worth a Thousand Words: The Images of Copyright*, 125 HARV. L. REV. 683 (2012); Justin Hughes, *The Photographer's Copyright—Photograph as Art, Photograph as Database*,

25 HARV. J.L. & TECH. 339 (2011–2012); Eva E. Subotnik, *Originality Proxies: Toward a Theory of Copyright and Creativity*, 76 BROOK. L. REV. 1487 (2011).

8. *Copyright Protection for Maps*. Recall that the first federal copyright statute expressly included maps and charts (e.g., nautical maps) within the scope of copyright protection. Under the present statute, copyright protection extends to maps under the definition of "pictorial, graphic and sculptural works." Can a map satisfy the originality requirement set forth in *Feist*? Isn't a map by its nature predominantly if not entirely driven by functional considerations (i.e., accurate representation of geographic information)?

In *Mason v. Montgomery Data, Inc.*, 967 F.2d 135 (5th Cir. 1992), a case decided after *Feist*, the court held that a series of real estate maps of a Texas county were eligible for copyright protection. The court found the maps original in two distinct respects: (1) Mason had exercised "sufficient creativity in [] the selection, coordination and arrangement of the facts that [the maps] depict"; and (2) the graphic artistry of the maps themselves was sufficiently original to qualify for protection. Are either of these elements truly original in the typical map? For example, what if the map includes every publicly accessible road? How many ways are there to accurately depict the United States and its 50 states? Should copyright depend on something as trivial as the colors chosen for each political subdivision? *Cf. Darden v. Peters*, 488 F.3d 277 (4th Cir. 2007) (upholding refusal of the Copyright Office to register standard census maps with the addition of color, shading, and labels using standard fonts and shapes as insufficiently original).

PROBLEMS

Problem IV-1. Central Bell, the local telephone utility, distributes both a "white pages" telephone book and a "yellow pages," which lists businesses that have chosen to advertise there. Bell's yellow pages are organized alphabetically by subject matter of the business and alphabetically within each subject. Bell itself created the subject headings with input from its advertisers. Bell also sells larger advertisements to certain companies for more money. Christopher Publications decides to create and distribute its own yellow pages directory to compete with Bell. Christopher does this by taking a copy of Bell's yellow pages and calling every business that advertises there and asking each if it would like to advertise in Christopher's publication. Christopher places the resulting ads in its own subject matter listings (which do overlap somewhat with Bell's). Many of the advertisements themselves (which are submitted by the advertisers) are identical to those in the Bell directory. Bell sues Christopher for copyright infringement. Who should prevail?

Problem IV-2. Harry Historian had always been curious about the cause of the Hindenburg disaster, the explosion of a German zeppelin in 1938. After carefully investigating records and news accounts of the disaster and interviewing witnesses, Harry concluded that the disaster was caused by a disgruntled crew member who sabotaged the dirigible so as to embarrass the Nazi regime. He then wrote a book developing his hypothesis. The book contained rich descriptions of the events leading up to the disaster, including detailed accounts of German beer hall revelry and the passionate patriotism of German nationals (as expressed in their enthusiastic singing of the German national anthem). Without obtaining the movie rights to Harry's book, Capitalistic Studios produced a movie of the disaster which featured a crewman-saboteur and many of the richly detailed scenes in Harry's book. Does Harry have a valid copyright infringement claim? Should he have such a claim?

Problem IV-3. Assume that West Publishing Company, which has published both official and unofficial reports of federal and state court decisions for over 100 years, and Mead Data Central are the only competitors in the market for computer legal research databases. Because cases (especially in the federal courts) are cited by West's volume and page number, Mead decides to copy West's pagination in its computer database. West sues, arguing that the arrangement of its cases in its reporters is copyrighted. Does West have a valid copyright?

Problem IV-4. The Bond News and Investor's World are both financial reporting services. Each provides to its subscribers a weekly update of all municipal bonds that have been "called" by the city, and several pieces of information about the bonds: the bond series, the call price, the date of the call, and the address and phone number of the calling agency. Bond obtains this information by having researchers cull through published notices in 250 newspapers nationwide each day. Bond, suspecting that Investor's is copying its data rather than conducting a similar search, plants false information in its updates. When Investor's publishes the same false information in its updates, Bond sues. Investor's admits copying the data but claims that it had a right to do so because the data were not copyrightable. Who should prevail?

Problem IV-5. In December 2010, the U.S. Postal Service issued a new stamp commemorating the Statue of Liberty. The press release announced "[t]he statue, located on Liberty Island in New York Harbor, was designed by French sculptor Frederic-Auguste Bartholdi."

Statue of Liberty
New York City

Statue of Liberty Replica
Las Vegas

In 1996, the New York-New York Hotel & Casino paid Robert Davidson $385,000 to sculpt the Las Vegas statue. Rather than replicate the New York Harbor Statue of Liberty precisely, he improvised a more contemporary female face. The eyes, eyelids and eyebrows on the replica appear more sharply defined than on the original statue. The lips on the replica are sultry and the hair is more modern.

Several months later, stamp collectors noticed that the image depicted on the stamp was based on a photograph not of the Statue of Liberty in New York Harbor, but rather a half-sized replica of the famous statue at the New York-New York Hotel & Casino on the Las Vegas strip. Upon learning of the U.S. Postal Service's mistake, Mr. Davidson, filed suit a copyright infringement suit against the U.S. Postal Service in the Court of Claims. Between 2010 and 2014, when the Statue of Liberty stamp was retired, the U.S. Postal Service sold more than 5 billion stamps for more than $2 billion, earning more than $70 million for the federal government.

Does Davidson have copyright protection for his sculpture?

2. Fixation in a Tangible Medium of Expression

17 U.S.C. § 101

A work is "fixed" in a tangible medium of expression when its embodiment in a copy or phonorecord, by or under the authority of the author, is sufficiently permanent or stable to permit it to be perceived, reproduced, or otherwise communicated for a period of more than transitory duration. A work consisting of sounds, images, or both, that are being transmitted, is "fixed" for purposes of this title if a fixation of the work is being made simultaneously with its transmission.

H.R. REP. NO. 94-1476
94th Cong., 2d Sess. 52–53 (1976)

As a basic condition of copyright protection, the bill [the Copyright Act of 1976] perpetuates the existing requirement that a work be fixed in a "tangible medium of expression," and adds that this medium may be one "now known or later developed," and that the fixation is sufficient if the work "can be perceived, reproduced, or otherwise communicated, either directly or with the aid of a machine or device." This broad language is intended to avoid the artificial and largely unjustifiable distinctions, derived from cases such as *White-Smith [Music] Publishing Co. v. Apollo Co.*, 209 U.S. 1 (1908), under which statutory copyrightability in certain cases has been made to depend upon the form or medium in which the work is fixed. Under the bill it makes no difference what the form, manner, or medium of fixation may be; whether it is in words, numbers, notes, sounds, pictures, or any other graphic or symbolic indicia; whether embodied in a physical object in written, printed, photographic, sculptural, punched, magnetic, or any other stable form; and whether it is capable of perception directly or by means of any machine or device "now known or later developed."

Under the bill, the concept of fixation is important since it not only determines whether the provisions of the statute apply to a work, but it also represents the dividing line between common law and statutory protection. As will be noted in more detail in connection with section 301, an unfixed work of authorship, such as an improvisation or an unrecorded choreographic work, performance, or broadcast, would continue to be subject to protection under State common law or statute, but would not be eligible for federal statutory protection under section 102.

The bill seeks to resolve, through the definition of "fixation" in section 101, the status of live broadcasts—sports, news coverage, live performances of music, etc.—that are reaching the public in unfixed form but that are simultaneously being recorded. When a football game is being covered by four television cameras, with a director guiding the activities of the four cameramen and choosing which of their electronic images are sent out to the public and in what order, there is little doubt that what the cameramen and the director are doing constitutes "authorship." The further question to be considered is whether there has been a fixation. If the images and sounds to be broadcast are first recorded (on a video tape, film, etc.) and then transmitted, the recorded work would be considered a "motion picture" subject to statutory protection against unauthorized reproduction or retransmission of the broadcast. If the program content is transmitted live to the public while being recorded at the same time, the case would be treated the same; the copyright owner would not be forced to rely on common law rather than statutory rights in proceeding against an infringing user of the live broadcast.

Thus, assuming it is copyrightable—as a "motion picture" or "sound recording," for example—the content of a live transmission should be accorded statutory protection if it is being recorded simultaneously with its transmission. On the other hand, the definition of "fixation" would exclude from the concept purely evanescent or transient reproductions such as those projected briefly on a screen, shown electronically on a television or other cathode ray tube, or captured momentarily in the "memory" of a computer.

Under the first sentence of the definition of "fixed" in section 101, a work would be considered "fixed in a tangible medium of expression" if there has been an authorized embodiment in a copy or phonorecord and if that embodiment "is sufficiently permanent or stable" to permit the work "to be perceived, reproduced, or otherwise communicated for a period of more than transitory duration." The second sentence makes clear that, in the case of "a work consisting of sounds, images, or both, that are being transmitted," the work is regarded as "fixed" if a fixation is being made at the same time as the transmission.

Under this definition "copies" and "phonorecords" together will comprise all of the material objects in which copyrightable works are capable of being fixed. The definitions of these terms in section 101, together with their usage in section 102 and throughout the bill, reflect a fundamental distinction between the "original work" which is the product of "authorship" and the multitude of material objects in which it can be embodied. Thus, in the sense of the bill, a "book" is not a work of authorship, but is a particular kind of "copy." Instead, the author may write a literary "work," which in turn can be embodied in a wide range of "copies" and "phonorecords," including books, periodicals, computer punch cards, microfilm, tape recordings, and so forth. It is possible to have an "original work of authorship" without having a "copy" or "phonorecord" embodying it, and it is also possible to have a "copy" or "phonorecord" embodying something that does not qualify as an "original work of authorship." The two essential elements—original work and tangible object—must merge through fixation in order to produce subject matter copyrightable under the statute.

COMMENTS AND QUESTIONS

1. The fixation requirement arises in two separate portions of the Copyright Act. First, it is a requirement for copyright protection. Section 102(a) of the Copyright Act provides that "[c]opyright protection subsists . . . in original works of authorship *fixed in any tangible medium of expression,* now known or later developed, from which they

can be perceived, reproduced, or otherwise communicated, either directly or with the aid of a machine or device" (emphasis added). Unless and until a work of authorship is so fixed, it does not qualify for copyright protection.

Fixation also plays a role in determining whether a defendant has infringed a copyright. Section 106(1) of the act provides that the copyright owner has the exclusive right to "reproduce the copyrighted work in copies or phonorecords." Section 101 of the act defines "copies" as "material objects . . . in which a work is *fixed*. . . ." (emphasis added). Thus, a defendant does not infringe the right to reproduce unless she has reproduced the copyrighted work in fixed form.

2. *Constitutional Mandate? Anti-Bootlegging Legislation.* As with the originality requirement, the Supreme Court has indicated that fixation is a constitutional requirement based on the Founders' use of the term "Writings" in art. I, § 8, cl. 8. *See Goldstein v. California*, 412 U.S. 546, 561 (1973) (interpreting "Writings" to mean "physical rendering[s]" of expression). The reach of this proposition as well as the interrelationship between the Intellectual Property Clause and the Commerce Clause was tested by the 1994 amendments to the Copyright Act, 17 U.S.C. § 1101 (civil) and § 2319A (criminal), allowing performers to sue and prosecutors to indict makers and distributors of bootleg recordings. Defendants in several cases asserted that this provision was unconstitutional on the ground that such performances were not "fixed." *See United States v. Martignon*, 492 F.3d 140 (2d Cir. 2007); *United States v. Moghadam*, 175 F.3d 1269 (11th Cir. 1999) (upholding anti-bootlegging statute under the Commerce Clause). The Second Circuit in *Martignon* determined that although the anti-bootlegging provisions could find no constitutional support under the Intellectual Property Clause, they could be validated under the Commerce Clause so long as they don't violate limits of the Intellectual Property Clause. Addressing only the criminal law provision—which was the only issue before it—the court determined that § 2319A merely authorizes the government to prosecute offenders and does not create rights, and therefore is not a copyright law. As a result, § 2319A was not enacted under the Intellectual Property Clause and therefore does not violate it. The implication, however, is that the civil provision may be unconstitutional. Note that the civil anti-bootlegging provision is also arguably infirm under the "Limited Times" clause of the Intellectual Property Clause since it contains no durational limit. *See* Chapter IV(D)(2).

3. *Policy Rationale(s) for a Fixation Requirement.* Why have a fixation requirement at all? One explanation for fixation lies in a view of copyright as intended to protect communication. *See* David G. Luettgen, *Functional Usefulness vs. Communicative Usefulness: Thin Copyright Protection for the Nonliteral Elements of Computer Programs*, 4 TEX. INTELL. PROP. L.J. 233 (1996). Certainly, the original copyright laws—and the Constitution—speak of authors and writings, which we associate with relatively direct communication between writer and audience. On this view, material that does not communicate (directly) to people is undeserving of copyright protection. Is there any necessary connection between whether a work is "fixed" and whether it communicates directly with an audience? Compare an extemporaneous public speech (unfixed, but communicative) with an individual's private diary (fixed, but private).

Another argument for the fixation requirement relates to the practical requirements of copyright litigation. Fixation helps in proving authorship. *See* Douglas Lichtman, *Copyright as a Rule of Evidence*, 52 DUKE L.J. 683, 716–35 (2003). If any expression could be copyrighted, the law might face a large number of frivolous infringement suits that would be virtually impossible to verify—along the lines of "I gave them the idea (or rather the expression of the idea) for that book!" Analogous rules exist in other areas of law. Consider the statute of frauds in contract law and the best evidence rule, requiring the use of original documents as evidence in trials so as to ensure authenticity. But these rules are subject to various exceptions. Couldn't the authenticity function of the fixation rule be accomplished by a heightened evidentiary requirement (e.g., corroborating evidence, eye- or earwitnesses, strong proof of access by the defendant) for unfixed works to be the basis for copyright infringement?

4. *Fixation in the Computer Context.* As noted above, a defendant does not infringe the right to reproduce unless she has fixed the work in a copy that persists for more than transitory duration. This issue takes on a technical dimension in computer cases. Does the act of loading a computer program in random access memory (RAM) constitute a copy? In *MAI v. Peak Computing*, 991 F.2d 511 (9th Cir. 1993), Peak performed maintenance on and repaired computers made by MAI. Peak needed to operate the computer and run MAI's copyrighted operating software to perform these functions. The Ninth Circuit found that because "the copy created in the RAM can be 'perceived, reproduced, or otherwise communicated,' [] the loading of software into the RAM creates a copy under the Copyright Act." But the court did not directly address the duration element. Distinguishing *MAI*, the Fourth Circuit held that electronic instantiations of data while in transit through an Internet service provider's routers were not fixed for more than transitory duration. *See CoStar Grp., Inc. v. LoopNet, Inc.*, 373 F.3d 544, 550–51 (4th Cir. 2004). Similarly, the Second Circuit in *Cartoon Network LP, LLLP v. CSC Holdings, Inc.*, 536 F.3d 121, 127–30 (2d Cir. 2008), held that data that resides in a buffer for no more than 1.2 seconds before being automatically overwritten is merely of transitory duration and hence does not constitute a "copy" for copyright purposes.

How long must information reside in computer memory before it is more than "merely transitory"? What if a computer is left on indefinitely?

5. *Natural Authorship and Fixation?* Chapman Kelley, a recognized landscape artist who designed and implemented two large elliptical wildflower plots in Chicago's Grant Park, brought an action against the park district under copyright law's moral rights provisions following its decision to substantially reduce and reconfigure his work. Under the moral rights provisions, which we explore in Chapter IV(E)(5), an artist of certain types of visual art has the right to prevent any distortion or modification of his work that would be "prejudicial to his . . . honor or reputation," and to recover for any such intentional distortion or modification undertaken without his consent. *See* 17 U.S.C. § 106A(a)(3)(A). In rejecting this claim, the Seventh Circuit concluded that

> [a] living garden like Wildflower Works is neither "authored" nor "fixed" in the senses required for copyright. . . .

Simply put, gardens are planted and cultivated, not authored. A garden's constituent elements are alive and inherently changeable, not fixed. Most of what we see and experience in a garden—the colors, shapes, textures, and scents of the plants—originates in nature, not in the mind of the gardener. At any given moment in time, a garden owes most of its form and appearance to natural forces, though the gardener who plants and tends it obviously assists. All this is true of Wildflower Works, even though it was designed and planted by an artist.

Of course, a human "author"—whether an artist, a professional landscape designer, or an amateur backyard gardener—determines the initial arrangement of the plants in a garden. This is not the kind of authorship required for copyright. To the extent that seeds or seedlings can be considered a "medium of expression," they originate in nature, and natural forces—not the intellect of the gardener—determine their form, growth, and appearance. Moreover, a garden is simply too changeable to satisfy the primary purpose of fixation; its appearance is too inherently variable to supply a baseline for determining questions of copyright creation and infringement. If a garden can qualify as a "work of authorship" sufficiently "embodied in a copy," at what point has fixation occurred? When the garden is newly planted? When its first blossoms appear? When it is in full bloom? How—and at what point in time—is a court to determine whether infringing copying has occurred?

In contrast, when a landscape designer conceives of a plan for a garden and puts it in writing—records it in text, diagrams, or drawings on paper or on a digital-storage device—we can say that his intangible intellectual property has been embodied in a fixed and tangible "copy." This writing is a sufficiently permanent and stable copy of the designer's intellectual expression and is vulnerable to infringing copying, giving rise to the designer's right to claim copyright. The same cannot be said of a garden, which is not a fixed copy of the gardener's intellectual property. Although the planting material is tangible and can be perceived for more than a transitory duration, it is not stable or permanent enough to be called "fixed." Seeds and plants in a garden are naturally in a state of perpetual change; they germinate, grow, bloom, become dormant, and eventually die. This life cycle moves gradually, over days, weeks, and season to season, but the real barrier to copyright here is not temporal but essential. The essence of a garden is its vitality, not its fixedness. It may endure from season to season, but its nature is one of dynamic change.

Kelley v. Chicago Park Dist., 635 F.3d 290, 304–05 (7th Cir. 2011). Landscape architects might disagree. Seeds and plants produce relatively predictable colors and shapes. Is the court's logic overly formalistic? Since this case arose in the context of moral rights and involved the alteration of a wildflower garden that had not been maintained, does it provide a strong foundation for evaluating a more conventional garden in a copyright infringement case?

6. *Fixation and Stand-Up Comedy.* "One day Milton Berle and Henny Youngman were listening to Joey Bishop tell a particularly funny gag. 'Gee, I wish I said that,' Berle whispered. 'Don't worry, Milton, [said Henny,] you will.'" MELVIN HELITZER, COMEDY WRITING SECRETS 4 (1987). Does stand-up comedy qualify for copyright protection? What would a comedian need to do to qualify? Is that a realistic solution to the problem of joke stealing? *See* Dotan Oliar & Christopher Sprigman, *There's No Free Laugh (Anymore): The Emergence of Intellectual Property Norms and the Transformation of Stand-Up Comedy*, 94 VA. L. REV. 1787 (2008) (suggesting that although formal legal protection for comedy routines may be weak, informal enforcement mechanisms (gossip, ostracism) and social norms may serve as a relatively effective substitute).

7. *State Law Protection for Unfixed Works.* Even when the fixation requirement bars federal copyright protection, common law protection may still be available. *See*, e.g., *Estate of Hemingway v. Random House*, 244 N.E.2d 250 (N.Y. 1968). The Copyright Act's preemption provision expressly retains state laws that protect unfixed expression. 17 U.S.C. § 301(b)(1).

PROBLEM

Problem IV-6. Comedy writer Alex Kaseberg posted the following joke on his website: "Tom Brady said he wants to give his M.V.P. truck to the man who won the game for the Patriots. So enjoy that truck, Pete Carroll." The next night, O'Brien opened his monologue by quipping: "Tom Brady said he wants to give the truck he was given as the Super Bowl M.V.P. to the guy who won the Super Bowl for the Patriots. So Brady is giving his truck to Seahawks Coach Pete Carroll."

Kaseberg sues O'Brien for copyright infringement. Does he have a valid copyright? What if instead of posting these jokes on his website, he had simply uttered them in a stand-up club? Would it matter whether Kaseberg scripts (i.e., writes out) his stand-up jokes?

---

3. Formalities

Copyright "formalities" are procedural requirements imposed on authors by the government that are necessary to obtain copyright protection but do not relate to the substance of the copyright. The United States has traditionally had four such formal requirements: (a) notice of copyright; (b) publication of the work; (c) registration of the work with the Copyright Office; and (d) deposit of a copy of the work with the Library of Congress. Over the past century, U.S. law has progressed from a regime in which failure to adhere to certain technical requirements resulted in forfeiture of copyright protection to the current regime in which formalities are largely voluntary and failure to comply does not risk forfeiture. The principal reason for this transformation was the decision by the United States to join the Berne Convention, which provides that copyright shall "not be subject to any formality." Nonetheless, copyright formalities have continuing relevance to the practice of copyright law, particularly for works created prior to January 1, 1978, the effective date of the 1976 Act.

i. Notice

U.S. copyright law has experienced three decreasingly restrictive notice regimes since the early part of the twentieth century:

1909 Act. Federal copyright law protected only those works that contained the following information in the appropriate form and location: the year of first publication; the word "Copyright," the abbreviation "Copr." or the symbol ©; and the name of the copyright holder.[3] 17 U.S.C. §§ 19, 20. Failure to satisfy the precise technical requirements of the 1909 Act, such as placing notice on the "title page or the page immediately following" of books or other printed publications, typically resulted in forfeiture of copyright protection and the work's falling into the public domain. Section 21 of the 1909 Act excused omissions due to "accident or mistake," although this provision has been interpreted narrowly.

1976 Act/Pre-Ratification of Berne Convention (January 1, 1978–March 1, 1989). The 1976 Act provided that copyright protection begins upon the creation of a work, not upon publication. Congress maintained a notice requirement, although it liberalized the rules governing form and location of notice, *see* §§ 401–03,[4] and it took much of the harshness out of the requirement, *see* §§ 405–06. Failure to give notice on a small number of copies would not result in forfeiture; nor would even large-scale omissions, so long as they were inadvertent and the copyright holder registered the work within five years after publication and made reasonable efforts to give notice after the omission was discovered.

Post-Ratification of the Berne Convention (since March 1, 1989). The Berne Convention Implementation Act, Pub. L. No. 100-568, 102 Stat. 2853 (1988), eliminated the notice requirement of U.S. copyright law prospectively. Thus, both the 1909 Act and 1976 Act (pre-Berne) regimes still apply to works publicly distributed without proper notice prior to March 1, 1989. Congress, however, *encouraged* voluntary notice by precluding alleged infringers from asserting "innocent infringement" (in mitigation of actual or statutory damages) unless the copies to which she had access lacked proper notice. § 401(d).

ii. Publication

a. 1909 Act

---

[3] Unpublished works were protectable at common law prior to the 1976 Act.

[4] The Copyright Office has issued regulations to accommodate different works by requiring only "reasonable" placement of the notice. In some cases, this may be on packaging, particularly where the user would not encounter the notice on the actual work (e.g., computer software object code) or where affixing the notice to the actual work would interfere with the work (e.g., sound recordings, some forms of visual art).

Federal copyright protection under the 1909 Act was triggered by the act of publishing a work. Unpublished works could be protected under state common law, or "constructively" published by registration with the Copyright Office. Despite the importance of "publication" to federal copyright protection, the 1909 Act did not specifically define the term. This gap spawned a rich and complex jurisprudence defining publication. Because of the grave consequences of publishing a work without proper notice—forfeiture of copyright protection—the courts developed a distinction between *divestive* publication, resulting in forfeiture (divestiture) of common law copyright protection, and *investive* publication, resulting in forfeiture of federal copyright protection if notice is inadequate. In a leading case, the Second Circuit observed that

> . . . courts apply different tests of publication depending on whether plaintiff is claiming protection because he did not publish and hence has a common law claim of infringement—in which case the distribution must be quite large to constitute "publication"—or whether he is claiming under the copyright statute—in which case the requirements for publication are quite narrow. In each case the courts appear so to treat the concept of "publication" as to prevent piracy.

American Visuals Corp. v. Holland, 239 F.2d 740, 744 (2d Cir. 1956). Thus, the extent of distribution required to divest common law copyright protection is substantially greater than that required to invest, i.e., require notice for, a federal copyrighted work. In *White v. Kimmell*, 193 F.2d 744, 746–47 (9th Cir. 1952), *cert. denied,* 343 U.S. 957 (1952), the court distinguished between "limited publication" whereby a distribution of copies to "a definitely selected group and for a limited purpose, and without the right of diffusion, reproduction, distribution or sale" did not constitute a publication for purposes of the 1909 Act, and "general publication," which operated to divest common law protection. In addition, courts generally found that public performance or display of a work did not constitute publication unless tangible copies of the work were distributed to the public. *See Ferris v. Frohman*, 223 U.S. 424 (1912) (applying pre-1909 Act law); *McCarthy v. White*, 259 F. 364 (S.D.N.Y. 1919) (public performance of musical work); *Estate of Martin Luther King, Jr., Inc. v. CBS, Inc.*, 194 F.3d 1211 (11th Cir. 1999) (holding that King's delivery of his renowned "I Have a Dream" speech in August 1963 to a large audience, along with the fact that sponsors of the event obtained live broadcasts on radio and television and extensive contemporary coverage of event in the news media, did not alone amount to general publication of the speech for copyright purposes and hence did not divest King of common law copyright protection for the speech); *King v. Mister Maestro, Inc.*, 224 F. Supp. 101 (S.D.N.Y. 1963) (same). Furthermore, courts determined that unauthorized distribution did not constitute publication. In these ways, courts alleviated some of the harsh effects of failure to adhere to the notice requirements.

Is a television broadcast a "publication" within the meaning of the 1909 Act? Does it matter whether permanent copies are made at the time of the broadcast?

b.   *1976 Act/Pre-Ratification of Berne Convention*

Under the 1976 Act, effective January 1, 1978–March 1, 1989, federal copyright protection is triggered by the act of creating a work fixed in a tangible medium of expression, and common law copyright is preempted. Hence publication no longer served to distinguish between statutory and common law copyright. Nonetheless, publication still served to determine when notice was required.

The 1976 Act clarified the copyright law by defining "publication" as

. . . the distribution of copies or phonorecords of a work to the public by sale or other transfer of ownership, or by rental, lease, or lending. The offering to distribute copies or phonorecords to a group of persons for purposes of further distribution, public performance, or public display, constitutes publication. A public performance or display of a work does not of itself constitute publication.

17 U.S.C. § 101. This definition largely codified the principal considerations that evolved through judicial interpretation of the 1909 Act. *See* H.R. REP. NO. 1476, 94th Cong., 2d Sess., 138 (1976). Publication turns on physical transfer of copies to the public generally without disclosure restrictions or to a narrower group for purposes of distribution or dissemination. The 1976 Act definition of publication expressly excludes public performance or display.

c.   *Post-Ratification of the Berne Convention*

With the elimination of a mandatory notice requirement, the act of publication is no longer a factor in determining the validity of works created after March 1, 1989. Nonetheless, publication still has relevance for works created after March 1, 1989 in the following respects:

- *Deposit.* Deposit at the Library of Congress is mandatory only for published works. § 407.
- *Works of Foreign Authors.* Whereas all unpublished works are protected regardless of nationality or domicile of the author, *published* works of foreign authors are protected only under the conditions described in § 104(b).
- *Duration of Copyright Protection.* The term of protection for entity owners and works for hire is 95 years from the year of first publication and 120 years from creation for unpublished works. § 302(c); *see also* § 302(d), (e).
- *Reproduction Rights of Libraries* depend on whether the work has been published. *See* § 108(b), (c).
- *Termination of Transfers. See* §203(a)(3).
- *Certain Performance Rights. See* §§ 110(9), 118(b), (d).
- *Establishing Prima Facie Evidence of Validity of Copyright.* Registration of copyright must occur within five years of first publication. § 410(c).

- *Damages.* Statutory damages and attorney's fees are available for published works only if registration preceded the infringement or if the work was registered within three months after publication. § 412.

PROBLEM

Problem IV-7. Which of the following acts constitute publication under the 1909 Act? the 1976 Act?

a. Penelope Poet brings copies of her latest three poems to the monthly meeting of the Philadelphia Aspiring Poets Society. She distributes copies to the eight people in attendance that month prior to reading the poems.

b. Professor Edgar Edifice assembles a course reader consisting of public domain materials and excerpts he wrote himself. Students in his Advanced Copyright Theory seminar purchase the reader for the cost of reproduction from the school's reprographics service.

c. Arnold Author recently completed a draft of his first novel. He sends a copy to his agent, whom he authorizes to distribute copies to publishing houses for consideration.

---

iii. Registration

Registration of a copyrighted work with the Copyright Office has been "voluntary" since the 1909 Act. Also unlike the notice requirement, the registration requirement remains in effect today with regard to works of U.S. origin, notwithstanding United States' adherence to the Berne Convention.[5]

a. 1909 Act

The term of a copyright for a 1909 Act work initially ran for 28 years, with the author having the right to renew the copyright for an additional 28 years. The Act did not require registration in order to obtain a copyright (publication with proper notice triggered protection), but it did require registration by the 28th year in order to renew the copyright.[6] Furthermore, registration of the work was a prerequisite to bringing an infringement action.

---

[5] As we will see in the international copyright law section, *see* Chapter IV(I), the Berne Convention does not mandate that nations jettison formalities entirely, only that they may not impose formalities as a prerequisite for copyright protection with respect to works of foreign origin. Nations remain free to discriminate against works of domestic origin.

[6] Pursuant to the Copyright Renewal Act of 1992, Congress made renewal automatic. Therefore, works published with proper notice after January 1, 1964 (1992 – 28 = 1964) receive the full duration available under the statute regardless of whether copyright was renewed. Nonetheless, Congress encouraged renewal registration by offering several benefits, such as automatic vesting, reversion rights in derivative works (§ 304(a)(4)(A), *see* Chapter IV(D(3)(iii) (discussion of *Abend*-rights)), evidentiary weight (renewal registration constitutes *prima facie* evidence of the facts asserted in the renewal certificate), and enhanced remedies.

b.   1976 Act/Pre-Ratification of Berne Convention

By shifting to a unitary term, the 1976 Act abolished renewal for works created after January 1, 1978, making copyright registration entirely optional for the maintenance of copyright protection. Duration of copyright protection no longer depends on registration. Nonetheless, Congress retained the registration system and encouraged its use through various incentives. First, successful registration constitutes *prima facie* evidence of the validity of the copyright. § 410. Second, a copyright holder must register the copyright before bringing an infringement action, § 411, so in practice an unregistered copyright is only a potential right rather than an actual right.[7] Finally, there is also a powerful incentive for *early* registration: a copyright holder can obtain statutory damages and attorneys' fees only for infringements that occurred after registration (or which occurred after publication if the work was registered within three months after publication).

Registration fees can add up, *see* https://www.copyright.gov/about/fees.html. although they pale in comparison to the cost of patents or trademarks. The basic fee for electronically registering a work is $45 for a single author, single work that was not done for hire; and $65 for other electronic filings. A paper filing costs $125. Fees vary for registration of databases, serials, unpublished works, and other types of works.

c.   Post-Ratification of the Berne Convention

To comply with the Berne Convention, Congress amended section 411 to eliminate the requirement that a copyright owner whose country of origin[8] is another Berne member nation must register his or her works prior to instituting suits. However, Congress retained the requirement of registration prior to suit for domestic works and works originating in non-Berne nations.

d.   Registration Must Be Made Prior to Filing Suit

Section 411(a) states that "no civil action for infringement of the copyright in any United States work shall be instituted until . . . registration of the copyright claim has been made in accordance with this title." The Supreme Court held in *Fourth Estate Public Benefit Corp. v. Wall-Street.com, LLC*, 139 S.Ct. 881 (2019), that "registration is akin to an administrative exhaustion requirement that the owner must satisfy before suing to enforce ownership rights." The Copyright Office takes approximately six months to process registration applications, which can delay the initiation of litigation. Applicants can, however, expedite registration to one week by paying a higher fee to obtain special handling. In addition, the Copyright Act provides for preregistration of classes of unpublished works that are prone to prerelease infringement (motion pictures,

---

[7] Interestingly, a copyright holder need only *file* for registration of copyright and obtain a response before bringing suit. The putative copyright owner is entitled to bring suit even if the Copyright Office rejects the registration application. *See* § 411(a).

[8] A work's country of origin is the country in which it was first published, or in the case of unpublished works, the country in which it was created.

sound recordings, musical compositions, literary works, computer programs, and advertising photographs). *See* Artists' Rights and Theft Prevention Act of 2005, Pub. L. No. 109-9, 119 Stat. 218 (Title I), codified at § 408(f).

iv. Deposit

Section 407 of the Copyright Act requires deposit of two copies of each work published in the United States[9] for which copyright is claimed within three months after publication. (Certain categories of works are exempted from the requirement.) The purpose of this requirement is to enhance the collection of the Library of Congress. Under the 1909 Act, the Register of Copyrights could demand compliance with this deposit requirement and failure to comply could result in forfeiture of the copyright. Under the 1976 Act, however, the Library deposit requirement—while still mandatory—does not affect the validity of a copyright or the author's right to bring suit. § 407. Failure to comply gives rise to a fine and stands in the way of completion of the registration process, which bars copyright enforcement actions. *See Geoscan, Inc. of Tex. v. Geotrace Techs., Inc.*, 226 F.3d 387 (5th Cir. 2000) (barring suit because the deposit was not a complete copy of the original source code as of the time that the lawsuit was filed).[10]

A separate deposit with the Copyright Office is also required for copyright registration by § 408. However, this requirement may generally be satisfied by § 407's Library deposit. Unlike the Library of Congress deposit requirement, failure to comply with the § 408 deposit requirement results in a refusal to register the copyright. The purpose behind registration deposit under § 408 is to enable the Copyright Office to know what it is registering. The § 407 Library of Congress deposit requirement promotes progress by making knowledge accessible.

4. Restoration of Foreign Copyrighted Works

The Berne Convention Implementation Act of 1988 brought U.S. copyright law formalities into compliance with the Berne Convention's minimum criteria on a prospective basis, but did not address the retrospective problem—that a number of foreign works that received copyright protection in their home country (and elsewhere in the world) entered the public domain in the United States because their authors failed to comply with then-applicable notice requirements of U.S. law. This problem was of more than technical or theoretical interest. Among the foreign works that were still under copyright protection in much of the rest of the world but in the public domain in the United States were many of the works of J.R.R. Tolkien, including *The Hobbit* and

---

[9] The provision limiting the Library deposit requirement to works published in the United States was added by the Berne implementing legislation in 1988.

[10] In amending the 1976 Act to adhere to the Berne Convention, Congress concluded that retention of the deposit requirement was not inconsistent with the Berne Convention because failure to comply with the deposit requirement did not result in forfeiture of any copyright protection. H.R. REP. No. 609, 100th Cong., 2d Sess. 44 (1988).

The Fellowship of the Ring. These works have been freely copyable in the United States but still received copyright protection elsewhere in the world.

Article 18 of the Berne Convention requires that new members protect all works of other member nations whose copyrights had not yet expired in their countries of origin. The United States complied with this provision in 1993 (with regard to works from Canada and Mexico as part of the North American Free Trade Agreement Act (NAFTA)) and in 1994 (with regard to all other Berne Convention nations as part of the Agreement on Trade-Related Aspects of Intellectual Property Rights (TRIPs) as part of the General Agreement on Tariffs and Trade (GATT) Uruguay Round). To comply with TRIPs, Congress added § 104A to the Copyright Act, restoring copyright protection for foreign works[11] from Berne Convention nations that had lost protection in the United States "due to noncompliance with formalities imposed. . . by United States copyright law." *See Dam Things from Den., a/k/a Troll Co. ApS v. Russ Berrie & Co., Inc.*, 290 F.3d 548 (3d Cir. 2002). In effect, these works are retrieved from the public domain in the United States and are treated in the same way as any other copyrighted works for purposes of duration, ownership, and so on. Under this law, copyrights in *The Hobbit*, *The Fellowship of the Ring*, and various other works of J.R.R. Tolkien were restored in the United States in 1996. *See* Library of Congress, Copyright Office, Copyright Restoration of Works in Accordance With the Uruguay Round Agreements Act, 61 Fed. Reg. 46,133 (Aug. 30, 1996).

Copyright restoration presents a number of potential problems and efforts to deal with them have made § 104A a complex provision. Copyright protection in restored works is not retroactive. However, the copyright owner does have the right to "cut off" future uses of the work after a limited grace period by giving the Copyright Office notice of her intention to enforce the copyright. More complex problems are presented by those who have created "derivative works" in reliance on the U.S. public domain status of a work of foreign origin. Should such authors be prevented from exploiting their creations following restoration of the underlying work's copyright? The Act provides that the authors of such derivative works may continue to exploit them, provided they pay "reasonable compensation" to the original copyright owner. *See* § 104A(d)(3)(B).

Does restoring copyright in works already in the public domain "promote the progress of science and the useful arts"? How? What additional incentive does such a right give to current authors? If it does not confer such an additional incentive, is it constitutional? Does copyright restoration violate First Amendment interests in the continued exploitation of public domain works? The Supreme Court rejected these lines of argument in *Golan v. Holder*, 565 U.S. 302 (2012), holding that the Intellectual Property Clause does not bar Congress from extending copyright protection to works that are already in the public domain. The Court reasoned that nothing in the text or history of the Copyright Clause confines the "Progress of Science" exclusively to "incentives for creation." The decision pointed to historical evidence, Congressional

---

[11] This provision excludes works of foreign authors that were first published in the United States without proper notice.

practice, and prior Supreme Court decisions suggesting that inducing the dissemination of existing works is an appropriate means to promote science. The Court also rejected the First Amendment argument on the ground that traditional limitations on copyright protection—such as the idea/expression dichotomy and fair use—serve as "built-in First Amendment accommodations."

C.   COPYRIGHTABLE SUBJECT MATTER

1.   The Domain and Scope of Copyright Protection

§ 102. Subject Matter of Copyright: In General

(a) Copyright protection subsists, in accordance with this title, in original works of authorship fixed in any tangible medium of expression, now known or later developed, from which they can be perceived, reproduced, or otherwise communicated, either directly or with the aid of a machine or device. Works of authorship include the following categories:

(1) literary works;

(2) musical works, including any accompanying words;

(3) dramatic works, including any accompanying music;

(4) pantomimes and choreographic works;

(5) pictorial, graphic, and sculptural works;

(6) motion pictures and other audiovisual works;

(7) sound recordings; and

(8) architectural works.[12]

H.R. REP. NO. 94-1476
94th Cong., 2d Sess. (1976)

The second sentence of section 102 lists [eight] broad categories which the concept of "works of authorship" is said to "include." The use of "include," as defined in section 101, makes clear that the listing is "illustrative and not limitative," and that the [eight] categories do not necessarily exhaust the scope of "original works of authorship" that the bill is intended to protect. Rather, the list sets out the general area of copyrightable subject matter, but with sufficient flexibility to free the courts from rigid and outmoded concepts of the scope of particular categories. The items are also overlapping in the sense that a work falling within one class may encompass works coming within some or all of the other categories. . . .

---

[12] The category of "architectural works" was added to section 102(a) by the Architectural Works Copyright Protection Act of 1990.

i. *Literary Works*

Section 101 of the Copyright Act defines "literary works" as "works, other than audiovisual works, expressed in words, numbers, or other verbal or numerical symbols or indicia, regardless of the nature of the material objects, such as books, periodicals, manuscripts, phonorecords, films, tapes, disks, or cards, in which they are embodied."

The legislative history notes that "[t]he term 'literary works' does not connote any criterion of literary merit or qualitative value: it includes catalogs, directories, and similar factual reference, or instructional works and compilations of data. It also includes computer databases, and computer programs to the extent that they incorporate authorship in the programmer's expression of original ideas, as distinguished from the ideas themselves." Copyright Law Revision, H.R. REP. NO. 94-1476, 94th Cong., 2d Sess. (1976). Although the domain of literary works is quite broad and the originality threshold for protection is low, the Copyright Office regulations state that "words and short phrases such as names, titles, and slogans" are not subject to copyright. 37 C.F.R. § 202.1.[13]

The scope of copyright protection for literary works extends not only to the literal text but also to non-literal elements of a work such as its structure, sequence, and organization. Thus, a second comer may not circumvent copyright law merely by paraphrasing an original text. As Judge Learned Hand has explained, were the rule otherwise, a "plagiarist would escape liability by immaterial variations" of the copyrighted work. *Nichols v. Universal Pictures*, 45 F.2d 119, 121 (2d Cir. 1930).

While the words of a story and other expressive elements of its text are clearly protectable, courts have struggled to delineate the scope of protection for other elements of literary works such as fictional characters. As we saw earlier, the scope of copyright protection is limited to expressive content and does not extend to the underlying ideas. To what extent, therefore, should an original literary description of a fictional character, such as James Bond or Superman, limit other authors' use of characters featuring similar attributes? In *Nichols*, Judge Learned Hand provided the following standard for determining the scope of protection for fictional characters:

> [W]e do not doubt that two plays may correspond in plot closely enough for infringement. How far that correspondence must go is another matter. Nor need we hold that the same may not be true as to the characters, quite independently of the "plot" proper, though, as far as we know, such a case has never arisen. If *Twelfth Night* were copyrighted, it is quite possible that a second comer might so closely imitate Sir Toby Belch or Malvolio as to infringe, but it would not be enough that for one of his characters he cast a riotous knight who kept wassail to the discomfort of the household, or a vain and foppish steward who became amorous of his mistress. These would be no more than Shakespeare's "ideas" in the play, as little capable of monopoly as Einstein's Doctrine of Relativity, or Darwin's theory of the Origin of Species. It follows

---

[13] Titles, names of characters, and phrases may, however, be protectable under trademark or unfair competition law. *See* Chapter 5.

that the less developed the characters, the less they can be copyrighted; that is the penalty an author must bear for marking them too indistinctly.

ii.   *Pictorial, Graphic, and Sculptural Works*

Section 101 of the Copyright Act defines "[p]ictorial, graphic, and sculptural [PGS] works" to include "two-dimensional and three-dimensional works of fine, graphic, and applied art, photographs, prints and art reproductions, maps, globes, charts, diagrams, models, and technical drawings, including architectural plans. . . ." As with literary works, courts are not authorized to judge the artistic merit of the work in deciding whether PGS works ought to qualify for copyright protection other than to determine that the threshold of original expression has been attained.

The most significant limitation placed on PGS works is the utilitarian function exception discussed below. Such works are not protectable to the extent that they have a utilitarian rather than artistic function. Thus, the useful article doctrine poses a significant limitation on the scope of protection for sculptural works.

As with literary works, the scope of protection for PGS works depends on the degree to which the author has delineated the subjects of the work. In some cases, particularly photographs, drawings and maps, the limited range of expressive choices necessarily limits the scope of protection afforded by copyright law.

PROBLEM

Problem IV-8. The New York Arrows, a professional soccer team, hired Sports Images, an advertising firm, to develop a logo to advertise the team. Sports Images developed the accompanying logo.

After a dispute with the team about fees, Sports Images submitted an application to the Copyright Office to register the work. Is the work copyrightable?

---

iii.   *Architectural Works*

Under the 1976 Act, architectural plans in the United States were protected as a species of PGS works. The protection afforded architectural works—actual structures— was therefore limited by the useful article doctrine and the idea/expression dichotomy.

As provided in the definition of PGS works in § 101, "the design of a useful article, as defined in this section, shall be considered a pictorial, graphic, or sculptural work only if, and only to the extent that, such design incorporates pictorial, graphic, or sculptural features that can be identified separately from, and are capable of existing independently of, the utilitarian aspects of the article." Hence architectural structures, as opposed to the drawings for them, had little if any protection under copyright law. *See Demetriades v. Kaufmann*, 690 F. Supp. 658 (S.D.N.Y. 1988) (holding that traced architectural plans infringed the originals, but that the construction of an identical building would not violate a copyright in architectural plans under the principles of *Baker v. Selden*).

In order to bring the United States into compliance with Article 2(1) of the Berne Convention, Congress passed the Architectural Works Copyright Protection Act of 1990. The Act specifically protects "the design of a building as embodied in any tangible medium of expression, including a building, architectural plans, or drawings. The work includes the overall form and elements in the design, but does not include individual standard features." § 101. The House Report states:

> By creating a new category of protectable subject matter in new section 102(a)(8), and therefore, by deliberately not encompassing architectural works as pictorial, graphic, or sculptural works in existing section 102(a)(5), the copyrightability of architectural works shall not be evaluated under the separability test applicable to pictorial, graphic, or sculptural works embodied in useful articles. There is considerable scholarly and judicial disagreement over how to apply the separability test, and the principal reason for not treating architectural works as pictorial, graphic, or sculptural works is to avoid entangling architectural works in this disagreement.

> The Committee does not suggest, though, that in evaluating the copyrightability or scope of protection for architectural works, the Copyright Office or the courts should ignore functionality. A two-step analysis is envisioned. First, an architectural work should be examined to determine whether there are original design elements present, including overall shape and interior architecture. If such design elements are present, a second step is reached to examine whether the design elements are functionally required. If the design elements are not functionally required, the work is protectable without regard to physical or conceptual separability. As a consequence, contrary to the Committee's report accompanying the 1976 Copyright Act with respect to industrial products, the aesthetically pleasing overall shape of an architectural work would be protected under this bill.

H.R. REP. NO. 101-735, 101st Cong., 2d Sess. 20-21 (1990).

The effective date for the Architectural Works Copyright Protection Act of 1990 is December 1, 1990, and it does not apply retroactively. Therefore, architectural works produced before that time are governed by the standard for PGS works. In addition, the protection of § 102(a)(8) is subject to two important limitations set forth in § 120:

(a) **Pictorial representations permitted.**—The copyright in an architectural work that has been constructed does not include the right to prevent the making, distributing, or public display of pictures, paintings, photographs, or other pictorial representations of the work, if the building in which the work is embodied is located in or ordinarily visible from a public place.

(b) **Alterations to and destruction of buildings.**—Notwithstanding the provisions of § 106(2), the owners of a building embodying an architectural work may, without the consent of the author or copyright owner of the architectural work, make or authorize the making of alterations to such building, and destroy or authorize the destruction of such building.

COMMENTS AND QUESTIONS

1. Is the distinction that Congress seeks to make between the conceptual separability analysis required for pictorial, graphic, and sculptural works and the two-step functionality limitation for architectural works coherent? In what circumstances do they produce different outcomes? What aspects of a house design are protectable?

2. *Distinguishing Architectural Works and Sculptural Structures.* The artist who designed the streetwall and courtyard space for a building in downtown Los Angeles sued the producers of the film *Batman Forever,* which featured this structure in the film (the building was the Second Bank of Gotham), for infringing the artist's copyright in its "sculptural work." The Ninth Circuit held that the work more properly constituted part of a larger architectural work comprising the building towers and hence could be photographed without authorization of the copyright owner under § 120(a). *See Leicester v. Warner Bros.*, 232 F.3d 1212 (9th Cir. 2000).

3. *Broadening the Pictorial Representation Limitation.* Section 120(a) enables other creators to film in the vicinity of publicly accessible architectural works. The transaction costs of having to negotiate licenses would be high, and it is difficult to imagine that architects' incentives to create would be much affected by not being able to control such uses. Couldn't a more general argument be made with regard to all publicly displayed sculpture, whether or not it is integrated into an architectural work? What about publicly visible artwork generally? Should it depend on the extent to which it is featured in the film or promotional advertising? Shouldn't filmmakers be allowed to capture that which is publicly viewable?

iv. *Musical Works and Sound Recordings*

Musical creativity manifests in various ways, including individual musical compositions, sound recordings of such compositions, dramatic works (such as operas and musical plays) incorporating music, motion pictures (sound tracks, musical performances), and audiovisual works (theme music, sound effects). Copyright law distinguishes among these aspects of musical creativity. We begin here with the basic building blocks: musical works (music, lyrics, and arrangements) and sound recordings.

Copyright law affords each of these different aspects of music protection in recognition of the distinctive skills and individuality involved in their creation. This distinction can have important ramifications. As we will discuss in more detail in section D on copyright ownership rights, U.S. copyright law accords owners of musical composition the full complement of rights (including the right to perform in public), whereas sound recordings do not receive a traditional performance right (although they now have a digital performance right). Therefore, when you hear a sound recording on traditional "over the air" radio broadcasts, the owner of the copyright in the musical composition typically is paid a royalty whereas the performer is not. Performers (and record labels) are paid, however, for satellite radio transmissions and digital streaming.

Congress first extended copyright protection for musical compositions in 1831 and added a performance right in 1897. Sound recordings did not receive federal copyright protection until 1972, and then only prospectively and without a public performance right. Congress afforded post-1972 sound recordings a digital performance right in 1995. Congress finally extended federal protection to pre-1972 sound recordings in 2018. Federal copyright protection does not extend to non-digital public performances, but such performances are eligible for state law protection.

The more limited right structure for sound recordings reflects the lobbying clout of broadcasters. They successfully resisted copyright protection for sound recordings for many years. When it finally gained enough momentum to pass, they were able to extract as a compromise that such protection would not include a performance right, thereby avoiding the burden of obtaining additional licenses.

Musical works can be written on paper, pressed onto a phonorecord, recorded on audiotape, represented in binary code on digital media, or otherwise fixed in a tangible medium of expression. The work must be original in its melody, harmony, or rhythm, individually or in combination. Sound recordings are magnetically or electronically recorded versions of a musical composition or any aural performance (such as spoken words, animal sounds, or sound effects). The definition of "sound recordings" excludes "the sounds accompanying a motion picture or other audiovisual work." § 101. Such recordings are protected as part of the motion picture or audiovisual work.

v.   *Dramatic, Pantomime, and Choreographic Works*

The protection afforded these three distinct copyrightable forms is similar in that each extends to written or otherwise fixed instructions for performing a work of art. A dramatic work portrays a story by means of dialogue or acting. "It gives direction for performance or actually represents all or a substantial portion of the action as actually occurring rather than merely being narrated or described." U.S. Copyright Office, Compendium II of Copyright Office Practices § 431. Distinguishing between literary, musical, and dramatic works can be important in practice. Although the three types of works are often captured in the same form, i.e., written text, performance and display rights may vary depending on whether the work is dramatic or nondramatic. *See*, e.g., §§ 110(2), 115.

Pantomime and choreographic works were first brought within copyright law by the 1976 Act. Copyright in such works inheres either in notation—such as Labanotation, a system of symbols for representing movements that can be related to a musical score—or (more commonly) in a film recording. Impromptu, unrecorded dancing is not a protectable work because it is not fixed in a tangible medium of expression.

Many of the rules governing dramatic, pantomime, and choreographic works parallel the law with regard to literary works. For example, copyright protection for choreographic works does not extend to simple dance steps, and protection for pantomimes does not extend to "conventional gestures." Both are akin to the "short phrases" denied protection among literary works. All three forms of work are entitled to protection not only against literal copying, but also against copying of their expressive elements, character, action, and dialogue. Should a series of yoga exercises be protectable? *See Bikram's Yoga College of India v. Evolation Yoga*, 803 F.3d 1032 (9th Cir. 2015) (affirming summary judgment of uncopyrightability of "Bikram yoga," a sequence of 26 yoga positions and two breathing exercises).

PROBLEM

Problem IV-9. At the 1995 Pan-World Figure Skating Championships in Denver, Colorado, skater Kurt Klutzinovich performed the first series of quadruple lutzes ever seen in competition. ABC sports commentator Bill McKay proclaimed it the "klutz," "Kurt's patented move." At the 1996 Championships, Kurt's coach threatens to bring a copyright infringement action against any other skater who performs a "klutz." Is Kurt's series of moves protectable as a choreographic work? If so, would another skater's performance of a klutz infringe Kurt's copyright?

---

vi. *Motion Pictures and Other Audiovisual Works*

The Copyright Act defines "audiovisual works" as

works that consist of a series of related images which are intrinsically intended to be shown by the use of machines or devices such as projectors, viewers, or electronic equipment, together with accompanying sounds, if any, regardless of the nature of the material objects, such as films or tapes, in which the works are embodied.

17 U.S.C. § 101. "Motion pictures" are a subset of audiovisual works "consisting of a series of related images, which, when shown in succession, impart an impression of motion, together with accompanying sounds, if any." § 101. Thus, sound tracks are treated as an integral part of the motion pictures that they accompany.

Protection for audiovisual works has taken on increased importance with the growth of computer software, particularly game and multimedia products.

vii. *Semiconductor Chips Designs (Mask Works)*

With the emergence of the semiconductors in the 1970s, the industry became increasingly concerned that competitors could duplicate the design of these works in a matter of months for a fraction of the development cost. Patent protection could protect the basic electronic circuitry if sufficiently novel and nonobvious, but such protection was perceived as inadequate to protect the painstaking work involved in designing semiconductor chips. The utilitarian nature of "mask works" arguably placed them outside of copyright protection. Responding to these concerns, Congress enacted a *sui generis* form of intellectual property for mask works in 1984 to fill the gap between patent and copyright protection. Although codified in the same Title of the U.S. Code housing the Copyright Act, *see* 17 U.S.C. §§ 901–14, the Semiconductor Chip Protection Act (SCPA) is "separate from and independent of the Copyright Act." *See* H.R. REP. NO. 98-781, at 5 (1984). Nonetheless, the SCPA reflects several principles of copyright law, such as the exclusion of protection for designs that are unoriginal, "staple, commonplace, or familiar in the semiconductor industry." Section 902(c) mirrors § 102(b) of the Copyright Act, barring protection for any "any idea, procedure, process, system, method of operation, concept, principle, or discovery." The SCPA also protects the right to reverse engineer mask works. In essence, this regime extends the lead-time of chip developers by deterring outright piracy of chip designs.

The regime has almost never been used because it largely codified industry norms and semiconductor industry changed their manufacturing process in the mid 1980s. There have only been two reported decisions involving copyright protection for mask works.

viii.   *Vessel Hull Designs*

After the Supreme Court struck down a Florida law protecting the design of boat hulls on the grounds that the Patent Act preempted state protection for innovation, *see Bonito Boats, Inc. v. Thunder Craft Boats, Inc.*, 489 U.S. 141 (1989), boat designers brought their concerns to Congress. They argued that competitors using "plug molding" could imitate boat hull designs in a fraction of the time and at a fraction of the cost that it took to design their works. In 1998, Congress passed the Vessel Hull Design Protection Act, codified at 17 U.S.C. §§ 1301–32, to fill this perceived gap in the intellectual property system. The contours of this *sui generis* regime significantly parallel the SCPA, including the bar on protection for utilitarian features modeled on copyright's useful article doctrine and § 102(b). *See* § 1302. One notable difference is that the issuance of a design patent for a vessel hull terminates copyright protection for such design. *Id.* at § 1329.

ix.   *Derivative Works and Compilations*

Section 103 of the Copyright Act provides protection for derivative works and compilations. The copyright in a derivative work or compilation "extends only to the material contributed by the author of such work, as distinguished from the preexisting material employed in the work." § 103(b).

A "derivative work" is

> based upon one or more preexisting works, such as a translation, musical arrangement, dramatization, fictionalization, motion picture version, sound recording, art reproduction, abridgment, condensation, or any other form in which a work may be recast, transformed, or adapted. A work consisting of editorial revisions, annotations, elaborations, or other modifications which, as a whole, represent an original work of authorship, is a "derivative work."

§ 101. We explore this definition in detail in Chapter IV(E)(1)(b), addressing the right to make derivative works.

Why should the copyright owner be entitled to a separate copyright in the derivative work, in addition to the copyright in the original work? There are at least two possible explanations for granting separate copyright protection to the original elements of a derivative work.

First, derivative works along a "chain" of related works may well entail significant new creativity beyond the original copyrighted work. For example, an author may produce a children's book, then a movie script based on the book, followed by a movie based on the script, and a series of stuffed animals based on characters from the movie. The stuffed animals at the end of this "chain" may bear little if any resemblance to identifiable characters in the original book. Allowing the derivative works to be copyrighted gives the copyright holder a stronger argument that each new step in the chain is in fact protectable as a derivative of the prior copyright. A second justification is that we may wish to protect new expression "derived" from works that are already in the public domain. *See* Paul Goldstein, *Derivative Rights and Derivative Works in Copyright*, 30 J. COPYRIGHT SOC'Y OF THE U.S.A. 209 (1983).

In addition, because derivative works often capture different markets, the copyright owner in the original work may wish to license to others the right to produce derivative works. Just because someone is a successful writer, for example, does not mean that he will be particularly successful at manufacturing and selling plush toys. Separating the copyright in original elements of a derivative work may facilitate the division of ownership between the original author and his licensees.

A "compilation" is a work "formed by the collection and assembling of preexisting materials or of data that are selected, coordinated, or arranged in such a way that the resulting work as a whole constitutes an original work of authorship. The term 'compilation' includes collective works." § 101. A "collective work" is a work, "such as a periodical issue, anthology, or encyclopedia, in which a number of contributions, constituting separate and independent works in themselves, are assembled into a collective whole." § 101.

The level of originality required for a compilation to be copyrightable has been a contentious issue in copyright law. Many fact-based works, such as telephone directories, require tremendous time, effort, and expense to compile. As we saw in the *Feist* case, however, there must be "some minimal degree of creativity" to garner copyright protection. Since neither the underlying material being compiled (names, which are factual) nor the method of arrangement (alphabetical order) were original, the compilation thus created was not copyrightable, regardless of how much effort was involved in producing the directory.

Many controversial copyright cases turn on whether a collection of uncopyrightable elements becomes copyrightable as a compilation. What is the threshold for originality in a compilation?

PROBLEM

Problem IV-10. Roth Greeting Card Company sells cute, clever, and sappy greeting cards comprising simple illustrations on the cover with very short segments of associated text (e.g., a character crying under the heading "I miss you already") as well as text inside the card (e.g., ". . . and you haven't even left.").

Some of the cards say nothing more than "I wuv you." United Card Company sells cards with different illustrations but identical text and arguably a similar style. Does Roth have a valid copyright in these cards? Under what theory?

---

2. **Limitations on Copyrightability: Distinguishing Function and Expression**

This section considers the fundamental doctrines that operate to channel protection for works between the patent and copyright regimes.

i.   *The Idea-Expression Dichotomy*

The most significant doctrine limiting the copyrightability of works is the "idea-expression" dichotomy, which is partially codified in § 102(b):

§ 102. Subject Matter of Copyright: In General

(b) In no case does copyright protection for an original work of authorship extend to any idea, procedure, process, system, method of operation, concept, principle, or discovery regardless of the form in which it is described, explained, illustrated, or embodied in such work.

The division between protectable expression and unprotectable ideas was explicated by the Supreme Court in the seminal case of *Baker v. Selden.*

Baker v. Selden
Supreme Court of the United States
101 U.S. 99 (1879)

MR. JUSTICE BRADLEY delivered the opinion of the court.

Charles Selden, the testator of the complainant in this case, in the year 1859 took the requisite steps for obtaining the copyright of a book, entitled "Selden's Condensed Ledger, or Book-keeping Simplified," the object of which was to exhibit and explain a peculiar system of book-keeping. In 1860 and 1861, he took the copyright of several other books, containing additions to and improvements upon the said system. The bill of complaint was filed against the defendant, Baker, for an alleged infringement of these copyrights. The latter, in his answer, denied that Selden was the author or designer of the books, and denied the infringement charged, and contends on the argument that the matter alleged to be infringed is not a lawful subject of copyright. . . .

The book or series of books of which the complainant claims the copyright consists of an introductory essay explaining the system of book-keeping referred to, to which are annexed certain forms or blanks, consisting of ruled lines, and headings, illustrating the system and showing how it is to be used and carried out in practice. This system effects the same results as book-keeping by double entry; but, by a peculiar arrangement of columns and headings, presents the entire operation, of a day, a week, or a month, on a single page, or on two pages facing each other, in an account-book. The defendant uses a similar plan so far as results are concerned; but makes a different arrangement of the columns, and uses different headings. If the complainant's testator had the exclusive right to the use of the system explained in his book, it would be difficult to contend that the defendant does not infringe it, notwithstanding the difference in his form of arrangement; but if it be assumed that the system is open to public use, it seems to be equally difficult to contend that the books made and sold by the defendant are a violation of the copyright of the complainant's book considered merely as a book explanatory of the system. Where the truths of a science or the methods of an art are the common property of the whole world, an author has the right to express the one, or explain and use the other, in his own way. As an author, Selden explained the system in a particular way. It may be conceded that Baker makes and uses account-books arranged on substantially the same system; but the proof fails to show that he has violated the copyright of Selden's book, regarding the latter merely as an explanatory work; or that he has infringed Selden's right in any way, unless the latter became entitled to an exclusive right in the system.

. . . [T]he question is, whether the exclusive property in a system of book-keeping can be claimed, under the law of copyright, by means of a book in which that system is explained? . . .

There is no doubt that a work on the subject of book-keeping, though only explanatory of well-known systems, may be the subject of a copyright; but, then, it is claimed only as a book. Such a book may be explanatory either of old systems, or of an entirely new system; and, considered as a book, as the work of an author, conveying information on the subject of book-keeping, and containing detailed explanations of the art, it may be a very valuable acquisition to the practical knowledge of the community. But there is a clear distinction between the book, as such, and the art which it is intended to illustrate. The mere statement of the proposition is so evident, that it requires hardly any argument to support it. The same distinction may be predicated of every other art as well as that of book-keeping. A treatise on the composition and use of medicines, be they old or new; on the construction and use of ploughs, or watches, or churns; or on the mixture and application of colors for painting or dyeing; or on the mode of drawing lines to produce the effect of perspective, would be the subject of copyright; but no one would contend that the copyright of the treatise would give the exclusive right to the art or manufacture described therein. The copyright of the book, if not pirated from other works, would be valid without regard to the novelty, or want of novelty, of its subject-matter. The novelty of the art or thing described or explained has nothing to do with the validity of the copyright. To give to the author of the book an exclusive property in the art described therein, when no examination of its novelty has ever been officially made, would be a surprise and a fraud upon the public. That is the province of letters-patent, not of copyright. The claim to an invention or discovery of an art or manufacture must be subjected to the examination of the Patent Office before an exclusive right therein can be obtained; and it can only be secured by a patent from the government.

The difference between the two things, letters-patent and copyright, may be illustrated by reference to the subjects just enumerated. Take the case of medicines. Certain mixtures are found to be of great value in the healing art. If the discoverer writes and publishes a book on the subject (as regular physicians generally do), he gains no exclusive right to the manufacture and sale of the medicine; he gives that to the public. If he desires to acquire such exclusive right, he must obtain a patent for the mixture as a new art, manufacture, or composition of matter. He may copyright his book, if he pleases; but that only secures to him the exclusive right of printing and publishing his book. So of all other inventions or discoveries. . . .

Of course, these observations are not intended to apply to ornamental designs, or pictorial illustrations addressed to the taste. Of these it may be said, that their form is their essence, and their object, the production of pleasure in their contemplation. This is their final end. They are as much the product of genius and the result of composition, as are the lines of the poet or the historian's periods. On the other hand, the teachings of science and the rules and methods of useful art have their final end in application and use; and this application and use are what the public derive from the publication of a book which teaches them. But as embodied and taught in a literary composition or book, their essence consists only in their statement. This alone is what is secured by the copyright. The use by another of the same methods of statement, whether in words or illustrations, in a book published for teaching the art, would undoubtedly be an infringement of the copyright.

Returning to the case before us, we observe that Charles Selden, by his books, explained and described a peculiar system of book-keeping, and illustrated his method by means of ruled lines and blank columns, with proper headings on a page, or on successive pages. Now, whilst no one has a right to print or publish his book, or any material part thereof, as a book intended to convey instruction in the art, any person may practice and use the art itself which he has described and illustrated therein. The use of the art is a totally different thing from a publication of the book explaining it. The copyright of a book on book-keeping cannot secure the exclusive right to make, sell, and use account-books prepared upon the plan set forth in such book. Whether the art might or might not have been patented, is a question which is not before us. It was not patented, and is open and free to the use of the public. And, of course, in using the art, the ruled lines and headings of accounts must necessarily be used as incident to it.

CONDENSED LEDGER.

Bro't Forw'd.		ON TIME.		DATE:		SUNDRIES to SUNDRIES	DISTRIBU-TION.		TOTAL.		BALANCE.	
DR.	CR.	DR.	CR.	DR.	CR.		DR.	CR.	DR.	CR.	DR.	CR.

CASH.

DR. | CR.

Carried Forward....

Selden's blank form for condensed ledger

The plausibility of the claim put forward by the complainant in this case arises from a confusion of ideas produced by the peculiar nature of the art described in the books which have been made the subject of copyright. In describing the art, the illustrations and diagrams employed happen to correspond more closely than usual with the actual work performed by the operator who uses the art. Those illustrations and diagrams consist of ruled lines and headings of accounts; and it is similar ruled lines and headings of accounts which, in the application of the art, the book-keeper makes with his pen, or the stationer with his press; whilst in most other cases the diagrams and illustrations can only be represented in concrete forms of wood, metal, stone, or some other physical embodiment. But the principle is the same in all. The description of the art in a book, though entitled to the benefit of copyright, lays no foundation for an exclusive claim to the art itself. The object of the one is explanation; the object of the other is use. The former may be secured by copyright. The latter can only be secured, if it can be secured at all, by letters-patent. . . .

The conclusion to which we have come is, that blank account books are not the subject of copyright; and that the mere copyright of Selden's book did not confer upon him the exclusive right to make and use account-books, ruled and arranged as designated by him and described and illustrated in said book.

The decree of the Circuit Court must be reversed, and the cause remanded with instructions to dismiss the complainant's bill; and it is

So ordered.

COMMENTS AND QUESTIONS

1. What is the Supreme Court's holding in this case? Did the Court rule that Selden's subject matter—accounting forms—are not copyrightable? Or that Selden's particular forms are not copyrightable? Alternatively, did the Court rule that Selden's forms are copyrightable but that the copyright does not prevent Baker's particular use of the forms, because such a result would in effect bestow upon Selden a monopoly over the system in question?

2. Professor Pamela Samuelson traces the history of this iconic case. *See* Pamela Samuelson, *The Story of* Baker v. Selden*: Sharpening the Distinction Between Authorship and Invention*, INTELLECTUAL PROPERTY STORIES (Jane C. Ginsburg and Rochelle C. Dreyfuss, eds. 2005) (noting that Selden had in fact unsuccessfully sought patent protection before trying copyright law).

3. Does the doctrine of *Baker v. Selden*—which establishes an idea-expression dichotomy—coherently channel intellectual property protection between the copyright and patent modes of protection? What differences between patentable subject matter (and the process of innovation) and copyrightable subject matter (and the process of artistic creativity) justify such a doctrine?

Consider the Seventh Circuit's discussion of copyright protection (or lack thereof) for recipes:

> The . . . recipes' directions for preparing the assorted dishes fall squarely within the class of subject matter specifically excluded from copyright protection by [§] 102(b). . . . The recipes at issue here describe a procedure by which the reader may produce many dishes featuring a specific yogurt. As such, they are excluded from copyright protection as either a "procedure, process, or system" [under §] 102(b).
>
> . . . Protection for ideas or processes is the purview of patent. . . .
>
> . . . [N]othing in our decision today runs counter to the proposition that recipes may be copyrightable. There are cookbooks in which the authors lace their directions for producing dishes with musings about the spiritual nature of cooking or reminiscences they associate with the wafting odors of certain dishes in various stages or preparation. . . . In other cases, recipes may be accompanied by tales of their historical or ethnic origin.

Publications Int'l v. Meredith Corp., 88 F.3d 473, 480–81 (7th Cir. 1996). What aspects of a cookbook are protectable?

4. *Distinguishing Idea from Expression.* The most challenging aspect of applying the idea-expression dichotomy is determining where to draw the line between idea and expression. Consider the work in question in *Baker v. Selden.* What was the "idea" behind Selden's book? Was it to describe a better system of accounting? Was it to describe a system of double-entry bookkeeping? Was it to describe the particular system he had invented? Or was it all of the above?

In the classic statement of how to draw the line between idea and expression, Judge Learned Hand stated the problem as follows:

> Upon any work, and especially upon a play, a great number of patterns of increasing generality will fit equally well, as more and more of the incident is left out. The last may perhaps be no more than the most general statement of what the play is about, and at times may consist only of its title; but there is a point in this series of abstractions where they are no longer protected, since otherwise the playwright could prevent the use of his "ideas" to which, apart from their expression, his property is never extended.

Nichols v. Universal Pictures Corp., 45 F.2d 119, 121 (2d Cir. 1930). Apply this reasoning to *Baker* itself. If the idea of Selden's book is to write a step-by-step guide explaining the use of his new forms (a low level of abstraction), even the detailed structure of the explanatory text may be unprotectable (because it is "necessary" to the idea). At a slightly higher level of abstraction, the Court considered the forms themselves unprotectable but gave Selden considerable latitude to protect his description of his system. At the highest levels of abstraction, had the Supreme Court determined that Selden's idea was to improve accounting, his double-entry bookkeeping forms might well have been considered simply one means of expressing that idea. In that case, Selden would presumably be entitled to copyright the forms.

How do courts determine the appropriate "level of abstraction" for distinguishing idea and expression? Paul Goldstein suggests that there are three categories of unprotectable ideas: the "animating concept" behind the work, the functional principles or "solutions" described or embodied in the work (such as Selden's forms), and the fundamental "building blocks" of creative expression (such as basic plot or character outlines in literary or dramatic works). 1 PAUL GOLDSTEIN, COPYRIGHT § 2.3.1.1 (1989). In his view, courts engage in a rough sort of balancing between the dangers of overprotecting and underprotecting a particular work in determining on which side of the idea/expression line the work falls.

5. *Blank Forms.* The Copyright Office considers the following works not copyrightable and hence ineligible for registration: "Blank forms, such as time cards, graph paper, account books, diaries, bank checks, scorecards, address books, report forms, order forms and the like, which are designed for recording information and do not in themselves convey information." 37 C.F.R. § 202(1)(c).

PROBLEMS

Problem IV-11. Mediforms designs and sells health care forms to doctors, who submit them to insurance carriers. The diagnosis checklist, pictured below, contains categories specified by the American Medical Association or government publications (including official code numbers). Mediforms offers a variety of forms, according to specialty, to reflect the illnesses and treatments most relevant to the particular doctor. The forms are personalized to include the doctor's name and address, the nature of the doctor's practice, and the hospitals or clinics at which the doctor performs services. Doctors may use the checklists provided or may customize their own checklists, which most doctors choose to do. The forms also contain brief instructions for filling in each blank and instructions explaining how to obtain insurance reimbursement. The forms were widely praised in the industry and were copied by competitors and individual doctors. Are the forms copyrightable? Should Mediforms be entitled at least to recoup its investment in developing the forms?

JOHN R. JOHNNSON, M.D.
Type of Practice or Specialty
1000 MAIN STREET, SUITE 10
SOME PLACE, USA 70000

STATE LIC. # 123456789
SOC. SEC. # 000-11-0000

TELEPHONE: (123) 234-5678

☐PRIVATE ☐BLUE CROSS ☐BLUE SHIELD ☐IND. ☐MEDICAID ☐MEDICARE ☐GOV'T.

PATIENT'S LAST NAME	FIRST			INITIAL	BIRTHDATE	SEX		TODAY'S DATE
					/ /	[ ]MALE [ ]FEMALE		/ /
ADDRESS	CITY	STATE	ZIP		RELATION TO SUBSCRIBER	REFERRING PHYSICIAN		
SUBSCRIBER OR POLICYHOLDER					INSURANCE CARRIER			
ADDRESS — IF DIFFERENT	CITY	STATE	ZIP	INS. ID		COVERAGE CODE		GROUP

DISABILITY RELATED TO: [ ]ILLNESS [ ]ACCIDENT [ ]IND. [ ]PREGNANCY [ ]	DATE SYMPTOMS APPEARED, INCEPTION OF PREGNANCY, OR ACCIDENT OCCURRED: / /	OTHER HEALTH COVERAGE? · [ ]NO [ ]YES · IDENTIFY

ASSIGNMENT: I hereby assign my insurance benefits to be paid directly to the undersigned physician. I am financially responsible for non-covered services.
SIGNED: (Patient or Parent If Minor)   Date:

RELEASE: I authorize the undersigned physician to release any information acquired in the course of my examination or treatment.
SIGNED: (Patient or Parent If Minor)   Date:

Family Practice

✓ DESCRIPTION	CPT4/MO	FEE	✓ DESCRIPTION	CPT4/MO	FEE	✓ DESCRIPTION	CPT4/MO	FEE
1. OFFICE VISIT	NEW EST.		**3. HOSP. SERVICES**	NEW EST.		**9. LABORATORY — IN OFFICE**		
Minimal	90030		Interm.(days) 90215 90260			Urine	81000	
Brief	90000 90040		Extended	90270		Occult Blood	89205	
Limited	90010 90050		Comprehensive	90220		ECG	93000	
Intermediate	90015 90060		Discharge 30 min. 1 hr					
Extended	90070		Detention Time 30 min. - 1 hr. 99150					
Comprehensive	90020 90080		Detention Time ___ Hrs. 99151			**10. SURGERY**		
			4. SPECIAL SERVICES			Anoscopy	46600	
			Called to ER - during ofc. hrs 99065			Sigmoidoscopy	45355	
2. INJECTIONS & IMMUNIZATIONS			Night Call - before 10 pm 99050					
Surgical Injection	206		Night Call - after 10 pm 99052					
DPT	90701		Sundays or Holidays 99054			Surgery Asst	-80	
DT	90702		**5. EMERGENCY ROOM**			**11. MISCELLANEOUS**		
Tetanus	90703			905		Booklet	99071	
OPV	90712		**6. HOUSE CALLS**			Special Reports	99080	
MMR	90707			901		Supplies, Ace Bandage	99070	
			7. EXTENDED CARE FACILITY			X-Ray		
				900				
			8. CONSULTATION					
				906				

DIAGNOSIS	ICD-9	☐ Condyloma Accuminata	078.1	☐ Hemorrhoids	455.6	☐ Paroxysmal Atrial Tachy.	427.2
☐ Abscess	682.9	☐ Conjunctivitis	372	☐ Hypertension	401.9	☐ Pediculosis Pubis-Scabies	133.0
☐ Abrasion-sup. Injury	919	☐ Contusion, Hematoma	924.9	☐ Influenza	487.1	☐ Pelvic Congestion	625.5
☐ Allergic Reaction	995.3	☐ Coronary Artery Dis.	414.9	☐ Ingrown Toenail	703.0	☐ Pharyngitis, Tonsil.-Acute	462
☐ Amenorrhea	626.0	☐ Cystitis-Pyelonaph	595.9/590.80	☐ Insomnia	780.52	☐ Pigmented Nevus	M8720/0
☐ Anemia	285.9	☐ Cephalgia-Migraine Tension	784.0	☐ Irritable Colon	564.1	☐ Post Nasal Drip	473.9
☐ Anxiety-Stress-Depression	309	☐ Dermatitis	692.0	☐ Jaundice-Hepatitis	782.4	☐ Pneumonitis-Pleuritis	486
☐ Arteriosclerosis	440.9	☐ Diabetes Mellitus	250.0	☐ Labyrinth.-Vertigo 386.30/780.4		☐ P.I.D.	614.9
☐ Arthralgia	719.4	☐ Duodenal Ulcer	532.9	☐ Laryngo-Tracheitis	464	☐ Prostatitis	601.9
☐ Arthrit.-Osteo Rheum. 716/714		☐ Duodenitis Gas	535.6	☐ Lipoma	214.9	☐ Puncture Wound	879.8
☐ Asthma Hayfever	493.0	☐ Dysmenorrhea	625.3	☐ Lipid Cholesterol Ab	272.7	☐ Renal Stone	592.0
☐ Bleeding Internal	626.6	☐ Emphysema-COPD	496	☐ Low Back Pain	724.2	☐ Sebaceous Cyst	706.2
☐ Bleeding Post Men	627.1	☐ Epicondylitis	726.32	☐ Lymphadenitis	289.3	☐ Seizure Disorder	780.3
☐ Boil-Carbuncle/Furuncle	680	☐ Epilepsy	345.9	☐ Lymphangitis	457.2	☐ Sinusitis	473.9
☐ Bronchitis-Acute/Chronic	490	☐ Eustachian Tube Congest.	381.50	☐ Menorrhagia	626.2	☐ Thyroid Disorder	246.9
☐ Bronchopneumonitis	485	☐ Exogenous Obesity	278.0	☐ Menopausal Syndrome	627.2	☐ Tinea Corpus-Pedis	110.5
☐ Bursitis	727	☐ Fatigue	780.7	☐ Myofascitis Tendonitis	729.1	☐ U.R.I. Viral Syndrome	480
☐ Cellulitis-Impetigo	682	☐ Foreign Body	879.8	☐ Muscle Strain/Sprain	848.9	☐ Urethritis-Cystitis	599.0
☐ Cerebral Con.	850.9	☐ Gastroenteritis	558.9	☐ Otitis-External Cerumen	382.9	☐ Vaginitis	616.10
☐ Cervicitis	616.0	☐ Heart Failure	428.0	☐ Otitis-Media Acute	382.9	☐ Weight Loss	783.2
☐ Cholecyst. & Cholelith. 575/574		☐ Hiatal Hernia	553.3	☐ Pain		☐	

DIAGNOSIS: (IF NOT CHECKED ABOVE)	SERVICES PERFORMED AT: [ ]Office [ ]Johnnson's Hospital 100 Main St. Some Place, USA 70000 [ ]E.R. [ ]N.H.	LAB SENT TO: [ ]State Hospital 200 State St. Some Place, USA 70001	DATES DISABLED: FROM: / / TO: / / OK TO RETURN TO WORK/SCHOOL / /

RETURN APPOINTMENT INFORMATION: 5 - 10 - 15 - 20 - 30 - 45 - 60	NEXT APPOINTMENT: M — T — W — TH — F — S	DOCTOR'S SIGNATURE/DATE
DAYS WKS. MOS. PRN PX.	DATE: / / TIME: AM PM	ACCEPT ASSIGNMENT? [ ]YES [ ]NO

INSTRUCTIONS TO PATIENT FOR FILING INSURANCE CLAIMS

1. COMPLETE UPPER PORTION OF THIS FORM.
2. SIGN & DATE.
3. MAIL THIS FORM DIRECTLY TO YOUR INSURANCE COMPANY. YOU MAY ATTACH YOUR OWN INSURANCE COMPANY'S FORM IF YOU WISH, ALTHOUGH IT IS NOT NECESSARY.

REC'D BY:	TOTAL TODAY'S FEE	
[ ]CASH	OLD BALANCE	
[ ]CR. CD.	TOTAL	
[ ]CHECK	AMT. REC'D. TODAY	
#_____	NEW BALANCE	

INSUR-A-BILL® • BIBBERO SYSTEMS, INC. • PETALUMA, CA. • © 3/84

Mediforms Medical Information Form

Problem IV-12. After years of research, Missy Chase Lapine wrote "The Sneaky Chef: Simple Strategies for Hiding Healthy Foods in Kids' Favorite Meals," which was published in April 2007. It includes dozens of recipes about how to camouflage purees of fruits and vegetables (such as spinach and sweet potatoes) into kids' favorite foods. Six months later, Jessica Seinfeld published "Deceptively Delicious: Simple Secrets to Getting Your Kids Eating Good Foods." It included many recipes with the same hidden purees: chocolate pudding (avocado); chocolate chip cookies (white bean); brownies (spinach); grilled cheese (sweet potato); French toast (sweet potato/carrot); meat sauce (sweet potato); chicken tenders (sweet potato); green eggs (spinach). Does Lapine have a valid copyright in the ingredient lists and proportions? What about the recipes and descriptive material? What about the arrangement of the recipes?

Lotus Development Corp. v. Borland International
United States Court of Appeals for the First Circuit
49 F.3d 807 (1st Cir. 1995),
aff'd by equally divided court, 526 U.S. 233 (1996)

STAHL, Circuit Judge.

This appeal requires us to decide whether a computer menu command hierarchy is copyrightable subject matter. In particular, we must decide whether, as the district court held, plaintiff-appellee Lotus Development Corporation's copyright in Lotus 1-2-3, a computer spreadsheet program, was infringed by defendant-appellant Borland International, Inc., when Borland copied the Lotus 1-2-3 menu command hierarchy into its Quattro and Quattro Pro computer spreadsheet programs. *See Lotus Dev. Corp. v. Borland Int'l, Inc.*, 788 F. Supp. 78 (D. Mass. 1992) ("Borland I"); *Lotus Dev. Corp. v. Borland Int'l, Inc.*, 799 F. Supp. 203 (D. Mass. 1992) ("Borland II"); *Lotus Dev. Corp. v. Borland Int'l, Inc.*, 831 F. Supp. 202 (D. Mass. 1993) ("Borland III"); *Lotus Dev. Corp. v. Borland Int'l, Inc.*, 831 F. Supp. 223 (D. Mass. 1993) ("Borland IV").

I. Background

Lotus 1-2-3 is a spreadsheet program that enables users to perform accounting functions electronically on a computer. Users manipulate and control the program via a series of menu commands, such as "Copy," "Print," and "Quit." Users choose commands either by highlighting them on the screen or by typing their first letter. In all, Lotus 1-2-3 has 469 commands arranged into more than 50 menus and submenus. [*See* picture below.]

Lotus 1-2-3, like many computer programs, allows users to write what are called "macros." By writing a macro, a user can designate a series of command choices with a single macro keystroke. Then, to execute that series of commands in multiple parts of the spreadsheet, rather than typing the whole series each time, the user only needs to type the single pre-programmed macro keystroke, causing the program to recall and perform the designated series of commands automatically. Thus, Lotus 1-2-3 macros shorten the time needed to set up and operate the program.

Borland released its first Quattro program to the public in 1987, after Borland's engineers had labored over its development for nearly three years. Borland's objective was to develop a spreadsheet program far superior to existing programs, including Lotus 1-2-3. In Borland's words, "from the time of its initial release . . . Quattro included enormous innovations over competing spreadsheet products."

									MENU;
Worksheet	Range	Copy	Move	File	Print	Graph	Data	Quit	
Global, Insert, Delete, Column-Width, Erase, Titles, Window, Status									
	A	B	C	D	E	F	G	H	
1									
2									
3									
4									
5									
6									
7									
8									
9									
10									
11									
12									
13									
14									
15									
16									
17									
18									
19									
20									

Facsimile of a Lotus 1-2-3 screen display

The district court found, and Borland does not now contest, that Borland included in its Quattro and Quattro Pro version 1.0 programs "a virtually identical copy of the entire 1-2-3 menu tree." *Borland III*, 831 F. Supp. at 212. In so doing, Borland did not copy any of Lotus's underlying computer code; it copied only the words and structure of Lotus's menu command hierarchy. Borland included the Lotus menu command hierarchy in its programs to make them compatible with Lotus 1-2-3 so that spreadsheet users who were already familiar with Lotus 1-2-3 would be able to switch to the Borland programs without having to learn new commands or rewrite their Lotus macros.

In its Quattro and Quattro Pro version 1.0 programs, Borland achieved compatibility with Lotus 1-2-3 by offering its users an alternate user interface, the "Lotus Emulation Interface." By activating the Emulation Interface, Borland users would see the Lotus menu commands on their screens and could interact with Quattro or Quattro Pro as if using Lotus 1-2-3, albeit with a slightly different looking screen and with many Borland options not available on Lotus 1-2-3. In effect, Borland allowed users to choose how they wanted to communicate with Borland's spreadsheet programs: either by using menu commands designed by Borland, or by using the commands and command structure used in Lotus 1-2-3 augmented by Borland-added commands.

Lotus filed this action against Borland in the District of Massachusetts on July 2, 1990, four days after a district court held that the Lotus 1-2-3 "menu structure, taken as a whole—including the choice of command terms [and] the structure and order of those terms," was protected expression covered by Lotus's copyrights. *Lotus Dev. Corp. v. Paperback Software Int'l*, 740 F. Supp. 37, 68, 70 (D. Mass. 1990) ("Paperback"). . . .

On July 31, 1992, the district court denied Borland's motion [for summary judgment] and granted Lotus's motion in part. The district court ruled that the Lotus menu command hierarchy was copyrightable expression because

> [a] very satisfactory spreadsheet menu tree can be constructed using different commands and a different command structure from those of Lotus 1-2-3. In fact, Borland has constructed just such an alternate tree for use in Quattro Pro's native mode. Even if one holds the arrangement of menu commands constant, it is possible to generate literally millions of satisfactory menu trees by varying the menu commands employed.

Borland II, 799 F. Supp. at 217. The district court demonstrated this by offering alternate command words for the ten commands that appear in Lotus's main menu. *Id.* For example, the district court stated that "the 'Quit' command could be named 'Exit' without any other modifications," and that "the 'Copy' command could be called 'Clone,' 'Ditto,' 'Duplicate,' 'Imitate,' 'Mimic,' 'Replicate,' and 'Reproduce,' among others." *Id.* Because so many variations were possible, the district court concluded that the Lotus developers' choice and arrangement of command terms, reflected in the Lotus menu command hierarchy, constituted copyrightable expression.

In granting partial summary judgment to Lotus, the district court held that Borland had infringed Lotus's copyright in Lotus 1-2-3. . . . *Borland II*, 799 F. Supp. at 223. The court nevertheless concluded that while the Quattro and Quattro Pro programs infringed Lotus's copyright, Borland had not copied the entire Lotus 1-2-3 user interface, as Lotus had contended. . . .

Immediately following the district court's summary judgment decision, Borland removed the Lotus Emulation Interface from its products. Thereafter, Borland's spreadsheet programs no longer displayed the Lotus 1-2-3 menus to Borland users, and as a result Borland users could no longer communicate with Borland's programs as if they were using a more sophisticated version of Lotus 1-2-3. Nonetheless, Borland's programs continued to be partially compatible with Lotus 1-2-3, for Borland retained what it called the "Key Reader" in its Quattro Pro programs. Once turned on, the Key Reader allowed Borland's programs to understand and perform some Lotus 1-2-3 macros. With the Key Reader on, the Borland programs used Quattro Pro menus for display, interaction, and macro execution, except when they encountered a slash ("/")

key in a macro (the starting key for any Lotus 1-2-3 macro), in which case they interpreted the macro as having been written for Lotus 1-2-3. Accordingly, people who wrote or purchased macros to shorten the time needed to perform an operation in Lotus 1-2-3 could still use those macros in Borland's programs. The district court permitted Lotus to file a supplemental complaint alleging that the Key Reader infringed its copyright.

The parties agreed to try the remaining liability issues without a jury. The district court held two trials, the Phase I trial covering all remaining issues raised in the original complaint (relating to the Emulation Interface) and the Phase II trial covering all issues raised in the supplemental complaint (relating to the Key Reader). . . .

In its Phase I trial decision, the district court found that "each of the Borland emulation interfaces contains a virtually identical copy of the 1-2-3 menu tree and that the 1-2-3 menu tree is capable of a wide variety of expression." *Borland III*, 831 F. Supp. at 218. The district court also rejected Borland's affirmative defenses of laches and estoppel. *Id.* at 218–23.

In its Phase II trial decision, the district court found that Borland's Key Reader file included "a virtually identical copy of the Lotus menu tree structure, but represented in a different form and with first letters of menu command names in place of the full menu command names." *Borland IV*, 831 F. Supp. at 228. In other words, Borland's programs no longer included the Lotus command terms, but only their first letters. The district court held that "the Lotus menu structure, organization, and first letters of the command names . . . constitute part of the protectable expression found in [Lotus 1-2-3]." *Id.* at 233. Accordingly, the district court held that with its Key Reader, Borland had infringed Lotus's copyright. *Id.* at 245. The district court also rejected Borland's affirmative defenses of waiver, laches, estoppel, and fair use. *Id.* at 235–45. The district court then entered a permanent injunction against Borland, *id.* at 245, from which Borland appeals. . . .

II. Discussion

On appeal, Borland does not dispute that it factually copied the words and arrangement of the Lotus menu command hierarchy. Rather, Borland argues that it "lawfully copied the unprotectable menus of Lotus 1-2-3." Borland contends that the Lotus menu command hierarchy is not copyrightable because it is a system, method of operation, process, or procedure foreclosed from protection by 17 U.S.C. § 102(b). Borland also raises a number of affirmative defenses.

A. Copyright Infringement Generally

. . . In this appeal, we are faced only with whether the Lotus menu command hierarchy is copyrightable subject matter in the first instance, for Borland concedes that Lotus has a valid copyright in Lotus 1-2-3 as a whole and admits to factually copying the Lotus menu command hierarchy. As a result, this appeal is in a very different posture from most copyright-infringement cases, for copyright infringement generally turns on whether the defendant has copied protected expression as a factual matter. Because of this different posture, most copyright-infringement cases provide only limited help to us in deciding this appeal. This is true even with respect to those copyright-infringement cases that deal with computers and computer software.

B. Matter of First Impression

Whether a computer menu command hierarchy constitutes copyrightable subject matter is a matter of first impression in this court. While some other courts appear to have touched on it briefly in dicta, *see, e.g., Autoskill, Inc. v. Nat'l Educ. Support Sys., Inc.*, 994 F.2d 1476, 1495 n.23 (10th Cir. 1993), we know of no cases that deal with the copyrightability of a menu command hierarchy standing on its own (i.e., without other elements of the user interface, such as screen displays, in issue). Thus we are navigating in uncharted waters.

Borland vigorously argues, however, that the Supreme Court charted our course more than 100 years ago when it decided *Baker v. Selden*, 101 U.S. 99 (1879). In *Baker v. Selden*, the Court held that Selden's copyright over the textbook in which he explained his new way to do accounting did not grant him a monopoly on the use of his accounting system. Borland argues: "The facts of *Baker v. Selden*, and even the arguments advanced by the parties in that case, are identical to those in this case. The only difference is that the 'user interface' of Selden's system was implemented by pen and paper rather than by computer." . . .

We do not think that *Baker v. Selden* is nearly as analogous to this appeal as Borland claims. Of course, Lotus 1-2-3 is a computer spreadsheet, and as such its grid of horizontal rows and vertical columns certainly resembles an accounting ledger or any other paper spreadsheet. Those grids, however, are not at issue in this appeal for, unlike *Selden*, Lotus does not claim to have a monopoly over its accounting system. Rather, this appeal involves Lotus's monopoly over the commands it uses to operate the computer. Accordingly, this appeal is not, as Borland contends, "identical" to *Baker v. Selden*. . . .

D. The Lotus Menu Command Hierarchy: A "Method of Operation"

Borland argues that the Lotus menu command hierarchy is uncopyrightable because it is a system, method of operation, process, or procedure foreclosed from copyright protection by 17 U.S.C. § 102(b). Section 102(b) states: "In no case does copyright protection for an original work of authorship extend to any idea, procedure, process, system, method of operation, concept, principle, or discovery, regardless of the form in which it is described, explained, illustrated, or embodied in such work." Because we conclude that the Lotus menu command hierarchy is a method of operation, we do not consider whether it could also be a system, process, or procedure.

We think that "method of operation," as that term is used in § 102(b), refers to the means by which a person operates something, whether it be a car, a food processor, or a computer. Thus a text describing how to operate something would not extend copyright protection to the method of operation itself; other people would be free to employ that method and to describe it in their own words. Similarly, if a new method of operation is used rather than described, other people would still be free to employ or describe that method.

We hold that the Lotus menu command hierarchy is an uncopyrightable "method of operation." The Lotus menu command hierarchy provides the means by which users control and operate Lotus 1-2-3. If users wish to copy material, for example, they use the "Copy" command. If users wish to print material, they use the "Print" command. Users must use the command terms to tell the computer what to do. Without the menu command hierarchy, users would not be able to access and control, or indeed make use of, Lotus 1-2-3's functional capabilities.

The Lotus menu command hierarchy does not merely explain and present Lotus 1-2-3's functional capabilities to the user; it also serves as the method by which the program is operated and controlled. . . . The Lotus menu command hierarchy is . . . different from the Lotus screen displays, for users need not "use" any expressive aspects of the screen displays in order to operate Lotus 1-2-3; because the way the screens look has little bearing on how users control the program, the screen displays are not part of Lotus 1-2-3's "method of operation." The Lotus menu command hierarchy is also different from the underlying computer code, because while code is necessary for the program to work, its precise formulation is not. In other words, to offer the same capabilities as Lotus 1-2-3, Borland did not have to copy Lotus's underlying code (and indeed it did not); to allow users to operate its programs in substantially the same way, however, Borland had to copy the Lotus menu command hierarchy. Thus the Lotus 1-2-3 code is not an uncopyrightable "method of operation."

The district court held that the Lotus menu command hierarchy, with its specific choice and arrangement of command terms, constituted an "expression" of the "idea" of operating a computer program with commands arranged hierarchically into menus and submenus. *Borland II*, 799 F. Supp. at 216. Under the district court's reasoning, Lotus's decision to employ hierarchically arranged command terms to operate its program could not foreclose its competitors from also employing hierarchically arranged command terms to operate their programs, but it did foreclose them from employing the specific command terms and arrangement that Lotus had used. In effect, the district court limited Lotus 1-2-3's "method of operation" to an abstraction.

Accepting the district court's finding that the Lotus developers made some expressive choices in choosing and arranging the Lotus command terms, we nonetheless hold that that expression is not copyrightable because it is part of Lotus 1-2-3's "method of operation." We do not think that "methods of operation" are limited to abstractions; rather, they are the means by which a user operates something. If specific words are essential to operating something, then they are part of a "method of operation" and, as such, are unprotectable. This is so whether they must be highlighted, typed in, or even spoken, as computer programs no doubt will soon be controlled by spoken words.

The fact that Lotus developers could have designed the Lotus menu command hierarchy differently is immaterial to the question of whether it is a "method of operation." In other words, our initial inquiry is not whether the Lotus menu command hierarchy incorporates any expression. Rather, our initial inquiry is whether the Lotus menu command hierarchy is a "method of operation." Concluding, as we do, that users operate Lotus 1-2-3 by using the Lotus menu command hierarchy, and that the entire

Lotus menu command hierarchy is essential to operating Lotus 1-2-3, we do not inquire further whether that method of operation could have been designed differently. The "expressive" choices of what to name the command terms and how to arrange them do not magically change the uncopyrightable menu command hierarchy into copyrightable subject matter.

Our holding that "methods of operation" are not limited to mere abstractions is bolstered by *Baker v. Selden*. In *Baker,* the Supreme Court explained that

> the teachings of science and the rules and methods of useful art have their final end in application and use; and this application and use are what the public derive from the publication of a book which teaches them. . . . The description of the art in a book, though entitled to the benefit of copyright, lays no foundation for an exclusive claim to the art itself. The object of the one is explanation; the object of the other is use. The former may be secured by copyright. The latter can only be secured, if it can be secured at all, by letters-patent.

Baker v. Selden, 101 U.S. at 104–05. Lotus wrote its menu command hierarchy so that people could learn it and use it. Accordingly, it falls squarely within the prohibition on copyright protection established in Baker v. Selden and codified by Congress in § 102(b).

In many ways, the Lotus menu command hierarchy is like the buttons used to control, say, a video cassette recorder ("VCR"). A VCR is a machine that enables one to watch and record video tapes. Users operate VCRs by pressing a series of buttons that are typically labelled "Record, Play, Reverse, Fast Forward, Pause, Stop/Eject." That the buttons are arranged and labeled does not make them a "literary work," nor does it make them an "expression" of the abstract "method of operating" a VCR via a set of labeled buttons. Instead, the buttons are themselves the "method of operating" the VCR.

When a Lotus 1-2-3 user chooses a command, either by highlighting it on the screen or by typing its first letter, he or she effectively pushes a button. Highlighting the "Print" command on the screen, or typing the letter "P," is analogous to pressing a VCR button labeled "Play."

Just as one could not operate a buttonless VCR, it would be impossible to operate Lotus 1-2-3 without employing its menu command hierarchy. Thus the Lotus command terms are not equivalent to the labels on the VCR's buttons, but are instead equivalent to the buttons themselves. Unlike the labels on a VCR's buttons, which merely make operating a VCR easier by indicating the buttons' functions, the Lotus menu commands are essential to operating Lotus 1-2-3. Without the menu commands, there would be no way to "push" the Lotus buttons, as one could push unlabeled VCR buttons. While Lotus could probably have designed a user interface for which the command terms were mere labels, it did not do so here. Lotus 1-2-3 depends for its operation on use of the precise command terms that make up the Lotus menu command hierarchy. . . .

Computer programs, unlike VCRs, are copyrightable as "literary works." 17 U.S.C. § 102(a). Accordingly, one might argue, the "buttons" used to operate a computer program are not like the buttons used to operate a VCR, for they are not subject to a useful-article exception. The response, of course, is that the arrangement of buttons on a VCR would not be copyrightable even without a useful-article exception, because the buttons are an uncopyrightable "method of operation." Similarly, the "buttons" of a computer program are also an uncopyrightable "method of operation."

That the Lotus menu command hierarchy is a "method of operation" becomes clearer when one considers program compatibility. Under Lotus's theory, if a user uses several different programs, he or she must learn how to perform the same operation in a different way for each program used. For example, if the user wanted the computer to print material, then the user would have to learn not just one method of operating the computer such that it prints, but many different methods. We find this absurd. The fact that there may be many different ways to operate a computer program, or even many different ways to operate a computer program using a set of hierarchically arranged command terms, does not make the actual method of operation chosen copyrightable; it still functions as a method for operating the computer and as such is uncopyrightable.

Consider also that users employ the Lotus menu command hierarchy in writing macros. Under the district court's holding, if the user wrote a macro to shorten the time needed to perform a certain operation in Lotus 1-2-3, the user would be unable to use that macro to shorten the time needed to perform that same operation in another program. Rather, the user would have to rewrite his or her macro using that other program's menu command hierarchy. This is despite the fact that the macro is clearly the user's own work product. We think that forcing the user to cause the computer to perform the same operation in a different way ignores Congress's direction in § 102(b) that "methods of operation" are not copyrightable. That programs can offer users the ability to write macros in many different ways does not change the fact that, once written, the macro allows the user to perform an operation automatically. As the Lotus menu command hierarchy serves as the basis for Lotus 1-2-3 macros, the Lotus menu command hierarchy is a "method of operation." . . .

We also note that in most contexts, there is no need to "build" upon other people's expression, for the ideas conveyed by that expression can be conveyed by someone else without copying the first author's expression. In the context of methods of operation, however, "building" requires the use of the precise method of operation already employed; otherwise, "building" would require dismantling, too. Original developers are not the only people entitled to build on the methods of operation they create; anyone can. Thus, Borland may build on the method of operation that Lotus designed and may use the Lotus menu command hierarchy in doing so.

Our holding that methods of operation are not limited to abstractions goes against *Autoskill,* 994 F.2d at 1495 n.23, in which the Tenth Circuit rejected the defendant's argument that the keying procedure used in a computer program was an uncopyrightable "procedure" or "method of operation" under § 102(b). The program at issue, which was designed to test and train students with reading deficiencies, *id.* at 1481, required students to select responses to the program's queries "by pressing the 1, 2, or 3 keys." *Id.* at 1495 n.23. The Tenth Circuit held that, "for purposes of the preliminary injunction, . . . the record showed that [this] keying procedure reflected at least a minimal degree of creativity," as required by Feist for copyright protection. *Id.* As an initial matter, we question whether a programmer's decision to have users select a response by pressing the 1, 2, or 3 keys is original. More importantly, however, we fail to see how "a student selecting a response by pressing the 1, 2, or 3 keys," *id.*, can be anything but an unprotectable method of operation. . . .

Reversed.

BOUDIN, Circuit Judge, concurring.

The importance of this case, and a slightly different emphasis in my view of the underlying problem, prompt me to add a few words to the majority's tightly focused discussion.

I.

Most of the law of copyright and the "tools" of analysis have developed in the context of literary works such as novels, plays, and films. In this milieu, the principal problem—simply stated, if difficult to resolve—is to stimulate creative expression without unduly limiting access by others to the broader themes and concepts deployed by the author. The middle of the spectrum presents close cases; but a "mistake" in providing too much protection involves a small cost: subsequent authors treating the same themes must take a few more steps away from the original expression.

The problem presented by computer programs is fundamentally different in one respect. The computer program is a means for causing something to happen; it has a mechanical utility, an instrumental role, in accomplishing the world's work. Granting protection, in other words, can have some of the consequences of patent protection in limiting other people's ability to perform a task in the most efficient manner. Utility does not bar copyright (dictionaries may be copyrighted), but it alters the calculus.

Of course, the argument for protection is undiminished, perhaps even enhanced, by utility: if we want more of an intellectual product, a temporary monopoly for the creator provides incentives for others to create other, different items in this class. But the "cost" side of the equation may be different where one places a very high value on public access to a useful innovation that may be the most efficient means of performing a given task. Thus, the argument for extending protection may be the same; but the stakes on the other side are much higher.

It is no accident that patent protection has preconditions that copyright protection does not—notably, the requirements of novelty and non-obviousness—and that patents are granted for a shorter period than copyrights. This problem of utility has sometimes manifested itself in copyright cases, such as *Baker v. Selden*, 101 U.S. 99 (1879), and been dealt with through various formulations that limit copyright or create limited rights to copy. But the case law and doctrine addressed to utility in copyright have been brief detours in the general march of copyright law.

Requests for the protection of computer menus present the concern with fencing off access to the commons in an acute form. A new menu may be a creative work, but over time its importance may come to reside more in the investment that has been made by users in learning the menu and in building their own mini-programs—macros—in reliance upon the menu. Better typewriter keyboard layouts may exist, but the familiar QWERTY keyboard dominates the market because that is what everyone has learned to use. *See* P. David, *CLIO and the Economics of QWERTY*, 75 AM. ECON. REV. 332 (1985). The QWERTY keyboard is nothing other than a menu of letters.

Thus, to assume that computer programs are just one more new means of expression, like a filmed play, may be quite wrong. The "form"—the written source code or the menu structure depicted on the screen—look hauntingly like the familiar stuff of copyright; but the "substance" probably has more to do with problems presented in patent law or, as already noted, in those rare cases where copyright law has confronted industrially useful expressions. Applying copyright law to computer programs is like assembling a jigsaw puzzle whose pieces do not quite fit. . . .

II.

In this case, the raw facts are mostly, if not entirely, undisputed. Although the inferences to be drawn may be more debatable, it is very hard to see that Borland has shown any interest in the Lotus menu except as a fall-back option for those users already committed to it by prior experience or in order to run their own macros using 1-2-3 commands. At least for the amateur, accessing the Lotus menu in the Borland Quattro or Quattro Pro program takes some effort.

Put differently, it is unlikely that users who value the Lotus menu for its own sake—independent of any investment they have made themselves in learning Lotus' commands or creating macros dependent upon them—would choose the Borland program in order to secure access to the Lotus menu. Borland's success is due primarily to other features. Its rationale for deploying the Lotus menu bears the ring of truth.

Now, any use of the Lotus menu by Borland is a commercial use and deprives Lotus of a portion of its "reward," in the sense that an infringement claim if allowed would increase Lotus' profits. But this is circular reasoning: broadly speaking, every limitation on copyright or privileged use diminishes the reward of the original creator. Yet not every writing is copyrightable or every use an infringement. The provision of reward is one concern of copyright law, but it is not the only one. If it were, copyrights would be perpetual and there would be no exceptions.

The present case is an unattractive one for copyright protection of the menu. The menu commands (e.g., "print," "quit") are largely for standard procedures that Lotus did not invent and are common words that Lotus cannot monopolize. What is left is the particular combination and sub-grouping of commands in a pattern devised by Lotus. This arrangement may have a more appealing logic and ease of use than some other configurations; but there is a certain arbitrariness to many of the choices.

If Lotus is granted a monopoly on this pattern, users who have learned the command structure of Lotus 1-2-3 or devised their own macros are locked into Lotus, just as a typist who has learned the QWERTY keyboard would be the captive of anyone who had a monopoly on the production of such a keyboard. Apparently, for a period Lotus 1-2-3 has had such sway in the market that it has represented the de facto standard for electronic spreadsheet commands. So long as Lotus is the superior spreadsheet—either in quality or in price—there may be nothing wrong with this advantage.

But if a better spreadsheet comes along, it is hard to see why customers who have learned the Lotus menu and devised macros for it should remain captives of Lotus because of an investment in learning made by the users and not by Lotus. Lotus has already reaped a substantial reward for being first; assuming that the Borland program is now better, good reasons exist for freeing it to attract old Lotus customers: to enable the old customers to take advantage of a new advance, and to reward Borland in turn for making a better product. If Borland has not made a better product, then customers will remain with Lotus anyway.

Thus, for me the question is not whether Borland should prevail but on what basis. Various avenues might be traveled, but the main choices are between holding that the menu is not protectable by copyright and devising a new doctrine that Borland's use is privileged. No solution is perfect and no intermediate appellate court can make the final choice.

To call the menu a "method of operation" is, in the common use of those words, a defensible position. After all, the purpose of the menu is not to be admired as a work of literary or pictorial art. It is to transmit directions from the user to the computer, i.e., to operate the computer. The menu is also a "method" in the dictionary sense because it is a "planned way of doing something," an "order or system," and (aptly here) an "orderly or systematic arrangement, sequence or the like." RANDOM HOUSE WEBSTER'S COLLEGE DICTIONARY 853 (1991).

A different approach would be to say that Borland's use is privileged because, in the context already described, it is not seeking to appropriate the advances made by Lotus' menu; rather, having provided an arguably more attractive menu of its own, Borland is merely trying to give former Lotus users an option to exploit their own prior investment in learning or in macros. The difference is that such a privileged use approach would not automatically protect Borland if it had simply copied the Lotus menu (using different codes), contributed nothing of its own, and resold Lotus under the Borland label.

The closest analogue in conventional copyright is the fair use doctrine. . . . [T]he doctrine of fair use was created by the courts and can be adapted to new purposes.

But a privileged use doctrine would certainly involve problems of its own. It might more closely tailor the limits on copyright protection to the reasons for limiting that protection; but it would entail a host of administrative problems that would cause cost and delay, and would also reduce the ability of the industry to predict outcomes. Indeed, to the extent that Lotus' menu is an important standard in the industry, it might be argued that any use ought to be deemed privileged.

In sum, the majority's result persuades me and its formulation is as good, if not better, than any other that occurs to me now as within the reach of courts. Some solutions (e.g., a very short copyright period for menus) are not options at all for courts but might be for Congress. In all events, the choices are important ones of policy, not linguistics, and they should be made with the underlying considerations in view.

COMMENTS AND QUESTIONS

1. The issues raised by the *Lotus* decision remain unsettled. The Supreme Court granted certiorari in the case, but it deadlocked 4-4 and therefore affirmed the First Circuit but produced no precedential opinion. *Lotus Dev. Corp. v. Borland Int'l*, 516 U.S. 233 (1996). Note that the First Circuit concedes that its opinion is at odds with the Tenth Circuit's decision in *Autoskill, Inc. v. National Educational Support Systems*, 994 F.2d 1476, 1495 n.23 (10th Cir. 1993), and dictum from the Ninth Circuit's decision in *Brown Bag Software v. Symantec Corp.*, 960 F.2d 1465, 1477 (9th Cir. 1992). On the other hand, the *Lotus* approach seems consistent with the legislative history of § 102(b). The House Report accompanying that section states: "Section 102(b) is intended, among other things, to make clear that the expression adopted by the programmer is the copyrightable element in a computer program, and that the actual processes or methods embodied in the program are not within the scope of the copyright law." H.R. REP. NO. 1476, 94th Cong., 2d Sess. 57 (1976), reprinted in 1976 U.S.C.C.A.N. 5659, 5670. Furthermore, most commentators agree with the ultimate result in *Lotus. See, e.g.*, Brief Amicus Curiae of Copyright Law Professors in Support of Respondent in Lotus v. Borland, No. 94-2003 (U.S. 1995) (brief submitted by 34 copyright professors urging affirmance for a variety of reasons); Dennis Karjala & Peter S. Menell, *Applying Fundamental Copyright Principles in* Lotus Development Corp. v. Borland International Inc., 10 HIGH TECH. L.J. 177 (1995); Mark A. Lemley, *Convergence in the Law of Software Copyright?*, 10 HIGH TECH. L.J. 1 (1995).

2. In the predecessor case to *Lotus v. Borland*, defendant Paperback Software argued that the command structure of the Lotus program is in essence a language. It can be used to create macros and run the spreadsheet. Is this a fair characterization? The district court attacked this analogy on two basic grounds: that Lotus 1-2-3 was not in fact a language, and that languages could be copyrightable. The first conclusion is certainly debatable; one's definition of a language (or alternatively a "system") will go a long way toward answering this question. But consider the court's second premise— that languages might be copyrightable. Is copyrighting "natural" (i.e., human) languages consistent with what you know of copyright law? Is a language functional or expressive? Does it matter whether the plaintiff is claiming the creation of certain words, on the one hand, or the entire system of grammar and interaction between words? Does the First Circuit's decision in *Lotus v. Borland* shed any light on this issue? Are languages "systems" or "methods of operation" which are denied protection under § 102(b)?

Is the QWERTY keyboard protectable by copyright? Why or why not? Does the answer depend on timing—whether the QWERTY keyboard has just been introduced, or whether it is well-established as the industry standard for typewriters? How would you apply § 102(b) in each case?

3. Both the majority and Judge Boudin's concurrence express concern over the harm that would be done to users of Lotus 1-2-3 if they could not copy their macros for use on Quattro Pro. Certainly, users have invested time and effort in using Lotus 1-2-3, and this may make them reluctant to change spreadsheet programs, even if Borland's program really is superior. But is this the sort of problem with which the copyright law should be concerned? Why isn't a customer preference for a known, trusted product part of the reward that the copyright owner is entitled to reap?

Courts have declined to find copyright protection (often on the grounds of merger) in cases where similarity in computer programs has been dictated by (a) standard practices in the industry for which the software programs are designed, (b) methods or practices that a large population has come to rely upon for daily activities, and (c) the need to operate on common hardware or with common software. *See* Peter S. Menell, *An Epitaph for Traditional Copyright Protection of Network Features of Computer Software*, 43 ANTITRUST BULL. 651 (1998); Peter S. Menell, *An Analysis of the Scope of Copyright Protection for Application Programs*, 41 STAN. L. REV. 1045, 1101–03 (1989) (arguing that a careful application of the merger doctrine can create incentives for the development of better computer application programs).

4. *Java Programming Language.* The copyrightability of application program interfaces (APIs) has reemerged. With the proliferation of programming environments in the 1990s, Sun Microsystems developed the Java object-oriented programming language with the goal and motto of "Write Once, Run Everywhere." Sun made most of its Java implementations available without charge, enabling Java to become a de facto standard. Many software developers use the Java language, as well as Oracle's API packages, to write applications (commonly referred to as "apps") for desktop and laptop computers, tablets, smartphones, and other devices.

The smartphone industry was poised for disruption in the early 2000 period. Blackberry and Palm were the market leaders. The industry focused on business users. In 2005, Google acquired Android, a mobile phone software start-up. In early 2007, Apple revolutionized the smartphone industry with the introduction of the iPhone. The iPhone vastly expanded the smartphone marketplace. Its iOS operating system and App Store catalyzed the software development community.

In developing a competing, more open, developer-friendly smartphone and app platform, Google chose to use the Java programming language. In addition, Google incorporated 11,500 lines of declarations associated with 37 of over 200 Java™ Platform, Standard Edition 7 API packages in the Android operating system. Google wrote its own implementation code for the 37 APIs. Nonetheless, due to the common programming language, coding conventions, and functional considerations, Google's implementation code for the 37 APIs possessed similarities to the overall structure, sequence, and organization of the Java implementation code. (Google introduced 129 additional APIs.)

Sun Microsystems initially hailed Google's decision to use Java for the Android mobile platform, but negotiations over a license to the APIs stalled because Google's Android platform wasn't fully interoperable with other Java implementations. Google chose to enter the market without a license to use the 37 Java APIs.

After Oracle Corporation acquired Sun Microsystems in 2010, Oracle sued Google alleging infringement of the 37 Java APIs. Google countered that there was only one way to write the Java method declarations and remain "interoperable" with Java and that the organization and structure of the 37 Java API packages constitute a "command structure" excluded from copyright protection under § 102(b). Judge Alsup agreed, holding that "[s]o long as the specific code used to implement a method is different, anyone is free under the Copyright Act to write his or her own code to carry out exactly the same function or specification of any methods used in the Java API. It does not matter that the declaration or method header lines are identical." *Oracle Am., Inc. v. Google Inc.*, 872 F. Supp. 2d 974, 976 (N.D. Cal. 2012). The district court held that the Java "command structure is a system or method of operation under § 102(b) of the Copyright Act and, therefore, cannot be copyrighted. Duplication of the command structure is necessary for interoperability." *Id.* at 977.

On appeal, the Federal Circuit reversed, holding that the "structure, sequence and organization" of an API was copyrightable and that even small amounts of literal copying was not de minimis. *See Oracle Am., Inc. v. Google Inc.*, 750 F.3d 1339 (Fed. Cir. 2014); *see generally* Peter S. Menell, *Rise of the API Copyright Dead?: An Updated Epitaph for Copyright Protection of Network and Functional Features of Computer Software*, 31 HARVARD J. L. & TECH. 305 (Special Issue: Software Interface Copyright, 2018) (tracing the history of software copyright jurisprudence and critiquing the Federal Circuit's decision); *see also* Peter S. Menell, *API Copyrightability Bleak House: Unraveling and Repairing the* Oracle v. Google *Jurisdictional Mess*, 31 BERKELEY TECH. L.J. 1515 (2016) (proposing that the Federal Circuit's jurisdiction be reformed so as to restore fidelity to regional circuit authority over copyright issues). The Federal Circuit remanded the case for a determination as to whether Google's use of the Java APIs constituted fair use, an issue on which the first jury deadlocked. In a second trial that concluded in May 2016, the jury ruled in Google's favor. The Federal Circuit reversed the district court again. *See Oracle Am., Inc. v. Google Inc.*, 886 F.3d 1179 (Fed. Cir. 2018). We explore the fair use aspect of the controversy in *Problem IV-56*.

Morrissey v. Procter & Gamble
United States Court of Appeals for the First Circuit
379 F.2d 675 (1st Cir. 1967)

ALDRICH, Chief Judge.

This is an appeal from a summary judgment for the defendant. The plaintiff, Morrissey, is the copyright owner of a set of rules for a sales promotional contest of the "sweepstakes" type involving the social security numbers of the participants. Plaintiff alleges that the defendant, Procter & Gamble Company, infringed, by copying almost precisely, Rule 1. In its motion for summary judgment, based upon affidavits and depositions, defendant denies that plaintiff's Rule 1 is copyrightable material, and denies access. The district court held for the defendant on both grounds. . . .

The second aspect of the case raises a more difficult question. Before discussing it we recite plaintiff's Rule 1, and defendant's Rule 1, the italicizing in the latter being ours to note the defendant's variations or changes.

> 1. Entrants should print name, address and social security number on a boxtop, or a plain paper. Entries must be accompanied by . . . boxtop or by plain paper on which the name . . . is copied from any source. Official rules are explained on . . . packages or leaflets obtained from dealer. If you do not have a social security number you may use the name and number of any member of your immediate family living with you. Only the person named on the entry will be deemed an entrant and may qualify for prize.
>
> Use the correct social security number belonging to the person named on entry. . . . [A] wrong number will be disqualified.

(Plaintiff's Rule)

> 1. Entrants should print name, address and Social Security number on a Tide boxtop, or *on* [a] plain paper. Entries must be accompanied by Tide boxtop *(any size)* or by plain paper on which the name "Tide" is copied from any source. Official rules are *available* on Tide Sweepstakes packages, or *on* leaflets *at* Tide dealers, *or you can send a stamped, self-addressed envelope to:* Tide "Shopping Fling" Sweepstakes, P.O. Box 4459, Chicago 77, Illinois.
>
> If you do not have a Social Security number, you may use the name and number of any member of your immediate family living with you. Only the person named on the entry will be deemed an entrant and may qualify for a prize.
>
> Use the correct Social Security number, belonging to the person named on *the* entry—wrong numbers will be disqualified.

(Defendant's Rule)

The district court, following an earlier decision, *Gaye v. Gillis*, D. Mass., 1958, 167 F. Supp. 416, took the position that since the substance of the contest was not copyrightable, which is unquestionably correct, *Baker v. Selden*, 101 U.S. 99 (1879); *Affiliated Enters. v. Gruber*, 86 F.2d 958 (1st Cir. 1936); *Chamberlin v. Uris Sales Corp.*, 150 F.2d 512 (2d Cir. 1945), and the substance was relatively simple, it must follow that plaintiff's rule sprung directly from the substance and "contains no original creative authorship." 262 F. Supp. at 738. This does not follow. Copyright attaches to form of expression, and defendant's own proof, introduced to deluge the court on the issue of access, itself established that there was more than one way of expressing even this simple substance. Nor, in view of the almost precise similarity of the two rules, could defendant successfully invoke the principle of a stringent standard for showing infringement which some courts apply when the subject matter involved admits of little variation in form of expression. . . .

Nonetheless, we must hold for the defendant. When the uncopyrightable subject matter is very narrow, so that "the topic necessarily requires," *Sampson & Murdock Co. v. Seaver-Radford Co.*, 140 F. 539, 541 (1st Cir. 1905); *cf.* KAPLAN, AN UNHURRIED VIEW OF COPYRIGHT, 64–65 (1967), if not only one form of expression, at best only a limited number, to permit copyrighting would mean that a party or parties, by copyrighting a mere handful of forms, could exhaust all possibilities of future use of the substance. In such circumstances it does not seem accurate to say that any particular form of expression comes from the subject matter. However, it is necessary to say that the subject matter would be appropriated by permitting the copyrighting of its expression. We cannot recognize copyright as a game of chess in which the public can be checkmated. *Cf. Baker v. Selden, supra.*

Upon examination the matters embraced in Rule 1 are so straightforward and simple that we find this limiting principle to be applicable. Furthermore, its operation need not await an attempt to copyright all possible forms. It cannot be only the last form of expression which is to be condemned, as completing defendant's exclusion from the substance. Rather, in these circumstances, we hold that copyright does not extend to the subject matter at all, and plaintiff cannot complain even if his particular expression was deliberately adopted.

Affirmed.

COMMENTS AND QUESTIONS

1. *The Merger Doctrine.* The *Morrissey* case applies what has come to be known as the "merger" doctrine: when there is only one or but a few ways of expressing an idea, then courts will find that the idea behind the work *merges* with its expression and the work is not copyrightable. The doctrine is an extension of the basic rationale of *Baker v. Selden.*

2. *Objective or Pragmatic Standard.* Application of the merger doctrine involves the same "levels of abstraction" problem described earlier. Characterizing the "idea" of a work at a lower level of abstraction brings the idea in close alignment with the expression, rendering that expression unprotectable. Logically, the doctrine follows the form, "categories (or genuses) are unprotectable; instances (or species) are protectable." The game then becomes to define what is the category or genus to which the work belongs. The more fine-grained and precise the definition of the category or genus, the more likely that the "expression" alleged to have been infringed is in fact an "idea."

Some courts have softened the harsh consequences of finding merger (i.e., no protection against copying) by finding that works with limited means of expression are copyrightable but that the scope of copyright protection for such works is "thin." In *Continental Casualty Co. v. Beardsley*, 253 F.2d 702 (2d Cir. 1958), the Second Circuit determined that the forms developed by the creator of a new type of insurance covering lost securities were copyrightable. The forms in question included explanatory information. The court reasoned that in the fields of insurance and commerce the use of specific language in forms and documents may be so essential to accomplish a desired result and so integrated with the use of a legal or commercial conception that the proper standard of infringement is one which will protect as far as possible the copyrighted language and yet allow free use of the thought beneath the language.

Since the competitor copied only the forms and not the explanatory language, however, the court determined that no infringement had occurred. Does this approach better comport with the objectives and structure of copyright law? Or might it force subsequent authors to use awkward variations in expression in order to make use of an unprotectable idea?

3. *Scenes à Faire.* Copyright protection does not extend to the "incidents, characters or settings which are as a practical matter indispensable, or at least standard, in the treatment of a given topic." *Atari, Inc. v. N. Am. Philips Consumer Elecs.*, 672 F.2d 607, 616 (7th Cir. 1982). To allow protection for such aspects of a work would unduly restrict subsequent authors in building their own works within general settings with which their audiences will relate.

4. *Revisiting the "Created Facts" Conundrum.* As noted previously, various forms of information—from part numbers to coin valuations to names and relationships among fictional characters (e.g., Fred Flintstone's wife)—represent an admixture of fact and creativity. Rather than apply *Feist*'s artificial definition of facts—things that are discovered and not created—would it be better to ground the resolution of disputes about created facts in the limiting doctrines—merger, idea-expression, *scenes à faire*, fair use, and implied license? *See* Justin Hughes, *Created Facts and the Flawed Ontology of Copyright Law*, 83 NOTRE DAME L. REV. 43 (2007).

PROBLEM

Problem IV-13. Insect Representations, Inc., sells a highly successful line of jewelry in the shape of various insects. One of its products is a stickpin in the shape of a bumblebee, made of gold veining and encrusted with a number of white gems. Animal Jewelry Corp. designs and markets a jeweled bee pin that also has gold veining and is encrusted with gems. However, Animal uses a different number of total gems, and some of its gems are colors other than white.

Insect Representations   **Animal Jewelry Corp.**

When Insect sues Animal for copyright infringement, Animal defends on the grounds that it has taken merely the "idea" of a jeweled bee pin. Who should prevail?

---

ii. The Useful Article Doctrine

Section 101 of the Copyright Act defines "pictorial, graphic, and sculptural [PGS] works," one of the categories of works protected under § 102, to include

> two-dimensional and three-dimensional works of fine, graphic, and applied art, photographs, prints and art reproductions, maps, globes, charts, diagrams, models, and technical drawings, including architectural plans. Such works shall include works of artistic craftsmanship insofar as their form but not their mechanical or utilitarian aspects are concerned; the design of a useful article, as defined in this section, shall be considered a pictorial, graphic, or sculptural work only if, and only to the extent that, such design incorporates pictorial, graphic, or sculptural features that can be identified separately from, and are capable of existing independently of, the utilitarian aspects of the article.

The Act defines a "useful article" as an "article having an intrinsic utilitarian function that is not merely to portray the appearance of the article or to convey information. An article that is normally a part of a useful article is considered a 'useful article.'" § 101.

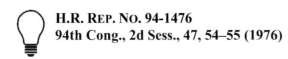

[T]he definition of "pictorial, graphic, and sculptural works" carries with it no implied criterion of artistic taste, aesthetic value, or intrinsic quality. The term is intended to comprise not only "works of art" in the traditional sense but also . . . works of "applied art." . . .

In accordance with the Supreme Court's decision in *Mazer v. Stein*, 347 U.S. 201 (1954), works of "applied art" encompass all original pictorial, graphic, and sculptural works that are intended to be or have been embodied in useful articles, regardless of factors such as mass production, commercial exploitation, and the potential availability of design patent protection. . . .

The Committee has added language to the definition of "pictorial, graphic, and sculptural works" in an effort to make clearer the distinction between works of applied art protectable under the bill and industrial designs not subject to copyright protection. The declaration that "pictorial, graphic, and sculptural works" include "works of artistic craftsmanship insofar as their form but not their mechanical or utilitarian aspects are concerned" is classic language: it is drawn from Copyright Office regulations promulgated in the 1940s and was expressly endorsed by the Supreme Court in the *Mazer* case.

The second part of the amendment states that "the design of a useful article . . . shall be considered a pictorial, graphic, or sculptural work only if, and only to the extent that, such design incorporates pictorial, graphic, or sculptural features that can be identified separately from, and are capable of existing independently of, the utilitarian aspects of the article." . . .

In adopting this amendatory language, the Committee is seeking to draw as clear a line as possible between copyrightable works of applied art and uncopyrighted works of industrial design. A two-dimensional painting, drawing, or graphic work is still capable of being identified as such when it is printed on or applied to utilitarian articles such as textile fabrics, wallpaper, containers, and the like. The same is true when a statue or carving is used to embellish an industrial product or, as in the *Mazer* case, is incorporated into a product without losing its ability to exist independently as a work of art. On the other hand, although the shape of an industrial product may be aesthetically satisfying and valuable, the Committee's intention is not to offer it copyright protection under the bill. Unless the shape of an automobile, airplane, ladies' dress, food processor, television set, or any other industrial product contains some element that, physically or conceptually, can be identified as separable from the utilitarian aspects of that article, the design would not be copyrighted under the bill. The test of separability and independence from "the utilitarian aspects of the article" does not depend upon the nature of the design—that is, even if the appearance of an article is determined by aesthetic (as opposed to functional) considerations, only elements, if any, which can be identified separately from the useful article as such are copyrightable. And, even if the three-dimensional design contains some such element (for example, a carving on the back of a chair or a floral relief design on silver flatware), copyright protection would extend only to that element, and would not cover the over-all configuration of the utilitarian article as such.

Star Athletica v. Varsity Brands
Supreme Court of the United States
137 S.Ct. 1002 (2017)

JUSTICE THOMAS delivered the opinion of the Court.

Congress has provided copyright protection for original works of art, but not for industrial designs. The line between art and industrial design, however, is often difficult to draw. This is particularly true when an industrial design incorporates artistic elements. Congress has afforded limited protection for these artistic elements by providing that "pictorial, graphic, or sculptural features" of the "design of a useful article" are eligible for copyright protection as artistic works if those features "can be identified separately from, and are capable of existing independently of, the utilitarian aspects of the article." 17 U.S.C. § 101.

We granted certiorari to resolve widespread disagreement over the proper test for implementing § 101's separate-identification and independent-existence requirements. We hold that a feature incorporated into the design of a useful article is eligible for copyright protection only if the feature (1) can be perceived as a two- or three-dimensional work of art separate from the useful article and (2) would qualify as a protectable pictorial, graphic, or sculptural work—either on its own or fixed in some other tangible medium of expression—if it were imagined separately from the useful article into which it is incorporated. Because that test is satisfied in this case, we affirm.

I

Respondents Varsity Brands . . . design, make, and sell cheerleading uniforms. Respondents have obtained or acquired more than 200 U.S. copyright registrations for two-dimensional designs appearing on the surface of their uniforms and other garments. These designs are primarily "combinations, positionings, and arrangements of elements" that include "chevrons . . . , lines, curves, stripes, angles, diagonals, inverted [chevrons], coloring, and shapes." At issue in this case are Designs 299A, 299B, 074, 078, and 0815.

Design 299A   Design 299B

Design 074   Design 078   Design 0815

Petitioner Star Athletica, L.L.C., also markets and sells cheerleading uniforms. Respondents sued petitioner for infringing their copyrights in the five designs. . . .

II

The first element of a copyright-infringement claim is "ownership of a valid copyright." A valid copyright extends only to copyrightable subject matter. . . .

The Copyright Act [] establishes a special rule for copyrighting a pictorial, graphic, or sculptural work incorporated into a "useful article," which is defined as "an article having an intrinsic utilitarian function that is not merely to portray the appearance of the article or to convey information." The statute does not protect useful articles as such. Rather, "the design of a useful article" is "considered a pictorial, graphical, or sculptural work only if, and only to the extent that, such design incorporates pictorial, graphic, or sculptural features that can be identified separately from, and are capable of existing independently of, the utilitarian aspects of the article." . . .

. . . In this case, our task is to determine whether the arrangements of lines, chevrons, and colorful shapes appearing on the surface of respondents' cheerleading uniforms are eligible for copyright protection as separable features of the design of those cheerleading uniforms. . . .

B

We must [] decide when a feature incorporated into useful article "can be identified separately from" and is "capable of existing independently of" "the utilitarian aspects" of the article. This is not a free-ranging search for the best copyright policy, but rather "depends solely on statutory interpretation." *Mazer v. Stein*, 347 U.S. 201, 214 (1954). "The controlling principle in this case is the basic and unexceptional rule that courts must give effect to the clear meaning of statutes as written." We thus begin and end our inquiry with the text, giving each word its "ordinary, contemporary, common meaning."

The statute provides that a "pictorial, graphic, or sculptural featur[e]" incorporated into the "design of a useful article" is eligible for copyright protection if it (1) "can be identified separately from," and (2) is "capable of existing independently of, the utilitarian aspects of the article." § 101. The first requirement—separate identification—is not onerous. The decisionmaker need only be able to look at the useful article and spot some two- or three-dimensional element that appears to have pictorial, graphic, or sculptural qualities.

The independent-existence requirement is ordinarily more difficult to satisfy. The decisionmaker must determine that the separately identified feature has the capacity to exist apart from the utilitarian aspects of the article. In other words, the feature must be able to exist as its own pictorial, graphic, or sculptural work as defined in § 101 once it is imagined apart from the useful article. If the feature is not capable of existing as a pictorial, graphic, or sculptural work once separated from the useful article, then it was not a pictorial, graphic, or sculptural feature of that article, but rather one of its utilitarian aspects.

Of course, to qualify as a pictorial, graphic, or sculptural work on its own, the feature cannot itself be a useful article or "[a]n article that is normally a part of a useful article" (which is itself considered a useful article). § 101. Nor could someone claim a copyright in a useful article merely by creating a replica of that article in some other medium—for example, a cardboard model of a car. Although the replica could itself be copyrightable, it would not give rise to any rights in the useful article that inspired it.

2

The statute as a whole confirms our interpretation. The Copyright Act provides "the owner of [a] copyright" with the "exclusive righ[t] . . . to reproduce the copyrighted work in copies." § 106(1). The statute clarifies that this right "includes the right to reproduce the [copyrighted] work in or on any kind of article, whether useful or otherwise." § 113(a). Section 101 is, in essence, the mirror image of § 113(a). Whereas

§ 113(a) protects a work of authorship first fixed in some tangible medium other than a useful article and subsequently applied to a useful article, § 101 protects art first fixed in the medium of a useful article. The two provisions make clear that copyright protection extends to pictorial, graphic, and sculptural works regardless of whether they were created as freestanding art or as features of useful articles. The ultimate separability question, then, is whether the feature for which copyright protection is claimed would have been eligible for copyright protection as a pictorial, graphic, or sculptural work had it originally been fixed in some tangible medium other than a useful article before being applied to a useful article.

3

This interpretation is also consistent with the history of the Copyright Act. . . .

Two of *Mazer*'s holdings are relevant here. First, the Court held that the respondents owned a copyright in the statuette even though it was intended for use as a lamp base. In doing so, the Court approved the Copyright Office's regulation extending copyright protection to works of art that might also serve a useful purpose.

Second, the Court held that it was irrelevant to the copyright inquiry whether the statuette was initially created as a freestanding sculpture or as a lamp base. . . .

C

In sum, a feature of the design of a useful article is eligible for copyright if, when identified and imagined apart from the useful article, it would qualify as a pictorial, graphic, or sculptural work either on its own or when fixed in some other tangible medium.

Applying this test to the surface decorations on the cheerleading uniforms is straightforward. First, one can identify the decorations as features having pictorial, graphic, or sculptural qualities. Second, if the arrangement of colors, shapes, stripes, and chevrons on the surface of the cheerleading uniforms were separated from the uniform and applied in another medium—for example, on a painter's canvas—they would qualify as "two-dimensional . . . works of . . . art," § 101. And imaginatively removing the surface decorations from the uniforms and applying them in another medium would not replicate the uniform itself. Indeed, respondents have applied the designs in this case to other media of expression—different types of clothing—without replicating the uniform. The decorations are therefore separable from the uniforms and eligible for copyright protection.[1]

The dissent argues that the designs are not separable because imaginatively removing them from the uniforms and placing them in some other medium of

---

[1] We do not today hold that the surface decorations are copyrightable. We express no opinion on whether these works are sufficiently original to qualify for copyright protection, see *Feist Publications, Inc. v. Rural Telephone Service Co.*, 499 U.S. 340–359 (1991), or on whether any other prerequisite of a valid copyright has been satisfied.

expression—a canvas, for example—would create "pictures of cheerleader uniforms."
. . .

This is not a bar to copyright. Just as two-dimensional fine art corresponds to the shape of the canvas on which it is painted, two-dimensional applied art correlates to the contours of the article on which it is applied. A fresco painted on a wall, ceiling panel, or dome would not lose copyright protection, for example, simply because it was designed to track the dimensions of the surface on which it was painted. Or consider, for example, a design etched or painted on the surface of a guitar. If that entire design is imaginatively removed from the guitar's surface and placed on an album cover, it would still resemble the shape of a guitar. But the image on the cover does not "replicate" the guitar as a useful article. Rather, the design is a two-dimensional work of art that corresponds to the shape of the useful article to which it was applied. The statute protects that work of art whether it is first drawn on the album cover and then applied to the guitar's surface, or vice versa. Failing to protect that art would create an anomaly: It would extend protection to two-dimensional designs that cover a part of a useful article but would not protect the same design if it covered the entire article. The statute does not support that distinction, nor can it be reconciled with the dissent's recognition that "artwork printed on a t-shirt" could be protected.

To be clear, the only feature of the cheerleading uniform eligible for a copyright in this case is the two-dimensional work of art fixed in the tangible medium of the uniform fabric. Even if respondents ultimately succeed in establishing a valid copyright in the surface decorations at issue here, respondents have no right to prohibit any person from manufacturing a cheerleading uniform of identical shape, cut, and dimensions to the ones on which the decorations in this case appear. They may prohibit only the reproduction of the surface designs in any tangible medium of expression—a uniform or otherwise.[2] . . .

D

. . .

1

. . . According to petitioner, if a feature of a useful article "advance[s] the utility of the article," then it is categorically beyond the scope of copyright. The designs here are not protected, it argues, because they are necessary to two of the uniforms' "inherent, essential, or natural functions"—identifying the wearer as a cheerleader and enhancing

---

[2] The dissent suggests that our test would lead to the copyrighting of shovels. But a shovel, like a cheerleading uniform, even if displayed in an art gallery, is "an article having an intrinsic utilitarian function that is not merely to portray the appearance of the article or to convey information." 17 U.S.C. § 101. It therefore cannot be copyrighted. A drawing of a shovel could, of course, be copyrighted. And, if the shovel included any artistic features that could be perceived as art apart from the shovel, and which would qualify as protectable pictorial, graphic, or sculptural works on their own or in another medium, they too could be copyrighted. But a shovel as a shovel cannot.

the wearer's physical appearance. Because the uniforms would not be equally useful without the designs, petitioner contends that the designs are inseparable from the "utilitarian aspects" of the uniform.

The Government . . . suggests that the appropriate test is whether the useful article with the artistic feature removed would "remai[n] *similarly* useful." In the view of the United States, however, a plain white cheerleading uniform is "similarly useful" to uniforms with respondents' designs.

The debate over the relative utility of a plain white cheerleading uniform is unnecessary. The focus of the separability inquiry is on the extracted feature and not on any aspects of the useful article that remain after the imaginary extraction. The statute does not require the decisionmaker to imagine a fully functioning useful article without the artistic feature. Instead, it requires that the separated feature qualify as a nonuseful pictorial, graphic, or sculptural work on its own.

Of course, because the removed feature may not be a useful article—as it would then not qualify as a pictorial, graphic, or sculptural work—there necessarily would be some aspects of the original useful article "left behind" if the feature were conceptually removed. But the statute does not require the imagined remainder to be a fully functioning useful article at all, much less an equally useful one. . . .

Because we reject the view that a useful article must remain after the artistic feature has been imaginatively separated from the article, we necessarily abandon the distinction between "physical" and "conceptual" separability, which some courts and commentators have adopted based on the Copyright Act's legislative history.

The statutory text indicates that separability is a conceptual undertaking. Because separability does not require the underlying useful article to remain, the physical-conceptual distinction is unnecessary.

2

Petitioner next argues that we should incorporate two "objective" components into our test to provide guidance to the lower courts: (1) "whether the design elements can be identified as reflecting the designer's artistic judgment exercised independently of functional influence," and (2) whether "there is [a] substantial likelihood that the pictorial, graphic, or sculptural feature would still be marketable to some significant segment of the community without its utilitarian function."

We reject this argument because neither consideration is grounded in the text of the statute. The statute's text makes clear that our inquiry is limited to how the article and feature are perceived, not how or why they were designed. See *Brandir Int'l, Inc. v. Cascade Pacific Lumber Co.*, 834 F. 2d 1142, 1152 (CA2 1987) (Winter, J., concurring in part and dissenting in part) (The statute "expressly states that the legal test is how the final article is perceived, not how it was developed through various stages").

The same is true of marketability. Nothing in the statute suggests that copyrightability depends on market surveys. Moreover, asking whether some segment of the market would be interested in a given work threatens to prize popular art over other forms, or to substitute judicial aesthetic preferences for the policy choices embodied in the Copyright Act.

3

Finally, petitioner argues that allowing the surface decorations to qualify as a "work of authorship" is inconsistent with Congress' intent to entirely exclude industrial design from copyright. Petitioner notes that Congress refused to pass a provision that would have provided limited copyright protection for industrial designs, including clothing, when it enacted the 1976 Act and that it has enacted laws protecting designs for specific useful articles—semiconductor chips and boat hulls—while declining to enact other industrial design statutes. From this history of failed legislation petitioner reasons that Congress intends to channel intellectual property claims for industrial design into design patents. It therefore urges us to approach this question with a presumption against copyrightability.

We do not share petitioner's concern. As an initial matter, "[c]ongressional inaction lacks persuasive significance" in most circumstances. Moreover, we have long held that design patent and copyright are not mutually exclusive. In any event, as explained above, our test does not render the shape, cut, and physical dimensions of the cheerleading uniforms eligible for copyright protection.

JUSTICE GINSBURG, concurring in the judgment.

I concur in the Court's judgment but not in its opinion. Unlike the majority, I would not take up in this case the separability test appropriate under 17 U.S.C. § 101. Consideration of that test is unwarranted because the designs at issue are not designs of useful articles. Instead, the designs are themselves copyrightable pictorial or graphic works *reproduced on* useful articles.

A pictorial, graphic, or sculptural work (PGS work) is copyrightable. § 102(a)(5). PGS works include "two dimensional and three-dimensional works of fine, graphic, and applied art." § 101. Key to this case, a copyright in a standalone PGS work "includes the right to reproduce the work in or on any kind of article, whether useful or otherwise." § 113(a). Because the owner of a copyright in a preexisting PGS work may exclude a would-be infringer from reproducing that work on a useful article, there is no need to engage in any separability inquiry to resolve the instant petition.

The designs here in controversy are standalone pictorial and graphic works that respondents Varsity Brands reproduce on cheerleading uniforms. Varsity's designs first appeared as pictorial and graphic works that Varsity's design team sketched on paper. Varsity then sought copyright protection for those two-dimensional designs, not for cheerleading costumes; its registration statements claimed "2-Dimensional artwork" and "fabric design (artwork)." Varsity next reproduced its two-dimensional graphic designs on cheerleading uniforms, also on other garments, including T-shirts and jackets.

In short, Varsity's designs are standalone PGS works that may gain copyright protection as such, including the exclusive right to reproduce the designs on useful articles.

JUSTICE BREYER, with whom JUSTICE KENNEDY joins, dissenting.

I agree with much in the Court's opinion. But I do not agree that the designs that Varsity Brands, Inc., submitted to the Copyright Office are eligible for copyright protection. Even applying the majority's test, the designs cannot "be perceived as . . . two- or three-dimensional work[s] of art separate from the useful article."

Look at the designs that Varsity submitted to the Copyright Office. You will see only pictures of cheerleader uniforms. And cheerleader uniforms are useful articles. A picture of the relevant design features, whether separately "perceived" on paper or in the imagination, is a picture of, and thereby "replicate[s]," the underlying useful article of which they are a part. Hence the design features that Varsity seeks to protect are not "capable of existing independently o[f] the utilitarian aspects of the article." 17 U.S.C. § 101.

I

The relevant statutory provision says that the "design of a useful article" is copyrightable "only if, and only to the extent that, such design incorporates pictorial, graphic, or sculptural features that can be identified separately from, and are capable of existing independently of, the utilitarian aspects of the article." But what, we must ask, do the words "identified separately" mean? The most direct, helpful aspect of the Court's opinion answers this question by stating:

> "Nor could someone claim a copyright in a useful article merely by creating a replica of that article in some other medium—for example, a cardboard model of a car. Although the replica could itself be copyrightable, it would not give rise to any rights in the useful article that inspired it."

Exactly so. These words help explain the Court's statement that a copyrightable work of art must be "perceived as a two- or three-dimensional work of art separate from the useful article." They help clarify the concept of separateness. They are consistent with Congress' own expressed intent.

Consider, for example, the explanation that the House Report for the Copyright Act of 1976 provides. It says:

> "Unless the shape of an automobile, airplane, ladies' dress, food processor, television set, or any other industrial product contains some element that, *physically or conceptually*, can be identified as separable from the utilitarian aspects of that article, the design would not be copyrighted . . . ." H. R. Rep., at 55 (emphasis added).

These words suggest two exercises, one physical, one mental. Can the design features (the picture, the graphic, the sculpture) be physically removed from the article (and considered separately), all the while leaving the fully functioning utilitarian object in place? If not, can one nonetheless conceive of the design features separately without replicating a picture of the utilitarian object? If the answer to either of these questions is "yes," then the design is eligible for copyright protection. Otherwise, it is not.

An example will help. Imagine a lamp with a circular marble base, a vertical 10-inch tall brass rod (containing wires) inserted off center on the base, a light bulb fixture emerging from the top of the brass rod, and a lampshade sitting on top. In front of the brass rod a porcelain Siamese cat sits on the base facing outward. Obviously, the Siamese cat is *physically separate* from the lamp, as it could be easily removed while leaving both cat and lamp intact. And, assuming it otherwise qualifies, the designed cat is eligible for copyright protection.

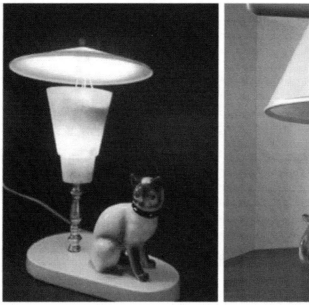 

Fig. 1   Fig. 2

Now suppose there is no long brass rod; instead the cat sits in the middle of the base and the wires run up through the cat to the bulbs. The cat is not physically separate from the lamp, as the reality of the lamp's construction is such that an effort to physically separate the cat and lamp will destroy both cat and lamp. The two are integrated into a single functional object, like the similar configuration of the ballet dancer statuettes that formed the lamp bases at issue in *Mazer v. Stein*, 347 U.S. 201 (1954). But we can easily imagine the cat on its own, as did Congress when conceptualizing the ballet dancer. *See* H.R. Rep., at 55 (the statuette in *Mazer* was "incorporated into a product without losing its ability to exist independently as a work of art"). In doing so, we do not create a mental picture of a lamp (or, in the Court's words, a "replica" of the lamp), which is a useful article. We simply perceive the cat separately, as a small cat figurine that could be a copyrightable design work standing alone that does not replicate the lamp. Hence the cat is conceptually separate from the utilitarian article that is the lamp. The pair of lamps pictured at Figures 1 and 2 illustrate this principle. . . .

By way of contrast, Van Gogh's painting of a pair of old shoes, though beautifully executed and copyrightable as a painting, would not qualify for a shoe design copyright. *See* 17 U.S.C. §§ 113(a)–(b).

Fig. 3: Vincent Van Gogh, "Shoes"

Courts have similarly denied copyright protection to objects that begin as three-dimensional designs, such as measuring spoons shaped like heart-tipped arrows, *Bonazoli v. R.S.V.P. Int'l, Inc.*, 353 F. Supp. 2d 218, 226–227 (D.R.I. 2005); candleholders shaped like sailboats, *Design Ideas, Ltd. v. Yankee Candle Co.*, 889 F. Supp. 2d 1119, 1128 (C.D. Ill. 2012); and wire spokes on a wheel cover, *Norris Industries, Inc. v. International Tel. & Tel. Corp.*, 696 F.2d 918, 922–924 (11th Cir. 1983). Why not? Because in each case the design is not separable from the utilitarian aspects of the object to which it relates. The designs cannot be physically separated because they themselves make up the shape of the spoon, candleholders, or wheel covers of which they are a part. And spoons, candleholders, and wheel covers are useful objects, as are the old shoes depicted in Van Gogh's painting. More importantly, one cannot easily imagine or otherwise conceptualize the design of the spoons or the candleholders or the shoes *without that picture, or image, or replica being a picture of spoons, or candleholders, or wheel covers, or shoes*. The designs necessarily bring along the underlying utilitarian object. Hence each design is not conceptually separable from the physical useful object.

The upshot is that one could copyright the floral design on a soupspoon but one could not copyright the shape of the spoon itself, no matter how beautiful, artistic, or esthetically pleasing that shape might be: A picture of the shape of the spoon is also a picture of a spoon; the picture of a floral design is not. See Compendium § 924.2(B).

To repeat: A separable design feature must be "capable of existing independently" of the useful article as a separate artistic work that is not itself the useful article. If the claimed feature could be extracted without replicating the useful article of which it is a part, and the result would be a copyrightable artistic work standing alone, then there is a separable design. But if extracting the claimed features would necessarily bring along the underlying useful article, the design is not separable from the useful article. In many or most cases, to decide whether a design or artistic feature of a useful article is conceptually separate from the article itself, it is enough to imagine the feature on its own and ask, "Have I created a picture of a (useful part of a) useful article?" If so, the design is not separable from the useful article. If not, it is.

In referring to imagined pictures and the like, I am not speaking technically. I am simply trying to explain an intuitive idea of what separation is about, as well as how I understand the majority's opinion. So understood, the opinion puts design copyrights in their rightful place. The law has long recognized that drawings or photographs of real world objects are copyrightable as drawings or photographs, but the copyright does not give protection against others making the underlying useful objects. That is why a copyright on Van Gogh's painting would prevent others from reproducing that painting, but it would not prevent others from reproducing and selling the comfortable old shoes that the painting depicts.

II

To ask this kind of simple question—does the design picture the useful article?—will not provide an answer in every case, for there will be cases where it is difficult to say whether a picture of the design is, or is not, also a picture of the useful article. But the question will avoid courts focusing primarily upon what I believe is an unhelpful feature of the inquiry, namely, whether the design can be imagined as a "two- or three-dimensional work of art." That is because virtually any industrial design can be thought of separately as a "work of art": Just imagine a frame surrounding the design, or its being placed in a gallery. Consider Marcel Duchamp's "readymades" series, the functional mass-produced objects he designated as art.

Fig. 4: Marcel Duchamp,
"In Advance of the Broken Arm"

What is there in the world that, viewed through an esthetic lens, cannot be seen as a good, bad, or indifferent work of art? What design features could not be imaginatively reproduced on a painter's canvas? Indeed, great industrial design may well include design that is inseparable from the useful article—where, as Frank Lloyd Wright put it, "form and function are one." FRANK LLOYD WRIGHT, AN AUTOBIOGRAPHY 146 (1943) (reprint 2005). Where they are one, the designer may be able to obtain 15 years of protection through a design patent. 35 U.S.C. §§ 171, 173; *see also* Mark P. McKenna & Katherine J. Strandburg, *Progress and Competition in Design*, 17 STAN. TECH. L. REV. 1, 48–51 (2013). But, if they are one, Congress did not intend a century or more of copyright protection.

III

The conceptual approach that I have described reflects Congress' answer to a problem that is primarily practical and economic. Years ago Lord Macaulay drew attention to the problem when he described copyright in books as a "tax on readers for the purpose of giving a bounty to writers." He called attention to the main benefit of copyright protection, which is to provide an incentive to produce copyrightable works and thereby "promote the Progress of Science and useful Arts." U.S. CONST., ART. I, § 8, cl. 8. But Macaulay also made clear that copyright protection imposes costs. Those costs include the higher prices that can accompany the grant of a copyright monopoly. They also can include (for those wishing to display, sell, or perform a design, film, work of art, or piece of music, for example) the costs of discovering whether there are previous copyrights, of contacting copyright holders, and of securing permission to copy. Sometimes, as Thomas Jefferson wrote to James Madison, costs can outweigh "the benefit even of limited monopolies." And that is particularly true in light of the fact that Congress has extended the "limited Times" of protection, from the "14 years" of Jefferson's day to potentially more than a century today.

The Constitution grants Congress primary responsibility for assessing comparative costs and benefits and drawing copyright's statutory lines. Courts must respect those lines and not grant copyright protection where Congress has decided not to do so. And it is clear that Congress has not extended broad copyright protection to the fashion design industry. *See, e.g.,* 1 NIMMER § 2A.08[H][3][c] (describing how Congress rejected proposals for fashion design protection within the 1976 Act and has rejected every proposed bill to this effect since then); *Esquire, Inc. v. Ringer,* 591 F. 2d 796, 800, n. 12 (CADC 1978) (observing that at the time of the 1976 Copyright Act, Congress had rejected every one of the approximately 70 design protection bills that had been introduced since 1914).

Congress' decision not to grant full copyright protection to the fashion industry has not left the industry without protection. Patent design protection is available. A maker of clothing can obtain trademark protection under the Lanham Act for signature features of the clothing. And a designer who creates an original textile design can receive copyright protection for that pattern as placed, for example, on a bolt of cloth, or anything made with that cloth.

The fashion industry has thrived against this backdrop, and designers have contributed immeasurably to artistic and personal self-expression through clothing. But a decision by this Court to grant protection to the design of a garment would grant the designer protection that Congress refused to provide. It would risk increased prices and unforeseeable disruption in the clothing industry, which in the United States alone encompasses nearly $370 billion in annual spending and 1.8 million jobs. That is why I believe it important to emphasize those parts of the Court's opinion that limit the scope of its interpretation. That language, as I have said, makes clear that one may not "claim a copyright in a useful article merely by creating a replica of that article in some other medium," which "would not give rise to any rights in the useful article that inspired it."

IV

If we ask the "separateness" question correctly, the answer here is not difficult to find. . . . Can the design features in Varsity's pictures exist separately from the utilitarian aspects of a dress? Can we extract those features as copyrightable design works standing alone, without bringing along, via picture or design, the dresses of which they constitute a part?

Consider designs 074, 078, and 0815. They certainly look like cheerleader uniforms. That is to say, they look like pictures of cheerleader uniforms, just like Van Gogh's old shoes look like shoes. I do not see how one could see them otherwise. Designs 299A and 2999B present slightly closer questions. They omit some of the dresslike context that the other designs possess. But the necklines, the sleeves, and the cut of the skirt suggest that they too are pictures of dresses. Looking at all five of Varsity's pictures, I do not see how one could conceptualize the design features in a way that does not picture, not just artistic designs, but dresses as well.

Were I to accept the majority's invitation to "imaginatively remov[e]" the chevrons and stripes as they are arranged on the neckline, waistline, sleeves, and skirt of each uniform, and apply them on a "painter's canvas," that painting would be of a cheerleader's dress. The esthetic elements on which Varsity seeks protection exist only as part of the uniform design—there is nothing to separate out but for dress-shaped lines that replicate the cut and style of the uniforms. Hence, each design is not physically separate, nor is it conceptually separate, from the useful article it depicts, namely, a cheerleader's dress. They cannot be copyrighted.

Varsity, of course, could have sought a design patent for its designs. Or, it could have sought a copyright on a textile design, even one with a similar theme of chevrons and lines.

But that is not the nature of Varsity's copyright claim. It has instead claimed ownership of the particular "'treatment and arrangement'" of the chevrons and lines of the design as they appear at the neckline, waist, skirt, sleeves, and overall cut of each uniform. The majority imagines that Varsity submitted something different—that is, only the surface decorations of chevrons and stripes, as in a textile design. As the majority sees it, Varsity's copyright claim would be the same had it submitted a plain rectangular space depicting chevrons and stripes, like swaths from a bolt of fabric. But considered on their own, the simple stripes are plainly unoriginal. Varsity, then, seeks to do indirectly what it cannot do directly: bring along the design and cut of the dresses by seeking to protect surface decorations whose "treatment and arrangement" *are coextensive with that design and cut.* As Varsity would have it, it would prevent its competitors from making useful three-dimensional cheerleader uniforms by submitting plainly unoriginal chevrons and stripes as cut and arranged on a useful article. But with that cut and arrangement, the resulting pictures on which Varsity seeks protection do not simply depict designs. They depict clothing. They depict the useful articles of which the designs are inextricable parts. And Varsity cannot obtain copyright protection that would give them the power to prevent others from making those useful uniforms, any more than Van Gogh can copyright comfortable old shoes by painting their likeness.

I fear that, in looking past the three-dimensional design inherent in Varsity's claim by treating it as if it were no more than a design for a bolt of cloth, the majority has lost sight of its own important limiting principle. One may not "claim a copyright in a useful article merely by creating a replica of that article in some other medium," such as in a picture. That is to say, one cannot obtain a copyright that would give its holder "any rights in the useful article that inspired it."

With respect, I dissent.

COMMENTS AND QUESTIONS

1. *Useful Article.* A threshold issue is whether a work is a useful article at all. According to § 101, a useful article is a work "having an intrinsic utilitarian function that is not merely to portray the appearance of the article or to convey information." Thus, a drawing of a rocket ship would not satisfy this definition, but the rocket ship itself would be a useful article. Nonetheless, the definition is difficult to apply as the degree of functionality wanes and the degree of fanciful and artistic expression rises. Consider the following examples:

- a distinctively decorated toy airplane
- clothing for a fashion doll
- an ornamental fireplace hearth that cannot burn wood

2. The majority claims that it is engaged merely in applying the plain meaning of § 101, but it does not discuss the entirety of the statutory definition. The definition of a pictorial, graphic, and sculptural work says that "[s]uch works shall include works of artistic craftsmanship insofar as their form but not their mechanical or utilitarian aspects are concerned." Is that true of the uniforms at issue in *Star Athletica*? Of other objects? Doesn't that language require some way of excluding the utilitarian aspects of a work from the scope of the copyright?

3. *Originality.* The Supreme Court remanded the case for a determination of whether the works at issue meet copyright law's originality standard. The case promptly settled. Do you think the works at issue possess the requisite "modicum of creativity"?

4. *The Conceptual Separability Test.* The conceptual separability test has been difficult to apply. Does *Star Athletica* simplify the inquiry? How is a court to separate the aesthetic from the useful elements in a useful article after *Star Athletica*?

Recall the Supreme Court's warning in *Bleistein* of the dangers of embroiling the courts in artistic value judgments. Is there any way to decide the separability question without rendering such a value judgment? *See* Rebecca Tushnet, *Worth a Thousand Words: The Images of Copyright*, 125 HARV. L. REV. 683 (2012); Alfred C. Yen, *Copyright Opinions and Aesthetic Theory*, 71 S. CAL. L. REV. 247 (1998).

5. *Binary Choice vs. Sliding Scale.* Court decisions treat separability of expression from utility to be a binary choice—the expression is either separable or not, with that determination largely determining liability. Could the philosophical indeterminacies of this doctrine be at least partially defused by employing a sliding scale, in which works lacking clear physical or conceptual separability but involving significant artistic creativity are subject to a higher standard for infringement (e.g., virtual identity) and narrow scope (so as not to interfere with competition for the functional elements of the article)? Would this approach jeopardize the supremacy of patent law in protecting utilitarian inventions? For a suggestion along these lines, see Mark A. Lemley & Mark P. McKenna, *Scope*, 57 WM. & MARY L. REV. 2197 (2016).

6. *Relation to Patent and Design Patent Protection.* Contrast the useful article doctrine with the idea-expression dichotomy. As discussed in *Baker v. Selden, supra*, the idea-expression dichotomy channels protection for functional works toward the

patent system, which applies a relatively high threshold for protection (novelty and nonobviousness), requires examination by a skilled examiner, and affords protection for only 20 years from the time an application is filed, thereby encouraging others to build upon patented advances following a relatively limited period of exclusive protection. Awarding protection for functional works through copyright law—with its low threshold for protection and much greater duration—would undermine the role of the patent system as the principal means for protecting utilitarian works and hinder the process of sequential innovation essential to technological progress. Does the useful article doctrine reflect a similar objective? Or does it show greater solicitude for the protection of artistic works? If so, what justifies the difference?

How is your analysis affected by Congress's statement in the legislative history to the Copyright Act of 1976 that copyright protection extends to works of "applied art" satisfying the separability requirement regardless of "the potential availability of design patent protection"? *In re Yardley*, 493 F.2d 1389 (C.C.P.A. 1974) (allowing a design patent for a copyrighted work). The Copyright Office regulations provide that "[t]he availability of protection or grant of protection under the law for a utility or design patent will not affect the registrability of a claim in an original work of pictorial, graphic, or sculptural authorship. *See* 37 C.F.R. § 202.10(a) (1995). Contrast copyright and design patents, Chapter III(H), in their protection for ornamental designs. What purpose is served by overlapping protection? Does copyright law do a better job of excluding functional features from protection?

Justice Breyer's dissent suggests that design patent protection might be available for design elements that are not separable from the utilitarian aspects of a PGS work. Doesn't this contradict the ornamentality/non-functionality limitation for design patents? *See* Peter S. Menell & Ella Corren, *The Design Patent Identity Crisis* (2020); Peter S. Menell & Daniel Yablon, Star Athletica*'s Fissure in the Intellectual Property Functionality Landscape*, 166 U. PA. L. REV. ONLINE 137 (2017) (tracing Justice Breyer's observation to questionable amici briefing and arguing that the logic of *Baker v. Selden*, rejecting copyright protection for functional features, applies equally to design patent and trade dress protection); *contra* Christopher J. Buccafusco, Mark A. Lemley, & Jonathan Masur, *Intelligent Design*, 68 DUKE L.J. 75 (2018) (explaining that the design patent functionality doctrine is different from and far more limited than the functionality doctrines in copyright law or trade dress law).

7. *Design Protection Legislation.* Congress has considered proposals to protect design by way of copyright at various times during the past century. Title II of the 1976 Copyright Revision Bill would have raised the threshold for originality (by excluding "staple or commonplace" designs) and required registration. Designs would have been protected for a term of ten years. The provision passed the Senate but failed to get out of committee in the House. Is such protection necessary to stimulate innovation in design given the availability of design patents? If so, what is the appropriate form of protection? *See generally* J.H. Reichman, *Design Protection and the Legislative Agenda*, 55 LAW & CONTEMP. PROBS. 281 (1992); Ralph Brown, *Design Protection: An Overview*, 34 UCLA L. REV. 1341 (1987).

Congress has passed two specialized design protection statutes: the Semiconductor Chip Protection Act of 1984 (SCPA) (codified at 17 U.S.C. §§ 901–14), and the Vessel Hull Design Protection Act, as part of the Digital Millennium Copyright Act of 1998 (codified at 17 U.S.C. §§ 1301–32). Although included in the same Title as the Copyright Act, these laws create *sui generis* forms of legal protection to fill in gaps in the intellectual property landscape. Both Acts provide relatively short periods of protection against piracy (ten years), registration requirements, and exclusions for utilitarian features. The SCPA expressly permits reverse engineering of mask works for the purposes of teaching, analyzing, or evaluating the concepts or techniques embodied in the mask work or in the circuitry, logic flow, or organization of its components. Such knowledge gained through reverse engineering may be embodied in original mask works.

8. *Fashion Designs*. Prior to *Star Athletica*, U.S. copyright protection did not extend to the design of clothing on the ground that clothing is a "useful article" ("an article having an intrinsic utilitarian function that is not merely to portray the appearance of the article or to convey information") and copyright in the design of a useful article may be claimed "only if, and only to the extent that, such design incorporates pictorial, graphic, or sculptural features that can be identified separately from, and are capable of existing independently of, the utilitarian aspects of the article."[14]

Due to advances in technology, knock-offs of the latest fashions are coming out of textile factories in East Asia within hours after the fashions first appear on fashion runways in Paris, Milan, and New York. In response, the high-end fashion industry has lobbied Congress to enact a relatively short (three years) term of protection against piracy of the non-utilitarian features of registered works. Do you believe that such protection is justified? Consider the analysis of Professors Kal Raustiala and Christopher Sprigman, who argue that the absence of copyright protection for fashion design has in fact spurred innovation by inducing obsolescence (copying diffuses designs into the mainstream, causing them to lose their appeal for fashion cognoscenti, which in turn spurs new fashion designs) and helping to anchor trends. *See The Piracy Paradox: Innovation and Intellectual Property in Fashion Design*, 92 VA. L. REV. 1687 (2006). Other scholars have questioned this analysis. *See* C. Scott Hemphill & Jeannie Suk, *The Law, Culture, and Economics of Fashion*, 61 STAN. L. REV. 1147 (2009); Randall Picker, *Of Pirates and Puffy Shirts*, VA. L. REV. IN BRIEF (2007); Susan Scafidi, *Intellectual Property and Fashion Design*, in INTELLECTUAL PROPERTY AND INFORMATION WEALTH: ISSUES AND PRACTICES IN THE DIGITAL AGE 115 (Peter K. Yu ed., 2007).

After *Star Athletica*, clothing design may get, not a few years of anti-piracy protection, but 95 years of protection.

---

[14] A print or design on a clothing garment is eligible for copyright protection if sufficiently original. Some courts have held that masquerade costumes may qualify for copyright protection. *See Entertainment Research Grp., Inc. v. Genesis Creative Grp., Inc.*, 122 F.3d 1211, 1221 (9th Cir. 1997).

PROBLEMS

Problem IV-14. The Walt Disney Company markets a line of telephones in the shape of the cartoon characters Mickey and Minnie Mouse. The telephones resemble the characters standing up, with push buttons on the torso and the telephone receiver resting on the hand. Are these designs copyrightable?

Mickey Mouse Phone

Problem IV-15. Armond Artist designs the "Vacquero" belt buckle, which sells for $1,000 (cast in silver) and $6,000 (cast in gold) at high-fashion jewelry stores. The design has been made a part of the permanent collection of the Metropolitan Museum of Art.

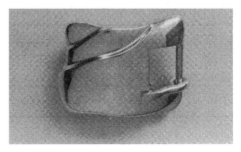

Vaquero Buckle

Is the buckle copyrightable?

Problem IV-16. Versace Fashion Display Inc. has developed a collection of original sculptural forms in the shape of the human torso. They are life-size and anatomically accurate, but without neck, arms, or a back. Versace supplies these forms to clothing retailers for the display of fashion clothing. These forms became popular in the market. Versace customers found the distinctive lines of the forms to be visually attractive and effective in selling blouses, shirts, and sweaters displayed on the forms. Discount Display, Inc., began to notice a decline in their mannequin sales after Versace entered the market. Thereafter, Discount Display expanded its catalog to include forms that it copied from Versace. In response, Versace registers its forms with the Copyright Office and sues Discount Display for copyright infringement.

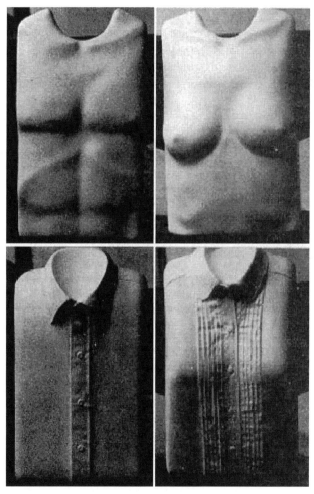

Torso Mannequins

How should a court resolve this dispute?

Problem IV-17. A growing number of city zoning ordinances require that building developers provide adequate bicycle racks to accommodate the growing number of bicycle commuters, ease traffic congestion, and reduce air pollution. The conventional bicycle racks available on the marketplace clashed with the architectural style of modern building designs. In response, Brandir International, an industrial design firm, developed a graceful, tubular steel "Ribbon Bike Rack." The Industrial Designers Society of America recognized the Brandir design for its "elegance and simplicity while providing functional security."

Brandir Bicycle Rack

Cascade Pacific Lumber Co., a building supply company, began offering its own ribbon-style bicycle rack. Brandir comes to you for advice following the *Star Athletica* decision. They would like to know whether the ribbon design is copyrightable. How would a court resolve this dispute?

iii. Government Works and Edicts

Works of the federal government are denied copyright protection under the express terms of the Copyright Act. Section 105 provides that copyright protection is not available "for any work of the United States Government, but the United States Government is not precluded from receiving and holding copyrights transferred to it by assignment, bequest, or otherwise." Section 101 defines "a work of the United States Government" as "a work prepared by an officer or employee of the United States Government as part of that person's official duties." The House Report notes that this definition should be construed in the same manner as the definition of "work made for hire." We focus on the "work for hire" doctrine in Chapter IV(D)(1)(i).

A potential problem arises where a federal government agency commissions a work by an independent contractor. The legislative history states:

The bill deliberately avoids making any sort of outright, unqualified prohibition against copyright in works prepared under Government contract or grant. There may well be cases where it would be in the public interest to deny copyright in the writings generated by Government research contracts and the like; it can be assumed that, where a government agency commissions a work for its own use merely as an alternative to having one of its own employees prepare the work, the right to secure a private copyright would be withheld. However, there are almost certainly many other cases where the denial of copyright protection would be unfair or would hamper the production and publication of important works. Where, under the particular circumstances, Congress or the agency involved finds that the need to have a work freely available outweighs the need of the private author to secure a copyright, the problem can be dealt with by specific legislation, agency regulations, or contractual restrictions.

H.R. REP. NO. 94-1476, 94th Cong., 2d Sess. 59 (1976).

By contrast, the Copyright Act and its accompanying legislative history say nothing about the availability of protection for works of state (and local) governments. The prevailing understanding is that state and local government bodies can obtain copyright for their works, subject to any state rules precluding or or restricting state copyright ownership.

A closely related issue involves the copyrightability of works produced by government actors or agencies in the exercise of their lawmaking authority, works that are commonly referred to as "government edicts." This is not an issue for works produced by federal lawmaking agencies, since such works constitute "work[s] of the U.S. Government" and are ineligible for protection. It nevertheless remains a consideration for many state and local governments.

The copyrightability of government edicts arose early in the history of the American republic. Wheaton, one of the Supreme Court's "official" reporters, asserted protection for his annotated compilations of Supreme Court opinions. Distinguishing between the reporter's work in annotating, editing, and condensing judicial opinions and the opinions themselves, the Supreme Court held that "no reporter has or can have any copyright in the written opinions delivered by this Court ; and that the judges thereof cannot confer on any reporter any such right." *Wheaton v. Peters*, 33 U.S. (8 Pet.) 591, 668 (1834).

Thus emerged what is commonly referred to as the "government edicts doctrine," which denies copyright protection to edicts of government. A few decades later, the Supreme Court reiterated the doctrine and applied it to the opinions of state court judges. *See Banks v. Manchester*, 128 U.S. 253 (1888); *Callaghan v. Meyers*, 128 U.S. 617 (1888). All the same, the Court concluded that annotations (and other parts of a case report) that are not prepared by a judge—but instead by an official court reporter— would be eligible for protection unless forbidden by state law. In due course, courts extended the government edicts doctrine came to official statutes, *Howell v. Miller*, 91

Fed. Rep. 129 (6th Cir. 1898), and more recently to model codes when enacted into law by a government body, *Veeck v. S. Bldg. Code Congress Int'l, Inc.*, 293 F.3d 791 (5th Cir. 2002) (en banc).

Most recently, the Supreme Court examined whether the government edicts doctrine would apply to annotations contained in an officially published compendium of state laws. *See Georgia v. Public.Resource.Org., Inc.*, 590 U.S. __ (2020). The annotations at issue were prepared by a private actor under the direct guidance and supervision of the state's Code Revision Commission, a branch of the state legislature. The state legislature then formally approved the annotations and merged them into the official code. The Court applied the government edicts doctrine to the official annotations, concluding that since "judges, acting as judges, cannot be 'authors' because of their authority to make and interpret the law, it follows that legislators, acting as legislators, cannot be either."

COMMENTS AND QUESTIONS

1. *Incentives to Develop Model Laws*. The dissent in *Veeck* asserted that copyright protection for model codes provides valuable incentives for creation of laws and model codes, noting that "unlike judges and legislators who are paid from public funds to issue opinions and draft laws, [defendant Southern Building Code Congress International] SBCCI is a private sector, not-for-profit organization which relies for its existence and continuing services, in significant part, on revenues from the sale of its model codes." *Veeck v. S. Bldg. Code Congress Int'l Inc.*, 293 F.3d 791, 815–17 (5th Cir. 2002) (dissenting opinion) (noting that "one third, or $3 million, of SBCCI's annual $9 million dollar revenue is generated by sales of model codes to contractors and other interested parties. The remaining revenue is mainly derived from the annual fees of voluntary members and member organizations. Voluntary members include scholars, builders, contractors, and governmental entities that have adopted the code.").

Professor Paul Goldstein disagrees: "It is difficult to imagine an area of creative endeavor in which the copyright incentive is needed less. Trade organizations have powerful reasons stemming from industry standardization, quality control, and self-regulation to produce these model codes; it is unlikely that, without copyright, they will cease producing them." *See* 1 GOLDSTEIN § 2.5.2

Who has the better of this argument? Is it appropriate for courts to be subjecting particular classes of works to this sort of open-ended analysis of whether copyright protection "promotes progress"? Doesn't the case turn on whether or not idea and expression merge in the wording of law? Should Congress amend the Copyright Act in order to resolve this issue one way or the other?

2. *Due Process*. Does the U.S. Constitution require that all edicts of government, such as judicial opinions, administrative rulings, legislative enactments, public ordinances, and similar official legal documents, whether federal, state, or local, are not copyrightable?

How would you evaluate the following types of works?

- *Public Safety Codes.* Such codes cover fire, electrical, building, plumbing, mechanical, fuel & gas, elevator, and boiler safety and many other topics and are mandated by law by cities, counties, states, and the federal government. Public.Resource.Org began posting state-mandated public safety codes online in 2008. It has received no objections.

- *Technical Standards Incorporated by Reference in the Code of Federal Regulations.* Public.Resource.Org began making these materials available in 2012. Several organizations sued: the American Society for Testing and Materials (ASTM) sued for posting federally mandated testing standards; the National Fire Protection Association (NFPA) for posting the National Electrical Code and other fire safety standards; and the American Society of Heating, Refrigerating, and Air-Conditioning Engineers (ASHRAE) for posting DOE-mandated energy standards. Jim Shannon, the President of NFPA, claimed that the posting of documents such as the National Electrical Code "threatens our future, our ability to continue our work, and the whole system of standards development that the public and governmental agencies rely on." *See American Society for Testing and Materials v. PublicResource.org*, 896 F.3d 437 (D.C. Cir. 2018) (overturning holding that industry standards are copyrightable and remanding for fair use determination).

3. Should the government edicts doctrine apply to "Restatements of Law"? The Restatements of Law are produced by a private organization, the American Law Institute (ALI), and attempt to synthesize case law and connected principles into concise "blackletter" rules for courts, lawyers and students to use and cite. In many common law areas, the Restatements have proven to be highly influential and authoritative, with courts routinely citing, quoting, and adopting entire blackletter provisions into their opinions. Does this render the "blackletter" of the Restatements similar to model codes? And are the Reporters' Notes and other accompanying material akin to the annotations at issue in *Georgia v. Public.Resource.Org., Inc.*?

4. Over the course of several decades, the American Medical Association developed the Physician's Current Procedural Terminology ("CPT"), a comprehensive classification system for identifying more than 6,000 medical procedures comprising a five-digit code and brief description for each procedure. The AMA revises the CPT each year to reflect new developments in medical procedures. In 1977, Congress instructed the Health Care Financing Administration to establish a uniform code for identifying physicians' services for use in completing Medicare and Medicaid claim forms. Rather than creating a new code, HCFA contracted with the AMA. The AMA gave HCFA a "non-exclusive, royalty free, and irrevocable license to use, copy, publish and distribute" the CPT on the conditions that the HCFA not "use any other system of procedure nomenclature . . . for reporting physicians' services" and require use of the CPT in programs administered by HCFA, by its agents, and by other agencies whenever possible. HCFA published notices in the Federal Register incorporating the CPT in HCFA's Common Procedure Coding System and adopted regulations requiring

applicants for Medicaid reimbursement to use the CPT. A publisher and distributor of medical books challenged the copyrightability of the CPT. Should this code be protectable? *See Practice Mgmt. Info. Corp. v. American Med. Ass'n*, 121 F.3d 516 (9th Cir. 1997) (upholding the AMA's copyright but finding that the AMA had misused its copyright rights), *amended by* 133 F.3d 1140 (1998).

PROBLEMS

Problem IV-18. To celebrate the bicentennial of the federal court system, the Administrative Office of the United States Courts commissioned KPBS, a public broadcasting station, to create a television series dramatizing famous early federal cases. The production contract assigned all copyright interests in the works to the federal government. The History Channel seeks to air these programs. Must it obtain a license from the federal government? Would your analysis differ if there were no assignment clause? What if a historian employed by the Administrative Office of the United States Courts served as a consultant to the television series? What if federal public officials—including Supreme Court Justices and the Solicitor General—provided commentaries about the famous cases?

Problem IV-19. You work in the intellectual property department of the law firm of Armatrading, Hendrix, and Clapton (AH&C), a 600-person firm with offices throughout the United States. The head of the litigation department just read a legal brief filed by opposing counsel that copied, almost verbatim, several paragraphs from a brief written by one of our firm's attorneys last year. Notwithstanding the adage that imitation is the sincerest form of flattery and that the purloined passages arise in the context of another litigation from the one in which our firm's attorney drafted the text in question, it infuriated the lawyers involved in the currently pending matter that legal work that our firm did (and for which a client of our firm paid dearly) is now being fobbed off on a court in the current matter as the work product of a cut-rate law firm (Dewey, Cheatem, and Howe (DC&H)).

After digging a bit more deeply into the matter, one of our paralegals determined that DC&H likely obtained the material from a new Eastlaw database: BRIEFS-ALL. It also found an advertisement in In-House Counsel, a journal targeting general counsels and other in-house lawyers, placed by DC&H which states: "Why pay exorbitant hourly rates for legal work—Our legal team charges on a per-project basis with costs tied to up-front estimates. Thanks to Eastlaw® Briefs-All® database, our attorneys have full access to the legal arguments being made by the highest priced firms."

According to an advertisement in the American Lawyer publication for the new database, Eastlaw makes available tens of thousands of briefs in an easily searchable form. Eastlaw's advertisement includes a note from the person heading up the operation: "It's pretty amazing what my team does here in Philadelphia. We harvest briefs from PACER and load them onto Eastlaw as downloadable Word documents. I tell you, I've never seen this much activity here at our operations!" Eastlaw does not obtain any licenses for this material. Does AH&C have a valid basis for bringing suit against DC&H or Eastlaw? What other considerations bear on pursuing this matter?

D.   OWNERSHIP AND DURATION

Copyrights today are in many ways like other forms of property interests. As we will see in Chapter IV(E), a copyright includes numerous distinct rights. Once a copyright is acquired, the entire bundle of rights may be assigned to others. Alternatively, the owner may divide and transfer particular rights. Nonetheless, there are significant differences between the ownership rules governing copyrights and those governing other property interests. The most important difference is that copyrights have limited duration. As required by the U.S. CONSTITUTION, copyrights enter the public domain after a statutorily determined limited time. Furthermore, Congress has differentiated the ownership, transfer, and termination of these rights in other ways as well. As you work through these provisions, consider how copyright ownership rules differ from the ownership rules for other forms of intellectual (e.g., patents) and real (e.g., land, chattel) property. What justifies these differences? More specifically, how do these differences promote the objectives of the copyright law?

This section first surveys the law that determines who initially acquires a copyright. This law includes the rules governing works for hire and jointly produced works. We then outline the rules governing the duration of copyright protection. These rules are complicated by the renewal process under the 1909 Act. We conclude with a discussion of the rules governing the division, transfer, and termination of transfers of copyright interests.

1.   Initial Ownership of Copyrights

As noted earlier, copyright law since the 1700s has vested copyright in authors and artists who create works satisfying the requirements of copyright law. Under current law, an individual who writes, composes, or paints an original work of authorship on her or his own acquires the copyright upon the work's creation. § 201(a). Since many works in our modern and increasingly interconnected economy, however, are produced in the employment context, commissioned by a production company or publisher, and/or result from collaborations among numerous authors, we begin our exploration of initial ownership with doctrines governing works made for hire and jointly created works.

i.   *Works Made for Hire*

The 1909 Act defined "the word 'author' [to] include an employer in the case of works made for hire," § 26, although the Act did not define the term "work made for hire." Courts took an expansive view of what constituted a work made for hire, presuming that any works created within the scope of employment or commissioned by independent contractors (at the "instance and expense" of the employer) vested in the employer. *See Marvel Characters, Inc. v. Kirby*, 726 F.3d 119 (2d Cir. 2013); *Brattleboro Publ'g Co. v. Winmill Publ'g Corp.*, 369 F.2d 565 (2d Cir. 1966); *Lin-Brook Builders Hardware v. Gertler*, 352 F.2d 298, 300 (9th Cir. 1965) ("when one person engages another, whether as employee or as an independent contractor, to produce a work of an artistic nature, [] in the absence of an express contractual reservation of the copyright in the artist, the presumption arises that the mutual intent of the parties is that the title to the copyright shall be in the person at whose instance and expense the work is done."). Nearly all circuits have adopted this test. *See* Meredith Annan House, Marvel v. Kirby: *A Clash of Comic Book Titans in the Work Made For Hire Arena*, 30 BERKELEY TECH. L.J. 933, 940–44 (2015).

The presumption can be overcome by an express agreement to the contrary or other evidence suggesting an alternative intention of the parties, such as industry custom or lack of supervision or creative control by the employer. Works created prior to January 1, 1978 remain subject to this test.

In the legislative process leading up to the 1976 Act, authors' representatives expressed concern that freelance authors lacked the bargaining power to reject contractual clauses designating their works as "works made for hire." The motion picture industry and other producers and publishers of works involving many creative contributors were concerned about holdout problems complicating commercial exploitation if they did not own copyrights in works they commissioned outright and for the entire duration of copyright protection. The ultimate compromise defines "work made for hire" to include: (1) a work prepared by an employee within the scope of his or her employment; or (2) a work falling within one of nine enumerated categories—a contribution to a collective work, a part of a motion picture or other audiovisual work, a translation, a supplementary work, a compilation, a test, answer material for a test, or an atlas—and evidenced by a written agreement signed by both parties expressly stating that the work is intended to be a "work made for hire." § 101. Disputes quickly arose as to what Congress intended by the term "employee."

Community for Creative Non-Violence et al. v. Reid
Supreme Court of the United States
490 U.S. 730 (1989)

Justice MARSHALL delivered the opinion of the Court.

In this case, an artist and the organization that hired him to produce a sculpture contest the ownership of the copyright in that work. To resolve this dispute, we must construe the "work made for hire" provisions of the Copyright Act of 1976 (Act or 1976 Act), 17 U.S.C. §§ 101 and 201(b), and in particular, the provision in § 101, which defines as a "work made for hire" a "work prepared by an employee within the scope of his or her employment" (hereinafter § 101(1)).

Petitioners are the Community for Creative Non-Violence (CCNV), a nonprofit unincorporated association dedicated to eliminating homelessness in America, and

Mitch Snyder, a member and trustee of CCNV. In the fall of 1985, CCNV decided to participate in the annual Christmastime Pageant of Peace in Washington, D.C., by sponsoring a display to dramatize the plight of the homeless. As the District Court recounted:

> Snyder and fellow CCNV members conceived the idea for the nature of the display: a sculpture of a modern Nativity scene in which, in lieu of the traditional Holy Family, the two adult figures and the infant would appear as contemporary homeless people huddled on a streetside steam grate. The family was to be black (most of the homeless in Washington being black); the figures were to be life-sized, and the steam grate would be positioned atop a platform "pedestal," or base, within which special-effects equipment would be enclosed to emit simulated "steam" through the grid to swirl about the figures. They also settled upon a title for the work—"Third World America"—and a legend for the pedestal: "and still there is no room at the inn." 652 F. Supp. 1453, 1454 (DC 1987).

Snyder made inquiries to locate an artist to produce the sculpture. He was referred to respondent James Earl Reid, a Baltimore, Maryland, sculptor. In the course of two telephone calls, Reid agreed to sculpt the three human figures. CCNV agreed to make the steam grate and pedestal for the statue. Reid proposed that the work be cast in bronze, at a total cost of approximately $100,000 and taking six to eight months to complete. Snyder rejected that proposal because CCNV did not have sufficient funds, and because the statue had to be completed by December 12 to be included in the pageant. Reid then suggested, and Snyder agreed, that the sculpture would be made of a material known as "Design Cast 62," a synthetic substance that could meet CCNV's monetary and time constraints, could be tinted to resemble bronze, and could withstand the elements. The parties agreed that the project would cost no more than $15,000, not including Reid's services, which he offered to donate. The parties did not sign a written agreement. Neither party mentioned copyright.

After Reid received an advance of $3,000, he made several sketches of figures in various poses. At Snyder's request, Reid sent CCNV a sketch of a proposed sculpture showing the family in a crechelike setting: the mother seated, cradling a baby in her lap; the father standing behind her, bending over her shoulder to touch the baby's foot. Reid testified that Snyder asked for the sketch to use in raising funds for the sculpture. Snyder testified that it was also for his approval. Reid sought a black family to serve as a model for the sculpture. Upon Snyder's suggestion, Reid visited a family living at CCNV's Washington shelter but decided that only their newly born child was a suitable model. While Reid was in Washington, Snyder took him to see homeless people living on the streets. Snyder pointed out that they tended to recline on steam grates, rather than sit or stand, in order to warm their bodies. From that time on, Reid's sketches contained only reclining figures.

Throughout November and the first two weeks of December 1985, Reid worked exclusively on the statue, assisted at various times by a dozen different people who were paid with funds provided in installments by CCNV. On a number of occasions, CCNV members visited Reid to check on his progress and to coordinate CCNV's construction of the base. CCNV rejected Reid's proposal to use suitcases or shopping bags to hold the family's personal belongings, insisting instead on a shopping cart. Reid and CCNV members did not discuss copyright ownership on any of these visits.

On December 24, 1985, 12 days after the agreed-upon date, Reid delivered the completed statue to Washington. There it was joined to the steam grate and pedestal prepared by CCNV and placed on display near the site of the pageant. Snyder paid Reid the final installment of the $15,000. The statue remained on display for a month. In late January 1986, CCNV members returned it to Reid's studio in Baltimore for minor repairs. Several weeks later, Snyder began making plans to take the statue on a tour of several cities to raise money for the homeless. Reid objected, contending that the Design Cast 62 material was not strong enough to withstand the ambitious itinerary. He urged CCNV to cast the statue in bronze at a cost of $35,000, or to create a master mold at a cost of $5,000. Snyder declined to spend more of CCNV's money on the project.

"Third World America," by James Earl Reid

In March 1986, Snyder asked Reid to return the sculpture. Reid refused. He then filed a certificate of copyright registration for "Third World America" in his name and announced plans to take the sculpture on a more modest tour than the one CCNV had proposed. Snyder, acting in his capacity as CCNV's trustee, immediately filed a competing certificate of copyright registration.

Snyder and CCNV then commenced this action against Reid and his photographer, Ronald Purtee, seeking return of the sculpture and a determination of copyright ownership. The District Court granted a preliminary injunction, ordering the sculpture's return. After a 2-day bench trial, the District Court declared that "Third World America" was a "work made for hire" under § 101 of the Copyright Act and that Snyder, as trustee for CCNV, was the exclusive owner of the copyright in the sculpture. 652 F. Supp., at 1457. The court reasoned that Reid had been an "employee" of CCNV within the meaning of § 101(1) because CCNV was the motivating force in the statue's production. Snyder and other CCNV members, the court explained, "conceived the idea of a contemporary Nativity scene to contrast with the national celebration of the season," and "directed enough of [Reid's] effort to assure that, in the end, he had produced what they, not he, wanted." *Id.*, at 1456.

The Court of Appeals for the District of Columbia Circuit reversed and remanded. . . .

II

A

The Copyright Act of 1976 provides that copyright ownership "vests initially in the author or authors of the work." 17 U.S.C. § 201(a). As a general rule, the author is the party who actually creates the work, that is, the person who translates an idea into a fixed, tangible expression entitled to copyright protection. § 102. The Act carves out an important exception, however, for "works made for hire." If the work is for hire, "the employer or other person for whom the work was prepared is considered the author" and owns the copyright, unless there is a written agreement to the contrary. § 201(b). Classifying a work as "made for hire" determines not only the initial ownership of its copyright, but also the copyright's duration, § 302(c), and the owners' renewal rights, § 304(a), termination rights, §203(a), and right to import certain goods bearing the copyright, § 601(b)(1). *See* 1 M. NIMMER & D. NIMMER, NIMMER ON COPYRIGHT § 5.03 [A], pp. 5–10 (1988). The contours of the work for hire doctrine therefore carry profound significance for freelance creators—including artists, writers, photographers, designers, composers, and computer programmers—and for the publishing, advertising, music, and other industries which commission their works.

Section 101 of the 1976 Act provides that a work is "for hire" under two sets of circumstances:

> (1) a work prepared by an employee within the scope of his or her employment; or

> (2) a work specially ordered or commissioned for use as a contribution to a collective work, as a part of a motion picture or other audiovisual work, as a translation, as a supplementary work, as a compilation, as an instructional text, as a test, as answer material for a test, or as an atlas, if the parties expressly agree in a written instrument signed by them that the work shall be considered a work made for hire.

Petitioners do not claim that the statue satisfies the terms of § 101(2). Quite clearly, it does not. Sculpture does not fit within any of the nine categories of "specially ordered or commissioned" works enumerated in that subsection, and no written agreement between the parties establishes "Third World America" as a work for hire.

The dispositive inquiry in this case therefore is whether "Third World America" is "a work prepared by an employee within the scope of his or her employment" under § 101(1). The Act does not define these terms. In the absence of such guidance, four interpretations have emerged. The first holds that a work is prepared by an employee whenever the hiring party retains the right to control the product. *See Peregrine v. Lauren Corp.*, 601 F. Supp. 828, 829 (Colo. 1985); *Clarkstown v. Reeder*, 566 F. Supp. 137, 142 (S.D.N.Y. 1983). Petitioners take this view. A second, and closely related, view is that a work is prepared by an employee under § 101(1) when the hiring party has actually wielded control with respect to the creation of a particular work. This approach was formulated by the Court of Appeals for the Second Circuit, *Aldon Accessories Ltd. v. Spiegel, Inc.*, 738 F.2d 548 (2d Cir. 1984), and adopted by the Fourth Circuit, *Brunswick Beacon, Inc. v. Schock-Hopchas Publishing Co.*, 810 F.2d 410 (1987), the Seventh Circuit, *Evans Newton, Inc. v. Chicago Systems Software*, 793 F.2d 889 (1986), and, at times, by petitioners. A third view is that the term "employee" within § 101(1) carries its common-law agency law meaning. This view was endorsed by the Fifth Circuit in *Easter Seal Society for Crippled Children and Adults of Louisiana, Inc. v. Playboy Enterprises*, 815 F.2d 323 (1987), and by the Court of Appeals below. Finally, respondent and numerous amici curiae contend that the term "employee" only refers to "formal, salaried" employees. *See, e.g.*, Brief for Respondent 23–24; Brief for Register of Copyrights as Amicus Curiae 7. The Court of Appeals for the Ninth Circuit recently adopted this view. *See Dumas v. Gommerman*, 865 F.2d 1093 (1989).

The starting point for our interpretation of a statute is always its language. *Consumer Product Safety Comm'n v. GTE Sylvania, Inc.*, 447 U.S. 102, 108 (1980). The Act nowhere defines the terms "employee" or "scope of employment." It is, however, well established that "where Congress uses terms that have accumulated settled meaning under . . . the common law, a court must infer, unless the statute otherwise dictates, that Congress means to incorporate the established meaning of these terms." *NLRB v. Amax Coal Co.*, 453 U.S. 322, 329 (1981). In the past, when Congress has used the term "employee" without defining it, we have concluded that Congress intended to describe the conventional master-servant relationship as understood by common-law agency doctrine. *See, e.g., Kelley v. Southern Pacific Co.*, 419 U.S. 318, 322–323 (1974). Nothing in the text of the work for hire provisions indicates that Congress used the words "employee" and "employment" to describe anything other than "'the conventional relation of employer and employee.'" *Kelley, supra*, at 323, quoting *Robinson*; compare *NLRB v. Hearst Publications, Inc.*, 322 U.S. 111, 124–132 (1944) (rejecting agency law conception of employee for purposes of the National Labor Relations Act where structure and context of statute indicated broader definition). On the contrary, Congress' intent to incorporate the agency law definition is suggested by § 101(1)'s use of the term, "scope of employment," a widely used term of art in agency law. *See* RESTATEMENT (SECOND) OF AGENCY § 228 (1958) (hereinafter RESTATEMENT).

. . . We thus agree with the Court of Appeals that the term "employee" should be understood in light of the general common law of agency.

In contrast, neither test proposed by petitioners is consistent with the text of the Act. The exclusive focus of the right to control the product test on the relationship between the hiring party and the product clashes with the language of § 101(1), which focuses on the relationship between the hired and hiring parties. The right to control the product test also would distort the meaning of the ensuing subsection, § 101(2). Section 101 plainly creates two distinct ways in which a work can be deemed for hire: one for works prepared by employees, the other for those specially ordered or commissioned works which fall within one of the nine enumerated categories and are the subject of a written agreement. The right to control the product test ignores this dichotomy by transforming into a work for hire under § 101(1) any "specially ordered or commissioned" work that is subject to the supervision and control of the hiring party. Because a party who hires a "specially ordered or commissioned" work by definition has a right to specify the characteristics of the product desired, at the time the commission is accepted, and frequently until it is completed, the right to control the product test would mean that many works that could satisfy § 101(2) would already have been deemed works for hire under § 101(1). Petitioners' interpretation is particularly hard to square with § 101(2)'s enumeration of the nine specific categories of specially ordered or commissioned works eligible to be works for hire, e.g., "a contribution to a collective work," "a part of a motion picture," and "answer material for a test." The unifying feature of these works is that they are usually prepared at the instance, direction, and risk of a publisher or producer. By their very nature, therefore, these types of works would be works by an employee under petitioners' right to control the product test. . . .

We therefore conclude that the language and structure of § 101 of the Act do not support either the right to control the product or the actual control approaches.[8] The structure of § 101 indicates that a work for hire can arise through one of two mutually exclusive means, one for employees and one for independent contractors, and ordinary canons of statutory interpretation indicate that the classification of a particular hired party should be made with reference to agency law.

This reading of the undefined statutory terms finds considerable support in the Act's legislative history. . . .

We turn, finally, to an application of § 101 to Reid's production of "Third World America." In determining whether a hired party is an employee under the general common law of agency, we consider the hiring party's right to control the manner and means by which the product is accomplished. Among the other factors relevant to this inquiry are the skill required; the source of the instrumentalities and tools; the location of the work; the duration of the relationship between the parties; whether the hiring party has the right to assign additional projects to the hired party; the extent of the hired party's discretion over when and how long to work; the method of payment; the hired party's role in hiring and paying assistants; whether the work is part of the regular

---

[8] We also reject the suggestion of respondent and amici that the § 101(1) term "employee" refers only to formal, salaried employees. While there is some support for such a definition in the legislative history, *see* VARMER, WORKS MADE FOR HIRE 130, the language of § 101(1) cannot support it. The Act does not say "formal" or "salaried" employee, but simply "employee." . . .

business of the hiring party; whether the hiring party is in business; the provision of employee benefits; and the tax treatment of the hired party. *See* RESTATEMENT § 220(2) (setting forth a nonexhaustive list of factors relevant to determining whether a hired party is an employee). No one of these factors is determinative. *See Ward*, 362 U.S., at 400; *Hilton Int'l Co. v. NLRB*, 690 F.2d 318, 321 (CA2 1982).

Examining the circumstances of this case in light of these factors, we agree with the Court of Appeals that Reid was not an employee of CCNV but an independent contractor. 846 F.2d, at 1494, n.11. True, CCNV members directed enough of Reid's work to ensure that he produced a sculpture that met their specifications. 652 F. Supp., at 1456. But the extent of control the hiring party exercises over the details of the product is not dispositive. Indeed, all the other circumstances weigh heavily against finding an employment relationship. Reid is a sculptor, a skilled occupation. Reid supplied his own tools. He worked in his own studio in Baltimore, making daily supervision of his activities from Washington practicably impossible. Reid was retained for less than two months, a relatively short period of time. During and after this time, CCNV had no right to assign additional projects to Reid. Apart from the deadline for completing the sculpture, Reid had absolute freedom to decide when and how long to work. CCNV paid Reid $15,000, a sum dependent on "completion of a specific job, a method by which independent contractors are often compensated." *Holt v. Winpisinger*, 811 F.2d 1532, 1540 (1987). Reid had total discretion in hiring and paying assistants. "Creating sculptures was hardly 'regular business' for CCNV." 846 F.2d, at 1494, n.11. Indeed, CCNV is not a business at all. Finally, CCNV did not pay payroll or Social Security taxes, provide any employee benefits, or contribute to unemployment insurance or workers' compensation funds.

Because Reid was an independent contractor, whether "Third World America" is a work for hire depends on whether it satisfies the terms of § 101(2). This petitioners concede it cannot do. Thus, CCNV is not the author of "Third World America" by virtue of the work for hire provisions of the Act. However, as the Court of Appeals made clear, CCNV nevertheless may be a joint author of the sculpture if, on remand, the District Court determines that CCNV and Reid prepared the work "with the intention that their contributions be merged into inseparable or interdependent parts of a unitary whole." 17 U.S.C. § 101. In that case, CCNV and Reid would be co-owners of the copyright in the work. *See* § 201(a).

For the aforestated reasons, we affirm the judgment of the Court of Appeals for the District of Columbia Circuit.

It is so ordered.

COMMENTS AND QUESTIONS

1. What policies underlie the work made for hire doctrine? From which philosophical perspectives do these policies flow? Does the court's analysis and holding in *CCNV* comport with these policies?

We learned earlier that copyright law, while originally aimed at shielding publishers from the threat of piracy, has since the early days of English law been focused on protecting authors. Does the "work made for hire" provision in the 1976 Act defeat this purpose? In the case of works made for hire, § 101 automatically vests copyright in employers, not the particular employees who author the work. This result is somewhat surprising, especially in light of patent law's approach of considering the individual inventor to be the patentee (at least nominally). Why is this so? Why are inventors always people, whereas authors can be companies? In view of assignability rules in patent law, does the distinction make a difference? Unlike copyright law, patent law has no termination of transfer rule or other provision safeguarding inventors against unremunerative transfers.

A principal justification for the work made for hire doctrine is the reduction of transaction costs. A work made for hire is deemed to be a corporate creation, so it need not be assigned. The doctrine essentially "preassigns" a work to the employer. This has the important effect of eliminating the costs of negotiating and executing assignment agreements. In addition, as we will see in Chapter IV(D)(1)(i), the work made for hire doctrine avoids the inalienability of the termination of transfer right. The work belongs to the employer *ab initio*, i.e., from the moment of creation, rather than by assignment. Such treatment solves a potentially large "holdout" problem in compilations, multimedia, motion pictures, and other works involving numerous contributors. Are the works listed in the second part of § 101's definition of work made for hire the types of works for which holdout problems are most likely? Are there any other works that ought to be included? In 1999, the recording industry persuaded Congress to add sound recordings to this list by modifying the statute without fanfare in a "technical amendments" bill. When the change was discovered, artists objected, and Congress undid the change in 2000. *See* David Nimmer & Peter S. Menell, *Sound Recordings, Works for Hire, and the Termination-of-Transfers Time Bomb*, 49 J. COPYRIGHT SOC'Y 387 (2001).

2. *The Restatement of Agency (Second) Factors*. Based on the RESTATEMENT (SECOND) OF AGENCY, the *Reid* Court identifies the following factors to be considered in determining whether an employment relationship exists:

- the skill required
- the source of the instrumentalities and tools
- the location of the work
- the duration of the relationship between the parties
- whether the hiring party has the right to assign additional projects to the hired party
- the extent of the hired party's discretion over when and how long to work
- the method of payment
- the hired party's role in hiring and paying assistants
- whether the work is part of the regular business of the hiring party

- whether the hiring party is in business
- the provision of employee benefits
- the tax treatment of the hired party

Note that these factors are not identical to the RESTATEMENT (SECOND) OF AGENCY factors. Some courts have augmented this list, considering the label (employee or contractor) that the parties apply to the relationship as well as the right to control the manner and means of the work, which is the RESTATEMENT's overarching test for employee status.

The Second Circuit in *Aymes v. Bonelli*, 980 F.2d 857 (2d Cir. 1992), cautioned that the "factors should not merely be tallied but should be weighed according to their significance in the case." The court emphasized the following factors as deserving of more weight: (1) the hiring party's right to control the manner and means of creation; (2) the skill required; (3) the provision of employee benefits; (4) the tax treatment of the hired party; and (5) whether the hiring party has the right to assign additional projects to the hired party. The court placed special emphasis on (3) and (4). Professor Ryan Vacca provides a systematic empirical analysis of the application of the *Reid* factors. *See* Ryan Vacca, *Works Made for Hire—Analyzing the Multifactor Balancing Test*, 42 FLA. ST. U. L. REV. 197 (2014). The following graphic illustrates his findings as to factor importance:

Least Important   **Most Important**

• Right to Control Manner & Means • Label • Hiring Party in Business	• Work Location • Hiring & Paying Assistants	• When & How Long to Work • Part of Regular Business of Hiring Party • Relationship Duration	• Additional Projects • Skill Required • Source of Instrumentalities & Tools	• Tax Treatment • Employee Benefits • Payment Method

In practice, the test has tilted toward the formal, salaried employee benchmark, which the Supreme Court declined to adopt. *See id.* at 234–35; I.T. Hardy, Copyright Law's Concept of Employment—What Congress Really Intended, 35 J. Copyright Soc'y U.S.A. 210 (1988).

3. *Within the Scope of Employment.* Even if a work is created by an employee, it must also be "within the scope of his or her employment" in order to be deemed a work made for hire. From the Supreme Court's instruction to apply the common law of agency, most courts reaching this issue have adopted the test set forth in RESTATEMENT (SECOND) OF AGENCY. An employee's work is deemed within the scope of his employment if:

a) it is within the kind he is employed to perform;

b) it occurs substantially within the authorized time and space limits; [and]

c) it is actuated, at least in part, by a purpose to serve the master.

RESTATEMENT (SECOND) OF AGENCY § 228 (1958). *See Quinn v. City of Detroit*, 988 F. Supp. 1044, 1049 (E.D. Mich. 1997).

4. *Copyright Shop Rights?* In the areas of trade secrets and patented inventions, courts have recognized a common law "shop right" which allows an employer to use an employee's invention to the extent necessary for its regular business where the employer contributed to the development of the invention, for example, by providing wages, tools, or a workplace. *See McElmurry v. Ark. Power & Light Co.*, 995 F.2d 1576, 1580 (Fed. Cir. 1993). In the negotiations leading up to the 1976 Act, screenwriters and film music composers advocated a comparable "shop right," whereby the employee would retain all other rights, subject to a covenant not to authorize competing uses. Congress rejected this proposal in favor of providing employers full copyright for works prepared within the scope of the worker's employment. H.R. REP. NO. 94-1476, at 121. What about works that the employee completes on the employer's time and using the employer's resources but fall outside of the employee's scope of employment? Should the employer be able to assert a shop right in this circumstance?

5. *Works of the U.S. Government.* As we saw earlier, works of the U.S. government are not copyrightable. Section 101 defines U.S. government works as works "prepared by an officer or employee of the United States government as part of that person's official duties." The legislative history makes clear that Congress intended this provision to parallel the scope of the work made for hire doctrine.

6. *Teacher Exception.* There is a significant exception to the work made for hire doctrine that prevents universities from claiming to own professors' works under the works made for hire doctrine. This exception is venerable, but lacks textual support in the 1976 Act. Some courts and commentators have concluded that the Act did in fact abolish the "teacher exception," but most work hard to find a way to keep the doctrine alive. *See Hays v. Sony Corp. of Am.*, 847 F.2d 412, 416 (7th Cir. 1988) (Posner, J.) (justifying the judge-made exception on the "havoc that [a contrary] conclusion would wreak in the settled practices of academic institutions, the lack of fit between the policy of the work-for-hire doctrine and the conditions of academic production, and the absence of any indication that Congress meant to abolish" the exception.); Rochelle Cooper Dreyfuss, *The Creative Employee and the Copyright Act of 1976*, 54 U. CHI. L. REV. 590, 597–98 (1987). Can you think of a way for the exception to survive the passage of the 1976 Act? Should it?

7. *The Role of Contract Law.* Regardless of whether a work is created within the confines of the Copyright Act's "work made for hire" provisions, parties are free to assign copyright interests through contract. Use of such instruments is quite common in the production of many commercial copyrighted works. There is, however, at least one important respect in which contract cannot substitute for "work made for hire" status. As we will discuss further below, the 1976 Act creates an inalienable right in authors to

terminate transfers of copyright in a 5-year window beginning 35 years after a transfer. *See* § 203(a). The only way that assignees can avoid this termination is by establishing that the copyright vested in their name *ab initio.* A non-author can satisfy this requirement only if the work falls within the definition of a "work made for hire." Assigned rights also differ from works made for hire in certain other respects, such as the duration of copyright protection.

8. *The Evolving Nature of Employers.* The precise language of the work made for hire doctrine is becoming increasingly important in a world of "network organizations." With the proliferation of consultants, "outsourcing," "downsizing," and "strategic partnering," businesses are placing much more emphasis on quasi-integration through contracts. This in turn makes for some interesting problems in view of the fact that copyright law was designed not for a complex, "organizationally promiscuous" world but a simple binary (big company vs. solo artist/author) world. How should this shift affect the interpretation of the work made for hire doctrine?

9. *AI Authors?* Artificial intelligence is now capable of generating works of music and art. Should those works be copyrightable? If so, who is the author? The machine itself? The original programmer? The people who trained the AI? The corporation that owns it?

PROBLEM

Problem IV-20. On April 27, 2006, Mannie Garcia, a photographer, covered an event at the National Press Club featuring actor George Clooney discussing his recent trip to war-torn Darfur. Among the attendees at the event was then-Senator Barack Obama, who had co-sponsored the Darfur Peace and Accountability Act. Several of the pictures shot by Mr. Garcia captured Senator Obama.

In the run-up to the 2008 presidential election, Shepard Fairey, a graphic artist, digitally altered one of the Garcia photographs to create an iconic campaign poster (emblazoned with the word "HOPE") for the Obama campaign. Fairey did not obtain a license to the underlying work and when furor arose that he had infringed the Associated Press's copyright, Fairey brought an action requesting that the HOPE poster be declared a fair use. (We will address the merits of this action in the fair use section.)

Along with its answer, the Associated Press filed a counterclaim for copyright infringement. As the basis for its claim, AP alleged that Mr. Garcia was a full-time salaried employee at the time that he took the photograph in question. Mr. Garcia disputes this allegation. In a motion to intervene in the Fairey-AP case, Garcia asserts that although he worked for the AP for a five-week period in the spring of 2006 when he took the photographs, he was never an AP employee: he received no benefits or vacation from AP; he used his own equipment; he was was free to and did work for other individuals and corporations during this time. Garcia also states that he never agreed to assign his copyrights to AP. Rather, he selected 16 of the 275 photographs that he shot at the Darfur event to transmit to AP. Who owns copyright in Garcia's Obama photograph? What if Garcia had signed a work-made-for-hire agreement?

ii.   *Joint Works*

The 1976 Act was the first to codify the law relating to joint works. It defines a joint work as "a work prepared by two or more authors with the intention that their contributions be merged into inseparable or interdependent parts of a unitary whole." 17 U.S.C. § 101. The House Report accompanying the Act elaborates further on this somewhat cryptic definition:

> [A] work is "joint" if the authors collaborated with each other, or if each of the authors prepared his or her contribution with the knowledge and intention that it would be merged with the contributions of other authors as "inseparable or interdependent parts of a unitary whole." The touchstone here is the intention, at the time the writing is done, that the parts be absorbed or combined into an integrated unit.

H.R. REP. No. 94-1476, at 120.

Once a work is found to be a joint work—and its authors therefore joint authors—copyright law treats them as "coowners" of the work. §102(a). On this question, the House Report notes that Congress intended to let the existing common law rules of coownership apply without any modification, which included treating the joint authors as "tenants in common" and affording each coowner the independent right to use or license the use of the work, subject to a duty to account to the other coowner(s). H.R. REP. No. 94-1476, at 121.

The Second Circuit was the first to interpret and apply the statute's understanding of joint works. In *Childress v. Taylor*, 945 F. 2d 500 (2d Cir. 1991), the court declined to treat mere "collaborat[ion]" as a separate basis for a joint work. The court interpreted the first sentence of the House Report quoted above to require an intention on the part of the contributors to be joint authors for the creation of a joint work. *Id.* at 505-06. *Childress* also adopted the position that each contributor needed to make a "copyrightable contribution" to the work, meaning that a non-copyrightable contribution (e.g., an idea) was insufficient, however significant it might be. *Id.* at 507. Lastly, the court concluded that the coownership among joint authors entitled each of coowner an "equal undivided interests in the work." *Id.* at 508.

Childress is commonly credited with having developed a two-pronged test for joint works: (i) a copyrightable contribution by each joint author; and (ii) a mutual intent in each of them to be joint authors. *See Erickson v. Trinity Theatre, Inc.*, 13 F. 3d 1061, 1068-69 (7th Cir. 1994). To establish the mutual intent requirement, courts have since come to develop what are known as "objective indicia", where they look to how the parties carried themselves before, during, and after the collaboration—both vis-à-vis each other and towards third parties--to discern the existence of the intention. Such indicia have included decision-making authoring, billing, and crediting, and agreements with third parties, among others. *See Thomson v. Larson*, 147 F. 3d 195, 203-05 (2d Cir. 1998).

In the case that follows, the Ninth Circuit adopts a different approach to the joint works doctrine.

Aalmuhammed v. Lee
United States Court of Appeals for the Ninth Circuit
202 F.3d 1227 (9th Cir. 2000)

KLEINFELD, Circuit Judge:

This is a copyright case involving a claim of coauthorship of the movie *Malcolm X.* We reject the "joint work" claim but remand for further proceedings on a quantum meruit claim.

I. Facts

In 1991, Warner Brothers contracted with Spike Lee and his production companies to make the movie *Malcolm X,* to be based on the book, *The Autobiography of Malcolm X.* Lee co-wrote the screenplay, directed, and co-produced the movie, which starred Denzel Washington as Malcolm X. Washington asked Jefri Aalmuhammed to assist him in his preparation for the starring role because Aalmuhammed knew a great deal about Malcolm X and Islam. Aalmuhammed, a devout Muslim, was particularly knowledgeable about the life of Malcolm X, having previously written, directed, and produced a documentary film about Malcolm X.

Aalmuhammed joined Washington on the movie set. The movie was filmed in the New York metropolitan area and Egypt. Aalmuhammed presented evidence that his involvement in making the movie was very extensive. He reviewed the shooting script for Spike Lee and Denzel Washington and suggested extensive script revisions. Some of his script revisions were included in the released version of the film; others were filmed but not included in the released version. Most of the revisions Aalmuhammed made were to ensure the religious and historical accuracy and authenticity of scenes depicting Malcolm X's religious conversion and pilgrimage to Mecca.

Aalmuhammed submitted evidence that he directed Denzel Washington and other actors while on the set, created at least two entire scenes with new characters, translated Arabic into English for subtitles, supplied his own voice for voice-overs, selected the proper prayers and religious practices for the characters, and edited parts of the movie during post production. Washington testified in his deposition that Aalmuhammed's contribution to the movie was "great" because he "helped to rewrite, to make more authentic." Once production ended, Aalmuhammed met with numerous Islamic organizations to persuade them that the movie was an accurate depiction of Malcolm X's life.

Aalmuhammed never had a written contract with Warner Brothers, Lee, or Lee's production companies, but he expected Lee to compensate him for his work. He did not intend to work and bear his expenses in New York and Egypt gratuitously. Aalmuhammed ultimately received a check for $25,000 from Lee, which he cashed, and a check for $100,000 from Washington, which he did not cash.

During the summer before *Malcolm X*'s November 1992 release, Aalmuhammed asked for a writing credit as a co-writer of the film, but was turned down. When the film was released, it credited Aalmuhammed only as an "Islamic Technical Consultant," far down the list. In November 1995, Aalmuhammed applied for a copyright with the U.S. Copyright Office, claiming he was a co-creator, co-writer, and co-director of the movie. The Copyright Office issued him a "Certificate of Registration," but advised him in a letter that his "claims conflict with previous registrations" of the film.

On November 17, 1995, Aalmuhammed filed a complaint against Spike Lee, his production companies, and Warner Brothers (collectively "Lee"). . . . The suit sought declaratory relief and an accounting under the Copyright Act. . . .

II. Analysis

A. Copyright Claim

Aalmuhammed claimed that the movie *Malcolm X* was a "joint work" of which he was an author, thus making him a co-owner of the copyright. . . .

Aalmuhammed argues that he established a genuine issue of fact as to whether he was an author of a "joint work," *Malcolm X.* The Copyright Act does not define "author," but it does define "joint work":

A "joint work" is a work prepared by two or more authors with the intention that their contributions be merged into inseparable or interdependent parts of a unitary whole.

"When interpreting a statute, we look first to the language." The statutory language establishes that for a work to be a "joint work" there must be (1) a copyrightable work, (2) two or more "authors," and (3) the authors must intend their contributions be merged into inseparable or interdependent parts of a unitary whole. A "joint work" in this circuit "requires each author to make an independently copyrightable contribution" to the disputed work. *Malcolm X* is a copyrightable work, and it is undisputed that the movie was intended by everyone involved with it to be a unitary whole. It is also undisputed that Aalmuhammed made substantial and valuable contributions to the movie, including technical help, such as speaking Arabic to the persons in charge of the mosque in Egypt, scholarly and creative help, such as teaching the actors how to pray properly as Muslims, and script changes to add verisimilitude to the religious aspects of the movie. Speaking Arabic to persons in charge of the mosque, however, does not result in a copyrightable contribution to the motion picture. Coaching of actors, to be copyrightable, must be turned into an expression in a form subject to copyright. The same may be said for many of Aalmuhammed's other activities. Aalmuhammed has, however, submitted evidence that he rewrote several specific passages of dialogue that appeared in *Malcolm X,* and that he wrote scenes relating to Malcolm X's Hajj pilgrimage that were enacted in the movie. If Aalmuhammed's evidence is accepted, as it must be on summary judgment, these items would have been independently copyrightable. Aalmuhammed, therefore, has presented a genuine issue of fact as to whether he made a copyrightable contribution. All persons involved intended that Aalmuhammed's contributions would be merged into interdependent parts of the movie as a unitary whole. Aalmuhammed maintains that he has shown a genuine issue of fact for each element of a "joint work."

But there is another element to a "joint work." A "joint work" includes "two or more authors." Aalmuhammed established that he contributed substantially to the film, but not that he was one of its "authors." We hold that authorship is required under the statutory definition of a joint work, and that authorship is not the same thing as making a valuable and copyrightable contribution. We recognize that a contributor of an expression may be deemed to be the "author" of that expression for purposes of determining whether it is independently copyrightable. The issue we deal with is a different and larger one: is the contributor an author of the joint work within the meaning of § 101.

By statutory definition, a "joint work" requires "two or more authors." The word "author" is taken from the traditional activity of one person sitting at a desk with a pen and writing something for publication. It is relatively easy to apply the word "author" to a novel. It is also easy to apply the word to two people who work together in a fairly traditional pen-and-ink way, like, perhaps, Gilbert and Sullivan. In the song, "I Am the Very Model of a Modern Major General," Gilbert's words and Sullivan's tune are inseparable, and anyone who has heard the song knows that it owes its existence to both men, Sir William Gilbert and Sir Arthur Sullivan, as its creative originator. But as the number of contributors grows and the work itself becomes less the product of one or two individuals who create it without much help, the word is harder to apply.

Who, in the absence of contract, can be considered an author of a movie? The word is traditionally used to mean the originator or the person who causes something to come into being, or even the first cause, as when Chaucer refers to the "Author of Nature." For a movie, that might be the producer who raises the money. Eisenstein thought the author of a movie was the editor. The "auteur" theory suggests that it might be the director, at least if the director is able to impose his artistic judgments on the film. Traditionally, by analogy to books, the author was regarded as the person who writes the screenplay, but often a movie reflects the work of many screenwriters. Grenier suggests that the person with creative control tends to be the person in whose name the money is raised, perhaps a star, perhaps the director, perhaps the producer, with control gravitating to the star as the financial investment in scenes already shot grows. Where the visual aspect of the movie is especially important, the chief cinematographer might be regarded as the author. And for, say, a Disney animated movie like *The Jungle Book,* it might perhaps be the animators and the composers of the music.

The Supreme Court dealt with the problem of defining "author" in new media in *Burrow-Giles Lithographic Co. v. Sarony*. The question there was, who is the author of a photograph: the person who sets it up and snaps the shutter, or the person who makes the lithograph from it. Oscar Wilde, the person whose picture was at issue, doubtless offered some creative advice as well. The Court decided that the photographer was the author, quoting various English authorities: "the person who has superintended the arrangement, who has actually formed the picture by putting the persons in position, and arranging the place where the people are to be—the man who is the effective cause of that"; "'author' involves originating, making, producing, as the inventive or master mind, the thing which is to be protected"; "the man who really represents, creates, or gives effect to the idea, fancy, or imagination." The Court said that an "author," in the sense that the Founding Fathers used the term in the CONSTITUTION, was "'he to whom anything owes its origin; originator; maker; one who completes a work of science or literature.'"

Answering a different question, what is a copyrightable "work," as opposed to who is the "author," the Supreme Court held in *Feist Publications* that "some minimal level of creativity" or "originality" suffices. But that measure of a "work" would be too broad and indeterminate to be useful if applied to determine who are "authors" of a movie. So many people might qualify as an "author" if the question were limited to whether they made a substantial creative contribution that that test would not distinguish one from another. Everyone from the producer and director to casting director, costumer, hairstylist, and "best boy" gets listed in the movie credits because all of their creative contributions really do matter. It is striking in *Malcolm X* how much the person who controlled the hue of the lighting contributed, yet no one would use the word "author" to denote that individual's relationship to the movie. A creative contribution does not suffice to establish authorship of the movie.

Burrow-Giles, in defining "author," requires more than a minimal creative or original contribution to the work. *Burrow-Giles* is still good law, and was recently reaffirmed in *Feist Publications. Burrow-Giles* and *Feist Publications* answer two distinct questions; who is an author, and what is a copyrightable work. *Burrow-Giles* defines author as the person to whom the work owes its origin and who superintended the whole work, the "master mind." In a movie this definition, in the absence of a contract to the contrary, would generally limit authorship to someone at the top of the screen credits, sometimes the producer, sometimes the director, possibly the star, or the screenwriter—someone who has artistic control. After all, in *Burrow-Giles* the lithographer made a substantial copyrightable creative contribution, and so did the person who posed, Oscar Wilde, but the Court held that the photographer was the author.

The Second and Seventh Circuits have likewise concluded that contribution of independently copyrightable material to a work intended to be an inseparable whole will not suffice to establish authorship of a joint work.[15] Although the Second and Seventh Circuits do not base their decisions on the word "authors" in the statute, the practical results they reach are consistent with ours. These circuits have held that a person claiming to be an author of a joint work must prove that both parties intended each other to be joint authors. In determining whether the parties have the intent to be joint authors, the Second Circuit looks at who has decision making authority, how the parties bill themselves, and other evidence.

In *Thomson v. Larson*, an off-Broadway playwright had created a modern version of *La Boheme,* and had been adamant throughout its creation on being the sole author.

---

[15] *Thomson v. Larson*, 147 F.3d 195 (2d Cir. 1998); *Erickson v. Trinity Theatre, Inc.*, 13 F.3d 1061 (7th Cir. 1994); *Childress v. Taylor*, 945 F.2d 500 (2d Cir. 1991

He hired a drama professor for "dramaturgical assistance and research," agreeing to credit her as "dramaturg" but not author, but saying nothing about "joint work" or copyright. The playwright tragically died immediately after the final dress rehearsal, just before his play became the tremendous Broadway hit, *Rent*. The dramaturg then sued his estate for a declaratory judgment that she was an author of *Rent* as a "joint work," and for an accounting. The Second Circuit noted that the dramaturg had no decision making authority, had neither sought nor was billed as a co-author, and that the defendant entered into contracts as the sole author. On this reasoning, the Second Circuit held that there was no intent to be joint authors by the putative parties and therefore it was not a joint work.

Considering *Burrow-Giles*, the recent cases on joint works (especially the thoughtful opinion in *Thomson v. Larson*), and the Gilbert and Sullivan example, several factors suggest themselves as among the criteria for joint authorship, in the absence of contract. First, an author "superintend[s]" the work by exercising control. This will likely be a person "who has actually formed the picture by putting the persons in position, and arranging the place where the people are to be—the man who is the effective cause of that," or "the inventive or master mind" who "creates, or gives effect to the idea." Second, putative coauthors make objective manifestations of a shared intent to be coauthors, as by denoting the authorship of *The Pirates of Penzance* as "Gilbert and Sullivan." We say objective manifestations because, were the mutual intent to be determined by subjective intent, it could become an instrument of fraud, were one coauthor to hide from the other an intention to take sole credit for the work. Third, the audience appeal of the work turns on both contributions and "the share of each in its success cannot be appraised." Control in many cases will be the most important factor.

The best objective manifestation of a shared intent, of course, is a contract saying that the parties intend to be or not to be coauthors. In the absence of a contract, the inquiry must of necessity focus on the facts. The factors articulated in this decision and the Second and Seventh Circuit decisions cannot be reduced to a rigid formula, because the creative relationships to which they apply vary too much. Different people do creative work together in different ways, and even among the same people working together the relationship may change over time as the work proceeds.

Aalmuhammed did not at any time have superintendence of the work. Warner Brothers and Spike Lee controlled it. Aalmuhammed was not the person "who has actually formed the picture by putting the persons in position, and arranging the place. . . ." Spike Lee was, so far as we can tell from the record. Aalmuhammed, like Larson's dramaturg, could make extremely helpful recommendations, but Spike Lee was not bound to accept any of them, and the work would not benefit in the slightest unless Spike Lee chose to accept them. Aalmuhammed lacked control over the work, and absence of control is strong evidence of the absence of coauthorship. Also, neither Aalmuhammed, nor Spike Lee, nor Warner Brothers, made any objective manifestations of an intent to be coauthors. Warner Brothers required Spike Lee to sign a "work for hire" agreement, so that even Lee would not be a coauthor and co-owner with Warner Brothers. It would be illogical to conclude that Warner Brothers, while not wanting to permit Lee to own the copyright, intended to share ownership with individuals like Aalmuhammed who worked under Lee's control, especially ones who at the time had made known no claim to the role of coauthor. No one, including Aalmuhammed, made any indication to anyone prior to litigation that Aalmuhammed was intended to be a coauthor and co-owner.

Aalmuhammed offered no evidence that he was the "inventive or master mind" of the movie. He was the author of another less widely known documentary about Malcolm X, but was not the master of this one. What Aalmuhammed's evidence showed, and all it showed, was that, subject to Spike Lee's authority to accept them, he made very valuable contributions to the movie. That is not enough for coauthorship of a joint work. . . .

COMMENTS AND QUESTIONS

1. *Originality and Joint Authorship.* As we saw in *Feist*, copyright law applies a low threshold for meeting the requirement of originality. Courts generally do not judge the "quality" of a contribution for purposes of determining whether the originality hurdle has been cleared. In the words of Justice Holmes, "It would be a dangerous undertaking for persons trained only to the law to constitute themselves final judges of the work of pictorial illustrations, outside the narrowest and most obvious limits." *Bleistein v. Donaldson Lithographing Co.*, 188 U.S. 239, 251 (1903). By contrast, the courts have developed a much higher threshold and more searching inquiry (subjective intent of the putative authors) for determining joint authorship. Does this make sense? *See* Mary K. LaFrance, *Authorship, Dominance, and the Captive Collaborator: Preserving the Rights of Joint Authors*, 50 EMORY L.J. 193 (2001). Can the complex collaborative projects made possible in today's increasingly interconnected world be realistically sorted out in this manner? *See generally* Rochelle Cooper Dreyfuss, *Collaborative Research: Conflicts on Authorship, Ownership, and Accountability*, 53 VAND. L. REV. 1161 (2000).

2. *Requirement of Independently Copyrightable Expression.* The Ninth Circuit, as well as others, *see, e.g.*, *Thomson v. Larson*, 147 F. 3d 195, 200-01 (2d Cir. 1998), requires that each joint author must make not just a copyrightable contribution, but instead an "independently copyrightable contribution" to a joint work. This implies that each joint author must have (a) contributed copyrightable expression to the work and (b) that such expression was independently protectable. Is the requirement of "independently copyrightable expression" compatible with the text of the statute and its legislative history?

Writing for the Seventh Circuit, Judge Posner takes a less rigid approach, which would dispense with the requirement of a copyrightable contribution altogether:

> [W]here two or more people set out to create a character jointly in such mixed media as comic books and motion pictures and succeed in creating a copyrightable character, it would be paradoxical if though the result of their joint labors had more than enough originality and creativity to be copyrightable,

no one could claim copyright. That would be peeling the onion until it disappeared. The decisions that say, rightly in the generality of cases, that each contributor to a joint work must make a contribution that if it stood alone would be copyrightable weren't thinking of the case in which it couldn't stand alone because of the nature of the particular creative process that had produced it.

Here is a typical case from academe. One professor has brilliant ideas but can't write; another is an excellent writer, but his ideas are commonplace. So they collaborate on an academic article, one contributing the ideas, which are not copyrightable, and the other the prose envelope, and . . . they sign as coauthors. Their intent to be the joint owners of the copyright in the article would be plain, and that should be enough to constitute them joint authors within the meaning of 17 U.S.C. § 201(a). This is the valid core of the Nimmers' heretical suggestion that "if authors A and B work in collaboration, but A's contribution is limited to plot ideas that standing alone would not be copyrightable, and B weaves the ideas into a completed literary expression, it would seem that A and B are joint authors of the resulting work." 1 NIMMER & NIMMER § 6.07.

Gaiman v. McFarlane, 360 F.3d 644, 658–59 (7th Cir. 2004).

3. *Contracting Authorship?* The *Aalmuhamed* decision notes that "[s]everal factors suggest themselves as among the criteria for joint authorship, *in the absence of contract.*" (Emphasis added.) This framing mistakenly suggests that joint authorship can be determined by parties contractually. While copyright *ownership* can usually be contracted—but not always: note that the termination of transfer is inalienable—joint authorship is always a matter of copyright law, since a court is obligated to ascertain the parties' relevant intent at the time of creating the work before it can find them to be joint authors. *See* Shyamkrishna Balganesh, *Unplanned Coauthorship*, 100 VA. L. REV. 1683, 1748-49 (2014).

4. *Actors.* Cindy Lee Garcia landed a minor role in a low-budget film entitled *Desert Warrior* which she was led to believe by Mark Basseley Youseff, the film's producer and writer, was going to be an action-adventure thriller set in ancient Arabia. Garcia spent three and a half days on set and was paid $500. *Desert Warrior* was never released, but her scene was included in *Innocence of Muslims*, a film depicting the Prophet Mohammed as "a murderer, pedophile, and homosexual." Youseff dubbed Garcia's voice with the lines: "Is your Mohammed a child molester? Our daughter is but a child."

A trailer for *Innocence of Muslim*, including Garcia's scene, was released on YouTube, generating protest, condemnation, and death threats against Garcia. Fearing for her life, Garcia filed a request pursuant to the Digital Millennium Copyright Act for YouTube to takedown the trailer. We explore this feature of digital copyright law in Chapter IV(F)(2). As we will see, only copyright owners have authority to force an Online Service Provider, such as YouTube, to takedown content.

Although Garcia did not assert joint authorship of *Innocence of Muslims*, she alleged that her performance included in the film was independently copyrightable and that she retained an interest in that copyright. YouTube denied the takedown request on the ground that Garcia did not have a copyright interest. Garcia filed a motion for a temporary restraining order five months later. Applying the heightened scrutiny for a request for affirmative relief, the district court rejected the motion. On appeal, a split Ninth Circuit ordered that the trailer be taken down. The majority found that an individual contribution to an integrated work could be independently copyrightable. Thus, Garcia, as the author of her performance, likely retained a copyright interest in her performance, "even when the work ha[d] been contributed to a joint work." *Garcia v. Google*, 743 F.3d 1258, 1265 (9th Cir. 2014).

The Ninth Circuit granted *en banc* review and overturned the panel decision. Its decision severely limits if not eliminates actors' copyright claim to film footage in which they appear. *Garcia v. Google, Inc.*, 786 F.3d 733 (9th Cir. 2015). Building on *Aalmuhammed v. Lee*, the Ninth Circuit emphasized that authorship in a collaborative project requires more than a "substantial creative contribution." To allow each and every contributor to films or other complex works a copyright interest would "make Swiss cheese of copyrights." The court ruled that the only work is the film and unless Garcia qualifies as a joint author, she has no copyright interest.

This decision is unlikely to have a significant effect on filmmaking since motion pictures are among the works eligible for work-made-for-hire status and studios routinely require actors to execute work-made-for-hire agreements. Thus, like *Aalmuhammed v. Lee*, *Garcia v. Google* is an outlier resulting from the producer's failure to get a work-made-for-hire agreements signed. Nonetheless, the decision negates actors' claims to copyright in film projects. Is this decision faithful to copyright's protection scheme? Were there other ways to avoid such an extreme result as the panel decision in *Garcia*? Are work-made-for-hire agreements even necessary after the *Garcia* decision?

5. *Directors.* In 2010, Robert Krakovski purchased the rights to a screenplay entitled *Heads Up* and hired Alex Merkin to direct the film. With input from Merkin, Krakovski assembled the cast and crew. Notwithstanding their failure to reach a work-made-for-hire agreement, Merkin began work directing *Heads Up*. After filming was completed, Krakovski gave Merkin a hard drive of the raw footage of the film. The parties did, however, enter into a Media Agreement under which Merkin would edit but not license, sell, or copy the footage for any purpose without the permission of Casa Duse, Krakovski's production entity. Unbeknownst to Krakovski, Merkin registered copyright to the raw footage for *Heads Up* in his own name. Merkin subsequently sought to block Krakovski's screening of the film. Krakovski brought an action to establish that Case Duse, and not Merkin, owned the copyright in the film footage.

Drawing on the Ninth Circuit's *en banc* Garcia decision, the Second Circuit held that a contributor to a creative work whose contribution is inseparable from, and integrated into, a work does not maintain a copyright interest in his or her contribution alone. *See 16 Casa Duse, LLC v. Merkin*, 791 F.3d 247, 254 (2d Cir. 2015). The court concluded that although the Copyright Act protects "motion pictures," the constituent parts of a motion picture or any other integrated work are not separately copyrightable.

The court supported its conclusion by reference to the Act's treatment of joint works—works prepared by multiple authors "with the intention that their contributions be merged into inseparable or interdependent parts of a unitary whole." The court doubted that Congress aimed to fill films with "thousands of standalone copyrights."

Applying this interpretation to the production of *Heads Up*, the court determined that Casa Duse was the dominant author of the film. First, Krakovski had the most control over the project—from initiating the project to executing all agreements with cast, crew, and third parties. Second, although Merkin had significant control as to the direction and creative elements of the film, Krakovski had the final authority. Moreover, "Casa Duse initiated the project; acquired the rights to the screenplay; selected the cast, crew, and director; controlled the production schedule; and coordinated (or attempted to coordinate) the film's publicity and release." *Id.* at 260.

Does this outcome square with the *Aalmuhammed* decision? Does it eviscerate directors' copyright interest in films that they direct absent "final cut" authority?

6. *Implied License?* Notwithstanding the "work made for hire" device for working around the joint authorship problem in films and other collaborative works, there is still a risk that a contributor to a project falls outside of the "work made for hire" designation. As in the *Aalmuhammed* case, studio lawyers may fail to get all contributors to a project to sign a "work made for hire" agreement. Although such a disaster was avoided in the *Aalmuhammed* case through the application of a relatively high joint authorship hurdle, what should a court do in a case where a relatively modest contributor to a major production who has not signed "work made for hire" agreement clears the joint authorship hurdle? *Cf.* F. Jay Dougherty, *Not a Spike Lee Joint? Issues in the Authorship of Motion Pictures Under U.S. Copyright Law*, 49 UCLA L. REV. 225, 317–33 (2001) (arguing that courts should find an implied license enabling the film producer to exploit the work without liability for damages absent a showing by the author that the use exceeded that which was reasonably foreseeable). Does *Garcia v. Google* put this concern to rest?

7 *Co-Ownership of Jointly Authored Works: Tenancy-in-Common.* The law treats joint authors as tenants-in-common, which courts have understood to require that in the absence of an agreement to the contrary, each of the co-owners has an equal, undivided ownership interest in the entire work,[16] even where it is clear that their respective contributions to the joint work are not equal. *Community for Creative Non-Violence v. Reid*, 846 F.2d 1485, 1498 (D.C. Cir. 1988), *aff'd*, 490 U.S. 730 (1989). Each owner can use the work and license others to do so,[17] subject to a duty to account to the others for profits. Had Aalmuhammed been deemed a joint author of the film Malcolm X, he would have been entitled to half of all profits from the film. He also would have had freedom to license the work to another film distribution studio, theaters, television

---

[16] Upon the death of each joint owner, the decedent's respective share of the joint work goes to his heirs. Joint authors can, however, agree to a right of survivorship or some other ownership arrangement.

[17] All joint owners must agree in writing to transfer of the copyright or an exclusive license. § 204(a).

broadcasters, or DVD distributors, so long as he provided Warner Brothers with half of the profits. Might this help explain why the court came out the way it did?

iii.   *Collective Works*

Section 201(c) provides:

> Copyright in each separate contribution to a collective work is distinct from copyright in the collective work as a whole, and vests initially in the author of the contribution. In the absence of an express transfer of the copyright or of any rights under it, the owner of copyright in the collective work is presumed to have acquired only the privilege of reproducing and distributing the contribution as part of that particular collective work, any revision of that collective work, and a later collective work in the same series.

> Section 101 defines a "collective work" as "a work, such as a periodical issue, anthology, or encyclopedia, in which a number of contributions, constituting separate and independent works in themselves, are assembled into a collective whole."

iv.   *The Rights of Authors and Publishers in Electronic Compilations*

Section 201(c) of the Copyright Act provides that when a copyrighted work is contributed to a collective work, the copyright in the collective work (held by its publisher) is separate from the copyright in the component works (held in the first instance by the authors). The statute provides that unless the parties agree otherwise, "the owner of the copyright in the collective work is presumed to have acquired only the privilege of reproducing and distributing the contribution as part of that particular collective work, any revision of that collective work, and any later collective work in the same series." § 201(c).

What happens when a collective work such as a magazine or law review is made available on the Internet through a searchable database? At least until recently, most publication contracts did not address this possibility. Nonetheless, publishers have treated the electronic version of their publication as if it were the same as the print version. That is, they have acted as though they had the rights to authorize the online use or reproduction of articles from their magazine. Digital dissemination of previously licensed works has resulted in the principal area of dispute.

In *New York Times Co., Inc. v. Tasini*, 533 U.S. 483 (2001), freelance authors of articles previously published in the New York Times, Newsday, and Sports Illustrated sued to enjoin these publications (and LEXIS/NEXIS) from distributing their articles through online databases and CD-ROM products.[18] The litigation focused on a relatively technical issue of statutory interpretation: whether distribution of the freelancers' articles falls within § 201(c) of the Act, which affords publishers of

---

[18] These authors operated under oral contracts with the publishers and hence the publishers cannot be deemed to be the owners of the works under the "work made for hire" doctrine. *See* § 101 (definition of "works made for hire").

collective works a limited privilege to publish any *revision* of that collective work and any later collective work in the same series without the permission of the authors. The Supreme Court found for the freelance authors, holding that removing articles from their context as part of a collective work and placing them into searchable databases as separate files went beyond the § 201(c) privilege.

Freelance photographers brought a similar lawsuit against the National Geographic Society when it produced "The Complete National Geographic" (CNG), a 30-disc CD-ROM product containing each monthly issue of the Magazine, as it was originally published, for the more than 100 years of the Magazine. Stories can be retrieved through the table of contents of each magazine or by using an electronic search engine. The search engine allows a user to find stories containing certain words or phrases within the texts of articles; descriptions of articles, including title, contributors, date, and major related subjects; advertisements; cover and page images; and page maps. To view a particular story, a user must insert the disk containing the issue in which the story appeared. The Second and Eleventh Circuits held that this republication of the magazines—including the freelance photographer photographs—constituted a privileged revision under § 201(c). *See Faulkner v. Nat'l Geographic Enters. Inc.*, 409 F.3d 26, 36 (2d Cir. 2005); *Greenberg v. Nat'l Geographic Soc'y*, 533 F.3d 1244 (11th Cir. 2008) (en banc). In addition, the CNG includes a short opening montage and a computer program that allows users to search the CNG, zoom in to particular pages, and print. The Eleventh Circuit held that this feature of the CNG fell outside of the § 201(c) privilege and remanded that issue for consideration of other defenses that had not yet been litigated. 533 F.3d at 1258, n.21.

What advice would you offer publishers about how they could continue to offer the works of freelance contributors through online databases and CD-ROM products without obtaining consent? What advice would you provide about how they could avoid such problems in the future? *Cf.* Amy Terry, Note, Tasini *Aftermath: The Consequence of the Freelancers' Victory*, 14 DePaul-LCA J. Art & Ent. L. & Pol'y 231 (2004) (arguing that publishers have responded in various ways to undermine the freelancers' victory in *Tasini*). What are the larger policy implications with regard to incentives to create and equity to authors posed by digital technology and online distribution channels? Does new technology favor publishers or authors, or does it improve or hurt the lots of both groups?

PROBLEMS

Problem IV-21. Smith, a graphic artist, is employed full time by ADCO to design and flesh out illustrations for advertising campaigns. In his spare time, at home and using no materials taken from work, Smith designs an ad campaign for another company on a freelance basis. Who owns the copyright in Smith's freelance work?

Problem IV-22. Edwards, a playwright, wrote three short plays to be produced by a community theater company. The plays were written on a tight budget, and Edwards made a number of revisions to the script during rehearsals. Some of the changes, including the reconstruction of two scenes, were made at the suggestion of actors during rehearsals, and the new scenes were worked out largely by consensus. After a creative disagreement, the theater company performs the plays without Edwards' permission. Edwards sues for copyright infringement, and the actors claim that they are joint authors with a right to perform the work. Who should prevail?

Problem IV-23. Bable comes up with an idea for a toy car with an integrated circuit that responds to commands as well as speaking and singing songs. Bable founds a company called Up and Running, Inc. to market her "talking car" concept. Bable finds several people to record some new material for the talking car.

a. The first is Sally Singer, who agrees to record a children's song she has written called "Red Light Go, Green Light Stop—Whoops!" for use on the car. Bable has Sally sign an agreement giving Up and Running "all ownership in the song." The song becomes a hit, and Bable licenses the song to Warner Kids Records for inclusion on an album of children's songs. Sally protests, saying she had planned to release her own album featuring the song.

b. The second is Telly Talker, a multilingual kids' storyteller who enters into a "long-term requirements employment" contract with Up and Running. Telly's job is to record translations of the songs and slogans that the toy car says into as many languages as Bable requires. The Japanese version of the toy car becomes a big hit, and Telly informs Bable that he is planning to license his recorded voice to a third party, Toyco, for use in their Japanese talking bear product.

c. The third is Gary Guitar, a musician who records guitar music for Up and Running. His practice is to record a snippet of music in whatever genre (bluegrass, jazz, etc.) Bable requests. Bable then sends a check with a standard form legend saying "cashing this check confirms your employment relationship with Up and Running, Inc., and the latter's ownership of the copyright in the music paid for hereby."

Who owns what copyrights in the car's songs and slogans?

Problem IV-24. After graduating from law school and passing the bar examination in 1994, George Jones joined the law firm of Blaketree, Hickman, and Charles (BH&C). He signed a standard associate employment contract stating that he would provide legal services on behalf of BH&C in exchange for a compensation package (salary plus bonus tied to billable hours, bar dues, health benefits, and contribution to retirement plan). George rotated among a variety of practice areas during his first two years—IP litigation, trademark prosecution, and corporate transactions. He received solid evaluations. He particularly liked the trademark group and requested to specialize in that department. Glenda Elston, the lead attorney in the department, viewed George favorably and he joined the department full-time early in his third year with the firm.

Six months into his third year, George recognized that many aspects of his work—validity analysis, record keeping, correspondence, etc.—could be usefully automated through the use of computer macros. In addition, he felt that the efficiency of the office could be vastly improved by creating an integrated database that all members of the trademark department (and clients) could access and use. He mentioned this idea at a department lunch and received mixed reactions. A few members of the group liked the idea and wanted to hear more about it. Glenda noted that there was a tremendous work load and that she did not want this type of project to distract George from his prosecution responsibilities. Without discussing the matter further with his colleagues, George decided to pursue the project in his spare time. He had taken some computer classes while in college and had kept up with advances in web-based computing, JAVA, and HTML. He began chipping away at this project at home. Using his own computer and software he purchased with his own funds, George developed a prototype of the program over the next year. He worked around the clock, putting in regular hours at the office and then spending evenings and weekends in his home office on his software project. George occasionally accessed the law firm's website and files in developing the program and eventually ported a version of the program onto his office machine. He also tested the program with his office files. As the program components reached the operational stage, George began using (and refining) the program at the office. His productivity increased, as did his enjoyment of work. The challenge of automating his practice brought tremendous satisfaction. After more than a year of effort, George completed a prototype for what he called "TM Prosecution Toolkit." The program stores general information on clients and their applications, provides a checklist/expert system for assessing the applicability of § 2 bars to registration, identifies necessary actions for trademark prosecution, records information on actions taken, generates draft forms and correspondence for use in prosecution, calculates prosecution deadline dates, and alerts responsible individuals to impending deadlines.

George demonstrated the program to the trademark group on February 12, 2000, at a department-wide planning retreat. By that point in time, the department had grown to almost 10 attorneys. Everyone was duly impressed. Glenda recommended that the system be implemented throughout the department immediately. BH&C touted the use of the program on its website and promotional materials. The materials referred to the program as "BH&C's innovative TM Prosecution ToolkitTM." Steven Roland, the firm's Information Technology specialist, adapted aspects of George's program so that clients and attorneys could access the TM Prosecution ToolkitTM database through a password protected portal. The firm touted this new service as its TM FileshareSM. George received a particularly large bonus the following December. He was initially pleased by the firm's and colleagues' reaction, but was dismayed when the firm registered the copyright and trademark in the program under the firm's name and began marketing the technology to other law firms and trademark consulting firms. Glenda invited George to serve on a committee that she was forming to guide Steve Roland and the firm's computer staff on improving the products and services.

George has come to you for advice. (You work at another IP law firm in town.) A prominent trademark search firm, TMs r Us, has approached George about acquiring the software. In addition, Shiply and Elrod, another law firm in town specializing in IP is interested in bringing George on board in a lucrative "Of Counsel" capacity, which would allow George to develop a business around the TM Prosecution Toolkit. (Although George still enjoys practicing law, the past two years have surfaced a latent entrepreneurial streak. The Shiply and Elrod opportunity provides what he considers to be an ideal mix of legal practice and entrepreneurship. In addition, his income would go up significantly.) Shiply and Elrod would, however, want George to license the program (on an exclusive basis) to the firm.

    a. Who owns copyright in "TM Prosecution Toolkit"? "TM Fileshare"?

    b. Could George prevent BH&C from further use of the programs?

2.   Duration and Renewal

The duration of copyright protection has evolved significantly over the past century, generally moving in the direction of a longer term of protection.

i.   *1909 Act*

The 1909 Act employed a dual term of protection, granting a first term of 28 years from the date of first publication (with proper notice) that could be renewed in the final year for a second term of 28 years. Failure to renew registration of copyright in that last year resulted in the work falling into the public domain.

ii.   *1976 Act*

The 1976 Act moved to a unitary term of protection lasting for the life of the author plus 50 years[19] (or, in the case of corporate, anonymous, or pseudonymous entities, or works made for hire, 75 years from publication or 100 years from creation, whichever occurred first). The 1976 Act also extended the renewal term for works for 1909 Act works to 47 years. For purposes of administrative convenience, the 1976 Act provided that copyright terms shall run until the end of the calendar year in which they would otherwise expire, thereby adding an additional period of up to one year. 1992 legislation made renewal registration optional on a prospective basis. As a result, works not yet in their renewal term (i.e., those published after 1964 (1992 minus 28 years)) no longer risked falling into the public domain prematurely. Section 106A(d) governs the duration of certain moral rights of visual artists.

iii.   *Sonny Bono Copyright Term Extension Act of 1998*

With copyrights from the 1920s and 1930s set to expire, heirs of music composers (such as George and Ira Gershwin) as well as major content companies (such as the Walt Disney Corporation, which feared the loss of protection for Mickey Mouse) lobbied Congress to extend copyright protection for an additional 20 years. The fact that the European Union had added 20 years just a few years earlier worked in their favor.

---

[19] In the case of joint works, the term of copyright protection is measured from the death of the last surviving author. 17 U.S.C. § 302(b).

The legislation was passed without organized opposition. It was named in memory of Representative Sonny Bono, a successful songwriter and recording artist from the 1960s who had died earlier that year in a skiing accident and who reportedly said that copyright should last forever.

Sections 302–05 of the Act govern copyright duration. Table 4-1 summarizes the principal features.

TABLE 4-1
Duration of Copyright Protection*

Works First Published in U.S.	*Term of Protection* (all terms of copyright run through the end of the calendar year in which they would otherwise expire)
Before 1925	In the public domain
1925–1963	If published without proper notice, then in public domain
	If published with proper notice but not renewed, then in public domain
	If published with proper notice and renewed, then 95 years after publication date
1964–1977	If published without proper notice, then in public domain
	If published with proper notice, then 95 years after publication date (note: automatic renewal applies if no actual renewal)
1978–Mar. 1, 1989	If created after 1977 and published with notice, 70 years after the death of author. If a work of corporate authorship, 95 years from publication or 120 years from creation, whichever expires first
	If created before 1978 and first published with notice in the specified period, the greater of the term specified in the previous entry or 31 December 2047

Mar. 1, 1989–2002	If created after 1977, 70 years after the death of author. If a work of corporate authorship, 95 years from publication or 120 years from creation, whichever expires first Created before 1978 and first published in this period, the greater of the term specified in the previous entry or 31 December 2047
After 2002	Life of the author + 70 years (if anonymous works, pseudonymous works, or works made for hire, 95 years from publication, or 120 years from creation, whichever is less)

Sound Recordings First Published in U.S.	
Before 1923	Enters the public domain on Jan. 1, 2022
1923–1946	100 years from publication
1947–1956	110 years from publication
1957–Feb. 14,1972	Through Feb. 15, 2067
Feb. 15,1972-Dec. 31, 1977	If published without proper notice, in the public domain
	If published with proper notice, 95 years from publication (and at least until 2068)
1978–Mar. 1, 1989	If published without proper notice and without subsequent registration, in the public domain
	If published with proper notice, life of the author + 70 years (if anonymous works, pseudonymous works, or works made for hire, 95 years from publication, or 120 years from creation, whichever is less)
After Mar. 1, 1989	Life of the author + 70 years (if anonymous works, pseudonymous works, or works made for hire, 95 years from publication, or 120 years from creation, whichever is less)

Architectural Works (architectural plans may also be protected as pictorial or graphic works)	
Prior to Dec. 1, 1990	If constructed by Dec. 1, 1990, protected only as drawings
	If constructed between Nov. 30, 1990 and Dec. 31, 2002, structure is protected for life or the author + 70 years (if anonymous works, pseudonymous works, or works made for hire, 95 years from publication, or 120 years from creation, whichever is less)
After Dec. 1, 1990	Life or the author + 70 years (if anonymous works, pseudonymous works, or works made for hire, 95 years from publication, or 120 years from creation, whichever is less)

Unpublished, Never Registered Works	
Unpublished works	Life of the author + 70 years; works from authors who died before 1950 are in the public domain
Unpublished anonymous and pseudonymous works, and works made for hire (corporate authorship)	120 years from date of creation; works created before 1900 are in the public domain
Unpublished works when the death date of the author is not known	120 years from date of creation; works created before 1900 are in the public domain

* This table is based on Copyright Term and the Public Domain of the United States, *http://copyright.cornell.edu/resources/publicdomain.cfm*. That chart includes further details, including copyright duration for works first published abroad and unpublished sound recordings.

COMMENTS AND QUESTIONS

1. *Determining the Optimal Duration of Copyright Protection.* In Art. 1, § 8, cl. 8 of the U.S. CONSTITUTION, Congress is authorized to provide limited terms of protection in order to promote progress in science and the useful arts. Does the duration of copyright protection effectuate the appropriate balance between reward to authors and enrichment of the public domain so as to best promote progress in the arts? Why is the term so much longer than for patents? Determining the appropriate balance requires consideration of a broad range of variables, each of which is difficult to assess and measure.

The optimal duration of copyright protection from a utilitarian perspective requires a balancing of the costs and benefits of lengthening protection. Benefits presumably come in the form of an enhanced incentive for authors and artists to create, while the costs imposed are the limitations on the rights of subsequent creators to make use of copyrighted works in their creative efforts and the social cost from monopoly pricing. Unfortunately, there is no good empirical data on this trade-off. Using cost and other data from publishing companies, Professor (now Justice) Stephen Breyer questioned the need for copyright protection of books in view of the lead time advantages and the threat of retaliation in the form of competitive pricing against later market entrants. *See* Stephen Breyer, *The Uneasy Case for Copyright: A Study in Copyright of Books, Photocopies and Computer Programs*, 84 HARV. L. REV. 281 (1970). Although Professor Breyer's conclusion that any copyright protection for books may be too long arguably overstates what his data can support, *see* Barry W. Tyerman, *The Economic Rationale for Copyright Protection for Published Books: A Reply to Professor Breyer*, 18 UCLA L. REV. 1100 (1971); Stephen Breyer, *Copyright: A Rejoinder*, 20 UCLA L. REV. 75 (1972), he certainly raises serious qualms about lengthening the duration of copyright protection. Copyright Office records show that copyright renewal rates gradually rose from 3.5% in 1883 to 15% in 1959, with musical compositions constituting nearly half of renewals and books only 7%. *See* Barbara Ringer, *Renewal of Copyright*, Copyright Office Study No. 31, App. C (1960), *reprinted in* 1 OMNIBUS COPYRIGHT REVISION LEGISLATIVE HISTORY: COPYRIGHT LAW REVISION STUDIES 20–34 (George S. Grossman ed., 2001).

2. Consider the following argument for significantly limiting copyright protection: At a qualitative level, there would seem little basis for protecting most copyrightable works longer than 10 to 15 years. This observation is supported by the renewal data discussed above. Casebooks, for example, are rarely marketable after 5 years unless they are revised. Similarly, the public's interest in many works of literature and art tends to follow popular waves of a decade or less. Moreover, one can argue that after 25 years, the main interest in most literary works is historical. The public would be served by allowing historians the ability to draw upon such works in creating new works of history and social commentary. With regard to those relatively few works that have enduring commercial value beyond a decade or two, there is little question that such works generate substantial revenue for their authors. Therefore the public would be best served by limiting copyright protection for literary works to 25 years. Are you persuaded by

this argument? What counterarguments would you offer? What philosophical basis or bases underlie your arguments? *See* William M. Landes & Richard A. Posner, *Indefinitely Renewable Copyright*, 70 U. CHI. L. REV. 471 (2003); Peter S. Menell, *Tailoring Legal Protection for Computer Software*, 39 STAN. L. REV. 1329, 1354–67, 1371–72 (1987) (recommending a short duration for computer software (as well as other adjustments to deal with functionality and network effects); Brief of George A. Akerlof et al. as Amici Curiae in Support of Petitioners, *Eldred v. Ashcroft*, 537 U.S. 186 (2003) (No. 01-618).

3. *Happy Birthday to You.* For decades, Warner/Chappell Music has asserted copyright ownership of the iconic song "Happy Birthday to You." Since the 1990s, the music publisher earned has over $1 million per year licensing the song. Moreover, many film producers and restaurants steered clear of the song so as to avoid liability. When rumors circulated that copyright in this composition may well have expired, Professor Robert Brauneis set out to trace the song's copyright provenance. *See* Robert Brauneis, *Copyright and the World's Most Popular Song*, 56 J. COPYRIGHT SOC'Y U.S.A. 335 (2009). He discovered that the music was originally composed by Mildred Jane Hill and Patty Smith Hill in the early 1890s as a children's song and was first published in 1893 as "Good Morning to All." The "Happy Birthday to You" lyrics were developed some time later (and likely by someone other than the Hills). The song's appearance in a scene in Irving Berlin's show "As Thousands Cheer" in 1933 led to a lawsuit, and in 1935 the copyright for "Happy Birthday to You" was registered by the Clayton F. Summy Co., the Hill sisters' publisher. Warner/Chappell acquired the rights as part of a 1988 publishing deal.

Jennifer Nelson set out to make a documentary about the song in 2013 and ran into a problem. Warner/Chappell charged her $1,500 to use the composition. She and others brought a declaratory relief class action to establish that "Happy Birthday to You" was in the public domain. The litigation produced a trove of evidence casting doubt on copyright subsistence in the song. At a minimum, the documents established that Warner/Chappell did not own copyright in the "Happy Birthday to You" lyrics. *See Rupa Marya v. Warner/Chappell Music*, 131 F. Supp. 3d 975 (C.D. Cal. 2015). And since the melody was in the public domain, Warner/Chappell had no leg to stand on in court. Warner/Chappell ultimately agreed to pay $14 million to settle the class action lawsuit. *See* Matt Hamilton, *"Happy Birthday" Lawsuit: Tentative Settlement Puts Song in Public Domain*, L.A. TIMES, Feb. 9, 2016.

4. *The Political Economy of Copyright Term Extension.* Who benefits most from the extension of the copyright term? Does extension of the copyright term pose a significant threat to the public? What reasons might explain the lack of public concern about this type of legislation? *See* William Patry, *The Failure of the American Copyright System: Protecting the Idle Rich*, 72 NOTRE DAME L. REV. 907 (1997).

5. *Constitutionality of Copyright Term Extensions.* Shortly after the passage of the Sonny Bono Copyright Term Extension Act of 1998 (CTEA), various entities seeking to republish and distribute works that would otherwise have fallen into the public domain challenged the CTEA on three constitutional grounds: (1) that it violates the

First Amendment by unduly restraining speech; (2) that it violates the originality requirement of the Intellectual Property Clause, Art. I, § 8, cl. 8, by conferring additional protection to works that already exist; and (3) that it exceeds the "limited Times" constraint upon Congress's authority to enact copyright legislation. In a 7-2 decision, the Supreme Court upheld the CTEA as within Congress's broad discretion to prescribe "limited Times" and not at odds with the First Amendment. *See Eldred v. Ashcroft*, 537 U.S. 186 (2003). Emphasizing nearly two centuries of evolution of intellectual property law, the Court determined that Congress could extend protection for extant works consistent with the Intellectual Property Clause: "Congress could rationally seek to 'promote . . . Progress' by including in every copyright statute an express guarantee that authors would receive the benefit of any later legislative extension of the copyright term." Not surprisingly, Justice Breyer dissented, reiterating the themes of his 1970 article. Given the Court's deferential standard, are there any constitutional limitations on the duration of copyright protection or is this a matter solely for the legislative branch?

6. *Political Reform?* The CTEA and the *Eldred* case have served to rally various entities opposed to the ever-expanding nature of intellectual property protection. Various proposals have surfaced, including the reintroduction of a copyright maintenance fee, aimed at accelerating growth of the public domain. *See, e.g.,* Christopher Sprigman, *Reform(aliz)ing Copyright*, 57 STAN. L. REV. 485 (2004); William M. Landes & Richard A. Posner, *Indefinitely Renewable Copyright*, 70 U. CHI. L. REV. 471 (2003). The Public Domain Enhancement Act, H.R. 2601, 108th Cong. (2003), would have required U.S. authors to renew their copyrights for the modest fee of $1 after 50 years and again at 10-year intervals until the copyright expired. Since relatively few works were renewed under the 1909 Act regime, this statute would mean that most older works would likely become available after 50 years and the registration system would make it easier to trace ownership for those works that remain protected. Should the United States adopt this reform? What reforms would you recommend?

7. *Copyright Expiration.* The Sonny Bono Copyright Extension Act of 1998 postponed works entering the public domain for 20 years. Beginning on January 1, 2019, works once again began entering the public domain. Among the notable works entering the public domain in 2019 were:

- Cecil B. DeMille's (first, less famous, silent version of) *The Ten Commandments*
- Short films by Chaplin, Keaton, Laurel and Hardy, and Our Gang (later Little Rascals)
- Cartoons including Felix the Cat (the character first appeared in a 1919 cartoon)
- Robert Frost's poem *Nothing Gold Can Stay*
- Igor Stravinsky's *Octet for Wind Instruments*
- JEAN TOOMER, CANE
- KAHLIL GIBRAN, THE PROPHET
- SIGMUND FREUD, THE EGO AND THE ID

- LE CORBUSIER, TOWARDS A NEW ARCHITECTURE
- Constantin Brâncuși's sculpture *Bird in Space*
- Artistic works by M. C. Escher, Pablo Picasso, Wassily Kandinsky, Max Ernst, and Man Ray

---

PROBLEMS

Problem IV-25. Determine the duration of copyright in the following cases (viewing each fact pattern in isolation):

a. Arnold Author completes his novel YOU'LL BE MINE 'TIL THE END OF TIME on February 28, 1996. The next day, February 29th, Arnold is hit by a bus and dies instantly. On what day does his copyright expire?

b. While working for THE NEW ENGLANDER MAGAZINE, Arnold Author writes a story entitled "You'll Always Be Mine." The story is finally published by THE NEW ENGLANDER in 2010. When does the copyright expire?

c. Arnold Author began work on his greatest novel, TIME IS ON MY SIDE, in 1990. In 1991, he completes the first three chapters. In 1992, he writes the middle three chapters. In 1993, he completes the final three chapters. In 1995, he signs an agreement with Time/Life Books to publish the novel. The contract assigns all copyright interests to Time/Life Books in exchange for 20 percent royalties based on the wholesale price. The book is finally published on January 1, 1996. Arnold dies on February 29, 1996. On what day does the copyright expire? Does your answer change if you assume that Arnold entered into a contract with Time/Life Books before writing the novel?

d. At the time of his death on February 29, 1996, Arnold Author has completed three fourths of his novel TIME LIVES ON. His will leaves all his property to his spouse, Angela Author, who is also a writer. She plans to complete the novel by 1999. Time/Life Books has agreed to publish the completed manuscript in the year 2000. Assuming that all goes according to plan, when will copyright in TIME LIVES ON expire?

Problem IV-26. What is the duration of copyright in the following cases?

a. Loretta Wrighter composed and sent a letter to her friend, Emily Johnson, in 1961. Emily has saved the letter in her correspondence file since that time. Loretta died in 1970. What is the term of protection for this work?

b. Stephen Morris published his first novel, CHILD'S PLAY, at the age of 6 in 1924. Remarkably, he is still alive today. What is the term of protection for this work?

c. Anita Author published (with proper notice) her novel entitled THE WINDS OF CHANGE in 1970. She died three years later. What is the term of protection for this work?

d. Penelope Painter painted her masterpiece entitled "Garden of Wildflowers" in 1953. She distributed copies with notice of copyright in 1955. She renewed the copyright in 1982. She died the next year. When does the copyright expire?

3.   Division, Transfer, and Reclaiming of Copyrights

The preceding section has explored one important difference between copyright interests and the traditional fee simple absolute in real property law: the limited duration of protection. Copyrights, therefore, can be analogized to a hybrid of a term of years and life estate in that the owner has control of the rights of copyright for a defined and limited period of time (life plus 70 years), after which such rights fall to the public at large.

Another important aspect of copyright ownership is the distinction between ownership of the material object on which the work of authorship is fixed—the book manuscript or oil canvas—and ownership of the copyright interests themselves. Section 202 states:

> Ownership of a copyright, or of any of the exclusive rights under a copyright, is distinct from ownership of any material object in which the work is embodied. Transfer of ownership of any material object, including the copy or phonorecord in which the work is first fixed, does not of itself convey any rights in the copyrighted work embodied in the object; nor, in the absence of an agreement, does transfer of ownership of a copyright or of any exclusive rights under a copyright convey property rights in any material object.

Thus, the author of a letter retains her copyright interests in the writing even though she sends the letter to the addressee. The addressee thereby obtains ownership of the material object but may not infringe the copyright interests of the author. The addressee may view the material object and he may show it to others, but he may not make copies, prepare derivative works, distribute the work, or perform or display the work publicly.

Two other elements of real property interests are the rights of property owners and the alienability of such rights. This section discusses the division, transfer, and termination of transfer rights of copyright holders. In the real property domain, the owner of a fee interest may freely divide and alienate the various rights of property ownership. For example, a property owner can divide her lot and sell a portion to another person. Alternatively, she may sell one particular right within the bundle of rights, such as the right to use a path running across the property (an easement). Moreover, such transfers are generally not terminable unless so specified in the transfer agreement. Thus, a property owner who creates an easement across her land cannot unilaterally terminate that right at a later time unless she reserved that power.

By contrast, copyright law restricts the alienability of the rights of copyright owners in certain ways. As you study these materials, scrutinize the reasons for restricting the alienability of copyright interests.

i.   *Division and Transfer of Copyright Interests Under the 1909 Act*

Courts interpreted the 1909 Act to preclude the formal divisibility of the rights comprising a copyright. A copyright owner could assign the entire copyright to another, but a transfer of any lesser interest was considered a license. This doctrine of indivisibility simplified the notice requirement. As noted earlier, failure to provide proper notice could result in forfeiture of copyright protection. The "owner" of the copyright (or "proprietor"), whether the author or the assignee of the entire copyright, was the appropriate name to be included in the copyright notice. One consequence of the doctrine of indivisibility was that only proprietors had standing to bring suit to enforce the copyright. Thus, a licensee would have to join the proprietor in order to protect his or her rights. In practice, however, courts' decisions interpreting the 1909 Act limited the effect of the indivisibility rule.

ii. *Division and Transfer of Copyright Interests Under the 1976 Act*

The 1976 Act eliminated restrictions on the formal divisibility of copyright interests. Section 201(d) provides:

The ownership of a copyright may be transferred in whole or in part by any means of conveyance or by operation of law, and may be bequeathed by will or pass as personal property by the applicable laws of intestate succession.

Any of the exclusive rights comprised in a copyright, including any subdivision of any of the rights specified by § 106, may be transferred as provided by clause (1) and owned separately. The owner of any particular exclusive right is entitled, to the extent of that right, to all of the protection and remedies accorded to the copyright owner by this title.

Section 101 defines "transfer of copyright ownership" to include an assignment or an *exclusive* license of any of the exclusive rights comprised in a copyright. The divisibility of copyright ownership enables any owner of an exclusive right to bring an infringement suit without having to join the copyright proprietor.

Section 204 requires transfers of copyright ownership to be executed in writing and signed by the copyright owner. Section 205 provides for the voluntary recordation of transfers with the Copyright Office. It also sets forth priority rules for resolving cases of conflicting transfers.

iii. *Reclaiming Copyrights*

Under the 1909 Act, authors could reclaim copyright interests that they had licensed at the time of renewal. This opportunity to reclaim copyright upon renewal proved unavailing in most commercial circumstances as book and music publishers routinely insisted upon assignment of the initial copyright term and the advance assignment of the renewal term in exchange for publishing a work. The Supreme Court upheld the enforceability of such contingent (upon the author's survival until renewal) advance assignment clauses. *See Fred Fisher Music Co. v. M. Witmark & Sons*, 318 U.S. 643 (1943).

While it eliminated the renewal regime, the 1976 Act created a much more potent means for authors and their survivors to reclaim copyright interests at a later time: an inalienable right to terminate transfers of copyright between the thirty-fifth and fortieth year from the execution of the transfer of rights for works created after 1977. § 203(a)(3). With respect to works in their second renewal term prior to 1978, § 304(c) allows authors and their families to terminate transfers between the fifty-sixth and sixty-first year of copyright protection for such works so as to allow them to profit from the 19 years of protection for such works added by the 1976 Act. A comparable right was bestowed upon authors in the Sonny Bono Copyright Term Extension Act of 1998, ensuring that they may reclaim the 20 years added to their copyrights. Termination of transfer rights may not be assigned in advance. Congress enacted these provisions to better ensure that authors and their families are able to reap a fair portion of the benefits of the author's creative efforts. Congress was concerned that authors had "unequal bargaining power" in negotiating rights with publishers and marketers "resulting in part from the impossibility of determining a work's value until it has been exploited." H.R. REP. NO. 1476, 94th Cong., 2d Sess. 124 (1976).

As noted in the discussion of the "works made for hire" doctrine, the only way for a transferee to prevent a termination of transfer is by establishing that the work was "made for hire" and therefore owned by the employer or commissioning party *ab initio* (from the outset). With regard to commissioned works (works prepared by independent contractors as opposed to "employees"), Congress limited this exception to the termination of transfer provision in two ways: by allowing only certain enumerated categories of works to be treated as works made for hire and by requiring that the parties specifically agree in writing that the work shall be treated as a "work made for hire." The film, magazine, newspaper, and textbook industries foresaw that the termination of transfer provision could seriously disrupt their operations and persuaded Congress to include "motion picture[s]" and "contribution[s] to collective works" among the enumerated categories.

COMMENTS AND QUESTIONS

1. *Renewal and Derivative Works: Abend Rights.* Cornell Woolrich's story, "It Had to Be Murder," was published by DIME DETECTIVE MAGAZINE in 1942. Woolrich retained all other rights in the story and in 1945 assigned the motion picture rights—for both the initial term of copyright and the contingent renewal term—to DeSylva Productions. In 1953, DeSylva assigned the story rights to Jimmy Stewart and Alfred Hitchcock, who together produced the film *Rear Window*, in 1954. Just prior to the renewal period for the story, Woolrich died, leaving the property in trust. The trustee renewed the copyright and assigned the renewal term to Sheldon Abend, an enterprising author's representative, in exchange for $650 plus 10 percent of any proceeds from exploitation of the story. Abend then sued Stewart, Hitchcock, and the distributor of *Rear Window*, alleging that further exploitation of the film without his consent infringed his copyright in the underlying story. The Supreme Court agreed, resting its decision on two critical interpretations of the 1909 Act: (1) when an author dies before the renewal period vests, the renewal right passes to the author's statutory successors and any advance assignments of rights in the renewal term go "unfulfilled"; and (2) that during the renewal term, continued exploitation of derivative works made with permission of the owners of underlying works during the original term of copyright nonetheless requires continued authorization to utilize such underlying copyrighted elements during

the renewal term. *See Stewart v. Abend*, 495 U.S. 207 (1990). Shortly thereafter, the parties settled the dispute, enabling *Rear Window* to be exploited and Abend to license a remake for worldwide distribution. What drove the settlement was that Abend would not have been able to exploit a remake outside the United States without consent of the owners of the copyright in Hitchcock's version of the film. In this sense, the Supreme Court's decision created a blocking right structure.

When Congress amended the Copyright Act in 1992 to provide for automatic renewal, it held out the carrot of so-called *Abend* rights as an incentive for renewal registration. Failure to file a renewal registration forfeited any claim to *Abend* rights.

2. *Termination of Transfers and Derivative Works*. When Congress added 19 years to the term of pre-1978 works in the 1976 Act and an additional 20 years in the CTEA in 1998, it expressly authorized continued exploitation of derivative works. *See* §§ 203(b)(1); 304(c)(6)(A).

3. *Circumventing Inalienability—Rescission and Regrant.* In 1930, A.A. Milne, author of the iconic children's book series featuring Winnie-the-Pooh, entered into an agreement granting Stephen Slesinger exclusive merchandising based on the Pooh works in the United States and Canada "for and during the respective periods of copyright and of any renewal thereof to be had under the Copyright Act." In 1956, the author passed away, bequeathed all beneficial interests in the Pooh works to a trust for the benefit of his widow during her lifetime ("Milne Trust"), and, after her death, to other beneficiaries ("Pooh Properties Trust"), which included his son, Christopher Robin, and his daughter, Clare. In 1971, the author's widow passed away and, in 1972, her beneficial interests under the Milne Trust were assigned to the Pooh Properties Trust. In 1983, faced with the possibility that Christopher might seek to terminate rights, the licensees and Christopher rescinded the earlier agreement and regranted the rights in exchange for a more lucrative deal for the Trust. Christopher passed away in 1996. In 2002, Clare Milne set out to recapture the 20 years added by the Copyright Term Extension Act. Notwithstanding the clear language in the 1976 Act stating that "[t]ermination of the grant may be effected notwithstanding *any* agreement to the contrary," § 304(c)(5) (emphasis added), the Ninth Circuit upheld the contract rescinding and regranting the copyright license on the ground that Christopher had— and knew that he had—the right to vest copyright in himself at the very time he revoked the prior grants and leveraged his termination rights to secure the benefits of the copyrighted works. *See Milne v. Stephen Slesinger, Inc.*, 430 F.3d 1036, 1046 (9th Cir. 2005). Christopher could not, however, have anticipated that Congress would add an additional 20 years in 1998 (and intended such extensions to benefit the original authors and their statutory successors).

In 2008, the Second Circuit followed a similar logic in upholding a 1994 agreement executed by Elaine Steinbeck, John Steinbeck's widow, canceling and superseding the author's 1938 license to the publisher. This "new agreement for continued publication" effectively eliminated the termination right of Steinbeck's children from a prior marriage. *See Penguin Grp. (USA) Inc. v. Steinbeck*, 537 F.3d 193 (2d Cir. 2008). Taking a cramped view of what constitutes an "agreement to the contrary" under

§ 304(c)(5), the Second Circuit viewed the result in this case as furthering Congress' intent by affording Steinbeck's widow leverage to renegotiate the contract. These decisions, however, overlook the broader legislative framework (which affords termination rights to a class of statutory successors) and raise serious concerns about the fidelity to the express language and meaning of the statute. *See* Peter S. Menell & David Nimmer, *Pooh-Poohing Copyright Law's "Inalienable" Termination Rights*, 57 J. COPYRIGHT SOC'Y 799 (2010).

4. *Sound Recordings and Works Made for Hire.* When the "work made for hire" provision of the 1976 Act was being hammered out in the early to mid-1960s, sound recordings were not yet a part of the Copyright Act. Record industry representatives were understandably focused on getting federal protection for their works. Furthermore, at that time many record labels considered recording artists to be employees. Therefore, there was not much attention focused on getting sound recordings included within the "work made for hire" exception to termination of transfer rule. Over the next two decades, the record industry underwent substantial changes. Recording artists became more independent, making the "employee" classification dubious.

Fearing that some of its prize assets might be vulnerable to notice of termination beginning in 2003 (Congress allowed for a ten-year window for notifying transferees) and actual termination in 2013 of works transferred in 1978, the sound recording industry surreptitiously persuaded Congress to insert "sound recordings" into the Act through a "technical amendment" buried within the Satellite Home Viewer Improvement Act of 1999. After this legislation was signed into law and word of the change became widely known, recording artists protested the backroom deal. Soon thereafter, Congress held hearings at which the Register of Copyrights acknowledged that the change was more than a "technical amendment." The industry defended its actions on the ground that record albums constitute "collective works" and hence sound recordings contained therein are owned by record companies as "contributions to collective works," one of the enumerated categories. Do you agree with this reading of the Copyright Act?

In an effort to clean the slate, the recording industry and recording artist representatives drafted a compromise bill repealing the 1999 provision and restoring the *status quo ante. See* Work Made for Hire and Copyright Corrections Act of 2000, Pub. L. No. 106-379, § 1, 114 Stat. 1444 (2000); David Nimmer & Peter S. Menell, *Sound Recordings, Works for Hire, and the Termination-of-Transfers Time Bomb*, 49 J. COPYRIGHT SOC'Y 387 (2001). Whether sound recordings should be deemed "works made for hire" awaits judicial resolution[20] or further legislation. How should sound

---

[20] Scattered district court rulings have reached the unremarkable conclusion that a work cannot qualify as commissioned if the basis is that it is a sound recording. *See Bucciarelli-Tieger v. Victory Records, Inc.*, 488 F. Supp. 2d 702 (N.D. Ill. 2007) (observing that "[s]ound recordings are notably exempt for the the list of works that can be specially commission as works-for-hire"); *Ballas v. Tedesco*, 41 F. Supp. 2d 531, 541 (D.N.J. 1999); *Staggers v. Real Authentic Sound*, 77 F. Supp. 2d 57 (D.D.C. 1999). In another context (determining the size of a statutory damages award), the Second Circuit held that particular record albums fit within the Copyright Act's definition of "compilation." *See Bryant v. Media Right Prods.,Inc.*, 603 F.3d

recordings be handled? Will the exploitation of sound recordings become a legal morass due to a multiplicity of claimants? Who is eligible to terminate in the case of a typical popular record—record producer, arranger, featured artists, band members, background musicians, recording engineer, remixing engineer? Are they all joint authors?

4. *Policy Analysis of the Termination of Transfers*. Will the termination of transfers provision alleviate the problem of "unremunerative transfers" that Congress sought to address through the creation of an inalienable termination right? Do you agree with Congress's premise that authors are at a serious bargaining disadvantage in negotiating the rights to their works? Is making the power of reverter inalienable necessary to address this concern?

What problems might arise as a result of the power to terminate copyright transfers? What alternative means might Congress have used to protect the interests of authors and their families short of an inalienable power of reverter?

E.   RIGHTS AND INFRINGEMENT

Copyright law grants a complex array of rights to enable owners to exploit their works, protect non-economic interests, and limit unauthorized activities. Copyright law also limits these rights in numerous and complex ways that can vary by types of works, users of works, and a range of other factors. As a result, it is necessary to study each of the rights separately. Note that we postpone consideration of fair use of copyrighted works until Chapter IV(F)(1).

Copyright infringement may occur by two distinct sets of actors: (1) those who directly infringe the rights of copyright holders; and (2) those who encourage or assist a third party to infringe. We explore direct infringement of the various copyright rights before turning to the indirect infringement doctrines.

1.   Direct Infringement

As noted in the introduction to this chapter, copyright law has for much of its history focused upon the protection of expressive works fixed in analog media—books, vinyl, tapes, film, and over-the-air broadcasting. This section begins with the bundle of rights that has grown up around these technology platforms. We then explore the protection of moral rights (rights of attribution and integrity) and limited pockets of state and common law protection of expressive works. The final subsection addresses the extensions of new rights relating to digital technology, most notably the anti-circumvention protections and limitations).

---

135 (2d Cir. 2010). It is not clear whether that classification would govern the determination of whether sound recordings could be works made for hire.

i.   *Traditional Copyright Rights*

§ 106. Exclusive Rights in Copyrighted Works

Subject to sections 107 through 118, the owner of copyright under this title has the exclusive rights to do and to authorize any of the following:

(1) to reproduce the copyrighted work in copies or phonorecords;

(2) to prepare derivative works based on the copyrighted work;

(3) to distribute copies or phonorecords of the copyrighted work to the public by sale or other transfer of ownership, or by rental, lease, or lending;

(4) in the case of literary, musical, dramatic, and choreographic works, pantomimes, and motion pictures and other audiovisual works, to perform the copyright work publicly;

(5) in the case of literary, musical, dramatic, and choreographic works, pantomimes, and pictorial, graphic, or sculptural works, including the individual images of a motion picture or other audiovisual work, to display the copyrighted work publicly; and

(6) in the case of sound recordings, to perform the copyrighted work publicly by means of a digital audio transmission. [This right was added in 1995.]

Anyone who "violates any of the exclusive rights of the copyright owner as provided by sections 106 through 122" is liable for copyright infringement. § 501(a).

a.   *The Right to Make Copies*

There is a close relationship between the rights in subsections (1), (2), and (3) of § 106. The right to "reproduce" is the most fundamental of the rights granted to the copyright owner. It includes all rights to fix a work in a tangible medium of expression, including the right to make phonorecords.

The right to reproduce granted by § 106(1) is not limited to literal reproduction (such as "copying" a disk or making a photocopy). Rather, it protects against the unauthorized making of "substantially similar" reproductions of protected expression.

The doctrines governing direct infringement of copyright address two distinct aspects: (1) proving copying; and (2) improper appropriation, which entails assessing substantiality of copying protected expression.

The first aspect relates to proving whether someone has actually copied the work of another. In contrast to patent protection, which prohibits making, using, selling, offering to sell, or importing the patent invention whether or not the accused infringed *copied* the patentee's technology, copyright law only prohibits *copying*. Thus, copyright protection does not bar independent creation. The fact that two composers produce similar musical compositions does not necessarily mean that one copied from the other. They may have independently composed similar songs. Ideally, a court would like to have direct proof of copying—e.g., eyewitness testimony, records indicating that one author obtained the work from another, videotape of direct copying, or distinctive flaws (such as unusual errors that are common to the two works). In many cases, however, such evidence is not available. Nonetheless, the circumstances surrounding the works may point inexorably toward a finding of copying, for example, where a work has been widely disseminated and a second author produces a nearly identical work.

The second aspect relates to the quantum of copying. The legislative history to § 106 provides the following guidance:

> [A] copyrighted work would be infringed by reproducing it *in whole or in any substantial part,* and by duplicating it exactly or by imitation or simulation. Wide departures or variations from the copyrighted works would still be an infringement as long as the author's "expression" rather [than] merely the author's "ideas" are taken.

H.R. REP. NO. 94-1476, 94th Cong., 2d Sess. 61 (1976) (emphasis added). As suggested by this passage, the inquiry into whether the defendant has violated a plaintiff's copyright is often complicated by the fact that many copyrightable works intermingle original expression with public domain materials, ideas, facts, stock literary elements, *scenes à faire,* and other nonprotectable elements. Thus, even when a defendant acknowledges having developed his or her work with knowledge of the plaintiff's work, she can defend on the grounds that her work is not *substantially similar* to the copyright owner's *protected expression.* Hence courts have had to develop an infringement filter that adequately protects the interests of copyright owners but at the same time does not interfere with the public's right to use unprotected elements.

Some courts confusingly use the term "substantial similarity" in discussing both actual copying and improper appropriation. *See* Alan Latman, *"Probative Similarity" as Proof of Copying: Toward Dispelling Some Myths in Copyright Infringement*, 90 COLUM. L. REV. 1187 (1990). The Ninth Circuit explained the confusion in *Skidmore v. Led Zeppelin*, 952 F.3d 1051, 1064 (9th Cir. 2020) (en banc):

> [The] infringement analysis contains two separate components: "copying" and "unlawful appropriation." . . . Although these requirements are too often referred to in shorthand lingo as the need to prove "substantial similarity," they are distinct concepts.
>
> Because independent creation is a complete defense to copyright infringement, a plaintiff must prove that a defendant copied the work. In the absence of direct evidence of copying, which is the case here, the plaintiff 'can attempt to prove it circumstantially by showing that the defendant had access to the plaintiff's work and that the two works share similarities probative of copying.' This type of probative or striking similarity shows that the similarities between the two works are due to 'copying rather than . . . coincidence, independent creation, or prior common source.'
>
> On the other hand, the hallmark of 'unlawful appropriation' is that the works share *substantial* similarities. . . .

As you study these materials, pay special attention to the context in which the courts are referring to "substantial similarity."

1. Copying

Arnstein v. Porter
United States Court of Appeals for the Second Circuit
154 F.2d 464 (2d Cir. 1946)

FRANK, Circuit Judge.

[Ira B. Arnstein sued Cole Porter for infringement of copyrights in various of plaintiff's musical compositions. He sought a jury trial. Plaintiff alleged that the defendant's "Begin the Beguine" had been plagiarized from plaintiff's "The Lord Is My Shepherd" and "A Mother's Prayer" and that defendant's "My Heart Belongs to Daddy" had been plagiarized from "A Mother's Prayer." Plaintiff testified in deposition that both works had been published and that about 2,000 copies of "The Lord Is My Shepherd" and over a million copies of "A Mother's Prayer" had been sold. Plaintiff offered no direct proof that defendant saw or heard these compositions. Plaintiff further testified that defendant's "Night and Day" had been plagiarized from plaintiff's "I Love You Madly" and that although the latter composition had not been published, it had been performed publicly over the radio. In addition, plaintiff averred that a copy of the song had been stolen from his room. Plaintiff alleged that some other songs of the defendant had been plagiarized from the plaintiff's unpublished works. He suggested in deposition that the defendant had gained access to these songs either through publishers or a movie producer who were sent copies or through "stooges" who defendant had hired to follow, watch, and live with the plaintiff (and who may have been responsible for the ransacking of his room). When asked how he knew that defendant had anything to do with the "burglaries," plaintiff testified "I don't know that he had to do with it, but I only know that he could have." Defendant testified in depositions that he had never seen nor heard the plaintiff's compositions and that he did not have any connection to the alleged theft of such works.

The district court granted defendant's motion for summary judgment.]

. . . The principal question on this appeal is whether the lower court, under Rule 56, properly deprived plaintiff of a trial of his copyright infringement action. The answer depends on whether "there is the slightest doubt as to the facts." In applying that standard here, it is important to avoid confusing two separate elements essential to a plaintiff's case in such a suit: (a) that defendant copied from plaintiff's copyrighted work and (b) that the copying (assuming it to be proved) went so far as to constitute improper appropriation.

As to the first—copying—the evidence may consist (a) of defendant's admission that he copied or (b) of circumstantial evidence—usually evidence of access—from which the trier of the facts may reasonably infer copying. Of course, if there are no similarities, no amount of evidence of access will suffice to prove copying. If there is evidence of access and similarities exist, then the trier of the facts must determine whether the similarities are sufficient to prove copying. On this issue, analysis ("dissection") is relevant, and the testimony of experts may be received to aid the trier of the facts. If evidence of access is absent, the similarities must be so striking as to preclude the possibility that plaintiff and defendant independently arrived at the same result.

If copying is established, then only does there arise the second issue, that of illicit copying (unlawful appropriation). On that issue (as noted more in detail below) the test is the response of the ordinary lay hearer; accordingly, on that issue, "dissection" and expert testimony are irrelevant.

In some cases, the similarities between the plaintiff's and defendant's work are so extensive and striking as, without more, both to justify an inference of copying and to prove improper appropriation. But such double-purpose evidence is not required; that is, if copying is otherwise shown, proof of improper appropriation need not consist of similarities which, standing alone, would support an inference of copying.

Each of these two issues—copying and improper appropriation—is an issue of fact. If there is a trial, the conclusions on those issues of the trier of the facts—of the judge if he sat without a jury, or of the jury if there was a jury trial—bind this court on appeal, provided the evidence supports those findings, regardless of whether we would ourselves have reached the same conclusions. But a case could occur in which the similarities were so striking that we would reverse a finding of no access, despite weak evidence of access (or no evidence thereof other than the similarities); and similarly as to a finding of no illicit appropriation.

We turn first to the issue of copying. After listening to the compositions as played in the phonograph recordings submitted by defendant, we find similarities; but we hold that unquestionably, standing alone, they do not compel the conclusion, or permit the inference, that defendant copied. The similarities, however, are sufficient so that, if there is enough evidence of access to permit the case to go to the jury, the jury may properly infer that the similarities did not result from coincidence.

Summary judgment was, then, proper if indubitably defendant did not have access to plaintiff's compositions. Plainly that presents an issue of fact. On that issue, the district judge, who heard no oral testimony, had before him the depositions of plaintiff and defendant. The judge characterized plaintiff's story as "fantastic"; and, in the light of the references in his opinion to defendant's deposition, the judge obviously accepted defendant's denial of access and copying. Although part of plaintiff's testimony on deposition (as to "stooges" and the like) does seem "fantastic," yet plaintiff's credibility, even as to those improbabilities, should be left to the jury. If evidence is "of a kind that greatly taxes the credulity of the judge, he can say so, or, if he totally disbelieves it, he may announce that fact, leaving the jury free to believe it or not." If, said Winslow, J., "evidence is to be always disbelieved because the story told seems remarkable or impossible, then a party whose rights depend on the proof of some facts out of the usual course of events will always be denied justice simply because his story is improbable."

We should not overlook the shrewd proverbial admonition that sometimes truth is stranger than fiction.

But even if we were to disregard the improbable aspects of plaintiff's story, there remain parts by no means "fantastic." On the record now before us, more than a million copies of one of his compositions were sold; copies of others were sold in smaller quantities or distributed to radio stations or band leaders or publishers, or the pieces were publicly performed. If, after hearing both parties testify, the jury disbelieves defendant's denials, it can, from such facts, reasonably infer access. It follows that, as credibility is unavoidably involved, a genuine issue of material fact presents itself. With credibility a vital factor, plaintiff is entitled to a trial where the jury can observe the witnesses while testifying. . . .

Assuming that adequate proof is made of copying, that is not enough; for there can be "permissible copying," copying which is not illicit. Whether (if he copied) defendant unlawfully appropriated presents, too, an issue of fact. The proper criterion on that issue is not an analytic or other comparison of the respective musical compositions as they appear on paper or in the judgment of trained musicians. The plaintiff's legally protected interest is not, as such, his reputation as a musician but his interest in the potential financial returns from his compositions which derive from the lay public's approbation of his efforts. The question, therefore, is whether defendant took from plaintiff's works so much of what is pleasing to the ears of lay listeners, who comprise the audience for whom such popular music is composed, that defendant wrongfully appropriated something which belongs to the plaintiff.

Surely, then, we have an issue of fact which a jury is peculiarly fitted to determine. Indeed, even if there were to be a trial before a judge, it would be desirable (although not necessary) for him to summon an advisory jury on this question.

We should not be taken as saying that a plagiarism case can never arise in which absence of similarities is so patent that a summary judgment for defendant would be correct. Thus suppose that Ravel's *Bolero* or Shostakovitch's *Fifth Symphony* were alleged to infringe "When Irish Eyes Are Smiling." But this is not such a case. For, after listening to the playing of the respective compositions, we are, at this time, unable to conclude that the likenesses are so trifling that, on the issue of misappropriation, a trial judge could legitimately direct a verdict for defendant.

At the trial, plaintiff may play, or cause to be played, the pieces in such manner that they may seem to a jury to be inexcusably alike, in terms of the way in which lay listeners of such music would be likely to react. The plaintiff may call witnesses whose testimony may aid the jury in reaching its conclusion as to the responses of such audiences. Expert testimony of musicians may also be received, but it will in no way be controlling on the issue of illicit copying, and should be utilized only to assist in determining the reactions of lay auditors. The impression made on the refined ears of musical experts or their views as to the musical excellence of plaintiff's or defendant's works are utterly immaterial on the issue of misappropriation; for the views of such persons are caviar to the general—and plaintiff's and defendant's compositions are not caviar. . . .

CLARK, Circuit Judge (dissenting).

[A]fter repeated hearings of the records, I could not find therein what my brothers found. The only thing definitely mentioned seemed to be the repetitive use of the note e, in certain places by both plaintiff and defendant, surely too simple and ordinary a device of composition to be significant. In our former musical plagiarism cases we have, naturally, relied on what seemed the total sound effect; but we have also analyzed the music enough to make sure of an intelligible and intellectual decision. Thus in *Arnstein v. Edward B. Marks Music Corp.*, 2 Cir., 82 F.2d 275, 277, Judge L. Hand made quite an extended comparison of the songs, concluding, inter alia: ". . . the seven notes available do not admit of so many agreeable permutations that we need be amazed at the re-appearance of old themes, even though the identity extend through a sequence of twelve notes." *See also* the discussion in *Marks v. Leo Feist, Inc.*, 2 Cir., 290 F. 959, and *Darrell v. Joe Morris Music Co.*, 2 Cir., 113 F.2d 80, where the use of six similar bars and of an eight-note sequence frequently repeated were respectively held not to constitute infringement, and *Wilkie v. Santly Bros.*, 2 Cir., 91 F.2d 978, where use of eight bars with other similarities amounting to over three-quarters of the significant parts was held infringement.

It is true that in *Arnstein v. Broadcast Music, Inc.*, 2 Cir., 137 F.2d 410, 412, we considered "dissection" or "technical analysis" not the proper approach to support a finding of plagiarism, and said that it must be "more ingenuous, more like that of a spectator, who would rely upon the complex of his impressions." But in its context that seems to me clearly sound and in accord with what I have in mind. Thus one may look to the total impression to repulse the charge of plagiarism where a minute "dissection" might dredge up some points of similarity. Hence one cannot use a purely theoretical disquisition to supply a tonal resemblance which does not otherwise exist. Certainly, however, that does not suggest or compel the converse—that one must keep his brain in torpor for fear that otherwise it would make clear differences which do exist. Music is a matter of the intellect as well as the emotions; that is why eminent musical scholars insist upon the employment of the intellectual faculties for a just appreciation of music.

Consequently I do not think we should abolish the use of the intellect here even if we could. When, however, we start with an examination of the written and printed material supplied by the plaintiff in his complaint and exhibits, we find at once that he does not and cannot claim extensive copying, measure by measure, of his compositions. He therefore has resorted to a comparative analysis—the "dissection" found unpersuasive in the earlier cases—to support his claim of plagiarism of small detached portions here and there, the musical fillers between the better known parts of the melody. And plaintiff's compositions, as pointed out in the cases cited above, are of the simple and trite character where small repetitive sequences are not hard to discover. It is as though we found Shakespeare a plagiarist on the basis of his use of articles, pronouns, prepositions, and adjectives also used by others. The surprising thing, however, is to note the small amount of even this type of reproduction which plaintiff by dint of extreme dissection has been able to find.

. . . The usual claim seems to be rested upon a sequence of three, of four, or of five—never more than five—identical notes, usually of different rhythmical values. Nowhere is there anything approaching the twelve-note sequence of the *Marks* case. . . .

In the light of these utmost claims of the plaintiff, I do not see a legal basis for the claim of plagiarism. So far as I have been able to discover, no earlier case approaches the holding that a simple and trite sequence of this type, even if copying may seem indicated, constitutes proof either of access or of plagiarism. . . .

COMMENTS AND QUESTIONS

1. *Infringement Analysis: Copying + Improper Appropriation.* The *Arnstein* majority articulates both elements needed to establish infringement: (a) copying and (b) improper (or unlawful) appropriation ("whether defendant took from plaintiff's works so much of what is pleasing to the ears of lay listeners, who comprise the audience for whom such popular music is composed, that defendant wrongfully appropriated something which belongs to the plaintiff"). We explore the former stage in these comments and problems and the latter stage in the next section.

2. *Circumstantial Proof of Copying: Access + Similarity.* The majority opinion in *Arnstein* articulates the leading test for establishing copying by way of circumstantial evidence. The court suggests a sliding scale: "[I]f there are no similarities, no amount of evidence of access will suffice to prove copying. If there is evidence of access and similarities exist, then the trier of the facts must determine whether the similarities are sufficient to prove copying. . . . If evidence of access is absent, the similarities must be so striking as to preclude the possibility that plaintiff and defendant independently arrived at the same result."

As reflected in *Arnstein,* courts began to examine the questions of access and probative similarity along a sliding scale. In this formulation, which came to be known as the *inverse ratio rule*, the stronger the evidence of access, the less compelling the similarities between the two works need be in order to give rise to an inference of copying.

Some courts failed to maintain the distinction between substantial similarity (unlawful appropriation) and probative similarity, and in the process came to incorrectly apply the inverse ratio rule to both factual copying and improper appropriation. *See, e.g., Three Boys Music Corp. v. Bolton*, 212 F. 3d 477, 485 (9th Cir. 2000). Responding to this confusion, the Ninth Circuit ruled *en banc* in *Skidmore*:

> Because the inverse ratio rule, which is not part of the copyright statute, defies logic, and creates uncertainty for the courts and the parties, we take this opportunity to abrogate the rule in the Ninth Circuit and overrule our prior cases to the contrary.

The circuits are split over the inverse ratio rule, but the majority of those that have considered the rule declined to adopt it. The Second, Fifth, Seventh, and Eleventh Circuits have rejected the rule. . . .

But even within our circuit, our embrace and application of the rule have had a 'checkered application.' 4 NIMMER § 13.03[D]. The very nature of the rule spawned uncertainty in its application. . . .

The lack of clear guidance is likely due in no small part to our use of the term 'substantial similarity,' both in the context of copying and unlawful appropriation, muddying the waters as to what part of the infringement analysis the rule applies.

As we struggled with the inverse ratio rule over the years, the Second Circuit rejected it as early as 1961, describing the idea as a 'superficially attractive apophthegm which upon examination confuses more than it clarifies.' Arc Music, 296 F.2d at 187. The court reasoned that 'access will not supply [similarity's] lack, and an undue stress upon that one feature can only confuse and even conceal this basic requirement.' *Id.* at 187-88. Importantly, the Second Circuit noted that there is 'no such principle' in 'the federal law of copyright.' *Id.* at 187....

The flaws in the rule can be seen in the inconsistent ways in which we have applied the rule within our circuit, the logic of the circuits that have rejected the rule, and analysis by academics and commentators. . . .

As a practical matter, the concept of "access" is increasingly diluted in our digitally interconnected world. Access is often proved by the wide dissemination of the copyrighted work. *See* Loomis v. Cornish, 836 F.3d 991, 995 (9th Cir. 2016). Given the ubiquity of ways to access media online, from YouTube to subscription services like Netflix and Spotify, access may be established by a trivial showing that the work is available on demand. *See* Brooks Barnes, *The Streaming Era Has Finally Arrived. Everything Is About to Change.*, N.Y. TIMES, Nov. 18, 2019 (In addition to Netflix, which 'entertain[s] more than 158 million subscribers worldwide,' there are currently '271 online video services available in the United States').

To the extent 'access' still has meaning, the inverse ratio rule unfairly advantages those whose work is *most* accessible by lowering the standard of proof for similarity. Thus the rule benefits those with highly popular works, like *The Office,* which are also highly accessible. But nothing in copyright law suggests that a work deserves stronger legal protection simply because it is more popular or owned by better-funded rights holders.

Finally, the inverse ratio rule improperly dictates how the jury should reach its decision. The burden of proof in a civil case is preponderance of the evidence. Yet this judge-made rule could fittingly be called the 'inverse burden rule.'

Although we are cautious in overruling precedent—as we should be—the constellation of problems and inconsistencies in the application of the inverse ratio rule prompts us to abrogate the rule. Access does not obviate the requirement that the plaintiff must demonstrate that the defendant actually copied the work. By rejecting the inverse ratio rule, we are not suggesting that access cannot serve as circumstantial evidence of actual copying in all cases; access, however, in no way can prove substantial similarity. We join the majority of our sister circuits that have considered the inverse ratio rule and have correctly chosen to excise it from copyright analysis. In light of this holding, the district court did not err in failing to instruct the jury on the inverse ratio rule.

Skidmore v. Led Zeppelin, 952 F.3d 1051, 1065-69 (9th Cir. 2020).

If evidence of access continues to serve as circumstantial evidence of factual copying, doesn't *Skidmore* effectively retain a narrower version of the sliding scale inference—only applicable to factual copying and not to improper appropriation—that the inverse ratio rule served?

3. *Subconscious Copying of a Work.* Robert Mack composed the song "He's So Fine," which The Chiffons recorded in 1962. It enjoyed popular success, rising to No. 1 on the U.S. billboard charts for five weeks in 1963; it was among the top hits in England for about seven weeks in 1963 as well. In 1970, George Harrison, formerly of The Beatles, wrote the song "My Sweet Lord." Both songs consisted of four repetitions of a very short basic musical phrase, "sol-me-ri," followed by four (or three) repetitions of another short basic musical phrase, "sol-la-do-la-do." In addition, the second use of the "sol-la-do-la-do" in both compositions include a grace note making the phrase go "sol-la-do-la-re-do." While neither phrase is novel (or uncommon), Harrison's expert acknowledged that the pattern of juxtaposing four (or four and three) repetitions of each phrase was unique, especially with the inclusion of the grace note. George Harrison testified at trial that he had composed the song while in Copenhagen, Denmark, while on a gig. He recalled "vamping" some guitar chords while singing "Hallelujah" and "Hare Krishna." The song developed further as he improvised with the other musicians in his entourage. In assessing copying, the court determined that George Harrison had not deliberately reproduced Mack's work. Nonetheless, the court found infringement on the grounds that "'My Sweet Lord' is the very same song as 'He's So Fine' with different words, and Harrison had access to 'He's So Fine.' This is, under the law, infringement of copyright, and is no less so even though subconsciously accomplished." *Bright Tunes Music Corp. v. Harrisongs Music, Ltd.*, 420 F. Supp. 177, 181 (S.D.N.Y. 1976) *Sheldon v. Metro-Goldwyn Pictures Corp.*, 81 F.2d 49, 54 (2d Cir. 1936) (L. Hand, J.) ("Yet unconscious plagiarism is actionable quite as much as deliberate.").

4. *Proof of Copying by Deliberate Error or Common Mistake.* Creators of fact works often deliberately plant minor errors in their works to trap copyists. We saw an example of this in *Feist,* Chapter IV(B)(1), where a telephone company placed false names in a telephone directory. Cartographers also frequently bury erroneous or misspelled place names in their maps for this reason. In addition, accidental

misspellings and other mistakes common to both works have aided copyright owners in establishing copying.

5. *Techniques for Reducing the Risk of Infringement: Returning Unopened Submissions and Clean Rooms.* Potential copyright defendants sometimes go to great lengths to avoid having access to works that might influence them. For example, many movie studios and television producers routinely return unsolicited scripts unopened. In the computer industry, program developers occasionally prepare new programs in "clean rooms," in which procedures are established to regulate the entry and exit of material from the location where the work is being created and the creative process is carefully documented so as to be able to prove that a program was independently created without access to code written by others.

PROBLEM

Problem IV-27. Scooter, a ventriloquist, performs a traveling show with a dummy that vocalizes the catchphrase "You Got the Right One, Uh-Huh." Scooter has performed this show since 1984. His performances have primarily been at elementary schools and Job Corps camps, but he did have a pavilion at the 1984 World's Fair in which he used the phrase. Scooter also attempted to promote his show by mailing unsolicited information packets to corporate executives. Included in these packets were letters that referred to his catchphrase. He mailed one such packet to a Pepsi executive in Baltimore in 1988, but the executive cannot recall ever receiving it.

In 1991, Pepsi starts a massive advertising campaign using Ray Charles singing "You Got the Right One Baby, Uh-Huh" with similar voice inflections. Scooter sues for copyright infringement. Does he have a case?

---

2. Improper Appropriation

The second problem that arises in assessing infringement is determining whether the defendant has copied sufficient protected expression to violate the plaintiff's copyright interests. Judge Learned Hand's opinion in *Nichols v. Universal Pictures, Corp.*, decided more than 80 years ago, remains the seminal case framing this inquiry. As you study this opinion, pay close attention to the manner in which the court distinguishes protected and unprotected expression and how it determines whether the defendant has improperly appropriated the plaintiff's work.

Nichols v. Universal Pictures Corporation
United States Court of Appeals for the Second Circuit
45 F.2d 119 (2d Cir. 1930)

L. HAND, Circuit Judge.

The plaintiff is the author of a play, "Abie's Irish Rose," which it may be assumed was properly copyrighted under section five, subdivision (d), of the Copyright Act, 17 USCA § 5(d). The defendant produced publicly a motion picture play, "The Cohens and

The Kellys," which the plaintiff alleges was taken from it. As we think the defendant's play too unlike the plaintiff's to be an infringement, we may assume, arguendo, that in some details the defendant used the plaintiff's play, as will subsequently appear, though we do not so decide. It therefore becomes necessary to give an outline of the two plays.

"Abie's Irish Rose" presents a Jewish family living in prosperous circumstances in New York. The father, a widower, is in business as a merchant, in which his son and only child helps him. The boy has philandered with young women, who to his father's great disgust have always been Gentiles, for he is obsessed with a passion that his daughter-in-law shall be an orthodox Jewess. When the play opens the son, who has been courting a young Irish Catholic girl, has already married her secretly before a Protestant minister, and is concerned to soften the blow for his father, by securing a favorable impression of his bride, while concealing her faith and race. To accomplish this he introduces her to his father at his home as a Jewess, and lets it appear that he is interested in her, though he conceals the marriage. The girl somewhat reluctantly falls in with the plan; the father takes the bait, becomes infatuated with the girl, concludes that they must marry, and assumes that of course they will, if he so decides. He calls in a rabbi, and prepares for the wedding according to the Jewish rite.

Meanwhile the girl's father, also a widower, who lives in California, and is as intense in his own religious antagonism as the Jew, has been called to New York, supposing that his daughter is to marry an Irishman and a Catholic. Accompanied by a priest, he arrives at the house at the moment when the marriage is being celebrated, but too late to prevent it and the two fathers, each infuriated by the proposed union of his child to a heretic, fall into unseemly and grotesque antics. The priest and the rabbi become friendly, exchange trite sentiments about religion, and agree that the match is good. Apparently out of abundant caution, the priest celebrates the marriage for a third time, while the girl's father is inveigled away. The second act closes with each father, still outraged, seeking to find some way by which the union, thus trebly insured, may be dissolved.

The last act takes place about a year later, the young couple having meanwhile been abjured by each father, and left to their own resources. They have had twins, a boy and a girl, but their fathers know no more than that a child has been born. At Christmas each, led by his craving to see his grandchild, goes separately to the young folks' home, where they encounter each other, each laden with gifts, one for a boy, the other for a girl. After some slapstick comedy, depending upon the insistence of each that he is right about the sex of the grandchild, they become reconciled when they learn the truth, and that each child is to bear the given name of a grandparent. The curtain falls as the fathers are exchanging amenities, and the Jew giving evidence of an abatement in the strictness of his orthodoxy.

"The Cohens and The Kellys" presents two families, Jewish and Irish, living side by side in the poorer quarters of New York in a state of perpetual enmity. The wives in both cases are still living, and share in the mutual animosity, as do two small sons, and even the respective dogs. The Jews have a daughter, the Irish a son; the Jewish father is in the clothing business; the Irishman is a policeman. The children are in love with each other, and secretly marry, apparently after the play opens. The Jew, being in great financial straits, learns from a lawyer that he has fallen heir to a large fortune from a great-aunt, and moves into a great house, fitted luxuriously. Here he and his family live in vulgar ostentation, and here the Irish boy seeks out his Jewish bride, and is chased away by the angry father. The Jew then abuses the Irishman over the telephone, and both become hysterically excited. The extremity of his feelings make[s] the Jew sick, so that he must go to Florida for a rest, just before which the daughter discloses her marriage to her mother.

On his return the Jew finds that his daughter has borne a child; at first he suspects the lawyer, but eventually learns the truth and is overcome with anger at such a low alliance. Meanwhile, the Irish family who have been forbidden to see the grandchild, go to the Jew's house, and after a violent scene between the two fathers in which the Jew disowns his daughter, who decides to go back with her husband, the Irishman takes her back with her baby to his own poor lodgings. The lawyer, who had hoped to marry the Jew's daughter, seeing his plan foiled, tells the Jew that his fortune really belongs to the Irishman, who was also related to the dead woman, but offers to conceal his knowledge, if the Jew will share the loot. This the Jew repudiates, and, leaving the astonished lawyer, walks through the rain to his enemy's house to surrender the property. He arrives in great dejection, tells the truth, and abjectly turns to leave. A reconciliation ensues, the Irishman agreeing to share with him equally. The Jew shows some interest in his grandchild, though this is at most a minor motive in the reconciliation, and the curtain falls while the two are in their cups, the Jew insisting that in the firm name for the business, which they are to carry on jointly, his name shall stand first.

It is of course essential to any protection of literary property, whether at common-law or under the statute, that the right cannot be limited literally to the text, else a plagiarist would escape by immaterial variations. That has never been the law, but, as soon as literal appropriation ceases to be the test, the whole matter is necessarily at large, so that, as was recently well said by a distinguished judge, the decisions cannot help much in a new case. *Fendler v. Morosco*, 253 N.Y. 281, 292, 171 N.E. 56. When plays are concerned, the plagiarist may excise a separate scene; or he may appropriate part of the dialogue. Then the question is whether the part so taken is "substantial," and therefore not a "fair use" of the copyrighted work; it is the same question as arises in the case of any other copyrighted work. But when the plagiarist does not take out a block in suit, but an abstract of the whole, decision is more troublesome. Upon any work, and especially upon a play, a great number of patterns of increasing generality will fit equally well, as more and more of the incident is left out. The last may perhaps be no more than the most general statement of what the play is about, and at times might consist only of its title; but there is a point in this series of abstractions where they are no longer protected, since otherwise the playwright could prevent the use of his "ideas," to which, apart from their expression, his property is never extended. Nobody has ever been able to fix that boundary, and nobody ever can. In some cases the question has been treated as though it were analogous to lifting a portion out of the copyrighted work;

but the analogy is not a good one, because, though the skeleton is a part of the body, it pervades and supports the whole. In such cases we are rather concerned with the line between expression and what is expressed. As respects plays, the controversy chiefly centers upon the characters and sequence of incident, these being the substance.

We did not in *Dymow v. Bolton*, 11 F.2d 690, hold that a plagiarist was never liable for stealing a plot; that would have been flatly against our ruling in *Dam v. Kirk La Shelle Co.*, 175 F. 902, and *Stodart v. Mutual Film Co.*, 249 F. 513, affirming my decision in (D.C.) 249 F. 507; neither of which we meant to overrule. We found the plot of the second play was too different to infringe, because the most detailed pattern, common to both, eliminated so much from each that its content went into the public domain; and for this reason we said, "this mere subsection of a plot was not susceptible of copyright." But we do not doubt that two plays may correspond in plot closely enough for infringement. How far that correspondence must go is another matter. Nor need we hold that the same may not be true as to the characters, quite independently of the "plot" proper, though, as far as we know such a case has never arisen. If Twelfth Night were copyrighted, it is quite possible that a second comer might so closely imitate Sir Toby Belch or Malvolio as to infringe, but it would not be enough that for one of his characters he cast a riotous knight who kept wassail to the discomfort of the household, or a vain and foppish steward who became amorous of his mistress. These would be no more than Shakespeare's "ideas" in the play, as little capable of monopoly as Einstein's Doctrine of Relativity, or Darwin's theory of the Origin of Species. It follows that the less developed the characters, the less they can be copyrighted; that is the penalty an author must bear for marking them too indistinctly.

In the two plays at bar we think both as to incident and character, the defendant took no more—assuming that it took anything at all—than the law allowed. The stories are quite different. One is of a religious zealot who insists upon his child's marrying no one outside his faith; opposed by another who is in this respect just like him, and is his foil. Their difference in race is merely an obligato to the main theme, religion. They sink their differences through grandparental pride and affection. In the other, zealotry is wholly absent; religion does not even appear. It is true that the parents are hostile to each other in part because they differ in race; but the marriage of their son to a Jew does no[t] apparently offend the Irish family at all, and it exacerbates the existing animosity of the Jew, principally because he has become rich, when he learns it. They are reconciled through the honesty of the Jew and the generosity of the Irishman; the grandchild has nothing whatever to do with it. The only matter common to the two is a quarrel between a Jewish and an Irish father, the marriage of their children, the birth of grandchildren and a reconciliation.

If the defendant took so much from the plaintiff, it may well have been because her amazing success seemed to prove that this was a subject of enduring popularity. Even so, granting that the plaintiff's play was wholly original, and assuming that novelty is not essential to a copyright, there is no monopoly in such a background. Though the plaintiff discovered the vein, she could not keep it to herself; so defined, the theme was too generalized an abstraction from what she wrote. It was only a part of her "ideas."

Nor does she fare better as to her characters. It is indeed scarcely credible that she should not have been aware of those stock figures, the low comedy Jew and Irishman. The defendant has not taken from her more than their prototypes have contained for many decades. If so, obviously so to generalize her copyright, would allow her to cover what was not original with her. But we need not hold this as matter of fact, much as we might be justified. Even though we take it that she devised her figures out of her brain de novo, still the defendant was within its rights.

There are but four characters common to both plays, the lovers and the fathers. The lovers are so faintly indicated as to be no more than stage properties. They are loving and fertile; that is really all that can be said of them, and anyone else is quite within his rights if he puts loving and fertile lovers in a play of his own, wherever he gets the cue. The plaintiff's Jew is quite unlike the defendant's. His obsession is his religion, on which depends such racial animosity as he has. He is affectionate, warm and patriarchal. None of these fit the defendant's Jew, who shows affection for his daughter only once, and who has none but the most superficial interest in his grandchild. He is tricky, ostentatious and vulgar, only by misfortune redeemed into honesty. Both are grotesque, extravagant and quarrelsome; both are fond of display; but these common qualities make up only a small part of their simple pictures, no more than any one might lift if he chose. The Irish fathers are even more unlike; the plaintiff's a mere symbol for religious fanaticism and patriarchal pride, scarcely a character at all. Neither quality appears in the defendant's, for while he goes to get his grandchild, it is rather out of a truculent determination not to be forbidden, than from pride in his progeny. For the rest he is only a grotesque hobbledehoy, used for low comedy of the most conventional sort, which any one might borrow, if he chanced not to know the exemplar.

The defendant argues that the case is controlled by my decision in *Fisher v. Dillingham*, (D.C.) 298 F. 145. Neither my brothers nor I wish to throw doubt upon the doctrine of that case, but it is not applicable here. We assume that the plaintiff's play is altogether original, even to an extent that in fact it is hard to believe. We assume further that, so far as it has been anticipated by earlier plays of which she knew nothing, that fact is immaterial. Still, as we have already said, her copyright did not cover everything that might be drawn from her play; its content went to some extent into the public domain. We have to decide how much, and while we are as aware as any one that the line, wherever it is drawn, will seem arbitrary, that is no excuse for not drawing it; it is a question such as courts must answer in nearly all cases. Whatever may be the difficulties a priori, we have no question on which side of the line this case falls. A comedy based upon conflicts between Irish and Jews, into which the marriage of their children enters, is no more susceptible of copyright than the outline of Romeo and Juliet.

The plaintiff has prepared an elaborate analysis of the two plays, showing a "quadrangle" of the common characters, in which each is represented by the emotions which he discovers. She presents the resulting parallelism as proof of infringement, but the adjectives employed are so general as to be quite useless. Take for example the attribute of "love" ascribed to both Jews. The plaintiff has depicted her father as deeply attached to his son, who is his hope and joy; not so, the defendant, whose father's conduct is throughout not actuated by any affection for his daughter, and who is merely once overcome for the moment by her distress when he has violently dismissed her lover. "Anger" covers emotions aroused by quite different occasions in each case; so do "anxiety," "despondency" and "disgust." It is unnecessary to go through the catalogue for emotions are too much colored by their causes to be a test when used so broadly. This is not the proper approach to a solution; it must be more ingenuous, more like that of a spectator, who would rely upon the complex of his impressions of each character. . . .

Decree affirmed.

COMMENTS AND QUESTIONS

1. *Test for Improper Appropriation.* Some decisions in the Ninth Circuit have bifurcated the analysis into an extrinsic test and an intrinsic test. *See, e.g., Shaw v. Lindheim*, 919 F.2d 1353 (9th Cir. 1990). The extrinsic test analytically dissects the objective manifestations of creativity (plots, themes, dialogue, mood, setting, pace, sequence, characters) in the plaintiff's work in order to determine the elements that are protectable under copyright law. In the second stage of analysis the trier of fact, applying a purely subjective perspective, determines whether the defendant's work improperly appropriates the plaintiff's protected expression.

Does this bifurcated approach make sense? How can the trier of fact compare the two works without relying on the objective approach to determine what is protectable? For criticism of this approach, *see* Mark A. Lemley, *Our Bizarre System for Proving Copyright Infringement*, 57 J. COPYRIGHT SOC'Y U.S.A. 719 (2010).

2. *Framing the Subjective Analysis Comparison.* A key issue in applying the intrinsic or subjective stage of analysis is delineating what the fact-finder compares in deciding whether two works are substantially similar. Does the fact-finder compare the two works as a whole or only those elements that are protectable? Courts have differed in their treatment of this critical issue. Some courts have held that the fact-finder shall compare the entirety of the two works, including the "unprotectable" elements. *See, e.g., Roth Greeting Cards v. United Card Co.*, 429 F.2d 1106 (9th Cir. 1970); *Sheldon v. Metro-Goldwyn Pictures Corp.*, 81 F.2d 49 (2d Cir. 1936). Other courts have excluded unprotectable elements from the comparison. *See, e.g., Hoehling v. Universal City Studios, Inc.*, 618 F.2d 972 (2d Cir. 1980); *Comput. Assocs. Int'l v. Altai, Inc.*, 982 F.2d 693 (2d Cir. 1992) (addressing the protection of computer code). Which view comports best with copyright principles? Should the answer depend on whether the basis for the copyright infringement claim is particular elements (in which case there would be no need to compare the works as whole) or a compilation of elements (in which case the fact-finder would need a wider lens)?

3. *How Much Must Be Taken to Constitute Improper Appropriation?* A copyright owner need not prove that all or nearly all of his or her work has been appropriated to establish infringement. Although the quantum necessary depends on the nature of the work, recall that the legislative history to § 106 provides that "a copyrighted work

would be infringed by reproducing it *in whole or in any substantial part,* and by duplicating it exactly or by imitation or simulation. Wide departures or variations from the copyrighted works would still be an infringement as long as the author's 'expression' rather than merely the author's 'ideas' are taken." H.R. REP. NO. 94-1476, 94th Cong., 2d Sess. 61 (1976) (emphasis added). Thus, courts have held that "[e]ven a small amount of the original, if it is qualitatively significant, may be sufficient to be an infringement. . . ." *Horgan v. Macmillan, Inc.*, 789 F.2d 157, 162 (2d Cir. 1986).

Determining the threshold for infringement is particularly difficult in those cases in which a defendant has copied distinct literal elements of the plaintiff's work and incorporated them into a larger work of his or her own. This class of cases has been referred to as *fragmented literal similarity. See* MELVILLE B. NIMMER & DAVID NIMMER, NIMMER ON COPYRIGHT § 13.03[A][2]. Nimmer writes:

> The question in each case is whether the similarity relates to matter which constitutes a substantial portion of plaintiff's work—not whether such material constitutes a substantial portion of defendant's work. The quantitative relation of the similar material to the total material contained in plaintiff's work is certainly of importance. However, even if the similar material is quantitatively small, if it is qualitatively important the trier of fact may properly find substantial similarity. In such circumstances the defendant may not claim immunity on the grounds the infringement "is such a little one." If, however, the similarity is only as to nonessential matters, then a finding of no substantial similarity should result.

4. *The Sliding Scale and the Virtual Identity Test.* As courts have increasingly recognized, "more similarity is required when less protectable matter is at issue." NIMMER ON COPYRIGHT § 13.03(A). Therefore, many courts now require "virtual identity" when dealing with works in which copyright protection is "thin"—i.e., works involving unprotectable elements and/or where the range of creative expression is limited. *See, e.g., Mattel, Inc. v. MGA Entertainment, Inc.*, 616 F.3d 904, 914–15 (9th Cir. 2010) (doll designs); *Incredible Technologies, Inc. v. Virtual Technologies*, 400 F.3d 1007 (7th Cir. 2005) (screen displays for video golf game); *Data East USA, Inc. v. Epyx, Inc.*, 862 F.2d 204 (9th Cir. 1988) (screen displays for video karate game); *Satava v. Lowry*, 323 F.3d 805, 811 (9th Cir. 2003) (glass sculptures encasing jellyfish); *Harper House, Inc. v. Thomas Nelson, Inc.*, 889 F.2d 197 (9th Cir. 1989) (day planner calendar); *cf. Jacobsen v. Deseret Book Co.*, 287 F.3d 936 (10th Cir. 2002) (noting that "[b]ecause fact-based works differ as to the relative proportion of fact and fancy [ranging from 'sparsely embellished maps and directories' to 'elegantly written biography'], the quantum of similarity required to establish infringement differs in each case").

5. *Substantial Similarity in Music Cases.* Although the Copyright Act does not limit protection in musical works to melody, many music composition infringement cases have focused on melodic elements and downplayed arrangements, bass lines, percussion, and other features. *See* Joseph Fishman, *Music as a Matter of Law*, 131 HARV. L. REV. 1861 (2018). This might reflect, in part, the use of sheet music for registering musical compositions prior to 1978. (After 1978, the Copyright Office

permitted musical composers to use sound recordings to register the underlying musical composition.)

The scope of copyright protection for musical compositions gained notoriety in litigation surrounding the 2013 best-selling single "Blurred Lines," composed by Pharrell Williams and Robin Thicke. The estate of Marvin Gaye alleged that "Blurred Lines" infringed Gaye's 1977 hit "Got to Give It Up." While promoting "Blurred Lines," Thicke stated that "Pharrell and I were in the studio and . . . I was like, 'Damn, we should make something like ["Got to Give It Up"], something with that groove.' Then he started playing a little something and we literally wrote the song in about half an hour and recorded it." Although the melodies of the two compositions differed, the songs featured similar arrangements of percussion and bass elements. The Ninth Circuit affirmed the jury's finding that the two compositions were substantially similar. *Williams v. Gaye*, 885 F.3d 1150 (9th Cir. 2018). Drawing on *Swirsky v. Carey*, 376 F.3d 841, 849 (9th Cir. 2004), the court held that musical creativity is not confined to a narrow range of expression.

6. *The* De Minimis *Doctrine—In General.* Copyright recognizes the maxim *de minimis non curat lex*—the law does not concern itself with trifles. The cases applying this principle use it as a shorthand for lack of substantial similarity—where "the copying of the protected material is so trivial 'as to fall below the quantitative threshold of substantial similarity.'" *Gordon v. Nextel Commc'ns and Mullen Adver., Inc.*, 345 F.3d 922, 924 (6th Cir. 2003) (quoting *Ringgold v. Black Entm't Television Inc.*, 126 F.3d 70, 74 (2d Cir. 1997)); *Fisher v. Dees*, 794 F.2d 432, 435 (9th Cir. 1986) (noting that *de minimis* copying "is so meager and fragmentary that the average audience would not recognize the appropriation"); *Warner Bros., Inc. v. Am. Broad. Cos.*, 720 F.2d 231, 242 (2d Cir. 1983) (holding that the *de minimis* doctrine allows "literal copying of a small and usually insignificant portion of the plaintiff's work"). Courts will not apply the doctrine, however, without attention to qualitative considerations. *See CyberMedia, Inc. v. Symantec Corp.*, 19 F. Supp. 2d 1070, 1077 (N.D. Cal. 1998) (holding that "even if a copied portion be relatively small in proportion to the entire work, if qualitatively important, the finder of fact may properly find substantial similarity").

7. De Minimis *Copying and Digital Sampling.* The rap and hip-hop genres have built new compositions upon digital samples (literal copying) of existing sound recordings. Several early cases held that such copying infringed copyrights in the underlying musical compositions on the basis of fragmented literal similarity. *See Grand Upright Music, Ltd. v. Warner Bros. Records, Inc.*, 780 F. Supp. 182 (S.D.N.Y. 1991); *Jarvis v. A & M Records*, 827 F. Supp. 282 (D.N.J. 1993). In the first appellate case to squarely address digital samples of sound recordings, the Sixth Circuit ruled that the Copyright Act bars application of the *de minimis* doctrine in this class of works, with the result that even the copying of a single note could constitute copyright infringement. *See Bridgeport Music, Inc. v. Dimension Films*, 410 F.3d 792, 800–01 (6th Cir. 2005). That court reasoned that:

> Section 114(b) provides that "[t]he exclusive right of the owner of copyright in a sound recording under clause (2) of § 106 is limited to the right

to prepare a derivative work in which the actual sounds fixed in the sound recording are rearranged, remixed, or otherwise altered in sequence or quality." Further, the rights of sound recording copyright holders under clauses (1) and (2) of § 106 "do not extend to the making or duplication of another sound recording that consists *entirely* of an independent fixation of other sounds, even though such sounds imitate or simulate those in the copyrighted sound recording." 17 U.S.C. § 114(b) (emphasis added). The significance of this provision is amplified by the fact that the Copyright Act of 1976 added the word "entirely" to this language. Compare Sound Recording Act of 1971, Pub. L. 92-140, 85 Stat. 391 (Oct. 15, 1971) (adding subsection (f) to former 17 U.S.C. § 1) ("does not extend to the making or duplication of another sound recording that is an independent fixation of other sounds"). In other words, a sound recording owner has the exclusive right to "sample" his own recording.

Id. at 800–01.

In view of the fact that Congress could not have had digital sampling in mind when it drafted the Sound Recording Act of 1971 or the Copyright Act of 1976, does this strike you as a reasonable interpretation? Do you think that Congress intended to override the *de minimis* doctrine through this language? *See VMG Salsoul, LLC v. Ciccone*, 824 F.3d 871, 880–87 (9th Cir. 2016) (rejecting the 6th Circuit's statutory interpretation and holding the *de minimis* doctrine applies across the classes of copyrightable works).

The Sixth Circuit bolstered its analysis on policy grounds, asserting that such a bright line rule ("Get a license or do not sample") would ease enforcement and would not stifle creativity because a well-functioning sampling market currently exists and because artists are free to record a *de minimis* "riff" in the studio. Do you agree? In any case, is it likely to matter much in practice? The *Bridgeport* case does not preclude a finding of fair use. *See id.* at 805. The Second Circuit has held that small samples may be fair use as a matter of law. *See Oyewole v. Ora*, 291 F. Supp. 3d 422 (S.D.N.Y. 2018), *aff'd* (2d Cir. 2019).

A case involving the rap song "Pass the Mic" presents another variation on this theme. The Beastie Boys obtained a sampling license from ECM, the record label controlling rights to noted jazz flutist James Newton's recording of his composition "Choir," to use a six-second clip from the song's opening as a backdrop for their sound recording. Newton sued, alleging that the Beastie Boys also needed a license to the underlying musical composition, for which he held the copyright. The court held that although the sound recording of the six-second sample may well have qualified for copyright protection due to the complexity of the performance, copying of the underlying musical composition—involving a three-note sequence sung above a finger-held C note to be played in a "largo/senza-misura" (slowly/without measure) tempo while overblowing the background C note—was not actionable under the *de minimis* doctrine. *Newton v. Diamond*, 349 F.3d 591 (9th Cir. 2003), *amended* 388 F.3d 1189 (9th Cir. 2004). Note that this case does not contradict the *Bridgeport* ruling because it involves copying of the musical composition and not the sound recording. Does it make sense to treat the scope of musical composition and sound recording copyrights differently in this way?

8. *The Role of Expert Testimony in Determining Improper Appropriation.* The court in *Arnstein* held that expert opinion is "utterly immaterial" to the determination of improper appropriation. Does this limitation on evidence make sense with regard to all works? Expert testimony would seem essential in assessing appropriation with regard to technically complex material written for specialized audiences. The issue arises frequently in the context of computer software copyright cases. Is it desirable to assess similarities in two database programs from the standpoint of the ordinary person on the street rather than the ordinary user of database programs? Isn't expert testimony on the extent to which programming elements are common in the trade essential to determining improper appropriation?

9. *The Appropriate Perspective for Assessing Substantial Similarity: The Ordinary Observer.* The Second Circuit has defined "substantial similarity" as whether the "ordinary observer, unless he set out to detect the disparities [between two works], would be disposed to overlook them, and regard their aesthetic appeal as the same." *Peter Pan Fabrics, Inc. v. Martin Weiner Corp.*, 274 F.2d 487, 489 (2d Cir. 1960).

A number of cases have narrowed the "ordinary observer" perspective by focusing on the impressions of the target audience for the work in question. For example, in *Original Appalachian Artworks, Inc. v. Blue Box Factory (USA) Ltd.*, 577 F. Supp. 625 (S.D.N.Y. 1983), involving copyright protection for a popular line of dolls called "Cabbage Patch Kids," the court allowed expert evidence about how the works would be perceived by children. In *Data East USA, Inc. v. Epyx, Inc.*, 862 F.2d 204 (9th Cir. 1988), the court assessed substantial similarity of two karate video games from the perspective of a "discerning 17.5 year-old boy," based on the district court's finding that "the average age of individuals purchasing 'Karate Champ' is 17.5 years, that the purchasers are predominantly male, and comprise a knowledgeable, critical, and discerning group."

Should the "ordinary observer" test be tailored to the target audience for the works? Is the "ordinary observer" perspective, even if tailored to reflect the target audience for the work, likely to distinguish between the protectable and nonprotectable elements of a work in assessing infringement?

PROBLEMS

Problem IV-28. Dinopets markets a line of stuffed animal toys for children. The line includes five popular dinosaurs with exaggerated facial features (e.g., large droopy eyes, long teeth, rounded noses), cheerful pastel colors (pink, lemon, lime), distinctive stitching, and a soft cuddly cotton texture. About a year after Dinopets were on the market, Gigatoys, Inc., a leading toy manufacturer, developed a line of stuffed dinosaur toys. Its line, the Dinomites, featured the five dinosaurs in the Dinopets line as well as three others. Dinomites are about 25 percent larger than comparable Dinopets. Dinomites feature cute facial features (including droopy eyes and long teeth) and come in earth-tone colors (light brown, clay, sand, and stone). They are made of a suede-like material (somewhat coarser than the Dinopets). Dinopets sues Gigatoys, alleging copyright infringement. How would the analysis be conducted? What result?

Problem IV-29. Gregg Gillis, who performs as Girl Talk, "mashes up" popular sound recordings into distinctive mosaic tracks. A typical Girl Talk song combines numerous (20 to 30) short to medium (3 to 40 second) clips into a frenetic, overlapping, winding, and often surprising work cutting across numerous musical styles (rap, hip hop, heavy metal, and pop). Has Gillis infringed the copyright on any of the songs he samples? On all of them? (Focus only on the infringement inquiry. We will return to this problem after we have covered the fair use defense.)

Problem IV-30. In preparing a biography of the reclusive author J.D. Salinger, Ian Hamilton gained access to letters Salinger wrote to a number of notable people that had been donated to university libraries. Through these letters and other sources, Hamilton constructed his biography of Salinger's life. Out of concern for copyright infringement, Hamilton quotes barely more than 200 words from the letters throughout the entire biography. Nonetheless, the letters are paraphrased or otherwise drawn upon in approximately 40 percent of the 192-page biography. To accurately describe events and emotions, impart some of Salinger's distinctive style, and avoid "pedestrian" reporting, Hamilton follows some of the passages from the letters closely.

The following examples illustrate Hamilton's use of the letters to present Salinger's life. In a 1943 letter to Whit Burnett, Salinger's friend, teacher, and editor at Story magazine, Salinger expressed his disapproval of the marriage of Oona O'Neill, with whom Salinger had been romantically involved, and Charlie Chaplin, the silent screen film star.

Salinger's Letter	*Hamilton's Biography*
I can see them at home evenings. Chaplin squatting grey and nude, atop his chiffonier, swinging his thyroid around his head by his bamboo cane, like a dead rat. Oona in an aquamarine gown, applauding madly from the bathroom. Agnes (her mother) in a Jantzen bathing suit, passing between them with cocktails. I'm facetious, but I'm sorry. Sorry for anyone with a profile as young and lovely as Oona's.	At one point in a letter to Whit Burnett, he provides a pen portrait of the Happy Hour Chez Chaplin: the comedian, ancient and unclothed, is brandishing his walking stick—attached to the stick, and horribly resembling a lifeless rodent, is one of Chaplin's vital organs. Oona claps her hands in appreciation and Agnes, togged out in a bathing suit, pours drinks. Salinger goes on to say he's sorry—sorry not for what he has just written, but for

> Oona: far too youthful and exquisite for such a dreadful fate.
>
> In another letter to Burnett, Salinger expresses his disfavor of presidential candidate Wendell Wilkie.
>
> | *Salinger's Letter* | *Hamilton's Biography* |
> | --- | --- |
> | He looks to me like a guy who makes his wife keep a scrapbook for him. | [Salinger] had fingered [Wilkie] as the sort of fellow who makes his wife keep an album of his press cuttings. |
>
> In another letter describing Parisians' adulation of American soldiers at the liberation of Paris, Salinger writes that the Parisians would have said "What a charming custom!" if:
>
> | *Salinger's Letter* | *Hamilton's Biography* |
> | --- | --- |
> | we had stood on top of the jeep and taken a leak. | the conquerors had chosen to urinate from the roofs of their vehicles. |
>
> Has Hamilton infringed Salinger's copyright in his letters?

Problem IV-31. Saul Steinberg, a noted graphic artist, prepared "A View of the World from 9th Avenue" (pictured below), which, after it appeared on the cover of the New Yorker magazine on March 29, 1976, became one of the best known illustrations of New York City. In 1984, Columbia Pictures released "Moscow on the Hudson," a comedy about a Russian musician who defects from the Soviet Union on a visit to the United States. To advertise the film, Columbia Pictures designed the movie poster depicted below. Saul Steinberg sued for copyright infringement. How would you analyze this claim? Try using Learned Hand's levels of abstraction framework in structuring your analysis.

Saul Steinberg, A view of the world from 9th Avenue, 1976

***Moscow on the Hudson* poster**

3. The Special Case of Computer Software

Computer software, by its very nature as written work intended to serve utilitarian purposes, defies easy categorization within our intellectual property system. The copyright law has traditionally served as the principal source of legal protection for literary and artistic work, while the patent system and trade secret law have been the primary means for protecting utilitarian works. Faced with the difficult challenge of fitting computer and other new information technologies under the existing umbrella of intellectual property protection, Congress in 1974 established the National Commission on New Technological Uses of Copyrighted Works (CONTU) to study the implications of the new technologies and recommend revisions to federal intellectual property law. After conducting extensive hearings and receiving expert reports, a majority of the blue-ribbon panel of copyright authorities and interest group representatives comprising CONTU concluded in 1978 that the intellectual work embodied in computer software should be protected under copyright law, notwithstanding the fundamental principle that copyright cannot protect "any idea, procedure, process, system, method of operation, concept, principle, or discovery." § 102(b).

CONTU explained that while "one is always free to make a machine perform any conceivable process (in the absence of a patent), [] one is not free to take another's program," subject to copyright's limiting doctrines—originality and the idea/expression dichotomy. CONTU, Final Report 20 (1978). "Section 102(b) is intended, among other things, to make clear that the expression adopted by the programmer is the copyrightable element in a computer program, and that the actual processes or methods embodied in the program are not within the scope of the copyright law." *Id.* at 19. "The way copyright affects games and game-playing is closely analogous: one may not adopt and republish or redistribute copyrighted game rules, but the copyright owner has no power to prevent others from playing the game." *Id.* at 20.

Congress adopted CONTU's recommendations in 1980, passing legislation almost identical to that suggested in the Final Report. In light of the computer software industry's relative youth and anticipated rapid growth, CONTU's rough empirical judgment that copyright would best promote the invention, development, and diffusion of new and better software products was, by necessity, speculative. As CONTU recognized, it was impossible in 1978 to establish a precise line between copyrightable expression of computer programs and the uncopyrightable processes that they implement. Yet the location of this line—the idea/expression dichotomy—was critical to the rough cost-benefit analysis that guided CONTU's recommendation. Drawing the line too liberally in favor of copyright protection would bestow strong monopolies upon those who develop operating systems that become industry standards and upon the first to write programs performing specific applications and would thereby inhibit other creators from developing improved programs and computer systems. Drawing the line too conservatively would allow programmers' efforts to be copied easily, thus discouraging the creation of all but modest incremental advances. The wisdom of Congress's decision to bring computer programs within the scope of copyright law thus depends critically upon where courts draw this line.

Computer Associates International v. Altai, Inc.
United States Court of Appeals for the Second Circuit
982 F.2d 693 (2d Cir. 1992)

WALKER, Circuit Judge:

. . . This appeal comes to us from the United States District Court for the Eastern District of New York, the Honorable George C. Pratt, Circuit Judge, sitting by designation. By Memorandum and Order entered August 12, 1991, Judge Pratt found that defendant Altai, Inc.'s ("Altai") OSCAR 3.4 computer program had infringed plaintiff Computer Associates' ("CA") copyrighted computer program entitled CA-SCHEDULER. Accordingly, the district court awarded CA $364,444 in actual damages and apportioned profits. Altai has abandoned its appeal from this award. With respect to CA's second claim for copyright infringement, Judge Pratt found that Altai's OSCAR 3.5 program was not substantially similar to a portion of CA-SCHEDULER called ADAPTER, and thus denied relief. . . .

II. FACTS

. . . The subject of this litigation originates with one of CA's marketed programs entitled CA-SCHEDULER. CA-SCHEDULER is a job scheduling program designed for IBM mainframe computers. Its primary functions are straightforward: to create a schedule specifying when the computer should run various tasks, and then to control the computer as it executes the schedule. CA-SCHEDULER contains a sub-program entitled ADAPTER, also developed by CA. ADAPTER is not an independently marketed product of CA; it is a wholly integrated component of CA-SCHEDULER and has no capacity for independent use.

Nevertheless, ADAPTER plays an extremely important role. It is an "operating system compatibility component," which means, roughly speaking, it serves as a translator. An "operating system" is itself a program that manages the resources of the computer allocating those resources to other programs as needed. The IBM System 370 family of computers, for which CA-SCHEDULER was created, is, depending upon the computer's size, designed to contain one of three operating systems: DOS/VSE, MVS, or CMS. As the district court noted, the general rule is that "a program written for one operating system, e.g., DOS/VSE, will not, without modification, run under another operating system such as MVS." *Comput. Assocs.*, 775 F. Supp. at 550. ADAPTER's function is to translate the language of a given program into the particular language that the computer's own operating system can understand. . . .

A program like ADAPTER, which allows a computer user to change or use multiple operating systems while maintaining the same software, is highly desirable. It saves the user the costs, both in time and money, that otherwise would be expended in purchasing new programs, modifying existing systems to run them, and gaining familiarity with their operation. The benefits run both ways. The increased compatibility afforded by an

ADAPTER-like component, and its resulting popularity among consumers, makes whatever software in which it is incorporated significantly more marketable.

Starting in 1982, Altai began marketing its own job scheduling program entitled ZEKE. The original version of ZEKE was designed for use in conjunction with a VSE operating system. By late 1983, in response to customer demand, Altai decided to rewrite ZEKE so that it could be run in conjunction with an MVS operating system.

[At that time, James P. Williams, then an employee of Altai and now its President, recruited Claude F. Arney, III, a long-standing friend and computer programmer who worked for CA, to assist Altai in designing an MVS version of ZEKE. Unknown to Williams, Arney was intimately familiar with CA's ADAPTER program and he took VSE and MVS source code versions of ADAPTER with him when he left CA to join Altai. Without disclosing his knowledge of ADAPTER, Arney persuaded Williams that the best way to modify ZEKE to run on an MVS operating system was to introduce a "common system interface" component, an approach that stemmed from Arney's familiarity with ADAPTER. Arney subsequently developed a component-program named OSCAR using the ADAPTER source code. Approximately 30 percent of the first generation of OSCAR was copied from CA's ADAPTER program. In mid-1988, CA discovered the copying from ADAPTER and brought this copyright infringement and trade secret action. Altai learned of the copying from the complaint.]

Upon advice of counsel, Williams initiated OSCAR's rewrite. The project's goal was to save as much of OSCAR 3.4 as legitimately could be used, and to excise those portions which had been copied from ADAPTER. Arney was entirely excluded from the process, and his copy of the ADAPTER code was locked away. Williams put eight other programmers on the project, none of whom had been involved in any way in the development of OSCAR 3.4. Williams provided the programmers with a description of the ZEKE operating system services so that they could rewrite the appropriate code. The rewrite project took about six months to complete and was finished in mid-November 1989. The resulting program was entitled OSCAR 3.5.

From that point on, Altai shipped only OSCAR 3.5 to its new customers. . . .

DISCUSSION

[The district court concluded that version 3.5 was not substantially similar to CA's ADAPTER.]

I. COPYRIGHT INFRINGEMENT

. . . As a general matter, and to varying degrees, copyright protection extends beyond a literary work's strictly textual form to its non-literal components. As we have said, "[i]t is of course essential to any protection of literary property that the right cannot be limited literally to the text, else a plagiarist would escape by immaterial variations." *Nichols v. Universal Pictures Co.*, 45 F.2d 119, 121 (2d Cir. 1930) (L. Hand, J.). Thus, where "the fundamental essence or structure of one work is duplicated in another," 3 NIMMER, § 13.03(A][1], at 13–24, courts have found copyright infringement. . . . This black letter proposition is the springboard for our discussion.

A. Copyright Protection for the Non-literal Elements of Computer Programs

It is now well settled that the literal elements of computer programs, i.e., their source and object codes, are the subject of copyright protection. . . . Here, as noted earlier, Altai admits having copied approximately 30% of the OSCAR 3.4 program from CA's ADAPTER source code, and does not challenge the district court's related finding of infringement.

In this case, the hotly contested issues surround OSCAR 3.5. As recounted above, OSCAR 3.5 is the product of Altai's carefully orchestrated rewrite of OSCAR 3.4. After the purge, none of the ADAPTER source code remained in the 3.5 version; thus, Altai made sure that the literal elements of its revamped OSCAR program were no longer substantially similar to the literal elements of CA's ADAPTER.

According to CA, the district court erroneously concluded that Altai's OSCAR 3.5 was not substantially similar to its own ADAPTER program. CA argues that this occurred because the district court "committed legal error in analyzing [its] claims of copyright infringement by failing to find that copyright protects expression contained in the non-literal elements of computer software." We disagree.

CA argues that, despite Altai's rewrite of the OSCAR code, the resulting program remained substantially similar to the structure of its ADAPTER program. As discussed above, a program's structure includes its non-literal components such as general flow charts as well as the more specific organization of inter-modular relationships, parameter lists, and macros. In addition to these aspects, CA contends that OSCAR 3.5 is also substantially similar to ADAPTER with respect to the list of services that both ADAPTER and OSCAR obtain from their respective operating systems. We must decide whether and to what extent these elements of computer programs are protected by copyright law.

[The court determines that the nonliteral elements of computer programs are entitled to copyright protection as literary works.]

1) Idea vs. Expression Dichotomy

It is a fundamental principle of copyright law that a copyright does not protect an idea, but only the expression of the idea. . . .

Drawing the line between idea and expression is a tricky business. Judge Learned Hand noted that "[n]obody has ever been able to fix that boundary, and nobody ever can," *Nichols*, 45 F.2d at 121. Thirty years later his convictions remained firm. "Obviously, no principle can be stated as to when an imitator has gone beyond copying the 'idea,' and has borrowed its 'expression,'" Judge Hand concluded. "Decisions must therefore inevitably be ad hoc." *Peter Pan Fabrics, Inc. v. Martin Weiner Corp.*, 274 F.2d 487, 489 (2d Cir. 1960).

The essentially utilitarian nature of a computer program further complicates the task of distilling its idea from its expression. *See SAS Inst.*, 605 F. Supp. at 829; *cf. Englund*, at 893. In order to describe both computational processes and abstract ideas, its content "combines creative and technical expression." *See* [Peter G.] Spivack, [Comment, *Does*

Form Follow Function? The Idea/Expression Dichotomy in Copyright Protection of Computer Software, 35 U.C.L.A. L. REV. 723,] 755 [(1988)]. The variations of expression found in purely creative compositions, as opposed to those contained in utilitarian works, are not directed towards practical application. For example, a narration of Humpty Dumpty's demise, which would clearly be a creative composition, does not serve the same ends as, say, a recipe for scrambled eggs—which is a more process oriented text. Thus, compared to aesthetic works, computer programs hover even more closely to the elusive boundary line described in § 102(b).

[The court reviewed the facts and holding of *Baker v. Selden*].

To the extent that an accounting text and a computer program are both "a set of statements or instructions . . . to bring about a certain result," 17 U.S.C. § 101, they are roughly analogous. In the former case, the processes are ultimately conducted by human agency; in the latter, by electronic means. In either case, as already stated, the processes themselves are not protectable. But the holding in *Baker* goes farther. The Court concluded that those aspects of a work, which "must necessarily be used as incident to" the idea, system or process that the work describes, are also not copyrightable. 101 U.S. at 104. Selden's ledger sheets, therefore, enjoyed no copyright protection because they were "necessary incidents to" the system of accounting that he described. *Id.* at 103. From this reasoning, we conclude that those elements of a computer program that are necessarily incidental to its function are similarly unprotectable.

While *Baker v. Selden* provides a sound analytical foundation, it offers scant guidance on how to separate idea or process from expression, and moreover, on how to further distinguish protectable expression from that expression which "must necessarily be used as incident to the work's underlying concept." In the context of computer programs, the Third Circuit's noted decision in *Whelan* [*Associates, Inc. v. Jaslow Dental Laboratory, Inc.*, 797 F.2d 1222 (3d Cir. 1986)] has, thus far, been the most thoughtful attempt to accomplish these ends.

The court in *Whelan* faced substantially the same problem as is presented by this case. There, the defendant was accused of making off with the non-literal structure of the plaintiff's copyrighted dental lab management program, and employing it to create its own competitive version. In assessing whether there had been an infringement, the court had to determine which aspects of the programs involved were ideas, and which were expression. In separating the two, the court settled upon the following conceptual approach:

[T]he line between idea and expression may be drawn with reference to the end sought to be achieved by the work in question. In other words, the purpose or function of a utilitarian work would be the work's idea, and everything that is not necessary to that purpose or function would be part of the expression of the idea. . . . Where there are various means of achieving the desired purpose, then the particular means chosen is not necessary to the purpose; hence, there is expression, not idea.

797 F.2d at 1236 (citations omitted). The "idea" of the program at issue in *Whelan* was identified by the court as simply "the efficient management of a dental laboratory." *Id.* at n.28.

So far, in the courts, the *Whelan* rule has received a mixed reception. While some decisions have adopted its reasoning, *see, e.g., Bull HN Info. Sys., Inc. v. American Express Bank, Ltd.*, 1990 Copyright Law Dec. (CCH) ¶ 26,555 at 23,278 (S.D.N.Y. 1990); *Dynamic Solutions, Inc. v. Planning & Control, Inc.*, 1987 Copyright Law Dec. (CCH) ¶ 26,062 at 20,912 (S.D.N.Y. 1987); *Broderbund Software Inc. v. Unison World, Inc.*, 648 F. Supp. 1127, 1133 (N.D. Cal. 1986), others have rejected it. *See Plains Cotton Co-op v. Goodpasture Computer Serv. Inc.*, 807 F.2d 1256, 1262 (5th Cir. 1987); *cf. Synercom Technology, Inc. v. University Computing Co.*, 462 F. Supp. 1003, 1014 (N.D. Tex. 1978) (concluding that order and sequence of data on computer input formats was idea not expression).

Whelan has fared even more poorly in the academic community, where its standard for distinguishing idea from expression has been widely criticized for being conceptually overbroad. *See, e.g.,* [Steven R.] Englund[, Note, *Idea, Process, or Protected Expression?: Determining the Scope of Copyright Protection of the Structure of Computer Programs*, 88 MICH. L. REV. 866,] 881 [(1990)]; [Peter S.] Menell[, *An Analysis of the Scope of Copyright Protection for Application Programs*, 41 STAN. L. REV. 1045,] 1074 [(1989)]. The leading commentator in the field has stated that, "[t]he crucial flaw in [*Whelan*'s] reasoning is that it assumes that only one 'idea,' in copyright law terms, underlies any computer program, and that once a separable idea can be identified, everything else must be expression." 3 NIMMER § 13.03[F], at 13-62.34. This criticism focuses not upon the program's ultimate purpose but upon the reality of its structural design. As we have already noted, a computer program's ultimate function or purpose is the composite result of interacting subroutines. Since each subroutine is itself a program, and thus, may be said to have its own "idea," *Whelan*'s general formulation that a program's overall purpose equates with the program's idea is descriptively inadequate.

Accordingly, we think that Judge Pratt wisely declined to follow *Whelan*. *See Computer Assocs.*, 775 F. Supp. at 558–60. In addition to noting the weakness in the *Whelan* definition of "program-idea," mentioned above, Judge Pratt found that *Whelan*'s synonymous use of the terms "structure, sequence, and organization," *see Whelan,* 797 F.2d at 1224 n.1, demonstrated a flawed understanding of a computer program's method of operation. *See Computer Assocs.*, 775 F. Supp. at 559–60 (discussing the distinction between a program's "static structure" and "dynamic structure"). Rightly, the district court found *Whelan*'s rationale suspect because it is so closely tied to what can now be seen—with the passage of time—as the opinion's somewhat outdated appreciation of computer science.

2) Substantial Similarity Test for Computer Program Structure: Abstraction-Filtration-Comparison

We think that *Whelan*'s approach to separating idea from expression in computer programs relies too heavily on metaphysical distinctions and does not place enough emphasis on practical considerations. *Cf. Apple Computer*, 714 F.2d at 1253 (rejecting certain commercial constraints on programming as a helpful means of distinguishing idea from expression because they did "not enter into the somewhat metaphysical issue of whether particular ideas and expressions have merged"). As the cases that we shall discuss demonstrate, a satisfactory answer to this problem cannot be reached by resorting, *a priori,* to philosophical first principles.

As discussed herein, we think that district courts would be well-advised to undertake a three-step procedure, based on the abstractions test utilized by the district court, in order to determine whether the non-literal elements of two or more computer programs are substantially similar. This approach breaks no new ground; rather, it draws on such familiar copyright doctrines as merger, *scenes à faire,* and public domain. In taking this approach, however, we are cognizant that computer technology is a dynamic field which can quickly outpace judicial decisionmaking. Thus, in cases where the technology in question does not allow for a literal application of the procedure we outline below, our opinion should not be read to foreclose the district courts of our circuit from utilizing a modified version.

In ascertaining substantial similarity under this approach, a court would first break down the allegedly infringed program into its constituent structural parts. Then, by examining each of these parts for such things as incorporated ideas, expression that is necessarily incidental to those ideas, and elements that are taken from the public domain, a court would then be able to sift out all non-protectable material. Left with a kernel, or possibly kernels, of creative expression after following this process of elimination, the court's last step would be to compare this material with the structure of an allegedly infringing program. The result of this comparison will determine whether the protectable elements of the programs at issue are substantially similar so as to warrant a finding of infringement. It will be helpful to elaborate a bit further.

Step One: Abstraction

As the district court appreciated, *see Computer Assocs.*, 775 F. Supp. at 560, the theoretic framework for analyzing substantial similarity expounded by Learned Hand in the *Nichols* case is helpful in the present context. In *Nichols*, we enunciated what has now become known as the "abstractions" test for separating idea from expression:

> Upon any work . . . a great number of patterns of increasing generality will fit equally well, as more and more of the incident is left out. The last may perhaps be no more than the most general statement of what the [work] is about, and at times might consist only of its title; but there is a point in this series of abstractions where they are no longer protected, since otherwise the [author] could prevent the use of his "ideas," to which, apart from their expression, his property is never extended.

Nichols, 45 F.2d at 121.

While the abstractions test was originally applied in relation to literary works such as novels and plays, it is adaptable to computer programs. In contrast to the *Whelan* approach, the abstractions test "implicitly recognizes that any given work may consist of a mixture of numerous ideas and expressions." 3 NIMMER § 13.03[F] at 13-62.34-63.

As applied to computer programs, the abstractions test will comprise the first step in the examination for substantial similarity. Initially, in a manner that resembles reverse engineering on a theoretical plane, a court should dissect the allegedly copied program's structure and isolate each level of abstraction contained within it. This process begins with the code and ends with an articulation of the program's ultimate function. Along the way, it is necessary essentially to retrace and map each of the designer's steps—in the opposite order in which they were taken during the program's creation.

As an anatomical guide to this procedure, the following description is helpful:

At the lowest level of abstraction, a computer program may be thought of in its entirety as a set of individual instructions organized into a hierarchy of modules. At a higher level of abstraction, the instructions in the lowest-level modules may be replaced conceptually by the functions of those modules. At progressively higher levels of abstraction, the functions of higher-level modules conceptually replace the implementations of those modules in terms of lower-level modules and instructions, until finally, one is left with nothing but the ultimate function of the program. . . . A program has structure at every level of abstraction at which it is viewed. At low levels of abstraction, a program's structure may be quite complex; at the highest level it is trivial.

Englund, at 897–98.

Step Two: Filtration

Once the program's abstraction levels have been discovered, the substantial similarity inquiry moves from the conceptual to the concrete. Professor Nimmer suggests, and we endorse, a "successive filtering method" for separating protectable expression from non-protectable material. *See generally* 3 NIMMER § 13.03[F]. This process entails examining the structural components at each level of abstraction to determine whether their particular inclusion at that level was "idea" or was dictated by considerations of efficiency, so as to be necessarily incidental to that idea; required by factors external to the program itself; or taken from the public domain and hence is non-protectable expression. *See also* [Mark T.] Kretschmer[, Note, *Copyright Protection For Software Architecture: Just Say No!*, 1988 COLUM. BUS. L. REV. 823,] 844–45 [(1988)] (arguing that program features dictated by market externalities or efficiency concerns are unprotectable). The structure of any given program may reflect some, all, or none of these considerations. Each case requires its own fact specific investigation.

Strictly speaking, this filtration serves "the purpose of defining the scope of plaintiff's copyright." *Brown Bag Software v. Symantec Corp.*, 960 F.2d 1465, 1475 (9th Cir.) (endorsing "analytic dissection" of computer programs in order to isolate protectable expression). By applying well developed doctrines of copyright law, it may ultimately leave behind a "core of protectable material." 3 NIMMER § 13.03[F](5), at 13-72. Further explication of this second step may be helpful.

(a) *Elements Dictated by Efficiency*

The portion of *Baker v. Selden*, discussed earlier, which denies copyright protection to expression necessarily incidental to the idea being expressed, appears to be the cornerstone for what has developed into the doctrine of merger. *See Morrissey v. Procter & Gamble Co.*, 379 F.2d 675, 678–79 (1st Cir. 1967) (relying on *Baker* for the proposition that expression embodying the rules of a sweepstakes contest was inseparable from the idea of the contest itself, and therefore were not protectable by copyright); *see also Digital Communications,* 659 F. Supp. at 457. The doctrine's underlying principle is that "[w]hen there is essentially only one way to express an idea, the idea and its expression are inseparable and copyright is no bar to copying that expression." *Concrete Machinery Co. v. Classic Lawn Ornaments. Inc.*, 843 F.2d 600, 606 (1st Cir. 1988). Under these circumstances, the expression is said to have "merged" with the idea itself. In order not to confer a monopoly of the idea upon the copyright owner, such expression should not be protected. *See Herbert Rosenthal Jewelry Corp. v. Kalpakian*, 446 F.2d 738, 742 (9th Cir. 1971).

CONTU recognized the applicability of the merger doctrine to computer programs. In its report to Congress it stated that:

[C]opyrighted language may be copied without infringing when there is but a limited number of ways to express a given idea. . . . In the computer context, this means that when specific instructions, even though previously copyrighted, are the only and essential means of accomplishing a given task, their later use by another will not amount to infringement.

CONTU Report at 20. While this statement directly concerns only the application of merger to program code, that is, the textual aspect of the program, it reasonably suggests that the doctrine fits comfortably within the general context of computer programs.

Furthermore, when one considers the fact that programmers generally strive to create programs "that meet the user's needs in the most efficient manner," Menell, at 1052, the applicability of the merger doctrine to computer programs becomes compelling. In the context of computer program design, the concept of efficiency is akin to deriving the most concise logical proof or formulating the most succinct mathematical computation. Thus, the more efficient a set of modules are, the more closely they approximate the idea or process embodied in that particular aspect of the program's structure.

While, hypothetically, there might be a myriad of ways in which a programmer may effectuate certain functions within a program—i.e., express the idea embodied in a given subroutine—efficiency concerns may so narrow the practical range of choice as to make only one or two forms of expression workable options. *See* 3 NIMMER § 13.03[F](2), at 13-63; *see also Whelan,* 797 F.2d at 1243 n.43 ("It is true that for certain tasks there are only a very limited number of file structures available, and in such cases the structures might not be copyrightable." . . .) Of course, not all program structure is informed by efficiency concerns. *See* Menell, at 1052 (besides efficiency, simplicity related to user accommodation has become a programming priority). It follows that, in order to determine whether the merger doctrine precludes copyright protection to an aspect of a program's structure that is so oriented, a court must inquire "whether the use of *this particular set of modules* is necessary efficiently to implement that part of the program's process" being implemented. Englund, at 902. If the answer is yes, then the expression represented by the programmer's choice of a specific module or group of modules has merged with their underlying idea and is unprotected. *Id.* at 902–03.

Another justification for linking structural economy with the application of the merger doctrine stems from a program's essentially utilitarian nature and the competitive forces that exist in the software marketplace. *See* Kretschmer, at 842. Working in tandem, these factors give rise to a problem of proof which merger helps to eliminate. Efficiency is an industry-wide goal. Since, as we have already noted, there may be only a limited number of efficient implementations for any given program task, it is quite possible that multiple programmers, working independently, will design the identical method employed in the allegedly infringed work. Of course, if this is the case, there is no copyright infringement. *See Roth Greeting Cards v. United Card Co.*, 429 F.2d 1106, 1110 (9th Cir. 1970); *Sheldon*, 81 F.2d at 54.

Under these circumstances, the fact that two programs contain the same efficient structure may as likely lead to an inference of independent creation as it does to one of copying. *See* 3 NIMMER § 13.03[F][2], at 13-65; *cf. Herbert Rosenthal Jewelry Corp.*, 446 F.2d at 741 (evidence of independent creation may stem from defendant's standing as a designer of previous similar works). Thus, since evidence of similarly efficient structure is not particularly probative of copying, it should be disregarded in the overall substantial similarity analysis. *See* 3 NIMMER § 13.03[F][2], at 13-65. . . .

(b) *Elements Dictated by External Factors*

We have stated that where "it is virtually impossible to write about a particular historical era or fictional theme without employing certain 'stock' or standard literary devices," such expression is not copyrightable. *Hoehling v. Universal Studios, Inc.*, 618 F.2d 972, 979 (2d Cir. 1980). . . .

Professor Nimmer points out that "in many instances it is virtually impossible to write a program to perform particular functions in a specific computing environment without employing standard techniques." 3 NIMMER § 13.03[F][3], at 13-65. This is a result of the fact that a programmer's freedom of design choice is often circumscribed by extrinsic considerations such as (1) the mechanical specifications of the computer on which a particular program is intended to run; (2) compatibility requirements of other programs with which a program is designed to operate in conjunction; (3) computer manufacturers' design standards; (4) demands of the industry being serviced; and (5) widely accepted programming practices within the computer industry. *Id.* at 13-65-71. . . .

(c) *Elements Taken from the Public Domain*

Closely related to the non-protectability of *scenes à faire,* is material found in the public domain. Such material is free for the taking and cannot be appropriated by a single author even though it is included in a copyrighted work. We see no reason to make an exception to this rule for elements of a computer program that have entered the public domain by virtue of freely accessible program exchanges and the like. *See* 3 NIMMER § 13.03[F][14]; *see also Brown Bag Software*, 960 F.2d at 1473 (affirming the district court's finding that "[p]laintiffs may not claim copyright protection of an . . . expression that is, if not standard, then commonplace in the computer software industry."). Thus, a court must also filter out this material from the allegedly infringed program before it makes the final inquiry in its substantial similarity analysis.

Step Three: Comparison

The third and final step of the test for substantial similarity that we believe appropriate for non-literal program components entails a comparison. Once a court has sifted out all elements of the allegedly infringed program which are "ideas" or are dictated by efficiency or external factors, or taken from the public domain, there may remain a core of protectable expression. In terms of a work's copyright value, this is the golden nugget. *See Brown Bag Software*, 960 F.2d at 1475. At this point, the court's substantial similarity inquiry focuses on whether the defendant copied any aspect of this protected expression, as well as an assessment of the copied portion's relative importance with respect to the plaintiff's overall program. *See* 3 NIMMER § 13.03[F][5]; *Data East USA*, 862 F.2d at 208 ("To determine whether similarities result from unprotectable expression, analytic dissection of similarities may be performed. If . . . all similarities in expression arise from use of common ideas, then no substantial similarity can be found.").

3) Policy Considerations

We are satisfied that the three step approach we have just outlined not only comports with, but advances the constitutional policies underlying the Copyright Act. Since any method that tries to distinguish idea from expression ultimately impacts on the scope of copyright protection afforded to a particular type of work, "the line [it draws] must be a pragmatic one, which also keeps in consideration 'the preservation of the balance between competition and protection. . . .'" *Apple Computer*, 714 F.2d at 1253 (citation omitted).

CA and some amici argue against the type of approach that we have set forth on the grounds that it will be a disincentive for future computer program research and development. At bottom, they claim that if programmers are not guaranteed broad copyright protection for their work, they will not invest the extensive time, energy and funds required to design and improve program structures. While they have a point, their argument cannot carry the day. The interest of the copyright law is not in simply conferring a monopoly on industrious persons, but in advancing the public welfare through rewarding artistic creativity, in a manner that permits the free use and development of non-protectable ideas and processes.

In this respect, our conclusion is informed by Justice Stewart's concise discussion of the principles that correctly govern the adaptation of the copyright law to new circumstances. In *Twentieth Century Music Corp. v. Aiken*, he wrote:

> The limited scope of the copyright holder's statutory monopoly, like the limited copyright duration required by the Constitution, reflects a balance of competing claims upon the public interest: Creative work is to be encouraged and rewarded, but private motivation must ultimately serve the cause of promoting broad public availability of literature, music, and the other arts. The immediate effect of our copyright law is to secure a fair return for an "author's" creative labor. But the ultimate aim is, by this incentive, to stimulate artistic creativity for the general public good. . . . When technological change has rendered its literal terms ambiguous, the Copyright Act must be construed in light of this basic purpose.

422 U.S. 151, 156 (1975) (citations and footnotes omitted).

Recently, the Supreme Court has emphatically reiterated that "[t]he primary objective of copyright is not to reward the *labor* of authors. . . ." *Feist Publications, Inc. v. Rural Tel. Serv. Co.*, 499 U.S. 340, 349 (1991) (emphasis added). While the *Feist* decision deals primarily with the copyrightability of purely factual compilations, its underlying tenets apply to much of the work involved in computer programming. *Feist* put to rest the "sweat of the brow" doctrine in copyright law. *Id.* at 359. The rationale of that doctrine "was that copyright was a reward for the hard work that went into compiling facts." *Id.* at 351. The Court flatly rejected this justification for extending copyright protection, noting that it "eschewed the most fundamental axiom of copyright law—that no one may copyright facts or ideas." *Id.*

Feist teaches that substantial effort alone cannot confer copyright status on an otherwise uncopyrightable work. As we have discussed, despite the fact that significant labor and expense often goes into computer program flow-charting and debugging, that process does not always result in inherently protectable expression. Thus, *Feist* implicitly undercuts the *Whelan* rationale, "which allow[ed] copyright protection beyond the literal computer code . . . [in order to] provide the proper incentive for programmers by protecting their most valuable efforts. . . ." *Whelan*, 797 F.2d at 1237 (footnote omitted). We note that *Whelan* was decided prior to *Feist* when the "sweat of the brow" doctrine still had vitality. In view of the Supreme Court's recent holding, however, we must reject the legal basis of CA's disincentive argument.

Furthermore, we are unpersuaded that the test we approve today will lead to the dire consequences for the computer program industry that plaintiff and some amici predict. To the contrary, serious students of the industry have been highly critical of the sweeping scope of copyright protection engendered by the *Whelan* rule, in that it "enables first comers to 'lock up' basic programming techniques as implemented in programs to perform particular tasks." Menell, at 1087.

To be frank, the exact contours of copyright protection for non-literal program structure are not completely clear. We trust that as future cases are decided, those limits will become better defined. Indeed, it may well be that the Copyright Act serves as a relatively weak barrier against public access to the theoretical interstices behind a program's source and object codes. This results from the hybrid nature of a computer program, which, while it is literary expression, is also a highly functional, utilitarian component in the larger process of computing.

Generally, we think that copyright registration—with its indiscriminating availability—is not ideally suited to deal with the highly dynamic technology of computer science. Thus far, many of the decisions in this area reflect the courts' attempt to fit the proverbial square peg in a round hole. The district court, *see Computer Assocs.*, 775 F. Supp. at 560, and at least one commentator have suggested that patent registration, with its exacting up-front novelty and non-obviousness requirements, might be the more appropriate rubric of protection for intellectual property of this kind. *See* Randell M. Whitmeyer, Comment, *A Plea for Due Processes: Defining the Proper Scope of Patent Protection for Computer Software*, 85 Nw. U. L. Rev. 1103, 1123–25 (1991). In any event, now that more than 12 years have passed since CONTU issued its final report, the resolution of this specific issue could benefit from further legislative investigation—perhaps a CONTU II.

In the meantime, Congress has made clear that computer programs are literary works entitled to copyright protection. Of course, we shall abide by these instructions, but in so doing we must not impair the overall integrity of copyright law. While incentive based arguments in favor of broad copyright protection are perhaps attractive from a pure policy perspective, *see Lotus Dev. Corp.*, 740 F. Supp. at 58, ultimately, they have a corrosive effect on certain fundamental tenets of copyright doctrine. If the test we have outlined results in narrowing the scope of protection, as we expect it will, that result flows from applying, in accordance with Congressional intent, long-standing principles of copyright law to computer programs. Of course, our decision is also informed by our concern that these fundamental principles remain undistorted.

B. *The District Court Decision*

. . .

2) Evidentiary Analysis

The district court had to determine whether Altai's OSCAR 3.5 program was substantially similar to CA's ADAPTER. . . .

The district court took the first step in the analysis set forth in this opinion when it separated the program by levels of abstraction. The district court stated:

> As applied to computer software programs, this abstractions test would progress in order of "increasing generality" from object code, to source code, to parameter lists, to services required, to general outline. In discussing the particular similarities, therefore, we shall focus on these levels.

Computer Assocs., 775 F. Supp. at 560. While the facts of a different case might require that a district court draw a more particularized blueprint of a program's overall structure, this description is a workable one for the case at hand.

Moving to the district court's evaluation of OSCAR 3.5's structural components, we agree with Judge Pratt's systematic exclusion of non-protectable expression. With respect to code, the district court observed that after the rewrite of OSCAR 3.4 to OSCAR 3.5, "there remained virtually no lines of code that were identical to ADAPTER." *Id.* at 561. Accordingly, the court found that the code "present[ed] no similarity at all." *Id.* at 562.

Next, Judge Pratt addressed the issue of similarity between the two programs' parameter lists and macros. He concluded that, viewing the conflicting evidence most favorably to CA, it demonstrated that "only a few of the lists and macros were similar to protected elements in ADAPTER; the others were either in the public domain or dictated by the functional demands of the program." *Id.* As discussed above, functional elements and elements taken from the public domain do not qualify for copyright protection. With respect to the few remaining parameter lists and macros, the district court could reasonably conclude that they did not warrant a finding of infringement given their relative contribution to the overall program. *See Warner Bros., Inc. v. American Broadcasting Cos., Inc.*, 720 F.2d 231, 242 (2d Cir. 1983) (discussing *de minimis* exception which allows for literal copying of a small and usually insignificant portion of the plaintiff's work); 3 NIMMER § 13.03[F][5], at 13-74. In any event, the district court reasonably found that, for lack of persuasive evidence, CA failed to meet its burden of proof on whether the macros and parameter lists at issue were substantially similar. *See Computer Assocs.*, 775 F. Supp. at 562.

The district court also found that the overlap exhibited between the list of services required for both ADAPTER and OSCAR 3.5 was "determined by the demands of the operating system and of the applications program to which it [was] to be linked through ADAPTER or OSCAR. . . ." *Id.* In other words, this aspect of the program's structure was dictated by the nature of other programs with which it was designed to interact and, thus, is not protected by copyright.

Finally, in his infringement analysis, Judge Pratt accorded no weight to the similarities between the two programs' organizational charts, "because [the charts were] so simple and obvious to anyone exposed to the operation of the program[s]." *Id.* CA argues that the district court's action in this regard "is not consistent with copyright law"—that "obvious" expression is protected, and that the district court erroneously failed to realize this. However, to say that elements of a work are "obvious," in the manner in which the district court used the word, is to say that they "follow naturally from the work's theme rather than from the author's creativity." 3 NIMMER § 13.03[F][3], at 1365. This is but one formulation of the *scenes à faire* doctrine, which we have already endorsed as a means of weeding out unprotectable expression. . . .

Since we accept Judge Pratt's factual conclusions and the results of his legal analysis, we affirm his dismissal of CA's copyright infringement claim based upon

OSCAR 3.5. We emphasize that, like all copyright infringement cases, those that involve computer programs are highly fact specific. The amount of protection due structural elements, in any given case, will vary according to the protectable expression found to exist within the program at issue. . . .

COMMENTS AND QUESTIONS

1. How does the *Altai* court distinguish idea from expression? How would *Baker v. Selden* be decided under the *Altai* approach?

2. *Altai* asks courts to analytically dissect a computer program to determine what is protectable and copied and compare this to the entire program, rather than to the protectable uncopied elements, to determine substantial similarity. Does this suggest that programs with relatively little protectable material can be freely copied?

3. The *Altai* test was rapidly adopted by most courts. Judicial convergence on the abstraction-filtration-comparison test has been so complete that every court to confront the issue since 1992 has chosen the *Altai* approach. In addition, courts in Canada, the United Kingdom, and France have endorsed the *Altai* filtration analysis.

Not all of these courts have approached the abstraction-filtration-comparison analysis in precisely the same way. The Tenth Circuit decision in *Gates Rubber Co. v. Bando Chemical Industry*, 9 F.3d 823 (10th Cir. 1993) is particularly notable for its elaboration of the test beyond the parameters of *Altai*. In that case, the court acknowledged that "[a]pplication of the abstractions test will necessarily vary from case-to-case and program-to-program. Given the complexity and ever-changing nature of computer technology, we decline to set forth any strict methodology for the abstraction of computer programs." Nonetheless, the court identified six levels of "generally declining abstraction": (1) the main purpose of the computer program, (2) the structure or architecture of a program, generally as represented in a flowchart, (3) "modules" that comprise particular program operations or types of stored data, (4) individual algorithms or data structures employed in each of the modules, (5) the source code that instructs the computer to carry out each necessary operation on each data structure, and (6) the object code that is actually read by the computer. The court used these levels of abstraction to facilitate its analysis of the program at issue.

The *Gates Rubber* court also gave further content to the filtration part of the *Altai* analysis. The court filtered out six unprotectable elements: ideas, the processes or methods of the computer program, facts, material in the public domain, expression that has "merged" with an idea or process, and expression that is so standard or common as to be a "necessary incident" to an idea or process (i.e., the *scenes à faire* doctrine). Finally, the court indicated that comparison of the protected elements of a program should be done on a case-by-case basis, with an eye toward determining whether a substantial portion of the protectable expression of the original work has been copied.

Is this analysis consistent with *Altai*? Is a court applying *Gates Rubber* likely to give more or less protection to a computer program than would the *Altai* court?

PROBLEM

Problem IV-32. Demento Corporation ("Demento") produces Demento II, the leading home video game system. The Demento II consists of a console, which runs game cartridges and attaches to a monitor or standard television, and a control device, which enables the user to manipulate characters or other images of particular games on the screen. Demento licenses a limited number of games per year.

To prevent unauthorized game producers from manufacturing games to run on the Demento II console, Demento developed a "lock out" device that governs access to the console. The console includes a "master chip" or "lock" that will run only game cartridges that contain an appropriate "slave chip" or "key." When a user inserts an authorized game cartridge into the Demento II, the slave chip transmits an arbitrary data stream "key" that is received by the master chip and unlocks the console, allowing the game to be played. The unlocking device is a sophisticated software program encoded in the master and slave chips. There are a multitude of different programs capable of generating the data stream that unlocks the console, although it would be almost impossible to decipher the "key" by trial and error. It would be like trying to find a needle in a haystack.

The rapid growth of the home video game market eroded the revenue base of Mutant Corporation ("Mutant"), a leading maker of arcade video games. Mutant sought to license the right to produce game cartridges for the Demento II system, but it was put off by the limits on the number of new games that Demento would license per year and the high cost of each license. Mutant decided instead to develop its own slave chip that would unlock the Demento II game cartridge.

Mutant engineers first chemically peeled the layers of the Demento II chips to allow microscopic examination of the circuitry. Through this means, they were able to decipher the object code. After that, they were able to construct the series of pulsating signals that unlocked the master chip. Mutant discovered that only a relatively small portion of the coded message was necessary to unlock the Demento II console. From this information, Mutant software designers built a slave chip that successfully unlocked the Demento II console and enabled Mutant's game cartridges to run. It included the entire coded message for fear that Demento might later alter new versions of the Demento II system in such a way as to make Mutant's cartridges inoperable on newer units seeking the fuller coded message. To differentiate its product, the Mutant slave program was written in a different computer language and employed a different microprocessor than the Demento II system. Since the Mutant microprocessor operated at a faster speed than the Demento II chip, the Mutant program included numerous pauses.

Despite these differences, Demento promptly sued Mutant for copyright infringement after Mutant introduced its first game cartridge for the Demento II system. What is the unprotectable idea of the Demento II system? What is the protectable expression? Is the lockout code functional? How would this case be resolved?

4. Limitations on the Exclusive Right to Copy

In general, the standard for copyright infringement does not turn on the intent of the copyist. The copyright laws do not apply only to copying for a commercial purpose or to large-scale copying, but to any copying. There are, however, several statutory exceptions to this general rule:

Archival Copies for Public Libraries. Section 108 exempts from copyright liability a public "library or archives" which makes only one copy of a work at a time, assuming the copy is made for specified purposes. Copies may be made for the preservation and replacement of existing works, but only if the work cannot be replaced by purchase at a "fair price." Libraries can also make single copies for noncommercial users, as long as the library does not engage in the "systematic reproduction or distribution" of such copies. Finally, libraries are not liable for copyright violations by their patrons (even those using on-site photocopiers), as long as the library posts conspicuous warnings notifying users of the copyright laws.

Ephemeral Copies by Broadcasters. Sections 112 and 118(d) permit broadcasters to make "ephemeral" or "ancillary" copies of certain performances and displays during the course of broadcasting. For example, broadcasters are permitted to make a copy during the course of retransmitting a program. We discuss these exceptions in more detail when we consider performance and display rights.

Reproduction for People with Disabilities. Section 121 provides that "it is not an infringement of copyright for an authorized entity to reproduce or to distribute copies or phonorecords of a previously published, nondramatic literary work if such copies or phonorecords are reproduced or distributed in specialized formats exclusively for use by blind or other persons with disabilities."

Noncommercial Copies of Musical Compositions and Sound Recordings. Section 1008, added by the Audio Home Recording Act of 1992 (AHRA), authorizes "consumers" to make copies of sound recordings for "non-commercial use." The immunity for home taping is part of a broader compromise that resolved issues surrounding the use of "digital audio tape" (DAT) technology, which was thought in 1992 to be the wave of the future. In return for this immunity from suit, manufacturers of DAT decks and tapes must pay a royalty to the Copyright Office for distribution to copyright owners. Furthermore, the Act outlaws the sale of DAT decks that can copy copies. We discuss the AHRA in Chapter IV(E)(1)(d)(i).

Running Computer Software. Section 117(a) provides that:

it is not an infringement for the owner of a copy of a computer program to make or authorize the making of another copy or adaptation of that computer program provided:

(1) that such a new copy or adaptation is created as an essential step in the utilization of the computer program in conjunction with a machine and that it is used in no other manner, or

(2) that such new copy or adaptation is for archival purposes only and that all archival copies are destroyed in the event that continued possession of the computer program should cease to be rightful.

Maintaining Computer Software. Section 117(c) provides that an owner or lessee of a computer may make or authorize "the making of a copy of a computer program if such copy is made solely by virtue of the activation of a machine that lawfully contains an authorized copy of the computer program, for purposes only of maintenance or repair of that machine."

Fair Use. The fair use doctrine provides a defense in many instances of copying. We consider fair use in detail in Chapter IV(F).

5. Compulsory Licensing of Musical Compositions

As discussed in Section IV(C)(1)(iv), copyright protection for music comes in two forms: (1) musical compositions; and (2) sound recordings. Congress extended copyright protection to musical compositions in 1831. Federal copyright protection for sound recordings—derivative works based on musical compositions—dates to 1972. The rights surrounding music are especially complex. In 2018, Congress substantially reformed copyright protection for music in response to the enormous changes in music creation, reproduction, distribution, and public performance wrought by digital technology and the internet. This section discusses the compulsory licensing regimes applicable to musical compositions. We address the other changes in later sections.

i. Mechanical Compulsory License I: Cover License

The history of the mechanical compulsory license and the explanation for the term "mechanical" compulsory license trace back to the introduction of the player piano at the turn of 20th century. *See* Howard B. Abrams, *Copyright's First Compulsory License*, 26 SANTA CLARA HIGH TECH. L.J. 215 (2009). The Aeolian Company sought to monopolize the industry by entering into exclusive licenses with owners of copyrights in popular musical compositions for the reproduction on those compositions on piano rolls. Its strategy hinged on the ability to block sales of piano rolls for non-Aeolian player pianos. This turned on an interpretive question: whether a piano roll constituted an infringing "copy" of a musical composition. Based upon a literal reading of copyright statutes and English precedents, the Supreme Court ruled that a piano roll was not a "copy" because it could not be understood by the human eye. *See White-Smith Music Publishing Co. v. Apollo Co.*, 209 U.S. 1, 17-18 (1908). In a concurring opinion, Justice Holmes questioned the logic of the decision, suggesting that the statute ought to be amended "except so far as some extraneous consideration of policy may oppose." *Id.* at 20.

The following year Congress legislatively overturned the Supreme Court's *White-Smith* decision along the lines that Justice Holmes suggested. The Copyright Act of 1909 subjected mechanical reproductions of musical compositions to copyright liability, but "as a condition of extending the copyright control to such mechanical reproductions," established a mechanical compulsory license after the copyright owner made or authorized the making of "parts of instruments serving to reproduce mechanically the musical work" available to any other person "upon the payment to the copyright proprietor of a royalty of two cents on each such part manufactured." 1909 Act §1(e). The statute required the licensee to file a notice of intention (NOI) with the Copyright Office to obtain a compulsory license. Thus, the statute prevented the Aeolian Company, or any other musical composition licensee, from obtaining the exclusive right to make mechanical reproductions of musical compositions.

The mechanical compulsory reproduction license had important ramifications for a far more important and lasting emerging technology: phonograms and phonorecords, Performing artists could record their own versions or "covers" of musical compositions after a recording was released with the musical composition owner's authorization by filing an NOI and paying the compulsory license rate for each copy of the record sold. The Harry Fox Agency, founded in 1927 by the National Music Publishers Association, emerged as the leading mechanical rights administrator. Over the ensuing years, musical composers advocated repeal of the compulsory license, complaining that the royalty rate was outdated and pointing out that the monopoly concern that led to the establishment of the compulsory mechanical license was no longer present. Record companies countered that the cover license promoted competition and a broader variety of sound recordings.

Congress ultimately retained the mechanical compulsory license in the 1976 Act, with reforms to adjust royalty rates over time. Section 115 of the Act permits anyone to record a musical composition that has previously been distributed to the public under the authority of the copyright owner upon the payment of a compulsory license determined by a formula specified in the statute. The compulsory license rate has risen since that time to the greater of 9.1¢ (or 1.75¢ per minute of playing time) per recording. Furthermore, § 115 docs not permit cover artists to change the "basic melody or fundamental character of the work." The copyright law does not prohibit close imitations of an artist's sound recording, so-called "sound-alike" versions. *See* § 114(b).

In a revealing exploration of the interplay of race and intellectual property law, Professor Robert Brauneis traces the development of the sound-alike provision to the disenfranchisement of African American recording artists in the mid 20th century. *See* Robert Brauneis, *Copyright Music and Race: The Case of Mirror Cover Recordings* (2020). By the 1920s, record companies began marketing along racial and social lines: "race" records by and for African Americans; "hillbilly" or "old-time" records by and for white, rural Southerners; and "popular" records, the largest category, by and for whites. As black rhythm and blues (R&B) releases on small, independent, and sometimes black-owned record companies showed promise on the "race" chart, large, white-owned major record company with national distribution used the cover license to market these compositions to the large "popular" music marketplace. "The white version was not so much a cover as a *copy*, an attempted *duplication* of not only the melody of the song but the musical voicings and rhythmic quality of the arrangement, plus the singer's distinctive vocal style as well in many cases." *See* JAMES M. SALEM, THE LATE GREAT JOHNNY ACE AND THE TRANSITION FROM R&B TO ROCK N' ROLL 168 (1999). Much of the rock n' roll music genre traces its roots to "race" music pioneers.

In 1948, African American-owned Supreme Records sued Decca Records and Capitol Records over cover versions of "A Little Bird Told Me," composed by Harvey Oliver Brooks, sang and performed on piano by Paula Watson, arranged by bandleader Leroy Whyte, and performed by instrumentalists and vocalists Albert Patrick, Leroy Whyte, Tiny Webb, Jesse Sailes, Chuck Hamilton, Maxwell Davis, and Pete Peterson, all African Americans. At that time, copyright law did not yet protect sound recordings. It only protected musical compositions, for which Decca and Capitol could license rights for 2¢ per record sold pursuant to the mechanical license provision of the 1909 Act. Lacking a clear copyright cause of action, Supreme Records asserted that the cover versions constituted unfair competition by appropriating "an introduction, overlaps and handclapping, choral responses, a certain verbal deviation from the wording of the song, and the introduction of [several] bars of music at about the middle of the song." *Supreme Records v. Decca Records*, 90 F. Supp. 904, 911 (S.D. Cal. 1950). The Supreme recording sold well in the "race" category, reaching 250,000 copies. However, this paled into comparison to Decca sales of two million copies of the sound-alike recording in the "popular" marketplace.

BILLBOARD reported that Decca "put its big legal guns" to work on the case "because of its importance as a precedent-setting suit." BILLBOARD, May 13, 1950, at 12. The court rejected Decca's claim, opining that "a mere recording of an arrangement of a musical composition by one who is not the author of the composition is [not] a property right which should be given recognition in equity." 90 F. Supp. at 908. The effect of the decision was to decision to "ope[n] the floodgates for cover versions during the 50s." LARRY STARR & CHRISTOPHER WATERMAN, AMERICAN POPULAR MUSIC FROM MINSTRELS TO MTV 196-197 (2003). Congress ultimately codified the freedom to produce sound-alikes as part of the 1976 Act. See § 114(b); *Newton v. Diamond*, 388 F.3d 1189 (9th Cir. 2003). As we explore in Chapter VI(D), such recordings can run afoul of the right of publicity and the Federal Trade Commission's unfair trade practice guidelines under limited circumstances in modern jurisprudence. *See Midler v. Ford Motor Co.*, 849 F.2d 460 (9th Cir. 1988).

ii.   Mechanical Compulsory License II: Digital Phonorecord Delivery (DPD)

As part of the legislation to facilitate digital music distribution in 1995 (Digital Performance Rights in Sound Recording Act (DPRSRA)), Congress expanded the § 115 compulsory license to include "digital phonorecord deliveries" or DPDs. *See* § 115(d). This provision authorized the Copyright Royalty Board (CRB) to establish compulsory license rates for delivery of DPDs. The Act distinguished between incidental DPDs ("where the reproduction is incidental to the transmission which constitutes the [DPD]"—i.e., the transmission recipient does not retain the phonorecord for subsequent playback) and general DPDs (where the recipient possesses a permanent copy of the phonorecord). The legislative history indicated that the royalty rate for incidental DPDs could be less than for general DPDs, but Congress left the details and the scope of what constituted a DPD unresolved. The online music industry, which was rapidly developing with a variety of download, limited download, webcasting, noninteractive streaming, and interactive streaming services, devolved into chaos.

In 2006, the Copyright Office construed the DPRSRA to encompass ringtones with compulsory license provisions. The legislation left the royalty rates for DPDs to be resolved through industry negotiations or arbitration by Copyright Royalty Judges. Although real-time transmissions—where no reproduction of a sound recording is made for the purposes of the transmission—did not constitute a DPD, composers, publishers, record labels and high-tech companies nonetheless reached an agreement in May 2008 establishing royalty rates and terms covering limited downloads, interactive streaming, and "all known incidental DPDs." *See* Copyright Royalty Board, Library of Congress, *Mechanical and Digital Phonorecord Delivery Rate Determination Proceeding*, 73 FED. REG. 57,033 (Oct. 1, 2008) (providing for a mechanical royalty of 10.5% of revenue, minus any amounts owed for performance royalties). When the musical composition copyright owners and record labels failed to reach agreement on royalty rates, the Copyright Royalty Judges stepped in and set rates of 24¢ per ringtone and the greater of 9.1¢ (or 1.75¢ per minute of playing time) for permanent digital downloads (e.g., iTunes). *See Recording Industry Ass'n of America, Inc. v. Librarian of Congress*, 608 F.3d 861 (D.C. Cir. 2010).

Over the ensuing decade, online streaming services such as Spotify and Pandora came to dominate the music distribution marketplace. Music composers complained bitterly about low royalty rates. Performing artists complained about the lack of federal copyright protection for pre-1972 sound recordings. Streaming services complained about the difficulties of tracking down songwriters to get permission. And class action lawsuits alleging failure to file NOIs against streaming services threatened massive exposure for copyright infringement.[21]

These pressures culminated in Congress's passage of the Music Modernization Act (MMA) in 2018, which revamped the § 115 DPD compulsory license, brought pre-1972 recordings within federal copyright protection, and sought to afford music producers a share of § 114 performance right royalties. We summarize the major adjustments to the § 115 DPD compulsory license here. Section IV(E)(1)(i)(d)(2) addresses performance rights in musical compositions and sound recordings. Section IV(E)(iii) discusses the treatment of pre-1972 sound recordings.

The MMA provides for an expansive DPD blanket license (§ 115(a), (b), (d)) for online music streaming, the formation of a mechanical licensing collective to administer

---

[21] The lawsuits sought $150,000 in statutory damages per work for willful copyright infringement of thousands of musical compositions based on alleged failure to file NOIs with the Copyright Office. The streaming services countered that the licenses were secured through the Harry Fox Agency.

the blanket license (§ 115(d)), the establishment of a musical works database (§ 115(d)(3)), and a royalty rate setting mechanism (§ 115(c)). The new regime uses a willing buyer/willing seller standard for rate setting rather than setting a "reasonable rate" based on maximizing public availability of creative works, affording copyright owners a fair return and licensees fair income, and minimizing industry disruption. The MMA also limits infringement liability for online services that make good faith efforts to comply with the compulsory licensing provisions (§ 115(d)(10)(A) (barring statutory damages)) and exempts copyright owners and online services from antitrust liability for negotiating compulsory licenses (§ 115(d)(11)(B)). Online services also retain freedom to negotiate licenses directly with musical composition owners.

Advocates of the MMA hope that it will reduce transaction costs, encourage registration of musical compositions and sound recordings, eliminate statutory damages windfalls, tilt royalty distribution toward parity between composers and performing artists, and promote licensing rather than litigation. The MMA includes detailed transition provisions. Many of the details of this regime will be worked out through rulemaking by the Copyright Office over the coming years. The blanket license goes into effect on January 1, 2021.

b. The Right to Prepare Derivative Works

In its early form, copyright law protected only against the production of substantially similar copies in the same medium. It did not protect against translations or dramatic renditions of a novel. Over time, copyright law has expanded to afford the copyright protection in a wide range of derivative media. George Lucas pioneered exploitation of the derivative work right by selling merchandise and licenses to turn a popular motion picture series (*Star Wars*) into a commercial juggernaut. Just as sports icons like Steph Curry or Jordan Speith can earn more money off the playing field through endorsements than through actual salary or tournament winnings, many authors today—such as John Grisham (*The Firm, The Pelican Brief*), Michael Crichton (*Jurassic Park, Disclosure*), and J.K. Rowling (*Harry Potter* series)—can earn far greater returns from movie and commercial tie-ins than from the novels on which these works are based. Disney and Universal Studios have been particularly effective in leveraging their copyrights in characters and films to television series, toys, commercial tie-ins, and theme parks.

Building upon the foundation laid by the 1909 Act and subsequent court decisions expanding the uses and media protected by copyright law, the 1976 Act provides the copyright owner the exclusive right "to prepare derivative works based upon the copyrighted work." § 106(2). The Act defines a "derivative work" as "a work based on one or more preexisting works, such as a translation, musical arrangement, dramatization, fictionalization, motion picture version, sound recording, art reproduction, abridgement, condensation, or any other form in which a work may be recast, transformed, or adapted." It also includes "a work consisting of editorial revisions, annotations, elaborations, or other modifications which, as a whole, represent an original work of authorship." As the following case reflects, this right structure can operate like a "prospect," *cf.* Edmund W. Kitch, *The Nature and Function of the Patent System*, 20 J.L. & ECON. 265 (1977); Mark A. Lemley, *The Economics of Improvement in Intellectual Property Law*, 75 TEX. L. REV. 989 (1997), affording the original author a broad opportunity to exploit new markets and incremental improvements in his or her work.

Anderson v. Stallone
United States District Court for the Central District of California
11 U.S.P.Q.2d 1161 (C.D. Cal. 1989)

KELLER, District Judge:

. . .

Factual Background

The movies *Rocky I*, *II*, and *III* were extremely successful motion pictures. Sylvester Stallone wrote each script and played the role of Rocky Balboa, the dominant character in each of the movies. In May of 1982, while on a promotional tour for the movie *Rocky III*, Stallone informed members of the press of his ideas for *Rocky IV*. Although Stallone's description of his ideas would vary slightly in each of the press conferences, he would generally describe his ideas as follows:

> I'd do it [*Rocky IV*] if Rocky himself could step out a bit. Maybe tackle world problems. . . . So what would happen, say, if Russia allowed her boxers to enter the professional ranks? Say Rocky is the United States' representative and the White House wants him to fight with the Russians before the Olympics. It's in Russia with everything against him. It's a giant stadium in Moscow and everything is Russian Red. It's a fight of astounding proportions with 50 monitors sent to 50 countries. It's the World Cup—a war between 2 countries.

WACO TRIBUNE-HERALD, May 28, 1982; Section D, pg. 1. In June of 1982, after viewing the movie *Rocky III*, Timothy Anderson wrote a thirty-one page treatment entitled "*Rocky IV*" that he hoped would be used by Stallone and MGM-UA Communications Co. (hereinafter "MGM") as a sequel to *Rocky III*. The treatment incorporated the characters created by Stallone in his prior movies and cited Stallone as a co-author.

In October of 1982, Mr. Anderson met with Art Linkletter, who was a member of MGM's board of directors. Mr. Linkletter set up a meeting on October 11, 1982, between Mr. Anderson and Mr. Fields, who was president of MGM at the time. Mr. Linkletter was also present at this October 11, 1982 meeting. During the meeting, the parties discussed the possibility that plaintiff's treatment would be used by defendants as the script for *Rocky IV*. At the suggestion of Mr. Fields, the plaintiff, who is a lawyer and was accompanied by a lawyer at the meeting, signed a release that purported to relieve MGM from liability stemming from use of the treatment. Plaintiff alleges that Mr. Fields told him and his attorney that "if they [MGM and Stallone] use his stuff [Anderson's treatment] it will be big money, big bucks for Tim."

On April 22, 1984, Anderson's attorney wrote MGM requesting compensation for the alleged use of his treatment in the forthcoming *Rocky IV* movie. On July 12, 1984, Stallone described his plans for the *Rocky IV* script on the Today Show before a national television audience. Anderson, in his deposition, states that his parents and friends called him to tell him that Stallone was telling "his story" on television. . . .

Stallone completed his *Rocky IV* script in October of 1984. *Rocky IV* was released in November of 1985. The complaint in this action was filed on January 29, 1987.

Conclusions of Law

. . .

IV.   Defendants Are Entitled to Summary Judgment on Anderson's Copyright Infringement Claims

. . .

A. Defendants Are Entitled to Summary Judgment Because Anderson's Treatment Is an Infringing Work That Is Not Entitled to Copyright Protection

The Court finds that Anderson's treatment is not entitled to copyright protection. This finding is based upon the following determinations that will be delineated further below: (a) the Rocky characters developed in *Rocky I, II* and *III* constitute expression protected by copyright independent from the story in which they are contained; (b) Anderson's treatment appropriated these characters and created a derivative work based upon these characters without Stallone's permission in violation of § 106(2); (c) no part of Anderson's treatment is entitled to copyright protection as his work is pervaded by the characters of the first three *Rocky* movies that are afforded copyright protection.

1. Visually Depicted Characters Can Be Granted Copyright Protection

The precise legal standard this Court should apply in determining when a character may be afforded copyright protection is fraught with uncertainty. The Second Circuit has followed Judge Learned Hand's opinion in *Nichols v. Universal Pictures*, 45 F.2d 119 (2d Cir. 1930). Judge Hand set forth a test, simple in theory but elusive in application, to determine when a character should be granted copyright protection. Essentially, under this test, copyright protection is granted to a character if it is developed with enough specificity so as to constitute protectable expression. *Id.* at 121.

This circuit originally created a more rigorous test for granting copyright protection to characters. In *Warner Bros. Pictures, Inc. v. Columbia Broadcasting System, Inc.* (hereinafter the "Sam Spade" opinion), this circuit held that the literary character Sam Spade was not copyrightable, opining that a character could not be granted copyright protection unless it "constituted the story being told." 216 F.2d 945, 950 (9th Cir. 1954). The Sam Spade case has not been explicitly overruled by this circuit and its requirement that a character "constitute the story being told" appears to greatly circumscribe the protection of characters in this circuit.

Subsequent decisions in the Ninth Circuit cast doubt on the reasoning and implicitly limit the holding of the Sam Spade case. In *Walt Disney Productions v. Air Pirates*, this circuit held that several Disney comic characters were protected by copyright. 581 F.2d 751, 755 (9th Cir. 1978). In doing so the Court of Appeals reasoned that because "comic book characters . . . are distinguishable from literary characters, the *Warner Bros.* language does not preclude protection of Disney's characters." *Id. Air Pirates* can be interpreted as either attempting to harmonize granting copyright protection to graphic characters with the "story being told" test enunciated in the Sam Spade case or narrowing the "story being told" test to characters in literary works. . . .

2. The Rocky Characters Are Entitled to Copyright Protection as a Matter of Law

. . . The Rocky characters are one of the most highly delineated group of characters in modern American cinema. The physical and emotional characteristics of Rocky Balboa and the other characters were set forth in tremendous detail in three Rocky movies before Anderson appropriated the characters for his treatment. The interrelationships and development of Rocky, Adrian, Apollo Creed, Clubber Lang, and Paulie are central to all three movies. Rocky Balboa is such a highly delineated character that his name is the title of all four of the Rocky movies and his character has become identified with specific character traits ranging from his speaking mannerisms to his physical characteristics. This Court has no difficulty ruling as a matter of law that the Rocky characters are delineated so extensively that they are protected from bodily appropriation when taken as a group and transposed into a sequel by another author. Plaintiff has not and cannot put before this Court any evidence to rebut the defendants' showing that Rocky characters are so highly delineated that they warrant copyright protection.

Plaintiff's unsupported assertions that Rocky is merely a stock character, made in the face of voluminous evidence that the Rocky characters are copyrightable, do not bar this Court from granting summary judgment on this issue. If any group of movie characters is protected by copyright, surely the Rocky characters are protected from bodily appropriation into a sequel which merely builds on the relationships and characteristics which these characters developed in the first three Rocky movies. No reasonable jury could find otherwise.

This Court need not and does not reach the issue of whether any single character alone, apart from Rocky, is delineated with enough specificity so as to garner copyright protection. . . .

This Court also finds that the Rocky characters were so highly developed and central to the three movies made before Anderson's treatment that they "constituted the story being told." All three Rocky movies focused on the development and relationships of the various characters. The movies did not revolve around intricate plots or story lines. Instead, the focus of these movies was the development of the Rocky characters. The same evidence which supports the finding of delineation above is so extensive that it also warrants a finding that the Rocky characters—Rocky, Adrian, Apollo Creed,

Clubber Lang, and Paulie—"constituted the story being told" in the first three Rocky movies.

3. Anderson's Work Is an Unauthorized Derivative Work

Under 17 U.S.C. § 106(2), the holder of a copyright has the exclusive right to prepare derivative works based upon his copyrighted work. In this circuit a work is derivative *"only if it would be considered an infringing work if* the material which it had derived from a prior work had been taken without the consent of the copyright proprietor of the prior work." *Litchfield v. Spielberg*, 736 F.2d 1352, 1354 (9th Cir. 1984) (emphasis in original), citing *United States v. Taxe*, 540 F.2d 961, 965 n.2 (9th Cir. 1976). This Court must now examine whether Anderson's treatment is an unauthorized derivative work under this standard.

Usually a court would be required to undertake the extensive comparisons under the *Krofft* substantial similarity test to determine whether Anderson's work is a derivative work. However, in this case, Anderson has bodily appropriated the *Rocky* characters in his treatment. This Court need not determine whether the characters in Anderson's treatment are substantially similar to Stallone's characters, as it is uncontroverted that the characters were lifted lock, stock, and barrel from the prior *Rocky* movies. Anderson retained the names, relationships and built on the experiences of these characters from the three prior *Rocky* movies. His characters are not merely substantially similar to Stallone's, they *are* Stallone's characters. As Professor Nimmer stated, "Where there is literal similarity . . . [i]t is not necessary to determine the level of abstraction at which similarity ceases to consist of an 'expression of ideas' since literal similarity by definition is always a similarity as to the expression of ideas." 3 M. NIMMER, § 13.03[3]. Anderson's bodily appropriation of these characters infringes upon the protected expression in the *Rocky* characters and renders his work an unauthorized derivative work. By bodily appropriating the significant elements of protected expression in the *Rocky* characters, Anderson has copied protected expression and his treatment infringes on Stallone's copyrighted work.

4. Since Anderson's Work Is an Unauthorized Derivative Work, No Part of the Treatment Can Be Granted Copyright Protection

Stallone owns the copyrights for the first three *Rocky* movies. Under 17 U.S.C. section 106(2), he has the exclusive right to prepare derivative works based on these copyrighted works. This Court has determined that Anderson's treatment is an unauthorized derivative work. Thus, Anderson has infringed upon Stallone's copyright. *See* 17 U.S.C. section 501(a).

Nevertheless, plaintiff contends that his infringing work is entitled to copyright protection and he can sue Stallone for infringing upon his treatment. Plaintiff relies upon 17 U.S.C. section 103(a) as support for his position that he is entitled to copyright protection for the non-infringing portions of his treatment. 17 U.S.C. section 103(a) reads:

The subject matter of copyright as specified by section 102 includes compilations and derivative works, but protection for a work employing preexisting material in which copyright subsists does not extend to any part of the work in which the material has been used unlawfully.

Plaintiff has not argued that section 103(a), on its face, requires that an infringer be granted copyright protection for the non-infringing portions of his work. He has not and cannot provide this Court with a single case that has held that an infringer of a copyright is entitled to sue a third party for infringing the original portions of his work. Nor can he provide a single case that stands for the extraordinary proposition he proposes here, namely, allowing a plaintiff to sue the party whose work he has infringed upon for infringement of his infringing derivative work.

Instead, Anderson alleges that the House Report on section 103(a) indicates that Congress intended protection for the non-infringing portions of derivative works such as his treatment. The House Report for section 103(a) first delineates the differences between compilations and derivative works. H.R. No. 1476, 94th Cong., 2d Sess. at 57–58 (1976). The House Report then reads as follows:

> The second part of the sentence that makes up section 103(a) deals with the status of a compilation or derivative work unlawfully employing preexisting copyrighted material. In providing that protection does not extend to "any part of the work in which such material has been used unlawfully," the bill prevents an infringer from benefiting, through copyright protection, from committing an unlawful act, but preserves protection for those parts of the work that do not employ the preexisting work. Thus, an unauthorized translation of a novel could not be copyrighted at all, but the owner of copyright in an anthology of poetry could sue someone who infringed the whole anthology, even though the infringer proves that publication of one of the poems was unauthorized.
>
> . . .

Plaintiff has written a treatment which is an unauthorized derivative work. This treatment infringes upon Stallone's copyrights and his exclusive right to prepare derivative works which are based upon these movies. 17 U.S.C. § 106(2). Section 103(a) was not intended to arm an infringer and limit the applicability of section 106(2) on unified derivative works. . . . Section 103(a) allows an author whose authorship essentially is the arrangement or ordering of several independent works to keep the copyright for his arrangement even if one of the underlying works he arranged is found to be used unlawfully. The infringing portion would be easily severable and the scope of the compilation author's own work would be easily ascertainable. Even if this Court were to interpret section 103(a) as allowing an author of an infringing derivative work to sue third parties based on the non-infringing portions of his work, section 106(2) most certainly precludes the author of an unauthorized infringing derivative work from suing the author of the work which he has already infringed. Thus, the Court HOLDS that the defendants are entitled to summary judgment on plaintiff's copyright claims as the plaintiff cannot gain copyright protection for any portion of his work under section

103(a). In addition, Anderson is precluded by section 106(2) from bringing an action for copyright infringement against Stallone and the other defendants. . . .

COMMENTS AND QUESTIONS

1. Why protect derivative works under § 106(2) at all? The Nimmer treatise refers to § 106(2)'s right to prepare derivative works as "completely superfluous." 2 NIMMER ON COPYRIGHT § 8.09[A], at 8–114. It reasons that infringement of the right to prepare derivative works necessarily also infringes either the right to make copies or the right to perform works, so there is no reason to have both. If derivative works must be "substantially similar" to the underlying work to infringe the § 106(2) right, does it add anything to the protections granted elsewhere in the Copyright Act?

Professor Paul Goldstein suggests that protecting derivative works is necessary in some instances to ensure that adequate incentives are given to copyright holders to develop new works. He argues that the author of a book should own the rights to a movie made out of that book, for example. *See* Paul Goldstein, *Derivative Rights and Derivative Works in Copyright*, 30 J. COPYRIGHT SOC'Y 209 (1982). But why are derivative rights necessary to accomplish this? In most such situations, the movie (or sequel) will of necessity copy places and characters exactly from the original. This seems to be a clear case of direct infringement of protected expression. If, on the other hand, expression from the original is *not* copied, but only general ideas or themes, is copyright protection desirable?

2. Were Stallone to lose this case, what would prevent prospective authors from generating numerous potential plot permutations for future James Bond films, publicizing them on the Internet, and then waiting to sue when MGM eventually selects one of these story lines? What counterarguments could you offer to this scenario? Is this risk really significant? What could MGM do to protect itself against such potential plaintiffs? On the other hand, does it seem fair that Stallone is free to take original work written by others without compensation?

3. *The Originality Requirement for Derivative Works.* In *Gracen v. Bradford Exchange*, 698 F.2d 300, 304 (7th Cir. 1983), MGM had licensed Bradford Exchange to use characters and scenes from the movie *The Wizard of Oz* in a series of collectors' plates. Bradford invited artists to submit paintings of Dorothy as played by Judy Garland, with the understanding that the artist who submitted the best painting would be offered a contract for the entire series. Bradford supplied contestants with photographs from the movie and the following instruction: "We do want *your* interpretation of these images, but your interpretation must evoke all the warm feeling the people have for the film and its actors. So, *your* Judy/Dorothy must be very recognizable as everybody's Judy/Dorothy." Jorie Gracen submitted a painting of Dorothy skipping along the yellow brick road that closely resembled two still images from the film. It integrated and embellished on the original scenes by, for example, adding a rainbow in the background, placing Toto under Dorothy's arm, and altering the lighting in the scene. After Gracen won the contest, Bradford offered her a contract for the plate series. Gracen declined the offer, after which Bradford hired another artist

to produce the series. Bradford provided the artist with a copy of Gracen's entry, from which he produced a similar representation. Gracen sued Bradford for copyright infringement. In finding against Gracen, Judge Posner reasoned that a derivative work must be substantially different from the underlying work to be copyrightable. Otherwise, the court would lack a plausible basis for determining whether a derivative work is based on the original or a prior derivate work. *Cf. L. Batlin & Son, Inc. v. Snyder*, 536 F.2d 486 (2d Cir. 1976) (en banc) (requiring substantial variation); *Pickett v. Prince*, 207 F.3d 402 (7th Cir. 2000). Should the threshold for originality be higher for derivative works?

4. *Economic Incentives.* Does a broad right to control derivative works comport with the economic incentive approach to intellectual property protection? Proponents of an incentive-based view of copyright might well challenge the assumption that authors should receive royalties from derivative works. Do authors really create under the assumption that their works will be translated into different forms? (Some do, certainly; Disney markets its animated films with an eye toward selling T-shirts and stuffed animals as well as movie tickets.) From a strict incentive perspective, should we reward authors in markets they did not originally enter? To what extent does your answer depend on assumptions about the capacity of authors and artists to develop other applications of their work? To what extent does your answer depend on assumptions about the transaction costs of licensing?

The economic rationale for derivative works may break down where the derivative right is used to preclude defendants from developing their own creative works in a market the plaintiff has not herself exploited, but which depends somehow on the plaintiff's work. Something of this sort may have happened in *Castle Rock Entertainment v. Carol Publishing Group*, 150 F.3d 132 (2d Cir. 1998). There the court enjoined the publication of a *Seinfeld* trivia book called the *Seinfeld Aptitude Test*. The court reasoned that the book infringed the copyright in the *Seinfeld* television series because it took numerous "facts" from the episodes created by the copyright owner. Because *Seinfeld* was fictional, the court concluded that these "facts" constituted copyrightable expression, and the defendants could not prevail on a fair use defense.

Do you find the result in the *Seinfeld* case convincing? What if the book in question had been an unauthorized biography of Jerry Seinfeld? A news report about a particularly controversial episode? What light, if any, does the case shed on the appropriate limits of the derivative work right?

5. *Comparison to Patent Scope.* Copyright law appears to afford the copyright proprietor broad control of all extensions of their original expression. Section 103(b) extends protection only to new expression, and not to preexisting material included in the derivative work. Only the original author or a licensee is entitled to a copyright in the derivative work. This means that if a filmmaker makes a movie out of a copyrighted book without authorization, adding substantial expression of her own in the process, she is not entitled to a copyright in any portion of the movie in which infringing material appears. *See Pickett v. Prince*, 207 F.3d 402 (7th Cir. 2000) (artisan who made a guitar in the shape of recording artist Prince's original love symbol infringed the copyright in

Prince's symbol and therefore lacked originality for the guitar shape); *Sobhani v. @Radical.Media Inc.*, 257 F. Supp. 2d 1234 (C.D. Cal. 2003).

Does this result make sense? If only new expression is copyrightable as part of a derivative work, why assign that new expression (as distinguished from the original expression) exclusively to the original author?

Compare this result with the "blocking patents" situation in patent law. As Professor Merges explains, this doctrine permits a second inventor to obtain a patent on his improvement even though that improvement also infringes another patent. Robert P. Merges, *Intellectual Property Rights and Bargaining Breakdown: The Case of Blocking Patents*, 62 TENN. L. REV. 74 (1994). Historically, this circumstance has led to enhanced bargaining, but the social costs of occasional bargaining breakdown justify a sort of "patent fair use" principle (the "reverse doctrine of equivalents"). Fortunately, although such situations are serious given that they often involve significant new technologies, they are relatively rare. In the great run of cases, the ingenious institution of blocking patents balances the rights of original creators and subsequent improvers rather nicely.

No such institution exists in the law of copyrights. *See* Mark A. Lemley, *The Economics of Improvement in Intellectual Property Law*, 75 TEX. L. REV. 989 (1997). Copyright doctrine prohibits a follow-on creator from appropriating and adding to the copyrighted material of an original creator. Professor Goldstein has argued that the cases provide no compelling reason to deny the derivative artist a copyright in his additional creative efforts:

> The rule [denying copyrightability for unauthorized derivative works] is, however, hard to justify when applied to derivative works such as the motion picture in *Sheldon v. MGM* [309 U.S. 390 (1940)] in which the underlying work represents only a small part of the value of the derivative work but, because it underlies the whole, will defeat copyright protection for the entire derivative work. Just as an injunction against the motion picture gave plaintiff there a greater return than was needed to induce his investment in the underlying work, so depriving the motion picture owner of all protection against others will give it far less return than is needed to justify investment in the derivative work."

Paul Goldstein, *Derivative Rights and Derivative Works in Copyright*, 30 J. COPYRIGHT SOC'Y U.S.A. 209 (1982); *see also* Wendy Gordon, *Toward a Jurisprudence of Benefits: The Norms of Copyright and the Problem of Private Censorship*, 57 U. CHI. L. REV. 1009 (1990). Perhaps the best explanation for the lack of a doctrine of "blocking copyrights" is copyright law's policy favoring the reputational interest of authors: by requiring ex ante licensing of anyone who wishes to incorporate a copyrighted work into another work, the law encourages authorial control. The law of derivative works is one way in which a personality or "moral rights" aspect creeps into U.S. copyright law. In effect, the strong protection given derivative works affords the original copyright owner control over alterations or "improvements" upon her work. *See* ROBERT P. MERGES, JUSTIFYING INTELLECTUAL PROPERTY 254 (2011).

Professor Joseph Fishman offers another rationale. By constraining cumulative creators, he contends that copyright law encourages a wider range of and bolder new creative works. *See* Joseph Fishman, *Creating Around Copyright*, 128 HARV. L. REV. 1333 (2015). He notes that George Lucas developed the first *Star Wars* film only after he failed to get a license for a remake of Flash Gordon. The developers of Donkey Kong and Mario were led to build something new after being denied use of Popeye.

Because there is no blocking copyrights doctrine, copyright law is left with a vacuum in certain cases. What should be done with the hypothetical infringer who creates otherwise protectable new expression? Should that new expression be unprotectable because it derives from an infringement? Should it be in the public domain? Should it be deemed "captured" by the original copyright holder?

6. *Video Game "Enhancements."* The House Report to the 1976 Act notes that the § 106(2) right to adapt is "broader" than the § 106(1) reproduction right "in the sense that reproduction requires fixation in copies or phonorecords, whereas the preparation of a derivative work, such as a ballet, pantomime, or improvised performance, may be an infringement even though nothing is ever fixed in tangible form." See H.R. Rep. No. 94-1476, 94th Cong., 2d Sess. 62 (1976). A series of cases involving video games has addressed whether add-on devices and software designed to enhance the playing experience constitute derivative works. In *Midway Mfg. Co. v. Arctic Int'l, Inc.*, 704 F.2d 1009 (7th Cir. 1983), the defendant sold printed circuit boards that sped up the play of plaintiff's Galaxian and Pac-Man video games. Interpreting the definition of "derivative work" in § 101 of the Act, the court explained that

> [i]t is not obvious from this language whether a speeded-up video game is a derivative work. A speeded-up phonograph record probably is not. *Cf. Shapiro, Bernstein & Co. v. Jerry Vogel Music Co.*, 73 F. Supp. 165, 167 (S.D.N.Y. 1947) ("The change in time of the added chorus, and the slight variation in the base of the accompaniment, there being no change in the tune or lyrics, would not be 'new work'"); 1 NIMMER ON COPYRIGHT § 3.03 (1982). But that is because the additional value to the copyright owner of having the right to market separately the speeded-up version of the recorded performance is too trivial to warrant legal protection for that right. A speeded-up video game is a substantially different product from the original game. As noted, it is more exciting to play and it requires some creative effort to produce. For that reason, the owner of the copyright on the game should be entitled to monopolize it on the same theory that he is entitled to monopolize the derivative works specifically listed in Section 101. The current rage for video games was not anticipated in 1976, and like any new technology the video game does not fit with complete ease the definition of derivative work in Section 101 of the 1976 Act. But the amount by which the language of Section 101 must be stretched to accommodate speeded-up video games is, we believe, within the limits within which Congress wanted the new Act to operate.

Midway Mfg. Co., 704 F.2d at 1014. Do you agree? Note that the defendant is not creating a new copy of the video game, since the sped-up version is not fixed in a tangible medium of expression. Should that matter in deciding whether the new version is a derivative work? *See Lewis Galoob Toys., Inc. v. Nintendo of America, Inc.*, 964 F.2d 965 (9th Cir. 1992) (requiring some instantiation short of fixation); *Micro Star v. Formgen, Inc.*, 154 F.3d 1107 (9th Cir. 1998) (same).

7. *Content Filtering.* In 2002, ClearPlay introduced a technology that allows consumers to activate film-specific filters to black out violent and sexual scenes and to mute profanity for DVDs. In order to accomplish this functionality, ClearPlay wrote software masks that run in parallel with DVDs that instruct the player to skip over particular scenes and mute specific segments. Motion picture studios brought suit, alleging that such scripts constituted unauthorized derivative works. Do such scripts constitute derivative works? Surely a consumer can fast-forward through scenes and press the mute button without violating the rights of the copyright owner. Should the owner of the copyright in the work have the exclusive right to provide add-on technologies to assist the consumer in these efforts?

After several years of litigation, Congress settled this dispute by passing the Family Entertainment and Copyright Act of 2005 (FECA), which immunizes:

> the making imperceptible, by or at the direction of a member of a private household, of limited portions of audio or video content of a motion picture, during a performance in or transmitted to that household for private home viewing, from an authorized copy of the motion picture, or the creation or provision of a computer program or other technology that enables such making imperceptible and that is designed and marketed to be used, at the direction of a member of a private household, for such making imperceptible, if no fixed copy of the altered version of the motion picture is created by such computer program or other technology.

17 U.S.C. § 110(11).

In 2014, VidAngel sought refuge under this provision for its platform that allowed customers with streaming accounts (Netflix, HBO, Amazon Prime) to select filters to remove scenes containing nudity, profanity, and graphic violence. After being denied licenses from motion picture studios, VidAngel developed a library of edited motion pictures by circumventing the copy-protection features of DVDs and Blu-ray discs. When major studios sued for copyright infringement, VidAngel defended on the ground that because it "begins its filtering process with an authorized copy"—a lawfully purchased disc—"any subsequent filtered stream" is also "from" that authorized copy, and therefore its service fell within FECA. The Ninth Circuit rejected this argument based on the statutory text ("from an authorized copy of a motion picture") and legislative history explaining that FECA in not a defense to the Copyright Act's anticircumvention provisions. *See Disney Enterprises, Inc. v. VidAngel, Inc.*, 869 F.3d 848, 857-60 (9th Cir. 2017). VidAngel was ultimately held liable for $62 million in damages. Should Congress expand FECA to authorize such activity?

8. *Software Guides "for Dummies."* Are *Windows for Dummies*, *Excel for Dummies*, and *Word for Dummies* derivative works? Whereas Hollywood seems to go

after derivative uses vigorously, the software industry has been much more welcoming of guides for software products. How would you explain this difference?

PROBLEMS

Problem IV-33. Garamon, a French author, wrote a successful novel in French. The novel is copyrighted in France in 1954. Garamon authorized an English translation of his novel but failed to comply with the formalities then required under U.S. law to obtain a U.S. copyright in the translation. Thus, the translation fell into the public domain. Subsequently, Oaktree Press photocopied and distributed the English translation of the novel in the United States. Garamon sues for infringement, not of the translation, but of the copyright on the underlying French novel. Who should prevail?

Problem IV-34. A graphic artist for WORLD ENQUIRER magazine is asked to produce a seamless integration of two photographs so that it appears that two figures from separate photographs were in the same picture. He scans the photographs and merges into an integrated graphic work using Adobe Photoshop. Assume one picture was copyrighted and the other was in the public domain. What rights do the owner of the copyrighted photograph and World Enquirer have in the resulting image?

Problem IV-35. In 1989, NBC introduced *Seinfeld*, a television sitcom featuring a standup comic and revolving around his quirky group of friends living in New York City. After a slow start, the show went on to enormous success, dominating television ratings throughout the 1990s and ending its run in 1998 at the top. In 1994, NBC launched *Friends*, another sitcom that revolved around a quirky group of friends living in New York City. It also went on to tremendous popular success.

In 2003, Jerry Seinfeld playfully accused *Friends* of being a *Seinfeld* rip-off. In a 2016 interview, the interviewer raised the issue: "It's been suggested that *Friends* is *Seinfeld* with the hugging and learning." Jerry responded: "No it's [our show] with better looking people."

How would you evaluate a hypothetical copyright infringement action by the producers of *Seinfeld* against the producers of *Friends*?

Problem IV-36. In 1951, J.D. Salinger's novel CATCHER IN THE RYE was published to critical acclaim. The first-person narrative of Holden Caulfield, a rebellious, awkward, and conflicted teenager following his expulsion from a college preparatory school, became required reading in many high school and college literature curricula. Millions of teenagers and young adults experienced coming of age through the eyes of Salinger's antihero, who became a symbol of teenage liberation and defiance. More than 65 million copies have been sold cumulatively, with sales still reaching a quarter of million per year, making it one of the bestselling books of all time. J.D. Salinger himself rebelled from the publicity generated by his success, becoming a recluse and withdrawing from publishing literary works.

In 2009, Fredrik Colting, writing under the pseudonym John David California ("J.D. California"), published the novel, 60 YEARS LATER: COMING THROUGH THE RYE. Referring to the protagonist only as C, the author weaves a story that is unmistakably modeled after Salinger's protagonist. Beyond the obvious effort to revive Caulfield, there is little else directly copied from Catcher in the Rye. Salinger brought suit, alleging that 60 YEARS LATER is an unauthorized sequel to his 1951 work. What arguments would you make for Salinger? Colting? How should a court rule on the copyright infringement claim? (Note: We will revisit this scenario when get to the fair use doctrine, so reserve those arguments for later.)

c. The Distribution Right

Section 106(3) grants copyright owners the "exclusive right to do and to authorize" the following: "to distribute copies or phonorecords of the copyrighted work to the public by sale or other transfer of ownership, or by rental, lease, or lending." This right grows out of the historic rights "to publish" and "to vend" recognized by earlier copyright statutes. This distribution right is closely allied with the right to copy, since reproduction has been the principal means of exploiting works of authorship for most of copyright's history. Thus, copying and selling a copyright owner's work without authorization violates both the right to copy and the right to distribute. As a corollary, both the copier who never does anything with his or her copies and the unknowing distributor of unauthorized copies are liable for copyright infringement.

Section 602 of the Copyright Act augments the distribution right by affording copyright owners the right to block importation or exportation of copies, subject to limited exceptions. See § 602(a)(3) (exceptions for government use (but not including schools), personal copies for private use, and scholarly, education, or religious purposes (but not more than five copies). Section 602(b) prohibits any importation of infringing copies.

1. The Scope of the Distribution Right: Does It Encompass Making a Work Available?

Prior to the emergence of file-sharing technology, the Copyright Act's distribution right was largely dormant. Most enforcement actions were premised upon violations of the reproduction right and the relatively rare cases invoking the distribution right but not the reproduction right involved arcane scenarios. With the proliferation of filesharing over the Internet, direct enforcement of the Copyright Act against filesharers has brought the scope of the distribution right to center stage, because many individual defendants are charged with allowing access to their computer drives containing copyrighted files, but others actually download those files.

Whereas the 1909 Act expressly protected the rights to "publish" and "vend," the 1976 Act speaks of a right to "distribute." Interpreting "distribute" narrowly, some courts have held that copyright owners must prove that a sound recording placed in a share folder was actually downloaded to establish violation of the distribution right. Other courts held that merely making a sound recording available violates the distribution right.

The ramifications for copyright enforcement in the Internet age are substantial. Under the narrow interpretation, the relative anonymity of Internet transmissions in combination with privacy concerns make enforcement costly and difficult. A broad interpretation exposes millions of filesharers to potentially crushing statutory damages.

In exploring the 1976 Act's voluminous legislative history, Professor Menell argues that Congress did not intend to narrow the 1909 Act's publish and vend rights. *See* Peter S. Menell, *In Search of Copyright's Lost Ark: Interpreting the Right to Distribute in the Internet Age*, 59 J. COPYRIGHT SOC'Y U.S.A. 1 (2011). Rather, the drafters expressly intended to broaden the reach of those rights. The reason for the change in terminology was to avoid some of the confusing jurisprudence that had formed around the meaning of "publication," most notably judicial efforts to avoid copyright forfeiture resulting from defective copyright notice. *See* Chapter IV(A)(3)(ii)(a) (discussing distinctions among general and limited publication and divestive and investive publication).

The courts remain divided over the proper interpretation of the distribution right in filesharing cases. *Compare Diversey v. Schmidly*, 738 F.3d 1196, 1202 n.7 (10th Cir. 2013) *with London-Sire Records, Inc. v. Doe*, 542 F. Supp. 2d 153 (D. Mass. 2008). The divergence reflects more general division over the role of legislative history in statutory interpretation. Based on extensive hearings and study, the Copyright Office concluded that § 106(3) embodies a making available right, i.e., that merely making a work available infringes § 106(3). *See* U.S. COPYRIGHT OFFICE, THE MAKING AVAILABLE RIGHT IN THE UNITED STATES: A REPORT OF THE REGISTER (Feb. 2016). Other courts have found otherwise. *See Atlantic Recording Corp. v. Howell*, 554 F. Supp. 2d 976 (D. Ariz. 2008); *London-Sire*, 542 F. Supp. 2d at 168. Even courts that have come to this interpretation nonetheless have allowed plaintiffs to prove violation of the distribution right through circumstantial evidence. Thus, the fact that a forensic expert hired by the copyright owner was able to find the copyrighted work in a filesharing folder controlled by the defendant relatively easily—by, for example, searching for a work's title or artist on widely available search engines—is sufficient to establish that it was more probable than not that the work was actually distributed. *See e.g., London-Sire Records*, 542 F. Supp. 2d at 169, 176–77; *see generally* Robert Kasunic, *Making Circumstantial Proof of Distribution Available*, 18 FORDHAM INTELL. PROP. MEDIA & ENT. L.J. 1145 (2008).

COMMENTS AND QUESTIONS

1. Why is this interpretive question of such importance in the digital age? Should those who share the latest Beyoncé release, *Star Wars* film, or independent artist project on the Internet without authorization be able to defend their actions on the ground that the copyright owner can't identify a specific downloader? What purpose is served by

requiring the copyright owner to show more than the fact that someone had uploaded the file to web-accessible platform? Note that under the 1909 Act, liability extended to anyone who published or sold a copyrighted work without authorization, whether or not anyone purchased an unauthorized copy. Should the same rules apply to individuals who make available infringing works simply by opening their computer drives to other individuals, with no expectation of profit?

Does a bookstore "distribute" copies of a work by putting it on a shelf for sale, even if no one buys it?

2. *Interpretation of Prior Licensing Deals in the Wake of New Distribution Platforms.* Whenever new technologies for distributing works of authorship emerge, the question inevitably arises whether older contracts extend to such new distribution channels. Rosetta Books, one of the first companies to distribute electronic books ("eBooks"), obtained permission from well-known authors Kurt Vonnegut, William Styron, and Robert B. Parker to distribute some of their classic titles (*Slaughterhouse-Five*, *Sophie's Choice*, and *Promised Land*) in eBook form. Their works became available for downloading on Rosetta Books' website shortly thereafter. Random House, the exclusive U.S. publisher of the print versions of these books, promptly sued, claiming that its book publishing agreements with these authors to "print, publish, and sell the work in book form" dating back to the 1960s, extended to this new medium. This litigation is reminiscent of prior waves of cases following the development of other new distribution media. *See Bartsch v. Metro-Goldwyn-Mayer*, 391 F.2d 150 (2d Cir. 1950) (whether license to exhibit motion pictures extends to television broadcasts); *Boosey & Hawkes Music Publishers v. Walt Disney*, 145 F.3d 481 (2d Cir. 1998) (whether license to record musical composition for use in a motion picture extends to video cassettes); *Bourne v. Walt Disney*, 68 F.3d 621 (2d Cir. 1995) (same). Applying a narrow interpretation of the contractual language, the district court denied Random House's motion for a preliminary injunction, and the Second Circuit affirmed. *See Random House, Inc. v. Rosetta Books LLC*, 150 F. Supp. 2d 613 (S.D.N.Y. 2001), *aff'd*, 283 F.3d 490 (2d Cir. 2002). Should a court interpret the terms of such contracts narrowly (limiting the contract to the literal media described in the agreement) or more expansively, seeking to gauge the larger intent and bargaining positions of the parties and consider knowledge available at the time of interpretation?

Publishers that have had to deal with these cases have responded by drafting extremely broad language, such as that conferring "all rights in any medium now known or later conceived anywhere in the known universe."

2. Limitations on the Distribution Right: The First Sale Doctrine

Congress carved out an important limitation on the exclusive right to distribute: the "first sale doctrine."

> Notwithstanding the provisions of section 106(3), the owner of a particular copy or phonorecord lawfully made under this title, or any person authorized

by such owner, is entitled, without the authority of the copyright owner, to sell
or otherwise dispose of the possession of that copy or phonorecord.

17 U.S.C. § 109(a). This doctrine parallels the Patent Act's "exhaustion principle." The
purchaser/recipient of an authorized copy may resell, lease, donate, or dispose of it
without restriction, but may not copy it. In response to the availability of home copying
technologies (cassette tape recorders and microcomputers), Congress limited the first
sale doctrine by prohibiting the rental of phonorecords and computer programs for
profit, fearing that the primary effect of such rentals was to encourage piracy. *See*
§ 109(b).

Courts have struggled with the interplay of the first sale doctrine with the § 602
import right. Manufacturers often sell goods in multiple national markets, sometimes
pricing goods differently depending upon supply (e.g., cost of manufacturing locally,
advertising expense, provision of repair or other services) and demand conditions (e.g.,
income, tastes, availability of substitutes). Copyright owners believed that § 602
afforded them the ability to preserve this ability to maintain price differentials across
national borders by prohibiting the importation of authorized sales in foreign markets.
But can purchasers of authorized copyrighted goods in foreign countries invoke the first
sale doctrine to bring them into the United States for resale? An enterprising graduate
student from Thailand tested this proposition.

Kirtsaeng v. John Wiley & Sons, Inc.
Supreme Court of the United States
568 S.Ct. 519 (2013)

JUSTICE BREYER delivered the opinion of the Court.

Section 106 of the Copyright Act grants "the owner of copyright under this title"
certain "exclusive rights," including the right "to distribute copies . . . of the copyrighted
work to the public by sale or other transfer of ownership." 17 U.S.C. § 106(3). These
rights are qualified, however, by the application of various limitations set forth in the
next several sections of the Act, §§ 107 through 122. Those sections, typically entitled
"Limitations on exclusive rights," include, for example, the principle of "fair use"
(§ 107), permission for limited library archival reproduction, (§ 108), and the doctrine
at issue here, the "first sale" doctrine (§ 109).

Section 109(a) sets forth the "first sale" doctrine as follows:

"Notwithstanding the provisions of section 106(3) [the section that grants
the owner exclusive distribution rights], the owner of a particular copy or
phonorecord *lawfully made under this title* . . . is entitled, without the authority
of the copyright owner, to sell or otherwise dispose of the possession of that
copy or phonorecord." (Emphasis added.)

Thus, even though § 106(3) forbids distribution of a copy of, say, the copyrighted
novel Herzog without the copyright owner's permission, § 109(a) adds that, once a copy
of Herzog has been lawfully sold (or its ownership otherwise lawfully transferred), the
buyer of *that copy* and subsequent owners are free to dispose of it as they wish. In

copyright jargon, the "first sale" has "exhausted" the copyright owner's § 106(3) exclusive distribution right.

What, however, if the copy of Herzog was printed abroad and then initially sold with the copyright owner's permission? Does the "first sale" doctrine still apply? Is the buyer, like the buyer of a domestically manufactured copy, free to bring the copy into the United States and dispose of it as he or she wishes?

To put the matter technically, an "importation" provision, § 602(a)(1), says that

"[i]mportation into the United States, without the authority of the owner of copyright under this title, of copies . . . of a work that have been acquired outside the United States is an infringement of the exclusive right to distribute copies . . . *under section 106*. . . ." (emphasis added).

Thus § 602(a)(1) makes clear that importing a copy without permission violates the owner's exclusive distribution right. But in doing so, § 602(a)(1) refers explicitly to the § 106(3) exclusive distribution right. As we have just said, § 106 is by its terms "[s]ubject to" the various doctrines and principles contained in §§ 107 through 122, including § 109(a)'s "first sale" limitation. Do those same modifications apply—in particular, does the "first sale" modification apply—when considering whether § 602(a)(1) prohibits importing a copy?

[W]e ask whether the "first sale" doctrine applies to protect a buyer or other lawful owner of a copy (of a copyrighted work) lawfully manufactured abroad. Can that buyer bring that copy into the United States (and sell it or give it away) without obtaining permission to do so from the copyright owner? Can, for example, someone who purchases, say at a used bookstore, a book printed abroad subsequently resell it without the copyright owner's permission?

In our view, the answers to these questions are, yes. We hold that the "first sale" doctrine applies to copies of a copyrighted work lawfully made abroad.

I

A

Respondent, John Wiley & Sons, Inc., publishes academic textbooks. Wiley obtains from its authors various foreign and domestic copyright assignments, licenses and permissions—to the point that we can, for present purposes, refer to Wiley as the relevant American copyright owner. Wiley often assigns to its wholly owned foreign subsidiary, John Wiley & Sons (Asia) Pte Ltd., rights to publish, print, and sell Wiley's English language textbooks abroad. Each copy of a Wiley Asia foreign edition will likely contain language making clear that the copy is to be sold only in a particular country or geographical region outside the United States. . . .

Petitioner, Supap Kirtsaeng, a citizen of Thailand, moved to the United States in 1997. . . . While he was studying in the United States, Kirtsaeng asked his friends and family in Thailand to buy copies of foreign edition English-language textbooks at Thai book shops, where they sold at low prices, and mail them to him in the United States.

Kirtsaeng would then sell them, reimburse his family and friends, and keep the profit. . . .

II

We must decide whether the words "lawfully made under this title" restrict the scope of § 109(a)'s "first sale" doctrine geographically. The Second Circuit, the Ninth Circuit, Wiley, and the Solicitor General (as *amicus*) all read those words as imposing a form of *geographical* limitation. The Second Circuit held that they limit the "first sale" doctrine to particular copies "made in territories *in which the Copyright Act is law*," which (the Circuit says) are copies "manufactured domestically," not "outside of the United States." (emphasis added). . . .

Under [this] geographical interpretation[], § 109(a)'s "first sale" doctrine would not apply to the Wiley Asia books at issue here. And, despite an American copyright owner's permission to *make* copies abroad, one who *buys* a copy of any such book or other copyrighted work—whether at a retail store, over the Internet, or at a library sale— could not resell (or otherwise dispose of) that particular copy without further permission.

Kirtsaeng, however, reads the words "lawfully made under this title" as imposing a *non*-geographical limitation. He says that they mean made "in accordance with" or "in compliance with" the Copyright Act. In that case, § 109(a)'s "first sale" doctrine would apply to copyrighted works as long as their manufacture met the requirements of American copyright law. In particular, the doctrine would apply where, as here, copies are manufactured abroad with the permission of the copyright owner. *See* § 106 (referring to the owner's right to authorize).

In our view, § 109(a)'s language, its context, and the common-law history of the "first sale" doctrine, taken together, favor a *non*-geographical interpretation. We also doubt that Congress would have intended to create the practical copyright-related harms with which a geographical interpretation would threaten ordinary scholarly, artistic, commercial, and consumer activities. We consequently conclude that Kirt-saeng's nongeographical reading is the better reading of the Act.

A

The language of § 109(a) read literally favors Kirtsaeng's nongeographical interpretation, namely, that "lawfully made under this title" means made "in accordance with" or "in compliance with" the Copyright Act. The language of § 109(a) says nothing about geography. The word "under" can mean "[i]n accordance with." 18 Oxford English Dictionary 950 (2d ed. 1989). *See also* Black's Law Dictionary 1525 (6th ed. 1990) ("according to"). And a nongeographical interpretation provides each word of the five-word phrase with a distinct purpose. The first two words of the phrase, "lawfully made," suggest an effort to distinguish those copies that were made lawfully from those that were not, and the last three words, "under this title," set forth the standard of "lawful[ness]." Thus, the nongeographical reading is simple, it promotes a traditional copyright objective (combatting piracy), and it makes word-by-word linguistic sense.

The geographical interpretation, however, bristles with linguistic difficulties. It gives the word "lawfully" little, if any, linguistic work to do. (How could a book be *un*lawfully "made under this title"?) It imports geography into a statutory provision that says nothing explicitly about it. And it is far more complex than may at first appear.

To read the clause geographically, Wiley . . . must first emphasize the word "under." Indeed, Wiley reads "under this title" to mean "in conformance with the Copyright Act *where the Copyright Act is applicable.*" Wiley must then take a second step, arguing that the Act "is applicable" only in the United States. . . .

One difficulty is that neither "under" nor any other word in the phrase means "where." It might mean "subject to," but as this Court has repeatedly acknowledged, the word evades a uniform, consistent meaning. *See Kucana v. Holder*, 558 U.S. 233, 245 (2010) ("'under' is chameleon"); *Ardestani v. INS*, 502 U.S. 129, 135 (1991) ("under" has "many dictionary definitions" and "must draw its meaning from its context"). . . .

B

Both historical and contemporary statutory context indicate that Congress, when writing the present version of § 109(a), did not have geography in mind. In respect to history, we compare § 109(a)'s present language with the language of its immediate predecessor. That predecessor said:

> "[N]othing in this Act shall be deemed to forbid, prevent, or restrict the transfer of any copy of a copyrighted work *the possession of which has been lawfully obtained.*" Copyright Act of 1909, § 41, 35 Stat. 1084 (emphasis added).

The predecessor says nothing about geography (and Wiley does not argue that it does). So we ask whether Congress, in changing its language implicitly *introduced* a geographical limitation that previously was lacking.

A comparison of language indicates that it did not. The predecessor says that the "first sale" doctrine protects "the transfer of any copy *the possession of which has been lawfully obtained.*" The present version says that "*the owner* of a particular copy or phonorecord lawfully made under this title is entitled to sell or otherwise dispose of the possession of that copy or phonorecord." . . .

Section 109(a) now makes clear that a lessee of a copy will *not* receive "first sale" protection but one who *owns* a copy *will* receive "first sale" protection, *provided,* of course, that the copy was "*lawfully made*" and not pirated. . . .

Finally, we normally presume that the words "lawfully made under this title" carry the same meaning when they appear in different but related sections. But doing so here produces surprising consequences. Consider:

(1) Section 109(c) says that, despite the copyright owner's exclusive right "to display" a copyrighted work (provided in § 106(5)), the owner of a particular copy "lawfully made under this title" may publicly display it without further authorization. To interpret these words geographically would mean that one who buys a copyrighted work of art, a poster, or even a bumper sticker, in Canada, in Europe, in Asia, could not display it in America without the copyright owner's further authorization.

(2) Section 109(e) specifically provides that the owner of a particular copy of a copyrighted video arcade game "lawfully made under this title" may "publicly perform or display that game in coin-operated equipment" without the authorization of the copyright owner. To interpret these words geographically means that an arcade owner could not ("without the authority of the copyright owner") perform or display arcade games (whether new or used) originally made in Japan.

(3) Section 110(1) says that a teacher, without the copyright owner's authorization, is allowed to perform or display a copyrighted work (say, an audiovisual work) "in the course of face-to-face teaching activities"—unless the teacher knowingly used "a copy that was not lawfully made under this title." To interpret these words geographically would mean that the teacher could not (without further authorization) use a copy of a film during class if the copy was lawfully made in Canada, Mexico, Europe, Africa, or Asia.

(4) In its introductory sentence, § 106 provides the Act's basic exclusive rights to an "owner of a copyright under this title." The last three words cannot support a geographic interpretation.

Wiley basically accepts the first three readings, but argues that Congress intended the restrictive consequences. And it argues that context simply requires that the words of the fourth example receive a different interpretation. Leaving the fourth example to the side, we shall explain in Part II-D why we find it unlikely that Congress would have intended these, and other related consequences.

C

A relevant canon of statutory interpretation favors a nongeographical reading. "[W]hen a statute covers an issue previously governed by the common law," we must presume that "Congress intended to retain the substance of the common law." *Samantar v. Yousuf*, 560 U.S. 305, 320, n.13 (2010). . . .

The "first sale" doctrine is a common-law doctrine with an impeccable historic pedigree. In the early 17th century Lord Coke explained the common law's refusal to permit restraints on the alienation of chattels. . . .

. . . Coke emphasizes the importance of leaving buyers of goods free to compete with each other when reselling or otherwise disposing of those goods. American law too has generally thought that competition, including freedom to resell, can work to the advantage of the consumer. *See, e.g., Leegin Creative Leather Products, Inc. v. PSKS, Inc.,* 551 U.S. 877, 886 (2007) (restraints with "manifestly anticompetitive effects" are *per se* illegal; others are subject to the rule of reason (internal quotation marks omitted)); 1 P. AREEDA & H. HOVENKAMP, ANTITRUST LAW ¶ 100, p. 4 (3d ed. 2006) ("[T]he principal objective of antitrust policy is to maximize consumer welfare by encouraging firms to behave competitively").

The "first sale" doctrine also frees courts from the administrative burden of trying to enforce restrictions upon difficult-to-trace, readily movable goods. And it avoids the selective enforcement inherent in any such effort. Thus, it is not surprising that for at least a century the "first sale" doctrine has played an important role in American copyright law. *See Bobbs-Merrill Co. v. Straus*, 210 U.S. 339 (1908); Copyright Act of 1909, § 41, 35 Stat. 1084. . . .

The common-law doctrine makes no geographical distinctions; nor can we find any in *Bobbs-Merrill* (where this Court first applied the "first sale" doctrine) or in § 109(a)'s predecessor provision, which Congress enacted a year later. . . .

D

Associations of libraries, used-book dealers, technology companies, consumer goods retailers, and museums point to various ways in which a geographical interpretation would fail to further basic constitutional copyright objectives, in particular "promot[ing] the Progress of Science and useful Arts." U.S. CONST., Art. I, § 8, cl. 8.

The American Library Association tells us that library collections contain at least 200 million books published abroad (presumably, many were first published in one of the nearly 180 copyright-treaty nations and enjoy American copyright protection under 17 U.S.C. § 104); that many others were first published in the United States but printed abroad because of lower costs; and that a geographical interpretation will likely require the libraries to obtain permission (or at least create significant uncertainty) before circulating or otherwise distributing these books.

How, the American Library Association asks, are the libraries to obtain permission to distribute these millions of books? How can they find, say, the copyright owner of a foreign book, perhaps written decades ago? . . . Are the libraries to stop circulating or distributing or displaying the millions of books in their collections that were printed abroad?

Used-book dealers tell us that, from the time when Benjamin Franklin and Thomas Jefferson built commercial and personal libraries of foreign books, American readers have bought used books published and printed abroad. The dealers say that they have "operat[ed] . . . for centuries" under the assumption that the "first sale" doctrine applies. But under a geographical interpretation a contemporary tourist who buys, say, at Shakespeare and Co. (in Paris), a dozen copies of a foreign book for American friends might find that she had violated the copyright law. . . .

Technology companies tell us that "automobiles, microwaves, calculators, mobile phones, tablets, and personal computers" contain copyrightable software programs or packaging. Many of these items are made abroad with the American copyright holder's permission and then sold and imported (with that permission) to the United States. A geographical interpretation would prevent the resale of, say, a car, without the permission of the holder of each copyright on each piece of copyrighted automobile software. . . .

Art museum directors ask us to consider their efforts to display foreign-produced works by, say, Cy Twombly, René Magritte, Henri Matisse, Pablo Picasso, and others. A geographical interpretation, they say, would require the museums to obtain permission from the copyright owners before they could display the work—even if the copyright owner has already sold or donated the work to a foreign museum. What are the museums to do, they ask, if the artist retained the copyright, if the artist cannot be found, or if a group of heirs is arguing about who owns which copyright?

These examples, and others previously mentioned, help explain *why* Lord Coke considered the "first sale" doctrine necessary to protect "Trade and Traffi[c], and bargaining and contracting," and they help explain *why* American copyright law has long applied that doctrine.

Neither Wiley nor any of its many *amici* deny that a geographical interpretation could bring about these "horribles"—at least in principle. . . .

For these reasons we conclude that the considerations supporting Kirtsaeng's nongeographical interpretation of the words "lawfully made under this title" are the more persuasive. The judgment of the Court of Appeals is reversed, and the case is remanded for further proceedings consistent with this opinion.

It is so ordered.

JUSTICE GINSBURG, with whom JUSTICE KENNEDY joins, and with whom JUSTICE SCALIA joins except as to Parts III and V-B-1, dissenting.

"In the interpretation of statutes, the function of the courts is easily stated. It is to construe the language so as to give effect to the intent of Congress." Instead of adhering to the Legislature's design, the Court today adopts an interpretation of the Copyright Act at odds with Congress' aim to protect copyright owners against the unauthorized importation of low-priced, foreign-made copies of their copyrighted works. The Court's bold departure from Congress' design is all the more stunning, for it places the United States at the vanguard of the movement for "international exhaustion" of copyrights— a movement the United States has steadfastly resisted on the world stage.

To justify a holding that shrinks to insignificance copyright protection against the unauthorized importation of foreign-made copies, the Court identifies several "practical problems." The Court's parade of horribles, however, is largely imaginary. Congress' objective in enacting 17 U.S.C. § 602(a)(1)'s importation prohibition can be honored without generating the absurd consequences hypothesized in the Court's opinion. I dissent from the Court's embrace of "international exhaustion." . . .

Because economic conditions and demand for particular goods vary across the globe, copyright owners have a financial incentive to charge different prices for copies of their works in different geographic regions. Their ability to engage in such price discrimination, however, is undermined if arbitrageurs are permitted to import copies from low-price regions and sell them in high-price regions. The question in this case is whether the unauthorized importation of foreign-made copies constitutes copyright infringement under U.S. law. . . .

The text of the Copyright Act demonstrates that Congress intended to provide copyright owners with a potent remedy against the importation of foreign-made copies of their copyrighted works. . . .

The Court's point of departure is similar to mine. According to the Court, the phrase "'lawfully made under this title' means made 'in accordance with' or 'in compliance with' the Copyright Act." But the Court overlooks that, according to the very dictionaries it cites, the word "under" commonly signals a relationship of subjection, where one thing is governed or regulated by another. *See* BLACK'S LAW DICTIONARY 1525 (6th ed. 1990) ("under" frequently means "inferior" or "subordinate"; 18 OXFORD ENGLISH DICTIONARY 950 (2d ed. 1989) ("under" means, among other things, "[i]n accordance with (*some regulative power or principle*)" (emphasis added)). Only by disregarding this established meaning of "under" can the Court arrive at the conclusion that Wiley's foreign-manufactured textbooks were "lawfully made under" U.S. copyright law, even though that law did not govern their creation. It is anomalous, however, to speak of particular conduct as "lawful" under an inapplicable law. For example, one might say that driving on the right side of the road in England is "lawful" under U.S. law, but that would be so only because U.S. law has nothing to say about the subject. The governing law is English law, and English law demands that driving be done on the left side of the road. . . .

The Court . . . interprets § 109(a) as applying only to copies whose making actually complied with Title 17, or would have complied with Title 17 had Title 17 been applicable (*i.e.*, had the copies been made in the United States). Congress, however, used express language when it called for such a counterfactual inquiry in 17 U.S.C. §§ 602(a)(2) and (b). *See* § 602(a)(2) ("Importation into the United States or exportation from the United States, without the authority of the owner of copyright under this title, of copies or phonorecords, the making of which either constituted an infringement of copyright, or *which would have constituted an infringement of copyright if this title had been applicable,* is an infringement of the exclusive right to distribute copies or phonorecords under section 106." (emphasis added)); § 602(b) ("In a case where the making of the copies or phonorecords *would have constituted an infringement of copyright if this title had been applicable,* their importation is prohibited." (emphasis added)). Had Congress intended courts to engage in a similarly hypothetical inquiry under § 109(a), Congress would presumably have included similar language in that section. *See Russello v. United States,* 464 U.S. 16, 23 (1983) ("'[W]here Congress includes particular language in one section of a statute but omits it in another section of the same Act, it is generally presumed that Congress acts intentionally and purposely in the disparate inclusion or exclusion.'").

Not only does the Court adopt an unnatural construction of the § 109(a) phrase "lawfully made under this title." Concomitantly, the Court reduces § 602(a)(1) to insignificance. As the Court appears to acknowledge, the only independent effect § 602(a)(1) has under today's decision is to prohibit unauthorized importations carried out by persons who merely have possession of, but do not own, the imported copies. *See* 17 U.S.C. § 109(a) (§ 109(a) applies to any "*owner* of a particular copy or phonorecord lawfully made under this title" (emphasis added)). If this is enough to avoid rendering § 602(a)(1) entirely "superfluous," it hardly suffices to give the owner's importation right the scope Congress intended it to have. Congress used broad language in § 602(a)(1); it did so to achieve a broad objective. Had Congress intended simply to provide a copyright remedy against larcenous lessees, licensees, consignees, and bailees of films and other copyright-protected goods, it likely would have used language tailored to that narrow purpose. . . .

III

The history of § 602(a)(1) reinforces the conclusion I draw from the text of the relevant provisions: § 109(a) does not apply to copies manufactured abroad. Section 602(a)(1) was enacted as part of the Copyright Act of 1976. . . .

"Section 602 [deals] with two separate situations: importation of 'piratical' articles (that is, copies or phonorecords made without any authorization of the copyright owner), and unauthorized importation of copies or phonorecords that were lawfully made. *The general approach of section 602 is to make unauthorized importation an act of infringement in both cases,* but to permit the Bureau of Customs to prohibit importation only of 'piratical' articles." S. REP. NO. 94–473, p. 151 (1975) (emphasis added). *See also* H.R. REP. NO. 94–1476, p. 169 (1976) (same).

In sum, the legislative history of the Copyright Act of 1976 is hardly "inconclusive." To the contrary, it confirms what the plain text of the Act conveys: Congress intended § 602(a)(1) to provide copyright owners with a remedy against the unauthorized importation of foreign-made copies of their works, even if those copies were made and sold abroad with the copyright owner's authorization.

IV

Unlike the Court's holding, my position is consistent with the stance the United States has taken in international-trade negotiations. . . .

V

I turn now to the Court's justifications for a decision difficult to reconcile with the Copyright Act's text and history. . . .

B

The Court sees many "horribles" following from a holding that the § 109(a) phrase "lawfully made under this title" does not encompass foreign-made copies. If § 109(a) excluded foreign-made copies, the Court fears, then copyright owners could exercise perpetual control over the downstream distribution or public display of such copies. A ruling in Wiley's favor, the Court asserts, would shutter libraries, put used-book dealers out of business, cripple art museums, and prevent the resale of a wide range of consumer goods, from cars to calculators. Copyright law and precedent, however, erect barriers to the anticipated horribles.

1

Recognizing that foreign-made copies fall outside the ambit of § 109(a) would not mean they are forever free of the first sale doctrine. . . .

Under the logic of *Bobbs-Merrill*, the sale of a foreign-manufactured copy in the United States carried out with the copyright owner's authorization would exhaust the copyright owner's right to "vend" that copy. The copy could thenceforth be resold, lent out, or otherwise redistributed without further authorization from the copyright owner. . . .

2

Other statutory prescriptions provide further protection against the absurd consequences imagined by the Court. For example, § 602(a)(3)(C) permits "an organization operated for scholarly, educational, or religious purposes" to import, without the copyright owner's authorization, up to five foreign-made copies of a non-audiovisual work—notably, a book—for "library lending or archival purposes."

The Court also notes that *amici* representing art museums fear that a ruling in Wiley's favor would prevent museums from displaying works of art created abroad. . . .

Limiting § 109(c) to U.S.-made works, however, does not bar art museums from lawfully displaying works made in other countries. Museums can, of course, seek the copyright owner's permission to display a work. Furthermore, the sale of a work of art to a U.S. museum may carry with it an implied license to publicly display the work. . . .

The Court worries about the resale of foreign-made consumer goods "contain[ing] copyrightable software programs or packaging." For example, the Court observes that a car might be programmed with diverse forms of software, the copyrights to which might be owned by individuals or entities other than the manufacturer of the car. Must a car owner, the Court asks, obtain permission from all of these various copyright owners before reselling her car? Although this question strays far from the one presented in this case and briefed by the parties, principles of fair use and implied license (to the extent that express licenses do not exist) would likely permit the car to be resold without the copyright owners' authorization. . . .

COMMENTS AND QUESTIONS

1. How would you characterize each of the opinion writer's approach to statutory interpretation? Does Justice Breyer adequately address Justice Ginsburg's analysis of the Copyright Act's text (e.g., § 602)) and legislative history? Who has the better policy argument? Is the Supreme Court the appropriate institution to resolve the policy question?

2. *Interaction of the First Sale Doctrine and the Right to Prepare Derivative Works: Art Tiles.* Can the purchaser of cards and books containing artwork mount and affix the pictures to ceramic tiles for later sale? The Ninth Circuit has held that the process of attaching art from a book onto ceramic tiles constituted the preparation of a derivative work. *See Mirage Editions, Inc. v. Albuquerque A.R.T. Co.*, 856 F.2d 1341 (9th Cir. 1988). In rejecting a first sale defense, the court recognized that the defendant could purchase a copy of the plaintiff's book and subsequently alienate its ownership in that book. "However, the right to transfer applies only to the particular copy of the book which appellant has purchased and nothing else. The mere sale of the book to the

appellant without a specific transfer by the copyright holder of its exclusive right to prepare derivative works, does not transfer that right to appellant. The derivative works right remains unimpaired and with the copyright proprietors." *Id.* at 1344. On nearly identical facts involving the same defendant, the Seventh Circuit reached a contrary result, holding that the mere mounting of pictures on tiles did not rise to the level of originality required to create a derivative work and that the first sale doctrine immunizes the defendants from liability for unauthorized distribution. *See Lee v. A.R.T. Company*, 125 F.3d 580 (7th Cir. 1997).

Do you agree with the reasoning of the Seventh Circuit or Ninth Circuit in the A.R.T. cases? Is it possible to envision circumstances under which framing a work of art involves original, creative expression? Even if it is, should the copyright owner be entitled to control how the work is framed once it has been sold?

3. *Software Marketing and "License versus Sale."* As a means of controlling post-transaction use of software programs, many software vendors have characterized the distribution of their products as "licenses" rather than "sales" and argued that the first sale doctrine accordingly does not apply. Should the rights conferred by copyright turn on the title given to the agreement? In *Softman Products Co., LLC v. Adobe Systems, Inc.*, 171 F. Supp. 2d 1075 (C.D. Cal. 2001), a software distributor had lawfully acquired a retail collection of Adobe software products and then unbundled them for later sale in violation of the terms of an End User Licensing Agreement (EULA), which prohibited the distribution of individual software titles that were originally distributed as part of a collection. Looking to the "economic realities of the exchange" by which Softman acquired the Adobe product, the court determined that "a single payment giving the buyer an unlimited period in which it has a right to possession . . . is a sale." As such, the court found that the first sale doctrine superseded the EULA. *See* Nancy S. Kim, *The Software Licensing Dilemma*, 2008 B.Y.U. L. REV. 1103 (2008); David A. Rice, *Licensing the Use of Computer Program Copies and the Copyright Act First Sale Doctrine*, 30 JURIMETRICS J. 157, 172 (1990) (noting the following factors in characterizing a software transaction as a sale rather than a license: temporally unlimited possession; absence of time limits on copy possession; pricing and payment schemes that are unitary, not serial; subsequent transfer is neither prohibited nor conditioned on obtaining the licensor's prior approval; and the principal purpose of the use restrictions is to protect intangible copyrightable subject matter and not to preserve property interests in individual program copies).

By contrast, in *Vernor v. Autodesk Inc.*, 621 F.3d 1102 (9th Cir. 2010), the court found that Autodesk had licensed, not sold, copies of its software, and so the first sale doctrine did not apply. The court focused particular attention on whether the agreement imposed restrictions on the use and transfer of the software:

> We hold today that a software user is a licensee rather than an owner of a copy where the copyright owner (1) specifies that the user is granted a license; (2) significantly restricts the user's ability to transfer the software; and (3) imposes notable use restrictions.

Id. at 1111. The court pointed to limitations on transfer in the license agreement. Should it matter whether those limitations are ever enforced? After *Vernor*, can a software company always draft an agreement that will avoid the first sale doctrine? Does *Vernor* survive the *Kirtsaeng* decision?

4. *Does Distribution of Promotional Copies Trigger the First Sale Doctrine?* Record labels and textbook publishers routinely distribute free copies of their copyrighted works to radio stations and university professors as a way of promoting air play and adoption for classroom use. But they do not want to have those copies resold, as such copies could displace direct sales. They have sought to preclude that result by including a notice on the promotional goods stating "Promotional Use Only—Not for Sale." In *UMG Recordings, Inc. v. Augusto*, 628 F.3d 1175 (9th Cir. 2011), the court rejected UMG's argument that such notice labels create a "license" that is not subject to the first sale doctrine. Looking to the "economic realities" of the transaction—including the effective passage of title, the fact that UMG does not expect to regain possession of the goods, the absence of a recurring benefit to UMG—the court found that UMG's distribution of the CDs was properly characterized as a gift or sale to which the first sale doctrine applied. Hence, the recipient was free to resell or distribute the copy.

5. *Digital Exhaustion.* As the digital revolution unfolds, a growing portion of information goods—from music to books and even the software that runs automobiles—comes to consumers digitally. Such information is typically licensed and increasingly updated automatically and remotely. Should such information goods be subject to the first sale doctrine? Should music downloads be resellable? How would the copyright owner be able to verify that a digital good had been erased from the seller's device? *See Capitol Records, LLC v. ReDigi, Inc.*, 910 F.3d 649 (2d Cir. 2018) (holding that ReDigi, a "used" digital download reseller, and its customers were not protected by the first sale doctrine because ReDigi's process for transferring files effectuates an unlawful reproduction of the copyrighted work). The Court of Justice of the European Union held the same in 2019. *See Nederlands Uitgeversverbond v. Tom Kabinet Internet BV*, C-263/18 (C.J.E.U. 2019).

The role of the first sale doctrine in the digital age has generated robust policy debate. *See* U.S. DEPARTMENT OF COMMERCE INTERNET POLICY TASK FORCE, WHITE PAPER ON REMIXES, FIRST SALE, AND STATUTORY DAMAGES (Jan. 2016); U.S. COPYRIGHT OFFICE, LIBRARY OF CONG., THE MAKING AVAILABLE RIGHT IN THE UNITED STATES 22, n.94 (2016); AARON PERZANOWSKI & JASON SCHULTZ, THE END OF OWNERSHIP: PERSONAL PROPERTY IN THE DIGITAL ECONOMY (2018); John F. Duffy & Richard Hynes, *Statutory Domain and the Commercial Law of Intellectual Property*, 102 VA. L. REV. 1 (2016).

PROBLEM

Problem IV-37. Lee, a law student, attends an expensive private school. After buying the books for his first-year classes, he underlines key passages in the books and takes some notes in the margins. At the end of the first year of law school, Lee sells his books back to the law school bookstore. The bookstore in turn sells them to incoming law students the next fall as "used books." Under what theory might Lee or the bookstore be liable for copyright infringement? Should they be?

---

d. Public Performance Right

The Copyright Act grants owners of literary, musical, dramatic, and choreographic works, pantomimes, and motion pictures and other audiovisual works the exclusive right to perform their works publicly. *See* § 106(4).

1. What Constitutes a "Public Performance"?

Section 101 defines "perform" broadly:

To "perform" a work means to recite, render, play, dance, or act it, either directly or by means of any device or process or, in the case of a motion picture or other audiovisual work, to show its images in any sequence or to make the sounds accompanying it audible.

The limitation to "public" performances, however, prevents many commonplace activities from infringing performance and display rights. The definition of a public performance or display is set forth in § 101:

To perform or display a work "publicly" means—

(1) to perform or display it at a place open to the public or at any place where a substantial number of persons outside of a normal circle of a family and its social acquaintances is gathered; or

(2) to transmit or otherwise communicate a performance or display of the work to a place specified by clause (1) or to the public, by means of any device or process, whether the members of the public capable of receiving the performance or display receive it in the same place or in separate places and at the same time or at different times.

Under this definition, you can probably have a (small) party at which you play a lawfully-acquired CD or video. Large parties—if they go beyond the amorphous category of your "social acquaintances"—may pose problems. Furthermore, if the place of performance or display is "open to the public," it does not appear to matter how many people actually view the performance. Clause (2) appears to cover all broadcasts to the "public" even if members of the public do not view the copyrighted work at the same place or time. Thus, a television broadcast is a performance, even though no one may watch it at all, or if people watch it only in the privacy of their own homes.

American Broadcasting Companies, Inc. v. Aereo, Inc.
U.S. Supreme Court
134 S.Ct. 2498 (2014)

JUSTICE BREYER delivered the opinion of the Court.

The Copyright Act of 1976 gives a copyright owner the "exclusive righ[t]" to "perform the copyrighted work publicly." 17 U.S.C. § 106(4). The Act's Transmit Clause defines that exclusive right as including the right to

> "transmit or otherwise communicate a performance . . . of the [copyrighted] work . . . to the public, by means of any device or process, whether the members of the public capable of receiving the performance . . . receive it in the same place or in separate places and at the same time or at different times." § 101.

We must decide whether respondent Aereo, Inc., infringes this exclusive right by selling its subscribers a technologically complex service that allows them to watch television programs over the Internet at about the same time as the programs are broadcast over the air. We conclude that it does.

I

A

For a monthly fee, Aereo offers subscribers broadcast television programming over the Internet, virtually as the programming is being broadcast. Much of this programming is made up of copyrighted works. Aereo neither owns the copyright in those works nor holds a license from the copyright owners to perform those works publicly.

Aereo's system is made up of servers, transcoders, and thousands of dime-sized antennas housed in a central warehouse. It works roughly as follows: First, when a subscriber wants to watch a show that is currently being broadcast, he visits Aereo's website and selects, from a list of the local programming, the show he wishes to see.

Second, one of Aereo's servers selects an antenna, which it dedicates to the use of that subscriber (and that subscriber alone) for the duration of the selected show. A server then tunes the antenna to the over-the-air broadcast carrying the show. The antenna begins to receive the broadcast, and an Aereo transcoder translates the signals received into data that can be transmitted over the Internet.

Third, rather than directly send the data to the subscriber, a server saves the data in a subscriber-specific folder on Aereo's hard drive. In other words, Aereo's system creates a subscriber-specific copy—that is, a "personal" copy—of the subscriber's program of choice.

Fourth, once several seconds of programming have been saved, Aereo's server begins to stream the saved copy of the show to the subscriber over the Internet. (The subscriber may instead direct Aereo to stream the program at a later time, but that aspect of Aereo's service is not before us.) The subscriber can watch the streamed program on the screen of his personal computer, tablet, smart phone, Internet-connected television, or other Internet-connected device. The streaming continues, a mere few seconds behind the over-the-air broadcast, until the subscriber has received the entire show.

Aereo emphasizes that the data that its system streams to each subscriber are the data from his own personal copy, made from the broadcast signals received by the particular antenna allotted to him. . . .

B

Petitioners are television producers, marketers, distributors, and broadcasters who own the copyrights in many of the programs that Aereo's system streams to its subscribers. . . .

II

This case requires us to answer two questions: First, in operating in the manner described above, does Aereo "perform" at all? And second, if so, does Aereo do so "publicly"? We address these distinct questions in turn. . . .

A

History makes plain that one of Congress' primary purposes in amending the Copyright Act in 1976 was to overturn this Court's determination that community antenna television (CATV) systems (the precursors of modern cable systems) fell outside the Act's scope. [The Court reviewed Fortnightly Corp. v. United Artists Television, Inc., 392 U.S. 390 1176 (1968), and Teleprompter Corp. v. Columbia Broadcasting System, Inc., 415 U.S. 394 (1974), both of which held that CATV systems were more analogous to viewers who amplify a signal, and hence do not perform copyrighted works, than broadcasters, who exercise significant creativity in choosing what to air and hence perform copyrighted works).]

B

In 1976 Congress amended the Copyright Act in large part to reject the Court's holdings in *Fortnightly* and *Teleprompter*. *See* H.R. REP. NO. 94-1476, pp. 86–87 (1976) (hereinafter H.R. Rep.). Congress enacted new language that erased the Court's line between broadcaster and viewer, in respect to "perform[ing]" a work. The amended statute clarifies that to "perform" an audiovisual work means "to show its images in any sequence or to make the sounds accompanying it audible." § 101; *see ibid.* (defining "[a]udiovisual works" as "works that consist of a series of related images which are intrinsically intended to be shown by the use of machines . . . , together with accompanying sounds"). Under this new language, both the broadcaster and the viewer of a television program "perform," because they both show the program's images and make audible the program's sounds. *See* H.R. Rep., at 63 ("[A] broadcasting network is performing when it transmits [a singer's performance of a song] . . . and any individual is performing whenever he or she . . . communicates the performance by turning on a receiving set").

Congress also enacted the Transmit Clause, which specifies that an entity performs publicly when it "transmit[s] . . . a performance . . . to the public." § 101; *see ibid.* (defining "[t]o 'transmit' a performance" as "to communicate it by any device or process whereby images or sounds are received beyond the place from which they are sent"). Cable system activities, like those of the CATV systems in *Fortnightly* and *Teleprompter*, lie at the heart of the activities that Congress intended this language to cover. *See* H.R. Rep., at 63 ("[A] cable television system is performing when it retransmits [a network] broadcast to its subscribers"); *see also ibid.* ("[T]he concep[t] of public performance . . . cover[s] not only the initial rendition or showing, but also any further act by which that rendition or showing is transmitted or communicated to the public"). The Clause thus makes clear that an entity that acts like a CATV system itself performs, even if when doing so, it simply enhances viewers' ability to receive broadcast television signals.

Congress further created a new section of the Act to regulate cable companies' public performances of copyrighted works. *See* § 111. Section 111 creates a complex, highly detailed compulsory licensing scheme that sets out the conditions, including the payment of compulsory fees, under which cable systems may retransmit broadcasts. H.R. Rep., at 88 (Section 111 is primarily "directed at the operation of cable television systems and the terms and conditions of their liability for the retransmission of copyrighted works").

Congress made these three changes to achieve a similar end: to bring the activities of cable systems within the scope of the Copyright Act.

C

This history makes clear that Aereo is not simply an equipment provider. Rather, Aereo, and not just its subscribers, "perform[s]" (or "transmit[s]"). Aereo's activities are substantially similar to those of the CATV companies that Congress amended the Act to reach. *See id.*, at 89 ("[C]able systems are commercial enterprises whose basic retransmission operations are based on the carriage of copyrighted program material"). Aereo sells a service that allows subscribers to watch television programs, many of which are copyrighted, almost as they are being broadcast. In providing this service, Aereo uses its own equipment, housed in a centralized warehouse, outside of its users' homes. By means of its technology (antennas, transcoders, and servers), Aereo's system "receive[s] programs that have been released to the public and carr[ies] them by private channels to additional viewers." *Fortnightly*, 392 U.S., at 400. It "carr[ies] . . . whatever programs [it] receive[s]," and it offers "all the programming" of each over-the-air station it carries. *Id.*, at 392, 400.

Aereo's equipment may serve a "viewer function"; it may enhance the viewer's ability to receive a broadcaster's programs. It may even emulate equipment a viewer could use at home. But the same was true of the equipment that was before the Court, and ultimately before Congress, in *Fortnightly* and *Teleprompter*.

We recognize, and Aereo and the dissent emphasize, one particular difference between Aereo's system and the cable systems at issue in *Fortnightly* and *Teleprompter*.

The systems in those cases transmitted constantly; they sent continuous programming to each subscriber's television set. In contrast, Aereo's system remains inert until a subscriber indicates that she wants to watch a program. Only at that moment, in automatic response to the subscriber's request, does Aereo's system activate an antenna and begin to transmit the requested program.

This is a critical difference, says the dissent. It means that Aereo's subscribers, not Aereo, "selec[t] the copyrighted content" that is "perform[ed]," and for that reason they, not Aereo, "transmit" the performance. Aereo is thus like "a copy shop that provides its patrons with a library card." A copy shop is not directly liable whenever a patron uses the shop's machines to "reproduce" copyrighted materials found in that library. *See* § 106(1) ("exclusive righ[t] . . . to reproduce the copyrighted work"). And by the same token, Aereo should not be directly liable whenever its patrons use its equipment to "transmit" copyrighted television programs to their screens.

In our view, however, the dissent's copy shop argument, in whatever form, makes too much out of too little. Given Aereo's overwhelming likeness to the cable companies targeted by the 1976 amendments, this sole technological difference between Aereo and traditional cable companies does not make a critical difference here. . . . Here the signals pursue their ordinary course of travel through the universe until today's "turn of the knob"—a click on a website—activates machinery that intercepts and reroutes them to Aereo's subscribers over the Internet. But this difference means nothing to the subscriber. It means nothing to the broadcaster. We do not see how this single difference, invisible to subscriber and broadcaster alike, could transform a system that is for all practical purposes a traditional cable system into "a copy shop that provides its patrons with a library card."

In other cases involving different kinds of service or technology providers, a user's involvement in the operation of the provider's equipment and selection of the content transmitted may well bear on whether the provider performs within the meaning of the Act. But the many similarities between Aereo and cable companies, considered in light of Congress' basic purposes in amending the Copyright Act, convince us that this difference is not critical here. We conclude that Aereo is not just an equipment supplier and that Aereo "perform[s]."

III

Next, we must consider whether Aereo performs petitioners' works "publicly," within the meaning of the Transmit Clause. Under the Clause, an entity performs a work publicly when it "transmit[s] . . . a performance . . . of the work . . . to the public." § 101. Aereo denies that it satisfies this definition. It reasons as follows: First, the "performance" it "transmit[s]" is the performance created by its act of transmitting. And second, because each of these performances is capable of being received by one and only one subscriber, Aereo transmits privately, not publicly. Even assuming Aereo's first argument is correct, its second does not follow.. . .

We assume arguendo that Aereo's first argument is correct. Thus, for present purposes, to transmit a performance of (at least) an audiovisual work means to communicate contemporaneously visible images and contemporaneously audible sounds of the work. *Cf. United States v. American Soc. of Composers, Authors and Publishers*, 627 F.3d 64, 73 (C.A.2 2010) (holding that a download of a work is not a performance because the data transmitted are not "contemporaneously perceptible"). When an Aereo subscriber selects a program to watch, Aereo streams the program over the Internet to that subscriber. Aereo thereby "communicate[s]" to the subscriber, by means of a "device or process," the work's images and sounds. § 101. And those images and sounds are contemporaneously visible and audible on the subscriber's computer (or other Internet-connected device). So under our assumed definition, Aereo transmits a performance whenever its subscribers watch a program.

But what about the Clause's further requirement that Aereo transmit a performance "to the public"? As we have said, an Aereo subscriber receives broadcast television signals with an antenna dedicated to him alone. Aereo's system makes from those signals a personal copy of the selected program. It streams the content of the copy to the same subscriber and to no one else. One and only one subscriber has the ability to see and hear each Aereo transmission. The fact that each transmission is to only one subscriber, in Aereo's view, means that it does not transmit a performance "to the public."

In terms of the Act's purposes, these differences do not distinguish Aereo's system from cable systems, which do perform "publicly." Viewed in terms of Congress' regulatory objectives, why should any of these technological differences matter? They concern the behind-the-scenes way in which Aereo delivers television programming to its viewers' screens. They do not render Aereo's commercial objective any different from that of cable companies. Nor do they significantly alter the viewing experience of Aereo's subscribers. Why would a subscriber who wishes to watch a television show care much whether images and sounds are delivered to his screen via a large multisubscriber antenna or one small dedicated antenna, whether they arrive instantaneously or after a few seconds' delay, or whether they are transmitted directly or after a personal copy is made? And why, if Aereo is right, could not modern CATV systems simply continue the same commercial and consumer-oriented activities, free of copyright restrictions, provided they substitute such new technologies for old? Congress would as much have intended to protect a copyright holder from the unlicensed activities of Aereo as from those of cable companies.

The text of the Clause effectuates Congress' intent. Aereo's argument to the contrary relies on the premise that "to transmit . . . a performance" means to make a single transmission. But the Clause suggests that an entity may transmit a performance through multiple, discrete transmissions. . . .

The Transmit Clause must permit this interpretation, for it provides that one may transmit a performance to the public "whether the members of the public capable of receiving the performance . . . receive it . . . at the same time or at different times." § 101. Were the words "to transmit . . . a performance" limited to a single act of communication, members of the public could not receive the performance communicated "at different times." Therefore, in light of the purpose and text of the

Clause, we conclude that when an entity communicates the same contemporaneously perceptible images and sounds to multiple people, it transmits a performance to them regardless of the number of discrete communications it makes. . . .

Moreover, the subscribers to whom Aereo transmits television programs constitute "the public." Aereo communicates the same contemporaneously perceptible images and sounds to a large number of people who are unrelated and unknown to each other. This matters because, although the Act does not define "the public," it specifies that an entity performs publicly when it performs at "any place where a substantial number of persons outside of a normal circle of a family and its social acquaintances is gathered." The Act thereby suggests that "the public" consists of a large group of people outside of a family and friends.

Neither the record nor Aereo suggests that Aereo's subscribers receive performances in their capacities as owners or possessors of the underlying works. This is relevant because when an entity performs to a set of people, whether they constitute "the public" often depends upon their relationship to the underlying work. When, for example, a valet parking attendant returns cars to their drivers, we would not say that the parking service provides cars "to the public." We would say that it provides the cars to their owners. We would say that a car dealership, on the other hand, does provide cars to the public, for it sells cars to individuals who lack a pre-existing relationship to the cars. Similarly, an entity that transmits a performance to individuals in their capacities as owners or possessors does not perform to "the public," whereas an entity like Aereo that transmits to large numbers of paying subscribers who lack any prior relationship to the works does so perform.

Finally, we note that Aereo's subscribers may receive the same programs at different times and locations. This fact does not help Aereo, however, for the Transmit Clause expressly provides that an entity may perform publicly "whether the members of the public capable of receiving the performance . . . receive it in the same place or in separate places and at the same time or at different times." In other words, "the public" need not be situated together, spatially or temporally. For these reasons, we conclude that Aereo transmits a performance of petitioners' copyrighted works to the public, within the meaning of the Transmit Clause.

IV

Aereo and many of its supporting *amici* argue that to apply the Transmit Clause to Aereo's conduct will impose copyright liability on other technologies, including new technologies, that Congress could not possibly have wanted to reach. We agree that Congress, while intending the Transmit Clause to apply broadly to cable companies and their equivalents, did not intend to discourage or to control the emergence or use of different kinds of technologies. But we do not believe that our limited holding today will have that effect.

For one thing, the history of cable broadcast transmissions that led to the enactment of the Transmit Clause informs our conclusion that Aereo "perform[s]," but it does not determine whether different kinds of providers in different contexts also "perform." For another, an entity only transmits a performance when it communicates contemporaneously perceptible images and sounds of a work. . . .

Further, we have interpreted the term "the public" to apply to a group of individuals acting as ordinary members of the public who pay primarily to watch broadcast television programs, many of which are copyrighted. We have said that it does not extend to those who act as owners or possessors of the relevant product. And we have not considered whether the public performance right is infringed when the user of a service pays primarily for something other than the transmission of copyrighted works, such as the remote storage of content. . . .

We also note that courts often apply a statute's highly general language in light of the statute's basic purposes. Finally, the doctrine of "fair use" can help to prevent inappropriate or inequitable applications of the Clause. *See Sony Corp. of America v. Universal City Studios, Inc.*, 464 U.S. 417 (1984).

We cannot now answer more precisely how the Transmit Clause or other provisions of the Copyright Act will apply to technologies not before us. We agree with the Solicitor General that "[q]uestions involving cloud computing, [remote storage] DVRs, and other novel issues not before the Court, as to which 'Congress has not plainly marked [the] course,' should await a case in which they are squarely presented." And we note that, to the extent commercial actors or other interested entities may be concerned with the relationship between the development and use of such technologies and the Copyright Act, they are of course free to seek action from Congress. *Cf.* Digital Millennium Copyright Act, 17 U.S.C. § 512. . . .

JUSTICE SCALIA, with whom JUSTICE THOMAS and JUSTICE ALITO join, dissenting.

[The dissent contended that direct copyright infringement can only occur through volitional conduct. It would have left open the potential for indirect liability. It concluded by criticizing the majority opinion for adopting a "guilt by resemblance" argument.]

[E]ven accepting that the 1976 amendments had as their purpose the overruling of our cable-TV cases, what they were meant to do and how they did it are two different questions—and it is the latter that governs the case before us here. The injury claimed is not violation of a law that says operations similar to cable TV are subject to copyright liability, but violation of § 106(4) of the Copyright Act. And whatever soothing reasoning the Court uses to reach its result ("this looks like cable TV"), the consequence of its holding is that someone who implements this technology *"perform[s]"under that provision*. That greatly disrupts settled jurisprudence which, before today, applied the straightforward, bright-line test of volitional conduct directed at the copyrighted work. If that test is not outcome determinative in this case, presumably it is not outcome determinative elsewhere as well. And it is not clear what the Court proposes to replace it. Perhaps the Court means to adopt (invent, really) a two-tier version of the Copyright Act, one part of which applies to "cable companies and their equivalents" while the other governs everyone else. . . .

Making matters worse, the Court provides no criteria for determining when its cable-TV-lookalike rule applies. Must a defendant offer access to live television to qualify? If similarity to cable-television service is the measure, then the answer must be yes. But consider the implications of that answer: Aereo would be free to do exactly what it is doing right now so long as it built mandatory time-shifting into its "watch" function. Aereo would not be providing live television if it made subscribers wait to tune in until after a show's live broadcast ended. A subscriber could watch the 7 p.m. airing of a 1-hour program any time after 8 p.m. Assuming the Court does not intend to adopt such a do-nothing rule (though it very well may), there must be some other means of identifying who is and is not subject to its guilt-by-resemblance regime.

Two other criteria come to mind. One would cover any automated service that captures and stores live television broadcasts at a user's direction. That can't be right, since it is exactly what remote storage digital video recorders (RS-DVRs) do, see *Cartoon Network*, 536 F.3d, at 124–25, and the Court insists that its "limited holding" does not decide the fate of those devices. The other potential benchmark is the one offered by the Government: The cable-TV-lookalike rule embraces any entity that "operates an integrated system, substantially dependent on physical equipment that is used in common by [its] subscribers." The Court sensibly avoids that approach because it would sweep in Internet service providers and a host of other entities that quite obviously do not perform.

That leaves as the criterion of cable-TV-resemblance nothing but th'ol' totality-of-the-circumstances test (which is not a test at all but merely assertion of an intent to perform test-free, ad hoc, case-by-case evaluation). It will take years, perhaps decades, to determine which automated systems now in existence are governed by the traditional volitional-conduct test and which get the Aereo treatment. (And automated systems now in contemplation will have to take their chances.) The Court vows that its ruling will not affect cloud-storage providers and cable-television systems, but it cannot deliver on that promise given the imprecision of its result-driven rule. Indeed, the difficulties inherent in the Court's makeshift approach will become apparent in this very case. Today's decision addresses the legality of Aereo's "watch" function, which provides nearly contemporaneous access to live broadcasts. On remand, one of the first questions the lower courts will face is whether Aereo's "record" function, which allows subscribers to save a program while it is airing and watch it later, infringes the Networks' public-performance right. The volitional-conduct rule provides a clear answer to that question: Because Aereo does not select the programs viewed by its users, it does not perform. But it is impossible to say how the issue will come out under the Court's analysis, since cable companies did not offer remote recording and playback services when Congress amended the Copyright Act in 1976. . . .

COMMENTS AND QUESTIONS

1. Much of the media attention surrounding the *Aereo* case focused on whether Aereo's disruptive technology worked around copyright text drafted in the analog age, yet the ultimate decision turned on deciphering the larger legislative context and broad text animating the public performance right. It took nearly two decades for the Copyright Act of 1976 to emerge, with the battle over cable television proving to be the largest roadblock. That may explain why the Supreme Court devotes so much effort to parsing legislative history in addressing Aereo's efforts to circumvent the Copyright Act's public performance right. *See* Peter S. Menell & David Nimmer, *Aereo, Disruptive Technology, and Statutory Interpretation*, SCOTUSBLOG (Jun. 26, 2014), http://www.scotusblog.com/2014/06/symposium-aereo-disruptive-technology-and-statutory-interpretation/.

2. *Public Access to Over-the-Air Broadcasts and Technological Disruption.* Aereo had a potent policy argument for why copyright law ought not to stand in the way of technology that expands access to over-the-air broadcasts. Yet the history surrounding the drafting of the 1976 Act in general and the Transmit Clause and Section 111 in particular reveals that Congress rejected a similar appeal nearly half a century ago in a different context. Community antenna television (CATV, now known as cable TV) emerged as a way for people in outlying communities to pool resources to erect antennas capable of receiving distant broadcast signals. These non-profit entities served democratic, speech-promoting purposes. The signals themselves were available for free so long as one had a strong enough antenna. The programming being broadcast was funded by commercial advertising, not subscriptions. Therefore, the expanded market for such content increased the value of commercial advertising to broadcasters and owners of copyrights in the programming being broadcast. And consumers lacked the ability to skip the ads. The CATV non-profit cooperatives merely enabled distant consumers to receive signals that they were each entitled to receive if they had erected their own antenna. And the Supreme Court held that CATV entities did not require licenses under the 1909 Act to retransmit the signal to their local areas in the *Fortnightly* and *Teleprompter* cases. Volumes of legislative history from the mid-1960s through passage of the 1976 Act are replete with studies and reports explaining why CATV retransmission ought to be permitted without licenses.

Congress compromised. It chose to deny cable networks license-free retransmission, but also denied copyright owners the right to an injunction in favor of a compulsory license. Fast forward to 2014. Aereo is a for-profit company that charges for retransmission of over-the-air broadcasts. Whether or not you agree with the policy ramifications of the *Aereo* decision, it is difficult to contend that the majority did not capture the intention underlying the 1976 regime. On the other hand, Aereo is capturing a signal the TV stations voluntarily distributed over the airwaves for free, and – unlike cable – is distributing that signal to one person at their request, not to a group.

Should Congress revisit that determination today? Should Congress expand the § 111 compulsory license to include Aereo-type services? How should the compulsory license rate be determined? On remand, Aereo sought a license under § 111 but was denied on the grounds that it was too similar to a cable company to avoid liability but not similar enough to a cable company to take advantage of the statutory license. To what extent should the added technological capability for consumers or automated DVRs to skip commercials affect your analysis?

3. *Cord Cutting and Local Broadcasting.* In January 2018, Locast, a non-profit entity, launched a free online digital translator service for streaming local broadcast television signals using internet-connected devices. Locast is a non-profit organization that funds its operation through donations. They request that users contribute $5 per month. Locast asserts that its operation is legal under the exemption set forth in § 111(a)(5). Do you agree?

4. *A Volition Requirement?* Justice Scalia invokes lower court rulings holding that direct copyright infringement can only occur through volitional conduct. The doctrine traces its roots to *Religious Technology Center v. Netcom On-Line Communication Services, Inc.*, 907 F. Supp. 1361 (N.D. Cal. 1995), a pre-DMCA Internet case holding that "[a]lthough copyright is a strict liability statute, there should still be some element of volition or causation which is lacking where a defendant's system is merely used to create a copy by a third party." Although early drafts of the DMCA online service provider safe harbor (§ 512) provision would have codified the volition doctrine, the ultimate statutory formulation took a different path. *See* 4 NIMMER ON COPYRIGHT § 12B.06[B][2][b]. Nonetheless, other district and appellate decisions have invoked the volition doctrine, including the Second Circuit in *Aereo* and *Cartoon Network LP, LLLP v. CSC Holdings, Inc.*, 536 F.3d 121, 130 (2d Cir. 2008).

Does the majority opinion in *Aereo* provide any clues as to whether volition is a requirement for direct infringement? The Court suggests that merely pressing the button doesn't indicate that you are in charge of the recording. How will that conclusion affect remote-storage DVRs like the one at issue in *Cartoon Network*? What about services like Sling that permit a user to access and view recorded content remotely over the Internet? *Cf. Fox Broadcasting Co. v. Dish Network LLC*, 2015 WL 1137593 (CD Cal. 2015) (recognizing that while "[t]he Supreme Court did not expressly address the general volitional conduct requirement for direct liability under the Copyright Act [in *Aereo*, the] volitional conduct doctrine is a significant and long-standing rule . . ."). The Supreme Court suggests that the fact that the user selects the content she will watch is not enough to make the user the relevant actor for copyright purposes. What more is required?

5. *Other Workarounds.* Following the *Aereo* decision, other disruptive technologies see opportunities to fill the void. Simple.TV sells an antenna and a set-top box that enables users to record over-the-air broadcasts. It also sells a premium service that provides automatic recording and remote access. Roku, Sling Media, TiVo, and Mohu also sell hardware enabling users to stream television to digital devices or watch web video on television sets. *See* Emily Steel, *After Supreme Court Ruling, Aereo's Rivals in TV Streaming Seize Opening*, N.Y. TIMES B1 (June 30, 2014). Are these technologies vulnerable under the Court's opinion?

6. *Public Place Clause*. Courts have grappled with the problem of when a performance occurs in a public place. The Third Circuit has held that video rental stores cannot provide viewing rooms for customers, because the performance of a rented movie in such a room is "public" (even though the room is rented only to one group at a time). The Third Circuit explained its rationale in terms that interpret the phrase "public performance" very broadly:

> The Copyright Act speaks of performances at a place open to the public. It does not require that the public place be actually crowded with people. A telephone booth, a taxi cab, and even a pay toilet are commonly regarded as "open to the public," even though they are usually occupied only by one party at a time.

Columbia Pictures v. Aveco, Inc., 800 F.2d 59, 63 (3d Cir. 1986); *accord Columbia Pictures v. Redd Horne*, 749 F.2d 154, 158 (3d Cir. 1984) (finding that small rental booths in video stores, seating up to four, were "open to the public" for purposes of public performance analysis). The Ninth Circuit distinguished these cases from the situation in which hotels rent their guests videocassettes and provide in-room videocassette players. "While the hotel may indeed be 'open to the public,' a guest's hotel room, once rented, is not." *Columbia Pictures v. Professional Real Estate Investors, Inc.*, 866 F.2d 278, 281 (9th Cir. 1989).

PROBLEMS

Problem IV-38. Cablevision, a large cable television provider, has seen interest in its set-top digital video recorders (DVR) and its video-on-demand (VOD) service increase. To better serve its customers, it has developed the capability to provide a server-based DVR, what it calls a Remote Storage DVR (RS-DVR). With the new RS-DVR, Cablevision would split the single stream of data that it has traditionally broadcast into two streams. The first would be routed immediately to customers as before. The second stream would flow into a device which would buffer the data stream, reformat it, and send it to the "Arroyo Server," which includes high-capacity hard disks for each RS-DVR customer. The server would automatically inquire as to whether any customers want to record any of that programming. If a customer has requested a particular program, the data for that program would move onto their designated hard disk. Like with a set-top DVR, as new data flows into their hard disk, old data would be overwritten if the disk was at capacity.

To the customer, the processes of recording and playback on the RS-DVR would be similar to that of a standard set-top DVR. Using a remote control, the customer could record programming by selecting a program in advance from an on-screen guide, or by pressing the record button while viewing a given program. A customer could not, however, record the earlier portion of a program once it has begun. To begin playback, the customer would select the show from an on-screen list of previously recorded programs. The principal difference in operation is that, instead of sending signals from the remote to an on-set box, the viewer sends signals from the remote, through the cable, to the Arroyo Server at Cablevision's central facility. In this respect, RS-DVR more closely resembles a Video on Demand (VOD) service, whereby a cable subscriber uses his or her remote and cable box to request transmission of content, such as a movie, stored on computers at the cable company's facility. But unlike a VOD service, RS-DVR users could only play content that they previously requested to be recorded.

Content providers—television and motion picture studios—worry that Cablevision is circumventing its VOD license, which would result in substantial loss of revenues. Cablevision argues that the remote DVR appears to the user just like a local video recorder of the type consumers have long used without additional payment. Does Cablevision need a public performance license from content providers to operate the RS-DVR service?

Problem IV-39. Ralston Hotels, a national hotel chain, offers guests an "in-room video rental" service. A menu is displayed on the guest's interactive television screen, and the guest can select both a movie and a starting time by using his remote control. Portland Pictures, a major movie producer that owns the video rental rights to its movies, sues Ralston, alleging that each selected movie is a "public performance" and demanding royalties. Who should prevail? Would your answer differ if Ralston made particular movies available only at certain times?

2. Blanket Public Performance Licenses and Collecting Societies

The challenges of enforcing musical composition public performance rights led to the formation of the American Society of Composers, Authors, and Publishers (ASCAP) in 1914. This consortium of leading musical composition authors and owners shared the costs of enforcing public performance rights in their compositions. ASCAP initially focused on live performances of musical compositions in theater, restaurants, and other public establishments. The consortium brought litigation to expand the interpretation of the public performance right, economized on enforcement activities, and innovated efficient licensing practices such as the blanket license. ASCAP played a central role in licensing musical compositions for radio and television broadcasts.

> ASCAP's big break came with the advent of radio technology in the early 1920s. At first, ASCAP allowed radio stations free use of members' compositions. By 1925, however, the "free sample" era ended and a series of lawsuits began. These were directed at early commercial users of radio—mostly large retail stores and hotels—and helped ASCAP establish the right for compensation to all music played over the radio. By 1940, the radio broadcasting industry had gross revenues of close to $200,000,000. Of this amount, ASCAP collected a reported $4,000,000, which represented two-thirds of ASCAP's gross revenue.

Robert P. Merges, *Contracting into Liability Rules: Intellectual Property and Collective Rights Organizations*, 84. CAL. L. REV. 1293, 1333 (1996). ASCAP works with both composers and publishers. Early in its development, ASCAP instituted a policy of splitting payouts equally between the two groups.

ASCAP's success brought antitrust scrutiny and competition. The Department of Justice sued ASCAP for antitrust violations in the early 1940s, resulting in the imposition of a consent decree that still governs today. That decree, and the associated rate-setting court, is overseen by the U.S. District Court for the Southern District of New York. ASCAP's practices led radio broadcasters to boycott ASCAP musical compositions during a ten month period in 1941 and form Broadcast Music Inc. (BMI), a rival collecting society.

ASCAP and BMI remain vital institutions today. SESAC, originally the Society of European Stage Authors and Composers, and Global Music Rights (GMR), formed in 2013, also serve as collecting societies (or performance rights organization) today. Analogous collecting societies function in many nations around the world.

PROBLEM

Problem IV-40. Buford, the owner of the Pumpwell service station located on a busy commercial street, receives approximately 20 calls each day from customers. Because of the volume of repair work that Pumpwell does, it frequently must put callers on hold. Buford decides to provide those callers with music while they are holding, so he patches his radio into the telephone. When a call is placed on hold, the caller hears a station selected by Buford until the call is picked up again. ASCAP sues Pumpwell for copyright infringement, claiming that Pumpwell is publicly performing its songs. Does ASCAP have a meritorious case?

---

3.   Treatment of Sound Recordings

Sound recordings, PGS (pictorial, graphic, or sculptural) works, and architectural works are conspicuously absent from § 106(4). The latter two categories are understandable. It is not clear what it would mean to "perform" a PGS or architectural work.

One of the most important means of exploiting a sound recording is to perform it publicly—for example, by broadcasting the recording on the radio. The explanation for this exclusion reveals a lot about the politics of copyright reform.

When Congress set out in the mid-1950s to overhaul the 1909 Act, the recording industry put the establishment of federal copyright protection for sound recordings at the top of their wishlist. By that point in time, however, the radio broadcasting industry was well-established and had significant political clout. Based on cases orchestrated by the American Society of Composers, Authors and Publishers (ASCAP), *see, e.g., Jerome H. Remick & Co. v. General Electric Co.*, 16 F.2d 829 (S.D.N.Y. 1926), radio broadcasters were already on the hook for musical composition licenses. By the late 1940s, these payments were handled through blanket licenses from ASCAP and BMI, another collective rights organizations founded by radio stations. Radio stations strenuously opposed paying another set of copyright owners for public performance. In addition, ASCAP and BMI worried that these additional licensing fees would come, at least in part, from their royalty streams. Furthermore, record labels realized that radio play was essential to marketing their works. Many in fact made illegal "payola" payments to get their records on the air.

With record piracy mounting by the late 1960s, record labels were willing to compromise. The Sound Recording Amendments Act of 1971 established federal protection for sound recordings, but without a public performance right. That compromise was carried over to the 1976 Act, although record labels and recording artists continued to fight for a public performance right for sound recordings. *See* Matthew S. DelNero, *Long Overdue? An Exploration of the Status and Merit of a General Public Performance Right in Sound Recordings*, 51 J. COPYRIGHT SOC'Y U.S.A. 473 (2004).

The emergence of the Internet created the conditions for partially addressing this gap in copyright protection. Terrestrial radio stations worried that webcasters posed a competitive threat. This produced an unlikely coalition among record labels, recording artists, and radio stations which led to the Digital Performance Right in Sound Recordings Act of 1995 (DPRSRA). The ultimate compromise amended §§ 106 and 114 of the Copyright Act to establish an exclusive right to perform sound recordings "publicly by means of a digital audio transmission." § 106(6). The DPRSRA also created a complex compulsory license regime for digital performances, later amended by the DMCA and the MMA.

4.   Statutory Limits on Performance and Display Rights

There are a number of specific statutory exceptions that limit the scope of the performance and display rights. We summarize each briefly; you are encouraged to study the statutory provisions at issue. The provisions are of two basic types: (1) public interest exemptions; and (2) compulsory licenses.

i.   Public Interest Exemptions

Section 110 of the Copyright Act exempts many "public interest" performances and displays from the reach of §§ 106(4) and (5). Thus, most live educational performances and displays are exempt under § 110(1), as are distance learning broadcasts (including via webcasts) made by accredited, nonprofit educational institutions (subject to various conditions). § 110(2). Religious performances and displays are exempt from the Act under § 110(3). Face-to-face performances of "nondramatic literary or musical works" for free or for charitable purposes are exempt, reviving in part the "for profit" requirement of the 1909 Act. § 110(4). Record stores may play records without charge to promote their sale under § 110(7), although the analogous performance of videos in video stores without permission appears to be prohibited.

After many years of complaints by small business and restaurant owners and performing rights societies over the collection of public performance royalties for broadcast and other recorded music played in these establishments, Congress passed the Fairness in Music Licensing Act in 1998. Due to the political strength of retailers and restaurant owners, Congress substantially broadened an exemption for home listening of transmitted performances to extend to small businesses (less than 2,000 square feet), restaurants (less than 3,750 square feet), and larger establishments conforming to limitations on the number of loudspeakers and television screen size. § 110(5). These establishments would still need a public performance license from the musical composition owner to host live or taped performances. § 513.

In May 2000, a World Trade Organization (WTO) panel found the Fairness in Music Licensing Act to be in violation of the Agreement on Trade Related Aspects of Intellectual Property Rights (TRIPS) and the Berne Convention for the Protection of Literary and Artistic Works requiring that member nations afford copyright owners minimum levels of protection. WTO Dispute Panel Report on Section 110(5) of the U.S. Copyright Act, WT/DS160/R § 7.1, at 69 (June 15, 2000). Although these accords allow member nations to craft limited exceptions that "do not conflict with a normal exploitation of the work and do not unreasonably prejudice the legitimate interests of the right holder," the WTO panel concluded that § 110(5) operated on too large a scale. A Congressional Research Service showed that 65.2 percent of all eating establishments, 71.8 percent of all drinking establishments, and 27 percent of all retail establishments qualified for the exemption. Rather than appeal the WTO decision, the United States has indicated its intention to amend § 110(5) and has agreed to pay approximately $1.1 million in damages per year until it brings its law into compliance. The United States and the European Community reached a mutually satisfactory temporary agreement in June 2003. The United States has yet to change the law to comply with the Berne Convention.

Given that the music being played in a bar or restaurant often comes over the radio, and the copyright owner has already been paid for the public performance over the radio, does § 110(5) really "conflict with a normal exploitation of the work"?

ii.   Compulsory Licenses

Cable Retransmission. As discussed in *Aereo*, § 111 authorizes television broadcast relays, or "secondary transmissions," under a variety of circumstances where they are not for profit and are not content-controlled. For example, the owner of an apartment building with a single reception antenna may relay its signal to residents of the building without charge. Cable systems are also entitled to retransmit television broadcasts over their networks and charge a fee for the service, provided that the cable network registers its intent to do so and pays a royalty based on the revenues it receives from subscribers. The royalty rate, a percentage of the cable system's gross receipts (as set forth in the statute), is based on the cable system's retransmission of distant *non-network* programming. Congress determined that content owners could fully recover the value of retransmission of their shows through their contracts with the networks. After all, retransmission in the local market for network programming enhanced advertising revenue, which would be passed through to content owners through the market for shows. Any loss to content owners would come from retransmission to distant markets as such programming lost the opportunity to license their content into the local network media channels. Cable companies cannot delay or alter the programming they relay from local television broadcasts.

Until 1993, the royalties paid to content owners were collected, calculated, and distributed under the supervision of the Copyright Royalty Tribunal, a governmental entity. From 1993 through 2004, distribution disputes were resolved privately or through ad hoc arbitration panels (Copyright Arbitration Royalty Panels (CARPs)). A 2004 law replaced the CARP process with three Copyright Royalty Judges (CRJ), full-time employees of the Library of Congress appointed for six-year terms with an opportunity for reappointment.

Satellite Retransmission. Section 119 provides a similar right to a compulsory license for satellite transmission to "unserved households"—that is, households that do not receive the normal transmission signal from a particular network or other station, either through broadcast or cable. Satellites may broadcast the signal of those stations to subscribing recipients upon the payment of a royalty. Unlike § 111, however, § 119 does not specify the royalty rate. Rather, the rate is subject to voluntary negotiation or compulsory arbitration between the satellite owner and the individual stations or networks.

Jukeboxes. Section 116 authorizes owners of jukeboxes ("coin-operated phonorecord players," in the words of the statute) to publicly perform the musical works contained in the jukebox subject to a compulsory license. This compulsory license, like that in § 111, is fixed by statute.

Public Broadcasting. Section 118 authorizes public broadcasting stations to transmit musical and artistic (but not literary or audiovisual) works upon payment of a compulsory license. This section does not, however, set royalty rates. Rather, it requires public broadcasters and the owners of such works to negotiate a rate every five years under the supervision of the Librarian of Congress.

Non-interactive Streaming. In establishing the § 106(6) digital performance right in sound recordings in 1995, Congress provided a compulsory license for non-interactive streaming services (such as webcasters, SiriusXM, and Pandora). The DPRSRA created a three-tiered system: (1) "exempt transmissions," including nonsubscription digital broadcast transmissions, largely by traditional broadcasters, are exempt from the digital performance right;[22] (2) non-interactive subscription digital transmissions meeting specified statutory criteria[23] are subject to the new right but are granted a compulsory license; and (3) interactive or user-selected streaming of music are ineligible for the

---

[22] Traditional television and radio broadcasters may continue to perform sound recordings without being subject to this new right, even if they convert their signal to digital form. *See* 17 U.S.C. § 114(d)(1). In addition, various secondary transmissions of exempt primary transmissions and transmissions within business establishments (such as MUZAK) do not implicate the digital performance right.

[23] See § 114(d)(2), (j)(13). In essence, non-interactive services mimic traditional radio stations. Users do not choose the tracks or artists and there are no pre-published playlists.

compulsory license and hence require consent of or a license from the sound recording copyright owner.

Section 114(f) provides for the compulsory license rate to be set by the Copyright Royalty Board in the absence of voluntary agreement among record labels and online services. Congress authorized SoundExchange, a non-profit collective rights management organization, to distribute the compulsory license royalties. Section 114(g) allocates 50% of the compulsory license royalties to be paid to record labels, 45% to featured vocalists and musicians, and 5% to non-featured performers. The MMA requires SoundExchange to "adopt and reasonably implement a policy that provides . . . for acceptance of instructions from" either sound recording copyright owners or featured artists, directing the collective to pay a portion of their share of royalties to "a producer, mixer, or sound engineer who was part of the creative process that created a sound recording." § 114(g)(5)(A). The statute does not specify any particular share of royalties to be paid to producers, mixers, and sound engineers. Section 114(g)(6) provides for mandatory payments to producers, mixers, and sound engineers who meet specified criteria.

e.   Public Display Right

The Copyright Act grants owners of "literary, musical, dramatic, and choreographic works, pantomimes, and pictorial, graphic, or sculptural works, including the individual images of a motion picture or other audiovisual work," the exclusive right to display such works. *See* § 106(5). Section 101 defines "display" broadly: "to show a copy of [the work], either directly or by means of a film, slide, television image, or any other device or process or, in the case of a motion picture or other audiovisual work, to show individual images nonsequentially."

Section 109(c) provides an exception to the public display right that is particularly important:

> the owner of a particular copy lawfully made under this title, or any person authorized by such owner, is entitled, without the authority of the copyright owner, to display that copy publicly, either directly or by the projection of no more than one image at a time, to viewers present at the place where the copy is located.

This limitation allows most common displays of a physical work, including works fixed at a single location (say, a museum) where they are visible to the public. As a result, there is far less litigation over public display than over public performance. Public display cases tend to involve the depiction of a copyrighted work through a television broadcast or over a computer network. *See* R. Anthony Reese, *The First Sale Doctrine in the Era of Digital Networks*, 44 B.C. L. REV. 577 (2003).

ii.   Moral Rights

Moral rights extend beyond ownership of economic control of works of authorship to encompass protections of the "personality" of the author. They include the right to have one's name associated with one's work (right of attribution) and the right to protect one's works from mutilation or distortion (right of integrity). Moral rights derive from the continental European "author's rights" tradition, which differs in many ways from the Anglo-American tradition emphasizing the economic function of intellectual property.

The carrot of joining the Berne Convention ultimately led the United States to bring moral rights protection into the Copyright Act. Article 6*bis*(1) of the Berne Convention requires that "even after the transfer of [copyrighted works], the author shall have the right to claim authorship of the work, and to object to any distortion, mutilation or other modification of, or other derogatory action in relation to the said work, which would be prejudicial to his honor or reputation." After initially taking the position that a patchwork of existing federal and state protections discharged its moral rights obligations under the Convention,[24] Congress passed the Visual Artists Rights Act of 1990 (VARA), which directly recognizes moral rights of visual artists. Compared to moral rights protections in Europe, U.S. protections apply quite narrowly (only to "work[s] of visual art") and are subject to significant exceptions.

Works Protected. A "work of visual art" is defined to include paintings, drawings, prints, still photographs (signed by the authors), and sculptures, existing in a single copy or in limited edition (200 or fewer copies). § 101.

Exclusions. A work of visual art does not include (i) "any poster, map, globe, chart, technical drawing, diagram, model, applied art, motion picture or other audiovisual work, book, magazine, newspaper, periodical, data base, electronic information service, electronic publication, or similar publication"; (ii) "any merchandising item or advertising, promotional, descriptive, covering, or packaging material or container"; or (iii) any work made for hire. § 101.

Rights. An author of a work of visual art has a right to claim authorship of the work, to prevent the use of her name on works she did not create, and to prevent the use of her name on works that have been modified or distorted. Authors of works of "recognized stature" have the right to prevent destruction of such works. § 106A(a)(3).

Duration. For works created on or after June 1, 1991, moral rights subsist for the life of the author (or the life of the last surviving artist in the case of joint works). § 106A(d)(3). As a result of legislative confusion about reconciling House and Senate versions of VARA, moral rights protection for works created prior to June 1, 1991 for

---

[24] The legislative history of the Berne Convention Implementation Act of 1988 pointed to rights under § 106; § 115(a)(2) (relating to distortions of musical works under the compulsory license); section 203 (termination of transfers); § 43(a) of the Lanham Act (relating to false designation of origin and false descriptions); state and local laws relating to publicity, contract, fraud and misrepresentation, unfair competition, defamation, and invasion of privacy; and new state statutes in eight states protecting rights of integrity and paternity in certain works of art. H.R. REP. NO. 609, 100th Cong., 2d Sess. 33–34 (1988). It is doubtful, however, that this collection of protections fully discharged U.S. obligations under the Berne Convention. *See* Jane C. Ginsburg & John M. Kernochan, *One Hundred and Two Years Later: the U.S. Joins the Berne Convention*, 13 COLUM.-VLA J. L. & ARTS 1, 27–38 (1988–89).

which the artist retained a copy or copies lasts for the life of the author plus 70 years. If the artist did not retain a copy, then no moral rights exist whatsoever.

Transfer and Waiver. Moral rights are personal to the artist and may be exercised only by the author. Such rights are not transferable, but may be waived (in a writing identifying the work and signed by the author). § 106A(b), (e).

Exceptions. A work that changes as a result of the passage of time or conservation measures does not trigger liability. In the case of works of visual art incorporated into buildings in such a way that removing the work will cause harm to the work, VARA seeks to strike a balance between the economic interests of property owners and the moral rights of authors. The integrity right does not apply to the extent that the artist consented to the installation of the work in the building (and acknowledged that such installation "may subject the work to destruction, distortion, mutilation, or other modification, by reason of its removal"). § 113(d).

Remedies. Violations of moral rights are subject to the full extent of civil copyright remedies, although not to criminal sanctions. Artists need not register their works in order to recover statutory damages or attorney's fees.

Castillo v. G&M Realty L.P.
United States Court of Appeals for the Second Circuit
950 F.3d 155 (2d Cir. 2020)

BARRINGTON D. PARKER, Circuit Judge:

. . .

The facts as found by the district court established that in 2002, Wolkoff undertook to install artwork in a series of dilapidated warehouse buildings that he owned in Long Island City, New York. Wolkoff enlisted Appellee Jonathan Cohen, a distinguished aerosol artist, to turn the warehouses into an exhibition space for artists. Cohen and other artists rented studio spaces in the warehouses and filled the walls with aerosol art, with Cohen serving as curator. Under Cohen's leadership, the site, known as 5Pointz, evolved into a major global center for aerosol art. it attracted thousands of daily visitors, numerous celebrities, and extensive media coverage.

"Creative destruction" was an important feature of the 5Pointz site. Some art at the site achieved permanence, but other art had a short lifespan and was repeatedly painted over. An elaborate system of norms—including Cohen's permission and often consent of the artist whose work was overpainted—governed the painting process. Cohen divided the walls into "short-term rotating walls," where works would generally last for days or weeks, and "longstanding walls," which were more permanent and reserved for the best works at the site. During its lifespan, 5Pointz was home to a total of approximately 10,650 works of art.

In May 2013, Cohen learned that Wolkoff had sought municipal approvals looking to demolish 5Pointz and to build luxury apartments on the site. seeking to prevent that destruction, Cohen applied to the New York City Landmark Preservation Commission to have 5Pointz designated a site of cultural significance. The application was unsuccessful, as were Cohen's efforts to raise money to purchase the site.

At that point, Cohen, joined by numerous 5Pointz artists, sued under VARA to prevent destruction of the site. VARA, added to the copyright laws in 1990, grants visual artists certain "moral rights" in their work. *See* 17 U.S.C. §106A(a). specifically, the statute prevents modifications of artwork that are harmful to artists' reputations. *Id.* § 106A(a)(3)(A). The statute also affords artists the right to prevent destruction of their work if that work has achieved "recognized stature" and carries over this protection even after the work is sold. *Id.* § 106A(a)(3)(B). Under §§ 504(b) and (c) an artist who establishes a violation of VARA may obtain actual damages and profits or statutory damages, which are enhanced if the artist proves that a violation was willful.

Early in the litigation, Plaintiffs applied for a temporary restraining order to prevent the demolition of the site, which the district court granted. As the TRO expired, Plaintiffs applied for a preliminary injunction. On November 12, 2013, the court denied the application in a minute order but told the parties that a written opinion would soon follow.

That night, Wolkoff began to destroy the artwork. He banned the artists from the site and refused them permission to recover any work that could be removed. Several nights later (and before the district court's written opinion could issue), Wolkoff deployed a group of workmen who, at his instruction, whitewashed the art.

On November 20, 2013, the district court issued its opinion denying the preliminary injunction. Judge Block concluded that, although some of the 5Pointz paintings may have achieved recognized stature, resolution of that question was best reserved for trial. The court also decided that, given the transitory nature of much of the work, preliminary injunctive relief was inappropriate and that the monetary damages available under VARA could remediate any injury proved at trial.

Following the destruction of the art, nine additional artists sued Wolkoff. . . .

On February 12, 2018, the district court issued its findings of fact and conclusions of law. Drawing on a vast record, the court found that 45 of the works had achieved recognized stature, that Wolkoff had violated VARA by destroying them, and that the violation was willful. More specifically, the court observed that the works "reflect[ed] striking technical and artistic mastery and vision worthy of display in prominent museums if not on the walls of 5Pointz." The findings emphasized Cohen's prominence in the world of aerosol art, the significance of his process of selecting the artists who could exhibit at 5Pointz, and the fact that, while much of the art was temporary, other works were on display for several years. Judge Block credited the artists' evidence of outside recognition of the 5Pointz works and expert testimony as to the works' stature. The court declined to impose liability with respect to the four remaining works because they had not achieved long-term preservation, were insufficiently discussed outside of 5Pointz, and were not modified to the detriment of the artists' reputations.

Where a violation of VARA is established, the statute permits the injured party to recover either actual damages and profits or statutory damages. 17 U.S.C. § 504. . . . Ultimately, the district court concluded that it could not reliably fix the market value of the destroyed paintings and, for that reason, declined to award actual damages.

Nonetheless, the court did award statutory damages. It determined that statutory damages would serve to sanction Wolkoff's conduct and to vindicate the policies behind VARA. In addition, and in accord with the advisory jury's verdict, the court found that Wolkoff had acted willfully. This finding was based on Wolkoff's awareness of the ongoing VARA litigation and his refusal to afford the artists the 90-day opportunity provided by the statute to salvage their artwork, some of which was removable. *See* 17 U.S.C. § 113(d)(2)(B). Judge Block was unpersuaded by Wolkoff's assertion that he whitewashed the artwork to prevent the artists from engaging in disruption and disorderly behavior at the site. Instead, he found that Wolkoff acted out of "pure pique and revenge for the nerve of the plaintiffs to sue to attempt to prevent the destruction of their art." Judge Block awarded the maximum amount of statutory damages: $150,000 for each of the 45 works, for a total of $6.75 million. . . .

DISCUSSION

. . .

I.

VARA creates a scheme of moral rights for artists. "The right of attribution generally consists of the right of an artist to be recognized by name as the author of his work or to publish anonymously or pseudonymously . . . ." *Carter v. Helmsley-Spear, Inc.*, 71 F.3d 77, 81 (2d Cir. 1995). It further includes the right to prevent the artist's work from being attributed to another and to prevent the use of the artist's name on works created by others. *Id.* "The right of integrity allows the [artist] to prevent any deforming or mutilating changes to his work, even after title in the work has been transferred."

Most importantly for this appeal, VARA gives "the author of a work of visual art" the right "to prevent any destruction of a work of recognized stature" and provides that "any intentional or grossly negligent destruction of that work is a violation of that right." 17 U.S.C. § 106A(a)(3)(B); *see also Carter*, 71 F.3d at 83. VARA further permits the artist "to prevent any intentional distortion, mutilation, or other modification of [his or her work] which would be prejudicial to his or her honor or reputation," and provides that "any intentional distortion, mutilation, or modification of that work is a violation of that right." 17 U.S.C. § 106A(a)(3)(A). The latter provision applies regardless of a work's stature. These rights may not be transferred, but they "may be waived if the author expressly agrees to such waiver in a written instrument signed by the author." *Id.* § 106A(e)(1).

Additionally, the statute contains specific provisions governing artwork incorporated into a building. If the artwork is incorporated "in such a way that removing the work from the building will cause the destruction, distortion, mutilation, or other modification of the work," then the artist's rights may be waived if and only if he "consented to the installation of the work in the building . . . in a written instrument." *Id.* § 113(d)(1). This instrument must be "signed by the owner of the building and the author" and must "specif[y] that the installation of the work may subject the work to destruction, distortion, mutilation, or other modification, by reason of its removal." *Id.* However, "[i]f the owner of a building wishes to remove a work of visual art which is a part of such building and which can be removed from the building without the destruction, distortion, mutilation, or other modification of the work," then the artist's rights prevail unless one of two things has occurred. *Id.* § 113(d)(2). First, the building's owner "has made a diligent, good faith attempt without success to notify the author of the owner's intended action affecting the work of visual art." *Id.* or second, the owner has "provide[d] such notice in writing and the person so notified failed, within 90 days after receiving such notice, either to remove the work or to pay for its removal." *Id.*

Damages for violations of VARA's rights of attribution and integrity are governed by general copyright law and include both actual and statutory damages. Statutory damages may range from $750 to $30,000 per work "as the court considers just." *Id.* § 504(c)(1). However, if "the [artist] sustains the burden of proving, and the court finds, that [a violation of VARA] was committed willfully, the court in its discretion may increase the award of statutory damages to a sum of not more than $150,000 [per work]." *Id.* § 504(c)(2).

II.

The crux of the parties' dispute on this appeal is whether the works at 5Pointz were works of "recognized stature," thereby protected from destruction under § 106A(a)(3)(B). We conclude that a work is of recognized stature when it is one of high quality, status, or caliber that has been acknowledged as such by a relevant community. *See Carter v. Helmsley-Spear, Inc.*, 861 F. Supp. 303, 324-25 (S.D.N.Y. 1994), *aff'd in part, vacated in part, rev'd in part*, 71 F.3d 77; *see also, e.g., Martin v. City of Indianapolis*, 192 F.3d 608, 612 (7th Cir. 1999). A work's high quality, status, or caliber is its stature, and the acknowledgement of that stature speaks to the work's recognition.

The most important component of stature will generally be artistic quality. The relevant community will typically be the artistic community, comprising art historians, art critics, museum curators, gallerists, prominent artists, and other experts. Since recognized stature is necessarily a fluid concept, we can conceive of circumstances under which, for example, a "poor" work by an otherwise highly regarded artist nonetheless merits protection from destruction under VARA. This approach helps to ensure that VARA protects "the public interest in preserving [the] nation"s culture," *Carter*, 71 F.3d at 81. This approach also ensures that the personal judgment of the court is not the determinative factor in the court's analysis. *See* Christopher J. Robinson, *The "Recognized Stature" Standard in the Visual Artists Rights Act*, 68 FORDHAM L. REV. 1935, 1945 n.84 (2000).

After all, we are mindful of Justice Holmes's cautionary observation that "[i]t would be a dangerous undertaking for persons trained only to the law to constitute themselves final judges of the worth of [visual art]," *Bleistein v. Donaldson Lithographing Co.*, 188 U.S. 239, 251 (1903); *accord Pollara v. Seymour*, 344 F.3d 265, 271 (2d Cir. 2003) ("We steer clear of an interpretation of VARA that would require courts to assess . . . the worth of a purported work of visual art . . . ."). For that reason, aside from the rare case where an artist or work is of such prominence that the issue of recognized stature need not be tried, expert testimony or substantial evidence of non-expert recognition will generally be required to establish recognized stature.

III.

Accordingly, to establish a violation of VARA in this case, the artists were required to demonstrate that their work had achieved recognized stature. Judge Block found that they did so. He concluded that "the plaintiffs adduced such a plethora of exhibits and credible testimony, including the testimony of a highly regarded expert, that even under the most restrictive of evidentiary standards almost all of the plaintiffs' works easily qualify as works of recognized stature." [The Court found substantial evidence supported that conclusion].

Initially, Wolkoff contends that the great majority of the works in question were temporary ones which, for that reason, could not meet the recognized stature requirement. We disagree. We see nothing in VARA that excludes temporary artwork from attaining recognized stature. Unhelpful to this contention is the fact that Wolkoff's own expert acknowledged that temporary artwork can achieve recognized stature.

The statute does not adopt categories of "permanent" and "temporary" artwork, much less include a definition of these terms. VARA is distinctive in that "[a] work of visual art is defined by the Act in terms both positive (what it is) and negative (what it is not)." *Carter*, 71 F.3d at 84. In narrowing the scope of the statute, Congress adopted a highly specific definition of visual art. *See* 17 U.S.C. § 101. In light of this specificity, we see no justification for adopting an additional requirement not included by Congress, even if that requirement is styled as a component of recognized stature. To do so would be to upset the balance achieved by the legislature.

Additionally, at least as recently as 2005, New York City saw a clear instance where temporary artwork achieved recognized stature. That winter, artists Christo Vladimirov Javacheff and Jeanne-Claude Denat, known collectively as "Christo," installed 7,503 orange draped gates in Central Park. This work, known as "The Gates," lasted only two weeks but was the subject of significant critical acclaim and attention, not just from the art world but also from the general public. *See* Richard Chused, *Moral Rights: The Anti-Rebellion Graffiti Heritage of 5Pointz*, 41 COLUM. J.L. & ARTS 583, 597-98 (2018). As Wolkoff concedes, "The Gates" achieved recognized stature and would have been protected under VARA.

In recent years, "street art," much of which is "temporary," has emerged as a major category of contemporary art. As one scholar has noted, "street art" has "blossomed into far more than spray-painted tags and quickly vanishing pieces . . . painted by rebellious urbanites. in some quarters, it has become high art." *Id.* at 583. For example, noted street artist Banksy has appeared alongside President Barack Obama and Apple founder Steve Jobs on *Time* magazine's list of the world's 100 most influential people. Though often painted on building walls where it may be subject to overpainting, Banksy's work is nonetheless acknowledged, both by the art community and the general public, as of significant artistic merit and cultural importance. Famously, Banksy's *Girl with a Balloon* self-destructed after selling for $1.4 million at Sotheby's, but, as with Banksy's street art, the temporary quality of this work has only added to its recognition.

A Banksy painting at 5Pointz would have possessed recognized stature, even if it were temporary. Even if "The Gates" had been replaced with another art exhibit, that work would have maintained its recognized stature. Although a work's short lifespan means that there will be fewer opportunities for the work to be viewed and evaluated, the temporary nature of the art is not a bar to recognized stature.

The district court correctly observed that when Congress wanted to impose durational limits on work subject to VARA, it knew how to do so. For example, the statute provides that "[t]he modification of a work of visual art which is a result of the passage of time or the inherent nature of the materials is not a distortion, mutilation, or other modification described in subsection (a)(3)(A)." 17 U.S.C. § 106A(c)(1). For that reason, the gradual erosion of outdoor artwork exposed to the elements or the melting of an ice sculpture does not threaten liability. Congress also imposed a durational limit insofar as the statute protects only works that are "fixed"—"sufficiently permanent . . . to be perceived. . . for a period of more than transitory duration." *Id.* §§ 101, 102(a). We have held that a work that exists for only 1.2 seconds is of merely transitory duration but have noted with approval cases holding that a work "embodied . . . for at least several minutes" is of more than transitory duration. *Cartoon Network LP, LLLP v. CSC Holdings, Inc.*, 536 F.3d 121, 127-28 (2d Cir. 2008). It is undisputed that the 5Pointz works survived far longer than this and therefore satisfied the statute's minimal durational requirement.

As a variation on the theme that temporary artwork does not merit VARA protection, Wolkoff contends that because the artists were aware that the 5Pointz buildings might eventually be torn down, they should have expected their work to be destroyed. The district court correctly observed, however, that VARA accounts for this possibility. Under § 113(d), if the art at 5Pointz was incorporated into the site such that it could not be removed without being destroyed, then Wolkoff was required to obtain "a written instrument . . . that [was] signed by the owner of the building and the [artist] and that specifie[d] that installation of the work may subject the work to destruction, distortion, mutilation, or other modification, by reason of its removal." 17 U.S.C. § 113(d)(1)(B). It is undisputed that no such instrument was executed. If, on the other hand, the 5Pointz art could have been safely removed, then Wolkoff was required to provide written notice of the planned demolition and to allow the artists 90 days to remove the work or to pay for its removal. *See id.* § 113(d)(2)(B). Again, it is undisputed that Wolkoff did none of this. . . .

Finally, Wolkoff contends that the district court erroneously focused on the stature of the 5Pointz site rather than the individual 5Pointz works. Yet again we see no error. The district court did not focus exclusively on the stature of the site. The court considered the individual works at the site and determined that some were not of recognized stature. Setting that aside, we easily conclude that the site of a work is relevant to its recognition and stature and may, in certain cases, render the recognition and stature of a work beyond question. Appearance at a major site—*e.g.*, the Louvre or the Prado—ensures that a work will be recognized, that is, seen and appreciated by the public and the art community. The appearance of a work of art at a curated site such as a museum or 5Pointz means that the work has been deemed meritorious by the curator and therefore is evidence of stature. When the curator is distinguished, his selection of the work is especially probative. Consequently, we see no error when the district court considered the 5Pointz site itself as some evidence of the works' recognized stature. . . .
.

V.

. . .

We review the district court's finding of willfulness for clear error, and we see none. *See 4 Pillar Dynasty LLC v. N.Y. & Co., Inc.*, 933 F.3d 202, 209 (2d Cir. 2019). As Judge Block found, Wolkoff admitted his awareness, prior to destroying 5Pointz, that the artists were pressing VARA claims. Additionally, VARA contains provisions limiting artists' rights vis-à-vis building owners when owners give them 90 days' notice and the opportunity to remove their artwork, 17 U.S.C. § 113(d)(2), but Wolkoff testified that, although he was advised by counsel both before and after the destruction, he chose "to hire people to whitewash[] it in one shot instead of *waiting for three months*," (alteration in original). The district court found that this testimony evinced a deliberate choice to violate VARA rather than to follow the statutory notice procedures.

Wolkoff did not help his cause when he later reminded the district court that he "would make the same decision today."

Most troubling to the district court and to us is Wolkoff's decision to whitewash the artwork at all. Nothing in the record indicates that it was necessary to whitewash the artwork before beginning construction of the apartments. . . .

. . . The district court was entitled to conclude, based on this record, that Wolkoff acted willfully and was liable for enhanced statutory damages. . . .

COMMENTS AND QUESTIONS

1. *Comparison to Moral Rights Protection in Continental Europe.* Significant constraints on moral rights protection built into § 106A make it much more limited than artist protection in Europe. Consider the case involving Picasso's painting "Trois Femmes." Two art investors cut the painting into one-inch squares, which they then marketed as "original Picassos." Daniel Grant, *Before You Cut Up That Picasso . . .*, WORLD MONITOR, Feb. 1992, at 58–59. This mutilation is illegal in France. Because Picasso was dead when this occurred, however, § 106A would not prohibit it in the United States. § 106A(d)(1). In addition, § 106A does not extend to a host of works, such as films, that are protected under European moral rights regimes. *Cf.* John Huston—*Asphalt Jungle* Case, reported at 22 INT'L REV. IND. PROP. & COPYRIGHT L. 121 (1991) (describing French court's decision to bar showing of "colorized" version of film made in black and white by director John Huston).

Moral rights in the continental tradition are normally thought to be "inalienable." Certainly, the Berne Convention speaks of an author retaining such rights even after relinquishing the copyright. And Sarraute refers to the "inalienable, unbarrable, and perpetual nature of the French moral right." Raymond Sarraute, *Current Theory on the Moral Right of Authors and Artists Under French Law*, 16 AM. J. COMP. L. 465, 485 (1968); *but see* Neil W. Netanel, *Alienability Restrictions and the Enhancement of Author Autonomy in United States and Continental Copyright Law*, 12 CARDOZO ARTS & ENT. L.J. 1 (1994) (suggesting that the extent of inalienability in continental moral rights law has been overstated). Should moral rights be subject to sale or waiver by contract? If so, what good are they?

2. Recall *Mirage Editions v. Albuquerque A.R.T.*, discussed in Chapter IV(E)(1)(c). The court there held that altering a copyrighted work created an infringing derivative work, even though the alteration did not involve the making of a new copy. Does this rule serve to protect the moral rights of artists by allowing them to prevent alterations of their works even after the artists have sold the work? Does it matter that the copyright owner, rather than the original author, is the one with the power to exercise this right?

3. *State Moral Rights.* In some states, VARA is augmented by separate state moral rights statutes. The state statutes generally provide more and broader rights to artists and restrict their alienability. *See, e.g.,* 107 N.M. Stat. Ann. § 13-4B-2(B), 3(B) (work of fine art is "any original work of visual or graphic art of any media . . . of recognized quality."); R.I. Gen. Laws § 5-62-2(e); Conn. Gen. Stat. Ann. § 42-116t; Cal. Civ. Code

§§ 987–990; Pa. Stat. Ann. title 73, §§ 2101–10; Mass. Gen. Laws Ann. ch. 231, § 85S. The New York moral rights statute takes a different tack. It emphasizes the value of an artist's reputation, rather than the intrinsic value of the work itself. Under this statute, for example, display of a mutilated original art work (or a copy for limited-run works) is prohibited only if the artist's name is associated with it. *See* N.Y. ARTS AND CULTURAL AFFAIRS LAW § 14.03 (1994).

The enforceability of these state protections has been cast into question by the passage of VARA. Due to federal preemption, VARA provides the exclusive vehicle for asserting "all legal or equitable rights that are equivalent to any of the" attribution and integrity rights as of June 1, 1991. State laws remain enforceable, however, to the extent that they create legal or equitable rights that are not equivalent to VARA's attribution and integrity rights or extend beyond the life of the author. Given the ambiguity surrounding the scope of federal preemption, it remains to be seen whether VARA's passage expands or contracts protection of visual artists' moral rights in the United States.

4. *Resale Royalties ("Droit de Suite")*. The *droit de suite* permits an artist to benefit from appreciation in the value of her works by entitling her to a percentage of all subsequent sales. The California Resale Royalty Act provides that a 5 percent royalty shall be paid on each sale of a work. *See* Cal. Civ. Code § 986(a). The Ninth Circuit, however, struck down this statute with respect to sales occurring outside of California under the dormant Commerce Clause. *See Sam Francis Foundation v. Christies, Inc.*, 784 F.3d 1320 (9th Cir. 2015) (en banc). The dormant Commerce Clause restricts state regulations that improperly burden or discriminate against interstate commerce. A later panel held that the statute was preempted by the 1976 Copyright Act. *See Close v. Sotheby's, Inc.*, 909 F.3d 1204 (9th Cir. 2018).

5. *Policy Analysis*. Moral rights remain controversial in the United States. They raise a host of difficult philosophical and implementation questions: Should U.S. law offer general protections to authors and artists against alteration or misattribution of their works? Do such rights interfere with the free licensing of works of intellectual property by giving the creator a continual "veto power" over editing and publication? Should moral rights extend beyond the first sale of a book or work of art, preventing its owner from (for example) destroying or mutilating that particular copy? Is it desirable for an artist to be able to control what the owner of a piece of art does with it? Even in the privacy of her own home? The statutes speak of "defacement, mutilation, or destruction" of works of art, but also prevent mere "alteration" and "modification." Who should make this determination? The artist? The courts? What might constitute actionable alteration of a work of art? Moving it? *Cf. Pollara v. Seymour*, 344 F.3d 265 (2d Cir. 2003).

iii.   *State and Common Law Copyrights*

The 1976 Act largely preempted state and common law copyright protection. *See* § 301. Congress carved out a few particular areas in which state or common law protection may still apply to works of authorship fixed in a tangible medium of expression. Most notably, § 301(c) preserves protection for sound recordings fixed before February 15, 1972.

This is a particularly active area of litigation. Record labels and recording artists have filed a raft of cases against Pandora, Spotify, and XM Radio seeking damages for public performance of pre-1972 sound recordings. The plaintiffs allege that either state statutes (in the case of California) or common law doctrines afford sound recording owners a public performance right. Interestingly, there is a Pennsylvania Supreme Court decision so holding. *See Waring v. WDAS Broadcasting Station*, 327 Pa. 433 (Penn. S.Ct. 1937) (reasoning that "[j]ust as the birth of the printing press made it necessary for equity to inaugurate a protection for literary and intellectual property, so these latter-day inventions [sound recording and broadcasting] make demands upon the creative and ever-evolving energy of equity to extend that protection so as adequately to do justice under current conditions of life"); *but cf. RCA Manufacturing Co. v. Whiteman*, 114 F.2d 86 (2d Cir. 1940) (holding that any "common-law property" in performances ended with sale of the records).

Notwithstanding the *Waring* decision, there was little effort to enforce a state or common law public performance right in sound recordings until this recent spate of cases. The defendants in the contemporary cases have pointed to this long period of non-enforcement to suggest that a common law public performance right was not thought to exist. On the other hand, there are plausible reasons for record companies to have stayed their hand. First, the record companies may well have also owned an interest in the underlying musical compositions through their music publishing divisions and hence stood to gain through the ASCAP or BMI license. Second, radio play promoted record sales. With the demise of record sales in the Internet Age, sound recording owners see getting a piece of the streaming revenue stream to be the best strategy.

The New York's Court of Appeals (its highest state court) ruled that there is no public performance right in sound recordings under New York's common law. *Flo & Eddie, Inc. v. Sirius XM Radio, Inc.*, 28 N.Y.3d 583 (Ct. App. 2016). The majority concluded that "[i]t would would be illogical to conclude that the right of public performance would have existed for decades without the courts recognizing such a right as a matter of state common law, and in the absence of any artist or record company attempting to enforce that right in this state until now." *Id.* at 605. Furthermore, "[b]ecause the consequences of doing so could be extensive and far-reaching, and there are many competing interests at stake, . . . the recognition of such a right should be left to the legislature." *Id.* at 605–06. The Supreme Court of Florida agreed. *See Flo & Eddie, Inc. v. Sirius XM Radio, Inc.*, 229 So. 3d 305 (Fla. S.Ct. 2017). An analogous case is pending in California.

Congress extended federal copyright protection to pre-1972 sound recordings in the Music Modernization Act. *See* § 1401. Federal protection extends for 95 years from first publication with a 3 to 15 years transition period. Congress granted owners of sound recordings rights under §§ 106(1), 106(2), 106(3), 106(6), 602, 1201, and 1202, subject to the § 107 fair use defense, § 108's library exemptions, the § 109(a) first sale doctrine, §110's exemptions for small shops and some non-profit uses, § 112's limitation for ephemeral recordings, and the § 512 online service provider safe harbor. The legislation also provides for noncommercial use of orphan works. *See* § 1401(c). The copyright remedies apply, with modest caveats. *See* § 1401(f)(5).

iv.   Digital Rights

a.   Audio Home Recording Act

As analog recording technology improved during the 1980s, the sound recording industry became particularly concerned about the inevitable arrival of digital recording technology. While listeners had been recording off the airwaves since the introduction of the audio cassette tape, copyright owners feared that digital equipment could produce the viral spread of high quality copies. By the mid-1980s, just a few years after the release of the record labels' catalogs in unencrypted digital format (on CDs), consumer electronics companies sought to introduce a host of new products that would enable consumers to make digital copies of audio recordings. These technologies, DAT and mini-disc (DCC), made it possible to produce identical copies of copyrighted works without any significant degradation of quality. As occurred with the introduction of video cassette recording technology in the early 1980s, copyright owners sued the principal manufacturer of this technology, the Sony Corporation. *See Cahn v. Sony Corp.*, 90 Civ. 4537 (S.D.N.Y. Jul. 9, 1990).

In the shadow of costly and uncertain litigation (and following Sony's acquisition of CBS Records, one of the leading record labels, in 1987), the various interests resolved their differences through negotiations which culminated in Congress's passage of the Audio Home Recording Rights Act of 1992 (codified at 17 U.S.C. §§ 1001–10). For the first time in the history of copyright, the government imposed technological design constraints on the manufacture of copying devices. This legislation also established a royalty on the sale of devices and blank recording media. Section 1002(a) prohibits the importation, manufacture, and distribution of any digital audio recording device that does not incorporate technological controls (Serial Copy Management System or functional equivalents) that block second-generation digital copying. This technology control allowed users to make copies directly from a compact disc, but not from digital copies made using this technology. In so doing, the AHRA sought to limit the viral spread of copies. Consumers could make first-generation copies, but no further copies could be made from those copies.

To compensate copyright owners for the copying that could result from these new technologies, the Act requires manufacturers and importers of digital audio recording equipment and blank tapes, disks, or other storage media to pay a percentage of their transfer prices (2 percent for digital audio devices and 3 percent for storage media) into a royalty pool, which is distributed to owners of musical compositions (one-third) and sound recordings (two-thirds) based on prior year sales and air time. *See* §§ 1003–07.[25]

---

[25] Note that the AHRA applies only to "digital audio recording device[s]" and "medi[a]," to the exclusion of personal computers, hard drives, memory cards–and cars. *See Alliance of Artists & Recording*

This compensation mechanism is administered by the Register of Copyright, with provisions for arbitration of disputes. Section 1008 affords immunity for the manufacture, importation, and distribution of digital audio devices meeting the § 1002 design requirements, any analog audio recording devices, and any recording media. It also immunizes consumers from infringement liability for the noncommercial use of analog or qualifying digital devices for making copies. Violations of the AHRA are not copyright violations. Rather, the AHRA contains its own enforcement, remedy, and dispute resolution provisions. *See* §§ 1009–10.

b. *Anti-Circumvention Provisions*

In the mid-1990s, content owners came to see encryption and other digital rights management technologies as a means of "self-help" in the effort to discourage unauthorized distribution of their works. They recognized, however, that such technologies would be vulnerable to hacking—unauthorized circumvention of technological protection measures. As a result, they sought to expand copyright protection beyond its traditional prohibitions against infringement to include limits on the decrypting or circumventing of technological protection systems and the trafficking in such decryption tools. They argued to Congress that without such protection, they would be unwilling to release content onto the Internet, which in turn would hamper the adoption of broadband services. Various other interests—ranging from ISPs and telecommunications companies to consumer electronics manufacturers, library associations, computer scientists, and copyright professors—expressed concern about chilling effects of such an expansion of copyright law upon those who transmit content and wish to make "fair use" of copyrighted works. The resulting legislation—the Digital Millennium Copyright Act of 1998 (DMCA)—responded to the core concerns of the content owners by enacting anti-circumvention and anti-trafficking bans, while assuaging the fears of the most powerful opposing interest group coalition—ISPs and telecom companies—by creating a series of online service provider safe harbors.

Somewhat like the AHRA, Title I of the DMCA goes beyond traditional copyright protections in order to address the threat of unauthorized reproduction and distribution of copyrighted works in the digital age.[26] But rather than mandating specific technology controls,[27] the DMCA focuses on ensuring the efficacy of technological control measures put in place by copyright owners. The statute divides technological protection measures (TPMs) into two functional categories: (1) those that control *access* to copyrighted works—e.g., password protection governing access to an eBook; and (2)

Cos. v. Denso Int'l, 947 F.3d 849 (D.C. Cir. 2020) (holding that since the "primary purpose" of cars is not to record music, they do not constitute digital audio recording devices even thought they can record music).

[26] Although codified as part of Title 17 of the U.S. Code, violations of the DMCA do not constitute copyright infringements. *See* §§ 1203–04 (specifying civil and criminal remedies for violations of the DMCA's anticircumvention and anti-trafficking provisions).

[27] While generally eschewing technology mandates, *see* § 1201(c)(3) (the "no mandate" provision), the DMCA does impose limited technology controls on some videocassette recorders. *See* § 1201(k) (requiring future analog VCRs to incorporate new anticopying technology).

those that permit access but control *copying (or some other right)* of copyrighted works—e.g., a digital rights management system that authorizes the user to view a film during a 24-hour period.[28] With regard to the first category (TPMs that prevent *access*), § 1201(a) prohibits both specific acts to circumvent the technological measure[29] and the manufacture, importation, trafficking in, and marketing of devices that: (1) are primarily designed or produced for the purpose of circumventing a technological measure that effectively "controls access to" a copyrighted work; (2) have only limited commercially significant purpose or use other than to circumvent such technological protection measures; or (3) are marketed for use in circumventing such technological protection measures. § 1201(a)(2). With regard to TPMs regulating *copying (or exercise of other copyright rights)* of a work where access has been lawfully obtained, § 1201(b) does not prohibit the act of circumvention but only trafficking in and marketing of circumvention devices. This more limited protection was purportedly designed so as not to impair users' ability to make fair use of content to which they have been given access.[30] This limitation, however, provides little solace to advocates of broad fair use standards because although it allows circumvention of use controls, the ban on trafficking of circumvention devices (including instructions) puts the means for such access beyond the reach of all but the most technically adept—those possessing the ability to decrypt restricted works unaided.

Section 1202 further bolsters encryption efforts by prohibiting the falsification, removal, or alteration of "copyright management information," such as digital

---

[28] It is unclear where DVD encryption falls in this typology. *See* NIMMER ON COPYRIGHT, § 12A.06. If the DVD encryption system, content scrambling system (CSS), limits playback on an authorized compliant player (an access TPM) and prevents copying of the content to another medium (a copying TPM), then both sections 1201(a) and 1201(b) could be implicated by decryption of CSS. But if CSS-encrypted DVDs can be freely copied, but just cannot be viewed without a compliant machine, then only section 1201(a) is implicated by decryption. *See Universal City Studios, Inc. v. Corley*, 273 F.3d 429 (2d Cir. 2001). The Court there provides this explication of section 1201's meaning:

Subsection 1201(b)(1) is similar to subsection 1201(a)(2), except that subsection 1201(a)(2) covers those who traffic in technology that can circumvent "a technological measure that effectively controls access to a work protected under" Title 17, whereas subsection 1201(b)(1) covers those who traffic in technology that can circumvent "protection afforded by a technological measure that *effectively protects a right of a copyright owner* under" Title 17. *Id.* § 1201(a)(2), (b)(1) (emphases added). In other words, although both subsections prohibit trafficking in a circumvention technology, the focus of subsection 1201(a)(2) is circumvention of technologies designed to *prevent access* to a work, and the focus of subsection 1201(b)(1) is circumvention of technologies designed to *permit access* to a work but *prevent copying* of the work or some other act that infringes a copyright. *See* S. REP. NO. 105-190, at 11–12 (1998). Subsection 1201(a)(1) differs from both of these anti-trafficking subsections in that it targets the use of a circumvention technology, not the trafficking in such a technology.

Id. at 441.

[29] § 1201(a)(1). To circumvent a technological measure is defined as descrambling a scrambled work, decrypting an encrypted work, or "otherwise to avoid, bypass, remove, deactivate, or impair a technological measure, without the authority of the copyright owner." § 1201(a)(3)(A).

[30] *See* H.R. REP. NO. 105-551, pt. 1, at 18 (1998); Exemption to Prohibition on Circumvention of Copyright Protection Systems for Access Control Technologies, 65 Fed. Reg. 64,557 (2000) (codified at 37 C.F.R. § 201).

watermarks and identifying information, when done with the intent to encourage or conceal infringement.

The DMCA addresses the many objections and concerns raised by various groups through a complex series of narrow exemptions. Detailed exemptions exist for law enforcement activities, radio and television broadcasters, libraries, encryption researchers, filtering of content to prevent access by minors, and protection for personally identifying information. *See* §§ 1201(d), (e), (h), (i). To reduce adverse effects of § 1201 upon fair use of copyrighted works, the DMCA authorizes the Librarian of Congress to exempt any classes of copyrighted works where persons making non-infringing uses are likely to be adversely affected by the anticircumvention ban. Perhaps of most significance, the DMCA authorizes the circumvention of technological protection measures for purposes of reverse engineering of computer programs for the "sole purpose of identifying and analyzing those elements of the program that are necessary to achieve interoperability of an independently created computer program." § 1201(f)(1).

COMMENTS AND QUESTIONS

1. *Stream Capture Technology.* One of the first tests of the anticircumvention prohibitions arose with regard to technology for streaming music and video over the Internet. RealNetworks developed technology that allows Internet users to access protected content encoded in its RealMedia formats using its RealPlayer software. The user cannot, however, store the content on their computer (unless the content provider activated the download capability). Streambox began offering its "VCR" and "Ripper" technologies. The Streambox VCR product enables users to access and download copies of RealMedia files that are streamed over the Internet by mimicking the operation of RealPlayer software. It then circumvents the authentication procedure in order to gain access to streamed content. Unlike the RealPlayer, however, the Streambox VCR bypasses the copy switch so that users can download content, even if the content owner had intended that it only be streamed. Once downloaded, the content can then be accessed, copied, and distributed at the user's discretion. Streambox's Ripper technology enables users to convert files from RealMedia (.RMA) format to other formats such as .WAV (a format commonly used for music editing), .WMA (Windows Media Player), and .MP3.

RealNetworks sued Streambox for violating the DMCA's anticircumvention prohibitions. On RealNetworks's motion for a preliminary injunction, the court held that aspects of the Streambox VCR were likely to violate the new law. *See RealNetworks, Inc. v. Streambox, Inc.*, 2000 WL 127311 (W.D. Wash. 2000). In particular, the court found that the authentication process used to establish a handshake between the RealPlayer and a RealNetworks server constitutes a "technological measure" that "effectively controls access" to copyrighted works. The Streambox VCR's means of establishing access and then bypassing the copy switch circumvents the technological protection measures. The court further found that it had no significant commercial purpose other than to enable users to access and record protected content.

The court rejected Streambox's defense that its software allows consumers to make "fair use" copies, such as to time or space shift access to content. It distinguished the *Sony* case on two grounds: (1) many of the copyright owners there authorized or would not have objected to having their content time-shifted whereas all of the content owners using the RealNetworks' technology to stream their works specifically chose not to authorize downloading; and (2) *Sony* did not address the new protections afforded by the DMCA.[31] The court declined to enjoin Streambox's Ripper software, raising doubts as to whether the .RMA format constituted a "technological protection measure" within the meaning of the DMCA and noting that Ripper could serve significant legitimate purposes.

2. *Constitutionality of the DMCA's Anticircumvention Provisions.* In a series of high-profile cases, the content industries pursued publishers of decryption code who have asserted as a defense that the DMCA interferes with their freedom of expression protected by the First Amendment. The courts upheld the anticircumvention provisions under the intermediate scrutiny test applied to content-neutral constraints on speech. Under this standard, the courts determined that the ban on distributing decryption code were adequately justified by the substantial governmental interest in restraining unauthorized distribution of copyrighted works in the digital age, were not related to the suppression of free expression, and did not burden substantially more speech than necessary to further the interest in preventing piracy. *See Universal City Studios, Inc. v. Corley*, 273 F.3d 429 (2d Cir. 2001); *see also United States v. Elcom, Ltd.*, 203 F. Supp. 2d 1111 (N.D. Cal. 2002).

3. *Circumventing Fair Use?* As noted above, violations of the DMCA are not acts of copyright infringement, but separate offenses. As a result, some courts have held that the defenses available under the Copyright Act, including fair use, simply don't apply to a DMCA claim. *321 Studios v. Metro-Goldwyn-Mayer, Inc.*, 307 F. Supp. 2d 1085 (N.D. Cal. 2004) (holding liable a provider of software that decrypted a DVD but allowed owners of a DVD only to make a single backup copy, notwithstanding the fair use claim for the making of that copy). While § 1201(c)(1) of the DMCA provides that "nothing in this law" shall interfere with "fair use," among other defenses, the courts coming to this conclusion have reasoned that the DMCA doesn't interfere with fair use, but merely renders it irrelevant by allowing copyright owners to bring a non-copyright claim. On the other hand, in *Chamberlain Group, Inc. v. Skylink Tech., Inc.*, 381 F.3d 1178 (Fed. Cir. 2004), the court engaged in a tortured interpretation of the statute in order to conclude that the fair use defense did apply to anticircumvention claims.

---

[31] The court cited NIMMER ON COPYRIGHT for the proposition that "those who manufacture equipment and products generally can no longer gauge their conduct as permitted or forbidden by reference to the *Sony* doctrine. For a given piece of machinery might qualify as a staple item of commerce, with a substantial noninfringing use, and hence be immune from attack under *Sony*'s construction of the Copyright Act—but nonetheless still be subject to suppression under Section 1201." 1 NIMMER ON COPYRIGHT (1999 Supp.), § 12A.18[B]. As such, "[e]quipment manufacturers in the twenty-first century will need to vet their products for compliance with Section 1201 in order to avoid a circumvention claim, rather than under *Sony* to negate a copyright claim." *Id.*

4. *Exemption Process.* As noted above, the anticircumvention provisions impinge upon fair use of copyrighted works. In addition to the narrow exceptions and limitations specified in the DMCA, Congress instructed the Copyright Office to conduct triennial rulemaking proceedings to consider whether additional categorical exemptions should be made. In the first such proceeding, conducted in 2000, the Copyright Office interpreted its authority narrowly. Its final rule exempted only two narrow classes of works from the anticircumvention ban: (1) literary works whose storage formats had malfunctioned or become obsolete; and (2) lists of filtering criteria employed by software vendors to screen undesirable Internet content. *See* U.S. Copyright Office, *Exemption to Prohibition on Circumvention of Copyright Protection Systems for Access Control Technologies*, 83 FED. REG. 54010 (2018). Moreover, the Copyright Office has streamlined the renewal process by interpreting its statutory authority "to permit determinations to be based upon evidence drawn from prior proceedings, but only upon a conclusion that this evidence remains reliable to support granting an exemption in the current proceeding." U.S. COPYRIGHT OFFICE, SECTION 1201 REPORT 143 (2017). . Since that time, the Copyright Office has vastly expanded the range of exemptions.

5. *Control of Aftermarket Products.* The general wording of the DMCA's anticircumvention provisions has produced an unanticipated wave of litigation involving the use of technological protection measures to exclude competitors from "aftermarkets"—goods or services supplied for a durable product (e.g., a printer) after its initial sale, such as replacement ink. Several companies embedded digital code into their products and aftermarket components that must interoperate in order to function as a means of exerting control over such aftermarkets. When competitors in these aftermarkets decrypted such digital code in order to manufacture their own components, these durable product manufacturers sued, alleging violation of the anticircumvention provisions of the DMCA. The courts declined to find liability, emphasizing that the careful balance that Congress sought to achieve between the "interests of content creators and information users," H.R .REP. NO. 105-551, pt. 1, at 26, would be upset if the anticircumvention prohibitions could be applied to activities that did not facilitate copyright infringement. *See Chamberlain Group, Inc. v. Skylink Tech., Inc.*, 381 F.3d 1178 (Fed. Cir. 2004) (holding that access to the copyrighted work was in fact authorized and that "section 1201 prohibits only forms of access that bear a reasonable relationship to the protections that the Copyright Act otherwise affords copyright owners"); *Lexmark Int'l, Inc. v. Static Control Components, Inc.*, 387 F.3d 522 (6th Cir. 2005) (holding that the lock-out technology at issue did not effectively control access to a copyrighted work); *see also Storage Technology Corp. v. Custom Hardware Engineering*, 421 F.3d 1307 (Fed. Cir. 2005) (decryption (by third party software repair entity) in order to perform software maintenance activities not actionable). Are these claims legitimate uses of the DMCA? Or are they a form of "bootstrapping," alleging that the lockout code is itself the copyrighted work that the code is nominally designed to protect?

2. Indirect Infringement

As technological advances provide ever more powerful means for reproducing, adapting, distributing, and performing copyrighted works, the contours of liability for those who contribute to, induce, or profit from the infringing acts of others, or who merely sell products that others can use to infringe, has taken center-stage in copyright law and policy. To understand these contours, we need to trace the development of copyright law. We begin with the analog age and then turn to the digital age.

i. The Analog Age

Copyright infringement standards developed from an austere statutory foundation. The 1790 Act provided that "any person or persons who shall print or publish any manuscript, without the consent and approbation of the author or proprietor thereof . . . shall be liable to suffer and pay to the said author or proprietor all damages occasioned by such injury." The Act did not provide a formal definition of infringement. The 1909 Act did not elucidate copyright's reach any further, stating simply that any person who "shall infringe the copyright in any work protected under the copyright laws of the United States . . . shall be liable" for various remedies. *See* 17 U.S.C. § 25 (1909 Act), recodified § 101 (1912 Act); *see also* H. Committee Print, 89th Cong., 1st Sess., Copyright Law Revision Part 6, Supplementary Report of the Register of Copyrights on the General Revision of the U.S. Copyright Law; 1965 Revision Bill (May 1965), chapter 7 (Copyright Infringement and Remedies) at 131 ("It seems strange, though not very serious, that the present law lacks any statement or definition of what constitutes an infringement.").

Against this bare legislative backdrop and drawing upon general principles of civil liability (tort law), courts recognized that copyright liability extends not just to those who infringe directly but also to those who contribute to or control the infringing acts of others. As noted more than a century ago, "[t]he evidence shows that the defendants bought the pictures from the complainants, furnished them to the photogravure company, ordered the copies made, and gave general directions as to how the work should be done. They are therefore liable as joint tort feasors." *Fishel v. Lueckel*, 53 F. 499 (S.D.N.Y. 1892); *see also Kalem Co. v. Harper Brothers*, 222 U.S. 55, 62–63 (1911) (observing that contributory liability is a principle "recognized in every part of the law").

a. Respondeat Superior

Courts readily recognized that employers should be liable for the infringing acts of their employees under traditional master-servant principles:

> Neither does the fact, if it is a fact, that young Williams, the operator of the player piano, borrowed this music without the direction, knowledge, or consent of the owner or manager of the theater affect the question. The rule of the common law applies, to wit, that the master is civilly liable in damages for the wrongful act of his servant in the transaction of the business which he was

employed to do, although the particular act may have been done without express authority from the master, or even against his orders.

M. Witmark & Sons v. Calloway, 22 F.2d 412, 415 (D. Tenn. 1927).

b. Vicarious Liability

Even outside of the master-servant context, courts extended liability to those who profit from infringing activity where an enterprise has the right and ability to prevent infringement.

> [T]he owner of a dance hall at whose place copyrighted musical compositions are played in violation of the rights of the copyright holder is liable, if the playing be for the profit of the proprietor of the dance hall. And this is so even though the orchestra be employed under a contract that would ordinarily make it an independent contractor.

Dreamland Ball Room v. Shapiro, Bernstein & Co., 36 F.2d 354, 355 (7th Cir. 1929); *see also Gershwin Publ'g Corp. v. Columbia Artists Mgmt.*, 443 F.2d 1159 (2d Cir. 1971) ("When the right and ability to supervise coalesce with an obvious and direct financial interest in the exploitation of copyrighted material—even in the absence of actual knowledge . . . —the purposes of copyright law may be best effectuated by the imposition of liability upon the beneficiary of that exploitation."). By contrast, courts did not extend liability to landlords who leased premises to a direct infringer for a fixed rental and did not participate directly in organizing or soliciting the infringing activity. *See Deutsch v. Arnold*, 98 F.2d 686 (2d Cir. 1938). *Cf. Fonovisa v. Cherry Auction*, 76 F.3d 259 (9th Cir. 1996) (extending liability to the operator of a swap meet who repeatedly leased booth space to concessionaires selling infringing tapes).

In discussing the infringement section, the House Report includes the following explanation:

Vicarious liability for infringing performances

> The committee has considered and rejected an amendment to this section intended to exempt the proprietors of an establishment, such as a ballroom or night club, from liability for copyright infringement committed by an independent contractor, such as an orchestra leader. A well-established principle of copyright law is that a person who violates any of the exclusive rights of the copyright owner is an infringer, including persons who can be considered related or vicarious infringers. To be held a related or vicarious infringer in the case of performing rights, a defendant must either actively operate or supervise the operation of the place wherein the performances occur, or control the content of the infringing program, and expect commercial gain from the operation and either direct or indirect benefit from the infringing performance. The committee has decided that no justification exists for changing existing law, and causing a significant erosion of the public performance right.

H.R. REP. NO. 94-1478 at 159–60. The Ninth Circuit declined to extend vicarious liability to a company that hired a contractor that used images copied from the Internet without authorization to design the company's website. The court emphasized that the hiring firm received no direct financial benefit from thee infringing activity. *See Erickson Prods. v. Kast*, 921 F.3d 822 (9th Cir. 2019).

c. *Contributory Liability*

"[O]ne who, with knowledge of the infringing activity, induces, causes, or materially contributes . . . may be held liable as a 'contributory' infringer." *Gershwin Publ'g Corp. v. Columbia Artists Mgmt.*, 443 F.2d 1159, 1162 (2d Cir. 1971). Thus, in *Elektra Records v. Gem Elec. Distribs.*, 360 F. Supp. 821 (E.D.N.Y. 1973), an electronics store which sold blank tapes and made available both pre-recorded tapes of copyrighted works and a high speed, coin-operated "Make-A-Tape" system was held contributorily liable for the infringing activities of its customers.

One of the studies commissioned for what ultimately became the 1976 Act reviewed the jurisprudence of indirect liability. *See* Alan Latman & William S. Tager, Liability of Innocent Infringers of Copyrights (Study No. 25 1958), reprinted in Subcomm. on Patents, Trademarks, and Copyrights, Senate Comm. on the Judiciary, 86th Cong., Copyright Law Revision: Studies 22–25, at 135 (Comm. Print 1960). The comments largely endorsed what the courts had done in extending copyright liability upstream. None of the many participants in the decade and a half of legislative hearings advocated change in the way such liability was addressed under the 1909 Act.

The principal reports accompanying the final version of the 1976 Act confirm that Congress intended to perpetuate indirect copyright liability. In explaining the general scope of copyright, the House Report recognizes contributory liability:

> The exclusive rights accorded to a copyright owner under section 106 are "to do and to authorize" any of the activities specified in the five numbered clauses. Use of the phrase "to authorize" is intended to avoid any questions as to the liability of *contributory* infringers. For example, a person who lawfully acquires an authorized copy of a motion picture would be an infringer if he or she engages in the business of renting it to others for purposes of unauthorized public performance.

H.R. REP. NO. 94-1478 at 61 (emphasis added).

Not long after the passage of the 1976 Act, the scope of contributory infringement liability was tested in a case in which the copyright owners claimed that the sale of a recording device—the video cassette recorder (VCR)—illegally contributed to infringement.

Sony Corporation of America v. Universal City Studios, Inc.
Supreme Court of the United States
464 U.S. 417 (1984)

JUSTICE STEVENS delivered the opinion of the Court.

[The respondents, a group of movie studios, sued the makers of video cassette recorders ("VCRs," or "VTR's" in the opinion), alleging that they were liable for contributory copyright infringement because consumers bought VCRs and used them to tape movies and other programming broadcast by television stations. In order for there to be indirect liability, there must direct infringement. We address the Court's treatment of indirect liability in this section and return to this case in section (E)(2), discussing whether time-shifting by VCR users is fair use.]

II

Article I, Sec. 8 of the Constitution provides that:

The Congress shall have Power . . . to Promote the Progress of Science and useful Arts, by securing for limited Times to Authors and Inventors the exclusive Right to their respective Writings and Discoveries.

The monopoly privileges that Congress may authorize are neither unlimited nor primarily designed to provide a special private benefit. Rather, the limited grant is a means by which an important public purpose may be achieved. It is intended to motivate the creative activity of authors and inventors by the provision of a special reward, and to allow the public access to the products of their genius after the limited period of exclusive control has expired.

The copyright law, like the patent statute, makes reward to the owner a secondary consideration. In *Fox Film Corp. v. Doyal*, 286 U.S. 123, 127, Chief Justice Hughes spoke as follows respecting the copyright monopoly granted by Congress, "The sole interest of the United States and the primary object in conferring the monopoly lie in the general benefits derived by the public from the labors of authors." It is said that reward to the author or artist serves to induce release to the public of the products of his creative genius.

United States v. Paramount Pictures, 334 U.S. 131, 158.

As the text of the Constitution makes plain, it is Congress that has been assigned the task of defining the scope of the limited monopoly that should be granted to authors or to inventors in order to give the public appropriate access to their work product. Because this task involves a difficult balance between the interests of authors and inventors in the control and exploitation of their writings and discoveries on the one hand, and society's competing interest in the free flow of ideas, information, and commerce on the other hand, our patent and copyright statutes have been amended repeatedly.[10]

---

[10] In its report accompanying the comprehensive revision of the Copyright Act in 1909, the Judiciary Committee of the House of Representatives explained this balance:

From its beginning, the law of copyright has developed in response to significant changes in technology. Indeed, it was the invention of a new form of copying equipment—the printing press—that gave rise to the original need for copyright protection. Repeatedly, as new developments have occurred in this country, it has been the Congress that has fashioned the new rules that new technology made necessary. . . .

The judiciary's reluctance to expand the protections afforded by the copyright without explicit legislative guidance is a recurring theme. *See, e.g., Teleprompter Corp. v. CBS*, 415 U.S. 394 (1974); *Fortnightly Corp. v. United Artists*, 392 U.S. 390 (1968); *White-Smith Music Publishing Co. v. Apollo Co.*, 209 U.S. 1 (1908); *Williams and Wilkins v. United States*, 487 F.2d 1345 (1973), affirmed by an equally divided court, 420 U.S. 376 (1975). Sound policy, as well as history, supports our consistent deference to Congress when major technological innovations alter the market for copyrighted materials. Congress has the constitutional authority and the institutional ability to accommodate fully the varied permutations of competing interests that are inevitably implicated by such new technology.

In a case like this, in which Congress has not plainly marked our course, we must be circumspect in construing the scope of rights created by a legislative enactment which never contemplated such a calculus of interests. In doing so, we are guided by Justice Stewart's exposition of the correct approach to ambiguities in the law of copyright:

> The limited scope of the copyright holder's statutory monopoly, like the limited copyright duration required by the Constitution, reflects a balance of competing claims upon the public interest: Creative work is to be encouraged and rewarded, but private motivation must ultimately serve the cause of promoting broad public availability of literature, music, and the other arts. The immediate effect of our copyright law is to secure a fair return for an "author's" creative labor. But the ultimate aim is, by this incentive, to stimulate artistic creativity for the general public good. "The sole interest of the United States and the primary object in conferring the monopoly," this Court has said, "lie in the general benefits derived by the public from the labors of authors." *Fox Film Corp. v. Doyal*, 286 U.S. 123, 127. When technological change has rendered its literal terms ambiguous, the Copyright Act must be construed in light of this basic purpose.

The enactment of copyright legislation by Congress under the terms of the Constitution is not based upon any natural right that the author has in his writings, . . . but upon the ground that the welfare of the public will be served and progress of science and useful arts will be promoted by securing to authors for limited periods the exclusive rights to their writings.

***

In enacting a copyright law Congress must consider . . . two questions: First, how much will the legislation stimulate the producer and so benefit the public, and, second, how much will the monopoly granted be detrimental to the public? The granting of such exclusive rights, under the proper terms and conditions, confers a benefit upon the public that outweighs the evils of the temporary monopoly.

H.R. REP. NO. 2222, 60th Cong., 2d Sess. 7 (1909).

Twentieth Century Music Corp. v. Aiken, 422 U.S. 151, 156 (footnotes omitted). . . .

The Copyright Act provides the owner of a copyright with a potent arsenal of remedies against an infringer of his work, including an injunction to restrain the infringer from violating his rights, the impoundment and destruction of all reproductions of his work made in violation of his rights, a recovery of his actual damages and any additional profits realized by the infringer or a recovery of statutory damages, and attorney's fees.

The two respondents in this case do not seek relief against the Betamax users who have allegedly infringed their copyrights. Moreover, this is not a class action on behalf of all copyright owners who license their works for television broadcast, and respondents have no right to invoke whatever rights other copyright holders may have to bring infringement actions based on Betamax copying of their works. As was made clear by their own evidence, the copying of the respondents' programs represents a small portion of the total use of VTR's. It is, however, the taping of respondents own copyrighted programs that provides them with standing to charge Sony with contributory infringement. To prevail, they have the burden of proving that users of the Betamax have infringed their copyrights and that Sony should be held responsible for that infringement.

III

The Copyright Act does not expressly render anyone liable for infringement committed by another. In contrast, the Patent Act expressly brands anyone who "actively induces infringement of a patent" as an infringer, 35 U.S.C. § 271(b), and further imposes liability on certain individuals labeled "contributory" infringers, § 271(c). The absence of such express language in the copyright statute does not preclude the imposition of liability for copyright infringements on certain parties who have not themselves engaged in the infringing activity. For vicarious liability is imposed in virtually all arcas of the law, and the concept of contributory infringement is merely a species of the broader problem of identifying the circumstances in which it is just to hold one individual accountable for the actions of another.

Such circumstances were plainly present in *Kalem Co. v. Harper Brothers*, 222 U.S. 55 (1911), the copyright decision of this Court on which respondents place their principal reliance. In *Kalem*, the Court held that the producer of an unauthorized film dramatization of the copyrighted book Ben Hur was liable for his sale of the motion picture to jobbers, who in turn arranged for the commercial exhibition of the film. . . .

Respondents argue that *Kalem* stands for the proposition that supplying the "means" to accomplish an infringing activity and encouraging that activity through advertisement are sufficient to establish liability for copyright infringement. This argument rests on a gross generalization that cannot withstand scrutiny. The producer in *Kalem* did not merely provide the "means" to accomplish an infringing activity; the producer supplied the work itself, albeit in a new medium of expression. Petitioners in the instant case do not supply Betamax consumers with respondents' works; respondents do. Petitioners supply a piece of equipment that is generally capable of copying the entire range of programs that may be televised: those that are uncopyrighted, those that are copyrighted but may be copied without objection from the copyright holder, and those that the copyright holder would prefer not to have copied. The Betamax can be used to make authorized or unauthorized uses of copyrighted works, but the range of its potential use is much broader than the particular infringing use of the film Ben Hur involved in *Kalem*. *Kalem* does not support respondents' novel theory of liability.

. . . The only contact between Sony and the users of the Betamax that is disclosed by this record occurred at the moment of sale. The District Court expressly found that "no employee of Sony . . . had either direct involvement with the allegedly infringing activity or direct contact with purchasers of Betamax who recorded copyrighted works off-the-air." And it further found that "there was no evidence that any of the copies made by . . . individual witnesses in this suit were influenced or encouraged by [Sony's] advertisements."

If vicarious liability is to be imposed on petitioners in this case, it must rest on the fact that they have sold equipment with constructive knowledge of the fact that their customers may use that equipment to make unauthorized copies of copyrighted material. There is no precedent in the law of copyright for the imposition of vicarious liability on such a theory. The closest analogy is provided by the patent law cases to which it is appropriate to refer because of the historic kinship between patent law and copyright law.[19] . . .

In the Patent Code both the concept of infringement and the concept of contributory infringement are expressly defined by statute. The prohibition against contributory infringement is confined to the knowing sale of a component especially made for use in connection with a particular patent. There is no suggestion in the statute that one patentee may object to the sale of a product that might be used in connection with other patents. Moreover, the Act expressly provides that the sale of a "staple article or commodity of commerce suitable for substantial noninfringing use" is not contributory infringement.

When a charge of contributory infringement is predicated entirely on the sale of an article of commerce that is used by the purchaser to infringe a patent, the public interest in access to that article of commerce is necessarily implicated. A finding of contributory infringement does not, of course, remove the article from the market altogether; it does, however, give the patentee effective control over the sale of that item. Indeed, a finding of contributory infringement is normally the functional equivalent of holding that the disputed article is within the monopoly granted to the patentee.[21]

---

[19] *E.g., United States v. Paramount Pictures*, 334 U.S. 131, 158 (1948); *Fox Film Corp. v. Doyal*, 286 U.S. 123, 131 (1932); *Wheaton and Donaldson v. Peters and Grigg*, 33 U.S. (8 Pet.) 591, 657–658 (1834). The two areas of the law, naturally, are not identical twins, and we exercise the caution which we have expressed in the past in applying doctrine formulated in one area to the other. *See generally, Mazer v. Stein*, 347 U.S. 201, 217–218 (1954); *Bobbs-Merrill Co. v. Straus*, 210 U.S. 339, 345 (1908).

[21] It seems extraordinary to suggest that the Copyright Act confers upon all copyright owners collectively, much less the two respondents in this case, the exclusive right to distribute VTR's simply because they may be used to infringe copyrights. That, however, is the logical implication of their claim.

For that reason, in contributory infringement cases arising under the patent laws the Court has always recognized the critical importance of not allowing the patentee to extend his monopoly beyond the limits of his specific grant. These cases deny the patentee any right to control the distribution of unpatented articles unless they are "unsuited for any commercial noninfringing use." Unless a commodity "has no use except through practice of the patented method," the patentee has no right to claim that its distribution constitutes contributory infringement. "To form the basis for contributory infringement the item must almost be uniquely suited as a component of the patented invention." P. ROSENBERG, PATENT LAW FUNDAMENTALS § 17.02[2] (1982). "[A] sale of an article which though adapted to an infringing use is also adapted to other and lawful uses, is not enough to make the seller a contributory infringer. Such a rule would block the wheels of commerce." *Henry v. A.B. Dick Co.*, 224 U.S. 1, 48 (1912), overruled on other grounds, *Motion Picture Patents Co. v. Universal Film Mfg. Co.*, 243 U.S. 502, 517 (1917).

We recognize there are substantial differences between the patent and copyright laws. But in both areas the contributory infringement doctrine is grounded on the recognition that adequate protection of a monopoly may require the courts to look beyond actual duplication of a device or publication to the products or activities that make such duplication possible. The staple article of commerce doctrine must strike a balance between a copyright holder's legitimate demand for effective—not merely symbolic—protection of the statutory monopoly, and the rights of others freely to engage in substantially unrelated areas of commerce. Accordingly, the sale of copying equipment, like the sale of other articles of commerce, does not constitute contributory infringement if the product is widely used for legitimate, unobjectionable purposes. Indeed, it need merely be capable of substantial noninfringing uses.

IV

[The court found that a substantial portion of the public's use of VCRs did not implicate copyright at all, and also that the most common use—time-shifting—was a fair use.] The Betamax is, therefore, capable of substantial noninfringing uses. Sony's sale of such equipment to the general public does not constitute contributory infringement of respondent's copyrights.

V

"The direction of Art. I is that Congress shall have the power to promote the progress of science and the useful arts. When, as here, the Constitution is permissive, the sign of how far Congress has chosen to go can come only from Congress." *Deepsouth Packing Co. v. Laitram Corp.*, 406 U.S. 518, 530 (1972).

The request for an injunction below indicates that respondents seek, in effect, to declare VTR's contraband. Their suggestion in this Court that a continuing royalty pursuant to a judicially created compulsory license would be an acceptable remedy merely indicates that respondents, for their part, would be willing to license their claimed monopoly interest in VTR's to petitioners in return for a royalty.

One may search the Copyright Act in vain for any sign that the elected representatives of the millions of people who watch television every day have made it unlawful to copy a program for later viewing at home, or have enacted a flat prohibition against the sale of machines that make such copying possible.

It may well be that Congress will take a fresh look at this new technology, just as it so often has examined other innovations in the past. But it is not our job to apply laws that have not yet been written. Applying the copyright statute, as it now reads, to the facts as they have been developed in this case, the judgment of the Court of Appeals must be reversed.

It is so ordered.

COMMENTS AND QUESTIONS

1. *Statutory Interpretation or Judicial Legislation?* How would you characterize the Court's interpretive methodology? Given that Congress had comprehensively revised the Copyright Act just a few years earlier, was the Court justified in transplanting an express provision of the 1952 Patent Act into the Copyright Act? How else might the Court have determined the appropriate liability standard in the absence of Congressional guidance?

2. The Court notes that "[t]he judiciary's reluctance to expand the protections afforded by the copyright without explicit legislative guidance is a recurring theme." Yet, it was the judiciary, and not Congress, that brought doctrines of indirect liability into copyright law, and Congress endorsed that approach in the 1976 Act. By contrast, the principal cases on which the Court relies for its comment about "judicial reluctance" addressed whether a statutory definition—created by Congress—applied to a new activity.

3. *Exploring the "Historic Kinship."* The Supreme Court justifies its transplantation of a categorical safe harbor from the patent statute into copyright law on the basis of a terse characterization of a rather complex historical relationship. Consider the following effort to delve more deeply into that relationship:

> While central to both patent and copyright law, technology plays very different roles in the two regimes. In patent law, technological innovation is the end to which the system is directed. . . . The staple article of commerce doctrine arose as a way of balancing contributory liability and patent misuse (antitrust-like limits on the leveraging of patent rights). . . .

> By contrast, in copyright law, technology serves as a means to the end of promoting creation and dissemination of works of authorship—art, music, literature, film, and other expressive works. Technology provides the platforms for instantiation, reproduction, and distribution on which creative expression flourishes and commerce occurs. When new technology platforms threaten the economic infrastructure supporting creative expression, copyright law seeks to protect the system that supports the creative arts.

. . . If, contrary to the Court's findings, VCRs did pose a serious threat to the "golden goose" of creative expression, then copyright law would have required a very different analytical perspective. Rather than look to patent law—which seeks to delineate the proper scope of exclusive rights in order to promote technological advance and freedom to use that which is not protected—the Court might have been better served by looking to statutory and common law regimes aimed at protecting interests threatened by technologies that can produce harmful side effects—such as tort law (nuisance, product defect) and environmental law. Thus, when a court enjoins a factory that spews noxious chemicals under nuisance or statutory environmental law, it would be misleading to characterize such a result as giving pollution victims "exclusive rights" over the factory's technology. A more apt characterization would be that society does not believe that the activity should be permitted in its current form. Such a perspective would not necessarily mean that the factory should be shut down permanently. But it might mean that it would have to install filters to limit the adverse effects on neighbors.

Similarly, copyright law has long constrained technologies and business practices that jeopardize the system that supports creative expression. In *Jerome H. Remick & Co. v. General Electric Co.*, 16 F.2d 829 (S.D.N.Y. 1926), a lawsuit pitting music publishers against the newly-emerging radio industry, the court had little difficulty finding that the defendant's broadcast of plaintiff's copyrighted musical composition constituted copyright infringement, despite the fact that such a holding conferred a measure of "control" over the nascent radio broadcasting industry. What that case established was that radio broadcasters would have to obtain valid copyright licenses if they were going to build the popularity of their medium using copyrighted content.[3] This decision did not "shut down" the radio industry. Rather it led to the development of institutions for monitoring of broadcasts and compensation of artists—such as the ASCAP blanket license—which have fostered both commercial broadcasting and the creative arts.

Brief of Professors Peter S. Menell, David Nimmer, Robert P. Merges & Justin Hughes, as Amici Curiae in Support of Petitioners, *Metro-Goldwyn-Mayer Studios Inc., et al. v. Grokster, Ltd.*, et al., No. 04-480 (2005), reprinted in 20 BERKELEY TECH. L.J. 511 (2005); *see also* Peter S. Menell & David Nimmer, *Unwinding Sony*, 95 CAL. L. REV. (2007).

Should the Court have looked to tort law or patent law as the default regime for determining the scope of indirect copyright liability? If it looked to tort law, should all services or technologies—from Internet service providers (ISPs) to general purpose computers and iPods—be subject to scrutiny? (We explore the statutory online service

---

[3] The dance hall cases can also be characterized in this way. . . . Dance halls, like radio . . . can be used for infringing and non-infringing uses. The dance hall cases established that the proprietors of such facilities bore some responsibility to ensure that their clubs were not used for infringing uses. In the end, most clubs complied with the law by obtaining blanket licenses through ASCAP and BMI.

provider safe harbor in Chapter V(F)(2).) Should the manufacturers of computers have to pay damages (including statutory damages) because some people misuse those computers? Should it matter that computer manufacturers, unlike dance hall owners, generally have no control over what purchasers do with their products? To what extent should copyright law, like tort law, encourage product manufacturers to consider the social harm of their design decisions?

Should the analysis focus on the entire product or be conducted on a feature-by-feature basis? Is there an argument that even if the VCR had substantial noninfringing uses, particular parts of its design didn't (e.g., the fast-forward button)? *Cf. Universal Music Australia v. Sharman License Holdings* ([2005] FCA 1242) (Australia) (requiring provider of file-sharing software to implement a keyword filtering technology that excludes copyrighted music from search results).

Since we are dealing with indirect liability, should the economics of enforcement factor into the equation? Are you comforted by the suggestion that copyright owners might not be entitled to block technologies that contribute to infringement altogether, but instead request that courts order design changes to counteract demonstrated piracy-causing effects? Consider that, as the *Sony* Court noted, copyright owners do not all see eye to eye. Would all copyright owners have to agree to allow a new technology? Most of them?

4. *"Capable of Substantial Noninfringing Use."* The Patent Act defines the staple article of commerce safe harbor as "suitable for substantial noninfringing use," 35 U.S.C. § 271(c), whereas the *Sony* decision speaks of "capable" of noninfringing use. What explains this difference? It appears that the Court wanted to get at both present and future uses. Are courts able to gauge such possibilities? Note in this regard that Hollywood was wrong to predict imminent disaster if Sony were allowed to continue making VCRs. *See* Mark A. Lemley, *Is the Sky Falling on the Content Industries?*, 9 J. TELECOM. & HIGH TECH. L. 125 (2011) (chronicling consistently wrong predictions by copyright owners that a new technology would destroy their market over the past 125 years). Does this suggest that courts should be cautious about using copyright law to screen markets for technology?

On the other hand, Professor Peter Menell suggests that the difficulty of enforcing copyright law in the Internet Age has adversely affected several key content industries significantly and that better crafted indirect copyright liability could encourage the development of more symbiotic platforms and services without jeopardizing technological innovation. *See* Peter S. Menell, *Infringement Conflation*, 64 STAN. L. REV. 1551 (2012).

Will allowing technology to continue without judicial intervention ultimately work to the benefit of copyright owners? Those technologies often turn out to provide new ways for copyright owners to get paid. YouTube's ContentID, for instance, allows copyright owners to authorize user-generated content employing their work and uses the carrot of sharing advertising revenues.

ii.   The Digital Age

The amount of content available over the Internet took a massive leap in late 1999 with the introduction of Napster's peer-to-peer network technology. This technology vastly expanded the effective storage and exchange capacity of the Internet by enabling computer users running Napster's software to search the hard drives of millions of other users for files encoded in the MP3 compression format commonly used for music files. Napster's server contained the labels of MP3 files, typically some combination of band names and song titles, which could be searched by Napster users. Searches produced a list of Internet addresses of computers containing the search term. Software running on the user's computer would then form a connection through the Internet to the particular computer containing the file, establish a link, and quickly transfer the file to the searcher's hard drive. In essence, the Napster platform converted every computer running the software and connected to Napster into a "servent"—enabling it to function as both a server and a client. It became the fastest adopted software application in the history of computer technology, attaining 70 million users within its relatively brief period of operation.

The trial court and the Ninth Circuit ultimately concluded that Napster's direct knowledge of copyright infringement by users of its software and its ability to control such activities through the index of file names maintained on its central servers created a responsibility to remove links to infringing content and engage in efforts to police its network. *See A&M Records, Inc. v. Napster, Inc.*, 239 F.3d 1004 (9th Cir. 2001). Furthermore, the district court required that Napster be 100 percent accurate, ensuring that no infringing files at all were indexed on the system. The burden of this responsibility and the prospect of crushing liability ultimately pushed Napster into bankruptcy. During the pendency of this litigation, a new generation of peer-to-peer software providers entered the market, prompting further legal battles.

 MGM Studios Inc. v. Grokster, Ltd.
Supreme Court of the United States
545 U.S. 913 (2005)

JUSTICE SOUTER delivered the opinion of the Court.

The question is under what circumstances the distributor of a product capable of both lawful and unlawful use is liable for acts of copyright infringement by third parties using the product. We hold that one who distributes a device with the object of promoting its use to infringe copyright, as shown by clear expression or other affirmative steps taken to foster infringement, is liable for the resulting acts of infringement by third parties.

I

A

Respondents, Grokster, Ltd., and StreamCast Networks, Inc., defendants in the trial court, distribute free software products that allow computer users to share electronic files through peer-to-peer networks, so called because users' computers communicate directly with each other, not through central servers. The advantage of peer-to-peer networks over information networks of other types shows up in their substantial and growing popularity. Because they need no central computer server to mediate the exchange of information or files among users, the high-bandwidth communications capacity for a server may be dispensed with, and the need for costly server storage space is eliminated. Since copies of a file (particularly a popular one) are available on many users' computers, file requests and retrievals may be faster than on other types of networks, and since file exchanges do not travel through a server, communications can take place between any computers that remain connected to the network without risk that a glitch in the server will disable the network in its entirety. Given these benefits in security, cost, and efficiency, peer-to-peer networks are employed to store and distribute electronic files by universities, government agencies, corporations, and libraries, among others.

Other users of peer-to-peer networks include individual recipients of Grokster's and StreamCast's software, and although the networks that they enjoy through using the software can be used to share any type of digital file, they have prominently employed those networks in sharing copyrighted music and video files without authorization. A group of copyright holders (MGM for short, but including motion picture studios, recording companies, songwriters, and music publishers) sued Grokster and StreamCast for their users' copyright infringements, alleging that they knowingly and intentionally distributed their software to enable users to reproduce and distribute the copyrighted works in violation of the Copyright Act, 17 U.S.C. § 101 et seq. (2000 ed. and Supp. II). MGM sought damages and an injunction.

Discovery during the litigation revealed the way the software worked, the business aims of each defendant company, and the predilections of the users. Grokster's eponymous software employs what is known as FastTrack technology, a protocol developed by others and licensed to Grokster. StreamCast distributes a very similar product except that its software, called Morpheus, relies on what is known as Gnutella technology. A user who downloads and installs either software possesses the protocol to send requests for files directly to the computers of others using software compatible with FastTrack or Gnutella. On the FastTrack network opened by the Grokster software, the user's request goes to a computer given an indexing capacity by the software and designated a supernode, or to some other computer with comparable power and capacity to collect temporary indexes of the files available on the computers of users connected to it. The supernode (or indexing computer) searches its own index and may communicate the search request to other supernodes. If the file is found, the supernode discloses its location to the computer requesting it, and the requesting user can download the file directly from the computer located. The copied file is placed in a designated sharing folder on the requesting user's computer, where it is available for other users to download in turn, along with any other file in that folder.

In the Gnutella network made available by Morpheus, the process is mostly the same, except that in some versions of the Gnutella protocol there are no supernodes. In these versions, peer computers using the protocol communicate directly with each other. When a user enters a search request into the Morpheus software, it sends the request to computers connected with it, which in turn pass the request along to other connected peers. The search results are communicated to the requesting computer, and the user can download desired files directly from peers' computers. As this description indicates, Grokster and StreamCast use no servers to intercept the content of the search requests or to mediate the file transfers conducted by users of the software, there being no central point through which the substance of the communications passes in either direction.

Although Grokster and StreamCast do not therefore know when particular files are copied, a few searches using their software would show what is available on the networks the software reaches. MGM commissioned a statistician to conduct a systematic search, and his study showed that nearly 90% of the files available for download on the FastTrack system were copyrighted works. Grokster and StreamCast dispute this figure, raising methodological problems and arguing that free copying even of copyrighted works may be authorized by the rightholders. They also argue that potential noninfringing uses of their software are significant in kind, even if infrequent in practice. Some musical performers, for example, have gained new audiences by distributing their copyrighted works for free across peer-to-peer networks, and some distributors of unprotected content have used peer-to-peer networks to disseminate files, Shakespeare being an example. Indeed, StreamCast has given Morpheus users the opportunity to download the briefs in this very case, though their popularity has not been quantified.

As for quantification, the parties' anecdotal and statistical evidence entered thus far to show the content available on the FastTrack and Gnutella networks does not say much about which files are actually downloaded by users, and no one can say how often the software is used to obtain copies of unprotected material. But MGM's evidence gives reason to think that the vast majority of users' downloads are acts of infringement, and because well over 100 million copies of the software in question are known to have been downloaded, and billions of files are shared across the FastTrack and Gnutella networks each month, the probable scope of copyright infringement is staggering.

Grokster and StreamCast concede the infringement in most downloads, and it is uncontested that they are aware that users employ their software primarily to download copyrighted files, even if the decentralized FastTrack and Gnutella networks fail to reveal which files are being copied, and when. From time to time, moreover, the companies have learned about their users' infringement directly, as from users who have sent e-mail to each company with questions about playing copyrighted movies they had downloaded, to whom the companies have responded with guidance. And MGM notified the companies of 8 million copyrighted files that could be obtained using their software.

Grokster and StreamCast are not, however, merely passive recipients of information about infringing use. The record is replete with evidence that from the moment Grokster and StreamCast began to distribute their free software, each one clearly voiced the objective that recipients use it to download copyrighted works, and each took active steps to encourage infringement.

After the notorious file-sharing service, Napster, was sued by copyright holders for facilitation of copyright infringement, *A & M Records, Inc. v. Napster, Inc.*, 114 F. Supp. 2d 896 (N.D. Cal. 2000), *aff'd in part, rev'd in part*, 239 F.3d 1004 (9th Cir. 2001), StreamCast gave away a software program of a kind known as OpenNap, designed as compatible with the Napster program and open to Napster users for downloading files from other Napster and OpenNap users' computers. Evidence indicates that "[i]t was always [StreamCast's] intent to use [its OpenNap network] to be able to capture email addresses of [its] initial target market so that [it] could promote [its] StreamCast Morpheus interface to them," App. 861; indeed, the OpenNap program was engineered "'to leverage Napster's 50 million user base,'" *Id.*, at 746.

StreamCast monitored both the number of users downloading its OpenNap program and the number of music files they downloaded. It also used the resulting OpenNap network to distribute copies of the Morpheus software and to encourage users to adopt it. Internal company documents indicate that StreamCast hoped to attract large numbers of former Napster users if that company was shut down by court order or otherwise, and that StreamCast planned to be the next Napster. A kit developed by StreamCast to be delivered to advertisers, for example, contained press articles about StreamCast's potential to capture former Napster users and it introduced itself to some potential advertisers as a company "which is similar to what Napster was." It broadcast banner advertisements to users of other Napster-compatible software, urging them to adopt its OpenNap. An internal e-mail from a company executive stated: "'We have put this network in place so that when Napster pulls the plug on their free service . . . or if the Court orders them shut down prior to that . . . we will be positioned to capture the flood of their 32 million users that will be actively looking for an alternative.'"

Thus, StreamCast developed promotional materials to market its service as the best Napster alternative. One proposed advertisement read: "Napster Inc. has announced that it will soon begin charging you a fee. That's if the courts don't order it shut down first. What will you do to get around it?" *Id.* at 897. Another proposed ad touted StreamCast's software as the "# 1 alternative to Napster" and asked "[w]hen the lights went off at Napster . . . where did the users go?" *Id.* at 836 (ellipsis in original).[7] StreamCast even planned to flaunt the illegal uses of its software; when it launched the OpenNap network, the chief technology officer of the company averred that "[t]he goal is to get in trouble with the law and get sued. It's the best way to get in the new[s]." *Id.* at 916.

The evidence that Grokster sought to capture the market of former Napster users is sparser but revealing, for Grokster launched its own OpenNap system called Swaptor and inserted digital codes into its Web site so that computer users using Web search engines to look for "Napster" or "[f]ree filesharing" would be directed to the Grokster

---

[7] The record makes clear that StreamCast developed these promotional materials but not whether it released them to the public. Even if these advertisements were not released to the public and do not show encouragement to infringe, they illuminate StreamCast's purposes.

Web site, where they could download the Grokster software. *Id.*, at 992–993. And Grokster's name is an apparent derivative of Napster.

StreamCast's executives monitored the number of songs by certain commercial artists available on their networks, and an internal communication indicates they aimed to have a larger number of copyrighted songs available on their networks than other file-sharing networks. *Id.*, at 868. The point, of course, would be to attract users of a mind to infringe, just as it would be with their promotional materials developed showing copyrighted songs as examples of the kinds of files available through Morpheus. *Id.*, at 848. Morpheus in fact allowed users to search specifically for "Top 40" songs, *Id.*, at 735, which were inevitably copyrighted. Similarly, Grokster sent users a newsletter promoting its ability to provide particular, popular copyrighted materials.

In addition to this evidence of express promotion, marketing, and intent to promote further, the business models employed by Grokster and StreamCast confirm that their principal object was use of their software to download copyrighted works. Grokster and StreamCast receive no revenue from users, who obtain the software itself for nothing. Instead, both companies generate income by selling advertising space, and they stream the advertising to Grokster and Morpheus users while they are employing the programs. As the number of users of each program increases, advertising opportunities become worth more. *Cf.* App. 539, 804. While there is doubtless some demand for free Shakespeare, the evidence shows that substantive volume is a function of free access to copyrighted work. Users seeking Top 40 songs, for example, or the latest release by Modest Mouse, are certain to be far more numerous than those seeking a free Decameron, and Grokster and StreamCast translated that demand into dollars.

Finally, there is no evidence that either company made an effort to filter copyrighted material from users' downloads or otherwise impede the sharing of copyrighted files. Although Grokster appears to have sent e-mails warning users about infringing content when it received threatening notice from the copyright holders, it never blocked anyone from continuing to use its software to share copyrighted files. *Id.*, at 75–76. StreamCast not only rejected another company's offer of help to monitor infringement, *Id.*, at 928–929, but blocked the Internet Protocol addresses of entities it believed were trying to engage in such monitoring on its networks, *Id.*, at 917–922.

B

After discovery, the parties on each side of the case cross-moved for summary judgment. The District Court limited its consideration to the asserted liability of Grokster and StreamCast for distributing the current versions of their software, leaving aside whether either was liable "for damages arising from past versions of their software, or from other past activities." The District Court held that those who used the Grokster and Morpheus software to download copyrighted media files directly infringed MGM's copyrights, a conclusion not contested on appeal, but the court nonetheless granted summary judgment in favor of Grokster and StreamCast as to any liability arising from distribution of the then current versions of their software. Distributing that software gave rise to no liability in the court's view, because its use did not provide the distributors with actual knowledge of specific acts of infringement.

The Court of Appeals affirmed. 380 F.3d 1154 (9th Cir. 2004). In the court's analysis, a defendant was liable as a contributory infringer when it had knowledge of direct infringement and materially contributed to the infringement. But the court read *Sony Corp. of America v. Universal City Studios, Inc.*, 464 U.S. 417, as holding that distribution of a commercial product capable of substantial noninfringing uses could not give rise to contributory liability for infringement unless the distributor had actual knowledge of specific instances of infringement and failed to act on that knowledge. The fact that the software was capable of substantial noninfringing uses in the Ninth Circuit's view meant that Grokster and StreamCast were not liable, because they had no such actual knowledge, owing to the decentralized architecture of their software. . . .

The Ninth Circuit also considered whether Grokster and StreamCast could be liable under a theory of vicarious infringement. The court held against liability because the defendants did not monitor or control the use of the software, had no agreed-upon right or current ability to supervise its use, and had no independent duty to police infringement. We granted certiorari.

II

A

MGM and many of the *amici* fault the Court of Appeals's holding for upsetting a sound balance between the respective values of supporting creative pursuits through copyright protection and promoting innovation in new communication technologies by limiting the incidence of liability for copyright infringement. The more artistic protection is favored, the more technological innovation may be discouraged; the administration of copyright law is an exercise in managing the trade-off. *See Sony Corp. v. Universal City Studios, supra*, at 442; *see generally* Ginsburg, *Copyright and Control Over New Technologies of Dissemination*, 101 COLUM. L. REV. 1613 (2001); Lichtman & Landes, *Indirect Liability for Copyright Infringement: An Economic Perspective*, 16 HARV. J. L. & TECH. 395 (2003).

The tension between the two values is the subject of this case, with its claim that digital distribution of copyrighted material threatens copyright holders as never before, because every copy is identical to the original, copying is easy, and many people (especially the young) use file-sharing software to download copyrighted works. This very breadth of the software's use may well draw the public directly into the debate over copyright policy, Peters, *Brace Memorial Lecture: Copyright Enters the Public Domain*, 51 J. COPYRIGHT SOC. 701, 705–717 (2004) (address by Register of Copyrights), and the indications are that the ease of copying songs or movies using software like Grokster's and Napster's is fostering disdain for copyright protection, Wu, *When Code Isn't Law*, 89 VA. L. REV. 679, 724–726 (2003). As the case has been presented to us, these fears are said to be offset by the different concern that imposing liability, not only on infringers but on distributors of software based on its potential for unlawful use, could limit further development of beneficial technologies. *See, e.g.*, Lemley & Reese, *Reducing Digital Copyright Infringement Without Restricting Innovation*, 56 STAN. L. REV. 1345, 1386–1390 (2004); Brief for Innovation Scholars and Economists as *Amici Curiae* 15–20; Brief for Emerging Technology Companies as *Amici Curiae* 19–25; Brief for Intel Corporation as *Amicus Curiae* 20–22.

The argument for imposing indirect liability in this case is, however, a powerful one, given the number of infringing downloads that occur every day using StreamCast's and Grokster's software. When a widely shared service or product is used to commit infringement, it may be impossible to enforce rights in the protected work effectively against all direct infringers, the only practical alternative being to go against the distributor of the copying device for secondary liability on a theory of contributory or vicarious infringement. *See In re Aimster Copyright Litigation*, 334 F.3d 643, 645–646 (C.A.7 2003).

One infringes contributorily by intentionally inducing or encouraging direct infringement, *see Gershwin Pub. Corp. v. Columbia Artists Management, Inc.*, 443 F.2d 1159, 1162 (C.A.2 1971), and infringes vicariously by profiting from direct infringement while declining to exercise a right to stop or limit it, *Shapiro, Bernstein & Co. v. H.L. Green Co.*, 316 F.2d 304, 307 (C.A.2 1963). Although "[t]he Copyright Act does not expressly render anyone liable for infringement committed by another," *Sony Corp. v. Universal City Studios*, 464 U.S., at 434, these doctrines of secondary liability emerged from common law principles and are well established in the law.

In the present case MGM has argued a vicarious liability theory, which allows imposition of liability when the defendant profits directly from the infringement and has a right and ability to supervise the direct infringer, even if the defendant initially lacks knowledge of the infringement. Because we resolve the case based on an inducement theory, there is no need to analyze separately MGM's vicarious liability theory.

B

Despite the currency of these principles of secondary liability, this Court has dealt with secondary copyright infringement in only one recent case, and because MGM has tailored its principal claim to our opinion there, a look at our earlier holding is in order. In *Sony Corp. v. Universal City Studios*, this Court addressed a claim that secondary liability for infringement can arise from the very distribution of a commercial product. There, the product, novel at the time, was what we know today as the videocassette recorder or VCR. Copyright holders sued Sony as the manufacturer, claiming it was contributorily liable for infringement that occurred when VCR owners taped copyrighted programs because it supplied the means used to infringe, and it had constructive knowledge that infringement would occur. At the trial on the merits, the evidence showed that the principal use of the VCR was for "'time-shifting,'" or taping a program for later viewing at a more convenient time, which the Court found to be a fair, not an infringing, use. There was no evidence that Sony had expressed an object of bringing about taping in violation of copyright or had taken active steps to increase its profits from unlawful taping. Although Sony's advertisements urged consumers to buy the VCR to "'record favorite shows'" or "'build a library'" of recorded programs, neither of these uses was necessarily infringing.

On those facts, with no evidence of stated or indicated intent to promote infringing uses, the only conceivable basis for imposing liability was on a theory of contributory infringement arising from its sale of VCRs to consumers with knowledge that some would use them to infringe. But because the VCR was "capable of commercially significant noninfringing uses," we held the manufacturer could not be faulted solely on the basis of its distribution.

This analysis reflected patent law's traditional staple article of commerce doctrine, now codified, that distribution of a component of a patented device will not violate the patent if it is suitable for use in other ways. 35 U.S.C. § 271(c); *Aro Mfg. Co. v. Convertible Top Replacement Co.*, 377 U.S. 476, 485 (1964) (noting codification of cases). The doctrine was devised to identify instances in which it may be presumed from distribution of an article in commerce that the distributor intended the article to be used to infringe another's patent, and so may justly be held liable for that infringement. "One who makes and sells articles which are only adapted to be used in a patented combination will be presumed to intend the natural consequences of his acts; he will be presumed to intend that they shall be used in the combination of the patent." *New York Scaffolding Co. v. Whitney*, 224 F. 452, 459 (C.A.8 1915).

In sum, where an article is "good for nothing else" but infringement, there is no legitimate public interest in its unlicensed availability, and there is no injustice in presuming or imputing an intent to infringe, *see Henry v. A.B. Dick Co.*, 224 U.S. 1, 48 (1912), overruled on other grounds, *Motion Picture Patents Co. v. Universal Film Mfg. Co.*, 243 U.S. 502 (1917). Conversely, the doctrine absolves the equivocal conduct of selling an item with substantial lawful as well as unlawful uses, and limits liability to instances of more acute fault than the mere understanding that some of one's products will be misused. It leaves breathing room for innovation and a vigorous commerce. See *Sony Corp. v. Universal City Studios, supra*, at 442; *Dawson Chemical Co. v. Rohm & Haas Co.*, 448 U.S. 176, 221 (1980); *Henry v. A.B. Dick Co., supra*, at 48.

The parties and many of the *amici* in this case think the key to resolving it is the *Sony* rule and, in particular, what it means for a product to be "capable of commercially significant noninfringing uses." MGM advances the argument that granting summary judgment to Grokster and StreamCast as to their current activities gave too much weight to the value of innovative technology, and too little to the copyrights infringed by users of their software, given that 90% of works available on one of the networks was shown to be copyrighted. Assuming the remaining 10% to be its noninfringing use, MGM says this should not qualify as "substantial," and the Court should quantify *Sony* to the extent of holding that a product used "principally" for infringement does not qualify. As mentioned before, Grokster and StreamCast reply by citing evidence that their software can be used to reproduce public domain works, and they point to copyright holders who actually encourage copying. Even if infringement is the principal practice with their software today, they argue, the noninfringing uses are significant and will grow.

We agree with MGM that the Court of Appeals misapplied *Sony*, which it read as limiting secondary liability quite beyond the circumstances to which the case applied. *Sony* barred secondary liability based on presuming or imputing intent to cause infringement solely from the design or distribution of a product capable of substantial lawful use, which the distributor knows is in fact used for infringement. The Ninth Circuit has read *Sony*'s limitation to mean that whenever a product is capable of substantial lawful use, the producer can never be held contributorily liable for third parties' infringing use of it; it read the rule as being this broad, even when an actual purpose to cause infringing use is shown by evidence independent of design and distribution of the product, unless the distributors had "specific knowledge of infringement at a time at which they contributed to the infringement, and failed to act upon that information." Because the Circuit found the StreamCast and Grokster software capable of substantial lawful use, it concluded on the basis of its reading of *Sony* that neither company could be held liable, since there was no showing that their software, being without any central server, afforded them knowledge of specific unlawful uses.

This view of *Sony*, however, was error, converting the case from one about liability resting on imputed intent to one about liability on any theory. Because *Sony* did not displace other theories of secondary liability, and because we find below that it was error to grant summary judgment to the companies on MGM's inducement claim, we do not revisit *Sony* further, as MGM requests, to add a more quantified description of the point of balance between protection and commerce when liability rests solely on distribution with knowledge that unlawful use will occur. It is enough to note that the Ninth Circuit's judgment rested on an erroneous understanding of *Sony* and to leave further consideration of the *Sony* rule for a day when that may be required.

C

Sony's rule limits imputing culpable intent as a matter of law from the characteristics or uses of a distributed product. But nothing in *Sony* requires courts to ignore evidence of intent if there is such evidence, and the case was never meant to foreclose rules of fault-based liability derived from the common law. *Sony Corp. v. Universal City Studios*, 464 U.S., at 439 ("If vicarious liability is to be imposed on Sony in this case, it must rest on the fact that it has sold equipment with constructive knowledge" of the potential for infringement). Thus, where evidence goes beyond a product's characteristics or the knowledge that it may be put to infringing uses, and shows statements or actions directed to promoting infringement, *Sony*'s staple-article rule will not preclude liability.

The classic case of direct evidence of unlawful purpose occurs when one induces commission of infringement by another, or "entic[es] or persuad[es] another" to infringe, BLACK'S LAW DICTIONARY 790 (8th ed. 2004), as by advertising. Thus at common law a copyright or patent defendant who "not only expected but invoked [infringing use] by advertisement" was liable for infringement "on principles recognized in every part of the law." *Kalem Co. v. Harper Brothers*, 222 U.S., at 62–63 (copyright infringement).

The rule on inducement of infringement as developed in the early cases is no different today. Evidence of "active steps . . . taken to encourage direct infringement," *Oak Industries, Inc. v. Zenith Electronics Corp.*, 697 F. Supp. 988, 992 (N.D. Ill. 1988), such as advertising an infringing use or instructing how to engage in an infringing use, show an affirmative intent that the product be used to infringe, and a showing that infringement was encouraged overcomes the law's reluctance to find liability when a defendant merely sells a commercial product suitable for some lawful use, *see, e.g.*, *Water Technologies Corp. v. Calco, Ltd.*, 850 F.2d 660, 668 (C.A. Fed. 1988) (liability for inducement where one "actively and knowingly aid[s] and abet[s] another's direct infringement" (emphasis omitted)); *Fromberg, Inc. v. Thornhill*, 315 F.2d 407, 412–413 (C.A.5 1963) (demonstrations by sales staff of infringing uses supported liability for inducement); *Haworth Inc. v. Herman Miller Inc.*, 37 U.S.P.Q.2d 1080, 1090 (W.D. Mich. 1994) (evidence that defendant "demonstrate[d] and recommend[ed] infringing configurations" of its product could support inducement liability); *Sims v. Mack Trucks, Inc.*, 459 F. Supp. 1198, 1215 (E.D. Pa. 1978) (finding inducement where the use "depicted by the defendant in its promotional film and brochures infringes the . . . patent"), overruled on other grounds, 608 F.2d 87 (C.A.3 1979). *Cf.* W. KEETON, D. DOBBS, R. KEETON & D. OWEN, PROSSER AND KEETON ON LAW OF TORTS 37 (5th ed. 1984) ("There is a definite tendency to impose greater responsibility upon a defendant whose conduct was intended to do harm, or was morally wrong").

For the same reasons that *Sony* took the staple-article doctrine of patent law as a model for its copyright safe-harbor rule, the inducement rule, too, is a sensible one for copyright. We adopt it here, holding that one who distributes a device with the object of promoting its use to infringe copyright, as shown by clear expression or other affirmative steps taken to foster infringement, is liable for the resulting acts of infringement by third parties. We are, of course, mindful of the need to keep from trenching on regular commerce or discouraging the development of technologies with lawful and unlawful potential. Accordingly, just as *Sony* did not find intentional inducement despite the knowledge of the VCR manufacturer that its device could be used to infringe, 464 U.S., at 439, n.19, mere knowledge of infringing potential or of actual infringing uses would not be enough here to subject a distributor to liability. Nor would ordinary acts incident to product distribution, such as offering customers technical support or product updates, support liability in themselves. The inducement rule, instead, premises liability on purposeful, culpable expression and conduct, and thus does nothing to compromise legitimate commerce or discourage innovation having a lawful promise.

II

A

The only apparent question about treating MGM's evidence as sufficient to withstand summary judgment under the theory of inducement goes to the need on

MGM's part to adduce evidence that StreamCast and Grokster communicated an inducing message to their software users. The classic instance of inducement is by advertisement or solicitation that broadcasts a message designed to stimulate others to commit violations. MGM claims that such a message is shown here. It is undisputed that StreamCast beamed onto the computer screens of users of Napster-compatible programs ads urging the adoption of its OpenNap program, which was designed, as its name implied, to invite the custom of patrons of Napster, then under attack in the courts for facilitating massive infringement. Those who accepted StreamCast's OpenNap program were offered software to perform the same services, which a factfinder could conclude would readily have been understood in the Napster market as the ability to download copyrighted music files. Grokster distributed an electronic newsletter containing links to articles promoting its software's ability to access popular copyrighted music. And anyone whose Napster or free file-sharing searches turned up a link to Grokster would have understood Grokster to be offering the same file-sharing ability as Napster, and to the same people who probably used Napster for infringing downloads; that would also have been the understanding of anyone offered Grokster's suggestively named Swaptor software, its version of OpenNap. And both companies communicated a clear message by responding affirmatively to requests for help in locating and playing copyrighted materials.

In StreamCast's case, of course, the evidence just described was supplemented by other unequivocal indications of unlawful purpose in the internal communications and advertising designs aimed at Napster users ("When the lights went off at Napster . . . where did the users go?" App. 836 (ellipsis in original)). Whether the messages were communicated is not to the point on this record. The function of the message in the theory of inducement is to prove by a defendant's own statements that his unlawful purpose disqualifies him from claiming protection (and incidentally to point to actual violators likely to be found among those who hear or read the message). Proving that a message was sent out, then, is the preeminent but not exclusive way of showing that active steps were taken with the purpose of bringing about infringing acts, and of showing that infringing acts took place by using the device distributed. Here, the summary judgment record is replete with other evidence that Grokster and StreamCast, unlike the manufacturer and distributor in *Sony*, acted with a purpose to cause copyright violations by use of software suitable for illegal use.

Three features of this evidence of intent are particularly notable. First, each company showed itself to be aiming to satisfy a known source of demand for copyright infringement, the market comprising former Napster users. StreamCast's internal documents made constant reference to Napster, it initially distributed its Morpheus software through an OpenNap program compatible with Napster, it advertised its OpenNap program to Napster users, and its Morpheus software functions as Napster did except that it could be used to distribute more kinds of files, including copyrighted movies and software programs. Grokster's name is apparently derived from Napster, it too initially offered an OpenNap program, its software's function is likewise comparable to Napster's, and it attempted to divert queries for Napster onto its own

Web site. Grokster and StreamCast's efforts to supply services to former Napster users, deprived of a mechanism to copy and distribute what were overwhelmingly infringing files, indicate a principal, if not exclusive, intent on the part of each to bring about infringement.

Second, this evidence of unlawful objective is given added significance by MGM's showing that neither company attempted to develop filtering tools or other mechanisms to diminish the infringing activity using their software. While the Ninth Circuit treated the defendants' failure to develop such tools as irrelevant because they lacked an independent duty to monitor their users' activity, we think this evidence underscores Grokster's and StreamCast's intentional facilitation of their users' infringement.[12]

Third, there is a further complement to the direct evidence of unlawful objective. It is useful to recall that StreamCast and Grokster make money by selling advertising space, by directing ads to the screens of computers employing their software. As the record shows, the more the software is used, the more ads are sent out and the greater the advertising revenue becomes. Since the extent of the software's use determines the gain to the distributors, the commercial sense of their enterprise turns on high-volume use, which the record shows is infringing. This evidence alone would not justify an inference of unlawful intent, but viewed in the context of the entire record its import is clear.

The unlawful objective is unmistakable.

B

In addition to intent to bring about infringement and distribution of a device suitable for infringing use, the inducement theory of course requires evidence of actual infringement by recipients of the device, the software in this case. As the account of the facts indicates, there is evidence of infringement on a gigantic scale, and there is no serious issue of the adequacy of MGM's showing on this point in order to survive the companies' summary judgment requests. Although an exact calculation of infringing use, as a basis for a claim of damages, is subject to dispute, there is no question that the summary judgment evidence is at least adequate to entitle MGM to go forward with claims for damages and equitable relief.

* * *

In sum, this case is significantly different from *Sony* and reliance on that case to rule in favor of StreamCast and Grokster was error. *Sony* dealt with a claim of liability based solely on distributing a product with alternative lawful and unlawful uses, with knowledge that some users would follow the unlawful course. The case struck a balance between the interests of protection and innovation by holding that the product's

---

[12] Of course, in the absence of other evidence of intent, a court would be unable to find contributory infringement liability merely based on a failure to take affirmative steps to prevent infringement, if the device otherwise was capable of substantial noninfringing uses. Such a holding would tread too close to the *Sony* safe harbor.

capability of substantial lawful employment should bar the imputation of fault and consequent secondary liability for the unlawful acts of others.

MGM's evidence in this case most obviously addresses a different basis of liability for distributing a product open to alternative uses. Here, evidence of the distributors' words and deeds going beyond distribution as such shows a purpose to cause and profit from third-party acts of copyright infringement. If liability for inducing infringement is ultimately found, it will not be on the basis of presuming or imputing fault, but from inferring a patently illegal objective from statements and actions showing what that objective was.

There is substantial evidence in MGM's favor on all elements of inducement, and summary judgment in favor of Grokster and StreamCast was error. On remand, reconsideration of MGM's motion for summary judgment will be in order. . . .

JUSTICE GINSBURG, with whom THE CHIEF JUSTICE and JUSTICE KENNEDY join, concurring.

I concur in the Court's decision, which vacates in full the judgment of the Court of Appeals for the Ninth Circuit and write separately to clarify why I conclude that the Court of Appeals misperceived, and hence misapplied, our holding in *Sony*. . . .

This case differs markedly from *Sony*. Here, there has been no finding of any fair use and little beyond anecdotal evidence of noninfringing uses. . . .

[W]hen the record in this case was developed, there was evidence that Grokster's and StreamCast's products were, and had been for some time, overwhelmingly used to infringe and that this infringement was the overwhelming source of revenue from the products. Fairly appraised, the evidence was insufficient to demonstrate, beyond genuine debate, a reasonable prospect that substantial or commercially significant noninfringing uses were likely to develop over time. . . .[3]

If, on remand, the case is not resolved on summary judgment in favor of MGM based on Grokster and StreamCast actively inducing infringement, the Court of Appeals, I would emphasize, should reconsider, on a fuller record, its interpretation of *Sony*'s product distribution holding. . . .

---

[3] Justice Breyer finds support for summary judgment in this motley collection of declarations and in a survey conducted by an expert retained by MGM. That survey identified 75% of the files available through Grokster as copyrighted works owned or controlled by the plaintiffs, and 15% of the files as works likely copyrighted. As to the remaining 10% of the files, "there was not enough information to form reasonable conclusions either as to what those files even consisted of, and/or whether they were infringing or non-infringing." Even assuming, as Justice Breyer does, that the *Sony* Court would have absolved Sony of contributory liability solely on the basis of the use of the Betamax for authorized time-shifting, summary judgment is not inevitably appropriate here. *Sony* stressed that the plaintiffs there owned "well below 10%" of copyrighted television programming, and found, based on trial testimony from representatives of the four major sports leagues and other individuals authorized to consent to home-recording of their copyrighted broadcasts, that a similar percentage of program copying was authorized. Here, the plaintiffs allegedly control copyrights for 70% or 75% of the material exchanged through the Grokster and StreamCast software and the District Court does not appear to have relied on comparable testimony about authorized copying from copyright holders.

JUSTICE BREYER, with whom JUSTICE STEVENS and JUSTICE O'CONNOR join, concurring.

I agree with the Court that the distributor of a dual-use technology may be liable for the infringing activities of third parties where he or she actively seeks to advance the infringement. I further agree that, in light of our holding today, we need not now "revisit" *Sony*. Other Members of the Court, however, take up the *Sony* question: whether Grokster's product is "capable of 'substantial' or 'commercially significant' noninfringing uses." And they answer that question by stating that the Court of Appeals was wrong when it granted summary judgment on the issue in Grokster's favor. I write to explain why I disagree with them on this matter. . . .

When measured against *Sony*'s underlying evidence and analysis, the evidence now before us shows that Grokster passes *Sony*'s test—that is, whether the company's product is capable of substantial or commercially significant noninfringing uses. For one thing, petitioners' (hereinafter MGM) own expert declared that 75% of current files available on Grokster are infringing and 15% are "likely infringing." That leaves some number of files near 10% that apparently are noninfringing, a figure very similar to the 9% or so of authorized time-shifting uses of the VCR that the Court faced in *Sony*. . . .

Importantly, *Sony* also used the word "capable," asking whether the product is "capable of" substantial noninfringing uses. Its language and analysis suggest that a figure like 10%, if fixed for all time, might well prove insufficient, but that such a figure serves as an adequate foundation where there is a reasonable prospect of expanded legitimate uses over time. *See ibid.* (noting a "significant potential for future authorized copying"). And its language also indicates the appropriateness of looking to potential future uses of the product to determine its "capability."

Here the record reveals a significant future market for noninfringing uses of Grokster-type peer-to-peer software. . . .

And that is just what is happening. Such legitimate noninfringing uses are coming to include the swapping of: research information (the initial purpose of many peer-to-peer networks); public domain films (e.g., those owned by the Prelinger Archive); historical recordings and digital educational materials (e.g., those stored on the Internet Archive); digital photos (OurPictures, for example, is starting a P2P photo-swapping service); "shareware" and "freeware" (e.g., Linux and certain Windows software); secure licensed music and movie files (Intent MediaWorks, for example, protects licensed content sent across P2P networks); news broadcasts past and present (the BBC Creative Archive lets users "rip, mix and share the BBC"); user-created audio and video files (including "podcasts" that may be distributed through P2P software); and all manner of free "open content" works collected by Creative Commons (one can search for Creative Commons material on StreamCast). I can find nothing in the record that suggests that this course of events will not continue to flow naturally as a consequence of the character of the software taken together with the foreseeable development of the Internet and of information technology.

There may be other now-unforeseen noninfringing uses that develop for peer-to-peer software, just as the home-video rental industry (unmentioned in *Sony*) developed for the VCR. But the foreseeable development of such uses, when taken together with an estimated 10% noninfringing material, is sufficient to meet *Sony*'s standard. . . .

COMMENTS AND QUESTIONS

1. At first blush, the unanimous Supreme Court in *Grokster* would appear to be a significant victory for content providers over peer-to-peer companies. But what will be the long-term impact of this decision on the distribution of file-sharing technology and enforcement of copyrights on the Internet? Could a new entrant into the file-sharing marketplace offering the very same functionality as Grokster or Streamcast shield itself from liability by avoiding statements encouraging infringement?

2. What light does the *Grokster* decision shed on contributory or vicarious liability in copyright law? How would you advise a client developing peer-to-peer technology (or other technology that could be used for copyright infringement) about the scope and predictability of the *Sony* safe harbor? Has this case clarified the scope of contributory or vicarious liability to any significant degree (and if so, in what direction)? Do the concurrences enhance or detract from the clarity of the *Sony* standard? Does the *Sony* standard matter now that copyright owners can bring a claim based on inducement even if the only conduct is selling a product capable of substantial noninfringing uses, so long as they can allege bad intent?

3. *BitTorrent Protocol.* Just as Grokster and Streamcast emerged during the litigation over Napster, BitTorrent, a powerful new generation of file-sharing technology, became available during the pendency of the *Grokster* litigation. BitTorrent breaks files into smaller pieces and provides users information about the location of the various pieces. This program allows rapid distribution of very large files and is used for full-length feature films, software, and music, as well as Linux upgrades and podcasts. BitTorrent is an open source program that is available for free (and does not earn any income from advertising). How would this technology fare under the *Grokster* decision?

In *Columbia Pictures Indus., Inc. v. Fung*, 710 F.3d 1020, 1039 (9th Cir. 2013), major film studios alleged that websites maintained by Gary Fung induced end users to download infringing copies of the studios' copyrighted works. Fung developed websites, such as isohunt.com and torrentbox.com, that organized torrent files into various categories such as "Top 20 TV Shows," "Top 20 Movies," and "Top 20 Most Active Torrents."

The Ninth Circuit interpreted *Grokster* to require proof of four elements: (1) the distribution of a device or product, which could include Fung's websites; (2) acts of infringement—statistical evidence established that more than 90% of the content associated with the torrent files available on Fung's websites was infringing; (3) an object of promoting its use to infringe copyright—"the record is replete with instances of Fung responding personally to queries for assistance in: uploading torrent files corresponding to obviously copyrighted material, finding particular copyrighted movies and television shows, getting pirated material to play properly, and burning the infringing content onto DVDs for playback on televisions"; and (4) causation—"acts of infringement by third parties" were caused by Fung's service. The court stopped short, however, of holding that Fung's failure to implement filtering tools or sale of advertising space on his websites would, on their own, establish the third (mental state) element. Nonetheless, such evidence corroborated the conclusion that Fung "acted with a purpose to cause copyright violations by use of" their services.

4. The Ninth Circuit held that AT&T was not secondarily liable for copyright infringement resulting from customer forwarding of multimedia messages. The court determined that AT&T had limited ability to control and supervise the content of messages and derived no direct financial benefit. *See Luvdarts, L.L.C. v. AT & T Mobility, L.L.C.*, 710 F.3d 1068 (9th Cir. 2013).

5. *Indirect Copyright Liability and Technological Innovation.* Following the Supreme Court's *Grokster* decision, Professor Lessig predicted that the decision would gravely hamper innovation in digital technology. *See* Robert Hof, *Ten Years of Chilled Innovation*, BUSINESS WEEK, June 29, 2005. The causal relationship that Professor Lessig and others draw reflects plausible logic. If those who develop technology that can be used to infringe copyrights are exposed to potentially crushing liability—such as what befell Napster, MP3.com's MyMP3 music locker service, ReplayTV's digital video recorder, and Grokster—it seems reasonable to surmise that digital technology innovators would, certainly at the margin, invest their resources and energies elsewhere. At the same time, however, there is no shortage of evidence suggesting that digital innovation and commercialization that contribute to copyright infringement are far from in retreat. Each month brings new digital technologies—iPod, image search engines, MySpace, YouTube, Facebook, Google's Book Search, BitTorrent, iPhone, Twitter, Kindle 2.0—many of which could be (and have been) portrayed as facilitating copyright infringement. The development and commercialization of these technologies suggests that the cloud of liability has not throttled the digital innovation pipeline. This conclusion makes intuitive sense as well. The upside of developing the next "killer app" is massive and well publicized. On the other hand, many of those new technologies, including image search, book search, ringtone making, and online video sites, have themselves been met with suits alleging copyright infringement. The threat of copyright litigation now figures into the business model of any new technology in the digital media space, and has arguably skewed innovation toward larger companies that can afford the cost of copyright litigation.

This debate raises several critical questions:

- What should be the goal of policy in this area—to promote technological innovation regardless of its effects on the enforceability of copyright law, to promote copyright law regardless of its effect on innovation, or to channel technological innovation so as to balance competing effects? Does "channeling innovation" come with its own costs?
- What is the proper rule or standard for public policy?
- Are courts the appropriate institutions for addressing these questions?

Compare Mark A. Lemley & R. Anthony Reese, *Reducing Digital Copyright Infringement Without Restricting Innovation*, 56 STAN. L. REV. 1345, 1390 (2004) (arguing that the social benefits of improved distribution platforms substantially outweigh better enforcement of copyright law, anything less immunizing than the *Sony* rule will significantly harm innovation, and that courts are ill-suited to making complex decisions requiring changes in technology design); *with* Peter S. Menell, *Indirect Copyright Liability and Technological Innovation*, 32 COLUM. J.L. & ARTS 375 (2009) (arguing that countervailing forces, such as the relatively modest capital requirements, research and social norms, risk- and liability-insulating institutions, and the importance of technological advance in fields unaffected by copyright liability dampen the effects of indirect copyright liability on innovation in distribution technologies).

6. *Policy Analysis.* As a venture capitalist remarked in a discussion with Napster's developers, "You've distributed more music [in your first year of operation] than the whole record industry since it came into existence." JOSEPH MENN, ALL THE RAVE 161 (2003). Doesn't it seem peculiar that the copyright system's treatment of the most dramatic advance in the means for reproducing and distributing works of authorship since the printing press is being decided by the courts reasoning from a pre-digital age technology (VCR) rather than expert bodies and democratic institutions? Various proposals have been floated on how to reform copyright law in the wake of peer-to-peer technology. Consider the following:

- replace the staple article of commerce standard with a predominant use standard that considers: (1) whether noninfringing uses can be achieved for most consumers through other means without significant added expense, inconvenience, or loss of functionality; (2) the extent to which copyright owners can protect themselves against infringements without undue cost (e.g., through encryption); and (3) the cost and efficacy of enforcement against direct infringers. This was the standard proposed by the dissent in *Sony*; they would have read it to make the VCR illegal.
- abolish indirect liability entirely and make it easier to enforce copyrights against direct infringers.
- abolish liability for noncommercial filesharing and impose a levy on Internet users designed to compensate copyright owners for estimated losses due to unauthorized copying.

These and related proposals are discussed in Peter S. Menell, *Design for Symbiosis: Promoting More Harmonious Paths for Technological Innovators and Expressive Creators in the Internet Age*, 55 COMMUNICATIONS OF THE ASSOCIATION OF COMPUTING MACHINERY 30 (May 2012); Mark A. Lemley & R. Anthony Reese, *Reducing Digital Copyright Infringement Without Restricting Innovation*, 56 STAN. L. REV. 1345 (2004); Robert P. Merges, *Compulsory Licensing v. the Three "Golden Oldies": Property Rights, Contracts, and Markets*, 508 CATO POLICY ANALYSIS (2004); Neil W. Netanel, *Impose a Noncommercial Use Levy to Allow Free Peer-to-Peer File Sharing*, 17 HARV. J.L. & TECH. 1 (2003).

7. *Seizing "Rogue" Websites.* Advances in streaming technology, expanded broadband coverage, and the growth of online advertising networks have led to the emergence of cyberlocker sites that earn sizeable profits from distributing copyrighted materials without authorization. Many of these websites are hosted outside of the United States although accessible from within the United States. The content industries pushed legislation in 2011 to target those sites. Called the Stop Online Piracy Act (SOPA), this legislation would have authorized courts to bar advertising networks and payment facilities from conducting business with infringing websites, prevent search engines from linking to the sites, and require Internet service providers to cease passing Internet traffic to particular sites. SOPA would also have expanded existing criminal laws to include unauthorized streaming of copyrighted content, imposing a maximum penalty of five years in prison. SOPA was shelved after an unprecedented uprising of Internet users in 2012, with over ten million people contacting Congress to express opposition on a single day in January. Even without this legislation, the U.S. Department of Justice and U.S. Immigration and Customs Enforcement (ICE) have launched a series of enforcement actions against foreign websites accused of fostering infringement of copyrighted works. These actions have included the seizure of domain names, effectively shutting down the entire site, raising First Amendment concerns.

PROBLEMS

Problem IV-41. Industrial Music Co. (IM) develops and produces the DJ Remixer, a digital music computer for home and personal use. The DJ Remixer allows individuals to edit and "remix" sound clips—their own and those derived from copyrighted sound recordings—to produce mashups. IM markets its device for amateur and professional DJs who want to edit their own works, but IM knows that many, if not most, of the devices it sells are used for "sampling" or otherwise copying copyrighted works without authorization. In fact, it has come to IM's attention that Girl Talk (*see Problem IV-29*) uses a DJ Remixer device. Is IM guilty of contributory infringement? If so, with every sale, or only with some sales? What if IM were to advertise that Girl Talk uses a DJ Remixer? Can the sale of the DJ Remixer be enjoined?

Problem IV-42. ReplayTV has introduced a digital video recorder (DVR), a digital version of the VCR. Thanks to digital technology, the ReplayTV 4500 offers consumers the ability to instantly skip over commercials with the click of a 30-second advance fast forward button. In addition, the large storage capacity of the ReplayTV 4500 hard drive enables consumers to store up to 60 hours of content, making archiving of content much more convenient than on VCRs. A survey of DVR owners finds that 35 percent say they never watch commercials while nearly 60 percent say they watch them only occasionally. The television industry fears that these capabilities will make advertisers much less willing to support their broadcasts. They sue to enjoin sale of ReplayTV's DVR. How should the court rule on this case?

ReplayTV allows consumers to connect their device to the Internet and send files of television broadcasts to other overs of ReplayTV devices. How should this feature be analyzed? Does it depend on whether any premium channel content (e.g., HBO) can be distributed in this manner?

F. DEFENSES

Beyond the many exceptions, compulsory licenses, and other limitations on copyright protection, copyright law establishes important defenses and safe harbors. This section begins with the fair use doctrine. It then explores the online service provider safe harbors created by the DMCA. The final exception summarizes a variety of other copyright defenses and limitations.

1. Fair Use

The fair use doctrine, developed over centuries of jurisprudence, has served two vital functions: (1) balancing the interests of pioneering authors and those who use their work as an input for cumulative creativity; and (2) as a safety valve for freedom of expression, *see* Neil Weinstock Netanel, *Locating Copyright within the First Amendment Skein*, 54 STAN. L. REV. 1 (2001). The doctrine has evolved substantially over the course of copyright's history and undoubtedly will continue to adapt to changes in the creative arts and the broader society. There are hundreds of decisions effectuating and adapting the fair use balance.

i.   *The Formative Era*

Although the Copyright Act of 1790 did not expressly establish a fair use defense, Justice Joseph Story, to whom we trace patent law's experimental use doctrine, *see Whittemore v. Cutter*, 29 Fed. Cas. 1120 (C.C.D. Mass. 1813), played a similarly formative role in the development of the fair use doctrine. *See Folsom v. Marsh*, 9 F. Cas. 342 (C.C.D. Mass. 1841).

Folsom v. Marsh involved the copying of the private letters of George Washington. Justice Story, sitting as a circuit judge, explained that

> [p]atents and copyrights approach, nearer than any other class of cases belonging to forensic discussions, to what may be called the metaphysics of the law, where the distinctions are, or at least may be, very subtile [sic] and refined, and, sometimes, almost evanescent. . . . [I]n cases of copyright, . . . the identity of the two works in substance, and the question of piracy, often depend upon a nice balance of the comparative use made in one of the materials of the other; the nature, extent, and value of the materials thus used; the objects of each work; and the degree to which each writer may be fairly presumed to have resorted to the same common sources of information, or to have exercised the same common diligence in the selection and arrangement of the materials. Thus, for example, no one can doubt that a reviewer may fairly cite largely from the original work, if his design be really and truly to use the passages for the purposes of fair and reasonable criticism. On the other hand, it is as clear, that if he thus cites the most important parts of the work, with a view, not to criticise,

but to supersede the use of the original work, and substitute the review for it, such a use will be deemed in law a piracy. A wide interval might, of course, exist between these two extremes, calling for great caution and involving great difficulty. . . .

Id. at 344–45. Although ultimately determining that Washington's letters could not be reproduced in substantial part without authorization, the case provided the foundation for one of copyright law's most important safety valves for promoting cumulative creativity and free expression.

Numerous cases refined, elaborated, and applied this doctrine, although such efforts have failed to bring about predictable results. Thus, nearly a century after Justice Story conceptualized the fair use doctrine, the great copyright jurist Learned Hand characterized it as "the most troublesome in the whole law of copyright." *Dellar v. Samuel Goldwyn, Inc.*, 104 F.2d 661, 662 (2d Cir. 1939).

ii. *Codification and Early Post-Codification Interpretation*

Congress sought to bring some clarity to this doctrine in its comprehensive codification of copyright law in 1976:

17 U.S.C. § 107. Limitations on Exclusive Rights: Fair Use (1976)

Notwithstanding the provisions of sections 106 and 106A, the fair use of a copyrighted work, including such use by reproduction in copies or phonorecords or by any other means specified by that section, for purposes such as criticism, comment, news reporting, teaching (including multiple copies for classroom use), scholarship, or research, is not an infringement of copyright. In determining whether the use made of a work in any particular case is a fair use the factors to be considered shall include—

(1) the purpose and character of the use, including whether such use is of a commercial nature or is for nonprofit educational purposes;

(2) the nature of the copyrighted work;

(3) the amount and substantiality of the portion used in relation to the copyrighted work as a whole; and

(4) the effect of the use upon the potential market for or value of the copyrighted work.

In the accompanying report, Congress stated the "general intention" behind the provision:

The statement of the fair use doctrine in section 107 offers some guidance to users in determining when the principles of the doctrine apply. However, the endless variety of situations and combinations of circumstances that can rise in particular cases precludes the formulation of exact rules in the statute. The bill endorses the purpose and general scope of the judicial doctrine of fair use, but there is no disposition to freeze the doctrine in the statute, especially during a period of rapid technological change. Beyond a very broad statutory explanation of what fair use is and some of the criteria applicable to it, the courts must be free to adapt the doctrine to particular situations on a case-by-case basis. Section 107 is intended to restate the present judicial doctrine of fair use, not to change, narrow, or enlarge it in any way.

H.R. REP. NO. 94-1476, at 66. Therefore, the many fair use decisions continue to provide the backdrop for applying this doctrine and courts are permitted to further evolve these principles.

As a result of the vast fair use landscape, it is essential to understand the development of the modern regime and to appreciate its principal contours. We provide this foundation through summarizing the critical influences in historical context and through a sampling of the most influential and current cases.

a.   *Sony Corp. of America v. Universal City Studios, Inc. (1984)*

The Supreme Court's first encounter with the 1976 Act's fair use formulation came in *Sony Corp. of America v. Universal City Studios, Inc.*, 464 U.S. 417 (1984), which we encountered in exploring the scope of indirect infringement. As we saw there and in *Limelight Networks, Inc. v. Akamai Technologies*, Inc., 134 S.Ct. 2111 (2014), *see* Chapter III(D)(1)(b)(iii), in order for a party to be indirectly liable, there must be direct infringement.

The record showed that most consumers used Sony's product for "time shifting"— recording shows for later viewing. Relatively few consumers engaged in "archiving"— recording and storing programs in a library. As summarized by the district court, "[a]ccording to plaintiffs' survey, 75.4% of the VTR [video tape recorder] owners use their machines to record for time-shifting purposes half or most of the time. Defendants' survey showed that 96% of the Betamax owners had used the machine to record programs they otherwise would have missed. . . . When plaintiffs asked interviewees how many cassettes were in their library, 55.8% said there were 10 or fewer. In defendants' survey, of the total programs viewed by interviewees in the past month, 70.4% had been viewed only that one time and for 57.9%, there were no plans for further viewing." 480 F. Supp. at 438. Both activities constituted copying of protected expression. The critical question was therefore whether these activities fell within the fair use exception. If not, then Sony could not be held indirectly liable.

In framing the analysis, the Court noted that fair use was "an equitable rule of reason," quoting H.R. REP. NO. 94-1476 at 65. The Court interpreted the first factor— "the commercial or nonprofit character of an activity"—as establishing a presumption that commercial use was presumptively unfair.[32] The Court held, however, that a contrary presumption applied to this case because home use is a noncommercial, nonprofit activity. Furthermore, because time-shifting merely allows the viewer to see freely-broadcast television signals at a more convenient time, the fact that the entire work is reproduced does not weigh against a finding of fair use. As regards the fourth

---

[32] As we will see below, the Supreme Court's decision in *Campbell v. Acuff-Rose Music, Inc.*, 510 U.S. 569 (1994), rejected this presumption.

fair use factor—the effect of the use upon the potential market for or value of the copyrighted work—the court noted that many sports, religious, and educational copyright owners consented to copying of their programs and that plaintiffs acknowledged that no actual harm to their copyrighted had yet occurred. Any potential future harm, possibly through a decline in measured live audience ratings used in advertising payments, was speculative. Viewing these considerations together, the Court upheld the district court's finding that concluded that the use of the Betamax for time-shifting constituted fair use. The Court did not, however, reach a conclusion on whether home archiving of shows was fair use, which is why it considered indirect liability.

COMMENTS AND QUESTIONS

1. The Court never directly addresses whether consumers who do not merely time shift but use their VCRs to archive—i.e., develop large collections of recorded movies and television shows—would also fall within the ambit of the fair use doctrine. Such a use became fairly common in the late 1980s, but waned as the DVD player replaced the VCR, and then as the digital video recorder (DVR) with its limited storage space became the recording medium of choice. Is archiving a fair use? Why or why not?

2. Would the fair use analysis of time shifting have changed if the plaintiffs had presented evidence that most consumers fast forwarded through television commercials? *See* Peter S. Menell & David Nimmer, *Unwinding Sony*, 95 CALIF. L. REV. 941, 968 (2007) (discovering that Justice O'Connor, the swing vote in the *Sony* 5-4 decision, had communicated to her colleagues that "timeshifting *with all advertisements preserved*" ought to be fair use in the absence of any evidence of harm to the copyright owners (emphasis added)).

3. What about the fact that the widespread availability of VCRs (and later DVDs) vastly expanded the marketplace for films and television content for several decades? Does the fact that a technology the copyright owners sought to ban soon accounted for a significant revenue source suggest that we should not trust copyright owners to decide what innovations should and should not be permissible? *See* Mark A. Lemley, *Is the Sky Falling on the Content Industries?*, 9 J. TELECOM. & HIGH TECH. L. 125 (2011).

In the end, both video cassette/DVD and P2P technologies faded as more symbiotic platforms—such as authorized streaming services with effective digital rights management, such as Netflix, Spotify, Hulu, and Amazon Prime, and YouTube's Content ID system for identifying, screening, and monetizing copyrighted content—produced a more balanced ecosystem that both supports creators and serves consumers. *See* Peter S. Menell, *Design for Symbiosis: Promoting More Harmonious Paths for Technological Innovators and Expressive Creators in the Internet Age*, 55 COMMUNICATIONS OF THE ACM, No. 5, 30-32 (May 2012).

4. *Sony* focused on the nature of the "public benefit" conferred by home taping. Public benefits are not expressly listed as a factor in § 107, although the "purpose and

character" of the use is one of the four factors. Is there a public benefit to home taping? If so, what is it and how should it be factored into the analysis?

PROBLEM

Problem IV-43. Refer back to *Problem IV-42*. Suppose that television production studios conducted a study finding that 85% of homes with the ReplayTV 4500 device regularly skip television commercials using the device's automated commercial-skipping features. They also obtained declarations from advertising executives stating that they have significantly reduced what they will pay for over-the-air advertising because of rampant commercial skipping and that many advertisers have either exited the broadcast television advertising marketplace or favor embedded advertising (integrating advertisements in television programs). How would these differences affect the fair use analysis of time-shifting?

---

b. *Harper & Row, Publishers, Inc. v. Nation Enterprises (1985)*

The Supreme Court addressed fair use the following year in *Harper & Row, Publishers, Inc. v. Nation Enterprises*, 471 U.S. 539 (1985). Following his defeat in the 1976 presidential election, Gerald Ford entered into a contract to publish a memoir, A TIME TO HEAL, with Harper & Row. Harper & Row entered into an agreement with TIME MAGAZINE for the weekly periodical to publish excerpts from the forthcoming memoir prior to the book's release. Just as TIME was preparing the excerpts, THE NATION obtained a purloined copy of Mr. Ford's manuscript and published a 300 word excerpt detailing President Ford's rationale for pardoning President Nixon, the most salient aspect of the memoir. As a result of THE NATION's scoop, TIME refused to pay the remaining $12,500 for the right to publish a 7,500 excerpt of the book prior to publication of the full manuscript. President Ford's publisher, Harper and Row, sued for copyright infringement. THE NATION defended on fair use grounds, emphasizing the newsworthiness of the information, its factual character of the material, the relatively small amount of copying, and freedom of speech.

Notwithstanding these important considerations, the Supreme Court placed substantial emphasis on the fact that President Ford's memoir had not yet been published and that THE NATION's article displaced a similar article for which TIME had agreed to pay. Quoting the NIMMER treatise, the Court observed that "it has never been seriously disputed that 'the fact that the plaintiff's work is unpublished . . . is a factor tending to negate the defense of fair use." The Court also noted language in the legislative history of the 1976 Act according the copyright owner the "right to control the first public distribution" of his work. Consequently, the scope the scope of fair use is narrower with respect to unpublished works. The Court also resisted the argument that the writings of public figures are excluded from copyright protection.

With these additional considerations in mind, the Court assessed the four § 107 factors as follows:

1. *Purpose and Character of the Use*: Although THE NATION "has every right to seek to be the first to publish information," it "went beyond simply reporting uncopyrightable information and actively sought to exploit the headline value of its infringement, making a 'news event' out of its unauthorized first publication of a noted figure's copyrighted expression."

2. *Nature of the Copyrighted Work*: The Court characterized the work as "unpublished historical narrative or autobiography." It emphasized that the excerpted portions went beyond conveying facts and merged idea and expression (such as Mr. Ford's characterization of the White House tapes as the "smoking gun") to include "subjective descriptions and portraits of public figures whose power lies in the author's individualized expression."

3. *Amount and Substantiality of the Portion Used*: While the THE NATION excerpted an "insubstantial portion" of A TIME TO HEAL, it took the "heart of the book"—what a TIME editor described as "the most interesting and moving parts of the entire manuscript." The Court noted that "a taking may not be excused merely because it is insubstantial with respect to the infringing work," citing *Sheldon v. Metro-Goldwyn Pictures Corp.*, 81 F.2d 49, 56 (2d Cir. 1936) (observing that "no plagiarist can excuse the wrong by showing how much of his work he did not pirate"). The Court further noted that "the direct takings from the unpublished manuscript constitute at least 13% of [THE NATION's] infringing article." The Court concluded by emphasizing the value of the excerpts and their key role in the infringing work.

4. *Effect on the Market*: The Court noted that the effect on the potential market is "undoubtedly the single more important element of fair use." The infringement directly caused the cancellation of TIME's pre-publication serialization of A TIME TO HEAL and the loss of the $12,500.

The Court concluded that "extensive prepublication quotations from an unreleased manuscript without the copyright owner's consent poses substantial potential for damage to the marketability of first serialization rights in general" and hence is not fair use.

COMMENTS AND QUESTIONS

1. A spirited dissent in *Harper & Row* argued that THE NATION had taken no more than was necessary to report the story, and that most of what was taken reflected ideas rather than expression. Given the newsworthiness of this information, shouldn't such use fit within the fair use doctrine?

2. *Unclean Hands*. In characterizing the fair use defense, as an equitable doctrine, the majority considered the "propriety of [a] defendant's conduct" relevant to the fair use determination. But should a defendant's bad faith be disqualifying?

3. *Copyright and Time*. Suppose THE NATION had published its article two weeks after the *Time* magazine article. Would the court reach a different result? Should it? What about a biographer who quotes extensively from Ford's memoirs 30 years later?

Several scholars have suggested that copyright can both ensure adequate primary incentives (appropriability) and better promote creativity by allowing greater use of copyrighted works as they age. *See* Justin Hughes, *Fair Use Across Time*, 50 UCLA L. REV. 775 (2003); Joseph P. Liu, *Copyright and Time: A Proposal*, 101 MICH. L. REV. 409 (2002).

4. *Unpublished Works.* As with other intellectual property regimes, the basic theory behind copyright law is that protection will promote more creation and the public will therefore benefit. What does this suggest for copyrighted works that are kept private? Should they be entitled to more or less protection? The *Harper & Row* Court seems to believe that such works are entitled to more protection because the privacy of the author is implicated. Can an argument be made to the contrary, particularly where, as here, the work is about to be released? Do we really want the monopoly provided to copyright holders to be extended to "monopoly reporting" of news events by the media?

In recognition of concern that strong protection for unpublished works could adversely affect historical research and other important values reflected in the fair use doctrine, Congress amended § 107 in 1992 to add the following caveat: "The fact that a work is unpublished shall not itself bar a finding of fair use if such finding is made upon consideration of all of [the § 107] factors." 102 Pub. L. No. 492, 106 Stat. 3145 (1992). The extent to which this provision re-equilibrates the balance in favor of the use of unpublished works remains unclear. The House Report accompanying this bill expressly approved the statement in *Harper & Row* that the unpublished nature of the work is a "key though not necessarily determinative factor tending to negate the defense of fair use." *See* H.R .REP. NO. 836, 102d Cong., 2d Sess. 9 (1992).

5. *Nature of the Infringed Work.* The copyrighted work in *Harper & Row* was an autobiography, which is a factual work. As we discovered earlier, the copyright protection afforded factual works is much "thinner" than for works of fiction, because the facts themselves cannot be protected. Should the Court have distinguished between factual and protectable material in determining the extent of copying by THE NATION? Would such an analysis have changed the result? The dissent in the case argued that there could be no copyright infringement because THE NATION took only ideas, and not protectable expression, from Ford's book.

6. *Percentage of the Potentially Infringing Work?* The percentage of the potentially infringing work is particularly noteworthy in suits against the makers of movies and television shows alleging that the movie or show infringes the copyright of a work that is shown briefly in the background of the film. In these cases, the copyrighted work (a chair, a sculpture, a poster, or a song) may be "taken" in its entirety, but it is generally a minuscule portion of the defendant's work. Courts dealing with these cases have come to different conclusions under the fair use doctrine. For example, in *Woods v. Universal City Studios*, 920 F. Supp. 62 (S.D.N.Y. 1996), the court enjoined the distribution of the film *12 Monkeys* because three scenes in the film featured a distinctive futuristic torture chamber modeled after a graphic work in the plaintiff's book. And in *Ringgold v. Black Entertainment Television Inc.*, 126 F.3d 70 (2d Cir. 1997), the court held that the use of an artistic poster as part of the background scenery that appeared for less than 30

seconds of a television sitcom was not fair use. By contrast, the depiction of background art for 60 seconds was held to be fair use in *Jackson v. Warner Bros.*, 993 F. Supp. 585 (E.D. Mich. 1997). *Cf. Sandoval v. New Line Cinema Corp.*, 147 F.3d 215 (2d Cir. 1998) (holding unpublished photographs appearing in the background of the movie *Seven* for less than 30 seconds constituted only *de minimis* copying, obviating fair use analysis).

7. *Fair Use as a Solution to Market Failure.* Wendy Gordon argues that the fair use doctrine can and does serve to remedy market failures.

> Though the copyright law has provided a means for excluding nonpurchasers and thus has attempted to cure the public goods problem, and though it has provided mechanisms to facilitate consensual transfers, at times bargaining may be exceedingly expensive or it may be impractical to obtain enforcement against nonpurchasers, or other market flaws might preclude achievement of desirable consensual exchanges. In those cases, the market cannot be relied on to mediate public interests in dissemination and private interests in remuneration. . . .

> Fair use should be awarded to the defendant in a copyright infringement action when (1) market failure is present; (2) transfer of the use to defendant is socially desirable; and (3) an award of fair use would not cause substantial injury to the incentives of the plaintiff copyright owner. The first element of this test ensures that market bypass will not be approved without good cause. The second element of the test ensures that the transfer of a license to use from the copyright holder to the unauthorized user effects a net gain in social value. The third element ensures that the grant of fair use will not undermine the incentive-creating purpose of the copyright law.

Wendy Gordon, *Fair Use as Market Failure: A Structural and Economic Analysis of the Betamax Case and Its Predecessors*, 82 COLUM. L. REV. 1600 (1982). The *Harper & Row* majority appears to endorse such a framework, citing the Gordon article and noting that "there is a fully functioning market that encourages the creation and dissemination of memoirs of public figures." *See Harper & Row*, 471 U.S. at 566 n.9. But is that the right question? Is the relevant market here the one for memoirs, or for articles like THE NATION's? If the latter, is there a "fully functioning market" for excerpts of this nature? For critical reviews of memoirs?

Does a focus on market failure and licensing unreasonably limit the scope of the fair use doctrine? If the point of the fair use doctrine is merely to avoid transaction costs, is it ever likely to play a role in a case that is litigated, where the parties have already shown a willingness to pay hundreds of thousands of dollars (for attorney's fees)? Should some copying be allowed without the copyist having to pay a royalty, even if the copyright owner would have demanded one? In a subsequent article, Gordon argues that her paper has been read too narrowly. *See* Wendy J. Gordon, *Excuse and Justification in the Law of Fair Use: Transactions Costs Have Always Been Only Part of the Story*, 50 J. COPYRIGHT SOC'Y 149 (2003).

8. Judge Kozinski of the Ninth Circuit Court of Appeals has proposed eliminating the fair use doctrine and injunctive relief altogether in favor of liability rules—essentially a form of judicially imposed compulsory licensing. *See* Alex Kozinski & Christopher Newman, *What's So Fair About Fair Use?*, 46 J. COPYRIGHT SOC'Y U.S.A. 513 (1999); *see also* Jane C. Ginsburg, *Fair Use for Free, or Permitted-But-Paid*, 29 BERKELEY TECH L.J. 1383 (2014). Does this strike you as a fairer regime? Would it better serve the purposes that Congress has sought to effectuate through § 107? What would be the effects of such a regime on licensing activity, royalty rates, court dockets, and freedom of expression?

PROBLEMS

Problem IV-44. A home movie taken by a witness named Zales captures the shooting of President John F. Kennedy in Dallas in 1963. Only days after the shooting, EARTH magazine buys the exclusive rights to the Zales film. It subsequently publishes some Zales frames in a magazine special on the assassination. The Zales frames are also appended to a government report by the Whitewash Commission on the assassination. Stone, a writer who is convinced that the Whitewash Report is flawed, unsuccessfully seeks permission from EARTH to reprint the Zales pictures in his book alleging a conspiracy to kill the president. Undaunted by EARTH's refusal, Stone breaks into EARTH's offices and photocopies the pictures, which he then publishes in his book. EARTH sues for copyright infringement. Stone defends on grounds of fair use, and offers to turn over all profits from his book to EARTH. What result?

Problem IV-45. Garrison, a scholar who believes that Lee Harvey Oswald acted alone, is incensed by Stone's (*Problem IV-44*) book. Garrison publishes a book that he entitles A REBUTTAL TO STONE. In it, Garrison follows Stone's organization in detail, presenting and refuting each of Stone's arguments. In doing so, Garrison quotes liberally from Stone's work. Garrison does not, however, use the Zales pictures. Stone sues for copyright infringement. Is Garrison's work fair use?

Problem IV-46. Refer back to the Salinger/Hamilton case (*Problem IV-30*). Can Hamilton successfully argue a fair use defense?

---

c.   The "Transformative" Turn

Pierre N. Leval, Toward a Fair Use Standard
103 HARV. L. REV. 1105 (1990)

. . . The doctrine of fair use need not be so mysterious or dependent on intuitive judgments. Fair use should be perceived not as a disorderly basket of exceptions to the rules of copyright, nor as a departure from the principles governing that body of law, but rather as a rational, integral part of copyright, whose observance is necessary to achieve the objectives of that law. . . .

I believe the answer to the question of justification turns primarily on whether, and to what extent, the challenged use is transformative. The use must be productive and must employ the quoted matter in a different manner or for a different purpose from the original. A quotation of copyrighted material that merely repackages or republishes the original is unlikely to pass the test . . . If, on the other hand, the secondary use adds value to the original—if the quoted matter is used as raw material, transformed in the creation of new information, new aesthetics, new insights and understandings—this is the very type of activity that the fair use doctrine intends to protect for the enrichment of society. . . .

We can [] gain a better understanding of fair use and greater consistency and predictability of court decisions by disciplined focus on the utilitarian, public-enriching objectives of copyright—and by resisting the impulse to import extraneous policies. Fair use is not a grudgingly tolerated exception to the copyright owner's rights of private property, but a fundamental policy of the copyright law. The stimulation of creative thought and authorship for the benefit of society depends assuredly on the protection of the author's monopoly. But it depends equally on the recognition that the monopoly must have limits. Those limits include the public dedication of facts (notwithstanding the author's efforts in uncovering them); the public dedication of ideas (notwithstanding the author's creation); and the public dedication of the right to make fair use of material covered by the copyright.

COMMENTS AND QUESTIONS

1. Judge Leval suggests that transformative works promote copyright's core utilitarian purpose. Judge Frank Easterbrook has questioned such an emphasis on statutory interpretation grounds: "[A]sking exclusively whether something is 'transformative' not only replaces the list in § 107 but also could override § 106(2), which protects derivative works. To say that a new use transforms the work is precisely to say that it is derivative and thus, one might suppose, protected under § 106(2). [Cases focusing on transformativeness] do not explain how every "transformative use" can be "fair use" without extinguishing the author's rights under § 106(2)." *Kienitz v. Sconnie Nation*, 766 F.3d 756 (7th Cir. 2014). Judge Easterbook thinks it best to focus on § 107's four factors, "of which the most important usually is the fourth (market effect)."

2. *False Factors*. Judge Leval question the characterization of fair use as a general equitable balance. "The temptation [to consider the mental state of the defendant] has been particularly strong in dealing with the difficult issue of fair use. This practice is, however, misguided. It produces anomalies that conflict with the goals of copyright and adds to the confusion surrounding the doctrine." In his view, fair use analysis should "maximize the creation and publication of socially useful material" by focusing on whether the secondary user's creation "is of the type that should receive those benefits." But doesn't this inquiry place judges in the role of art critic that Justice Holmes resisted in *Bleistein*?

Similarly, Judge Leval cautions against weighing artistic integrity (moral rights) or privacy concerns in the fair use balance. While recognizing the social interest in these concerns, Judge Leval contends that copyright law is poorly suited to addressing these issues and doing so jeopardizes copyright law's core purpose.

3. Is fair use a question of fact or law? Who should decide—judge or jury? Is it amenable to summary judgment? In *Oracle Corp. v. Google LLC*, 886 F.3d 1179 (Fed. Cir. 2018), the Federal Circuit, having remanded the case for a second trial on fair use, concluded that it owed no deference to the jury's verdict because legal, not factual, issues predominate in the fair use inquiry. The Supreme Court has granted review of this case. *See Google LLC v. Oracle America, Inc.*, 140 S.Ct. 520 (2019).

 Campbell v. Acuff-Rose Music, Inc.
Supreme Court of the United States
510 U.S. 569 (1994)

JUSTICE SOUTER delivered the opinion of the Court.

We are called upon to decide whether 2 Live Crew's commercial parody of Roy Orbison's song, "Oh, Pretty Woman," may be a fair use within the meaning of the Copyright Act of 1976, 17 U.S.C. § 107. Although the District Court granted summary judgment for 2 Live Crew, the Court of Appeals reversed, holding the defense of fair use barred by the song's commercial character and excessive borrowing. Because we hold that a parody's commercial character is only one element to be weighed in a fair use enquiry, and that insufficient consideration was given to the nature of parody in weighing the degree of copying, we reverse and remand.

I

In 1964, Roy Orbison and William Dees wrote a rock ballad called "Oh, Pretty Woman" and assigned their rights in it to respondent Acuff-Rose Music, Inc. Acuff-Rose registered the song for copyright protection.

Petitioners Luther R. Campbell, Christopher Wongwon, Mark Ross, and David Hobbs are collectively known as 2 Live Crew, a popular rap music group. In 1989, Campbell wrote a song entitled "Pretty Woman," which he later described in an affidavit as intended, "through comical lyrics, to satirize the original work. . . ." On July 5, 1989, 2 Live Crew's manager informed Acuff-Rose that 2 Live Crew had written a parody of "Oh, Pretty Woman," that they would afford all credit for ownership and authorship of the original song to Acuff-Rose, Dees, and Orbison, and that they were willing to pay a fee for the use they wished to make of it. Enclosed with the letter were a copy of the lyrics and a recording of 2 Live Crew's song. Acuff-Rose's agent refused permission, stating that "I am aware of the success enjoyed by 'The 2 Live Crews,' but I must inform you that we cannot permit the use of a parody of 'Oh, Pretty Woman.'" Nonetheless, in June or July 1989, 2 Live Crew released records, cassette tapes, and compact discs of "Pretty Woman" in a collection of songs entitled "As Clean As They Wanna Be." The albums and compact discs identify the authors of "Pretty Woman" as Orbison and Dees and its publisher as Acuff-Rose.

Almost a year later, after nearly a quarter of a million copies of the recording had been sold, Acuff-Rose sued 2 Live Crew and its record company, Luke Skyywalker Records, for copyright infringement. The District Court granted summary judgment for 2 Live Crew, reasoning that the commercial purpose of 2 Live Crew's song was no bar to fair use; that 2 Live Crew's version was a parody, which "quickly degenerates into a play on words, substituting predictable lyrics with shocking ones" to show "how bland and banal the Orbison song" is; that 2 Live Crew had taken no more than was necessary to "conjure up" the original in order to parody it; and that it was "extremely unlikely that 2 Live Crew's song could adversely affect the market for the original." The District Court weighed these factors and held that 2 Live Crew's song made fair use of Orbison's original.

The Court of Appeals for the Sixth Circuit reversed and remanded. 972 F.2d 1429, 1439 (1992). Although it assumed for the purpose of its opinion that 2 Live Crew's song was a parody of the Orbison original, . . . the court concluded that its "blatantly commercial purpose . . . prevents this parody from being a fair use."

We granted certiorari to determine whether 2 Live Crew's commercial parody could be a fair use.

II

It is uncontested here that 2 Live Crew's song would be an infringement of Acuff-Rose's rights in "Oh, Pretty Woman," under the Copyright Act of 1976, 17 U.S.C. § 106, but for a finding of fair use through parody. From the infancy of copyright protection, some opportunity for fair use of copyrighted materials has been thought necessary to fulfill copyright's very purpose, "to promote the Progress of Science and useful Arts. . . ." U.S. CONST., Art. I, § 8, cl. 8. For as Justice Story explained, "in truth, in literature, in science and in art, there are, and can be, few, if any, things, which in an abstract sense, are strictly new and original throughout. Every book in literature, science and art, borrows, and must necessarily borrow, and use much which was well known and used before." *Emerson v. Davies*, 8 F. Cas. 615, 619 (No. 4,436) (CCD Mass. 1845). Similarly, Lord Ellenborough expressed the inherent tension in the need simultaneously to protect copyrighted material and to allow others to build upon it when he wrote, "while I shall think myself bound to secure every man in the enjoyment of his copyright, one must not put manacles upon science." *Carey v. Kearsley*, 4 Esp. 168, 170, 170 Eng. Rep. 679, 681 (K.B. 1803). In copyright cases brought under the Statute of Anne of 1710, English courts held that in some instances "fair abridgements" would not infringe an author's rights, *see* W. PATRY, THE FAIR USE PRIVILEGE IN COPYRIGHT LAW 6–17 (1985) (hereinafter Patry); Leval, *Toward a Fair Use Standard*, 103 HARV. L. REV. 1105, 1105 (1990) (hereinafter Leval), and although the First Congress enacted our initial copyright statute, Act of May 31, 1790, 1 Stat. 124, without any explicit reference to "fair use," as it later came to be known, the doctrine was recognized by the American courts nonetheless. . . .

A

The first factor in a fair use enquiry is "the purpose and character of the use, including whether such use is of a commercial nature or is for nonprofit educational purposes." § 107(1). This factor draws on Justice Story's formulation, "the nature and objects of the selections made." *Folsom v. Marsh*, 9 F. Cas., at 348. The enquiry here may be guided by the examples given in the preamble to § 107, looking to whether the use is for criticism, or comment, or news reporting, and the like, *see* § 107. The central purpose of this investigation is to see, in Justice Story's words, whether the new work merely "supersedes the objects" of the original creation, *Folsom v. Marsh, supra*, at 348; *accord, Harper & Row, supra*, at 562 ("supplanting" the original), or instead adds something new, with a further purpose or different character, altering the first with new expression, meaning, or message; it asks, in other words, whether and to what extent the new work is "transformative." Leval 1111. Although such transformative use is not absolutely necessary for a finding of fair use, the goal of copyright, to promote science and the arts, is generally furthered by the creation of transformative works. Such works thus lie at the heart of the fair use doctrine's guarantee of breathing space within the confines of copyright, and the more transformative the new work, the less will be the significance of other factors, like commercialism, that may weigh against a finding of fair use.

[P]arody has an obvious claim to transformative value, as Acuff-Rose itself does not deny. Like less ostensibly humorous forms of criticism, it can provide social benefit, by shedding light on an earlier work, and, in the process, creating a new one. We thus line up with the courts that have held that parody, like other comment or criticism, may claim fair use under § 107.

The germ of parody lies in the definition of the Greek parodeia, quoted in Judge Nelson's Court of Appeals dissent, as "a song sung alongside another." 972 F.2d, at 1440, quoting 7 ENCYCLOPEDIA BRITANNICA 768 (15th ed. 1975). Modern dictionaries accordingly describe a parody as a "literary or artistic work that imitates the characteristic style of an author or a work for comic effect or ridicule," or as a "composition in prose or verse in which the characteristic turns of thought and phrase in an author or class of authors are imitated in such a way as to make them appear ridiculous." For the purposes of copyright law, the nub of the definitions, and the heart of any parodist's claim to quote from existing material, is the use of some elements of a prior author's composition to create a new one that, at least in part, comments on that author's works. If, on the contrary, the commentary has no critical bearing on the substance or style of the original composition, which the alleged infringer merely uses to get attention or to avoid the drudgery in working up something fresh, the claim to fairness in borrowing from another's work diminishes accordingly (if it does not vanish), and other factors, like the extent of its commerciality, loom larger.[14] Parody

---

[14] A parody that more loosely targets an original than the parody presented here may still be sufficiently aimed at an original work to come within our analysis of parody. If a parody whose wide dissemination in the market runs the risk of serving as a substitute for the original or licensed derivatives

needs to mimic an original to make its point, and so has some claim to use the creation of its victim's (or collective victims') imagination, whereas satire can stand on its own two feet and so requires justification for the very act of borrowing.

The fact that parody can claim legitimacy for some appropriation does not, of course, tell either parodist or judge much about where to draw the line. Like a book review quoting the copyrighted material criticized, parody may or may not be fair use, and petitioner's suggestion that any parodic use is presumptively fair has no more justification in law or fact than the equally hopeful claim that any use for news reporting should be presumed fair, *see Harper & Row*, 471 U.S., at 561. The Act has no hint of an evidentiary preference for parodists over their victims, and no workable presumption for parody could take account of the fact that parody often shades into satire when society is lampooned through its creative artifacts, or that a work may contain both parodic and non-parodic elements. Accordingly, parody, like any other use, has to work its way through the relevant factors, and be judged case by case, in light of the ends of the copyright law.

Here, the District Court held, and the Court of Appeals assumed, that 2 Live Crew's "Pretty Woman" contains parody, commenting on and criticizing the original work, whatever it may have to say about society at large. . . .

We have less difficulty in finding that critical element in 2 Live Crew's song than the Court of Appeals did, although having found it we will not take the further step of evaluating its quality. The threshold question when fair use is raised in defense of parody is whether a parodic character may reasonably be perceived.[16] Whether, going beyond that, parody is in good taste or bad does not and should not matter to fair use. As Justice Holmes explained, "it would be a dangerous undertaking for persons trained only to the law to constitute themselves final judges of the worth of [a work], outside of the narrowest and most obvious limits. At the one extreme some works of genius would be sure to miss appreciation. Their very novelty would make them repulsive until the public had learned the new language in which their author spoke." *Bleistein v. Donaldson Lithographing Co.*, 188 U.S. 239, 251 (1903) (circus posters have copyright protection); *cf. Yankee Publishing Inc. v. News America Publishing, Inc.*, 809 F. Supp. 267, 280 (S.D.N.Y. 1992) (Leval, J.) ("First Amendment protections do not apply only to those who speak clearly, whose jokes are funny, and whose parodies succeed") (trademark case).

(*see infra*, discussing factor four), it is more incumbent on one claiming fair use to establish the extent of transformation and the parody's critical relationship to the original. By contrast, when there is little or no risk of market substitution, whether because of the large extent of transformation of the earlier work, the new work's minimal distribution in the market, the small extent to which it borrows from an original, or other factors, taking parodic aim at an original is a less critical factor in the analysis, and looser forms of parody may be found to be fair use, as may satire with lesser justification for the borrowing than would otherwise be required.

[16] The only further judgment, indeed, that a court may pass on a work goes to an assessment of whether the parodic element is slight or great, and the copying small or extensive in relation to the parodic element, for a work with slight parodic element and extensive copying will be more likely to merely "supersede the objects" of the original.

While we might not assign a high rank to the parodic element here, we think it fair to say that 2 Live Crew's song reasonably could be perceived as commenting on the original or criticizing it, to some degree. 2 Live Crew juxtaposes the romantic musings of a man whose fantasy comes true, with degrading taunts, a bawdy demand for sex, and a sigh of relief from paternal responsibility. The later words can be taken as a comment on the naiveté of the original of an earlier day, as a rejection of its sentiment that ignores the ugliness of street life and the debasement that it signifies. It is this joinder of reference and ridicule that marks off the author's choice of parody from the other types of comment and criticism that traditionally have had a claim to fair use protection as transformative works.[17]

The Court of Appeals, however, immediately cut short the enquiry into 2 Live Crew's fair use claim by confining its treatment of the first factor essentially to one relevant fact, the commercial nature of the use. The court then inflated the significance of this fact by applying a presumption ostensibly culled from *Sony*, that "every commercial use of copyrighted material is presumptively . . . unfair. . . ." *Sony*, 464 U.S., at 451. In giving virtually dispositive weight to the commercial nature of the parody, the Court of Appeals erred.

The language of the statute makes clear that the commercial or non profit educational purpose of a work is only one element of the first factor enquiry into its purpose and character. . . .

B

The second statutory factor, "the nature of the copyrighted work," § 107(2), draws on Justice Story's expression, the "value of the materials used." *Folsom v. Marsh*, 9 F. Cas., at 348. This factor calls for recognition that some works are closer to the core of intended copyright protection than others, with the consequence that fair use is more difficult to establish when the former works are copied. *See, e.g., Stewart v. Abend*, 495 U.S., at 237–238 (contrasting fictional short story with factual works); *Harper & Row*, 471 U.S., at 563–564 (contrasting soon-to-be-published memoir with published speech); *Sony*, 464 U.S., at 455, n.40 (contrasting motion pictures with news broadcasts); *Feist*, 499 U.S., at 348–351 (contrasting creative works with bare factual compilations); 3 M. NIMMER & D. NIMMER, NIMMER ON COPYRIGHT § 13.05[A][2] (1993); Leval 1116. We agree with both the District Court and the Court of Appeals that use of the Orbison original's creative expression for public dissemination falls within the core of the copyright's protective purposes. This fact, however, is not much help in this case, or ever likely to help much in separating the fair use sheep from the infringing goats in a parody case, since parodies almost invariably copy publicly known, expressive works.

---

[17] We note in passing that 2 Live Crew need not label its whole album, or even this song, a parody in order to claim fair use protection, nor should 2 Live Crew be penalized for this being its first parodic essay. Parody serves its goals whether labeled or not, and there is no reason to require parody to state the obvious (or even the reasonably perceived).

C

The third factor asks whether "the amount and substantiality of the portion used in relation to the copyrighted work as a whole," § 107(3) (or, in Justice Story's words, "the quantity and value of the materials used," *Folsom v. Marsh*, *supra*, at 348) are reasonable in relation to the purpose of the copying. Here, attention turns to the persuasiveness of a parodist's justification for the particular copying done, and the enquiry will harken back to the first of the statutory factors, for, as in prior cases, we recognize that the extent of permissible copying varies with the purpose and character of the use. *See Sony*, 464 U.S., at 449–450 (reproduction of entire work "does not have its ordinary effect of militating against a finding of fair use" as to home videotaping of television programs); *Harper & Row*, 471 U.S., at 564 ("Even substantial quotations might qualify as fair use in a review of a published work or a news account of a speech" but not in a scoop of a soon-to-be-published memoir). The facts bearing on this factor will also tend to address the fourth, by revealing the degree to which the parody may serve as a market substitute for the original or potentially licensed derivatives. *See* Leval 1123.

The District Court considered the song's parodic purpose in finding that 2 Live Crew had not helped themselves overmuch. The Court of Appeals disagreed, stating that "while it may not be inappropriate to find that no more was taken than necessary, the copying was qualitatively substantial. . . . We conclude that taking the heart of the original and making it the heart of a new work was to purloin a substantial portion of the essence of the original." 972 F.2d, at 1438. . . .

Where we part company with the court below is in applying [this factor] to parody, and in particular to parody in the song before us. Parody presents a difficult case. Parody's humor, or in any event its comment, necessarily springs from recognizable allusion to its object through distorted imitation. Its art lies in the tension between a known original and its parodic twin. When parody takes aim at a particular original work, the parody must be able to "conjure up" at least enough of that original to make the object of its critical wit recognizable. What makes for this recognition is quotation of the original's most distinctive or memorable features, which the parodist can be sure the audience will know. Once enough has been taken to assure identification, how much more is reasonable will depend, say, on the extent to which the song's overriding purpose and character is to parody the original or, in contrast, the likelihood that the parody may serve as a market substitute for the original. But using some characteristic features cannot be avoided.

We think the Court of Appeals was insufficiently appreciative of parody's need for the recognizable sight or sound when it ruled 2 Live Crew's use unreasonable as a matter of law. It is true, of course, that 2 Live Crew copied the characteristic opening bass riff (or musical phrase) of the original, and true that the words of the first line copy the Orbison lyrics. But if quotation of the opening riff and the first line may be said to go to the "heart" of the original, the heart is also what most readily conjures up the song for parody, and it is the heart at which parody takes aim. Copying does not become excessive in relation to parodic purpose merely because the portion taken was the original's heart. If 2 Live Crew had copied a significantly less memorable part of the original, it is difficult to see how its parodic character would have come through.

This is not, of course, to say that anyone who calls himself a parodist can skim the cream and get away scot free. In parody, as in news reporting, context is everything, and the question of fairness asks what else the parodist did besides go to the heart of the original. It is significant that 2 Live Crew not only copied the first line of the original, but thereafter departed markedly from the Orbison lyrics for its own ends. 2 Live Crew not only copied the bass riff and repeated it, but also produced otherwise distinctive sounds, interposing "scraper" noise, overlaying the music with solos in different keys, and altering the drum beat. This is not a case, then, where "a substantial portion" of the parody itself is composed of a "verbatim" copying of the original. It is not, that is, a case where the parody is so insubstantial, as compared to the copying, that the third factor must be resolved as a matter of law against the parodists.

Suffice it to say here that, as to the lyrics, we think the Court of Appeals correctly suggested that "no more was taken than necessary," but just for that reason, we fail to see how the copying can be excessive in relation to its parodic purpose, even if the portion taken is the original's "heart." As to the music, we express no opinion whether repetition of the bass riff is excessive copying, and we remand to permit evaluation of the amount taken, in light of the song's parodic purpose and character, its transformative elements, and considerations of the potential for market substitution sketched more fully below.

D

The fourth fair use factor is "the effect of the use upon the potential market for or value of the copyrighted work." § 107(4). It requires courts to consider not only the extent of market harm caused by the particular actions of the alleged infringer, but also "whether unrestricted and widespread conduct of the sort engaged in by the defendant . . . would result in a substantially adverse impact on the potential market" for the original. NIMMER § 13.05[A][4], p. 13-102.61 (footnote omitted); accord *Harper & Row*, 471 U.S., at 569; Senate Report, p. 65; *Folsom v. Marsh*, 9 F. Cas., at 349. The enquiry "must take account not only of harm to the original but also of harm to the market for derivative works." *Harper & Row, supra*, at 568.

Since fair use is an affirmative defense, its proponent would have difficulty carrying the burden of demonstrating fair use without favorable evidence about relevant markets. In moving for summary judgment, 2 Live Crew left themselves at just such a disadvantage when they failed to address the effect on the market for rap derivatives, and confined themselves to uncontroverted submissions that there was no likely effect on the market for the original. They did not, however, thereby subject themselves to the evidentiary presumption applied by the Court of Appeals. In assessing the likelihood of significant market harm, the Court of Appeals quoted from language in *Sony* that "'if the intended use is for commercial gain, that likelihood may be presumed. But if it is for a noncommercial purpose, the likelihood must be demonstrated.'" 972 F.2d, at 1438, quoting *Sony*, 464 U.S., at 451. The court reasoned that because "the use of the copyrighted work is wholly commercial, . . . we presume a likelihood of future harm to Acuff-Rose exists." In so doing, the court resolved the fourth factor against 2 Live Crew, just as it had the first, by applying a presumption about the effect of commercial use, a presumption which as applied here we hold to be error.

No "presumption" or inference of market harm that might find support in *Sony* is applicable to a case involving something beyond mere duplication for commercial purposes. *Sony*'s discussion of a presumption contrasts a context of verbatim copying of the original in its entirety for commercial purposes, with the non-commercial context of *Sony* itself (home copying of television programming). In the former circumstances, what *Sony* said simply makes common sense: when a commercial use amounts to mere duplication of the entirety of an original, it clearly "supersedes the objects," *Folsom v. Marsh*, 9 F. Cas., at 348, of the original and serves as a market replacement for it, making it likely that cognizable market harm to the original will occur. *Sony*, 464 U.S., at 451. But when, on the contrary, the second use is transformative, market substitution is at least less certain, and market harm may not be so readily inferred. Indeed, as to parody pure and simple, it is more likely that the new work will not affect the market for the original in a way cognizable under this factor, that is, by acting as a substitute for it ("superseding [its] objects"). *See* Leval 1125. This is so because the parody and the original usually serve different market functions.

We do not, of course, suggest that a parody may not harm the market at all, but when a lethal parody, like a scathing theater review, kills demand for the original, it does not produce a harm cognizable under the Copyright Act. Because "parody may quite legitimately aim at garroting the original, destroying it commercially as well as artistically," B. KAPLAN, AN UNHURRIED VIEW OF COPYRIGHT 69 (1967), the role of the courts is to distinguish between "biting criticism [that merely] suppresses demand [and] copyright infringement[, which] usurps it." *Fisher v. Dees*, 794 F.2d, at 438.

This distinction between potentially remediable displacement and unremediable disparagement is reflected in the rule that there is no protectable derivative market for criticism. The market for potential derivative uses includes only those that creators of original works would in general develop or license others to develop. Yet the unlikelihood that creators of imaginative works will license critical reviews or lampoons of their own productions removes such uses from the very notion of a potential licensing market. "People ask . . . for criticism, but they only want praise." S. MAUGHAM, OF HUMAN BONDAGE 241 (Penguin ed. 1992). Thus, to the extent that the opinion below may be read to have considered harm to the market for parodies of "Oh, Pretty Woman," the court erred. Accord, *Fisher v. Dees*, 794 F.2d, at 437; Leval 1125.

In explaining why the law recognizes no derivative market for critical works, including parody, we have, of course, been speaking of the later work as if it had nothing but a critical aspect (i.e., "parody pure and simple"). But the later work may have a more complex character, with effects not only in the arena of criticism but also in protectable markets for derivative works, too. In that sort of case, the law looks beyond the criticism to the other elements of the work, as it does here. 2 Live Crew's song comprises not only parody but also rap music, and the derivative market for rap music is a proper focus of enquiry, *see Harper & Row*, 471 U.S., at 568; NIMMER § 13.05[B]. Evidence of substantial harm to it would weigh against a finding of fair use, because the licensing of derivatives is an important economic incentive to the creation of originals. *See* 17 U.S.C. § 106(2) (copyright owner has rights to derivative works). Of course, the only harm to derivatives that need concern us, as discussed above, is the harm of market substitution. The fact that a parody may impair the market for derivative uses by the very effectiveness of its critical commentary is no more relevant under copyright than the like threat to the original market.

Although 2 Live Crew submitted uncontroverted affidavits on the question of market harm to the original, neither they, nor Acuff-Rose, introduced evidence or affidavits addressing the likely effect of 2 Live Crew's parodic rap song on the market for a non-parody, rap version of "Oh, Pretty Woman." . . . It is impossible to deal with the fourth factor except by recognizing that a silent record on an important factor bearing on fair use disentitled the proponent of the defense, 2 Live Crew, to summary judgment. The evidentiary hole will doubtless be plugged on remand.

III

It was error for the Court of Appeals to conclude that the commercial nature of 2 Live Crew's parody of "Oh, Pretty Woman" rendered it presumptively unfair. No such evidentiary presumption is available to address either the first factor, the character and purpose of the use, or the fourth, market harm, in determining whether a transformative use, such as parody, is a fair one. The court also erred in holding that 2 Live Crew had necessarily copied excessively from the Orbison original, considering the parodic purpose of the use. We therefore reverse the judgment of the Court of Appeals and remand for further proceedings consistent with this opinion.

It is so ordered.

APPENDIX A	**APPENDIX B**
"Oh, Pretty Woman" *by Roy Orbison and William Dees*	*"Pretty Woman" by 2 Live Crew*
Pretty Woman, walking down the street,	Pretty woman walkin' down the street
Pretty Woman, the kind I like to meet,	Pretty woman girl you look so sweet
Pretty Woman, I don't believe you, you're not the truth,	Pretty woman you bring me down to that knee
No one could look as good as you Mercy	Pretty woman you make me wanna beg please Oh, pretty woman
Pretty Woman, won't you pardon me,	Big hairy woman you need to shave that stuff

Pretty Woman, I couldn't help but see,	Big hairy woman you know I bet it's tough
Pretty Woman, that you look lovely as can be . . .	Big hairy woman all that hair it ain't legit 'Cause you look like 'Cousin It' Big hairy woman . . .

COMMENTS AND QUESTIONS

1. *Burden of Proof.* 2 Live Crew was successful in persuading the Supreme Court to reverse the Court of Appeals and reduce the significance of the presumption that commercial uses are unfair. But the Supreme Court did not simply affirm the district court's ruling that 2 Live Crew was entitled to summary judgment. Instead, the Court remanded the case for a determination of the parody's effect on the market for (non-parodic) rap derivatives of "Pretty Woman." Furthermore, the Court assumed that it was 2 Live Crew's burden to show that its parody had no such effect. Is 2 Live Crew—or any defendant—likely to be able to present such evidence and thus to prevail on summary judgment? Is it appropriate to assign the burden of proof to defendants on this issue? To what extent is *Sony*'s presumption that commercial use is unfair still applicable?

Is fair use a defense, or part of the plaintiff's affirmative case? *Campbell* treats it as an affirmative defense. But the Copyright Act says that fair use "is not an infringement of copyright." § 107; *see Lenz v. Universal Music Corp.*, 815 F.3d 1145 (9th Cir. 2015) (observing that § 107 "expressly authorizes fair use" and thus "labeling it as an affirmative defense that excuses conduct is a misnomer").

2. *Relevance of Intent.* Must the alleged infringer's primary intent be to parody the work? Arguably, 2 Live Crew simply wanted to engage in satire. Their song is arguably only obliquely directed at Orbison's. Can a work ever be a parody if the author did not intend it to be? Note that 2 Live Crew originally asserted that their song was a *cover* of the original, and was therefore eligible for a compulsory license under § 115. This argument failed because 2 Live Crew substantially changed the song from its original version.

The Supreme Court downplayed the role of the defendant's state of mind. The fact that 2 Live Crew was denied permission has no bearing on whether its use was fair. *Campbell*, 510 U.S. at 585 n.18; *see also* Pierre N. Leval, *Toward a Fair Use Standard*, 103 HARV. L. REV. 1105, 1126–28 (1990) (arguing that good faith is irrelevant to fair use analysis and conflicts with the policy interests underlying copyright and fair use protections).

3. *Scope of the Derivative Work Right.* The debate over parodies reflects a larger copyright issue that the Court does not directly address. Does the copyright owner have the right to prevent derivative works from being created, or only the right to receive royalties from derivative works produced by others? Traditionally, copyright law has assumed that the copyright owner has the right to prevent others from publishing a work at all without his or her permission. But the Court in *Campbell* seems to assume the

reverse—that copyright owners are expected to license their rights in order to promote the widespread distribution of information (a key policy underlying copyright law). *See* footnote 10 of the Court's opinion.

Are copyright owners likely to allow parodies voluntarily? Because many parodies lampoon the original, the authors of the original are often unwilling to permit a parody to be prepared at any price. Professor Merges has described this reluctance as the "bargaining breakdown" problem—noneconomic factors prevent the parties from agreeing to what might be an efficient license (in purely economic terms). *See* Robert P. Merges, *Are You Making Fun of Me? Notes on Market Failure and the Parody Defense in Copyright*, 21 AIPLA Q.J. 305 (1993). *Cf.* Richard A. Posner, *When Is Parody Fair Use?*, 21 J. LEGAL STUD. 79 (1992). In particular, in this case, Acuff-Rose refused to negotiate a mutually advantageous transfer because they didn't like the defendant's song. Does the breakdown of bargaining justify fair use treatment of parodies? Does the policy of encouraging dissemination do so? Note that some parodists like Weird Al Yankovic do succeed in getting licenses for their work, although the resulting parodies might be less critical than those produced without a license.

5. *Parody or Satire?* The problems with the parody/satire distinction were put into sharp relief by the Ninth Circuit's decision in *Dr. Seuss Enterprises v. Penguin Books*, 109 F.3d 1394 (9th Cir. 1997). In that case, the defendant published a book making fun of the O.J. Simpson murder trial. Called "The Cat NOT in the Hat," the poem copied the graphic artistic style and lyric structure of Theodore Geisel's famous children's book *The Cat in the Hat.* The Ninth Circuit rejected the defendant's claim of fair use. It held that the defendant's work was satire, not parody, because his intent was to poke fun at the O.J. Simpson trial and not at the Dr. Seuss book, and therefore was not within the scope of fair use.

Does *Dr. Seuss* misread *Campbell* in suggesting that satire can never be fair use? The defendant's work seems precisely the sort of transformative use that *Campbell* seemed to encourage, and there is no way to create such a work without relying on Geisel's preexisting work.

6. Margaret Mitchell's 1936 novel, GONE WITH THE WIND, has become one of the best-selling books in the world. The Mitchell Trust has actively managed the copyright, authorizing derivative works and a variety of commercial items. Alice Randall decided to retell this classic story of the pre-Civil War South from the perspective of Cyana, the illegitimate daughter of the plantation owner and the slave who cared for his children. Randall's book, THE WIND DONE GONE, contains many of the characters, settings, plot devices, and scenes from Mitchell's work, although viewed from a very different perspective. Randall's publisher, Houghton and Mifflin, no doubt familiar with the *Campbell* case, billed the work as a "provocative literary parody that explodes the mythology perpetrated by a Southern classic." Suntrust, the Trustee of the Mitchell Trust, sued to halt publication of Randall's book. The trial court issued a preliminary injunction, finding that the plaintiff was likely to prevail on both substantial similarity and lack of fair use. *Suntrust Bank v. Houghton Mifflin Co.*, 136 F. Supp. 2d 1357, 1364 (N.D. Ga. 2001).

On appeal, the Eleventh Circuit reversed the injunction. It agreed that the works were substantially similar, but held that Randall's book would likely prevail on its fair use defense. 268 F.3d 1257 (11th Cir. 2001). With respect to the first factor, the purpose and character of the work, the court found Randall's work to criticize and transform the original, stripping away the romantic portrait of the antebellum South painted by GONE WITH THE WIND and reversing the race roles originally portrayed. Besides tipping the first factor in favor of fair use, the work's highly transformative nature meant that it would not compete with the original or harm the market for derivatives under the fourth factor. With respect to the third factor, the court acknowledged that THE WIND DONE GONE borrowed heavily from the original, but noted, citing *Campbell*, that parodies need to copy substantially in order to conjure up the original. It also noted that the second factor, nature of the copyrighted work, had little bearing since parodies nearly always copy expressive works. Thus, based principally on its analysis of factors one and four, coupled with First Amendment concerns about prior restraints on speech, the appellate court concluded that THE WIND DONE GONE would likely prevail on a fair use defense, and overturned the lower court's preliminary injunction. *Cf.* Jed Rubenfeld, *The Freedom of Imagination: Copyright's Constitutionality*, 112 YALE L.J. 1 (2002); Zahr Said Stauffer, *'Po-Mo Karaoke' or Postcolonial Pastiche? What Fair Use Analysis Could Draw from Literary Criticism*, 31 COLUM. J.L. & ARTS 43 (2007); Christina Bohannan, *Copyright Harm, Foreseeability, and Fair Us*e, 85 WASH. U.L. REV. 969 (2007). The parties settled the case in a manner that allowed Randall's book to remain on the market.

7. *Reputational Injury*. It is obvious why copyright owners do not want people to make fun of them. But can transformations destroy the market for the original, not by poking fun at it, but by associating it with undesirable elements? In *Furie v. Infowars, LLC*, 401 F. Supp. 3d 952 (C.D. Cal. 2019), the plaintiff sued after his cartoon design Pepe the Frog became adopted by white nationalists as a racist meme. The court held that whether this repurposing was fair use presented a disputed question of fact.

Should an artist have control over the ways in which his image is used to support causes he abhors? Or would giving that control impede free speech? Could Margaret Mitchell's estate have made the same argument against THE WIND DONE GONE?

PROBLEMS

Problem IV-47. Recall *Problem IV-36* relating to J.D. Salinger's lawsuit against Fredrik Colting over the novel "60 Years Later: Coming through the Rye." Colting seeks shelter under the fair use doctrine, arguing that his novel is a parody under the Campbell decision. How should a court rule?

Problem IV-48. Air Pirates, a publisher of counter-culture adult comic books, developed a series of comic books cynically depicting popular children's cartoon characters, including Mickey and Minnie Mouse, Donald Duck, and Goofy, as promiscuous, drug-dealing rogues. Here is one of the magazine covers:

Should Air Pirates' use be considered fair?

iii.   The Modern Fair Use Landscape

Fair use analysis is among the most rich and varied fields of jurisprudence. As Justice Story observed in 1841, it is not easy "to lay down any general principles applicable to all cases." As a result, lawyers must inevitably review dozens of cases in evaluating whether a use is fair. They must also deal with the fact that their client could be sued in any regional circuit, or if a patent issue in play, the Federal Circuit. They must also deal with the uncertainty of which judge or panel will hear their case. How a parody will come out may well depend on whether the judge "gets" the joke? How a technology-oriented case is decided can depend on the court's technological sophistication? How an art case is viewed can depend on the subjective tastes of the jurist(s)? The challenge is daunting. Fair use analysis, like many aspect of legal analysis, is a form of applied risk analysis.

Fortunately, distinctive patterns have begun to emerge in the fair use landscape. We suggest three main contours for navigating the modern fair use landscape: (i) conventional; (ii) contextual; and (iii) functional.

a.   Conventional

Many fair use cases fit within the examples provided in the § 107 preamble: "criticism, comment, news reporting, teaching (including multiple copies for classroom use), scholarship, or research." Several of these categories relate to First Amendment protections. Yet it would be a mistake to assume that simply being in these categories resolves the fair use question. As the Supreme Court's *Campbell* decision illustrates, the fair use balance must be applied to critical or parodic works. And academic publishers have been able to prevent unauthorized reproduction of journal articles and books in various contexts.

American Geophysical Union v. Texaco Inc.
United States Court of Appeals for the Second Circuit
60 F.3d 913 (2d Cir. 1994)

Jon O. NEWMAN, Chief Judge:

. . . Plaintiffs American Geophysical Union and 82 other publishers of scientific and technical journals (the "publishers") brought a class action claiming that Texaco's unauthorized photocopying of articles from their journals constituted copyright infringement. Among other defenses, Texaco claimed that its copying was fair use under section 107 of the Copyright Act. . . .

Although Texaco employs 400 to 500 research scientists, of whom all or most presumably photocopy scientific journal articles to support their Texaco research, the parties stipulated—in order to spare the enormous expense of exploring the photocopying practices of each of them—that one scientist would be chosen at random as the representative of the entire group. The scientist chosen was Dr. Donald H. Chickering, II, a scientist at Texaco's research center in Beacon, New York. For consideration at trial, the publishers selected from Chickering's files photocopies of eight particular articles from the JOURNAL OF CATALYSIS. . . .

Chickering, a chemical engineer at the Beacon research facility, has worked for Texaco since 1981 conducting research in the field of catalysis, which concerns changes in the rates of chemical reactions. To keep abreast of developments in his field, Chickering must review works published in various scientific and technical journals related to his area of research. Texaco assists in this endeavor by having its library circulate current issues of relevant journals to Chickering when he places his name on the appropriate routing list.

The copies of the eight articles from CATALYSIS found in Chickering's files that the parties have made the exclusive focus of the fair use trial were photocopied in their entirety by Chickering or by other Texaco employees at Chickering's request. Chickering apparently believed that the material and data found within these articles would facilitate his current or future professional research. The evidence developed at trial indicated that Chickering did not generally use the CATALYSIS articles in his research immediately upon copying, but placed the photocopied articles in his files to have them available for later reference as needed. Chickering became aware of six of the photocopied articles when the original issues of CATALYSIS containing the articles were circulated to him. He learned of the other two articles upon seeing a reference to them in another published article. As it turned out, Chickering did not have occasion to make use of five of the articles that were copied. . . .

I. The Nature of the Dispute

. . .

A. Fair Use and Photocopying

. . . As with the development of other easy and accessible means of mechanical reproduction of documents, the invention and widespread availability of photocopying technology threatens to disrupt the delicate balances established by the Copyright Act. As a leading commentator astutely notes, the advent of modern photocopying technology creates a pressing need for the law "to strike an appropriate balance between the authors' interest in preserving the integrity of copyright, and the public's right to enjoy the benefits that photocopying technology offers." 3 NIMMER ON COPYRIGHT § 13.05[E][1], at 13-226.

Indeed, if the issue were open, we would seriously question whether the fair use analysis that has developed with respect to works of authorship alleged to use portions of copyrighted material is precisely applicable to copies produced by mechanical means. The traditional fair use analysis, now codified in section 107, developed in an effort to adjust the competing interests of authors—the author of the original copyrighted work and the author of the secondary work that "copies" a portion of the original work in the course of producing what is claimed to be a new work. Mechanical "copying" of an entire document, made readily feasible and economical by the advent of xerography, is obviously an activity entirely different from creating a work of authorship. Whatever social utility copying of this sort achieves, it is not concerned with creative authorship. . . .

II. The Enumerated Fair Use Factors of Section 107

. . .

A. First Factor: Purpose and Character of Use

The first factor listed in section 107 is "the purpose and character of the use, including whether such use is of a commercial nature or is for nonprofit educational purposes." § 107(1). Especially pertinent to an assessment of the first fair use factor are the precise circumstances under which copies of the eight CATALYSIS articles were made. After noticing six of these articles when the original copy of the journal issue containing each of them was circulated to him, Chickering had them photocopied, at least initially, for the same basic purpose that one would normally seek to obtain the original—to have it available on his shelf for ready reference if and when he needed to look at it. The library circulated one copy and invited all the researchers to make their own photocopies. It is a reasonable inference that the library staff wanted each journal issue moved around the building quickly and returned to the library so that it would be available for others to look at. Making copies enabled all researchers who might one day be interested in examining the contents of an article in the issue to have the article readily available in their own offices. In Chickering's own words, the copies of the articles were made for "my personal convenience," since it is "far more convenient to have access in my office to a photocopy of an article than to have to go to the library each time I wanted to refer to it." Significantly, Chickering did not even have occasion to use five of the photocopied articles at all, further revealing that the photocopies of the eight Catalysis articles were primarily made just for "future retrieval and reference."

It is true that photocopying these articles also served other purposes. The most favorable for Texaco is the purpose of enabling Chickering, if the need should arise, to go into the lab with pieces of paper that (a) were not as bulky as the entire issue or a bound volume of a year's issues, and (b) presented no risk of damaging the original by exposure to chemicals. And these purposes might suffice to tilt the first fair use factor in favor of Texaco if these purposes were dominant. For example, if Chickering had asked the library to buy him a copy of the pertinent issue of Catalysis and had placed it on his shelf, and one day while reading it had noticed a chart, formula, or other material that he wanted to take right into the lab, it might be a fair use for him to make a photocopy, and use that copy in the lab (especially if he did not retain it and build up a mini-library of photocopied articles). This is the sort of "spontaneous" copying that is part of the test for permissible nonprofit classroom copying. *See* Agreement on Guidelines for Classroom Copying in Not-For-Profit Educational Institutions, quoted in PATRY, THE FAIR USE PRIVILEGE, at 308. But that is not what happened here as to the six items copied from the circulated issues.

As to the other two articles, the circumstances are not quite as clear, but they too appear more to serve the purpose of being additions to Chickering's office "library" than to be spontaneous copying of a critical page that he was reading on his way to the lab. One was copied apparently when he saw a reference to it in another article, which was in an issue circulated to him. The most likely inference is that he decided that he ought to have copies of both items—again for placement on his shelf for later use if the need arose. The last article was copied, according to his affidavit, when he saw a reference to it "elsewhere." What is clear is that this item too was simply placed "on the shelf." As he testified, "I kept a copy to refer to in case I became more involved in support effects research."

The photocopying of these eight CATALYSIS articles may be characterized as "archival"—i.e., done for the primary purpose of providing numerous Texaco scientists (for whom Chickering served as an example) each with his or her own personal copy of each article without Texaco's having to purchase another original journal. The photocopying "merely 'supersedes the objects' of the original creation," *Campbell*, 114 S.Ct. at 1171 (quoting *Folsom v. Marsh*, 9 F. Cas. 342, 348 (C.C.D. Mass. 1841) (No. 4,901)), and tilts the first fair use factor against Texaco. We do not mean to suggest that no instance of archival copying would be fair use, but the first factor tilts against Texaco in this case because the making of copies to be placed on the shelf in Chickering's office is part of a systematic process of encouraging employee researchers to copy articles so as to multiply available copies while avoiding payment.

Texaco criticizes three aspects of the District Court's analysis of the first factor. . . .

1. Commercial Use. We generally agree with Texaco's contention that the District Court placed undue emphasis on the fact that Texaco is a for-profit corporation conducting research primarily for commercial gain. Since many, if not most, secondary users seek at least some measure of commercial gain from their use, unduly emphasizing the commercial motivation of a copier will lead to an overly restrictive view of fair use. . . .

We do not consider Texaco's status as a for-profit company irrelevant to the fair use analysis. Though Texaco properly contends that a court's focus should be on the use of the copyrighted material and not simply on the user, it is overly simplistic to suggest that the "purpose and character of the use" can be fully discerned without considering the nature and objectives of the user.

Ultimately, the somewhat cryptic suggestion in section 107(1) to consider whether the secondary use "is of a commercial nature or is for nonprofit educational purposes" connotes that a court should examine, among other factors, the value obtained by the secondary user from the use of the copyrighted material. *See Rogers*, 960 F.2d at 309 ("The first factor . . . asks whether the original was copied in good faith to benefit the public or primarily for the commercial interests of the infringer."); *MCA, Inc. v. Wilson*, 677 F.2d 180, 182 (2d Cir. 1981) (court is to consider "whether the alleged infringing use was primarily for public benefit or for private commercial gain"). The commercial/nonprofit dichotomy concerns the unfairness that arises when a secondary user makes unauthorized use of copyrighted material to capture significant revenues as a direct consequence of copying the original work. *See Harper & Row*, 471 U.S. at 562 ("The crux of the profit/nonprofit distinction is . . . whether the user stands to profit from exploitation of the copyrighted material without paying the customary price.").

Consistent with these principles, courts will not sustain a claimed defense of fair use when the secondary use can fairly be characterized as a form of "commercial exploitation," i.e., when the copier directly and exclusively acquires conspicuous financial rewards from its use of the copyrighted material. . . . Conversely, courts are more willing to find a secondary use fair when it produces a value that benefits the broader public interest. . . . The greater the private economic rewards reaped by the secondary user (to the exclusion of broader public benefits), the more likely the first factor will favor the copyright holder and the less likely the use will be considered fair.

As noted before, in this particular case the link between Texaco's commercial gain and its copying is somewhat attenuated: the copying, at most, merely facilitated Chickering's research that might have led to the production of commercially valuable products. Thus, it would not be accurate to conclude that Texaco's copying of eight particular Catalysis articles amounted to "commercial exploitation," especially since the immediate goal of Texaco's copying was to facilitate Chickering's research in the sciences, an objective that might well serve a broader public purpose. *See Twin Peaks*, 996 F.2d at 1375; *Sega Enterprises*, 977 F.2d at 1522. Still, we need not ignore the for-profit nature of Texaco's enterprise, especially since we can confidently conclude that Texaco reaps at least some indirect economic advantage from its photocopying. As the publishers emphasize, Texaco's photocopying for Chickering could be regarded simply as another "factor of production" utilized in Texaco's efforts to develop profitable products. Conceptualized in this way, it is not obvious why it is fair for Texaco to avoid having to pay at least some price to copyright holders for the right to photocopy the original articles.

2. *Transformative Use.* The District Court properly emphasized that Texaco's photocopying was not "transformative." After the District Court issued its opinion, the Supreme Court explicitly ruled that the concept of a "transformative use" is central to a proper analysis under the first factor, *see Campbell*, 114 S.Ct. at 1171–73. The Court explained that though a "transformative use is not absolutely necessary for a finding of fair use, . . . the more transformative the new work, the less will be the significance of other factors, like commercialism, that may weigh against a finding of fair use." *Id.* at 1171. . . .

[T]o the extent that the secondary use "adds something new, with a further purpose or different character," the value generated goes beyond the value that inheres in the original and "the goal of copyright, to promote science and the arts, is generally furthered." *Campbell*, 114 S.Ct. at 1171; *see also* Pierre N. Leval, *Toward a Fair Use Standard*, 103 HARV. L. REV. 1105, 1111 (1990). It is therefore not surprising that the "preferred" uses illustrated in the preamble to section 107, such as criticism and comment, generally involve some transformative use of the original work. *See* 3 NIMMER ON COPYRIGHT § 13.05[A][1][b], at 13-160.

Texaco suggests that its conversion of the individual CATALYSIS articles through photocopying into a form more easily used in a laboratory might constitute a transformative use. However, Texaco's photocopying merely transforms the material object embodying the intangible article that is the copyrighted original work. *See* 17 U.S.C. §§ 101, 102 (explaining that copyright protection in literary works subsists in the original work of authorship "regardless of the nature of the material objects . . . in which they are embodied"). Texaco's making of copies cannot properly be regarded as a transformative use of the copyrighted material. . . .

On balance, we agree with the District Court that the first factor favors the publishers, primarily because the dominant purpose of the use is "archival." . . .

B. Second Factor: Nature of Copyrighted Work

The second statutory fair use factor is "the nature of the copyrighted work." 17 U.S.C. § 107(2). . . . Ultimately the manifestly factual character of the eight articles precludes us from considering the articles as "within the core of the copyright's protective purposes," *Campbell*, 114 S.Ct. at 1175; *see also Harper & Row*, 471 U.S. at 563 ("The law generally recognizes a greater need to disseminate factual works than works of fiction or fantasy."). Thus, in agreement with the District Court, we conclude that the second factor favors Texaco.

C. Third Factor: Amount and Substantiality of Portion Used

The third statutory fair use factor is "the amount and substantiality of the portion used in relation to the copyrighted work as a whole." 17 U.S.C. § 107(3). The District

Court concluded that this factor clearly favors the publishers because Texaco copied the eight articles from CATALYSIS in their entirety. [The Court of Appeals agreed.]

D. Fourth Factor: Effect Upon Potential Market or Value

The fourth statutory fair use factor is "the effect of the use upon the potential market for or value of the copyrighted work." 17 U.S.C. § 107(4). Assessing this factor, the District Court detailed the range of procedures Texaco could use to obtain authorized copies of the articles that it photocopied and found that "whatever combination of procedures Texaco used, the publishers' revenues would grow significantly." The Court concluded that the publishers "powerfully demonstrated entitlement to prevail as to the fourth factor," since they had shown "a substantial harm to the value of their copyrights" as the consequence of Texaco's copying. . . .

In analyzing the fourth factor, it is important (1) to bear in mind the precise copyrighted works, namely the eight journal articles, and (2) to recognize the distinctive nature and history of "the potential market for or value of" these particular works. Specifically, though there is a traditional market for, and hence a clearly defined value of, journal issues and volumes, in the form of per-issue purchases and journal subscriptions, there is neither a traditional market for, nor a clearly defined value of, individual journal articles. As a result, analysis of the fourth factor cannot proceed as simply as would have been the case if Texaco had copied a work that carries a stated or negotiated selling price in the market.

Like most authors, writers of journal articles do not directly seek to capture the potential financial rewards that stem from their copyrights by personally marketing copies of their writings. Rather, like other creators of literary works, the author of a journal article "commonly sells his rights to publishers who offer royalties in exchange for their services in producing and marketing the author's work." *Harper & Row*, 471 U.S. at 547. In the distinctive realm of academic and scientific articles, however, the only form of royalty paid by a publisher is often just the reward of being published, publication being a key to professional advancement and prestige for the author, *see Weissmann*, 868 F.2d at 1324 (noting that "in an academic setting, profit is ill-measured in dollars. Instead, what is valuable is recognition because it so often influences professional advancement and academic tenure."). The publishers in turn incur the costs and labor of producing and marketing authors' articles, driven by the prospect of capturing the economic value stemming from the copyrights in the original works, which the authors have transferred to them. Ultimately, the monopoly privileges conferred by copyright protection and the potential financial rewards therefrom are not directly serving to motivate authors to write individual articles; rather, they serve to motivate publishers to produce journals, which provide the conventional and often exclusive means for disseminating these individual articles. It is the prospect of such dissemination that contributes to the motivation of these authors. . . .

1. Sales of Additional Journal Subscriptions, Back Issues, and Back Volumes. Since we are concerned with the claim of fair use in copying the eight individual articles from CATALYSIS, the analysis under the fourth factor must focus on the effect of Texaco's photocopying upon the potential market for or value of these individual articles. Yet, in their respective discussions of the fourth statutory factor, the parties initially focus on the impact of Texaco's photocopying of individual journal articles upon the market for Catalysis journals through sales of CATALYSIS subscriptions, back issues, or back volumes. . . .

On this record [], the evidence is not resounding for either side. The District Court specifically found that, in the absence of photocopying, (1) "Texaco would not ordinarily fill the need now being supplied by photocopies through the purchase of back issues or back volumes . . . [or] by enormously enlarging the number of its subscriptions," but (2) Texaco still "would increase the number of subscriptions somewhat." 802 F. Supp. at 19. This moderate conclusion concerning the actual effect on the marketability of journals, combined with the uncertain relationship between the market for journals and the market for and value of individual articles, leads us to conclude that the evidence concerning sales of additional journal subscriptions, back issues, and back volumes does not strongly support either side with regard to the fourth factor. *Cf. Sony*, 464 U.S. at 451–55 (rejecting various predictions of harm to value of copyrighted work based on speculation about possible consequences of secondary use). At best, the loss of a few journal subscriptions tips the fourth factor only slightly toward the publishers because evidence of such loss is weak evidence that the copied articles themselves have lost any value.

2. Licensing Revenues and Fees. The District Court, however, went beyond discussing the sales of additional journal subscriptions in holding that Texaco's photocopying affected the value of the publishers' copyrights. Specifically, the Court pointed out that, if Texaco's unauthorized photocopying was not permitted as fair use, the publishers' revenues would increase significantly since Texaco would (1) obtain articles from document delivery services (which pay royalties to publishers for the right to photocopy articles), (2) negotiate photocopying licenses directly with individual publishers, and/or (3) acquire some form of photocopying license from the Copyright Clearance Center Inc. ("CCC"). *See* 802 F. Supp. at 19. Texaco claims that the District Court's reasoning is faulty because, in determining that the value of the publishers' copyrights was affected, the Court assumed that the publishers were entitled to demand and receive licensing royalties and fees for photocopying. Yet, continues Texaco, whether the publishers can demand a fee for permission to make photocopies is the very question that the fair use trial is supposed to answer.

It is indisputable that, as a general matter, a copyright holder is entitled to demand a royalty for licensing others to use its copyrighted work, *see* 17 U.S.C. § 106 (copyright owner has exclusive right "to authorize" certain uses), and that the impact on potential licensing revenues is a proper subject for consideration in assessing the fourth factor, *see, e.g.*, *Campbell*, 114 S.Ct. at 1178; *Harper & Row*, 471 U.S. at 568–69.

However, not every effect on potential licensing revenues enters the analysis under the fourth factor. Specifically, courts have recognized limits on the concept of "potential licensing revenues" by considering only traditional, reasonable, or likely to be developed markets when examining and assessing a secondary use's "effect upon the potential market for or value of the copyrighted work." *See Campbell*, 114 S.Ct. at 1178 ("The market for potential derivative uses includes only those that creators of original works would in general develop or license others to develop."); *Harper & Row*, 471 U.S. at 568 (fourth factor concerned with "use that supplants any part of the *normal* market for a copyrighted work") (emphasis added) (quoting S. REP. NO. 473, 94th Cong., 1st Sess. 65 (1975)); *see also Mathieson v. Associated Press*, 23 U.S.P.Q.2d 1685, 1690–91 (S.D.N.Y. 1992) (refusing to find fourth factor in favor of copyright holder because secondary use did not affect any aspect of the normal market for copyrighted work). . . .

Though the publishers still have not established a conventional market for the direct sale and distribution of individual articles, they have created, primarily through the CCC, a workable market for institutional users to obtain licenses for the right to produce their own copies of individual articles via photocopying. The District Court found that many major corporations now subscribe to the CCC systems for photocopying licenses. 802 F. Supp. at 25. Indeed, it appears from the pleadings, especially Texaco's counterclaim, that Texaco itself has been paying royalties to the CCC. Since the Copyright Act explicitly provides that copyright holders have the "exclusive rights" to "reproduce" and "distribute copies" of their works, *see* 17 U.S.C. § 106(1) & (3), and since there currently exists a viable market for licensing these rights for individual journal articles, it is appropriate that potential licensing revenues for photocopying be considered in a fair use analysis.

Despite Texaco's claims to the contrary, it is not unsound to conclude that the right to seek payment for a particular use tends to become legally cognizable under the fourth fair use factor when the means for paying for such a use is made easier. This notion is not inherently troubling: it is sensible that a particular unauthorized use should be considered "more fair" when there is no ready market or means to pay for the use, while such an unauthorized use should be considered "less fair" when there is a ready market or means to pay for the use. The vice of circular reasoning arises only if the availability of payment is conclusive against fair use. Whatever the situation may have been previously, before the development of a market for institutional users to obtain licenses to photocopy articles, *see Williams & Wilkins*, 487 F.2d at 1357–59, it is now appropriate to consider the loss of licensing revenues in evaluating "the effect of the use upon the potential market for or value of" journal articles. It is especially appropriate to do so with respect to copying of articles from CATALYSIS, a publication as to which a photocopying license is now available. We do not decide how the fair use balance would be resolved if a photocopying license for CATALYSIS articles were not currently available. . . .

Primarily because of lost licensing revenue, and to a minor extent because of lost subscription revenue, we agree with the District Court that "the publishers have demonstrated a substantial harm to the value of their copyrights through [Texaco's] copying," 802 F. Supp. at 21, and thus conclude that the fourth statutory factor favors the publishers. . . .

The order of the District Court is affirmed.

JACOBS, Circuit Judge, dissenting:

The stipulated facts crisply present the fair use issues that govern the photocopying of entire journal articles for a scientist's own use, either in the laboratory or as part of a personal file assisting that scientist's particular inquiries. I agree with much in the majority's admirable review of the facts and the law. Specifically, I agree that, of the four nonexclusive considerations bearing on fair use enumerated in section 107, the second factor (the nature of the copyrighted work) tends to support a conclusion of fair use, and the third factor (the ratio of the copied portion to the whole copyrighted work) militates against it. I respectfully dissent, however, in respect of the first and fourth factors. As to the first factor: the purpose and character of Dr. Chickering's use is integral to transformative and productive ends of scientific research. As to the fourth factor: the adverse effect of Dr. Chickering's use upon the potential market for the work, or upon its value, is illusory. For these reasons, and in light of certain equitable considerations and the overarching purpose of the copyright laws, I conclude that Dr. Chickering's photocopying of the Catalysis articles was fair use. . . .

The critical facts adduced by the majority are that Dr. Chickering is a chemical engineer employed at a corporate research facility who keeps abreast of developments in his field by reviewing specialized scientific and technical journals, and who photocopies individual journal articles in the belief that doing so will facilitate his current or future professional research. 60 F.3d at 915. I agree with the majority that the immediate goal of the photocopying was "to facilitate Chickering's research in the sciences, an objective that might well serve a broader public purpose." 60 F.3d at 922–23. The photocopying was therefore integral to ongoing research by a scientist. In my view, all of the statutory factors organize themselves around this fact. The four factors listed in section 107 (and reviewed one by one in the majority opinion) are considerations that bear upon whether a particular use is fair; but those factors are informed by a preamble sentence in section 107 that recites in pertinent part that "the fair use of a copyrighted work, including such use by reproduction in copies . . . for purposes such as . . . scholarship, or research, is not an infringement of copyright." . . .

Consider what Dr. Chickering actually does with scientific journals. As a research scientist, he routinely sifts through the latest research done by his peers, much of which is printed in journals such as *Catalysis.* He determines which articles potentially assist his specific trains of thought and lines of inquiry, and he photocopies them. Relative to the volume of articles in each issue, his photocopying is insubstantial. He then files the articles for possible future use or study. As the majority observes, "[b]efore modern photocopying, Chickering probably would have converted the original article into a more serviceable form by taking notes, whether cursory or extended; today he can do so with a photocopying machine." 60 F.3d at 923–24. The majority[] questions whether or not a scholar's handwritten copy of a full work is "necessarily" a fair use. As the majority adds, however, *Williams & Wilkins* says:

> [I]t is almost unanimously accepted that a scholar can make a handwritten copy of an entire copyrighted article for his own use, and in the era before photoduplication it was not uncommon (and not seriously questioned) that he

could have his secretary make a typed copy for his personal use and files. These customary facts of copyright-life are among our givens.

Williams & Wilkins, 487 F.2d at 1350. What Dr. Chickering does is simply a technologically assisted form of note-taking, such as has long been customary among researchers: the photocopy machine saves Dr. Chickering the toil and time of recording notes on index cards or in notebooks, and improves the accuracy and range of the data, charts, and formulas he can extract from the passing stream of information; but the note-taking purpose remains the same. . . .

In this case the only harm to a market is to the supposed market in photocopy licenses. The CCC scheme is neither traditional nor reasonable; and its development into a real market is subject to substantial impediments. There is a circularity to the problem: the market will not crystallize unless courts reject the fair use argument that Texaco presents; but, under the statutory test, we cannot declare a use to be an infringement unless (assuming other factors also weigh in favor of the secondary user) there is a market to be harmed. At present, only a fraction of journal publishers have sought to exact these fees. I would hold that this fourth factor decisively weighs in favor of Texaco, because there is no normal market in photocopy licenses, and no real consensus among publishers that there ought to be one.

COMMENTS AND QUESTIONS

1. Is the majority's reasoning in *Texaco* circular? Isn't the issue to be resolved whether or not Texaco has to pay a license fee in order to photocopy journal articles? The answer to that question depends on whether Texaco's copies constitute a "fair use." But the court hinges the fair use inquiry on whether or not the copyright owners have lost licensing revenue from Texaco. Does this make sense?

The majority suggests that the "vice of circularity" can be avoided by considering "only traditional, reasonable, or likely to be developed markets" when considering a challenged use upon a potential market. Do you agree? *See* James Gibson, *Risk Aversion and Rights Accretion in Intellectual Property Law*, 116 YALE L.J. 882 (2007) (arguing that risk-aversion on the part of potential defendants will cause them to pay even for uses they had a legal right to make).

2. *From Borrowed Passages to Mechanically Reproduced Works*. Judge Newman questions whether the fair use doctrine, which initially developed to allow use of portions of copyrighted material as part of new works, should have been extended to allow copying of entire documents through the use of xerography at all. Does this perspective look too narrowly at creativity, focusing on the output and overlooking the research process? Judge Leval, the trial court judge in the case (who now sits on the Second Circuit), noted that the effect of requiring permissions would be that Texaco would have to buy more copies of journals it wished to circulate (or at least would have to pay more money to the CCC for permission to make photocopies). Assuming a budget constraint, Texaco will purchase a narrower range of journals, since it must buy more copies of the more widely used journals. Does this promote "the progress of science and

the useful arts"? Is it a result the authors of journal articles would applaud? At the least, isn't the loss of information transfer that results from these decisions a factor to be considered in determining the issue of fair use? Alternatively, might Texaco allocate its research acquisition budget more broadly by allowing researchers to acquire articles on a pay-as-you-read/download basis? In the end, determining actual market effects can be quite difficult.

Most people today would agree that making a single photocopy of a single academic article for research purposes—whether by the NIH or by a commercial group—promotes the scholarly enterprise and falls within the fair use privilege. But at what point do such individual fair uses become a collective infringement of copyright? Would a well-functioning licensing market—such as that envisioned by the CCC and encouraged by Judge Newman—serve to promote both primary and cumulative creativity? Or would it simply add another transaction cost to scientific research?

3. *Coursepacks.* Copyright owners have brought a number of cases against "copy shops" that reproduce course readers. *See e.g., Cambridge Univ. Press v. Georgia State University*, 769 F.32 1232 (11th Cir. 2014) (holding that use of extensive excerpts in course readers was not transformative, but that the first factor favored the non-profit user; that a fixed 10% of the original or one chapter rule is erroneous; and fair use must be done on a work-by-work basis); *Princeton Univ. Press v. Michigan Document Servs.*, 99 F.3d 1381 (6th Cir. 1996) (en banc) (holding as a matter of law that the for-profit copying of academic readers could not be a fair use); *Basic Books v. Kinko's Graphics Corp.*, 758 F. Supp. 1522 (S.D.N.Y. 1991) (holding photocopier shop liable for printing coursepacks that included excerpts from books); *but cf. Great Minds v. Office Depot, Inc.*, 945 F.3d 1106 (9th Cir. 2019) (holding that school that was licensed to make copies for nonprofit use could contract to make copies for a for-profit company).

4. *Copyright Law Driving Social Change and Market Formation.* Prior to the coursepack decisions, many university teachers and copy shops ignored copyright law. *See* ROBERT ELLICKSON, ORDER WITHOUT LAW 258–64 (1991) (documenting how informal norms among professors "trump" the formal law of copyright as regards photocopying articles for course packets). In less than a decade, the *Texaco* and coursepack decisions swung social practices 180 degrees. Most university bookstores will not distribute unauthorized course readers. As a result, the CCC has become well known and well used.

Does the existence of licensing transactions vindicate Professor Merges's conjecture about strong property rules producing effective licensing institutions? *See* Robert P. Merges, *Contracting into Liability Rules: Intellectual Property Rights and Collective Rights Organizations*, 84 CALIF. L. REV. 1293 (1996). To the extent that licensing markets function well—i.e., producing efficient, low-cost access to scholarly works—is fair use needed? Note that had the court found fair use, it would have deflated the CCC's sails by making private licensing of these copies unnecessary. Does this one-way ratchet suggest that courts should be cautious in finding fair use? Or has society lost something important by moving from a system under which people were free to make copies for academic research to one in which the ability to make those copies exists only at the collective sufferance of a host of copyright owners?

The rise of the Internet has offered a new model for creating coursepacks. Some professors now use links on course websites to "distribute" course readings. In many cases, these works are freely available, although licensing sometimes plays a role. Should this electronic distribution be illegal absent a license from the CCC? Does *Texaco* compel that result? The Second Circuit backed off of its licensing market holding in *Bill Graham Archives v. Dorling Kindersley Ltd.*, 448 F.3d 605 (2d Cir. 2006), at least where the defendant did more than make an identical copy. *Cf.* Mark A. Lemley, *Should a Licensing Market Require Licensing?*, 70 LAW & CONTEMP. PROBS. 185 (2007) (arguing that plaintiffs in such cases should be entitled to actual damages but not punitive damages or an injunction).

4. *Academic Journal Publishing*. The *Texaco* court focuses on the market effects of Texaco's practices on the publication of academic research. Yet the authors of such works—principally university professors and scientists—typically assign their copyrights in exchange for publication and do not receive royalties. Subscription (and licensing) fees go to the publisher. This practice makes sense within the traditional copyright system, since without print journals the spread of knowledge and research would suffer.

The Internet now offers an open source alternative, which is generating pressure on traditional print publishers whose prices have continued to rise, straining the budgets of their principal customers—university libraries. New online publishing markets—such as the Public Library of Science (PLoS), the California Digital Library, the Social Science Research Network (SSRN), the Berkeley Economics Press (BePress)—offer zero- or lower-cost alternatives for the distribution of academic research. Google Scholar now offers powerful search tools for identifying research online. Professors are increasingly seeking rights to post their published works in free and open online archives. Until now, most professors have preferred the higher prestige print journals, but that preference is waning as online alternatives develop reputations and speed works into circulation. Will technology ultimately solve the problems raised by *Texaco* by bringing about fundamental change in the organization of academic publishing? *Cf.* Gabe Bloch, *Transformation in Publishing: Modeling the Effect of New Media*, 20 BERKELEY TECH. L.J. 647 (2005). Does the existence of a new, low-cost means of distribution of ideas mean that there is less need for economic support of the publishing industry through copyright?

5. *Classroom Guidelines*. In 1975, the House Judiciary Subcommittee considering reform of the Copyright Act urged publishers, educators, librarians, and other interested parties to develop guidelines for reproduction of materials for educational purposes. The meetings resulted in the Agreement on Guidelines for Classroom Copying in Not-For-Profit Educational Institutions, available at http://www.copyright.gov/circs/circ21.pdf (*see* pages 6–8). The guidelines do not provide much leeway for the types of customized coursepacks that have become common. For example, prose works are limited to "either a complete article, story or essay of less than 2,500 words" or "an excerpt from any

prose work of not more than 1,000 words or 10% of the work, whichever is less, but in any event a minimum of 500 words."

Section 108 exempts libraries from liability for copies made on their premises as long as they post a copyright warning notice as specified in 37 C.F.R. § 201.14. Is there a justification for this difference in treatment between photocopier businesses and libraries?

7. *The Orphan Work Problem.* The CCC regime works reasonably well for licensing the many works available through this licensing clearinghouse. But what about works that are still under copyright for which the owners cannot be located? As universities and copy shops increasingly police the assemblage of coursepacks, it has become more difficult and in some cases impossible to get permissions to copy rare or out-of-print works. The scaling back of formalities in copyright law means that copyright owners have no obligation to maintain contact information in any central repository. Should the fair use standard be lower in such circumstances? What about where a licensor refuses to license or only on exorbitant terms? *Cf.* William F. Patry & Richard A. Posner, *Fair Use and Statutory Reform in the Wake of* Eldred, 92 CAL. L. REV. 1639 (2004). The Copyright Office has initiated a project aimed at studying ways of alleviating the orphan work problem. *See* U.S. Copyright Office, REPORT ON ORPHAN WORKS: A REPORT OF THE REGISTER OF COPYRIGHTS (Jan. 2006); *see also* U.S. Copyright Office, ORPHAN WORKS AND MASS DIGITIZATION (Jun. 2015).

8. *Just the Facts.* The Second Circuit gave short shrift to the second factor, finding that the factual nature of the works copied favored Texaco but that it did not weigh heavily. Elsewhere, the Second Circuit has suggested that the factual nature of the works copied may *never* determine the outcome of a fair use case. *Fox News Network, LLC v. TVEyes, Inc.*, 883 F.3d 169 (2d Cir. 2018). By contrast, the D.C. Circuit held that the verbatim copying of industry standards that had been adopted into law by a public interest group was likely fair use in significant part because of the second factor. *American Soc'y for Testing & Materials v. Public Resource.org*, 896 F.3d 437 (D.C. Cir. 2018).

Should it matter that Dr. Chickering likely cared about the unprotectable facts in the articles he copied, not the copyrighted expression? *See* Mark A. Lemley & Bryan Casey, *Fair Learning*, 99 Tex. L. Rev. (2021) (arguing that fair use should encompass "fair learning" by those who copy the expressive works only as a path to getting access to unprotectable facts).

PROBLEM

Problem IV-49. Steve Vander Ark, a school librarian, became an enormous fan of the Harry Potter book series. In 1999, while reading the second book in the series, Vander Ark began tracking characters, spells, creatures, and objects in the story. He started a website—the Harry Potter Lexicon—with hyperlinks to cross-referenced entries. This evolved into an alphabetical index that attracted substantial interest among Potter enthusiasts. With each new edition, the Lexicon expanded, as did its popularity.

Even J.K. Rowling, the author of the series, and her publisher, extolled the value of the Lexicon website as a reference tool.

In 2007, Vander Ark entered into an agreement with RDR Books to publish the Lexicon as a print book—an encyclopedia of Harry Potter. As slated for publication, the book contains over 2,000 entries, all of which are derived from the Harry Potter books, many of which include page references, and some of which include passages drawn directly from or paraphrased from Harry Potter books (usually without quotation marks). The Lexicon also summarizes many plot elements in the books. Nonetheless, the majority of the Lexicon is not text taken from the Potter books, but text written by Vander Ark. Does this work fall within the fair use doctrine?

b.   *Contextual/Different Purpose*

Digital technology now provides tools that enable authors, artists, and musicians to engage in all manner of projects that would have been prohibitively expensive just a few decades ago. Musicians can sample tracks in composing rap and hip-hop sound recordings. Graphic artists can easily find, edit, and compose images. High school students can put together documentary films for history projects. And the Internet provides powerful tools—from YouTube to file sharing—for distributing these works to the world at large.

In the pre-digital world, only professional enterprises—motion picture studios, record labels, publishers—were in a position to support these projects and to bring them to the mass marketplace. They employed or had access to lawyers and other business professionals trained to secure rights in underlying copyrighted works that were incorporated into these projects. The democratization of these tools has brought fair use doctrine to the fore like never before. Whereas a Hollywood studio typically erred on the side of caution in "remixing" underlying copyrighted inputs, many new wave artists, authors, and musicians are less circumspect (or less aware of the legal standards and licensing institutions). As a result, courts are increasingly confronting a new generation of fair use cases.

In *Bill Graham Archives v. Dorling Kindersley Ltd.*, 448 F.3d 605 (2d Cir. 2006), the owner of copyrights in concert posters, ticket illustrations, and other memorabilia from the Grateful Dead sued the publisher of GRATEFUL DEAD: THE ILLUSTRATED TRIP ("ILLUSTRATED TRIP"). The 480-page coffee table book tells the story of the Grateful Dead along a timeline running continuously through the book, chronologically combining over 2000 images representing dates in the Grateful Dead's history with explanatory text. A typical page of the book features a collage of images, text, and graphic art designed to simultaneously capture the eye and inform the reader.

The book's publisher, Dorling Kindersley (DK) initially sought permission from Bill Graham Archives ("BGA") to reproduce several concert posters in the book. After negotiations over licensing fees broke down, DK proceeded with publication of ILLUSTRATED TRIP with inclusion of seven artistic images from Grateful Dead event posters and tickets. The images were displayed in significantly reduced form and accompanied by captions describing the concerts they represent. BGA sued for infringement.

The Second Circuit panel drew heavily upon Judge Leval's transformative framing of fair use in concluding that these uses, even of the entire, expressive images, constituted fair use. The court emphasized that the defendant's use of the images as part of an illustrated timeline was "plainly different from the original purpose for which they were created," noting that the "works are displayed to commemorate historic events, arranged in a creative fashion, and displayed in significantly reduced form." The defendant's book augmented some of the images with biographical text. The book

> minimized the expressive value of the reproduced images by combining them with a prominent timeline, textual material, and original graphical artwork, to create a collage of text and images on each page of the book. To further this collage effect, the images are displayed at angles and the original graphical artwork is designed to blend with the images and text. Overall, DK's layout ensures that the images at issue are employed only to enrich the presentation of the cultural history of the Grateful Dead, not to exploit copyrighted artwork for commercial gain.

Moreover, the court viewed BGA's images as an inconsequential portion of ILLUSTRATED TRIP. The book is 480 pages long, while the BGA images appear on only seven pages. Although the original posters range in size from 13" × 19" to more than 19" × 27", the largest reproduction of a BGA image in ILLUSTRATED TRIP is less than 3" × 4 1/2", less than 1/20 the size of the original. No BGA image took up more than one-eighth of a page in a book or is given more prominence than any other image on the page. In total, the images account for less than one-fifth of one percent of the book. Furthermore, although DK is a commercial enterprise, it "did not exploit BGA's images in its commercial advertising or in any other way to promote the sale of the book. ILLUSTRATED TRIP merely uses pictures and text to describe the life of the Grateful Dead. By design, the use of BGA's images is incidental to the commercial biographical value of the book."

As regards the critical fourth factor—the effect of the use on the market for the original works—the court found that defendant's use did not affect BGA's primary market for the sale of the poster images. BGA stressed, however, that DK's unauthorized use interfered with the market for licensing its images for use in books. Nonetheless, the court determined that DK's transformative use did not impair a traditional licensed use. BGA's direct evidence of its license revenues involved markedly different uses.

♀ **Blanch v. Koons**
United States Court of Appeals for the Second Circuit
467 F.3d 244 (2d Cir. 2006)

SACK, Circuit Judge.

This appeal presents the question whether an artist's appropriation of a copyrighted image in a collage painting is, under the circumstances, protected "fair use" under the copyright law. *See* 17 U.S.C. § 107.

On commission from defendants Deutsche Bank and The Solomon R. Guggenheim Foundation, defendant Jeff Koons created a collage painting, initially for display in Berlin, Germany, in which he copied, but altered the appearance of, part of a copyrighted photograph taken by the plaintiff Andrea Blanch. . . .

Background

Jeff Koons is a visual artist. His work has been exhibited widely in museums and commercial galleries and has been the subject of much critical commentary. He is known for incorporating into his artwork objects and images taken from popular media and consumer advertising, a practice that has been referred to as "neo-Pop art" or (perhaps unfortunately in a legal context) "appropriation art." His sculptures and paintings often contain such easily recognizable objects as toys, celebrities, and popular cartoon figures.

Koons has been the subject of several previous lawsuits for copyright infringement. In the late 1980s, he created a series of sculptures for an exhibition entitled the "Banality Show" ("Banality"). In doing so, he commissioned large three-dimensional reproductions of images taken from such sources as commercial postcards and syndicated comic strips. Although many of the source images were copyrighted, Koons did not seek permission to use them. In separate cases based on three different sculptures from "Banality," this Court and two district courts concluded that Koons's use of the copyrighted images infringed on the rights of the copyright holders and did not constitute fair use under the copyright law. *See Rogers v. Koons,* 960 F.2d 301 (2d Cir.), *cert. denied,* (1992); *Campbell v. Koons,* 1993 WL 97381 (S.D.N.Y. 1993); *United Feature Syndicate v. Koons,* 817 F. Supp. 370 (S.D.N.Y.1993). . . .

Koons's Painting

To create the "Easyfun-Ethereal" paintings, Koons culled images from advertisements or his own photographs, scanned them into a computer, and digitally superimposed the scanned images against backgrounds of pastoral landscapes. He then printed color images of the resulting collages for his assistants to use as templates for applying paint to billboard-sized, 10' × 14' canvasses. . . .

One of the "Easyfun-Ethereal" paintings, "Niagara," is the subject of this action. Like the other paintings in the series, "Niagara" consists of fragmentary images collaged against the backdrop of a landscape. The painting depicts four pairs of women's feet and lower legs dangling prominently over images of confections—a large chocolate fudge brownie topped with ice cream, a tray of donuts, and a tray of apple danish pastries—with a grassy field and Niagara Falls in the background. The images of the legs are placed side by side, each pair pointing vertically downward and extending from the top of the painting approximately two-thirds of the way to the bottom. Together, the four pairs of legs occupy the entire horizontal expanse of the painting. . . .

In an affidavit submitted to the district court, Koons states that he was inspired to create "Niagara" by a billboard he saw in Rome, which depicted several sets of women's lower legs. By juxtaposing women's legs against a backdrop of food and landscape, he says, he intended to "comment on the ways in which some of our most basic appetites—for food, play, and sex—are mediated by popular images." "By re-contextualizing these fragments as I do, I try to compel the viewer to break out of the conventional way of experiencing a particular appetite as mediated by mass media."

Blanch's Photograph

Koons drew the images in "Niagara" from fashion magazines and advertisements. One of the pairs of legs in the painting was adapted from a photograph by the plaintiff Andrea Blanch, an accomplished professional fashion and portrait photographer. During her career of more than twenty years, Blanch has published her photographs in commercial magazines, including *Details*, *G.Q.*, *Vogue*, and *Allure*; in photography periodicals and collections; and in advertisements for clients selling products under such widely recognized names as Revlon, Universal Films, Johnny Walker, and Valentino. She is also the author of a book of photographs and interviews entitled *Italian Men: Love & Sex*.

The Blanch photograph used by Koons in "Niagara" appeared in the August 2000 issue of *Allure* magazine. Entitled "Silk Sandals by Gucci" ("'Silk Sandals'"), it depicts a woman's lower legs and feet, adorned with bronze nail polish and glittery Gucci sandals, resting on a man's lap in what appears to be a first-class airplane cabin. The legs and feet are shot at close range and dominate the photograph. *Allure* published "Silk Sandals" as part of a six-page feature on metallic cosmetics entitled "Gilt Trip." . . .

Blanch photographed "Silk Sandals" at a "shoot" organized by Condé Nast Publications, *Allure*'s publisher. According to Blanch's deposition testimony, Paul Cavaco, the creative director of *Allure*, suggested the model, sandals, and nail polish to be used in the photograph. Blanch participated in their selection and retained control over the camera, the film, the lighting, and the composition of the photographs. She testified that it was her idea to use an airplane interior as a backdrop and to place the female model's feet on the male model's lap. She explained that she wanted to "show some sort of erotic sense[;] . . . to get . . . more of a sexuality to the photographs."

Koons's Use of Blanch's Photograph

While working on the "Easyfun-Ethereal" series, Koons saw "Silk Sandals" in *Allure*. According to Koons, "certain physical features of the legs [in the photograph] represented for me a particular type of woman frequently presented in advertising." He considered this typicality to further his purpose of commenting on the "commercial images . . . in our consumer culture."

Koons scanned the image of "Silk Sandals" into his computer and incorporated a version of the scanned image into "Niagara." He included in the painting only the legs and feet from the photograph, discarding the background of the airplane cabin and the man's lap on which the legs rest. Koons inverted the orientation of the legs so that they dangle vertically downward above the other elements of "Niagara" rather than slant upward at a 45-degree angle as they appear in the photograph. He added a heel to one of the feet and modified the photograph's coloring. The legs from "Silk Sandals" are second from the left among the four pairs of legs that form the focal images of "Niagara." Koons did not seek permission from Blanch or anyone else before using the image.

Blanch's *Allure* Magazine photograph

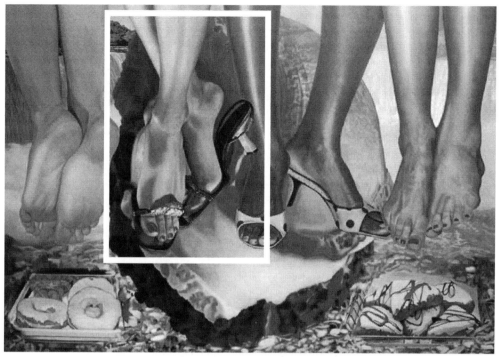

Koon's "Niagara" painting with Blanch's photograph indicated

The Parties' Economic Gains and Losses

Deutsche Bank paid Koons $2 million for the seven "Easyfun-Ethereal" paintings. Koons reports that his net compensation attributable to "Niagara" was $126,877. Deutsche Bank received gross revenues of approximately $100,000 from the exhibition of the "Easyfun-Ethereal" paintings at the Deutsche Guggenheim Berlin, a total that includes admission fees and catalogue and postcard sales. The record does not reflect Deutsche Bank's expenses for that exhibition other than the commission of the paintings.

The subsequent exhibition of the paintings at the Solomon R. Guggenheim Museum in New York sustained a net loss, although when profits from catalogue and postcard sales are taken into account, Guggenheim estimates that it earned a profit of approximately $2,000 from "Niagara." In 2004, the auction house Sotheby's reportedly appraised "Niagara" at $1 million. The work has not, however, been sold, nor does the record indicate that it or any other painting commissioned by Deutsche Bank has been offered for sale or been the subject of a bid.

Allure paid Blanch $750 for "Silk Sandals." Although Blanch retains the copyright to the photograph, she has neither published nor licensed it subsequent to its appearance in *Allure.* Indeed, Blanch does not allege that she has ever licensed any of her photographs for use in works of graphic art or other visual art. At her deposition, Blanch testified that Koons's use of the photograph did not cause any harm to her career or upset any plans she had for "Silk Sandals" or any other photograph in which she has rights. She also testified that, in her view, the market value of "Silk Sandals" did not decrease as the result of Koons's alleged infringement. . . .

Discussion

. . .

II. Fair Use

. . . "The ultimate test of fair use . . . is whether the copyright law's goal of 'promoting the Progress of Science and useful Arts,' U.S. CONST., art. I, § 8, cl. 8, 'would be better served by allowing the use than by preventing it.'" *Castle Rock Entm't*, 150 F.3d at 141.

A. First Factor: The Purpose and Character of the Use

The first statutory factor in the fair-use inquiry is "the purpose and character of the use, including whether such use is of a commercial nature or is for nonprofit educational purposes." 17 U.S.C. § 107(1).

1. "Transformative" Use. . . . Koons does not argue that his use was transformative solely because Blanch's work is a photograph and his a painting, or because Blanch's photograph is in a fashion magazine and his painting is displayed in museums. He would have been ill advised to do otherwise. . . .

But Koons asserts—and Blanch does not deny—that his purposes in using Blanch's image are sharply different from Blanch's goals in creating it. *Compare* Koons Aff. at ¶ 4 ("I want the viewer to think about his/her personal experience with these objects, products, and images and at the same time gain new insight into how these affect our lives.") *with* Blanch Dep. at 112–113 ("I wanted to show some sort of erotic sense[;] . . . to get . . . more of a sexuality to the photographs."). The sharply different objectives that Koons had in using, and Blanch had in creating, "Silk Sandals" confirms the transformative nature of the use. *See Bill Graham Archives*, 448 F.3d at 609 (finding transformative use when defendant's purpose in using copyrighted concert poster was "plainly different from the original purpose for which they were created"); *see also* 17 U.S.C. § 107(1) (first fair-use factor is the "*purpose* and character of the use" (emphasis added)).

Koons is, by his own undisputed description, using Blanch's image as fodder for his commentary on the social and aesthetic consequences of mass media. His stated objective is thus not to repackage Blanch's "Silk Sandals," but to employ it "'in the creation of new information, new aesthetics, new insights and understandings.'" *Castle Rock Entm't*, 150 F.3d at 142 (quoting Leval, *Toward a Fair Use Standard*, 103 HARV. L. REV. 1105, 1111 (1990)). When, as here, the copyrighted work is used as "raw material," *Castle Rock Entm't*, 150 F.3d at 142, in the furtherance of distinct creative or communicative objectives, the use is transformative. *Id.*; *see also Bill Graham Archives*, 448 F.3d at 609 (use of concert posters "as historical artifacts" in a biography was transformative); *Leibovitz v. Paramount Pictures Corp.*, 137 F.3d 109, 113 (2d Cir. 1998) (parody of a photograph in a movie poster was transformative when "the ad [was] not merely different; it differ[ed] in a way that may reasonably be perceived as commenting" on the original).

The test for whether "Niagara's" use of "Silk Sandals" is "transformative," then, is whether it "merely supersedes the objects of the original creation, or instead adds something new, with a further purpose or different character, altering the first with new expression, meaning, or message." *Campbell*, 510 U.S. at 579. The test almost perfectly describes Koons's adaptation of "Silk Sandals": the use of a fashion photograph created for publication in a glossy American "lifestyles" magazine—with changes of its colors, the background against which it is portrayed, the medium, the size of the objects pictured, the objects' details and, crucially, their entirely different purpose and meaning—as part of a massive painting commissioned for exhibition in a German art-gallery space. We therefore conclude that the use in question was transformative.

2. Commercial Use. Koons made a substantial profit from the sale of "Niagara." . . .

It can hardly be said [] that the defendants' economic gains from "Niagara" were "to the exclusion of broader public benefits." *Am. Geophysical Union*, 60 F.3d at 921–22. Notwithstanding the fact that artists are sometimes paid and museums sometimes earn money, the public exhibition of art is widely and we think properly considered to "have value that benefits the broader public interest." *Id.* at 922; *see also* 20 U.S.C. § 951 (stating that "access to the arts and the humanities" fosters "wisdom and vision" and makes citizens "masters of their technology and not its unthinking servants").

3. Parody, Satire, and Justification for the Copying. The secondary work in *Campbell* was a parody, and some of the language in the opinion, and some of the cases following it, *see, e.g.*, *Leibovitz v. Paramount Pictures Corp.*, *supra*, are specifically about parody. "Niagara," on the other hand, may be better characterized for these purposes as satire—its message appears to target the genre of which "Silk Sandals" is typical, rather than the individual photograph itself. *See Rogers*, 960 F.2d at 310 (concluding that a previous work by Koons was not a parody because "the copied work must be, at least in part, an object of the parody" and it was "difficult to discern [in Koons's work] any parody of the photograph . . . itself"); *Campbell*, 510 U.S. at 581 n.15 ("Satire has been defined as a work 'in which prevalent follies or vices are assailed with ridicule,' 14 OXFORD ENGLISH DICTIONARY, . . . at 500, or are 'attacked through irony, derision, or wit,' AMERICAN HERITAGE DICTIONARY . . . at 1604.").

We have applied Campbell in too many non-parody cases to require citation for the proposition that the broad principles of Campbell are not limited to cases involving parody. But the satire/parody distinction may nevertheless be relevant to the application of these principles. As the Campbell Court observed, "[p]arody needs to mimic an original to make its point, and so has some claim to use the creation of its victim's (or collective victims') imagination, whereas satire can stand on its own two feet and so requires justification for the very act of borrowing." *Id.* at 580–81.

It is not, of course, our job to judge the merits of "Niagara," or of Koons's approach to art. *See Campbell*, 510 U.S. at 582 ("'[I]t would be a dangerous undertaking for persons trained only to the law to constitute themselves final judges of the worth of a work, outside of the narrowest and most obvious limits.'" (quoting *Bleistein v. Donaldson Lithographing Co.*, 188 U.S. 239, 251 (1903) (Holmes, J.))). The question is whether Koons had a genuine creative rationale for borrowing Blanch's image, rather than using it merely "to get attention or to avoid the drudgery in working up something fresh." *Id.* at 580. Although it seems clear enough to us that Koons's use of a slick fashion photograph enables him to satirize life as it appears when seen through the prism of slick fashion photography, we need not depend on our own poorly honed artistic sensibilities. Koons explained, without contradiction, why he used Blanch's image:

> Although the legs in the ALLURE MAGAZINE photograph ["Silk Sandals"] might seem prosaic, I considered them to be necessary for inclusion in my painting rather than legs I might have photographed myself. The ubiquity of the photograph is central to my message. The photograph is typical of a certain style of mass communication. Images almost identical to them can be found in almost any glossy magazine, as well as in other media. To me, the legs depicted in the Allure photograph are a fact in the world, something that everyone experiences constantly; they are not anyone's legs in particular. By using a fragment of the ALLURE photograph in my painting, I thus comment upon the culture and attitudes promoted and embodied in ALLURE MAGAZINE. By using an existing image, I also ensure a certain authenticity or veracity that enhances my commentary—it is the difference between quoting and paraphrasing—and ensure that the viewer will understand what I am referring to.

We conclude that Koons thus established a "justif[ication for] the very act of [his] borrowing." *Campbell*, 510 U.S. at 581. Whether or not Koons could have created "Niagara" without reference to "Silk Sandals," we have been given no reason to question his statement that the use of an existing image advanced his artistic purposes.

4. "Bad Faith." Much has been written about whether good faith was de-emphasized by the advent of *Campbell* or essentially written out of the first part of the fair-use test. . . . In any event, the only act of bad faith alleged here is that Koons used Blanch's photograph without first asking her permission. We are aware of no controlling authority to the effect that the failure to seek permission for copying, in itself, constitutes bad faith. And as the Campbell Court noted by way of dictum, "If the use is otherwise fair, then no permission need be sought or granted." *Campbell*, 510 U.S. at 585 n.18. In light of that statement by the Supreme Court, it can hardly be said to have been an act of bad faith for Koons to have neither "sought [n]or [been] granted" permission for the use of "Silk Sandals" if, as we find, the use is "otherwise fair."

5. Conclusions as to the First Factor. Because Koons's appropriation of Blanch's photograph in "Niagara" was intended to be—and appears to be—"transformative," because the creation and exhibition of the painting cannot fairly be described as commercial exploitation and the "commerciality" of the use is not dispositive in any event, and because there is insufficient indication of "bad faith," we agree with the district court that the first fair-use factor strongly favors the defendants.

B. Second Factor: Nature of the Copyrighted Work

The second statutory factor is "the nature of the copyrighted work." 17 U.S.C. § 107(2). It "calls for recognition that some works are closer to the core of intended copyright protection than others, with the consequence that fair use is more difficult to establish when the former works are copied." *Campbell*, 510 U.S. at 586.

> Two types of distinctions as to the nature of the copyrighted work have emerged that have figured in the decisions evaluating the second factor: (1) whether the work is expressive or creative, such as a work of fiction, or more factual, with a greater leeway being allowed to a claim of fair use where the work is factual or informational, and (2) whether the work is published or unpublished, with the scope for fair use involving unpublished works being considerably narrower.

2 HOWARD B. ABRAMS, THE LAW OF COPYRIGHT, § 15:52 (2006).

As noted, Blanch's "Silk Sandals" was published. Under the second of the two considerations mentioned by Abrams, that fact favors the defendants.

As for the first consideration, we disagree with the district court's characterization of Blanch's photograph as "banal rather than creative." Accepting that "Silk Sandals" is a creative work, though, it does not follow that the second fair-use factor, even if it somewhat favors Blanch, has significant implications for on our overall fair-use analysis. As we recently explained, although "the creative nature of artistic images typically weighs in favor of the copyright holder," "the second factor may be of limited usefulness where the creative work of art is being used for a transformative purpose." *Bill Graham Archives*, 448 F.3d at 612; *cf. Campbell*, 510 U.S. at 586 (stating that the second factor is rarely "likely to help much in separating the fair use sheep from the infringing goats in a parody case"). To paraphrase *Bill Graham Archives*, the second fair-use factor has limited weight in our analysis because Koons used Blanch's work in a transformative manner to comment on her image's social and aesthetic meaning rather than to exploit its creative virtues.

C. Third Factor: Amount and Substantiality of the Portion Used

The third factor bearing on fair use is "the amount and substantiality of the portion used in relation to the copyrighted work as a whole." 17 U.S.C. § 107(3). The question is whether "'the quantity and value of the materials used,' are reasonable in relation to the purpose of the copying." *Campbell*, 510 U.S. at 586. . . .

As we have discussed . . . above, Koons asserts that his artistic goals led him to incorporate preexisting images such as Blanch's photograph into his paintings in order to reference certain "fact[s] in the world." . . . The question is whether, once he chose to copy "Silk Sandals," he did so excessively, beyond his "justified" purpose for doing so in the first place—whether the use was "reasonable in relation to the purpose of the copying." *Campbell*, 510 U.S. at 586.

It seems to us that Koons's copying of "Silk Sandals" was indeed reasonable when measured in light of his purpose, to convey the "fact" of the photograph to viewers of the painting, and in light of the quantity, quality, and importance of the material used. He did not copy those aspects of "Silk Sandals" "whose power lies in [Blanch's] individualized expression." *Harper & Row*, 471 U.S. at 563. As Blanch testified in her deposition, her key creative decisions in the shoot were the choice of an airplane cabin as a setting and her placement of the female model's legs on the male model's lap. But neither the airplane background nor the man's lap appear in "Niagara." It depicts only the woman's legs and sandal-clad feet. In light of Koons's choice to extract the legs, feet, and sandals in "Silk Sandals" from their background, we find his statement that he copied only that portion of the image necessary to evoke "a certain style of mass communication" to be persuasive. We conclude that the amount and substantiality of Koons's copying was "reasonable in relation to the purpose of the copying." *Campbell*, 510 U.S. at 586. The district court said that "[t]he third factor is neutral as between the parties"; we think that it weighs distinctly in Koons's favor. This modest difference in our views, however, does not alter our ultimate conclusion on fair use.

D. Fourth Factor: Market Effects

The fourth and final statutory factor is "the effect of the use upon the potential market for or value of the copyrighted work." 17 U.S.C. § 107(4). "In considering the fourth factor, our concern is not whether the secondary use suppresses or even destroys the market for the original work or its potential derivatives, but whether the secondary use usurps the market of the original work." *NXIVM Corp.*, 364 F.3d at 481–82. "The market for potential derivative uses includes only those that creators of original works would in general develop or license others to develop." *Campbell*, 510 U.S. at 592.

Blanch acknowledges that she has not published or licensed "Silk Sandals" subsequent to its appearance in *Allure*, that she has never licensed any of her photographs for use in works of graphic or other visual art, that Koons's use of her photograph did not cause any harm to her career or upset any plans she had for "Silk Sandals" or any other photograph, and that the value of "Silk Sandals" did not decrease as the result of Koons's alleged infringement. In light of these admissions, it is plain that "Niagara" had no deleterious effect "upon the potential market for or value of the copyrighted work." 17 U.S.C. § 107(4). The fourth fair-use factor greatly favors Koons.

Conclusion

Having explored the statutory factors and weighed them together in light of the purposes of copyright, *Campbell*, 510 U.S. at 78, we think that the district court's conclusion was correct—that copyright law's goal of "promoting the Progress of Science and useful Arts," U.S. Const., art. I, § 8, cl. 8, would be better served by allowing Koons's use of "Silk Sandals" than by preventing it. We therefore conclude that neither he nor the other defendants engaged in or are liable for copyright infringement.

COMMENTS AND QUESTIONS

1. A literal interpretation of "transformative" would seem to require that the work itself be altered. The appellate panel in *Bill Graham Archives* concludes that reproducing a work in a smaller format and as part of a mosaic of images is "transformative." The Ninth Circuit has come to a similar conclusion in finding "thumbnail" images used in Internet search engines to be transformative. *See Kelly v. Ariba Soft*, 336 F.3d 811 (9th Cir. 2003). And the appellate panel in *Koons* focuses upon the purpose of the use, rather than physical alteration. *See also Oyewole v. Ora*, 291 F. Supp. 3d 422 (S.D.N.Y. 2018), *aff'd* (2d Cir. 2019) (holding that the sampling of music in a particular rap song is transformative as a matter of law because it placed the sample in a new context). Might it be more useful to have a broader vocabulary for fair uses?

2. *Does (Should) Refusal to License on Fair Terms Affect the Fair Use Balance?* The court in *Bill Graham Archives* notes in its background section that DK initially sought permission from BGA and that BGA was receptive, but that the bargaining reached an impasse. Given the modest use of BGA images, might DK's offer to license and BGA's ultimate rejection of the overture have influenced the court's decision? Inversely, if DK had been cavalier about the use of BGA's images, might the court have been less sympathetic? If so, this would suggest that those wishing to make use of copyrighted works in "gray area" works might want to make reasonable offers to license before going ahead with the use. Should courts bear this consideration in mind, at least in non-parody contexts? Would it promote or undermine private resolution of disputes? Would it promote greater fairness in this area? Recall the suggestion that there be no fair use doctrine, but rather compulsory licensing. *See* Alex Kozinski & Christopher Newman, *What's So Fair About Fair Use?*, 46 J. COPYRIGHT SOC'Y U.S.A. 513 (1999); *see also* Peter S. Menell & Ben Depoorter, *Using Fee Shifting to Promote Fair Use and Fair Licensing*, 102 CAL. L. REV. 53 (2014) (proposing that courts award attorney's fees to defendants who make reasonable offers to license copyrighted works).

3. *Reasonable Observer Standard.* Over the course of six years, Photographer Patrick Cariou living among Rastafarians in Jamaica. He gained their trust and was allowed to take their portraits. PowerHouse Books published a YES, RASTA, large format book of his collection, in 2000. The book retailed for $60 and sold approximately 6,000 copies, netting Cariou about $8,000. Cariou was in negotiations with a Manhattan gallery for exhibits of 30 to 40 photographs, with multiple prints to be sold for $3000 to $20,000 each.

About that time, Richard Prince opened his Canal Zone exhibition at one of the Manhattan Gagosian galleries, a leading contemporary art gallery (that also features the work of Jeffrey Koons). The Canal Zone exhibition was largely built around Cariou photographs, which were greatly enlarged and combined with other pictures (some from Cariou's collection as well as nude women). In some works, Prince superimposed oval-shaped "lozenges" over the Rastafarian facial features, creating a gas mask appearance. In one work, Prince placed an electric guitar image over the portrait subject's torso. Prince's works sold for upwards more than $1,000,000. Cariou's planned exhibition fell through as a result of the publicity surrounding the Prince exhibition.

Here are representative images from Cariou's book and Prince's exhibition:

PATRICK CARIOU,
YES RASTA! 118 (2000)

Richard Prince, Graduation (2008)
Collage, inkjet, and acrylic on canvas,
72 ¾" x 52 ½"

PATRICK CARIOU,
YES RASTA! 53 (2000)

Richard Prince,
Back to the Garden (2008)
Collage, inkjet, and acrylic on canvas
80" x 120"

Cariou sued Prince as well as the Gagosian Gallery for copyright infringement. Prince and the Gagosian Gallery asserted fair use. Prince testified that his purpose in appropriating other people's originals for use in his artwork is that doing so helps him "get as much fact into [his] work and reduce[] the amount of speculation." As a result, Judge Batts found that he did not intend to transform Cariou's work and concluded that the works did not qualify for fair use. The Second Circuit reversed, holding that the critical question of transformativness is how the works appear to a reasonable observer. *See Cariou v. Prince*, 714 F.3d 694 (2d Cir. 2013). The court concluded that most of the works were fair use as a matter of law and remanded on a subset of less transformative images. The case settled before the district court took up the remand. *Compare Brammer v. Violent Hues Prods.*, 922 F.3d 255, 266 (4th Cir. 2019) (holding that simply cropping a picture for use does not transform it).

What is the appropriate perspective for judging transformativeness? Should it turn on the artist's subjective intent? A reasonable observer? The judge? The jury?

4. *Free Culture.* Professor Lawrence Lessig has called attention to the threat that strict interpretation of the fair use doctrine (as well as other provisions) pose to cumulative creativity made increasingly more possible in the digital age. *See* LAWRENCE LESSIG, FREE CULTURE (2004); LAWRENCE LESSIG, REMIX: MAKING ART AND COMMERCE THRIVE IN THE HYBRID ECONOMY (2008). Lessig worries that a "permission culture" will stifle non-traditional sources of creativity, such as user-generated content, that do not have copyright lawyers on retainer to obtain needed permissions. Do *Bill Graham Archives*, *Blanch*, and *Cariou* suggest that courts may be providing a wider berth for "remix" creativity? To what extent have changes in art and music resulting from digital technology influenced the evolution of the fair use doctrine?

5. *Creative Commons.* In addition to advocating broad interpretation of the fair use doctrine (and shorter duration for copyright protection), Professor Lessig has inspired a social movement that offers an alternative to the "permission culture" of traditional media industries. Creative Commons provides tools to assist authors in promoting the reuse and remixing of their works at the time of creation by opting into a different set of defaults than those provided by the Copyright Act. Creative Commons licenses distinguish among four categories of permissions: (1) attribution—requires users to attribute the original author; (2) modification—the author can designate whether the work can be modified; (3) share and share alike—anyone using the work agrees to make the resulting work available on the same basis; and (4) noncommercial use—the work may be used for noncommercial purposes. Creative Commons provides tools to assist creators in finding licensed works that can be shared, remixed, or reused.

PROBLEMS

Problem IV-50. Recall *Problem IV-20*, relating to the Obama HOPE poster produced by Shepard Fairey. We have reproduced below the poster as well as the photograph on which Fairey based it. While Fairey donated copies of this poster to the Obama campaign and authorized them to copy it, he retained the originals and the copyright and commercialized the poster, resulting in substantial profits. Does the fair use defense shield Fairey from copyright liability? Should it?

AP/Garcia Obama Photograph and Shepard Fairey HOPE Poster

Problem IV-51. Richard Prince has a new project: enlarging Instagram selfie images, adding his name and some text, and selling the resulting work for upwards of $100,000.

How would you advise doedeere (pictured) regarding a possible copyright infringement claim?

Problem IV-52. Dr. Seuss Enterprises ("DSE") is the owner of the copyrights to the works of Theodor S. Geisel, the author and illustrator of the books written under the pseudonym "Dr. Seuss." Mr. Geisel wrote and illustrated OH, THE PLACES YOU'LL GO! ("GO!"). DSE oversees a robust publishing program, working closely with publishers to release anniversary editions, reissues in new formats and sizes, and updated editions of the iconic Dr. Seuss books.

DSE also licenses authors and illustrators to publish additional works under the Dr. Seuss brand. DSE has also licensed the publication of several books that are derivative of GO!. These books continue the style of the original Dr. Seuss books, and DSE provides close quality control to ensure consistency of style and quality.

While most Dr. Seuss books are marketed principally to children, adults buy them as well. Some Dr. Seuss works are aimed at teenagers and adults. GO! is an especially popular gift for high school and college graduates.

In 2016, David Gerrold, Ty Templeton, and Glenn Hauman formed ComicMix to develop a *Star Trek* primer. (*Star Trek* is a widely successful science fiction space travel franchise. An entire subculture has grown up around the show. The best-known line from the series describes the mission of the U.S.S. Enterprise: "to boldly go where no [one] has gone before.") Gerrold wrote episodes for the *Star Trek* television series. Templeton is a skilled illustrator.

ComicMix eventually developed a Seuss-style book featuring *Star Trek* backgrounds, characters, and themes: OH THE PLACES YOU'LL BOLDLY GO! (BOLDLY). ComicMix included a disclaimer on the BOLDLY copyright page: "This is a work of fair use, and is not associated with or endorsed by CBS Studio or Dr. Seuss Enterprises." The following comparison illustrates the similarities of and differences between the two works:

OH THE PLACES YOU'LL GO!   OH THE PLACES YOU'LL BOLDLY GO!

DSE sued for copyright infringement. How should a court rule on the fair use defense? How would your answer differ if CBS sued for infringement of the copyrights in Star Trek?

Problem IV-53. Recall *Problem IV-29*, relating to Girl Talk's mashups of copyrighted musical compositions and sound recordings.

Do Girl Talk's mashups fall within the scope of the fair use defense?

The Coalition for Fair Sampling (CFS) has proposed that Congress adopt the Remix Compulsory License Act (RCLA) modeled on the cover license in § 115 of the Copyright Act. Under the RCLA, a remix artist seeking to develop a sound recording that comprises more than 5 existing sound recordings would be eligible for a compulsory license by paying the § 115 statutory license rate (currently 9.1¢ for a 5 minute song (or less); with escalations for longer songs) into the RCLA Fund. The basic idea is that the remixer would be building his or her work on both musical composition and sound recording works and hence the baseline for the entire work should be double the musical composition cover license rate. By making the compulsory license rate 100 percent of the baseline for just the musical composition copyright, the remixer would effectively be credited with half of the total value of the remixed work (assuming that the musical composition and sound recording copyrights were treated symmetrically). Thus, by paying 9.1¢, the remixer could clear all sample licenses needed for a mashup of 5 minutes (or less).

In order to obtain the compulsory license, the remix artist would be required to register the remixed work with the Copyright Office along with a detailed, per-second explication of what prior musical compositions and sound recordings were used. The Copyright Office would, through notice and comment rulemaking, develop a formula for dividing revenue among the musical composition and sound recording owners. (The Copyright Office would also work with the music publishing and sound recording industries to develop a comprehensive database of protected works and tools for identifying owners of tracks that are sampled.) SoundExchange—which administers statutory licenses for sound recording copyrights and allocates revenues—would be responsible for allocating the RCLA Fund to eligible musical composition and sound recording owners.

In order to make this new regime effective, the RCLA would create some categorical fair use safe harbors and limitations. In particular, the RCLA would categorically exempt any sample of less than 5 seconds from liability. Thus, no copyright owner could sue over digital samples (or loops of digital samples) of less than 5 seconds. Such copyright owners would not participate in the distribution of the RCLA Fund. At the same time, the RCLA would categorically exempt from the fair use defense any digital sample of greater than 5 seconds unless the remix artist could establish that such sample was a parody or for political purposes. The purposes of these fair use safe harbors and limitations would be to channel remix artists into the RCLA and to vastly simplify litigation over remix works.

Do you think that this is a constructive approach? Why or why not?

c. Functional/Technological Purpose

As reflected in the Sony Betamax case, the fair use doctrine plays a critical role in accommodating advances in reproduction and distribution technologies. In the congressional report accompanying the 1976 Act,

Congress recognized the important role that courts play in adapting fair use during periods of rapid technological change. H.R. REP. NO. 94-1476, at 66. The past two decades have witnessed a torrential technological advance, both literally and figuratively. There have been several important pockets of fair use jurisprudence addressing technological change.

Reverse Engineering of Computer Software to Develop Interoperable Products. Many software companies distribute their products solely in object code so as to discourage imitation. Companies seeking to decipher the software so as to build interoperable projects must engage in the tedious and time-consuming process of reverse engineering the code. This typically involves making numerous copies of the object code. Several courts have held that this experimental process to decipher software logic and develop interoperable software products falls within the fair use privilege. *See e.g., Sony Computer Entertainment, Inc. v. Connectix Corp.*, 203 F.3d 596 (9th Cir. 2000); *DSC Communications v. DGI Technologies*, 81 F.3d 597, 601 (5th Cir. 1996); *Bateman v. Mnemonics, Inc.*, 79 F.3d 1532, 1539 n.18 (11th Cir. 1995); *Atari Games Corp. v. Nintendo of America*, 975 F.2d 832, 843–44 (Fed. Cir. 1992); *Sega Enterprises Ltd. v. Accolade, Inc.*, 977 F.2d 1510 (9th Cir. 1992) (basing its conclusion that copying the entirety of a computer program for purposes of deciphering unprotected elements is fair use on the principle that "functional requirements for compatibility with the Genesis [video game console are] aspects of Sega's programs that are not protected by copyright. 17 U.S.C. § 102(b)."); Pamela Samuelson & Suzanne Scotchmer, *The Law and Economics of Reverse Engineering*, 111 YALE L.J. 1575 (2002); Peter S. Menell, *An Epitaph for Traditional Copyright Protection of Network Features of Computer Software*, 43 ANTITRUST BULL. 651 (1998); *LaST Frontier Conference Report on Copyright Protection of Computer Software*, 30 JURIMETRICS J. 15, 24–25 (1989) (conference consensus statement).

Search. Search engines scour and index the Internet so as to provide users with a ranking of the most relevant web sites for text or images. The courts have generally been receptive to this search tools even though they inevitably involve copying of copyrighted works. *See Perfect 10, Inc. v. Amazon.com, Inc.*, 487 F.3d 701 (9th Cir. 2007) (holding that the use of copyrighted thumbnail images in internet search results was transformative because the thumbnail copies served a different function from the original copyrighted images); *accord Kelly v. Arriba Soft Corp.*, 336 F.3d 811 (9th Cir. 2003).

In a related vein, authors and publishers have been engaged in a long-standing struggle with Google over its book search project. The aspiration behind Google's project is nearly as old as civilization itself. At the beginning of the third century B.C.E., Ptolemy II set out to collect and house the world's knowledge in the Library of

Alexandria. At its peak, the library is believed to have stored 400,000 to 700,000 parchment scrolls, between 30 and 70 percent of all books then in existence. Although ultimately destroyed by fire, the library reflects early societal interest in collecting and preserving knowledge, goals that are reflected in various aspects of copyright law. *See generally* Peter S. Menell, *Knowledge Access and Preservation Policy in the Digital Age*, 44 HOUS. L. REV. 1013 (2007).

In late 2004, Google set out to accomplish a similar feat—"to organize the world's information and make it universally accessible and useful." In conjunction with leading university and public libraries, Google undertook to scan all of or portions of the major book collections in the world with the goal of making those texts searchable. For works in the public domain, users would be able to access the entire book. For books still under copyright, users would be able to receive only a few lines of text ("snippets") surrounding their search term. The service would help users discover books and provide information about where to obtain a complete copy if the book is not in the public domain. Google would, however, earn a return on this investment. It would deliver advertisements along with search results, in much the way that its search engine and e-mail products function.

Soon after the project was announced, the Association of American Publishers (AAP) castigated Google for posing a risk of "systematic infringement of copyright on a massive scale." The Authors' Guild, a group representing writers, filed a class-action lawsuit to stop or modify the Google Book Search Project.

After the litigation was filed, Google provided an opt-out whereby any copyright owner could request Google not to scan his or her book into its database. Copyright owners could also opt into the Partner Program, through which they could share revenue with Google. Virtually all publishers participate in this program, meaning that the copyright fight is largely over works that are out of print but still in copyright, and particularly over "orphan works" whose owner cannot be found. After a settlement agreement with many authors and publishers was rejected by the court, the litigation went forward. In a fitting conclusion to a decade of litigation, Judge Leval had the final word.

Authors Guild v. Google, Inc.
United States Court of Appeals for the Second Circuit
804 F.3d 202 (2015)

LEVAL, Circuit Judge:

This copyright dispute tests the boundaries of fair use. Plaintiffs, who are authors of published books under copyright, sued Google, Inc. ("Google") for copyright infringement . . . .

Google defended on the ground that its actions constitute "fair use," which, under 17 U.S.C. § 107, is "not an infringement." . . . The district court agreed. *Authors Guild, Inc. v. Google Inc.*, 954 F. Supp. 2d 282, 294 (S.D.N.Y.2013). Plaintiffs brought this appeal.

Plaintiffs contend the district court's ruling was flawed in several respects. They argue: (1) Google's digital copying of entire books, allowing users through the snippet function to read portions, is not a "transformative use" within the meaning of *Campbell v. Acuff-Rose Music, Inc.*, 510 U.S. 569, 578–585 (1994), and provides a substitute for Plaintiffs' works; (2) notwithstanding that Google provides public access to the search and snippet functions without charge and without advertising, its ultimate commercial profit motivation and its derivation of revenue from its dominance of the world-wide Internet search market to which the books project contributes, preclude a finding of fair use; (3) even if Google's copying and revelations of text do not infringe plaintiffs' books, they infringe Plaintiffs' derivative rights in search functions, depriving Plaintiffs of revenues or other benefits they would gain from licensed search markets; (4) Google's storage of digital copies exposes Plaintiffs to the risk that hackers will make their books freely (or cheaply) available on the Internet, destroying the value of their copyrights; and (5) Google's distribution of digital copies to participant libraries is not a transformative use, and it subjects Plaintiffs to the risk of loss of copyright revenues through access allowed by libraries. We reject these arguments and conclude that the district court correctly sustained Google's fair use defense.

Google's making of a digital copy to provide a search function is a transformative use, which augments public knowledge by making available information about Plaintiffs' books without providing the public with a substantial substitute for matter protected by the Plaintiffs' copyright interests in the original works or derivatives of them. The same is true, at least under present conditions, of Google's provision of the snippet function. Plaintiffs' contention that Google has usurped their opportunity to access paid and unpaid licensing markets for substantially the same functions that Google provides fails, in part because the licensing markets in fact involve very different functions than those that Google provides, and in part because an author's derivative rights do not include an exclusive right to supply information (of the sort provided by Google) about her works. Google's profit motivation does not in these circumstances justify denial of fair use. Google's program does not, at this time and on the record before us, expose Plaintiffs to an unreasonable risk of loss of copyright value through incursions of hackers. Finally, Google's provision of digital copies to participating libraries, authorizing them to make non-infringing uses, is non-infringing, and the mere speculative possibility that the libraries might allow use of their copies in an infringing manner does not make Google a contributory infringer. Plaintiffs have failed to show a material issue of fact in dispute.

We affirm the judgment. . . .

COMMENTS AND QUESTIONS

1. The Google Books decision follows in the wake of *Authors Guild, Inc. v. HathiTrust*, 755 F.3d 87 (2d Cir. 2014). Google collaborated with HathiTrust, a consortium of universities, to establish the HathiTrust Digital Library ("HDL"). The HDL repository provides a Boolean searchable catalog to all patrons, full access to copyrighted works to patrons with certified "print disabilities" (blindness or disabilities

that prevent a person from holding a book or turning pages), and preservation of copyrighted books. The HDL stores digital copies of the works in four different locations. Drawing on Judge Leval's framework, the Second Circuit concluded that the indexing/search and print disabilities features were fair use. The court emphasized that HDL had effective security measures in place to prevent unauthorized access to the copyrighted works. The court further held that the plaintiffs lacked standing to challenge the preservation function because the plaintiffs had failed to establish a non-speculative risk that the HDL might create replacement copies of their copyrighted works.

2. Transformativeness has become a central element of fair use analysis.

The Transformative Use Doctrine in Unreversed District Court Preliminary Injunctions, Bench Trials, and Crossed Motions for Summary Judgment			
	1995–2000	**2001–2005**	**2006–2010**
(1) Considers Transformativeness	70.45%	77.27%	95.83%
(2) Finds that use is transformative	22.72%	31.81%	50.00%
(3) Defendant wins when court considers transformativeness	32.14%	47.06%	60.87%
(4) Defendant wins when court finds that use is transformative	88.89%	100%	100%
(5) Overall defendant wins	22.73%	40.91%	58.33%

Neil Netanel, *Making Sense of Fair Use*, 15 LEWIS & CLARK L. REV. 715, 755 (2011).

3. It remains to be seen how fair use will further evolve. *Cf.* Pamela Samuelson, *Possible Futures of Fair Use*, 90 WASH. L. REV. 815 (2015).

PROBLEMS

Problem IV-54. HonorCode.biz has developed and operates an online plagiarism detection service designed to detect plagiarism by high school and college students. Its software scours the web to identify academic articles, term papers, and other materials on topics commonly assigned in high school and college classes. It downloads those materials into a proprietary database. HonorCode.biz offers its service in various packages to high schools, colleges, publishers, film production studios, and others interested in determining the authenticity of written materials.

TermPaper.com sells term papers written by its team of college graduates. It offers a broad range of papers on commonly assigned topics—from Shakespeare to history.

TermPaper.com discovered that some of its term papers have been used to detect plagiarism by HonorCode.biz. HonorCode requires its customers to upload papers submitted for evaluation into HonorCode's database. Apparently, some of TermPaper.com's customers have submitted papers to schools utilizing HonorCode's plagiarism detection service. As a result, papers "purchased" from TermPaper's archive are now used by HonorCode's plagiarism detection service.

TermPaper.com sues HonorCode.biz for copyright infringement. Please analyze their likelihood of success.

Problem IV-55. TVEyes operates a media-monitoring service enables its subscribers to track when keywords on television or radio. Using speech-to-text recognition technology, TVEyes records the entire content of hundreds of television and radio outlets, including Fox News, and creates a searchable database of that content. This is how the Daily Show identifies clips from other news outlets for its programming. Many other businesses also subscribe, including Bloomberg, Goldman Sachs, and the Association of Trial Lawyers. The service is also used by the White House, over 100 members of Congress, and police departments.

TVEyes' subscribers gain access to a customized Watch List Page, which monitors all of the subscriber's desired keywords and terms. Subscribers can set up email alerts for specific keywords or terms. TVEyes' responses provide a thumbnail image of the show, a snippet of transcript, and a short video clip beginning 14 seconds before the keyword was used. The TVEyes User Agreement limits use of downloaded clips to internal purposes. When TVEyes users ask how to obtain rights to publicly post or disseminate clips, TVEyes refers the inquirer to the broadcaster.

TVEyes is a for-profit company with annual revenues of $10 million. Subscribers pay a monthly fee of $500. TVEyes advertises in its marketing materials that its users can "watch live TV, 24/7;" "monitor Breaking News;" and "download unlimited clips" of television programming in high definition. It also highlights that subscribers can play unlimited clips from television broadcasts, "email unlimited clips to unlimited recipients," "post an unlimited number of clips" to social media, and enjoy "unlimited storage [of clips] on TVEyes servers." TVEyes also advertises that subscribers can edit unlimited radio and television clips and download edited clips to their hard drive or to a compact disk. The TVEyes User Manual states that its Media Snapshot feature "allows you to watch live-streams of everything we are recording. This is great for Crisis Communications, monitoring Breaking News, as well as for Press Conferences."

Fox News is an international television news organization. It makes about 16% of its television broadcast content available online, and is concerned that a broader dissemination would weaken its viewer-base or create a substitute for viewing Fox News on television cable and satellite. Fox News provides clips of segments of its programs within an hour of airing. Visitors to Fox News' websites are shown a pre-reel advertisement, before watching news clips. Visitors to Fox News' websites can also copy and paste URLs of specific clips to share on social media platforms. Fox News also allows website visitors to search the video clip content on its website, and provide keywords for that purpose. Fox News restricts the use of the video clips provided on the websites, requiring that they are to be used for "personal use only and [the content] may not be used for commercial purposes." Visitors to Fox News' websites are not permitted to download any of the video clips. Fox News licenses third party websites, including Yahoo!, Hulu, and YouTube, to store and show video clips of segments of its program on their websites, thereby generating another stream of income by the license fees Fox

News charges. Fox News also distributes video clips through its exclusive clip-licensing agent, ITN Source. Overall, Fox News has made approximately $2 million in licensing fees through ITN Source.

Fox News has sued TVEyes, alleging direct and indirect copyright infringement. TVEyes claims that its service makes fair use of Fox News content. How would you analyze the following TVEyes features:

- recording and indexing
- keyword search
- enabling subscribers to download broadcast content onto a local hard drive
- enabling subscribers to email clips

Problem IV-56. In the mid-1990s, Sun Microsystems developed the *Java Programming Language* with the goal of establishing an interoperable programming environment. It promoted Java as "Write Once, Run Everywhere." Sun made most of its Java implementations available without charge, enabling Java to become a de facto standard. Many software developers use the Java language, as well as the Java API packages, to write applications (commonly referred to as "apps") for desktop and laptop computers, tablets, smartphones, and other devices.

In early 2007, Apple revolutionized the smartphone industry with the introduction of the iPhone. The iPhone vastly expanded the smartphone marketplace. Its iOS operating system platform and App Store catalyzed the software development community.

In developing a competing, more open, developer-friendly, smartphone and app platform, Google chose to use the Java programming language. In addition, Google incorporated 7,000 lines of declaration code (or headers) associated with 37 Java API packages in developing the Android operating system. (The Java™ Platform, Standard Edition 7 API Specification contains over 200 API packages.) Google optimized the Android code along several dimensions: size, features, and ease of use for programmers. The overall Android operating system contains 166 API packages.

In writing Android code, Google literally copied only the *declaration code* or headers. Headers are not executable code; they are labels for functions of a particular library or chapter of executable code. The 7,000 lines of declaration code that Google copied represented about 3 percent of the lines of code in the Android version of the 37 APIs (and a far smaller percentage of full Android code base).

Google wrote the *implementing code* for the 37 Java API packages using a clean room process. Nonetheless, due to the common programming language, coding conventions, and functional considerations, Google's implementation code possessed similarities to the overall structure, sequence, and organization of Sun's implementation code.

Sun Microsystems initially hailed Google's decision to use Java for the Android platform, but negotiations over a license to the APIs stalled when Google declined to implement a fully interoperable implementation. Google chose to enter the market without a license to use the 37 Java APIs.

After Oracle Corporation acquired Sun Microsystems in 2010, Oracle sued Google alleging infringement of the Java APIs. Google countered that there was only one way to write the Java method declarations and remain "interoperable" with Java and that the organization and structure of the 37 Java API packages constitute a "command structure" excluded from copyright protection under § 102(b). On appeal from a district court decision finding for Google, the Federal Circuit reversed, holding that the "structure, sequence and organization" of an API was copyrightable and that even small amounts of literal copying was not de minimis. *See Oracle Am., Inc. v. Google Inc.*, 750 F.3d 1339 (Fed. Cir. 2014). The case was remanded for a determination as to whether Google's use of the Java APIs constituted fair use. (The jury in the first trial deadlocked on that issue.)

At the trial following remand, Oracle argued that the declaration code as well as the structure, sequence, and organization of the 37 APIs were original and creative, Google's copying was commercial, Android competes with Sun/Oracle's Java mobile platform, and Android has undermined interoperability. Google asserted fair use on the following grounds: that the overwhelming majority of Google's implementing code is not infringing; that under § 102(b) and other limiting doctrines, declaring code is functional and hence not protectable; and Oracle's struggles to establish a Java mobile operating system platform are not attributable to Android's use of the 37 APIs but rather to Sun/Oracle's open licensing choices and inadequate feature set.

The jury held for Google, but the Federal Circuit reversed, holding that Google's use of Oracle's APIs was commercial in nature, was not transformative, and adversely affected the market for Oracle's Java platform, and hence was not fair use. *See Oracle America, Inc. v. Google*, 886 F.3d 1179 (Fed. Cir. 2018). Google seeks review at the Supreme Court. How would you argue the appeal for Oracle? for Google? What is the proper resolution?

2. Online Service Provider Safe Harbors

As the Internet emerged as a communications and commercial medium in the mid 1990s, new commercial enterprises providing access to the Internet found themselves in a precarious situation. Did the emerging Online Service Provider (OSP) industry face liability for hosting websites containing infringing content and transmitting copyrighted works without authorization?

In *Religious Technology Center v. Netcom On-Line Communication Services, Inc.*, 907 F. Supp. 1361 (N.D. Cal. 1995), a copyright owner sued an Internet access provider (Netcom) and its subscriber, a computer bulletin board service (BBS) hosting a Usenet newsgroup, for direct and indirect copyright liability on the basis of material posted to the newsgroup by a user. Netcom employed an automated system for relaying messages on Usenet groups without any monitoring or control of content. The court determined that "[a]lthough copyright is a strict liability statute, there should still be some element of volition or causation which is lacking where a defendant's system is merely used to create a copy by a third party." To hold otherwise would "also result in liability for every single Usenet server in the worldwide link of computers transmitting [the poster's infringing] message to every other computer." With regard to contributory liability, the court held that when a BBS cannot reasonably verify a claim of infringement—because of "the copyright holder's failure to provide the necessary documentation to show that there is a likely infringement" or otherwise—then the knowledge element of contributory infringement should be deemed lacking. As to participation, the court concluded that "it is fair, assuming Netcom is able to take simple measures to prevent further damage to plaintiffs' copyrighted works, to hold Netcom liable for contributory infringement where Netcom has knowledge of [the poster's] infringing postings yet continues to aid in the accomplishment of [the infringer's] purpose of publicly distributing the postings" by taking volitional acts. Other courts adopted the *Netcom* approach. *See, e.g., ALS Scan, Inc. v. RemarQ Cmtys., Inc.*, 239 F.3d 619 (4th Cir. 2001); *Marobie-Fl, Inc. v. National Ass'n of Fire and Equipment Distributors*, 983 F. Supp. 1167 (N.D. Ill. 1997).

Controversy over the scope of OSP liability fed directly into negotiations over the Digital Millennium Copyright Act (DMCA) taking shape in Congress in 1998. OSPs, such as America Online (AOL) and Yahoo!, warned that failure to incorporate immunity directly into the Copyright Act could severely impair the rapidly emerging OSP industry and impede the growth of economic activity on the Internet. At their urging (and over the resistance of the major content industries—publishing, motion pictures, sound recording), Congress established a series of safe harbors insulating OSPs from liability for transmitting, storing, or linking to unauthorized content.

Viacom Int'l, Inc. v. YouTube
United States Court of Appeals for the Second Circuit
676 F.3d 19 (2d Cir. 2012)

CABRANES, Circuit Judge.

. . . The plaintiffs alleged direct and secondary copyright infringement based on the public performance, display, and reproduction of approximately 79,000 audiovisual "clips" that appeared on the YouTube website between 2005 and 2008. They demanded, inter alia, statutory damages pursuant to 17 U.S.C. § 504(c) or, in the alternative, actual damages from the alleged infringement, as well as declaratory and injunctive relief.

In a June 23, 2010 Opinion and Order (the "June 23 Opinion"), the District Court held that the defendants were entitled to DMCA safe harbor protection primarily because they had insufficient notice of the particular infringements in suit. In construing the statutory safe harbor, the District Court concluded that the "actual knowledge" or "aware[ness] of facts or circumstances" that would disqualify an online service provider from safe harbor protection under § 512(c)(1)(A) refer to "knowledge of specific and identifiable infringements." The District Court further held that item-specific knowledge of infringing activity is required for a service provider to have the "right and ability to control" infringing activity under § 512(c)(1)(B). Finally, the District Court held that the replication, transmittal, and display of videos on YouTube constituted activity "by reason of the storage at the direction of a user" within the meaning of § 512(c)(1).

These related cases present a series of significant questions of statutory construction. We conclude that the District Court correctly held that the § 512(c) safe harbor requires knowledge or awareness of specific infringing activity, but we vacate the order granting summary judgment because a reasonable jury could find that YouTube had actual knowledge or awareness of specific infringing activity on its website. We further hold that the District Court erred by interpreting the "right and ability to control" provision to require "item-specific" knowledge. . . .

BACKGROUND

A. The DMCA Safe Harbors

"The DMCA was enacted in 1998 to implement the World Intellectual Property Organization Copyright Treaty." Title II of the DMCA, separately titled the "Online Copyright Infringement Liability Limitation Act" (OCILLA), was designed to "clarif[y] the liability faced by service providers who transmit potentially infringing material over their networks." S. REP. No. 105–190 at 2 (1998). But "[r]ather than embarking upon a wholesale clarification" of various copyright doctrines, Congress elected "to leave current law in its evolving state and, instead, to create a series of 'safe harbors[]' for certain common activities of service providers." *Id.* at 19. To that end, OCILLA established a series of four "safe harbors" that allow qualifying service providers to limit their liability for claims of copyright infringement based on (a) "transitory digital network communications," (b) "system caching," (c) "information residing on systems or networks at [the] direction of users," and (d) "information location tools." 17 U.S.C. §§ 512(a)–(d).

To qualify for protection under any of the safe harbors, a party must meet a set of threshold criteria. First, the party must in fact be a "service provider," defined, in pertinent part, as "a provider of online services or network access, or the operator of facilities therefor." 17 U.S.C. § 512(k)(1)(B). A party that qualifies as a service provider must also satisfy certain "conditions of eligibility," including the adoption and reasonable implementation of a "repeat infringer" policy that "provides for the termination in appropriate circumstances of subscribers and account holders of the service provider's system or network." *Id.* § 512(i)(1)(A). In addition, a qualifying service provider must accommodate "standard technical measures" that are "used by copyright owners to identify or protect copyrighted works." *Id.* §§ 512(i)(1)(B), (i)(2).

Beyond the threshold criteria, a service provider must satisfy the requirements of a particular safe harbor. In this case, the safe harbor at issue is § 512(c), which covers infringement claims that arise "by reason of the storage at the direction of a user of material that resides on a system or network controlled or operated by or for the service provider." *Id.* § 512(c)(1). The § 512(c) safe harbor will apply only if the service provider:

> (A)(i) does not have actual knowledge that the material or an activity using the material on the system or network is infringing;
>
> (ii) in the absence of such actual knowledge, is not aware of facts or circumstances from which infringing activity is apparent; or
>
> (iii) upon obtaining such knowledge or awareness, acts expeditiously to remove, or disable access to, the material;
>
> (B) does not receive a financial benefit directly attributable to the infringing activity, in a case in which the service provider has the right and ability to control such activity; and
>
> (C) upon notification of claimed infringement as described in paragraph (3), responds expeditiously to remove, or disable access to, the material that is claimed to be infringing or to be the subject of infringing activity.

Id. §§ 512(c)(1)(A)–(C). Section 512(c) also sets forth a detailed notification scheme that requires service providers to "designate[] an agent to receive notifications of claimed infringement," *Id.* § 512(c)(2), and specifies the components of a proper notification, commonly known as a "takedown notice," to that agent, *see id.* § 512(c)(3). Thus, actual knowledge of infringing material, awareness of facts or circumstances that make infringing activity apparent, or receipt of a takedown notice will each trigger an obligation to expeditiously remove the infringing material.

With the statutory context in mind, we now turn to the facts of this case.

B. Factual Background

YouTube was founded in February 2005 by Chad Hurley ("Hurley"), Steve Chen ("Chen"), and Jawed Karim ("Karim"), three former employees of the internet company Paypal. When YouTube announced the "official launch" of the website in December 2005, a press release described YouTube as a "consumer media company" that "allows people to watch, upload, and share personal video clips at www.YouTube.com." Under the slogan "Broadcast yourself," YouTube achieved rapid prominence and profitability, eclipsing competitors such as Google Video and Yahoo Video by wide margins. In November 2006, Google acquired YouTube in a stock-for-stock transaction valued at $1.65 billion. By March 2010, at the time of summary judgment briefing in this litigation, site traffic on YouTube had soared to more than 1 billion daily video views, with more than 24 hours of new video uploaded to the site every minute.

The basic function of the YouTube website permits users to "upload" and view video clips free of charge. Before uploading a video to YouTube, a user must register and create an account with the website. The registration process requires the user to accept YouTube's Terms of Use agreement, which provides, inter alia, that the user "will not submit material that is copyrighted . . . unless [he is] the owner of such rights or ha[s] permission from their rightful owner to post the material and to grant YouTube all of the license rights granted herein." When the registration process is complete, the user can sign in to his account, select a video to upload from the user's personal computer, mobile phone, or other device, and instruct the YouTube system to upload the video by clicking on a virtual upload "button."

Uploading a video to the YouTube website triggers a series of automated software functions. During the upload process, YouTube makes one or more exact copies of the video in its original file format. YouTube also makes one or more additional copies of the video in "Flash" format, a process known as "transcoding." The transcoding process ensures that YouTube videos are available for viewing by most users at their request. The YouTube system allows users to gain access to video content by "streaming" the video to the user's computer in response to a playback request. YouTube uses a computer algorithm to identify clips that are "related" to a video the user watches and display links to the "related" clips. . . .

DISCUSSION

. . .

A. Actual and "Red Flag" Knowledge: § 512(c)(1)(A)

The first and most important question on appeal is whether the DMCA safe harbor at issue requires "actual knowledge" or "aware[ness]" of facts or circumstances indicating "specific and identifiable infringements," Viacom, 718 F. Supp. 2d at 523. We consider first the scope of the statutory provision and then its application to the record in this case.

1. The Specificity Requirement

"As in all statutory construction cases, we begin with the language of the statute," *Barnhart v. Sigmon Coal Co.*, 534 U.S. 438, 450 (2002). Under § 512(c)(1)(A), safe harbor protection is available only if the service provider:

(i) does not have actual knowledge that the material or an activity using the material on the system or network is infringing;

(ii) in the absence of such actual knowledge, is not aware of facts or circumstances from which infringing activity is apparent; or

(iii) upon obtaining such knowledge or awareness, acts expeditiously to remove, or disable access to, the material. . . .

17 U.S.C. § 512(c)(1)(A). As previously noted, the District Court held that the statutory phrases "actual knowledge that the material . . . is infringing" and "facts or circumstances from which infringing activity is apparent" refer to "knowledge of specific and identifiable infringements." *Viacom*, 718 F. Supp. 2d at 523. For the reasons that follow, we substantially affirm that holding.

Although the parties marshal a battery of other arguments on appeal, it is the text of the statute that compels our conclusion. In particular, we are persuaded that the basic operation of § 512(c) requires knowledge or awareness of specific infringing activity. Under § 512(c)(1)(A), knowledge or awareness alone does not disqualify the service provider; rather, the provider that gains knowledge or awareness of infringing activity retains safe-harbor protection if it "acts expeditiously to remove, or disable access to, the material." 17 U.S.C. § 512(c)(1)(A)(iii). Thus, the nature of the removal obligation itself contemplates knowledge or awareness of specific infringing material, because expeditious removal is possible only if the service provider knows with particularity which items to remove. Indeed, to require expeditious removal in the absence of specific knowledge or awareness would be to mandate an amorphous obligation to "take commercially reasonable steps" in response to a generalized awareness of infringement. Viacom Br. 33. Such a view cannot be reconciled with the language of the statute, which requires "expeditious[]" action to remove or disable " *the material* " at issue. 17 U.S.C. § 512(c)(1)(A)(iii) (emphasis added).

On appeal, the plaintiffs dispute this conclusion by drawing our attention to § 512(c)(1)(A)(ii), the so-called "red flag" knowledge provision. *See id.* § 512(c)(1)(A)(ii) (limiting liability where, "in the absence of such actual knowledge, [the service provider] is not aware of facts or circumstances from which infringing activity is apparent"). In their view, the use of the phrase "facts or circumstances" demonstrates that Congress did not intend to limit the red flag provision to a particular type of knowledge. The plaintiffs contend that requiring awareness of specific infringements in order to establish "aware[ness] of facts or circumstances from which infringing activity is apparent," 17 U.S.C. § 512(c)(1)(A)(ii), renders the red flag provision superfluous, because that provision would be satisfied only when the "actual knowledge" provision is also satisfied. For that reason, the plaintiffs urge the Court to hold that the red flag provision "requires less specificity" than the actual knowledge provision.

This argument misconstrues the relationship between "actual" knowledge and "red flag" knowledge. It is true that "we are required to 'disfavor interpretations of statutes that render language superfluous.'" *Conn. ex rel. Blumenthal v. U.S. Dep't of the Interior*, 228 F.3d 82, 88 (2d Cir. 2000) (quoting *Conn. Nat'l Bank v. Germain*, 503 U.S. 249, 253, 112 S.Ct. 1146, 117 L.Ed.2d 391 (1992)). But contrary to the plaintiffs' assertions, construing § 512(c)(1)(A) to require actual knowledge or awareness of specific instances of infringement does not render the red flag provision superfluous. The phrase "actual knowledge," which appears in § 512(c)(1)(A)(i), is frequently used to denote subjective belief. *See, e.g., United States v. Quinones*, 635 F.3d 590, 602 (2d Cir. 2011) ("[T]he belief held by the defendant need not be reasonable in order for it to defeat . . . actual knowledge."). By contrast, courts often invoke the language of "facts or circumstances," which appears in § 512(c)(1)(A)(ii), in discussing an objective reasonableness standard. *See, e.g., Maxwell v. City of New York*, 380 F.3d 106, 108 (2d Cir. 2004) ("Police officers' application of force is excessive . . . if it is objectively unreasonable in light of the facts and circumstances confronting them, without regard to their underlying intent or motivation." (internal quotation marks omitted)).

The difference between actual and red flag knowledge is thus not between specific and generalized knowledge, but instead between a subjective and an objective standard. In other words, the actual knowledge provision turns on whether the provider actually or "subjectively" knew of specific infringement, while the red flag provision turns on whether the provider was subjectively aware of facts that would have made the specific infringement "objectively" obvious to a reasonable person. The red flag provision, because it incorporates an objective standard, is not swallowed up by the actual knowledge provision under our construction of the § 512(c) safe harbor. Both provisions do independent work, and both apply only to specific instances of infringement.

The limited body of case law interpreting the knowledge provisions of the § 512(c) safe harbor comports with our view of the specificity requirement. Most recently, a panel of the Ninth Circuit addressed the scope of § 512(c) in *UMG Recordings, Inc. v. Shelter Capital Partners LLC*, 667 F.3d 1022 (9th Cir. 2011), a copyright infringement case against Veoh Networks, a video-hosting service similar to YouTube. As in this case, various music publishers brought suit against the service provider, claiming direct and secondary copyright infringement based on the presence of unauthorized content on the website, and the website operator sought refuge in the § 512(c) safe harbor. The Court of Appeals affirmed the district court's determination on summary judgment that the website operator was entitled to safe harbor protection. With respect to the actual knowledge provision, the panel declined to "adopt[] a broad conception of the knowledge requirement," *id.* at 1038, holding instead that the safe harbor "[r]equir[es] specific knowledge of particular infringing activity," *id.* at 1037. The Court of Appeals "reach[ed] the same conclusion" with respect to the red flag provision, noting that "[w]e do not place the burden of determining whether [materials] are actually illegal on a service provider." *Id.* at 1038 (alterations in original) (quoting *Perfect 10, Inc. v. CCBill LLC*, 488 F.3d 1102, 1114 (9th Cir. 2007)).

Although *Shelter Capital* contains the most explicit discussion of the § 512(c) knowledge provisions, other cases are generally in accord. *See, e.g.*, *Capitol Records, Inc. v. MP3tunes, LLC*, 821 F. Supp. 2d 627, 635 (S.D.N.Y. 2011) ("Undoubtedly, MP3tunes is aware that some level of infringement occurs. But, there is no genuine dispute that MP3tunes did not have specific 'red flag' knowledge with respect to any particular link. . . ."); *UMG Recordings, Inc. v. Veoh Networks, Inc.*, 665 F. Supp. 2d 1099, 1108 (C.D.Cal.2009) ("UMG II") ("[I]f investigation of 'facts and circumstances' is required to identify material as infringing, then those facts and circumstances are not 'red flags.'"). While we decline to adopt the reasoning of those decisions in toto, we note that no court has embraced the contrary proposition—urged by the plaintiffs—that the red flag provision "requires less specificity" than the actual knowledge provision.

Based on the text of § 512(c)(1)(A), as well as the limited case law on point, we affirm the District Court's holding that actual knowledge or awareness of facts or circumstances that indicate specific and identifiable instances of infringement will disqualify a service provider from the safe harbor.

2. The Grant of Summary Judgment

The corollary question on appeal is whether, under the foregoing construction of § 512(c)(1)(A), the District Court erred in granting summary judgment to YouTube on the record presented. For the reasons that follow, we hold that although the District Court correctly interpreted § 512(c)(1)(A), summary judgment for the defendants was premature.

i. Specific Knowledge or Awareness

The plaintiffs argue that, even under the District Court's construction of the safe harbor, the record raises material issues of fact regarding YouTube's actual knowledge or "red flag" awareness of specific instances of infringement. To that end, the plaintiffs draw our attention to various estimates regarding the percentage of infringing content on the YouTube website. For example, Viacom cites evidence that YouTube employees conducted website surveys and estimated that 75–80% of all YouTube streams contained copyrighted material. The class plaintiffs similarly claim that Credit Suisse, acting as financial advisor to Google, estimated that more than 60% of YouTube's content was "premium" copyrighted content—and that only 10% of the premium content was authorized. These approximations suggest that the defendants were conscious that significant quantities of material on the YouTube website were infringing. *See Viacom Int'l*, 718 F. Supp. 2d at 518 ("[A] jury could find that the defendants not only were generally aware of, but welcomed, copyright-infringing material being placed on their website."). But such estimates are insufficient, standing alone, to create a triable issue of fact as to whether YouTube actually knew, or was aware of facts or circumstances that would indicate, the existence of particular instances of infringement.

Beyond the survey results, the plaintiffs rely upon internal YouTube communications that do refer to particular clips or groups of clips. The class plaintiffs argue that YouTube was aware of specific infringing material because, *inter alia*, YouTube attempted to search for specific Premier League videos on the site in order to gauge their "value based on video usage." In particular, the class plaintiffs cite a February 7, 2007 e-mail from Patrick Walker, director of video partnerships for Google and YouTube, requesting that his colleagues calculate the number of daily searches for the terms "soccer," "football," and "Premier League" in preparation for a bid on the global rights to Premier League content. On another occasion, Walker requested that any "clearly infringing, official broadcast footage" from a list of top Premier League clubs—including Liverpool Football Club, Chelsea Football Club, Manchester United Football Club, and Arsenal Football Club—be taken down in advance of a meeting with the heads of "several major sports teams and leagues." YouTube ultimately decided not to make a bid for the Premier League rights—but the infringing content allegedly remained on the website.

The record in the *Viacom* action includes additional examples. For instance, YouTube founder Jawed Karim prepared a report in March 2006 which stated that, "[a]s of today[,] episodes and clips of the following well-known shows can still be found [on YouTube]: Family Guy, South Park, MTV Cribs, Daily Show, Reno 911, [and] Dave Chapelle [sic]." Karim further opined that, "although YouTube is not legally required to monitor content . . . and complies with DMCA takedown requests, we would benefit from *preemptively* removing content that is blatantly illegal and likely to attract criticism." He also noted that "a more thorough analysis" of the issue would be required. At least some of the TV shows to which Karim referred are owned by Viacom. A reasonable juror could conclude from the March 2006 report that Karim knew of the presence of Viacom-owned material on YouTube, since he presumably located specific clips of the shows in question before he could announce that YouTube hosted the content "[a]s of today." A reasonable juror could also conclude that Karim believed the clips he located to be infringing (since he refers to them as "blatantly illegal"), and that YouTube did not remove the content from the website until conducting "a more thorough analysis," thus exposing the company to liability in the interim.

Furthermore, in a July 4, 2005 e-mail exchange, YouTube founder Chad Hurley sent an e-mail to his co-founders with the subject line "budlight commercials," and stated, "we need to reject these too." Steve Chen responded, "can we please leave these in a bit longer? another week or two can't hurt." Karim also replied, indicating that he "added back in all 28 bud videos." Similarly, in an August 9, 2005 e-mail exchange, Hurley urged his colleagues "to start being diligent about rejecting copyrighted / inappropriate content," noting that "there is a cnn clip of the shuttle clip on the site today, if the boys from Turner would come to the site, they might be pissed?" Again, Chen resisted:

> but we should just keep that stuff on the site. i really don't see what will happen. what? someone from cnn sees it? he happens to be someone with power? he happens to want to take it down right away. he gets in touch with cnn legal. 2 weeks later, we get a cease & desist letter. we take the video down.

And again, Karim agreed, indicating that "the CNN space shuttle clip, I like. we can remove it once we're bigger and better known, but for now that clip is fine."

Upon a review of the record, we are persuaded that the plaintiffs may have raised a material issue of fact regarding YouTube's knowledge or awareness of specific instances of infringement. The foregoing Premier League e-mails request the identification and removal of "clearly infringing, official broadcast footage." The March 2006 report indicates Karim's awareness of specific clips that he perceived to be "blatantly illegal." Similarly, the Bud Light and space shuttle e-mails refer to particular clips in the context of correspondence about whether to remove infringing material from the website. On these facts, a reasonable juror could conclude that YouTube had actual knowledge of specific infringing activity, or was at least aware of facts or circumstances from which specific infringing activity was apparent. *See* § 512(c)(1)(A)(i)–(ii). Accordingly, we hold that summary judgment to YouTube on all clips-in-suit, especially in the absence of any detailed examination of the extensive record on summary judgment, was premature. . . .

ii. "Willful Blindness"

The plaintiffs further argue that the District Court erred in granting summary judgment to the defendants despite evidence that YouTube was "willfully blind" to specific infringing activity. On this issue of first impression, we consider the application of the common law willful blindness doctrine in the DMCA context.

"The principle that willful blindness is tantamount to knowledge is hardly novel." *Tiffany (NJ) Inc. v. eBay, Inc.*, 600 F.3d 93, 110 n. 16 (2d Cir. 2010) (collecting cases); *see In re Aimster Copyright Litig.*, 334 F.3d 643, 650 (7th Cir. 2003) ("Willful blindness is knowledge, in copyright law . . . as it is in the law generally."). A person is "willfully blind" or engages in "conscious avoidance" amounting to knowledge where the person "'was aware of a high probability of the fact in dispute and consciously avoided confirming that fact.'" *United States v. Aina-Marshall*, 336 F.3d 167, 170 (2d Cir. 2003) (quoting *United States v. Rodriguez*, 983 F.2d 455, 458 (2d Cir. 1993)); *cf. Global-Tech Appliances, Inc. v. SEB S.A.*, 131 S.Ct. 2060, 2070–71 (2011) (applying the willful blindness doctrine in a patent infringement case). Writing in the trademark infringement context, we have held that "[a] service provider is not . . . permitted willful blindness. When it has reason to suspect that users of its service are infringing a protected mark, it may not shield itself from learning of the particular infringing transactions by looking the other way." *Tiffany*, 600 F.3d at 109.

The DMCA does not mention willful blindness. As a general matter, we interpret a statute to abrogate a common law principle only if the statute "speak[s] directly to the question addressed by the common law." *Matar v. Dichter*, 563 F.3d 9, 14 (2d Cir. 2009) (internal quotation marks omitted). The relevant question, therefore, is whether the DMCA "speak[s] directly" to the principle of willful blindness. *Id.* (internal quotation marks omitted). The DMCA provision most relevant to the abrogation inquiry is § 512(m), which provides that safe harbor protection shall not be conditioned on "a service provider monitoring its service or affirmatively seeking facts indicating infringing activity, except to the extent consistent with a standard technical measure complying with the provisions of subsection (i)." 17 U.S.C. § 512(m)(1). Section 512(m) is explicit: DMCA safe harbor protection cannot be conditioned on affirmative monitoring by a service provider. For that reason, § 512(m) is incompatible with a broad common law duty to monitor or otherwise seek out infringing activity based on general awareness that infringement may be occurring. That fact does not, however, dispose of the abrogation inquiry; as previously noted, willful blindness cannot be defined as an affirmative duty to monitor. *See Aina-Marshall*, 336 F.3d at 170 (holding that a person is "willfully blind" where he "was aware of a high probability of the fact in dispute and consciously avoided confirming that fact"). Because the statute does not "speak[] directly" to the willful blindness doctrine, § 512(m) limits—but does not abrogate—the doctrine. Accordingly, we hold that the willful blindness doctrine may be applied, in appropriate circumstances, to demonstrate knowledge or awareness of specific instances of infringement under the DMCA.

The District Court cited § 512(m) for the proposition that safe harbor protection does not require affirmative monitoring, *Viacom*, 718 F. Supp. 2d at 524, but did not expressly address the principle of willful blindness or its relationship to the DMCA safe harbors. As a result, whether the defendants made a "deliberate effort to avoid guilty knowledge," *In re Aimster*, 334 F.3d at 650, remains a fact question for the District Court to consider in the first instance on remand.

B. Control and Benefit: § 512(c)(1)(B)

Apart from the foregoing knowledge provisions, the § 512(c) safe harbor provides that an eligible service provider must "not receive a financial benefit directly attributable to the infringing activity, in a case in which the service provider has the right and ability to control such activity." 17 U.S.C. § 512(c)(1)(B). The District Court addressed this issue in a single paragraph, quoting from § 512(c)(1)(B), the so-called "control and benefit" provision, and concluding that "[t]he 'right and ability to control' the activity requires knowledge of it, which must be item-specific." *Viacom*, 718 F. Supp. 2d at 527. For the reasons that follow, we hold that the District Court erred by importing a specific knowledge requirement into the control and benefit provision, and we therefore remand for further fact-finding on the issue of control.

1. "Right and Ability to Control" Infringing Activity

On appeal, the parties advocate two competing constructions of the "right and ability to control" infringing activity. 17 U.S.C. § 512(c)(1)(B). Because each is fatally flawed, we reject both proposed constructions in favor of a fact-based inquiry to be conducted in the first instance by the District Court.

The first construction, pressed by the defendants, is the one adopted by the District Court, which held that "the provider must know of the particular case before he can control it." *Viacom*, 718 F. Supp. 2d at 527. The Ninth Circuit recently agreed, holding that "until [the service provider] becomes aware of specific unauthorized material, it cannot exercise its 'power or authority' over the specific infringing item. In practical terms, it does not have the kind of ability to control infringing activity the statute contemplates." *UMG Recordings, Inc. v. Shelter Capital Partners LLC*, 667 F.3d 1022, 1041 (9th Cir. 2011). The trouble with this construction is that importing a specific knowledge requirement into § 512(c)(1)(B) renders the control provision duplicative of § 512(c)(1)(A). Any service provider that has item-specific knowledge of infringing activity and thereby obtains financial benefit would already be excluded from the safe harbor under § 512(c)(1)(A) for having specific knowledge of infringing material and failing to effect expeditious removal. No additional service provider would be excluded by § 512(c)(1)(B) that was not already excluded by § 512(c)(1)(A). Because statutory interpretations that render language superfluous are disfavored, Conn. ex rel. Blumenthal, 228 F.3d at 88, we reject the District Court's interpretation of the control provision.

The second construction, urged by the plaintiffs, is that the control provision codifies the common law doctrine of vicarious copyright liability. The common law imposes liability for vicarious copyright infringement "[w]hen the right and ability to supervise coalesce with an obvious and direct financial interest in the exploitation of copyrighted materials—even in the absence of actual knowledge that the copyright mono[poly] is being impaired." *Shapiro, Bernstein & Co. v. H.L. Green Co.*, 316 F.2d

304, 407 (2d Cir. 1963); *cf. Metro–Goldwyn–Mayer Studios Inc. v. Grokster, Ltd.*, 545 U.S. 913, 930 n. 9 (2005). To support their codification argument, the plaintiffs rely on a House Report relating to a preliminary version of the DMCA: "The 'right and ability to control' language ... codifies the second element of vicarious liability. . . . Subparagraph (B) is intended to preserve existing case law that examines all relevant aspects of the relationship between the primary and secondary infringer." H.R .REP. NO. 105–551(I), at 26 (1998). In response, YouTube notes that the codification reference was omitted from the committee reports describing the final legislation, and that Congress ultimately abandoned any attempt to "embark[] upon a wholesale clarification" of vicarious liability, electing instead "to create a series of 'safe harbors' for certain common activities of service providers." S. REP. NO. 105–190, at 19.

Happily, the future of digital copyright law does not turn on the confused legislative history of the control provision. The general rule with respect to common law codification is that when "Congress uses terms that have accumulated settled meaning under the common law, a court must infer, unless the statute otherwise dictates, that Congress means to incorporate the established meaning of those terms." *Neder v. United States*, 527 U.S. 1, 21 (1999) (ellipsis and internal quotation marks omitted). Under the common law vicarious liability standard, "'[t]he ability to block infringers' access to a particular environment for any reason whatsoever is evidence of the right and ability to supervise.'" *Arista Records LLC v. Usenet.com, Inc.*, 633 F. Supp. 2d 124, 157 (S.D.N.Y.2009) (alteration in original) (quoting *A & M Records, Inc. v. Napster, Inc.*, 239 F.3d 1004, 1023 (9th Cir. 2001)). To adopt that principle in the DMCA context, however, would render the statute internally inconsistent. Section 512(c) actually presumes that service providers have the ability to "block ... access" to infringing material. *Id.* at 157; *see Shelter Capital*, 667 F.3d at 1042–43. Indeed, a service provider who has knowledge or awareness of infringing material or who receives a takedown notice from a copyright holder is required to "remove, or disable access to, the material" in order to claim the benefit of the safe harbor. 17 U.S.C. §§ 512(c)(1)(A)(iii) & (C). But in taking such action, the service provider would—in the plaintiffs' analysis—be admitting the "right and ability to control" the infringing material. Thus, the prerequisite to safe harbor protection under §§ 512(c)(1)(A)(iii) & (C) would at the same time be a disqualifier under § 512(c)(1)(B).

Moreover, if Congress had intended § 512(c)(1)(B) to be coextensive with vicarious liability, "the statute could have accomplished that result in a more direct manner." *Shelter Capital*, 667 F.3d at 1045.

> It is conceivable that Congress . . . intended that [service providers] which receive a financial benefit directly attributable to the infringing activity would not, under any circumstances, be able to qualify for the subsection (c) safe harbor. But if that was indeed their intention, it would have been far simpler and much more straightforward to simply say as much.

Id. (alteration in original) (quoting *Ellison v. Robertson*, 189 F. Supp. 2d 1051, 1061 (C.D. Cal. 2002), *aff'd in part and rev'd in part on different grounds*, 357 F.3d 1072 (9th Cir. 2004)).

In any event, the foregoing tension—elsewhere described as a "predicament" and a "catch22"—is sufficient to establish that the control provision "dictates" a departure from the common law vicarious liability standard, *Neder*, 527 U.S. at 21. Accordingly, we conclude that the "right and ability to control" infringing activity under § 512(c)(1)(B) "requires something more than the ability to remove or block access to materials posted on a service provider's website." *MP3tunes, LLC*, 2011 WL 5104616, at *14; *accord Wolk v. Kodak Imaging Network, Inc.*, 821 F. Supp. 2d at 645. The remaining—and more difficult—question is how to define the "something more" that is required.

To date, only one court has found that a service provider had the right and ability to control infringing activity under § 512(c)(1)(B). In *Perfect 10, Inc. v. Cybernet Ventures, Inc.*, 213 F. Supp. 2d 1146 (C.D. Cal. 2002), the court found control where the service provider instituted a monitoring program by which user websites received "detailed instructions regard[ing] issues of layout, appearance, and content." *Id.* at 1173. The service provider also forbade certain types of content and refused access to users who failed to comply with its instructions. *Id.* Similarly, inducement of copyright infringement under *Metro-Goldwyn-Mayer Studios Inc. v. Grokster, Ltd.*, 545 U.S. 913 (2005), which "premises liability on purposeful, culpable expression and conduct," *Id.* at 937, might also rise to the level of control under § 512(c)(1)(B). Both of these examples involve a service provider exerting substantial influence on the activities of users, without necessarily—or even frequently—acquiring knowledge of specific infringing activity.

In light of our holding that § 512(c)(1)(B) does not include a specific knowledge requirement, we think it prudent to remand to the District Court to consider in the first instance whether the plaintiffs have adduced sufficient evidence to allow a reasonable jury to conclude that YouTube had the right and ability to control the infringing activity and received a financial benefit directly attributable to that activity.

C. "By Reason of" Storage: § 512(c)(1)

The § 512(c) safe harbor is only available when the infringement occurs "by reason of the storage at the direction of a user of material that resides on a system or network controlled or operated by or for the service provider." 17 U.S.C. § 512(c)(1). In this case, the District Court held that YouTube's software functions fell within the safe harbor for infringements that occur "by reason of" user storage, noting that a contrary holding would "confine[] the word 'storage' too narrowly to meet the statute's purpose." *Viacom*, 718 F. Supp. 2d at 526. For the reasons that follow, we affirm that holding with respect to three of the challenged software functions—the conversion (or "transcoding") of videos into a standard display format, the playback of videos on "watch" pages, and the "related videos" function. We remand for further fact-finding with respect to a fourth software function, involving the third-party syndication of videos uploaded to YouTube. . . .

COMMENTS AND QUESTIONS

1. *The Red Flag Test.* Are you persuaded by the Second Circuit's reading of the red flag provision?

The legislative history explains that

[t]he "red flag" test has both a subjective and an objective element. In determining whether the service provider was aware of a "red flag," the subjective awareness of the service provider of the facts or circumstances in question must be determined. However, in deciding whether those facts or circumstances constitute a "red flag"—in other words, whether infringing activity would have been apparent to a reasonable person operating under the same or similar circumstances—an objective standard should be used.

Commerce Rep. (DMCA) H.R .REP. NO. 105-551, Part 2, 105th Cong., 2d Sess. (July 22, 1998) p. 44. Does this square with the Second Circuit's interpretation? The Ninth Circuit has adopted the same reading. *See UMG Recordings v. Shelter Capital Partners*, 667 F.3d 1022 (9th Cir. 2013).

2. *Statutory Interpretation and Technological Change.* Professor Menell suggests that the court's narrow interpretation reflected discomfort with applying a regime that was designed for the web circa 1998—where OSPs hosted websites actively managed by webmasters—to Web 2.0 functionality, such as Veoh and YouTube, that use automated processes to continually upload user-generated content. The imposition of statutory damages—ranging up to $150,000 per work if infringement was found to be willful—could produce disproportionate, crushing liability. *See* Peter S. Menell, *Judicial Regulation of Digital Copyright Windfalls: Making Interpretive and Policy Sense of* Viacom v. YouTube *and* UMG Recordings v. Shelter Capital Partners (2012) http://papers.ssrn.com/sol3/papers.cfm?abstract_id=2049445.

3. *Willful Blindness.* The Second Circuit holds that the DMCA does not abrogate the willful blindness doctrine. Based on the information reflected in the opinion, do you think that YouTube willfully blinded itself to specific instances of infringing content on its website? What do you make of the fact that Viacom allegedly uploaded clips from some its shows for promotional purposes?

Record companies pursued similar allegations against Vimeo, a website offering user-generated content like YouTube. In *Capitol Records, LLC v. Vimeo, LLC*, 826 F.3d 78 (2d Cir. 2016), the Second Circuit ruled that "learn[ing] facts raising a *suspicion* of infringement (as opposed to facts making infringement *obvious*)" (emphasis in original) does not trigger an obligation to investigate possible infringement; to do so would vitiate § 512(m)'s "no duty to monitor" limitation on liability. The court further reasoned that sporadic instances (amongst millions of posted videos) in which Vimeo employees may have encouraged users to post infringing videos cannot support an allegation of generalized encouragement of infringement that would strip Vimeo of § 512(m)'s "no duty to monitor" limitation.

4. *"At the Direction of the User."* Some social media platforms invite users to develop their own channels or thematic communities. Do unpaid "moderators" bring

such websites outside of the § 512(c) safe harbor? How should courts determine whether web-postings are "at the direction of the user" as opposed to the OSP? *See Mavrix Photographs, LLC v. LiveJournal, Inc.*, 853 F.3d 1020 (9th Cir. 2017) (applying common law agency principles to assess whether unpaid website moderators who ran thematic communities and made discretionary judgments about what to post were agents of the LiveJournal platform); *cf. Ventura Content, Ltd. v. Motherless, Inc.*, 885 F.3d 597 (9th Cir. 2018) (holding that review of uploaded material uploaded solely for compliance with legal requirements (and without any discretionary judgment) does not bar access to the § 512(c) safe harbor on the ground that the material is not posted at the direction of users).

5. *Reconciling Vicarious Liability with* § 512(c)(1)(B). The court concludes that the "right and ability to control" infringing activity under § 512(c)(1)(B) must "require[] something more than the ability to remove or block access to materials posted on a service provider's website." Otherwise it would be coextensive with common law vicarious liability, making its inclusion in the statute superfluous. But what is the something more?

6. *Volition Requirement: Does § 512 Codify or Supplant* Netcom? Although an early draft of the DMCA safe harbor provisions incorporated "*Netcom*'s protections," *see CoStar Group, Inc. v. LoopNet, Inc.*, 373 F.3d 544, 554 n.* (4th Cir. 2004) (citing legislative history), the § 512 provisions ultimately enacted differentiate among four distinct protected activities, each with their own eligibility requirements. *See* NIMMER ON COPYRIGHT § 12B.06[B]. The statute expressly contemplates volition in the transmission (§ 512(a)) and caching (§ 512(b)) activities, but does not discuss volition as it applies to the storage (§ 512(c)) and linking (§ 512(d)) safe harbors. Thus, the continuing applicability of *Netcom*'s volitional requirement as a shield to OSP liability for storing infringing material and linking to infringing material is open to question. *See* Robert C. Denicola, *Volition and Copyright Infringement*, 37 CARDOZO L. REV. 1259, 1270–84 (2016). But courts have treated volition as an element of copyright infringement, which must be shown for liability whether or not the safe harbor applies. *See, e.g., Perfect 10, Inc. v. Giganews, Inc.*, 847 F.3d 657 (9th Cir. 2017). Under this logic, a company not engaged in volitional acts is not infringing copyright and does not need a safe harbor.

The issue had direct bearing on *Cartoon Network LP, LLLP v. CSC Holdings, Inc.*, 536 F.3d 121 (2d Cir. 2008), where motion picture copyright owners alleged that Cablevision, a cable television provider, directly infringed their works by storing copies on a server-based (remote storage) digital video recorder system (RS-DVR). Cablevision offered customers the option of recording television programs for later viewing in its cloud-based storage system. It defended the infringement action on the ground that the system was automated and hence the content owners could not establish volition on Cablevision's part.[33] The Second Circuit agreed: "We do not believe that an

---

[33] Cartoon Network did not allege indirect infringement out of concern that a court might rule that consumers were insulated from liability by the *Sony* staple article of commerce doctrine.

RS-DVR customer is sufficiently distinguishable from a VCR user to impose liability as a direct infringer on a different party for copies that are made automatically upon that customer's command . . . [V]olitional conduct is an important element of direct liability." 536 F.3d at 131.

More recently, the operator of a photograph-sharing website (Polyvore.com) asserted that it could not be held liable for direct copyright infringement of celebrity photographs posted by users on the ground that it did not act "volitionally": the images appear on "Polyvore's website 'without any interaction by Polyvore's employees' and that '[a]ny subsequent indexing, storage or display . . . is the result of an automated process that stems from the user's initial upload.'" The district court granted Polyvore's motion for summary judgment based on lack of volition under *Cartoon Network*. On appeal, the Second Circuit vacated the district court's decision on the ground there remained dispute whether Polyvore created multiple copies of the plaintiff's photographs that were not requested by Polyvore users. See *BWP Media USA Inc. v. Polyvore, Inc.*, 922 F.3d 42, 44 (2d Cir. 2019). The panel grappled with but ultimately sidestepped whether volition is a separate requirement for direct copyright infringement or an aspect of a causation inquiry. Each panel member filed a concurring opinion discussing the volition issue.

Judge Jon O. Newman framed the question as follows:

> The ultimate issue on this appeal, of increasing importance in the age of digital transmissions, concerns the circumstances under which a developer or operator of a computer system or program, activated by its customers, can be liable for direct infringement of a copyright. . . .

> An initial issue posed by *Netcom*'s "volition or causation" phrase is whether the words "volition" and "causation" are synonyms or alternatives. Long before *Netcom*, there was no doubt that when the identity of a person liable for direct infringement was disputed, it was necessary to prove who caused the infringement. Infringement is a tort, as this Court long ago recognized, *see American Code Co. v. Bensinger*, 282 F. 829, 834 (2d Cir. 1922); *Ted Browne Music Co. v. Fowler*, 290 F. 751, 754 (2d Cir. 1923), and no person may be held liable for any tort unless that person (alone or with others) has caused the injury for which a claim is made. "Volition" in Judge Whyte's phrase is best understood to mean a concept essentially reflecting tort law causation. *See* 4 NIMMER ON COPYRIGHT § 13.08[C][1], at 13-290.6 ("*Netcom* simply stands for the unremarkable proposition that proximate causation historically underlines copyright infringement liability no less than other torts."). . . . [A]s the NIMMER treatise makes clear, "causation," in the context of copyright infringement, is tort law "proximate cause," rather than "but for" causation. *See id.*; Robert C. Denicola, *Volition and Copyright Infringement*, 37 CARDOZO L. REV. 1259, 1268 (2016). However, in this context, "[u]nlike 'legal' or 'proximate' cause, 'causation' is not invoked in *Netcom* to evaluate the connection between the tort and the plaintiff's harm, but instead to analyze the connection between the defendant's actions and the commission of the tort. Judge Whyte was concerned

with whether the defendants 'caused' the infringement, not whether the infringement 'caused' the plaintiff's injury." *Id.* at 1269. . . .

[T]here is language in *Cartoon Network* that I question: "In determining who actually 'makes' a copy, a significant difference exists between making a request *to a human employee*, who then volitionally operates the copying system to make the copy, and issuing a command directly to a system, which automatically obeys commands and engages in no volitional conduct." *Id.* at 131 (emphasis added). I agree there is a difference, but the stark alternatives posed by this sentence create the risk that it will be overread to mean that only a human being who operates a copying system, for example, in a copy shop, can satisfy the volition/causation requirement and render the copy shop liable for infringement, and that the person or entity that designs and or operates a system that makes one or more copies when it "automatically obeys commands" cannot be liable for infringement. . . .

Pertinent to the possible infringement liability of the operator of a system that facilitates automatic copying, the legislative history of the 1976 Copyright Act recognized that "where the work was infringed by two or more tort feasors [*sic*], the bill would make them jointly and severally liable." "There is no rule of copyright law that would preclude the imposition of direct liability on both parties [i.e., the system operator and the user]." Denicola, 37 CARDOZO L. REV. at 1273.

However, tort law principles of causation do not necessarily apply in the copyright field exactly as they apply with respect to torts generally or joint tortfeasor liability in particular. In addition to assuring protection for the rights of copyright owners in order to promote creativity, copyright law, especially in the digital age, must avoid such an expansive regime of protection that developers of computer programs and system operators are unduly deterred from making socially useful contributions to widespread access to information.

The caselaw has not yet developed clear principles for determining when the developer or operator of a system, activated automatically by a user, is jointly liable with the user for direct infringement. . . .

I disagree with Judge Walker's opinion when it appears to indicate that all developers or operators of systems that make copies, at a customer's keystroke command, of copyrighted materials selected by the customer should be insulated from direct liability for infringement. Selection by the customer may well be relevant to determining whether system developers or operators share direct liability with a customer, but is not necessarily determinative.

BWP Media USA Inc. v. Polyvore, Inc., 922 F.3d 42, 61-67 (2d Cir. 2019) (Newman, J., concurring).

Judge John Walker defended the volition requirement in his concurrence. He noted that volition has textual underpinnings in the Copyright Act, *see id.* at 53 (citing *Aereo*, 573 U.S. at 453 (Scalia, J., dissenting)), and emphasized that "direct liability is not the only avenue for recovery against an ISP for copyright infringement. Secondary liability exists precisely to impose liability on defendants who, while not directly responsible for infringing conduct, still should be held liable." *Id.* He noted that "[t]he distinction between direct and secondary liability would collapse if there were not a clear rule for determining whether the defendant committed the infringing act. The volitional-conduct requirement supplies that rule; its purpose is not to excuse defendants from accountability, but to channel the claims against them into the correct analytical track." *Id.* at 54 (quoting *Aereo*, 573 U.S. at 455 ((Scalia, J., dissenting)). Judge Rosemary Pooler opined that "volitional-conduct analysis must enter the landscape of multiple devices, mindful of both our copy-shop past and the realities of functional website design in our present."

7. *User-Generated Content Principles.* Several content owners and UGC sites jointly announced the Principles for UGC Services as a voluntary, market-based approach to limiting online piracy in 2007. *See* PRINCIPLES FOR USER GENERATED CONTENT SERVICES http://www.ugcprinciples.com. This set of best practices includes the use of "effective content identification technology ("Identification Technology") with the goal of eliminating from . . . infringing user-uploaded audio and video content for which Copyright Owners have provided Reference Material." Although Google did not formally join this initiative, the ContentID system that it implemented for YouTube largely follows the UGC Principles model. For this reason, the *Viacom* lawsuit did not seek prospective relief, although they were seeking roughly $10 billion in statutory damages. Rather, it only sought damages for the period prior to implementation of these measures. Given YouTube's prominence and the use of filtering technology by other UGC websites, can it now be said that content identification is now a "standard technical measure," one of the requirements for eligibility for the § 512(c) safe harbor? Section 512(i) defines a "standard technical measure" as a:

> technical measure[] that [is] used by copyright owners to identify or protect copyrighted works and—
>
> > (A) ha[s] been developed pursuant to a broad consensus of copyright owners and service providers in an open, fair, voluntary, multi-industry standards process;
> >
> > (B) [is] available to any person on reasonable and nondiscriminatory terms; and
> >
> > (C) do[es] not impose substantial costs on service providers or substantial burdens on their systems or networks.

See Lauren G. Gallo, *Note, The (Im)possibility of "Standard Technical Measures" for UGC Websites*, 34 COLUM. J.L. & ARTS 283 (2011). Content identification technology is available from several vendors. Professors Sonia K. Katyal and Jason M. Schultz question whether technological filters can adequately balance fair use concerns. *See* Sonia K. Katyal & Jason M. Schultz, *The Unending Search for the Optimal Infringement Filter*, 12 COLUM. L. REV. SIDEBAR 83 (2012). But can the failure to use any such technology be responsible under today's conditions? *See* Peter S. Menell,

Jumping the Grooveshark: A Case Study in DMCA Safe Harbor Abuse (Dec. 2011), http://papers.ssrn.com/sol3/papers.cfm?abstract_id=1975579. If so, it may be difficult for some startups to enter the market, since they cannot easily develop the expensive monitoring systems designed by large companies like YouTube, whose ContentID system cost hundreds of millions of dollars. Or they may need to license filtering technology from other start-ups, such as Audible Magic.

8. *Terminating Repeat Infringers.* The DMCA imposes responsibilities upon OSPs that seek to obtain the benefits of the specified safe harbors. In addition to meeting the three threshold requirements, they must reasonably implement a policy of terminating repeat infringers. Several cases explore the ambiguities of the statute, including the problematic question of who is a repeat infringer. *See BMG Rights Management (US) LLC v. Cox Communications, Inc.*, 881 F.3d 293 (4th Cir. 2018) (holding that ISP did not implement its repeat infringer policy in a consistent or meaningful way, thereby losing protection of the § 512 safe harbor); *Ellison v. Robertson*, 357 F.3d 1072 (9th Cir. 2004); *see generally* David Nimmer, *Repeat Infringers*, 52 J. COPYRIGHT SOC'Y U.S.A. 167 (2005).

9. *Counter Notification and Putback.* OSPs are exempt from liability for the good faith removal of allegedly infringing material. This immunity is subject to their compliance with the notification and counter-notification procedure. In order to protect users' rights, the OSP must promptly notify users that material has been blocked or removed. The user may then provide a "counter notification" stating that the material may properly be stored, which the OSP must promptly pass along to the copyright owner. If the user provides a counter notification contesting the takedown request, the OSP is required to replace the disputed content unless the copyright owner sues the uploader within 14 days of the counter notification. If the copyright owner does not file suit against the uploader within a designated period, the OSP must restore the material. It may replace the disputed material after 10 days if the copyright owner has not filed a lawsuit but is required to restore it within 14 business days of the counter notification if no lawsuit is filed against the uploader. § 512(g)(2). In practice, however, an OSP may disregard the counter notification and instead rely on its terms of service to shield itself from liability to its customer.

10. *Erroneous Takedown Notices—§ 512(f).* The DMCA has aroused concern that copyright owners might use overly aggressive tactics or misrepresentations to suppress free speech or other legal activities. *See* Jennifer M. Urban, Joe Karaganis and Brianna L. Schofield, *Notice and Takedown in Everyday Practice* (Mar. 29, 2016), (noting "surprisingly high percentages of [takedown] notices of questionable validity, with mistakes made by both 'bots' and humans"). To deter such misuse of the takedown procedure, § 512(f) provides for damages, including costs and attorney's fees, for knowing misrepresentation that material or activity is infringing. Courts apply a subjective standard for determining whether a takedown notice was propounded in "good faith." *Rossi v. Motion Picture Association of America*, 391 F.3d 1000, 1004 (9th Cir. 2004); *Online Policy Group v. Diebold, Inc.*, 337 F. Supp. 2d 1195 (N.D. Cal. 2004) (finding "knowing misrepresentation" in takedown request and awarding damages and

attorney's fees pursuant to § 512(f)). A copyright owner must consider whether the use is fair under § 107 before filing a takedown request. *See Lenz v. Universal Music Corp.*, 572 F. Supp. 2d 1150 (9th Cir. 2015). Liability for misrepresentation turns on the copyright owner's subjective good faith belief that the use is not fair, not an objective "reasonableness" standard. *See id.*

11. *Applicability of the DMCA Safe Harbor to Pre-1972 Sound Recordings.* The Second Circuit held that notwithstanding the § 301 preservation of state law protections for pre-1972 source recordings, the DMCA's online service provider safe harbors insulate service providers for liability for state law copyright violations. *See Capitol Records, LLC v. Vimeo, LLC*, 826 F.3d 78 (2d Cir. 2016). While recognizing the Copyright Office's expertise in copyright law, the court nonetheless declined to follow the Copyright Office's contrary interpretation of the DMCA. *See* UNITED STATES COPYRIGHT OFFICE, FEDERAL COPYRIGHT PROTECTION FOR PRE-1972 SOUND RECORDINGS 5 (2011), available at http://copyright.gov/docs/sound/pre-72-report.pdf.

PROBLEM

Problem IV-57. Real Estate Net offers local independent real estate agents an inexpensive means for posting real estate listings to a large searchable online database. To post a listing, subscribers fill out an online form and agree to "Terms and Conditions" that include a promise not to post copies of photographs without authorization. The subscriber then transmits the text of the listing and any applicable photographs to Real Estate Net. The text gets posted immediately, while the photograph goes into a temporary folder. Within 48 hours, a Real Estate Net employee reviews the photograph to determine whether the photograph in fact depicts commercial real estate and to identify any obvious evidence, such as a copyright notice, that the photograph may have been copyrighted by another. If the photograph fails either one of these criteria, the employee deletes the photograph and notifies the subscriber. Otherwise, the employee clicks an "accept" button that uploads the photograph to Real Estate Net's website.

National Realtors, Inc. (NRI) maintains a large online database of real estate information, including photographs to which it holds copyright. NRI's online customers agree not to post its photographs on other websites. Notwithstanding such agreements, NRI discovered approximately 100 of its copyrighted photographs among the nearly 50,000 photographs posted on Real Estate Net's website. With regard to 25 of the photographs in question, NRI has sent letters to Real Estate Net demanding that the specific works be removed, to which Real Estate Net has promptly complied. NRI has also made general allegations of infringement and mentioned the names of several real estate agents that have posted photographs without authorization.

Please advise Real Estate Net on any potential copyright liability based on the above facts. In addition, please identify any steps that Real Estate Net might take to reduce its exposure to liability in the future.

3. Other Defenses

In addition to statutory defenses (§§ 108–18) and the fair use doctrine (§ 107), there are a number of other defenses against a claim of copyright infringement. Many of these are straightforward, and the reader has no doubt encountered similar defenses elsewhere in the law. The most significant defenses include:

i. *Independent Creation*

A defendant may present evidence to prove that he or she created the work independently.

ii. *Consent/License*

A defendant may defend a copyright action on the ground that he or she has the copyright owner's permission to make use of the protected material. Note that § 204 requires transfers of copyright ownership to be executed in writing and signed by the copyright owner. Nonexclusive licenses, however, need not be in writing.

iii. *Inequitable Conduct*

Closely related to copyright invalidity, the inequitable conduct doctrine parallels the patent law defense of inequitable conduct discussed in Chapter III. Inequitable conduct occurs when a copyright owner obtains a copyright through fraud or other deceptive conduct on the Copyright Office—for example, by failing to disclose the owner's own plagiarism of a prior work. Circumstances that give rise to inequitable conduct generally also render copyrights invalid, but the defense is distinct because some of the consequences may be different.

iv. *Copyright Misuse*

As copyright has expanded into the realm of technological products   most notably, computer software—courts have become increasingly sensitive to the ways in which copyright protection may be leveraged to undermine free competition. In 1990, a court held that a software licensing agreement that prohibited a licensee from developing any kind of computer-assisted die-making software for a term of 99 years constituted misuse, rendering the copyright unenforceable until the improper effects of the overreaching had been purged. *See Lasercomb America, Inc. v. Reynolds*, 911 F.2d 970 (4th Cir. 1990); *see also DSC, Inc. v. DGI, Inc.*, 81 F.3d 597 (5th Cir. 1996); *Practice Management Info. Corp. v. American Medical Ass'n*, 121 F.3d 516 (9th Cir. 1997); *Alcatel v. DGI Technologies*, 166 F.3d 772 (5th Cir. 1999); *Assessment Technologies of WI, LLC v. WIREdata, Inc.*, 350 F.3d 640 (7th Cir. 2003); *but see Bellsouth Advertising & Pub. Corp. v. Donnelley Information Pub., Inc.*, 933 F.2d 952, 961 (11th Cir. 1991) (declining to follow *Lasercomb*). Copyright misuse is a blend of antitrust policies and copyright-specific policies against the improper extension of copyrights.

v.   Immoral/Illegal/Obscene Works

Although some early cases refused to enforce copyrights in obscene or otherwise antisocial works, the modern trend rejects such a defense. *See Mitchell Bros. Film Group v. Adult Cinema Theater*, 604 F.2d 852 (9th Cir. 1980) (pornography); *Belcher v. Tarbox*, 486 F.2d 1087 (9th Cir. 1973) (racing forms).

vi.   Statute of Limitations

Section 507 provides a three-year statute of limitations "after the claim accrued." The Supreme Court held in *Petrella v. MGM Inc.*, 134 S.Ct. 1962 (2014) that the doctrine of laches does not generally bar copyright actions, notwithstanding an 18-year delay in filing suit. Therefore, a copyright owner can bring an action for a continuing infringement at any time and recover injunctive relief and damages for three years. The Court noted, however, laches may, "in extraordinary circumstances," curtail the award of equitable relief. The Court cited *Chirco v. Crosswinds Communities, Inc.*, 474 F.3d 227 (2007), where owners of a copyrighted architectural design, although aware of an allegedly infringing housing project, delayed suit until the project was substantially constructed and partially occupied. An order mandating destructin of the project in those circumstances would not be tolerable. The *Petrella* decision rekindles the potential for many copyright infringement actions previously thought barred by laches.

PROBLEM

Problem IV-58. Randy Wolfe was a guitar prodigy. In the summer of 1966, at the age of 15, he performed alongside Jimi Hendrix in Jimi's band, Jimmy James and the Blue Flames, in Greenwich Village clubs. Jimi gave Randy, who hailed from Los Angeles, the nickname Randy "California," which became his stage name. In 1967, Randy formed the psychedelic rock band Spirit. The next year, Randy penned *Taurus*, an instrumental plucked guitar song with a hypnotical sound eerily like Led Zeppelin's iconic *Stairway to Heaven*. Yet Led Zeppelin would not release the rock 'n roll classic until 1971.

Perhaps it was a coincidence. But Spirit in fact played four shows in North America with Led Zeppelin in 1968 and 1969. In fact, Led Zeppelin opened for Spirit at the Denver show. Spirit never hit it big. California expressed his frustration over *Stairway to Heaven* in a 1997 LISTENER MAGAZINE interview: "I [would] say it was a ripoff, . . . [a]nd the guys made millions of bucks on it and never said [t]hank you, never said, '[c]an we pay you some money for it?' It [is] kind of a sore point with me. Maybe someday their conscience will make them do something about it." Unfortunately, Randy died later that year rescuing his 12-year old son from a rip current in Hawaii.

Randy California's estate seeks your advice on bringing a copyright infringement action against Led Zeppelin, their record label, their music publisher, and anyone else profiting from *Stairway to Heaven*.

G. REMEDIES

Copyright law provides for injunctive relief, monetary remedies, and attorney's fees. Furthermore, copyright law includes criminal penalties for intentional acts of infringement for financial gain.

1.   Injunctions

The Copyright Act authorizes courts to issue "temporary" (or preliminary) injunctions and permanent injunctions "on such terms as [they] may deem reasonable to prevent or restrain infringement of a copyright." § 502(a). Furthermore, courts may order the seizure or impoundment of allegedly infringing articles while a copyright case is pending under the authority of § 503(a) (in civil cases) or 18 U.S.C. § 2323 (civil and criminal cases). Those articles may be destroyed or forfeited to the United States after judgment.

Until 2006, courts routinely granted injunctive relief in copyright cases. Preliminary injunctions were generally granted as a matter of course where a plaintiff convinced the court that a finding of infringement was likely. Courts typically presumed the inadequacy of legal remedies on the theory that it would be difficult to "close the door" after an infringing work has been publicly distributed.

This relatively automatic approach to injunctive relief in copyright cases has been replaced by a searching, equitable balancing framework after *eBay*. The Supreme Court pointed in this direction a century ago in affirming a decision refusing to award injunctive relief. *See Dun v. Lumbermen's Credit Ass'n*, 209 U.S. 20, 23–24 (1908). The Supreme Court's decision in *Campbell v. Acuff-Rose Music*, 510 U.S. 569 (1994), emphasized the discretionary nature of injunctive remedies in copyright cases:

> Because the fair use enquiry often requires close questions of judgment as to the extent of permissible borrowing in cases involving parodies (or other critical works), courts may also wish to bear in mind that the goals of the copyright law, "to stimulate the creation and publication of edifying matter," Leval[, *Toward a Fair Use Standard*, 103 HARV. L. REV. 1105,] 1134 [(1990)], are not always best served by automatically granting injunctive relief when parodists are found to have gone beyond the bounds of fair use. *See* 17 U.S.C. § 502(a) (court " *may* . . . grant . . . injunctions on such terms as it may deem reasonable to prevent or restrain infringement") (emphasis added); Leval 1132 (while in the "vast majority of cases, [an injunctive] remedy is justified because most infringements are simple piracy," such cases are "worlds apart from many of those raising reasonable contentions of fair use" where "there may be a strong public interest in the publication of the secondary work [and] the copyright owner's interest may be adequately protected by an award of damages for whatever infringement is found"); *Abend v. MCA, Inc.*, 863 F.2d 1465, 1479 (9th Cir. 1988) (finding "special circumstances" that would cause "great injustice" to defendants and "public injury" were injunction to issue), *aff'd sub nom. Stewart v. Abend*, 495 U.S. 207 (1990).

510 U.S. at 578 n.10. The Supreme Court reinforced this approach in *New York Times Co., Inc. v. Tasini, Inc.*, 533 U.S. 483, 505 (2001) (noting that "it hardly follows from today's decision that an injunction against the inclusion of these Articles in the Databases (much less all freelance articles in any databases) must issue"); *see also Broadcast Music, Inc. v. Columbia Broadcasting System, Inc.*, 441 U.S. 1, 4–6, 10–12 (1979) (recounting history of blanket music licensing regimes and consent decrees governing their operation); *Silverstein v. Penguin Putnam, Inc.*, 368 F.3d 77, 80 (2d Cir. 2004) ("Even if Silverstein's creative contribution to the selection of Mrs. Parker's previously uncollected poems is non-trivial, and even if Penguin's appropriation of it was deliberate, enforcement of his rights by a preliminary or permanent injunction that stops publication of Complete Poems is an abuse of discretion.").

The First Amendment supplies a second principle limiting the award of injunctive relief in copyright cases. Scholars have pointed out the inconsistency between First Amendment prior restraint jurisprudence—barring preliminary injunctions in libel and obscenity cases as unconstitutional—and the availability of such relief in copyright cases. *See* Rebecca Tushnet, *Copy This Essay: How Fair Use Doctrine Harms Free Speech and How Copying Serves It*, 114 YALE L.J. 535 (2004); Jed Rubenfeld, *The Freedom of Imagination: Copyright's Constitutionality*, 112 YALE L.J. (2002); Mark A. Lemley & Eugene Volokh, *Freedom of Speech and Injunctions in Intellectual Property Cases*, 48 DUKE L.J. 147 (1998).

Courts pay heed to this interplay. For example, the court in *Suntrust Bank v. Houghton Mifflin Co.*, 268 F.3d 1257 (11th Cir. 2001), overturned a preliminary injunction against a retelling of the literary classic, GONE WITH THE WIND, from the standpoint of slaves on the Tara plantation in part on this ground. *See also Elvis Presley Enterprises, Inc. v. Passport Video*, 357 F.3d 896, 899 (9th Cir. 2004) ("In a case of this kind involving the biography of a man with an immense following, it is necessary for a court to keep in mind that injunctions are a device of equity and are to be used equitably, and that a court suppressing speech must be aware that it is trenching on a zone made sacred by the First Amendment.").

The Supreme Court's decision in *eBay, Inc. v. MercExchange, LLC*, 547 U.S. 388 (2006), addressing the availability of injunctive relief under the Patent Act, reinforces the essential role of equitable balancing in copyright cases as well:

> According to well-established principles of equity, a plaintiff seeking a permanent injunction must satisfy a four-factor test before a court may grant such relief. A plaintiff must demonstrate: (1) that it has suffered an irreparable injury; (2) that remedies available at law, such as monetary damages, are inadequate to compensate for that injury; (3) that, considering the balance of hardships between the plaintiff and defendant, a remedy in equity is warranted; and (4) that the public interest would not be disserved by a permanent injunction. . . .

> This approach is consistent with our treatment of injunctions under the Copyright Act. Like a patent owner, a copyright holder possesses "the right to

exclude others from using his property." *Fox Film Corp. v. Doyal*, 286 U.S. 123, 127 (1932); *see also id.*, at 127–128 ("A copyright, like a patent, is at once the equivalent given by the public for benefits bestowed by the genius and meditations and skill of individuals, and the incentive to further efforts for the same important objects" (internal quotation marks omitted)). Like the Patent Act, the Copyright Act provides that courts "may" grant injunctive relief "on such terms as it may deem reasonable to prevent or restrain infringement of a copyright." 17 U.S.C. § 502(a). And as in our decision today, this Court has consistently rejected invitations to replace traditional equitable considerations with a rule that an injunction automatically follows a determination that a copyright has been infringed. *See*, e.g., *New York Times Co. v. Tasini*, 533 U.S. 483, 505 (2001) (citing *Campbell v. Acuff-Rose Music, Inc.*, 510 U.S. 569, 578, n.10 (1994)); *Dun v. Lumbermen's Credit Assn.*, 209 U.S. 20, 23–24 (1908).

eBay Inc. v. MercExchange, LLC, 547 U.S. 388, 391–92 (2006); *see also Perfect 10, Inc. v. Google, Inc.*, 653 F.3d 976, 981 (9th Cir. 2011) (concluding that the circuit's "longstanding rule that '[a] showing of a reasonable likelihood of success on the merits in a copyright infringement claim raises a presumption of irreparable harm' 'is clearly irreconcilable with the reasoning' of the [Supreme] Court's decision in *eBay* and has therefore been 'effectively overruled'" in favor of the traditional four-factor framework (citations omitted)); *Salinger v. Colting*, 607 F.3d 68, 75, 79 (2d Cir. 2010) (same); *TD Bank v. Hill*, 928 F.3d 259 (3d Cir. 2019) (same).

As in the patent field, the Supreme Court's *eBay* decision has produced a sea change in the consideration of requests for injunctive relief in the copyright field. *See* Richard Dannay, *Copyright Injunctions and Fair Use: Enter* eBay—*Four-Factor Fatigue or Four-Factor Freedom?*, 55 J. COPYRIGHT SOC'Y U.S.A. 449 (2008). This does not mean, however, that injunctive relief will become the exception in copyright cases. Injunctions will remain readily available in "simple piracy" cases, although less likely where there the defendant contributes transformative creativity or engages in political or social commentary. This may be especially true where the copyright owner refuses to license his or her work.

PROBLEMS

Problem IV-59. Lebbeus, a writer and artist, writes a surrealist novel that features an elaborate, futuristic torture chamber with a distinctive chair attached to moving rails on a wall. He draws a picture of the chair and uses it to illustrate the cover of his novel. Pinnacle Entertainment, a major movie studio, releases *Seven Apes*, a science-fiction movie whose plot is entirely unlike Lebbeus's novel, but which in one 90-second scene features a chair on rails strikingly similar to the one on the book cover. Assume that the court determines that Pinnacle has copied the chair from Lebbeus, and that it has no legal defense. What is the appropriate remedy? Should Lebbeus be entitled to enjoin distribution of *Seven Apes*? How would a court determine the appropriate share of profits from the movie?

Problem IV-60. Recall *Problem IV-30* addressing alleged infringement of J.D. Salinger's letters by biographer, Ian Hamilton. Suppose that the court found the biography to infringe Salinger's letters. Salinger steadfastly refused to license use of the letters. How should a court rule on Salinger's request for a permanent injunction barring publication of Hamilton's biography in the aftermath of the eBay decision?

Problem IV-61. Margaret Wise Brown wrote and Clement Hurd illustrated GOODNIGHT MOON, a children's bedtime story, in 1947. It became a timeless classic, easing generation after generation of children to sleep. Its refrain "Goodnight room. Goodnight moon. Goodnight cow jumping over the moon. Goodnight light, and the red balloon . . ." will bring instant recognition and a smile to millions of parents and children. It is featured in the 1990 film Kindergarten Cop, where Arnold Schwarzenegger as Detective John Kimble reads this book to the kids in kindergarten before their afternoon nap. In the closing year of the Bush Administration, Erich Origen and Gan Golan wrote GOODNIGHT BUSH (2008), exploring the travails of the George W. Bush administration. Suppose the copyright owners sue to enjoin the book and that a district court in the Ninth Circuit, applying the precedent set in *Dr. Seuss Enters., L.P. v. Penguin Books USA, Inc.*, 109 F.3d 1394 (9th Cir. 1997) (drawing a stark line in fair use analysis between parody, in the copyrighted work is the target (and hence use is necessary for commentary), and satire, in which the copyrighted work is merely a vehicle to poke fun at another target (and hence requires greater justification for borrowing)), determines that GOODNIGHT BUSH infringes GOODNIGHT MOON and does not qualify as fair use. What remedy should the court award?

Problem IV-62. Suppose that a documentary filmmaker finds a photograph for use in her project. After painstaking efforts to identify the copyright owner prove unsuccessful, she incorporates the image in her film. It provides the backdrop for critical elements of the work. Upon release of the film, which draws critical acclaim, the photographer surfaces and sues to enjoin use of the image. Assuming that the use is found to be infringing and not a fair use, what remedy should be ordered? Does your analysis or conclusion change if the filmmaker made no effort to identify the copyright owner?

2. Damages

Not all aspects of copyright law follow the property rule model. As we have seen, the fair use doctrine absolves the defendant of any responsibility to compensate the copyright owner, although the amount of harm plays a role in determining whether the defense succeeds. As we also have discussed, there are a number of other provisions for compulsory licensing in copyright law.

Where injunctions are replaced by a liability rule, or where the defendant has infringed before an injunction can be entered, copyright law authorizes the copyright owner to collect either actual damages and profits (defined as the loss to the copyright holder plus additional profits made by the infringer) or statutory damages. § 504.

i. *Actual Damages and Profits*

Actual damages can include lost revenue and indirect damage attributable to the infringing conduct, both of which can be difficult to prove. As a result, copyright owners often seek to disgorge the defendants' profits or, where the work has been timely registered, elect statutory damages. The following case lays out the principal framework and burdens in establishing the infringer's profits.

Sheldon v. Metro-Goldwyn Pictures Corp.
Supreme Court of the United States
309 U.S. 390 (1940)

MR. CHIEF JUSTICE HUGHES delivered the opinion of the Court.

The questions presented are whether, in computing an award of profits against an infringer of a copyright, there may be an apportionment so as to give to the owner of the copyright only that part of the profits found to be attributable to the use of the copyrighted material as distinguished from what the infringer himself has supplied, and, if so, whether the evidence affords a proper basis for the apportionment decreed in this case.

Petitioners' complaint charged infringement of their play "Dishonored Lady" by respondents' motion picture "Letty Lynton," and sought an injunction and an accounting of profits. The Circuit Court of Appeals, reversing the District Court, found and enjoined the infringement and directed an accounting. 81 F.2d 49. Thereupon the District Court confirmed with slight modifications the report of a special master which awarded to petitioners all the net profits made by respondents from their exhibitions of the motion picture, amounting to $587,604.37. 26 F. Supp. 134, 136. The Circuit Court of Appeals reversed, holding that there should be an apportionment and fixing petitioners' share of the net profits at one-fifth. 106 F.2d 45, 51. In view of the importance of the question, which appears to be one of first impression in the application of the copyright law, we granted certiorari. December 4, 1939.

Petitioners' play "Dishonored Lady" was based upon the trial in Scotland, in 1857, of Madeleine Smith for the murder of her lover,—a *cause celebre* included in the series of "Notable British Trials" which was published in 1927. The play was copyrighted as an unpublished work in 1930, and was produced here and abroad. Respondents took the title of their motion picture "Letty Lynton" from a novel of that name written by an English author, Mrs. Belloc Lowndes, and published in 1930. That novel was also based upon the story of Madeleine Smith and the motion picture rights were bought by respondents. There had been negotiations for the motion picture rights in petitioners' play, and the price had been fixed at $30,000, but these negotiations fell through.

As the Court of Appeals found, respondents in producing the motion picture in question worked over old material; "the general skeleton was already in the public demesne. A wanton girl kills her lover to free herself for a better match; she is brought to trial for the murder and escapes." [106 F.2d 50.] But not content with the mere use of that basic plot, respondents resorted to petitioners' copyrighted play. They were not innocent offenders. From comparison and analysis, the Court of Appeals concluded that they had "deliberately lifted the play"; their "borrowing was a deliberate plagiarism." It is from that standpoint that we approach the questions now raised.

Respondents contend that the material taken by infringement contributed in but a small measure to the production and success of the motion picture. They say that they themselves contributed the main factors in producing the large net profits; that is, the popular actors, the scenery, and the expert producers and directors. Both courts below have sustained this contention.

The District Court thought it "punitive and unjust" to award all the net profits to petitioners. The court said that, if that were done, petitioners would receive the profits that the "motion picture stars" had made for the picture "by their dramatic talent and the drawing power of their reputations." "The directors who supervised the production of the picture and the experts who filmed it also contributed in piling up these tremendous net profits." The court thought an allowance to petitioners of 25 percent of these profits "could be justly fixed as a limit beyond which complainants would be receiving profits in no way attributable to the use of their play in the production of the picture." But, though holding these views, the District Court awarded all the net profits to petitioners, feeling bound by the decision of the Court of Appeals in *Dam v. Kirk La Shelle Co.*, 175 F. 902, 903, a decision which the Court of Appeals has now overruled.

The Court of Appeals was satisfied that but a small part of the net profits was attributable to the infringement, and, fully recognizing the difficulty in finding a satisfactory standard, the court decided that there should be an apportionment and that it could fairly be made. The court was resolved "to avoid the one certainly unjust course of giving the plaintiffs everything, because the defendants cannot with certainty compute their own share." The court would not deny "the one fact that stands undoubted," and, making the best estimate it could, it fixed petitioners' share at one-fifth of the net profits, considering that to be a figure "which will favor the plaintiffs in every reasonable chance of error."

Petitioners stress the provision for recovery of "all" the profits, but this is plainly qualified by the words "which the infringer shall have made from such infringement." This provision in purpose is cognate to that for the recovery of "such damages as the copyright proprietor may have suffered due to the infringement." The purpose is thus to provide just compensation for the wrong, not to impose a penalty by giving to the copyright proprietor profits which are not attributable to the infringement.

Prior to the Copyright Act of 1909, there had been no statutory provision for the recovery of profits, but that recovery had been allowed in equity both in copyright and patent cases as appropriate equitable relief incident to a decree for an injunction. *Stevens v. Gladding*, 17 How. 447, 455. That relief had been given in accordance with the principles governing equity jurisdiction, not to inflict punishment but to prevent an unjust enrichment by allowing injured complainants to claim "that which, *ex aequo et bono*, is theirs, and nothing beyond this." *Livingston v. Woodworth*, 15 How. 546, 560. *See Root v. Railway Co.*, 105 U.S. 189, 194, 195. Statutory provision for the recovery of profits in patent cases was enacted in 1870. The principle which was applied both prior to this statute and later was thus stated in the leading case of *Tilghman v. Proctor*, 125 U.S. 136, 146:

> The infringer is liable for actual, not for possible gains. The profits, therefore, which he must account for, are not those which he might reasonably have made, but those which he did make, by the use of the plaintiff's invention; or, in other words, the fruits of the advantage which he derived from the use of that invention, over what he would have had in using other means then open to the public and adequate to enable him to obtain an equally beneficial result. If there was no such advantage in his use of the plaintiff's invention, there can be no decree for profits, and the plaintiff's only remedy is by an action at law for damages. . . .

Petitioners stress the point that respondents have been found guilty of deliberate plagiarism, but we perceive no ground for saying that in awarding profits to the copyright proprietor as a means of compensation, the court may make an award of profits which have been shown not to be due to the infringement. That would be not to do equity but to inflict an unauthorized penalty. To call the infringer a trustee *ex maleficio* merely indicates "a mode of approach and an imperfect analogy by which the wrongdoer will be made to hand over the proceeds of his wrong." *Larson Co. v. Wrigley Co.*, 277 U.S. 97, 99, 100. He is in the position of one who has confused his own gains with those which belong to another. *Westinghouse Co. v. Wagner Co., supra*, p. 618. He "must yield the gains begotten of his wrong." *Duplate Corp. v. Triplex Co.*, 298 U.S. 448, 457. Where there is a commingling of gains, he must abide the consequences, unless he can make a separation of the profits so as to assure to the injured party all that justly belongs to him. When such an apportionment has been fairly made, the copyright proprietor receives all the profits which have been gained through the use of the infringing material and that is all that the statute authorizes and equity sanctions.

Both courts below have held in this case that but a small part of the profits were due to the infringement, and, accepting that fact and the principle that an apportionment may be had if the evidence justifies it, we pass to the consideration of the basis of the actual apportionment which has been allowed.

The controlling fact in the determination of the apportionment was that the profits had been derived, not from the mere performance of a copyrighted play, but from the exhibition of a motion picture which had its distinctive profit-making features, apart from the use of any infringing material, by reason of the expert and creative operations involved in its production and direction. In that aspect the case has a certain resemblance to that of a patent infringement, where the infringer has created profits by the addition of non-infringing and valuable improvements. And, in this instance, it plainly appeared that what respondents had contributed accounted for by far the larger part of their gains. . . .

COMMENTS AND QUESTIONS

1. Does *Sheldon* unfairly prevent copyright owners from prohibiting access to their works? Consider the case of private diaries that are published. Might not the injury to the author in some cases exceed the profits of the publisher? Section 504(a) attempts to take care of this problem by allowing the copyright owner to recover both his actual losses and any additional profits incurred by the infringer, so long as the copyright owner does not thereby obtain a "double recovery."

2. Is it reasonable to draw a distinction between "counterfeiting" a work—that is, copying it in its entirety for profit—and infringing the copyright through another means (say, by writing a substantially similar screenplay)? Should counterfeiting be punished more severely than other forms of infringement? In 1982, Congress passed the Piracy and Counterfeiting Amendments Act, 18 U.S.C. §§ 2318–19. The Act makes it a felony to "knowingly traffic" in counterfeit phonorecords or audiovisual works and sets fines of up to $250,000 and prison terms of up to five years.

3. *Imputed License Fee/Reasonable Royalty.* As we saw earlier, the Patent Act sets a lower bound for damages at a reasonable royalty. 35 U.S.C. § 284. The Copyright Act contains no analogous provision. Yet in cases where the copyright owner could not adequately prove actual damages or gain to the infringer and the copyright owner did not timely register the work (and hence could not elect statutory damages), they have sought to recover an imputed license fee. The court in *Deltak, Inc. v. Advanced Systems, Inc.*, 767 F.2d 357 (7th Cir. 1985), interpreted actual damages to include the "value of use" to the defendant so as to avoid the harsh result of no recovery. The Second Circuit, after initially questioning that theory, *see Business Trends Analysts, Inc. v. Freedonia Group, Inc.*, 887 F.2d 399 (2d Cir. 1989), has now approved it, *see Davis v. The Gap, Inc.*, 246 F.3d 152, 161 (2d Cir. 2001). The Ninth Circuit in *Mackie v. Rieser*, 296 F.3d 909 (9th Cir. 2002), held that the market value at the time of infringement is determined by answering the hypothetical query concerning "what a willing buyer would have been reasonably required to pay to a willing seller" for the infringed work. *See also Oracle Corp. v. SAP AG*, 765 F.3d 1081 (9th Cir. 2014) (rejecting argument that the plaintiff must show that the copyright holder would have agreed to license the work in order to claim a lost licensing fee; noting that "[h]ypothetical-license damages assume rather than require the existence of a willing seller and buyer"); *Polar Bear Prods., Inc. v. Timex Corp.*, 384 F.3d 700, 709 (9th Cir. 2004) (sustaining a jury verdict of $315,000 in lost license fees, renewal fees, and lost profits as within the range of reasonable market value where the infringer declined to pay the copyright owner a fee of $37,500 for video footage).

Recall the problems that have arisen in the calculation of reasonable royalties in the patent context. *See* Chapter III(G)(ii)(2). Does determination of reasonable royalties in copyright cases pose the same sorts of problems?

4. *Punitive Damages.* Almost all courts have held that punitive damages are not available for copyright infringement. Such a requirement goes beyond the restitutionary nature of copyright law. *See Bucklew v. Hawkins, Ash, Baptie & Co.*, 329 F.3d 923,

931–32 (7th Cir. 2003). "The public policy rationale for punitive damages of punishing and preventing malicious conduct can be properly accounted for in the provisions for increasing a maximum statutory damage award" in cases of willful infringement. *Id.* at 177. The one case to leave open the possibility of punitive damages, *TVT Records v. Island Def Jam Music Group*, 262 F. Supp. 2d 185, 187 (S.D.N.Y. 2003), rests on a questionable foundation. But in some cases the availability of statutory damages may have the same effect, since a plaintiff can recover up to $150,000 per work infringed even if the work in question was worth only a few dollars and was copied only once.

ii.   *Statutory Damages*

From the nation's founding, Congress has provided for the award of statutory damages for copyright infringements. As Congress explained in the lead-up to the 1976 Copyright Act, the "need for this special remedy arises from the acknowledged inadequacy of actual damages and profits in many cases" due to the inherent difficulties of detecting and proving copyright damages. *See* U.S. Copyright Office, REPORT OF THE REGISTER OF COPYRIGHTS ON THE GENERAL REVISION OF THE U.S. COPYRIGHT LAW 102 (July 1961). Congress focused on the challenges faced by music composers and publishers in enforcing their public performance rights. *See id.* at 103 ("[i]n many cases, especially those involving public performances, the only direct loss that could be proven is the amount of a license fee. An award of such an amount would be an invitation to infringe with no risk to the infringer.") The threat of statutory damages motivated public performance venues to obtain ASCAP, BMI, and SESAC blanket licenses.

Copyright owners who register their copyright prior to infringement (or within three months of publication) may elect, at any time prior to the entry of judgment, to forgo recovering actual damages and profits and obtain statutory damages. §§ 412, 504(c)(1).

With the growing risk of online infringement, Congress ramped up statutory damage levels. *See* Digital Theft Deterrence and Copyright Damages Improvement Act of 1999, Pub. L. No. 106-160, 113 Stat. 1774. Under current law, copyright owners who register their copyright prior to infringement (or within three months of publication) may elect, at any time prior to the entry of judgment, to forgo recovering actual damages and profits and obtain statutory damages. Where the plaintiff has not proved that the defendant intentionally infringed, the court must award between $750 and $30,000 per infringed work. § 504(c)(1). The lower bound falls to $200 where the infringer establishes that he or she was not aware and had no reason to believe that his or her acts constituted infringement. § 504(c)(2). Where willful infringement is established, the upper bound rises to $150,000 per infringed work. § 504(c)(2).

The statute provides little in the way of guidelines for determining the statutory damage level. In practice, judges have based the statutory damage award on various factors, such as the harm to the copyright owner and gain to the defendant. Courts tend to increase these levels where the defendant willfully infringed and decrease from this level when the defendant acted innocently. The uncertainty surrounding these awards has been magnified by the Supreme Court's ruling in *Feltner v. Columbia Pictures*

Television, 523 U.S. 340 (1998), holding that under the Seventh Amendment, copyright owners have a right to a jury determination of the statutory damages amount.

COMMENTS AND QUESTIONS

1. *Statutory Damages in the Internet Age.* The statutory damages provision, enacted prior to the Internet age, has become controversial in an era where potentially thousands of works can be infringed at the press of a button. This can produce massive monetary rewards in contexts in which actual harm and profits are disproportionately modest. For example, in *UMG Recordings, Inc. v. MP3.com, Inc.*, 92 F. Supp. 2d 349 (S.D.N.Y. 2000), the court assessed a streaming music locker service (MyMP3.com)—which enabled subscribers to develop a virtual online music locker from which they could access sound recordings copied and stored on MP3.com's servers from any Internet portal through a password protected user interface—$25,000 per CD copied, resulting in an total award of over $100 million, even though the defendant's service had just begun operating and there was little if any evidence of actual harm. This decision is often cited as chilling innovation in Internet technology and business models. For arguments against applying statutory damages in certain situations, *see* Mark A. Lemley, *Should a Licensing Market Require Licensing?*, 70 LAW & CONTEMP. PROBS. 185 (2007); Peter S. Menell, *This American Copyright Life: Reflections on Re-Equilibrating Copyright for the Internet Age*, 61 J. COPYRIGHT SOC'Y U.S.A. 235, 298–317 (2014) (recommending distinguishing between non-commercial, small-scale infringers and commercial, large-scale infringers and adjusting statutory damage limits for each category); Pamela Samuelson & Tata Wheatland, *Statutory Damages in Copyright Law: A Remedy in Need of Reform*, 51 WM. & MARY L. REV. 439 (2009). The Department of Commerce has called attention for statutory reform. *See* Department of Commerce, Internet Policy Task Force, WHITE PAPER ON REMIXES, FIRST SALE, AND STATUTORY DAMAGES: COPYRIGHT POLICY, CREATIVITY, AND INNOVATION IN THE DIGITAL ECONOMY 85–94 (Jan. 2016) (recommending (1) incorporating a list of factors for courts and juries to consider when determining the amount of a statutory damages award; (2) expanding eligibility for the lower "innocent infringement" statutory damages awards; and (3) affording courts wider discretion in cases involving non-willful secondary liability for online services offering a large number of works).

2. *The Teacher-Librarian-Broadcaster Exception.* Section 504(d) of the Copyright Act exempts teachers, librarians, and broadcasters from statutory damages if they believed, and had reasonable grounds for believing, that their infringing conduct constituted fair use.

PROBLEM

Problem IV-63. Like thousands of other Internet users, Jammie Thomas-Rasset received a cease-and-desist letter and settlement offer from the RIAA alleging that she was engaging in unauthorized sharing of copyrighted sound recordings. After Ms. Thomas-Rasset refused to settle, several record companies brought suit for copyright infringement. At trial, plaintiffs presented evidence that the defendant had shared over 1,000 sound recordings. They sought statutory damages for 24 particular recordings. Other evidence at trial indicated that the defendant had destroyed her hard drive just prior to her deposition, that her distinctive online alias was associated with the sharing of the files in question, and that she had changed her story on several occasions. The jury found that the defendant had knowingly infringed the plaintiff's worked and assessed $80,000 per song, resulting in a total award of $1.92 million.

1. You are the trial judge. The defendant seeks to overturn this verdict as grossly excessive and hence in violation of the Due Process Clause of the U.S. Constitution. Her counsel relies upon *BMW of North America, Inc. v. Gore*, 517 U.S. 559 (1996), where the Supreme Court struck down as grossly excessive a punitive damage award of $2 million for a distributor's failure to disclose that an automobile had been repainted after being damaged prior to delivery. The Court emphasized the low level of reprehensibility of conduct and 500 to 1 ratio between the award and the actual harm suffered. What would do you rule? What factors guide your determination? To what extent should deterrence and the difficulty of detecting online infringers affect your analysis?

2. You are a legislator. Does this verdict indicate that the statutory damage provision of the Copyright Act requires reform for the Internet age? If so, what adjustments would you make?

3. Attorney's Fees and Costs

Section 505 of the Copyright Act authorizes the award of attorney's fees in the discretion of the court to "prevailing parties." This provision bars courts from awarding attorney's fees "as a matter of course." *Fogerty v. Fantasy, Inc.*, 510 U.S. 517, 533 (1994). It must use its reasoned discretion in making an award of attorney's fees. Furthermore, courts must treat prevailing plaintiffs and defendants on an equal basis. *Id.* at 527. The Supreme Court identified several nonexclusive factors to be considered in weighing a fee award: frivolousness, motivation, objective unreasonableness, and the need in particular circumstances to advance considerations of compensation and deterrence. *Id.* at 534, n.19. In *Kirtsaeng v. John Wiley & Sons, Inc.*, 136 S.Ct. 1979 (2016), the Court identified objective reasonableness of a party's position as substantial factor in assessing the need for a fee award, but cautioned that it is not the only or controlling factor. Rather, courts should consider the range of pertinent factors in a particular case and could award fees against a party asserting a reasonable position where, for example, it engages in litigation misconduct or overaggressive assertion of copyright protection.

The Supreme Court's reasoning in rejecting a "dual standard" that favored plaintiffs in *Fogerty v. Fantasy* is instructive on the issue of appropriate copyright incentives:

> [T]he policies served by the Copyright Act are more complex, more measured, than simply maximizing the number of meritorious suits for copyright infringement. . . .

Because copyright law ultimately serves the purpose of enriching the general public through access to creative works, it is peculiarly important that the boundaries of copyright law be demarcated as clearly as possible. To that end, defendants who seek to advance a variety of meritorious copyright defenses should be encouraged to litigate them to the same extent that plaintiffs are encouraged to litigate meritorious claims of infringement. In the case before us, the successful defense of "The Old Man Down the Road" increased public exposure to a musical work that could, as a result, lead to further creative pieces. Thus a successful defense of a copyright infringement action may further the policies of the Copyright Act every bit as much as a successful prosecution of an infringement claim by the holder of a copyright.

510 U.S. at 526–27.

Section 505 of the Copyright Act also authorizes the award of "full costs" in the court's discretion. The Supreme Court ruled in *Rimini Street, Inc. v. Oracle USA, Inc.*, 139 S.Ct. 873 (2019), however, that "[a] statute awarding 'costs' will not be construed as authorizing an award of litigation expenses beyond the six categories listed in [28 U.S.C.] §§ 1821 and 1920, absent an explicit statutory instruction to that effect." *Id.* at 878. As a result, the Court excluded recovery of expert witness fees, e-discovery expenses, and jury consultant fees.

4. Criminal Enforcement

Throughout most of its history, copyright's enforcement regime has centered on private enforcement. In many contexts, the principal impacts of copyright infringement affected one or a few copyright owners and the law used tort-based remedies as the enforcement driver. Where there were economies of scale and scope in enforcement, as in the case of musical compositions, authors and publishers joined forces to police violations and enforce copyright protection. *See* Robert P. Merges, *Contracting into Liability Rules: Intellectual Property Rights and Collective Rights Organizations*, 84 CAL. L. REV. 1293 (1996) (discussing the emergence of ASCAP as a collective enforcement institution.

Nonetheless, criminal copyright law provisions date back more than a century. *See generally* Peter S. Menell, *This American Copyright Life: Reflections on Re-Equilibrating Copyright for the Internet Age*, 61 J. COPYRIGHT SOC'Y U.S.A. 235, 317–39 (2014) (tracing the history of public enforcement of copyright law and recommending ways to better tailor public enforcement for the Internet Age). Congress established criminal liability for willful, commercial exploitation of dramatic and musical compositions in 1897 to address the difficulty of enforcement of copyright protection against traveling performers. Congress expanded criminal liability to all willful copyright infringements for profit in the 1909 Act, but criminal copyright prosecutions were only rarely pursued. Congress included criminal penalties in the Sound Recording Act of 1971, and largely carried the 1909 Act's criminal enforcement provisions to the 1976 Act with increased sanctions. Section 506 provides for criminal enforcement and penalties for copyright infringement. Criminal enforcement targets willful infringement for commercial advantage or private financial gain.

As advances in digital technology in the 1990s greatly expanded the scale, modalities, and complexity of copyright infringement, Congress expanded criminal copyright liability to deal with the threats. At the urging of the computer software industry, Congress passed the Copyright Felony Act of 1992, significantly expanding criminal sanctions for willful infringement of all copyrighted works.

In one of the first criminal Internet copyright infringement cases, *United States v. LaMacchia*, 871 F. Supp. 535 (D. Mass. 1994), the government sought to use the wire fraud statute, 18 U.S.C. § 1343 (2012), rather than the Copyright Act to pursue the operator of a computer bulletin board service distributing copies of copyrighted software. The reason for this strategy was that the defendant lacked a profit motive. The court characterized David LaMacchia, a twenty-one year old MIT student, as a computer hacker—implying that he was merely following a hacker credo of sharing code. Prior to the Internet, such Robin Hood-type activity could not reach a global audience. Judge Stearns sensed that such behavior posed a serious threat to the copyright system.

Nonetheless, the court granted the defendant's motion to dismiss the case, relying on the Supreme Court's decision in *Dowling v. United States*, 473 U.S. 207 (1985), holding that the wire fraud statute could not be interpreted to encroach on copyright's domain without clear indication that Congress so intended.[34] While praising the government's purpose in prosecuting LaMacchia, Judge Stearns nonetheless noted that the government's interpretation of the wire fraud statute would "criminalize the conduct of not only persons like LaMacchia, but also the myriad of home computer users who succumb to the temptation to copy even a single software program for private use." He invited Congress to address this issue, observing that "[c]riminal as well as civil penalties should probably attach to willful, multiple infringements of copyrighted software even absent a commercial motive on the part of the infringer. One can envision ways that the copyright law could be modified to permit such prosecution. But, "'[i]t is the legislature, not the Court which is to define a crime, and ordain its punishment.'"

Notwithstanding concerns about bringing the activities of college pranksters within the felony realm, Congress closed the "LaMacchia loophole" in the No Electronic Theft Act of 1997. Pub. L. No. 105-147, 111 Stat. 2678–80 (codified as amended at 17 U.S.C. § 506, 18 U.S.C. § 2319, and 28 U.S.C. § 994). This so-called "NET Act" extended criminal infringement to willful "reproduction or distribution [of copyrighted works], including by electronic means, during any 180-day period, of 1 or more copies or phonorecords of 1 or more copyrighted works, which have a total retail value of more than $1,000," which removes any mens rea (motive) component. It also stiffened the

---

[34] The Supreme Court in *Dowling* rejected an attempt by the government to prosecute copyright infringement as transportation of stolen property. The Court reasoned that the specific statutory scheme of § 506 was meant to replace, not supplement, general laws that were not written with intellectual property in mind.

criminal penalties applicable to copyright infringement committed through electronic means. Congress viewed prosecutorial discretion in whether to pursue the matter and judicial restraint in sentencing as critical to achieving appropriate enforcement.

In the first NET Act prosecution, completed in November 1999, federal prosecutors proceeded against a college student who had posted MP3 files, movie clips, and software on his website. Although a plea bargain kept the student out of jail, the case received substantial publicity. The more general problem of computer crime—fraud and the spreading of computer viruses—has led the United States Department of Justice to establish specialized cybercrime units throughout the nation. In December 2001, federal agents carried out raids in 27 cities as part of effort to break up a particularly notorious software piracy ring known by the name "DrinkorDie."

In response to the growing availability of movies on peer-to-peer networks soon after (and in some cases, even before) their theatrical release, Congress passed the Artists' Rights and Theft (ART) Prevention Act of 2005. The ART Act prohibits the unauthorized, knowing use or attempted use of a video camera or similar device to transmit or make a copy of a motion picture in movie theaters. The so-called camcorder law authorizes movie theater employees to detain those suspected of committing an offense in a reasonable manner and imposes imprisonment and stiff fines for violations. Several states also ban cameras and other recording devices such as image-capturing cell phones in theaters. The ART Act also establishes criminal penalties for willful copyright infringement by the distribution of a computer program, musical work, motion picture or other audiovisual work, or sound recording being prepared for commercial distribution by making it available on a computer network accessible to members of the public if the person knew or should have known that the work was intended for commercial distribution. On the civil side, the ART Act provides for preregistration of a work that is being prepared for commercial distribution to allow copyright owners to recover statutory damages and attorney's fees for infringement of works in the production pipeline.

Congress added additional criminal provisions in the Prioritizing Resources and Organization for Intellectual Property Act of 2008. The PRO-IP Act provides stiffer penalties for piracy and counterfeiting activities, harmonizes forfeiture procedures for intellectual property offenses, makes it illegal to export counterfeit goods, and eliminates loopholes that might prevent enforcement of otherwise validly registered copyrights.

The PRO-IP Act established an Intellectual Property Enforcement Coordinator (IPEC) office within the Executive Office of the President to coordinate anti-piracy efforts across relevant Federal agencies (Department of Justice, Office of Management and Budget, Department of Homeland Security, Federal Bureau of Investigation (FBI), Immigration and Custom Enforcement (ICE), Customs and Border Protection, the Patent and Trademark Office, the Office of the U.S. Trade Representative, and the U.S. Copyright Office), foreign governments, private companies, and public interest groups to implement the best strategies to foster and protect invention and creativity. The IPEC has been responsible for developing and implementing a Joint Strategic Plan to combat counterfeiting and piracy.

As part of these efforts, the IPEC coordinated "Operation in Our Sites," leading the ICE and the Department of Homeland Security to seize hundreds of websites alleged to traffic in unauthorized copyright content and counterfeit goods. *See* Karen Kopel, *Operation Seizing Our Sites: How the Federal Government Is Taking Domain Names Without Prior Notice*, 28 BERKELEY TECH. L.J. 859 (2013). The seizure of domains containing allegedly infringing copyrighted materials proceeds according to the following steps: (1) ICE agents download or stream suspicious content; (2) ICE agents then check with rights holders to verify that the content is protected; (3) ICE and NIPRCC present this evidence to the Department of Justice, which determines whether there is adequate basis to obtain a seizure order for the website in question; (4) investigators determine whether the domain name is registered in the United States; (5) ICE and NIPRCC present affidavits to a federal magistrate judge; (6) the federal magistrate judge determines whether there is probable cause to support infringement; (7) the magistrate judge grants a seizure order that is served on the domain name registry (as opposed to the website operator); (8) the domain name registry must restrain and lock the domain name pending completion of the forfeiture proceeding and transfer the domain name's title, rights, and interests to the U.S. government; and (9) the registry must redirect the domain to a web page operated by the U.S. government displaying a plaque stating that the website has been seized. Among the factors that the Department of Justice considers in determining whether to seize a website are the popularity of the site, whether it is commercial in nature, whether it is profitable, and whether seizure would have a substantial impact on piracy.

These seizures have raised concerns about freedom of expression, due process, and chilling effects on technological innovation. The owner of a website that has been seized under this process cannot challenge the decision until after the website has been transferred to the government. Only then is the website owner afforded an opportunity to challenge the validity of the affidavit supporting the seizure. The government bears the burden of proof in such proceeding. The website owner may also demand return of the property by writing directly to ICE. If ICE does not return the website within fifteen days, the owner can petition the U.S. District Court in which the seizure warrant was issued or executed.

Several ICE domain seizures illustrate the due process, free expression, and overbreadth problems. In November 2010, the government seized eighty-two domains alleged to be engaged in the sale and distribution of counterfeit goods and pirated works. The seizures included several rap and hip hop blogs showcasing new artists tagged by an RIAA representative as pirate sites. Dajaz1.com allegedly posted pre-release songs owned by RIAA member labels. Yet these songs had apparently been "leaked" by record label promotional representatives for marketing and publicity. Thus, the website seized had authorization to post the works. Even after this mistake was revealed within a few weeks by the NEW YORK TIMES, *see* Ben Sisario, *Piracy Fight Shuts Down Music Blogs*, N.Y. TIMES (Dec. 13, 2010) the government delayed more than year before unceremoniously returning the domain. The owner and users of the blog lost more than a year of activity without justification. *See* Nate Anderson, *Government Admits Defeat, Gives Back Seized Rojadirecta Domains*, ARSTECHNICA (Aug. 28, 2012). Something similar happened with rojadirecta.com, a Spanish sports streaming site. The government seized the domain name in the days before the Super Bowl because of the fear that the game would be streamed on the site. Rojadirecta challenged the seizure, pointing out that streaming of live sporting events was lawful in Europe and that most of the content posted by users was European. Rojadirecta also argued that the seizure of domain names in advance of any determination of copyright infringement was a prior restraint of speech in violation of the First Amendment. Eighteen months after the seizure, while the Second Circuit was considering the prior restraint issue, the government again decided to give back the domain, mooting the dispute. Thus, while ICE seizures continue unabated, their legality has never been definitively litigated.

H. INTERNATIONAL COPYRIGHT LAW

Although copyright protection, like patent protection, is territorial (country-specific) in nature, the lack of formalities in copyright law today along with widespread ratification of international treaties affording authors of signatory countries national treatment has resulted in nearly universal protection for copyrighted works. Therefore, U.S. copyright owners can enforce their rights in the courts of most nations in the world without even registering their works. The effectiveness of such efforts in stemming piracy, however, varies significantly on the basis of local conditions. Similarly, most foreign authors of works first published just about anywhere in the world can enforce their copyrights against infringement in the United States in U.S. courts.

This near-global copyright protection has not always been the case. Our purpose in this section is to provide a concise history of U.S. involvement in the international copyright system and survey the principal contours of international copyright law. Students interested in delving more deeply into the subject should consult one of the comprehensive international copyright treatises. *See* NIMMER ON COPYRIGHT chs. 17, 18; PAUL GOLDSTEIN & P. BERNT HUGENHOLZ, INTERNATIONAL COPYRIGHT: PRINCIPLES, LAW, AND PRACTICE (3d ed. 2012); LIONEL BENTLY, INTERNATIONAL COPYRIGHT LAW AND PRACTICE (2015).

1. Evolution of the International Copyright System and U.S. Participation

Early copyright laws did not afford protection to the works of foreign nationals. As printing businesses grew and literacy expanded, nations came to recognize the common interest in affording protection to authors from other nations. Without protection for works of foreign authors, publishers of domestic authors would have to compete with publishers of foreign works without any royalty obligations. Furthermore, domestic authors lost out on foreign royalty streams unless they could obtain protection abroad. As a solution, by the mid-nineteenth century, several European countries entered into bilateral treaties or passed legislation affording the works of foreign nationals protection on a reciprocal basis (i.e., where works of that nation's authors were afforded protection in the courts of the foreign national's home country). This movement eventually led most of the nations of Western Europe, as well as a few other nations, to adopt the Berne Convention for the Protection of Literary and Artistic Works in 1886. In order to join the convention, a nation's copyright law had to meet specified minimum criteria for protection. Authors from signatory nations obtained "national treatment"—i.e., the same rights as domestic authors—in each member nation. Over the course of the next century, most nations of the world would join this treaty.

The United States long took an isolationist position in the development of international copyright law. *See generally* Hamish R. Sandison, *The Berne Convention and the Universal Copyright Convention: The American Experience*, 11 COLUM.-V.L.A. J.L. & ARTS 89 (1986). This in part reflected the relatively undeveloped nature of the arts in the early republic and the protectionist political influences of American publishers. England produced many of the popular English-language authors well into the nineteenth century, and U.S. publishers had much to gain from being able to copy the works of British novelists and poets. During a visit to the United States in 1842, Charles Dickens bemoaned "the exquisite [in]justice of never deriving sixpence from an enormous American sale of all my books" and castigated American publishers for undermining the flourishing of native literary talent. As aptly noted by a later commentator, "American readers were less inclined to read the novels of Cooper or Hawthorne for a dollar when they could buy a novel of Scott or Dickens for a quarter." Max Kampelman, *The United States and International Copyright*, 41 AM. J. INT'L L. 406, 413 (1947). To the disappointment of Dickens, as well as many foreign and U.S. authors at the time, domestic publishers successfully blocked protection for foreign works until the late nineteenth century.

The United States grudgingly yielded to protection for works of foreign authors with the passage of the International Copyright Act of 1891 (the Chace Act). The U.S. insisted upon compliance with U.S. notice, registration, and deposit requirements and erected a further protectionist measure: a requirement that any printed book or periodical in the English language, as well as any printed book or periodical of domestic origin in any language, had to be printed from type set in the United States. This manufacturing clause continued until July 1, 1986. By complying with these requirements, foreign authors whose nations provided reciprocal protection to American nationals could obtain protection for their works in the United States. Following the Chace Act, the United States also began to enter into bilateral copyright reciprocity agreements with a growing number of nations. As an alternative to Berne, from which the U.S. was barred by its formalities and protectionist policies, the United States became a charter member of the less demanding, but also less widely adopted, Universal Copyright Convention (U.C.C.) in 1955. For the next three decades, the U.C.C. and bilateral treaties afforded American authors the ability to enforce their copyrights in much of the world. Furthermore, U.S. copyright owners could obtain "back door" protection for their works under the Berne Convention by publishing their works simultaneously in the United States and a Berne signatory nation.

Nonetheless, by the mid-1980s, as the global content marketplace expanded to unprecedented levels and piracy of copyrighted works in many corners of the world increased, the U.S. government came to believe that Berne membership was essential if the U.S. was to persuade other nations to join the international copyright system and exert its influence on the reform of global copyright protection. Notwithstanding reluctance to jettison formalities and revise its domestic copyright system to satisfy Berne's minimum criteria, the United States joined the Berne Convention in 1989. (We have discussed throughout this chapter the myriad changes aimed at achieving Berne compliance—including eliminating formalities for foreign authors, creating moral rights, expanding protection for architectural works, and restoring copyrights for foreign works that were lost as a result of failure to comply with U.S. formalities.) In so doing, U.S. copyright proprietors gained the ability to protect their works directly in two dozen additional nations and the United States gained a seat at the Berne negotiation table. The Berne Convention now includes over 150 nations.

Soon thereafter, the United States and other developed nations elevated the role of intellectual property on the global stage by placing the formation of a new, more readily enforceable treaty mandating minimum intellectual property standards on the agenda for the ongoing multilateral trade negotiations as part of the Uruguay Round of the General Agreement on Tariffs and Trade (GATT) (reconstituted in 1995 as the World Trade Organization (WTO)).[35] These negotiations resulted in the Agreement on Trade-Related Aspects of Intellectual Property Rights (TRIPs), a treaty signed by more than 100 nations that entered into force on January 1, 1995. That treaty set minimum standards for copyright protection required of each member nation, and also for the first time set expectations regarding enforcement of those legal rules. Developed nations had one year to bring their domestic laws into compliance; developing nations and ex-communist states were afforded an additional grace period of up to ten years.

Rapid advances in digital technology fueled continuing international negotiations over copyright standards. In 1996, under the auspices of the World Intellectual Property Organization (WIPO), an arm of the United Nations which administers the Berne Convention, national representatives reached agreement on two supplementary agreements—the WIPO Copyright Treaty and the WIPO Performances and Phonograms Treaty. These treaties strengthen copyright protection along several dimensions. Of most significance (and controversy) were provisions aimed at protecting copyrights in the digital age. It was pursuant to these treaties that the United States adopted the anticircumvention, protection of copyright management information, and online service provider safe harbor provisions of the Digital Millennium Copyright Act. These treaties entered into force in 2002, upon ratification by 30 nations, although their implementation awaits domestic action in many WIPO nations.

---

[35] In addition, the United States, Canada, and Mexico entered into the North American Free Trade Agreement (NAFTA) in 1993. This agreement mandates that each of the member nations afford minimum standards for protection, most notably the availability of preliminary injunctive relief, and provides an enforcement mechanism for addressing disputes among the member nations.

2. International Copyright Treaties

This section summarizes the main features of the Berne Convention and the TRIPs treaty, the principal international copyright conventions operating today.[36]

i. *Berne Convention for the Protection of Literary and Artistic Works*

The Berne Convention has undergone several revisions over its long history. The latest text, to which most Berne signatories adhere, was negotiated in Paris in 1971. The Berne Convention was structured so that members were not required to adhere to revisions as a condition of membership. As a result, several nations still adhere to prior versions, such as the Rome (1928) or Brussels (1948) text. With China's and the Russian Federation's accession in 1992 and 1995, respectively, the Berne Convention includes all of the most significant economies in the world.

The Berne Convention is built upon two pillars: (1) national treatment—member nations must afford works of nationals of other Berne member nations the same protections as works of domestic authors (Article 5(1)); and (2) minimum standards— the copyright laws of member nations must satisfy the following minimum criteria:

Works Covered (Article 2). The convention covers "literary and artistic works," which is defined broadly to include "every production in the literary, scientific and artistic domain, whatever may be the mode or form of expression." It also includes derivative works and collective works, but excludes newsworthy facts. Although initially considered outside of the copyright domain, recent developments such as the E.C. Software Directive, TRIPs, and the WIPO Copyright Treaty indicate that computer programs are to be protected as "literary works" within the meaning of the Berne Convention. By contrast, commentary and national practice suggest that the Berne Convention does not extend to phonograms (sound recordings), which are commonly accorded rights outside the United States under the rubric of "neighboring" rights. Several other treaties apply to these works.[37]

Limitations on Formalities (Article 5(2)). "The enjoyment and the exercise of [copyright] shall not be subject to any formality . . . other than in the country of origin of the work." Thus, Berne prohibits only those formalities that would operate to preclude copyright protection for works from other member states. A Berne member may impose formalities upon works of its own authors and may impose formalities as a condition to certain types of remedies (e.g., statutory damages, attorneys' fees), compulsory licenses, or exemptions.

---

[36] The Universal Copyright Convention and bilateral agreements have a continuing role with regard to the protection of U.S. works published prior to U.S. entry into Berne or TRIPs in countries that are not Berne signatories.

[37] *See* International Convention for the Protection of Performers, Producers of Phonograms and Broadcasting Organizations (1961) (Rome Convention); Convention for the Protection of Producers of Phonograms Against Unauthorized Duplication of Their Phonograms (1971) (Geneva Phonograms Convention); Convention Relating to the Distribution of Programme-Carrying Signals Transmitted by Satellite (1974) (Brussels Satellite Convention); WIPO Performances and Phonogram Treaty (1996).

Duration (Article 7). Berne members must afford protection for no less than life of the author plus 50 years or 50 years from publication in the case of motion pictures and anonymous or pseudonymous works. Photographic works and applied art shall receive no less than 25 years of protection from the time of creation.

Exclusive Rights (Articles 8, 9, 11, 12, and 14). The Berne Convention requires that member nations afford exclusive rights to make and authorize translation, reproduction, public performance, and adaptation of their works. Any exceptions to Berne's right of reproduction must meet a three-step test: "It shall be a matter for legislation in the countries of the Union [1] to permit the reproduction of such works in certain special cases, provided that such reproduction [2] does not conflict with a normal exploitation of the work and [3] does not unreasonably prejudice the legitimate interests of the author." Art. 9(2). In contrast to U.S. law, the Berne Convention does not include display and distribution among the exclusive rights that must be accorded.

Moral Rights (Article 6*bis*). The Berne Convention provides:

Independently of the author's economic rights, and even after the transfer of the said rights, the author shall have the right to claim authorship of the work and to object to any distortion, mutilation or other modification of, or other derogatory action in relation to, the said work, which would be prejudicial to his honor or reputation.

The rights granted to the author in accordance with the preceding paragraph shall, after his death, be maintained, at least until the expiry of the economic rights . . .

The means of redress for safeguarding the rights granted by this Article shall be governed by the legislation of the country where protection is claimed.

Exceptions (Articles 2*bis*, 10, 10*bis*). Berne members may limit protection for political speeches, allow the press broader rights to reproduce public lectures, and carve out a fair use privilege.

Restoration of Rights (Article 18). The Convention applies to "all works which, at the moment of its coming into force, have not yet fallen into the public domain in the country of origin through the expiry of the term of protection."

ii.   *Agreement on Trade-Related Aspects of Intellectual Property Rights (TRIPs)*

The TRIPs Agreement incorporates and expands upon the Berne foundation. By its terms, all WTO Member Countries must enforce all requirements of the Berne Convention, save the moral rights provisions (Article 9). Furthermore, WTO Members must adhere to requirements set forth in the agreement relating to neighboring rights, but not extending to prior conventions (Article 14). TRIPs specifies more extensive civil and criminal enforcement obligations and incorporates the new WTO dispute-settlement process for resolving disputes among the member nations. It was pursuant to this procedure that the U.S. Fairness in Music Licensing Act was held to be in violation of TRIPs and the Berne Convention. *See* United States—Section 110(5) of the U.S.

Copyright Act, Report of the Panel, World Trade Organization, WT/DS160/R Jun. 15, 2000. Subject to several exemptions, TRIPs (Article 4) also goes beyond the Berne framework by requiring that members afford all foreign authors the same protections as those offered to authors from the "most favored nation." In most cases, such treatment will be the same as national treatment—that which a nation affords its own authors.

TRIPs expands on the minimum criteria of the Berne Convention in several respects:

Works Covered (Article 10). TRIPs requires that member nations afford protection for computer programs as literary works under the Berne Convention. Original selection or arrangement of databases must also be protected.

Exclusive Rights (Article 11). Member nations must afford copyright owners the right to authorize or prohibit rental of computer programs and films. The same provision, however, authorizes nations to permit movie rental "unless such rental has led to widespread copying of such works which is materially impairing the exclusive right of reproduction conferred in that Member on authors and their successors in title."

Exceptions (Article 13). TRIPs limits exceptions to Berne's exclusive rights by requiring that Members "confine limitations or exceptions to exclusive rights to certain special cases which do not conflict with a normal exploitation of the work and do not unreasonably prejudice the legitimate interests of the right holder." Unlike the Berne three-step test governing exceptions to the right of reproduction, the TRIPs three-step test applies to all of the exclusive rights.

COMMENTS AND QUESTIONS

1. *Global Copyright Governance*. Certainly by comparison to the patent field, international copyright protection would seem to be a model of global governance. The nearly universal reach of the Berne Convention in combination with the World Trade Organization's formal dispute resolution mechanism have brought about a reasonably well-coordinated system for the protection of copyrights throughout the world. Given the challenges facing copyright owners in the digital age, it could be said that these developments could not have come about at a more opportune time.

2. *Political Economy of International Copyright Law and Policy*. Political economists and advocates for the public domain tend to view international developments in the copyright arena somewhat more cynically. *See* MICHAEL P. RYAN, KNOWLEDGE DIPLOMACY: GLOBAL COMPETITION AND THE POLITICS OF INTELLECTUAL PROPERTY (1998); Pamela Samuelson, *The Copyright Grab*, WIRED 4.01 (Jan. 1996). They see the TRIPs Agreement and the WIPO Copyright Treaties as the product of well-coordinated content industry lobbyists seeking ever stronger protection, quite possibly at the expense of lesser developed nations and the public at large. Are these industries using their superior organizational skills and political influence unjustly, or are they rightly concerned to be advocating for enhanced protections in the face of digital technologies that threaten to undermine the legal

institutions supporting creative expression? Is it possible that both are true? Have new interest groups formed in the global arena to counterbalance the protectionist bias?

iii. Other Copyright Treaties

WIPO adopted the Beijing Treaty on Audiovisual Performances at the Beijing Diplomatic Conference in 2012. The Beijing Treaty grants performers four kinds of economic rights for audiovisual fixations of performances, such as motion pictures: (i) the right of reproduction; (ii) the right of distribution; (iii) the right of rental; and (iv) the right of making available. It also grants performers three kinds of economic rights in unfixed (live) performances: (i) the right of broadcasting (except in the case of rebroadcasting); (ii) the right of communication to the public (except where the performance is a broadcast performance); and (iii) the right of fixation. The Beijing Treaty also grants performers several moral rights: (i) the right to claim to be identified as the performer (except where such an omission would be dictated by the manner of the use of the performance); and (ii) the right to object to any distortion, mutilation or other modification that would be prejudicial to the performer's reputation, taking into account the nature of the audiovisual fixations. Article 13 of the Beijing Treaty incorporates the so-called "three-step" test to determine limitations and exceptions, as provided for in Article 9(2) of the Berne Convention, extending its application to all rights. The Beijing Treaty will enter into force three months after 30 eligible parties have deposited their instruments of ratification or accession.

WIPO adopted the Marrakesh Treaty to Facilitate Access to Published Works for Persons Who Are Blind, Visually Impaired or Otherwise Print Disabled in 2013. It requires contracting parties to introduce a standard set of limitations and exceptions to copyright rules in order to permit reproduction, distribution and making available of published works in formats designed to be accessible to visually impaired and otherwise print disabled persons, and to permit exchange of these works across borders by organizations that serve those beneficiaries. Its entry into force requires the deposit of 20 instruments of ratification or accession by eligible parties.

The United States has also negotiated a series of bilateral and multilateral trade agreements with particular blocks of nations that include copyright provisions. Those agreements often compel U.S. trading partners to more aggressively enforce copyrights. The Trans-Pacific Partnership (TPP), signed in 2015, is the latest example. Many of these agreements have proved controversial, as much for the secrecy with which they were negotiated as for the substantive provisions they contain.

3. Protection of U.S. Works Against Infringement Abroad

International copyright law incorporates the doctrine of "territoriality." This doctrine embodies three precepts. First, a nation's laws apply only within its territorial boundaries. Second, nations may exercise jurisdiction over those within its boundaries. And third, principles of comity caution against any nation state applying its laws in such a way as to interfere with the sovereignty interests of other nations. Stated another way, U.S. copyright law does not apply extraterritorially. *See Subafilms, Ltd. v. MGM-Pathe*

Communications Co., 24 F.3d 1088, 1095 (9th Cir. 1994) (en banc) (noting "eighty years of consistent jurisprudence").

As a result, U.S. copyright owners must look to the law of the nation in which infringement occurs to obtain redress. This poses the question whether a U.S. copyright owner possesses enforceable rights in another nation, which turns on whether the nation is party to a multi-lateral treaty (such as TRIPs, Berne, or U.C.C.) or whether a bilateral agreement with the United States which confers protection upon U.S. copyright owners or the nation extends protection to foreign copyright owners on some other basis.[38] Just a few decades ago, analysis of the complexity of international accords arose with some frequency. The nearly universal reach of Berne today makes 1989, the year in which the U.S. joined this convention, an historic dividing point in the protection U.S. copyright interests enjoy abroad.

Due to the widespread adoption of Berne, U.S. works—both post-1989 and pre-1989—receive national treatment in most nations of the world. That does not, however, ensure that an enforcement action by a U.S. copyright owner can proceed in a foreign court. A threshold question of standing arises: does the foreign country (commonly referred to as the "protecting country") recognize the party seeking to enforce a copyright interest as the owner of rights in the work? The proper test depends upon choice of law rules, which determine whether U.S. law or the law of the protecting country governs. United States courts apply the law of the state with the "most significant relationship" to the work to determine ownership. *See Itar-Tass Russian News Agency v. Russian Kurrier*, 153 F.3d 82 (2d Cir. 1998) (finding that some of the plaintiffs lacked standing because they were not owners of an exclusive right under Russian copyright law). Other nations may apply their own law. If the putative U.S. copyright owner is not recognized as such by the protecting state, then it will not be permitted to proceed.

Once the standing hurdle is cleared, there remains the determination whether and to what extent the foreign country protects the work for which enforcement is sought. Although the Berne Convention (now augmented by TRIPs) establishes minimum standards for protection, U.S. copyright protection extends beyond these limits in several respects (and arguably falls short in other areas, such as protection of moral rights). For example, whereas the United States protects sound recordings under copyright law, many other countries treat such works under neighboring rights regimes that fall outside of the Berne Convention. Lastly, liability and remedies must be determined. Reflecting the territoriality doctrine, most nations, including the United States, apply the conflicts principle of *lex loci delicti* ("the law of the place where the tort or other wrong was committed") to infringement analysis and determination of remedies.

Furthermore, there is an important exception to national treatment relating to duration of copyright protection for works of foreign origin. Under Article 7(8) of the

---

[38] Germany and France, for example, extend protection universally. U.S. copyright law protects all unpublished works irrespective of the author's nationality.

Berne Convention, the duration of protection may be the shorter of the duration as between the protecting country and the country of origin, unless the law of the protecting country chooses otherwise. The rule of the shorter term applies in most countries of the world. The E.C. Term Directive requires that member countries adhere to the rule of the shorter term.

COMMENTS AND QUESTIONS

1. *The Rule of the Shorter Term and Duration of U.S. Copyrights Under the 1909 Act.* Under the Berne Convention, what is the duration of U.S. copyright protection for pre-1976 Act U.S. works which lost (or never received) copyright protection for failure to comply with required formalities (publication with proper notice)? What about those works for which renewal was not sought or successfully attained? In an "informal" advisory opinion, a WIPO official took the position that in the case of "those works, which, due to the non-compliance with formalities (such as the requirement of publication of notice), have never been protected, it is clear that they have not fallen into the public . . . through the expiry of the term of protection since there has been no term of protection applicable for them." For works that received only one term of protection under the 1909 Act, the WIPO official opined that the term should be ninety-five years from publication, the term which would had been available had renewal been successfully obtained (and applicable term extensions been added), because this is the duration that the owner would have enjoyed had formalities "been fulfilled (or would not have existed)." *See* Letter of Shozo Uemura, Deputy Director General, World Intellectual Property Organization, reprinted in 47 J. COPYRIGHT OFF. SOC'Y 91 (1999). It can certainly be argued, however, that U.S. works for which no renewal registration was made fell into the public domain through the "expiry of the term of protection."

2. *Protection of U.S. Works Outside of Berne/TRIPs Member Nations.* In one of the relatively few nations not party to Berne or TRIPs, a U.S. copyright owner can enforce its rights only if that nation extends protection to foreign copyright owners directly or if that nation is party to a bilateral agreement with the United States conferring copyright protection upon each nation's copyright owners. If a basis for protection is identified, the U.S. copyright owner's standing to sue and substantive rights would be determined under the protecting nation's copyright and choice of law regime.

3. *Combating Foreign Infringing Activities in U.S. Courts.* Notwithstanding the territoriality doctrine, U.S. copyright owners can pursue remedies in U.S. courts for foreign infringement in several circumstances:

- Where an "act" of infringement occurs within the United States even though the infringement is completed abroad, the copyright owner can sometimes pursue remedies under U.S. copyright law. *See Ortman v. Stanray Corp.*, 163 U.S.P.Q. 331 (N.D. Ill. 1969). Nonetheless, a defendant cannot be held liable under U.S. law for merely authorizing conduct that occurred overseas that would constitute copyright infringement if it occurred in the United States. *See Subafilms, Ltd. v. M.G.M.-Pathe Communications*, 24 F.3d 1088 (9th Cir. 1994) (en banc).

- Sections 602 and 603 of the U.S. Copyright Act prohibit the importation of infringing articles. *See also* 19 U.S.C. § 337 (providing for exclusion of infringing articles through an International Trade Commission proceeding).
- A U.S. copyright owner, or any copyright owner for that matter, may be able to sue for infringement occurring elsewhere in the world if personal jurisdiction over the defendant can be obtained in an American court under a theory that copyright infringement constitutes a transitory cause of action. *Cf.* Curtis Bradley, *Territorial Intellectual Property Rights in an Age of Globalism*, 37 VA. J. INT'L L. 505 (1997). 28 U.S.C. § 1332(a)(2) confers jurisdiction in federal court where there is diversity of citizenship (including citizens of a State and subjects of a foreign state) and at least $75,000 in dispute. The U.S. court would apply the law of the country in which the alleged infringement occurred. *See London Film Prods. Ltd. v. Intercontinental Communications, Inc.*, 580 F. Supp. 47 (S.D.N.Y. 1984). There are, however, potential legal and practical impediments to such a course of action. The defendant may persuade the court to dismiss the action under the *forum non conveniens* doctrine. *See, e.g., Murray v. British Broad. Corp.*, 81 F.3d 287 (2d Cir. 1996); *but cf. Boosey & Hawkes Music Publishers, Ltd. v. Walt Disney Co.*, 145 F.3d 481 (2d Cir. 1998) (overturning dismissal of an action under this doctrine); *Armstrong v. Virgin Records, Ltd.*, 91 F. Supp. 2d 628, 637–38 (S.D.N.Y. 2000). Furthermore, to the extent that the plaintiff seeks injunctive or other relief that is available only in the nation in which the infringement is occurring, then she will still have to pursue enforcement abroad.
- If copyright infringement occurs within the United States, the plaintiff can recover the defendant's profits from overseas sales or use of infringing works. *See Los Angeles News Service v. Reuters Television, Int'l*, 149 F.3d 987 (9th Cir. 1998). Does this make sense? What if liability would differ under the laws of other jurisdictions? Note that in *Computer Associates Int'l v. Altai, Inc.*, 126 F.3d 365 (2d Cir. 1997), the court held that a copyright owner that had lost its claim in the United States could bring the same claim in France under French law. Is it fair that if a copyright owner wins in the U.S. they can get worldwide damages, but if they lose in the United States they are free to try again elsewhere?

4. *Other Means for Combating Foreign Piracy of U.S. Copyrighted Works.* Under § 301 of the Trade Act of 1974, as amended (including "Special 301" authority), the U.S. Trade Representative monitors the protection of U.S. intellectual property rights abroad and uses the threat of trade sanctions as a means of promoting greater enforcement by other nations. U.S. administrations have used this provision to put countries on a "priority watch list" if they do not adequately enforce intellectual property rights and to obtain a series of bilateral treaty concessions on intellectual property rights from those countries. Some scholars argue that Special 301 is an efficient means of enforcing intellectual property rights. *See* Tara Kalagher Giunta & Lily H. Shang, *Ownership of Information in a Global Economy*, 27 GEO. WASH. J. INT'L L. &

ECON. 327 (1994). Many nations, however, have criticized the procedure as discriminatory and at odds with multilateral dispute resolution mechanisms such as the World Trade Organization's process. *See* Lina M. Montén, *The Inconsistency Between Section 301 and TRIPS: Counterproductive with Respect to the Future of International Protection of Intellectual Property Rights?*, 9 MARQ. INTELL. PROP. L. REV. 387 (2005).

5. *Enforcing Infringements of U.S. Copyrights Abroad.* In *Lucasfilm v. Ainsworth*, [2011] UKSC 39, the producer and owner of the Star Wars films sought to prevent a contractor who manufactured the Stormtrooper costumes for the first Star Wars film (from detailed copyrighted paintings owned by Lucasfilm) from selling the costumes to U.S. and U.K. customers. Although the U.K. Supreme Court ruled that the Stormtrooper costumes were no longer protected in the U.K. because they were industrial designs for which protection lasted only 25 years, it nonetheless held that U.K. courts could adjudicate claims for violation of U.S. copyright law for sales to the United States.

6. *The Territoriality Doctrine and the Internet.* Will the territoriality doctrine function effectively in cyberspace? For example, courts in several nations have come to diametrically opposed conclusions in resolving copyright disputes relating to file-sharing activities that cross international boundaries. In the United States and in Australia, distributors of peer-to-peer file-sharing software have been held liable for copyright infringement, but in the Netherlands the same defendants have been held not to be liable. Which rule should govern? It seems difficult to say that a web site can be shut down in one country but can continue to operate in another. Especially given the possible res judicata ramifications, *but cf. Computer Associates Int'l v. Altai*, 126 F.3d 365 (2d Cir. 1997) (refusing to enjoin the French suit under principles of res judicata or collateral estoppel, reasoning that the application of French law to conduct occurring in France presented a separate issue from the one litigated in the U.S. case), cyberspace copyright disputes could fuel races to courthouses in several nations and produce friction among nations. *See* Peter P. Swire, *Elephants and Mice Revisited: Law and Choice of Law on the Internet*, 153 U. PA. L. REV. 1975 (2005) (suggesting that such conflict has not yet manifested on a large scale due to technology's ability to trump law, lack of jurisdiction over defendants, harmonization of substantive law, and the existence of self-regulatory and other systems that suppress choice-of-law conflicts for transactions); *see generally Symposium: Copyright's Long Arm: Enforcing U.S. Copyrights Abroad*, 24 LOY. L.A. ENT. L. REV. 45 (2004); Paul Schiff Berman, *The Globalization of Jurisdiction*, 151 U. PA. L. REV. 311 (2002). As the problem of unauthorized distribution of copyrighted works on the Internet escalates and nations' legal decisions and legislation diverge, will we see an increase in conflicts of law problems or will copyright owners direct their efforts toward enforcement within separate countries in combination with efforts to harmonize legal regimes through multilateral treaty negotiations?

4. Protection of Foreign Works Against Infringement in the United States

The framework for analyzing protection for foreign works in the United States mirrors the framework applied to the protection of U.S. works abroad. The United States affords protection for all works of Berne and TRIPs members for which copyright subsists in their country of origin, irrespective of when such nations joined these treaties. *See* §§ 104(a), 104A (restoration of copyright in works of foreign origin). The United States does not apply the rule of the shorter term, and therefore foreign copyright owners may obtain the full benefit of the U.S. term of copyright protection even if protection has expired in the country of origin. Works receiving the benefit of Berne protection that would otherwise have fallen into the public domain in the United States on the basis of a notice defect may be enforced.

CHAPTER V:
TRADEMARK LAW

A. Introduction   891
    1. Historical Background   891
    2. Trademark Theory   892
    3. The Basic Economics of Trademarks and Advertising   894
B. What can be protected as a trademark?   900
    1. Trademarks, Trade Names, and Service Marks   901
    2. Certification and Collective Marks   902
    3. Trade Dress and Product Configurations   904
C. Establishment of Trademark Rights   905
    1. Distinctiveness   905
        i.   Classification of Terms and Requirements for Protection   905
        ii.   Genericness   919
        iii. Distinctiveness of Trade Dress and Product Configuration   933
        iv.   Product Configuration   940
        v.   Functionality   955
    2. Priority   967
        i.   Actual Use in Commerce   967
        ii.   Intent-to-Use Application Process   975
        iii. Geographic Limitations on Trademark Use   977
        iv.   Secondary Meaning and Priority   979
        v.   Priority and Trademark Theory   983
        a.   Reducing Search Costs   983
            b.   Incentives to Create Trademarks   983
            c.   Priority and the Prevention of Trademark Races   985
    3. Trademark Office Procedures   988
        i.   Principal vs. Supplemental Register   988
        ii.   Grounds for Refusing Registration   989
            a.   Immoral, Scandalous, or Disparaging Marks   991
            b.   Geographic Marks   993
        iii. Marks Which Are "Primarily Merely a Surname"   997
        iv.   Opposition   1001
        v.   Cancellation   1001
        vi.   Concurrent Registration   1002
    4. Incontestability   1003
D. Trademark Liability Analysis   1008
    1. Threshold Issue: Trademark Use   1008
    2. Trademark Infringement and Related Doctrines   1017
        i.   Confusion-Based Infringement   1017
            a.   General Multi-Factor "Likelihood of Confusion" Test   1018

3.   Types of Confusion   1026
    i.   Confusion as to Source   1026
    ii.   Confusion as to Sponsorship   1027
       a.   Trademarks and Organizational Forms: The Growth of Franchising   1029
       b.   Merchandising   1030
    iii.   Reverse Confusion   1042
    iv.   Timing of Confusion   1043
       a.   Initial Interest Confusion   1043
       b.   Post-Sale Confusion   1054
    v.   Dilution   1057
4.   Cybersquatting   1075
5.   Indirect Infringement   1077
6.   False Advertising   1089
E.   Defenses   1108
   1.   Abandonment   1108
    i.   Cessation of Use   1108
    ii.   Unsupervised Licenses   1116
    iii.   Assignments in Gross   1121
   2.   Exhaustion/First Sale   1123
    i.   Resale Without Requisite Quality Control   1123
    ii.   Repackaged Goods   1124
    iii.   Repaired and Reconditioned Goods   1124
   3.   Fair Use   1125
    i.   Descriptive/"Classic" Fair Use   1125
    ii.   Nontrademark (or Nominative) Use, Parody, and the First Amendment   1130
   4.   Other Defenses   1144
    i.   Laches   1144
    ii.   Unclean Hands   1145
       a.   Fraud in Obtaining Trademark Registration   1146
       b.   Trademark Misuse   1146
F.   Remedies   1147
   1.   Injunctions   1147
   2.   Damages   1152
    i.   Infringer's Gain and Mark Owner's Loss   1152
    ii.   Corrective Advertising   1158
       a.   Note on the Trademark Counterfeiting Act of 1984   1165
G.   International Issues   1166
   1.   U.S. Trademarks Abroad: The New Internationalization   1167
   2.   Foreign Trademarks in the United States: Limited Internationalization   1168
   3.   Note on the "Gray Market"   1169
   4.   Worldwide Famous Marks   1171

A.   INTRODUCTION

1.   Historical Background

Trademarks have existed for almost as long as trade itself. Once human economies progressed to the point where a merchant class specialized in making goods for others, the people who made and sold clothing or pottery began to "mark" their wares with a word or symbol to identify the maker. Such marks—often no more than the name of the maker—have been discovered on goods from China, India, Persia, Egypt, Rome, Greece, and elsewhere, and date back as much as 4,000 years. *See* WILLIAM H. BROWNE, A TREATISE ON THE LAW OF TRADEMARKS 1–14 (1885). These early marks served several purposes. First, they were a form of advertising, allowing makers to get their name in front of potential customers. Second, they may have been used to prove that the goods were sold by a particular merchant, thus helping to resolve ownership disputes. Third, the marks served as a guarantee of quality, since a merchant who identifies herself with her goods puts her reputation on the line.

These functions coalesced in modern practice, where trademarks are widely viewed as devices that help to reduce information and transaction costs by allowing customers to estimate the nature and quality of goods before purchase.

Consumers rely most on trademarks when it is difficult to inspect a product quickly and cheaply to determine its quality. Many products fit this description: cars, computers, electronic equipment, even food and toys. In precisely these cases, unscrupulous competitors may be tempted to copy the trademark of a rival producer known for superior quality. After all, it is easier to copy a trademark than to duplicate production techniques, quality assurance programs, and the like. Early trademark cases reflect an awareness of the need to provide a legal remedy against counterfeiting. *See, e.g.*, *Sykes v. Sykes*, 107 Eng. Rep. 834 (1824) (entitling first user of a trademark to prevent subsequent use of the same mark by others selling the same types of goods).

In the United States, federal statutory trademark protection emerged relatively late by comparison to patent and copyright protection. This reflected the gradual path of economic development.

> [T]rademark law . . . was relatively undeveloped in [the early nineteenth century]. No trademark infringement case was decided in the United States before 1825. Joseph Story granted the first injunction for trademark infringement, in 1844, to protect the makers of "Taylor's Persian Thread." Congress provided neither guidance nor any machinery for registration. Legal protection for designers of trademarks had to be forged in the rough mills of the courts. The economy was still deeply rooted in land and its produce. Intellectual property, despite the name, was not valued for intellectual reasons at all, but because of mercantile and industrial applications. As such, this property was not a central concern of the law until the full-blown factory age.

LAWRENCE FRIEDMAN, A HISTORY OF AMERICAN LAW 257 (2d ed. 1985).

Trademarks in the eighteenth century were protected only by the common law of fraud. *See* Kenneth J. Vandevelde, *The New Property of the Nineteenth Century: The Development of the Modern Concept of Property*, 29 BUFF. L. REV. 325, 341 (1980). "[I]n the American colonies laws passed to maintain the quality of manufactured articles came to form the basis of the country's subsequent trademark legislation. . . . [B]ut not until the late 1840s was the first state law passed to 'prevent fraud in the use of false stamps and labels.' . . . ." Mira Wilkins, *The Neglected Intangible Asset: The Influence of the Trademark on the Rise of the Modern Corporation*, 34 BUS. & HIST. 66, 72 (1992). Beginning with *Millington v. Fox*, 3 My. & Cr. 338, 40 Eng. Rep. 956 (Ch. 1838), where a tradesman was permanently enjoined from using another's mark, dicta suggested that marks were a form of property.

Congress enacted federal trademark protection in 1870. That statute, which grounded protection for trademark rights in the IP Clause of the Constitution, however, was short-lived. The Supreme Court struck down the establishment of trademark protection under a legislative power to protect "inventions and discoveries in the arts and sciences, or with the writings of authors." *Trade-Mark Cases*, 100 U.S. 82, 93–94 (1879). As the Court noted, "[t]he ordinary trade-mark has no necessary relation to invention or discovery." *Id.* at 94. Nor do they reflect "*the fruits of intellectual labor*, embodied in the form of books, prints, engravings, and the like." *Id.* (emphasis in original).

The Supreme Court suggested that the Commerce Clause provided a proper foundation for trademark protection. *Id.* at 94–95. Congress followed this guidance, reenacting limited federal trademark protection in the Act of 1881. As a result, the use of a mark in commerce has long served as a requirement for trademark protection. The 1881 Act, however, was limited to use of marks in foreign commerce. Congress expanded protection to interstate commerce in the Act of 1905. The modern statutory codification dates to the Lanham Act, 15 U.S.C. § 1051, et seq., enacted in 1946.

The history of federal trademark protection reflects expansion of trademark owner rights. The Act of 1905 eliminated the requirements of identity and intention to deceive, substituting instead the more fluid test of likelihood of confusion. The Lanham Act further broadened trademark law by providing advantages to registration of trademarks and introducing a separate statutory prohibition against "unfair methods of competition" that afforded protection even to unregistered marks. 15 U.S.C. § 1125(a). Congress added protection against dilution—blurring and tarnishment—of famous marks in 1996. It added protection for domain names in 1999. The result is that a broad class of "marks" now qualify for Lanham Act protection, and a small subset of famous marks have protection beyond confusing uses.

2. Trademark Theory

Trademarks differ in fundamental ways from the other types of intellectual property protection we have studied thus far. Patents, copyrights, and trade secrets are designed to protect and/or reward something new, inventive, or creative, whether it be an idea, discovery, , or expressive work. A trademark, by contrast, does not "depend upon novelty, invention, discovery, or any work of the brain. It requires no fancy or imagination, no genius, no laborious thought." *Trade-Mark Cases*, 100 U.S. at 94. Rather, trademark protection is awarded merely to those who were the first to use a distinctive mark in commerce. In trademark parlance, the senior (that is, first) user of a mark may prevent junior (subsequent) users from employing the same or a similar mark where there is a "likelihood of confusion" between the two marks.

Traditionally, there has been nothing in trademark law analogous to the desire to encourage invention or creation that underlies (at least in part) patent and copyright law. There is no explicit federal policy to encourage the creation of more trademarks. Rather, the fundamental principles of trademark law have essentially been ones of tort: unfair competition and the tort of deception of the consumer.[1] *See* Mark McKenna, *The Normative Foundations of Trademark Law*, 82 NOTRE DAME L. REV. 1839 (2007). In this sense, trademarks may not be thought of as analogous to "property rights" at all. *See, e.g., Hanover Star Milling Co. v. Metcalf*, 240 U.S. 403 (1916), and cases cited therein. Rather, they are rights acquired with the use of a trademark in commerce, and they continue only so long as that use continues. Nonetheless, some aspects of trademark law and some recent trends in the law are best explained by thinking of trademarks as property rights.

Early cases (and statutes) took a narrow view of trademark protection. Trademark infringement originally was limited to the use of a name or mark identical to the trademark in the sale of identical goods, where the infringer's use was intended to deceive consumers. These cases were essentially an extension of common law misrepresentation principles that allowed a consumer to sue.

Consumers are not the only ones injured when a company passes its goods off as being made by another. The authentic source of the goods is hurt too. One reading of trademark law is that it conflates these discrete harms into a single cause of action—one that can only be brought by the competitor, not the consumer. Doing so increased the likelihood that these causes of action would be brought in the first place. Individual consumers are isolated, and each one generally purchases only a few of a given trademarked item. An individual consumer has very little incentive to police trademark infringements. The difficulty of forming a class for purposes of class action remedies is simply too great. This is an example of the collective action problem.

Competitors have a much greater incentive to police misuse of their marks. In this view, the legitimate trademark user's lower transaction costs in policing the mark are harnessed to the original, fundamental consumer protection rationale to obtain the mod-

---

[1] These are two very different interests held by different parties, both protected by a trademark granted to one of the parties. This combination of producer and consumer interests in trademark protection is significant, and this theme runs throughout the chapter.

ern trademark infringement suit. Trademark "ownership," in this view, essentially begins as something like a legal fiction that gives the trademark owner a cause of action he would not otherwise have, in order to benefit consumers and the competitive process.

Giving the originator of a mark the right to police counterfeiting also serves to protect investment in advertising and promoting the product in association with the mark and product-related investments such as high-quality raw materials, production equipment, and quality assurance techniques. This theory is closer to a traditional IP story, but unlike patents and copyrights, the investment the law is protecting is not in the thing being protected.

3. The Basic Economics of Trademarks and Advertising

Economic analysis of seller-provided information (advertising and trademarks) grows out of several fields of economic research and has evolved significantly over the past century. Early industrial organization economists were critical of advertising (and hence branding) on the ground that such activities "unnaturally" stimulated demand, thereby fostering and perpetuating oligopoly through "artificial" product differentiation. Edward Chamberlin viewed trademarks as a means for reinforcing monopoly power by differentiating products and thereby excluding others from using the differentiating characteristic, even if only a mark. *See* EDWARD CHAMBERLIN, THE THEORY OF MONOPOLISTIC COMPETITION (1933). By generating a downward sloping demand curve for its brand, trademark owners could generate monopoly rents (and resulting deadweight loss). Drawing on this literature, Professor Ralph Brown tied the analysis of trade symbols to the larger context of commercial advertising, which he considered to serve both useful (informative) and wasteful (persuasive—intended to suggest that one product is superior to a similar if not identical alternative) ends. *See* Ralph S. Brown, Jr,, *Advertising and the Public Interest: Legal Protection of Trade Symbols*, 47 YALE L.J. 1165 (1948). This led him to approach trademark protection with skepticism.

There is something to this concern. Certainly, advertising may have the effect of differentiating in the minds of consumers products that are in fact similar or identical. The result of this brand differentiation may be that the trademark owner obtains some power over price. An example is over-the-counter drugs, where brand-name drugs regularly sell for twice the price of their "generic" equivalents, even though the two drugs are chemically identical. Thus, one could argue that advertising actually hurts rather than helps consumers.

Nonetheless, the information economics literature of the 1960s and 1970s offered a more positive view of advertising and trademarks. *See* Jack Hirshleifer, *Where Are We in the Theory of Information?*, 63 AMER. ECON. REV. 31 (1973); Phillip Nelson, *Advertising as Information*, 82 J. POL. ECON. 729 (1974); George J. Stigler, *The Economics of Information*, 69 J. POL. ECON. 213 (1961). They reasoned that trademarks, as a concise and unequivocal indicator of the source (e.g., Apple) and nature (e.g., iPhone) of particular goods, facilitate consumer search. Consumers can readily assess observable product characteristics, such as price, color, shape. Experience characteristics, such as taste or durability, are more difficult to assess. By communicating the source of the goods, trademarks signal product reliability and quality characteristics associated with the reputation of the manufacturer. Thus, they can counteract the "market for lemons" problem—the unreliability of some goods—by communicating to consumers the enterprise which is responsible for the goods and, in some cases, the specifications of the goods. *See* George A. Ackerlof, *The Market for 'Lemons': Quality Uncertainty and the Market Mechanism*, 84 Q.J. ECON. 488 (1970).

The brand name Coca-Cola, for example, informs the consumer of the maker of the soft drink beverage as well as the taste that they can expect. If the product lives up to or exceeds expectations, then the trademark owner gains a loyal customer who will be willing to pay a premium in future transactions; if the product disappoints, then the trademark owner will have more difficulty making future sales to that consumer (or will have to offer a discount to attract their business). In this way, trademarks implicitly communicate unobservable characteristics about the quality of branded products, thereby fostering incentives for firms to invest in product quality, even when such attributes are not directly observable prior to a purchasing decision. Sellers who enter the high quality segment of the market must initially invest in building a strong reputation. Only after consumers become acquainted with the attributes of their brand can they recoup these costs. In equilibrium, therefore, high quality items sell for a premium above their costs of production to compensate for the initial investment in reputation. Trademarks also facilitate efficient new business models, such as franchising, which generate economies of scale and scope in marketing and facilitate rapid business diffusion across vast geographic areas.

The branding of products also creates incentives for disreputable sellers to pass off their own wares as the goods of better respected manufacturers. Trademark law (as well as false advertising and unfair competition laws more generally) harnesses the incentives of sellers in the marketplace to police the use of marks and advertising claims of competitors. Sellers often have the best information about the quality of products in the marketplace; they also have a direct stake in preventing competitors from free riding on their brand, reputation, and consumer loyalty. By creating private causes of action, trademark and false advertising law take advantage of this informational base and incentive structure as well as the vast decentralized enforcement resources of trademark owners to regulate the informational marketplace, effectively in the name of consumers.

Under this now widely accepted view of consumer information economics, trademarks economize on consumer search costs. Consumers benefit from concise and effective designations of the source of products. For example, consumers can quickly assess the attributes of a computer made by Lenovo® featuring an Intel® Pentium® processor and Microsoft®'s Windows® operating system. If such trademarks were not available or could not be relied upon, the consumer would have to incur substantial additional costs in shopping for a computer. The ability to establish and maintain reliable trademarks reinforces firms' desire to develop and maintain consistent quality standards. It also fosters competition among firms over a wide quality and variety spectrum.

In general, consumers distinguish among three types of product features: search attributes, such as color and price, which can be inspected prior to purchase; experience attributes, such as taste, which can only be verified through use of the product (typically after purchase); and credence attributes, such as durability, which can only be verified over time (or through the use of surrogate sources of information—e.g., CONSUMER REPORTS). Brands signal experience and credence attributes. Branded dealers are more likely to carry products for which quality was more difficult to verify and to serve customers who place a higher value on search.

Some trademarks also serve a more ambiguous function: signaling status or identity for some consumers. Some have referred to such commodities as "Veblen" goods, reflecting Thorstein Veblen's theory of conspicuous consumption. *See* THORSTEIN VEBLEN, THE THEORY OF THE LEISURE CLASS: AN ECONOMIC STUDY OF INSTITUTIONS (1899). This theory posits that demand for status goods rise with increases in price. Purchasers of such goods may be interested in being associated with a particular brand—such as a Rolex watch, a t-shirt with the name and colors of a particular university, or a corporate brand—possibly apart from whether it is authentic or the quality associated with the authentic good. *See* Rochelle C. Dreyfuss, *Expressive Genericity: Trademarks as Language in the Pepsi Generation*, 65 NOTRE DAME L. REV. 397 (1990). Some purchasers of such goods may well prefer a less expensive, counterfeit version. They presumably would not be confused when purchasing such goods (e.g., a "Rolex" watch sold on a street corner for $10). A brand evokes an image, and consumers adopt the brand because they feel attached to the image or want to be associated with it. Note that when a trademark serves as an indicator of a brand, it is primarily associated with general qualities and attributes, as opposed to specific features of specific products. Thus Ralph Lauren, Martha Stewart, and Nike may have originated as traditional trademarks indicating the source of specific products (such as luxury clothing, housewares, or running shoes), but they have over time become something much more: a signal of values, attributes and even a particular lifestyle. When a trademark reaches this status, it can be attached to many different types of products. It still indicates that the goods it is attached to emanate from an "authorized source," but it is doing something quite distinct from the traditional function of trademarks. It is understood that a brand is widely licensed, and that the trademark owner does not itself manufacture all the goods to which the brand/mark are attached. The brand serves rather as an indication that the things it is attached to embody in some way the values and lifestyle signal associated with the brand. *See* Susan Fournier, *Consumers and Their Brands: Developing Relationship Theory in Consumer Research*, 24 J. CONSUMER RESEARCH 343 (1998).

The marketing of less expensive, lower quality imitations of status goods has different effects on the sellers and purchasers of authentic goods. The availability of counterfeit articles could conceivably divert some consumers who would otherwise purchase the authentic article even though they know it is not genuine, although this effect is likely to be relatively small due to the large price differential and the availability of the authentic goods for those who are interested. The lower quality of the counterfeit goods could, however, erode the goodwill associated with the authentic manufacturer through post-sale confusion—on-lookers who mistake the shoddier counterfeit good for the authentic good and may be less inclined to purchase the authentic version by the trademark owner, thereby reducing sales by the trademark owner. In addition, due to the proliferation of non-easily recognized "fakes," prior and potential purchasers of the authentic "status" goods may be less interested in owning a much less rare commodity. The value of ownership may be sullied. In essence, status goods exhibit a negative network externality, whereby proliferation of such goods erodes the value to prior purchasers. The significance of these harms is speculative, and should perhaps be weighed against the expressive benefits to those who want to associate themselves with a brand without paying the price. *See* Jeremy Sheff, *Veblen Brands*, 96 MINN. L. REV. 769 (2012); Barton Beebe, *Intellectual Property Law and the Sumptuary Code*, 123 HARV. L. REV. 809 (2010).

Notwithstanding the general benefits afforded by trademarks, protection entails several types of costs. Protection of generic or descriptive terms as trademark can increase search costs and impair competition by raising the marketing costs of competitors. For example, if a cookie manufacturer were to obtain a trademark on the word "cookie," then other companies interested in selling cookies would have a much more difficult time communicating the nature of their goods to consumers. If, however, the trademark was to "Mrs. Fields Cookies" and any protection for "cookies" was disclaimed, then potential competitors would be able to describe their products in the most easily recognized manner and would be able to develop their own marks—such as "ACME Cookies." At a minimum, trademark protection for descriptive terms significantly reduces the effective range of terms that may be used others.

A complicating factor in the protection of trademarks is the endogeneity of the usage and meaning of terms and symbols over time. Even a distinctive term can become "generic" (common) if consumers come to associate marks with a particular product (as opposed to its manufacturer). The evolution of the use of the term "thermos" illustrates this phenomenon. At the turn of the twentieth century, the original manufacturer of vacuum-insulated flasks selected the term "Thermos"—derived from the word "therme" meaning "heat"—to brand its product. At the time that it was adopted, Thermos was distinctive and not associated with any particular product. The American Thermos Bottle Company, which acquired the U.S. patent rights for this technology, undertook advertising and educational campaigns that tended to make "thermos" a generic term descriptive of vacuum-insulated flasks rather than of its origin. After the patents expired, other manufacturers began using this term to describe their own vacuum insulated flask products. As we will discuss further below, use of the term became generic in the eyes of consumers, and hence the law, and the original manufacturer of the product (and developer of the mark) lost trademark protection. *King-Seeley Thermos Co. v. Aladdin Industries, Inc.*, 321 F.2d 577 (2d Cir. 1963).

As with other modes of intellectual property, trademark protection also involves administrative and maintenance costs. Although the cost of acquiring trademark protection is relatively low, mark owners must police their marks to prevent unauthorized use and supervise licensees to ensure that quality standards are maintained. As a mark enters common parlance and becomes associated in the minds of consumers with a general product category as opposed to the manufacturing source—as in the Thermos example—the owner must invest in advertising to clarify that the mark is associated with a particular supplier in order to prevent "genericide"—the death of a trademark due its becoming generic. For many years, Xerox spent large sums on advertising to discourage generic usage of the term "xerox" as noun or verb for photocopying. (Such advertising, however, may well serve a more traditional marketing function: reminding consumers that Xerox is a dominant source and brand.) Google faces a similar exposure today.

Trademark law has been expanding in recent decades. Trade dress, anti-dilution protection, anti-cybersquatting protection, and other developments are all part of the trend. This expansion has moved trademark's conceptual center of gravity well beyond its traditional moorings in "consumer confusion."

> [M]any courts and commentators succumbed to "property mania"—the belief that expanded trademark protection was necessarily desirable so long as the result could be characterized as "property." The result has been a radical and ongoing expansion of trademark protection, both in terms of what can be owned as a trademark and in terms of what trademark ownership entails. This expansion, and its associated reinterpretation of trademark's underlying policies, presents a serious threat to social welfare and has placed at risk the competitive balance that deception-based trademark law originally established. Like deception-based trademark protection, property-based trademark protection can enable a trademark owner to differentiate her product and exclude others from using the differentiating feature. It can thereby cede control over distinct product markets to individual producers and generate for a trademark owner the downward sloping demand curve of a monopolist. However, unlike deception-based trademark, property-based trademark has only a tenuous relationship to consumer deception, and therefore lacks the offsetting efficiency advantages associated with deception-based trademark's quality control and certification functions. As a result, property-based trademark appears presumptively anticompetitive—it generates market power and associated efficiency losses without the offsetting efficiency gains that are thought to justify deception-based trademark.

Glynn S. Lunney, Jr., *Trademark Monopolies*, 48 EMORY L.J. 367, 372 (1999); *see* Mark A. Lemley, *The Modern Lanham Act and the Death of Common Sense*, 108 YALE L.J. 1687 (1999). Critics of expansive trademark law address one form of trademark expansion: the strengthening of the bundle of rights associated with a particular trademark. However, trademark owners often engage in another type of expansion: once a trademark is established for one type of product, they try to "leverage the brand" by selling other products under the same trademark. Marketing evidence, however, suggests that consumers are quite good at keeping different products using the same brand separate in their minds. *See* Mark P. McKenna, *Testing Modern Trademark Law's Theory of Harm*, 95 IOWA L. REV. 63 (2009).

Those costs are greater still when trademark law protects not words, but the characteristics of the products themselves. Preventing a competitor from using the word "cookie" to describe its products would put them (and consumers) to some inconvenience, forcing them to find another word consumers would understand. But if the trademark owner can claim that their decision to include chocolate chips in their cookies is a trademark because people identify chocolate chip cookies with them, competitors will be unable to make similar products under any name

Trademark protection can also interfere with both communicative and creative expression. Broad exclusive trademark rights would limit the ability of others (including non-competitors) to comment on and poke fun at trademarks and their owners. *See generally* Rebecca Tushnet, *Trademark as Commercial Speech Regulation*, 58 S. C. L. REV. 737 (2007). Various doctrines limit such adverse effects. But as trademark protection has expanded beyond the traditional core–for example, to encompass a broad conception of connection to, sponsorship, and affiliation with a trademark owner–it becomes more difficult to assess the boundaries, leading film and television production companies, for example, to tread carefully (and increasingly incur the costs of licensing transactions) in the use of trademarks in their works.

COMMENTS AND QUESTIONS

1. Note how the two economic approaches to trademarks—the older product differentiation theory (trademarks bad) and the newer product information theory (trademarks good)—follow from differing views of the economic role of advertising and promotional expenditure in general. Do you think advertising (1) communicates valuable price/quality information; (2) artificially creates demand for nonessential product features and product "image"; or (3) some combination of the two? *See* Barton Beebe, *Search and Persuasion in Trademark Law*, 103 MICH. L. REV. 2020 (2005) (arguing that people's views of trademark law largely depend on inconsistent assumptions about whether advertising helps or manipulates consumers).

2. Why is a legal remedy necessary for false representations about the origins of consumer goods? If you hire a carpenter to fix your roof and he does a bad job, you will not hire him again. What are the differences between this scenario and products purchased less often from more diverse sources? *See* Akerlof, *supra*, (observing that under some conditions markets for goods such as used cars may not function effectively because buyers find it difficult to test the quality of the goods offered, giving sellers an incentive to sell poor quality items, with a resultant diminution of activity across the entire market). Akerlof concludes that one way to stop the "market for lemons" dynamic, where bad (low quality) sellers drive out good ones, is through the use of brand names.

> Brand names not only indicate quality but also give the consumer means of retaliation if the quality does not meet expectations. For the consumer will then curtail future purchases. Often too, new products are associated with old brand names. This ensures the prospective consumer of the quality of the product.

Id. Akerlof identifies other institutions that serve the same purpose: guarantees; chain stores; and government licensing, as of doctors. Could all trademark law be eliminated by mandatory warranty terms? Would consumers necessarily trust them? Would such terms lower search costs as much as brand names? How about government certification programs—e.g., "U.S. Grade A Refrigerators"? If the idea is that consumers need certification of quality levels, why wouldn't they prefer independent, third party certification? Under what circumstances do consumers demand just that? Do they do so, e.g., for airlines, doctors, lawyers? Why in some cases and not others? (Consider the costs of a bad product choice.)

Alternatively, private organizations might be expected to spring up to provide unbiased evaluation of products for a fee. Such organizations exist. Groups like Consumer's Union sell their evaluations of products, and their reputation depends on continued accuracy and integrity in product investigation. Other examples of private, third-party certification include Good Housekeeping magazine and Underwriters Laboratories, both of which give "seals of approval" to certain products and services that meet their quality standards.

B.   WHAT CAN BE PROTECTED AS A TRADEMARK?

As noted above, the first trademarks were simply names or identifying symbols attached to goods. Names, symbols, and logos remain important trademarks, but they have been joined by a host of other sorts of trademarks. Company names now exist alongside product names. Slogans or phrases qualify for protection as trademarks. The design of a product itself or its packaging may be distinctive "trade dress" entitled to protection under the Lanham Act.

As with patent and copyright law, various doctrines restrict what terms and symbols are eligible for trademark protection. Suppose, for example, that Ford owned the exclusive right to describe its products as "cars" or "automobiles." Customers looking for automated means of ground transportation offered by other companies might encounter difficulty in knowing what to ask for. *See* Kenneth L. Port, *Foreword: Symposium on Intellectual Property Law Theory*, 68 CHI.-KENT L. REV. 585, 596–98 (1993).

To avoid this problem, only some terms and symbols are eligible for trademark protection. Whether an identifying name or phrase may be protected as a trademark, and the degree of protection accorded to it, both depend on the "strength" of the mark. This in turn depends on, among other things, the "classification" of the term as either (1) arbitrary or fanciful, (2) suggestive, (3) descriptive, or (4) generic. An arbitrary or fanciful mark is a word or phrase that bears no relationship whatsoever to the product it describes. "Exxon" is a good example of a fanciful mark. Arbitrary and fanciful marks are the strongest, because any value they possess in terms of name recognition obviously comes from the corporate use of the name, rather than the natural association in people's minds between a name and a product. The other three categories decrease in strength as they increase in natural association: "suggestive" marks suggest a product in people's minds; "descriptive" terms, including geographic designations and personal names, describe the product or service offered. They only garner trademark protection upon acquiring source-identifying meaning to consumers. "Generic" terms are so associated with a particular product class that they have become the natural way to refer to that type of product, and hence are ineligible for trademark protection.

1. Trademarks, Trade Names, and Service Marks

To the layperson, trademarks are often thought of as the public name of a producer or other business. The Lanham Act distinguishes among several different types of marks. "Trademarks" are the words, phrases, logos, and symbols that producers use to identify their goods:

> **Trademark.** The term "trademark" includes any word, name, symbol, or device, or any combination thereof—
>
> > (1) used by a person, or
> >
> > (2) which a person has a bona fide intention to use in commerce and applies to register on the principal register established by this Act,
>
> to identify and distinguish his or her goods, including a unique product, from those manufactured or sold by others and to indicate the source of the goods, even if that source is unknown.

Lanham Act § 45, 15 U.S.C. § 1127.

The term "trademark" does not cover another closely associated type of business identifier, the service mark. Service marks serve the same purposes as trademarks, but they are used to identify services rather than goods. The Act defines service marks as follows:

> **Service Mark.** The term "service mark" means any word, name, symbol, or device, or any combination thereof—
>
> > (1) used by a person, or
> >
> > (2) which a person has a bona fide intention to use in commerce and applies to register on the principal register established by this Act,
>
> to identify and distinguish the services of one person, including a unique service, from the services of others and to indicate the source of the services, even if that source is unknown. Titles, character names, and other distinctive features of radio and television programs may be registered as service marks notwithstanding that they, or the programs, may advertise the goods of the sponsor.

Lanham Act § 45, 15 U.S.C. § 1127. In general, service marks are subject to the same rules as trademarks. *See, e.g., Martahus v. Video Duplication Servs., Inc.*, 3 F.3d 417 (Fed. Cir. 1993) (cancellation of service mark on grounds that similar service mark had priority).

One issue that sometimes arises involves attempts to register marks for services that are closely related to the sale of goods. In general, services that are "expected or routine" in connection with particular goods are not eligible for service mark registration. This exclusion serves to reduce proliferation of closely related marks on the principal register. *See, e.g., In re Dr. Pepper Co.*, 836 F.2d 508 (Fed. Cir. 1987) (affirming trademark office rejection of service mark for conducting contests in connection with sale of soft drinks).

Unlike trademarks and service marks, trade names—the names of the businesses themselves rather than the products or services they provide—cannot be registered under the Lanham Act unless they function to identify the source of particular goods or services, rather than merely identifying a company. *See Bell v. Streetwise Records, Ltd.*, 761 F.2d 67, 75 (1st Cir. 1985). State trademark registration offices permit trade name registration even without association with particular goods or services. State and federal common law provide protection against confusingly similar company names, however.

2. Certification and Collective Marks

For the most part, the "source" identified by a trademark is a single company or individual. But for two special types of marks—certification and collective marks—this is not the case.

Certification Mark. The term "certification mark" means any word, name, symbol, or device, or any combination thereof—

(1) used by a person other than its owner, or

(2) which its owner has a bona fide intention to permit a person other than the owner to use in commerce and files an application to register on the principal register established by this chapter,

to certify regional or other origin, material, mode of manufacture, quality, accuracy, or other characteristics of such person's goods or services or that the work or labor on the goods or services was performed by members of a union or other organization.

Lanham Act § 45, 15 U.S.C. § 1127. Certification marks are generally used by trade associations or other commercial groups to identify a particular type of goods. For example, the city of Roquefort, France, holds a certification mark in "Roquefort" as a sheep's milk cheese cured in the limestone caves of Roquefort, France. *See Community of Roquefort v. William Faehndrich, Inc.*, 303 F.2d 494 (2d Cir. 1962) (enjoining use of the term "Imported Roquefort Cheese" on cheese not made in Roquefort, France). Certification marks cannot be limited to a single producer; they must be open to anyone who meets the standards set forth for certification.

Certification marks certify conformity with centralized standards. *See, e.g., Levy v. Kosher Overseers Association of America Inc.*, 36 U.S.P.Q.2d 1724 (S.D.N.Y. 1995), *rev'd*, 104 F.3d 38 (2d Cir. 1997) (involving Organized Kashruth Laboratories' well-known kosher certification mark, signified by the "circle K" mark). Many early trademarks grew out of trade guilds, which had much the same quality-control function; hence certification marks were among the first true modern trademarks. *See* FRANK SCHECHTER, THE HISTORICAL FOUNDATIONS OF THE LAW RELATING TO TRADEMARKS 47 (1925).

Certification marks are meant to bear the "seal of approval" of a central organization, so they can be cancelled on the ground that the organization no longer exercises sufficient control over its members to ensure consistent product standards. *See* Lanham Act § 14, 15 U.S.C. § 1064 (providing that a certification mark may be cancelled if not policed effectively).

> ***Collective Mark.*** The term "collective mark" means a trademark or service mark—
>
> (1) used by the members of a cooperative, an association, or other collective group or organization, or
>
> (2) which such cooperative, association, or other collective group or organization has a bona fide intention to use in commerce and applies to register on the principal register established by this chapter, and includes marks indicating membership in a union, an association, or other organization.

Lanham Act § 45, 15 U.S.C. § 1127. Collective marks can be usefully divided into two categories:

Type of Collective Mark	Characteristics	Examples
(1) Identification of Member Goods or Services	• The mark is used by collective members to identify that the source is a member of the collective. • The collective neither sells goods nor performs services under the collective mark, but may advertise or otherwise promote the goods or services sold or rendered by its members under the mark.	• National Turkey Federation (advertises under the mark "Turkey. The Perfect Protein."); members use the mark to distinguish their products from those of non-members. • Florists' Transworld Delivery Association (FTD)
(2) Identification of Membership within the Collective Organization	• Neither the collective nor its members uses the collective membership mark to identify and distinguish goods or services • The sole function of the mark is to indicate that the person displaying the mark is a member of the organized collective group.	• Professional Golf Association (PGA) • American Automobile Association (AAA) • Members of a fraternal organization display the mark by wearing pins upon which the mark appears or by carrying membership cards bearing the mark.

A collective group may itself be engaged in the marketing of its own goods or services under a particular mark, in which case the mark is not a collective mark but is rather a trademark for the collective's goods or service mark for the collective's services. For the most part, these types of collective marks are treated the same as conventional trademarks.

3. Trade Dress and Product Configurations

Words or phrases that serve to identify a product are not all that the Lanham Act protects. The act also protects "trade dress," the design and packaging of materials, and even the design and shape of a product itself, if the packaging or the product configuration serve the same source-identifying function as trademarks. It is possible to register both trade dress and product configurations as "trademarks" under the Lanham Act. (Indeed, such a registration was at issue in the *Qualitex Co. v. Jacobson Products Co., Inc.*, 514 U.S. 159 (1995), excerpted below.) However, because of the complexities of trade dress protection, many companies forgo registration of trade dress and look to § 43(a) of the Lanham Act, 15 U.S.C. § 1125(a), to enforce their claims.

§ 1125 [Lanham Act § 43]. False Designations of Origin and False Descriptions Forbidden

(a)(1) Any person who, on or in connection with any goods or services, or any container for goods, uses in commerce any word, term, name, symbol, or device, or any combination thereof, or any false designation of origin, false or misleading description of fact, or false or misleading representation of fact, which—

(A) Is likely to cause confusion, or to cause mistake, or to deceive as to the affiliation, connection, or association of such person with another person, or as to the origin, sponsorship, or approval of his or her goods, services, or commercial activities by another person, or

(B) in commercial advertising or promotion, misrepresents the nature, characteristics, qualities, or geographic origin of his or her or another person's goods, services, or commercial activities, shall be liable in a civil action by any person who believes that he or she is or is likely to be damaged by such act.

Section 43(a) is commonly referred to as providing "federal common law" protection for trademarks and related source identifiers.

C.   ESTABLISHMENT OF TRADEMARK RIGHTS

1.   Distinctiveness

i.   *Classification of Terms and Requirements for Protection*

When a term is immediately capable of identifying a unique source, rights to the term are determined solely by priority of use. *See* Chapter V(C)(2). Terms such as these are labeled "inherently distinctive," although for analytical completeness they are further subdivided into sub-categories: arbitrary and fanciful, or suggestive. For all other terms—those deemed not inherently distinctive—the Lanham Act requires proof of an additional element to secure trademark rights: secondary or acquired meaning.

The most important type of word or symbol requiring proof of secondary meaning is a *descriptive* term. A descriptive mark is "[a] word, picture, or other symbol that directly describes something about the goods or services in connection with which it is used as a mark." J. THOMAS MCCARTHY, MCCARTHY'S DESK ENCYCLOPEDIA OF INTELLECTUAL PROPERTY 119 (2d ed. 1995). Examples include: Tender Vittles for cat food, Arthriticare for arthritis treatment, and Investacorp for financial services.

In addition to descriptive terms, several other types of terms require secondary meaning to acquire legal protection: most notably *geographic* terms (such as Nantucket soft drinks) and *personal names* (such as O'Malley's beer).[2]

A descriptive term garners trademark protection when it reaches a threshold of acquired or secondary meaning associated with a single source of products. Thus, the descriptive term "Tender Vittles"—consisting of the adjective "tender" (referring to softness of food) and "vittles" (referring to food)—is protectable as a trademark only once an appreciable number of consumers associate it with a brand of cat food. To be sure, Tender Vittles retains its primary meaning as a product descriptor. But proof that it has acquired a secondary meaning as a source identifier elevates it to trademark status.

It is important to understand the nature of this secondary meaning. It does not mean that buyers need to know the *identity* of the source, only that the product or service comes from a *single* source. The phrase "single source" may thus be understood to mean "single though anonymous source." *See A.J. Canfield Co. v. Honickman*, 808 F.2d 291 (3d Cir. 1986).

Zatarain's, Inc. v. Oak Grove Smokehouse, Inc.
United States Court of Appeals for the Fifth Circuit
698 F.2d 786 (5th Cir. 1983)

GOLDBERG, Circuit Judge:

This appeal of a trademark dispute presents us with a menu of edible delights sure to tempt connoisseurs of fish and fowl alike. At issue is the alleged infringement of two trademarks, "Fish-Fri" and "Chick-Fri," held by appellant Zatarain's, Inc. ("Zatarain's"). The district court held that the alleged infringers had a "fair use" defense to any asserted infringement of the term "Fish-Fri" and that the registration of the term "Chick-Fri" should be cancelled. We affirm.

I.   Facts and Proceedings Below

A.   The Tale of the Town Frier

Zatarain's is the manufacturer and distributor of a line of over one hundred food products. Two of these products, "Fish-Fri" and "Chick-Fri," are coatings or batter mixes used to fry foods. These marks serve as the entree in the present litigation.

Zatarain's "Fish-Fri" consists of 100% corn flour and is used to fry fish and other seafood. "Fish-Fri" is packaged in rectangular cardboard boxes containing twelve or twenty-four ounces of coating mix. The legend "Wonderful FISH-FRI™" is displayed prominently on the front panel, along with the block Z used to identify all Zatarain's

---

[2] In addition, the following require proof of secondary meaning: titles of single literary works; descriptive titles of literary series; non-inherently distinctive designs and symbols; non-inherently distinctive trade dress and packaging; and product and container shapes. MCCARTHY, TRADEMARKS AND UNFAIR COMPETITION §15.01[2].

products. The term "Fish-Fri" has been used by Zatarain's or its predecessor since 1950 and has been registered as a trademark since 1962.

Zatarain's "Chick-Fri" is a seasoned corn flour batter mix used for frying chicken and other foods. The "Chick-Fri" package, which is very similar to that used for "Fish-Fri," is a rectangular cardboard container labelled "Wonderful CHICK-FRI." Zatarain's began to use the term "Chick-Fri" in 1968 and registered the term as a trademark in 1976.

Zatarain's products are not alone in the marketplace. At least four other companies market coatings for fried foods that are denominated "fish fry" or "chicken fry." Two of these competing companies are the appellees here, and therein hangs this fish tale.

Appellee Oak Grove Smokehouse, Inc. ("Oak Grove") began marketing a "fish fry" and a "chicken fry" in March 1979. Both products are packaged in clear glassine packets that contain a quantity of coating mix sufficient to fry enough food for one meal. The packets are labelled with Oak Grove's name and emblem, along with the words "FISH FRY" or "CHICKEN FRY." Oak Grove's "FISH FRY" has a corn flour base seasoned with various spices; Oak Grove's "CHICKEN FRY" is a seasoned coating with a wheat flour base.

B. Out of the Frying Pan, Into the Fire

Zatarain's first claimed foul play in its original complaint filed against Oak Grove on June 19, 1979, in the United States District Court for the Eastern District of Louisiana. The complaint alleged trademark infringement and unfair competition under the Lanham Act §§ 32(1), 43(a), 15 U.S.C. §§ 1114(1), 1125(a) (1976), and La. Rev. Stat. Ann. § 51:1405(A) (West Supp. 1982).

The district court found that Zatarain's trademark "Fish-Fri" was a descriptive term with an established secondary meaning, but held that Oak Grove and Visko's had a "fair use" defense to their asserted infringement of the mark. The court further found that Zatarain's trademark "Chick-Fri" was a descriptive term that lacked secondary meaning, and accordingly ordered the trademark registration cancelled.

Battered, but not fried, Zatarain's appeals from the adverse judgment on several grounds. First, Zatarain's argues that its trademark "Fish-Fri" is a suggestive term and therefore not subject to the "fair use" defense. Second, Zatarain's asserts that even if the "fair use" defense is applicable in this case, appellees cannot invoke the doctrine because their use of Zatarain's trademarks is not a good faith attempt to describe their products. Third, Zatarain's urges that the district court erred in cancelling the trademark registration for the term "Chick-Fri" because Zatarain's presented sufficient evidence to establish a secondary meaning for the term. For these reasons, Zatarain's argues that the district court should be reversed. . . .

III.   The Trademark Claims

A.   Basic Principles

1.   *Classifications of Marks*

The threshold issue in any action for trademark infringement is whether the work or phrase is initially registerable or protectable. Courts and commentators have traditionally divided potential trademarks into four categories. A potential trademark may be classified as (1) generic, (2) descriptive, (3) suggestive, or (4) arbitrary or fanciful. These categories, like the tones in a spectrum, tend to blur at the edges and merge together. The labels are more advisory than definitional, more like guidelines than pigeonholes. Not surprisingly, they are somewhat difficult to articulate and to apply. *Soweco, Inc. v. Shell Oil* Co., 617 F.2d 1178, 1183 (5th Cir. 1980); *Vision Center*, 596 F.2d at 115.

A generic term is "the name of a particular genus or class of which an individual article or service is but a member." *Vision Center*, 596 F.2d at 115; *Abercrombie & Fitch Co. v. Hunting World, Inc.*, 537 F.2d 4, 9 (2d Cir. 1976). A generic term connotes the "basic nature of articles or services" rather than the more individualized characteristics of a particular product. *American Heritage*, 494 F.2d at 11. Generic terms can never attain trademark protection. *William R. Warner & Co. v. Eli Lilly & Co.*, 265 U.S. 526, 528 (1924). Further, if at any time a registered trademark becomes generic as to a particular product or service, the mark's registration is subject to cancellation. Lanham Act § 14, 15 U.S.C. § 1064(c) (1976). Such terms as aspirin and cellophane have been held generic and therefore unprotectable as trademarks. *See Bayer Co. v. United Drug Co.*, 272 F. 505 (S.D.N.Y. 1921) (aspirin); *Du Pont Cellophane Co. v. Waxed Products Co.*, 85 F.2d 75 (2d Cir. 1936) (cellophane).

A descriptive term "identifies a characteristic or quality of an article or service," *Vision Center*, 596 F.2d at 115, such as its color, odor, function, dimensions, or ingredients. *American Heritage*, 494 F.2d at 11. Descriptive terms ordinarily are not protectable as trademarks, Lanham Act § 2(e)(1), 15 U.S.C. § 1052(e)(1) (1976); they may become valid marks, however, by acquiring a secondary meaning in the minds of the consuming public. *See id.* § 2(f), 15 U.S.C. § 1052(f). Examples of descriptive marks would include "Alo" with reference to products containing gel of the aloe vera plant, *Aloe Creme Laboratories, Inc. v. Milsan, Inc.*, 423 F.2d 845 (5th Cir. 1970), and "Vision Center" in reference to a business offering optical goods and services, *Vision Center*, 596 F.2d at 117. As this court has often noted, the distinction between descriptive and generic terms is one of degree. *Soweco*, 617 F.2d at 1184; *Vision Center*, 596 F.2d at 115 n.11 (citing 3 R. CALLMAN, THE LAW OF UNFAIR COMPETITION, TRADEMARKS AND MONOPOLIES § 70.4 (3d ed. 1969)). The distinction has important practical consequences, however; while a descriptive term may be elevated to trademark status with proof of secondary meaning, a generic term may never achieve trademark protection. *Vision Center*, 596 F.2d at 115 n.11.

A suggestive term suggests, rather than describes, some particular characteristic of the goods or services to which it applies and requires the consumer to exercise the imagination in order to draw a conclusion as to the nature of the goods and services. *Soweco*, 617 F.2d at 1184. A suggestive mark is protected without the necessity for proof of secondary meaning. The term "Coppertone" has been held suggestive in regard to sun tanning products. *See Douglas Laboratories, Inc. v. Copper Tan*, Inc., 210 F.2d 453 (2d Cir. 1954).

Arbitrary or fanciful terms bear no relationship to the products or services to which they are applied. Like suggestive terms, arbitrary and fanciful marks are protectable without proof of secondary meaning. The term "Kodak" is properly classified as a fanciful term for photographic supplies, *see Eastman Kodak Co. v. Weil*, 137 Misc. 506, 243 N.Y.S. 319 (1930) ("Kodak"); "Ivory" is an arbitrary term as applied to soap. *Abercrombie & Fitch*, 537 F.2d at 9 n.6.

2. Secondary Meaning

As noted earlier, descriptive terms are ordinarily not protectable as trademarks. They may be protected, however, if they have acquired a secondary meaning for the consuming public. The concept of secondary meaning recognizes that words with an ordinary and primary meaning of their own "may [after] long use with a particular product, come to be known by the public as specifically designating that product." *Volkswagenwerk Aktiengesellschaft v. Rickard*, 492 F.2d 474, 477 (5th Cir. 1974). In order to establish a secondary meaning for a term, a plaintiff "must show that the primary significance of the term in the minds of the consuming public is not the product but the producer." *Kellogg Co. v. National Biscuit Co.*, 305 U.S. 111, 118 (1938). The burden of proof to establish secondary meaning rests at all times with the plaintiff; this burden is not an easy one to satisfy, for "[a] high degree of proof is necessary to establish secondary meaning for a descriptive term." *Vision Center*, 596 F.2d at 118 (quoting 3 R. CALLMAN, *supra*, § 77.3, at 359). Proof of secondary meaning is an issue only with respect to descriptive marks; suggestive and arbitrary or fanciful marks are automatically protected upon registration, and generic terms are unprotectable even if they have acquired secondary meaning. *See Soweco*, 617 F.2d at 1185 n.20.

3. The "Fair Use" Defense

Even when a descriptive term has acquired a secondary meaning sufficient to warrant trademark protection, others may be entitled to use the mark without incurring liability for trademark infringement. When the allegedly infringing term is "used fairly and in good faith only to describe to users the goods or services of [a] party, or their geographic origin," Lanham Act § 33(b)(4), 15 U.S.C. § 1115(b)(4) (1976), a defendant in a trademark infringement action may assert the "fair use" defense. The defense is available only in actions involving descriptive terms and only when the term is used in its descriptive sense rather than its trademark sense. *Soweco*, 617 F.2d at 1185; *see Venetianaire Corp. v. A & P Import Co.*, 429 F.2d 1079, 1081–1082 (2d Cir. 1970). In essence, the fair use defense prevents a trademark registrant from appropriating a descriptive term for its own use to the exclusion of others, who may be prevented thereby from accurately describing their own goods. *Soweco*, 617 F.2d at 1185. The holder of a protectable descriptive mark has no legal claim to an exclusive right in the primary, descriptive meaning of the term; consequently, anyone is free to use the term in its primary, descriptive sense so long as such use does not lead to customer confusion as to the source of the goods or services. *See* 1 J. MCCARTHY, TRADEMARKS AND UNFAIR COMPETITION § 11.17, at 379 (1973).

4. Cancellation of Trademarks

Section 37 of the Lanham Act, 15 U.S.C. § 1119 (1976), provides as follows:

> In any action involving a registered mark the court may determine the right to registration, order the cancellation of registrations, in whole or in part, restore cancelled registrations, and otherwise rectify the register with respect to the registrations of any party to the action. Decrees and orders shall be certified by the court to the Commissioner, who shall make appropriate entry upon the records of the Patent Office, and shall be controlled thereby.

This circuit has held that when a court determines that a mark is either a generic term or a descriptive term lacking secondary meaning, the purposes of the Lanham Act are well served by an order cancelling the mark's registration. *American Heritage*, 494 F.2d at 14.

We now turn to the facts of the instant case.

B. "FISH-FRI"[3]

1. Classification

Throughout this litigation, Zatarain's has maintained that the term "Fish-Fri" is a suggestive mark automatically protected from infringing uses by virtue of its registration in 1962. Oak Grove and Visko's assert that "fish fry" is a generic term identifying a class of foodstuffs used to fry fish; alternatively, Oak Grove and Visko's argue that "fish fry" is merely descriptive of the characteristics of the product. The district court found that "Fish-Fri" was a descriptive term identifying a function of the product being sold. Having reviewed this finding under the appropriate "clearly erroneous" standard, we affirm. *See Vision Center*, 596 F.2d at 113.

We are mindful that "[t]he concept of descriptiveness must be construed rather broadly." 3 R. CALLMAN, *supra*, § 70.2. Whenever a word or phrase conveys an immediate idea of the qualities, characteristics, effect, purpose, or ingredients of a product or service, it is classified as descriptive and cannot be claimed as an exclusive trademark. *Id.* § 71.1; *see Stix Products, Inc. v. United Merchants & Manufacturers, Inc.*, 295 F. Supp. 479, 488 (S.D.N.Y. 1968). Courts and commentators have formulated a number of tests to be used in classifying a mark as descriptive.

A suitable starting place is the dictionary, for "[t]he dictionary definition of the word is an appropriate and relevant indication 'of the ordinary significance and meaning of

---

[3] We note at the outset that Zatarain's use of the phonetic equivalent of the words "fish fry"—that is, misspelling it—does not render the mark protectable. *Soweco*, 617 F.2d at 1186 n.24.

words' to the public." *American Heritage*, 494 F.2d at 11 n.5. WEBSTER'S THIRD NEW INTERNATIONAL DICTIONARY 858 (1966) lists the following definitions for the term "fish fry": "1. a picnic at which fish are caught, fried, and eaten; . . . 2. fried fish." Thus, the basic dictionary definitions of the term refer to the preparation and consumption of fried fish. This is at least preliminary evidence that the term "Fish-Fri" is descriptive of Zatarain's product in the sense that the words naturally direct attention to the purpose or function of the product.

The "imagination test" is a second standard used by the courts to identify descriptive terms. This test seeks to measure the relationship between the actual words of the mark and the product to which they are applied. If a term "requires imagination, thought and perception to reach a conclusion as to the nature of goods," *Stix Products*, 295 F. Supp. at 488, it is considered a suggestive term. Alternatively, a term is descriptive if standing alone it conveys information as to the characteristics of the product. In this case, mere observation compels the conclusion that a product branded "Fish-Fri" is a prepackaged coating or batter mix applied to fish prior to cooking. The connection between this merchandise and its identifying terminology is so close and direct that even a consumer unfamiliar with the product would doubtless have an idea of its purpose or function. It simply does not require an exercise of the imagination to deduce that "Fish-Fri" is used to fry fish. *See Vision Center*, 596 F.2d at 116–17. Accordingly, the term "Fish-Fri" must be considered descriptive when examined under the "imagination test."

A third test used by courts and commentators to classify descriptive marks is "whether competitors would be likely to need the terms used in the trademark in describing their products." *Union Carbide Corp. v. Ever-Ready, Inc.*, 531 F.2d 366, 379 (7th Cir. 1976). A descriptive term generally relates so closely and directly to a product or service that other merchants marketing similar goods would find the term useful in identifying their own goods. *Vision Center*, 596 F.2d at 116–17. Common sense indicates that in this case merchants other than Zatarain's might find the term "fish fry" useful in describing their own particular batter mixes. While Zatarain's has argued strenuously that Visko's and Oak Grove could have chosen from dozens of other possible terms in naming their coating mix, we find this position to be without merit. As this court has held, the fact that a term is not the only or even the most common name for a product is not determinative, for there is no legal foundation that a product can be described in only one fashion. *Vision Center*, 596 F.2d at 117 n.17. There are many edible fish in the sea, and as many ways to prepare them as there are varieties to be prepared. Even piscatorial gastronomes would agree, however, that frying is a form of preparation accepted virtually around the world, at restaurants starred and unstarred. The paucity of synonyms for the words "fish" and "fry" suggests that a merchant whose batter mix is specially spiced for frying fish is likely to find "fish fry" a useful term for describing his product.

A final barometer of the descriptiveness of a particular term examines the extent to which a term actually has been used by others marketing a similar service or product. *Vision Center*, 596 F.2d at 117. This final test is closely related to the question whether competitors are likely to find a mark useful in describing their products. As noted above, a number of companies other than Zatarain's have chosen the word combination "fish fry" to identify their batter mixes. Arnaud's product, "Oyster Shrimp and Fish Fry," has been in competition with Zatarain's "Fish-Fri" for some ten to twenty years. When companies from A to Z, from Arnaud to Zatarain's, select the same term to describe their similar products, the term in question is most likely a descriptive one.

The correct categorization of a given term is a factual issue, *Soweco*, 617 F.2d at 1183 n.12; consequently, we review the district court's findings under the "clearly erroneous" standard of Fed. R. Civ. P. 52. *See Vision Center*, 596 F.2d at 113. The district court in this case found that Zatarain's trademark "Fish-Fri" was descriptive of the function of the product being sold. Having applied the four prevailing tests of descriptiveness to the term "Fish-Fri," we are convinced that the district court's judgment in this matter is not only not clearly erroneous, but clearly correct. . . .

2. *Secondary Meaning*

Descriptive terms are not protectable by trademark absent a showing of secondary meaning in the minds of the consuming public.[5] To prevail in its trademark infringement action, therefore, Zatarain's must prove that its mark "Fish-Fri" has acquired a secondary meaning and thus warrants trademark protection. The district court found that Zatarain's evidence established a secondary meaning for the term "Fish-Fri" in the New Orleans area. We affirm.

The existence of secondary meaning presents a question for the trier of fact, and a district court's finding on the issue will not be disturbed unless clearly erroneous. The burden of proof rests with the party seeking to establish legal protection for the mark— the plaintiff in an infringement suit. The evidentiary burden necessary to establish secondary meaning for a descriptive term is substantial.

In assessing a claim of secondary meaning, the major inquiry is the consumer's attitude toward the mark. The mark must denote to the consumer "a single thing coming from a single source," *Coca-Cola Co. v. Koke Co.*, 254 U.S. 143, 146 (1920), to support a finding of secondary meaning. Both direct and circumstantial evidence may be relevant and persuasive on the issue.

Factors such as amount and manner of advertising, volume of sales, and length and manner of use may serve as circumstantial evidence relevant to the issue of secondary meaning. *See, e.g., Vision Center*, 596 F.2d at 119. While none of these factors alone will prove secondary meaning, in combination they may establish the necessary link in

---

[5] A mark that has become "incontestable" under section 15 of the Lanham Act, 15 U.S.C. § 1065 (1976), cannot be challenged as lacking secondary meaning, although it is subject to seven statutory defenses. *See id.* § 33(b), 15 U.S.C. § 1115(b). In order for a registrant's mark to be deemed "incontestable," the registrant must use the mark for five continuous years following the registration date and must file certain affidavits with the Commissioner of Patents. *Id.* § 15, 15 U.S.C. § 1065. No evidence in the record indicates that Zatarain's has satisfied the requirements of "incontestability"; consequently, we must determine whether proof of secondary meaning otherwise exists.

the minds of consumers between a product and its source. It must be remembered, however, that "the question is not the extent of the promotional efforts, but their effectiveness in altering the meaning of [the term] to the consuming public." *Aloe Creme Laboratories*, 423 F.2d at 850.

Since 1950, Zatarain's and its predecessor have continuously used the term "Fish-Fri" to identify this particular batter mix. Through the expenditure of over $400,000 for advertising during the period from 1976 through 1981, Zatarain's has promoted its name and its product to the buying public. Sales of twelve-ounce boxes of "Fish-Fri" increased from 37,265 cases in 1969 to 59,439 cases in 1979. From 1964 through 1979, Zatarain's sold a total of 916,385 cases of "Fish-Fri." The district court considered this circumstantial evidence of secondary meaning to weigh heavily in Zatarain's favor.

In addition to these circumstantial factors, Zatarain's introduced at trial two surveys conducted by its expert witness, Allen Rosenzweig. In one survey, telephone interviewers questioned 100 women in the New Orleans area who fry fish or other seafood three or more times per month. Of the women surveyed, twenty-three percent specified Zatarain's "Fish-Fri" as a product they "would buy at the grocery to use as a coating" or a "product on the market that is especially made for frying fish." In a similar survey conducted in person at a New Orleans area mall, twenty-eight of the 100 respondents answered "Zatarain's 'Fish-Fri'" to the same questions. . . .

The authorities are in agreement that survey evidence is the most direct and persuasive way of establishing secondary meaning. *Vision Center*, 596 F.2d at 119; 1 J. MCCARTHY, *supra*, § 15.12(D). The district court believed that the survey evidence produced by Zatarain's, when coupled with the circumstantial evidence of advertising and usage, tipped the scales in favor of a finding of secondary meaning. Were we considering the question of secondary meaning de novo, we might reach a different conclusion than did the district court, for the issue is close.

Mindful, however, that there is evidence in the record to support the finding below, we cannot say that the district court's conclusion was clearly erroneous. Accordingly, the finding of secondary meaning in the New Orleans area for Zatarain's descriptive term "Fish-Fri" must be affirmed.

3. *The "Fair Use" Defense*

Although Zatarain's term "Fish-Fri" has acquired a secondary meaning in the New Orleans geographical area, Zatarain's does not now prevail automatically on its trademark infringement claim, for it cannot prevent the fair use of the term by Oak Grove and Visko's. The "fair use" defense applies only to descriptive terms and requires that the term be "used fairly and in good faith only to describe to users the goods or services of such party, or their geographic origin." Lanham Act § 33(b), 15 U.S.C. § 1115(b)(4) (1976). The district court determined that Oak Grove and Visko's were entitled to fair use of the term "fish fry" to describe a characteristic of their goods; we affirm that conclusion.

Zatarain's term "Fish-Fri" is a descriptive term that has acquired a secondary meaning in the New Orleans area. Although the trademark is valid by virtue of having acquired a secondary meaning, only that penumbra or fringe of secondary meaning is given legal protection. Zatarain's has no legal claim to an exclusive right in the original, descriptive sense of the term; therefore, Oak Grove and Visko's are still free to use the words "fish fry" in their ordinary, descriptive sense, so long as such use will not tend to confuse customers as to the source of the goods. *See* 1 J. MCCARTHY, *supra*, § 11.17.

The record contains ample evidence to support the district court's determination that Oak Grove's and Visko's use of the words "fish fry" was fair and in good faith. Testimony at trial indicated that the appellees did not intend to use the term in a trademark sense and had never attempted to register the words as a trademark. Oak Grove and Visko's apparently believed "fish fry" was a generic name for the type of coating mix they manufactured. In addition, Oak Grove and Visko's consciously packaged and labelled their products in such a way as to minimize any potential confusion in the minds of consumers. The dissimilar trade dress of these products prompted the district court to observe that confusion at the point of purchase—the grocery shelves—would be virtually impossible. Our review of the record convinces us that the district court's determinations are correct. We hold, therefore, that Oak Grove and Visko's are entitled to fair use of the term "fish fry" to describe their products; accordingly, Zatarain's claim of trademark infringement must fail.

C. "CHICK-FRI"

1. *Classification*

Most of what has been said about "Fish-Fri" applies with equal force to Zatarain's other culinary concoction, "Chick-Fri." "Chick-Fri" is at least as descriptive of the act of frying chicken as "Fish-Fri" is descriptive of frying fish. It takes no effort of the imagination to associate the term "Chick-Fri" with Southern fried chicken. Other merchants are likely to want to use the words "chicken fry" to describe similar products, and others have in fact done so. Sufficient evidence exists to support the district court's finding that "Chick-Fri" is a descriptive term; accordingly, we affirm.

2. *Secondary Meaning*

The district court concluded that Zatarain's had failed to establish a secondary meaning for the term "Chick-Fri." We affirm this finding. The mark "Chick-Fri" has been in use only since 1968; it was registered even more recently, in 1976. In sharp contrast to its promotions with regard to "Fish-Fri," Zatarain's advertising expenditures for "Chick-Fri" were mere chickenfeed; in fact, Zatarain's conducted no direct advertising campaign to publicize the product. Thus the circumstantial evidence presented in support of a secondary meaning for the term "Chick-Fri" was paltry.

Allen Rosenzweig's survey evidence regarding a secondary meaning for "Chick-Fri" also "lays an egg." The initial survey question was a "qualifier": "Approximately how many times in an average month do you, yourself, fry fish or other seafood?" Only if respondents replied "three or more times a month" were they asked to continue the survey. This qualifier, which may have been perfectly adequate for purposes of the "Fish-Fri" questions, seems highly unlikely to provide an adequate sample of potential consumers of "Chick-Fri." This survey provides us with nothing more than some data regarding fish friers' perceptions about products used for frying chicken. As such, it is entitled to little evidentiary weight.[10]

It is well settled that Zatarain's, the original plaintiff in this trademark infringement action, has the burden of proof to establish secondary meaning for its term. *Vision Center*, 596 F.2d at 118. This it has failed to do. The district court's finding that the term "Chick-Fri" lacks secondary meaning is affirmed.

COMMENTS AND QUESTIONS

1. *Geographic Scope of Secondary Meaning.* Note that in *Zatarain*'s, the survey sample is drawn from a relatively small area—the New Orleans metropolitan region. Should secondary meaning in this area permit a descriptive mark to be enforced anywhere, or only in this area? Is this in effect a geographic limitation on the scope of a trademark that is not apparent from the statute—which provides ostensibly national protection for registered marks? How does this geographic limitation interact with the doctrines governing the conflict between junior common law users of a mark and a senior, federally registered mark owner? To achieve registration and therefore nationwide protection, the Trademark Office has generally required applicants for federal registration (which confers presumptively nationwide protection) to show more than secondary meaning in a limited area. *See Philip Morris, Inc. v. Liggett & Myers Tobacco Co.*, 139 U.S.P.Q. 240 (TTAB 1963).

Trademark law limits trademark protection for unregistered descriptive marks to the geographic scope of secondary meaning. Lou Adray opened a discount electronics store in Orange County, bordering Los Angeles County, in 1968. Other members of the family operated other "Adray's" discount electronics stores in Southern California until 1979, when they sold their businesses, including the right to use the "Adray's" name, to Adry–Mart, which has since operated several "Adray's" stores in Los Angeles County. When Adry-Mart opened another "Adray's" store about five miles from Orange County, Lou Adray sought a preliminary injunction. The Ninth Circuit held that the district court was correct in instructing the jury that for Lou to receive damages he must show secondary meaning in the market areas in which Adry-Mart operated its Orange County stores. *Adray v. Adry-Mart, Inc.*, 76 F.3d 984 (9th Cir. 1996), *amending* 68 F.3d 362 (9th Cir. 1995). The court observed that there was no possibility that Lou could show national secondary meaning. The court further held that it was clear error for the district court to find that Adry-Mart's market included all of Los Angeles County; the evidence

---

[10] Even were we to accept the results of the survey as relevant, the result would not change. In the New Orleans area, only 11 of the 100 respondents in the telephone survey named "Chick-Fri," "chicken fry," or Zatarain's "Chick-Fri" as a product used as a coating for frying chicken. Rosenzweig himself testified that this number was inconclusive for sampling purposes. Thus the survey evidence cannot be said to establish a secondary meaning for the term "Chick-Fri."

established that in some parts of the county Lou Adray had a bigger market share than Adry-Mart. The court remanded the case for reconsideration of the geographic scope of each business's geographic scope.

The *Adray* court distinguished *Fuddruckers, Inc. v. Doc's B.R. Others, Inc.*, 826 F.2d 837 (9th Cir. 1987), where the Ninth Circuit held that Fuddrucker's, a national chain, was not required to establish secondary meaning in a particular disputed area if it could "show that its trade dress had acquired secondary meaning among some substantial portion of consumers nationally." The court explained that "restaurant customers travel" and "Fuddruckers should be permitted to show that its trade dress had acquired secondary meaning among some substantial portion of consumers nationally." *Id.* at 844. The court also noted that the defendants adopted their trade dress in bad faith. They opened their similarly designed restaurant after negotiations with Fuddrucker's to open a licensed franchise had collapsed.

2. *Should Suggestive Marks Be Treated as Inherently Distinctive? Compare M2 Software, Inc. v. Madacy Entm't*, 421 F.3d 1073, 1081 (9th Cir. 2005) (stating that suggestive marks, like descriptive marks, are "conceptually weak"), *with Pizzeria Uno Corp. v. Temple*, 747 F.2d 1522, 1527 (4th Cir. 1984) (stating that suggestive marks are considered "strong" as well as "presumptively valid" (quoting *Del Labs., Inc. v. Alleghany Pharmacal Corp.*, 516 F. Supp. 777, 780 (S.D.N.Y. 1981)); *see generally* Jake Linford, *The False Dichotomy Between Suggestive and Descriptive Trademarks*, 76 OHIO ST. L.J. 1367, 1402-21 (2015) (arguing that suggestive marks should be required to establish secondary meaning).

3. *Proving Secondary Meaning.* The test of "secondary meaning" is very fact-specific and relies on the reactions of consumers to a term, generally as tested through consumer surveys. The Federal Circuit set forth a representative group of factors:

> the considerations to be assessed in determining whether a mark has acquired secondary meaning can be described by the following six factors: (1) association of the trade dress with a particular source by actual purchasers (typically measured by customer surveys); (2) length, degree, and exclusivity of use; (3) amount and manner of advertising; (4) amount of sales and number of customers; (5) intentional copying; and (6) unsolicited media coverage of the product embodying the mark. . . . All six factors are to be weighed together in determining the existence of secondary meaning.

Converse, Inc. v. International Trade Comm'n, 909 F.3d 1110 (Fed. Cir. 2018).

What is the proper role of "circumstantial evidence" of secondary meaning, such as advertising expenditures, the commercial success of the product, and attempts at imitation? Such evidence is generally allowed by courts in cases where secondary meaning is at issue. But should it be? If it is clear, for example, that advertising expenditures have been completely ineffective in swaying the public, is the fact of such expenditures relevant? The answer may depend on your views as to why we are protecting trademarks.

If our goal is to provide incentives for businesses to invest in marks (and therefore in quality control), we may want to encourage such expenditures directly.

4. *Fair use*. The court refers to the "fair use defense." The trademark fair use doctrine differs from the copyright fair use doctrine. Trademark fair use refers to the right of competitors to use a term for its ordinary meaning to describe a product or service. *See Sunmark, Inc. v. Ocean Spray Cranberries, Inc.*, 64 F.3d 1055 (7th Cir. 1995) (upholding use of the term "sweet-tart" to describe the flavor of a cranberry juice drink as fair notwithstanding trademark protection of "Sweettarts" for candy). In *KP Permanent Make-up, Inc. v. Lasting Impression I, Inc.*, 543 U.S. 111 (2004), the Supreme Court held that "some possibility of consumer confusion must be compatible with fair use." The availability of the defense depends on a balance of factors, including the extent of any likely consumer confusion, accuracy of use, commercial justification, and mark strength. *See* RESTATEMENT OF UNFAIR COMPETITION § 28. We explore this defense in more detail in Chapter V(E)(3).

5. *Foreign Descriptive Terms*. In some circumstances, it may not even be clear that a term is descriptive. Consider the problem of terms that are descriptive in a language other than English. The doctrine of foreign equivalents holds that foreign words must be translated into English for purposes of determining their protectability. Application of this doctrine, however, has been uneven. Is "La Posada" (Spanish for "inn") descriptive of lodging services? Does it matter whether a substantial portion of the clientele speaks Spanish? *See In re Pan Tex Hotel Corp.*, 190 U.S.P.Q. 109 (TTAB 1976) (La Posada is not descriptive because it is unlikely that consumers will translate the name into English); *Palm Bay Imports v. Veuve Clicquot*, 396 F.3d 1369 (Fed. Cir. 2005) ("Veuve Clicquot" not confusingly similar to "The Widow," since most American consumers won't know that "veuve" is French for "widow"; "[t]he doctrine of foreign equivalents is not an absolute rule and should be viewed merely as a guideline. . . applied only when it is likely that the ordinary American purchaser would stop and translate the word into its English equivalent."). *Compare In re Hag Aktiengesellschaft*, 155 U.S.P.Q. 598 (TTAB 1967) ("Kaba," meaning coffee in Arabic, is descriptive of coffee). Similarity of meaning in translation is important, but not determinative, in deciding the issue of descriptiveness. The relation in sight and sound between the English and foreign terms is also important; "a much closer approximation [between the meaning of the foreign term and the English equivalent] is necessary to justify a refusal to register on that basis alone where the marks otherwise are totally dissimilar." *In re Sarkli, Ltd.*, 220 U.S.P.Q. 111, 113 (Fed. Cir. 1983).

The quantitative measure of how many consumers are confused is also important with respect to the doctrine of "foreign equivalents." This rule comes into play when a foreign word or phrase is sought to be registered, and the word is said to be descriptive in the language from which it is drawn, or is said to indicate a geographic origin that is not in fact true. For example, in a case where a company selling vodka sought to register "Moskovskaya" for vodka, the PTO refused registration; Moskovskaya in Russian means literally "of or from Moscow," and the vodka was not manufactured there. The

Federal Circuit reversed the PTO, holding that it had misinterpreted the provision on marks that are "primarily geographically deceptively misdescriptive" under 15 U.S.C. § 1052(e)(3). *In re Spirits Int'l, N.V.*, 563 F.3d 1347, 1349 (Fed. Cir. 2009) "[T]he appropriate inquiry," the Federal Circuit said, "is whether a substantial portion of the relevant consumers is likely to be deceived, not whether any absolute number or particular segment of the relevant consumers (such as foreign language speakers) is likely to be deceived." *Id.*, at 1353. The court remanded for a finding concerning whether the vodka was aimed primarily at Russian speakers. If so, a "substantial" number of consumers might be deceived. If it was aimed at the general population, however, where only 0.25% speak Russian, it would not be deceptive. *Id.*, at 1357; *see also In re New Yorker Cheese Co.*, 130 U.S.P.Q. 120 (TTAB 1961) (mark in Polish unprotectable for canned ham marketed toward the Polish community).

Whatever the logic of the foreign translation rule, it is inconsistently applied. The TTAB, for instance, has concluded that Le Sorbet is a foreign equivalent that must be translated and is therefore descriptive but that La Yogurt is not. *Compare In re Le Sorbet, Inc.*, 228 U.S.P.Q. 27 (TTAB 1985) (finding combination of foreign-language term preceded by foreign-language article to be descriptive) *with In re Johanna Farms Inc.*, 8 U.S.P.Q.2d 1408 (TTAB 1988) (reasoning that the combination of an English generic noun and a French article creates the impression of a brand name rather than a descriptive term).

6. *Acronyms.* One possible way around a finding that a term is descriptive (or generic) is to alter the term, either by misspelling it or by using an acronym. This, and not an intrinsic aversion to proper spelling, explains the profusion of product names with words like "EZ," "Klear," and "Fri." But misspelling does not work. As long as the meaning of the term is clear, as with fish fri, it will be treated as a descriptive term.

Acronyms are occasionally, but not normally, effective in creating a distinctive mark. The relevant question for the courts is whether the misspelling or acronym has the same connotation as the original descriptive or generic term. If it does, the acronym is not entitled to protection. Thus, ROM has been held to be generic because it conveys the same meaning to the listener as "read-only memory." *Intel Corp. v. Radiation, Inc.*, 184 U.S.P.Q. 54 (TTAB 1984). By contrast, "L.A." was not merely descriptive of "low alcohol" beer. *Anheuser-Busch, Inc. v. Stroh Brewery Co.*, 750 F.2d 631 (8th Cir. 1984) ("[I]f some operation of the imagination is required to connect the initials with the product, the initials cannot be equated with the generic phrase, but are suggestive in nature, thereby rendering them protectable."). *See generally* MCCARTHY, TRADEMARKS AND UNFAIR COMPETITION 12-72–12-75 (1993).

7. *Personal Names.* Like descriptive terms, personal names (e.g., "Jones Antiques") need to acquire secondary meaning in order to obtain trademark protection. That is true whether or not the name is actually that of the person making the product or is fictitious ("McDonald's"), so long as it is recognized by the public as "primarily merely a surname." Lanham Act § 2(a)(e)(4), 15 U.S.C. § 1052(a)(e)(4). But does the acquisition of trademark status of a personal name by one enterprise preclude a second comer from

using his or her own name? Although early cases recognized an absolute right to use one's name in business, "the more recent trend is to forbid any use of the name as part of the proprietor's trademark, permitting use only in a subsidiary capacity, and . . . with the first name attached [in equal size]. . . . In either event, the junior user has almost uniformly been bound to display negative disclaimers." *Basile, S.p.A. v. Basile*, 899 F.2d 35, 38 (D.C. Cir. 1990). Thus, the courts have developed a limited fair use defense tailored to personal names along the general contours of the fair use defense for descriptive terms discussed in *Zatarain's*.

8. *Geographic Terms.* Geographic terms must also generally establish secondary meaning in order to garner trademark protection. The issue of what constitutes a geographic term, however, raises various complications. For example, is Philadelphia Cream Cheese a geographic term if the product is not made in or sold primarily in Philadelphia? The Trademark Office and the courts have developed an elaborate structure distinguishing between descriptive, misdescriptive, and deceptive geographic names. We will examine these doctrines in detail. *See* Chapter V(C)(3).

Even beyond the threshold for protection, can the establishment of trademark protection in a geographic term through secondary meaning (e.g., "New York Times") prevent other companies from using geographic designations? As with descriptive names and personal names, the courts have developed a fair use doctrine for analyzing such uses, balancing a merchant's interest in accurately describing its location against the interest of the senior users and the consumer. The junior user must confine and adapt geographical usage so as to avoid likelihood of confusion. Courts will often accommodate these competing interests by requiring junior users to employ disclaimers, prefixes, suffixes, and other means of reducing confusion. *See generally* MᴄCᴀʀᴛʜʏ, Tʀᴀᴅᴇ-ᴍᴀʀᴋs ᴀɴᴅ Uɴғᴀɪʀ Cᴏᴍᴘᴇᴛɪᴛɪᴏɴ § 14.07.

9. *Prefixes.* The Trademark Trial and Appeal Board has held that use of the letter "e" as a prefix in front of a commonly known and understood word—such as "eFashion"—yields a descriptive term for an online retailer. *See In re Styleclick*, 57 U.S.P.Q.2d 1445 (TTAB 2000). In a companion case, the TTAB held that use of the word "virtual" in front of a common word—as in "Virtual Fashion"—also results in a descriptive term. *See In re Styleclick*, 57 U.S.P.Q.2d 1523 (TTAB 2000).

ii.   *Genericness*

For a term to serve the purpose of a trademark, it must point to a unique source. When a term refers instead to a general class of products, it is deemed "generic" and cannot serve as a trademark. "Toyota" is a source of products, a species; "car" is a class of products—a genus.

Generic terms are either "born generic," i.e., refused registration on the Principal Register because they are generic *ab initio, see, e.g., Schwan's IP, LLC v. Kraft Pizza Co.*, 379 F. Supp. 2d 1016 (D. Minn. 2005), *aff'd* (8th Cir. 2006) ("Brick Oven Pizza" was generic) or they become generic over time through a process called "genericide." In *United States Patent & Trademark Office v. Booking.com*, __ S.Ct. __ (2020), the

Court held that the test for genericness was the same regardless of whether a term was alleged to be born generic or to have become generic through usage. The Court defined the basic principles for determining genericness:

> [S]everal guiding principles are common ground. First, a "generic" term names a "class" of goods or services, rather than any particular feature or exemplification of the class. *See* §§1127, 1064(3), 1065(4) (referring to "the generic name for the goods or services"); *Park 'N Fly*, 469 U. S., at 194 ("A generic term is one that refers to the genus of which the particular product is a species."). Second, for a compound term, the distinctiveness inquiry trains on the term's meaning as a whole, not its parts in isolation. *See Estate of P. D. Beckwith, Inc. v. Commissioner of Patents*, 252 U. S. 538, 545–546 (1920). Third, the relevant meaning of a term is its meaning to consumers. *See Bayer Co. v. United Drug Co.*, 272 F. 505, 509 (SDNY 1921) (Hand, J.) ("What do the buyers understand by the word for whose use the parties are contending?"). Eligibility for registration, all agree, turns on the mark's capacity to "distinguis[h]" goods "in commerce." §1052. Evidencing the Lanham Act's focus on consumer perception, the section governing cancellation of registration provides that "[t]he primary significance of the registered mark to the relevant public . . . shall be the test for determining whether the registered mark has become the generic name of goods or services." §1064(3).

Elliott v. Google Inc.
United States Court of Appeals for the Ninth Circuit
860 F.3d 1151 (9th Cir. 2017)

TALLMAN, Circuit Judge:

I.

Between February 29, 2012, and March 10, 2012, Chris Gillespie used a domain name registrar to acquire 763 domain names that included the word "google." Each of these domain names paired the word "google" with some other term identifying a specific brand, person, or product—for example, "googledisney.com," "googlebarackobama.net," and "googlenewtvs.com."

Google, Inc. ("Google") objected to these registrations and promptly filed a complaint with the National Arbitration Forum ("NAF"), which has authority to decide certain domain name disputes under the registrar's terms of use. Google argued that the registrations violate the Uniform Domain Name Dispute Resolution Policy, which is included in the registrar's terms of use, and amount to domain name infringement, colloquially known as "cybersquatting." Specifically, Google argued that the domain names are confusingly similar to the GOOGLE trademark and were registered in bad faith. The NAF agreed, and transferred the domain names to Google on May 10, 2012.

Shortly thereafter, David Elliott filed, and Gillespie later joined, an action in the Arizona District Court. Elliott petitioned for cancellation of the GOOGLE trademark under the Lanham Act, which allows cancellation of a registered trademark if it is primarily understood as a "generic name for the goods or services, or a portion thereof, for which it is registered." 15 U.S.C. § 1064(3). Elliott petitioned for cancellation on the ground that the word "google" is primarily understood as "a generic term universally used to describe the act[ ] of internet searching."

On September 23, 2013, the parties filed cross-motions for summary judgment on the issue of genericness. Elliott requested summary judgment because (1) it is an indisputable fact that a majority of the relevant public uses the word "google" as a verb—i.e., by saying "I googled it," and (2) verb use constitutes generic use as a matter of law. Google maintained that verb use does not automatically constitute generic use, and that Elliott failed to create even a triable issue of fact as to whether the GOOGLE trademark is generic. Specifically, Google argued that Elliott failed to present sufficient evidence to support a jury finding that the relevant public primarily understands the word "google" as a generic name for internet search engines. The district court agreed with Google and its framing of the relevant inquiry, and granted summary judgment in its favor.

. . . For the reasons described below, we reject both of Elliott's arguments and affirm summary judgment for Google.

II.

. . .

Over time, the holder of a valid trademark may become a "victim of 'genericide.'" *Freecycle Network, Inc. v. Oey*, 505 F.3d 898, 905 (9th Cir. 2007) (quoting J. Thomas McCarthy, McCarthy on Trademarks and Unfair Competition § 12:1 (4th ed. 1998) [hereinafter McCarthy]). Genericide occurs when the public appropriates a trademark and uses it as a generic name for particular types of goods or services irrespective of its source. For example, ASPIRIN, CELLOPHANE, and ESCALATOR were once protectable as arbitrary or fanciful marks because they were primarily understood as identifying the source of certain goods. But the public appropriated those marks and now primarily understands aspirin, cellophane, and escalator as generic names for those same goods. The original holders of the ASPIRIN, CELLOPHANE, and ESCALATOR marks are thus victims of genericide.

The question in any case alleging genericide is whether a trademark has taken the "fateful step" along the path to genericness. The mere fact that the public sometimes uses a trademark as the name for a unique product does not immediately render the mark generic. See 15 U.S.C. § 1064(3). Instead, a trademark only becomes generic when the "primary significance of the registered mark to the relevant public" is as the name for a particular type of good or service irrespective of its source. Id.

We have often described this as a "who-are-you/what-are-you" test. *See Yellow Cab Co. of Sacramento v. Yellow Cab of Elk Grove, Inc.*, 419 F.3d 925, 929 (9th Cir. 2005) (quoting *Filipino Yellow Pages, Inc.*, 198 F.3d at 1147). If the relevant public primarily understands a mark as describing "who" a particular good or service is, or where it comes from, then the mark is still valid. But if the relevant public primarily understands a mark as describing "what" the particular good or service is, then the mark has become generic. In sum, we ask whether "the primary significance of the term in the minds of the consuming public is [now] the product [and not] the producer." *Kellogg Co. v. Nat'l Biscuit Co.*, 305 U.S. 111, 118 (1938).

A.

On appeal, Elliott claims that he has presented sufficient evidence to create a triable issue of fact as to whether the GOOGLE trademark is generic, and that the district court erred when it granted summary judgment for Google. . . .

We conclude that Elliott's proposed inquiry is fundamentally flawed for two reasons. First, Elliott fails to recognize that a claim of genericide must always relate to a particular type of good or service. Second, he erroneously assumes that verb use automatically constitutes generic use. For similar reasons, we conclude that the district court did not err in its formulation of the relevant inquiry under the primary significance test.

First, we take this opportunity to clarify that a claim of genericide or genericness must be made with regard to a particular type of good or service. . . . Elliott claims that the word "google" has become a generic name for "the act" of searching the internet, and argues that the district court erred when it focused on internet search engines. We reject Elliott's criticism and conclude that the district court properly recognized the necessary and inherent link between a claim of genericide and a particular type of good or service.

This requirement is clear from the text of the Lanham Act, which allows a party to apply for cancellation of a trademark when it "becomes the generic name for the *goods or services . . .* for which it is registered." 15 U.S.C. § 1064(3) (emphasis added). The Lanham Act further provides that "[i]f the registered mark becomes the generic name for less than all of the goods or services for which it is registered, a petition to cancel the registration for only those *goods or services* may be filed." *Id.* (emphasis added). Finally, the Lanham Act specifies that the relevant question under the primary significance test is "whether the registered mark has become the generic name of [certain] *goods or services.*" *Id.* (emphasis added). In this way, the Lanham Act plainly requires that a claim of genericide relate to a particular type of good or service.

We also note that such a requirement is necessary to maintain the viability of arbitrary marks as a protectable trademark category. By definition, an arbitrary mark is an existing word that is used to identify the source of a good with which the word otherwise has no logical connection. If there were no requirement that a claim of genericide relate to a particular type of good, then a mark like IVORY, which is "arbitrary as applied to soap," could be cancelled outright because it is "generic when used to describe a product made from the tusks of elephants." *Abercrombie & Fitch Co. v. Hunting World, Inc.*, 537 F.2d 4, 9 n.6 (2d Cir. 1976). This is not how trademark law operates: Trademark law recognizes that a term may be unprotectable with regard to one type of good, and protectable with regard to another type of good. In this way, the very existence of arbitrary marks as a valid trademark category supports our conclusion that a claim of genericide must relate to a particular type of good or service.

Second, Elliott's alternative inquiry fails because verb use does not automatically constitute generic use. Elliott claims that a word can only be used in a trademark sense when it is used as an adjective. He supports this claim by comparing the definitions of adjectives and trademarks, noting that both adjectives and trademarks serve descriptive functions.

Once again, Elliott's semantic argument contradicts fundamental principles underlying the protectability of trademarks. When Congress amended the Lanham Act to specify that the primary significance test applies to claims of genericide, it specifically acknowledged that a speaker might use a trademark as the name for a product, i.e., as a noun, and yet use the mark with a particular source in mind, i.e., as a trademark. It further explained that:

> A trademark can serve a dual function—that of [naming] a product while at the same time indicating its source. Admittedly, if a product is unique, it is more likely that the trademark adopted and used to identify that product will be used as if it were the identifying name of that product. But this is not conclusive of whether the mark is generic.

S. REP. NO. 98-627, at 5 (1984). In this way, Congress has instructed us that a speaker might use a trademark as a noun and still use the term in a source-identifying trademark sense.

Moreover, we have already implicitly rejected Elliott's theory that only adjective use constitutes trademark use. In *Coca-Cola Co. v. Overland, Inc.*, 692 F.2d 1250 (9th Cir. 1982), the Coca-Cola Company sued a local restaurant for trademark infringement because its servers regularly and surreptitiously replaced customer orders for "a coke" with a non-Coca-Cola beverage. The restaurant defended on the basis of genericide, arguing that the COKE trademark had become a generic name for all cola beverages. To support its claim, the restaurant presented employee affidavits stating that the employees believed that customers who ordered "a coke" were using the term in a generic sense. We rejected these affidavits because they were not based on personal knowledge. More significant to the issue at hand, we also noted that the mere fact that customers ordered "a coke," i.e., used the mark as a noun, failed to show "what . . . customers [were] thinking," or whether they had a particular source in mind. *Id.* at 1255.

If Elliott were correct that a trademark can only perform its source-identifying function when it is used as an adjective, then we would not have cited a need for evidence regarding the customers' inner thought processes. Instead, the fact that the customers used the trademark as a noun and asked for "a coke" would prove that they had no particular source in mind. In this way, we have implicitly rejected Elliott's theory that a trademark can only serve a source-identifying function when it is used as an adjective.

For these reasons, the district court correctly rejected Elliott's theory that verb use automatically constitutes generic use. . . . We have already acknowledged that a customer might use the noun "coke" in an indiscriminate sense, with no particular cola beverage in mind; or in a discriminate sense, with a Coca-Cola beverage in mind. In the same way, we now recognize that an internet user might use the verb "google" in an indiscriminate sense, with no particular search engine in mind; or in a discriminate sense, with the Google search engine in mind. . . .

B.

. . .

A party applying for cancellation of a registered trademark bears the burden of proving genericide by a preponderance of the evidence. Moreover, the holder of a registered trademark benefits from a presumption of validity and has "met its [initial] burden of demonstrating" the lack of "a genuine issue of material fact" regarding genericide. *Coca-Cola Co.*, 692 F.2d at 1254. Therefore, in light of the relevant inquiry under the primary significance test, Elliott was required to identify sufficient evidence to support a jury finding that the primary significance of the word "google" to the relevant public is as a name for internet search engines generally and not as a mark identifying the Google search engine in particular.

At summary judgment, the district court assumed that a majority of the public uses the verb "google" to refer to the act of "searching on the internet without regard to [the] search engine used." In other words, it assumed that a majority of the public uses the verb "google" in a generic and indiscriminate sense. The district court then concluded that this fact, on its own, cannot support a jury finding of genericide under the primary significance test. We agree.

As explained above, a claim of genericide must relate to a particular type of good. Even if we assume that the public uses the verb "google" in a generic and indiscriminate sense, this tells us nothing about how the public primarily understands the word itself, irrespective of its grammatical function, with regard to internet search engines. As explained below, we also agree that Elliott's admissible evidence only supports the favorable but insufficient inference already drawn by the district court—that a majority of the public uses the verb "google" in a generic sense. Standing in isolation, this fact is insufficient to support a jury finding of genericide. The district court therefore properly granted summary judgment for Google. . . .

[The court ruled that although consumer surveys may be used to support a genericide claim, two of Elliott's surveys were inadmissible because they were not conducted by a qualified expert and the third went no further than the favorable inference (finding that consumers use the verb "google" in a generic or indiscriminate sense) that the district court had drawn.]

We next consider Elliott's examples of alleged generic use by the media and by consumers. Documented examples of generic use might support a claim of genericide if they reveal a prevailing public consensus regarding the primary significance of a registered trademark. *See* MCCARTHY § 12:13 (explaining that generic use by the media is a "strong indication of the general public's perception") (quoting *Murphy Door Bed Co. v. Interior Sleep Sys., Inc.*, 874 F.2d 95, 101 (2d Cir. 1989)). However, if the parties offer competing examples of both generic and trademark use, this source of evidence is typically insufficient to prove genericide. *See id.*

Initially, we note that Elliott's admissible examples are only examples of verb use. . . .

Next, we consider Elliott's proffered dictionary evidence. *See* MCCARTHY § 12:13 (noting that dictionary definitions are "sometimes persuasive in determining public usage"). Elliott does not present any examples where "google" is defined as a generic name for internet search engines. Instead, Elliott presents secondary definitions where google is defined as a verb. *See, e.g.*, Google, CollinsEnglishDictionary.com, https://www.collinsdictionary.com/dictionary/english/google (last visited Apr. 15, 2017) (defining google primarily as a "trademark" but secondarily as a verb meaning "to search for (something on the internet) using a search engine"); Google, Dictionary.com, http://dictionary.reference.com/browse/google (last visited Apr. 15, 2017) (defining google primarily as the "brand name of a leading Internet search engine" but secondarily as a verb meaning "to search the Internet for information about [something]"). Once again, Elliott's proffered dictionary evidence only supports the favorable inference already drawn by the district court.

Next, we consider Elliott's claim that Google has used its own trademark in a generic sense. Generic use of a mark by the holder of that mark can support a finding of genericide. *See* MCCARTHY § 12:13. However, Elliott has not presented an example of generic use by Google. Instead, Elliott has presented an email from Google cofounder Larry Page, which encourages recipients to "[h]ave fun and keep googling!" Once again, Elliott relies on an example of verb use. . . .

Finally, we consider Elliott's claim that there is no efficient alternative for the word "google" as a name for "the act" of searching the internet regardless of the search engine used. Once again, a claim of genericide must relate to a particular type of good or service. In order to show that there is no efficient alternative for the word "google" as a generic term, Elliott must show that there is no way to describe "internet search engines" without calling them "googles." Because not a single competitor calls its search engine "a google," and because members of the consuming public recognize and refer to different "internet search engines," Elliott has not shown that there is no available substitute for the word "google" as a generic term. *Compare, e.g.,* Q-*Tips, Inc. v. Johnson & Johnson*, 108 F. Supp. 845, 863 (D.N.J. 1952) (concluding that "medical swab" and "cotton-tipped applicator" are efficient alternatives for Q-Tips); with *Bayer Co.*, 272 F. at 505 (concluding that there is no efficient substitute for the generic term "aspirin" because consumers do not know the term "acetyl salicylic acid"); *see also Softbelly's Inc.*, 353 F.3d at 531 (explaining that genericide does not typically occur "until the trademark has gone so far toward becoming the exclusive descriptor of the product that sellers of competing brands cannot compete effectively without using the name"). . . .

III.

. . . We agree that Elliott has failed to present sufficient evidence to support a jury finding that the relevant public primarily understands the word "google" as a generic name for internet search engines and not as a mark identifying the Google search engine in particular. We therefore affirm the district court's grant of summary judgment. . . .

AFFIRMED.

WATFORD, J., concurring:

I join the court's well-reasoned opinion with one caveat. To resolve this appeal, we need not decide whether evidence of a trademark's "indiscriminate" verb use could ever tell us something about whether the public primarily thinks of the mark as the generic name for a type of good or service. To the extent the court's opinion can be read as taking a position on that question, I decline to join that aspect of its reasoning.

We don't need to resolve whether evidence of indiscriminate verb use is categorically irrelevant in an action alleging that a trademark has become generic because, on this record, no rational jury could find in the plaintiffs' favor even taking into account the flimsy evidence of indiscriminate verb use they produced. In support of its motion for summary judgment, Google produced overwhelming evidence that the public primarily understands the word "Google" as a trademark for its own search engine, not the name for search engines generally. In Google's consumer survey, 93% of respondents identified "Google" as a brand name, rather than a common name for search engines. In every dictionary in the record, the first entry for "Google" or "google" refers to Google's search engine. Google extracted concessions from the plaintiffs' expert linguists that Google functions as a trademark for Google's search engine. Google also submitted evidence showing that it uses its trademark to refer only to its own search engine, that it polices infringement by others, and that its competitors refrain from using the trademark to refer to their own search engines. Finally, Google offered evidence showing that major media outlets use "Google" to refer exclusively to Google's search engine. . . .

COMMENTS AND QUESTIONS

1. *Descriptive + Corporate Designation = Generic.* In *Goodyear's India Rubber Glove Mfg. Co. v. Goodyear Rubber Co.*, 128 U. S. 598, 602 (1888), the Supreme Court ruled that a generic corporate designation added to a generic term does not confer trademark eligibility was not "capable ofexclusive appropriation." Standing alone, the term "Goodyear Rubber" could not serve as a trademark because it referred, at that time, to "well-known classes of goods produced by the process known as Goodyear's invention." *Id.* "[A]ddition of the word 'Company'" supplied no protectable meaning, the Court concluded, because adding "Company" "only indicates that parties have formed an association or partnership to deal in such goods." *Id.*

2. *Generic.com.* Many domain names (e.g., pets.com) begin as descriptive or generic terms with a generic suffix (.com) but then build source identification and goodwill over time because of the uniqueness of the cyberspace address. Drawing on the common-law principle reflected in *Goodyear's India Rubber Glove Mfg. Co. v. Goodyear Rubber Co.*, 128 U. S. 598, 602 (1888), the U.S. PTO rejected registrations of generic terms followed by ".com." The Supreme Court overturned this categorical rule in *United States Patent & Trademark Office v. Booking.com*, __ S.Ct. __ (2020). It held that the fact that a .com domain resolved to a particular website meant that consumers could come to associate the generic words "booking" and ".com" with that website, and if they did the law should protect that association. *But see id.* at __ (Breyer, J., dissenting) (noting that the exclusivity of booking.com was already protected by the uniqueness of its domain name, and that the only purpose for giving booking.com a trademark in that name was to allow it to sue others using similar generic terms, such as "eBooking.com").

3. *Preventing and Policing Genericide.* Companies often fight vigorously to prevent their trademarks from becoming generic through casual usage. Consider the strong message sent by Xerox Corporation in the following advertisement.

Apart from general advertising such as this, firms also police the uses of their marks via lawsuits. *See, e.g., Selchow & Righter Co. v. McGraw-Hill Book Co.*, 580 F.2d 25 (2d Cir. 1978) (granting Scrabble trademark holder preliminary injunction against publisher of "The Scrabble Dictionary," on grounds that publication would cause irreparable injury by possibly rendering trademark generic); Elliot Staffin, *The Dilution Doctrine: Towards a Reconciliation with the Lanham Act*, 6 FORDHAM INTELL. PROP. MEDIA & ENT. L.J. 105, 117 (1995) (collecting cases finding that dilution causes of action may lie against those employing a trademark in a way that threatens to make it generic). *Cf.* Ralph H. Folsom & Larry L. Teply, *Trademarked Generic Words*, 89 YALE L.J. 1323, 1346–47 n.110 (1980) (describing organized efforts of trademark attorneys to pressure dictionary publishers into excluding trademarked words and/or including disclaimers, and arguing that inclusion in a dictionary should not bear on genericide issue). This latter form of policing may explain a finding in William M. Landes & Richard A. Posner, *Trademark Law: An Economic Perspective*, 30 J.L. & ECON. 265, 296 (1987) ("Thus, although words held to be generic are more likely to show up in the dictionary than those held not to be generic, the difference in probabilities is small—54% versus 41%.").

Trademark lawyers also seek to prevent their clients' terms from being used as nouns or verbs, fearing that this will lead to their use as the generic term. Perhaps surprisingly, no court has ever held a mark generic for being used as a verb, and many companies actually encourage such use in their advertising slogans (e.g., "Do you Yahoo!?"). The real question is whether people are using the trademark as a verb to refer only to use of the company's product or to signify the action by any enterprise.

Allowing trademark owners broad enforcement powers to police their marks against genericide—for example, by constraining the use of marks by the public, advertisers, and newspapers so as to prevent "dilution by genericization"—potentially conflicts with competition (comparative advertisement, consumer product reviews) and First Amendment values (news reporting, free speech).

4. In *Kellogg Co. v. National Biscuit Co.*, 305 U.S. 111, 116–18 (1938), Justice Brandeis set out a classic discussion of "genericide," though one infused also with elements of functionality and descriptiveness/secondary meaning:

> The plaintiff has no exclusive right to the use of the term "Shredded Wheat" as a trade name. For that is the generic term of the article, which describes it with a fair degree of accuracy; and is the term by which the biscuit in pillow-shaped form is generally known by the public. Since the term is generic, the original maker of the product acquired no exclusive right to use it. As Kellogg Company had the right to make the article, it had, also, the right to use the term by which the public knows it. . . . Ever since 1894 the article has been known to the public as shredded wheat. For many years, there was no attempt to use the term "Shredded Wheat" as a trade-mark. . . .

Moreover, the name "Shredded Wheat," as well as the product, the process and the machinery employed in making it, has been dedicated to the public. The basic patent for the product and for the process of making it, and many other patents for special machinery to be used in making the article, issued to Perky. In those patents the term "shredded" is repeatedly used as descriptive of the product. The basic patent expired October 15, 1912; the others soon after. Since during the life of the patents "Shredded Wheat" was the general designation of the patented product, there passed to the public upon the expiration of the patent, not only the right to make the article as it was made during the patent period, but also the right to apply thereto the name by which it had become known. As was said in *Singer Mfg. Co. v. June Mfg. Co.*, 163 U.S. 169, 185:

> It equally follows from the cessation of the monopoly and the falling of the patented device into the domain of things public, that along with the public ownership of the device there must also necessarily pass to the public the generic designation of the thing which has arisen during the monopoly. . . . To say otherwise would be to hold that, although the public had acquired the device covered by the patent, yet the owner of the patent or the manufacturer of the patented thing had retained the designated name which was essentially necessary to vest the public with the full enjoyment of that which had become theirs by the disappearance of the monopoly.

It is contended that the plaintiff has the exclusive right to the name "Shredded Wheat," because those words acquired the "secondary meaning" of shredded wheat made at Niagara Falls by the plaintiff's predecessor. There is no basis here for applying the doctrine of secondary meaning. The evidence shows only that due to the long period in which the plaintiff or its predecessor was the only manufacturer of the product, many people have come to associate the product, and as a consequence the name by which the product is generally known, with the plaintiff's factory at Niagara Falls. But to establish a trade name in the term "shredded wheat" the plaintiff must show more than a subordinate meaning which applies to it. It must show that the primary significance of the term in the minds of the consuming public is not the product but the producer. This it has not done. The showing which it has made does not entitle it to the exclusive use of the term shredded wheat but merely entitles it to require that the defendant use reasonable care to inform the public of the source of its product.

The Court cites *Singer Mfg. Co. v. June Mfg. Co.*, 163 U.S. 169, 185 (1896), for the proposition that once a patent on a device expires, the name by which that device has been sold also enters the public domain. Surely that is not always the case. Numerous products that once were patented are still sold under the same trademark. And this result—that patent expiration does not automatically end trademark protection—is also consistent with the purposes behind the two laws, which are very different. The key to *Singer*'s holding may lie in its expressed concern that "the owner of the patent. . . had retained the designated name which was essentially necessary to vest the public with the full enjoyment of" the product. Thus, it is only when the name itself is "essentially necessary" to sales of the product—that is, when the name is generic—that trademark protection should not survive the expiration of a patent.

5. *Generic Trade Dress*. While most genericness cases involve word marks, trade dress and product configurations can also be generic. *See, e.g., Kendall-Jackson Winery v. E. & J. Gallo Winery*, 150 F.3d 1042 (9th Cir. 1998), where the court held that an autumnal grape leaf featured on both plaintiff's and defendant's wine bottles was generic in the wine industry.

6. When a court declares a term generic, it can destroy a right built up with considerable investment. Is this the same as instances where government decrees destroy private property; that is, should "just compensation" be paid for this "taking" under the Fifth Amendment to the U.S. Constitution? Does your answer depend on whether trademarks are viewed as property or instead as an unfair competition or consumer protection right? *See* Stephen L. Carter, *Does It Matter Whether Intellectual Property Is Property?*, 68 CHI.-KENT L. REV. 715 (1993) (speculating about the desirability of such an arrangement); *cf. Ruckelshaus v. Monsanto Co.*, 467 U.S. 986 (1984) (requiring just compensation for government disclosure of a trade secret).

The Second Circuit holds that even generic terms are entitled to protection against some forms of unfair competition. *See, e.g., Genesee Brewing Co. v. Stroh Brewing Co.*, 124 F.3d 137, 150 (2d Cir. 1997) (although plaintiff's used the generic term "Honey Brown Ale" to refer to its product, the defendant could nonetheless be liable if it did not use "every reasonable means to prevent confusion" as to the source of its products); *Forschner Group Inc. v. Arrow Trading Co.*, 124 F.3d 402 (2d Cir. 1997); *Home Builders Ass'n of Greater St. Louis v. L & L Exhibition Mgmt., Inc.*, 226 F.3d 944 (8th Cir. 2000) (holding that a generic mark that has acquired secondary meaning may require that other users take steps to avoid confusion). Does it defeat the point of genericness if defendants can be liable under unfair competition law for using generic terms? *See* Stacey L. Dogan & Mark A. Lemley, *A Search-Costs Theory of Limiting Doctrines in Trademark Law*, 97 TRADEMARK REP. 1223 (2007) (arguing that refusing to give any protection to a generic term can hurt consumers who associate that term with a particular company).

5. *Reversing Genericide*. If a mark is generic, can it ever be protected? Before 2020, most courts would have said no. But the Supreme Court strongly suggested in *United States Patent & Trademark Office v. Booking.com*, __ S.Ct. __ (2020), that the answer is yes. It held that a combination of two generic terms ("booking" for travel booking services and ".com" for a website) could become protectable as long as consumers viewed it as source-identifying.7. *Expressive versus Competitive Genericide*. Some trademarks serve an expressive role in public discourse beyond commercial source identification. The communicative content of trademarks such as Barbie, Marlboro, or Whac-a-Mole—the unique images and associations these terms call to mind—are a by-

product of the advertisers' commercially motivated saturation campaigns. But they result from statements and associations made by the public, not by the trademark owner. Rochelle Dreyfuss questions whether trademark doctrine has kept up with these developments in popular culture. *See* Rochelle C. Dreyfuss, *Expressive Genericity: Trademarks as Language in the Pepsi Generation*, 65 NOTRE DAME L. REV. 397 (1990). She suggests extending traditional concepts of genericness to encompass the realm of expressive (as opposed to commercial, or what she calls "competitive") uses of trademarks. "If [a] mark is found to be rhetorically unique within its context, it would be considered expressively—but not necessarily competitively—generic, and the trademark owner would not be permitted to suppress its utilization in that context." This would permit courts to expressive significance of the mark as opposed to consumer confusion.

8. Terms that were once trademarks but have since become generic include aspirin, elevator, escalator, and thermos. More recent rulings have held "bottled at the source" generic for bottled water, *CG Roxane LLC v. Fiji Water Co.*, 569 F. Supp. 2d 1019 (N.D. Cal. 2008), "Texas Toast" generic for croutons, *T. Marzetti Co. v. Roskam Baking Co.*, 680 F.3d 629 (6th Cir. 2012); and "duck tours" generic for amphibious city tours, *Boston Duck Tours, LP v. Super Duck Tours, LLC*, 531 F.3d 1 (1st Cir. 2008).

9. *Standardization and Network Effects.* Does it make sense that the very success of an invented trademark should be its undoing? The success of marks that become generic is perhaps attributable more to the collective labor of the users than to the labor of the trademark originator. The efforts of the users in learning a new word, rather than the efforts of the creator in designing the work, account for the success of these kinds of marks. Wendy Gordon argues:

> Giving ownership in intellectual products that have come to serve as standards, such as West citations or generic [terms], would not ordinarily leave "enough, and as good" [in the Lockean sense]. There may be room in the world for only one of a given type of thing, or a long-lived artifice may become a mode of communication. It is the nature of a standard that nothing "as good" is available. For these reasons, the [Lockean] proviso would be violated if the courts gave those who create standards in nonfungible goods a right to prevent people from utilizing them.

Wendy J. Gordon, *A Property Right in Self-Expression: Equality and Individualism in the Natural Law of Intellectual Property*, 102 YALE L.J. 1533, 1600 (1993) (footnote omitted). *See also* Peter S. Menell, *Economic Analysis of Network Effects and Intellectual Property*, 34 BERKELEY TECH. L.J. 219, 275-79 (2019); Justin Hughes, *The Philosophy of Intellectual Property*, 77 GEO. L.J. 287, 315-23 (1988) (suggesting that ownership of most intellectual products will easily satisfy the Lockean proviso, though "extraordinary ideas" like generic terms should remain open for all to use). The public contributes to the success of strong trademarks. *See* Steven Wilf, *Who Authors Trademarks?*, 17 CARDOZO ARTS & ENT. L.J. 1 (1999). Should they have an ownership interest too? How would the legal system administer intellectual property rights that emerge from collective efforts? *See* Robert P. Merges, *Locke for the Masses: Property Rights and the Products of Collective Creativity*, 36 HOFSTRA L. REV. 1179 (2008).

Professor Gordon's argument extends the network externalities argument to individual words. When a word comes to describe a genus or class of goods, i.e., enters general use, it takes on some of the properties of a computer protocol. Requiring consumers and competitors to use this second-best descriptor entails costs. *See* Ralph H. Folsom & Larry L. Teply, *Trademarked Generic Words*, 89 YALE L.J. 1323, 1340–41 (1980). Consider the example of "plexiglas." The next best alternative to this well-known descriptor might be: "unbreakable clear plastic sheets of window material." That is not only a mouthful; it is more expensive to advertise (because it is longer), harder to remember, and prone to mistakes and confusion. Thus, it is not hard to see why "plexiglas" became the preferred shorthand for it. Consequently, although the originator of this term might have put substantial effort into creating it and encouraging its use, there is a good argument that it has become a standard name (or descriptor)—and hence generic. *But Cf. Rohm & Haas Co. v. Polycast Technology Corp.*, 172 U.S.P.Q. 167 (D. Del. 1971) (enjoining defendant's use of Plexiglas mark). As another example, consider "Yo-Yo"; how would you describe this kind of toy without using the word *yo-yo*? *Cf. Donald F. Duncan, Inc. v. Royal Tops Mfg. Co.*, 343 F.2d 655 (7th Cir. 1965) (holding "yo-yo" generic, besides being descriptive in a Filipino language (Ilocano)).

Folsom & Teply, 89 YALE L.J. at 1354, contend that *policing costs* (as reflected in Xerox advertisement) wasted resources and therefore should not be considered in determining whether a trademark has become generic. Can you defend expenditures to keep a mark from becoming generic on the basis that they are attempts to provide alternative "standards" that will thereby retain the source-indicating function of threatened trademarks? If consumers accept the premise of the ads and faithfully refer to the "copier" instead of the "Xerox," are consumers harmed? And do such expenditures show that the cost of informing the public about alternative product descriptors is worth it to the firm, given its investment in its trademark? *Cf. E.I. du Pont de Nemours & Co. v. Yoshida Int'l, Inc.*, 393 F. Supp. 502, 523–24 (E.D.N.Y. 1975) ("Teflon" not generic, in part because of du Pont's vigorous education and policing campaign). It may be impossible, however, to resist genericide due to rapid and widespread use. *Cf. Du Pont Cellophane Co. v. Waxed Prods. Co.*, 85 F.2d 75 (2d Cir. 1936) (holding "cellophane" generic despite vigorous policing efforts). Does such rapid acceptance indicate that the next best alternative descriptor is significantly less effective? *Cf.* Folsom & Teply, *supra*, at 1344 (noting that some alternative terms are better than others; comparing "lip balm" as alternative to "Chap Stick"; with "dextro-amphetamine sulphate" as alternative to "Dexadrine"); Comment, *Trademarks and Generic Words: An Effect-on-Competition Test*, 51 U. CHI. L. REV. 868, 884–85 (1984) (advocating use of antitrust-like cross-elasticities of demand analysis to determine degree of substitutability between terms).

Can you see a less benign motive for expenditures to maintain the trademark status of a word that has become a widely used name for a product class? *See* Folsom & Teply, *supra*, at 1337 (suggesting two: (1) to maintain entry barriers to competition; and (2) to obtain "free advertising" every time someone uses the trademarked word to refer to a product class). This perspective points away from a per se rule that significant policing expenditures alone can preserve the trademark status of a term. Moreover, to the extent that firms attempt to police the noncommercial use of marks, there may be a significant effect on the free flow of information and ideas. *See* Leah Chan Grinvald, *Policing the Cease and Desist Letter*, 49 U.S.F. L. REV. 411 (2015) (noting the role of trademark policing in over-enforcement and in terrorem threats against legitimate uses) The First Amendment, comes into play in these situations, but only if defendants choose to fight rather than capitulate.

10. *Born generic?* Can a term start out generic? Common sense says yes; even an invented term like "smartphone" or "automobile" may be understood from the outset to refer to a class of things. Somewhat surprisingly, however, one court has said no. *San Diego Comic Convention v. Dan Farr Productions*, 2017 WL 3732081 (S.D. Cal. Aug. 30, 2017) (concluding that there was no category of marks "generic ab initio" and that defendants had not proven that the term "comic-con" had become generic), *aff'd in pertinent part,* 807 F.3d 674 (9th Cir. 2020).

PROBLEM

Problem V-1. Apple's iPhone is extremely popular, in large part because of the many third party applications (or "apps") users can buy to run on the iPhone. Apple sells those apps through an icon on the iPhone labeled "App Store." Apple applies to register the term "app store" and seeks to prevent competing smartphone manufacturers from describing their application marketplaces as "app stores."

Is the term "app store" generic?

---

iii.   *Distinctiveness of Trade Dress and Product Configuration*

Two Pesos, Inc. v. Taco Cabana, Inc.
Supreme Court of the United States
505 U.S. 763 (1992)

JUSTICE White delivered the opinion of the Court.

The issue in this case is whether the trade dress[1] of a restaurant may be protected under § 43(a) of the Trademark Act of 1946 (Lanham Act), 60 Stat. 441, 15 U.S.C.

---

[1] The District Court instructed the jury: "'Trade dress' is the total image of the business. Taco Cabana's trade dress may include the shape and general appearance of the exterior of the restaurant, the identifying sign, the interior kitchen floor plan, the decor, the menu, the equipment used to serve food, the servers' uniforms and other features reflecting on the total image of the restaurant." The Court of Appeals accepted this definition and quoted from *Blue Bell Bio-Medical v. Cin-Bad, Inc.*, 864 F.2d 1253, 1256 (CA5 1989): "The 'trade dress' of a product is essentially its total image and overall appearance." *See* 932 F.2d 1113, 1118 (CA5 1991). It "involves the total image of a product and may include features such as size, shape, color or color combinations, texture, graphics, or even particular sales techniques." *John H. Harland Co. v.*

§ 1125(a) (1982 ed.), based on a finding of inherent distinctiveness, without proof that the trade dress has secondary meaning.

I

Respondent Taco Cabana, Inc., operates a chain of fast-food restaurants in Texas. The restaurants serve Mexican food. The first Taco Cabana restaurant was opened in San Antonio in September 1978, and five more restaurants had been opened in San Antonio by 1985. Taco Cabana describes its Mexican trade dress as "a festive eating atmosphere having interior dining and patio areas decorated with artifacts, bright colors, paintings and murals. The patio includes interior and exterior areas with the interior patio capable of being sealed off from the outside patio by overhead garage doors. The stepped exterior of the building is a festive and vivid color scheme using top border paint and neon stripes. Bright awnings and umbrellas continue the theme." 932 F.2d 1113, 1117 (CA5 1991).

In December 1985, a Two Pesos, Inc., restaurant was opened in Houston. Two Pesos adopted a motif very similar to the foregoing description of Taco Cabana's trade dress. Two Pesos restaurants expanded rapidly in Houston and other markets, but did not enter San Antonio. In 1986, Taco Cabana entered the Houston and Austin markets and expanded into other Texas cities, including Dallas and El Paso where Two Pesos was also doing business.

In 1987, Taco Cabana sued Two Pesos in the United States District Court for the Southern District of Texas for trade dress infringement under § 43(a) of the Lanham Act, 15 U.S.C. § 1125(a) (1982 ed.), and for theft of trade secrets under Texas common law. The case was tried to a jury, which was instructed to return its verdict in the form of answers to five questions propounded by the trial judge. The jury's answers were: Taco Cabana has a trade dress; taken as a whole, the trade dress is nonfunctional; the trade dress is inherently distinctive; the trade dress has not acquired a secondary meaning in the Texas market; and the alleged infringement creates a likelihood of confusion on the part of ordinary customers as to the source or association of the restaurant's goods or services. Because, as the jury was told, Taco Cabana's trade dress was protected if it either was inherently distinctive or had acquired a secondary meaning, judgment was entered awarding damages to Taco Cabana. In the course of calculating damages, the trial court held that Two Pesos had intentionally and deliberately infringed Taco Cabana's trade dress.

The Court of Appeals ruled that the instructions adequately stated the applicable law and that the evidence supported the jury's findings. In particular, the Court of Appeals rejected petitioner's argument that a finding of no secondary meaning contradicted a finding of inherent distinctiveness.

II

Clarke Checks, Inc., 711 F.2d 966, 980 (CA11 1983). RESTATEMENT (THIRD) OF UNFAIR COMPETITION RESTATEMENT (THIRD) OF UNFAIR COMPETITION § 16, Comment a (Tent. Draft No. 2, Mar. 23, 1990).

The Lanham Act was intended to make "actionable the deceptive and misleading use of marks" and "to protect persons engaged in . . . commerce against unfair competition." § 45, 15 U.S.C. § 1127. Section 43(a) "prohibits a broader range of practices than does § 32," which applies to registered marks, *Inwood Laboratories, Inc. v. Ives Laboratories, Inc.*, 456 U.S. 844, 858 (1982), but it is common ground that § 43(a) protects qualifying unregistered trademarks and that the general principles qualifying a mark for registration under § 2 of the Lanham Act are for the most part applicable in determining whether an unregistered mark is entitled to protection under § 43(a). *See A.J. Canfield Co. v. Honickman*, 808 F.2d 291, 299, n.9 (CA3 1986); *Thompson Medical Co. v. Pfizer Inc.*, 753 F.2d 208, 215–216 (CA2 1985).

Exterior Views of Two Pesos Restaurant and Taco Cabana Restaurant

The Court of Appeals determined that the District Court's instructions were consistent with the foregoing principles and that the evidence supported the jury's verdict. Both courts thus ruled that Taco Cabana's trade dress was not descriptive but rather inherently distinctive, and that it was not functional. None of these rulings is before us in this case, and for present purposes we assume, without deciding, that each of them is correct. In going on to affirm the judgment for respondent, the Court of Appeals, following its prior decision in *Chevron*, held that Taco Cabana's inherently distinctive trade dress was entitled to protection despite the lack of proof of secondary meaning. It is this issue that is before us for decision, and we agree with its resolution by the Court of Appeals. There is no persuasive reason to apply to trade dress a general requirement of secondary meaning which is at odds with the principles generally applicable to infringement suits under § 43(a). Petitioner devotes much of its briefing to arguing issues that are not before us, and we address only its arguments relevant to whether proof of secondary meaning is essential to qualify an inherently distinctive trade dress for protection under § 43(a). Petitioner argues that the jury's finding that the trade dress has not acquired a secondary meaning shows conclusively that the trade dress is not inherently distinctive. The Court of Appeals' disposition of this issue was sound:

> Two Pesos' argument—that the jury finding of inherent distinctiveness contradicts its finding of no secondary meaning in the Texas market—ignores the law in this circuit. While the necessarily imperfect (and often prohibitively difficult) methods for assessing secondary meaning address the empirical question

of current consumer association, the legal recognition of an inherently distinctive trademark or trade dress acknowledges the owner's legitimate proprietary interest in its unique and valuable informational device, regardless of whether substantial consumer association yet bestows the additional empirical protection of secondary meaning.

932 F.2d, at 1120 n.7. . . .

This brings us to the line of decisions by the Court of Appeals for the Second Circuit that would find protection for trade dress unavailable absent proof of secondary meaning, a position that petitioner concedes would have to be modified if the temporary protection that it suggests is to be recognized. In *Vibrant Sales, Inc. v. New Body Boutique, Inc.*, 652 F.2d 299 (1981), the plaintiff claimed protection under § 43(a) for a product whose features the defendant had allegedly copied. The Court of Appeals held that unregistered marks did not enjoy the "presumptive source association" enjoyed by registered marks and hence could not qualify for protection under § 43(a) without proof of secondary meaning. *Id.* at 303, 304. The court's rationale seemingly denied protection for unregistered but inherently distinctive marks of all kinds, whether the claimed mark used distinctive words or symbols or distinctive product design. The court thus did not accept the arguments that an unregistered mark was capable of identifying a source and that copying such a mark could be making any kind of a false statement or representation under § 43(a).

This holding is in considerable tension with the provisions of the Act. If a verbal or symbolic mark or the features of a product design may be registered under § 2, it necessarily is a mark "by which the goods of the applicant may be distinguished from the goods of others," 60 Stat. 428, and must be registered unless otherwise disqualified. Since § 2 requires secondary meaning only as a condition to registering descriptive marks, there are plainly marks that are registrable without showing secondary meaning. These same marks, even if not registered, remain inherently capable of distinguishing the goods of the users of these marks. Furthermore, the copier of such a mark may be seen as falsely claiming that his products may for some reason be thought of as originating from the plaintiff. . . .

The Fifth Circuit was quite right in *Chevron,* and in this case, to follow the *Abercrombie* classifications consistently and to inquire whether trade dress for which protection is claimed under § 43(a) is inherently distinctive. If it is, it is capable of identifying products or services as coming from a specific source and secondary meaning is not required. This is the rule generally applicable to trademark, and the protection of trademarks and trade dress under § 43(a) serves the same statutory purpose of preventing deception and unfair competition. There is no persuasive reason to apply different analysis to the two. The "proposition that secondary meaning must be shown even if the trade dress is a distinctive, identifying mark, [is] wrong, for the reasons explained by Judge Rubin for the Fifth Circuit in *Chevron.*" *Blau Plumbing, Inc. v. S.O.S. Fix-it, Inc.,* 781 F.2d 604, 608 (CA7 1986). The Court of Appeals for the Eleventh Circuit also follows *Chevron, Ambrit, Inc. v. Kraft, Inc.,* 805 F.2d 974, 979 (1986), and the Court of

Appeals for the Ninth Circuit appears to think that proof of secondary meaning is superfluous if a trade dress is inherently distinctive. *Fuddruckers, Inc. v. Doc's B.R. Others, Inc.*, 826 F.2d 837, 843 (1987).

It would be a different matter if there were textual basis in § 43(a) for treating inherently distinctive verbal or symbolic trademarks differently from inherently distinctive trade dress. But there is none. The section does not mention trademarks or trade dress, whether they be called generic, descriptive, suggestive, arbitrary, fanciful, or functional. Nor does the concept of secondary meaning appear in the text of § 43(a). Where secondary meaning does appear in the statute, 15 U.S.C. § 1052 (1982 ed.), it is a requirement that applies only to merely descriptive marks and not to inherently distinctive ones. We see no basis for requiring secondary meaning for inherently distinctive trade dress protection under § 43(a) but not for other distinctive words, symbols, or devices capable of identifying a producer's product.

Engrafting onto § 43(a) a requirement of secondary meaning for inherently distinctive trade dress also would undermine the purposes of the Lanham Act. Protection of trade dress, no less than of trademarks, serves the Act's purpose to "secure to the owner of the mark the goodwill of his business and to protect the ability of consumers to distinguish among competing producers. National protection of trademarks is desirable, Congress concluded, because trademarks foster competition and the maintenance of quality by securing to the producer the benefits of good reputation." *Park 'N Fly,* 469 U.S., at 198, citing S. REP. NO. 1333, 79th Cong., 2d Sess., 3–5 (1946) (citations omitted). By making more difficult the identification of a producer with its product, a secondary meaning requirement for a nondescriptive trade dress would hinder improving or maintaining the producer's competitive position.

Suggestions that under the Fifth Circuit's law, the initial user of any shape or design would cut off competition from products of like design and shape are not persuasive. Only nonfunctional, distinctive trade dress is protected under § 43(a). The Fifth Circuit holds that a design is legally functional, and thus unprotectable, if it is one of a limited number of equally efficient options available to competitors and free competition would be unduly hindered by according the design trademark protection. *See Sicilia Di R. Biebow & Co. v. Cox*, 732 F.2d 417, 426 (CA5 1984). This serves to assure that competition will not be stifled by the exhaustion of a limited number of trade dresses.

On the other hand, adding a secondary meaning requirement could have anticompetitive effects, creating particular burdens on the start-up of small companies. It would present special difficulties for a business, such as respondent, that seeks to start a new product in a limited area and then expand into new markets. Denying protection for inherently distinctive nonfunctional trade dress until after secondary meaning has been established would allow a competitor, which has not adopted a distinctive trade dress of its own, to appropriate the originator's dress in other markets and to deter the originator from expanding into and competing in these areas.

As noted above, petitioner concedes that protecting an inherently distinctive trade dress from its inception may be critical to new entrants to the market and that withholding protection until secondary meaning has been established would be contrary to the goals of the Lanham Act. Petitioner specifically suggests, however, that the solution is to dispense with the requirement of secondary meaning for a reasonable, but brief period at the outset of the use of a trade dress. If § 43(a) does not require secondary meaning at the outset of a business' adoption of trade dress, there is no basis in the statute to support the suggestion that such a requirement comes into being after some unspecified time.

III

We agree with the Court of Appeals that proof of secondary meaning is not required to prevail on a claim under § 43(a) of the Lanham Act where the trade dress at issue is inherently distinctive, and accordingly the judgment of that court is affirmed.

COMMENTS AND QUESTIONS

1. *Two Pesos* reverses several circuit court decisions that had held § 43(a) action for trade dress infringement required proof of secondary meaning even if the trade dress at issue was inherently distinctive. *See, e.g., Ferrari S.p.A. v. Roberts*, 944 F.2d 1235, 1239 (6th Cir. 1991).

2. Focus for a moment on the policy justifications the Court offers in support of its ruling. Two such justifications appear: that protecting distinctive trade dress will enable companies to appropriate their own goodwill, and that small companies may be unable to protect their trade dress from larger infringers if they are required to establish secondary meaning. Are these justifications persuasive? Should the Court focus on the rights of the trademark holder to protect its goodwill, or on the rights of the public to accurate product information? Are these two goals likely to come into conflict here?

3. Does the Court adopt either the "incentive" or property-rights theory of trademark law? *See* Stephen L. Carter, *Does It Matter Whether Intellectual Property Is Property?*, 68 CHI.-KENT L. REV. 715, 721–22 (1993) (arguing that *Two Pesos* is indicative of a trend strengthening the "property" nature of intellectual property). Certainly, the Court expresses a concern that seems consistent with the incentive theory: "protecting an inherently distinctive trade dress from its inception may be critical to new entrants to the market." Early protection encourages the development of new marks, in the Court's view.

A moral argument can also be made in favor of protecting inherently distinctive trade dress, at least against intentional copying. Such an argument asserts that the infringer can make no valid moral claim to copy the trade dress, so a right to it ought to reside in its creator. This is different from saying that the originator of the trade dress has earned it; it says that he gets it by default, because no one else has a superior claim. *See* LAWRENCE BECKER, PROPERTY RIGHTS: PHILOSOPHIC FOUNDATIONS 41 (1977) ("It is not so much that the producers *deserve* the produce of their labors. It is rather that no one else does. . . ."); *see also* Robert C. Denicola, *Institutional Publicity Rights: An Analysis of the Merchandising of Famous Trade Symbols*, 62 N.C. L. REV. 603, 640–41 (1984) (arguing no one has better claim to trademark's commercial value than its producer). Arguably, though, this approach misses the point. Isn't the question not *who* should own the right to a mark, but whether *anyone* should have exclusive rights to it?

Judge Posner gives an economic answer to this question; he says that in some situations we declare property rights merely to prevent wasteful dissipation of the value of the asset covered by the right. He explicitly applies this to the right of publicity. *See* RICHARD POSNER, ECONOMIC ANALYSIS OF LAW 43 (4th ed. 1992):

> [W]hatever information value a celebrity's endorsement has to consumers would be lost if every advertiser can use the celebrity's name and picture. . . . The existence of a congestion externality provides an argument that rights of publicity should be perpetual and thus inheritable (a matter of legal controversy today). We don't want this form of information or expression to be in the public domain, because it will be less valuable there, whether the celebrity is dead or alive.

Is this such a situation? What waste would occur if other restaurants were permitted to duplicate the Taco Cabana décor? For a contrary argument, that the copying of product design should be permitted in a market economy unless society needs to subsidize the creation of such designs, *see* Robert C. Denicola, *Freedom to Copy*, 108 YALE L.J. 1661 (1999); Mark A. Lemley, *Ex Ante Versus Ex Post Justifications for Intellectual Property*, 71 U. CHI. L. REV. 147 (2004).

4. Should trade dress protection extend to the décor of a restaurant? Is the restaurant layout, design, color scheme, etc., the same as packaging for other types of products? If so, what product (or service) is being packaged? Does *Two Pesos* open the door to a wide variety of claims that a particular style of doing business is protectable trade dress? An extreme example of a trade dress claim allowed in the wake of *Two Pesos* is *Toy Mfrs. of America v. Helmsley-Spear, Inc.*, 960 F. Supp. 673 (S.D.N.Y. 1997), where the court held that the plaintiff's "unique" registration process, forms, and location for a toy fair (taken together) constituted protectable trade dress and was infringed by the defendants.

Even if restaurant décor or product packaging can serve a trademark function, how do we know whether they are actually doing so? Sometimes the color or design of a package (or a restaurant) is just ornamental. In *Seabrook Foods v. Bar-Well Foods*, 568 F.2d 1342 (C.C.P.A. 1977), the court held that product packaging must signal to consumers that it is a trademark rather than just ornamentation in order to qualify for protection. Does Taco Cabana's décor meet that standard?

PROBLEM

Problem V-2. Recall Problem IV-52 regarding ComicMix's mashup of Dr Seuss's OH THE PLACES YOU'LL GO! with the *Star Trek* series: OH THE PLACES YOU'LL BOLDLY GO!. The mashup title picks up on *Star Trek*'s visionary line: "To boldly go where no man has gone before." Is Dr. Seuess's cover design entitled to trademark protection? What about *Star Trek*'s "boldy" phrase or depiction of the Starship Enterprise? What about the artwork depicted in Problem IV-52?

---

iv.   *Product Configuration*

Qualitex Co. v. Jacobson Products Co., Inc.
Supreme Court of the United States
514 U.S. 159 (1995)

JUSTICE Breyer delivered the opinion of the Court.

The question in this case is whether the Lanham Trademark Act . . . permits the registration of a trademark that consists, purely and simply, of a color. We conclude that, sometimes, a color will meet ordinary legal trademark requirements. And, when it does so, no special legal rule prevents color alone from serving as a trademark.

I

The case before us grows out of petitioner Qualitex Company's use (since the 1950's) of a special shade of green-gold color on the pads that it makes and sells to dry cleaning firms for use on dry cleaning presses. In 1989 respondent Jacobson Products (a Qualitex rival) began to sell its own press pads to dry cleaning firms; and it colored those pads a similar green-gold. In 1991 Qualitex registered the special green-gold color on press pads with the Patent and Trademark Office as a trademark. Registration No. 1,633,711 (Feb. 5, 1991). Qualitex subsequently added a trademark infringement count . . . in a lawsuit it had already filed challenging Jacobson's use of the green-gold color.

Qualitex won the lawsuit in the District Court. 21 U.S.P.Q.2d 1457 (CD Cal. 1991). But, the Court of Appeals for the Ninth Circuit set aside the judgment in Qualitex's favor on the trademark infringement claim because, in that Circuit's view, the Lanham Act does not permit Qualitex, or anyone else, to register "color alone" as a trademark. 13 F.3d 1297, 1300, 1302 (1994).

The courts of appeals have differed as to whether or not the law recognizes the use of color alone as a trademark. *Compare NutraSweet Co. v. Stadt Corp.*, 917 F.2d 1024, 1028 (CA7 1990) (absolute prohibition against protection of color alone), with *In re Owens-Corning Fiberglas Corp.*, 774 F.2d 1116, 1128 (CA Fed. 1985) (allowing registration of color pink for fiberglass insulation). . . .Therefore, this Court granted certiorari. . . . We now hold that there is no rule absolutely barring the use of color alone, and we reverse the judgment of the Ninth Circuit.

II

The Lanham Act gives a seller or producer the exclusive right to "register" a trademark . . . and to prevent his or her competitors from using that trademark. . . . Both the language of the Act and the basic underlying principles of trademark law would seem to include color within the universe of things that can qualify as a trademark. The language of the Lanham Act describes that universe in the broadest of terms. It says that trademarks "includ[e] any word, name, symbol, or device, or any combination thereof." § 1127. Since human beings might use as a "symbol" or "device" almost anything at all that is capable of carrying meaning, this language, read literally, is not restrictive. The courts and the Patent and Trademark Office have authorized for use as a mark a particular shape (of a Coca-Cola bottle), a particular sound (of NBC's three chimes), and even a particular scent (of plumeria blossoms on sewing thread). *See, e.g.*, Registration No. 696,147 (Apr. 12, 1960); Registration Nos. 523,616 (Apr. 4, 1950) and 916,522 (July 13, 1971); *In re Clarke*, 17 U.S.P.Q.2d 1238, 1240 (TTAB 1990). If a shape, a sound, and a fragrance can act as symbols why, one might ask, can a color not do the same?

. . . True, a product's color is unlike "fanciful," "arbitrary," or "suggestive" words or designs, which almost automatically tell a customer that they refer to a brand. . . . *[S]ee Two Pesos, Inc. v. Taco Cabana, Inc.*, 112 S.Ct. 2753, 2757 (1992). The imaginary word "Suntost," or the words "Suntost Marmalade," on a jar of orange jam immediately would signal a brand or a product "source"; the jam's orange color does not do so. But, over time, customers may come to treat a particular color on a product or its packaging (say, a color that in context seems unusual, such as pink on a firm's insulating material or red on the head of a large industrial bolt) as signifying a brand. And, if so, that color would have come to identify and distinguish the goods—i.e. to "indicate" their "source"—much in the way that descriptive words on a product (say, "Trim" on nail clippers or "Car-Freshner" on deodorizer) can come to indicate a product's origin. . . . In this circumstance, trademark law says that the word (e.g., "Trim"), although not inherently distinctive, has developed "secondary meaning." *See Inwood Laboratories, Inc. v. Ives Laboratories, Inc.*, 456 U.S. 844, 851, n.11 (1982) ("secondary meaning" is acquired when "in the minds of the public, the primary significance of a product feature . . . is to identify the source of the product rather than the product itself"). Again, one might ask, if trademark law permits a descriptive word with secondary meaning to act as a mark, why would it not permit a color, under similar circumstances, to do the same?

We cannot find in the basic objectives of trademark law any obvious theoretical objection to the use of color alone as a trademark, where that color has attained "secondary meaning" and therefore identifies and distinguishes a particular brand (and thus indicates its "source"). In principle, trademark law, by preventing others from copying a source-identifying mark, "reduce[s] the customer's costs of shopping and making purchasing decisions," 1 J. MCCARTHY, MCCARTHY ON TRADEMARKS AND UNFAIR COMPETITION § 2.01[2], p. 2–3 (3d ed. 1994) (hereinafter MCCARTHY), for it quickly and easily assures a potential customer that this item—the item with this mark—is made by the same producer as other similarly marked items that he or she liked (or disliked) in the past. At the same time, the law helps assure a producer that it (and not an imitating competitor) will reap the financial, reputation-related rewards associated with a desirable product. The law thereby "encourage[s] the production of quality products," *ibid.*, and simultaneously discourages those who hope to sell inferior products by capitalizing on a consumer's inability quickly to evaluate the quality of an item offered for sale. . . . It is the source-distinguishing ability of a mark—not its ontological status as color, shape, fragrance, word, or sign—that permits it to serve these basic purposes. *See* Landes & Posner, *Trademark Law: An Economic Perspective*, 30 J. LAW & ECON. 265, 290 (1987). And, for that reason, it is difficult to find, in basic trademark objectives, a reason to disqualify absolutely the use of a color as a mark.

Neither can we find a principled objection to the use of color as a mark in the important "functionality" doctrine of trademark law. The functionality doctrine prevents trademark law, which seeks to promote competition by protecting a firm's reputation, from instead inhibiting legitimate competition by allowing a producer to control a useful product feature. It is the province of patent law, not trademark law, to encourage invention by granting inventors a monopoly over new product designs or functions for a limited time, 35 U.S.C. §§ 154, 173, after which competitors are free to use the innovation. If a product's functional features could be used as trademarks, however, a monopoly over such features could be obtained without regard to whether they qualify as patents and could be extended forever (because trademarks may be renewed in perpetuity). *See Kellogg Co. v. National Biscuit Co.*, 305 U.S. 111, 119–120 . . . (1938) (Brandeis, J.); *Inwood Laboratories, Inc.*, *supra*, 456 U.S., at 863 (White, J., concurring in result) ("A functional characteristic is 'an important ingredient in the commercial success of the product,' and, after expiration of a patent, it is no more the property of the originator than the product itself") (citation omitted). Functionality doctrine therefore would require, to take an imaginary example, that even if customers have come to identify the special illumination-enhancing shape of a new patented light bulb with a particular manufacturer, the manufacturer may not use that shape as a trademark, for doing so, after the patent had expired, would impede competition—not by protecting the reputation of the original bulb maker, but by frustrating competitors' legitimate efforts to produce an equivalent illumination-enhancing bulb. *See, e.g., Kellogg Co.*, *supra*, 305 U.S., at 119–120 (trademark law cannot be used to extend monopoly over "pillow" shape of shredded wheat biscuit after the patent for that shape had expired). This Court consequently has explained that, "[i]n general terms, a product feature is functional," and cannot serve as a trademark, "if it is essential to the use or purpose of the article or if it affects the cost or quality of the article," that is, if exclusive use of the feature would put competitors at a significant non-reputation-related disadvantage. *Inwood Laboratories, Inc.*, 456 U.S., at 850, n.10. Although sometimes color plays an important role (unrelated to source identification) in making a product more desirable, sometimes it does not. And, this latter fact—the fact that sometimes color is not essential to a product's use or purpose and does not affect cost or quality—indicates that the doctrine of "functionality" does not create an absolute bar to the use of color alone as a mark. *See Owens-Corning*, 774 F.2d, at 1123 (pink color of insulation in wall "performs no nontrademark function").

It would seem, then, that color alone, at least sometimes, can meet the basic legal requirements for use as a trademark. It can act as a symbol that distinguishes a firm's goods and identifies their source, without serving any other significant function. . . . Indeed, the District Court, in this case, entered findings (accepted by the Ninth Circuit) that show Qualitex's green-gold press pad color has met these requirements. The green-gold color acts as a symbol. Having developed secondary meaning (for customers identified the green-gold color as Qualitex's), it identifies the press pads' source. And, the green-gold color serves no other function. (Although it is important to use some color on press pads to avoid noticeable stains, the court found "no competitive need in the press pad industry for the green-gold color, since other colors are equally usable." 21 U.S.P.Q.2d, at 1460, 1991 WL 318798.) Accordingly, unless there is some special reason that convincingly militates against the use of color alone as a trademark, trademark law would protect Qualitex's use of the green-gold color on its press pads.

III

Respondent Jacobson Products says that there are four special reasons why the law should forbid the use of color alone as a trademark. We shall explain, in turn, why we, ultimately, find them unpersuasive.

First, Jacobson says that, if the law permits the use of color as a trademark, it will produce uncertainty and unresolvable court disputes about what shades of a color a competitor may lawfully use. Because lighting (morning sun, twilight mist) will affect perceptions of protected color, competitors and courts will suffer from "shade confusion" as they try to decide whether use of a similar color on a similar product does, or does not, confuse customers and thereby infringe a trademark. Jacobson adds that the "shade confusion" problem is "more difficult" and "far different from" the "determination of the similarity of words or symbols." . . .

We do not believe, however, that color, in this respect, is special. Courts traditionally decide quite difficult questions about whether two words or phrases or symbols are sufficiently similar, in context, to confuse buyers. They have had to compare, for example, such words as "Bonamine" and "Dramamine" (motion-sickness remedies); "Huggies" and "Dougies" (diapers); "Cheracol" and "Syrocol" (cough syrup); "Cyclone" and "Tornado" (wire fences); and "Mattres" and "1-800-Mattres" (mattress franchisor telephone numbers). . . . Legal standards exist to guide courts in making such comparisons. *See, e.g.*, 2 MCCARTHY § 15.08; 1 MCCARTHY §§ 11.24–11.25 ("[S]trong" marks, with greater secondary meaning, receive broader protection than "weak" marks). We do not see why courts could not apply those standards to a color, replicating, if necessary, lighting conditions under which a colored product is normally sold. . . .

Second, Jacobson argues, as have others, that colors are in limited supply. *See, e.g.*, *NutraSweet Co.*, 917 F.2d, at 1028; *Campbell Soup Co. v. Armour & Co.*, 175 F.2d 795, 798 (CA3 1949). Jacobson claims that, if one of many competitors can appropriate a particular color for use as a trademark, and each competitor then tries to do the same, the supply of colors will soon be depleted. Put in its strongest form, this argument would concede that "[h]undreds of color pigments are manufactured and thousands of colors can be obtained by mixing." L. CHESKIN, COLORS: WHAT THEY CAN DO FOR YOU 47 (1947). But, it would add that, in the context of a particular product, only some colors are usable. By the time one discards colors that, say, for reasons of customer appeal, are not usable, and adds the shades that competitors cannot use lest they risk infringing a similar, registered shade, then one is left with only a handful of possible colors. And, under these circumstances, to permit one, or a few, producers to use colors as trademarks will "deplete" the supply of usable colors to the point where a competitor's inability to find a suitable color will put that competitor at a significant disadvantage.

This argument is unpersuasive, however, largely because it relies on an occasional problem to justify a blanket prohibition. When a color serves as a mark, normally alternative colors will likely be available for similar use by others. *See, e.g.*, *Owens-Corning*, 774 F.2d, at 1121 (pink insulation). Moreover, if that is not so—if a "color depletion" or "color scarcity" problem does arise—the trademark doctrine of "functionality" normally would seem available to prevent the anticompetitive consequences that Jacobson's argument posits, thereby minimizing that argument's practical force.

The functionality doctrine, as we have said, forbids the use of a product's feature as a trademark where doing so will put a competitor at a significant disadvantage because the feature is "essential to the use or purpose of the article" or "affects [its] cost or quality." *Inwood Laboratories, Inc.*, 456 U.S., at 850, n.10. The functionality doctrine thus protects competitors against a disadvantage (unrelated to recognition or reputation) that trademark protection might otherwise impose, namely their inability reasonably to replicate important non-reputation-related product features. For example, this Court has written that competitors might be free to copy the color of a medical pill where that color serves to identify the kind of medication (e.g., a type of blood medicine) in addition to its source. *See id.*, at 853, 858, n.20 ("[S]ome patients commingle medications in a container and rely on color to differentiate one from another"); *see also* J. GINSBURG, D. GOLDBERG, & A. GREENBAUM, TRADEMARK AND UNFAIR COMPETITION LAW 194–195 (1991) (noting that drug color cases "have more to do with public health policy" regarding generic drug substitution "than with trademark law"). And, the federal courts have demonstrated that they can apply this doctrine in a careful and reasoned manner, with sensitivity to the effect on competition. Although we need not comment on the merits of specific cases, we note that lower courts have permitted competitors to copy the green color of farm machinery (because customers wanted their farm equipment to match) and have barred the use of black as a trademark on outboard boat motors (because black has the special functional attributes of decreasing the apparent size of the motor and ensuring compatibility with many different boat colors). . . . The RESTATEMENT (THIRD) OF UNFAIR COMPETITION adds that, if a design's "aesthetic value" lies in its ability to "confe[r] a significant benefit that cannot practically be duplicated by the use of alternative designs," then the design is "functional." RESTATEMENT (THIRD) OF UNFAIR COMPETITION § 17, Comment c, pp. 175–176 (1995). The "ultimate test of aesthetic functionality," it explains, "is whether the recognition of trademark rights would significantly hinder competition." *Id.*, at 176.

The upshot is that, where a color serves a significant nontrademark function—whether to distinguish a heart pill from a digestive medicine or to satisfy the "noble instinct for giving the right touch of beauty to common and necessary things," G.K. CHESTERTON, SIMPLICITY AND TOLSTOY 61 (1912)—courts will examine whether its use as a mark would permit one competitor (or a group) to interfere with legitimate (nontrademark-related) competition through actual or potential exclusive use of an important product ingredient. That examination should not discourage firms from creating aesthetically pleasing mark designs, for it is open to their competitors to do the same. *See, e.g., W. T. Rogers Co. v. Keene*, 778 F.2d 334, 343 (CA7 1985) (Posner, J.). But, ordinarily, it should prevent the anticompetitive consequences of Jacobson's hypothetical "color depletion" argument, when, and if, the circumstances of a particular case threaten "color depletion."

Third, Jacobson points to many older cases—including Supreme Court cases—in support of its position. [The Court distinguishes these as arising before the Lanham Act of 1946.]

Fourth, Jacobson argues that there is no need to permit color alone to function as a trademark because a firm already may use color as part of a trademark, say, as a colored circle or colored letter or colored word, and may rely upon "trade dress" protection, under § 43(a) of the Lanham Act, if a competitor copies its color and thereby causes consumer confusion regarding the overall appearance of the competing products or their packaging, *see* 15 U.S.C. § 1125(a) (1988 ed., Supp. V). The first part of this argument begs the question. One can understand why a firm might find it difficult to place a usable symbol or word on a product (say, a large industrial bolt that customers normally see from a distance); and, in such instances, a firm might want to use color, pure and simple, instead of color as part of a design. Neither is the second portion of the argument convincing. Trademark law helps the holder of a mark in many ways that "trade dress" protection does not. *See* 15 U.S.C. § 1124 (ability to prevent importation of confusingly similar goods); § 1072 (constructive notice of ownership); § 1065 (incontestable status); § 1057(b) (prima facie evidence of validity and ownership). Thus, one can easily find reasons why the law might provide trademark protection in addition to trade dress protection.

IV

Having determined that a color may sometimes meet the basic legal requirements for use as a trademark and that respondent Jacobson's arguments do not justify a special legal rule preventing color alone from serving as a trademark (and, in light of the District Court's here undisputed findings that Qualitex's use of the green-gold color on its press pads meets the basic trademark requirements), we conclude that the Ninth Circuit erred in barring Qualitex's use of color as a trademark. For these reasons, the judgment of the Ninth Circuit is

Reversed.

COMMENTS AND QUESTIONS

1. The Court mentions "NBC's three chimes" as an example of a sound that is registered as a trademark under the Lanham Act. Another famous example is MGM's "lion's roar," usually heard at the beginning of an MGM film. *See also Harley Wants Roar of Engine Protected by a Trademark*, SACRAMENTO BEE, Mar. 27, 1996, at D6 (describing Harley-Davidson trademark application for engine sound opposed by competitors). Compare this with § 43(a) cases alleging imitation of famous voices, *e.g., Midler v. Ford Motor Co.*, 849 F.2d 460 (9th Cir. 1988); *see* Chapter VI(D).

Play-Doh recently succeeded in registering a mark for the smell of its dough, which has remained unchanged since 1956.

2. The Court says that color does not automatically receive protection, but can be protected on a showing of secondary meaning. But how much evidence of secondary meaning is required? In *In re General Mills IP Holdings II, LLC*, No. 86757390 (TTAB Aug. 22, 2017), the TTAB held that the color yellow standing alone was not sufficiently associated with Cheerios cereal to warrant trademark registration.

Is the Court's problem with color anywhere or with the fact that the trademark is on the color of the product itself? Would a green-gold logo or packaging raise the same concerns? *See McNeil Nutrition v. Heartland Sweeteners*, 566 F. Supp. 2d 378 (E.D. Pa. 2008) (finding that the yellow packaging of Splenda sugar substitute was arbitrary and thus inherently distinctive). Consider the next case.

PROBLEM

Problem V-3. AlertFive makes medical alert bracelets. The bracelets are designed to monitor an aspect of the wearer's medical condition, and trigger an alarm if the measurement indicates a dangerous condition. For example, AlertFive makes a bracelet that monitors heart rate and sounds an alarm if the heart rate goes above or below a certain range.

Aware that people in the modern world are bombarded by sounds, and can come to tune them out, AlertFive sought to make the alarm associated with its bracelets unusual and memorable. Rejecting a standard beeping noise, it selected a trilling sound that increases in volume as it goes up the scale. AlertFive advertises its product on daytime television, and the ads feature a patient being saved in the nick of time because one of its bracelet alarms went off. Can AlertFive prevent a competitor from selling a bracelet that makes a similar noise to alert a patient to an abnormal heart rate?

Wal-Mart Stores, Inc. v. Samara Brothers, Inc.
Supreme Court of the United States
529 U.S. 205 (2000)

JUSTICE SCALIA delivered the opinion of the Court.

In this case, we decide under what circumstances a product's design is distinctive, and therefore protectible, in an action for infringement of unregistered trade dress under § 43(a) of the Trademark Act of 1946 (Lanham Act), 60 Stat. 441, as amended, 15 U.S.C. § 1125(a).

I

Respondent Samara Brothers, Inc., designs and manufactures children's clothing. Its primary product is a line of spring/summer one-piece seersucker outfits decorated with appliques of hearts, flowers, fruits, and the like. A number of chain stores, including JCPenney, sell this line of clothing under contract with Samara.

Petitioner Wal-Mart Stores, Inc., is one of the nation's best known retailers, selling among other things children's clothing. In 1995, Wal-Mart contracted with one of its suppliers, Judy-Philippine, Inc., to manufacture a line of children's outfits for sale in the 1996 spring/summer season. Wal-Mart sent Judy-Philippine photographs of a number of garments from Samara's line, on which Judy-Philippine's garments were to be based; Judy-Philippine duly copied, with only minor modifications, 16 of Samara's garments, many of which contained copyrighted elements. In 1996, Wal-Mart briskly sold the so-called knockoffs, generating more than $1.15 million in gross profits. . . .

After sending cease-and-desist letters, Samara brought this action in the United States District Court for the Southern District of New York against Wal-Mart, Judy-Philippine, Kmart, Caldor, Hills, and Goody's for copyright infringement under federal law, consumer fraud and unfair competition under New York law, and—most relevant for our purposes—infringement of unregistered trade dress under § 43(a) of the Lanham Act, 15 U.S.C. § 1125(a). . . .

After a weeklong trial, the jury found in favor of Samara on all of its claims. . . . The Second Circuit affirmed. . ., and we granted certiorari. . . .

II

The Lanham Act provides for the registration of trademarks, which it defines in § 45 to include "any word, name, symbol, or device, or any combination thereof [used or intended to be used] to identify and distinguish [a producer's] goods . . . from those manufactured or sold by others and to indicate the source of the goods. . . . " 15 U.S.C. § 1127. . . . In addition to protecting registered marks, the Lanham Act, in § 43(a), gives a producer a cause of action for the use by any person of "any word, term, name, symbol, or device, or any combination thereof . . . which . . . is likely to cause confusion . . . as to the origin, sponsorship, or approval of his or her goods. . . . " 15 U.S.C. § 1125(a). It is the latter provision that is at issue in this case.

The breadth of the definition of marks registrable under § 2, and of the confusion-producing elements recited as actionable by § 43(a), has been held to embrace not just word marks, such as "Nike," and symbol marks, such as Nike's "swoosh" symbol, but also "trade dress"—a category that originally included only the packaging, or "dressing," of a product, but in recent years has been expanded by many courts of appeals to encompass the design of a product. *See, e.g., Ashley Furniture Industries, Inc. v. Sangiacomo N.A., Ltd.*, 187 F.3d 363 (C.A.4 1999) (bedroom furniture); *Knitwaves, Inc. v. Lollytogs, Ltd.*, 71 F.3d 996 (C.A.2 1995) (sweaters); *Stuart Hall Co., Inc. v. Ampad Corp.*, 51 F.3d 780 (C.A.8 1995) (notebooks). These courts have assumed, often without discussion, that trade dress constitutes a "symbol" or "device" for purposes of the relevant sections, and we conclude likewise. "Since human beings might use as a 'symbol' or 'device' almost anything at all that is capable of carrying meaning, this language, read literally, is not restrictive." *Qualitex Co. v. Jacobson Products Co.*, 514 U.S. 159, 162 (1995). This reading of § 2 and § 43(a) is buttressed by a recently added subsection of § 43(a), § 43(a)(3), which refers specifically to "civil action[s] for trade dress infringement under this chapter for trade dress not registered on the principal register." 15 U.S.C.A. § 1125(a)(3) (Oct. 1999 Supp.).

The text of § 43(a) provides little guidance as to the circumstances under which unregistered trade dress may be protected. It does require that a producer show that the allegedly infringing feature is not "functional," *see* § 43(a)(3), and is likely to cause confusion with the product for which protection is sought, *see* § 43(a)(1)(A), 15 U.S.C. § 1125(a)(1)(A). Nothing in § 43(a) explicitly requires a producer to show that its trade dress is distinctive, but courts have universally imposed that requirement, since without distinctiveness the trade dress would not "cause confusion . . . as to the origin, sponsorship, or approval of [the] goods," as the section requires. Distinctiveness is, moreover, an explicit prerequisite for registration of trade dress under § 2, and "the general principles qualifying a mark for registration under § 2 of the Lanham Act are for the most part applicable in determining whether an unregistered mark is entitled to protection under § 43(a)." *Two Pesos, Inc. v. Taco Cabana, Inc.*, 505 U.S. 763, 768 (1992) (citations omitted).

In evaluating the distinctiveness of a mark under § 2 (and therefore, by analogy, under § 43(a)), courts have held that a mark can be distinctive in one of two ways. First, a mark is inherently distinctive if "[its] intrinsic nature serves to identify a particular source." *Ibid.* In the context of word marks, courts have applied the now-classic test originally formulated by Judge Friendly, in which word marks that are "arbitrary" ("Camel" cigarettes), "fanciful" ("Kodak" film), or "suggestive" ("Tide" laundry detergent) are held to be inherently distinctive. *See Abercrombie & Fitch Co. v. Hunting World, Inc.*, 537 F.2d 4, 10–11 (C.A.2 1976). Second, a mark has acquired distinctiveness, even if it is not inherently distinctive, if it has developed secondary meaning, which occurs when, "in the minds of the public, the primary significance of a [mark] is to identify the source of the product rather than the product itself." *Inwood Laboratories, Inc. v. Ives Laboratories, Inc.*, 456 U.S. 844, 851 n.11 (1982).

The judicial differentiation between marks that are inherently distinctive and those that have developed secondary meaning has solid foundation in the statute itself. Section 2 requires that registration be granted to any trademark "by which the goods of the applicant may be distinguished from the goods of others"—subject to various limited exceptions. 15 U.S.C. § 1052. It also provides, again with limited exceptions, that "nothing in this chapter shall prevent the registration of a mark used by the applicant which has become distinctive of the applicant's goods in commerce"—that is, which is not inherently distinctive but has become so only through secondary meaning. § 2(f), 15 U.S.C. § 1052(f). Nothing in § 2, however, demands the conclusion that *every* category of mark necessarily includes some marks "by which the goods of the applicant may be distinguished from the goods of others" *without* secondary meaning—that in every category some marks are inherently distinctive.

Indeed, with respect to at least one category of mark—colors—we have held that no mark can ever be inherently distinctive. *See Qualitex,* 514 U.S., at 162–163. In *Qualitex,* petitioner manufactured and sold green-gold dry-cleaning press pads. After respondent began selling pads of a similar color, petitioner brought suit under § 43(a), then added a claim under § 32 after obtaining registration for the color of its pads. We held that a color could be protected as a trademark, but only upon a showing of secondary meaning. Reasoning by analogy to the *Abercrombie & Fitch* test developed for word marks, we noted that a product's color is unlike a "fanciful," "arbitrary," or "suggestive" mark, since it does not "almost *automatically* tell a customer that [it] refer[s] to a brand," *ibid.*, and does not "immediately . . . signal a brand or a product 'source,'" *Id.*, at 163. However, we noted that, "over time, customers may come to treat a particular color on a product or its packaging . . . as signifying a brand." *Id.*, at 162–163. Because a color, like a "descriptive" word mark, could eventually "come to indicate a product's origin," we concluded that it could be protected *upon a showing of secondary meaning. Ibid.*

It seems to us that design, like color, is not inherently distinctive. The attribution of inherent distinctiveness to certain categories of word marks and product packaging derives from the fact that the very purpose of attaching a particular word to a product, or encasing it in a distinctive packaging, is most often to identify the source of the product. Although the words and packaging can serve subsidiary functions—a suggestive word mark (such as "Tide" for laundry detergent), for instance, may invoke positive connotations in the consumer's mind, and a garish form of packaging (such as Tide's squat, brightly decorated plastic bottles for its liquid laundry detergent) may attract an otherwise indifferent consumer's attention on a crowded store shelf—their predominant function remains source identification. Consumers are therefore predisposed to regard those symbols as indication of the producer, which is why such symbols "almost *automatically* tell a customer that they refer to a brand," *Id.*, at 162–163, and "immediately . . . signal a brand or a product 'source,'" *Id.*, at 163. And where it is not reasonable to assume consumer predisposition to take an affixed word or packaging as indication of source—where, for example, the affixed word is descriptive of the product ("Tasty" bread) or of a geographic origin ("Georgia" peaches)—inherent distinctiveness will not be found. That is why the statute generally excludes, from those word marks that can be registered as inherently distinctive, words that are "merely descriptive" of the goods, § 2(e)(1), 15 U.S.C. § 1052(e)(1), or "primarily geographically descriptive of them," *see* § 2(e)(2), 15 U.S.C. § 1052(e)(2). In the case of product design, as in the case of color, we think consumer predisposition to equate the feature with the source does not exist. Consumers are aware of the reality that, almost invariably, even the most unusual of product designs—such as a cocktail shaker shaped like a penguin—is intended not to identify the source, but to render the product itself more useful or more appealing.

The fact that product design almost invariably serves purposes other than source identification not only renders inherent distinctiveness problematic; it also renders application of an inherent-distinctiveness principle more harmful to other consumer interests. Consumers should not be deprived of the benefits of competition with regard to the utilitarian and esthetic purposes that product design ordinarily serves by a rule of law that facilitates plausible threats of suit against new entrants based upon alleged inherent distinctiveness. How easy it is to mount a plausible suit depends, of course, upon the clarity of the test for inherent distinctiveness, and where product design is concerned we have little confidence that a reasonably clear test can be devised. Respondent and the United States as *amicus curiae* urge us to adopt for product design relevant portions of the test formulated by the Court of Customs and Patent Appeals for product packaging in *Seabrook Foods, Inc. v. Bar-Well Foods, Ltd.*, 568 F.2d 1342 (1977). That opinion, in determining the inherent distinctiveness of a product's packaging, considered, among other things, "whether it was a 'common' basic shape or design, whether it was unique or unusual in a particular field, [and] whether it was a mere refinement of a commonly-adopted and well-known form of ornamentation for a particular class of goods viewed by the public as a dress or ornamentation for the goods." *Id.*, at 1344 (footnotes omitted). Such a test would rarely provide the basis for summary disposition of an anticompetitive strike suit. Indeed, at oral argument, counsel for the United States quite understandably would not give a definitive answer as to whether the test was met in this very case, saying only that "[t]his is a very difficult case for that purpose."

It is true, of course, that the person seeking to exclude new entrants would have to establish the nonfunctionality of the design feature, *see* § 43(a)(3), 15 U.S.C.A. § 1125(a)(3) (Oct. 1999 Supp.)—a showing that may involve consideration of its esthetic appeal, *see Qualitex,* 514 U.S., at 170. Competition is deterred, however, not merely by successful suit but by the plausible threat of successful suit, and given the unlikelihood of inherently source-identifying design, the game of allowing suit based upon alleged inherent distinctiveness seems to us not worth the candle. That is especially so since the producer can ordinarily obtain protection for a design that *is* inherently source identifying (if any such exists), but that does not yet have secondary meaning, by securing a design patent or a copyright for the design—as, indeed, respondent did for certain elements of the designs in this case. The availability of these other protections greatly reduces any harm to the producer that might ensue from our conclusion that a product design cannot be protected under § 43(a) without a showing of secondary meaning.

Respondent contends that our decision in *Two Pesos* forecloses a conclusion that product-design trade dress can never be inherently distinctive. . . . *Two Pesos* unquestionably establishes the legal principle that trade dress can be inherently distinctive, *See, e.g., Id.,* at 773, but it does not establish that *product-design* trade dress can be. *Two Pesos* is inapposite to our holding here because the trade dress at issue, the decor of a restaurant, seems to us not to constitute product *design*. It was either product packaging—which, as we have discussed, normally *is* taken by the consumer to indicate origin—or else some tertium quid that is akin to product packaging and has no bearing on the present case.

Respondent replies that this manner of distinguishing *Two Pesos* will force courts to draw difficult lines between product-design and product-packaging trade dress. There will indeed be some hard cases at the margin: a classic glass Coca-Cola bottle, for instance, may constitute packaging for those consumers who drink the Coke and then discard the bottle, but may constitute the product itself for those consumers who are bottle collectors, or part of the product itself for those consumers who buy Coke in the classic glass bottle, rather than a can, because they think it more stylish to drink from the former. We believe, however, that the frequency and the difficulty of having to distinguish between product design and product packaging will be much less than the frequency and the difficulty of having to decide when a product design is inherently distinctive. To the extent there are close cases, we believe that courts should err on the side of caution and classify ambiguous trade dress as product design, thereby requiring secondary meaning. The very closeness will suggest the existence of relatively small utility in adopting an inherent-distinctiveness principle, and relatively great consumer benefit in requiring a demonstration of secondary meaning. . . .

We hold that, in an action for infringement of unregistered trade dress under § 43(a) of the Lanham Act, a product's design is distinctive, and therefore protectible, only upon a showing of secondary meaning. The judgment of the Second Circuit is reversed, and the case is remanded for further proceedings consistent with this opinion.

It is so ordered.

COMMENTS AND QUESTIONS

1. *Trade Dress Classification*. The Supreme Court establishes three categories for determining whether a product's trade dress is protectable: (1) product packaging; (2) product design; and (3) a "tertium quid" (defined in the OXFORD ENGLISH DICTIONARY as "[s]omething (indefinite or left undefined) related in some way to two (definite or known) things, but distinct from both."). Product *packaging* can be inherently distinctive (as in the *Taco Cabana* case, above), while product design cannot. But how is one to distinguish the two? Should close cases (such as the Coca-Cola bottle) be characterized as product design and hence subject to the higher threshold of secondary meaning? Is the real problem that the Court's assumption in *Two Pesos* that the décor of a Mexican restaurant was inherently distinctive was ill-advised? Further, the Court leaves unresolved who decides on the classification of trade dress. *Two Pesos* seems to suggest that

this question is for the jury, whereas *Samara* emphasizes summary adjudication. Who should decide?

2. Does the classification scheme established for word marks help to distinguish descriptive from inherently distinctive trade dress? In *Rock and Roll Hall of Fame and Museum, Inc. v. Gentile Productions*, 134 F.3d 749 (6th Cir. 1998), the owner of the Rock and Roll Hall of Fame building in Cleveland, Ohio, sued a photographer who marketed pictures of the building set against the Cleveland skyline, alleging that the photographer was infringing the building's trade dress. The district court issued a preliminary injunction, but the Sixth Circuit reversed. The majority and the dissent battled over the proper classification of the museum. The majority agreed that the design of the museum was "fanciful" but denied that it was "fanciful in a trademark sense." It concluded that the design of the museum itself did not function as a trademark and that the public did not recognize it as such. Important to the court's determination was the trademark owner's inconsistent use of the museum's design as a source-identifying function:

> [A]lthough the Museum has used drawings or pictures of its building design on various goods, it has not done so with any consistency. As museum director Robert Bosak stated in his affidavit, "the Museum has used versions of the building shape trademark on . . . a wide variety of products." Several items marketed by the Museum display only the rear of the Museum's building, which looks dramatically different from the front. Drawings of the front of the Museum on the two T-shirts in the record are similar, but they are quite different from the photograph featured in the Museum's poster. And, although the photograph from the poster is also used on a postcard, another postcard displays various close-up photographs of the Museum which, individually and perhaps even collectively, are not even immediately recognizable as photographs of the Museum. In this regard, this case is similar to those in which a party has claimed trademark rights in a famous person's likeness. *In Estate of Presley* [*v. Russen*, 513 F. Supp. 1339, 1363–64 (D.N.J. 1981)], the court concluded that, although one particular image of [Elvis] Presley had been used consistently as a mark, "the available evidence [did] not support [the estate's] broad position" that all images of Presley served such a function.

134 F.3d 749, 754–55.

In another case, the Sixth Circuit had little difficulty in applying *Samara*'s classification scheme to furniture. *See Herman Miller v. Palazzetti Imports and Exports, Inc.*, 270 F.3d 298 (6th Cir. 2001) (finding genuine issue of material fact as to whether lounge chair and ottoman had acquired secondary meaning); *see also Weber-Stephen Products LLC v. Sears Holding Corp.*, No., 2015 WL 5161347, at *1 (N.D. Ill. Sept. 1, 2015) (denying defendant Sears's summary judgment motion in part on the basis that secondary meaning in shape of plaintiff's grills can be inferred from defendant's intentional copying of grill shape, in the "hop[e] that consumers would look at them and 'think of the market share leader, Weber'").

3. *Can color-based trade dress packaging ever be inherently distinctive?* In *In re Forney Industries, Inc.*, 955 F.3d 940 (Fed. Cir. 2020), the Federal Circuit held that while color is usually perceived as ornamentation as opposed to source identification, color-based packaging can indicate the source of goods to consumers and therefore can be inherently distinctive. In the case before the court, the product packaging for pressure gauges featured a solid black stripe at the top with the color yellow gradually fading into orange and then red at the bottom. Does this square with your reading of *Qualitex*, *Two Pesos*, and *Samara*? Does this progression of colors communicate the function of a pressure gauge, thereby affording the trademark owner an advantage in communicating the attributes of its product? Might other color gradients work as well as yellow to red?

4. *Product Configurations and Overlapping Intellectual Property Rights.* An old rule of intellectual property law called the "principle of election" used to limit an author to one type of intellectual property protection. That doctrine was rejected in *In re Yardley*, 493 F.2d 1389 (C.C.P.A. 1974). *Yardley* involved a design patent application for a watch which featured a caricature of then-Vice President of the United States Spiro Agnew. The patent examiner rejected the application on the ground that Yardley had already received several copyright registrations for the watch. The Court of Customs and Patent Appeals reversed, concluding that the principle of election was in direct conflict with the patent, copyright and trademark statutes. The court reasoned that because each statute strikes its own "coverage" balance, a work that qualifies for protection under more than one statute is entitled to the protection of each.

Nonetheless, where Congress has not expressly dictated the principles for channeling protection among the various modes of intellectual property, the courts have construed the scope of protection in order to effectuate the larger policies of federal intellectual property law. In general, utility patent protection trumps all other modes of intellectual property with regard to the functional features of products. The courts recognize that patent law imposes high thresholds for protection (novelty, nonobviousness, and disclosure) and an examination process and affords a relatively short duration of protection in order to balance the short-run hampering of free competition with the longer-term benefits of innovation. Were copyright law or trademark law to afford protection for utilitarian features of products, patent law would be unnecessary and competition would give way to monopolization by the first to design a product, regardless of the effort that went into the design. In order to minimize this threat, the Supreme Court in *Baker v. Selden* foreclosed competition under copyright law for accounting systems. (Congress reinforced this limitation in the 1976 Copyright Act, *see* 17 U.S.C. § 102(b).) The Supreme Court acknowledged a similarly high burden for establishing that a product feature or configuration that has been the subject of a utility patent can ever qualify for trade dress protection. *See TrafFix Devices, Inc. v. Marketing Displays, Inc.*, 532 U.S. 23 (2001), excerpted below (functionality defense); Christopher Buccafusco, Mark A. Lemley, & Jonathan Masur, *Intelligent Design*, 68 DUKE L.J. 75(2018) (suggesting a return to the doctrine of election).

The Supreme Court took a sharply different tack from *Yardley* in its most recent treatment of the issue. In *Dastar Corp. v. Twentieth Century Fox Film Corp.*, 539 U.S. 23 (2003), defendant Dastar produced and sold its own copies of plaintiff's video series, in which the copyright had expired. Fox sued on the grounds that Dastar was misrepresenting the origin of the goods in violation of the Lanham Act. The Court rejected that argument, construing "origin" narrowly to mean only the physical source of the videotapes, not who had actually filmed or produced them. In so holding, the Court was expressly concerned to avoid reading the Lanham Act to conflict with copyright law, which would permit such copying. It warned "against misuse or over-extension of trademark and related protections into areas traditionally occupied by patent or copyright," and explained that "allowing a cause of action under § 43(a) for that representation would create a species of mutant copyright law that limits the public's federal right to copy and to use expired copyrights." *Id.* at 34. The Court seems quite concerned with channeling protection between the copyright and trademark regimes and unwilling to permit much overlap between the two.

5. *Promoting Progress in Fashion Design.* Some have argued that the fashion design industry has thrived in part because formal intellectual property protection does not extend the cut of clothing and the shape of many fashion items and that the absence of significant protection accelerates fashion design cycles. *See* KAL RAUSTIALA AND CHRISTOPHER SPRIGMAN, THE KNOCKOFF ECONOMY (2012); *but see* C. Scott Hemphill and Jeannie Suk, *The Law, Culture, and Economics of Fashion*, 61 STAN. L. REV. 1147, 1183 (2009) ("In fact, many [fashion] designers are vocal advocates against copying, and . . . make use of the currently limited legal tools available to curb copyists."); Susan Scafidi, *F.I.T.: Fashion as Information Technology*, 59 SYR. L. REV. 69 (2008).

As reflected in *L.A. Gear*, Chapter III(H), design patents can cover shoe design. Until 2017, copyright law denied protection for the cut of dress designs, although not original print designs on clothing. The Supreme Court's decision in *Star Athletica, see* Chapter IV(C)(2)(ii), muddied that distinction. To what extent does trade dress protect fashion design? While not excluding trade dress protection for dress designs, the *Samara* decision reflects a concern for not unduly hindering competition. The Court noted that product design "almost invariably serves purposes other than source identification," such as making products more useful or appealing. The Court also stated that application of the inherently distinctive test in product design cases could deprive consumers of "the benefits of competition with regard to the utilitarian and esthetic purposes that product design ordinarily serves." *See also Samara Bros., Inc. v. Wal-Mart Stores, Inc.*, 165 F.3d 120, 133 (2d Cir. 1999) (Newman, dissenting) (noting that "we must construe the Lanham Act 'in the light of a strong federal policy in favor of vigorously competitive markets'"; "courts are to 'exercise[] particular caution when extending [trademark] protection to product designs'"; "'just as copyright law does not protect ideas but only their concrete expression, neither does trade dress law protect an idea, a concept, or a generalized type of appearance.'").6. Should "Tide's squat, brightly decorated plastic bottles for its liquid laundry detergent" be deemed inherently distinctive, as Justice Scalia seems to suggest?

PROBLEM

Problem V-4. Alice Richland, a gourmet chef world-renowned for her chocolate desserts, designs a new line of chocolate products. Called "Chocolate Shells," these products are made of dark chocolate flavored in special ways with a combination of ingredients Alice hit upon after months of work in her kitchens. The use of the special ingredients imparts a unique flavor to the Shells, and has the additional property of making the usually soft chocolate feel sandy or grainy to the touch. The Shells are made in the shapes of different seashells native to the Florida coast, and each shell is colored in a different, unusual pattern. On the advice of her lawyer, Alice files a trademark application seeking to register each of her shell designs. What aspects of the Shells are entitled to registration? To § 43(a) protection?

---

v.   Functionality

 TrafFix Devices, Inc. v. Marketing Displays, Inc.
Supreme Court of the United States
532 U.S. 23 (2001)

JUSTICE KENNEDY delivered the opinion of the Court.

Temporary road signs with warnings like "Road Work Ahead" or "Left Shoulder Closed" must withstand strong gusts of wind. An inventor named Robert Sarkisian obtained two utility patents for a mechanism built upon two springs (the dual-spring design) to keep these and other outdoor signs upright despite adverse wind conditions. The holder of the now-expired Sarkisian patents, respondent Marketing Displays, Inc. (MDI), established a successful business in the manufacture and sale of sign stands incorporating the patented feature. MDI's stands for road signs were recognizable to buyers and users (it says) because the dual-spring design was visible near the base of the sign.

This litigation followed after the patents expired and a competitor, TrafFix Devices, Inc., sold sign stands with a visible spring mechanism that looked like MDI's. MDI and TrafFix products looked alike because they were. When TrafFix started in business, it sent an MDI product abroad to have it reverse engineered, that is to say copied. Complicating matters, TrafFix marketed its sign stands under a name similar to MDI's. MDI used the name "WindMaster," while TrafFix, its new competitor, used "WindBuster.".

. .

I

. . . The District Court ruled against MDI on its trade dress claim. 971 F. Supp. 262 (E.D. Mich. 1997). After determining that the one element of MDI's trade dress at issue was the dual-spring design, *Id.*, at 265, it held that "no reasonable trier of fact could determine that MDI has established secondary meaning" in its alleged trade dress, *Id.*, at 269. In other words, consumers did not associate the look of the dual-spring design with MDI. As a second, independent reason to grant summary judgment in favor of TrafFix, the District Court determined the dual-spring design was functional. . . .

The Court of Appeals for the Sixth Circuit reversed the trade dress ruling. 200 F.3d 929 (1999). . . . In its criticism of the District Court's ruling on the trade dress question, the Court of Appeals took note of a split among Courts of Appeals in various other Circuits on the issue whether the existence of an expired utility patent forecloses the possibility of the patentee's claiming trade dress protection in the product's design. 200 F.3d, at 939. *Compare Sunbeam Products, Inc. v. West Bend Co.*, 123 F.3d 246 (C.A.5 1997) (holding that trade dress protection is not foreclosed), *Thomas & Betts Corp. v. Panduit Corp.*, 138 F.3d 277 (C.A.7 1998) (same), *and Midwest Industries, Inc. v. Karavan Trailers, Inc.*, 175 F.3d 1356 (C.A. Fed. 1999) (same), *with Vornado Air Circulation Systems, Inc. v. Duracraft Corp.*, 58 F.3d 1498, 1500 (C.A.10 1995) ("Where a product configuration is a significant inventive component of an invention covered by a utility patent . . . it cannot receive trade dress protection"). To resolve the conflict, we granted certiorari.

II

It is well established that trade dress can be protected under federal law. The design or packaging of a product may acquire a distinctiveness which serves to identify the product with its manufacturer or source; and a design or package which acquires this secondary meaning, assuming other requisites are met, is a trade dress which may not be used in a manner likely to cause confusion as to the origin, sponsorship, or approval of the goods. In these respects protection for trade dress exists to promote competition. . . . Congress confirmed this statutory protection for trade dress by amending the Lanham Act to recognize the concept. Title 15 U.S.C. § 1125(a)(3) (1994 ed., Supp. V) provides: "In a civil action for trade dress infringement under this chapter for trade dress not registered on the principal register, the person who asserts trade dress protection has the burden of proving that the matter sought to be protected is not functional." This burden of proof gives force to the well-established rule that trade dress protection may not be claimed for product features that are functional. *Qualitex, supra*, at 164–165; *Two Pesos, Inc. v. Taco Cabana, Inc.*, 505 U.S. 763, 775 (1992). And in *Wal-Mart, supra*, we were careful to caution against misuse or over-extension of trade dress. We noted that "product design almost invariably serves purposes other than source identification." *Id.*, at 213.

Trade dress protection must subsist with the recognition that in many instances there is no prohibition against copying goods and products. In general, unless an intellectual property right such as a patent or copyright protects an item, it will be subject to copying. As the Court has explained, copying is not always discouraged or disfavored by the laws which preserve our competitive economy. *Bonito Boats, Inc. v. Thunder Craft Boats, Inc.*, 489 U.S. 141, 160 (1989). Allowing competitors to copy will have salutary effects in many instances. "Reverse engineering of chemical and mechanical articles in the public domain often leads to significant advances in technology." *Ibid.*

The principal question in this case is the effect of an expired patent on a claim of trade dress infringement. A prior patent, we conclude, has vital significance in resolving the trade dress claim. A utility patent is strong evidence that the features therein claimed are functional. If trade dress protection is sought for those features the strong evidence of functionality based on the previous patent adds great weight to the statutory presumption that features are deemed functional until proved otherwise by the party seeking trade dress protection. Where the expired patent claimed the features in question, one who seeks to establish trade dress protection must carry the heavy burden of showing that the feature is not functional, for instance by showing that it is merely an ornamental, incidental, or arbitrary aspect of the device.

In the case before us, the central advance claimed in the expired utility patents (the Sarkisian patents) is the dual-spring design; and the dual-spring design is the essential feature of the trade dress MDI now seeks to establish and to protect. The rule we have explained bars the trade dress claim, for MDI did not, and cannot, carry the burden of overcoming the strong evidentiary inference of functionality based on the disclosure of the dual-spring design in the claims of the expired patents.

The dual springs shown in the Sarkisian patents were well apart (at either end of a frame for holding a rectangular sign when one full side is the base) while the dual springs at issue here are close together (in a frame designed to hold a sign by one of its corners). As the District Court recognized, this makes little difference. The point is that the springs are necessary to the operation of the device. . . .

The dual-spring design serves the important purpose of keeping the sign upright even in heavy wind conditions; and, as confirmed by the statements in the expired patents, it does so in a unique and useful manner. As the specification of one of the patents recites, prior art "devices, in practice, will topple under the force of a strong wind." U.S. Patent No. 3,662,482, col. 1. The dual-spring design allows sign stands to resist toppling in strong winds. . . .

III

In finding for MDI on the trade dress issue the Court of Appeals gave insufficient recognition to the importance of the expired utility patents, and their evidentiary significance, in establishing the functionality of the device. The error likely was caused by its misinterpretation of trade dress principles in other respects. As we have noted, even if there has been no previous utility patent the party asserting trade dress has the burden to establish the nonfunctionality of alleged trade dress features. MDI could not meet this burden. Discussing trademarks, we have said "'[i]n general terms, a product feature is functional,' and cannot serve as a trademark, 'if it is essential to the use or purpose of the article or if it affects the cost or quality of the article.'" *Qualitex,* 514 U.S., at 165 (quoting *Inwood Laboratories, Inc. v. Ives Laboratories, Inc.,* 456 U.S. 844, 850, n.10 (1982)). Expanding upon the meaning of this phrase, we have observed that a functional feature is one the "exclusive use of [which] would put competitors at a significant non-reputation-related disadvantage." 514 U.S. at 165. The Court of Appeals in the instant case seemed to interpret this language to mean that a necessary test for functionality is "whether the particular product configuration is a competitive necessity." 200 F.3d at 940. *See* also *Vornado,* 58 F.3d, at 1507 ("Functionality, by contrast, has been defined both by our circuit, and more recently by the Supreme Court, in terms of competitive need"). This was incorrect as a comprehensive definition. As explained in *Qualitex, supra,* and *Inwood, supra,* a feature is also functional when it is essential to the use or purpose of the device or when it affects the cost or quality of the device. The *Qualitex* decision did not purport to displace this traditional rule. Instead, it quoted the rule as *Inwood* had set it forth. It is proper to inquire into a "significant non-reputation-related disadvantage" in cases of aesthetic functionality, the question involved in *Qualitex.* Where the design is functional under the *Inwood* formulation there is no need to proceed further to consider if there is a competitive necessity for the feature. In *Qualitex,* by contrast, aesthetic functionality was the central question, there having been no indication that the green-gold color of the laundry press pad had any bearing on the use or purpose of the product or its cost or quality.

The Court has allowed trade dress protection to certain product features that are inherently distinctive. *Two Pesos,* 505 U.S., at 774. In *Two Pesos,* however, the Court at the outset made the explicit analytic assumption that the trade dress features in question (decorations and other features to evoke a Mexican theme in a restaurant) were not functional. *Id.*, at 767, n.6. The trade dress in those cases did not bar competitors from copying functional product design features. In the instant case, beyond serving the purpose of informing consumers that the sign stands are made by MDI (assuming it does so), the dual-spring design provides a unique and useful mechanism to resist the force of the wind. Functionality having been established, whether MDI's dual-spring design has acquired secondary meaning need not be considered.

There is no need, furthermore, to engage, as did the Court of Appeals, in speculation about other design possibilities, such as using three or four springs which might serve the same purpose. 200 F.3d, at 940. Here, the functionality of the spring design means that competitors need not explore whether other spring juxtapositions might be used. The dual-spring design is not an arbitrary flourish in the configuration of MDI's product; it is the reason the device works. Other designs need not be attempted.

Because the dual-spring design is functional, it is unnecessary for competitors to explore designs to hide the springs, say by using a box or framework to cover them, as suggested by the Court of Appeals. *Ibid.* The dual-spring design assures the user the device will work. If buyers are assured the product serves its purpose by seeing the operative mechanism that in itself serves an important market need. It would be at cross-purposes to those objectives, and something of a paradox, were we to require the manufacturer to conceal the very item the user seeks.

In a case where a manufacturer seeks to protect arbitrary, incidental, or ornamental aspects of features of a product found in the patent claims, such as arbitrary curves in the legs or an ornamental pattern painted on the springs, a different result might obtain. There the manufacturer could perhaps prove that those aspects do not serve a purpose within the terms of the utility patent. The inquiry into whether such features, asserted to be trade dress, are functional by reason of their inclusion in the claims of an expired utility patent could be aided by going beyond the claims and examining the patent and its prosecution history to see if the feature in question is shown as a useful part of the invention. No such claim is made here, however. MDI in essence seeks protection for the dual-spring design alone. The asserted trade dress consists simply of the dual-spring design, four legs, a base, an upright, and a sign. MDI has pointed to nothing arbitrary about the components of its device or the way they are assembled. The Lanham Act does not exist to reward manufacturers for their innovation in creating a particular device; that is the purpose of the patent law and its period of exclusivity. The Lanham Act, furthermore, does not protect trade dress in a functional design simply because an investment has been made to encourage the public to associate a particular functional feature with a single manufacturer or seller. The Court of Appeals erred in viewing MDI as possessing the right to exclude competitors from using a design identical to MDI's and to require those competitors to adopt a different design simply to avoid copying it. MDI cannot gain the exclusive right to produce sign stands using the dual-spring design by asserting that consumers associate it with the look of the invention itself. Whether a utility patent has expired or there has been no utility patent at all, a product design which has a particular appearance may be functional because it is "essential to the use or purpose of the article" or "affects the cost or quality of the article." *Inwood,* 456 U.S., at 850 n.10.

TrafFix and some of its *amici* argue that the Patent Clause of the Constitution, Art. I, § 8, cl. 8, of its own force, prohibits the holder of an expired utility patent from claiming trade dress protection. We need not resolve this question. If, despite the rule that functional features may not be the subject of trade dress protection, a case arises in which trade dress becomes the practical equivalent of an expired utility patent, that will be time enough to consider the matter. The judgment of the Court of Appeals is reversed, and the case is remanded for further proceedings consistent with this opinion.

It is so ordered.

COMMENTS AND QUESTIONS

1. *Channeling Principles of Intellectual Property Law.* This case addresses the interplay of the patent and trademark domains. Functionality serves much the same role as *Baker v. Selden*, Chapter IV(C)(2), which channels works between the patent and copyright regimes. *See generally Kellogg Co. v. National Biscuit Co.*, 305 U.S. 111, 122 (1938) (suggesting that lapse of patent on shredded wheat cereal, together with widespread use and lax policing of the mark, obviate trademark status of "Shredded Wheat"); *cf. Trade-Mark Cases*, 100 U.S. 82 (1879) (trademark statute cannot be predicated upon the patent and copyright clause of the Constitution). These cases bolster the primacy of the patent system as the means for protecting exclusive rights for functional features of products.

Had MDI been able to protect its spring design for road signs as trade dress, it would have the equivalent of a perpetual patent through the "back door" of trademark law. The social welfare loss of perpetual protection of functional features could be substantial. The right to exclude others from making, using, selling, or importing a design during the patent term enables the patentee to build source identification in the marketplace for its distinctive (and functional) design. The rule articulated in *TrafFix* ensures that the patent quid pro quo—disclosure in exchange for protection of *limited* duration—continues to operate. *Cf.* Theodore H. Davis, Jr., *Copying in the Shadow of the Constitution: The Rational Limits of Trade Dress Protection*, 80 MINN. L. REV. 595 (1996). But does this balance potentially come at a cost in terms of consumer confusion? Should society's interest in free competition (after the expiration of a patent) trump some confusion as to the source of products?

2. Congress codified functionality as a basis to refuse registration, as well as a ground for opposition and cancellation and a defense to incontestability. *See* 15 U.S.C. §§ 1052, 1064, 1091, 1115 (1998).

3. *Definition of "Functional."* The Court states that a product design appearance is functional if it is "essential to the use or purpose of the article" or "affects the cost or

quality of the article." The "cost or quality" prong swallows the rest; an "essential" design feature surely must affect the "cost or quality" of the product. A particular design choice need not be the only option to be functional. *See Sportvision v. SportsMedia Tech Corp.*, 2005 WL 1869350 (N.D. Cal. Aug. 4, 2005) (holding that the color yellow was functional for an electronic line superimposed on a football field to indicate how far a team needed to travel to make a first down. While yellow was not the only possible color, it was easier than other colors for viewers to see.). What if a feature is both functional but also recognized as signaling source (say, the shape of a distinctive sports car)?

Courts resolve disputes over whether trade dress is functional by weighing five factors:

> (1) the existence of a utility patent, expired or unexpired, that involves or describes the functionality of an item's design element; (2) the utilitarian properties of the item's unpatented design elements; (3) advertising of the item that touts the utilitarian advantages of the item's design elements; (4) the dearth of, or difficulty in creating, alternative designs for the item's purpose; (5) the effect of the design feature on an item's quality or cost.

Georgia-Pacific Consumer Prods. v. Kimberly-Clark Corp., 647 F.3d 723, 727–28 (7th Cir. 2011) (quoting *Specialized Seating, Inc. v. Greenwich Industries, L.P.*, 472 F.Supp. 2d 999, 1011 (N.D. Ill. 2007); *but cf. Eppendorf-Netheler-Hinz GmbH v. Ritter GmbH*, 289 F.3d 351 (5th Cir. 2002) (if a product feature is "essential" to the product's use or purpose, then there is no need to consider whether there are competitive alternatives since the product feature, in being "essential," would be found to be functional even if there are competitive alternatives).

4. *Functional Word Marks.* While most functionality cases involve trade dress, the functionality doctrine also extends to word marks if they serve a function. Can you think of situations in which names, words, or other forms of traditional registered trademarks might be functional? How would a functional name differ from a generic name? In *United States Patent & Trademark Office v. Booking.com*, __ S.Ct. __ (2020), the Supreme Court rejected the argument that a ".com" suffix is a functional characteristic of the Internet: "Booking.com lays no claim to the use of unique domain names generally. Nor does the PTO contend that the particulardomain name 'Booking.com' is essential to the use or purpose of online hotel-reservation services, affects these services' cost or quality, or is otherwise necessary for competitors to use." *Id.* at ___, n.5.

5. *Separability of Functional and Distinctive Elements.* The fact that a product or feature has been patented does not necessarily mean that all of its aspects are functional. Many patented products have distinctive features that can be separated from the functional elements. What should courts do about designs that are partially distinctive and partially functional (a category which includes most, if not all, designs)? Should there be a threshold (say, 80 percent functional) below which defendants are free to copy the design? Or must copiers attempt to parse the functional from the non-functional? (Compare in this regard the copyright rules, which allow the copying of ideas but not their expression.) Suppose the two cannot be separated? *See* Christopher J. Buccafusco &

Mark A. Lemley, *Functionality Screens*, 103 VA. L. REV. 1293 (2017) (arguing that trademark, unlike copyright or design patent, denies all protection in that circumstance); *cf.* Peter S. Menell & Daniel Yablon, Star Athletica*'s Fissure in the Intellectual Property Functionality Landscape*, 166 U. PA. L. REV. ONLINE 137 (2017) (cautioning against affording protection to functional designs or features outside of the auspices of the utility patent system and applauding the parsimonious approaches reflected in *TrafFix* and *Samara*).

The *TrafFix* case addresses the separability problem through the use of a legal presumption: "Where the expired patent claimed the features in question, one who seeks to establish trade dress protection must carry the heavy burden of showing that the feature is not functional, for instance by showing that it is merely an ornamental, incidental, or arbitrary aspect of the device." Is this standard any more determinative than the conceptual separability standard in copyright law?

Even if individual features are functional, the unique combination of those features may be protectable if there is no reason that combination affects the cost or quality of the product. *See Bodum USA v. A Top New Casting Inc.*, 927 F.3d 486 (7th Cir. 2019) (holding that plaintiff's overall design for a French coffee press was not functional even though individual elements were).

Note on Aesthetic Functionality

. In *TrafFix,* the Supreme Court characterizes its prior decision in *Qualitex* (allowing protection of green-gold color for dry cleaning press pads) as centering on the question of "aesthetic functionality." In so doing, the Court confined its references to "competitive need" and putting competitors at "significant non-reputation-related disadvantage" in that case to the "aesthetic functionality" cases. If a feature is found to be utilitarian because it affects the cost or quality of the article, it can be freely copied regardless of whether competitors have alternative means of competing effectively.

The concept of "aesthetic functionality" has long troubled courts and commentators. *See* A. Samuel Oddi, *The Functions of "Functionality" in Trademark Law*, 22 HOUS. L. REV. 925, 963 (1985). Section 742 of the Restatement of Torts (1938) captured the concept in the following manner: "[w]hen goods are bought largely for their aesthetic value, their features may be functional." The Restatement gave as an example a red heart-shaped box for chocolates. *Id.* (comment *a*). Such a shape is no better at holding chocolates than a rectangular box (and hence cannot properly be characterized as utilitarian), but it is easy to see why the heart-shaped box would be particularly appealing to consumers, especially on Valentine's Day. The aesthetic functionality doctrine aims to ensure that aesthetically desirable characteristics are not monopolized in the absence of copyright protection.

But what if a design is both aesthetically pleasing and an indication of source? The shape of products such as cars will regularly combine utilitarian design elements, aesthetic elements, and source-identifying elements. How can courts limit the scope of protection for product configurations to only those parts of a product that are nonfunctional?

Courts originally sought to ensure that trademark protection would not extend to design elements that were valued because they were aesthetically pleasing as well as source-identifying. *Pagliero v. Wallace China Co.*, 198 F.2d 339 (9th Cir. 1952). But more recent decisions have relaxed the *Pagliero* standard (no trade dress protection if a design enhances the appeal of a product to consumers) by focusing on the extent to which trade dress protection forecloses alternative designs. *See Moldex-Metric, Inc. v. McKeon Prods.*, 891 F.3d 878 (9th Cir. 2018) (holding that aesthetic functionality must consider the availability of alternative designs); *Wallace Int'l Silversmiths, Inc. v. Godinger Silver Art Co., Inc.*, 916 F.2d 76 (2d Cir. 1990); *Maker's Mark Distillery, Inc., v. Diageo N. Am., Inc.*, 679 F.3d 410 (6th Cir. 2012) (holding a dripping red wax seal protected on a bourbon bottle because people associated it with Maker's Mark); RESTATEMENT (THIRD) UNFAIR COMPETITION § 17, comment *c* (stating that a feature is aesthetically functional only if it "confers a significant benefit that cannot practically be duplicated by the use of alternative designs"); *see generally* Graeme B. Dinwoodie, *The Death of Ontology: A Teleological Approach to Trademark Law*, 84 IOWA L. REV. 611, 692–93 (1999).

In *TrafFix*, the Supreme Court suggests a broader view of aesthetic functionality, asking only whether the inability to copy the design would put the defendant at a significant disadvantage for reasons not related to reputation. Nonetheless, courts today extend protection to aesthetically pleasing aspects of a design if they also signal source. *See Blumenthal Distributing, Inc. v. Herman Miller, Inc.*, __ F.3d __ (9th Cir. 2020) (holding that iconic Eames and Aeron chairs were protectable even though individual elements were functional because the overall combination of those elements did not affect the cost or quality of the article). *Blumenthal* stated the test as follows:

> In *TrafFix Devices, Inc. v. Marketing Displays, Inc.*, the Supreme Court split functionality into two types, each with its own legal test. 532 U.S. 23, 32–33 (2001). The two types are "utilitarian functionality," which is based on how well the product works, and "aesthetic functionality," which is based on how good the product looks. *See Au-Tomotive Gold, Inc. v. Volkswagen of Am., Inc.*, 457 F.3d 1062, 1067 (9th Cir. 2006) ("'utilitarian' functionality . . . relates to the performance of the product in its intended purpose); *see id.* at 1073–74 (aesthetic functionality is based on "'intrinsic' aesthetic appeal"). If the claimed trade dress has either type of functionality, it is unprotectable. *See id.* at 1072.
>
> . . . A claimed trade dress has aesthetic functionality if it serves "an aesthetic purpose wholly independent of any source identifying function," such that the trade dress's protection under trademark law "would impose a significant non-reputation-related competitive disadvantage" on its owner's competitors. *Id.* at 1129, 1131 (*quoting AuTomotive Gold*, 457 F.3d at 1072, 1073). This requirement aims to ensure that trademark law protects fair competition between sellers, and does not sanction sellers' poaching their competitors' su-

perior reputations. *See Au-Tomotive Gold*, 457 F.3d at 1073–74. Thus, the inquiry is whether, if one seller were given exclusive rights to use the claimed trade dress, other sellers would be forced to use alternative designs that make their products more costly to sell, or for which consumers' willingness to pay would be lower for reasons having nothing to do with the reputation of any source (e.g., the alternative designs would not have as much intrinsic aesthetic appeal). If such competitive disadvantages would be significant, then this second requirement for aesthetic functionality is satisfied.

COMMENTS AND QUESTIONS

1. The retreat from the *Pagliero* standard and the emphasis on the utilitarian functionality doctrine (which prevents backdoor patents) overlooks an analogous concern with backdoor copyrights. Aesthetic functionality controversies do not arise nearly as frequently as utilitarian functionality disputes for a number of reasons, including the more limited market power typically associated with copyright protection and the ease with which copyright claims can be asserted (relative to patent protection).[3] Now that copyright protection is not subject to forfeiture as a result of failure to observe formalities, as occurred in *Pagliero*, trademark protection for aesthetic features seems unnecessary. Relative to trademark concerns, the primacy of copyright law in the protection of creative expression rests on a comparable footing to the primacy of patent law in the protection of utilitarian features. Therefore, when a copyright has expired (or protection lost), the developer of an expressive work should not be able to gain protection for such expression through the backdoor of trademark law. Further, engaging courts in the determination of whether copying an aesthetic design foreclosed competition may well be unworkable, *see Kohler Co. v. Moen, Inc.*, 12 F.3d 632, 649 (7th Cir. 1993) (Cudahy, J., dissenting) (noting that "the attempt to categorize product features as 'essential' or 'nonessential' for competition is perplexing and ultimately vain"); *see also* MCCARTHY, TRADEMARK AND UNFAIR COMPETITION § 7.81, and improperly transmutes trademark law into design protection, *see Krueger Int'l Inc. v. Nightingale*, 915 F. Supp. 595, 606 (S.D.N.Y. 1996) (criticizing aesthetic functionality doctrine on the grounds that it denied protection for design features "whose only sin was to delight the sense").

Professor Justin Hughes proposes that "aesthetic functionality should only be found by courts when the product feature at issue triggers a positive cognitive, psychological, or aesthetic response among a substantial composite of the relevant consumers *and* that response predates the trademark owner's activities." *See* Justin Hughes, *Cognitive and Aesthetic Functionality in Trademark Law*, 36 CARDOZO L. REV. 1227, 1230 (2015) (emphasis in original). Does that approach make sense? Or would it provide automatic

---

[3] The *Pagliero* case was brought as a trademark dispute because Wallace had failed to provide copyright notice upon the first publication of designs on its plates and hence forfeited copyright protection. Hence, trade dress protection served as an alternative theory for recovery. Had the plates been published after U.S. accession to the Berne Convention, Wallace would have been able to pursue a copyright cause of action even if notice had not been provided when the plates were "published."

protection to a trademark owner who happens to be the first to create something beautiful?

2. Why might courts be inclined to the view that utilitarian functionality represents a higher hurdle to overcome than aesthetic functionality (requiring proof of a "significant non-reputation-related disadvantage" that is "wholly independent" of reputation)? Could the problem be solved through remedies—e.g., allowing free competition in expressive designs so long as the copyist used reasonable indications of source (and possibly disclaimers) to minimize consumer confusion? Or should courts expressly balance trademark interests (avoiding consumer confusion) against the threat to free competition (where copyright does not afford protection)?

3. *Artistic Style.* Can artistic style serve as a trademark? Courts have been skeptical. *See, e.g., Dr. Seuss Ents. v. ComicMix LLC*, 256 F. Supp. 3d 1099 (S.D. Cal. 2017) (dismissing the trademark cause of action based on First Amendment concerns and the failure to allege consumer confusion); *Whitehead v. CBS/Viacom, Inc.*, 315 F. Supp. 2d 1, 13 (D.D.C. 2004) ("in the context of a literary work, the Lanham Act protects the distinctive source-distinguishing mark, not the work as a whole.").

PROBLEMS

Problem V-5. Ferrari is a world-famous maker of upscale sports cars. It limits the number of cars it produces, and each car costs approximately $200,000. Ferrari's cars have the same general features as normal cars—wheels, chassis, etc.—but they also have a distinctive look that is easily recognized. They are sleek and low to the ground, a fact that may make them accelerate more quickly and that makes them more attractive to look at.

Roberts sells a fiberglass kit that replicates the exterior features of a Ferrari, though not the engine or performance. When sued for trade dress infringement, Roberts defends on the grounds that the Ferrari design is functional. Is it?

Problem V-6. Eighteen years ago, Spartan Laboratories invented and patented a new pain-relieving drug called asperol. During the term of the patent, Spartan retained the exclusive right to sell asperol, which it manufactured in bright orange capsules. After the Spartan patent expired, a number of other companies began making generic asperol. Each of these companies sells the generic asperol in the same bright orange capsules as Spartan. Although the orange capsules are not visible inside the manufacturers' boxes (which do not resemble each other), asperol is sold only by prescription, and pharmacists invariably remove the drug from its original packaging and repackage it in their own bottles. The result is that the consumer sees only the name "asperol" and the orange capsules, regardless of who makes the drug.

Spartan filed suit under § 43(a) of the Lanham Act, alleging that the other manufacturers had infringed its trade dress protection by coloring the capsules orange. At trial, Spartan proves that the color orange is protectable because it is distinctive and because, over the 17 years of the patent, pharmacists and customers had come to equate orange with Spartan's asperol. The generic manufacturers defend the suit on the grounds that the color is functional. In support of this claim, they present survey evidence that patients, particularly elderly patients, may become upset if the color of the drug is changed, and may refuse to believe that the drug is in fact asperol. The generic manufacturers present further evidence that pharmacists rely in part on color in making sure that they have packaged and labelled drugs correctly. Is the color orange functional?

Problem V-7. Christian Louboutin designs high fashion women's footwear. Since 1992, Louboutin's high-heeled shoes have featured shiny, red-lacquered soles for which the brand is known in the fashion in industry. (Previously, soles were generally black or tan, and weren't considered part of the ornamentation of the shoe.) These shoes sell for as much as $1,000 a pair and are favorites for film stars and A-list notables. They even feature in Jennifer Lopez's song "Louboutins" (Epic Records 2009) ("Boy, watch me walk it out . . . Walk this right up out the house I'm throwin' on my Louboutins"). The PTO awarded a trademark with Registration No. 3,361,597 (the "Red Sole Mark") to Louboutin on January 1, 2008.

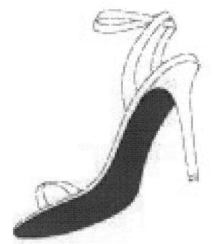

FOR: WOMEN'S HIGH FASHION DESIGNER FOOTWEAR, IN CLASS 25 (U.S. CLS. 22 AND 39).

FIRST USE 0–0–1992; IN COMMERCE 0–0–1992.

THE COLOR(S) RED IS/ARE CLAIMED AS A FEATURE OF THE MARK.

THE MARK CONSISTS OF A LACQUERED RED SOLE ON FOOTWEAR. THE DOTTED LINES ARE NOT PART OF THE MARK BUT ARE INTENDED ONLY TO SHOW PLACEMENT OF THE MARK.

When Yves Saint Laurent began selling shoes with soles in a number of colors, including red, Christian Louboutin sued for infringement. YSL counter-claimed to cancel Louboutin's registration for red-soled fashion shoes. What are the best arguments on each side? Who should prevail?

2.   Priority

As in patent law, trademark protection turns on timing. Section 45(a) of the Lanham Act requires that the mark either be (1) "used in commerce" or (2) registered with a bona fide intention to use it in commerce. Both at common law and under the traditional Lanham Act registration procedures, determining who owned a trademark meant determining who was first to use it to identify her goods.

The requirement of "use in commerce" reflects the constitutional basis for federal trademark laws, which unlike the patent and copyright statutes, rely on congressional power to regulate foreign and interstate commerce. This requirement also goes hand-in-hand with the basic trademark theory—the protection of consumer associations of a brand with a particular product, which can arise only after a trademark is placed on goods sold in commerce.

But just what constitutes use of a term as a designation of source? And how much use is enough to secure legal protection for the term? We explore these questions on multiple levels: (i) what constitutes use in commerce; (ii) the intent-to-use application process; (iii) geographic limitations on trademark use; (iv) the interplay of secondary meaning and priority; and (v) priority and trademark theory.

i.   *Actual Use in Commerce*

Zazu Designs v. L'Oreal, S.A.
United States Court of Appeals for the Seventh Circuit
979 F.2d 499 (7th Cir. 1992)

EASTERBROOK, Circuit Judge.

In 1985, Cosmair, Inc., concluded that young women craved pink and blue hair. To meet the anticipated demand, Cosmair developed a line of "hair cosmetics"—hair coloring that is easily washed out. These inexpensive products, under the name ZAZU, were sold in the cosmetic sections of mass merchandise stores. Apparently the teenagers of the late 1980s had better taste than Cosmair's marketing staff thought. The product flopped, but its name gave rise to this trademark suit. Cosmair is the United States licensee of L'Oreal, S.A., a French firm specializing in perfumes, beauty aids, and related products. Cosmair placed L'Oreal's marks on the bottles and ads. . . .

L'Oreal hired Wordmark, a consulting firm, to help it find a name for the new line of hair cosmetics. After checking the United States Trademark Register for conflicts, Wordmark suggested 250 names. L'Oreal narrowed this field to three, including ZAZU, and investigated their availability. This investigation turned up one federal registration of ZAZU as a mark for clothing and two state service mark registrations including that word. One of these is Zazu Hair Designs; the other was defunct.

Zazu Hair Designs is a hair salon in Hinsdale, Illinois, a suburb of Chicago. We call it "ZHD" to avoid confusion with the ZAZU mark. . . . The salon is a partnership between Raymond R. Koubek and Salvatore J. Segretto, hairstylists who joined forces in

1979. ZHD registered ZAZU with Illinois in 1980 as a trade name for its salon. L'Oreal called the salon to find out if ZHD was selling its own products. The employee who answered reported that the salon was not but added, "we're working on it." L'Oreal called again; this time it was told that ZHD had no products available under the name ZAZU.

L'Oreal took the sole federal registration, held by Riviera Slacks, Inc., as a serious obstacle. Some apparel makers have migrated to cosmetics, and if Riviera were about to follow Ralph Lauren (which makes perfumes in addition to shirts and skirts) it might have a legitimate complaint against a competing use of the mark. *Sands, Taylor & Wood Co. v. Quaker Oats Co.*, 24 U.S.P.Q.2d 1001, 1011 (7th Cir. 1992). Riviera charged L'Oreal $125,000 for a covenant not to sue if L'Oreal used the ZAZU mark on cosmetics. In April 1986, covenant in hand and satisfied that ZHD's state trade name did not prevent the introduction of a national product, L'Oreal made a small interstate shipment of hair cosmetics under the ZAZU name. It used this shipment as the basis of an application for federal registration, filed on June 12, 1986. By August L'Oreal had advertised and sold its products nationally.

Unknown to L'Oreal, Koubek and Segretto had for some time aspired to emulate Vidal Sassoon by marketing shampoos and conditioners under their salon's trade name. In 1985 Koubek began meeting with chemists to develop ZHD's products. Early efforts were unsuccessful; no one offered a product that satisfied ZHD. Eventually ZHD received acceptable samples from Gift Cosmetics, some of which Segretto sold to customers of the salon in plain bottles to which he taped the salon's business card. Between November 1985 and February 1986 ZHD made a few other sales. Koubek shipped two bottles to a friend in Texas, who paid $13. He also made two shipments to a hair stylist friend in Florida—40 bottles of shampoo for $78.58. These were designed to interest the Floridian in the future marketing of the product line. These bottles could not have been sold to the public, because they lacked labels listing the ingredients and weight. *See* 21 U.S.C. § 362(b); 15 U.S.C. §§ 1452, 1453(a); 21 CFR §§ 701.3, 701.13(a). After L'Oreal's national marketing was under way, its representatives thrice visited ZHD and found that the salon still had no products for sale under the ZAZU name. Which is not to say that ZHD was supine. Late in 1985 ZHD had ordered 25,000 bottles silkscreened with the name ZAZU. Later it ordered stick-on labels listing the ingredients of its products. In September 1986 ZHD began to sell small quantities of shampoo in bottles filled (and labeled) by hand in the salon. After the turn of the year ZHD directed the supplier of the shampoo and conditioner to fill some bottles; the record does not reveal how many.

After a bench trial the district court held that ZHD's sales gave it an exclusive right to use the ZAZU name nationally for hair products. 9 U.S.P.Q.2d 1972 (N.D. Ill. 1988). The court enjoined L'Oreal from using the mark (a gesture, since the product had bombed and L'Oreal disclaimed any interest in using ZAZU again). It also awarded ZHD $100,000 in damages on account of lost profits and $1 million more to pay for corrective advertising to restore luster to the ZAZU mark. [The final judgment also included a $1 million punitive damage award for "oppressive and deceitful" tactics used in the litigation.]

Federal law permits the registration of trademarks and the enforcement of registered marks. Through § 43(a) of the Lanham Act, 15 U.S.C. § 1125(a), a provision addressed to deceit, it also indirectly allows the enforcement of unregistered marks. But until 1988 federal law did not specify how one acquired the rights that could be registered or enforced without registration. That subject fell into the domain of state law, plus federal common law elaborating on the word "use" in § 43(a). . . . At common law, "use" meant sales to the public of a product with the mark attached. *Trade-Mark Cases*, 100 U.S. 82, 94–95 (1879). *See* also *Hanover Star Milling Co. v. Metcalf*, 240 U.S. 403, 414 (1916); *United Drug Co. v. Theodore Rectanus Co.*, 248 U.S. 90, 97 (1918).

"Use" is neither a glitch in the Lanham Act nor a historical relic. By insisting that firms use marks to obtain rights in them, the law prevents entrepreneurs from reserving brand names in order to make their rivals' marketing more costly. Public sales let others know that they should not invest resources to develop a mark similar to one already used in the trade. *Blue Bell, Inc. v. Farah Manufacturing Co.*, 508 F.2d 1260, 1264–65 (5th Cir. 1975); *see also* William M. Landes and Richard A. Posner, *Trademark Law: An Economic Perspective*, 30 J.L. & ECON. 265, 281–84 (1987). Only active use allows consumers to associate a mark with particular goods and notifies other firms that the mark is so associated.

Under the common law, one must win the race to the marketplace to establish the exclusive right to a mark. *Blue Bell v. Farah; La Societe Anonyme des Parfums LeGalion v. Jean Patou, Inc.*, 495 F.2d 1265, 1271–74 (2d Cir. 1974). Registration modifies this system slightly, allowing slight sales plus notice in the register to substitute for substantial sales without notice. 15 U.S.C. § 1051(a). (The legislation in 1988 modifies the use requirement further, but we disregard this.) ZHD's sales of its product are insufficient use to establish priority over L'Oreal. A few bottles sold over the counter in Hinsdale, and a few more mailed to friends in Texas and Florida, neither link the ZAZU mark with ZHD's product in the minds of consumers nor put other producers on notice. As a practical matter ZHD had no product, period, until months after L'Oreal had embarked on its doomed campaign.

In finding that ZHD's few sales secured rights against the world, the district court relied on cases such as *Department of Justice v. Calspan Corp.*, 578 F.2d 295 (C.C.P.A. 1978), which hold that a single sale, combined with proof of intent to go on selling, permit the vendor to register the mark. *See also Axton-Fisher Tobacco Co. v. Fortune Tobacco Co.*, 82 F.2d 295 (C.C.P.A. 1936); *Maternally Yours, Inc. v. Your Maternity Shop, Inc.*, 234 F.2d 538, 542 (2d Cir. 1956). . . . But use sufficient to register a mark that soon is widely distributed is not necessarily enough to acquire rights in the absence of registration. The Lanham Act allows only trademarks "used in commerce" to be registered. 15 U.S.C. § 1051(a). Courts have read "used" in a way that allows firms to seek protection for a mark before investing substantial sums in promotion. *See Fort Howard*

Paper Co. v. Kimberly-Clark Corp., 390 F.2d 1015 (C.C.P.A. 1968); *Cf. Jim Dandy Co. v. Martha White Foods, Inc.*, 458 F.2d 1397, 1399 (C.C.P.A. 1972) (party may rely on advertising to show superior registration rights); *But see Weight Watchers International, Inc. v. I. Rokeach & Sons, Inc.*, 211 U.S.P.Q. 700, 709 (T.M.T.A.B. 1981) (more than minimal use is required to register because the statute allows only "owner[s]" to register, and ownership of a mark depends on commercial use). Liberality in registering marks is not problematic, because the registration gives notice to latecomers, which token use alone does not. Firms need only search the register before embarking on development. Had ZHD registered ZAZU, the parties could have negotiated before L'Oreal committed large sums to marketing.

ZHD applied for registration of ZAZU after L'Oreal not only had applied to register the mark but also had put its product on the market nationwide. Efforts to register came too late. At oral argument ZHD suggested that L'Oreal's knowledge of ZHD's plan to enter the hair care market using ZAZU establishes ZHD's superior right to the name. Such an argument is unavailing. Intent to use a mark, like a naked registration, establishes no rights at all. *Hydro-Dynamics, Inc. v. George Putnam & Co.*, 811 F.2d 1470, 1472 (Fed. Cir. 1987). Even under the 1988 amendments (*see* note), which allow registration in advance of contemplated use, an unregistered plan to use a mark creates no rights. Just as an intent to buy a choice parcel of land does not prevent a rival from closing the deal first, so an intent to use a mark creates no rights a competitor is bound to respect. A statute granting no rights in bare registrations cannot plausibly be understood to grant rights in "intents" divorced from either sales or registrations. Registration itself establishes only a rebuttable presumption of use as of the filing date. *Rolley, Inc. v. Younghusband*, 204 F.2d 209, 211 (9th Cir. 1953). ZHD made first use of ZAZU in connection with hair services in Illinois, but this does not translate to a protectable right to market hair products nationally. The district court construed L'Oreal's knowledge of ZHD's use of ZAZU for salon services as knowledge "of [ZHD's] superior rights in the mark." 9 U.S.P.Q.2d at 1978. ZHD did not, however, have superior rights in the mark as applied to hair products, because it neither marketed such nor registered the mark before L'Oreal's use. Because the mark was not registered for use in conjunction with hair products, any knowledge L'Oreal may have had of ZHD's plans is irrelevant. *Cf. Weiner King, Inc. v. Wiener King Corp.*, 615 F.2d 512 (C.C.P.A. 1980).

Imagine the consequences of ZHD's approach. Businesses that knew of an intended use would not be entitled to the mark even if they made the first significant use of it. Businesses with their heads in the sand, however, could stand on the actual date they introduced their products, and so would have priority over firms that intended to use a mark but had not done so. Ignorance would be rewarded—and knowledgeable firms might back off even though the rivals' "plans" or "intent" were unlikely to come to fruition. Yet investigations of the sort L'Oreal undertook prevent costly duplication in the development of trademarks and protect consumers from the confusion resulting from two products being sold under the same mark. *See Natural Footwear Ltd. v. Hart, Shaffner & Marx*, 760 F.2d 1383, 1395 (3d Cir. 1985). L'Oreal should not be worse off because it made inquiries and found that, although no one had yet used the mark for hair products, ZHD intended to do so. Nor should a potential user have to bide its time until it learns whether other firms are serious about marketing a product. The use requirement rewards those who act quickly in getting new products in the hands of consumers. Had L'Oreal discovered that ZHD had a product on the market under the ZAZU mark or that ZHD had registered ZAZU for hair products, L'Oreal could have chosen another mark before committing extensive marketing resources. Knowledge that ZHD planned to use the ZAZU mark in the future does not present an obstacle to L'Oreal's adopting it today. *Selfway, Inc. v. Travelers Petroleum, Inc.*, 579 F.2d 75, 79 (C.C.P.A. 1978).

Occasionally courts suggest that "bad faith" adoption of a mark defeats a claim to priority. *See California Cedar Products Co. v. Pine Mountain Corp.*, 724 F.2d 827, 830 (9th Cir. 1984); *Stern Electronics, Inc. v. Kaufman*, 669 F.2d 852, 857 (2d Cir. 1982); *Blue Bell v. Farah*, 508 F.2d at 1267. Although ZHD equates L'Oreal's knowledge of its impending use with "bad faith," the cases use the term differently. In each instance the court applied the label "bad faith" to transactions designed merely to reserve a mark, not to link the name to a product ready to be sold to the public. In California Cedar Products, for example, two firms sprinted to acquire the abandoned DURAFLAME mark. One shipped some of its goods in the abandoning company's wrapper with a new name pasted over it. Two days later the other commenced bona fide sales under the DURAFLAME mark. The court disregarded the first shipment, calling it "both prema-ture and in bad faith," 724 F.2d at 830, and held that the first firm to make bona fide sales to customers was the prior user. "Bad faith" was no more than an epithet stapled to the basic conclusion: that reserving a mark is forbidden, so that the first producer to make genuine sales gets the rights. If these cases find a parallel in our dispute, ZHD occupies the place of the firm trying to reserve a mark for "intended" exploitation. ZHD doled out a few samples in bottles lacking labeling necessary for sale to the public. Such transactions are the sort of pre-marketing maneuvers that these cases hold insufficient to establish rights in a trademark.

The district court erred in equating a use sufficient to support registration with a use sufficient to generate nationwide rights in the absence of registration. Although whether ZHD's use is sufficient to grant it rights in the ZAZU mark is a question of fact on which appellate review is deferential, *California Cedar Products*, 724 F.2d at 830 . . . , the extent to which ZHD used the mark is not disputed. ZHD's sales of hair care products were insufficient as a matter of law to establish national trademark rights at the time L'Oreal put its electric hair colors on the market.

[In a forcefully stated section of the opinion, the court also reversed the punitive damages holding.]

Reversed and remanded.

Cudahy, C.J., dissenting:

On the important issue of good faith, L'Oreal's conduct here merits a very hard look. In the case of Riviera, a men's clothing retailer, L'Oreal was careful to pay

$125,000 for an agreement not to sue. Yet men's clothing and hair cosmetics marketed to women hardly seem related at all. On the other hand, a women's hair salon developing a line of hair care products is a purveyor of goods and services that seem closely related to hair cosmetics. Therefore, L'Oreal's knowledge of ZHD's use defeats any claim L'Oreal may have to priority.

One of the keys here seems to be the use of ZAZU as a service mark connected with the provision of salon services by ZHD. A service mark can be infringed by its use on a closely related product. . . . [*See*] 2 J. THOMAS MCCARTHY, TRADEMARK AND UN-FAIR COMPETITION § 24:6, at 71 (2d ed. 1984 & Supp. 1991) (stating that "[w]here the services consist of retail sales services, likelihood of confusion is found when another mark is used on goods which are commonly sold through such a retail outlet"). A service and a product are related if buyers are likely to assume a common source or sponsor-ship. . . . The salon services and hair products at issue in this case, which are nearly as kindred as a service and product can be, offer the paradigmatic illustration of things that are closely related. Thus the majority's disregard for ZHD's substantial use of ZAZU in connection with salon services is unfounded. . . .

In this case, ZHD's use of the ZAZU mark, both in its highly successful salon ser-vice business, which drew some out-of-state clients, and in its local and interstate prod-uct sales to customers and to a potential marketer, surely is more than de minimis. The extensive evidence of ZHD's intent to step up hair product sales—such as its order for 25,000 ZAZU-emblazoned bottles and its inquiry about advertising rates in a national magazine—bolsters this assessment. Even if ZHD did fail to demonstrate more than a de minimis market penetration nationally, at the very least it successfully established exclusive rights within its primary area of operation. The salon's substantial advertising, increasing revenue and staff and preliminary product sales indicate sufficient market penetration to afford trademark protection in that region. *See Natural Footwear Ltd. v. Hart, Schaffner & Marx*, 760 F.2d 1383 (3d Cir.) (senior user can establish common law rights in geographic areas where it achieved market penetration). . . .

L'Oreal concedes that ZHD has exclusive rights to use ZAZU for salon services in the Hinsdale area. Those exclusive rights also preclude L'Oreal from using the mark on hair products in the local area because of the likelihood of confusion between those products and ZHD's salon services, even apart from any confusion between the two parties' products. Given the deferential standard of review on the factual question of use, therefore, I think it clear that ZHD has achieved market penetration and exclusive rights to the ZAZU mark at the very least in the Chicago area.

ZHD's contention that its rights in the ZAZU mark extend beyond the local area is enhanced by evidence that L'Oreal did not, as we have noted, act in good faith. The majority's consideration of the good faith issue minimizes the important role good faith plays in trademark disputes, particularly disputes involving unregistered marks. . . . *See, e.g., A. J. Canfield Co. v. Honickman*, 808 F.2d 291 (3d Cir. 1986) (stating the doctrine that a senior user "has enforceable rights against any junior user who adopted the mark with knowledge of its senior use"). . . . Contrary to the majority's narrow characterization of bad faith as a concept employed solely to deter attempts to reserve marks prior to genuine sales, courts have examined junior users' good faith in a variety of contexts. In fact, this court has held that a good faith junior user is simply one that begins using a mark without knowledge that another party already is using it. *The Money Store v. Harriscorp Finance, Inc.*, 689 F.2d 666, 674 (7th Cir. 1982); *see* 2 McCARTHY, *supra*, § 26:4 at 292 (equating good faith to "the junior user's lack of knowledge"). And while such knowledge may not automatically negate good faith, only the most unusual situations encompass both knowledge and good faith. . . .

COMMENTS AND QUESTIONS

1. *Notice.* Consider this passage from Judge Easterbrook's opinion: "Liberality in registering marks is not problematic, because the registration gives notice to latecomers, which token use alone does not. Firms need only search the register before embarking on development. Had ZHD registered ZAZU, the parties could have negotiated before L'Oreal committed large sums to marketing."

But ZHD *did* register Zazu—not as a federal trademark, but as a business (trade name) in the State of Illinois. Why is this any different from the *federal* registration contemplated by Easterbrook? Does it provide less opportunity for negotiating prior to large investments? Recall the evidence in the case, which established not only that L'Oreal found the ZHD trade name in its trademark search, but also that L'Oreal contacted ZHD and learned it was planning a hair product line. Standard trademark search services generally find all state and federal registrations, together with many "common law" (i.e., nonregistered) uses. Given this evidence, why was state registration any less of a basis for negotiation than federal registration? *See Malcolm Nicol & Co. v. Witco Corp.*, 881 F.2d 1063, 1065 (Fed. Cir. 1989) (a trade name, even one that lacks any independent trademark or service mark significance, may bar registration of a trademark or service mark that is confusingly similar to that trade name).

2. *Scarcity of Terms.* Judge Easterbrook says that through the use requirement, "the law prevents entrepreneurs from reserving brand names in order to make their rivals' marketing more costly." Could a rival reserve all the potential trademarks that would allow a firm to identify its products? *Cf.* Stephen L. Carter, *The Trouble with Trademarks*, 99 YALE L.J. 759, 760 (1990) (suggesting that if the supply of limited supply of desirable terms is limited, then "allowing protection of marks devoid of market significance may raise substantial barriers to entry by competitors")

Barton Beebe and Jeanne Fromer suggest that trademarks may be more scarce than we might imagine. They find that nearly all of the ten thousand most common English words have been registered as trademarks in most or all classes. Barton Beebe & Jeanne Fromer, *Are We Running Out of Trademarks? An Empirical Study of Trademark Depletion and Congestion*, 131 HARV. L. REV. 945 (2018).

Note that another rationale for the use requirement stems not from rivals' costs, but from the desire not to encourage firms to specialize in identifying and registering potential trademarks. *See* Chapter V(C)(2)(v) (Priority and Trademark Theory).

3. *Bad Faith. Blue Bell, Inc. v. Farah Mfg. Co.*, 508 F.2d 1260 (5th Cir. 1975), teaches that although the race is to the swift in trademark law, the race must be run cleanly if a firm wants to prevail. In the case, Farah's management settled on the name "Time Out" for a new line of blue jeans on May 16. Sample tags using the new name were drawn up on June 27, and on July 3 Farah sent out 12 pair of jeans bearing the new mark to its regional sales managers. More extensive shipments occurred on July 11. Meanwhile Blue Bell management decided on the name "Time Out" for *its* new line of jeans on June 18. Blue Bell commissioned several hundred sample tags (bearing the new logo) that were attached over the top of existing tags on a large shipment of jeans sent out on July 5. By October, both firms had received substantial orders for their respective new lines of jeans. The court ruled (1) that Blue Bell's "secondary" use of the new logo was in "bad faith," and therefore its July 5 shipment did not establish priority and (2) that Farah's minimal shipments on July 3 also did not establish priority. This left Farah's July 11 shipment as the first substantial use of the new mark in commerce—so Farah won.

When Blue Bell slapped new labels on old jeans, the court condemned it as "a bad faith attempt to reserve a mark." What if, subsequent to the relabeling but before Farah's first shipments, Blue Bell had made actual sales to consumers? Would their prior bad faith deprive them of priority? Should it? Why did the court not characterize Farah's sales of pants to employees as an attempt to "reserve a mark"?

As we will see, bad faith also comes into play in trademark law in infringement analysis and the defense of abandonment.

4. *Sports Team Relocation.* Can advertising or other "promotional activities" ever form the basis for priority? The general answer in the law is no; actual sales are required. But there are exceptions.

A dispute involving the move of the Los Angeles Rams to St. Louis highlights some of the issues accompanying the birth of a mark following the relocation of an existing team to a new locale. On January 17, 1995, St. Louis Mayor Freeman Bosley and Georgia Frontiere, owner of the Los Angeles Rams Football Company, announced that the Los Angeles Rams football franchise intended to relocate to St. Louis, Missouri. By early February of 1995, the Rams organization had received over 72,000 personal seat license applications for the St. Louis stadium where the Rams would play. On February 22, 1995, Johnny Blastoff, a corporation in the business of creating and marketing cartoon characters, filed a trademark application in Wisconsin for the name of a fictional cartoon sports team named the "St. Louis Rams." On March 10, 1995, Blastoff filed two federal intent-to-use trademark applications for the "St. Louis Rams" mark. One month later, the Rams' move to St. Louis was approved by the National Football League. Although a number of vendors began selling unlicensed merchandise bearing the mark "St. Louis Rams" in January of 1995, officially licensed vendors began using the "St. Louis

Rams" mark in a wide variety of merchandise sales in April of 1995. In March 1997, Blastoff filed a declaratory judgment against the Rams football organization, the NFL, and others, alleging that he did not infringe the NFL defendants' trademark rights. In determining that the Rams first appropriated the mark through use as a designation of origin, the court placed emphasis on the nature of franchise relocations, *see Indianapolis Colts, Inc. v. Metropolitan Baltimore Football Club Ltd.*, 34 F.3d 410, 413 (7th Cir. 1994) (finding a strong presumption of franchise owner priority in a team mark when a franchise relocates to a new city), and the role of "advertising brochures, catalogs, newspaper ads, and articles in newspapers and trade publications" and use on television and radio in establishing public identification of a mark with a product or service, *see T.A.B. Systems v. Pactel Teletrac*, 77 F.3d 1372, 1375 (Fed. Cir. 1996); *In re Owens-Corning Fiberglas Corp.*, 774 F.2d 1116, 1125 (Fed. Cir. 1985); *see also Johnny Blastoff, Inc. v. Los Angeles Rams Football Co.*, 188 F.3d 427 (7th Cir. 1999); *Maryland Stadium Authority v. Becker*, 806 F. Supp. 1236 (D. Md. 1992), *aff'd,* 36 F.3d 1093 (4th Cir. 1994),. Ironically, in 2016 the Rams moved *back* to Los Angeles, perhaps setting off another chapter in the trademark relocation saga.

5. *The Territoriality Principle and the Famous-Mark Doctrine.* In *Buti v. Impressa Perosa S.R.L.*, 139 F.3d 98 (2d Cir. 1998), the "Fashion Café," based in Milan, Italy, advertised its business in the United States just before Buti began using the same mark for restaurants in the United States. The court held that the Italian restaurant could not obtain United States trademark rights through its advertising because the services it was providing were not themselves offered in commerce in the United States. *See also ITC Ltd. v. Punchgini, Inc.*, 482 F.3d 135, 165 (2d Cir. 2007) (declining to adopt famous marks doctrine); *Societe de Developpements et d'Innovations des Marches Agricoles et Alimentaires-Sodima Union de Cooperatives Agricoles v. International Yogurt*, 662 F. Supp. 839, 847 (D. Or. 1987) ("An axiom of trademark law is: no trade, no trademark."). These cases reflect the territoriality principle: "[p]riority of trademark rights in the United States depends solely upon priority of use in the United States, not on priority of use anywhere in the world." *See* J. THOMAS MCCARTHY, MCCARTHY ON TRADEMARKS AND UNFAIR COMPETITION § 29:2. The Ninth Circuit has recognized a narrow exception to the territoriality principle where a well-known mark outside of the United States (Mexico) had developed secondary meaning in the United States (just north of the border in the San Diego area). *See Grupo Gigante S.A. de C.V. v. Dallo & Co.*, 391 F.3d 1088 (9th Cir. 2004). We further explore the international law aspects of the "famous marks" doctrine in Chapter V(G)(4).

ii.   *Intent-to-Use Application Process*

The *Zazu* case was decided under pre-1989 federal trademark law. In 1988, Congress authorized an "intent to use" registration process. *See* Trademark Law Revision Act of 1988 (hereinafter TLRA), codified at 15 U.S.C. § 1051. Under pre-1989 law, *actual* use in commerce, prior to application for registration, was a requirement for registration. This requirement spurred prospective applicants to ship and/or sell a small batch of goods in order to secure trademark protection, a practice that came to be known as "token use."

Among other things, the TLRA provided that "[a] person who has a bona fide intention, under circumstances showing the good faith of such person, to use a trademark in commerce may apply to register the trademark . . . on the principal register." Assuming an application based on an intention to use a mark is otherwise allowable, the Trademark Office will issue a "notice of allowance" to the trademark owner (rather than simply registering the mark on the Principal Register). 15 U.S.C. § 1063(b)(2). After the notice of allowance is granted, the trademark owner has six months (extendable to one year automatically and to three years for good cause shown) to submit a verified statement that the trademark has in fact been used in commerce, at which point it is entered on the Principal Register. If the trademark owner does not submit such a statement, the trademark is considered abandoned. 15 U.S.C. § 1051(d). Assuming that the intent-to-use registrant does eventually use the mark, however, the initial application will be considered "constructive use," entitling the registrant to nationwide priority from the date of the application. 15 U.S.C. § 1057(c).

The TLRA brought United States law closer harmony with the law in the rest of the world. No other country required actual use before a mark could be registered. Because international treaties required the United States to give full credit to foreign applicants who had registered marks outside the United States, the United States use requirement in practice meant that *only* U.S. citizens were required to show use in commerce in order to register a mark in the United States. At the same time, U.S. law remains different than the law elsewhere. While applicants can now file an application in the U.S. based on an intent to use a mark, they must show actual use of the mark in commerce before that application will ultimately be approved.

The TLRA also eliminated "token use" by raising the standard for determining when a mark has been "use[d] in commerce." Consider, for example, the case of *Paramount Pictures Corp. v. White*, 31 U.S.P.Q.2d 1768 (TTAB 1994), *aff'd*, 108 F.3d 1392 (Fed Cir. 1997) (unpub.), where Paramount opposed registration of "The Romulans" for a connect-the-dots game distributed by White, leader of a rock group called The Romulans. One ground for the opposition was that the mark had not been used in commerce; in particular, that the distribution of connect-the-dots games on promotional fliers for the band was not a statutory use in commerce justifying registration. In commenting on the magnitude of use, the Trademark Trial and Appeal Board stated: "The legislative history of the Trademark Law Revision Act reveals that the purpose of the amendment was to eliminate 'token use' as a basis for registration, and that the new stricter standard contemplates instead commercial use of the type common to the particular industry in question." 31 U.S.P.Q.2d at 1774. Footnote 8 of the Board's opinion quotes from the Congressional Record of November 19, 1987, p. 196–97:

> Amendment of the definition of "use in commerce" is one of the most far-reaching changes the legislation contains. Revised to eliminate the commercially-transparent practice of token use, which becomes unnecessary with the

legislation's provision for an intent-to-use application system, it will have a measurable effect on improving the accuracy of the register. . . . The committee intends that the revised definition of "use in commerce" be interpreted to mean commercial use which is typical in a particular industry.

Id.; but cf. Allard Enters., Inc. v. Advanced Programming Resources, Inc., 146 F.3d 350 (6th Cir. 1998) (plaintiff's somewhat extensive "word-of-mouth" campaign to popularize "APR" mark for computer professional placement service established priority under post-TLRA law). For an example of the pre-1989 rule, *see Fort Howard Paper v. Kimberly Clark Corp.*, 390 F.2d 1015 (C.C.P.A. 1968) (very limited use sufficient to establish priority); *but cf. La Societe Anonyme des Parfums LeGalion v. Jean Patou, Inc.*, 495 F.2d 1265 (2d Cir. 1974) (token sales program not sufficient use to avoid abandonment); *Procter & Gamble v. Johnson & Johnson, Inc.*, 485 F. Supp. 1185 (S.D.N.Y. 1979), *aff'd without opinion*, 636 F.2d 1203 (2d Cir. 1980) ("minor brands program" not sufficient use).

Could it be argued in the *Zazu* case that ZHD's shipments of hair products were only a "token use"? How might the TLRA have affected the dissent in *Zazu*? Would L'Oreal's good faith still be an issue under the TLRA? *Cf. M.Z. Berger & Co. v. Swatch AG*, 787 F.3d 1368 (Fed. Cir. 2015) (upholding TTAB cancellation of mark on grounds that the intent to use registration lacked good faith).

iii.   *Geographic Limitations on Trademark Use*

At common law (and today for unregistered marks), ownership of a trademark does not necessarily confer nationwide protection. Rather, common law trademarks are protected only in the areas where the marked products are sold or advertised. Thus, the owner of an unregistered trademark for goods sold in Oregon and Washington, but not elsewhere, is entitled to prevent others from using that mark for similar goods only in Oregon and Washington. The rationale is that trademarks are not intended to confer a broad property right but merely to protect the goodwill the trademark owner has invested in the mark. Because no one outside Oregon or Washington could associate the mark with the owner, there is no reason to protect it elsewhere. Thus a seller of similar goods in New York can use the same name for the goods without conflict.

There are two exceptions to this common law rule, both based on concerns that the trademark owner's goodwill will be unfairly taken. First, a trademark owner is entitled to the exclusive use of her mark in any geographic area in which the mark's reputation has been established, even if the product is not sold in that geographic area. Such a broader geographic reputation might be established, for example, by national advertising or media coverage of a local business such as a restaurant. Further, the trademark owner is entitled to protect the mark in a territory which he is expected to reach in the normal expansion of his business, even if there is no current likelihood of confusion in that area. *See Hanover Star Milling Co. v. Metcalf*, 240 U.S. 403 (1916). Second, a trademark owner is entitled to prevent anyone from intentionally trading on her goodwill, even outside her established geographic area. Only innocent (or "good faith") use of the same mark is protected. But does good faith mean no knowledge of the senior mark at all or just no effort to trade on its goodwill? The circuits are split. *Compare Stone Creek, Inc. v. Omnia Italian Design, Inc.*, 875 F.3d 426 (9th Cir. 2017) (knowledge of a remote senior user precludes good faith) *with GTE Corp. v. Williams*, 904 F.2d 536, 541 (10th Cir. 1990); *see C.P. Interests, Inc. v. Cal. Pools, Inc.*, 238 F.3d 690, 700 (5th Cir. 2001) (knowledge does not preclude good faith).

One of the principal advantages of trademark registration is that it automatically confers nationwide protection of the mark, retroactive to the date of the trademark application, even if the goods for which the mark is used are sold or advertised in only a small part of the country. Thus, trademark registration is vital to protect businesses that plan to expand geographically, as well as those that fear a large national company might use the same name.

What happens, then, if two parties use the same mark for the same goods? If neither party registers its mark, then the common law rule applies. Each party is entitled to exclusive use of the mark in the areas where it has established goodwill. Should the two marks come into conflict in a particular geographic area, the conflict will be resolved in favor of the earliest user *in that area.* If one party registers her mark and the other does not, the registrant will generally be entitled to the exclusive right to use the mark throughout the country. However, the non-registering party may assert a "limited area" defense. This defense allows the non-registering party to claim priority in those geographic areas where he has made continuous use of the mark since *before* the registering party filed her application. The non-registering party is "frozen" in the use of his mark, however, and cannot expand it outside his existing territory or a natural "zone of expansion." *See Weiner King, Inc. v. Wiener King Corp.*, 615 F.2d 512 (C.C.P.A. 1980).

Finally, if the parties agree, or if the Trademark Board determines that registration of both marks is unlikely to cause confusion, it is possible that both marks may be registered for "concurrent use." If two or more marks are registered concurrently, however, the Trademark Office will impose whatever restrictions on the use of the marks are necessary to prevent confusion among consumers.

COMMENTS AND QUESTIONS

1. Compare the current U.S. trademark system to the various schemes for filing patent applications. You will recall that the United States long used a "first to invent" rule for determining who is entitled to obtain a patent, while the rest of the world grants a patent to the "first to file." Is there a similar distinction in trademark law, between "first to use" and "first to file"? If so, does the Trademark Law Revision Act turn the United States into a "first to file" system?

2. Why should the user of an arbitrary or suggestive but unregistered trademark be limited to protection in a particular geographic area? The asserted justification is that the trademark owner has established goodwill only in that limited area. But why should that matter? Distinctive marks, unlike descriptive marks, are entitled to automatic pro-

tection under trademark law without proof that the public associates them with a particular product. *See* Chapter V(C)(1). Isn't it inconsistent to limit the scope of that protection to geographic areas in which the public has formed such an association?

3. Priority disputes are often resolved by the Trademark Trial and Appeal Board through oppositions. Section 13 of the Lanham Act, 15 U.S.C. § 1063, provides that "[a]ny person who believes that he would be damaged by the registration of a mark upon the principal register may . . . file an opposition in the Patent and Trademark Office, stating the grounds therefor." Further, 15 U.S.C. § 1062(a) expressly provides that trademark applications be published before issuance, so that interested parties may have the opportunity to search for and oppose potentially damaging applications. Applications may be opposed by showing that the mark is not entitled to registration, for example because others had made use of it before the applicant did.

4. Return to the *Two Pesos* case discussed above. The Court's opinion turned on whether Taco Cabana's trade dress was inherently distinctive. But it was unregistered. Given that, why didn't Two Pesos have a legitimate claim to be the first to use that trade dress in Houston? Is Houston in a reasonable "zone of expansion" for a fast food restaurant from San Antonio, 200 miles away?

iv.   Secondary Meaning and Priority

Consider how the doctrine of priority interacts with the doctrine of secondary meaning. Under trademark priority rules, the trademark is presumptively owned by the first person to use it in commerce (barring a federal registration). But the secondary meaning doctrine provides that *descriptive* marks are not entitled to protection until their owner can prove secondary meaning in the minds of consumers. So when does a trademark owner obtain priority of use in a descriptive mark? When she first uses the mark? Or only after she can establish secondary meaning?

This issue has arisen in a number of cases where the defendant is accused of quickly adopting a plaintiff's descriptive mark before the plaintiff can establish secondary meaning. In *Laureyssens v. Idea Group, Inc.*, 964 F.2d 131 (2d Cir. 1992), the court considered a trade dress infringement suit by the makers of "Happy Cube" 3-D puzzles against the makers of "Snafooz" puzzles.

Laureyssens v. Idea Group, Inc.
United States Court of Appeals for the Second Circuit
964 F.2d 131 (2d Cir. 1992)

OAKES, Chief Judge:

. . . The district court found that there was no serious question whether *actual* secondary meaning exists in the HAPPY CUBE trade dress. We think this conclusion is sound given the weak sales of the HAPPY CUBE puzzles, low expenditures for advertising and promotion, minimal unsolicited media coverage, and the brief period of exclusive use of the HAPPY CUBE trade dress.[4] And, while there was evidence of intentional imitation as to the puzzles themselves, there was no evidence of copying of the trade dress.

The district court concluded, however, that Laureyssens satisfied the requirement of secondary meaning by raising a serious question whether the flat-form, shrink-wrapped HAPPY CUBE trade dress should be protected under the doctrine of secondary meaning in the making.

In *Metro Kane Imports, Ltd. v. Federated Dept. Stores, Inc.*, 625 F. Supp. 313, 316 (S.D.N.Y. 1985), *aff'd*, 800 F.2d 1128 (2d Cir. 1986), Judge Sweet explained that a trade dress will be "protected against intentional, deliberate attempts to capitalize on a distinctive product" where "secondary meaning is 'in the making' but not yet fully developed." *See also Jolly Good Industries, Inc. v. Elegra, Inc.*, 690 F. Supp. 227, 230–31 (S.D.N.Y. 1988) (indicating that the theory has been "well-received by commentators" and citing as an example, 3 R. CALLMAN, THE LAW OF UNFAIR COMPETITION, TRADEMARKS AND MONOPOLIES § 77.3, at 356 (3d ed. 1971)).[5] The supposed doctrine seeks to prevent pirates from intentionally siphoning off another's nascent consumer recognition and goodwill. *See, e.g., Jolly Good*, 690 F. Supp. at 230–31.

In this case, Judge Sweet found that although Idea Group offered evidence that the SNAFOOZ packaging was developed without prior knowledge of the HAPPY CUBE trade dress, "the evidence does not indicate when [Idea Group] developed its flat-form shrink wrapped package, and therefore Plaintiffs have barely established a serious question of [Idea Group's] 'intentional deliberate attempts' to copy their trade dress." 768 F. Supp. at 1048.

We are, then, squarely presented for the first time with the question whether the doctrine of secondary meaning in the making should be recognized under the Lanham Act. . . .

"The doctrine, if taken literally, is inimical to the purpose of the secondary meaning requirement." Restatement, *supra*, § 13 reporter's note, comment *e* at 53. The secondary meaning requirement exists to insure that something worth protecting exists—an association that has developed in the purchasing public's mind between a distinctive trade dress and its producer—before trademark law applies to limit the freedom of a competitor to compete by copying. As the drafters of the Restatement, *supra*, § 17 comment b at 104–05, explain:

> The freedom to copy product and packaging features is limited by the law of trademarks only when the copying is likely to confuse prospective purchasers

---

[4] The record indicates that the HAPPY CUBE trade dress was adopted in 1990, and for some of that time Idea Group was marketing its puzzles in the allegedly infringing trade dress.

[5] The subsequent edition of Callman's treatise, however, contains no language expressing approval for the doctrine of secondary meaning in the making. *See* 3 R. CALLMAN, THE LAW OF UNFAIR COMPETITION, TRADEMARKS, AND MONOPOLIES § 19.27 (4th ed. 1989).

as to the source or sponsorship of the goods. The imitation or even complete duplication of another's product or packaging creates no risk of confusion unless some aspect of the duplicated appearance is identified with a particular source. Unless a design is distinctive . . . and thus distinguishes the goods of one producer from those of others, it is ineligible for protection as a trademark.

See also Norwich Pharmacal Co. v. Sterling Drug, Inc., 271 F.2d 569, 572 (2d Cir. 1959) ("Absent confusion, imitation of certain successful features in another's product is not unlawful and to that extent a 'free ride' is permitted."); *Perfect Fit Industries, Inc. v. Acme Quilting Co.*, 618 F.2d 950, 952–53 (2d Cir. 1980). The so-called doctrine of secondary meaning in the making, by affording protection before prospective purchasers are likely to associate the trade dress with a particular sponsor, constrains unnecessarily the freedom to copy and compete.

The Eighth Circuit previously recognized the improper focus of the concept of secondary meaning in the making in *Black & Decker Mfg. v. Ever-Ready Appliance Mfg.*, 684 F.2d 546, 550 (8th Cir. 1982):

> Such a theory focuses solely upon the intent and actions of the seller of the product to the exclusion of the consuming public; but the very essence of secondary meaning is the association in the mind of the public of particular aspects of trade dress with a particular product and producer.

See also Scagnelli, *Dawn of a New Doctrine?—Trademark Protection for Incipient Secondary Meaning*, 71 TRADEMARK REP. 527, 542–43 (1981).

The argument in favor of permitting development of a doctrine of secondary meaning in the making, offered by Laureyssens, rests principally on the supposition that, without such a doctrine, there will be strong incentives for pirates to capitalize on products that have not yet developed secondary meaning. This argument, however, underestimates the level of protection afforded under existing law to prevent piracy in the early stages of product development. *See* Scagnelli, *supra*, at 543–49. For example, intentional copying is "persuasive evidence" of secondary meaning. *Coach Leatherware*, 933 F.2d at 169 (noting, however, that "conscious replication alone does not establish secondary meaning"); *see also* RESTATEMENT, *supra*, § 17 comment b at 106. Furthermore, secondary meaning can develop quickly to preclude knock-off artists from infringing. *See Maternally Yours, Inc. v. Your Maternity Shop, Inc.*, 234 F.2d 538, 541 (2d Cir. 1956) (secondary meaning acquired in mark MATERNALLY YOURS for maternity apparel store in the 11 months preceding defendant's opening of store named YOUR MATERNITY SHOP). Finally, under New York's common law of unfair competition, a producer's trade dress is protected without proof of secondary meaning against practices imbued with an odor of bad faith. *See Saratoga Vichy Spring Co. v. Lehman*, 625 F.2d 1037, 1044 (2d Cir. 1980). These practices include palming off, actual deception, appropriation of another's property, *see Norwich Pharmacal*, 271 F.2d at 570–71; *Upjohn Co. v. Schwartz*, 246 F.2d 254, 261–62 (2d Cir. 1957), or deliberate copying. *See Morex S.P.A. v. Design Inst. of Am., Inc.*, 779 F.2d 799, 801–02 (2d Cir. 1985); *Perfect Fit Indus.*, 618 F.2d at 952–54; Restatement, *supra*, § 16 reporter's note at 115.

Therefore, true innovators, at least under New York law, have adequate means of recourse against free-riders.

For these reasons, we reject the doctrine of secondary meaning in the making under section 43(a) of the Lanham Act. Accordingly, we reverse the district court's decision to grant a preliminary injunction against Idea Group based on section 43(a) of the Lanham Act. Given our holding, we need not address the likelihood of confusion which may have been created by the SNAFOOZ trade dress. . . .

COMMENTS AND QUESTIONS

1. Courts have been virtually unanimous in rejecting secondary meaning in the making as inconsistent with the idea that descriptive marks are not protected. Indeed, many courts expressly require that a trademark plaintiff obtain secondary meaning before the defendant begins any use of the term. *See* McCarthy, Trademarks and Unfair Competition § 16.12, at 16-40 to 16-43 (collecting cases). *Cf. Fuddruckers, Inc. v. Doc's B.R. Others, Inc.*, 826 F.2d 837 (9th Cir. 1987) (plaintiff was entitled to protect restaurant with trade dress nationally recognized among travelers against infringement by restaurant in Arizona, even though plaintiff had not established secondary meaning in Arizona directly).

What happens to trademarks that acquire secondary meaning too late? Are they wholly unprotectable? Or can they be asserted against a third party who uses the mark after secondary meaning is acquired? Note that the Trademark Office will register a descriptive mark that is first to acquire secondary meaning, regardless of when other users began use without secondary meaning. Presumably, that registration confers some rights, at least against subsequent adopters. But does it make sense that earlier users are "grandfathered" into the market and can continue to use the mark in competition with its owner?

2. What is wrong with protecting secondary meaning "in the making"? Suppose that in *Laureyssens,* the plaintiff had proven that Idea Group copied its descriptive packaging exactly because it knew that Laureyssens was advertising its product heavily and that Idea Group intended to trade on Laureyssens' expected success in making its packaging distinctive. Is it really fair to permit Idea Group to borrow Laureyssens' future goodwill merely because Laureyssens hasn't yet succeeded in establishing that goodwill? The court acknowledges this argument but contends that the doctrine of secondary meaning adequately protects against "piracy in the early stages of product development." Is the court's argument persuasive?

3. *Secondary Meaning and Registration.* The owner of a descriptive mark can register the mark if it can show secondary meaning. But secondary meaning where? Interestingly, while the secondary meaning needs to be in in more than a small area, *Philip Morris, Inc. v. Liggett & Myers Tobacco*, 139 U.S.P.Q. 240 (T.T.A.B. 1963), it does not need to be nationwide. But registration will confer nationwide priority, even in regions where the mark has not established secondary meaning.

v.   *Priority and Trademark Theory*

a.   *Reducing Search Costs*

Do any of the tests for priority discussed so far make sense in terms of lowering consumer search costs? Consider: if a second user can freely appropriate a mark, then consumers who have begun to rely on the association between the mark and the first user's product will be thwarted. This situation not only destroys that particular association with the first user's product; it may also make consumers less likely to establish such associations in the future. The upshot is that unless we protect the rights of the first user, more consumers will spend more time searching for goods.

On the other hand, many priority cases involve very limited uses in commerce; these cases typically occur early in the life of a new product or marketing campaign. As a consequence, very few consumers will, at the time of the litigation, have come to associate the mark in question with any goods. Where this is so, we might consider issues other than absolute priority to be important. For example, we might ask whether the first or second user was better positioned to distribute the goods bearing the mark. If the second user was in a better position—e.g., was larger, had more money to spend on advertising, etc.—why not let it use the mark? If consumer search costs are the key, why not take into account the interests of *future* consumers, who may be better served by allowing a search-cost-reducing trademark to fall into the hands of a large company that can make best use of it?

Then again, if the second user can really make better use of the mark, wouldn't it buy the trademark from the first user? When this is so, an award of priority to the first user will give it a share of the value of the market that will ultimately be served by the second user. Perhaps the payment to the first user will compensate it to some extent for the effort expended in coming up with a mark that, in the second user's hands, has real commercial value. (Notice that if this is so, it is a far cry from the consumer protection theory of trademark protection; it comes closer to the property theory described in the Introduction. No one is paying the consumers whose expectations are dashed.)

b. *Incentives to Create Trademarks*

Recall the respective efforts of Zazu Hair Design (ZHD), the plaintiff in the case that begins this section, and Wordmark, the consulting firm that L'Oreal hired to help identify a catchy name for its new hair coloring products. Why should ZHD potentially receive rights to the trademark when it appears that Wordmark thought to use Zazu as a product name first? (ZHD had only been using it as a trade name.) In other words, why doesn't the law grant rights to firms that specialize in creating new trademarks? Why must a mark be "used in commerce," as the statute phrases it, to receive legal protection? An argument for abolishing this requirement was made by Stephen Carter in his article, *Does It Matter Whether Intellectual Property Is Property?*, 68 CHI.-KENT L. REV. 715, 721 (1993): "But perhaps we should say, So what? How simple and elegant it would be to conclude that secondary meaning is unnecessary because the first to appropriate the mark owns it; owns it not because of its representational nature, but because it is a product of the mind."

Consider some counterarguments. In a seminal article written more than 60 years ago, Ralph S. Brown, Jr. highlighted the dual nature of trademark as serving both private and public interests. *See* Ralph S. Brown, Jr., *Advertising and the Public Interest: Legal Protection of Trade Symbols*, 57 YALE L.J. 1165, 1167 (1948). Expanding on this theme, Professor Wendy Gordon observes that:

> Promotional value, good will, popularity, and similar elements of value are joint products of both the public and the creator to a greater extent than are intellectual products themselves. True, even standard intellectual products—collocations of words, music, scenes—will be beneficial only if someone appreciates them; labor is never the only source of value, even for Locke. But with standard intellectual products the active role of the producer and the comparatively passive role of the public makes it easier to assign the resulting value primarily to the laborer. By contrast, with products such as popularity and "commercial magnetism," the chain of causality and responsibility is much harder to trace. . . . Usually a trademark is not purposely created for its own sake; the "benefit" purposely created is the good will of the owning entity (such as its reputation for manufacturing high-quality products), which the trademark merely happens to represent.

Wendy J. Gordon, *A Property Right in Self-Expression: Equality and Individualism in the Natural Law of Intellectual Property*, 102 YALE L.J. 1533, 1588 n.277 (1993); *Cf.* HAL MORGAN, SYMBOLS OF AMERICA (1987) (noting broad cultural impact of well-known trademarks). Note the skepticism Professor Gordon apparently feels regarding the claim that trademarks are brought about by legal incentives. This skepticism is shared by Rochelle Dreyfuss. *See* Rochelle C. Dreyfuss, *Expressive Genericity: Trademarks as Language in the Pepsi Generation*, 65 NOTRE DAME L. REV. 397, 399 (1990) ("[T]here is little need to create economic incentives to encourage businesses to develop a vocabulary with which to conduct commerce. . . .").

What do you think would happen if the law did give rights to firms such as Wordmark? Would it deplete the "stock" of potential trademarks available to actual manufacturers and sellers? *See* Beebe & Fromer, *supra* (showing that the Principal Register is surprisingly full). Would it be burdensome if many firms who wanted to start a business had to go first to a firm like Wordmark to "shop for a trademark"? How would the parties agree on a fair price for a trademark?

Keep in mind when thinking about these issues that even though firms such as Wordmark are not granted a legal right under the Lanham Act, such firms exist anyway. Indeed, from published reports, it would appear that the image/identity industry is thriving. Is this a good argument against a system that granted rights to these firms?

Do you suppose ZHD would have a cause of action against Wordmark? How about L'Oreal, on the grounds that Wordmark chose a trademark that wound up in costly litigation? Perhaps in the contract specifying Wordmark's services, Wordmark expressly disclaims liability for subsequent litigation.

c. Priority and the Prevention of Trademark Races

Why should the law grant rights to the first user of a mark, no matter how obscure the use, rather than the first to be recognized as a brand? Consider the alternative: if two entities have to "race" to establish nationwide recognition for their mark, will they spend more money widely distributing their new product—and advertising it—than they would otherwise? Would such extensive, early promotional efforts be wasteful? Is the role of trademark priority to forestall such wasteful expenditures and instead promote a more rational product "rollout" nationwide? Should the parties ever be able to divide up the nation?

Some guidance may be gleaned from a prominent justification for secure title in real property holdings. It has been argued that without secure property rights, assigned in advance, those seeking use of a resource will make wasteful expenditures seeking to claim it. The idea is that the orderly, rational development of the resource will be distorted by the absence of property rights. For example, consider "land rushes," such as the famous Oklahoma Land Rush. *See* Terry L. Anderson & Peter J. Hill, *The Race for Property Rights*, 33 J.L. & ECON. 177 (1990); R. Taylor Dennen, *Some Efficiency Effects of Nineteenth-Century Federal Land Policy: A Dynamic Analysis*, 51 AGRIC. HIST. 718 (1977); David D. Haddock, *First Possession Versus Optimal Timing: Limiting the Dissipation of Economic Value*, 64 WASH. U. L. REV. 775 (1986). Economic historians have detected evidence of wasteful spending by prospective claimants to real property. *See generally* GARY D. LIBECAP, CONTRACTING FOR PROPERTY RIGHTS (1989). Instead of allocating early expenditures rationally—e.g., some money for land, some for seeds, fertilizer, and building materials—people put all their money into the pursuit of land claims. The upshot was that the land was not utilized in an efficient manner. (Compare this line of reasoning to the "prospect theory" of patents. *See* Chapter III(A)(3).)

If the analogy between land development and trademark investment makes sense, why not go all the way to a pure registration system, under which virtually no expenditures need be made to secure trademark rights?

As another branch of economic theory would predict, "pure" registration systems—those where broad rights can be acquired without actual use in commerce—have been known to give rise to the scattershot acquisition of numerous trademarks solely for their resale value to real prospective users. In short, pure registration also invites "rent seeking." *Cf.* William M. Landes & Richard A. Posner, *Trademark Law: An Economic Perspective*, 30 J.L. & ECON. 265, 275 (1987). Consider the case of Robert Aries, who in 1965 had the foresight to register over 100 valuable American trademarks, including Pan American, NBC, Texaco, Monsanto, and Goodrich, with the National Trademark Office of Monaco. After registering the trademarks, Mr. Aries forced the American companies to buy their own marks back from him. Gerald D. O'Brien, *The Madrid Agreement Adherence Question*, 56 TRADEMARK REP. 326, 328 (1966). Similar practices were well known under French trademark law until the 1960s. *See, e.g.*, Andre Armengaud, *The New French Law on Trademarks*, 56 TRADEMARK REP. 430, 435–36 (1966):

> In France, during the last few years before the enactment of the 1964 Act, trademark registrations were becoming more and more numerous. This was due to the fact that many persons to whom a fancy name would come to mind, would register the name with the ulterior motive of obtaining some financial return from a possible subsequent user should the occasion arise. As a result, the area of choice for marks for new products was becoming narrower every day. Another drawback was that a merchant, or a manufacturer engaged in a particular trade area like hosiery for instance, would register his mark in all thirty-four classes. The relatively low cost of trademark registration in France, negligible as compared to the high costs a large company usually bears for advertising, made such practices possible. . . . [T]hese two practices . . . were responsible for the tremendous volume of trademark registration.

On the end of these practices in France, *see* Gerard Dassas, *Survey of Experience Under the French Trademark Law*, 66 TRADEMARK REP. 485, 491 (1976).

A similar phenomenon occurred in the 1990s with Internet domain names. The registration of domain names was initially handled by Network Solutions, Inc. (NSI) and is now overseen by a variety of domain name registries operating under the auspices of a nonprofit entity called the Internet Corporation for Assigned Names and Numbers (ICANN). These entities have allocated domain names on a first-come, first-served basis for a modest fee. During its initial period of operation, this system wreaked havoc among trademark holders as "cybersquatters" rushed in to register well-known trademarks held by others. These registrants would then offer to sell them to the trademark owners at exorbitant prices. Some companies even registered the marks of their competitors and used the sites to put up comparative product information. *See, e.g.*, Joshua Quittner, *Making a Name on the Internet*, NEWSDAY, Oct. 7, 1994, at A4 ("It['s] . . . like a gold rush: Two thousand requests a month are coming in to stake claim to a name on the Internet, nearly 10 times as many as a year ago."). Courts, ICANN, and legislatures developed rules and dispute resolution processes to curtail such extortionate rent seeking. The potential to profit from registering domain names closely related to the trademarks of others continues to occur, although the opportunities for extracting value from trademark owners have been greatly reduced and the penalties for crossing the line greatly enhanced. *See, e.g.*, *Shields v. Zuccarini*, 254 F.3d 476 (3d Cir. 2001) (enjoining "typo-squatting"—registering misspelled versions of trademarks—and imposing a large fine under the Anticybersquatting Consumer Protection Act).

There seems to be good reason to allow some sort of early claiming system (i.e., registration with national effect after minimal use) without going all the way to "pure" registration (which invites equally wasteful rent seeking). An alternative would be to allow pure registration with lapse for nonuse after some period of time. Notice that this quite adequately describes the current system of "intent to use" registration.

COMMENTS AND QUESTIONS

1. The *Zazu* case and its ilk center on what constitutes "use" for trademark purposes. But what happens when the "use" asserted by a plaintiff originates not with the seller of goods itself, but with the common parlance of consumers? Consider, for example, *Volkswagenwerk A.G. v. Advanced Welding & Mfg. Co.*, 193 U.S.P.Q. 673 (TTAB 1976), which concerned trademark rights in the word "Bug." To Volkswagen (VW), the official moniker for its classic economy car was "Type I," or, later, "Beetle." But in common parlance, this car was universally referred to as a "Bug." Importantly, it was the consuming public, and not VW, that originated this usage. Should trademark law protect the association between VW and "Bug," even though "Bug" originated with consumers themselves? Courts tend toward the view that consumer associations should be protected in this context. *See id.; see also National Cable Television Ass'n v. American Cinema Editors, Inc.*, 937 F.2d 1572 (Fed. Cir. 1991) (ACE used in common parlance as an acronym for association of film (cinema) editors). That reflects the "consumer protection" rationale for trademarks, as opposed to the incentive/property rationale. (Do you see why? How much did VW invest in creating the "Bug" mark?) One issue in cases such as these is that to prevent confusion, *someone* must have the right to stop third parties from using the distinctive name for other products; because "the consuming public" is a diffuse mass of people, there is no obvious representative who might be chosen to enforce rights in the distinctive name. *Cf.* Abraham Bell & Gideon Parchomovsky, *Copyright Trust*, 100 CORNELL L. REV. 1015 (2015) (proposing a solution to a loosely analogous collective action problem in copyright enforcement).

2. Difficult priority problems arise when a well-known trademark is abandoned by its original owner. The priority question involves a race among rivals to capture the mark. *See California Cedar Products Co. v. Pine Mountain Corp.*, 724 F.2d 827, 830 (9th Cir. 1984) (bad faith of first rival to claim abandoned Duraflame mark for ersatz fireplace logs negates its claim, leaving second rival to claim the mark with priority). Are the issues the same as when firms race to obtain rights to a new mark? Under a strict consumer protection rationale for trademarks, is there an argument that abandoned marks should be off-limits to rival firms, at least for a number of years? Why would a firm abandon a mark when it has value to rivals—why not sell it? *Cf.* Chapter V(B)(1)(ii)–(iii) (dealing with abandonment and restrictions on licensing and assignments).

PROBLEMS

Problem V-8. Preco Industries began using the term "Porcelaincote" for its porcelain resurfacing material in 1966. Preco concedes that, at the time it began use, the "Porcelaincote" mark was unprotectable because it was descriptive. Preco continued to use the mark for a relatively minor product line. In 1977, Ceramco began to use the identical mark for identical goods. [Both companies sell their products on a nationwide basis.] In 1979, Ceramco began a nationwide advertising campaign using the "Porcelaincote" mark. Shortly thereafter, in 1980, Preco began a similar campaign. In 1981, the parties filed complaints against each other for trademark infringement. The court determined at trial that Ceramco established secondary meaning in 1979, and that Preco established it in 1980.

Assume that neither party ever registered its mark. Who should prevail in the lawsuits? Does either party have rights against a third company that began using the name in 1990? Does your answer to either of these questions change if one or both parties registered its mark on the Principal Register?

Problem V-9. In May 1989, Shalom Children's Wear begins advertising and planning a line of clothes to be called "Body Gear." In November 1989, In-Wear Corp. files an intent-to-use application for the mark "Body Gear." Shalom files an intent-to-use application for the same mark in December 1989 and begins selling its products in February 1990. Is either party entitled to register the Body Gear mark? (Assume that the mark is otherwise protectable.) Does the result change if In-Wear fails to begin selling its clothes by November 1992?

3. Trademark Office Procedures

Administrative proceedings concerning trademarks in the United States are among the most stringent in the world. The U.S. Patent and Trademark Office (PTO) actively examines applications and—with the help of the courts—polices the trademark registers as well. In this section we review these administrative procedures.

i. *Principal vs. Supplemental Register*

Although registration is not a prerequisite to trademark protection, trademarks registered on the Principal Register enjoy a number of significant advantages. The primary advantages are: (1) nationwide constructive use and constructive notice, which cut off rights of other users of the same or similar marks, Lanham Act § 22 (15 U.S.C. § 1072) and Lanham Act § 7(c) (15 U.S.C. § 1057(c)), and (2) the possibility of achieving incontestable status after five years, which greatly enhances rights by eliminating a number of defenses, Lanham Act § 15 (15 U.S.C. § 1065).[4]

---

[4] Other advantages include: (1) the right to request customs officials to bar the importation of goods bearing infringing trademarks, Lanham Act § 42 (15 U.S.C. § 1124), and (2) provisions for treble damages,

Trademark applications are maintained in an index at the PTO and made available for public scrutiny soon after filing. This procedure is different from patent applications, the contents of which are kept secret for 18 months after filing in most cases.

The Supplemental Register was established by the 1946 Lanham Act "to enable persons in this country to domestically register trademarks so that they might obtain registration under the laws of foreign countries." MCCARTHY, TRADEMARKS AND UN-FAIR COMPETITION, § 19.09[1] (1996), at 19–68. Under the Paris Convention, foreign registration could not be granted in the absence of domestic registration. Because there are countries where trademark registration is granted to marks that would not qualify for the U.S. Principal Register, the Supplemental Register was created. Thus, even if a U.S. mark cannot gain the advantages of registration on the Principal Register, it may obtain protection in foreign countries.

To be eligible for the Supplemental Register a mark need only be capable of distinguishing goods or services. There is no need to prove that it actually functions in that capacity. The Supplemental Register is not available for clearly generic names, but it is available for the registration of trade dress.

Unlike the Principal Register, registration on the Supplemental Register confers no substantive trademark rights. *See, e.g., Clairol, Inc. v. Gillette Co.*, 389 F.2d 264 (2d Cir. 1968). Registration on the Supplemental Register has no evidentiary effects, it does not provide constructive notice of ownership, the mark cannot become incontestable, and it cannot be used as a basis for the Treasury Department to prevent the importation of infringing goods. However, a mark on the Supplemental Register may be litigated in federal court, may be cited by the PTO against a later applicant, and may provide notice to others that the mark is in use. *See In re Clorox Co.*, 578 F.2d 305 (C.C.P.A. 1978). Marks registered on the Supplemental Register are not subject to intent-to-use filings or opposition challenges, but may be canceled at any time by a court.

ii. *Grounds for Refusing Registration*

Section 2 of the Lanham Act provides the basis for many of the grounds for refusing registration on the Principal Register. Many, but not all, track the trademark protectability doctrines we have just discussed:

No trademark by which the goods of the applicant may be distinguished from the goods of others shall be refused registration on the principal register on account of its nature unless it—

(a) Consists of or comprises immoral, deceptive, or scandalous matter; or matter which may disparage or falsely suggest a connection with persons, living or dead, institutions, beliefs, or national symbols, or bring them into contempt, or disrepute.

---

attorney fees, and certain other remedies in civil infringement actions, Lanham Act §§ 34–38 (15 U.S.C. §§ 1116–1120).

(b) Consists of or comprises the flag or coat of arms or other insignia of the United States, or of any State or municipality, or of any foreign nation, or any simulation thereof.

(c) Consists of or comprises a name, portrait, or signature identifying a particular living individual except by his written consent, or the name, signature, or portrait, of a deceased President of the United States during the life of his widow, if any, except by the written consent of the widow.

(d) Consists of or comprises a mark which so resembles a mark registered in the Patent and Trademark Office, or a mark or trade name previously used in the United States by another and not abandoned, as to be likely, when used on or in connection with the goods of the applicant, to cause confusion, or to cause mistake, or to deceive: *Provided,* That, if the Commissioner determines [accordingly, concurrent registrations may be possible; see below].

(e) Consists of a mark which,

> (1) when used on or in connection with the goods of the applicant is merely descriptive or deceptively misdescriptive of them,

> (2) when used on or in connection with the goods of the applicant is primarily geographically descriptive of them, except as indications of regional origin may be registrable under section 1054 of this title,

> (3) when used on or in connection with the goods of the applicant is primarily geographically deceptively misdescriptive of them,

> (4) is primarily merely a surname, or

> (5) comprises any matter that, as a whole, is functional.

Lanham Act § 2, 15 U.S.C. § 1052. Marks rejected under subsection (e)(1), (2), and (4) may be registered if the applicant can demonstrate secondary meaning, however.

The prohibition on registering flags or coats of arms can arise in some surprising contexts. In *Re/Max LLC v. M.L. Jones & Assocs.*, 2014 WL 7405461 (E.D.N.C. Dec. 30, 2014), the court ordered the cancellation of real estate company Re/Max's trademark consisting of horizontal bands of red, white, and blue because it was identical to the flag of the Netherlands.

| **'048 Trademark** | **The Netherlands' Flag** |

a.   *Immoral, Scandalous, or Disparaging Marks*

From the establishment of the modern U.S. trademark registration system in the late 1940s until 2017, the Trademark Office applied Section 2(a) to bar federal registration for immoral, scandalous, or disparaging terms. The decisions were at times inconsistent. For example, the PTO denied registration to "MORMON WHISKY", and "HAVE YOU HEARD THAT SATAN IS A REPUBLICAN?" while allowing registration for STINKY GRINGO and THE DEVIL IS A DEMOCRAT. Scholars and civil liberties organizations have long questioned whether Section 2(a) violated the First Amendment's prohibition on laws abridging free expression. *See, e.g.,* Jeffrey Lefstin, *Does the First Amendment Bar Cancellation of REDSKINS?*, 52 STAN. L. REV. 665 (2000); Mark A. Lemley, *The Modern Lanham Act and the Death of Common Sense*, 108 YALE L.J. 1687, 1710–11 (1999).

The issue gained salience in recent years as litigants pressed the issue from both sides. Native American groups sought to cancel the Washington Redskins trademark as an offensive slur. On the other side, representatives of historically denigrated groups sought to reclaim terms that were previously considered vulgar, offensive, or disparaging. For example, a lesbian motorcycle club that participates in gay pride events successfully fought the PTO over "DYKES ON BIKES." Simon Tam, the lead singer of a rock band comprised of Asian Americans, challenged the PTO's refusal to register "THE SLANTS."

In *Matal v. Tam*, 137 U.S. 1744 (2017), the Supreme Court invalidated the Section 2(a) disparagement clause on First Amendment grounds, although the Court divided on the reasoning. All of the justices confirmed that the government can regulate or punish fraud, defamation, and incitement within constitutional bounds. Furthermore, the justices agreed that trademark registration did not constitute government speech, such as promoting particular policies, to which the First Amendment does not apply. As the Court noted, the Federal Government does not dream up these marks. "[I]if trademarks represent government speech, what does the Government have in mind when it advises Americans to "make.believe" (Sony), "Think different" (Apple), "Just do it" (Nike), or "Have it your way" (Burger King)? Was the Government warning about a coming disaster when it registered the mark "EndTime Ministries"? *Id.* at 1759.

The justices divided on how to address whether Section 2(a) could be upheld under the more relaxed First Amendment standards applicable to commercial speech. Justice Alito, Chief Justice Roberts, Justice Thomas, and Justice Breyer determined that there was no need to resolve the issue because the disparagement bar reaches well beyond the narrow purpose of driving out invidious discrimination. Rather, it "reaches any trademark that disparages *any person, group, or institution*. It applies to trademarks like the following: 'Down with racists,' 'Down with sexists,' 'Down with homophobes.' *Id.* at 1765 (emphasis in original). By contrast, Justices Kennedy, Ginsburg, Sotomayor, and Kagan considered the PTO's role in determining what is disparaging to be the root of the problem. In their view, Section 2(a) plainly represents a form of viewpoint discrimination—an "egregious form of content discrimination—which is "presumptively unconstitutional" regardless of whether the speech is commercial.

> To the extent trademarks qualify as commercial speech, they are an example of why that term or category does not serve as a blanket exemption from the First Amendment's requirement of viewpoint neutrality. . . . Here that real marketplace exists as a matter of state law and our common-law tradition, quite without regard to the Federal Government. These marks make up part of the expression of everyday life, as with the names of entertainment groups, broadcast networks, designer clothing, newspapers, automobiles, candy bars, toys, and so on. Nonprofit organizations—ranging from medical-research charities and other humanitarian causes to political advocacy groups—also have trademarks, which they use to compete in a real economic sense for funding and other resources as they seek to persuade others to join their cause. To permit viewpoint discrimination in this context is to permit Government censorship.

Id. at 1767–68.

In the aftermath of the *Tam* decision, the Supreme Court struck down the "immoral" and "scandalous" prongs of Section 2(a) as unconstitutional under the First Amendment because they were similarly viewpoint-based. *Iancu v. Brunetti*, 139 S.Ct. 2294 (2019) (holding that FUCT on a T-shirt, while vulgar, is registrable). Interestingly, while the result in *Tam* was unanimous, four Justices wrote separate opinions in *Brunetti* suggesting that while the statute was unconstitutionally overbroad, a more narrowly-drawn statute might constitutionally be able to ban profanity.

How would you categorize FUCT on the distinctiveness spectrum?

Scandalous trademark applications have skyrocketed since 2017, but registrations remain low. *See* Jeffrey Greene & Rose Kautz, *The State of Scandalous Trademarks Post-*Brunetti, Law360 (Apr. 16, 2020). A high percentage of these applications (50%) relate to the fashion industry. Industry commentators opine that fashion brands see scandalous marks as a way to attract consumers in an increasingly crowded marketplace. *See* Rachel Leah, *Prada, Gucci And Now Burberry: Are Brands Under Fire For Offensive Designs Doing It On Purpose?*, SALON (Feb. 20, 2019). Yet the Trademark Office is finding non-§2(a) ways to refuse these applications. For example, the Trademark Office routinely refusing registrations for slogans on t-shirts as ornamental, i.e., merely decoration and not source identifying. The Trademark Office has also rejected fashion brand applications on the ground that they are commonplace messages: "F*** You" is viewed in the same way as "Drive Safely" or "Proudly Made in the USA." Many of these applications also fail on the grounds that they create a likelihood of confusion with an earlier-filed application for registration.

While vindicating some First Amendment values, *Tam* raises serious social justice concerns. *See* Victoria F. Phillips, *Beyond Trademark: The Washington Redskins Case and the Search for Dignity*, 92 CHICAGO-KENT L. REV. 1061 (2018); ERIK STEGMAN & VICTORIA F. PHILLIPS, MISSING THE POINT—THE REAL IMPACT OF NATIVE MASCOTS AND TEAM NAMES ON AMERICAN INDIAN AND ALASKA NATIVE YOUTH, CENTER FOR AMERICAN PROGRESS (July 2014); Rita Heimes, *Trademarks, Identity, and Justice*, 11 J. MARSHALL REV. INTELL. PROP. L. 133, 158–65 (2011); K.J. Greene, *Trademark Law and Racial Subordination: From Marketing of Stereotypes to Norms of Authorship*, 58 SYRACUSE L. REV. 431, 436, 444 (2008) (discussing the role of trademarks in reinforcing racial stereotyping (noting the "Aunt Jemima" logo) and pointing out how what is considered offensive and disparaging shifts over time). In the aftermath of George Floyd's tragic death and the ascendancy of the Black Lives Matter movement, some companies have begun rethinking their use of offensive trademarks. *See* Emily Heil, *Quaker Is Dropping the Aunt Jemima Image and Name After Recognizing They Are 'Based on a Racial Stereotype'*, WASH. POST (Jun. 17, 2020); Alison Kosik, *Fedex Asks the Washington Redskins to Change Their Name After Pressure from Investor Groups*, CNN BUSINESS (Jul. 3, 2020).

b. *Geographic Marks*

In re Nantucket, Inc.
United States Court of Customs and Patent Appeals
677 F.2d 95 (C.C.P.A. 1982)

MARKEY, Chief Judge.

Nantucket, Inc. (Nantucket) appeals from a decision of the Trademark Trial and Appeal Board (board) affirming a refusal to register the mark NANTUCKET for men's shirts on the ground that it is "primarily geographically deceptively misdescriptive." *In re Nantucket, Inc.*, 209 U.S.P.Q. 868 (TTAB 1981). We reverse.

Background

. . . Nantucket, based in North Carolina, filed [an] application . . . for registration of NANTUCKET for men's shirts on the principal register in the Patent and Trademark Office (PTO). . . .

TMEP § 1208.02 indicates that a mark is primarily geographical, inter alia, if it "is the name of a place which has general renown to the public at large and which is a place from which goods and services are known to emanate as a result of commercial activity."

The examiner, citing a dictionary definition of "Nantucket" as an island in the Atlantic Ocean south of Massachusetts, concluded that the mark NANTUCKET was either primarily geographically descriptive or primarily geographically deceptively misdescriptive, depending upon whether Nantucket's shirts did or did not come from Nantucket Island.

Nantucket informed the PTO that its shirts "do not originate from Nantucket Island," and insisted that the mark would not be understood by purchasers as representing that the shirts were produced there because the island has no market place significance vis-à-vis men's shirts. . . . As applied to shirts, it was argued, NANTUCKET is arbitrary and nondescriptive, because there is no association in the public mind of men's shirts with Nantucket Island.

The examiner's final refusal was based on the view that, because the shirts did not come from Nantucket Island, NANTUCKET is "primarily geographically deceptively misdescriptive."

Before the board, Nantucket relied upon a number of cases, of which In re Circus Ices, Inc., 158 U.S.P.Q. 64 (TTAB 1968), is representative, for its asserted "public association" or "noted for" test. In that case, the board said:

> The term "HAWAIIAN," meaning of or pertaining to Hawaii or the Hawaiian Islands, possesses an obvious geographical connotation, but it does not necessarily follow therefrom that it is primarily geographically descriptive of applicant's product within the meaning of Section 2(e). In determining whether or not a geographical term is primarily geographically descriptive of a product, of primary consideration is whether or not there is an association in the public mind of the product with the particular geographical area, as for example perfumes and wines with France, potatoes with Idaho, rum with Puerto Rico, and beef with Argentina. . . . In the present case, it has not been made to appear that Hawaii or the Hawaiian Islands are noted for flavored-ice products or that the term "HAWAIIAN" is used by anyone to denote the geographical origin of such products. [. . .]

The board concluded that the "term NANTUCKET" has a readily recognizable geographic meaning, and . . . no alternative non-geographic significance . . . and hence falls within the proscription of Section 2(e)(2). *Id.*

The Board's Test

. . . The board's test rests mechanistically on the one question of whether the mark is recognizable, at least to some large segment of the public, as the name of a geographical area. NANTUCKET is such. That ends the board's test. Once it is found that the mark is the name of a known place, i.e., that it has "a readily recognizable geographic meaning," the next question, whether applicant's goods do or do not come from that place, becomes irrelevant under the board's test, for if they do, the mark is "primarily geographically descriptive"; if they don't, the mark is "primarily geographically deceptively misdescriptive."[5]

The Statute

One flaw in the board's test resides in its factoring out the nature of applicant's goods, in contravention of § 2(e)(2)'s requirement that the mark be evaluated "when applied to the goods of the applicant," and that registration be denied only when the mark is geographically descriptive or deceptively misdescriptive "of them" (the goods).

Another flaw in the board's test lies in its failure to give appropriate weight to the presence of "deceptively" in § 2(e)(2). If the goods do not originate in the geographic area denoted by the mark, the mark might in a vacuum be characterized as geographically misdescriptive, but the statutory characterization required for denial of registration is "geographically *deceptively* misdescriptive." (Emphasis supplied.) Before that statutory characterization may be properly applied, there must be a reasonable basis for believing that purchasers are likely to be deceived.[5] . . .

Geographic terms are merely a specific kind of potential trademark, subject to characterization as having a particular kind of descriptiveness or misdescriptiveness. Registration of marks that would be perceived by potential purchasers as describing or deceptively misdescribing the goods themselves may be denied under § 2(e)(1). Registration of marks that would be perceived by potential purchasers as describing or deceptively misdescribing the geographic origin of the goods may be denied under § 2(e)(2). In either case, the mark must be judged on the basis of its role in the marketplace.

As the courts have made plain, geographically deceptive misdescriptiveness cannot be determined without considering whether the public associates the goods with the place which the mark names. If the goods do not come from the place named, and the public makes no goods-place association, the public is not deceived and the mark is accordingly not geographically deceptively misdescriptive. . . .

In *National Lead Co. v. Wolfe*, 223 F.2d 195, 199, (CA 9 1955), the court held that neither DUTCH, nor DUTCH BOY, as applied to paint, was used "otherwise than in a fictitious, arbitrary and fanciful manner," and noted that "there is no likelihood that the use of the name 'Dutch' or 'Dutch Boy' in connection with the appellant's goods would be understood by purchasers as representing that the goods or their constituent materials were produced or processed in Holland or that they are of the same distinctive kind or quality as those produced, processed or used in that place."

---

[5] [Under the modern statute, primarily geographically descriptive marks can be registered if they have acquired secondary meaning. By contrast, geographically deceptively misdescriptive marks that mislead consumers about a material issue can never be registered. 15 U.S.C. § 1052(f).—Eds.]

[5] Reasonable persons are unlikely to believe that bananas labeled ALASKA originated or were grown in Alaska. On the other hand, reasonable persons are quite likely to believe that salmon labeled ALASKA originated in the waters of that state. The board recognized this decisional parameter in its references to French wine, Idaho potatoes, etc., in *Circus Ices*, 158 U.S.P.Q. at 64.

. . . There is no indication that the purchasing public would expect men's shirts to have their origin in Nantucket when seen in the market place with NANTUCKET on them. Hence buyers are not likely to be deceived, and registration cannot be refused on the ground that the mark is "primarily geographically deceptively misdescriptive."

Accordingly, the decision of the board is reversed.

COMMENTS AND QUESTIONS

1. In some cases prospective trademark registrants may be trying to seize on the descriptiveness of a term of geographic origin; "Napa" for wine would be an example. Another motivation is to seize on the good feelings engendered by a place name. *See, e.g., Singer Mfg. Co. v. Birginal-Bigsby Corp.*, 319 F.2d 273 (C.C.P.A. 1963) (American Beauty is primarily geographically deceptively misdescriptive when applied to sewing machines of Japanese origin). For example, a trademark applicant might try to register "Cuban" for cigars made in New Hampshire; this would very likely lead to a finding of deceptiveness (section 2(a)), and the application would be barred completely.

On the other hand, the use of a geographic term is not always forbidden. As the *Nantucket* case demonstrates, the question is whether the public connects the geographic indication with the source of goods. Thus, "Arctic" for vegetables is not geographically descriptive, because consumers would be unlikely to think it indicated that the vegetables came from the Arctic. For a questionable application of the deceptive misdescriptiveness doctrine, *see In re Broyhill Furn. Indus.*, 60 U.S.P.Q.2d 1511 (TTAB 2001) ("Toscana" primarily geographically deceptively misdescriptive for furniture).

If the public does not in fact associate the trademarked goods with the place, why would brand owners want to use that name? *See* Alan L. Durham, *Trademarks and the Landscape of Imagination*, 79 TEMPLE L. REV. 1181 (2006) (arguing that place names "evoke ideas with which the[] manufacturer would like to associate its brand" rather than the place of manufacture). Patagonia outdoor wear, for instance, may remind people of wild places rather than signal that the clothes are made there.

2. In many countries, geographic terms—usually for food or wine—serve also to certify composition, traditional preparation techniques, quality, and actual taste. In Europe, for example, so-called appellations of origin for wine—such as "Champagne," "Chablis," and "Chianti"—are protected by statute and administered by national authorities. *See Institut National des Appellations d'Origine v. Vintners Int'l Co.*, 958 F.2d 1574 (Fed. Cir. 1992) (affirming denial of opposition by plaintiff, French national authority for establishing and policing appellations of origin, for registration of "Chablis with a Twist" for citrus-flavored wine drink that did not originate in France).

As part of the GATT amendments in 1994, Congress (as a concession to European interests) adopted limited recognition of the appellations of origin concept.

Lanham Act § 2(a) [15 U.S.C. § 1052(a)]

No trademark . . . shall be refused registration on the principal register on account of its nature unless it—

> (a) Consists of or comprises . . . a geographical indication which, when used on or in connection with wines or spirits, identifies a place other than the origin of the goods and is first used on or in connection with wines or spirits by the applicant on or after one year after the date on which the WTO [World Trade Organization] Agreement (as defined in section 3501(9) of Title 19) enters into force with respect to the United States.

Section 2(e) has also long provided that appellations of origin registered under the Lanham Act § 4 (15 U.S.C § 1054) (collective and certification marks) are an exception to the prohibition on geographically descriptive trademarks. A certification mark is a guarantee of authenticity—"Belgian chocolates" must come from Belgium, for example. Certification marks may be registered without proof of secondary meaning but must be made available in a nondiscriminatory fashion to anyone who complies with the terms of the certification. *See Community of Roquefort v. William Faehndrich, Inc.*, 303 F.2d 494 (2d Cir. 1962) (French city of Roquefort was entitled to prevent use of the term "Roquefort" to describe cheese made in Hungary, based on United States certification mark). Note that group certification marks serve much the same quality assurance function as individual trademarks, but (assuming collective action problems are overcome) they may effectively protect small businesses who could not establish a well-known mark on their own.

For a spirited debate on appellations of origin, *see* Irene Calboli, *Time to Say Local Cheese and Smile at Geographical Indications of Origin? International Trade and Local Development in the United States*, 53 HOUS. L. REV. 373 (2015) (offering some possible compromises between European and American positions); Jim Chen, *A Sober Second Look at Appellations of Origin: How the United States Will Crash France's Wine and Cheese Party*, 5 MINN. J. GLOBAL TRADE 29 (1996) (arguing that appellations of origin are artificial market segmentation devices that detract from consumer welfare); Louis Lorvellec, *You've Got to Fight for Your Right to Party,* 5 MINN. J. GLOBAL TRADE 65 (1996) (begging to differ, from French perspective). .

3. Marks that are "deceptive" cannot be registered even if they are not geographic in nature. *See, e.g., Glendale Int'l Corp. v. PTO*, 374 F. Supp. 2d 479 (E.D. Va. 2005) (the mark "Titanium" was deceptive for a recreational vehicle that contained no titanium).

iii.   Marks Which Are "Primarily Merely a Surname"

Section 2 treats as "descriptive" marks that are "primarily merely a surname" in the minds of consumers, whether or not the mark actually represents the owner's surname. From *In re Garan, Inc.*, 3 U.S.P.Q.2d 1537, 1539–40 (TTAB 1987):

> That there are no other meanings of the name in the English language will not support refusal of registration of the surname under the "primarily merely a surname" statutory language unless the average member of the purchasing public would, upon seeing it used as a trademark, recognize it as a surname. This

rule was first announced by the late Assistant Commissioner Leeds in her landmark decision, *Ex parte Rivera Watch Corporation*, 106 U.S.P.Q. 145, 149 (Comr. Pats. 1955), as follows:

> There are some names which by their very nature have only a surname significance even though they are rare surnames. "Seidenberg," if rare, would be in this class. And there are others which have no meaning—well known or otherwise—and are in fact surnames which do not, when applied to goods as trademarks, create the impression of being surnames. It seems to me that the test to be applied in the administration of this provision in the Act is not the rarity of the name, nor whether it is the applicant's name, nor whether it appears in one or more telephone directories, nor whether it is coupled with a baptismal name or initials. The test should be: What is the primary significance to the purchasing public? . . .

Some twenty years later, in *In re Kahan & Weisz Jewelry Manufacturing Corp.*, 508 F.2d 831 (C.C.P.A. 1975), a case involving facts strikingly similar to those in the one now before us, the predecessor of the Court above expressly adopted the Rivera rule and it has since been consistently followed by the Board. *See, e.g., In re Pillsbury Co.*, 174 U.S.P.Q. 318 (TTAB 1972). . . .

Clearly, based on the above, we cannot stop with the directory listings and absence of other meanings, but must evaluate all of the relevant factors.

The six (or seven) directory and NEXIS listings of "Garan" as a surname have limited persuasive impact in view of the fact these were the only ones found in an enormous NEXIS database and some 43 directories of major population centers. In this context, we conclude that "Garan" is an extremely rare surname. While rare surnames may nevertheless be considered to be "primarily merely" surnames, e.g., *In re Possis Medical, Inc.*, 230 U.S.P.Q. 72, 74 (TTAB 1986), and cases cited therein, we agree with appellant that the degree of a surname's rareness should have material impact on the weight given the directory evidence. Here, since it appears that the directory and NEXIS evidence shows "Garan" to be an extremely rare surname, we conclude that the directory and NEXIS evidence only slightly supports the Office's position that GARAN is "primarily merely a surname."

On analysis, we find all of the other factors either neutral or supportive of appellant's position that GARAN would be perceived by purchasers as an arbitrary term or as the trademark and trade name of appellant.

COMMENTS AND QUESTIONS

1. The statutory hesitance to register surnames springs in part from an old common law policy in favor of the right to use one's name, a policy that still has some life. *Basile, S.p.A. v. Basile*, 899 F.2d 35 (D.C. Cir. 1990), for example, is a case where an Italian watchmaker by the name of Basile sought to use that name on watches in the United

States—against the wishes of an established company, well known for its watches sold under the same name. In his opinion reviewing the scope of the injunction granted by the district court in the case, Judge Williams of the D.C. Circuit summarized the common law rule and its more recent interpretation:

> A seller's right to use his family name might have carried the day against a risk of buyer confusion in an era when the role of personal and localized reputation gave the right a more exalted status. In *Burgess v. Burgess*, 3 De G.M. & G. 896, 903–904, 43 Eng. Rep. 351, 354 (1853), the plaintiff's son had followed him into the trade of making anchovy paste; Lord Justice Bruce said:
>
> > All the Queen's subjects have a right, if they will, to manufacture and sell pickles and sauces, and not the less that their fathers have done so before them. All the Queen's subjects have a right to sell these articles in their own names, and not the less so that they bear the same name as their fathers.
>
> *See also Brown Chemical Co. v. Meyer*, 139 U.S. 540, 544 (1891) ("[a] man's name is his own property, and he has the same right to its use and enjoyment as he has to that of any other species of property"); *Stix, Baer & Fuller Dry Goods Co. v. American Piano Co.*, 211 F. 271, 274 (8th Cir. 1913). But even quite old decisions have enjoined a second comer's use of his name where necessary to prevent confusion. *See, e.g., Thaddeus Davids Co. v. Davids Manufacturing Co.*, 233 U.S. 461, 472 (1914); *Hat Corp. of America v. D.L. Davis Corp.*, 4 F. Supp. 613, 623 (D. Conn. 1933). The commentators, moreover, have been scornful of protecting the second comer's right to use his name at the expense of customer confusion, anathematizing it as the "sacred rights" theory. *See* Milton Handler & Charles Pickett, *Trade-Marks and Trade Names—An Analysis and Synthesis*, 30 COLUM. L. REV. 168, 197–200 (1930). . . . Case Note, 38 HARV. L. REV. 405, 406 (1925). As the *Basile* court noted:
>
> > True, even recent decisions have invoked the right to use one's name, at least as an interest against which the senior user's are balanced. *See Taylor Wine* [*Co., Inc. v. Bully Hill Vineyards, Inc.*, 569 F.2d 731, 734 (2d Cir. 1978)] at 735. . . . But its weight has decidedly diminished. The courts are now consistent in imposing tighter restrictions on the second comer in the face of possible confusion . . . ; any residual protection of the second comer's use of his own name seems amply explained by the more general principle that an equitable remedy should be no broader than necessary to correct the wrong. . . . Where the second comer had established no reputation under his own name, one court did not even purport to "balance."
>
> > This trend in the law unsurprisingly reflects trends in the marketplace. In a world of primarily local trade, the goodwill of an anchovy paste seller may well have depended on his individual reputation within the community. Indeed, one elderly decision tells us that an entrepreneur's failure to use his family name once risked "the reproach of doing business under false colors." *Hat Corp.*, 4 F. Supp. at 623. By contrast, the court went on, "[i]n an age when by corporate

activity, mass production, and national distribution, the truly personal element has been so largely squeezed out of business, there is naturally less legitimate pecuniary value in a family name." *Id.*; *see also* Handler & Pickett, 30 COLUM. L. REV. at 199. That was in 1933 and the point is more obvious today. Other than understandable pride and sense of identity, the modern businessman loses nothing by losing the name. A junior user's right to use his name thus must yield to the extent its exercise causes confusion with the senior user's mark. . .

Here Francesco Basile's interest in the use of his name is peculiarly weak. He has no reputation in the United States as a watchmaker. . . . There is no suggestion that the watch industry is one where an individual proprietor's personal presentation of his wares plays a key commercial role, as may still be true of high fashion designers such as Yves St. Laurent and Christian Dior. Nor is it a business that has remained largely local in scope. Although none of these conditions would allow a second comer to use his own name at a serious cost of customer confusion, their absence means that Francesco's interest in his own name here is scarcely greater than his interest in the name Bulova. . . . [W]e think the only plausible motivation for his fight here is a wish to free-ride on Basile's goodwill, precisely what the law means to suppress.

Basile, 899 F.2d at 39–40.

2. Should it matter whether the surname sought to be registered is common or rare? That the senior trademark user is well known or obscure? *See* Spencer T. Smith, *Primarily Merely*, 63 TRADEMARK REP. 24 (1973).

3. The scope of injunctions shows the remnants of the common law concern with the right to use one's name. Courts are more likely to permit the junior use if the user disclaims any connection with the more famous senior user. *See Taylor Wine Co. v. Bully Hill Vineyards*, 569 F.2d 731 (2d Cir. 1978).

4. Should the nature of the defendant's use matter? One court has held that the restrictions applied to registering personal names should not apply where the name in question ("Niles") was used for a plush toy camel, since unlike personal names there was no strong business interest in using one's own name for a camel. *Peaceable Planet, Inc. v. Ty, Inc.*, 362 F.3d 986 (7th Cir. 2004).

PROBLEM

Problem V-10. Ernest and Julio Gallo are the nation's largest sellers of wine. They sell their wine under the "Gallo" label and have advertised that trademark heavily. Ernest and Julio's younger brother Joseph Gallo runs a company called Gallo Cattle Co. Gallo Cattle begins selling cheese and salami under the name "Gallo Cheese" and "Gallo Salami." If Ernest and Julio Gallo wish to stop their brother from marketing meat and cheese under the Gallo name, what must they be able to show at trial? If they win, how should a court craft the injunction granting relief? What should it forbid?

---

iv.   Opposition

Section 13(a) of the Lanham Act reads in part:

(a) Any person who believes that he would be damaged by the registration of a mark upon the principal register may, upon payment of the prescribed fee, file an opposition in the Patent and Trademark Office, stating the grounds therefor, within thirty days after the publication . . . of the mark sought to be registered.

Because potential opposers must become aware of the contested mark's future registration, opposition is meaningful protection only for firms possessing the resources to conduct frequent searches of the Official Gazette, where prospective trademarks are published.

An opposer must plead and prove that: (1) it is likely to be damaged by registration of the applicant's mark (this is the standing requirement); and (2) that there are valid legal grounds why the applicant is not entitled to register its claimed mark. The opposer is in the plaintiff position, and the applicant is in the defendant position. The opposer has the burden of proving that the applicant has no right to register the contested mark. In general, there has been a trend toward liberalization of the standing requirement. 3 MCCARTHY § 20.02[1][a] (1996). "To establish standing to oppose, the opposer need only be something more than a gratuitous interloper or a vicarious avenger of someone else's rights." *Id.*, at § 20.16.

Once the standing threshold has been crossed, the opposer may rely on any legal ground that negates the applicant's right to registration. *See, e.g., Estate of Biro v. Bic Corp.*, 18 U.S.P.Q.2d 1382 (TTAB 1991). For example, an opposer might argue that the applicant did not make sufficient use of the mark in interstate commerce to receive a use-based registration. Generally, opposers rely on one of the bars to registration described in Lanham Act section 2, with section 2(d) being the most common. Section 2(d) prohibits registration where the applicant's mark so resembles either (1) opposer's registered mark or (2) opposer's prior common law mark or trade name, as to be likely to cause confusion. The test for likelihood of confusion is the same used in general litigation. 3 MCCARTHY, *supra*, at § 20.24. It is described in detail in Chapter V(D)(1).

v.   Cancellation

If opposition is the first "backstop" to ex parte examination of trademarks, cancellation may be thought of as the second. Even after a trademark examiner is satisfied that a mark meets the requirements for registration and the mark is in fact registered, it may still be challenged in an inter partes proceeding. The Lanham Act allows one who "believes that he is or will be damaged by registration" to petition for cancellation of marks on either the Principal or Supplemental Register. Lanham Act § 18. Cancellation petitions are heard by the Trademark Trial and Appeal Board (TTAB). In civil suits where a federally registered mark is at issue, such as suits under Lanham Act § 2, the court may order cancellation of the registration.

The standing requirement for cancellation proceedings is quite similar to that for opposition. In both cases, the statute speaks in terms of the plaintiff's belief that he or she will be damaged.

Even after cancellation of the registration, a mark may still enjoy common law rights. *See, e.g., National Trailways Bus System v. Trailway Van Lines*, 269 F. Supp. 352 (E.D.N.Y. 1965).

vi.   Concurrent Registration

Concurrent use registration is provided for in Lanham Act § 2(d):

No trademark . . . shall be refused registration on the principal register . . . unless it—. . .

> (d) Consists of or comprises a mark which so resembles a mark . . . as to be likely. . . to cause confusion. . . : *Provided,* That if the Director determines that confusion, mistake, or deception is not likely to result from the continued use by more than one person of the same or similar marks under conditions and limitations as to the mode or place of use of the marks or the goods on or in connection with which such marks are used, concurrent registrations may be issued to such persons when they have become entitled to use such marks as a result of their concurrent lawful use in commerce prior to (1) the earliest of the filing dates of the applications pending or of any registration issued under this Act. . . .

Lanham Act § 2(d), 15 U.S.C. § 1052(d). Section 2(d) goes on to say that prior use may be waived by agreement of the parties seeking concurrent registration, and that the commissioner may also issue concurrent use registrations when ordered to do so by a court. *Id.*

The most important condition for approval of concurrent use registration is that such registration cannot be likely to cause confusion of buyers or others. *Application of Beatrice Foods Co.*, 429 F.2d 466 (C.C.P.A. 1970). In *Beatrice,* the senior user (Beatrice) had used a mark in 23 states and the junior user (Fairway) had used a mark in five states by the time the registration hearing commenced. Both had filed registration applications, and a concurrent use proceeding was instituted. The court established the general rule that the senior user can be awarded registration covering all parts of the United States except those regions where the subsequent (junior) user can establish existing rights in its actual area of use or zones of natural expansion. The junior user must show that confusion is not likely to result from the concurrent registration. The court then recognized three exceptions to this general rule: (1) the PTO is not required to grant registration contrary to an agreement between the parties that leaves some territory open; (2) where the junior user is the first to obtain federal registration, the junior user obtains nationwide rights subject only to the territorial limitations of the senior user (*See, e.g., Wiener King, Inc. v. Weiner King Corp.*, 615 F.2d 512 (C.C.P.A. 1980) (junior user who registered first and expanded after discovering the senior user was entitled to registration covering the entire United States with the exception of a small enclave encompassing the senior user's territory)); and (3) areas of mutual nonuse may be maintained if the mark, goods, and territories are such that this is the only way to avoid the likelihood of confusion.

COMMENTS AND QUESTIONS

Should an agreement settling a dispute between parties seeking concurrent registration—hence carving up the nation into exclusive territories—be scrutinized for antitrust issues? *See VMG Enters. Inc. v. F. Quesada & Franco Inc.*, 788 F. Supp. 648 (D.P.R. 1992). Absent intellectual property rights, an agreement among competitors to divide up markets would be illegal per se. *See Palmer v. BRG of Georgia*, 498 U.S. 46 (1990).

4. Incontestability

Park 'N Fly, Inc. v. Dollar Park and Fly, Inc.
Supreme Court of the United States
469 U.S. 189 (1985)

JUSTICE O'Connor delivered the opinion of the Court.

In this case we consider whether an action to enjoin the infringement of an incontestable trade or service mark may be defended on the grounds that the mark is merely descriptive. We conclude that neither the language of the relevant statutes nor the legislative history supports such a defense.

I

Petitioner operates long-term parking lots near airports. After starting business in St. Louis in 1967, petitioner subsequently opened facilities in Cleveland, Houston, Boston, Memphis, and San Francisco. Petitioner applied in 1969 to the United States Patent and Trademark Office (Patent Office) to register a service mark consisting of the logo of an airplane and the words "Park 'N Fly." The registration issued in August 1971. Nearly six years later, petitioner filed an affidavit with the Patent Office to establish the incontestable status of the mark. As required by § 15 of the Trademark Act of 1946 (Lanham Act), 60 Stat. 433, as amended, 15 U.S.C. § 1065, the affidavit stated that the mark had been registered and in continuous use for five consecutive years, that there had been no final adverse decision to petitioner's claim of ownership or right to registration, and that no proceedings involving such rights were pending. Incontestable status provides, subject to the provisions of § 15 and § 33(b) of the Lanham Act, "conclusive evidence of the registrant's exclusive right to use the registered mark. . . ." § 33(b), 15 U.S.C. § 1115(b).

Respondent also provides long-term airport parking services, but only has operations in Portland, Oregon. Respondent calls its business "Dollar Park and Fly." Petitioner filed this infringement action in 1978 in the United States District Court for the District of Oregon and requested the court permanently to enjoin respondent from using the words "Park and Fly" in connection with its business. Respondent counterclaimed and sought cancellation of petitioner's mark on the grounds that it is a generic term. *See* § 14(c), 15 U.S.C. § 1064(c). Respondent also argued that petitioner's mark is unenforceable because it is merely descriptive. *See* § 2(e), 15 U.S.C. § 1052(e). As two additional defenses, respondent maintained that it is in privity with a Seattle corporation that has used the expression "Park and Fly" since a date prior to the registration of petitioner's mark, *see* § 33(b)(5), 15 U.S.C. § 1115(b)(5), and that it has not infringed because there is no likelihood of confusion. *See* § 32(1), 15 U.S.C. § 1114(1). . . .

II

. . . This case requires us to consider the effect of the incontestability provisions of the Lanham Act in the context of an infringement action defended on the grounds that the mark is merely descriptive. Statutory construction must begin with the language employed by Congress and the assumption that the ordinary meaning of that language accurately expresses the legislative purpose. *See American Tobacco Co. v. Patterson*, 456 U.S. 63, 68 (1982). With respect to incontestable trade or service marks, § 33(b) of the Lanham Act states that "registration shall be conclusive evidence of the registrant's exclusive right to use the registered mark" subject to the conditions of § 15 and certain enumerated defenses. Section 15 incorporates by reference subsections (c) and (e) of § 14, 15 U.S.C. § 1064. An incontestable mark that becomes generic may be canceled at any time pursuant to § 14(c). That section also allows cancellation of an incontestable mark at any time if it has been abandoned, if it is being used to misrepresent the source of the goods or services in connection with which it is used, or if it was obtained fraudulently or contrary to the provisions of § 4, 15 U.S.C. § 1054, or §§ 2(a)–(c), 15 U.S.C. §§ 1052(a)–(c). . . .

The language of the Lanham Act also refutes any conclusion that an incontestable mark may be challenged as merely descriptive. A mark that is merely descriptive of an applicant's goods or services is not registrable unless the mark has secondary meaning. Before a mark achieves incontestable status, registration provides prima facie evidence of the registrant's exclusive right to use the mark in commerce. § 33(a), 15 U.S.C. § 1115(a). The Lanham Act expressly provides that before a mark becomes incontestable an opposing party may prove any legal or equitable defense which might have been asserted if the mark had not been registered. *Ibid.* Thus, § 33(a) would have allowed respondent to challenge petitioner's mark as merely descriptive if the mark had not become incontestable. With respect to incontestable marks, however, § 33(b) provides that registration is conclusive evidence of the registrant's exclusive right to use the mark, subject to the conditions of § 15 and the seven defenses enumerated in § 33(b) itself. Mere descriptiveness is not recognized by either § 15 or § 33(b) as a basis for challenging an incontestable mark.

The statutory provisions that prohibit registration of a merely descriptive mark but do not allow an incontestable mark to be challenged on this ground cannot be attributed to inadvertence by Congress. The Conference Committee rejected an amendment that would have denied registration to any descriptive mark, and instead retained the provisions allowing registration of a merely descriptive mark that has acquired secondary meaning. *See* H.R. CONF. REP. NO. 2322, 79th Cong., 2d Sess., 4 (1946) (explanatory statement of House managers). The Conference Committee agreed to an amendment providing that no incontestable right can be acquired in a mark that is a common descriptive, i.e., generic, term. *Id.*, at 5. Congress could easily have denied incontestability to merely descriptive marks as well as to generic marks had that been its intention.

The Court of Appeals in discussing the offensive/defensive distinction observed that incontestability protects a registrant against cancellation of his mark. 718 F.2d, at 331. This observation is incorrect with respect to marks that become generic or which otherwise may be canceled at any time pursuant to §§ 14(c) and (e). Moreover, as applied to marks that are merely descriptive, the approach of the Court of Appeals makes incontestable status superfluous. Without regard to its incontestable status, a mark that has been registered five years is protected from cancellation except on the grounds stated in §§ 14(c) and (e). Pursuant to § 14, a mark may be canceled on the grounds that it is merely descriptive only if the petition to cancel is filed within five years of the date of registration. § 14(a), 15 U.S.C. § 1064(a). The approach adopted by the Court of Appeals implies that incontestability adds nothing to the protections against cancellation already provided in § 14. The decision below not only lacks support in the words of the statute; it effectively emasculates § 33(b) under the circumstances of this case.

VI

We conclude that the holder of a registered mark may rely on incontestability to enjoin infringement and that such an action may not be defended on the grounds that the mark is merely descriptive. Respondent urges that we nevertheless affirm the decision below based on the "prior use" defense recognized by § 33(b)(5) of the Lanham Act. Alternatively, respondent argues that there is no likelihood of confusion and therefore no infringement justifying injunctive relief. The District Court rejected each of these arguments, but they were not addressed by the Court of Appeals. 718 F.2d, at 331–332, n.4. That court may consider them on remand. The judgment of the Court of Appeals is reversed, and the case is remanded for further proceedings consistent with this opinion. It is so ordered.

Justice STEVENS, dissenting.

In trademark law, the term "incontestable" is itself somewhat confusing and misleading because the Lanham Act expressly identifies over 20 situations in which infringement of an allegedly incontestable mark is permitted.[1] Moreover, in § 37 of the Act, Congress unambiguously authorized judicial review of the validity of the registration "in any action involving a registered mark." The problem in this case arises because

---

[1] Section 33(b) enumerates seven categories of defenses to an action to enforce an incontestable mark. *See* 15 U.S.C. § 1115(b), quoted ante, at 3, n.1. In addition, a defendant is free to argue that a mark should never have become incontestable for any of the four reasons enumerated in § 15. 15 U.S.C. § 1065. Moreover, § 15 expressly provides that an incontestable mark may be challenged on any of the grounds set forth in subsections (c) and (e) of § 14, 15 U.S.C. § 1064, and those sections, in turn, incorporate the objections to registrability that are defined in §§ 2(a), 2(b), and 2(c) of the Act. 15 U.S.C. §§ 1052(a), (b), and (c).

of petitioner's attempt to enforce as "incontestable" a mark that Congress has plainly stated is inherently unregistrable.

The mark "Park 'N Fly" is at best merely descriptive in the context of airport parking.[3] Section 2 of the Lanham Act plainly prohibits the registration of such a mark unless the applicant proves to the Commissioner of the Patent and Trademark Office that the mark "has become distinctive of the applicant's goods in commerce," or to use the accepted shorthand, that it has acquired a "secondary meaning." *See* 15 U.S.C. §§ 1052(e), (f). Petitioner never submitted any such proof to the Commissioner, or indeed to the District Court in this case. Thus, the registration plainly violated the Act.

The violation of the literal wording of the Act also contravened the central purpose of the entire legislative scheme. Statutory protection for trademarks was granted in order to safeguard the goodwill that is associated with particular enterprises. A mark must perform the function of distinguishing the producer or provider of a good or service in order to have any legitimate claim to protection. A merely descriptive mark that has not acquired secondary meaning does not perform that function because it simply "describes the qualities or characteristics of a good or service." No legislative purpose is served by granting anyone a monopoly in the use of such a mark. . . .

The word "incontestable" is not defined in the Act. Nor, surprisingly, is the concept explained in the Committee Reports on the bill that was enacted in 1946. The word itself implies that it was intended to resolve potential contests between rival claimants to a particular mark. And, indeed, the testimony of the proponents of the concept in the Committee hearings that occurred from time to time during the period when this legislation was being considered reveals that they were primarily concerned with the problem that potential contests over the ownership of registrable marks might present. No one ever suggested that any public purpose would be served by granting incontestable status to a mark that should never have been accepted for registration in the first instance.

COMMENTS AND QUESTIONS

1. Why should marks be allowed to become incontestable? Does this privilege reflect a judgment that judicial review of trademarks is unnecessary after a certain time? That the Trademark Office can be trusted to make the right decision in an ex parte proceeding? Certainly, no similar right is afforded the holders of patents, even though they

---

[3] In the Court of Appeals petitioner argued that its mark was suggestive with respect to airport parking lots. The Court of Appeals responded: "We are unpersuaded. Given the clarity of its first word, Park 'N Fly's mark seen in context can be understood readily by consumers as an offering of airport parking—imagination, thought, or perception is not needed. Simply understood, 'park and fly' is a clear and concise description of a characteristic or ingredient of the service offered—the customer parks his car and flies from the airport. We conclude that Park 'N Fly's mark used in the context of airport parking is, at best, a merely descriptive mark." 718 F.2d 327, 331 (CA9 1983). Although the Court appears to speculate that even though the mark is now merely descriptive it might not have been merely descriptive in 1971 when it was first registered. . . . I find such speculation totally unpersuasive. But even if the Court's speculation were valid, the entire rationale of its opinion is based on the assumption that the mark is in the "merely descriptive" category.

are in some sense a "stronger" intellectual property right. Professor Kenneth Port has advocated abolition of trademark incontestability. *See* Kenneth L. Port, *The Illegitimacy of Trademark Incontestability*, 26 IND. L. REV. 519 (1993). Professor Port reasons that trademark incontestability creates what is in effect a property right in trademarks, since 15 U.S.C. § 1115(b) speaks of a conclusive presumption of the trademark holder's "ownership of the mark." (Certainly, the Court's "quiet title" rationale smacks of real property law.) This property right, he asserts, is inconsistent with general principles of trademark law. He explains:

> Patent and copyright owners enjoy the "bundle of rights" notion of property. Their rights are divisible, freely alienable, and exclusive for the duration of statutory protection.
>
> Trademarks, on the other hand, enjoy none of the "bundle of rights" that other forms of property enjoy. Trademark holders possess only the right to exclude others from using that specific trademark on similar goods. Holders of marks possess the right to protect the sphere of interest in which they are using the mark by excluding others, but nothing more. Mark holders do not possess a property right in the mark itself, because trademarks are nothing when devoid of the goodwill they have come to represent or the product on which they are used.

26 IND. L. REV. at 553. Is this a fair criticism?

2. How does the dissent in *Park 'N Fly* deal with the majority's argument that "incontestability" would be worthless if a trademark holder could not use it to enforce his rights against an infringer? Is Justice Stevens's argument persuasive? If the owner of a descriptive mark improperly registered is not entitled to judicial enforcement of his "incontestable" trademark, why should he be entitled to Customs assistance in stopping the importation of goods? To registration of the invalid trademark in other countries? Further, why have incontestability at all? Wouldn't the legal system be better served by a rule that improperly issued trademarks could be cancelled at any time? Note that because generic trademarks can be challenged at any time, incontestable status makes the line between descriptive and generic trademarks even more important than usual. *See, e.g., Tiffany & Co. v. Costco Wholesale Corp.*, 994 F. Supp. 2d 474, 479 (S.D.N.Y. 2014) (refusing to grant summary judgment on question of whether incontestable mark is generic).

This debate was resurrected in *Shakespeare Co. v. Silstar Corp.*, 9 F.3d 1091 (4th Cir. 1993). There, the District Court cancelled plaintiff's registration for a color scheme on a fishing rod on the grounds that it was functional (apparently because it helped to catch fish). The Fourth Circuit reversed, noting that the mark had become incontestable and holding that incontestable marks cannot be cancelled for functionality because functionality was not specifically enumerated in section 1064. The dissent argued that federal courts should not enforce the mark, even if they could not cancel it.

The functionality problem raises an interesting question about incontestability. What happens when trade dress which is initially not functional *becomes* functional over time? (This may happen because of widespread adoption of the owner's trade dress. For example, a computer graphical user interface (GUI) may become so familiar to so many users that it becomes a "standard" in the industry, and it is a commercial advantage to use the standard product.) Would trademark defendants lose *any* opportunity to defeat the mark on functionality grounds? Apparently concerned by the result in *Shakespeare*, Congress revised the Lanham Act in 1998 to provide that functionality may be asserted even against an "incontestable" mark. 15 U.S.C. § 1064(3).

3. Note that the presumptions afforded registered trademarks differ in several ways from those given to issued patents. Registered trademarks, while entitled to a presumption of validity, are not entitled to the benefit of the "clear and convincing evidence" rule applied in patent cases. At the same time, there is no provision for incontestability of patents after a certain number of years. Is there any reason for these differing presumptions?

4. Patent law gives inventors no rights at all unless the Patent Office issues them a patent. By contrast, copyright law gives full protection to unregistered works as soon as they are created, and there are current legislative efforts to abolish the Copyright Office entirely. Trademark law appears to fall somewhere in between. Trademark owners are entitled to protection without registration, but there are still substantial benefits to registering a trademark. Can you think of any reason for the different administrative schemes? Which is preferable?

D. TRADEMARK LIABILITY ANALYSIS

The Lanham Act imposes liability on those who:

- create a likelihood of confusion (§ 32, 15 U.S.C. § 1114 (registered marks); § 43(a)(1), 15 U.S.C. § 1125(a)(1) (registered or unregistered marks);
- create a likelihood of dilution (§ 43(c), 15 U.S.C. § 1125(c));
- cybersquat (§ 43(d), 15 U.S.C. § 1125(d)); or
- engage in false advertising (§ 43(a)(1), 15 U.S.C. § 1125(a)(1)).

As noted at the outset of this chapter, the entire federal trademark protection scheme turns on use in commerce. Thus, we begin treatment of trademark liability analysis with the threshold issue of trademark use. We then turn to the specifics of each form of trademark liability.

1. Threshold Issue: Trademark Use

As we saw in earlier, a trademark owner must use a mark in commerce to establish rights in the mark. This follows from the Lanham Act's grounding in the Constitution's Commerce Clause. The concept of "use in commerce" also arises in proving trademark infringement. Both § 32 (relating to registered marks) and § 43(a) (relating to registered and unregistered marks) impose liability on those who "use [a protected mark] in commerce" "on or in connection with" goods and services.

In the definitions section, the Lanham Act provides:

The term "use in commerce" means the bona fide use of a mark in the ordinary course of trade, and not made merely to reserve a right in a mark. For purposes of this chapter, a mark shall be deemed to be in use in commerce—

(1) on goods when—

(A) it is placed in any manner on the goods or their containers or the dis-plays associated therewith or on the tags or labels affixed thereto, or if the nature of the goods makes such placement impracticable, then on documents associated with the goods or their sale, and

(B) the goods are sold or transported in commerce, and

(2) on services when it is used or displayed in the sale or advertising of services and the services are rendered in commerce, or the services are rendered in more than one State or in the United States and a foreign country and the person rendering the services is engaged in commerce in connection with the services.

Lanham Act § 45, 15 U.S.C. § 1127.

Traditional use of a mark by a defendant occurs when the defendant brands its own goods with a mark alleged to be too similar to the plaintiff's. But trademark owners are increasingly filing suit against a variety of other ways a defendant might employ a mark: mentioning it in a song or book, for instance, depicting it on a T-shirt, discussing it in a news article, or even teaching a trademark class. Are these uses "on or in connection with" the provision of goods and services? Or is there a requirement that the defendant use the plaintiff's mark as a mark?

Rescuecom Corp. v. Google, Inc.
United States Court of Appeals for the Second Circuit
562 F.3d 123 (2d Cir. 2009)

LEVAL, Circuit Judge:

. . .

Background

As this appeal follows the grant of a motion to dismiss, we must take as true the facts alleged in the Complaint and draw all reasonable inferences in favor of Rescuecom. Rescuecom is a national computer service franchising company that offers on-site computer services and sales. Rescuecom conducts a substantial amount of business over the Internet and receives between 17,000 to 30,000 visitors to its website each month. It also advertises over the Internet, using many web-based services, including those offered by Google. Since 1998, "Rescuecom" has been a registered federal trademark, and there is no dispute as to its validity.

Google operates a popular Internet search engine, which users access by visiting www.google.com. Using Google's website, a person searching for the website of a particular entity in trade (or simply for information about it) can enter that entity's name or trademark into Google's search engine and launch a search. Google's proprietary system responds to such a search request in two ways. First, Google provides a list of links to websites, ordered in what Google deems to be of descending relevance to the user's search terms based on its proprietary algorithms. Google's search engine assists the public not only in obtaining information about a provider, but also in purchasing products and services. If a prospective purchaser, looking for goods or services of a particular provider, enters the provider's trademark as a search term on Google's website and clicks to activate a search, within seconds, the Google search engine will provide on the searcher's computer screen a link to the webpage maintained by that provider (as well as a host of other links to sites that Google's program determines to be relevant to the search term entered). By clicking on the link of the provider, the searcher will be directed to the provider's website, where the searcher can obtain information supplied by the provider about its products and services and can perhaps also make purchases from the provider by placing orders.

The second way Google responds to a search request is by showing context-based advertising. When a searcher uses Google's search engine by submitting a search term, Google may place advertisements on the user's screen. Google will do so if an advertiser, having determined that its ad is likely to be of interest to a searcher who enters the particular term, has purchased from Google the placement of its ad on the screen of the searcher who entered that search term. What Google places on the searcher's screen is more than simply an advertisement. It is also a link to the advertiser's website, so that in response to such an ad, if the searcher clicks on the link, he will open the advertiser's website, which offers not only additional information about the advertiser, but also perhaps the option to purchase the goods and services of the advertiser over the Internet. Google uses at least two programs to offer such context-based links: AdWords and Keyword Suggestion Tool.

AdWords is Google's program through which advertisers purchase terms (or keywords). When entered as a search term, the keyword triggers the appearance of the advertiser's ad and link. An advertiser's purchase of a particular term causes the advertiser's ad and link to be displayed on the user's screen whenever a searcher launches a Google search based on the purchased search term. Advertisers pay Google based on the number of times Internet users "click" on the advertisement, so as to link to the advertiser's website. For example, using Google's AdWords, Company Y, a company engaged in the business of furnace repair, can cause Google to display its advertisement and link whenever a user of Google launches a search based on the search term, "furnace repair." Company Y can also cause its ad and link to appear whenever a user searches for the term "Company X," a competitor of Company Y in the furnace repair business.

Thus, whenever a searcher interested in purchasing furnace repair services from Company X launches a search of the term X (Company X's trademark), an ad and link would appear on the searcher's screen, inviting the searcher to the furnace repair services of X's competitor, Company Y. And if the searcher clicked on Company Y's link, Company Y's website would open on the searcher's screen, and the searcher might be able to order or purchase Company Y's furnace repair services.

In addition to Adwords, Google also employs Keyword Suggestion Tool, a program that recommends keywords to advertisers to be purchased. The program is designed to improve the effectiveness of advertising by helping advertisers identify keywords related to their area of commerce, resulting in the placement of their ads before users who are likely to be responsive to it. Thus, continuing the example given above, if Company Y employed Google's Keyword Suggestion Tool, the Tool might suggest to Company Y that it purchase not only the term "furnace repair" but also the term "X," its competitor's brand name and trademark, so that Y's ad would appear on the screen of a searcher who searched Company X's trademark, seeking Company X's website.

Once an advertiser buys a particular keyword, Google links the keyword to that advertiser's advertisement. The advertisements consist of a combination of content and a link to the advertiser's webpage. Google displays these advertisements on the search result page either in the right margin or in a horizontal band immediately above the column of relevance-based search results. These advertisements are generally associated with a label, which says "sponsored link." Rescuecom alleges, however, that a user might easily be misled to believe that the advertisements which appear on the screen are in fact part of the relevance-based search result and that the appearance of a competitor's ad and link in response to a searcher's search for Rescuecom is likely to cause trademark confusion as to affiliation, origin, sponsorship, or approval of service. This can occur, according to the Complaint, because Google fails to label the ads in a manner which would clearly identify them as purchased ads rather than search results. The Complaint alleges that when the sponsored links appear in a horizontal bar at the top of the search results, they may appear to the searcher to be the first, and therefore the most relevant, entries responding to the search, as opposed to paid advertisements.

Google's objective in its AdWords and Keyword Suggestion Tool programs is to sell keywords to advertisers. Rescuecom alleges that Google makes 97% of its revenue from selling advertisements through its AdWords program. Google therefore has an economic incentive to increase the number of advertisements and links that appear for every term entered into its search engine.

Many of Rescuecom's competitors advertise on the Internet. Through its Keyword Suggestion Tool, Google has recommended the Rescuecom trademark to Rescuecom's competitors as a search term to be purchased. Rescuecom's competitors, some responding to Google's recommendation, have purchased Rescuecom's trademark as a keyword in Google's AdWords program, so that whenever a user launches a search for the term "Rescuecom," seeking to be connected to Rescuecom's website, the competitors' advertisement and link will appear on the searcher's screen. This practice allegedly allows

Rescuecom's competitors to deceive and divert users searching for Rescuecom's website. According to Rescuecom's allegations, when a Google user launches a search for the term "Rescuecom" because the searcher wishes to purchase Rescuecom's services, links to websites of its competitors will appear on the searcher's screen in a manner likely to cause the searcher to believe mistakenly that a competitor's advertisement (and website link) is sponsored by, endorsed by, approved by, or affiliated with Rescuecom.

The District Court granted Google's 12(b)(6) motion and dismissed Rescuecom's claims. . . . The district court explained its decision saying that even if Google employed Rescuecom's mark in a manner likely to cause confusion or deceive searchers into believing that competitors are affiliated with Rescuecom and its mark, so that they believe the services of Rescuecom's competitors are those of Rescuecom, Google's actions are not a "use in commerce" under the Lanham Act because the competitor's advertisements triggered by Google's programs did not exhibit Rescuecom's trademark. The court rejected the argument that Google "used" Rescuecom's mark in recommending and selling it as a keyword to trigger competitor's advertisements because the court read *1-800* to compel the conclusion that this was an internal use and therefore cannot be a "use in commerce" under the Lanham Act.

Discussion

. . .

I.   Google's Use of Rescuecom's Mark Was a "Use in Commerce"

. . . Sections 32 and 43 of the Act, which we also refer to by their codified designations, 15 U.S.C. §§ 1114 & 1125, *inter alia*, impose liability for unpermitted "use in commerce" of another's mark which is "likely to cause confusion, or to cause mistake, or to deceive," § 1114, "as to the affiliation . . . or as to the origin, sponsorship or approval of his or her goods [or] services . . . by another person." § 1125(a)(1)(A). . . . [The definition of the term "use in commerce" in § 45] provides in part that "a mark shall be deemed to be in use in commerce . . . (2) on services when it is used or displayed in the sale or advertising of services and the services are rendered in commerce." 15 U.S.C. § 1127. Our court found that the plaintiff failed to show that the defendant made a "use in commerce" of the plaintiff's mark, within that definition.

. . . [W]hat Google is recommending and selling to its advertisers is Rescuecom's trademark. Second, . . . Google displays, offers, and sells Rescuecom's mark to Google's advertising customers when selling its advertising services. In addition, Google encourages the purchase of Rescuecom's mark through its Keyword Suggestion Tool. Google's utilization of Rescuecom's mark fits literally within the terms specified by 15 U.S.C. § 1127. According to the Complaint, Google uses and sells Rescuecom's mark "in the sale . . . of [Google's advertising] services . . . rendered in commerce." § 1127.

Google, supported by amici, argues that . . . the inclusion of a trademark in an internal computer directory cannot constitute trademark use. Several district court decisions in this Circuit appear to have reached this conclusion. *See e.g.*, *S&L Vitamins, Inc.*

v. Australian Gold, Inc., 521 F. Supp. 2d 188, 199–202 (E.D.N.Y. 2007) (holding that use of a trademark in metadata did not constitute trademark use within the meaning of the Lanham Act because the use "is strictly internal and not communicated to the public") . . . [R]egardless of whether Google's use of Rescuecom's mark in its internal search algorithm could constitute an actionable trademark use, Google's recommendation and sale of Rescuecom's mark to its advertising customers are not internal uses. . . . If we were to adopt Google and its amici's argument, the operators of search engines would be free to use trademarks in ways designed to deceive and cause consumer confusion.[4] This is surely neither within the intention nor the letter of the Lanham Act.

Google and its amici contend further that its use of the Rescuecom trademark is no different from that of a retail vendor who uses "product placement" to allow one vender to benefit from a competitors' name recognition. An example of product placement occurs when a store-brand generic product is placed next to a trademarked product to induce a customer who specifically sought out the trademarked product to consider the typically less expensive, generic brand as an alternative. Google's argument misses the point. From the fact that proper, non-deceptive product placement does not result in liability under the Lanham Act, it does not follow that the label "product placement" is a magic shield against liability, so that even a deceptive plan of product placement designed to confuse consumers would similarly escape liability. It is not by reason of absence of a use of a mark in commerce that benign product placement escapes liability; it escapes liability because it is a benign practice which does not cause a likelihood of consumer confusion. In contrast, if a retail seller were to be paid by an off-brand purveyor to arrange product display and delivery in such a way that customers seeking to purchase a famous brand would receive the off-brand, believing they had gotten the brand they were seeking, we see no reason to believe the practice would escape liability merely because it could claim the mantle of "product placement." The practices attributed to Google by the Complaint, which at this stage we must accept as true, are significantly different from benign product placement that does not violate the Act.

. . . [T]he practices here attributed to Google by Rescuecom's complaint are that Google has made use in commerce of Rescuecom's mark. Needless to say, a defendant must do more than use another's mark in commerce to violate the Lanham Act. The gist of a Lanham Act violation is an unauthorized use, which "is likely to cause confusion, or to cause mistake, or to deceive as to the affiliation, . . . or as to the origin, sponsorship, or approval of . . . goods [or] services." *See* 15 U.S.C. § 1125(a). We have no idea whether Rescuecom can prove that Google's use of Rescuecom's trademark in its AdWords program causes likelihood of confusion or mistake. Rescuecom has alleged that

---

[4] For example, instead of having a separate "sponsored links" or paid advertisement section, search engines could allow advertisers to pay to appear at the top of the "relevance" list based on a user entering a competitor's trademark—a functionality that would be highly likely to cause consumer confusion. Alternatively, sellers of products or services could pay to have the operators of search engines automatically divert users to their website when the users enter a competitor's trademark as a search term. Such conduct is surely not beyond judicial review merely because it is engineered through the internal workings of a computer program.

it does, in that would-be purchasers (or explorers) of its services who search for its website on Google are misleadingly directed to the ads and websites of its competitors in a manner which leads them to believe mistakenly that these ads or websites are sponsored by, or affiliated with Rescuecom. This is particularly so, Rescuecom alleges, when the advertiser's link appears in a horizontal band at the top of the list of search results in a manner which makes it appear to be the most relevant search result and not an advertisement. What Rescuecom alleges is that by the manner of Google's display of sponsored links of competing brands in response to a search for Rescuecom's brand name (which fails adequately to identify the sponsored link as an advertisement, rather than a relevant search result), Google creates a likelihood of consumer confusion as to trademarks. If the searcher sees a different brand name as the top entry in response to the search for "Rescuecom," the searcher is likely to believe mistakenly that the different name which appears is affiliated with the brand name sought in the search and will not suspect, because the fact is not adequately signaled by Google's presentation, that this is not the most relevant response to the search. Whether Google's actual practice is in fact benign or confusing is not for us to judge at this time. We consider at the 12(b)(6) stage only what is alleged in the Complaint. . . .

Conclusion

The judgment of the district court is vacated and the case is remanded for further proceedings.

APPENDIX

On the Meaning of "Use in Commerce" in Sections 32 and 43 of the Lanham Act

[In a detailed examination of the text and legislative history of the Lanham Act, the court concludes that Congress did not intend that the § 45 definition of "use in commerce" to serve as a threshold requirement for pursuing a trademark infringement action.]

. . . When one considers the entire definition of "use in commerce" set forth in § 1127, it becomes plainly apparent that this definition was intended to apply to the Act's use of that term in defining favored conduct, which qualifies to receive the protection of the Act." [By contrast, the term "use in commerce" in §§ 32, 43 to trigger liability was the result of amendments in 1962 and 1988 intended to expand liability.]

The Senate Report for the 1988 amendment confirms that the definition in § [45] was meant to apply only to registering a mark rather than infringing one. The Senate Report explained that the "revised [use in commerce] definition is intended to apply to all aspects of the trademark registration process," and that "[c]learly, however, use of *any type* will continue to be considered in an infringement action." *See* S. Rep. 100-515 100th Cong. at 45 (1988) (emphasis added). This, of course, is consistent with the Lanham Act's intent to make actionable the deceptive and misleading use of marks in commerce-an intent which has not changed since the Lanham Act was first enacted. *See* Lanham Act, 60 Stat. 427, § 45 (1946); 15 U.S.C. § 1127. According to the Senate Report, a purpose in amending this section was to add "a reference to make clear that the section applies only to acts or practices which occur in [or] affect commerce." *See* S. Rep. 100-515 100th Cong. at 41 (1988). The amendment left only one reference to commerce in § 1125(a), which was the "uses in commerce" language. This term was thus employed in the 1988 revision to make clear that liability would be imposed for acts that occur in or affect commerce, i.e. those within Congress's Commerce Clause power. Thus, the term "uses in commerce" in the current § [43](a) is intended to refer to a use that falls within Congress's commerce power, and not to the restrictive definition of "use in commerce," set forth in § 45 to define standards of qualification for an owner to register a mark and receive the benefits and protection of the Act.

It therefore appears that the history of the development of the Lanham Act confirms what is also indicated by a common-sense understanding of the provisions. The definition of the term "use in commerce" provided by § [45], was intended to continue to apply, as it did when the definition was conceived in the 1941 bill, to the sections governing qualification for registration and for the benefits of the Act. In that version, the term "use in commerce" did not appear in § 32, which established the elements of liability for infringing upon a federally registered mark. The eventual appearance of that phrase in that section did not represent an intention that the phrase carry the restrictive definition which defined an owner's entitlement to registration. The appearance rather resulted from happenstance pairing of the verb "use" with the term "in commerce," whose purpose is to claim the jurisdictional authority of the Commerce Clause. Section [45], as noted, does not prescribe that its definitions necessarily apply throughout the Act. They apply "unless the contrary is plainly apparent from the context." . . .

COMMENTS AND QUESTIONS

1. The Ninth Circuit has followed *Rescuecom. See Network Automation Inc. v. Advanced Systems Concepts Inc.*, 638 F.3d 1137, 1145 (9th Cir. 2011); *cf.* Graeme Dinwoodie & Mark D. Janis, *Confusion over Use: Contextualism in Trademark Law*, 92 IOWA L. REV. 1597 (2007). In the wake of *Rescuecom*, the Second Circuit has held that a defendant need not use content as a mark at all in order to be liable for trademark infringement. *See Kelly-Brown v. Winfrey*, 717 F.3d 295 (2d Cir. 2013) (Oprah Winfrey could be liable for putting the phrase "Own Your Power" on the cover of her magazine; the phrase was trademarked by the plaintiff for providing motivational services).

By contrast, several other circuits have applied a "trademark use" requirement, though most did so before *Rescuecom. See, e.g., DaimlerChrysler AG v. Bloom*, 315 F.3d 932 (8th Cir. 2003) (holding that a telecommunications company did not use the term "Mercedes" in a trademark sense merely by licensing a vanity phone number that spelled "1-800-MERCEDES" to Mercedes dealers); *Interactive Prods. Corp. v. A2Z Mobile Office Solutions, Inc.*, 326 F.3d 687, 695 (6th Cir. 2003) ("If defendants are only using [plaintiff's] trademark in a 'non-trademark' way—that is, in a way that does not identify the source of a product—then trademark infringement and false designation of origin laws do not apply.")

2. Should it matter that Google is making money by selling ads that appear when a user searches for "rescuecom"? Should it matter what the content of those ads is? Is "trading on the goodwill" associated with a trademark always illegal?

The court distinguishes product placement on grocery store shelves, calling it a "benign" act that is not infringing. How persuasive is this distinction? Does it matter that product makers pay grocery stores to get better shelf placement? To be placed next to their competitors? To print out coupons at the register when customers buy their competitors' products?

3. Professors Stacey Dogan and Mark Lemley argue that the trademark use doctrine serves an important limiting function:

> The speech-oriented objectives of the trademark use doctrine protect more than just intermediaries; they prevent trademark holders from asserting a generalized right to control language, an interest that applies equally—and sometimes especially—when the speaker competes directly with the trademark holder. The trademark use doctrine has broad application—because of it, newspapers aren't liable for using a trademarked term in a headline, even if the use is confusing or misleading. Writers of movies and books aren't liable for using trademarked goods in their stories. Makers of telephone directories aren't liable for putting all the ads for taxi services together on the same page. Marketing surveyors aren't liable for asking people what they think of a competitor's brand-name product. Magazines aren't liable for selling advertisements that relates to the content of their special issues, even when that content involves trademark owners. Gas stations and restaurants aren't liable for locating across the street from an established competitor, trading on the attraction the established company has created or benefiting from the size of the sign the established company has put up. Individuals aren't liable for their use of a trademark in conversation, even in an inaccurate or misleading way (referring to a Puffs brand facial tissue as a "Kleenex," or a competing cola as a "Coke," for example). Generic drug manufacturers aren't liable for placing their drugs near their brand-name equivalents on drug store shelves, and the stores aren't liable for accepting the placement. They may be making money from their "uses" of the trademark, and the uses may be ones the trademark owner objects to, but they are not *trademark* uses and therefore are not within the ambit of the statute.

Stacey L. Dogan & Mark A. Lemley, *Trademarks and Consumer Search Costs on the Internet*, 41 HOUS. L. REV. 777 (2004); *accord* Margreth Barrett, *Internet Trademark Suits and the Demise of Trademark Use*, 39 U.C. DAVIS L. REV. 371 (2006); *but see* 4 J. THOMAS MCCARTHY, TRADEMARKS AND UNFAIR COMPETITION § 11:15:50 (arguing that the doctrine does not exist, and that likelihood of confusion is the only requirement for infringement); Graeme Dinwoodie & Mark D. Janis, *Confusion over Use: Contextualism in Trademark Law*, 92 IOWA L. REV. 1597 (2007).

4. *Nontrademark Use Defense.* As we will see in Chapter V(E)(3)(ii), trademark law provides a nominative fair use defense that insulates certain types of free expression

from trademark liability. Other courts protect parodies from trademark liability using a special test. Some courts have also adopted a test designed to protect expressive uses from trademark liability. But these are individual defenses created by courts to protect particular acts the court considers valuable. Does it make sense for courts to create individual defenses on an ad hoc for particular uses they find desirable rather than a general doctrine that delineates trademark from non-trademark uses?

5. *Defendant's Use "in Connection with the Sale . . . of any Goods or Services."* Michael Kremer was dissatisfied with the hair restoration services performed by Bosley Medical Institute. He acquired the domain www.BosleyMedical.com and posted various items, such as investigative reports and testimonials criticizing Bosley Medical's activities. Bosley Medical sued for trademark infringement, as well as other causes of action. The Ninth Circuit dismissed the claim on the ground that Kremer's use of the Bosley trademark was not in connection with the sale, distribution, or advertising of any goods or services" because the gripe site did not sell or advertise anything. *See Bosley Medical Institute, Inc. v. Kremer*, 403 F.3d 672 (9th Cir. 2005). Is that still true after *Rescuecom*? Why isn't this a "use in commerce" under the Second Circuit's analysis? Would it matter if Kremer sold ads to pay the fees of maintaining the site? *Compare Nissan Motor Co. v. Nissan Comp. Corp.*, 378 F.3d 1002 (9th Cir. 2004) (owner of Nissan Computer Corp. could not use nissan.com to complain about prior trademark suit by Nissan Motor because it also used the site to collect ad revenue).

6. The Court engages in a detailed analysis of the statutory "use in commerce" language. But that language seems directed primarily at establishing that the *plaintiff* has established rights in a mark by using it in commerce. Does it make sense to apply the same language here? Or is the trademark use doctrine a judicially-created one, no different than many other doctrines in trademark law?

2. Trademark Infringement and Related Doctrines

As the principal branch of unfair competition law, the Lanham Act and trademark law more generally encompass a broad range of liability concepts: (i) confusion-based infringement; (ii) dilution; (iii) extension by contract (franchising and merchandising); (iv) domain names and cybersquatting; (v) indirect liability; and (vi) false advertising. Chapter VI covers the related area of right of publicity.

i. *Confusion-Based Infringement*

Growing out of the palming off tort, trademark law has focused on confusingly similar uses of source-identifying terms, images, and product designs. Section *a* presents the general "likelihood of confusion" multi-factor framework for determining direct trademark infringement. Section *b* explores the types of confusion considered: (1) source; (2) sponsorship; and (3) reverse confusion. Section *c* examines the timing of confusion: (1) initial interest; (2) point of sale; and (3) post-sale.

a.   General Multi-Factor "Likelihood of Confusion" Test

AMF Inc. v. Sleekcraft Boats
United States Court of Appeals for the Ninth Circuit
599 F.2d 341 (9th Cir. 1979)

ANDERSON, Circuit Judge.

In this trademark infringement action, the district court, after a brief non-jury trial, found appellant AMF's trademark was valid, but not infringed, and denied AMF's request for injunctive relief.

AMF and appellee Nescher both manufacture recreational boats. AMF uses the mark Slickcraft, and Nescher uses Sleekcraft. The crux of this appeal is whether concurrent use of the two marks is likely to confuse the public. The district judge held that confusion was unlikely. We disagree and remand for entry of a limited injunction.

I.   Facts

AMF's predecessor used the name Slickcraft Boat Company from 1954 to 1969 when it became a division of AMF. The mark Slickcraft was federally registered on April 1, 1969, and has been continuously used since then as a trademark for this line of recreational boats.

Slickcraft boats are distributed and advertised nationally. AMF has authorized over one hundred retail outlets to sell the Slickcraft line. For the years 1966–1974, promotional expenditures for the Slickcraft line averaged approximately $200,000 annually. Gross sales for the same period approached $50,000,000.

After several years in the boatbuilding business, appellee Nescher organized a sole proprietorship, Nescher Boats, in 1962. This venture failed in 1967. In late 1968 Nescher began anew and adopted the name Sleekcraft. Since then Sleekcraft has been the Nescher trademark. The name Sleekcraft was selected without knowledge of appellant's use. After AMF notified him of the alleged trademark infringement, Nescher adopted a distinctive logo and added the identifying phrase "Boats by Nescher" on plaques affixed to the boat and in much of its advertising. The Sleekcraft mark still appears alone on some of appellee's stationery, signs, trucks, and advertisements.

The Sleekcraft venture succeeded. Expenditures for promotion increased from $6,800 in 1970 to $126,000 in 1974. Gross sales rose from $331,000 in 1970 to over $6,000,000 in 1975. Like AMF, Nescher sells his boats through authorized local dealers.

Slickcraft boats are advertised primarily in magazines of general circulation. Nescher advertises primarily in publications for boat racing enthusiasts. Both parties exhibit their product line at boat shows, sometimes the same show. . . .

IV.   Likelihood of Confusion

When the goods produced by the alleged infringer compete for sales with those of the trademark owner, infringement usually will be found if the marks are sufficiently similar that confusion can be expected.[9] When the goods are related,[10] but not competitive, several other factors are added to the calculus. If the goods are totally unrelated, there can be no infringement because confusion is unlikely.

AMF contends these boat lines are competitive. Both lines are comprised of sporty, fiberglass boats often used for water skiing; the sizes of the boats are similar as are the prices. Nescher contends his boats are not competitive with Slickcraft boats because his are true high performance boats intended for racing enthusiasts.

The district court found that although there was some overlap in potential customers for the two product lines, the boats "appeal to separate sub-markets." Slickcraft boats are for general family recreation, and Sleekcraft boats are for persons who want high speed recreation; thus, the district court concluded, competition between the lines is negligible. Our research has led us to only one case in which a similarly fine distinction in markets has been recognized, *Sleeper Lounge Co. v. Bell Manufacturing Co.*, 253 F.2d 720 (CA 9 1958). Yet, after careful review of all the exhibits introduced at trial, we are convinced the district court's finding was warranted by the evidence.

The Slickcraft line is designed for a variety of activities: fishing, water skiing, pleasure cruises, and sunbathing. The promotional literature emphasizes family fun. Sleekcraft boats are not for families. They are low-profile racing boats designed for racing, high speed cruises, and water skiing. Seating capacity and luxury are secondary. Unlike the Slickcraft line, handling capability is emphasized. The promotional literature projects an alluring, perhaps flashier, racing image; absent from the pictures are the small children prominently displayed in the Slickcraft brochures.

Even though both boats are designed for towing water skiers, only the highly skilled enthusiast would require the higher speeds the Sleekcraft promises. We therefore affirm the district court's finding that, despite the potential market overlap, the two lines are not competitive. Accordingly, we must consider all the relevant circumstances in assessing the likelihood of confusion. *See Durox Co. v. Duron Paint Manufacturing Co.*, 320 F.2d 882, 885 (CA 4 1963).

V. Factors Relevant to Likelihood of Confusion

In determining whether confusion between related goods is likely, the following factors are relevant:[11]

1. strength of the mark;

2. proximity of the goods;

---

[9] The alleged infringer's intent in adopting the mark is weighed, both as probative evidence of the likelihood of confusion and as an equitable consideration.

[10] Related goods are those "products which would be reasonably thought by the buying public to come from the same source if sold under the same mark." *Standard Brands, Inc. v. Smidler*, 151 F.2d 34, 37 (CA 2 1945). *See Yale Electric Corp. v. Robertson*, 26 F.2d 972 (CA 2 1928).

[11] The list is not exhaustive. Other variables may come into play depending on the particular facts presented. *Triumph Hosiery Mills, Inc. v. Triumph Int'l Corp.*, 308 F.2d 196, 198 (CA 2 1962); RESTATEMENT OF TORTS § 729, Comment a (1938).

3.   similarity of the marks;

4.   evidence of actual confusion;

5.   marketing channels used;

6.   type of goods and the degree of care likely to be exercised by the purchaser;

7.   defendant's intent in selecting the mark; and

8.   likelihood of expansion of the product lines.

1.   Strength of the Mark . . .

[W]e hold that Slickcraft is a suggestive mark when applied to boats. . . . Although appellant's mark is protectable and may have been strengthened by advertising, . . . it is a weak mark entitled to a restricted range of protection. Thus, only if the marks are quite similar, and the goods closely related, will infringement be found. . . .

2.   Proximity of the Goods

For related goods, the danger presented is that the public will mistakenly assume there is an association between the producers of the related goods, though no such association exists. . . . The more likely the public is to make such an association, the less similarity in the marks is requisite to a finding of likelihood of confusion. . . . Thus, less similarity between the marks will suffice when the goods are complementary, . . . the products are sold to the same class of purchasers, . . . or the goods are similar in use and function. . . .

Although these product lines are non-competing, they are extremely close in use and function. In fact, their uses overlap. Both are for recreational boating on bays and lakes. Both are designed for water skiing and speedy cruises. Their functional features, for the most part, are also similar: fiberglass bodies, outboard motors, and open seating for a handful of people. Although the Sleekcraft boat is for higher speed recreation and its refinements support the market distinction the district court made, they are so closely related that a diminished standard of similarity must be applied when comparing the two marks. . . .

3.   Similarity of the Marks

The district court found that "the two marks are easily distinguishable in use either when written or spoken." Again, there is confusion among the cases as to whether review of this finding is subject to the clearly erroneous standard. . . .

Similarity of the marks is tested on three levels: sight, sound, and meaning. . . . Each must be considered as they are encountered in the marketplace. Although similarity is measured by the marks as entities, similarities weigh more heavily than differences. . . .

Standing alone the words Sleekcraft and Slickcraft are the same except for two inconspicuous letters in the middle of the first syllable. . . . To the eye, the words are similar.

In support of the district court's finding, Nescher points out that the distinctive logo on his boats and brochures negates the similarity of the words. We agree: the names appear dissimilar when viewed in conjunction with the logo, but the logo is often absent. The exhibits show that the word Sleekcraft is frequently found alone in trade journals, company stationery, and various advertisements.

Nescher also points out that the Slickcraft name is usually accompanied by the additional trademark AMF. As a result of this consistent use, Nescher argues, AMF has become the salient part of the mark indicative of the product's origin. . . .

Although Nescher is correct in asserting that use of a housemark can reduce the likelihood of confusion, . . . the effect is negligible here even though AMF is a well-known house name for recreational equipment. The exhibits show that the AMF mark is down-played in the brochures and advertisements; the letters AMF are smaller and skewed to one side. Throughout the promotional materials, the emphasis is on the Slickcraft name. Accordingly, we find that Slickcraft is the more conspicuous mark and serves to indicate the source of origin to the public. . . .

Sound is also important because reputation is often conveyed word-of-mouth. We recognize that the two sounds can be distinguishable, but the difference is only in a small part of one syllable. In *G. D. Searle & Co. v. Chas. Pfizer & Co.*, 265 F.2d 385 (CA 7 1959), the court reversed the trial court's finding that Bonamine sounded "unlike" Dramamine, stating that: "Slight differences in the sound of trademarks will not protect the infringer." *Id.* at 387. The difference here is even slighter. . . .

Neither expert testimony nor survey evidence was introduced below to support the trial court's finding that the marks were easily distinguishable to the eye and the ear. . . . The district judge based his conclusion on a comparison of the marks. After making the same comparison, we are left with a definite and firm conviction that his conclusion is incorrect. . . .

The final criterion reinforces our conclusion. Closeness in meaning can itself substantiate a claim of similarity of trademarks. *See, e.g., S.C. Johnson & Son, Inc. v. Drop Dead Co.*, 210 F. Supp. 816 (S.D. Cal. 1962), *aff'd*, 326 F.2d 87 (1963) (Pledge and Promise). Nescher contends the words are sharply different in meaning. This contention is not convincing; the words are virtual synonyms. WEBSTER'S NEW WORLD DICTIONARY OF THE AMERICAN LANGUAGE 1371 (1966).

Despite the trial court's findings, we hold that the marks are quite similar on all three levels.

4. *Evidence of Actual Confusion*

Evidence that use of the two marks has already led to confusion is persuasive proof that future confusion is likely. . . . Proving actual confusion is difficult, however, . . . and the courts have often discounted such evidence because it was unclear or insubstantial. . . .

AMF introduced evidence that confusion had occurred both in the trade and in the mind of the buying public. A substantial showing of confusion among either group might have convinced the trial court that continued use would lead to further confusion. . . .

The district judge found that in light of the number of sales and the extent of the parties' advertising, the amount of past confusion was negligible. We cannot say this finding is clearly erroneous though we might have viewed the evidence more generously.

5. Marketing Channels

Convergent marketing channels increase the likelihood of confusion. . . . There is no evidence in the record that both lines were sold under the same roof except at boat shows; the normal marketing channels used by both AMF and Nescher are, however, parallel. Each sells through authorized retail dealers in diverse localities. The same sales methods are employed. The price ranges are almost identical. Each line is advertised extensively though different national magazines are used; the retail dealers also promote the lines, by participating in smaller boat shows and by advertising in local newspapers and classified telephone directories. Although different submarkets are involved, the general class of boat purchasers exposed to the products overlap.

6. Type of Goods and Purchaser Care

Both parties produce high quality, expensive goods. According to the findings of fact, the boats "are purchased only after thoughtful, careful evaluation of the product and the performance the purchaser expects."

In assessing the likelihood of confusion to the public, the standard used by the courts is the typical buyer exercising ordinary caution. . . . Although the wholly indifferent may be excluded, . . . the standard includes the ignorant and the credulous. . . . When the buyer has expertise in the field, a higher standard is proper though it will not preclude a finding that confusion is likely. . . . Similarly, when the goods are expensive, the buyer can be expected to exercise greater care in his purchases; again, though, confusion may still be likely. . . .

The parties vigorously dispute the validity of the trial court's finding on how discriminating the average buyer actually is. Although AMF presented expert testimony to the contrary, the court's finding is amply supported by the record. The care exercised by the typical purchaser, though it might virtually eliminate mistaken purchases, does not guarantee that confusion as to association or sponsorship is unlikely.

The district court also found that trademarks are unimportant to the average boat buyer. Common sense and the evidence indicate this is not the type of purchase made only on "general impressions." . . . This inattention to trade symbols does reduce the possibilities for confusion. . . .

The high quality of defendant's boats is also relevant in another way. The hallmark of a trademark owner's interest in preventing use of his mark on related goods is the threat such use poses to the reputation of his own goods. . . . When the alleged infringer's goods are of equal quality, there is little harm to the reputation earned by the trademarked goods. Yet this is no defense, for present quality is no assurance of continued quality. . . . The wrong inheres in involuntarily entrusting one's business reputation to another business. . . . AMF, of course, cannot control the quality of Sleekcraft boats. . . . [Indeed, e]quivalence in quality may actually contribute to the assumption of a common connection.

7. Intent

The district judge found that Nescher was unaware of appellant's use of the Slickcraft mark when he adopted the Sleekcraft name. There was no evidence that anyone attempted to palm off the latter boats for the former. And after notification of the purported infringement, Nescher designed a distinctive logo. . . . We agree with the district judge: appellee's good faith cannot be questioned.

When the alleged infringer knowingly adopts a mark similar to another's, reviewing courts presume that the defendant can accomplish his purpose: that is, that the public will be deceived. . . . Good faith is less probative of the likelihood of confusion, yet may be given considerable weight in fashioning a remedy.

8. Likelihood of Expansion

Inasmuch as a trademark owner is afforded greater protection against competing goods, a "strong possibility" that either party may expand his business to compete with the other will weigh in favor of finding that the present use is infringing. . . . When goods are closely related, any expansion is likely to result in direct competition. . . . The evidence shows that both parties are diversifying their model lines. The potential that one or both of the parties will enter the other's submarket with a competing model is strong.

VI. Remedy

[A] limited mandatory injunction is warranted. Upon remand the district court should consider the above interests in structuring appropriate relief.

COMMENTS AND QUESTIONS

1. Why did AMF win? Which factor or factors were critical?

2. Each circuit has its own multi-factor test, although the factors largely overlap. *See, e.g., Boston Athletic Ass'n v. Sullivan*, 867 F.2d 22, 29 (1st Cir. 1989); *Pizzeria Uno Corp. v. Temple*, 747 F.2d 1522, 1527 (4th Cir. 1984); *Polaroid Corp. v. Polarad Elecs. Corp.*, 287 F.2d 492, 495 (2d Cir. 1961).

Are all of these factors (however many there may in fact be) equally important? Strength of the mark may obviously be significant for validity purposes as well as for showing likelihood of confusion, but its use in an infringement proceeding presumes that the mark has already been determined valid. Must a plaintiff prove all the factors? Only some of them? Are there some that must be proven in all cases? Conversely, can proof of one factor ever be sufficient by itself? The Ninth Circuit has backed off from its statement in *AMF* that totally dissimilar marks can never be confusing. *See Jada*

Toys, Inc. v. Mattel, Inc., 518 F.3d 628, 633–34 (9th Cir. 2008); *but see Converse, Inc. v. International Trade Comm'n*, 909 F.3d 1110, 1124 (Fed. Cir. 2018) (citing *Versa Prods. Co. v. Bifold Co. (Mfg.)*, 50 F.3d 189, 202 (3d Cir. 1995) ("[S]ubstantial similarity of appearance is necessarily a prerequisite to a finding of likelihood of confusion in product configuration cases.")).

3. An interesting case on proximity of goods (factor 2) is *Death Tobacco, Inc. v. Black Death USA*, 31 U.S.P.Q.2d 1899, 1903 (C.D. Cal. 1993):

> In this case, defendant's ["Black Death"] vodka and plaintiff's ["Death"] cigarettes are related products. They are, to some extent, complementary in that smoking and drinking are related vices that are often undertaken together. They are also somewhat similar in use and function. Cigarettes and vodka both have a mood altering effect and both are used for recreation and relaxation. . . .

> The most important factor in the determination of relatedness, here, is that the two items are sold to the same class of purchasers. Defendant introduced evidence that Black Death vodka and Death cigarettes are sold in the same package stores in both San Francisco and Los Angeles. Several store owners display the two products adjacent to one another on the shelf.

4. Proof of actual confusion among consumers can sometimes be offered anecdotally, particularly where both products have already been in the market for a significant period of time. But confused consumers are difficult to find, and if the infringement is challenged early enough there may not be very many of them at all. In those circumstances, courts generally allow the results of consumer surveys as evidence of "actual" confusion. *See, e.g.*, *Union Carbide v. Ever-Ready, Inc.*, 531 F.2d 366, 387–88 (7th Cir. 1976); *Mutual of Omaha Ins. Co. v. Novak*, 836 F.2d 397, 400–01 (8th Cir. 1987). Because of the importance of actual confusion in proving likelihood of confusion, however, and because of the potential for abuse of the survey process, courts are relatively strict about the surveys they allow, routinely rejecting or discounting surveys that are improperly designed or ask ambiguous or leading questions.

Professor Barton Beebe has shown that survey evidence plays a surprisingly small role in deciding actual cases. *See* Barton Beebe, *An Empirical Study of the Multifactor Tests for Trademark Infringement*, 94 CAL. L. REV. 1581 (2006). The most important factors are similarity of the marks and defendant's intent in choosing a mark.

5. Who must be likely to be confused? Obviously, the strictness with which this test is applied will determine the chances that a trademark plaintiff has of proving infringement. The consumer who is tested is the "reasonably prudent purchaser" of the products at issue. This standard allows for a great deal of flexibility in testing marks used with different products. For example, the reasonably prudent purchaser of fleets of commercial airplanes may be expected both to be more sophisticated and to pay more attention to the decision than the reasonably prudent purchaser of pencils for home use. In light of this, should trademark law offer more protection to the owner of a trademark for

pencils (and thus indirectly to the consumers of pencils) than to the owners of airplane trademarks?

A related question is how many consumers must be likely to be confused. The fact that the reasonably prudent consumer is at issue might suggest that at least half of the consuming public must be confused in order to constitute trademark infringement. After all, if the median consumer is not "reasonable," who is? But courts have not been willing to require such a strong showing from plaintiffs. Instead, likelihood of confusion is regularly found if as few as 10 to 15 percent of the consumers surveyed were confused. Is it reasonable to test infringement on the basis of the reactions of a small minority of the population? If not, how much confusion should be required? *See Mushroom Makers, Inc. v. R.G. Barry Corp.*, 580 F.2d 44, 47 (2d Cir. 1978) (testing the "likelihood that *an appreciable number of ordinarily prudent purchasers* will be misled, or indeed simply confused, as to the source of the goods in question") (emphasis added)).

6. What does it mean for two marks to be similar? The courts generally consider three kinds of similarity—sight, sound, and meaning. (Note that the second, and possibly the third, kind of similarity have little or no relevance to trade dress.) Similarity is generally tested by comparing the marks as a whole, rather than by dissecting them. This approach makes sense since consumers are likely to pay attention to the whole mark in context. On the other hand, dissection is appropriate if the aim is to prevent trademark owners from exercising control over generic, functional, or disclaimed portions of a trademark or trade dress. The trademark owner shouldn't be able to point to similarities between parts of a composite mark that are generic or disclaimed.

Because the perception of the consumer when exposed to the whole mark in context is the linchpin of trademark infringement, a defendant's use of a similar or even identical trademark on similar products may be ameliorated by other differences between the mark and the packaging. For example, similarities in trade dress might not confuse consumers if the packages contain very different product names in large, obvious letters on the front. Disclaimers can also be effective in reducing likelihood of confusion if consumers are likely to notice them. If consumers would nonetheless be confused, however, efforts to ameliorate the effects of similar marks will not avoid trademark infringement.

If the plaintiff holds a family of related marks (such as the use of the "Mc" prefix in various McDonald's products), courts may be more willing to find similarity where the defendant copies the common element in the family. *See Quality Inns v. McDonalds*, 695 F. Supp. 198 (D. Md. 1988) (enjoining McSleep for a cheap hotel chain).

7. What does the defendant's intent have to do with the likelihood that consumers will be confused by the two marks? Certainly, intentional copying is likely to be closer than accidental similarity, and therefore quite possibly more confusing, but isn't that adequately tested by the other factors that the court employs? Has the court slipped in a "fairness" factor to create what is in effect a presumption that counterfeiting (that is, intentional copying of a trademark) is illegal? Or is this factor, like secondary considerations in patent law' nonobviousness doctrine, a form of circumstantial evidence? Is a

presumption of likelihood of confusion where the defendant has intentionally copied a mark appropriate?

8. The fact that a trademark has been made incontestable precludes a defendant from challenging it on the basis of mere descriptiveness. *See Park 'N Fly v. Dollar Park and Fly, Inc.*, 469 U.S. 189 (1985). An incontestable mark, however, is not necessarily a *strong* mark for purposes of determining likelihood of confusion. In *Petro Stopping Centers v. James River Petroleum Inc.*, 130 F.3d 88 (4th Cir. 1997), the Fourth Circuit affirmed a district court conclusion that plaintiff's Petro mark was merely descriptive and therefore weak, despite the fact that it was incontestable. The court noted that validity and infringement are separate inquiries and that incontestability applies only to the validity of a trademark. *Accord Sports Authority Inc. v. Abercrombie & Fitch*, 965 F. Supp. 925 (E.D. Mich. 1997). *But see Sovereign Military Hospitaller Order of St. John of Jerusalem of Rhodes & Malta v. Fla. Priory of the Knights Hospitallers of the Sovereign Order of St. John of Jerusalem, Knights of Malta, the Ecumenical Order*, 809 F.3d 1171 (11ᵗʰ Cir. 2015) (following Eleventh Circuit precedent that incontestable marks are deemed strong, while noting that "the law in this Circuit is almost certainly incorrect" and that "the incontestability of a mark, by itself, says nothing about its strength.").

9. How does the Internet affect the analysis of "marketing channels"? Are two goods marketed in the same channels because they are both available on the Internet? Early cases suggested the answer was yes, *see, e.g., Brookfield Communications v. West Coast Entertainment Corp.*, 174 F.3d 1036 (9th Cir. 1999), but more recent decisions recognize that Internet consumers are more discerning, *see, e.g., Volkswagen AG v. Dorling Kindersley Publishing Inc.*, 2009 WL 909573 (E.D. Mich. Mar. 31, 2009) (finding that Volkswagen car accessories and a book about cars were not marketed in the same channels even though both were available on Amazon.com, albeit in different sections). And while marketing channels can affect the likelihood that the products overlap, trademark rights are not limited to sales in a particular marketing channel. *See Excelled Sheepskin & Leather Coat Corp. v. Oregon Brewing Co.*, 897 F.3d 413 (2d Cir. 2018).

3. Types of Confusion

The traditional case for consumer confusion is that consumers will believe the infringer's product is the same as the trademark owner's product because of the similarity between the marks. Presumably, this confusion will allow the infringer to take sales away from the trademark owner by trading on the latter's goodwill. Although such confusion is the central problem at which trademark law is aimed, it is only one of many different ways in which consumers may be confused by different marks. Consider the following types of consumer confusion actionable under the Lanham Act.

i. Confusion as to Source

The classic case of trademark infringement concerns passing off or palming off of goods as those of another source. Counterfeiting and knock-offs fall into this category.

Trademark confusion as to source can arise even when the infringer is offering differing goods than those sold by a trademark owner. Suppose that a competitor uses another's trademark on a product that the trademark owner does not sell. In that case, presumably, consumers cannot buy the infringer's products *instead of* the trademark owner's because the trademark owner does not sell the products at all. At the turn of the twentieth century, trademark protection was limited to competing goods and hence such deceptive acts were not actionable. *See, e.g., Borden Ice Cream v. Borden's Condensed Milk Co.*, 201 F. 510 (7th Cir. 1912) (use of identical trademark for different milk products does not constitute trademark infringement). At that time, most manufacturers sold a single product.

With the expansion and diversification of product manufacturing and marketing, courts came to recognize that identical (or even similar) trademarks can sometimes cause confusion *as to the source of the products* even in the absence of direct product competition. *See Yale Electric Corp. v. Robertson*, 26 F.2d 972 (2d Cir. 1928) (holding that the mark YALE for flashlights was confusingly similar to the plaintiff's use of YALE for locks). The scope of this doctrine ebbed and flowed through the mid-twentieth century as judges became concerned about barriers to entry and monopoly power. *See* Robert G. Bone, *Taking the Confusion Out of "Likelihood of Confusion": Toward a More Sensible Approach to Trademark Infringement*, 106 NW. U. L. REV. 1307, 1316–34 (2012). By the 1960s, the modern noncompeting goods doctrine emerged, as reflected in the multi-factor likelihood of confusion test. *See Polaroid Corp. v. Polarad Electronics Corp.*, 287 F.2d 492 (2d Cir. 1961) (pitting POLAROID, maker of optical and photography products, including some involving television uses, against POLARAD, seller of microwave devices and television studio equipment). For example, "Prell" is a trademark for a brand of shampoo and conditioner. If another company uses the term "Prell" for its hair coloring product, consumers may well believe that they are buying a product sold by the same company that sells Prell shampoo, particularly given the proximity of the two goods. While the infringer will not take sales of hair colors away from the trademark owner in this instance, the trademark owner may be hurt by this confusion in at least two ways. First, if the quality of the hair color is inferior, consumers may blame the maker of shampoo and stop buying Prell products altogether. *But cf.* Mark P. McKenna, *Testing Modern Trademark Law's Theory of Harm*, 95 IOWA L. REV. 63 (2009) (finding that marketing scholarship reports that this type of harm is rare). Second, it is possible that the trademark owner may wish to expand into the market for hair colors. If it does, confusion between the products will almost certainly result if both parties use the Prell mark.

The modern test encompasses both competing and noncompeting goods, although the similarity of the goods and likelihood of expansion are factors in the analysis.

ii. *Confusion as to Sponsorship*

Even in situations in which consumers will not believe that the trademark owner is the one selling the product, the use of a similar trademark may still confuse them by causing them to believe that the trademark owner is affiliated with or sponsors the infringer's products. For example, suppose that a company that sells soup uses the trade symbol of the United States Olympic Committee ("USOC") on its soup cans. Presumably, the USOC does not sell soup, and no reasonable consumer would be likely to conclude that she was in fact buying USOC soup. But consumers might well conclude that the infringer was somehow affiliated with the USOC (for example, as a contributor), or that one group had agreed to sponsor the other. This confusion as to affiliation or sponsorship is actionable under the Lanham Act, assuming the other requirements for protecting a mark are met.[6]

In cases of confusion either as to source or sponsorship, the essential question remains whether consumers are likely to be confused by the similarity of the marks. Because of this, many of the *Sleekcraft* factors apply with equal force to these inquiries. For example, proximity between the products sold by the parties, while not required, does tend to increase both the likelihood of confusion as to source and the chance that the parties will eventually be in direct competition. A similar analysis of infringement can be conducted to determine whether any of these types of confusion is likely.

Should it matter whether consumers are confused about the relationship between two unrelated companies if that confusion doesn't affect their purchasing decisions? Why or why not? *See* Mark A. Lemley & Mark P. McKenna, *Irrelevant Confusion*, 62 STAN. L. REV. 413 (2010) (arguing that trademark law ought to focus on confusion that is relevant to purchasing decisions).

Sponsorship confusion has the potential to dramatically expand the scope of trademark law because the parties no longer need to be in any sort of competitive relationship. Sponsorship cases have prevailed, for instance, on behalf of a maker of chocolate bars that sued a political candidate who shares its name for depicting the name too much like the candy bar. *See Hershey Co. v. Friends of Steve Hershey*, 33 F. Supp. 3d 588 (D. Md. 2014). And some courts have concluded that *consumers* don't have to be confused at all as long as *some* class of people are confused in a way that "presents a significant risk to the sales, goodwill, *or* reputation of the trademark owner." *Arrowpoint Cap. Corp. v. Arrowpoint Asset Mgmt.*, 793 F.3d 313 (3d Cir. 2015) (emphasis in original).

Sponsorship confusion comes up in two specific types of cases, which we discuss in detail in the sections that follow.

---

[6] Confusion as to affiliation or sponsorship is only expressly addressed in § 43(a) of the Lanham Act, which applies to unregistered marks. Jay Dratler has suggested that the protections afforded to unregistered marks under § 43(a) also apply to registered marks, whether under § 32 of the Lanham Act or under § 43(a). *See* JAY DRATLER, JR., INTELLECTUAL PROPERTY LAW: COMMERCIAL, CREATIVE, AND INDUSTRIAL PROPERTY § 10.01[1][i], at 10-5–10-6.

a. Trademarks and Organizational Forms: The Growth of Franchising

From its modern founding, trademark law has been at the service of emerging patterns in the organization of industry. In the beginning, that meant protecting emerging channels of trade in relatively local settings. Next came the great nationalization of the economy with the growth of large retail empires in the late nineteenth and early twentieth centuries. Today trademarks form an integral part of the variegated economic landscape of the industrialized world.

Professor Mira Wilkins, a business historian, explains:

> The legally-backed trade marks ... became essential intangible assets, providing the basis for the rise of the modern enterprise. ... The trade mark's fundamental contribution to the modern corporation was that it generated efficiency gains by creating for the firm the opportunity for large sales over long periods. ... Without the trade mark, the introduction and acceptance by buyers of modern products, produced with economies of scale or scope, and marketed over long distances, would have been impossible. ... The trade mark by reducing the costs of information led to efficiencies in production and distribution.

Mira Wilkins, *The Neglected Intangible Asset: The Influence of the Trademark on the Rise of the Modern Corporation*, 34 BUS. & HIST. 66, 87–88 (1992). Interestingly, Professor Wilkins also points out the role that trademarks play in facilitating organizational diversity, or making possible various alternative forms of production. The clearest and most important recent example is franchising.

Trademarks are the "cornerstone of a franchise system." *Susser v. Carvel Corp.*, 206 F. Supp. 636, 640 (S.D.N Y. 1962), *aff'd*, 332 F.2d 505 (1965). The trademark of the franchisor is the identifiable symbol of continuity; it indicates the presence of the national brand at each location. Thus, whatever the precise nature of the franchise, the franchisor and franchisee are very likely to be parties to a trademark license agreement.

Here again we see the stretching of traditional theory. The individual source from which the national brand emanates is the franchisor. This is often a remote corporate entity, whereas one could argue that the franchisee is the real "source" (at the local level) of the goods. To maintain uniformity (and stay on the good side of the abandonment issue; see below), the franchisor almost invariably imposes certain contractual requirements on the franchisee. Yet it is still the franchisee, in the last instance, who actually runs the establishment where the goods are sold. *See* James M. Treece, *Trademark Licensing and Vertical Restraints in Franchising Arrangements*, 116 U. PA. L. REV. 435 (1968); Lynn M. LoPucki, *Toward a Trademark-Based Liability System*, 49 UCLA L. REV. 1099 (2002) (suggesting that tort liability should follow the trademark rather than the franchisee).

In economic terms, franchising is an interesting mix of contractual and integrated governance characteristics—a kind of hybrid organization in which the franchisee is neither an employee of the franchisor nor an arm's-length buyer of the franchisor's goods. *See* James A. Brickley & Frederick H. Dark, *The Choice of Organizational Form: The Case of Franchising*, 18 J. FIN. ECON. 401, 403–07 (1987); Gillian K. Hadfield, *Problematic Relations: Franchising and the Law of Incomplete Contracts*, 42 STAN. L. REV. 927 (1990). The franchise trademark plays an interesting role in this relationship. It is one of the franchisor's great assets, one of the things it can sell to franchisees. Yet once a franchisee begins to use the trademark, he or she is in a position to harm the franchise's reputation by selling inferior quality goods. (Note that doing so hurts other franchisees as well.) Indeed, if many of the franchise's customers are travelers who come from afar and do not pass through often, a franchisee might be tempted to "free ride" off the quality investments of the franchisor and other franchisees by selling inferior goods. Many of the provisions in franchise agreements are directed at preventing such an outcome, e.g., agreements to purchase ingredients and other inputs from the franchisor, stipulations to frequent inspections, and profit-sharing arrangements. *See* Paul H. Rubin, *The Theory of the Firm and the Structure of the Franchise Contract*, 21 J.L. & ECON. 223 (1978). *Cf.* Patrick J. Kaufman & Francine Lafontaine, *Costs of Control: The Source of Economic Rents for McDonald's Franchisees*, 37 J.L. & ECON. 417 (1994) (finding substantial "rents" or profits left to the franchisee after the franchisor's "cut," indicating that incentive system in franchise contracts was working). In this complicated relationship, trademarks are a key strategic asset. Note also that in many states various aspects of franchise contracts—especially termination provisions—are closely regulated. *See, e.g.*, Thomas M. Pitegoff, *Franchise Relationship Laws: A Minefield for Franchisors*, 45 BUS. LAW. 289 (1989).

What significance does the growth of franchising have for trademark doctrine? Note that once franchising has become widespread, we can no longer assume that the trademark indicates the maker of goods. Licensing, sponsorship, and affiliation become more important in a franchised world, and designation of actual source less important. Should we be concerned about the disaggregation of trademarks from the goods they represent? Does the selling of trademarks without goods attached to them make trademark owners less able to use the mark as a guarantee of quality? Alternatively, does it suggest that the trademark owner will invest even more in quality assurance, since the value of the mark is all it has to offer? *See* Mark A. Lemley & Mark P. McKenna, *Owning Mark(et)s*, 109 MICH. L. REV. 137 (2010).

b.   *Merchandising*

Evidence is everywhere that a boom is under way in the licensing of trademarks. From sports team logos to university names to designer symbols, badges of affiliation and prestige are ever more common on products of all kinds. And, importantly, these badges come at a premium. As Robert Denicola has written,

> [a]t any sporting goods store one can find plain, unadorned shirts, shorts, and jackets in assorted styles and colors. They are usually near the rear. Closer to the front are items apparently similar in all respects except one—they are prominently decorated with a variety of words and symbols. Some bear the names of

athletic equipment manufacturers. Others display the names or insignia of professional sports teams, the name and seal of the state university, or the nickname and mascot of the local high school. They frequently cost significantly more than the items in the rear, yet they sell.

Robert C. Denicola, *Institutional Publicity Rights: An Analysis of the Merchandising of Famous Trade Symbols*, 62 N.C. L. REV. 603 (1983).

Turning logos into profit centers may make sense as a business strategy, but it poses problems for the legal system. The cases in this chapter highlight the fundamental problem: traditionally, trademarks were thought of as symbols representing products, rather than as products in and of themselves. Thus, traditional trademark law protects a trademark only because, and only insofar as, it is emblematic of the goodwill behind a product. The mark itself is not the point; it is simply a vehicle to convey useful information regarding a product's quality, prestige, and so on. The trademark guides the consumer to the transaction; sale of the underlying product is the "profit center."

All this changes when the trademark becomes the *subject* of the transaction rather than an adjunct to it. In such a transaction, the mark does not represent the product: it *is* the product. Consider the following case.

Board of Supervisors for Louisiana State University v. Smack Apparel Co.
United States Court of Appeals for the Fifth Circuit
550 F.3d 465 (5th Cir. 2008)

REAVLEY, Circuit Judge:

These consolidated appeals concern a trademark dispute between four universities and an apparel company and its principal. The Universities alleged in the district court that the defendants violated the Lanham Act and infringed their trademarks by selling t-shirts with the schools' color schemes and other identifying indicia referencing the games of the schools' football teams. The district court granted summary judgment to the Universities for trademark infringement and conducted a jury trial as to damages, with the jury returning a verdict favoring the plaintiffs. The defendants appeal the summary judgment order, and the Universities appeal the district court's denial of their post-verdict motion for attorneys' fees. We conclude that the colors, content, and context of the offending t-shirts are likely to cause confusion as to their source, sponsorship, or affiliation, and we AFFIRM.

Background

The plaintiffs are Louisiana State University (LSU), the University of Oklahoma (OU), Ohio State University (OSU), the University of Southern California (USC), and Collegiate Licensing Company (CLC), which is the official licensing agent for the schools.[1] The defendants are Smack Apparel Company and its principal, Wayne Curtiss (collectively Smack).

Each university has adopted a particular two-color scheme as its school colors (purple and gold for LSU, crimson and creme for OU, scarlet and gray for OSU, and cardinal and gold for USC). The Universities have used their respective color combinations for over one hundred years, and the color schemes are immediately recognizable to those who are familiar with the Universities. The schools use these color schemes in many areas associated with university life, including on campus signs and buildings, on printed brochures, journals, and magazines, and on materials sent to potential donors. The Universities also use the color schemes extensively in connection with their athletic programs, particularly on team uniforms, resulting in wide-spread recognition of the colors among college sports fans. Each university operates a successful collegiate football program, and the respective football teams have appeared on numerous occasions in nationally televised football games that have been viewed by millions of people.

The schools also grant licenses for retail sales of products, including t-shirts, that bear the university colors and trademarks. In recent years, the total annual sales volume of products bearing the school colors along with other identifying marks has exceeded $93 million for all the Universities combined. The Universities hold registered trademarks in their respective names and commonly used initials. They do not, however, possess registered trademarks in their color schemes.

Smack Apparel Company is located in Tampa, Florida. Since 1998 Smack has manufactured t-shirts targeted toward fans of college sports teams, and it uses school colors and printed messages associated with the Universities on its shirts. Smack sells some of the shirts over the Internet, but most are sold wholesale to retailers and t-shirt vendors. The shirts frequently appear alongside those that have been officially licensed by the Universities. The instant case involves six of Smack's t-shirt designs that concern the appearance of the OU and LSU football teams in the 2004 Sugar Bowl in New Orleans, Louisiana, and the number of national championships previously won by OSU and USC. The district court described these Smack shirt designs as follows:

• OU (2 shirt designs): (1) "Bourbon Street or Bust" (with the "ou" in "Bourbon" in a different typestyle) (front), "Show us your beads!" (with the "ou" in "your" in a different typestyle) and "Sweet as Sugar!" (back) (2) "Beat Socal" (front), "And Let's Make it Eight!" (back). These shirts refer to 2004 Sugar Bowl contest in New Orleans between the OU and LSU football teams. A victory in the Sugar Bowl could have given OU a claim to an eighth national football championship. One of OU's principal rivals to this claim was USC.

• LSU (2 shirt designs): (1) "Beat Oklahoma" (front), "And Bring it Back to the Bayou!" and "2003 College Football National Championship" (back) (2) "2003 College Football National Champions" (front), colored circular depiction of game scores, with "2003 College Football National Champions" and "Sweet as Sugar" (back). These shirts refer to the 2004 Sugar Bowl contest in New Orleans between OU and LSU, which was played to determine the Bowl Championship Series national football champion.

- OSU: "Got Seven?" (front), "We do! 7 Time National Champs," with depiction of the state of Ohio and a marker noting "Columbus Ohio" (back). This shirt refers to the seven college football national titles claimed by OSU.

- USC: "Got eight?" (front), "We Do! Home of the 8 Time National Champions!" and depiction of the state of California with a star marked "SoCal" (back). This design refers to USC's claim to eight college national football championships.

Bd. of Supervisors of LA State Univ. v. Smack Apparel Co. In addition to the messages described above, each shirt included Smack's own logo in a space approximately 2.5 inches wide and the words "Talkin' the Talk.". . .

The Universities claimed that Smack's products are similar to and competed with goods sold or licensed by the Universities and are sold directly alongside merchandise authorized by the plaintiffs at or near events referenced in the shirts. In this way, according to the Universities, the sale of Smack's products is likely to deceive, confuse, and mislead consumers into believing that Smack's products are produced, authorized, or associated with the plaintiff Universities. The Universities sought injunctive relief, lost profits, damages, costs, and attorneys' fees. . . .

II. Discussion

. . .

A. Protectable trademark and secondary meaning

. . . The parties correctly agree that a color scheme can be protected as a trademark when it has acquired secondary meaning and is non-functional. *Qualitex Co. v. Jacobson Prods. Co.* Although the parties discuss color at length in their briefs, the Universities do not claim that every instance in which their team colors appear violates their respective trademarks. Instead, the claimed trademark is in the colors on merchandise that combines other identifying indicia referring to the Universities. It is appropriate therefore to consider not only the color but also the entire context in which the color and other indicia are presented on the t-shirts at issue here.

Smack contends that the claimed marks are too broad to encompass a trademark because the concept of color along with other identifying indicia is not distinctive. We disagree. As noted, the statute contemplates that a trademark may include any word, name, or symbol "*or any combination thereof.*" The Supreme Court has recognized that the Lanham Act describes the universe of permissible marks "in the broadest of terms." Because the Court recognizes that trademarks may include color, we see no reason to exclude color plus other identifying indicia from the realm of protectable marks provided the remaining requirements for protection are met. Thus, the first step here is to ask whether the Universities' claimed marks have acquired secondary meaning. . . .

There is no dispute in this case that for a significant period of time the Universities have been using their color schemes along with other indicia to identify and distinguish themselves from others. Smack admits in its brief that the Universities' colors are well known among fans "as a shorthand nonverbal visual means of identifying the universities." But according to Smack, the longstanding use of the school colors to adorn licensed products is not the same as public recognition that the school colors identify the Universities as a unique source of goods. We think, however, that the factors for determining secondary meaning and an examination of the context in which the school colors are used and presented in this case support the conclusion that the secondary meaning of the marks is inescapable.

The record shows that the Universities have been using their color combinations since the late 1800s. The color schemes appear on all manner of materials, including brochures, media guides, and alumni materials associated with the Universities. Significantly, each university features the color schemes on merchandise, especially apparel connected with school sports teams, and such prominent display supports a finding of secondary meaning. The record also shows that sales of licensed products combining the color schemes with other references to the Universities annually exceed the tens of millions of dollars. As for advertising, the district court held that the Universities "advertise items with their school colors in almost every conceivable manner. . . ." It is not clear from the summary judgment evidence where and how the Universities advertise their merchandise, but they certainly do use their color schemes and indicia in numerous promotional materials aimed at students, faculty, alumni, and the public in general, which strengthens the conclusion that the color schemes and indicia viewed in context of wearing apparel also serves as an indicator of the Universities as the source or sponsor of the apparel. Furthermore, the district court correctly observed that the school color schemes have been referenced multiple times in newspapers and magazines and that the schools also frequently refer to themselves using the colors. The district court did not specifically refer to any consumer-survey evidence or direct consumer testimony, but it noted that Smack admitted it had incorporated the Universities' color schemes into its shirts to refer to the Universities and call them to the mind of the consumer. Thus, Smack itself believed that the Universities' color schemes had secondary meaning that could influence consumers, which further supports the conclusion that there is secondary meaning here.[35] Given the longstanding use of the color scheme marks and their prominent display on merchandise, in addition to the well-known nature of the colors as shorthand for the schools themselves and Smack's intentional use of the colors and other references, there is no genuine issue of fact that when viewed in the context of t-shirts

---

[35] *See also Thomas & Betts Corp. v. Panduit Corp.*, 65 F.3d 654, 663 (7th Cir.1995). We also note that the record does contain survey evidence compiled by the Universities indicating that approximately thirty percent of consumers interviewed believed two of Smack's t-shirts were produced or sponsored by the Universities. We have indicated that survey evidence often may be the most direct and persuasive evidence of secondary meaning. *Sugar Busters LLC v. Brennan,* 177 F.3d 258, 269 (5th Cir.1999). Nevertheless, Smack moved in limine to exclude the Universities' survey evidence, and the district court found it unnecessary to rule on the motion because of the other evidence in the record. Because no party has raised the issue, we express no opinion on the correctness of the district court's belief and merely note the presence of the survey evidence in the record.

or other apparel, the marks at issue here have acquired the secondary meaning of identifying the Universities in the minds of consumers as the source or sponsor of the products rather than identifying the products themselves. . . .

B. Likelihood of confusion

. . . Smack argues that there were genuine issues of material fact whether its t-shirt
designs were likely to cause confusion among consumers. We disagree. The first digit
[in the likelihood of confusion analysis], the type of mark, refers to the strength of the
mark. Generally, the stronger the mark, the greater the likelihood that consumers will
be confused by competing uses of the mark. We agree with the district court that the
plaintiffs' marks, which have been used for over one hundred years, are strong. . . .

Smack presented photographs of three businesses in Louisiana, eight businesses in
Ohio, and approximately 20 businesses in Oklahoma that incorporated in their signage
color schemes similar to the school colors of LSU, OSU, and OU, respectively. The
businesses included several restaurants and bars, a driving school, a pain management
clinic, a theater, a furniture store, a dry cleaners, a motel, a donut shop, an apartment
complex, and a car care company. All third-party use of a mark, not just use in the same
industry as a plaintiff, may be relevant to whether a plaintiff's mark is strong or weak.
But the key is whether the third-party use diminishes in the public's mind the association
of the mark with the plaintiff—surely lacking where colors are shown on a store wall.
See Univ. of Ga. Athletic Ass'n v. Laite. Smack's evidence falls far below that of extensive use, and the specific photographs of third-party use here fail to create an issue of
fact concerning the public's association between the plaintiffs and color schemes and
other indicia that clearly reference the Universities. We conclude that the Universities
possess strong marks in their use of color schemes and other identifying indicia on college sports-themed merchandise.

The second digit is the similarity of the marks. This factor requires consideration of
the marks' appearance, sound, and meaning. The district court held that the marks at
issue are virtually identical. Smack argues that there was no evidence that any of its
shirts were identical to any shirts licensed by the Universities and that its t-shirt designs
are not at all similar to any of the Universities' licensed products. Smack's contention
is belied by the record, and even a cursory comparison of Smack's designs with the
plaintiffs' licensed products reveals striking similarity.

For example, one of Smack's shirt designs in purple and gold is referred to as the
"sundial" shirt and was targeted toward LSU fans. The front of the shirt proclaims "2003
National Champions," and the back contains the scores from twelve games won by LSU.
The scores are arranged in a circle with a short phrase poking fun at each opponent. The
shirt also contains the final score of the 2004 Sugar Bowl, which LSU won, and the
phrase "Sweet as Sugar!" Although the shirt does not use the initials "LSU" anywhere,
its identification of LSU as the national champion is unmistakable from the colors and
from the references to the games in which LSU played. This shirt is strikingly similar
to LSU's own merchandise that also uses the purple and gold colors and proclaims LSU
as the national champion. Several of the official designs contain the scores of the games

from LSU's season and at least two designs present those scores in a circular arrangement. The official designs also contain the phrases "Ain't It Sweet!" and "Pour It On!"

Another Smack shirt directed at LSU fans is the "Beat Oklahoma" shirt. It states, "Bring it Back to the Bayou." This is very similar to two official designs that state in part "Bring It Home" and "We'll Have Big Fun on the Bayou."

The evidence of similarity is not limited to the shirts targeted toward LSU fans. For example, the "Bourbon Street or Bust!" shirt directed at OU fans highlights the letters "OU" in a different type face in the words "Bayou" and "your." It also states "Sweet as Sugar," references beads, and contains a picture of a mardi gras mask. OU presented evidence of official t-shirt designs that also highlight the letters "OU," contain phrases such as "Ain't Nothin' Sweeter" and "100% Pure Sugar," and contain depictions of mardi gras masks and beads. Another Smack OU design encourages, "Let's Make it Eight," while official designs proclaim "Sugar is Sweet But . . . 8 is Great!"

. . . We conclude that Smack's shirts and the Universities' products are similar in look, sound, and meaning, and contain very similar color schemes, words, and images. The similarities in design elements are overwhelming and weigh heavily in favor of a likelihood of confusion. The district court correctly held there is no genuine issue of material fact with respect to this digit of confusion.[54]

The third digit in the likelihood of confusion analysis is the similarity of the products or services. We disagree with Smack's assertion that the district court did not find a great deal of similarity between the plaintiffs' products and the t-shirts at issue, as the district court specifically held that "[i]t is undisputed that both Smack and the universities market shirts bearing the same color schemes, logos, and designs." The district court went on to reject Smack's argument that its t-shirts differed from the Universities' products because of the use of irreverent phrases or slang language, reasoning that Smack's use of such phrases and language was a misuse of the Universities' good will in its marks. Smack denies that it appropriated the Universities' good will, but it does not make an argument here that its shirts are distinguishable from those of the Universities because of particular language on its shirts. We therefore find this factor weighs in favor of a likelihood of confusion.

Smack concedes that the fourth factor of the analysis—identity of retail outlets and purchasers—weighs in favor of a likelihood of confusion because the Universities' licensed products are often sold wholesale to the same retailers who purchase Smack's products.

---

[54] Because we conclude that there is no issue of fact as to the similarity of the use of the marks in the t-shirt designs, we need not consider Smack's contention that the district court erroneously stated there had been instances where consumers actually believed Smack's shirts were affiliated with or sponsored by the Universities. Smack points to a stipulation by the parties at the summary judgment stage that there was no evidence any consumer purchased a Smack shirt believing it to be licensed by one of the Universities. Actual confusion on the part of a consumer is not required to find a likelihood of confusion, however. *Elvis Presley Enters.*, 141 F.3d at 203.

The fifth digit is the identity of advertising media. The district court found that Smack used the Universities' color schemes, logos, and designs in advertising its shirts at the same or similar venues as those used by the Universities. The court based its finding on Smack's admission that it participated in the same trade shows as the Universities and that it displayed its shirts at the trade shows. The Universities do not point us to evidence that trade shows are a significant advertising channel for the kinds of products at issue in this case. Although the t-shirts are sold to the public at the same retail outlets as officially licensed merchandise, Curtiss testified that beside limited sales on Smack's web site, Smack does not sell directly to the public and does not advertise. Curtiss testified that Smack sells mainly to wholesalers. Some of these wholesalers may include Smack's shirts in advertisements that promote their own business, but Curtiss was unable to provide much information about these ads. We conclude that this digit, based on trade show advertising, is minimally probative.

The sixth digit of confusion further supports a likelihood of confusion. Although not necessary to a finding of likelihood of confusion, a defendant's intent to confuse may alone be sufficient to justify an inference that there is a likelihood of confusion. As noted by the district court, Smack admitted that it "'used school colors and "other indicia" with the intent of identifying the university plaintiffs as the subject of the message expressed in the shirt design.'" Curtiss testified that it was "no coincidence" that Smack's shirts incorporated the color schemes of the plaintiff Universities and that he designed the shirts to make people think of the particular school that each shirt targeted. Smack asserts that its intent to copy is not the same as an intent to confuse. The circumstances of this case show, however, that Smack intended to capitalize on the potential for confusion. Smack knew that its shirts were sold in the same venues as and sometimes alongside officially licensed merchandise, and it intentionally incorporated color marks to create the kind of association with the Universities that would influence purchasers.

. . . Smack did not hope to sell its t-shirts because of some competitive difference in quality or design compared with the Universities' licensed products, but rather it intended to take advantage of the popularity of the Universities' football programs and the appearance of the school teams in the college bowl games. We have previously said that when a "mark was adopted with the intent of deriving benefit from the reputation of [the mark holder] that fact alone 'may be sufficient to justify the inference that there is confusing similarity.'" *Amstar Corp. v. Domino's Pizza, Inc.* We believe that Smack's admitted intent and the similarity in appearance between Smack's shirts and the Universities' licensed products is strong evidence of a likelihood of confusion.

Smack argues that an intent to confuse is negated by its use of its own logo and the words "Talkin' the Talk," which it maintains identifies it as the source of the shirt. We are not persuaded. Smack's logo appears in a space that is only 2.5 inches wide. We cannot conclude, without more, that this small and inconspicuous placement of the logo would disabuse consumers of a mistaken belief that the Universities sponsored, endorsed or were otherwise affiliated with the t-shirts. Smack has not pointed to evidence that its own logo is recognizable by consumers or that it was acting to trade off its own reputation as a producer of specialty t-shirts. Nor are we convinced that Smack's logo on the shirts acts as a disclaimer. The Universities point out that they require all licensed products to contain the licensee's name. Therefore, a consumer could believe that Smack's logo merely indicated that it was a licensee. We conclude that the intent digit weighs in favor of a conclusion that there is a likelihood of confusion.

The seventh digit is evidence of actual confusion. Evidence that consumers have been actually confused in identifying the defendant's use of a mark as that of the plaintiff may be the best evidence of a likelihood of confusion. It is well established, however, that evidence of actual confusion is not necessary for a finding of a likelihood of confusion. The district court did not resolve whether there was sufficient evidence of actual confusion, and because such evidence is not required we also find it unnecessary to pass on the question further.[69]

With respect to the eighth digit of confusion—the degree of care exercised by potential purchasers—the district court held that the t-shirts at issue are relatively inexpensive impulse items that are not purchased with a high degree of care. Where items are relatively inexpensive, a buyer may take less care in selecting the item, thereby increasing the risk of confusion. . . .

After reviewing the record, we conclude that there is no genuine issue of fact that Smack's use of the Universities' color schemes and other identifying indicia creates a likelihood of confusion as to the source, affiliation, or sponsorship of the t-shirts. As noted above, the digits of confusion—particularly the overwhelming similarity of the marks and the defendant's intent to profit from the Universities' reputation—compel this conclusion. This is so, we have noted, because Smack's use of the Universities' colors and indicia is designed to create the illusion of affiliation with the Universities and essentially obtain a "free ride" by profiting from confusion among the fans of the Universities' football teams who desire to show support for and affiliation with those teams. This creation of a link in the consumer's mind between the t-shirts and the Universities and the intent to directly profit therefrom results in "an unmistakable aura of deception" and likelihood of confusion.

Smack contends that there is no evidence that consumers care one way or the other whether t-shirts purchased for wear at a football game are officially licensed and that, absent evidence that consumers prefer licensed merchandise, it was error for the district court to conclude there was a likelihood of confusion. . . .

We hold that given the record in this case and the digits of confusion analysis discussed above—including the overwhelming similarity between the defendant's t-shirts and the Universities' licensed products, and the defendant's admitted intent to create an association with the plaintiffs and to influence consumers in calling the plaintiffs to

---

[69] The Universities contend that there was evidence of actual confusion consisting of consumer surveys concerning two of the six t-shirt designs and testimony from Curtiss that "I have had people come up and go-at the booth and go, 'Are these licensed?' " The evidence is arguably minimal, *see Amstar,* 615 F.2d at 263, but as discussed we need not resolve the matter.

mind—that the inescapable conclusion is that many consumers would likely be confused and believe that Smack's t-shirts were sponsored or endorsed by the Universities. The Universities exercise stringent control over the use of their marks on apparel through their licensing program. It is also undisputed that the Universities annually sell millions of dollars worth of licensed apparel. We further recognize the public's indisputable desire to associate with college sports teams by wearing team-related apparel. We are not persuaded that simply because some consumers might not care whether Smack's shirts are officially licensed the likelihood of confusion is negated. Whether or not a consumer *cares* about official sponsorship is a different question from whether that consumer would likely *believe* the product is officially sponsored. For the foregoing reasons, we conclude that a likelihood of confusion connecting the presence of the Universities' marks and the Universities' themselves was demonstrated in this case.

COMMENTS AND QUESTIONS

1. In what sense did Smack intend to confuse consumers? Does the court confuse an intent to "free ride"—to make money by reminding people of the plaintiff universities—with an intent to profit from confusion? Note in this regard that the plaintiffs introduced no evidence of actual confusion, and indeed what evidence there was suggested that consumers know the difference between licensed and unlicensed products.

Shouldn't it be possible to dispel that confusion with a sufficiently clear disclaimer? Does it matter that Smack's web site, where people must go to buy its T-shirts, says in large letters at the very top "Licensed ONLY by the First Amendment"?

2. The court says that "Whether or not a consumer *cares* about official sponsorship is a different question from whether that consumer would likely *believe* the product is officially sponsored." Why does it matter whether consumers think the shirts were (or legally had to be) licensed? Is the trademark owner injured if consumers think Smack had to get a license but don't care whether or not they bought licensed apparel? *See* Mark A. Lemley & Mark P. McKenna, *Irrelevant Confusion*, 62 STAN. L. REV. 413 (2010) (arguing that consumers should have to be confused about something they care about).

3. Smack was careful not to use the name of any university or its sports team. It also used, not the exact university colors, but a recognizable variant on those colors. Shouldn't that be enough? What could Smack do to sell a T-shirt to LSU fans that wouldn't run afoul of the court's ruling? Would the use of the words "Got 7? We do" without the school colors but sold near the school on the eve of the big game still signify a particular university to consumers?

4. How does printing the logo on T-shirts lower consumer search costs? Are universities in the business of making T-shirts? If the logo does not summarize product attributes such as quality, why protect it?

A university or sports team logo does not summarize information about the quality of the hat; it demonstrates loyalty to a team. Indeed, many if not most sports logos are licensed to a broad array of products, many of differing degrees of quality. The "high end" Red Sox cap ("just like the pros wear!") is a far different product—qua hat—than the cheap synthetic cap costing a few dollars and sold in discount stores. The same is true for sweatshirts and t-shirts emblazoned with the logos of college and professional teams. Similar examples can be drawn from other avenues of commerce. Thus, outdoor equipment companies with a certain consumer cachet have been known to lend their logos for application to sport-utility vehicles. Yet no one, or very few, can suppose that companies specializing in backpacks, long underwear, and hiking boots have suddenly taken up truck production.

In these cases, the consumer is buying an image. The trademark owner possesses rights in a symbol associated with certain qualities. Lending that symbol to diverse products connects those products to the feelings the symbol evokes. (The same thing happens outside commerce as well; consider the difference when the "stars and stripes" image is added to a plain object such as a flag or a tombstone.)

Outside the university and professional sports context, many people have sought to trademark a picture or slogan they put on a T-shirt. Trademark law doesn't protect those images because consumers are likely to view them as ornamental, not source-identifying. As one court put it in rejecting plaintiff's claim to own the phrase "Lettuce Turnip the Beet" becausee it sold T-shirts bearing that phrase, absent some preexisting well-known mark, "there is *no* evidence . . . that consumers seek to purchase products based on [the trademark owner's reputation]. . . . Rather, consumers are interested in purchasing products displaying the pun. . . . [W]hile a source-identifying trademark may embody a pun, no one can claim exclusive rights to use the pun merely by printing it on t-shirts . . . or other similar products and calling it a 'trademark.'" *LTTB, LLC v. Redbubble, Inc.*, 385 F. Supp. 3d 916 (N.D. Cal. 2019).

5. While many courts have ruled for plaintiffs in merchandising cases, particular where universities or professional sports teams are involved, not all courts do so. Professors Stacey Dogan and Mark Lemley review the cases and conclude that the majority refuse to protect trademarks on merchandise absent a showing of consumer confusion. Further, they point out that the Supreme Court has never recognized a merchandising right, and argue that the current Court is unlikely to do so given its many recent decisions limiting trademark protection. *See* Stacey L. Dogan & Mark A. Lemley, *The Merchandising Right: Fragile Theory or Fait Accompli?*, 54 EMORY L.J. 461 (2005).

Assuming that Professors Dogan and Lemley are right that a merchandising right doesn't fit well within existing trademark doctrine, what should happen if people have come to believe that only the Dallas Cowboys are permitted to sell Dallas Cowboys merchandise? Should the law expand over time to take account of changing consumer norms, or should it set the rules according to trademark principles and force consumer norms to adapt to those rules?

6. Should it matter that the merchandise is a joke? We discuss defenses for parody and nontrademark use in Section V(F)(3)(ii). But the humorous nature of merchandise

can also affect whether consumers are likely to be confused about sponsorship. In *Beyonce Knowles-Carter v. Feyonce, Inc.*, 347 F. Supp. 3d 217 (S.D.N.Y. 2018), the court denied summary judgment that "Feyonce" merchandise marketed to fiancés would confuse consumers into thinking it was sponsored by the musician Beyonce: "A rational jury might or might not conclude that the pun here is sufficient to dispel any confusion among the purchasing public." *Id.* at 221; *see also id.* at 226; *LTTB, LLC v. Redbubble, Inc.*, 385 F. Supp. 3d 916 (N.D. Cal. 2019).

PROBLEM

Problem V-11. A popular "cult" movie includes characters who have tattooed famous brand logos on various parts of their bodies. The practice quickly catches on, first among "avant-garde" artists, and then among college and high school students.

Post-Modern Concepts, Inc. (PMC), seeing an opportunity, opens a storefront tattoo parlor in a popular retail mall in the Midwest. Here PMC applies popular logos as tattoos. At first, customers are primarily interested in the ironic use of logos, as in the film; the logos are primarily used as a spoof or commentary on consumerism. One popular tattoo, for instance, includes the famous "Calvin Klein" wordmark and logo, drawn inside a red circle with a slash. Soon, however—perhaps predictably—the ironic intent of the original practice is lost as it becomes very chic to have a logo tattoo. Thus, many people begin to request tattoos without the red slash and circle. The most popular trademark logo tattoos are "Rolls Royce," "Nike," the original "Calvin Klein," and "Harley-Davidson."

Success is instantaneous. In response to torrid demand, PMC sets up franchises all over the country.

Owners of the trademarks begin to notice PMC. They are concerned primarily about lost revenues, because PMC has never taken out any trademark licenses. But some trademark owners are also concerned that pictures of people with logo tattoos are beginning to appear in the press. Even some famous celebrities, such as popular musicians and sports stars, have tattoos in prominent places. When their picture appears in the newspaper, the logo—or part of it—does too. Other trademark owners are concerned that logo tattoos are being applied on parts of the body traditionally covered by clothing. These owners fear that when pictures of people with logo tattoos in these places appear—sometimes in press outlets not fit for family viewing—the trademarks are denigrated.

What hurdles will the trademark owners have to clear to enforce their rights? (Are these marks attached to a product? Also, PMC will undoubtedly argue that sports team fanatics have long painted their faces in team colors, or drawn the team logo on their faces; and that even before PMC, some permanent tattoos consisting of corporate logos were popular, such as "Chevy," "Red Sox Forever," or, perhaps most common, "Harley Davidson.") Are there any risks to letting the practice continue without any enforcement efforts? Does PMC, or its customers, have a defense not based in trademark law?

iii.   *Reverse Confusion*

Trademark confusion ordinarily occurs when the junior user trades on the reputation of the trademark owner, confusing the public into thinking that its goods are associated with those of the senior trademark owner. At times, however, a large company will adopt the mark of a smaller trademark owner. In this case, the danger is presumably not that the junior user will trade on the smaller company's goodwill. The risk, instead, is that the public will come to associate the mark not with its true owner but with the infringer (who has spent a great deal of money to advertise it). Several courts have made it clear that reverse confusion is trademark infringement, and that the relative size of the companies does not matter. *See Uber Promotions, Inc. v. Uber Technologies, Inc.*, 162 F.Supp.3d 1253 (N.D. Fla. 2016). Indeed, companies have periodically been forced to halt or even retract major advertising campaigns because of reverse confusion problems. *See, e.g., Big O Tire Dealers, Inc. v. Goodyear Tire & Rubber Co.*, 561 F.2d 1365 (10th Cir. 1977); *Sands, Taylor & Wood v. Quaker Oaks*, 34 F.3d 1340 (7th Cir. 1994).

In *Illinois High School Ass'n v. GTE Vantage*, 99 F.3d 244 (7th Cir. 1996), Judge Posner developed a new branch of the doctrine where the public of the media plays a role in creating new meaning for an established mark. The plaintiffs were the owners of the trademark "March Madness" for their annual high school basketball tournament. After the media began using the term to describe the NCAA *college* basketball tournament, the NCAA and its various licensees adopted the term and used it in advertising their own products and services. The Illinois High School Association sued alleging reverse confusion—that their mark had been appropriated by the NCAA. The Seventh Circuit rejected this claim, creating a new trademark classification: the "dual use trademark." The court reasoned that where *the public,* not the defendant, had appropriated a trademark for use to describe another product or service, trademark law should not stand in the way.

Does this result make sense? Why isn't this an ordinary case of reverse confusion? Under the Seventh Circuit's opinion, presumably *both* the Illinois High School Association and the NCAA now have rights to the mark. Does this comport with the rationales for trademark protection? Who now has the right to sue infringers? To license the use of the mark?

A number of reverse confusion cases have come up in the context of plagiarism of works of authorship, where the author claims that the copier engaged in "reverse passing off"—that is, selling the plaintiff's work as her own rather than vice versa. In *Dastar Corp. v. Twentieth Century Fox Film Corp.*, 539 U.S. 23 (2003), however, the Supreme Court made it clear that Lanham Act § 43(a) does not prevent the uncredited copying of a work of authorship; any such rights must come from copyright law. *See* Jane C. Ginsburg, *The Right to Claim Authorship in U.S. Copyright and Trademark Laws*, 41 HOUS. L. REV. 263 (2004); David Nimmer, *The Moral Imperative Against Academic Plagiarism (Without a Moral Right Against Reverse Passing Off)*, 54 DEPAUL L. REV. 1 (2004). Note that a strong "right of attribution" is well-established in many foreign intellectual property systems, especially in Europe. *See* ROBERTA ROSENTHAL KWALL,

THE SOUL OF CREATIVITY: FORGING A MORAL RIGHTS LAW FOR THE UNITED STATES (2009) (proposing stronger recognition of moral rights in the U.S.).

iv. Timing of Confusion

The tort of palming off focused on confusion at the point of sale. As marketing methods and consumer search activities have expanded, especially with the Internet, the temporal dimension of confusion has widened.

a. Initial Interest Confusion

What happens when confusion is dispelled before a product is ever purchased? For example, suppose that Burger King erects a large McDonald's sign by a highway exit. There is no McDonald's at that exit, so consumers won't end up thinking they are buying from one. However, they might be lured into Burger King once they have left the highway. Should this sort of deliberate effort to confuse consumers, but not at the point of purchase, be actionable?

Infringement can be based upon confusion that creates initial customer interest, even though any confusion is dispelled before the point of sale. This doctrine traces back to *Grotrian, Helfferich, Schulz, Th. Steinweg Nachf. v. Steinway & Sons*, 365 F. Supp. 707, 717 (S.D.N.Y. 1973), *aff'd*, 523 F.2d 1331 (2d Cir. 1975), where the court found that a prospective piano purchaser may be lead to purchase a "Grotrian-Steinweg" piano because he was initially under the mistaken impression that the piano was affiliated with the "Steinway" brand: "Misled into an initial interest, a potential Steinway buyer may satisfy himself that the less expensive Grotrian-Steinweg is at least as good, if not better, than a Steinway. Deception and confusion thus work to appropriate [Steinway's] good will." *See id.* at 717. Thus, even though the buyer was not confused at the point of purchase, initial interest confusion affected the buyer's search and arguably influenced her purchasing decision.

The Seventh Circuit has explained that

[t]he Lanham Act forbids a competitor from luring potential customers away from a producer by initially passing off its goods as those of the producer's, even if confusion as to the source of the goods is dispelled by the time any sales are consummated. This "bait and switch" of producers, also known as initial interest confusion, will affect the buying decision of consumers in the market for the goods, effectively allowing the competitor to get its foot in the door by confusing consumers.

Dorr-Oliver, Inc. v. Fluid-Quip, Inc., 94 F.3d 376, 382 (7th Cir. 1996). .

Courts were initially drawn to initial interest theory during the early days of the Internet. *See, e.g., People for the Ethical Treatment of Animals v. Doughney*, 263 F.3d 359, 362 (4th Cir. 2001); *Brookfield Commc'ns, Inc. v. West Coast Entm't Corp.*, 174 F.3d 1036 (9th Cir. 1999). As the Internet has become more widely used and understood, the attraction to initial interest confusion on the Internet has waned. *See, e.g., Network*

Automation, Inc. v. Advanced Systems Concepts, Inc., 638 F.3d 1137 (9th Cir. 2011); *Lamparello v. Falwell*, 420 F.3d 309, 315–18 (4th Cir. 2005).

Multi Time Machine, Inc. v. Amazon.com, Inc.
United States Court of Appeals for the Ninth Circuit
804 F.3d 930 (9th Cir. 2015)

SILVERMAN, Circuit Judge:

In the present appeal, we must decide whether the following scenario constitutes trademark infringement: A customer goes online to Amazon.com looking for a certain military-style wristwatch—specifically the "MTM Special Ops"—marketed and manufactured by Plaintiff Multi Time Machine, Inc. The customer types "mtm special ops" in the search box and presses "enter." Because Amazon does not sell the MTM Special Ops watch, what the search produces is a list, with photographs, of several other brands of military style watches that Amazon *does* carry, specifically identified by their brand names—Luminox, Chase–Durer, TAWATEC, and Modus.

MTM brought suit alleging that Amazon's response to a search for the MTM Special Ops watch on its website is trademark infringement in violation of the Lanham Act. MTM contends that Amazon's search results page creates a likelihood of confusion, even though there is no evidence of any actual confusion and even though the other brands are clearly identified by name. The district court granted summary judgment in favor of Amazon, and MTM now appeals.

We affirm. "The core element of trademark infringement" is whether the defendant's conduct "is likely to confuse customers about the source of the products." *E. & J. Gallo Winery v. Gallo Cattle Co.,* 967 F.2d 1280, 1290 (9th Cir.1992). Because Amazon's search results page clearly labels the name and manufacturer of each product offered for sale and even includes photographs of the items, no reasonably prudent consumer accustomed to shopping online would likely be confused as to the source of the products. Thus, summary judgment of MTM's trademark claims was proper.

I. Factual and Procedural Background

MTM manufactures and markets watches under various brand names including MTM, MTM Special Ops, and MTM Military Ops. MTM holds the federally registered trademark "MTM Special Ops" for timepieces. MTM sells its watches directly to its customers and through various retailers. To cultivate and maintain an image as a high-end, exclusive brand, MTM does not sell its watches through Amazon.com. Further, MTM does not authorize its distributors, whose agreements require them to seek MTM's permission to sell MTM's products anywhere but their own retail sites, to sell MTM watches on Amazon.com. Therefore, MTM watches have never been available for sale on Amazon.com.

Amazon is an online retailer that purports to offer "Earth's Biggest Selection of products." Amazon has designed its website to enable millions of unique products to be sold by both Amazon and third party sellers across dozens of product categories.

Consumers who wish to shop for products on Amazon's website can utilize Amazon's search function. The search function enables consumers to navigate Amazon.com's large marketplace by providing consumers with relevant results in response to the consumer's query. In order to provide search results in which the consumer is most likely to be interested, Amazon's search function does not simply match the words in the user's query to words in a document, such as a product description in Amazon.com's catalog. Rather, Amazon's search function—like general purpose web search engines such as Google or Bing—employs a variety of techniques, including some that rely on user behavior, to produce relevant results. By going beyond exactly matching a user's query to text describing a product, Amazon's search function can provide consumers with relevant results that would otherwise be overlooked.

Consumers who go onto Amazon.com and search for the term "mtm special ops" are directed to a search results page. On the search results page, the search query used— here, "mtm special ops"—is displayed twice: in the search query box and directly below the search query box in what is termed a "breadcrumb." The breadcrumb displays the original query, "mtm special ops," in quotation marks to provide a trail for the consumer to follow back to the original search. Directly below the breadcrumb, is a "Related Searches" field, which provides the consumer with alternative search queries in case the consumer is dissatisfied with the results of the original search. Here, the Related Search that is suggested to the consumer is: "mtm special ops watch." Directly below the "Related Searches" field is a gray bar containing the text "Showing 10 Results." Then, directly below the gray bar is Amazon's product listings. The gray bar separates the product listings from the breadcrumb and the "Related Searches" field. The particular search results page at issue is displayed below:

MTM watches are not listed on the page for the simple reason that neither Amazon nor MTM sells MTM watches on Amazon. MTM filed a complaint against Amazon, alleging that Amazon's search results page infringes MTM's trademarks in violation of the Lanham Act. . . . The district court granted Amazon's motion for summary judgment. . . .

III. Discussion

To prevail on a claim of trademark infringement under the Lanham Act, "a trademark holder must show that the defendant's use of its trademark 'is likely to cause confusion, or to cause mistake, or to deceive.'" *Fortune Dynamic, Inc. v. Victoria's Secret Stores Brand Mgmt.*, 618 F.3d 1025, 1030 (9th Cir. 2010) (quoting 15 U.S.C. § 1125(a)(1)–(a)(1)(A)). "The test for likelihood of confusion is whether a 'reasonably prudent consumer' in the marketplace is likely to be confused as to the origin of the good or service bearing one of the marks." *Dreamwerks Prod. Group v. SKG Studio,*

142 F.3d 1127, 1129 (9th Cir. 1998). "The confusion must 'be probable, not simply a possibility.'" *Murray v. Cable NBC*, 86 F.3d 858, 861 (9th Cir.1996).

Here, the district court was correct in ruling that there is no likelihood of confusion. Amazon is responding to a customer's inquiry about a brand it does not carry by doing no more than stating clearly (and showing pictures of) what brands it does carry. . . .

In the present case, the eight-factor *Sleekcraft* test is not particularly apt. This is not surprising as the *Sleekcraft* test was developed for a different problem—i.e., for analyzing whether two competing brands' *marks* are sufficiently similar to cause consumer confusion. *See Sleekcraft*, 599 F.2d at 348. Although the present case involves *brands* that compete with MTM, such as Luminox, Chase–Durer, TAWATEC, and Modus, MTM does not contend that the *marks* for these competing brands are similar to its trademarks. Rather, MTM argues that the design of Amazon's search results page creates a likelihood of initial interest confusion because when a customer searches for MTM Special Ops watches on Amazon.com, the search results page displays the search term used—here, "mtm special ops"—followed by a display of numerous watches manufactured by MTM's competitors and offered for sale by Amazon, without explicitly informing the customer that Amazon does not carry MTM watches.

Thus, the present case focuses on a different type of confusion than was at issue in *Sleekcraft*. Here, the confusion is not caused by the design of the competitor's mark, but by the design of the web page that is displaying the competing mark and offering the competing products for sale. *Sleekcraft* aside, the ultimate test for determining likelihood of confusion is whether a "reasonably prudent consumer" in the marketplace is likely to be confused as to the origin of the goods. *Dreamwerks*, 142 F.3d at 1129. Our case can be resolved simply by an evaluation of the web page at issue and the relevant consumer. *Cf. Brookfield*, 174 F.3d at 1054 ("[I]t is often possible to reach a conclusion with respect to likelihood of confusion after considering only a subset of the factors."). Indeed, we have previously noted that "[i]n the keyword advertising context [i.e., where a user performs a search on the internet, and based on the keywords contained in the search, the resulting web page displays certain advertisements containing products or services for sale,] the 'likelihood of confusion will ultimately turn on what the consumer saw on the screen and reasonably believed, given the context.'" *Network Automation*, 638 F.3d at 1153. In other words, the case will turn on the answers to the following two questions: (1) Who is the relevant reasonable consumer?; and (2) What would he reasonably believe based on what he saw on the screen?

Turning to the first question, we have explained that "[t]he nature of the goods and the type of consumer is highly relevant to determining the likelihood of confusion in the keyword advertising context." *Network Automation*, 638 F.3d at 1152. "In evaluating this factor, we consider 'the typical buyer exercising ordinary caution.' " *Au–Tomotive Gold, Inc. v. Volkswagen of Am., Inc.*, 457 F.3d 1062, 1076 (9th Cir. 2006) (quoting *Sleekcraft*, 599 F.2d at 353). "Confusion is less likely where buyers exercise care and precision in their purchases, such as for expensive or sophisticated items." *Id.* Moreover, "the default degree of consumer care is becoming more heightened as the novelty of the

Internet evaporates and online commerce becomes commonplace." *Network Automation,* 638 F.3d at 1152.

The goods in the present case are expensive. It is undisputed that the watches at issue sell for several hundred dollars. Therefore, the relevant consumer in the present case "is a reasonably prudent consumer accustomed to shopping online." *Toyota Motor Sales, U.S.A., Inc. v. Tabari,* 610 F.3d 1171, 1176 (9th Cir. 2010).

Turning to the second question, as MTM itself asserts, the labeling and appearance of the products for sale on Amazon's web page is the most important factor in this case. This is because we have previously noted that clear labeling can eliminate the likelihood of initial interest confusion in cases involving Internet search terms. *See, e.g., Playboy Enters.,* 354 F.3d at 1030 n. 44 (explaining that clear labeling "might eliminate the likelihood of initial interest confusion that exists in this case"); *Network Automation,* 638 F.3d at 1154 (same). Indeed, MTM itself argues: "The common thread of [the Ninth Circuit's decisions in *Brookfield, Playboy,* and *Network Automation*] is that liability under the Lanham Act can only be avoided as a matter of law where there is clear labeling to avoid the possibility of confusion—including initial interest confusion—resulting from the use of another's trademark." Thus, MTM agrees that summary judgment of its trademark claims is appropriate if there is clear labeling that avoids likely confusion.

Here, the products at issue are clearly labeled by Amazon to avoid any likelihood of initial interest confusion by a reasonably prudent consumer accustomed to online shopping. When a shopper goes to Amazon's website and searches for a product using MTM's trademark "mtm special ops," the resulting page displays several products, all of which are clearly labeled with the product's name and manufacturer in large, bright, bold letters and includes a photograph of the item. In fact, the manufacturer's name is listed twice. For example, the first result is "Luminox Men's 8401 Black Ops Watch by Luminox." The second result is "Chase–Durer Men's 246.4BB7–XL–BR Special Forces 1000XL Black Ionic–Plated Underwater Demolition Team Watch by Chase–Durer." Because Amazon clearly labels each of the products for sale by brand name and model number accompanied by a photograph of the item, it is unreasonable to suppose that the reasonably prudent consumer accustomed to shopping online would be confused about the source of the goods.

. . . MTM argues that because Amazon lists the search term "mtm special ops" at the top of the page, a consumer might conclude that the products displayed are types of MTM watches. But, merely looking at Amazon's search results page shows that such consumer confusion is highly unlikely. None of these watches is labeled with the word "MTM" or the phrase "Special Ops," let alone the specific phrase "MTM Special Ops." Further, some of the products listed are not even watches. The sixth result is a book entitled "Survive!: The Disaster, Crisis and Emergency Handbook by Jerry Ahem." The tenth result is a book entitled "The Moses Expedition: A Novel by Juan Gómez–Jurado." No reasonably prudent consumer, accustomed to shopping online or not, would assume that a book entitled "The Moses Expedition" is a type of MTM watch or is in any way affiliated with MTM watches. Likewise, no reasonably prudent consumer accustomed to shopping online would view Amazon's search results page and conclude that the products offered are MTM watches. It is possible that someone, somewhere might be confused by the search results page. But, "[u]nreasonable, imprudent and inexperienced web-shoppers are not relevant." *Tabari,* 610 F.3d at 1176; *see also Network Automation,* 638 F.3d at 1153 ("[W]e expect consumers searching for expensive products online to be even more sophisticated."). To establish likelihood of confusion, MTM must show that confusion is *likely,* not just *possible. See Murray,* 86 F.3d at 861.

MTM argues that in order to eliminate the likelihood of confusion, Amazon must change its search results page so that it explains to customers that it does not offer MTM watches for sale before suggesting alternative watches to the customer. We disagree. The search results page makes clear to anyone who can read English that Amazon carries only the brands that are clearly and explicitly listed on the web page. The search results page is unambiguous—not unlike when someone walks into a diner, asks for a Coke, and is told "No Coke. Pepsi." *See Multi Time Mach., Inc. v. Amazon.com, Inc.,* 792 F.3d 1070, 1080–81 (9th Cir. 2015) (Silverman, J., dissenting).

In light of the clear labeling Amazon uses on its search results page, no reasonable trier of fact could conclude that Amazon's search results page would likely confuse a reasonably prudent consumer accustomed to shopping online as to the source of the goods being offered. *Cf. Playboy,* 354 F.3d at 1030 n. 44 (Clear labeling "might eliminate the likelihood of initial interest confusion that exists in this case."); *Network Automation,* 638 F.3d at 1154 (same). As Judge Berzon put it, "I do not think it is reasonable to find initial interest confusion when a consumer is never confused as to source or affiliation, but instead knows, or should know, from the outset that a product or web link is not related to that of the trademark holder because the list produced by the search engine so informs him." *Playboy,* 354 F.3d at 1034–35 (9th Cir. 2004) (Berzon, J., concurring). . . .

The likelihood of confusion is often a question of fact, but not always. In a case such as this, where a court can conclude that the consumer confusion alleged by the trademark holder is highly unlikely by simply reviewing the product listing/advertisement at issue, summary judgment is appropriate. *Cf. M2 Software,* 421 F.3d at 1085 (explaining that summary judgment of a trademark claim is appropriate where the plaintiff has failed to present "sufficient evidence to permit a rational trier of fact to find that confusion is 'probable,' not merely 'possible' ").

. . . However, if we were to evaluate each of the remaining *Sleekcraft factors,* those factors would not change our conclusion, here, because those factors are either neutral or unimportant.

"Actual confusion"—We have held that "[a] showing of actual confusion among significant numbers of consumers provides strong support for the likelihood of confusion." *Playboy,* 354 F.3d at 1026 (noting that a strong showing by the plaintiff in regard to this factor alone can reverse a grant of summary judgment). However, here, there is no evidence of actual confusion. The only "evidence" MTM presented to the district court of actual confusion is the deposition testimony of MTM's president stating that someone named Eric told him, in reference to Amazon's web page, "it's confusing." Hearsay problems aside, this testimony is too speculative to show actual confusion because there is no evidence showing that Eric was a potential consumer. Indeed, at oral argument, MTM conceded that it does not have evidence of actual consumer confusion. Therefore, this factor does not weigh in MTM's favor.

"Defendant's Intent"—We have also held that "[a] defendant's intent to confuse constitutes probative evidence of likely confusion: Courts assume that the defendant's intentions were carried out successfully." *Playboy,* 354 F.3d at 1028 (footnote omitted). MTM argues that the design of Amazon's search results page is evidence of its intent to cause confusion. The design, however, indisputably produces results that are clearly labeled as to the type of product and brand. Amazon has designed its results page to alleviate any possible confusion about the source of the products by clearly labeling each of its products with the product's name and manufacturer. Therefore, this factor also does not weigh in MTM's favor.

. . . [A]s we previously found in *Network Automation,* the remaining *Sleekcraft* factors are unimportant in a case, such as this, involving Internet search terms where the competing products are clearly labeled and the relevant consumer would exercise a high degree of care. *See Network Automation,* 638 F.3d at 1150–53 (finding "proximity of goods," "similarity of marks," "marketing channels," and "likelihood of expansion" to be unimportant in a trademark case involving Internet search terms where the advertisements are clearly labeled and the relevant consumers would exercise a high degree of care).

IV. Conclusion

In light of Amazon's clear labeling of the products it carries, by brand name and model, accompanied by a photograph of the item, no rational trier of fact could find that a reasonably prudent consumer accustomed to shopping online would likely be confused by the Amazon search results. Accordingly, we affirm the district court's grant of summary judgment in favor of Amazon.

AFFIRMED.

BEA, Circuit Judge, dissenting:

Today the panel holds that when it comes to internet commerce, judges, not jurors, decide what labeling may confuse shoppers. In so doing, the court departs from our own trademark precedent and from our summary judgment jurisprudence. Because I believe that an Amazon shopper seeking an MTM watch might well initially think that the watches Amazon offers for sale when he searches "MTM Special Ops" are affiliated with MTM, I must dissent.

If her brother mentioned MTM Special Ops watches, a frequent internet shopper might try to purchase one for him through her usual internet retail sites, perhaps Overstock.com, Buy.com, and Amazon.com. At Overstock's site, if she typed "MTM special ops," the site would respond "Sorry, your search: 'mtm special ops' returned no results."

Similarly, at Buy.com, she would be informed "0 results found. Sorry. Your search for mtm special ops did not return an exact match. Please try your search again."

Things are a little different over at "Earth's most customer-centric company," as Amazon styles itself. There, if she were to enter "MTM Special Ops" as her search request on the Amazon website, Amazon would respond with its page showing (1) MTM Special Ops in the search field (2) "MTM Specials Ops" again—in quotation marks—immediately below the search field and (3) yet again in the phrase "Related Searches: *MTM special ops watch,*" (emphasis in original) all before stating "Showing 10 Results." What the website's response will not state is the truth recognized by its competitors: that Amazon does not carry MTM products any more than do Over-stock.com or Buy.com. Rather, below the search field, and below the second and third mentions of "MTM Special Ops" noted above, the site will display aesthetically similar, multi-function watches manufactured by MTM's competitors. The shopper will see that Luminox and Chase–Durer watches are offered for sale, in response to her MTM query.

MTM asserts the shopper might be confused into thinking a relationship exists be-tween Luminox and MTM; she may think that MTM was acquired by Luminox, or that MTM manufactures component parts of Luminox watches, for instance. As a result of this initial confusion, MTM asserts, she might look into buying a Luminox watch, rather than junk the quest altogether and seek to buy an MTM watch elsewhere. MTM asserts that Amazon's use of MTM's trademarked name is likely to confuse buyers, who may ultimately buy a competitor's goods.

MTM may be mistaken. But whether MTM is mistaken is a question that requires a factual determination, one this court does not have authority to make. . . .

Capturing initial consumer attention has been recognized by our court to be a grounds for finding of infringement of the Lanham Act since 1997. *Dr. Seuss Enter-prises, L.P. v. Penguin Books USA, Inc.,* 109 F.3d 1394, 1405 (9th Cir. 1997) (identify-ing "initial consumer attention" as a basis for infringement). In 1999, citing *Dr. Seuss,* we expressly adopted the initial interest confusion doctrine in the internet context, and never repudiated it. *Brookfield Communications, Inc. v. West Coast Entertainment Corp.,* 174 F.3d 1036, 1062 (9th Cir. 1999). It may not apply where the competing goods or services are "clearly labeled" such that they cause only mere diversion, but whether such goods or services are clearly labeled so as to prevent a prudent internet shopper's initial confusion depends on the overall function and presentation of the web page. The issue is whether a prudent internet shopper who made the search request and saw the Amazon result—top to bottom—would more likely than not be affected by that "initial interest confusion." That is, an impression—when first shown the results of the re-quested MTM Special Ops search—that Amazon carries watches that have some con-nection to MTM, and that those watches are sold under the name Luminox or Chase–Durer. Whether there is likelihood of such initial interest confusion, I submit, is a jury question. Intimations in our case law that initial interest confusion is bad doctrine not-withstanding, it is the law of our circuit, and, I submit, the most fair reading of the Lanham Act.

... [T]he majority reads 15 U.S.C. § 1125 to apply only at point of sale—the majority writes that it is unreasonable to suppose that a reasonably prudent consumer accustomed to shopping online would be confused about the source of the goods where Luminox and Chase-Durer watches are labeled as such, but does not address the possibility that a reasonably prudent consumer might initially assume that those brands enjoyed some affiliation with MTM which, in turn, could cause such a shopper to investigate brands which otherwise would not have been of interest to her. . . .

On this record, a jury could infer that users who are confused by the search results are confused as to why MTM products are not listed. There is a question of fact whether users who are confused by the search result will wonder whether a competitor has acquired MTM or is otherwise affiliated with or approved by MTM. . . .

[T]he majority finds that Amazon's intent weighs in favor of Amazon. A defendant's intent is relevant because a "defendant's intent to confuse constitutes probative evidence of likely confusion." *Playboy,* 354 F.3d at 1029. MTM submitted evidence that Amazon vendors and customers had complained to Amazon because they did not understand why they received certain non-responsive search results when they searched for products that are not carried by Amazon. The evidence showed that Amazon employees did not take action to address the complaints by explaining to the public how its search function works. One Amazon employee noted that explaining [broad-based searching] to the public might draw customers' and vendors' unwanted scrutiny to the matter. Amazon did not disclose to shoppers that its search function responds to customer behavior.

As in *Playboy,* this evidence suggests, "at a minimum, that defendants do nothing to alleviate confusion . . . Although not definitive, this factor provides some evidence of an intent to confuse on the part of defendants." *Playboy,* 354 F.3d at 1029. From evidence that "Earth's most customer-centric company" took no action on these complaints, a jury could infer that Amazon intended to confuse its customers. . . .

COMMENTS AND QUESTIONS

1. Is Amazon engaged in "bait and switch" tactics? How difficult would it be for Amazon to indicate that it does not carry the brand indicated in the keyword search? What if Amazon's search results were to indicate: "We don't carry 'MTM Special Ops' brand, but we do have the following competing products"?

Could Amazon automate that process? How would its servers know when to generate such a statement? Consider that trademark owners might also sue if Amazon *did* carry their products but wrongly included a statement saying it did not.

2. Claims of initial interest confusion arise most frequently on the Internet. Early search engines categorized results in part by the site's use of "metatags," which are words on the page invisible to the user but which are read by computer search engines. Some companies began putting the names of their competitors' products (or even just

popular trademarks such as "Playboy") into their metatags in an effort to draw unsuspecting consumers to their site. Is the use of a competitor's trademark in a metatag infringement? The cases seem to turn on whether there was a legitimate reason to make reference to the trademark on the web page. *Compare Brookfield Commc'ns v. West Coast Entm't Corp.*, 174 F.3d 1036 (9th Cir. 1999) (use of plaintiff's trademark in a website "metatag" was trademark infringement where it contributed to customer confusion) *and People for the Ethical Treatment of Animals v. Doughney*, 263 F.3d 359 (4th Cir. 2001) *with Playboy Enters. v. Welles*, 279 F.3d 796 (9th Cir. 2002) (use of "Playmate of the Year" in a metatag to accurately describe defendant's resume was not illegal).

Most search engines no longer use metatags. Instead, the issue of initial interest confusion comes up in the context of search results and ads which may divert Internet users to sites other than the one they are searching for. Should the same analysis apply to ad text that diverts consumer attention away from their "intended" search result?

2. *Doughney* is a particularly interesting application of the idea of initial interest confusion concept. The plaintiff, People for the Ethical Treatment of Animals (PETA), is an advocacy group opposed to eating meat, wearing fur, and conducting research on animals. The defendant registered the Internet domain name peta.org, where he set up a page entitled "People Eating Tasty Animals" that was a parody of PETA and its goals. The Fourth Circuit found that using the domain name peta.org impermissibly caused initial-interest confusion, even though visitors to the site immediately discovered that it had no affiliation with PETA and even though Doughney was not competing with PETA in any commercial sense. Is this result correct? Or should initial interest confusion be limited to cases in which the parties are direct competitors, as the Third Circuit held in *Checkpoint Sys. v. Check Point Software Techs.*, 269 F.3d 270 (3d Cir. 2001)? *See* Stacey L. Dogan & Mark A. Lemley, *Trademarks and Search Costs on the Internet*, 41 HOUS. L. REV. 777 (2004) (making the latter argument).

3. Some commentators have been critical of the expansion of confusion doctrines, particularly as regards the Internet. *See, e.g.*, Eric Goldman, *Deregulating Relevancy in Internet Trademark Law*, 54 EMORY L.J. 507 (2005). They argue that attraction of initial interest is easy to reverse in the Internet context—the confused surfer simply clicks the "back" button on their Internet browser. As one court explained,

> what appears to concern Groeneveld is not so much initial-interest *confusion,* but initial interest, period. Groeneveld, in other words, simply does not want its customers to become interested in Lubecore as a potential competitor and possibly switch over. We cannot ascribe any other interpretation to Groeneveld's rather startling claim that evidence of diverted sales and declining revenues, which are the normal signs of a market opening up to competition, create "a reasonable inference of confusion and its likelihood." Groeneveld's desire to be the only game in town is perfectly natural; most companies would hope for that status. But Groeneveld cannot get any help from trade-dress law in suppressing lawful competition.

Groeneveld Tr. Efficiency, Inc. v. Lubecore Int'l, Inc., 730 F.3d 494, 519 (6th Cir. 2013).

4. Is there anything left of the initial interest confusion doctrine after *Multi-Time Machine*? Is accurately labeling the products you are selling always sufficient to avoid such confusion?

5. Some scholars note that much operative law in the contemporary economy is made in the first instance by large "platform" companies such as Amazon.com. *See, e.g.,* Jane K. Winn, *The Secession of the Successful: The Rise of Amazon as Private Global Consumer Protection Regulator*, 58 AZ. L. REV. 193 (2016). Not all companies selling goods on these companies have the resources to challenge platform company standard policy, and not all may want to for fear of repercussions. Should courts require informal, intra-company dispute resolution mechanisms in these instances? If so, how should courts review them for fairness, etc.?

b. *Post-Sale Confusion*

Suppose that consumers do not confuse two products at the point of purchase, but that third parties mistake the source of the purchased product from a distance (or stripped of identifying trademarks). This was the situation in *Lois Sportswear, U.S.A., Inc. v. Levi Strauss & Co.*, 799 F.2d 867 (2d Cir. 1986). There, Levi Strauss had registered not only its trade name and its jean labels, but also the pattern of stitching on the back pockets of its jeans. Lois Sportswear sold jeans with clearly different labels, but with an identical stitching pattern. The trial court found that there was no evidence of actual confusion by purchasers but that nonpurchasers, seeing the jeans "worn by a passer-by," would likely be confused. Should such "post-sale confusion" be actionable? The Second Circuit held that post-sale confusion constituted trademark infringement: "The confusion the Act seeks to prevent in this context is that a consumer seeing the familiar stitching pattern will associate the jeans with [Levi's] and that association will influence his buying decisions."

The district court also concluded that the Lois jeans were not of inferior quality. Given that, how is Levi Strauss & Co. hurt by any confusion that does arise? It will not lose sales, since customers themselves are not confused. Further, any confusion inures to the company's benefit, doesn't it? Whose interests are being protected by this decision?

Although some courts still require point of sale confusion, *see, e.g., Gibson Guitar Corp. v. Paul Reed Smith Guitars*, 423 F.3d 539 (6th Cir. 2005); *Beneficial Corp. v. Beneficial Capital Corp.*, 529 F. Supp. 445 (S.D.N.Y. 1982) (holding that trademark law protects only against mistaken purchasing decisions); *Nike, Inc. v. "Just Did It" Enters.*, 6 F.3d 1225 (7th Cir. 1993), many also recognize confusion after the sale of a product as actionable. In *Mastercrafters Clock & Radio Co. v. Vacheron & Constantin-Le Coultre Watches, Inc.*, 221 F.2d 464 (2d Cir. 1955), the junior user copied the distinctive appearance of the senior user's expensive "Atmos" clock. Judge Frank held that

> at least some customers would buy [the copier's] cheaper clock for the purpose of acquiring the prestige gained by displaying what many visitors at the customers' homes would regard as a prestigious article. [The copier's] wrong thus consisted of the fact that such a visitor would be likely to assume that the clock was an Atmos clock. . . . [T]he likelihood of such confusion suffices to render [the copier's] conduct actionable.

Id. at 466. This same problem arises in the sale of "knockoff" versions of high quality goods on street corners and flea markets. The purchaser of a "Rolex" branded watch for $25 on a street corner appreciates that he or she is not purchasing an authentic product. *See Rolex Watch U.S.A., Inc. v. Canner*, 645 F. Supp. 484 (S.D. Fla. 1986); *United States v. Torkington*, 812 F.2d 1347 (11th Cir. 1987). One might reasonably conclude, therefore, that there is no consumer confusion from counterfeiting. But courts have resisted that result. Some have pointed to a harm to the exclusivity of a luxury good:

> [t]he creation of confusion in the post-sale context can be harmful in that if there are too many knockoffs in the market, sales of the originals may decline because the public is fearful that what they are purchasing may not be an original. Furthermore, the public may be deceived in the resale market if it requires expertise to distinguish between an original and a knockoff. Finally, the purchaser of an original is harmed by the widespread existence of knockoffs because the high value of originals, which derives in part from their scarcity, is lessened.

See Hermes Int'l v. Lederer de Paris Fifth Ave., Inc., 219 F.3d 104, 108 (2d Cir. 2000). *See generally* MCCARTHY, TRADEMARKS AND UNFAIR COMPETITION § 23:7; Alex Kozinski, *Trademarks Unplugged*, 68 N.Y.U. L. REV. 960 (1993). Other courts simply fall back on the declaration that "it cannot be the case" that a defendant can get away with profiting from a mark owner's goodwill, whether or not the consumers are confused. *Coach, Inc. v. The Treasure Box, Inc.*, 2013 WL 2402922 (N.D. Ind. May 31, 2013).

How would one prove post-sale confusion? Who are the relevant consumers? *Compare General Motors Corp. v. Urban Gorilla LLC*, 500 F.3d 1222 (10th Cir. 2007) (denying injunction against company that made "body kits" that made another truck look like a Hummer; court found insufficient evidence of post-sale confusion) *with Ferrari S.p.A. v. Roberts*, 944 F.2d 1235, 1239 (6th Cir. 1991) (finding infringement in the sale of kit cars); *see* Kal Raustiala & Christopher Jon Sprigman, *Rethinking Post-Sale Confusion*, 108 TRADEMARK REP. 881, 903 (May-June 2018) (contending that post-sale confusion is rare and that courts should be required to show a clear connection between post-sale confusion and harm, and not just observer confusion; "and even if even if [post-sale] confusion is clearly established, defendants may be able to show that this confusion is, on balance, beneficial—or that a substantial chunk of it is beneficial, and hence any monetary award ought to be highly circumscribed.").

PROBLEMS

Problem V-12. Bristol-Myers, a major pharmaceutical company, markets "Excedrin" pain reliever. Since 1968, B-M has marketed "Excedrin PM," which is a pain reliever that does not interfere with sleep. Excedrin PM tablets are sold in a solid blue box whose color fades from dark at the top to light at the bottom. The box contains the words "Excedrin PM" in large white letters across the top third of the box. In the bottom right-hand corner of the box is a depiction of two tablets labeled "PM." B-M also sells Excedrin PM capsules, which are packaged identically except that the background is green and the two capsules in the picture read "Excedrin PM." Both the mark Excedrin PM and the dress of both boxes are registered with the Trademark Office.

In 1991, McNeil Pharmaceuticals introduced "Tylenol PM," a pain reliever chemically identical to Excedrin PM. Tylenol PM tablets are sold in a solid blue box whose color fades from dark at the top to light at the bottom. The box contains the words "Tylenol PM" in large white and yellow letters across the top third of the box. In the bottom right-hand corner of the box is a depiction of two tablets, one labeled "Tylenol" and the other labeled "PM." McNeil also sells Tylenol PM capsules, which are packaged identically except that the background is blue and the two capsules in the picture both read "Tylenol PM."

B-M sues McNeil, alleging that both its use of the term PM and its trade dress are likely to confuse consumers. Who should prevail?

Problem V-13. Ivory Soap is sold for approximately $1.00 a bar. It is a heavily advertised brand name, which identifies itself as "99.44% pure." Whitewash Soap Co. makes and sells counterfeit Ivory Soap bars, which are packaged identically to Ivory (using the Ivory name and trade dress) and which contain chemically identical bars of soap. These counterfeit "Ivory" bars are sold for $.50 each. If a consumer buys the Whitewash soap thinking it is Ivory, how has he been injured? Hasn't he benefited? Is there any reason to protect Ivory's trademark against infringement at the expense of consumer welfare?

v. *Dilution*

Nearly a century ago, Frank Schechter, a trademark practitioner, proposed to protect trademarks against loss of distinctiveness—what has come to be known as dilution. *See* Frank I. Schechter, *The Rational Basis of Trademark Protection*, 40 HARV. L. REV. 813 (1927). This theory departed from the standard confusion-based account of trademark protection. Schechter believed that dilution better fit the ways that marks functioned in the marketplace and that courts ought to recognize that reality.

The famous 1898 British case of Kodak bicycles illustrated Schechter's idea. *See Eastman Kodak Co. v. Kodak Cycle Co.*, 15 Rep. Pat. Cas. 105 (1898). The court there allowed the famous Kodak film company to stop the use of Kodak for bicycles, reasoning that Kodak would suffer harm from the use even if no one would think the film company was making bicycles. Schechter argued that "If 'Kodak' may be used for bath tubs and cakes . . . and 'Ritz-Carlton' for coffee, these marks must inevitably be lost in the commonplace words of the language, despite the originality and ingenuity in their contrivance, and the vast expenditures in advertising them which the courts concede should be protected to the same extent as plant and machinery." 40 HARV. L. REV. at 830.

The dilution theory did not attract much support in the years following Schechter's publication. *See* Robert G. Bone, *Schechter's Ideas in Historical Context and Dilution's Rocky Road*, 24 SANTA CLARA COMPUTER & HIGH TECH. L.J. 469 (2008). It was ignored in the formulation of the Lanham Act of 1946. Yet, beginning in 1947, a number of states passed anti-dilution statutes. Massachusetts led the way, followed over the next decade by Illinois, New York, and Georgia. In 1965, The U.S. Trademark Association adopted an anti-dilution provision to its Model State Trademark Bill.

The trademark dilution theory gradually gained salience and brand owners succeeded in persuading Congress to establish federal anti-dilution protection in the mid-1990s. The legislative history of the Federal Trademark Dilution Act of 1995, Pub. L. No. 104-98, codified at 15 U.S.C. § 1125(c), which added a new § 43(c) to the Lanham Act, explained that:

> [This bill would] create a federal cause of action to protect famous marks from unauthorized users that attempt to trade upon the goodwill and established renown of such marks and, thereby, dilute their distinctive quality. The provision is intended to protect famous marks where the subsequent, unauthorized commercial use of such marks by others dilutes the distinctiveness of the mark. The bill defines the term "dilution" to mean "the lessening of the capacity of a famous mark to identify and distinguish goods or services regardless of the presence or absence of (a) competition between the parties, or (b) likelihood of confusion, mistakes, or deception." Thus, for example, the use of DUPONT shoes, BUICK aspirin, and KODAK pianos would be actionable under this legislation. The protection of marks from dilution differs from the protection accorded marks from trademark infringement. Dilution does not rely upon the standard

test of infringement, that is, likelihood of confusion, deception or mistake. Rather, it applies when the unauthorized use of a famous mark reduces the public's perception that the mark signifies something unique, singular, or particular. As summarized in one decision:

> Dilution is an injury that differs materially from that arising out of the orthodox confusion. Even in the absence of confusion, the potency of a mark may be debilitated by another's use. This is the essence of dilution. Confusion leads to immediate injury, while dilution is an infection, which if allowed to spread, will inevitably destroy the advertising value of the mark.

Mortellito v. Nina of California, Inc., 335 F. Supp. 1288, 1296 (S.D.N.Y. 1972).

In 2003, the Supreme Court interpreted that statute to prevent only *actual* dilution rather than a likelihood of dilution. *Moseley v. V Secret Catalogue*, 537 U.S. 418 (2003). Congress overrode this interpretation in 2006 to require only a likelihood of, as well as to change the definition of dilution to make it harder to prove and to expand defenses to dilution. Section 43(c) of the Lanham Act now provides in part:

(c) Dilution by blurring; dilution by tarnishment

(1) Injunctive relief. Subject to the principles of equity, the owner of a famous mark that is distinctive, inherently or through acquired distinctiveness, shall be entitled to an injunction against another person who, at any time after the owner's mark has become famous, commences use of a mark or trade name in commerce that is likely to cause dilution by blurring or dilution by tarnishment of the famous mark, regardless of the presence or absence of actual or likely confusion, of competition, or of actual economic injury.

(2) Definitions

(A) For purposes of paragraph (1), a mark is famous if it is widely recognized by the general consuming public of the United States as a designation of source of the goods or services of the mark's owner. In determining whether a mark possesses the requisite degree of recognition, the court may consider all relevant factors, including the following:

(i) The duration, extent, and geographic reach of advertising and publicity of the mark, whether advertised or publicized by the owner or third parties.

(ii) The amount, volume, and geographic extent of sales of goods or services offered under the mark.

(iii) The extent of actual recognition of the mark.

(iv) Whether the mark was registered under the Act of March 3, 1881, or the Act of February 20, 1905, or on the principal register.

(B) For purposes of paragraph (1), "dilution by blurring" is association arising from the similarity between a mark or trade name and a famous mark that impairs the distinctiveness of the famous mark. In determining whether a mark or trade name is likely to cause dilution by blurring, the court may consider all relevant factors, including the following:

(i) The degree of similarity between the mark or trade name and the famous mark.

(ii) The degree of inherent or acquired distinctiveness of the famous mark.

(iii) The extent to which the owner of the famous mark is engaging in substantially exclusive use of the mark.

(iv) The degree of recognition of the famous mark.

(v) Whether the user of the mark or trade name intended to create an association with the famous mark.

(vi) Any actual association between the mark or trade name and the famous mark.

(C) For purposes of paragraph (1), "dilution by tarnishment" is association arising from the similarity between a mark or trade name and a famous mark that harms the reputation of the famous mark.

(3) Exclusions. The following shall not be actionable as dilution by blurring or dilution by tarnishment under this subsection:

(A) Any fair use, including a nominative or descriptive fair use, or facilitation of such fair use, of a famous mark by another person other than as a designation of source for the person's own goods or services, including use in connection with—

(i) advertising or promotion that permits consumers to compare goods or services; or

(ii) identifying and parodying, criticizing, or commenting upon the famous mark owner or the goods or services of the famous mark owner.

(B) All forms of news reporting and news commentary.

(C) Any noncommercial use of a mark.

Lanham Act § 43(c), 15 U.S.C. § 1125(c).

COMMENTS AND QUESTIONS

1. Schechter's proposal applied only to coined, fanciful, or arbitrary marks, only to situations in which the junior user's mark was identical to that of the senior user, and only to use of identical marks on noncompeting goods. 40 HARV. L. REV. at 825–30. Courts and commentators have since expanded the doctrine to include marks that have acquired secondary meaning, situations where the junior user's mark has substantial similarity to the senior user's mark, *see, e.g., Mead Data Central, Inc. v. Toyota Motor*

Sales, U.S.A., Inc., 875 F.2d 1026 (2d Cir. 1989), and to use of similar marks on competing goods, *see, e.g., Deere & Co. v. MTD Products, Inc.*, 41 F.3d 39 (2d Cir. 1994) (enjoining MTD, a manufacturer of tractors, from using an animated version of Deere's well-known leaping deer trademark in its television advertising campaign).

2. At least some commentators believe that anti-dilution law does not go far enough in protecting trademark owners. *See* Jerre B. Swann, *Dilution Redefined for the Year 2002*, 92 TRADEMARK REP. 585 (2002); Jerre B. Swann & Theodore H. Davis, Jr., *Dilution, An Idea Whose Time Has Gone: Brand Equity as Protectable Property, The New/Old Paradigm*, 1 J. INTELL. PROP. L. 219 (1994) (arguing for explicit property rights in brand equity, going beyond anti-dilution law). Other commentators contend it has gone too far. *See* Kenneth L. Port, *The "Unnatural" Expansion of Trademark Rights: Is a Federal Dilution Statute Necessary?*, 85 TRADEMARK REP. 525 (1995); *see also* Kenneth L. Port, *Trademark Extortion: The End of Trademark Law*, 65 WASH. & LEE L. REV. 585, 585 (2008) (arguing dilution statutes provide the means for effective strike suits by owners against new market entrants); Clarisa Long, *Dilution*, 106 COLUM. L. REV. 1029, 1032 (2006) (reporting judicial resistance to dilution).

Louis Vuitton Malletier S.A. v. Haute Diggity Dog, LLC
United States Court of Appeals for the Fourth Circuit
507 F.3d 252 (4th Cir. 2007)

NIEMEYER, Circuit Judge:

Louis Vuitton Malletier S.A., a French corporation located in Paris, that manufactures luxury luggage, handbags, and accessories, commenced this action against Haute Diggity Dog, LLC, a Nevada corporation that manufactures and sells pet products nationally, alleging trademark infringement under 15 U.S.C. § 1114(1)(a), trademark dilution under 15 U.S.C. § 1125(c), copyright infringement under 17 U.S.C. § 501, and related statutory and common law violations. Haute Diggity Dog manufactures, among other things, plush toys on which dogs can chew, which, it claims, parody famous trademarks on luxury products, including those of Louis Vuitton Malletier. The particular Haute Diggity Dog chew toys in question here are small imitations of handbags that are labeled "Chewy Vuiton" and that mimic Louis Vuitton Malletier's LOUIS VUITTON handbags.

On cross-motions for summary judgment, the district court concluded that Haute Diggity Dog's "Chewy Vuiton" dog toys were successful parodies of Louis Vuitton Malletier's trademarks, designs, and products, and on that basis, entered judgment in favor of Haute Diggity Dog on all of Louis Vuitton Malletier's claims.

On appeal, we agree with the district court that Haute Diggity Dog's products are not likely to cause confusion with those of Louis Vuitton Malletier and that Louis Vuitton Malletier's copyright was not infringed. On the trademark dilution claim, however, we reject the district court's reasoning but reach the same conclusion through a different analysis. Accordingly, we affirm.

I

Louis Vuitton Malletier S.A. ("LVM") is a well known manufacturer of luxury luggage, leather goods, handbags, and accessories, which it markets and sells worldwide. In connection with the sale of its products, LVM has adopted trademarks and trade dress that are well recognized and have become famous and distinct. Indeed, in 2006, BusinessWeek ranked LOUIS VUITTON as the 17th "best brand" of all corporations in the world and the first "best brand" for any fashion business.

LVM has registered trademarks for "LOUIS VUITTON," in connection with luggage and ladies' handbags (the "LOUIS VUITTON mark"); for a stylized monogram of "LV," in connection with traveling bags and other goods (the "LV mark"); and for a monogram canvas design consisting of a canvas with repetitions of the LV mark along with four-pointed stars, four-pointed stars inset in curved diamonds, and four-pointed flowers inset in circles, in connection with traveling bags and other products (the "Monogram Canvas mark"). In 2002, LVM adopted a brightly-colored version of the Monogram Canvas mark in which the LV mark and the designs were of various colors and the background was white (the "Multicolor design"), created in collaboration with Japanese artist Takashi Murakami. For the Multicolor design, LVM obtained a copyright in 2004. In 2005, LVM adopted another design consisting of a canvas with repetitions of the LV mark and smiling cherries on a brown background (the "Cherry design").

As LVM points out, the Multicolor design and the Cherry design attracted immediate and extraordinary media attention and publicity in magazines such as Vogue, W, Elle, Harper's Bazaar, Us Weekly, Life and Style, Travel & Leisure, People, In Style, and Jane. The press published photographs showing celebrities carrying these handbags, including Jennifer Lopez, Madonna, Eve, Elizabeth Hurley, Carmen Electra, and Anna Kournikova, among others. When the Multicolor design first appeared in 2003, the magazines typically reported, "The Murakami designs for Louis Vuitton, which were the hit of the summer, came with hefty price tags and a long waiting list." People Magazine said, "the wait list is in the thousands." The handbags retailed in the range of $995 for a medium handbag to $4500 for a large travel bag. The medium size handbag that appears to be the model for the "Chewy Vuiton" dog toy retailed for $1190. The Cherry design appeared in 2005, and the handbags including that design were priced similarly-in the range of $995 to $2740. LVM does not currently market products using the Cherry design.

The original LOUIS VUITTON, LV, and Monogram Canvas marks, however, have been used as identifiers of LVM products continuously since 1896.

During the period 2003–2005, LVM spent more than $48 million advertising products using its marks and designs, including more than $4 million for the Multicolor design. It sells its products exclusively in LVM stores and in its own in-store boutiques that are contained within department stores such as Saks Fifth Avenue, Bloomingdale's, Neiman Marcus, and Macy's. LVM also advertises its products on the Internet through the specific websites www.louisvuitton.com and www.eluxury.com.

Although better known for its handbags and luggage, LVM also markets a limited selection of luxury pet accessories—collars, leashes, and dog carriers—which bear the Monogram Canvas mark and the Multicolor design. These items range in price from approximately $200 to $1600. LVM does not make dog toys.

Haute Diggity Dog, LLC, which is a relatively small and relatively new business located in Nevada, manufactures and sells nationally—primarily through pet stores—a line of pet chew toys and beds whose names parody elegant high-end brands of products such as perfume, cars, shoes, sparkling wine, and handbags. These include—in addition to Chewy Vuiton (LOUIS VUITTON)—Chewnel No. 5 (Chanel No. 5), Furcedes (Mercedes), Jimmy Chew (Jimmy Choo), Dog Perignonn (Dom Perignon), Sniffany & Co. (Tiffany & Co.), and Dogior (Dior). The chew toys and pet beds are plush, made of polyester, and have a shape and design that loosely imitate the signature product of the targeted brand. They are mostly distributed and sold through pet stores, although one or two Macy's stores carries Haute Diggity Dog's products. The dog toys are generally sold for less than $20, although larger versions of some of Haute Diggity Dog's plush dog beds sell for more than $100.

Haute Diggity Dog's "Chewy Vuiton" dog toys, in particular, loosely resemble miniature handbags and undisputedly evoke LVM handbags of similar shape, design, and color. In lieu of the LOUIS VUITTON mark, the dog toy uses "Chewy Vuiton"; in lieu of the LV mark, it uses "CV"; and the other symbols and colors employed are imitations, but not exact ones, of those used in the LVM Multicolor and Cherry designs. . . .

[The court found that the Chewy Vuiton toys were successful parodies that were not likely to confuse consumers.]

III

LVM also contends that Haute Diggity Dog's advertising, sale, and distribution of the "Chewy Vuiton" dog toys dilutes its LOUIS VUITTON, LV, and Monogram Canvas marks, which are famous and distinctive, in violation of the Trademark Dilution Revision Act of 2006 ("TDRA"), 15 U.S.C.A. § 1125(c) (West Supp. 2007). It argues, "Before the district court's decision, Vuitton's famous marks were unblurred by any third party trademark use." "Allowing defendants to become the first to use similar marks will obviously blur and dilute the Vuitton Marks." It also contends that "Chewy Vuiton" dog toys are likely to tarnish LVM's marks because they "pose a choking hazard for some dogs."

Haute Diggity Dog urges that, in applying the TDRA to the circumstances before us, we reject LVM's suggestion that a parody "automatically" gives rise to "actionable dilution." Haute Diggity Dog contends that only marks that are "identical or substantially similar" can give rise to actionable dilution, and its "Chewy Vuiton" marks are not identical or sufficiently similar to LVM's marks. It also argues that "[its] spoof, like other obvious parodies," "'tends to increase public identification' of [LVM's] mark with [LVM]," quoting *Jordache* [*Enterprises, Inc. v. Hogg Wyld, Ltd.*, 828 F.2d 1482, 1490 (10th Cir. 1987)], rather than impairing its distinctiveness, as the TDRA requires. As for LVM's tarnishment claim, Haute Diggity Dog argues that LVM's position is at best based on speculation and that LVM has made no showing of a likelihood of dilution by tarnishment. . . .

[T]o state a dilution claim under the TDRA, a plaintiff must show:

(1) that the plaintiff owns a famous mark that is distinctive;

(2) that the defendant has commenced using a mark in commerce that allegedly is diluting the famous mark;

(3) that a similarity between the defendant's mark and the famous mark gives rise to an association between the marks; and

(4) that the association is likely to impair the distinctiveness of the famous mark or likely to harm the reputation of the famous mark.

In the context of blurring, distinctiveness refers to the ability of the famous mark uniquely to identify a single source and thus maintain its selling power. *See N.Y. Stock Exch. v. N.Y., N.Y. Hotel LLC*, 293 F.3d 550, 558 (2d Cir. 2002) (observing that blurring occurs where the defendant's use creates "the possibility that the [famous] mark will lose its ability to serve as a unique identifier of the plaintiff's product"). In proving a dilution claim under the TDRA, the plaintiff need not show actual or likely confusion, the presence of competition, or actual economic injury. *See* 15 U.S.C.A. § 1125(c)(1).

The TDRA creates three defenses based on the defendant's (1) "fair use" (with exceptions); (2) "news reporting and news commentary"; and (3) "noncommercial use." *Id.* § 1125(c)(3).

A

We address first LVM's claim for dilution by blurring.

The first three elements of a trademark dilution claim are not at issue in this case. LVM owns famous marks that are distinctive; Haute Diggity Dog has commenced using "Chewy Vuiton," "CV," and designs and colors that are allegedly diluting LVM's marks; and the similarity between Haute Diggity Dog's marks and LVM's marks gives rise to an association between the marks, albeit a parody. The issue for resolution is whether the association between Haute Diggity Dog's marks and LVM's marks is likely to impair the distinctiveness of LVM's famous marks.

In deciding this issue, the district court correctly outlined the six factors to be considered in determining whether dilution by blurring has been shown. *See* 15 U.S.C.A. § 1125(c)(2)(B). But in evaluating the facts of the case, the court did not directly apply those factors it enumerated. It held simply:

[The famous mark's] strength is not likely to be blurred by a parody dog toy product. Instead of blurring Plaintiff's mark, the success of the parodic use depends upon the continued association with LOUIS VUITTON.

Louis Vuitton Malletier, 464 F. Supp. 2d at 505. The amicus supporting LVM's position in this case contends that the district court, by not applying the statutory factors, misapplied the TDRA to conclude that simply because Haute Diggity Dog's product was a parody meant that "there can be no association with the famous mark as a matter of law." Moreover, the amicus points out correctly that to rule in favor of Haute Diggity Dog, the district court was required to find that the "association" did not impair the distinctiveness of LVM's famous mark.

LVM goes further in its own brief, however, and . . . suggests that any use by a third person of an imitation of its famous marks dilutes the famous marks as a matter of law. This contention misconstrues the TDRA.

The TDRA prohibits a person from using a junior mark that is likely to dilute (by blurring) the famous mark, and blurring is defined to be an impairment to the famous mark's distinctiveness. "Distinctiveness" in turn refers to the public's recognition that the famous mark identifies a single source of the product using the famous mark.

To determine whether a junior mark is likely to dilute a famous mark through blurring, the TDRA directs the court to consider all factors relevant to the issue, including six factors that are enumerated in the statute:

(i) The degree of similarity between the mark or trade name and the famous mark.

(ii) The degree of inherent or acquired distinctiveness of the famous mark.

(iii) The extent to which the owner of the famous mark is engaging in substantially exclusive use of the mark.

(iv) The degree of recognition of the famous mark.

(v) Whether the user of the mark or trade name intended to create an association with the famous mark.

(vi) Any actual association between the mark or trade name and the famous mark.

15 U.S.C.A. § 1125(c)(2)(B). Not every factor will be relevant in every case, and not every blurring claim will require extensive discussion of the factors. But a trial court must offer a sufficient indication of which factors it has found persuasive and explain why they are persuasive so that the court's decision can be reviewed. The district court did not do this adequately in this case. Nonetheless, after we apply the factors as a matter of law, we reach the same conclusion reached by the district court.

We begin by noting that parody is not automatically a complete defense to a claim of dilution by blurring where the defendant uses the parody as its own designation of source, i.e., as a trademark. Although the TDRA does provide that fair use is a complete defense and allows that a parody can be considered fair use, it does not extend the fair use defense to parodies used as a trademark. As the statute provides:

The following shall not be actionable as dilution by blurring or dilution by tarnishment under this subsection:

(A) Any fair use . . . *other than as a designation of source for the person's own goods or services*, including use in connection with . . . parodying. . . .

15 U.S.C.A. § 1125(c)(3)(A)(ii) (emphasis added). Under the statute's plain language, parodying a famous mark is protected by the fair use defense only if the parody is not "a designation of source for the person's own goods or services."

The TDRA, however, does not require a court to ignore the existence of a parody that is used as a trademark, and it does not preclude a court from considering parody as part of the circumstances to be considered for determining whether the plaintiff has made out a claim for dilution by blurring. Indeed, the statute permits a court to consider "all relevant factors," including the six factors supplied in § 1125(c)(2)(B).

Thus, it would appear that a defendant's use of a mark as a parody is relevant to the overall question of whether the defendant's use is likely to impair the famous mark's distinctiveness. Moreover, the fact that the defendant uses its marks as a parody is specifically relevant to several of the listed factors. For example, factor (v) (whether the defendant intended to create an association with the famous mark) and factor (vi) (whether there exists an actual association between the defendant's mark and the famous mark) directly invite inquiries into the defendant's intent in using the parody, the defendant's actual use of the parody, and the effect that its use has on the famous mark. While a parody intentionally creates an association with the famous mark in order to be a parody, it also intentionally communicates, if it is successful, that it is not the famous mark, but rather a satire of the famous mark. *See PETA*, 263 F.3d at 366. That the defendant is using its mark as a parody is therefore relevant in the consideration of these statutory factors.

Similarly, factors (i), (ii), and (iv)—the degree of similarity between the two marks, the degree of distinctiveness of the famous mark, and its recognizability—are directly implicated by consideration of the fact that the defendant's mark is a successful parody. Indeed, by making the famous mark an object of the parody, a successful parody might actually enhance the famous mark's distinctiveness by making it an icon. The brunt of the joke becomes yet more famous. *See Hormel Foods*, 73 F.3d at 506 (observing that a successful parody "tends to increase public identification" of the famous mark with its source); *see also Yankee Publ'g Inc. v. News Am. Publ'g Inc.*, 809 F. Supp. 267, 272–82 (S.D.N.Y. 1992) (suggesting that a sufficiently obvious parody is unlikely to blur the targeted famous mark).

In sum, while a defendant's use of a parody as a mark does not support a "fair use" defense, it may be considered in determining whether the plaintiff-owner of a famous mark has proved its claim that the defendant's use of a parody mark is likely to impair the distinctiveness of the famous mark.

In the case before us, when considering factors (ii), (iii), and (iv), it is readily apparent, indeed conceded by Haute Diggity Dog, that LVM's marks are distinctive, famous, and strong. The LOUIS VUITTON mark is well known and is commonly identified as a brand of the great Parisian fashion house, Louis Vuitton Malletier. So too are its other marks and designs, which are invariably used with the LOUIS VUITTON mark. It may not be too strong to refer to these famous marks as icons of high fashion.

While the establishment of these facts satisfies essential elements of LVM's dilution claim, *see* 15 U.S.C.A. § 1125(c)(1), the facts impose on LVM an increased burden to demonstrate that the distinctiveness of its famous marks is likely to be impaired by a successful parody. Even as Haute Diggity Dog's parody mimics the famous mark, it communicates simultaneously that it is not the famous mark, but is only satirizing it. *See PETA*, 263 F.3d at 366. And because the famous mark is particularly strong and distinctive, it becomes more likely that a parody will not impair the distinctiveness of the mark. In short, as Haute Diggity Dog's "Chewy Vuiton" marks are a successful parody, we conclude that they will not blur the distinctiveness of the famous mark as a unique identifier of its source.

It is important to note, however, that this might not be true if the parody is so similar to the famous mark that it likely could be construed as actual use of the famous mark itself. Factor (i) directs an inquiry into the "degree of similarity between the junior mark and the famous mark." If Haute Diggity Dog used the actual marks of LVM (as a parody or otherwise), it could dilute LVM's marks by blurring, regardless of whether Haute Diggity Dog's use was confusingly similar, whether it was in competition with LVM, or whether LVM sustained actual injury. *See* 15 U.S.C.A. § 1125(c)(1). Thus, "the use of DUPONT shoes, BUICK aspirin, and KODAK pianos would be actionable" under the TDRA because the unauthorized use of the famous marks themselves on unrelated goods might diminish the capacity of these trademarks to distinctively identify a single source. *Moseley*, 537 U.S. at 431 (quoting H.R. REP. NO. 104-374, at 3 (1995), as re-printed in 1995 U.S.C.C.A.N. 1029, 1030). This is true even though a consumer would be unlikely to confuse the manufacturer of KODAK film with the hypothetical producer of KODAK pianos.

But in this case, Haute Diggity Dog mimicked the famous marks; it did not come so close to them as to destroy the success of its parody and, more importantly, to diminish the LVM marks' capacity to identify a single source. Haute Diggity Dog designed a pet chew toy to imitate and suggest, but not use, the marks of a high-fashion LOUIS VUITTON handbag. It used "Chewy Vuiton" to mimic "LOUIS VUITTON"; it used "CV" to mimic "LV"; and it adopted imperfectly the items of LVM's designs. We conclude that these uses by Haute Diggity Dog were not so similar as to be likely to impair the distinctiveness of LVM's famous marks.

In a similar vein, when considering factors (v) and (vi), it becomes apparent that Haute Diggity Dog intentionally associated its marks, but only partially and certainly imperfectly, so as to convey the simultaneous message that it was not in fact a source of LVM products. Rather, as a parody, it separated itself from the LVM marks in order to make fun of them.

In sum, when considering the relevant factors to determine whether blurring is likely to occur in this case, we readily come to the conclusion, as did the district court, that

LVM has failed to make out a case of trademark dilution by blurring by failing to establish that the distinctiveness of its marks was likely to be impaired by Haute Diggity Dog's marketing and sale of its "Chewy Vuiton" products.

B

LVM's claim for dilution by tarnishment does not require an extended discussion. To establish its claim for dilution by tarnishment, LVM must show, in lieu of blurring, that Haute Diggity Dog's use of the "Chewy Vuiton" mark on dog toys harms the reputation of the LOUIS VUITTON mark and LVM's other marks. LVM argues that the possibility that a dog could choke on a "Chewy Vuiton" toy causes this harm. LVM has, however, provided no record support for its assertion. It relies only on speculation about whether a dog could choke on the chew toys and a logical concession that a $10 dog toy made in China was of "inferior quality" to the $1190 LOUIS VUITTON handbag. The speculation begins with LVM's assertion in its brief that "defendant Woofie's admitted that 'Chewy Vuiton' products pose a choking hazard for some dogs. Having prejudged the defendant's mark to be a parody, the district court made light of this admission in its opinion, and utterly failed to give it the weight it deserved," citing to a page in the district court's opinion where the court states:

> At oral argument, plaintiff provided only a flimsy theory that a pet may some day choke on a Chewy Vuiton squeak toy and incite the wrath of a confused consumer against LOUIS VUITTON.

Louis Vuitton Malletier, 464 F. Supp. 2d at 505. The court was referring to counsel's statement during oral argument that the owner of Woofie's stated that "she would not sell this product to certain types of dogs because there is a danger they would tear it open and choke on it." There is no record support, however, that any dog has choked on a pet chew toy, such as a "Chewy Vuiton" toy, or that there is any basis from which to conclude that a dog would likely choke on such a toy.

We agree with the district court that LVM failed to demonstrate a claim for dilution by tarnishment. *See Hormel Foods*, 73 F.3d at 507. . . .

The judgment of the district court is AFFIRMED.

COMMENTS AND QUESTIONS

1. Louis Vuitton also argued that people would be confused by the Chewy Vuiton dog toys, pointing out that Louis Vuitton sold upscale dog collars. Are consumers likely to be confused by the defendant's use of Chewy Vuiton for dog toys? If not, why doesn't that fact also dispose of the dilution case? Should a dilution claim be able to save a failed trademark infringement claim? If so, what role is there left for a trademark infringement claim in such a case? Is dilution a form of "super-trademark law"? In *Moseley v. V Secret Catalogue*, 537 U.S. 418 (2003), the court said:

> Unlike traditional infringement law, the prohibitions against trademark dilution are not the product of common-law development, and are not motivated by an interest in protecting consumers.

Is that right? If not protecting consumers, what purpose does dilution law serve?

2. Louis Vuitton continues to push the limits of trademark dilution law. In *Louis Vuitton Malletier, S.A. v. Hyundai Motor Am.*, 2012 WL 1022247 (S.D.N.Y. Mar. 22, 2012), the economy car manufacturer Hyundai aired a thirty-second commercial titled "Luxury," which included "a four-second scene of an inner-city basketball game played on a lavish marble court with a gold hoop." The scene also included a basketball bearing marks meant to evoke the Louis Vuitton Monogram. The Court rejected Hyundai's parody defense based in large part on deposition testimony from Hyundai representatives that conclusively established that the car company had no intention for the commercial to make any statement about Louis Vuitton at all. On that basis, the court concluded that Hyundai had "disclaimed any intention to parody, criticize or comment upon Louis Vuitton" and that the ad was only intended to make a "broader social comment" about "what it means for a product to be luxurious." The decision has been sharply criticized. *See* 4 McCarthy § 24:120.

3. Marks need not be identical to prove dilution. *See, e.g., Nabisco, Inc. v. PF Brands, Inc.*, 191 F.3d 208 (2d Cir. 1999) (applying dilution to goldfish-shaped cheddar crackers that were similar to the plaintiff's famous goldfish cheddar crackers). If the marks are not identical, how similar must they be? Obviously, the likelihood of confusion test cannot apply here. But there must be some degree of similarity, or consumers would not associate the defendant's mark with the plaintiff's. One court has held that the marks must be more similar for a finding of dilution than for a finding of consumer confusion. *AutoZone, Inc. v. Tandy Corp.*, 373 F.3d 786 (6th Cir. 2004) ("Powerzone" not similar enough to dilute "AutoZone"). Does this make sense? Consider what the Supreme Court said in *Moseley*:

> We do agree, however, with [the] conclusion that, at least where the marks at issue are not identical, the mere fact that consumers mentally associate the junior user's mark with a famous mark is not sufficient to establish actionable dilution. [S]uch mental association will not necessarily reduce the capacity of the famous mark to identify the goods of its owner, the statutory requirement for dilution under the FTDA. For even though Utah drivers may be reminded of the circus when they see a license plate referring to the "greatest *snow* on earth," it by no means follows that they will associate "the greatest show on earth" with skiing or snow sports, or associate it less strongly or exclusively with the circus. "Blurring" is not a necessary consequence of mental association. (Nor, for that matter, is "tarnishing.")

Moseley, 537 U.S. at 418. What more than association is required? How can the plaintiff prove it? *See Levi Strauss & Co. v. Abercrombie & Fitch Trading Co.*, 633 F.3d 1158 (9th Cir. 2011) (holding that marks need not be identical or nearly identical; it is sufficient if they are similar enough that one "is likely to impair the distinctiveness" of another).

4. *Nature of Harm Cognizable for Dilution Purposes.* Dilution doctrine, as developed by the courts, comprises two principal types of harms: blurring and tarnishment.

Nabisco, 191 F.3d at 208, illustrates the former: Nabisco's use of goldfish-shaped cheese crackers allegedly reduces the exclusive association that consumers have between the mark and Pepperidge Farm. But how is one to prove that a mark has been blurred? Is blurring something that we can identify only after the fact, once a term like Acme or Federal is in widespread use for a variety of goods?

Tarnishment arises where a junior user undermines the image that consumers hold of a famous mark by using the mark to advertise unsavory products. For example, the marketing of posters printed with the words "Enjoy Cocaine" featuring the same typeface and red and white color scheme as Coca-Cola's "Enjoy Coca-Cola" advertisements was found to tarnish Coca-Cola's famous mark. *See Coca-Cola Co. v. Gemini Rising, Inc.*, 346 F. Supp. 1183 (E.D.N.Y. 1972); *see also Dallas Cowboys Cheerleaders, Inc. v. Pussycat Cinema, Ltd.*, 604 F.2d 200 (2d Cir. 1979) (dilution to promote a pornographic movie by suggesting that Dallas Cowboys Cheerleaders were participants and to use actresses whose costumes resembled those of the Dallas Cowboys cheerleaders).

By contrast, using a mark to criticize the mark's owner is not tarnishment under the statute. Nor is it illegal to use the mark to display or refer to the plaintiff's own product, even if it is in a context the plaintiff might find repugnant. For example, in *Wham-O, Inc. v. Paramount Pictures Corp.*, 286 F. Supp. 2d 1254 (C.D. Cal. 2003), the owner of the Slip 'N Slide trademark sued the makers of the film *Dickie Roberts: Former Child Star* over a scene in which the fictional Roberts injured himself by misusing a Slip 'N Slide water slide. The court held that the film's depiction of the product was "silly" but could not tarnish the plaintiff's mark. *See also Caterpillar Inc. v. Walt Disney Co.*, 287 F. Supp. 2d 913 (N.D. Ill. 2003) (depicting plaintiff's bulldozers being used by a villain in a children's movie did not tarnish plaintiff's marks). Rather, tarnishment occurs only when the famous mark is used on the *defendant's* unsavory goods, causing the public to draw a connection between the plaintiff's goods and the defendant's.

5. *Fame.* The requirement of fame is designed as an important limitation on the reach of dilution protection. *See* Senate Judiciary Committee Report on S. 1883, S. REP. NO. 100-515, at 41–42 (Sept. 15, 1988) (noting that "Section 43(c) of the Act is to be applied selectively and is intended to provide protection only to those marks which are both truly distinctive and famous"); *TCPIP Holding Co., Inc. v. Haar Communic'ns, Inc.*, 244 F.3d 88 (2d Cir. 2001) ("It seems most unlikely that Congress intended to confer on marks that have enjoyed only brief fame in a small part of the country or among a small segment of the population, the power to enjoin all other users throughout the nation in all realms of commerce."); *see generally* MCCARTHY, TRADEMARKS AND UNFAIR COMPETITION § 24:112.

Following the Act's passage in 1995, numerous courts uncritically applied the "fame" requirement in an effort to snare cyber-pirates. Thus courts found a host of obscure marks to be famous. *See, e.g., Intermatic, Inc. v. Toeppen*, 947 F. Supp. 1227 (N.D. Ill. 1996) ("Intermatic"); *Teletech Customer Care Mgmt., Inc. v. Tele-Tech Company, Inc.*, 977 F. Supp. 1407 (C.D. Cal. 1997) ("Teletech"); *Panavision Int'l v. Toeppen*, 141 F. 3d 1316 (9th Cir. 1998) ("Panavision"); *Archdiocese of St. Louis v. Internet*

Entm't Grp., 34 F. Supp. 2d 1145 (E.D. Mo. 1999) ("Papal Visit 1999," "Pastoral Visit," "1999 Papal Visit Commemorative Official Commemorative Items," and "Papal Visit 1999, St. Louis"). *But see Avery Dennison Corp. v. Sumpton*, 189 F.3d 868 (9th Cir. 1999) (overturning a lower court decision finding "Avery" and "Dennison" to be famous trademarks).

Outside the domain name context, a few courts significantly reduced the standard for fame by finding that a mark can be "famous" in a narrow product market. *See Times Mirror Magazines v. Las Vegas Sporting News*, 212 F.3d 157 (3d Cir. 2000) (holding that "The Sporting News" is a famous mark).

When Congress revised the dilution statute in 2006, it tightened up the requirements to prove fame, in part by abolishing the concept of niche fame. The statute now requires that a mark be "widely recognized by the general consuming public of the United States." The result has been that far fewer trademarks qualify for dilution protection than did so before 2006, even marks that some would regard as well known within their niches. *See Coach Servs. v. Triumph Learning, LLC*, 668 F.3d 1356 (Fed. Cir. 2012) ("Coach" is famous enough to be considered a strong mark for confusion purposes, but has not been proven famous for dilution purposes); *Bd. of Regents, the Univ. of Tex. Sys. v. KST Electric, Ltd.*, 550 F. Supp. 2d 657 (W.D. Tex. 2008) (finding that the longhorn silhouette associated with the University of Texas at Austin was not famous outside the "niche" of college sporting events); *Milbank Tweed Hadley & McCloy LLP v. Milbank Holding Corp.*, 82 U.S.P.Q.2d 1583 (C.D. Cal. 2007) (New York law firm Milbank not famous outside niche market).

6. *Dual Requirements of Distinctiveness and Fame?* In *Nabisco, Inc. v. PF Brands*, 191 F.3d 208 (2d Cir. 1999), the court suggested that the FTDA requires proof of both distinctiveness of the plaintiff's mark and fame in order to receive federal protection. The practical effect of this interpretation was to exclude descriptive marks from dilution protection. McDonald's, United Airlines, Ace Hardware, and American Airlines would not have been eligible for federal dilution protection under the Second Circuit approach because they lack inherently distinctive marks (even though they could well meet the "fame" requirement).

The 2006 revisions to the dilution statute reversed this decision, making it clear in subsection (c)(1) that famous marks can be either inherently distinctive or have acquired distinctiveness.

Should the law extend dilution protection to descriptive marks? Is there a greater need for companies in other fields to use those marks than there is to use an inherently distinctive mark? Consider *Visa Int'l Serv. Ass'n v. JSL Corp.*, 610 F.3d 1088 (9th Cir. 2010) (holding that eVisa for an English language school in Japan diluted the famous Visa credit card mark; the court concluded that the term "visa" had only one meaning, and it was a credit card). Can the use of an English language term ("visa") dilute the brand significance of a mark even if the term is used in its descriptive sense? Could Apple Computer sue a seller of fruit that used the term "apple" prominently?

7. *Noncommercial and Nontrademark Uses.* The dilution statute requires that the defendant's use be use as a "mark or trade name," not simply use "otherwise than as a designation of source." Whatever the merits of a general trademark use requirement (discussed above), therefore, it seems that the defendant must engage in trademark use to be liable under the dilution statute. *See* Stacey L. Dogan & Mark A. Lemley, *The Trademark Use Requirement in Dilution Cases*, 24 SANTA CLARA COMPUT. & HIGH TECH. L.J. 571 (2008). Thus, mere registration of a trademark as a domain name does not constitute commercial use. As explained by one court,

> [w]hen a domain name is used only to indicate an address on the Internet, the domain name is not functioning as a trademark. . . . NSI's acceptance of domain name registrations is connected only with the names' technical function on the Internet to designate a set of computers. . . . Something more than the registration of the name is required before the use of a domain name is infringing.

Lockheed Martin Corp. v. Network Sols., Inc., 985 F. Supp. 949, 956–57 (C.D. Cal. 1997), *aff'd,* 141 F.3d 1316 (9th Cir. 1998).

Haute Diggity Dog's use was not a nontrademark use because the company was using the term Chewy Vuiton to brand and sell its own products. But as the Fourth Circuit noted, while such "brand parodies" are not automatically immune from a dilution claim, they can still survive if their parodic nature means that they are unlikely to blur the significance of the mark they make fun of. *See* Stacey L. Dogan & Mark A. Lemley, *Parody as Brand*, 47 U.C. DAVIS L. REV. 473 (2013). The TTAB, by contrast, rejects the Chewy Vuiton case outright, holding that "we find it virtually impossible to conceive of a situation where a parody defense to a dilution claim can succeed" when the defendant is itself using the parody as a mark. *New York Yankees P'ship v. IET Prods & Servs., Inc.*, No. 91189692 (TTAB May 8, 2015). The applicant there was prohibited from registering "The House That Juice Built" and an accompanying logo showing the New York Yankees top hat over a syringe. Despite the rather obvious intent to comment on the use of performance-enhancing drugs by Yankees players, the TTAB held that the applicant's mark would blur the significance of "The House that Ruth Built," a registered Yankees mark.

8. *Referential Uses; Comparative Advertising.* It is a defense to a dilution claim that the famous mark was used in lawful comparative advertising. In *Ty, Inc. v. Perryman*, 306 F.3d 509 (7th Cir. 2002), the court held that it also could not dilute a mark to use it to refer to the trademark owner. Ty, the maker of Beanie Babies, sued an individual who accurately advertised second-hand Beanie Babies for resale. Judge Posner's opinion explained that there was no blurring or tarnishment of the Beanie Baby mark here, since the use of the mark was only to refer accurately to the plaintiff's own goods. The court acknowledged Ty's argument that Perryman was free riding on the fame of its mark, but said that "in that attenuated sense of free riding, almost everyone in business is free riding." (We discuss this issue further in the section on nominative use. *See* Chapter V(E)(3)(ii).)

Subsection (3) of the statute creates a broad list of things exempt from the reach of the dilution statute, including all noncommercial uses, fair uses, nontrademark uses, comparative advertising, news reporting, parody, commentary, and criticism. Given these defenses, was there any need for Judge Posner to decide that there was no blurring or tarnishment in *Ty*?

9. *Categories of Marks Protected Against Dilution.* As reflected in the *Nabisco* case through its protection of the product configuration of Pepperidge Farms' cracker, the FTDA can protect trade dress as well as more traditional trademarks. *See also Sunbeam Prods. v. West Bend Co.*, 123 F.3d 246 (5th Cir. 1998). For criticism of this application of dilution, *see* Paul Heald, *Exposing the Malign Application of the Federal Dilution Statute to Product Configurations*, 5 J. INTELL. PROP. L. 415 (1995).

10. *International Scope of Dilution Protection.* The Paris Convention, including Article 6*bis*, is silent on the protection of trademarks against dilution. GATT-TRIPs signatory countries, however, must now provide some form of protection against dilution of a mark, at least if it is famous.

> Article 6*bis* of the Paris Convention (1967) shall apply, mutatis mutandis, to goods or services which are not similar to those in respect of which a trademark is registered, provided that use of that trademark in relation to those goods or services would indicate a connection between those goods and services and the owner of the registered trademark and provided that the interests of the owner of the registered trademark are likely to be damaged by such use.

Final Act Embodying the Results of the Uruguay Round of Multilateral Trade Negotiations, done at Marrakech, Morocco, Apr. 15, 1994, Annex 1C: Agreement on Trade-Related Aspects of Intellectual Property Rights (TRIPs), at Article 16(3). For congressional approval, *see* Uruguay Rounds Agreements Act, Pub. L. No. 103-465, Dec. 8, 1994. Why can a mark not currently used in a country be protected against dilution in another country? Does it matter whether the mark is registered? Should foreign marks be protected against dilution in anticipation of their possible entry into the market? This provision has been used to target "trademark pirates": individuals who identify famous trademarks not yet used in their country and register those marks in anticipation of the famous trademark owner's expansion abroad.

11. *Dilution and "Search Theory.* How would you define the harm that comes with dilution in terms of the consumer search rationale? As a consumer, is locating Coca-Cola in the store or picking out the Coke ad in a magazine more difficult if there are many unassociated products or ads that use the Coke name? As an experiment, try walking down the "generic" aisle in a supermarket, where all the boxes are plain black and white, trying to pick out the macaroni among the spaghetti, rigatoni, and so on. Would distinctive labels—all brightly colored, with striking designs—make a difference? From a certain distance, to take a different example, it is difficult to pick out a single marathon runner from the crowd of other runners, even though—or because—each runner is dressed in day-glo warmups, running shoes, and so on. The point is simply this: if many products share a similar label, the fact that the label is striking when viewed in isolation is irrelevant. It is as difficult to discern a single blazing orange poppy in a field full of them as it is to identify a lone grey pebble out of a rock pile.

If attention spans are truly taxed in the current era, with its barrage of information and images, dilution may be an even more important adjunct to traditional "consumer confusion" rationales for trademarks. Indeed, the harm that dilution seeks to address might best be described as a loss of consumer *attention* due to the proliferation of similar or identical symbols of trade. Professor Rebecca Tushnet documents this loss of attention, pointing to studies that show that it takes consumers longer to recognize dilute marks than unique ones. *See* Rebecca Tushnet, *Gone in Sixty Milliseconds: Trademark Law and Cognitive Science*, 86 TEX. L. REV. 507 (2008). The difference is measured in milliseconds, though. And, as she observes, not all the marks afforded protection against dilution are unique.

Trademark owners thus seek to protect the distinctiveness of their marks—first, to ensure a moment of unfettered attention, and then to indicate a unique connection between the mark and the seller's product. For an argument that prohibiting trademark dilution is consistent with the law's general focus on reducing consumer search costs, *see* Stacey L. Dogan & Mark A. Lemley, *The Merchandising Right: Fragile Theory or Fait Accompli?*, 54 EMORY L.J. 461 (2005). *But see* Tushnet, *supra* (arguing that if this attention deficit was indeed a problem, dilution law would have to prevent far more uses than in fact it does).

PROBLEMS

Problem V-14. Mead Data Central is the owner of the registered trademark LEXIS for a legal and business-related electronic database. The service is extremely well known among lawyers, but not among the general public.

A decade after the first use of the LEXIS mark, Toyota names its new luxury car the "Lexus." Mead sues for dilution of its LEXIS mark. What result? On what facts does your decision depend?

Problem V-15. My Other Bag, Inc. ("MOB") sells simple canvas tote bags with the text "My Other Bag ..." on one side and drawings meant to evoke iconic handbags by luxury designers, such as Louis Vuitton, Chanel, and Fendi, on the other. MOB's totes are a play on the classic "my other car . . ." novelty bumper stickers, which can be seen on inexpensive, beat up cars across the country informing passersby—with tongue firmly in cheek—that the driver's "other car" is a Mercedes (or some other luxury car brand). Whereas the Louis Vuitton bag depicted below retails for over $1200, the MOB canvas version sells for $38.

Louis Vuitton sues MOB for trademark dilution and trademark infringement. How should a court resolve the lawsuit?

Problem V-16. Starbucks is a famous trademark for gourmet coffee. The Black Bear Micro Roastery, a small coffee shop in New York, decides to sell a dark-roasted blend of coffee it calls "Charbucks Blend." The term Charbucks Blend is used under a prominent logo that reads Black Bear Micro Roastery.

Does Charbucks dilute Starbucks? Under what theory of dilution? What evidence would help you resolve the question?

Problem V-17. Between 1937 and 1949, J. R. R. Tolkein wrote THE LORD OF THE RINGS, which went on to become one of the best-selling novel series. Adaptations of the novels for radio, theatre, and film have expanded LOTR popularity. The Saul Zaentz Company acquired the intellectual property rights to the classic novels and licenses a wide range of merchandise associated with the iconic series.

In March 2017, Bro Gnarley opened "The Lord of the Dings," a surfboard repair shop in Malibu, California. In addition to repairing surfboards, Bro sells tee shirts featuring images of Frodo, Gandalf, and other LOTR characters on surfboards displayed above "The Lord of the Dings" in script reminiscent of the LOTR novels and motion picture posters. In July 2017, Alex Fender renamed his automotive repair shop in Sonoma, California, "The Lord of the Dings." He also sells promotional tee shirts featuring LOTR characters, automobile images, and "The Lord of the Dings" logo. In January 2018, Bruce Ellery opened a dent repair franchising company named "The Lord of the Dings." What advice would you provide The Saul Zaentz Company, Bro Gnarley, Alex Fender, and Bruce Ellery about trademark protection and liability?

4. Cybersquatting

The emergence of the Internet created a new problem for trademark owners: cybersquatting. By paying a modest registration fee, anyone could register an unregistered domain name. The only rule governing registration was first-come, first-served. And in the early days of the Internet, domain names—terms like "microsoft.com" that mapped to a particular Internet location—were the primary way people found companies they were looking for. This led to a flurry of registration–a veritable Internet gold rush. Several opportunists landed on the strategy of registering domains comprising well-known trademarks. They in turn offered them to the true trademark owner at a steep price. Some registrants threatened to post disparaging information on a website at the domain. *See, e.g., Virtual Works, Inc. v. Volkswagen of America, Inc.*, 238 F.3d 264 (4th Cir. 2001). Others registered the domain names of their competitors or political groups with which they disagreed.

Courts saw the injustice in this activity, but could not easily find a confusion-based trademark violation. With passage of the Federal Trademark Dilution Act of 1996, some courts used the newly-minted dilution theory. Many of these cases, however, distorted the dilution requirements, finding all manner of obscure trademarks famous. *See, e.g., Intermatic, Inc. v. Toeppen*, 947 F. Supp. 1227 (N.D. Ill. 1996) ("Intermatic"); *Teletech Customer Care Mgmt., Inc. v. Tele-Tech Company, Inc.*, 977 F. Supp. 1407 (C.D. Cal. 1997) ("Teletech"); *Panavision Int'l v. Toeppen*, 141 F. 3d 1316 (9th Cir. 1998) ("Panavision"); *Archdiocese of St. Louis v. Internet Entment Grp.*, 34 F. Supp. 2d 1145 (E.D. Mo. 1999) ("Papal Visit 1999," "Pastoral Visit," "1999 Papal Visit Commemorative Official Commemorative Items," and "Papal Visit 1999, St. Louis").

Congress addressed these concerns by passing the Anticybersquatting Consumer Protection Act of 1999 ("ACPA"). The statute added § 43(d) to the Lanham Act, which provides that:

A person shall be liable in a civil action by the owner of a mark, including a personal name which is protected as a mark under this section, if, without regard to the goods or services of the parties, that person—

(i) has a bad faith intent to profit from that mark, including a personal name which is protected as a mark under this section; and

(ii) registers, traffics in, or uses a domain name that—

(I) in the case of a mark that is distinctive at the time of registration of the domain name, is identical or confusingly similar to that mark;

(II) in the case of a famous mark that is famous at the time of registration of the domain name, is identical or confusingly similar to or dilutive of that mark; or

(III) is a trademark, word, or name protected by reason of section 706 of title 18 or section 220506 of title 36.

§ 43(d)(1)(A), 15 U.S.C. § 1125(d)(1)(A). The statute contains an *in rem* provision allows the trademark owner to proceed against the domain name itself in the judicial district where the domain name registrar, domain name registry, or other domain name authority registered or assigned the domain name is located. In this way, the trademark owner can gain cancellation or transfer of the domain name even if it cannot obtain *in personam* jurisdiction over the registrant.

The ACPA eliminated the strain on developing dilution law and provided an effective remedy for cybersquatting. Some cases emerged raising questions about whether the registrant had "bad faith intent to profit" or instead an intent to criticize or make fun. *Compare People for the Ethical Treatment of Animals v. Doughney*, 263 F.3d 359 (4th Cir. 2001) (finding an individual who set up a page entitled "People Eating Tasty Animals" at peta.org, the expected site of animal-rights group People for the Ethical Treatment of Animals, to be engaged in cybersquatting) *with Bosley Med. Inst. v. Kremer*, 403 F.3d 672 (9th Cir. 2005) (finding no violation of ACPA for operating a noncommercial gripe site); *Lamparello v. Falwell*, 420 F.3d 309 (4th Cir. 2005) (finding that no violation of the ACPA where a young gay man maintained a gripe site criticizing the Reverend Jerry Falwell at www.fallwell.com for his anti-gay preaching).

At nearly the same time that the ACPA was enacted, the Internet Corporation for Assigned Names and Numbers ("ICANN"), which oversees the Internet address system, established the Uniform Domain Name Dispute Resolution Policy ("UDRP"). All domain name registrants agree to be bound by ICANN policies, including the UDRP, when they register a domain. The UDRP parallels the ACPA in terms of its standard for transferring domain names. The UDRP's arbitration process, which relies upon a large pool of trademark and Internet attorneys, operates far more quickly and less expensively than federal court adjudication. As a result, the UDRP has largely supplanted the ACPA. Thousands of garden-variety domain name disputes have been resolved through the UDRP process. Any party, however, has the right to pursue a domain name dispute in federal court pursuant to the ACPA.

In recent years, the significance of the ACPA and the UDRP has somewhat faded because of changes in how people use the Internet. With the rise of effective search engines, Internet users increasingly find companies they are looking for the same way they find anything else—by typing the name into a search bar. Indeed, some browsers have now integrated the search function into the URL window, so typing in, say, www.microsoft.com runs the same search as typing "Microsoft" into Google's search bar. Nonetheless, domain names continue to exist as addresses and sources. For example, information about this book (and related information) can be conveniently remembered (and found) by going to IPNTA.com. (Notice how we slipped in that little advertisement.) Furthermore, the Internet Committee on Assigned Names and Numbers (ICANN) continues to release new top-level domains, creating more domains (and more opportunity for trademark disputes).

5.   Indirect Infringement

Tiffany Inc. v. eBay Inc.
United States Court of Appeals for the Second Circuit
600 F.3d 93 (2d Cir. 2010)

SACK, Circuit Judge:

eBay, Inc. ("eBay"), through its eponymous online marketplace, has revolutionized the online sale of goods, especially used goods. It has facilitated the buying and selling by hundreds of millions of people and entities, to their benefit and eBay's profit. But that marketplace is sometimes employed by users as a means to perpetrate fraud by selling counterfeit goods.

Plaintiffs Tiffany (NJ) Inc. and Tiffany and Company (together, "Tiffany") have created and cultivated a brand of jewelry bespeaking high-end quality and style. Based on Tiffany's concern that some use eBay's website to sell counterfeit Tiffany merchandise, Tiffany has instituted this action against eBay, asserting various causes of action—sounding in trademark infringement, trademark dilution and false advertising—arising from eBay's advertising and listing practices. For the reasons set forth below, we affirm the district court's judgment with respect to Tiffany's claims of trademark infringement and dilution but remand for further proceedings with respect to Tiffany's false advertising claim.

Background

. . .

eBay

eBay is the proprietor of www.ebay.com, an Internet-based marketplace that allows those who register with it to purchase goods from and sell goods to one another. It "connect[s] buyers and sellers and [ ] enable[s] transactions, which are carried out directly between eBay members." *Tiffany,* 576 F. Supp. 2d at 475. In its auction and listing services, it "provides the venue for the sale [of goods] and support for the transaction[s], [but] it does not itself sell the items" listed for sale on the site, nor does it ever take physical possession of them, Thus, "eBay generally does not know whether or when an item is delivered to the buyer."

eBay has been enormously successful. More than six million new listings are posted on its site daily. At any given time it contains some 100 million listings.

eBay generates revenue by charging sellers to use its listing services. For any listing, it charges an "insertion fee" based on the auction's starting price for the goods being sold and ranges from $0.20 to $4.80. For any completed sale, it charges a "final value fee" that ranges from 5.25% to 10% of the final sale price of the item. Sellers have the option of purchasing, at additional cost, features "to differentiate their listings, such as a border or bold-faced type." . . .

Tiffany

Tiffany is a world-famous purveyor of, among other things, branded jewelry. Since 2000, all new Tiffany jewelry sold in the United States has been available exclusively through Tiffany's retail stores, catalogs, and website, and through its Corporate Sales Department. It does not use liquidators, sell overstock merchandise, or put its goods on sale at discounted prices. It does not—nor can it, for that matter—control the "legitimate secondary market in authentic Tiffany silvery jewelry," i.e., the market for second-hand Tiffany wares. The record developed at trial "offere[d] little basis from which to discern the actual availability of authentic Tiffany silver jewelry in the secondary market."

Sometime before 2004, Tiffany became aware that counterfeit Tiffany merchandise was being sold on eBay's site. Prior to and during the course of this litigation, Tiffany conducted two surveys known as "Buying Programs," one in 2004 and another in 2005, in an attempt to assess the extent of this practice. Under those programs, Tiffany bought various items on eBay and then inspected and evaluated them to determine how many were counterfeit. Tiffany found that 73.1% of the purported Tiffany goods purchased in the 2004 Buying Program and 75.5% of those purchased in the 2005 Buying Program were counterfeit. The district court concluded, however, that the Buying Programs were "methodologically flawed and of questionable value," and "provide[d] limited evidence as to the total percentage of counterfeit goods available on eBay at any given time." The court nonetheless decided that during the period in which the Buying Programs were in effect, a "significant portion of the 'Tiffany' sterling silver jewelry listed on the eBay website . . . was counterfeit," and that eBay knew "that some portion of the Tiffany goods sold on its website might be counterfeit." The court found, however, that "a substantial number of authentic Tiffany goods are [also] sold on eBay." . . .

Anti-Counterfeiting Measures

Because eBay facilitates many sales of Tiffany goods, genuine and otherwise, and obtains revenue on every transaction, it generates substantial revenues from the sale of purported Tiffany goods, some of which are counterfeit. "eBay's Jewelry & Watches category manager estimated that, between April 2000 and June 2004, eBay earned $4.1 million in revenue from completed listings with 'Tiffany' in the listing title in the Jewelry & Watches category." Although eBay was generating revenue from all sales of goods on its site, including counterfeit goods, the district court found eBay to have "an interest in eliminating counterfeit Tiffany merchandise from eBay . . . to preserve the reputation of its website as a safe place to do business." The buyer of fake Tiffany goods might, if and when the forgery was detected, fault eBay. Indeed, the district court found that "buyers . . . complain[ed] to eBay" about the sale of counterfeit Tiffany goods. "[D]uring the last six weeks of 2004, 125 consumers complained to eBay about purchasing 'Tiffany' items through the eBay website that they believed to be counterfeit."

Because eBay "never saw or inspected the merchandise in the listings," its ability to determine whether a particular listing was for counterfeit goods was limited. Even had it been able to inspect the goods, moreover, in many instances it likely would not have had the expertise to determine whether they were counterfeit. *Id.* at 472 n.7 ("[I]n many instances, determining whether an item is counterfeit will require a physical inspection of the item, and some degree of expertise on the part of the examiner.").

Notwithstanding these limitations, eBay spent "as much as $20 million each year on tools to promote trust and safety on its website." For example, eBay and PayPal set up "buyer protection programs," under which, in certain circumstances, the buyer would be reimbursed for the cost of items purchased on eBay that were discovered not to be genuine. eBay also established a "Trust and Safety" department, with some 4,000 employees "devoted to trust and safety" issues, including over 200 who "focus exclusively on combating infringement" and 70 who "work exclusively with law enforcement."

By May 2002, eBay had implemented a "fraud engine," "which is principally dedicated to ferreting out illegal listings, including counterfeit listings." eBay had theretofore employed manual searches for keywords in listings in an effort to "identify blatant instances of potentially infringing . . . activity." "The fraud engine uses rules and complex models that automatically search for activity that violates eBay policies." In addition to identifying items actually advertised as counterfeit, the engine also incorporates various filters designed to screen out less-obvious instances of counterfeiting using "data elements designed to evaluate listings based on, for example, the seller's Internet protocol address, any issues associated with the seller's account on eBay, and the feedback the seller has received from other eBay users." In addition to general filters, the fraud engine incorporates "Tiffany specific filters," including "approximately 90 different keywords" designed to help distinguish between genuine and counterfeit Tiffany goods. During the period in dispute, eBay also "periodically conducted [manual] reviews of listings in an effort to remove those that might be selling counterfeit goods, including Tiffany goods."

For nearly a decade, including the period at issue, eBay has also maintained and administered the "Verified Rights Owner ('VeRO') Program"—a "'notice-and-takedown' system" allowing owners of intellectual property rights, including Tiffany, to "report to eBay any listing offering potentially infringing items, so that eBay could remove such reported listings." Any such rights-holder with a "good-faith belief that [a particular listed] item infringed on a copyright or a trademark" could report the item to eBay, using a "Notice Of Claimed Infringement form or NOCI form." During the period under consideration, eBay's practice was to remove reported listings within twenty-four hours of receiving a NOCI, but eBay in fact deleted seventy to eighty percent of them within twelve hours of notification.

On receipt of a NOCI, if the auction or sale had not ended, eBay would, in addition to removing the listing, cancel the bids and inform the seller of the reason for the cancellation. If bidding had ended, eBay would retroactively cancel the transaction. In the event of a cancelled auction, eBay would refund the fees it had been paid in connection with the auction.

In some circumstances, eBay would reimburse the buyer for the cost of a purchased item, provided the buyer presented evidence that the purchased item was counterfeit. During the relevant time period, the district court found, eBay "never refused to remove a reported Tiffany listing, acted in good faith in responding to Tiffany's NOCIs, and always provided Tiffany with the seller's contact information."

In addition, eBay has allowed rights owners such as Tiffany to create an "About Me" webpage on eBay's website "to inform eBay users about their products, intellectual property rights, and legal positions." eBay does not exercise control over the content of those pages in a manner material to the issues before us.

Tiffany, not eBay, maintains the Tiffany "About Me" page. With the headline **"BUYER BEWARE,"** the page begins: **"Most of the purported TIFFANY & CO. silver jewelry and packaging available on eBay is counterfeit."** It also says, *inter alia*:

> The only way you can be certain that you are purchasing a genuine TIFFANY & CO. product is to purchase it from a Tiffany & Co. retail store, via our website (www.tiffany.com) or through a Tiffany & Co. catalogue. Tiffany & Co. stores do not authenticate merchandise. A good jeweler or appraiser may be able to do this for you.

In 2003 or early 2004, eBay began to use "special warning messages when a seller attempted to list a Tiffany item." *Tiffany*[*(NJ) Inc. v. eBay, Inc.*, 576 F. Supp. 2d 463, 491 (S.D.N.Y.2008)]. These messages "instructed the seller to make sure that the item was authentic Tiffany merchandise and informed the seller that eBay 'does not tolerate the listing of replica, counterfeit, or otherwise unauthorized items' and that violation of this policy 'could result in suspension of [the seller's] account.'" The messages also provided a link to Tiffany's "About Me" page with its "buyer beware" disclaimer. If the seller "continued to list an item despite the warning, the listing was flagged for review."

In addition to cancelling particular suspicious transactions, eBay has also suspended from its website "'hundreds of thousands of sellers every year,' tens of thousands of whom were suspected [of] having engaged in infringing conduct." eBay primarily employed a "'three strikes rule'" for suspensions, but would suspend sellers after the first violation if it was clear that "the seller 'listed a number of infringing items,' and '[selling counterfeit merchandise] appears to be the only thing they've come to eBay to do.'" But if "a seller listed a potentially infringing item but appeared overall to be a legitimate seller, the 'infringing items [were] taken down, and the seller [would] be sent a warning on the first offense and given the educational information, [and] told that . . . if they do this again, they will be suspended from eBay.'"

By late 2006, eBay had implemented additional anti-fraud measures: delaying the ability of buyers to view listings of certain brand names, including Tiffany's, for 6 to 12 hours so as to give rights-holders such as Tiffany more time to review those listings; developing the ability to assess the number of items listed in a given listing; and restricting one-day and three-day auctions and cross-border trading for some brand-name items.

The district court concluded that "eBay consistently took steps to improve its technology and develop anti-fraud measures as such measures became technologically feasible and reasonably available." *Id.* at 493.

eBay's Advertising

At the same time that eBay was attempting to reduce the sale of counterfeit items on its website, it actively sought to promote sales of premium and branded jewelry, including Tiffany merchandise, on its site. Among other things, eBay "advised its sellers to take advantage of the demand for Tiffany merchandise as part of a broader effort to grow the Jewelry & Watches category." And prior to 2003, eBay advertised the availability of Tiffany merchandise on its site. eBay's advertisements trumpeted "Mother's Day Gifts!," a "Fall FASHION BRAND BLOWOUT," "Jewelry Best Sellers," "GREAT BRANDS, GREAT PRICES," or "Top Valentine's Deals," among other promotions. It encouraged the viewer to "GET THE FINER THINGS." These advertisements provided the reader with hyperlinks, at least one of each of which was related to Tiffany merchandise—"Tiffany," "Tiffany & Co. under $150," "Tiffany & Co," "Tiffany Rings," or "Tiffany & Co. under $50."

eBay also purchased sponsored-link advertisements on various search engines to promote the availability of Tiffany items on its website. *Tiffany,* 576 F. Supp. 2d at 480. In one such case, in the form of a printout of the results list from a search on Yahoo! for "tiffany," the second sponsored link read "**Tiffany** on eBay. Find **tiffany** items at low prices. With over 5 million items for sale every day, you'll find all kinds of unique [unreadable] Marketplace. www.ebay.com." Tiffany complained to eBay of the practice in 2003, and eBay told Tiffany that it had ceased buying sponsored links. The district court found, however, that eBay continued to do so indirectly through a third party.

. . . Tiffany appeals from the district court's judgment for eBay.

Discussion

. . .

I. Direct Trademark Infringement

. . . Tiffany alleges that eBay infringed its trademark in violation of section 32 of the Lanham Act. The district court described this as a claim of "direct trademark infringement," *Tiffany,* 576 F. Supp. 2d at 493, and we adopt that terminology. Under section 32, "the owner of a mark registered with the Patent and Trademark Office can bring a civil action against a person alleged to have used the mark without the owner's consent." *ITC Ltd. v. Punchgini, Inc.*, 482 F.3d 135, 145–46 (2d Cir. 2007). We analyze such a claim "under a familiar two-prong test. The test looks first to whether the plaintiff's mark is entitled to protection, and second to whether the defendant's use of the mark is likely to cause consumers confusion as to the origin or sponsorship of the defendant's goods." *Savin Corp. v. Savin Group,* 391 F.3d 439, 456 (2d Cir. 2004).In the district court, Tiffany argued that eBay had directly infringed its mark by using it on eBay's website and by purchasing sponsored links containing the mark on Google and Yahoo! *Tiffany,* 576 F. Supp. 2d at 494. Tiffany also argued that eBay and the sellers of the counterfeit goods using its site were jointly and severally liable. The district court rejected these arguments on the ground that eBay's use of Tiffany's mark was protected by the doctrine of nominative fair use. . . .

We agree with the district court that eBay's use of Tiffany's mark on its website and in sponsored links was lawful. eBay used the mark to describe accurately the genuine Tiffany goods offered for sale on its website. And none of eBay's uses of the mark suggested that Tiffany affiliated itself with eBay or endorsed the sale of its products through eBay's website. . . .

II. Contributory Trademark Infringement

The more difficult issue, and the one that the parties have properly focused our attention on, is whether eBay is liable for contributory trademark infringement—i.e., for culpably facilitating the infringing conduct of the counterfeiting vendors. Acknowledging the paucity of case law to guide us, we conclude that the district court correctly granted judgment on this issue in favor of eBay.

A. Principles

Contributory trademark infringement is a judicially created doctrine that derives from the common law of torts. *See, e.g.,* *Hard Rock Café Licensing Corp. v. Concession Servs., Inc.,* 955 F.2d 1143, 1148 (7th Cir. 1992); *cf. Metro-Goldwyn-Mayer Studios Inc. v. Grokster, Ltd.,* 545 U.S. 913, 930 (2005) ("[T]hese doctrines of secondary liability emerged from common law principles and are well established in the law."). The Supreme Court most recently dealt with the subject in *Inwood Laboratories, Inc. v. Ives Laboratories, Inc.,* 456 U.S. 844 (1982). There, the plaintiff, Ives, asserted that several drug manufacturers had induced pharmacists to mislabel a drug the defendants produced to pass it off as Ives'. According to the Court, "if a manufacturer or distributor intentionally induces another to infringe a trademark, or if it continues to supply its product to one whom it knows or has reason to know is engaging in trademark infringement, the manufacturer or distributor is contributorially [sic] responsible for any harm done as a result of the deceit." *Id.* at 854. The Court ultimately decided to remand the case to the Court of Appeals after concluding it had improperly rejected factual findings of the district court favoring the defendant manufacturers. *Id.* at 857–59.

Inwood's test for contributory trademark infringement applies on its face to manufacturers and distributors of goods. Courts have, however, extended the test to providers of services.

The Seventh Circuit applied *Inwood* to a lawsuit against the owner of a swap meet, or "flea market," whose vendors were alleged to have sold infringing Hard Rock Café T-shirts. *See Hard Rock Café,* 955 F.2d at 1148–49. The court "treated trademark infringement as a species of tort," *Id.* at 1148, and analogized the swap meet owner to a landlord or licensor, on whom the common law "imposes the same duty . . . [as *Inwood*] impose[s] on manufacturers and distributors," *Id.* at 1149; *see also Fonovisa, Inc. v. Cherry Auction, Inc.*, 76 F.3d 259 (9th Cir. 1996) (adopting *Hard Rock Café*'s reasoning and applying *Inwood* to a swap meet owner).

Speaking more generally, the Ninth Circuit concluded that *Inwood*'s test for contributory trademark infringement applies to a service provider if he or she exercises sufficient control over the infringing conduct. *Lockheed Martin Corp. v. Network Solutions, Inc.*, 194 F.3d 980, 984 (9th Cir. 1999); *see also id.* ("Direct control and monitoring of the instrumentality used by a third party to infringe the plaintiff's mark permits the expansion of *Inwood Lab.*'s 'supplies a product' requirement for contributory infringement."). . . .

B.   Discussion

. . .

2.   Is eBay Liable Under *Inwood*?

The question that remains, then, is whether eBay is liable under the *Inwood* test on the basis of the services it provided to those who used its website to sell counterfeit Tiffany products. As noted, when applying *Inwood* to service providers, there are two ways in which a defendant may become contributorially liable for the infringing conduct of another: first, if the service provider "intentionally induces another to infringe a trademark," and second, if the service provider "continues to supply its [service] to one whom it knows or has reason to know is engaging in trademark infringement." *Inwood,* 456 U.S. at 854. Tiffany does not argue that eBay induced the sale of counterfeit Tiffany goods on its website—the circumstances addressed by the first part of the *Inwood* test. It argues instead, under the second part of the *Inwood* test, that eBay continued to supply its services to the sellers of counterfeit Tiffany goods while knowing or having reason to know that such sellers were infringing Tiffany's mark.

The district court rejected this argument. First, it concluded that to the extent the NOCIs that Tiffany submitted gave eBay reason to know that particular listings were for counterfeit goods, eBay did not continue to carry those listings once it learned that they were specious. *Tiffany,* 576 F. Supp. 2d at 515–16. The court found that eBay's practice was promptly to remove the challenged listing from its website, warn sellers and buyers, cancel fees it earned from that listing, and direct buyers not to consummate the sale of the disputed item. The court therefore declined to hold eBay contributorially liable for the infringing conduct of those sellers. On appeal, Tiffany does not appear to challenge this conclusion. In any event, we agree with the district court that no liability arises with respect to those terminated listings.

Tiffany disagrees vigorously, however, with the district court's further determination that eBay lacked sufficient knowledge of trademark infringement by sellers behind other, non-terminated listings to provide a basis for *Inwood* liability. Tiffany argued in the district court that eBay knew, or at least had reason to know, that counterfeit Tiffany goods were being sold ubiquitously on its website. As evidence, it pointed to, *inter alia,* the demand letters it sent to eBay in 2003 and 2004, the results of its Buying Programs that it shared with eBay, the thousands of NOCIs it filed with eBay alleging its good faith belief that certain listings were counterfeit, and the various complaints eBay received from buyers claiming that they had purchased one or more counterfeit Tiffany items through eBay's website. Tiffany argued that taken together, this evidence established eBay's knowledge of the widespread sale of counterfeit Tiffany products on its website. Tiffany urged that eBay be held contributorially liable on the basis that despite that knowledge, it continued to make its services available to infringing sellers.

The district court rejected this argument. It acknowledged that "[t]he evidence produced at trial demonstrated that eBay had *generalized* notice that some portion of the Tiffany goods sold on its website might be counterfeit." *Id.* at 507. The court characterized the issue before it as "whether eBay's *generalized* knowledge of trademark infringement on its website was sufficient to meet the 'knowledge or reason to know' prong of the *Inwood* test." *Id.* at 508. eBay had argued that "such generalized knowledge is insufficient, and that the law demands more specific knowledge of individual instances of infringement and infringing sellers before imposing a burden upon eBay to remedy the problem." *Id.*

The district court concluded that "while eBay clearly possessed general knowledge as to counterfeiting on its website, such generalized knowledge is insufficient under the *Inwood* test to impose upon eBay an affirmative duty to remedy the problem." *Id.* at 508. The court reasoned that *Inwood*'s language explicitly imposes contributory liability on a defendant who "continues to supply its product[—in eBay's case, its service—]to *one* whom it knows or has reason to know is engaging in trademark infringement." *Id.* at 508. The court also noted that plaintiffs "bear a high burden in establishing 'knowledge' of contributory infringement," and that courts have

> been reluctant to extend contributory trademark liability to defendants where there is some uncertainty as to the extent or the nature of the infringement. In *Inwood,* Justice White emphasized in his concurring opinion that a defendant is not "require[d] . . . to refuse to sell to dealers who merely *might* pass off its goods."

Id. at 508–09 (quoting *Inwood,* 456 U.S. at 861) (White, J., concurring).

Accordingly, the district court concluded that for Tiffany to establish eBay's contributory liability, Tiffany would have to show that eBay "knew or had reason to know of specific instances of actual infringement" beyond those that it addressed upon learning of them. Tiffany failed to make such a showing.

On appeal, Tiffany argues that the distinction drawn by the district court between eBay's general knowledge of the sale of counterfeit Tiffany goods through its website, and its specific knowledge as to which particular sellers were making such sales, is a "false" one not required by the law. Tiffany posits that the only relevant question is "whether all of the knowledge, when taken together, puts [eBay] on notice that there is a substantial problem of trademark infringement. If so and if it fails to act, [eBay] is liable for contributory trademark infringement."

We agree with the district court. For contributory trademark infringement liability to lie, a service provider must have more than a general knowledge or reason to know that its service is being used to sell counterfeit goods. Some contemporary knowledge of which particular listings are infringing or will infringe in the future is necessary. . . .

We find helpful the Supreme Court's discussion of *Inwood* in a subsequent *copyright* case, *Sony Corp. of America v. Universal City Studios, Inc.*, 464 U.S. 417 (1984). There, defendant Sony manufactured and sold home video tape recorders. *Id.* at 419, 104 S.Ct. 774. Plaintiffs Universal Studios and Walt Disney Productions held copyrights on various television programs that individual television-viewers had taped using the defendant's recorders. The plaintiffs contended that this use of the recorders constituted copyright infringement for which the defendants should be held contributorily liable. *Id.* In ruling for the defendants, the Court discussed *Inwood* and the differences between contributory liability in trademark versus copyright law.

> If *Inwood*'s *narrow standard* for contributory trademark infringement governed here, [the plaintiffs'] claim of contributory infringement would merit little discussion. Sony certainly does not "intentionally induce[ ]" its customers to make infringing uses of [the plaintiffs'] copyrights, nor does it supply its products to *identified individuals known by it* to be engaging in continuing infringement of [the plaintiffs'] copyrights.

Id. at 439 n.19 (quoting *Inwood*, 456 U.S. at 855).

Thus, the Court suggested, had the *Inwood* standard applied in *Sony*, the fact that Sony might have known that some portion of the purchasers of its product used it to violate the copyrights of others would not have provided a sufficient basis for contributory liability. *Inwood*'s "narrow standard" would have required knowledge by Sony of "identified individuals" engaging in infringing conduct. Tiffany's reading of *Inwood* is therefore contrary to the interpretation of that case set forth in *Sony*.

Although the Supreme Court's observations in *Sony*, a copyright case, about the "knows or has reason to know" prong of the contributory trademark infringement test set forth in *Inwood* were dicta, they constitute the only discussion of that prong by the Supreme Court of which we are aware. We think them to be persuasive authority here.

Applying *Sony*'s interpretation of *Inwood*, we agree with the district court that "Tiffany's general allegations of counterfeiting failed to provide eBay with the knowledge required under *Inwood*." *Tiffany*, 576 F. Supp. 2d at 511. Tiffany's demand letters and

Buying Programs did not identify particular sellers who Tiffany thought were then offering or would offer counterfeit goods. And although the NOCIs and buyer complaints gave eBay reason to know that certain sellers had been selling counterfeits, those sellers' listings were removed and repeat offenders were suspended from the eBay site. Thus Tiffany failed to demonstrate that eBay was supplying its service to individuals who it knew or had reason to know were selling counterfeit Tiffany goods.

Accordingly, we affirm the judgment of the district court insofar as it holds that eBay is not contributorily liable for trademark infringement.

3. Willful Blindness

Tiffany and its amici express their concern that if eBay is not held liable except when specific counterfeit listings are brought to its attention, eBay will have no incentive to root out such listings from its website. They argue that this will effectively require Tiffany and similarly situated retailers to police eBay's website—and many others like it—"24 hours a day, and 365 days a year." They urge that this is a burden that most mark holders cannot afford to bear. . . .

But we are [] disposed to think, and the record suggests, that private market forces give eBay and those operating similar businesses a strong incentive to minimize the counterfeit goods sold on their websites. eBay received many complaints from users claiming to have been duped into buying counterfeit Tiffany products sold on eBay. The risk of alienating these users gives eBay a reason to identify and remove counterfeit listings. Indeed, it has spent millions of dollars in that effort.

Moreover, we agree with the district court that if eBay had reason to suspect that counterfeit Tiffany goods were being sold through its website, and intentionally shielded itself from discovering the offending listings or the identity of the sellers behind them, eBay might very well have been charged with knowledge of those sales sufficient to satisfy *Inwood*'s "knows or has reason to know" prong. *Tiffany*, 576 F. Supp. 2d at 513–14. A service provider is not, we think, permitted willful blindness. When it has reason to suspect that users of its service are infringing a protected mark, it may not shield itself from learning of the particular infringing transactions by looking the other way. *See, e.g., Hard Rock Café*, 955 F.2d at 1149 ("To be willfully blind, a person must suspect wrongdoing and deliberately fail to investigate."); *Fonovisa*, 76 F.3d at 265 (applying *Hard Rock Café*'s reasoning to conclude that "a swap meet can not disregard its vendors' blatant trademark infringements with impunity").[15] In the words of the Seventh Circuit, "willful blindness is equivalent to actual knowledge for purposes of the Lanham Act." *Hard Rock Café*, 955 F.2d at 1149.

---

[15] To be clear, a service provider is not contributorily liable under Inwood merely for failing to anticipate that others would use its service to infringe a protected mark. Inwood, 456 U.S. at 854 n.13 (stating that for contributory liability to lie, a defendant must do more than "reasonably anticipate" a third party's infringing conduct (internal quotation marks omitted)). But contributory liability may arise where a defendant is (as was eBay here) made aware that there was infringement on its site but (unlike eBay here) ignored that fact.

eBay appears to concede that it knew as a general matter that counterfeit Tiffany products were listed and sold through its website. Without more, however, this knowledge is insufficient to trigger liability under *Inwood.* The district court found, after careful consideration, that eBay was not willfully blind to the counterfeit sales. That finding is not clearly erroneous. eBay did not ignore the information it was given about counterfeit sales on its website.

III. Trademark Dilution

. . . The district court rejected Tiffany's dilution by blurring claim on the ground that "eBay never used the TIFFANY Marks in an effort to create an association with its own product, but instead, used the marks directly to advertise and identify the availability of authentic Tiffany merchandise on the eBay website." *Tiffany,* 576 F. Supp. 2d at 524. The court concluded that "just as the dilution by blurring claim fails because eBay has never used the [Tiffany] Marks to refer to eBay's own product, the dilution by tarnishment claim also fails."

We agree. There is no second mark or product at issue here to blur with or to tarnish "Tiffany."

Tiffany argues that counterfeiting dilutes the value of its product. Perhaps. But insofar as eBay did not itself sell the goods at issue, it did not itself engage in dilution.

Tiffany argued unsuccessfully to the district court that eBay was liable for contributory dilution. Assuming without deciding that such a cause of action exists, the court concluded that the claim would fail for the same reasons Tiffany's contributory trademark infringement claim failed. . . .

Conclusion

For the foregoing reasons, we affirm the judgment of the district court with respect to the claims of trademark infringement and dilution. [W]e return the cause to the district court for further proceedings with respect to Tiffany's false advertising claim.

COMMENTS AND QUESTIONS

1. Both patent law and copyright law have well-developed doctrines of indirect infringement. Defendants are liable for contributory infringement if, although they did not themselves infringe the patent or copyright, they assisted or encouraged others to infringe. Liability for contributory infringement extends to the makers and vendors of machines on which infringements are performed, but only if the machines are not capable of a substantial noninfringing use. As *Tiffany* suggests, the equivalent doctrine in trademark law is narrower. *Cf. Perfect 10, Inc. v. Visa Int'l Service Ass'n*, 494 F.3d 788, 806 (9th Cir. 2007) ("The tests for secondary trademark infringement are even more difficult to satisfy than those required to find secondary copyright infringement."). Why?

2. Courts have held that indirect infringement of trademarks extends to manufactures and distributors, as well as to flea market operators. In *Hard Rock Cafe Licensing*

Corp. v. Concession Services, Inc., 955 F.2d 1143, 1149 (7th Cir. 1992), the Seventh Circuit applied the *Inwood* test for contributory trademark liability to the operator of a flea market, and found that the operator would be liable for the copyright infringement of vendors it permits on its premises if it knows or has reason to know that the vendor "is acting or will act tortiously." However, it still "has no affirmative duty to take precautions against the sale of counterfeits." *Id.*

Is this result defensible? Does it extend to newspapers that print advertisements by counterfeiters? To graphics and print shops that print ads? To those who sell furniture or office supplies to counterfeiters?

3. Did the *Tiffany* court reach the correct result? Should the law take into account who can more efficiently bear the burden of policing for counterfeits? How does eBay's VeRO system compare to the DMCA safe harbors? *See generally* Stacey L. Dogan, *Principles Standards vs. Boundless Discretion: Approaches to Intermediary Trademark Liability Online*, 37 COLUM. J. L. & THE ARTS 503 (2014). Approaches to this problem vary across countries. In China, as in the U.S., the law generally favors online marketplace platforms. *See* Ying Du, *Secondary Liability for Trademark Infringement Online Legislation and Judicial Decisions in China*, 37 COLUM. J. L. & ARTS 541 (2014). In Europe, many countries are more protective of trademark owners, many of which are luxury brands with a long provenance. *See e.g.*, *S.A. Louis Vuitton Malletier v. eBay, Inc.*, Tribunal de Commerce de Paris, Premiere Chambre B. (Paris Commercial Court), Case No. 200677799 (June 30, 2008) (eBay violated Louis Vuitton trademarks by passively allowing infringers to sell goods online).

4. A number of trademark owners have sued Google and other Internet search engines, alleging that their ads (which are targeted based on Internet keywords selected by the advertiser) infringe their trademarks. In *GEICO v. Google*, 2005 WL 1903128 (E.D. Va. Aug. 8, 2005), the district court rejected such a claim, ruling that the plaintiff could not demonstrate that the mere sale of a keyword confused consumers. The court left open the possibility that the advertisers themselves might be liable for infringement if the text of the ads were confusing, and that Google might be liable for contributory infringement if it encouraged such confusion. *See also* Stacey L. Dogan & Mark A. Lemley, *Trademarks and Consumer Search Costs on the Internet*, 41 HOUS. L. REV. 777 (2004) (arguing for this approach). Does it make sense to distinguish between ads that are likely to confuse consumers and those that aren't? Or is the mere use of a trademark as a keyword problematic even if no one will be confused by the resulting ad? Even if an advertiser is liable for running a confusing ad, is Google contributing to that infringement? How? What could Google do to avoid liability, short of terminating its entire advertising program?

6. False Advertising

Section 43(a) of the Lanham Act includes a specific prohibition on false or misleading advertising:

(a)(1) Any person who, on or in connection with any goods or services, or any container for goods, uses in commerce any word, term, name, symbol, or device, or any combination thereof, or any false designation of origin, false or misleading description of fact, or false or misleading representation of fact, which— . . .

(B) in commercial advertising or promotion, misrepresents the nature, characteristics, qualities, or geographic origin of his or her or another person's goods, services, or commercial activities, shall be liable in a civil action by any person who believes that he or she is or is likely to be damaged by such act.

MillerCoors, LLC v. Anheuser-Busch Companies, LLC
United States District Court, Western District of Wisconsin
2019 WL 2250644 (2019)

WILLIAM M. CONLEY, District Judge:

During Super Bowl LIII, defendant Anheuser-Busch launched an advertising campaign highlighting plaintiff MillerCoors use of corn syrup in brewing Miller Lite and Coors Light, as compared to Anheuser-Busch's use of rice in its flagship light beer, Bud Light. This lawsuit followed, with MillerCoors asserting a claim of false advertising under the Lanham Act, 15 U.S.C. § 1125(a)(1)(B).

Before the court is plaintiff's motion for preliminary injunction.

UNDISPUTED FACTS

A. Relevant Light Beer Market

Miller Brewing Company was founded in 1855, and Coors Brewing Company was founded in 1873. Plaintiff MillerCoors, LLC was formed in 2008 as a U.S. joint venture between the owners of the Miller Brewing Company and the Coors Brewing Company. Miller Lite and Coors Light were both introduced to U.S. consumers in the 1970s. Defendant Anheuser-Busch Companies, LLC is a multinational beverage company that sells numerous products, including Bud Light beer. Currently, Bud Light has the largest market share of the U.S. market for light beers, while Miller Lite and Coors Light have the second and third-highest share of the U.S. market for light beer, respectively. . . .

B. Beer Brewing Process and Ingredients

The first step in brewing beer is to create a nutrient substrate, called "wort," that yeast needs for fermentation. The sugars in the wort are sourced from malt, or from a combination of malt and starchy grains like corn or rice. Plaintiff asserts that the sugar source is selected based on the style and taste characteristics, which defendant does not dispute, although pointing out that cost may also be a factor. Defendant further represents that corn syrup is less expensive than rice.

In its brewing process for Miller Lite and Coors Light beers, plaintiff contends that it uses "corn syrup, rather than another source of sugar, to aid fermentation because it does not mask or change the barley and hops flavors and aromas distinctive to Miller Lite and Coors Light beers." Defendant contends that plaintiff has also "publicly, attributed the taste of its beers, in part, to corn syrup, stating that 'corn syrup gives beer a milder and lighter-bodied flavor.'" There is no meaningful difference between using rice or corn syrup as an ingredient in terms of health or safety of the resulting beer product.

The yeast's natural fermentation process converts the corn syrup sugars into ethanol, flavors, aromas, carbon dioxide, heat and a next generation of yeast cells, leaving a small amount of residual sugars. Plaintiff represents—and defendant disputes only on the basis that it lacks information and knowledge—that "[n]o corn syrup appears in the Coors Light and Miller Lite products at the end of the fermentation." Moreover, MillerCoors does not add corn syrup or any other sweetener (including high-fructose corn syrup) to the finished Coors Light or Miller Lite products.

While defendant Anheuser-Busch uses corn syrup as an ingredient in fermentations of many of its other products, Bud Light uses rice as its sugar source. Presumably, no rice or any other sweetener appears in Bud Light at the end of the fermentation process either.

C. Super Bowl Commercials and Subsequent Advertisements

On February 3, 2019, during the television broadcast of Super Bowl LIII, Anheuser-Busch launched a nationwide advertising campaigning featuring claims that Miller Lite and Coors Light are "made with" or "brewed with" corn syrup. A 60-second commercial, titled "Special Delivery," first ran during the Super Bowl and has continued to run both in a full-length version, as well as shorter 15-second and 30-second "cut down" versions.

While defendant purports to dispute any description or paraphrasing of the "Special Delivery" advertisement, the commercial contains the following scenes in order:

- The Bud Light King, the Bud Light Knight and a wizard discuss how Bud Light is brewed, with four barrels behind them labeled, "Water," "Rice," "Hops," and "Barley".

- One of the Bud Light King's knights then enters with a large barrel labeled "Corn Syrup" and announces, "My King, this corn syrup was just delivered."

- The Bud Light King responds, "that's not ours. We don't brew Bud Light with corn syrup." The knight responds, "Miller Lite uses corn syrup," to which the King respond, "Let us take it to them at once."

- The party then embarks on an arduous journey to deliver the barrel of corn syrup to the Miller Lite Castle.

- Once the Bud Light party arrives at the Miller Lite Castle, the Bud Light King announces, "Oh brewers of Miller Lite, we received your corn syrup by mistake." The Miller Lite King, with a supply of Miller Lite at his side, responds, "That's not our corn syrup. We received our shipment this morning.... Try the Coors Light Castle. They also use corn syrup."

- The party then embarks on another arduous journey to deliver the barrel to the Coors Light Castle.

- Upon arrival, the Bud Light King again announces, "Oh brewers of Coors Light, is this corn syrup yours?" The Coors Light King answers, "Well, well, well. Looks like the corn syrup has come home to be brewed. To be clear, we brew Coors Light with corn syrup."

- The commercial closes with the written statement and voice over, "Bud Light, Brewed with no Corn Syrup."

Since the Superbowl, the "Special Delivery" commercial in its 30-second and 60-second versions has aired over 900 times on over 20 channels.

During the Super Bowl, Anheuser-Busch also aired two 15-second commercials, "Medieval Barbers" and "Trojan Horse Occupants." Collectively, these commercials, like Special Delivery, also state that Miller Lite and Coors Light are "made with corn syrup." Since the Super Bowl, these ads have aired 257 and 566 times, respectively.

This year's Super Bowl advertising commanded between $ 5.1 and $ 5.3 million per 30 seconds of media placement, not including production costs. The "Special De-livery" ad, in particular, "quickly became one of the night's most talked about ... with some observers hailing it as an advertising touchdown." . . .

In addition to these television commercials, Anheuser-Busch has also launched print-media and billboard campaigns, including three sequential billboards which read:

1. Bud Light 100% less corn syrup than Coors Light.

2. and . . . wait for it . . .

3. 100% less corn syrup than Miller Lite.

Anheuser-Busch has also used its Twitter account to further this campaign. Three days after the Super Bowl, Anheuser-Busch's Twitter account displayed the following image:

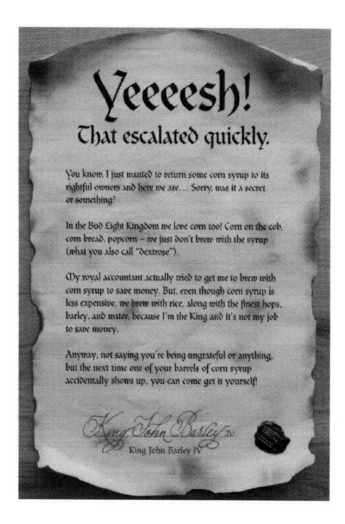

A few weeks later, Anheuser-Busch Natural Light's Twitter account contained the following image, displaying a Miller Lite can next to a Karo corn syrup bottle as if in a family portrait:

♡ 219   ↻ 456   ♡ 4.4K   ✉

[Annheuser-Busch ran additional advertisements poking fun at MillerCoors and highlighted the use of sugar in the MillerCoors lite beer. The NEW YORK TIMES quoted Anheuser-Busch's vice president of communications stating "We stand behind the Bud Light transparency campaign and have no plans to change the advertising."]

D. Anheuser-Busch's Intent in Launching Campaign

On February 7, 2019, Beer Business Daily reported that according to Andy Goeler, Anheuser-Busch's head of marketing for Bud Light, told its distributors that:

> [Anheuser-Busch] did focus-group the heck out of this [Special Delivery] ad, and found consumers generally don't differentiate between high fructose corn syrup and corn syrup, and that it is a major triggering point in choosing brands to purchase, particularly among women.

In an interview with Food and Wine Magazine, in response to the question, "What is wrong with corn syrup?," Goeler responded:

People started to react to corn syrup, they started to react to no preservatives, and they started to react to no artificial flavors. There are things that consumers on their own had perceptions -- for whatever reason -- that there were ingredients they preferred not to consume if they didn't have to. So it was pretty clear to us what to highlight. If you look at our packaging, we highlight all three of those. No corn syrup. No artificial flavors. No preservatives. It was purely driven by consumer desire.

The interviewer then noted that Anheuser-Busch had "decided to focus on corn syrup instead of no preservative or things like that," and asked Goeler why he thought "consumers see corn syrup as something they don't want?" (Id. at 4.) In response, Goeler explained, "I think it's probably an ingredient some prefer not to consume is the simple answer. . . . [S]ome consumers—for their own personal reasons—have concluded that they prefer not putting something like corn syrup, if they had a choice, into their body."
. . .

E. MillerCoors' Consumer Survey

In support of its motion for preliminary injunction, MillerCoors retained Dr. Yoram Wind, a professor at the University of Pennsylvania Wharton School of Business with expertise in consumer behavior and marketing, to conduct a survey of consumers. Wind surveyed 2,034 consumers who were shown either a test or control version of the "Mountain Folk" commercial described above. Of the total respondents, 1,016 were randomly assigned to view the test ad, and 1,018 were randomly assigned to view a control ad.

The control ad was the same commercial as the test ad, but with an added, prominent disclaimer: "While corn syrup is used during the brewing of Miller Lite and Coors Light, there is NO corn syrup in the Miller Lite and Coors Light you drink."

According to Wind's analysis, "61 percent of respondents who saw the test stimulus believe that corn syrup is in the Miller Lite and/or Coors Light you drink (3 percent who said 'In Drink' plus 58 percent who said 'Both Brewed with and in Drink'). In contrast, only 26 percent of respondents who saw the control stimulus (3 percent who said 'In Drink' plus 23 percent who said 'Both Brewed with and in Drink') have that belief." Wind, further opined, that the difference in perception of 35% of consumers "is both economically and statistically significant." Wind also concluded based on an analysis of open-ended responses that the phrase " 'made with' used in the Bud Light commercial to describe the relationship between Miller Lite and/or Coors Light and corn syrup is ambiguous."

In support of its motion, plaintiff contends that the advertisements exploit or further misconceptions about corn syrup and high fructose corn syrup ("HFCS"). The corn syrup MillerCoors uses in its brewing process is a distinct substance from HFCS. Dr. John S. White, a biochemist with industry experience in "products of the corn wet milling industry including starches, maltodextrins and corn syrups," represents that he "has worked extensively on the divisive [HFCS] issue for the past 15 years," and that "there is a common point of confusion about corn syrup and HFCS, despite the fact that they are very different products." With respect to the survey, Wind concluded that "more respondents who saw the test stimulus (24 percent) than who saw the control stimulus (19 percent) believed that the commercial says, suggests, or implies that corn syrup and high fructose corn syrup are the same."

F. Consumer Communications

In January 2019, before the launch of the advertising campaign at issue in this lawsuit, "MillerCoors had received virtually no consumer communications related to corn syrup." After the Super Bowl, through March 22, 2019, MillerCoors received 179 communications related to corn syrup. Defendant disputes the significance of these communications on the basis that "[t]his small number of communications after the Super Bowl consists of thoughts from a miniscule fraction of the overall relevant consumers, and Dr. Wind provided no evidence that his dataset of particular consumers who actively reached out to MillerCoors is representative of all potential MillerCoors consumers." Nevertheless, according to Wind's analysis, "[t]wenty-two percent of consumer communications noted that the presence of corn syrup will have an impact on their likelihood of purchasing Miller Lite and/or Coors Light, with 18 percent likely to end or decrease their purchases of Miller Lite and/or Coors Light and 4 percent noting a likelihood to begin or increase their purchases of Miller Lite and/or Coors Light."

G. Social Media Reaction to Campaign

[Following the Super Bowl, MillerCoors identified numerous posts on social media focusing on the presence of corn syrup in Miller Lite and Coors Light products.]

OPINION

. . .

I. Likelihood of Success on the Merits

"To prevail on a deceptive-advertising claim under the Lanham Act, a plaintiff must establish that (1) the defendant made a material false statement of fact in a commercial advertisement; (2) the false statement actually deceived or had the tendency to deceive a substantial segment of its audience; and (3) the plaintiff has been or is likely to be injured as a result of the false statement." *Eli Lilly & Co. v. Arla Foods, Inc.*, 893 F.3d 375, 381–82 (7th Cir. 2018) (citing *Hot Wax, Inc. v. Turtle Wax, Inc.*, 191 F.3d 813, 819 (7th Cir. 1999)). The Seventh Circuit recognizes two types of "false statements": (1) "those that are literally false" and (2) "those that are literally true but misleading." Id. at 382 (citing *Hot Wax*, 191 F.3d at 820).

The required proof varies based on which type of statement is at issue. A literally false statement is "an explicit representation of fact that on its face conflicts with reality." *Eli Lilly*, 893 F.3d at 382. The type of statements that fall into this category are "bald-faced, egregious, undeniable, [and] over the top." *Schering-Plough Healthcare Prods., Inc. v. Schwarz Pharma, Inc.*, 586 F.3d 500, 513 (7th Cir. 2009). As such, "[a] literally false statement will necessarily deceive consumers, so extrinsic evidence of actual consumer confusion is not required." *Eli Lilly*, 893 F.3d at 382.

For statements that are literally true but misleading, "the plaintiff ordinarily must produce evidence of actual consumer confusion in order to carry its burden to show that the challenged statement has 'the tendency to deceive a substantial segment of its audience.'" *Id.* at 382 (quoting *Hot Wax*, 191 F.3d at 819–20). At the preliminary injunction stage, however, a consumer survey or other "hard evidence of actual consumer confusion" is not required. *Id.* Instead, the Seventh Circuit instructs that district courts should analyze "the ads themselves, the regulatory guidance, and the evidence of decreased demand." *Id.*

In its brief, plaintiff argues that it may also demonstrate that an ad has the tendency to deceive a substantial segment by showing that the "defendant has intentionally set out to deceive the public, and the defendant's deliberate conduct in this regard is of an egregious nature." *Johnson & Johnson * Merck Consumer Pharm. Co. v. Smithkline Beecham Corp.*, 960 F.2d 294, 298–99 (2d Cir. 1992) ("J&J * Merck") Such evidence gives rise to a presumption "that consumers are, in fact, being deceived," and then "the burden shifts to the defendant to demonstrate the absence of consumer confusion." *Id.* (internal citation and quotations marks omitted). . . .

A. Misleading Statements

Recognizing that the alleged misleading statement must be considered in context of the full advertisement, *Hot Wax*, 191 F.3d at 820, plaintiff nonetheless focuses its argument around four misleading statements: (1) "made with," "brewed with" or "uses" corn syrup; (2) Bud Light has "100% less corn syrup than Miller Lite or Coors Light" or that it has "no corn syrup"; (3) referring to corn syrup as an "ingredient"; and (4) corn syrup is used to "save money" or is "less expensive."

1. "made with," "brewed with" or "uses"

There is no dispute that the statements that Miller Lite and Coors Light "use" or are "made with" or "brewed with" corn syrup are literally true. Instead, plaintiff argues that "when viewed as a whole, [the advertisements] deceive[ ] consumers into believing that Miller Lite and Coors Light final products actually contain corn syrup and thus are unhealthy and inferior to Bud Light." Plaintiff's argument also turns on its representation, grounded in expert opinion, that there is no corn syrup in either end product. . . .

For support of its argument that these statements are misleading, plaintiff directs the court to *Abbott Laboratories v. Mead Johnson & Company*, 971 F.3d 6 (7th Cir. 1992), in which the Seventh Circuit reversed the district court's denial of a preliminary injunction in a Lanham Act claim involving competing oral electrolyte maintenance solutions ("OES") products administered to prevent dehydration in infants suffering from acute diarrhea or vomiting. In Abbott Laboratories, the defendant introduced a new product "Ricelyte" into the market to compete with "Pedialyte." Pedialyte was a "glucose-based solution," whereas Ricelyte was manufactured from "rice syrup solids." In the advertisements at issue, defendant emphasized "that Ricelyte's carbohydrate components (i.e., rice syrup solids) come from rice, whereas Pedialyte's carbohydrate component is glucose."

As the district court found, however, the rice syrup solids are "hydrolytically derived from rice carbohydrates, [but] are not actually 'rice carbohydrates' as that term is used in the scientific and medical communities." In addition to finding that the description of Ricelyte as a "rice-based oral electrolyte solution" was literally false, the Seventh Circuit also concluded that the name Ricelyte

> implies more than the permissible message that Ricelyte is produced from rice or contains rice syrup solids derived from rice carbohydrates. It also implies that Ricelyte *actually contains* rice and rice carbohydrates—or at least we can say that Abbott has established a strong likelihood of so proving at trial.

Id. at 15 (emphasis added).

Here, plaintiff MillerCoors would grasp onto this distinction between a product being "derived from" an ingredient as compared to "actually contain[ing]" the ingredient. In particular, plaintiff argues that defendant's advertisements blur this line or, at minimum, this language "do[es] not foreclose the possibility in consumers['] minds that corn syrup is added as a finishing ingredient to the beer." As defendant points out, however, there is no affirmative duty to disclose or disclaim if the advertisement at issue is not false or misleading.

More to the point, unlike in *Abbott Laboratories*, viewing the "made with," "brewed with" or "uses" statements in the context of the full commercials here, there are no express or implicit messages that the corn syrup is actually in the finished product. In finding the use of the Ricelyte name misleading, the Abbott Laboratories court pointed to "[t]he product's label [which] places the name 'Ricelyte' directly above the phrase 'Rice-Based Oral Electrolyte Maintenance Solution,'" and "references, both verbal and pictorial, to rice in Mead's print advertisements and brochures." *Abbott Labs.*, 971 F.2d at 15. As described in detail above, the Bud Light commercials containing the "made with" or "brewed with" language show delivery of a large barrel of corn syrup, but do not show corn syrup being added to the finished Miller Lite or Coors Light products. Moreover, unlike Ricelyte, Bud Light is apparently brewed with grains of rice, not some derivative syrup.

Plaintiff also directs the court to *Eli Lilly and Company v. Arla Foods, Inc.*, 893 F.3d 375 (7th Cir. 2018), in which the Seventh Circuit affirmed the district court's entry of a preliminary injunction against a cheese manufacturer's advertisements implying that milk from recombinant bovine somatropin ("rbST")-treated cows was unwholesome. The advertisements at issue stated that "Arla cheese contains no 'weird stuff' or 'ingredients that you can't pronounce'—in particular, no milk from cows treated with [rbST]," and depicted rbST as "a cartoon monster with razor sharp horns and electric fur." Critically, at least at the preliminary injunction stage, the defendant cheese producer conceded that "rbST-derived dairy products are the same quality, nutrition, and safety as other dairy products."

The Seventh Circuit determined that the explicit statements were accurate: "RbST is an artificial growth hormone given to some cows, and Arla does not use milk from those cows." Id. at 382. The court, however, affirmed the district court's analysis of the evidence— "the ads themselves, the regulatory guidance, and the evidence of decreased demand"—to conclude that the advertisements were misleading. Specifically, the court explained:

> the ad campaign centers on disparaging dairy products made from milk supplied by rbST-treated cows. The ads draw a clear contrast between Arla cheese (high quality, nutritious) and cheese made from rbST-treated cows (impure, unwholesome). The use of monster imagery, "weird stuff" language, and child actors combine to colorfully communicate the message that responsible consumers should be concerned about rbST-derived dairy products.

Id. at 382–83.

Here, too, the *Eli Lilly* decision is distinguishable on the basis that the Bud Light "made with," "brewed with" or "uses" ads do not disparage corn syrup or otherwise expressly draw attention to any negative health consequences. (See Def.'s Opp'n 24 (distinguishing *Eli Lilly* and other comparative ads on the basis that the ads at issue here are "whimsical, humorous and no message of disgust or danger from drinking the beers are communicated verbally or in imagery").) In fairness, plaintiff's counsel rightly points out that this link may have been unnecessary here, since at least some consumers appear to associate corn syrup, and particularly high fructose corn syrup, with harmful health consequences, or certainly defendant hoped.

However, instead of analyzing the commercial or the advertising campaign more broadly in order to demonstrate that these statements are misleading, plaintiff relies on open-ended questions in Wind's consumer survey, in which consumers interpreted "'made with' to mean, for example 'contains,' 'uses,' 'has,' 'is made with,' 'is in,' or 'is added.'" As an initial matter, certain of the respondents' descriptions -- namely, "uses" and "is made with"— appear accurate, and contradict plaintiff's argument that "made with" or "brewed with" means "is contained" in the finished product. Indeed, responding that "made with" means "is made with" does not appear to be an interpretation of the phrase at all.

Putting aside these concerns about the quality of this proof, relying on survey evidence to find that an advertisement is "misleading" may well bring statements that merely are "susceptible to misunderstanding" within the scope of a Lanham Act violation, which the Seventh Circuit instructed is not appropriate in *Mead Johnson & Company v. Abbott Laboratories* ("*Mead Johnson I*"), 201 F.3d 883 (7th Cir. 2000). In that case, an infant formula manufacturer brought a Lanham Act action against a competitor, based on the competitor's use of the statement "1st Choice of Doctors" in its advertisements. The district court entered a preliminary injunction, in part, based on its finding that the statement "implies to consumers that a majority of physicians strongly prefer the product for strictly professional reasons," and the market research, while showing a plurality of support among physicians, did not show a majority of support. *Id.* at 884.

The Seventh Circuit rejected this conclusion and reversed the entry of a preliminary injunction, explaining that "it is all but impossible to call the claim of 'first choice' misleading . . . [u]nless the meaning of language is itself to be determined by survey evidence." Id. In other words, the Seventh Circuit rejected an attempt to solely rely on survey evidence to demonstrate that language is misleading.

In a subsequent opinion, denying a petition for rehearing, the Seventh Circuit clarified a portion of its prior opinion and order, explaining:

> Section 43(a)(1) forbids misleading as well as false claims, but interpreting "misleading" to include factual propositions that are susceptible to misunderstanding would make consumers as a whole worse off by suppressing truthful statements that will help many of them find superior products. A statement is misleading when, although literally true, it implies something that is false. *Abbott Laboratories v. Mead Johnson & Co.,* 971 F.2d 6, 13 (7th Cir. 1992). "Misleading" is not a synonym for "misunderstood," and this record does not support a conclusion that Abbott's statements implied falsehoods about Similac.

Mead Johnson & Co. v. Abbott Labs. ("*Mead Johnson II*"), 209 F.3d 1032, 1034 (7th Cir. 2000).

The court notes that *Mead Johnson* is not without its critics, and understandably so: how does one draw the line between an advertising statement that is susceptible to misunderstanding but not misleading?[15] . . .

[R]equiring plaintiff to point to some other aspect of the ad besides a truthful statement is entirely consistent with the approach of the Seventh Circuit and other courts in the cases cited by plaintiff. In finding a literally true statement misleading, courts consistently seem to rely on disparaging or derogatory references to the ingredients in the competitor's product, e.g., *Eli Lilly,* 893 F.3d at 379 (depicting rbST as a "cartoon monster with razor sharp horns and electric fur"); *Chobani, LLC v. Dannon Co., Inc.,* 157 F. Supp. 3d 190, (N.D.N.Y. 2016) (using "negative phrasing," e.g., "bad stuff," in reference to sucralose contained in defendant's yogurt); *Polar Corp. v. Coca-Cola Co.,* 871 F. Supp. 1520, 1521 (D. Mass. 1994) ("This Court finds that, by causing the polar bear to throw the can of Coke into a trash bin labeled 'Keep the Arctic Pure,' Polar has implied that Coke is not pure."), or references that suggest a quality not present in a product is in fact in the product, e.g., *Abbott Laboratories,* 971 F.2d at 10 (placing rice grains

---

[15] One scholar has suggested that this holding requires materiality in addition to a misunderstanding for a claim to be misleading. Rebecca Tushnet, *Running the Gamut from A to B: Federal Trademark and False Advertising Law,* 159 U. PA. L. REV. 1305, 1349 (2011). To illustrate, Tushnet explains, "One may misunderstand a fact in the abstract: I could be wrong about the size of a computer's hard drive. If I am misled, however, I am being led: induced, or at least potentially induced, to change my position based on my misunderstanding, as when I am more likely to buy a computer because of my belief about the size of the hard drive." *Id.* Even this language, however, suggests that something more overt is required on the part of the advertiser to find a true statement misleading.

prominently on advertisements). Consistent with these cases, plaintiff MillerCoors must point to something in the advertisement to allow a reasonable consumer to draw the inference that "brewed with," "made with" or "uses" corn syrup means that corn syrup is in the final product. . . .

For all these reasons, the court concludes that plaintiff has not demonstrated a likelihood of success in demonstrating that the advertisements solely using the language "brewed with," "made with," or "uses" corn syrup are misleading.

2. Bud Light has "100% less corn syrup than Miller Lite or Coors Light" or that it has "no corn syrup"

Plaintiff also contends that defendant's statements that Bud Light contains "100% less corn syrup" than Miller Lite and/or Coors Light and that Bud Light contains "no corn syrup" are misleading because they "highlight this false dichotomy in a way that suggests consumers should care about it for important reasons such as health concerns." (Pl.'s Br. (dkt. #9) 30.) Unlike the "made with" or "brewed with" statement, these statements, while also literally true, support a reasonable interpretation that Miller Lite and Coors Light contain corn syrup. Thus, the court agrees with plaintiff that it has a likelihood of success in demonstrating that these statements are misleading. The same is also true for the second Thespians commercial, a mock film preview, which contains the following frames:

These advertisements, unlike the ones described above, do not contain any reference to Miller Lite and Coors Light being "made with" or "brewed with" corn syrup; instead, these advertisements—either in stating what is not in Bud Light or in stating what is in Miller Lite or Coors Light—cross the line from simply being susceptible to misunderstanding to being misleading, or, at minimum, the court finds that plaintiff is likely to succeed in making such a showing.

3. Ingredient

Next, plaintiff points to references to "corn syrup" being an "ingredient." As an initial point, it is not clear what constitutes an "ingredient" in the context of beer. As the parties acknowledged during the hearing, there are no labeling requirements with respect to ingredients for beer. See 27 C.F.R. § 7.22 (requiring name, class, name and address of permit holder, net contents and alcohol content). Even in the food context, as far as this court could find, "ingredient" is not defined, but appears to cover items that are used in the production of a food product, even if not in the end product (e.g., leavening items). See 21 C.F.R. § 101.4 (setting for designation of ingredients for food labeling). . . .

[T]he use of "ingredient" must also be considered in context. In most of the advertisements, defendant uses the word ingredient or lists ingredients in conjunction with the "made with" or "brewed with" language. For example, in the Cave Explorers commercial, one character reads out-loud what is written on the inside of the cave, "Coors Light is made with barley, water, hop extract and corn syrup," followed by another character reading out-loud from a different writing, "Bud Light is made with barley, rice, water, hops and no corn syrup." The same is true for the first Thespians advertisement and the Mountain Folk advertisements. *See* ad transcript (using "made with" to list ingredients in Bud Light and Miller Lite); ad transcript (using "made with" to list ingredients in Bud Light, Miller Lite and Coors Light).)

There is one exception. In the most recent commercial, released March 20, 2019, the Bud Light King states,

> Miller, Miller, Miller. I've been made aware of your recent advertisement. I brought you your shipment of corn syrup, and this is how you repay me?

> Look if you're this set on imitating our kingdom, may I suggest also imitating us by putting an ingredients label on your packaging. People want to know *what ingredients are in their beer.*

> But what do I know? I'm just the king of a kingdom that doesn't brew beer with corn syrup.

(emphasis added). For the same reason that the "100% less corn syrup," "no corn syrup" or "corn syrup" language is problematic, the court also concludes that plaintiff is likely to succeed in demonstrating that this language is misleading because it crosses the line to encourage a reasonable consumer to believe that corn syrup is actually contained in the final product. . . .

B. Intent to Deceive

To date, plaintiff's strongest evidence is defendant's own statements indicating that in launching this campaign, it was both aware of and intended to exploit consumer concerns about corn syrup (and high fructose corn syrup in particular). As detailed above, defendant's head of marketing for Bud Light and senior director of corporation communications in various publications described the market research defendant engaged in before launching this campaign. Specifically, defendant found that "consumers generally don't differentiate between high fructose corn syrup and corn syrup, and that it is a major triggering point in choosing brands to purchase"; "consumers on their own had perceptions—for whatever reason—that there were ingredients they preferred not to consume if they didn't have to" and, therefore, "it was pretty clear to us what to highlight"; and that consumers "have concluded that they prefer not putting something like corn syrup, if they had a choice, into their body."

As the court indicated during the hearing, these statements support a finding that defendant was aware of consumer concerns about and the likelihood of confusion surrounding corn syrup and HFCS, and that defendant hoped consumers would interpret advertising statements about "made with corn syrup" or "brewed with corn syrup" as corn syrup actually being in the finished products. As acknowledged above, however, the Seventh Circuit has not yet embraced the doctrine that would create a rebuttable presumption of consumer confusion or deception based on an intent to deceive, though perhaps this evidence could serve to color the "made with" and "brewed with" statements to push them across the line to allow a reasonable finding that they are misleading, and not simply susceptible to misunderstanding. . . .

Moreover, as discussed above, at least the Second and Third Circuit require a showing of "egregious conduct" *in addition* to intent to deceive to give rise to this rebuttable presumption. . . .

As the Third Circuit explained in discussing competitor advertisements in the antacid market:

> Both the earlier Mylanta advertising and the Maalox advertising have tried to exploit the consumer confusion the FDA feared between the results of ANC tests and symptom relief. The advertisements tout the ANC strength, promise symptom relief, and invite consumers to make the connection. *Although there is evidence of intent to mislead, it is of a kind regrettably pervasive throughout the antacid industry and does not reach the egregious proportions that would warrant a presumption shifting the burden of proof.* Therefore, we need not decide whether to adopt the *Smithkline Beecham* presumption in case of clear and egregious conduct. In this case, the district court's failure to consider Johnson–Merck's evidence as to Rorer's intent was not error.

Johnson & Johnson-Merck Consumer Pharm., 19 F.3d at 132 (emphasis added); *see also Am. Home Prod. Corp. v. Procter & Gamble Co.*, 871 F. Supp. 739, 763 (D.N.J. 1994) ("Despite the great weight of the evidence demonstrating an intent to mislead, the court found that the actions of the defendant were simply not egregious.").

Because all advertising seems to be an effort to exploit consumer likes and dislikes, interests and fears, applying the Lanham Act to neutral, truthful statements intended to exploit or take advantage of consumer beliefs is problematic, especially in light of the arguable value of comparative advertisements in promoting intelligent consumer decision-making. Absent additional guidance from the Seventh Circuit, the court is unwilling, at this stage in the proceedings, to rely on intent as the hook to find plaintiff likely to succeed on demonstrating that the "made with," "brewed with," or "uses" corn syrup statements are misleading.

C. Evidence of Confusion

To demonstrate a likelihood of success on its Lanham Act claim, plaintiff must put forth evidence that a "substantial segment of its audience" was deceived by defendant's advertisements. *Eli Lilly*, 893 F.3d at 381–82. As detailed above, plaintiff offers evidence of confusion in the form of: (1) a consumer survey conducted by its expert Dr. White; (2) consumer communications mentioning corn syrup after the launch of the campaign during the Super Bowl; and (3) reactions on social media.

Plaintiff principally relies on the surveys finding that "a net (after account for the control group) of 35% of consumers were misled by the ad into thinking that Miller Lite and Coors Light contain corn syrup." Plaintiff directs the court to cases holding that survey evidence that "at least 15% of consumers have been misled" constitutes a "substantial percentage" for purposes of satisfying the second element of a Lanham Act claim. ((citing *Novartis Consumer Health, Inc. v. Johnson & Johnson-Merck Consumer Pharm., Co.*, 290 F.3d 578, 594 (3d Cir. 2002); *Eli Lilly Co. v. Arla Foods, Inc.*, 17-cv-703, 2017 WL 4570547, at *9 (E.D. Wis. June 15, 2017), *aff'd* 893 F.3d 375 (7th Cir. 2018)).)

In response, defendant, largely through a declaration of its own expert, John R. Hauser, Sc.D., offers several challenges to the reliability of the survey and this 35% figure. . . .

Perhaps these challenges cast some doubt on survey results showing a difference in perception between the control and test advertisement of 35% of consumers, but defendant and its expert fall short of providing a basis to reject the survey results out of hand. Moreover, as plaintiff points out and as described above, the Seventh Circuit has repeatedly rejected the notion that survey evidence is required to obtain a preliminary injunction. *See, e.g., Eli Lilly*, 893 F.3d at 382.

Plaintiff also relies on consumer communications, and Wind's analysis of those communications, finding that 18% indicated that they were "likely to end or decrease their purchases of Miller Lite and/or Coors Light" because of corn syrup. As defendant points out persuasively, this analysis was based on 32 total communications, out of the approximately 100 million people who watched the Super Bowl. Moreover, defendant points out that of the ten comments Wind highlights, a number of them accurately described that Miller Lite and Coors Light use or are brewed with corn syrup, rather than plaintiff's alleged mistaken belief that corn syrup is in the final product. Viewed in isolation, the court agrees that these statements are insufficient to prove that a substantial segment of consumers are likely to be deceived by the advertisements, but it is some anecdotal support for the survey results. . . .

In sum, the court finds that plaintiff's evidence is sufficient to support a finding at the preliminary injunction stage that it has some likelihood of success in proving defendant's advertisements deceived or have the tendency to deceive a substantial segment of consumers to believe that Miller Lite and Coors Light actually contain corn syrup. Of course, for the reasons explained above, these results are only relevant to those ads that the court concluded cross the line between susceptible to misunderstanding and misleading because of the language used and the context surrounding that language. . .

.

IV. Injunction

Based on the above discussion, the court will grant a limited injunction, enjoining defendant from using the following language in its commercials, print advertisements and social media:

- Bud Light contains "100% less corn syrup";
- Bud Light in direct reference to "no corn syrup" without any reference to "brewed with," "made with" or "uses";
- Miller Lite and/or Coors Light and "corn syrup" without including any reference to "brewed with," "made with" or "uses"; and
- Describing "corn syrup" as an ingredient "in" the finished product.

With reference to the above described advertisements, the court specifically intends to include, without limiting, defendant's display of the following advertisements:

- "100% less corn syrup" billboards
- Second Thespians commercial; and
- Bud Light King commercial.

COMMENTS AND QUESTIONS

1. The Second Circuit has taken the position that "[w]hether or not the statements made in the advertisements are literally true, § 43(a) of the Lanham Act encompasses more than blatant falsehoods. It embraces innuendo, indirect intimations, and ambiguous suggestions evidenced by the consuming public's misapprehension of the hard facts underlying an advertisement." *Vidal Sassoon, Inc. v. Bristol-Myers Co.*, 661 F.2d 272 (2d Cir. 1981) (comparison ad that misled consumers as to the extent and methodology of the survey conducted was actionable under § 43(a)).

In some cases, unlike *MilleCoors,* the advertisement is literally false on its face. In such cases, the courts will presume that consumers will be deceived by the statements, obviating the need for the plaintiff to prove that consumers are actually confused. *See, e.g., Southland Sod Farms v. Stover Seed Co.*, 108 F.3d 1134 (9th Cir. 1997); *Cashmere & Camel Hair Mfg. Inst. v. Saks Fifth Ave*, 284 F.3d 402 (1st Cir. 2002) (misrepresentation as to the percentage of cashmere in a sweater was literally false, and so was presumed to have deceived consumers). The Third Circuit has gone so far as to hold that a completely unsubstantiated advertising claim is necessarily literally false, triggering the presumption. *Novartis Consumer Health Inc. v. Johnson & Johnson-Merck Consumer Pharms. Co.*, 290 F.3d 578 (3d Cir. 2002).

Can we even be sure whether a statement is true? Consider representations that a food product is "organic." Can we assess the truth of these claims without knowing what consumers understand them to mean? What if consumers are not of one mind, so that the claim is considered accurate by some but inaccurate by others? For an exploration of these issues, *see* Rebecca Tushnet, *It Depends on What the Meaning of "False" Is: Falsity and Misleadingness in Commercial Speech Doctrine*, 41 LOY. L.A. L. REV. 227 (2007).

Most courts have created a third category—claims that are "literally false by necessary implication." These are claims that are literally true but that everyone would understand to mean something that is untrue. For instance, a claim that my tuna is "dolphin free" might be literally true if there are no dolphins in the can. But the public is sure to understand the statement as a claim that no dolphins were harmed in the catching of the tuna. If that implication is untrue, the statement is literally false by necessary implication. Notably, courts in these cases do not require proof of consumer perception or deception, instead grouping these claims with those that are actually false.

Both false and misleading statements must also be material. A claim about an irrelevant fact—say, a statement that my company employs 11,000 people when in fact it employs only 10,950—may be literally false, but it is unlikely to harm the plaintiff. Materiality can be shown by evidence that consumers care about the claim. Alternatively, claims about the intrinsic characteristics of either the plaintiff's or the defendant's product are automatically deemed material.

2. What did Anheuser-Busch do wrong in its initial advertisement? Did it say that Miller Lite was bad for consumers? Or did it simply rely on the fact that, for reasons of their own, people prefer to avoid beer brewed with corn syrup? The creation of often artificial brand distinctions is an integral part of product advertising. Is there anything wrong with creating such distinctions? Does it matter that, as here, the ad takes advantage of misinformed consumers rather than misleading them itself?

Suppose that Anheuser-Busch had never mentioned its own product or compared the two, but had merely questioned the wisdom of using corn syrup. Would MillerCoors have a cause of action under § 43(a)? Traditionally, the answer was no. Before the Trademark Law Revision Act of 1988, § 43(a) prohibited only false or misleading statements about the advertiser's *own* product. Disparagement of the plaintiff's product, while likely actionable under state law tort theories, did not violate the Lanham Act. *See Bernard Food Indus. v. Dietene Co.*, 415 F.2d 1279 (7th Cir. 1969). The 1988 Amendments to § 43 clearly reverse this rule, at least as to statements made in "commercial advertising or promotion." Should federal law provide a cause of action for disparagement of goods or competitors? Johnson & Johnson also sued under state law, specifically §§ 349, 350 of the New York General Business Law. These provisions cover, respectively, unfair trade practices in general and false advertising, and they are representative of state law false advertising statutes.

3. The Seventh Circuit largely affirmed the district court's decision:

> By choosing a word such as 'ingredients' with multiple potential meanings, Molson Coors brought this problem on itself. It is enough for us to hold that it is not 'false or misleading' (§ 1125(a)(1)) for a seller to say or imply, of a business rival, something that the rival says about itself. . . .

> The judgment is affirmed to the extent that it denies Molson Coors's request for an injunction . . . and reversed to the extent that the Bud Light advertising or packaging has been enjoined . . .

Molson Coors Beverage Company USA LLC v. Anheuser-Busch Companies, LLC, 957 F.3d 837, 839 (7th Cir. 2020).

4. While advertisements comparing products or attacking one product often come from a competitor in the market, this is not necessarily the case. Consumers' rights groups like Consumer's Union (publisher of the popular magazine *Consumer Reports*) regularly compare competing products against each other. Government agencies do the same on occasion, and irate consumers have been known to vent their frustration by advertising the defects of a product they are particularly unhappy with. Do these comparisons or disparagements—which presumably are made by neutral third parties rather than competitors—fall within the scope of § 43(a)? The legislative history suggests that § 43(a) was not intended to reach "consumer or editorial comment" by a group like Consumer's Union. Cong. Rec. H10420-21 (daily ed. Oct. 19, 1988) (statement of Rep. Kastenmeier). The dilution provisions of § 43(c) expressly exempt news reporting and comparative advertising from the reach of that section.

5. *What is "advertising"?* Certainly television and print advertisements fall within the scope of the false advertising prohibition. But what about flyers handed out on the street? Sales presentations? Letters to a customer? The general rule is that the Lanham Act does not apply to isolated statements or correspondence to individuals. But in *Seven-Up Co. v. Coca-Cola Co.*, 86 F.3d 1379 (5th Cir. 1996), the court concluded that a series of sales presentations made to bottlers qualified as advertising for purposes of the Lanham Act. *See also Champion Labs. v. Parker-Hannifin*, 2009 WL 1266924 (E.D. Mich. Apr. 30, 2009) (presentation to General Motors could be "commercial promotion" where GM was the only market for the product); *but see Sports Unlimited v. Lankford Enters.*, 275 F.3d 996 (10th Cir. 2002) (distribution of defamatory information to between two and seven people did not constitute "commercial advertising"); *First Health Grp. Corp. v. BCE Emergis Corp.*, 269 F.3d 800 (7th Cir. 2001) (person-to-person pitches aren't advertising).

6. The false advertising prohibition in § 43(a) is the most obviously consumer-oriented of the provisions in the Lanham Act. Protecting consumers from false information about products obviously furthers one of the key goals of trademark law—to ensure that

consumers have accurate information on which to make purchasing decisions. Given this, it is somewhat surprising that consumers do not have standing to sue for false advertising. The Supreme Court held in *Lexmark Int'l v. Static Control Components*, 572 U.S. 118, 132 (2014) that

> to come within the zone of interests in a suit for false advertising under § 1125(a), a plaintiff must allege an injury to a commercial interest in reputation or sales. A consumer who is hoodwinked into purchasing a disappointing product may well have an injury-in-fact cognizable under Article III, but he cannot invoke the protection of the Lanham Act—a conclusion reached by every Circuit to consider the question. Even a business misled by a supplier into purchasing an inferior product is, like consumers generally, not under the Act's aegis.

The court reasoned that the purpose of the false advertising provision of the Lanham Act, unlike the trademark provisions, was to protect against unfair competition, not to protect consumers specifically. Does that make sense?

7. Is private litigation by competitors necessary to ensure accuracy in advertising? *See* Lillian R. BeVier, *Competitor Suits for False Advertising Under Section 43(a) of the Lanham Act: A Puzzle in the Law of Deception*, 78 VA. L. REV. 1, 2–3 (1992) (describing most false advertising claims as "systematically trivial," and arguing that "competitors' incentives to sue are not correlated with the likelihood of consumer harm."). Professor BeVier argues that for the most part the market will discipline producers whose ads are misleading.

8. *Industry Self-Regulation*. Many industry trade associations have advertising codes, as do media and media associations. The National Advertising Division (NAD) of the Council of Better Business Bureaus has actively investigated advertising complaints since 1971. *See* Jeffrey S. Edelstein, *Self-Regulation of Advertising: An Alternative to Litigation and Government Action*, 43 IDEA 509 (2003); David H. Bernstein, *How to "Litigate" False Advertising Cases Before the NAD*, in STRATEGIES FOR LITIGATING COPYRIGHT, TRADEMARK & UNFAIR COMPETITION CASES 255 (2002). The NAD is funded by dues paid to the Council of Better Business Bureaus by advertisers and advertising agencies. Use of these institutions, however, is mixed and influenced by the major industry players.

9. *Public Enforcement*. The Federal Trade Commission (FTC) and state consumer protection agencies have taken a more active interest in policing various deceptive business practices. *See* Arthur Best, *Controlling False Advertising: A Comparative Study of Public Regulation, Industry Self-Policing and Private Litigation*, 20 GA. L. REV. 1 (1985) (comparing benefits of three different sources of ad regulation, and arguing for expansion of private litigation in various cases).

10. *Remedies*. Plaintiffs overwhelmingly seek injunctive relief in § 43(a) advertising cases. Damages can be difficult to prove and quickly stopping the false advertising is a high priority. In some cases, however, they seek—and obtain—damages. *See, e.g., U-*

Haul Int'l v. Jartran, Inc., 793 F.2d 1034 (9th Cir. 1986) (sustaining $40 million award of defendant's profits calculated with reference to defendant's advertising costs). Indeed, some courts will award some presumptive damages when claims are proven literally false. *See Southland Sod Farms v. Stover Seed Co.*, 108 F.3d 1134, 1146 (9th Cir. 1997). Other courts, however, require proof that the defendant has benefited from the false advertisements. *See Logan v. Burgers Ozark Country Cured Hams*, 263 F.3d 447 (5th Cir. 2001). At least one commentator has argued that damages ought to be more liberally awarded. *See* Arthur Best, *Monetary Damages for False Advertising*, 49 U. PITT. L. REV. 1 (1987) (advocating a presumption that ads cause economic injury, and that courts use a defendant's expenditures on the challenged ads as an approximate measure of the injury they caused plaintiff). Do we need enhanced damages remedies in these cases? Or does the nature of competition provide sufficient incentive for competitors to challenge false advertisements?

11. *First Amendment Limitations.* Suing a defendant for making false statements in the press raises obvious First Amendment concerns. *See* Rebecca Tushnet, *It Depends on What the Meaning of "False" Is: Falsity and Misleadingness in Commercial Speech Doctrine*, 41 LOY. L.A. L. REV. 227 (2007); C. Edwin Baker, *Advertising and the Democratic Process*, 140 U. PA. L. REV. 2097 (1992). Most of the cases involving independent testing agencies, as well as a number of the direct competitor disparagement cases, are litigated as First Amendment cases, in which the plaintiff must prove falsity plus actual malice if she is a public figure. *See, e.g., Bose Corp. v. Consumers Union of U.S., Inc.*, 466 U.S. 485 (1984). Chapter V(E)(3)(ii) discusses the interplay of parody and trademark protection.

E.   DEFENSES

Like patent and copyright law, trademark law has a broad range of defenses. We have already addressed invalidity, functionality, and genericness doctrines earlier in the chapter because they relate to protectability of the mark at all. This section explores other trademark defenses.

1.   Abandonment

i.   Cessation of Use

Major League Baseball Properties, Inc. v. Sed Non Olet Denarius, Ltd.
United States District Court for the Southern District of New York
817 F. Supp. 1103 (S.D.N.Y. 1993)

MOTLEY, District Judge.

I.   Introduction

Plaintiffs, Major League Baseball Properties, Inc. ("Properties") and Los Angeles Dodgers, Inc. ("Los Angeles"), allege in their Amended Complaint that the conduct of the . . . defendants [corporate operators of three restaurants, and their principals] (hereinafter collectively "The Brooklyn Dodger") . . . constitute: a) an infringement upon the rights of plaintiffs' trademarks in violation of 15 U.S.C. §§ 1114 and 1117; b) a wrongful appropriation of plaintiffs' trademarks in violation of 15 U.S.C. § 1125; c) a violation of plaintiffs' common law trademark and property rights; d) a violation of plaintiffs' rights under the New York General Business Law § 368-d; e) unfair competition; and f) the intentional use by defendants of a counterfeit mark in violation of 15 U.S.C. § 1117(b).

Each of these six causes of action is alleged to flow from defendants' use of the words "The Brooklyn Dodger" as the name and servicemark of the restaurants which defendants have operated in Brooklyn, New York, beginning in March 1988. Plaintiffs initially sought permanent injunctive relief, an accounting of profits, the destruction of physical items containing the allegedly infringing marks, monetary damages, and attorneys' fees.

By their Answer and Amended Answer defendants denied any infringement of plaintiffs' alleged right to use a "Brooklyn Dodger" trademark. Defendants also pleaded the defenses of abandonment by plaintiffs of any "Brooklyn Dodgers" mark which plaintiffs may have owned at one time, as well as laches. The abandonment defense was premised upon the plaintiffs' failure to make any commercial or trademark use of the "Brooklyn Dodgers" name for at least 25 years after Los Angeles left Brooklyn in 1958. The laches defense was premised upon the fact that plaintiffs waited for more than a year and a half after learning of defendants' use of the allegedly infringing trademark before advising defendants of any alleged infringement. During this period defendants expended substantial resources and monies in establishing their restaurants in Brooklyn, New York. . . .

Finally, in their Amended Answer, defendants counterclaimed for the cancellation of various trademark registrations for "Brooklyn Dodgers" filed by plaintiffs after defendants' application to register the "Brooklyn Dodger" servicemark was filed on April 28, 1988. . . .

II. Findings of Facts

. . .

Plaintiff Los Angeles is a corporation with offices and its principal place of business in Los Angeles, California. It is the owner of the Los Angeles Dodgers, a professional baseball team which, since 1958, has played baseball in Los Angeles, California under the name the "Los Angeles Dodgers." . . . Prior to 1958 the same professional baseball team played baseball in Brooklyn, New York and were known as the "Brooklyn Dodgers" or the "Dodgers."

In 1958, the team moved the site of its home games from Brooklyn to Los Angeles. . . . It pointedly changed its name to Los Angeles Dodgers, Inc. . . .

By agreement with the Major League Clubs, Properties has been granted the exclusive right to market, license, publish, publicize, promote nationally, and protect the trademarks owned by the Major League Clubs, including those owned by the Los Angeles Dodgers. . . .

. . . By 1991, retail sales of licensed Major League Baseball merchandise were in excess of $2 billion. [Plaintiffs estimate that of the total Dodgers merchandising revenue, only $9 million of 1991 sales carried the *Brooklyn* Dodgers name.]

. . . On March 17, 1988 SNOD began doing business as a restaurant under the name "The Brooklyn Dodger Sports Bar and Restaurant." . . .

It was the individual defendants' decision that their restaurants would emphasize the multiple themes of fun, sports and Brooklyn. Their intention was to create a nostalgic setting where Brooklynites could relax and reminisce about times gone by. . . .

They initially chose to name their establishment "Ebbets Field" after the former baseball park located in Brooklyn, New York in which a baseball team known as the "Brooklyn Dodgers" played baseball until October, 1957. . . .

[Defendants rejected the name "Ebbets Field" because of a conflict with a small restaurant elsewhere in New York.]

The defendants knew that the departure of the "Brooklyn Dodgers" in 1958 had been accompanied by monumental hard feelings in the Borough of Brooklyn. In fact the relocation was one of the most notorious abandonments in the history of sports. . . . At the time defendants selected their logo, they were aware that Los Angeles owned federal trademark registrations for the word "Dodgers." . . . However, at no time during their consideration of the "Brooklyn Dodger" name did the individual defendants have any reason to believe that "The Brooklyn Dodger" mark was being used by Los Angeles, and certainly not for restaurant or tavern services. . . . When considering the use of the "Brooklyn Dodger" mark, at no time was there any discussion among the individual defendants and Brian Boyle about trading on the goodwill of Los Angeles in Brooklyn. . . . Indeed, non-party witness Brian Boyle, a life-long Brooklyn resident, testified that, given the acrimonious abandonment of Brooklyn by Los Angeles, the idea of trading on Los Angeles' "goodwill" in Brooklyn is almost "laughable."

C. *Defendants' Use of the Trademark*

In connection with each of defendants' [three] "The Brooklyn Dodger" restaurants, defendants make and/or made prominent use of the "Dodger" name and the "Brooklyn Dodger" name, with the word "Dodger" in stylized script, in the color blue, and in blue script.

The defendants' composite design mark consisted of three words: "The," "Brooklyn" and "Dodger" are entwined with one another and with an impish character, . . . which was styled after the Charles Dickens' character, the "Artful Dodger" from the novel Oliver Twist, leaning against the "r" in "Dodger." . . . Defendants, however, make significant use of their logo without the cartoon character to promote their business, including on merchandise such as apparel, in advertisements, on their letterhead and as part of their servicemark.

Defendants' logo is similar to Los Angeles' trademarks. The name "Brooklyn Dodger" is similar to the name "Brooklyn Dodgers" as used by plaintiffs. The script used by the defendants in their logo is similar to that used in Los Angeles' trademarks. The color blue used by defendants is similar to the color blue used by and associated with Los Angeles' [team] in Brooklyn. The swash or tail of the word "Dodger" used by defendants is similar to that used in Los Angeles' trademarks in terms of style and length. . . . .

In selecting their logo, defendants intentionally sought to reproduce the Brooklyn Dodgers' trademarks. Indeed, the script for the defendants' logo was intentionally chosen by defendants to track the script used by the Brooklyn Dodgers. . . .

D. Plaintiffs' Use of the Trademark

. . .

Plaintiffs' use of the "Brooklyn Dodgers" mark was based upon its physical location, until October 1957, in Brooklyn, New York. However, in 1959, Los Angeles made prominent commercial use and reference to their Brooklyn heritage and trademarks in connection with the promotion of Roy Campanella Night, honoring the former Brooklyn Dodgers player and present employee. . . . Los Angeles made prominent use of their trademarks incorporating the word "Brooklyn" at their annual oldtimers games. . . . Oldtimers games are commercial baseball exhibitions at which former players are honored and perform so that older fans can recall the past and younger fans can learn about the history of the Club.

[The court describes extensive licensing and use of the Los Angeles Dodgers trademarks, including for food services and restaurants.]

While plaintiffs have from time to time made use of their former "Brooklyn Dodgers" mark occasionally and sporadically for historical retrospective[s] such as "Old Timer's Day" festivities, the documentary proof establishes that, following its departure from Brooklyn, Los Angeles' earliest licensing of the "Brooklyn Dodgers" mark occurred on April 6, 1981.

Between 1981 and March 17, 1988, the date of defendants' first use of their mark for restaurant and tavern services, plaintiffs used their "Brooklyn Dodgers" mark for a variety of purposes. Those uses were almost exclusively in the context of T-shirts, jackets, sportswear, sports paraphernalia and on various types of novelty items (i.e. on drinking mugs, cigarette lighters, pens, Christmas tree ornaments, wristbands, etc.). . . . However, none of these uses competes with defendants' use of the mark for restaurant and tavern services.

[The court describes several instances between 1981 and 1988 where businesses sought and received permission to use the "Brooklyn Dodgers" name and logo, including several that were restaurant-related.] . . .

III. Conclusions of Law

[The court concluded that plaintiffs had failed to prove a likelihood of confusion; for completeness, it then considered defenses.]

C.   Defendants' Affirmative Defenses

1.   *Abandonment*

Under the Lanham Act a federally registered trademark is considered abandoned if its "use has been discontinued with intent not to resume." *Cerveceria Centroamericana, S.A. v. Cerveceria India, Inc.*, 892 F.2d 1021, 1023 (Fed. Cir. 1989) (quoting Lanham Act, 15 U.S.C. § 1127 (1988)).

Abandonment is defined in the Lanham Act: "A mark shall be deemed 'abandoned'—(a) When its use has been discontinued with intent not to resume. Intent not to resume may be inferred from circumstances." 15 U.S.C. § 1127 (1988).

. . . The burden of proving abandonment falls upon the party seeking cancellation of a registered mark because a certificate of registration is "'prima facie evidence of the validity of the registration' and continued use." *Cerveceria India*, 892 F.2d at 1023 . . . .

. . . The party seeking cancellation must establish abandonment by a preponderance of the evidence. *See Cerveceria India*, 892 F.2d at 1023–24. The Lanham Act provides that "[n]onuse for two consecutive years shall be prima facie abandonment." 15 U.S.C. § 1127. . . . Prima facie abandonment establishes a rebuttable presumption of abandonment. . . . The evidence presented at trial established that between 1958 and 1981 plaintiffs made no commercial trademark use whatsoever of any "Brooklyn Dodgers" mark. Minor changes in a trademark that do not affect the overall commercial impression of the mark do not constitute abandonment. . . . However, Los Angeles' change, in this case, from "Brooklyn Dodgers" to "Los Angeles Dodgers" was not minor; it involved an essential element affecting the public's perception of the mark and the team.[19] . . .

Plaintiffs argue that their "Dodgers" mark without a geographical reference—that is, "Dodgers" alone—is a protected use infringed by defendants actions. However, in this context, "Brooklyn" is more than a geographic designation or appendage to the word "Dodgers." The "Brooklyn Dodgers" was a non-transportable cultural institution separate from the "Los Angeles Dodgers" or the "Dodgers" who play in Los Angeles. It is not simply the "Dodgers," (and certainly not the "Los Angeles Dodgers"), that defendants seek to invoke in their restaurant; rather defendants specifically seek to recall the nostalgia of the cultural institution that was the "Brooklyn Dodgers." It was the

---

[19]   While Los Angeles ceased commercial use of the trademark because of its relocation from Brooklyn to Los Angeles, its motive, justifiable or not, is irrelevant. *Stetson*, 955 F.2d at 851. Nevertheless, Los Angeles' nonuse in this case was voluntary. Courts have been more reluctant to find an absence of intent to resume where the trademark owner had an excusable reason for nonuse—that is, where nonuse was involuntary. *See, e.g., Defiance Button Machine Co. v. C & C Metal Products Corp.*, 759 F.2d 1053, 1059 (2d Cir. 1985) (no abandonment where cessation of business was involuntary); *American International Group, Inc. v. American International Airways, Inc.*, 726 F. Supp. 1470 (E.D. Pa. 1989) (where airline declared bankruptcy, remaining goodwill and lack of intent to abandon precluded finding abandonment).

"Brooklyn Dodgers" name that had acquired secondary meaning in New York in the early part of this century, prior to 1958. It was that cultural institution that Los Angeles abandoned.

. . . In this case, in order to maintain use of the mark, Los Angeles would have had to continue to use "Brooklyn Dodgers" as the name of its baseball team. Only in this way would the public continue to identify the name with the team. *Defiance Button Mach. Co. v. C & C Metal Products Corp.*, 759 F.2d 1053, 1059 (2d Cir. 1985). . . .

Rather than using the "Brooklyn Dodgers" mark in the ordinary course of trade, a more accurate description of Los Angeles' use of the mark, at least between 1958 and 1981, was given by its General Counsel in a 1985 letter to someone seeking to use it on a novelty item:

> Since the Dodgers moved to Los Angeles in 1958 the name "Brooklyn Dodgers" has been reserved strictly for use in conjunction with items of historical interest.

. . . Under the law, such warehousing is not permitted. . . . Rights in a trademark are lost when trademarks are "warehoused" as plaintiffs attempted to "warehouse" the "Brooklyn Dodgers" mark for more than two (2) decades. . . . Plaintiffs' failure to use the "Brooklyn Dodgers" trademark between 1958, when Los Angeles left Brooklyn, and 1981 constitutes abandonment of the trademark. . . .

Abandonment under the Lanham Act, however, requires both nonuse and intent not to resume use. . . .

Once prima facie abandonment has been proven, the trademark registrants—in this case plaintiffs—must carry their burden of producing evidence that there was an intent to resume use of the trademark. *Cerveceria India*, 892 F.2d at 1025–26. . . .

. . . Rather than merely proving that it did not intend to abandon its trademark, the trademark registrant must demonstrate that it intended to use or resume use. *See Exxon*, 695 F.2d at 99, 102–03 ("Stopping at an 'intent not to abandon' [rather than 'intent to resume'] tolerates an owner's protecting a mark with neither commercial use nor plans to resume commercial use. Such a license is not permitted by the Lanham Act"). . . .

. . . Plaintiffs have in no way demonstrated their intent to resume commercial use of the "Brooklyn Dodgers" mark within two years after Los Angeles left Brooklyn in 1958 or at anytime within the ensuing quarter century. . . .

2. Resumption

Having determined that plaintiffs abandoned the "Brooklyn Dodgers" mark, the next inquiry is to determine the effect of that abandonment, given that plaintiffs have recently resumed limited use of the trademark. . . .

. . . [I]f plaintiffs have any interest in a "Brooklyn Dodgers" mark, that interest arose in 1981 when commercial use of the mark resumed after a twenty-three (23) year hiatus. Plaintiffs' preemptive rights in the "Brooklyn Dodgers" mark would extend only to the precise goods on or in connection with which the trademark was used since its resumption (i.e. clothing, jewelry, novelty items).

In other words, the fact that plaintiffs resumed use prior to defendants' use does not mean that plaintiffs may preclude defendants' use of the mark in their restaurant business in Brooklyn. . . .

Accordingly, the court declines to enjoin defendants' very limited use of the "Brooklyn Dodger" mark by defendants for use in connection with its local restaurants directed toward older Brooklyn Dodgers fans in the Brooklyn community in the city of New York. . . .

COMMENTS AND QUESTIONS

1. Would the result change if "The Brooklyn Dodger" restaurant began selling Brooklyn Dodger t-shirts? Other memorabilia?

2. The Lanham Act defines abandonment as follows:

A mark shall be deemed to be "abandoned" when either of the following occurs:

(1) When its use has been discontinued with intent not to resume such use. Intent not to resume may be inferred from circumstances. Nonuse for three consecutive years shall be prima facie evidence of abandonment. "Use" of a mark means the bona fide use of such mark made in the ordinary course of trade, and not made merely to reserve a right in a mark.

(2) When any course of conduct of the owner, including acts of omission as well as commission, causes the mark to . . . lose its significance as a mark. . . .

Lanham Act § 45, 15 U.S.C. § 1127. The *Dawn Donut* case, *infra*, deals with the § 45(2) type of abandonment.

3. If trademark rights are essentially about protecting consumers from confusion, why does the legal standard require anything other than a showing that the mark's meaning has faded sufficiently so that it can now be "reclaimed" by another? Why does the statute settle for a presumption; why not a per se rule, perhaps based on a longer period—say ten years? *Cf.* Note, *The Song Is Over But the Melody Lingers On: Persistence of Goodwill and the Intent Factor in Trademark Abandonment*, 56 FORDHAM L. REV. 1003, 1006–07 (1988) ("[W]hen a trademark has persisting or residual goodwill, even after a period of nonuse, doubts should be resolved in favor of the trademark owner and against the competitor charging abandonment. . . . [Courts] should . . . make it as difficult as possible to find a trademark abandoned whenever goodwill in the mark persists."). What arguments can you think of in favor of this liberal rule? Against? Should there be an incentive to aggressively "recycle" marks that have shown some usefulness?

Do you think the association between the name "Brooklyn Dodgers" and the major league baseball team now located in Los Angeles had faded sufficiently for someone else to reclaim the name? What if the defendant had set up a baseball team with that name? Do the unusual facts in this case—especially the animosity between ex-Brooklyn Dodger fans and the Los Angeles Dodgers—suggest why a per se rule might not make sense in every case? Is the court right to assume the absence of "goodwill" here, where consumers recognize the Dodger mark but simply have bad associations with it? Or does the continual connection in the public's mind suggest an ongoing role for trademark law? Professors Dogan and Lemley argue that companies should not be permitted to race to grab up abandoned marks that still carry goodwill in the minds of consumers because those consumers will be injured when a new company starts selling different products under the same mark. *See* Stacey L. Dogan & Mark A. Lemley, *A Search-Costs Theory of Limiting Doctrines in Trademark Law*, 97 TRADEMARK REP. 1223 (2007).

4. Are there reasons to limit the abandonment doctrine where it may affect personal names that clearly seem to "belong" to the trademark owner? In *Abdul-Jabaar v. General Motors*, 85 F.3d 407, 411 (9th Cir. 1996), the court rejected defendant's claim that basketball star Kareem Abdul-Jabaar had abandoned his birth name, Lew Alcindor. The court established a per se rule: "A proper name thus cannot be deemed abandoned throughout its possessor's life, despite his failure to use it. . . ."

PROBLEMS

Problem V-18. Until 1972, the Humble Oil & Refining Co. was one of the largest producers and sellers of gasoline in the world. In that year, after a merger with Esso, Humble decided to change its name to Exxon, an arbitrary mark it had selected for the purpose. The company invested an enormous amount of money advertising the new name and placing its new brand on all its products, services, and correspondence. However, the new Exxon also started a "brand maintenance program," under which it continued to make a few sales every year under the Humble name. It sent certain invoices on Humble letterhead, and bulk oil was sometimes sold in Humble barrels. Exxon continued this program throughout the 1970s.

In 1975, a new oil exploration company decides to call itself the Humble Oil Exploration Co. The new company picked the Humble name because they hoped to trade on residual goodwill left in the name, and because they believed Exxon had abandoned its old name. Can the new company use the Humble name?

Problem V-19. IBM Corporation is a world-famous maker of computers and other business machines. For decades, people have informally referred to IBM as. "Big Blue," both in conversation and in published articles and papers about the company. However, IBM does not itself use or claim the name "Big Blue." It has never registered the name Big Blue, its employees are forbidden by company policy to use the name in referring to the company, and at one point an exasperated company spokesperson is reported to have said "We're not Big Blue—please don't call us that. We want nothing to do with the name." Nonetheless, the nickname persists.

In 1994, a small repair shop that specializes in fixing IBM computers decided to call itself the "Big Blue Repair Shop." After BBRS started using the name, IBM sent it a cease-and-desist letter alleging that IBM owned the rights to the name Big Blue, since people used it to refer to IBM. Who has priority in use of the Big Blue mark?

ii. *Unsupervised Licenses*

 Dawn Donut Company, Inc. v. Hart's Food Stores, Inc.
United States Court of Appeals for the Second Circuit
267 F.2d 358 (2d Cir. 1959)

[Dawn Donut, a Michigan wholesaler of doughnut mix, owned federally registered trademarks Dawn and Dawn Donut. Dawn brought a trademark infringement suit against defendant Hart's Food Stores ("Hart"), which used the mark "Dawn" in connection with its sale of doughnuts and baked goods in stores in and around Rochester, N.Y. Hart filed a counterclaim to cancel plaintiff's registrations, on the ground that plaintiff had abandoned its trademarks due to inadequate quality control and supervision on the part of its licensees—the retail bakeries that sold doughnuts made from Dawn's mix. The district court denied Dawn's request for an injunction and dismissed Hart's counterclaim. This appeal followed. In an omitted (and oft-cited) portion of this opinion, Circuit Judge Lumbard held that plaintiff was not entitled to any relief under the Lanham Act because there was no present likelihood that plaintiff would expand its retail use of its trademarks into defendant's market area. A majority of the panel also found that there was no abandonment by plaintiff of its registrations, and that therefore defendant was not entitled to have plaintiff's registrations of trademarks cancelled.]

LUMBARD, Circuit Judge [dissenting in part]. . . .

The final issue presented is raised by defendant's appeal from the dismissal of its counterclaim for cancellation of plaintiff's registration on the ground that the plaintiff failed to exercise the control required by the Lanham Act over the nature and quality of the goods sold by its licensees.

We are all agreed that the Lanham Act places an affirmative duty upon a licensor of a registered trademark to take reasonable measures to detect and prevent misleading uses of his mark by his licensees or suffer cancellation of his federal registration. The Act, 15 U.S.C.A. § 1064, provides that a trademark registration may be cancelled because the trademark has been "abandoned." And "abandoned" is defined in 15 U.S.C.A. § 1127 to include any act or omission by the registrant which causes the trademark to lose its significance as an indication of origin.

Prior to the passage of the Lanham Act many courts took the position that the licensing of a trademark separately from the business in connection with which it had been used worked an abandonment. *Reddy Kilowatt, Inc. v. MidCarolina Electric Cooperative, Inc.*, 4 Cir., 1957, 240 F.2d 282, 289; *American Broadcasting Co. v. Wahl Co.*, 2 Cir., 1941, 121 F.2d 412, 413; *Everett O. Fisk & Co. v. Fisk Teachers' Agency, Inc.*, 8 Cir., 1924, 3 F.2d 7, 9. The theory of these cases was that:

A trade-mark is intended to identify the goods of the owner and to safeguard his good will. The designation if employed by a person other than the one whose business it serves to identify would be misleading. Consequently, "a right to the use of a trade-mark or a trade-name cannot be transferred in gross."

American Broadcasting Co. v. Wahl Co., *supra*, 121 F.2d at page 413.

Other courts were somewhat more liberal and held that a trademark could be licensed separately from the business in connection with which it had been used provided that the licensor retained control over the quality of the goods produced by the licensee. *E.I. DuPont de Nemours & Co. v. Celanese Corporation of America*, 1948, 167 F.2d 484, 35 CCPA 1061. . . . But even in the *DuPont* case the court was careful to point out that naked licensing, viz. the grant of licenses without the retention of control, was invalid. *E.I. DuPont de Nemours & Co. v. Celanese Corporation of America, supra*, 167 F.2d at page 489.

The Lanham Act clearly carries forward the view of these latter cases that controlled licensing does not work an abandonment of the licensor's registration, while a system of naked licensing does. 15 U.S.C.A. § 1055 provides:

> Where a registered mark or a mark sought to be registered is or may be used legitimately by related companies, such use shall inure to the benefit of the registrant or applicant for registration, and such use shall not affect the validity of such mark or of its registration, provided such mark is not used in such manner as to deceive the public. . . .[7]

Without the requirement of control, the right of a trademark owner to license his mark separately from the business in connection with which it has been used would create the danger that products bearing the same trademark might be of diverse qualities. *See American Broadcasting Co. v. Wahl Co., supra; Everett O. Fisk & Co. v. Fisk Teachers' Agency, Inc., supra.* If the licensor is not compelled to take some reasonable steps to prevent misuses of his trademark in the hands of others the public will be deprived of its most effective protection against misleading uses of a trademark. The public is hardly in a position to uncover deceptive uses of a trademark before they occur and will be at best slow to detect them after they happen. Thus, unless the licensor exercises supervision and control over the operations of its licensees the risk that the public will be unwittingly deceived will be increased and this is precisely what the Act is in part designed to prevent. *See* SEN. REPORT NO. 1333, 79th Cong., 2d Sess. (1946). Clearly the only effective way to protect the public where a trademark is used by licensees is to place on the licensor the affirmative duty of policing in a reasonable manner the activities of his licensees.

---

[7] [Lanham Act § 45 now reads in relevant part: "The term 'related company' means any person whose use of a mark is controlled by the owner of the mark with respect to the nature and quality of the goods or services on or in connection with which the mark is used." 15 U.S.C. § 1127. The portion of 15 U.S.C. ß 1055 (Lanham Act § 5) quoted just above in the case has not changed.—EDS.]

The critical question on these facts therefore is whether the plaintiff sufficiently policed and inspected its licensees' operations to guarantee the quality of the products they sold under its trademarks to the public. The trial court found that: "By reason of its contacts with its licensees, plaintiff exercised legitimate control over the nature and quality of the food products on which plaintiff's licensees used the trademark 'Dawn.' Plaintiff and its licensees are related companies within the meaning of Section 45 of the Trademark Act of 1946." It is the position of the majority of this court that the trial judge has the same leeway in determining what constitutes a reasonable degree of supervision and control over licensees under the facts and circumstances of the particular case as he has on other questions of fact; and particularly because it is the defendant who has the burden of proof on this issue they hold the lower court's finding not clearly erroneous.

I dissent from the conclusion of the majority that the district court's findings are not clearly erroneous because while it is true that the trial judge must be given some discretion in determining what constitutes reasonable supervision of licensees under the Lanham Act, it is also true that an appellate court ought not to accept the conclusions of the district court unless they are supported by findings of sufficient facts. It seems to me that the only findings of the district judge regarding supervision are in such general and conclusory terms as to be meaningless. In the absence of supporting findings or of undisputed evidence in the record indicating the kind of supervision and inspection the plaintiff actually made of its licensees, it is impossible for us to pass upon whether there was such supervision as to satisfy the statute. There was evidence before the district court in the matter of supervision, and more detailed findings thereon should have been made.

Plaintiff's licensees fall into two classes: (1) those bakers with whom it made written contracts providing that the baker purchase exclusively plaintiff's mixes and requiring him to adhere to plaintiff's directions in using the mixes; and (2) those bakers whom plaintiff permitted to sell at retail under the "Dawn" label doughnuts and other baked goods made from its mixes although there was no written agreement governing the quality of the food sold under the Dawn mark.[6]

The contracts that plaintiff did conclude, although they provided that the purchaser use the mix as directed and without adulteration, failed to provide for any system of inspection and control. Without such a system plaintiff could not know whether these

---

[6] On cross-examination plaintiff's president conceded that during 1949 and 1950 the company in some instances, the number of which is not made clear by his testimony, distributed its advertising and packaging material to bakers with whom it had not reached any agreement relating to the quality of the goods sold in packages bearing the name "Dawn." It also appears from plaintiff's list of the 16 bakers who were operating as exclusive Dawn shops at the time of the trial that plaintiff's contract with 3 of these shops had expired and had not been renewed and that in the case of 2 other such shops the contract had been renewed only after a substantial period of time had elapsed since the expiration of the original agreement. The record indicates that these latter 2 bakers continued to operate under the name "Dawn" and purchase "Dawn" mixes during the period following the expiration of their respective franchise agreements with the plaintiff. Particularly damaging to plaintiff is the fact that one of the 2 bakers whose franchise contracts plaintiff allowed to lapse for a substantial period of time has also been permitted by plaintiff to sell doughnuts made from a mix other than plaintiff's in packaging labeled with plaintiff's trademark.

bakers were adhering to its standards in using the mix or indeed whether they were selling only products made from Dawn mixes under the trademark "Dawn."

The absence, however, of an express contract right to inspect and supervise a licensee's operations does not mean that the plaintiff's method of licensing failed to comply with the requirements of the Lanham Act. Plaintiff may in fact have exercised control in spite of the absence of any express grant by licensees of the right to inspect and supervise.

The question then, with respect to both plaintiff's contract and non-contract licensees, is whether the plaintiff in fact exercised sufficient control.

Here the only evidence in the record relating to the actual supervision of licensees by plaintiff consists of the testimony of two of plaintiff's local sales representatives that they regularly visited their particular customers and the further testimony of one of them, Jesse Cohn, the plaintiff's New York representative, that "in many cases" he did have an opportunity to inspect and observe the operations of his customers. The record does not indicate whether plaintiff's other sales representatives made any similar efforts to observe the operations of licensees.

Moreover, Cohn's testimony fails to make clear the nature of the inspection he made or how often he made one. His testimony indicates that his opportunity to observe a licensee's operations was limited to "those cases where I am able to get into the shop" and even casts some doubt on whether he actually had sufficient technical knowledge in the use of plaintiff's mix to make an adequate inspection of a licensee's operations.

The fact that it was Cohn who failed to report the defendant's use of the mark "Dawn" to the plaintiff casts still further doubt about the extent of the supervision Cohn exercised over the operations of plaintiff's New York licensees.

Thus I do not believe that we can fairly determine on this record whether plaintiff subjected its licensees to periodic and thorough inspections by trained personnel or whether its policing consisted only of chance, cursory examinations of licensees' operations by technically untrained salesmen. The latter system of inspection hardly constitutes a sufficient program of supervision to satisfy the requirements of the Act.

. . . I would direct the district court to order the cancellation of plaintiff's registrations if it should find that the plaintiff did not adequately police the operations of its licensees. . . .

The district court's denial of an injunction restraining defendant's use of the mark "Dawn" on baked and fried goods and its dismissal of defendant's [abandonment] counterclaim are affirmed.

COMMENTS AND QUESTIONS

1. Despite its age and the fact that it was a dissent, Judge Lumbard's discussion in *Dawn Donut* regarding licensee supervision and abandonment is still the standard in the area. *See* McCarthy, Trademarks and Unfair Competition § 26.14.

2. Trademark rights are regularly lost because of unsupervised licensing. *See, e.g., Stanfield v. Osborne Indus., Inc.*, 52 F.3d 867 (10th Cir. 1995) (denying plaintiff's advertising-related trademark claim because rights were lost due to unsupervised license); *Barcamerica Int'l USA Trust v. Tyfield Importers, Inc.*, 289 F.2d 589 (9th Cir. 2002) (finding lack of express contractual right to inspect and supervise licensee's operation as well as no actual supervision).

3. The *Celanese* case cited in *Dawn Donut, E.I. du Pont de Nemours & Co. v. Celanese Corporation*, 167 F.2d 484 (C.C.P.A. 1948), was one of the first cases to establish the legitimacy of trademark licensing over the objection that licensing necessarily entailed an abandonment. Obviously, the growth of franchising, character merchandising, and related practices depended on such a holding. Much modern business would be impossible if corporations could not expand their brand names in these ways. *See* Chapter V(D)(2)(i)(2)(a) (discussing franchising and merchandising).

Franchising requires sufficient exercise of control so that the customer receives a consistent experience:

> There is no rule that trademark proprietors must ensure "high quality" goods—or that "high quality" permits unsupervised licensing. "Kentucky Fried Chicken" is a valid mark, *see Kentucky Fried Chicken Corp. v. Diversified Packaging Corp.*, 549 F.2d 368 (5th Cir.1977), though neither that chain nor any other fast-food franchise receives a star (or even a mention) in the *Guide Michelin*. The sort of supervision required for a trademark license is the sort that produces *consistent* quality. "Trademarks [are] indications of consistent and predictable quality assured through the trademark owner's control over the use of the designation". RESTATEMENT § 33 comment b. *See also* WILLIAM M. LANDES & RICHARD A. POSNER, THE ECONOMIC STRUCTURE OF INTELLECTUAL PROPERTY LAW 166–68, 184–86 (2003).

> A person who visits one Kentucky Fried Chicken outlet finds that it has much the same ambiance and menu as any other. A visitor to any Burger King likewise enjoys a comforting familiarity and knows that the place will not be remotely like a Kentucky Fried Chicken outlet (and is sure to differ from Hardee's, Wendy's, and Applebee's too). The trademark's function is to tell shoppers what to expect—and whom to blame if a given outlet falls short. The licensor's reputation is at stake in every outlet, so it invests to the extent required to keep the consumer satisfied by ensuring a repeatable experience.

Eva's Bridal Ltd. v. Halanick Ents., Inc., 639 F.3d 788, 790 (7th Cir. 2011) (canceling trademark for naked licensing).

4. If a trademark owner wants to spend its own goodwill by licensing those who sell lower quality products, why not let it? *See* Pamela S. Chestek, *Let's Kill the "Naked License" Defense*, 104 TRADEMARK REP. 924 (2014); Irene Calboli, *The Sunset of "Quality Control" in Modern Trademark Licensing*, 57 AM. U. L. REV. 341 (2007). The company would surely be permitted to reduce the quality of the products it makes itself.

iii.   *Assignments in Gross*

The rule that unsupervised or "naked" licenses can amount to abandonment has a logical corollary: that outright assignments of trademarks are invalid. This common law rule was codified in the Lanham Act: "A registered mark or a mark for which application to register has been filed shall be assignable with the goodwill of the business in which the mark is used, or with that part of the goodwill of the business connected with the use of and symbolized by the mark." Lanham Act § 10, 15 U.S.C. § 1060.

Assignments of trademarks alone, without any underlying assets or "goodwill," are called "assignments in gross." They are invalid, *see* McCARTHY, TRADEMARKS AND UNFAIR COMPETITION § 18.01, a result said to follow from the fact that trademarks are only repositories and symbols of goodwill, rather than true property rights. *See American Steel Foundries v. Robertson*, 269 U.S. 372, 380 (1926). That case reasoned that consumers, having come to rely on a trademark to identify the characteristics of a product as manufactured and sold by Firm *A,* would be harmed if *A* simply sold the mark outright to Firm *B* without transferring any of the employees or production machinery that Firm *A* had used to make its product. *Id.* By the same reasoning, courts invalidated trademarks when sold to another firm for use on a different product. *See Filkins v. Blackman*, 9 Fed. Cas. 50, 51 (No. 4786) (C.C.D. Conn. 1876) ("The right to the use of a trademark cannot be so enjoyed by an assignee that he shall have the right to affix the mark to goods differing in character or species from the article to which it was originally attached.").

As originally applied, the rule against assignments in gross was quite strict; in general, a firm was required to assign tangible assets along with the trademark. *See, e.g., Pepsico, Inc. v. Grapette Co.*, 416 F.2d 285 (8th Cir. 1969) (invalidating the assignment of soft drink trademark (Peppy) for failure to transfer any assets including formula or process for making the beverage associated with the mark). More recently, however, the traditional rule has been relaxed, partly in recognition of the increased frequency and importance of trademark-related transactions. The contemporary rule can be seen operating in cases involving assignment of "soft" trademark-related assets, such as customer lists, production formulas (as opposed to machinery), and even amorphous "goodwill." *See, e.g., In re Roman Cleanser Co.*, 802 F.2d 207 (6th Cir. 1986) (validating transfer of trademark in satisfaction of security interest in it, together with formulas and customer lists); *Money Store v. Harriscorp Finance, Inc.*, 689 F.2d 666 (7th Cir. 1982) (assignment of Money Store trademark by senior user for $1 not invalid; nominal recitation of "goodwill" in assignment contract, without transfer of any other assets, was enough). *Cf.* WILLIAM M. LANDES & RICHARD A. POSNER, TRADEMARK LAW: AN ECONOMIC PERSPECTIVE, 30 J.L. & ECON. 265, 274–75 (1987) (arguing that the "assignment in gross" doctrine makes sense only in "final period" cases, where sellers of goods are leaving the market and hence do not care if consumers are disappointed by the low quality of the assignee's goods).

The rule against assignments in gross makes sense from the point of view of protecting consumer associations between a mark and an underlying product. If the symbol changes hands and is now used to "refer to" a different product, consumers might be confused. (Imagine if language experts decided to change the meaning of a common word, without telling anyone.) As Landes and Posner, *supra*, argue, the risk of confusion is greatest when the trademark assignor is leaving the market.

COMMENTS AND QUESTIONS

1. This rationale for the "No Assignment in Gross" doctrine assumes that consumers cannot perceive the lower quality of the assignee's product when they look at the product. What if the assignee uses the mark on a completely different type of product altogether? Wouldn't consumers understand that circumstances have changed if they see the mark attached to new goods? (On the other hand, if they would, why buy the mark at all for use on different goods?)

Should we encourage the transfer of trademarks that have proven effective? Why restrict transfers to those accompanied by underlying assets? *See* Irene Calboli, *Trademark Assignment "With Goodwill": A Concept Whose Time Has Gone*, 57 FLA. L. REV. 771 (2005); Allison Sell McDade, Note, *Trading in Trademarks—Why the Anti-Assignment in Gross Doctrine Should Be Abolished When Trademarks Are Used as Collateral*, 77 TEX. L. REV. 465 (1998) (focusing on the use of trademarks as security interests); *but see* Mark A. Lemley, *The Modern Lanham Act and the Death of Common Sense*, 108 YALE L.J. 1687 (1999) (supporting the doctrine as consistent with the consumer-oriented focus of trademark law). What would happen to consumer expectations if a lending company foreclosed on a trademark?

2. Does (or should) the law similarly prohibit the original trademark owner from significantly decreasing the quality of his or her goods, or from changing the type of product to which the mark is attached? *See* 2 J. THOMAS MCCARTHY, MCCARTHY ON TRADEMARKS AND UNFAIR COMPETITION § 17.09 (citing cases and arguing that this would amount to deceit under the Lanham Act). The latter may be an issue for registered marks, where the classification of goods is important.

3. Article 21 of the General Agreements on Tariffs and Trade, which entered into force in the United States in 1995, provides that "the owner of a registered trademark shall have the right to assign his trademark with or without the transfer of the business to which the trademark belongs." Does this article require the United States to abolish the rule against assignment in gross?

4. *Foreign Rejection of the "No Assignment in Gross" Doctrine.* Japan, for example, recognizes private property rights in the trademark itself. Therefore, assignments in gross are valid even if totally divorced from any goodwill. Trademark rights are also severable; they may be assigned by class, providing the goods of the remaining classification would not cause confusion with the goods of the class assigned. *See generally* Kazuko Matsuo, *Trademarks*, in 4 DOING BUSINESS IN JAPAN (Zentaro Kitagawa ed., 1991).

2. Exhaustion/First Sale

As with patent and copyright law, once a trademark owner or licensee sells a trade-marked good, the buyer of that good is free to resell the good without permission of the trademark owner. The IP protection governing that product is "exhausted" after the first authorized sale. As the Ninth Circuit has explained, "the right of a producer to control distribution of its trademarked product does not extend beyond the first sale of the product." *See Sebastian Int'l v. Longs Drug Stores Corp.*, 53 F.3d 1073 (9th Cir. 1995). The first sale doctrine, however, applies only to authorized sales of genuine products.

The exhaustion doctrine is subject to important limitations relating to resale of goods without requisite quality control requirements, repackaging of goods, and repair and reconditioning of goods. It also arises with regard to importation of goods.

i. *Resale Without Requisite Quality Control*

The resale of goods can violate quality control standards set by the trademark owner. Such sales interfere with the essential link between the source and the quality of the goods. In *Warner-Lambert Co. v. Northside Development Corp.*, 86 F.3d 3 (2d Cir. 1996), the maker of Halls® cough drops sought to enjoin a wholesaler from selling the product beyond its freshness expiration date. The court held that

> [d]istribution of a product that does not meet the trademark holder's quality control standards may result in the devaluation of the mark by tarnishing its image. If so, the non-conforming product is deemed for Lanham Act purposes not to be the genuine product of the holder, and its distribution constitutes trade-mark infringement.

Id. at 6; *see also Shell Oil Co. v. Commercial Petroleum, Inc.*, 928 F.2d 104 (4th Cir. 1991). Nonetheless, a broad application of this rule would enable trademark owners to nullify the exhaustion doctrine. The Third Circuit has warned that

> "quality control" is not a talisman the mere utterance of which entitles the trade-mark owner to judgment. . . . Rather, the test is whether the quality control procedures established by the trademark owner are likely to result in differences between the products such that consumer confusion regarding the sponsorship of the products could injure the trademark owner's goodwill.

Iberia Goods Corp. v. Romeo, 150 F.3d 298, 304 (1998). Notwithstanding that warning, one court has allowed claims that the resale of legitimate Williams-Sonoma product on Amazon.com by third-party sellers was not protected by the first sale doctrine because consumers might believe Williams-Sonoma authorized the sales. *See Williams-Sonoma, Inc. v. Amazon.com, Inc.*, 3:18-cv-07548 (N.D. Cal. May 2, 2019). If that is right, it may be impossible to resolve first sale issues on a motion to dismiss.

ii.   *Repackaged Goods*

Even where goods satisfy the legitimate quality concerns of a trademark owner, the repackaging or rebottling of the trademarked goods for sale by another entity could potentially undermine consumers' perception as to the nature and quality of trademarked goods. Nonetheless, the Supreme Court in *Prestonettes v. Coty*, 264 U.S. 359 (1924), held that "[w]hen the mark is used in such a way that does not deceive the public we see no such sanctity in the word as to prevent its being used to tell the truth. It is not taboo." The Court held that a repackager could resell the trademarked goods of an unaffiliated vendor so long there was no confusion, which could be accomplished through a suitable disclaimer indicating how the repackaged product had been altered and that the reseller was not affiliated with the source of the underlying trademarked product. Thus, courts hold that legitimate purchasers of trademarked goods can generally repackage and resell such goods with the original trademark so long as they (1) disclose that the product has been repackaged; (2) reveal their name; (3) disclaim any affiliation with the trademark owner; and (4) not give undue prominence to the trademark of the source of the repackaged good. Such safeguards balance the exhaustion principle, limiting consumer confusion, and protecting trademark owners' goodwill.

iii.   *Repaired and Reconditioned Goods*

Similar concerns can arise when purchasers of trademarked goods repair or recondition them for resale. As with repackaged goods, repaired and reconditioned goods can be resold under the original source's trademark so long as the reseller discloses the nature, quality, and source of the goods. *See Champion Spark Plug Co. v. Sanders*, 331 U.S. 125 (1947) (holding that a reseller of reconditioned spark plugs need not remove the original trademark so long as the repaired goods were stamped "repaired" or "used" on each plug and the cartons disclosed that the plugs were reconditioned and indicated the reseller's name). That is why the owner of, say, a Toyota Prius can resell it as a Toyota Prius even though it has been repaired. The Court noted, however, that trademark infringement might nonetheless occur where "the reconditioning or repair would be so extensive or basic that it would be a misnomer to call the article by its original name, even though the works 'used' or 'repaired' were added." *Id.* at 129. Thus, the Ninth Circuit enjoined a reconditioner of Rolex watches from using the Rolex trademark on repaired watches incorporating non-Rolex parts. *See Rolex Watch, U.S.A., Inc. v. Michel Co.*, 179 F.3d 704 (9th Cir. 1999). This rule, however, does not afford Rolex or any other original source with a monopoly in the market for replacement parts. *See Karl Storz Endoscopy-America, Inc. v. Fiber Tech Medical, Inc.*, 4 Fed. Appx. 128 (4th Cir. 2001) (holding that the Lanham Act does not prevent the owner of a trademarked product from choosing the source of repair parts so long as there is no misrepresentation of the repairer's source of part or affiliation with the trademark owner of the product in question).

3.   Fair Use

Trademark law features two "fair use" doctrines: (i) descriptive or "classic" fair use; and (ii) nontrademark or nominative fair use. Despite their similarity in name, the doctrines cover very different things. And both are distinct from the fair use doctrine in copyright law.

Trademark law's descriptive fair use doctrine derives from the limitations of descriptive marks. When there is only one or but a few ways to communicate effectively, trademark law permits competitors leeway. We don't want owners of descriptive marks to monopolize the power of descriptive terms. They may only leverage the secondary meaning that they have acquired. Hence, trademark law needs to strike a delicate balance in which some potential confusion is tolerated.

Trademark law's nominative fair use doctrine, also known as non-trademark use, concerns circumstances in which the defendant uses the plaintiff's mark, not to brand its own goods, but to talk about the plaintiff's goods.

i.   *Descriptive/"Classic" Fair Use*

We previewed the descriptive fair use doctrine in the *Zatarain's* case. But properly understood, fair use is a defense to a trademark infringement claim. As the following case explains, however, it has a complex procedural posture.

KP Permanent Make-up, Inc. v. Lasting Impression I, Inc.
Supreme Court of the United States
543 U.S. 111 (2004)

JUSTICE SOUTER delivered the opinion of the Court.

The question here is whether a party raising the statutory affirmative defense of fair use to a claim of trademark infringement, 15 U.S.C. § 1115(b)(4), has a burden to negate any likelihood that the practice complained of will confuse consumers about the origin of the goods or services affected. We hold it does not.

I

Each party to this case sells permanent makeup, a mixture of pigment and liquid for injection under the skin to camouflage injuries and modify nature's dispensations, and each has used some version of the term "micro color" (as one word or two, singular or plural) in marketing and selling its product. Petitioner KP Permanent Make-Up, Inc., claims to have used the single-word version since 1990 or 1991 on advertising flyers and since 1991 on pigment bottles. Respondents Lasting Impression I, Inc., and its licensee, MCN International, Inc. (Lasting, for simplicity), deny that KP began using the term that early, but we accept KP's allegation as true for present purposes. . . . The PTO registered the mark to Lasting in 1993, and in 1999 the registration became incontestable. § 1065.

It was also in 1999 that KP produced a 10-page advertising brochure using "micro-color" in a large, stylized typeface, provoking Lasting to demand that KP stop using the term. Instead, KP sued Lasting in the Central District of California, seeking, on more than one ground, a declaratory judgment that its language infringed no such exclusive right as Lasting claimed. Lasting counterclaimed, alleging, among other things, that KP had infringed Lasting's "Micro Colors" trademark.

KP sought summary judgment on the infringement counterclaim, based on the statutory affirmative defense of fair use, 15 U.S.C. § 1115(b)(4). After finding that Lasting had conceded that KP used the term only to describe its goods and not as a mark, the District Court held that KP was acting fairly and in good faith because undisputed facts showed that KP had employed the term "microcolor" continuously from a time before Lasting adopted the two-word, plural variant as a mark. Without inquiring whether the practice was likely to cause confusion, the court concluded that KP had made out its affirmative defense under § 1115(b)(4) and entered summary judgment for KP on Lasting's infringement claim.

On appeal, 328 F.3d 1061 (2003), the Court of Appeals for the Ninth Circuit thought it was error for the District Court to have addressed the fair use defense without delving into the matter of possible confusion on the part of consumers about the origin of KP's goods. The reviewing court took the view that no use could be recognized as fair where any consumer confusion was probable, . . . We now vacate the judgment of the Court of Appeals.

II

A

. . . The holder of a registered mark (incontestable or not) has a civil action against anyone employing an imitation of it in commerce when "such use is likely to cause confusion, or to cause mistake, or to deceive." § 1114(1)(a). Although an incontestable registration is "conclusive evidence . . . of the registrant's exclusive right to use the . . . mark in commerce," § 1115(b), the plaintiff's success is still subject to "proof of infringement as defined in section 1114," *ibid.* And that, as just noted, requires a showing that the defendant's actual practice is likely to produce confusion in the minds of consumers about the origin of the goods or services in question. *See Two Pesos, Inc. v. Taco Cabana, Inc.*, 505 U.S. 763, 780 (1992) (Stevens, J., concurring); RESTATEMENT (THIRD) OF UNFAIR COMPETITION § 21, Comment a (1995) (hereinafter RESTATEMENT). This plaintiff's burden has to be kept in mind when reading the relevant portion of the further provision for an affirmative defense of fair use, available to a party whose "use of the name, term, or device charged to be an infringement is a use, otherwise than as a mark, . . . of a term or device which is descriptive of and used fairly and in good faith only to describe the goods or services of such party, or their geographic origin. . . ." § 1115(b)(4).

Two points are evident. Section 1115(b) places a burden of proving likelihood of confusion (that is, infringement) on the party charging infringement even when relying on an incontestable registration. And Congress said nothing about likelihood of confusion in setting out the elements of the fair use defense in § 1115(b)(4).

Starting from these textual fixed points, it takes a long stretch to claim that a defense of fair use entails any burden to negate confusion. It is just not plausible that Congress would have used the descriptive phrase "likely to cause confusion, or to cause mistake, or to deceive" in § 1114 to describe the requirement that a markholder show likelihood of consumer confusion, but would have relied on the phrase "used fairly" in § 1115(b)(4) in a fit of terse drafting meant to place a defendant under a burden to negate confusion. . . .

Finally, a look at the typical course of litigation in an infringement action points up the incoherence of placing a burden to show nonconfusion on a defendant. If a plaintiff succeeds in making out a prima facie case of trademark infringement, including the element of likelihood of consumer confusion, the defendant may offer rebutting evidence to undercut the force of the plaintiff's evidence on this (or any) element, or raise an affirmative defense to bar relief even if the prima facie case is sound, or do both. But it would make no sense to give the defendant a defense of showing affirmatively that the plaintiff cannot succeed in proving some element (like confusion); all the defendant needs to do is to leave the factfinder unpersuaded that the plaintiff has carried its own burden on that point. A defendant has no need of a court's true belief when agnosticism will do. Put another way, it is only when a plaintiff has shown likely confusion by a preponderance of the evidence that a defendant could have any need of an affirmative defense, but under Lasting's theory the defense would be foreclosed in such a case." [I]t defies logic to argue that a defense may not be asserted in the only situation where it even becomes relevant." *Shakespeare Co. v. Silstar Corp.*, 110 F.3d, at 243. Nor would it make sense to provide an affirmative defense of no confusion plus good faith, when merely rebutting the plaintiff's case on confusion would entitle the defendant to judgment, good faith or not. . . .

B

Since the burden of proving likelihood of confusion rests with the plaintiff, and the fair use defendant has no free-standing need to show confusion unlikely, it follows (contrary to the Court of Appeals's view) that some possibility of consumer confusion must be compatible with fair use, and so it is. The common law's tolerance of a certain degree of confusion on the part of consumers followed from the very fact that in cases like this one an originally descriptive term was selected to be used as a mark, not to mention the undesirability of allowing anyone to obtain a complete monopoly on use of a descriptive term simply by grabbing it first. *Canal Co. v. Clark*, 13 Wall., at 323–324, 327. The Lanham Act adopts a similar leniency, there being no indication that the statute was meant to deprive commercial speakers of the ordinary utility of descriptive words. "If any confusion results, that is a risk the plaintiff accepted when it decided to identify its product with a mark that uses a well known descriptive phrase." *Cosmetically Sealed Industries, Inc. v. Chesebrough-Pond's USA Co.*, 125 F.3d, at 30. *See also Park 'N Fly,*

Inc. v. Dollar Park and Fly, Inc., 469 U.S. 189, 201 (1985) (noting safeguards in Lanham Act to prevent commercial monopolization of language); *Car-Freshner Corp. v. S.C. Johnson & Son, Inc.*, 70 F.3d 267, 269 (C.A.2 1995) (noting importance of "protect[ing] the right of society at large to use words or images in their primary descriptive sense"). This right to describe is the reason that descriptive terms qualify for registration as trademarks only after taking on secondary meaning as "distinctive of the applicant's goods,' 15 U.S.C. § 1052(f), with the registrant getting an exclusive right not in the original, descriptive sense, but only in the secondary one associated with the markholder's goods, 2 MCCARTHY, *supra*, § 11:45, p. 11–90 ("The only aspect of the mark which is given legal protection is that penumbra or fringe of secondary meaning which surrounds the old descriptive word").

While we thus recognize that mere risk of confusion will not rule out fair use, we think it would be improvident to go further in this case, for deciding anything more would take us beyond the Ninth Circuit's consideration of the subject. It suffices to realize that our holding that fair use can occur along with some degree of confusion does not foreclose the relevance of the extent of any likely consumer confusion in assessing whether a defendant's use is objectively fair. Two Courts of Appeals have found it relevant to consider such scope, and commentators and amici here have urged us to say that the degree of likely consumer confusion bears not only on the fairness of using a term, but even on the further question whether an originally descriptive term has become so identified as a mark that a defendant's use of it cannot realistically be called descriptive. *See Shakespeare Co. v. Silstar Corp.*, 110 F.3d, at 243 (" [T]o the degree that confusion is likely, a use is less likely to be found fair . . ." (emphasis deleted)); *Sunmark, Inc. v. Ocean Spray Cranberries, Inc.*, 64 F.3d, at 1059; RESTATEMENT § 28.

Since we do not rule out the pertinence of the degree of consumer confusion under the fair use defense, we likewise do not pass upon the position of the United States, as amicus, that the "used fairly" requirement in § 1115(b)(4) demands only that the descriptive term describe the goods accurately. Accuracy of course has to be a consideration in assessing fair use, but the proceedings in this case so far raise no occasion to evaluate some other concerns that courts might pick as relevant, quite apart from attention to confusion. The Restatement raises possibilities like commercial justification and the strength of the plaintiff's mark. RESTATEMENT § 28. As to them, it is enough to say here that the door is not closed.

III

In sum, a plaintiff claiming infringement of an incontestable mark must show likelihood of consumer confusion as part of the prima facie case, 15 U.S.C. § 1115(b), while the defendant has no independent burden to negate the likelihood of any confusion in raising the affirmative defense that a term is used descriptively, not as a mark, fairly, and in good faith, § 1115(b)(4).

Because we read the Court of Appeals as requiring KP to shoulder a burden on the issue of confusion, we vacate the judgment and remand the case for further proceedings consistent with this opinion.

COMMENTS AND QUESTIONS

1. *A Delicate, Contextual Balance.* The Supreme Court's decision highlights the ambivalent quality of trademark law's classic fair use doctrine: "some possibility of consumer confusion must be compatible with fair use." On remand, the Ninth Circuit held that while no longer determinative, consumer confusion was still relevant in deciding whether a use was fair. 408 F.3d 596 (9th Cir. 2005). The court endorsed the RE-STATEMENT (THIRD) OF UNFAIR COMPETITION § 28 cmt. b balancing test for applying the descriptive fair use defense:

> the strength of the plaintiff's mark and the extent of likely or actual confusion are important factors in determining whether a use is fair. Surveys and other evidence relating to the perceptions of prospective purchasers are thus relevant to the application of the defense, and a use that is likely to create substantial confusion will not ordinarily be considered a fair use. . . .

The court emphasized that "*to the degree* that confusion is likely, a use is less likely to be found fair." 408 F.3d at 607–08.

2. *Burden of Proof.* We usually think of defendants bearing the burden of proving a defense. Based on its interpretation of Lanham Act § 33(b), 15 U.S.C. § 1115(b), however, the Court found that the classic fair use defense is intertwined with the plaintiff's evidentiary burden to show that the defendant's actual practice is likely to confuse consumers as to the source of the goods or services in question. The Court notes that this burden must be borne in mind when interpreting the statute's affirmative defense to "use [] the name, term, or device charged to be an infringement is a use, otherwise than as a mark, . . . of a term or device which is descriptive of and used fairly and in good faith only to describe the goods or services of such party, or their geographic origin . . ." § 33(b)(4). The Court resolves this tension by holding that the defendant need not negate a showing of likelihood of confusion to prevail on its defense. This suggests that the plaintiff's effective burden in a case involving a classic fair use defense is higher than merely proving likelihood of confusion.

3. *Is the Classic Fair Use Defense Limited to Descriptive Marks?* While the statute speaks in terms of a defendant's use "to describe" an attribute of the defendant's product, both the Second and Ninth Circuits have held that the defense is available for inherently distinctive marks as well. *See Car-Freshner Corp. v. S.C. Johnson & Son*, 70 F.3d 267, 269 (2d Cir. 1995); *Brother Records, Inc. v. Jardine*, 318 F.3d 900, 907 (9th Cir. 2003); 1 J. MCCARTHY, TRADEMARKS AND UNFAIR COMPETITION § 11.17[1] (endorsing the application to inherently distinctive marks).

Does this make sense? How can someone use another's inherently distinctive mark to describe their own products? *See, e.g., Sazerac Brands LLC v. Peristyle, LLC*, 892 F.3d 853 (6th Cir. 2018) (holding that the defendant's accurate and good faith reference to the geographic fact that its bourbon is made in "the Former Old Taylor Distillery"—

named for Colonel Edmund Haynes Taylor, Jr., a famous distiller in the late 19th century—on its bourbon product was fair use notwithstanding the plaintiff's trademark on "Old Taylor" for its bourbon product).

4. *Classic Fair Use Rescues Romance.* In *Cosmetically Sealed Industries, Inc. v. Chesebrough-Pond's USA*, 125 F.3d 28 (2d Cir. 1997), the plaintiff had registered the trademark "Sealed With a Kiss" for a brand of long-lasting lipstick. Plaintiff sued after the defendant began an advertising campaign for its own brand of lipstick that encouraged users to place a lipstick "kiss" on a postcard and mail it to someone. The defendant's campaign used the phrase "Seal it with a Kiss!!" The court held that the phrase "sealed with a kiss" was in common use and that the defendant was not liable because it merely used that common phrase in its descriptive (rather than its trademark) sense.

That last point is important. Defendants who also seek to use a descriptive term as a mark won't be able to take advantage of the fair use defense. *See Lifeguard Licensing Corp. v. Ann Arbor T-shirt Co.*, 2018 WL 3364388 (S.D.N.Y. July 9, 2018).

ii. *Nontrademark (or Nominative) Use, Parody, and the First Amendment*

Mattel, Inc. v. MCA Records
United States Court of Appeals for the Ninth Circuit
296 F.3d 894 (9th Cir. 2002)

KOZINSKI, Circuit Judge:

If this were a sci-fi melodrama, it might be called Speech-Zilla meets Trademark Kong.

I.

Barbie was born in Germany in the 1950s as an adult collector's item. Over the years, Mattel transformed her from a doll that resembled a "German street walker," as she originally appeared, into a glamorous, long-legged blonde. Barbie has been labeled both the ideal American woman and a bimbo. She has survived attacks both psychic (from feminists critical of her fictitious figure) and physical (more than 500 professional makeovers). She remains a symbol of American girlhood, a public figure who graces the aisles of toy stores throughout the country and beyond. With Barbie, Mattel created not just a toy but a cultural icon.

With fame often comes unwanted attention. Aqua is a Danish band that has, as yet, only dreamed of attaining Barbie-like status. In 1997, Aqua produced the song Barbie Girl on the album *Aquarium*. In the song, one bandmember impersonates Barbie, singing in a high-pitched, doll-like voice; another bandmember, calling himself Ken, entices Barbie to "go party." (The lyrics are in the Appendix.) Barbie Girl singles sold well and, to Mattel's dismay, the song made it onto Top 40 music charts.

Mattel brought this lawsuit against the music companies who produced, marketed and sold Barbie Girl: MCA Records, Inc., Universal Music International Ltd. . . .

Mattel appeals the district court's ruling that Barbie Girl is a parody of Barbie and a nominative fair use [and] that MCA's use of the term Barbie is not likely to confuse consumers as to Mattel's affiliation with Barbie Girl or dilute the Barbie mark. . . .

III

A. A trademark is a word, phrase or symbol that is used to identify a manufacturer or sponsor of a good or the provider of a service. *See New Kids on the Block v. News Am. Publ'g, Inc.*, 971 F.2d 302, 305 (9th Cir. 1992). It's the owner's way of preventing others from duping consumers into buying a product they mistakenly believe is sponsored by the trademark owner. A trademark "inform[s] people that trademarked products come from the same source." *Id.* at 305 n.2. Limited to this core purpose—avoiding confusion in the marketplace—a trademark owner's property rights play well with the First Amendment. "Whatever first amendment rights you may have in calling the brew you make in your bathtub 'Pepsi' are easily outweighed by the buyer's interest in not being fooled into buying it." [Alex Kozinski,] *Trademarks Unplugged*, 68 N.Y.U. L. REV. 960, 973 (1993).

The problem arises when trademarks transcend their identifying purpose. Some trademarks enter our public discourse and become an integral part of our vocabulary. How else do you say that something's "the Rolls Royce of its class"? What else is a quick fix, but a Band-Aid? Does the average consumer know to ask for aspirin as "acetyl salicylic acid"*? See Bayer Co. v. United Drug Co.*, 272 F. 505, 510 (S.D.N.Y. 1921). Trademarks often fill in gaps in our vocabulary and add a contemporary flavor to our expressions. Once imbued with such expressive value, the trademark becomes a word in our language and assumes a role outside the bounds of trademark law.

Our likelihood-of-confusion test, *see AMF Inc. v. Sleekcraft Boats*, 599 F.2d 341, 348–49 (9th Cir. 1979), generally strikes a comfortable balance between the trademark owner's property rights and the public's expressive interests. But when a trademark owner asserts a right to control how we express ourselves—when we'd find it difficult to describe the product any other way (as in the case of aspirin), or when the mark (like Rolls Royce) has taken on an expressive meaning apart from its source-identifying function—applying the traditional test fails to account for the full weight of the public's interest in free expression.

The First Amendment may offer little protection for a competitor who labels its commercial good with a confusingly similar mark, but "[t]rademark rights do not entitle the owner to quash an unauthorized use of the mark by another who is communicating ideas or expressing points of view." *L.L. Bean, Inc. v. Drake Publishers, Inc.*, 811 F.2d 26, 29 (1st Cir. 1987). Were we to ignore the expressive value that some marks assume, trademark rights would grow to encroach upon the zone protected by the First Amendment. *See Yankee Publ'g, Inc. v. News Am. Publ'g, Inc.*, 809 F. Supp. 267, 276 (S.D.N.Y. 1992) ("[W]hen unauthorized use of another's mark is part of a communicative message and not a source identifier, the First Amendment is implicated in opposition to the trademark right."). Simply put, the trademark owner does not have the right to control public discourse whenever the public imbues his mark with a meaning beyond its source-identifying function. *See Anti-Monopoly, Inc. v. Gen. Mills Fun Group*, 611 F.2d 296, 301 (9th Cir. 1979) ("It is the source-denoting function which trademark laws protect, and nothing more.").

B. There is no doubt that MCA uses Mattel's mark: Barbie is one half of Barbie Girl. But Barbie Girl is the title of a song about Barbie and Ken, a reference that—at least today—can only be to Mattel's famous couple. We expect a title to describe the underlying work, not to identify the producer, and Barbie Girl does just that.

The Barbie Girl title presages a song about Barbie, or at least a girl like Barbie. The title conveys a message to consumers about what they can expect to discover in the song itself; it's a quick glimpse of Aqua's take on their own song. The lyrics confirm this: The female singer, who calls herself Barbie, is "a Barbie girl, in [her] Barbie world." She tells her male counterpart (named Ken), "Life in plastic, it's fantastic. You can brush my hair, undress me everywhere/Imagination, life is your creation." And off they go to "party." The song pokes fun at Barbie and the values that Aqua contends she represents. *See Cliffs Notes, Inc. v. Bantam Doubleday Dell Publ'g Group*, 886 F.2d 490, 495–96 (2d Cir. 1989). The female singer explains, "I'm a blond bimbo girl, in a fantasy world/Dress me up, make it tight, I'm your dolly."

The song does not rely on the Barbie mark to poke fun at another subject but targets Barbie herself. *See Campbell v. Acuff-Rose Music, Inc.*, 510 U.S. 569 (1994); *see also Dr. Seuss Ents., L.P. v. Penguin Books USA, Inc.*, 109 F.3d 1394, 1400 (9th Cir. 1997). This case is therefore distinguishable from *Dr. Seuss*, where we held that the book *The Cat NOT in the Hat!* borrowed Dr. Seuss's trademarks and lyrics to get attention rather than to mock *The Cat in the Hat!* The defendant's use of the Dr. Seuss trademarks and copyrighted works had "no critical bearing on the substance or style of *The Cat in the Hat!*, and therefore could not claim First Amendment protection. *Id.* at 1401. *Dr. Seuss* recognized that, where an artistic work targets the original and does not merely borrow another's property to get attention, First Amendment interests weigh more heavily in the balance. *See id.* at 1400–02; *see also Harley-Davidson, Inc. v. Grottanelli*, 164 F.3d 806, 812–13 (2d Cir. 1999) (a parodist whose expressive work aims its parodic commentary at a trademark is given considerable leeway, but a claimed parodic use that makes no comment on the mark is not a permitted trademark parody use).

The Second Circuit has held that "in general the [Lanham] Act should be construed to apply to artistic works only where the public interest in avoiding consumer confusion outweighs the public interest in free expression." *Rogers v. Grimaldi*, 875 F.2d 994, 999 (2d Cir. 1989); *see also Cliffs Notes*, 886 F.2d at 494 (quoting *Rogers*, 875 F.2d at 999). *Rogers* considered a challenge by the actress Ginger Rogers to the film *Ginger and Fred*. The movie told the story of two Italian cabaret performers who made a living by imitating Ginger Rogers and Fred Astaire. Rogers argued that the film's title created the false impression that she was associated with it.

At first glance, Rogers certainly had a point. Ginger was her name, and Fred was her dancing partner. If a pair of dancing shoes had been labeled Ginger and Fred, a dancer might have suspected that Rogers was associated with the shoes (or at least one of them), just as Michael Jordan has endorsed Nike sneakers that claim to make you fly through the air. But Ginger and Fred was not a brand of shoe; it was the title of a movie and, for the reasons explained by the Second Circuit, deserved to be treated differently.

A title is designed to catch the eye and to promote the value of the underlying work. Consumers expect a title to communicate a message about the book or movie, but they do not expect it to identify the publisher or producer. *See Application of Cooper*, 254 F.2d 611, 615–16 (C.C.P.A. 1958) (A "title . . . identifies a specific literary work, . . . and is not associated in the public mind with the . . . manufacturer." (internal quotation marks omitted)). If we see a painting titled "Campbell's Chicken Noodle Soup," we're unlikely to believe that Campbell's has branched into the art business. Nor, upon hearing Janis Joplin croon "Oh Lord, won't you buy me a Mercedes-Benz?," would we suspect that she and the carmaker had entered into a joint venture. A title tells us something about the underlying work but seldom speaks to its origin: Though consumers frequently look to the title of a work to determine what it is about, they do not regard titles of artistic works in the same way as the names of ordinary commercial products. Since consumers expect an ordinary product to be what the name says it is, we apply the Lanham Act with some rigor to prohibit names that misdescribe such goods. But most consumers are well aware that they cannot judge a book solely by its title any more than by its cover. *Rogers,* 875 F.2d at 1000 (citations omitted).

Rogers concluded that literary titles do not violate the Lanham Act "unless the title has no artistic relevance to the underlying work whatsoever, or, if it has some artistic relevance, unless the title explicitly misleads as to the source or the content of the work." *Id.* at 999 (footnote omitted). We agree with the Second Circuit's analysis and adopt the *Rogers* standard as our own.

Applying *Rogers* to our case, we conclude that MCA's use of Barbie is not an infringement of Mattel's trademark. Under the first prong of *Rogers,* the use of Barbie in the song title clearly is relevant to the underlying work, namely, the song itself. As noted, the song is about Barbie and the values Aqua claims she represents. The song title does not explicitly mislead as to the source of the work; it does not, explicitly or otherwise, suggest that it was produced by Mattel.

The only indication that Mattel might be associated with the song is the use of Barbie in the title; if this were enough to satisfy this prong of the *Rogers* test, it would render *Rogers* a nullity. We therefore agree with the district court that MCA was entitled to summary judgment on this ground. We need not consider whether the district court was correct in holding that MCA was also entitled to summary judgment because its use of Barbie was a nominative fair use.

IV

Mattel separately argues that, under the Federal Trademark Dilution Act ("FTDA"), MCA's song dilutes the Barbie mark in two ways: It diminishes the mark's capacity to identify and distinguish Mattel products, and tarnishes the mark because the song is inappropriate for young girls. *See* 15 U.S.C. § 1125(c). . . .

MCA's use of the mark is dilutive. MCA does not dispute that, while a reference to Barbie would previously have brought to mind only Mattel's doll, after the song's popular success, some consumers hearing Barbie's name will think of both the doll and the song, or perhaps of the song only. This is a classic blurring injury and is in no way diminished by the fact that the song itself refers back to Barbie the doll. To be dilutive, use of the mark need not bring to mind the junior user alone. The distinctiveness of the mark is diminished if the mark no longer brings to mind the senior user alone.[5] . . .

Such a reading of the statute would . . . create a constitutional problem, because it would leave the FTDA with no First Amendment protection for dilutive speech other than comparative advertising and news reporting. This would be a serious problem because the primary (usually exclusive) remedy for dilution is an injunction.[6] As noted above, tension with the First Amendment also exists in the trademark context, especially where the mark has assumed an expressive function beyond mere identification of a product or service. *See supra; New Kids on the Block,* 971 F.2d at 306–08. These concerns apply with greater force in the dilution context because dilution lacks two very significant limitations that reduce the tension between trademark law and the First Amendment.

First, depending on the strength and distinctiveness of the mark, trademark law grants relief only against uses that are likely to confuse. *See* 5 McCarthy § 30:3, at 30-8 to 30-11; Restatement § 35 cmt. c at 370. A trademark injunction is usually limited to uses within one industry or several related industries. Dilution law is the antithesis of trademark law in this respect, because it seeks to protect the mark from association in the public's mind with wholly unrelated goods and services. The more remote the good or service associated with the junior use, the more likely it is to cause dilution rather than trademark infringement. A dilution injunction, by contrast to a trademark injunction, will generally sweep across broad vistas of the economy.

Second, a trademark injunction, even a very broad one, is premised on the need to prevent consumer confusion. This consumer protection rationale—averting what is essentially a fraud on the consuming public—is wholly consistent with the theory of the First Amendment, which does not protect commercial fraud. *Cent. Hudson Gas & Elec. v. Pub. Serv. Comm'n,* 447 U.S. 557, 566 (1980); *see Thompson v. W. States Med. Ctr.,* 535 U.S. 357 (2002) (applying *Central Hudson*). Moreover, avoiding harm to consumers is an important interest that is independent of the senior user's interest in protecting its business.

Dilution, by contrast, does not require a showing of consumer confusion, 15 U.S.C. § 1127, and dilution injunctions therefore lack the built-in First Amendment compass of trademark injunctions. In addition, dilution law protects only the distinctiveness of

---

[5] Because we find blurring, we need not consider whether the song also tarnished the Barbie mark.

[6] The FTDA provides for both injunctive relief and damages, but the latter is only available if plaintiff can prove a willful intent to dilute. 15 U.S.C. § 1125(c)(2).

the mark, which is inherently less weighty than the dual interest of protecting trademark owners and avoiding harm to consumers that is at the heart of every trademark claim.

Fortunately, the legislative history of the FTDA suggests an interpretation of the "noncommercial use" exemption that both solves our interpretive dilemma and diminishes some First Amendment concerns: "Noncommercial use" refers to a use that consists entirely of noncommercial, or fully constitutionally protected, speech. *See* 2 JEROME GILSON ET AL., TRADEMARK PROTECTION AND PRACTICE § 5.12[1][c][vi], at 5–240 (this exemption "is intended to prevent the courts from enjoining speech that has been recognized to be [fully] constitutionally protected," "such as parodies"). Where, as here, a statute's plain meaning "produces an absurd, and perhaps unconstitutional, result[, it is] entirely appropriate to consult all public materials, including the background of [the statute] and the legislative history of its adoption." *Green v. Bock Laundry Mach. Co.*, 490 U.S. 504, 527 (1989) (Scalia, J., concurring).

. . . To determine whether Barbie Girl falls within this exemption, we look to our definition of commercial speech under our First Amendment caselaw. *See* H.R. REP. NO. 104-374, at 8, reprinted in 1995 U.S.C.C.A.N. 1029, 1035 (the exemption "expressly incorporates the concept of 'commercial' speech from the 'commercial speech' doctrine"); 141 Cong. Rec. S19306-10, S19311 (daily ed. Dec. 29, 1995) (the exemption "is consistent with existing [First Amendment] case law").

"Although the boundary between commercial and noncommercial speech has yet to be clearly delineated, the 'core notion of commercial speech' is that it 'does no more than propose a commercial transaction.'" *Hoffman v. Capital Cities/ABC, Inc.*, 255 F.3d 1180, 1184 (9th Cir. 2001) (quoting *Bolger v. Youngs Drug Prods. Corp.*, 463 U.S. 60, 66 (1983)). If speech is not "purely commercial"—that is, if it does more than propose a commercial transaction—then it is entitled to full First Amendment protection. *Id.* at 1185–86 (internal quotation marks omitted).

In *Hoffman,* a magazine published an article featuring digitally altered images from famous films. Computer artists modified shots of Dustin Hoffman, Cary Grant, Marilyn Monroe and others to put the actors in famous designers' spring fashions; a still of Hoffman from the movie "Tootsie" was altered so that he appeared to be wearing a Richard Tyler evening gown and Ralph Lauren heels. Hoffman, who had not given permission, sued under the Lanham Act and for violation of his right to publicity. *Id.* at 1183.

The article featuring the altered image clearly served a commercial purpose: "to draw attention to the for-profit magazine in which it appear[ed]" and to sell more copies. *Id.* at 1186. Nevertheless, we held that the article was fully protected under the First Amendment because it included protected expression: "humor" and "visual and verbal editorial comment on classic films and famous actors." *Id.* at 1185 (internal quotation marks omitted). Because its commercial purpose was "inextricably entwined with [these] expressive elements," the article and accompanying photographs enjoyed full First Amendment protection. *Id.*

Hoffman controls: Barbie Girl is not purely commercial speech, and is therefore fully protected. To be sure, MCA used Barbie's name to sell copies of the song. However, as we've already observed, see pp. 1189–90 *supra*, the song also lampoons the Barbie image and comments humorously on the cultural values Aqua claims she represents. Use of the Barbie mark in the song Barbie Girl therefore falls within the noncommercial use exemption to the FTDA. For precisely the same reasons, use of the mark in the song's title is also exempted. . . .

VI

After Mattel filed suit, Mattel and MCA employees traded barbs in the press. When an MCA spokeswoman noted that each album included a disclaimer saying that Barbie Girl was a "social commentary [that was] not created or approved by the makers of the doll," a Mattel representative responded by saying, "That's unacceptable. . . . It's akin to a bank robber handing a note of apology to a teller during a heist. [It n]either diminishes the severity of the crime, nor does it make it legal." He later characterized the song as a "theft" of "another company's property."

MCA filed a counterclaim for defamation based on the Mattel representative's use of the words "bank robber," "heist," "crime" and "theft." But all of these are variants of the invective most often hurled at accused infringers, namely "piracy." No one hearing this accusation understands intellectual property owners to be saying that infringers are nautical cutthroats with eyepatches and peg legs who board galleons to plunder cargo. In context, all these terms are nonactionable "rhetorical hyperbole," *Gilbrook v. City of Westminster*, 177 F.3d 839, 863 (9th Cir. 1999). The parties are advised to chill.

Affirmed.

Appendix

"Barbie Girl" by Aqua

- Hiya Barbie!
- Hi Ken!
- You wanna go for a ride?
- Sure, Ken!
- Jump in!
- Ha ha ha ha!
(CHORUS)
I'm a Barbie girl, in my Barbie world
Life in plastic, it's fantastic
You can brush my hair, undress me everywhere
Imagination, life is your creation
Come on Barbie, let's go party!
(CHORUS)
I'm a blonde bimbo girl, in a fantasy world
Dress me up, make it tight, I'm your dolly
You're my doll, rock and roll, feel the glamour in pink

Kiss me here, touch me there, hanky-panky
You can touch, you can play
If you say "I'm always yours," ooh ooh
(CHORUS)
(BRIDGE)
Come on, Barbie, let's go party, ah ah ah yeah
Come on, Barbie, let's go party, ooh ooh, ooh ooh
Come on, Barbie, let's go party, ah ah ah yeah
Come on, Barbie, let's go party, ooh ooh, ooh ooh
Make me walk, make me talk, do whatever you please
I can act like a star, I can beg on my knees
Come jump in, be my friend, let us do it again
Hit the town, fool around, let's go party
You can touch, you can play
You can say "I'm always yours"
You can touch, you can play
You can say "I'm always yours"
(BRIDGE)
(CHORUS ×2)
(BRIDGE)
- Oh, I'm having so much fun!
- Well, Barbie, we're just getting started!
- Oh, I love you Ken!

COMMENTS AND QUESTIONS

1. To similar effect is *Mattel v. Walking Mountain Prods.*, 353 F.3d 792 (9th Cir. 2003), where the court held that an artist who posed Barbie dolls nude in photographs in which they were attacked by vintage household appliances was not liable for trademark infringement or dilution, since his use of the term Barbie accurately stated the content of his works, he was criticizing or parodying Barbie, and his use was not commercial use.

2. *Nontrademark or "Nominative" Use.* In *New Kids on the Block v. News Am. Publ'g, Inc.*, 971 F.2d 302 (9th Cir. 1992), USA Today asked its readers: "Who's the best on the block?" This feature commented that "New Kids on the Block are pop's hottest group. Which of the five is your fave? Or are they a turn off? . . . Each call [to a 900 number] costs 50 cents. Results in Friday's Life Section." In finding that this use of the band's name did not infringe its trademark rights, Judge Kozinski articulated the contours and elements of the nominative use doctrine:

> [W]e may generalize a class of cases where the use of the trademark does not attempt to capitalize on consumer confusion or to appropriate the cachet of one product for a different one. Such nominative use of a mark—where the only

word reasonably available to describe a particular thing is pressed into service—lies outside the strictures of trademark law: Because it does not implicate the source-identification function that is the purpose of trademark, it does not constitute unfair competition; such use is fair because it does not imply sponsorship or endorsement by the trademark holder. "When the mark is used in a way that does not deceive the public we see no such sanctity in the word as to prevent its being used to tell the truth." *Prestonettes, Inc. v. Coty*, 264 U.S. 359, 368 (1924) (Holmes, J.).

To be sure, this is not the classic fair use case where the defendant has used the plaintiff's mark to describe the defendant's own product. Here, the New Kids trademark is used to refer to the New Kids themselves. We therefore do not purport to alter the test applicable in the paradigmatic fair use case. If the defendant's use of the plaintiff's trademark refers to something other than the plaintiff's product, the traditional fair use inquiry will continue to govern. But, where the defendant uses a trademark to describe the plaintiff's product, rather than its own, we hold that a commercial user is entitled to a nominative fair use defense provided he meets the following three requirements: First, the product or service in question must be one not readily identifiable without use of the trademark; second, only so much of the mark or marks may be used as is reasonably necessary to identify the product or service; and third, the user must do nothing that would, in conjunction with the mark, suggest sponsorship or endorsement by the trademark holder.

New Kids on the Block, 971 F.2d at 307–08.

How would the court rule if USA Today had used the band's logo in the feature? How would the court in *Mattel* have responded if MCA used the Barbie logo on the Aqua album cover? What if the Barbie logo had a red circle with a slash symbol ("no") through it? What if it merely had a Barbie look-alike on the cover? Does the 2006 Trademark Dilution Revision Act, which explicitly protects "identifying and parodying, criticizing, or commenting upon the famous mark owner or the goods" but only if used "otherwise than as a mark" change the court's analysis? *See* Stacey L. Dogan & Mark A. Lemley, *Parody as Brand*, 47 U.C. DAVIS L. REV. 473 (2013).

Is nominative use a defense to a trademark infringement case, or is it simply a different way of analyzing likelihood of confusion? As with the classic fair use doctrine, the practical effect of the characterization can be substantial: a defense applies even if consumers are confused.

The Third Circuit has rejected the *New Kids on the Block* formulation of nominative use, concluding that as a defense, nominative use should not depend on whether the use confuses some consumers. *See Century 21 Real Estate Corp. v. LendingTree, Inc.*, 425 F.3d 211 (3d Cir. 2006). Who is right? Does *KP Permanent* shed any light on the question? The First Circuit has also rejected the Ninth Circuit's requirement that the defendant's work take "no more of the mark than was necessary," holding that "a trademark holder has no right to police 'unnecessary' use of its mark. Whether necessary or not, a defendant's use of a mark must be confusing . . ." *Swarovski AG v. Building #19, Inc.*, 704 F.3d 44 (1st Cir. 2013). The Second Circuit has combined the traditional likelihood of confusion factors and the Ninth Circuit's factors into a single test. *See International Information Systems Security Certification Consortium, Inc. v. Security University, LLC*, 823 F.3d 153 (2d Cir. 2016).

3. How does the nontrademark use doctrine square with the merchandising rights in logos and university names that some courts have granted to trademark owners?

4. Terri Welles, Playboy Magazine's Playmate of the Year in 1981, created a website offering photographs of Welles (some for free, others for sale), membership in her photo club, and links to other commercial sites. Her website contained "playboy" and "playmate" in metatags, the phrase "Playmate of the Year 1981" on the masthead of the website and in banner advertisements, and the repeated use of the abbreviation "PMOY '81" as a watermark on the web pages. How should each of these uses be evaluated under the *New Kids on the Block* test? *See Playboy Enters., Inc. v. Welles*, 279 F.3d 796 (9th Cir. 2002) (Welles was free to use Playboy's trademarks to accurately advertise her affiliation with the magazine, but could not go beyond that to trade on those marks).

5. *Non-Dilution Parody Analysis.* Parody has been an effective defense not only against claims grounded in state dilution laws, but also against trademark infringement per se. But a parody that confuses consumers will not be immune from trademark infringement. *See Cliffs Notes, Inc. v. Bantam Doubleday Dell Publ'g Grp., Inc.*, 886 F.2d 490 (2d Cir. 1989). In *Mutual of Omaha Ins. Co. v. Novak*, 836 F.2d 397 (8th Cir. 1987), the court observed that

> [a] parody must convey two simultaneous—and contradictory—messages: that it is the original, but also that it is not the original and is instead a parody. To the extent that it does only the former but not the latter, it is not only a poor parody but also vulnerable under trademark law, since the customer will be confused.

Id. at 494 (affirming district court's finding of likelihood of confusion between plaintiff's famous "Mutual of Omaha" mark and defendant's anti-nuclear t-shirts, bearing funny picture and "Mutant of Omaha" legend).

In *Hormel Foods Corp. v. Jim Henson Prods., Inc.*, 73 F.3d 497 (2d Cir. 1996), the court held that defendant's use of a character named "SPA'AM" in a movie was an acceptable parody of the plaintiff's famous registered mark "SPAM" for meat-related products. The opinion treats the case strictly under "likelihood of confusion" principles. Although no confusion is found to be likely, and the parody is permitted, the First Amendment is never mentioned. Should the First Amendment protect even confusing parodies? *See* Steven M. Perez, *Confronting Biased Treatment of Trademark Parody Under the Lanham Act*, 44 EMORY L.J. 1451 (1995) (arguing that trademark-based "likelihood of confusion" analysis makes parody cases too unpredictable and inconsistent with free speech interests).

6. *Parody/Satire Distinction.* As we discussed in Chapter IV, courts distinguish between parody and satire in applying copyright's fair use doctrine, finding parody of a copyrighted work much more likely to fall within the scope of the doctrine than satirical treatment. The court in *Mattel* suggests that Congress intended to exclude "parody, satire, editorial and other forms of expression that are not a part of a commercial transaction" from the scope of the dilution cause of action. Should this clearer and broader exemption also apply to traditional (likelihood of confusion) trademark claims?

In *Elvis Presley Enterprises v. Capece*, 141 F.3d 188 (5th Cir. 1998), the Fifth Circuit imported the parody/satire distinction from copyright law into traditional trademark analysis. The court held that defendant's 1960s theme bar could not use the name "Velvet Elvis" because it infringed on the rights of Elvis Presley's estate. The owner of the bar claimed that he was engaged in a legitimate parody of the kitsch associated with certain aspects of the 1960s. The Fifth Circuit concluded that "parody is not a defense to trademark infringement," and that in any event the "Velvet Elvis" was engaged in satire and not parody because its statement did not require the use of the Elvis trademark.

Does it make sense to import copyright law's parody/satire distinction into trademark law? Aren't the purposes of the laws different? In any event, how likely is it that consumers will be confused by the use of the "Velvet Elvis" name? Contrast this case with *E.S.S. Entertainment 2000 v. Rock Star Videos*, 547 F.3d 1095 (9th Cir. 2008), which held that the First Amendment protected the depiction of a strip club in the video game Grand Theft Auto: San Andreas called the "Pig Pen" with a likeness similar to plaintiff's actual "Play Pen" strip club so long as the use had at least "some artistic relevance" and was not "expressly misleading."

7. *The* Rogers *Test.* The *Rogers v. Grimaldi* test discussed in *Mattel* offers substantially more protection to speech than does the parody/satire distinction. *Rogers* shields an expressive work from trademark liability ~~where~~ ^unless^ the defendant's use of the mark (1) is not artistically relevant to the work or (2) explicitly misleads consumers as to the source or the content of the work. Thus, artists can paint and video games can depict actual Alabama football players wearing team uniforms. *See Univ. of Alabama Bd. of Trs. v. New Life Art, Inc.*, 683 F.3d 1266 (11th Cir. 2012); *Brown v. Electronic Arts, Inc.*, 724 F.3d 1235 (9th Cir. 2013). And Fox can call its TV show about the music industry *Empire* even though there is an actual Empire record label, when Fox's show is about a fictional record label called Empire. *Twentieth Century Fox Television v. Empire Distrib. Inc.*, 2016 WL 685106 (C.D. Cal. Feb. 1, 2016); *but see Louis Vuitton Malletier, S.A. v. Hyundai Motor Am.*, 2012 WL 1022258 (S.D.N.Y. March 22, 2012) (holding that humorous ad criticizing unnecessary luxury by depicting a basketball featuring the Louis Vuitton logo on a marble court with a gold hoop infringed Vuitton's trademarks).

Gordon v. Drape Creative, Inc., 909 F.3d 257 (9th Cir. 2018), illustrates the outer limits of the *Rogers* test. Christopher Gordon created a popular YouTube video known for its catchphrases "Honey Badger Don't Care" and "Honey Badger Don't Give a S- -

-." He obtained trademarks on the phrases and commercialized various products, including greeting cards, mugs, and clothing, with the phrases. He brought a trademark infringement against a greeting card company for marketing greeting cards featuring the Honey Badger catchphrases. The district court granted summary judgment to the defendants pursuant to the *Rogers* test. On appeal, the Ninth Circuit held although that defendants' greeting cards are expressive works to which *Rogers* applies, there remained a genuine issue of material fact as to *Rogers*'s second prong—i.e., whether defendants' use of Gordon's mark in their greeting cards is explicitly misleading.

In applying this prong, courts examine a broad range of factors in balancing "the public interest in avoiding consumer confusion" against "the public interest in free expression." *Rogers*, 875 F.2d at 999. The *Gordon* court noted that

> In some instances, the use of a mark alone may explicitly mislead consumers about a product's source if consumers would ordinarily identify the source by the mark itself. If an artist pastes Disney's trademark at the bottom corner of a painting that depicts Mickey Mouse, the use of Disney's mark, while arguably relevant to the subject of the painting, could explicitly mislead consumers that Disney created or authorized the painting, even if those words do not appear alongside the mark itself.

909 F.3d at 270.

In overturning the district court's grant of summary judgment for the defendants, the Ninth Circuit emphasized two factors: (1) the degree to which the junior user uses the mark in the same way as the senior user; and (2) the extent to which the junior user has added his or her own expressive content to the work beyond the mark itself.

Does *Gordon* undo *Mattel* and the *Rogers* test? The court rejects any requirement that "explicitly misleading" uses of a mark be, well, explicit. If the use of a mark in the same way the plaintiff uses it can suffice, what is left of the rule that the use of the trademark alone can't satisfy the plaintiff's burden on the second prong? Aren't we just back to the general likelihood of confusion test? Could you argue that Barbie Girl was explicitly misleading under this test? How would you argue it? Would it matter if Mattel had licensed other people to make songs about Barbie? *See Stouffer v. National Geographic Partners*, 400 F. Supp. 3d 1161 (D. Colo. 2019) (reading *Gordon* as "back[ing] away" from its *Empire* decision and narrowing another case applying *Rogers* "to its factual context"). *Stouffer* rejects *Rogers* in favor of asking whether the defendant had "a genuine artistic motive" for using the trademark in its title.

One court has distinguished *Gordon* on step two even where the parties directly compete. In *Caiz v. Roberts*, 2019 WL 1755421 (C.D. Cal. 2019), Caiz, a rapper, owns the trademark rights to the term "Mastermind" and has used the name in the music industry since 1999. Caiz alleged that Roberts, commonly known as "Rick Ross," infringed Caiz's trademark by releasing an album, creating a tour, and adopting a persona called "Mastermind." The court rejected the claim on summary judgment. "In contrast to the defendants in Gordon using the Honey Badger catchphrase as the 'centerpiece' of their greeting cards, Roberts is using 'Mastermind' as one album title out of six albums throughout his career . . . [E]ven where the mark is used, it is through Roberts' own artistic expression," and in "every instance where [the mark] was used [by Roberts] it was accompanied by a clear indication that it is associated with 'Rick Ross.'" Is that distinction persuasive? Could Drape Creative make the same claims?

PROBLEMS

Problem V-20. Toho, Inc. is the owner of the copyrights in several Japanese "Godzilla" movies as well as the registered U.S. trademark "Godzilla." Toho granted a license to a major American movie company to use the name and the monster in its recent high-budget film and various related products and promotional efforts.

Capitalizing on the hype surrounding the new Godzilla film, Edgar publishes a book cataloguing the history of Godzilla in film and print. He titles his book "Godzilla" and places a picture of the monster on the cover. Toho sues for trademark infringement.

How should the court rule? Would it matter if Toho had licensed a different writer to produce an "authorized" history?

Problem V-21. Anheuser-Busch sells beer under a variety of brand names, including Michelob. As part of a general trend of brand proliferation in the beer industry, Busch introduced sub-brands of Michelob, including Michelob Dry, Michelob Lite, and Michelob Ice.

After an oil spill near an Anheuser-Busch plant, Balducci runs the following advertisement for "Michelob Oily" on the back of a humor magazine. The ad identifies itself as a parody in micro-print along the side. The pictures in the ad are takeoffs from those in actual Michelob commercials.

Anheuser-Busch sues Balducci for trademark infringement. At trial, Busch can show only a tiny percentage of consumers who thought Michelob Oily was a real product, but it proves that half the people surveyed believed Balducci should have to get permission from Busch to run the ad. Who should prevail?

Problem V-22. The Coca-Cola Co. maintains an extremely strong and well-recognized trademark in the word "Coke" for its soft drink, and in the phrase "Enjoy Coke," particularly when used in connection with its red and white patterned logo. Gemini Rising, Inc., which distributes commercial posters, designs a poster with font and colors identical to Coca-Cola's which reads "Enjoy Cocaine." After passersby who saw the poster complain to the local press, Coca-Cola brings suit against Gemini Rising. At trial, Coca-Cola offers evidence from a few members of the public who apparently believed that Coca-Cola had sponsored the posters, including one woman who threatened to organize a boycott of Coca-Cola products. What result?

Does your result change if Gemini Rising is a nonprofit political organization devoted to drug legalization? If it agrees to include a statement in medium-sized print at the bottom of the poster disclaiming any affiliation with the Coca-Cola Co.?

4.   Other Defenses

i.   *Laches*

As we saw in prior chapters, laches is a traditional defense to any request for injunctive relief. In the context of trademark infringement, courts have held that the defense can also be used to defeat a request for profits or damages arising from trademark infringement—although such remedies are traditionally deemed "legal" rather than equitable. The Lanham Act recognizes the defense, and declares it enforceable even against a federally registered mark that has become incontestable. Lanham Act § 33(b)(9), 15 U.S.C. § 1115(b)(9).

In order to establish the defense, the defendant must generally show that (1) the plaintiff had sufficient knowledge of the defendant's activities concerning the mark at issue; (2) the plaintiff delayed in bringing suit; and (3) the defendant will be prejudiced by allowing the plaintiff to assert its rights at this time. *See, e.g., Cuban Cigar Brands N. V. v. Upmann Intern., Inc.*, 457 F. Supp. 1090, 1096 (S.D.N.Y. 1978).

In determining whether a laches defense is applicable there are no bright line rules to determining whether there was a prejudicial delay. While many courts use a time period analogous to the state law statute of limitations as a starting point in their analysis, it is not determinative of unreasonable delay. Rather, most courts pay particular attention to the facts of the case at bar and balance the equities. In deciding whether a laches defense will succeed, the Ninth Circuit weighs six factors: (1) the strength of plaintiff's trademark; (2) plaintiff's diligence in enforcing the mark; (3) the harm to plaintiff if relief is denied; (4) whether defendant acted in good faith ignorance of plaintiff's rights; (5) competition between the parties; and (6) the harm suffered by defendant because of plaintiff's delay. *See E-Systems, Inc. v. Monitek, Inc.*, 720 F.2d 604, 607 (9th Cir. 1983). Laches will not protect a willful infringer.

Notably, the period of time required to trigger laches is much shorter in trademark than in copyright law. A delay of even several months in filing suit may bar a preliminary injunction, for instance.

Although the Lanham Act does not have its own statute of limitations, courts have used limitations periods contained in "related" contracts between the parties, limitations periods in "analogous" state statutes, and the doctrine of laches to determine when a claim in time-barred. In addition, a federal four-year "catch all" statute of limitations is applicable to cases arising under a federal law enacted after December 1, 1990.

ii.   Unclean Hands

Unclean hands is a traditional equitable defense based on significant misconduct by the trademark owner specifically related to the subject matter of the litigation. In such a case, a court will deny the plaintiff injunctive or other equitable relief.

The Lanham Act provides that traditional equitable defenses are available in trademark infringement actions, even against incontestable marks. Lanham Act § 33(b)(9), 15 U.S.C. § 1115(b)(9). The RESTATEMENT (THIRD) OF UNFAIR COMPETITION explains that

> [i]f a designation used as a trademark, trade name, collective mark, or certification mark is deceptive, or if its use is otherwise in violation of public policy, or if the owner of the designation has engaged in other substantial misconduct directly related to the owner's assertion of rights in the trademark, trade name, collective mark, or certification mark, the owner may be barred in part or whole from the relief that would otherwise be available. . . .

RESTATEMENT (THIRD) OF UNFAIR COMPETITION § 32.

The Supreme Court has explained that "[a]ny willful act concerning the cause of action which rightfully can be said to transgress equitable standards of conduct is sufficient cause for the invocation of the maxim." *Precision Instrument Mfg. Co. v. Automotive Maintenance Mach. Co.*, 324 U.S. 806, 815 (1945). There are, however, limits on the kind of conduct that can be labeled "unclean hands." The Third Circuit held that the conduct at issue must rise to the level of "egregious" misconduct: "Because a central concern in an unfair competition case is protection of the public from confusion, courts require clear, convincing evidence of 'egregious' misconduct before invoking the doctrine of unclean hands." *Citizens Financial Group, Inc. v. Citizens Nat. Bank of Evans City*, 383 F.3d 110, 129 (3d Cir. 2004). The Ninth Circuit has taken a similar position. It requires a balancing approach that weighs the plaintiff's conduct against the defendant's wrongs and the potential injury to the public resulting from the defendant's use of the mark:

> In the interests of right and justice the court should not automatically condone the defendant's infractions because the plaintiff is also blameworthy, thereby leaving the two wrongs unremedied and increasing the injury to the public. . . .

The relative extent of each party's wrong upon the other and upon the public should be taken into account and an equitable balance struck.

Republic Molding Corp. v. B.W. Photo Utilities, 319 F.2d 347, 350 (9th Cir. 1963).

a.   *Fraud in Obtaining Trademark Registration*

Fraud in the procurement of a federal trademark registration can serve as an affirmative defense to a charge of infringement of a registered mark (even if the registration has become incontestable. A party raising the defense generally must demonstrate that the registrant has: (1) knowingly made false statements or submissions to the PTO, and (2) that the registration would not have issued but for the false statements or submissions. Fraud is treated as a "disfavored defense." *Aveda Corp. v. Evita Marketing, Inc.*, 706 F. Supp. 1419, 1425 (D. Minn. 1989). Indeed, the Seventh Circuit has stated that:

> Fraud must be shown by *clear and convincing evidence* in order to provide a basis for either cancellation or damages. . . . Fraud will be deemed to exist only when there is a deliberate attempt to mislead the Patent [and Trademark] Office into registering the mark.

Money Store v. Harriscorp Finance, Inc., 689 F.2d 666, 670 (7th Cir. 1982) (emphasis added).

While fraudulent registration can defeat a claim of trademark infringement or a registered mark, the trademark owner is still free to sue for infringement under state law and under § 43(a) of the Lanham Act. *See Aveda Corp.*, 706 F. Supp. at 1425 ("Trademarks are created by use, not registration. Federal registration creates valuable substantive and procedural rights, but the com-mon law creates the underlying right to exclude. Thus, even if a plaintiff's registration is shown to be fraudulently obtained, the plaintiff's common law rights in the mark may still support an injunction against an infringing defendant."). The Lanham Act provides a separate civil cause of action available to anyone injured by another's fraudulent procurement of federal trade-mark registration. *See* Lanham Act § 38, 15 U.S.C. § 1120.

b.   *Trademark Misuse*

Early cases held that a plaintiff's alleged anticompetitive activity was no defense to a claim of trademark infringement. Later cases, however, have entertained the defense. *See, e.g., Forstmann Woolen Co. v. Murray Sices Corp.*, 10 F.R.D. 367 (D.N.Y. 1950); *Sanitized, Inc. v. S. C. Johnson & Sons, Inc.*, 23 F.R.D. 230 (S.D.N.Y. 1959); *Phi Delta Theta Fraternity v. J. A. Buchroeder & Co.*, 251 F. Supp. 968 (W.D. Mo. 1966); *Electrical Information Publications, Inc. v. C-M Periodicals, Inc.*, 163 U.S.P.Q. 624 (N.D. Ill. 1969); *Estee Lauder, Inc. v. Fragrance Counter, Inc.*, 189 F.R.D. 269 (S.D.N.Y. 1999).

Courts generally require that the defendant demonstrate not only that a trademark owner committed an antitrust violation, but also that the trade-mark itself was used to accomplish the violation. In the Zeiss case, which Thomas McCarthy has called "the most carefully reasoned case on the issue," MCCARTHY § 31:91, Judge Mansfield explained:

> Since denial of a plaintiff's exclusive right to the use of his trademark is not essential to the restoration of competition, it is not enough merely to prove that merchandise bearing a trademark, however valuable the trade-mark, has been used in furtherance of antitrust violations. If this is all that were required, any antitrust violation in the distribution of such merchandise would result in a forfeiture of the trademark with a consequent unnecessary frustration of the policy underlying trademark enforcement. An essential element of the antitrust misuse defense in a trademark case is proof that the mark itself has been the basic and fundamental vehicle required and used to accomplish the violation.

Carl Zeiss Stiftung v. VEB Carl Zeiss, Jena, 298 F. Supp. 1309, 1315 (S.D.N.Y. 1969), *modified*, 433 F.2d 6862d Cir. 1970).

The trademark misuse defense is rarely successful.

F.   REMEDIES

1.   Injunctions

Herb Reed Enterprises, LLC v. Florida Entertainment Management, Inc.
United States Court of Appeals for the Ninth Circuit
763 F.3d 1239 (9th Cir. 2013)

MCKEOWN, Circuit Judge:

"The Platters"—the legendary name of one of the most successful vocal performing groups of the 1950s—lives on. With 40 singles on the Billboard Hot 100 List, the names of The Platters' hits ironically foreshadowed decades of litigation—"Great Pretender," "Smoke Gets In Your Eyes," "Only You," and "To Each His Own." Larry Marshak and his company Florida Entertainment Management, Inc. (collectively "Marshak") challenge the district court's preliminary injunction in favor of Herb Reed Enterprises ("HRE"), enjoining Marshak from using the "The Platters" mark in connection with any vocal group with narrow exceptions. We consider an issue of first impression in our circuit: whether the likelihood of irreparable harm must be established—rather than presumed, as under prior Ninth Circuit precedent—by a plaintiff seeking injunctive relief in the trademark context. In light of Supreme Court precedent, the answer is yes, and we reverse the district court's order granting the preliminary injunction.

Background

The Platters vocal group was formed in 1953, with Herb Reed as one of its founders. Paul Robi, David Lynch, Zola Taylor, and Tony Williams, though not founders, have come to be recognized as the other "original" band members. The group became a "global sensation" during the latter half of the 1950s, then broke up in the 1960s as the original members left one by one. After the break up, each member continued to perform under some derivation of the name "The Platters."

Litigation has been the byproduct of the band's dissolution; there have been multiple legal disputes among the original members and their current and former managers over ownership of "The Platters" mark. . . .

Last year brought yet another lawsuit. HRE commenced the present litigation in 2012 against Marshak in the District of Nevada, alleging trademark infringement and seeking a preliminary injunction against Marshak's continued use of "The Platters" mark. . . . The district court found that HRE had established a likelihood of success on the merits, a likelihood of irreparable harm, a balance of hardships in its favor, and that a preliminary injunction would serve public interest. Accordingly, the district court granted the preliminary injunction . . . .

III. Preliminary Injunction

To obtain a preliminary injunction, HRE "must establish that [it] is likely to succeed on the merits, that [it] is likely to suffer irreparable harm in the absence of preliminary relief, that the balance of equities tips in [its] favor, and that an injunction is in the public interest." *Winter v. Natural Res. Def. Council, Inc.*, 555 U.S. 7, 20 (2008). . . .

B. Likelihood of Irreparable Harm

. . . As the district court acknowledged, two recent Supreme Court cases have cast doubt on the validity of this court's previous rule that the likelihood of "irreparable injury may be *presumed* from a showing of likelihood of success on the merits of a trademark infringement claim." *Brookfield Commc'ns, Inc. v. W. Coast Entm't Corp.*, 174 F.3d 1036, 1066 (9th Cir. 1999) (emphasis added). Since *Brookfield*, the landscape for benchmarking irreparable harm has changed with the Supreme Court's decisions in *eBay Inc. v. MercExchange, L.L.C.*, 547 U.S. 388, in 2006, and *Winter* in 2008.

In *eBay*, the Court held that the traditional four-factor test employed by courts of equity, including the requirement that the plaintiff must establish irreparable injury in seeking a permanent injunction, applies in the patent context. 547 U.S. at 391. Likening injunctions in patent cases to injunctions under the Copyright Act, the Court explained that it "has consistently rejected . . . a rule that an injunction automatically follows a determination that a copyright has been infringed," and emphasized that a departure from the traditional principles of equity "should not be lightly implied." *Id.* at 391–93 (citations omitted). The same principle applies to trademark infringement under the Lanham Act. Just as "[n]othing in the Patent Act indicates that Congress intended such a departure," so too nothing in the Lanham Act indicates that Congress intended a departure for trademark infringement cases. *Id.* at 391–92. Both statutes provide that injunctions may be granted in accordance with "the principles of equity." 35 U.S.C. § 283; 15 U.S.C. § 1116(a).

In *Winter*, the Court underscored the requirement that the plaintiff seeking a preliminary injunction "demonstrate that irreparable injury is *likely* in the absence of an injunction." 555 U.S. at 22 (emphasis in original) (citations omitted). The Court reversed a preliminary injunction because it was based only on a "possibility" of irreparable harm, a standard that is "too lenient." *Id. Winter*'s admonition that irreparable harm must be shown to be likely in the absence of a preliminary injunction also forecloses the presumption of irreparable harm here.

Following *eBay* and *Winter,* we held that likely irreparable harm must be demonstrated to obtain a preliminary injunction in a copyright infringement case and that actual irreparable harm must be demonstrated to obtain a permanent injunction in a trademark infringement action. *Flexible Lifeline Sys. v. Precision Lift, Inc.,* 654 F.3d 989, 998 (9th Cir. 2011); *Reno Air Racing Ass'n, Inc., v. McCord,* 452 F.3d 1126, 1137–38 (9th Cir. 2006). Our imposition of the irreparable harm requirement for a permanent injunction in a trademark case applies with equal force in the preliminary injunction context. *Amoco Prod. Co. v. Village of Gambell, AK,* 480 U.S. 531, 546 n. 12 (1987) (explaining that the standard for a preliminary injunction is essentially the same as for a permanent injunction except that "likelihood of" is replaced with "actual"). We now join other circuits in holding that the *eBay* principle—that a plaintiff must establish irreparable harm—applies to a preliminary injunction in a trademark infringement case. *See N. Am. Med. Corp. v. Axiom Worldwide, Inc.,* 522 F.3d 1211, 1228–29 (11th Cir. 2008); *Audi AG v. D'Amato,* 469 F.3d 534, 550 (6th Cir. 2006) (applying the requirement to a permanent injunction in a trademark infringement action).

Having anticipated that the Supreme Court's decisions in *eBay* and *Winter* signaled a shift away from the presumption of irreparable harm, the district court examined irreparable harm in its own right, explaining that HRE must "establish that remedies available at law, such as monetary damages, are inadequate to compensate" for the injury arising from Marshak's continuing allegedly infringing use of the mark. *Herb Reed Enters., LLC v. Fla. Entm't Mgmt., Inc.,* No. 2:12–cv–00560–MMD–GWF, 2012 WL 3020039, at *15 (D.Nev. Jul. 24, 2012). Although the district court identified the correct legal principle, we conclude that the record does not support a determination of the likelihood of irreparable harm.

Marshak asserts that the district court abused its discretion by relying on "unsupported and conclusory statements regarding harm [HRE] *might* suffer." We agree.

The district court's analysis of irreparable harm is cursory and conclusory, rather than being grounded in any evidence or showing offered by HRE. To begin, the court noted that it "cannot condone trademark infringement simply because it has been occurring for a long time and may continue to occur." The court went on to note that to do so "could encourage wide-scale infringement on the part of persons hoping to tread on the goodwill and fame of vintage music groups." Fair enough. Evidence of loss of control over business reputation and damage to goodwill could constitute irreparable harm. *See, e.g., Stuhlbarg Int'l Sales Co., Inc. v. John D. Brush and Co., Inc.,* 240 F.3d 832, 841 (9th Cir. 2001) (holding that evidence of loss of customer goodwill supports finding of irreparable harm). Here, however, the court's pronouncements are grounded in platitudes rather than evidence, and relate neither to whether "irreparable injury is *likely* in the absence of an injunction," *Winter,* 555 U.S. at 22, nor to whether legal remedies, such as money damages, are inadequate in this case. It may be that HRE could establish the likelihood of irreparable harm. But missing from this record is any such evidence.

In concluding its analysis, the district court simply cited to another district court case in Nevada "with a substantially similar claim" in which the court found that "the harm to Reed's reputation caused by a different unauthorized Platters group warranted a preliminary injunction." *HRE*, 2012 WL 3020039, at *15–16. As with its speculation on future harm, citation to a different case with a different record does not meet the standard of showing "likely" irreparable harm.

Even if we comb the record for support or inferences of irreparable harm, the strongest evidence, albeit evidence not cited by the district court, is an email from a potential customer complaining to Marshak's booking agent that the customer wanted Herb Reed's band rather than another tribute band. This evidence, however, simply underscores customer confusion, not irreparable harm.

The practical effect of the district court's conclusions, which included no factual findings, is to reinsert the now-rejected presumption of irreparable harm based solely on a strong case of trademark infringement. Gone are the days when "[o]nce the plaintiff in an infringement action has established a likelihood of confusion, it is ordinarily presumed that the plaintiff will suffer irreparable harm if injunctive relief does not issue." *Rodeo Collection, Ltd. v. W. Seventh*, 812 F.2d 1215, 1220 (9th Cir. 1987) (citing *Apple Computer, Inc. v. Formula International Inc.*, 725 F.2d 521, 526 (9th Cir. 1984)). This approach collapses the likelihood of success and the irreparable harm factors. Those seeking injunctive relief must proffer evidence sufficient to establish a likelihood of irreparable harm. As in *Flexible Lifeline*, 654 F.3d at 1000, the fact that the "district court made no factual findings that would support a likelihood of irreparable harm," while not necessarily establishing a lack of irreparable harm, leads us to reverse the preliminary injunction and remand to the district court.

In light of our determination that the record fails to support a finding of likely irreparable harm, we need not address the balance of equities and public interest factors.

REVERSED and REMANDED.

COMMENTS AND QUESTIONS

1. Like patent law and much of copyright law, trademark remedies have traditionally been organized around a property rule. This means that infringers have no "right" to use the trademark upon payment of damages; trademark owners were historically entitled to injunctions against infringement as a matter of course.

The application of a property rule makes sense in the trademark context because trademarks serve to protect a unique good—the plaintiff's business goodwill. Infringers who trade on or dilute (and thus appropriate or destroy) a plaintiff's goodwill cannot simply "buy back" that goodwill with money. Once it is dissipated, it is gone forever. Nor can consumers easily be "unconfused" once they are misled with counterfeit marks.

Trademark law, however, is not a typical property right. Owners of real property are entitled to sell it to whomever they wish. They may also let other people rent it for a fee. Trademark owners have no such unfettered rights to sell or license their trademarks. Both the sale and the licensing of trademarks are subject to significant legal restrictions. *See* Chapter V(E)(1). Having given trademark owners a property right to enable them to protect their goodwill, the government appears unwilling to allow trademark owners to do what they see fit with that right. Instead, restrictions on alienation of trademarks are designed to make sure that the trademark is in fact used to promote the goodwill of the associated business.

At the same time, the consumer stake in avoiding confusion means that the public interest will weigh more heavily in favor of injunctive relief in trademark cases than in other kinds of IP cases. Consumers, after all, don't benefit from damage awards to trademark plaintiffs, and it would seem odd for a court to conclude that the defendant was confusing consumers, but permit it to continue doing so. For an argument that courts should be more willing to grant injunctions in trademark than in patent or copyright cases, see Mark A. Lemley, *Did eBay Irreparably Injure Trademark Law?*, 92 NOTRE DAME L. REV. 1795 (2017).

2. The Supreme Court ruled in *eBay, Inc. v. MercExchange LLC*, 547 U.S. 388 (2006), that injunctions in patent cases were not available as a matter of course, but depended on the plaintiff satisfying a multi-factor equitable test focused on injury to the plaintiff and the public interest. Is *Herb Reed* right that the same rule should apply to trademark law, or is the interest of the public in avoiding deception sufficient to justify an injunction whether or not competitors have been irreparably injured? Most courts to consider the issue have concluded that *eBay* applies with full force to trademark cases. *See, e.g., Herb Reed Ents. v. Florida Ent. Mgm't*, 736 F.3d 1239 (9th Cir. 2013); *Voice of the Arab World, Inc. v. MDTV Medical News Now, Inc.*, 645 F.3d 26 (1st Cir. 2011); *North Am. Med. Corp. v. Axiom Worldwide*, 522 F.3d 1211 (11th Cir. 2008).

3. *eBay* made clear that its four factors were to be applied on a case-by-case basis, and that there were no categorical rules for deciding when to grant an injunction. Did *Herb Reed* faithfully follow that rule? Or did it create a new categorical rule, requiring proof of actual irreparable harm in every case? In *adidas Am. v. Skechers USA*, 890 F.3d 747 (9th Cir. 2018), the court held that Skechers infringed adidas's famous three-stripe mark on running shoes, but nonetheless reversed the grant of a preliminary injunction, concluding that post-sale confusion did not irreparably injure a trademark owner merely because the brand owner lost control over the use of its mark. While adidas argued that Skechers shoes were of lower quality, there was no way a third party could tell that merely by seeing other people wearing the shoes. But the court distinguished luxury goods for which the brand owner has created artificial scarcity. Judge Clifton, dissenting, would have limited *Herb Reed* to its facts. He cited the Third Circuit in distinguishing *Herb Reed*: "Although we no longer apply a presumption [of irreparable injury], the logic underlying the presumption can, and does, inform how we exercise

our equitable discretion . . ." *Groupe SEB USA v. Euro-Pro Operating LLC*, 774 F.3d 192, 205 n.8 (3d Cir. 2014).

2. Damages

i. *Infringer's Gain and Mark Owner's Loss*

While injunctions are the fundamental Lanham Act remedy, they are not the only one. Damages are also sometimes available in trademark infringement cases. Section 35(a) of the Lanham Act, 15 U.S.C. § 1117(a), provides that plaintiffs are entitled:

> to recover (1) defendant's profits, (2) any damages sustained by the plaintiff, and (3) the costs of the action. . . . In assessing profits the plaintiff shall be required to prove defendant's sales only; defendant must prove all elements of cost or deduction claimed. In assessing damages the court may enter judgment . . . for any sum above the amount found as actual damages, not exceeding three times such amount.

But damages play a much less significant role in trademark cases than in other areas of IP. *See* Lex Machina, TRADEMARK LITIGATION REPORT 2017 (finding that only 28% of plaintiff wins resulted in a damage award and that most of those were default judgments). .

ROMAG FASTENERS, INC. *v.* FOSSIL GROUP, INC..
United States Supreme Court
__ S.Ct. __ (2020)

JUSTICE GORSUCH delivered the opinion of the Court.

When it comes to remedies for trademark infringement, the Lanham Act authorizes many. A district court may award a winning plaintiff injunctive relief, damages, or the defendant's ill-gotten profits. Without question, a defendant's state of mind may have a bearing on what relief a plaintiff should receive. An innocent trademark violator often stands in very different shoes than an intentional one. But some circuits have gone further. These courts hold a plaintiff can win a profits remedy, in particular, only after showing the defendant *willfully* infringed its trademark. The question before us is whether that categorical rule can be reconciled with the statute's plain language.

The question comes to us in a case involving handbag fasteners. Romag sells magnetic snap fasteners for use in leather goods. Fossil designs, markets, and distributes a wide range of fashion accessories. Years ago, the pair signed an agreement allowing Fossil to use Romag's fasteners in Fossil's handbags and other products. Initially, both sides seemed content with the arrangement. But in time Romag discovered that the factories Fossil hired in China to make its products were using counterfeit Romag fasteners—and that Fossil was doing little to guard against the practice. Unable to resolve its concerns amicably, Romag sued. The company alleged that Fossil had infringed its trademark and falsely represented that its fasteners came from Romag. After trial, a jury agreed with Romag, and found that Fossil had acted "in callous disregard" of Romag's rights. At the same time, however, the jury rejected Romag's accusation that Fossil had acted willfully, as that term was defined by the district court.

For our purposes, the last finding is the important one. By way of relief for Fossil's trademark violation, Romag sought (among other things) an order requiring Fossil to hand over the profits it had earned thanks to its trademark violation. But the district court refused this request. The court pointed out that controlling Second Circuit precedent requires a plaintiff seeking a profits award to prove that the defendant's violation was willful. Not all circuits, however, agree with the Second Circuit's rule. We took this case to resolve that dispute over the law's demands.

Where does Fossil's proposed willfulness rule come from? The relevant section of the Lanham Act governing remedies for trademark violations, §35, 60Stat. 439–440, as amended, 15 U. S. C. §1117(a), says this:

> "When a violation of any right of the registrant of a mark registered in the Patent and Trademark Office, a violation under section 1125(a) or (d) of this title, or a willful violation under section 1125(c) of this title, shall have been established . . . , the plaintiff shall be entitled, subject to the provisions of sections 1111 and 1114 of this title, and subject to the principles of equity, to recover (1) defendant's profits, (2) any damages sustained by the plaintiff, and (3) the costs of the action."

Immediately, this language spells trouble for Fossil and the circuit precedent on which it relies. The statute does make a showing of willfulness a precondition to a profits award when the plaintiff proceeds under §1125(c). That section, added to the Lanham Act some years after its initial adoption, creates a cause of action for trademark dilution—conduct that lessens the association consumers have with a trademark. But Romag alleged and proved a violation of §1125(a), a provision establishing a cause of action for the false or misleading use of trademarks. And in cases like that, the statutory language has *never* required a showing of willfulness to win a defendant's profits. . . . Nor does this Court usually read into statutes words that aren't there. It's a temptation we are doubly careful to avoid when Congress has (as here) included the term in question elsewhere in the very same statutory provision.

A wider look at the statute's structure gives us even more reason for pause. The Lanham Act speaks often and expressly about mental states. Section 1117(b) requires courts to treble profits or damages and award attorney's fees when a defendant engages in certain acts *intentionally* and with specified *knowledge*. Section 1117(c) increases the cap on statutory damages from $200,000 to $2,000,000 for certain *willful* violations. Section 1118 permits courts to order the infringing items be destroyed if a plaintiff proves any violation of §1125(a) or a *willful* violation of §1125(c). Section 1114 makes certain *innocent* infringers subject only to injunctions. Elsewhere, the statute specifies certain *mens rea* standards needed to establish liability, before even getting to the question of remedies. See, *e.g.,* §§1125(d)(1)(A)(i), (B)(i) (prohibiting certain conduct only if undertaken with "bad faith intent" and listing nine factors relevant to ascertaining bad faith intent). Without doubt, the Lanham Act exhibits considerable care with *mens rea* standards. The absence of any such standard in the provision before us, thus, seems all the more telling.

So how exactly does Fossil seek to conjure a willfulness requirement out of §1117(a)? Lacking any more obvious statutory hook, the company points to the language indicating that a violation under §1125(a) can trigger an award of the defendant's profits "subject to the principles of equity." In Fossil's telling, equity courts historically required a showing of willfulness before authorizing a profits remedy in trademark disputes. Admittedly, equity courts didn't require so much in patent infringement cases and other arguably analogous suits. See, *e.g., Dowagiac Mfg. Co.* v. *Minnesota Moline Plow Co.,* 235 U.S. 641, 644, 650–651 (1915). But, Fossil says, trademark is different. There alone, a willfulness requirement was so long and universally recognized that today it rises to the level of a "principle of equity" the Lanham Act carries forward.

It's a curious suggestion. Fossil's contention that the term "principles of equity" includes a willfulness requirement would not directly contradict the statute's other, express *mens rea* provisions or render them wholly superfluous. But it would require us to assume that Congress intended to incorporate a willfulness requirement here obliquely while it prescribed *mens rea* conditions expressly elsewhere throughout the Lanham Act. That might be possible, but on first blush it isn't exactly an obvious construction of the statute.

Nor do matters improve with a second look. The phrase "principles of equity" doesn't readily bring to mind a substantive rule about *mens rea* from a discrete domain like trademark law. In the context of this statute, it more naturally suggests fundamental rules that apply more systematically across claims and practice areas. A principle is a "fundamental truth or doctrine, as of law; a comprehensive rule or doctrine which furnishes a basis or origin for others." BLACK'S LAW DICTIONARY 1417 (3d ed. 1933); Black's Law Dictionary 1357 (4th ed. 1951). And treatises and handbooks on the "principles of equity" generally contain transsubstantive guidance on broad and fundamental questions about matters like parties, modes of proof, defenses, and remedies. See, *e.g.,* E. MERWIN, PRINCIPLES OF EQUITY AND EQUITY PLEADING (1895); J. INDERMAUR & C. THWAITES, MANUAL OF THE PRINCIPLES OF EQUITY (7th ed. 1913); H. SMITH, PRACTICAL EXPOSITION OF THE PRINCIPLES OF EQUITY (5th ed. 1914); R. MEGARRY, SNELL'S PRINCIPLES OF EQUITY (23d ed. 1947). Our precedent, too, has used the term "principles of equity" to refer to just such transsubstantive topics. See, *e.g., eBay Inc.* v. *MercExchange, L. L. C.,* 547 U.S. 388, 391, 393 (2006); *Holmberg* v. *Armbrecht,* 327 U.S. 392, 395 (1946). Congress itself has elsewhere used "equitable principles" in just this way: An amendment to a different section of the Lanham Act lists "laches, estoppel, and acquiescence" as examples of "equitable principles." 15 U. S. C.

§1069. Given all this, it seems a little unlikely Congress meant "principles of equity" to direct us to a narrow rule about a profits remedy within trademark law.

But even if we were to spot Fossil that first essential premise of its argument, the next has problems too. From the record the parties have put before us, it's far from clear whether trademark law historically required a showing of willfulness before allowing a profits remedy. The Trademark Act of 1905—the Lanham Act's statutory predecessor which many earlier cases interpreted and applied—did not mention such a requirement. It's true, as Fossil notes, that some courts proceeding before the 1905 Act, and even some later cases following that Act, did treat willfulness or something like it as a pre-requisite for a profits award and rarely authorized profits for purely good-faith infringement. See, *e.g., Horlick's Malted Milk Corp.* v. *Horluck's, Inc.*, 51 F.2d 357, 359 (WD Wash. 1931) (explaining that the plaintiff "cannot recover defendant's profits unless it has been shown beyond a reasonable doubt that defendant was guilty of willful fraud in the use of the enjoined trade-name"); see also *Saxlehner* v. *Siegel-Cooper Co.*, 179 U.S. 42, 42–43 (1900) (holding that one defendant "should not be required to account for gains and profits" when it "appear[ed] to have acted in good faith"). But Romag cites other cases that expressly rejected any such rule. See, *e.g., Oakes* v. *Tonsmierre*, 49 F. 447, 453 (CC SD Ala. 1883); see also *Stonebraker* v. *Stonebraker*, 33 Md. 252, 268 (1870); *Lawrence-Williams Co.* v. *Societe Enfants Gombault et Cie*, 52 F.2d 774, 778 (CA6 1931). . . .

At the end of it all, the most we can say with certainty is this. *Mens rea* figured as an important consideration in awarding profits in pre-Lanham Act cases. This reflects the ordinary, transsubstantive principle that a defendant's mental state is relevant to assigning an appropriate remedy. That principle arises not only in equity, but across many legal contexts. See, *e.g., Smith* v. *Wade*, 461 U.S. 30, 38–51 (1983) (42 U. S. C. §1983); *Morissette* v. *United States*, 342 U.S. 246, 250–263 (1952) (criminal law); *Wooden-Ware Co.* v. *United States*, 106 U.S. 432, 434–435 (1882) (common law trespass). It's a principle reflected in the Lanham Act's text, too, which permits greater statutory damages for certain willful violations than for other violations. 15 U. S. C. §1117(c). And it is a principle long reflected in equity practice where district courts have often considered a defendant's mental state, among other factors, when exercising their discretion in choosing a fitting remedy. See, *e.g., L. P. Larson, Jr., Co.* v. *Wm. Wrigley, Jr., Co.*, 277 U.S. 97, 99–100 (1928); *Lander* v. *Lujan*, 888 F.2d 153, 155–156 (CADC 1989); *United States* v. *Klimek*, 952 F. Supp. 1100, 1117 (ED Pa. 1997). Given these traditional principles, we do not doubt that a trademark defendant's mental state is a highly important consideration in determining whether an award of profits is appropriate. But acknowledging that much is a far cry from insisting on the inflexible precondition to recovery Fossil advances.. . .

JUSTICE SOTOMAYOR, concurring in the judgment.

I agree that 15 U. S. C. §1117(a) does not impose a "willfulness" prerequisite for awarding profits in trademark infringement actions. Courts of equity, however, defined "willfulness" to encompass a range of culpable mental states—including the equivalent of recklessness, but excluding "good faith" or negligence. See 5 McCarthy on Trade-marks and Unfair Competition §30:62 (5th ed. 2019) (explaining that "willfulness" ranged from fraudulent and knowing to reckless and indifferent behavior); see also, *e.g., Lawrence-Williams Co.* v. *Societe Enfants Gombault et Cie*, 52 F.2d 774, 778 (CA6 1931); *Regis* v. *Jaynes*, 191 Mass. 245, 248–249, 77 N.E. 774, 776 (1906).

The majority suggests that courts of equity were just as likely to award profits for such "willful" infringement as they were for "innocent" infringement. But that does not reflect the weight of authority, which indicates that profits were hardly, if ever, awarded for innocent infringement. See, *e.g., Wood* v. *Peffer*, 55 Cal. App. 2d 116, 125 (1942) (explaining that "equity constantly refuses, for want of fraudulent intent, the prayer for an accounting of profits"); *Globe-Wernicke Co.* v. *Safe-Cabinet Co.*, 110 Ohio St. 609, 617, 144 N.E. 711, 713 (1924) ("By the great weight of authority, particularly where the infringement . . . was deliberate and willful, it is held that the wrongdoer is required to account for all profits realized by him as a result of his wrongful acts"); *Dickey* v. *Mutual Film Corp.*, 186 App. Div. 701, 702, 174 N.Y.S. 784 (1919) (declining to award profits because there was "no proof of any fraudulent intent upon the part of the defendant"); *Standard Cigar Co.* v. *Goldsmith*, 58 Pa. Super. 33, 37 (1914) (reasoning that a defendant "should be compelled to account for . . . profits" where "the infringement complained of was not the result of mistake or ignorance of the plaintiff 's right"). Nor would doing so seem to be consistent with longstanding equitable principles which, after all, seek to deprive only wrongdoers of their gains from misconduct. Cf. *Duplate Corp.* v. *Triplex Safety Glass Co.*, 298 U.S. 448, 456–457 (1936). Thus, a district court's award of profits for innocent or good-faith trademark infringement would not be consonant with the "principles of equity" referenced in §1117(a) and reflected in the cases the majority cites.

Because the majority is agnostic about awarding profits for both "willful" and innocent infringement as those terms have been understood, I concur in the judgment only.

Justice Alito, with whom Justice Breyer and Justice Kagan join, concurring.

We took this case to decide whether willful infringement is a prerequisite to an award of profits under 15 U. S. C. §1117(a). The decision below held that willfulness is such a prerequisite. That is incorrect. The relevant authorities, particularly pre-Lanham Act case law, show that willfulness is a highly important consideration in awarding profits under §1117(a), but not an absolute precondition. I would so hold and concur on that ground.

COMMENTS AND QUESTIONS

1. *History of Equitable Remedies.* Justice Sotomayor correctly characterizes the history of equitable remedies. For many years, courts unanimously followed the holding in *Champion Spark Plug* v. *Sanders*, 331 U.S. 125, 130–31 (1947), that an accounting is appropriate only when fraud or palming off is present, and that courts would grant an accounting of defendant's profits only if the defendant acted in bad faith. See *Western Diversified Servs.* v. *Hyundai Motor Am., Inc.*, 427 F.3d 1269 (10th Cir. 2005). The

three cases that the majority cites for the proposition that willfulness need not be proved to obtain disgorgement of the defendant's profits are more that 90 years old. *See,* Pamela Samuelson, John M. Golden, & Mark P. Gergen, *Recalibrating Disgorgement Awards in Intellectual Property Cases*, B.U. L. REV. (forthcoming 2021).

Nor is the majority correct that this is an aberration in trademark law. To the contrary, the equitable remedy of disgorgement of defendant's gains (as opposed to recovering plaintiff's own losses) has traditionally been limited to "conscious wrongdoers." *See* DAN B. DOBBS & CAPRICE L. ROBERTS, LAW OF REMEDIES 420 (3d ed. 2018) ("Serious and conscious wrongdoing should be required to justify a recovery of defendant's profits except when a different rule is imposed by statute."); DOUGLAS LAYCOCK, MODERN AMERICAN REMEDIES (5th ed. 2018). The theory is straightforward: requiring the defendant to pay more than the plaintiff lost makes sense only if the goal is to punish or deter the defendants by depriving them of their ill-gotten gains. Remedies jurisprudence has traditionally reserved such penalties for intentional acts. *See Mishawaka Rubber & Woolen Mfg. Co. v. S. S. Kresge Co.*, 316 U.S. 203, 206–07 (1942) (explaining that "[t]here may well be a windfall to the trade-mark owner where it is impossible to isolate the profits which are attributable to the use of the infringing mark. But to hold otherwise would give the windfall to the wrongdoer"). Perhaps *Romag* means that is no longer true, but if so, the Court has fundamentally rewritten longstanding remedies law.

2. *Statutory Drafting Accident.* Trademark law has long allowed the award of monetary relief "subject to principles of equity." 15 U.S.C. §1117(a). When Congress added the dilution law in 1996, though, it chose not to allow dilution plaintiffs *any* monetary relief, legal or equitable, unless the defendant acted willfully. But because Congress put the dilution remedies in the same section as the trademark infringement remedies, the section expressly says willfulness is required for dilution but is silent on willfulness for trademark infringement. The majority reads that addition as making a strong case that willfulness is no longer required. Does it? Should it matter that Congress clearly did not intend to change the longstanding rules of trademark infringement remedies? Note there is a perfectly reasonable way to read the statute to preserve that result: willfulness is required for *any* monetary relief under the dilution statute, but not for trademark infringement; trademark infringement allows the plaintiff to recover its losses, but permits disgorgement of defendant's gains only "subject to principles of equity."

3. The practical effect of *Romag* may be less dramatic than it seems. While the Court eliminates the requirement of willfulness, it says that "we do not doubt that a trademark defendant's mental state is a highly important consideration in determining whether an award of profits is appropriate." And the four concurring Justices seem to sign on only to that result, leaving willfulness, if not an absolute requirement, an important factor in disgorging profits. That may give cover to courts that do not want to upend longstanding remedies law.

4. Is an accounting for profits ever possible in a dilution case? If so, why? If the plaintiff is compensated for her losses caused by the dilution, does it make any sense to

take away the defendant's profits in an unrelated market as well? 15 U.S.C. § 1125(c) makes damages available in dilution cases only upon a showing of willful infringement.

5. Who should bear the burden of proof in determining profits? *See also Experience Hendrix L.L.C. v. Hendrixlicensing.com Ltd*, 762 F.3d 829, 843 (9th Cir. 2014) (holding that the trademark owner has burden of establishing both its lost profits and its expenses; but when infringer's profits are at issue, plaintiff need only show defendant's revenue, after which burden of proving expenses shifts to defendant).

Suppose that a defendant has established significant goodwill of its own between the time it adopted a mark and the time it is found to have infringed. If the plaintiff is entitled to an injunction, does the defendant have any way of recovering the value of its investment in goodwill? Is it at least entitled to a setoff against damages for its monetary losses as a result of the injunction? Does it matter if the case is a dilution case and the defendant is in a separate market?

6. The combination of *Herb Reed* and the fact that damages are hard to prove means that in some cases courts will find consumer confusion but award neither damages nor an injunction. Does that seem fair? What should happen in such a case?

ii. *Corrective Advertising*

Big O Tire Dealers, Inc. v. The Goodyear Tire & Rubber Company
United States Court of Appeals for the Tenth Circuit
561 F.2d 1365 (10th Cir. 1977)

LEWIS, Chief Judge.

This civil action was brought by Big O Tire Dealers, Inc. ("Big O") asserting claims of unfair competition against The Goodyear Tire & Rubber Co. ("Goodyear") based upon false designation of origin under 15 U.S.C. § 1125(a) and common law trademark infringement. After a ten-day trial and three days of deliberation, the jury returned the following verdict:

> We the jury in the above entitled cause, upon our oath do say that we find the following as our verdict herein:
>
> Upon the claim of liability for trademark infringement we find for Big O Inc.
>
> Upon the claim of liability for false designation of origin we find for Goodyear.
>
> Upon the claim for trademark disparagement we find for Big O Inc.
>
> We find that plaintiff has proven special compensatory damages in the amount of $None.
>
> We find that plaintiff has proven general compensatory damages in the amount of $2,800,000.
>
> We assess punitive or exemplary damages in the amount of $16,800,000.
>
> Dated September 4, 1975.

Filing a comprehensive post-trial opinion the United States District Court for the District of Colorado entered judgment on the jury's verdict, permanently enjoined Goodyear from infringing on Big O's trademark, and dismissed Goodyear's counter-claim for equitable relief. 408 F. Supp. 1219. Goodyear appeals that judgment.

Big O is a tire-buying organization which provides merchandising techniques, advertising concepts, operating systems, and other aids to approximately 200 independent retail tire dealers in 14 states who identify themselves to the public as Big O dealers. These dealers sell replacement tires using the Big O label on "private brand" tires. They also sell other companies' brands such as B.F. Goodrich and Michelin Tires. At the time of trial Big O's total net worth was approximately $200,000.

Goodyear is the world's largest tire manufacturer. In 1974 Goodyear's net sales totaled more than $5.25 billion and its net income after taxes surpassed $157 million. In the replacement market Goodyear sells through a nationwide network of company-owned stores, franchise dealers, and independent retailers.

In the fall of 1973 Big O decided to identify two of its lines of private brand tires as "Big O Big Foot 60" and "Big O Big Foot 70." These names were placed on the sidewall of the respective tires in raised white letters. The first interstate shipment of these tires occurred in February 1974. Big O dealers began selling these tires to the public in April 1974. Big O did not succeed in registering "Big Foot" as a trademark with the United States Patent and Trademark Office. . . .

In July 1974 Goodyear decided to use the term "Bigfoot" in a nationwide advertising campaign to promote the sale of its new "Custom Polysteel Radial" tire. The name "Custom Polysteel Radial" was molded into the tire's sidewall. Goodyear employed a trademark search firm to conduct a search for "Bigfoot" in connection with tires and related products. This search did not uncover any conflicting trademarks. After this suit was filed Goodyear filed an application to register "Bigfoot" as a trademark for tires but withdrew it in 1975. Goodyear planned to launch its massive, nationwide "Bigfoot" advertising campaign on September 16, 1974.

On August 24, 1974, Goodyear first learned of Big O's "Big Foot" tires. Goodyear informed Big O's president, Norman Affleck, on August 26 of Goodyear's impending "Bigfoot" advertising campaign. Affleck was asked to give Goodyear a letter indicating Big O had no objection to this use of "Bigfoot." When Affleck replied he could not make this decision alone, it was suggested Affleck talk with John Kelley, Goodyear's vice-president for advertising.

Affleck called Kelley and requested more information on Goodyear's impending advertising campaign. A Goodyear employee visited Affleck on August 30 and showed him rough versions of the planned Goodyear "Bigfoot" commercials and other promotional materials. On September 10, Affleck and two Big O directors met in New Orleans, with Kelley and Goodyear's manager of consumer market planning to discuss the problem further. At this time the Big O representatives objected to Goodyear using "Bigfoot" in connection with tires because they believed any such use would severely damage Big

O. They made it clear they were not interested in money in exchange for granting Goodyear the right to use the "Bigfoot" trademark, and asked Goodyear to wind down the campaign as soon as possible. Goodyear's response to this request was indefinite and uncertain.

During the trial several Goodyear employees conceded it was technically possible for Goodyear to have deleted the term "Bigfoot" from its television advertising as late as early September. However, on September 16, 1974, Goodyear launched its nation-wide "Bigfoot" promotion on ABC's Monday Night Football telecast. By August 31, 1975, Goodyear had spent $9,690,029 on its massive, saturation campaign.

On September 17 [1974] Affleck wrote Kelley a letter setting forth his understanding of the New Orleans meeting that Goodyear would wind up its "Bigfoot" campaign as soon as possible. Kelley replied on September 20, denying any commitment to discontinue use of "Bigfoot" and declaring Goodyear intended to use "Bigfoot" as long as it continued to be a helpful advertising device.

On October 9 Kelley told Affleck he did not have the authority to make the final decision for Goodyear and suggested that Affleck call Charles Eaves, Goodyear's executive vice-president. On October 10 Affleck called Eaves and Eaves indicated the possibility of paying Big O for the use of the term "Bigfoot." When Affleck stated no interest in the possibility Eaves told him Goodyear wished to avoid litigation but that if Big O did sue, the case would be in litigation long enough that Goodyear might obtain all the benefits it desired from the term "Bigfoot."

This was the final communication between the parties until Big O filed suit on November 27, 1974. The district court denied Big O's request for a temporary restraining order and a preliminary injunction. After judgment was entered on the jury's verdict for Big O, Goodyear appealed to this court. Goodyear's allegations of error are discussed below. . . .

IV

. . . Big O does not claim nor was any evidence presented showing Goodyear intended to trade on the goodwill of Big O or to palm off Goodyear products as being those of Big O. Instead, Big O contends Goodyear's use of Big O's trademark created a likelihood of confusion concerning the source of Big O's "Big Foot" tires.

The facts of this case are different from the usual trademark infringement case. As the trial judge stated, the usual trademark infringement case involves a claim by a plaintiff with a substantial investment in a well established trademark. The plaintiff would seek recovery for the loss of income resulting from a second user attempting to trade on the goodwill associated with that established mark by suggesting to the consuming public that his product comes from the same origin as the plaintiff's product. The instant case, however, involves reverse confusion wherein the infringer's use of plaintiff's mark results in confusion as to the origin of plaintiff's product. Only one reported decision involves the issue of reverse confusion. In *Westward Coach Mfg. Co. v. Ford Motor*

Co., 7 Cir., 388 F.2d 627, the court held reverse confusion is not actionable as a trademark infringement under Indiana law.

Consequently, Goodyear argues the second use of a trademark is not actionable if it merely creates a likelihood of confusion concerning the source of the first user's product. Since both parties agree Colorado law is controlling in this case, we must decide whether this so-called reverse confusion is actionable under Colorado law. To our knowledge, the Colorado courts have never considered whether a second use creating the likelihood of confusion about the source of the first user's products is actionable. However, the Colorado Court of Appeals in deciding a trade name infringement case involving an issue of first impression, cogently pointed out that the Colorado Supreme Court "has consistently recognized and followed a policy of protecting established trade names and preventing public confusion and the tendency has been to widen the scope of that protection." *Wood v. Wood's Homes Inc.*, 33 Colo. App. 285, 519 P.2d 1212, 1215–16.

Using that language as a guiding light in divining what Colorado law is on this issue of first impression, we hold that the Colorado courts, if given the opportunity, would extend its common law trademark infringement actions to include reverse confusion situations. Such a rule would further Colorado's "policy of protecting trade names and preventing public confusion" as well as having "the tendency [of widening] the scope of that protection."

The district court very persuasively answered Goodyear's argument that liability for trademark infringement cannot be imposed without a showing that Goodyear intended to trade on the goodwill of Big O or to palm off Goodyear products as being those of Big O's when it said:

> The logical consequence of accepting Goodyear's position would be the immunization from unfair competition liability of a company with a well established trade name and with the economic power to advertise extensively for a product name taken from a competitor. If the law is to limit recovery to passing off, anyone with adequate size and resources can adopt any trademark and develop a new meaning for that trademark as identification of the second user's products. The activities of Goodyear in this case are unquestionably unfair competition through an improper use of a trademark and that must be actionable.

408 F. Supp. at 1236.

Goodyear further argues there was no credible evidence from which the jury could have found a likelihood of reverse confusion. A review of the record demonstrates the lack of merit in this argument. Big O presented more than a dozen witnesses who testified to actual confusion as to the source of Big O's "Big Foot" tires after watching a Goodyear "Bigfoot" commercial. The jury could have reasonably inferred a likelihood of confusion from these witnesses' testimony of actual confusion. Moreover, two of Goodyear's executive officers, Kelley and Eaves, testified confusion was likely or even inevitable. . . .

VII

Finally, Goodyear challenges the jury's verdict awarding Big O $2.8 million in compensatory damages and $16.8 million in punitive damages. . . .

Big O also asserts the evidence provided the jury with a reasonable basis for determining the amount of damages. Big O claims the only way it can be restored to the position it was in before Goodyear infringed its trademark is to conduct a corrective advertising campaign. Big O insists it should be compensated for the advertising expenses necessary to dispel the public confusion caused by Goodyear's infringement. Goodyear spent approximately $10 million on its "Bigfoot" advertising campaign. Thus, Big O advances two rationales in support of the $2.8 million award: (1) there were Big O Tire Dealers in 28 percent of the states (14 of 50) and 28 percent of $10 million equals the amount of the award; and (2) the Federal Trade Commission generally orders businesses who engage in misleading advertising to spend approximately 25 percent of their advertising budget on corrective advertising and this award is roughly 25 percent of the amount Goodyear spent infringing on Big O's trademark. The district court used the first rationale in denying Goodyear's motion to set the verdict aside. The second rationale was presented by Big O at oral argument. . . .

There is precedent for the recovery of corrective advertising expenses incurred by a plaintiff to counteract the public confusion resulting from a defendant's wrongful conduct. . . . Unlike the wronged parties in those cases Big O did not spend any money prior to trial in advertising to counteract the confusion from the Goodyear advertising. It is clear from the record Big O did not have the economic resources to conduct an advertising campaign sufficient to counteract Goodyear's $9,690,029 saturation advertising campaign. We are thus confronted with the question whether the law should apply differently to those who have the economic power to help themselves concurrently with the wrong than to those who must seek redress through the courts. Under the facts of this case we are convinced the answer must be no. Goodyear contends the recovery of advertising expenses should be limited to those actually incurred prior to trial. In this case the effect of such a rule would be to recognize that Big O has a right to the exclusive use of its trademark but has no remedy to be put in the position it was in prior to September 16, 1974, before Goodyear effectively usurped Big O's trademark. The impact of Goodyear's "Bigfoot" campaign was devastating. The infringing mark was seen repeatedly by millions of consumers. It is clear from the record that Goodyear deeply penetrated the public consciousness. Thus, Big O is entitled to recover a reasonable amount equivalent to that of a concurrent corrective advertising campaign.

As the district court pointed out, the jury's verdict of $2.8 million corresponds to 28 percent of the approximately $10 million Goodyear spent infringing Big O's mark. Big O has dealers in 14 states which equals 28 percent of the 50 states. Big O also points out the jury's award is close to 25 percent of the amount Goodyear spent infringing on Big O's mark. Big O emphasizes that the Federal Trade Commission often requires businesses who engage in misleading advertising to spend 25 percent of their advertising budget on corrective advertising.

Taking cognizance of these two alternative rationales for the jury's award for compensatory damages we are convinced the award is not capable of support as to any amount in excess of $678,302. As the district court implied in attempting to explain the jury's verdict, Big O is not entitled to the total amount Goodyear spent on its nationwide campaign since Big O only has dealers in 14 states, thus making it unnecessary for Big O to run a nationwide advertising campaign. Furthermore, implicit in the FTC's 25 percent rule in corrective advertising cases is the fact that dispelling confusion and deception in the consuming public's mind does not require a dollar-for-dollar expenditure. In keeping with "'(t)he constant tendency of the courts . . . to find some way in which damages can be awarded where a wrong has been done,'" we hold that the maximum amount which a jury could reasonably find necessary to place Big O in the position it was in before September 16, 1974, vis-à-vis its "Big Foot" trademark, is $678,302. We arrive at this amount by taking 28 percent of the $9,690,029 it was stipulated Goodyear spent on its "Bigfoot" campaign, and then reducing that figure by 75 percent in accordance with the FTC rule, since we agree with that agency's determination that a dollar-for-dollar expenditure for corrective advertising is unnecessary to dispel the effects of confusing and misleading advertising.

[The court also awarded $4 million in punitive damages.]

COMMENTS AND QUESTIONS

1. How was Big O hurt by Goodyear's massive advertising campaign? If the products have the same name, and if Goodyear spends much more on advertising than Big O does, shouldn't sales of Big O Tires increase? One possible answer is that Big O feared that Goodyear's tires would be of lower quality than its own and that its public image would suffer as a result of being associated with Goodyear. But that doesn't seem to be the case here, since Goodyear was selling premium tires and Big O was selling off-brands. Can you envision any way in which Goodyear's advertising of the brand would reduce Big O's sales?

Is the public hurt by thinking that Big O is affiliated with Goodyear? How? Is Big O hurt? Should that matter?

2. In the *Big O Tires* case, the court ordered as a remedy that Goodyear pay $4 million in punitive damages plus $678,302—what it would cost in corrective advertising to "undo" the "damage" Goodyear had done in connecting itself with the Big O name.

This punitive damage award raises an interesting point. Is the court justified in ordering compensation—whether in the form of corrective advertising or a cash payment—beyond the point where advertising would have benefited Big O? If Goodyear benefits more from the advertising than Big O would have—as is perhaps shown by the fact that it costs more to restore the status quo for Big O—does this establish that the trademark is better left in Goodyear's hands? What if Goodyear realizes that it can make better use of a trademark currently held by a competitor; should we allow Goodyear to appropriate the mark by paying damages as set by the court? (Note that this is an example of a "liability rule." *See* Chapters III(G)(1); IV(G)(2).) What would be the effects of such a rule?

Further, consider that *any* spending is really a windfall to Big O, since it did not have the resources to shell out anything like $4 million in advertising. Is there any consumer interest served by corrective advertising in a reverse confusion case? Won't it just confuse consumers more? Note that the court did not actually order the corrective advertising, just the payment of a typical sum of money that might be spent in such advertising. *See also PODS Enterprises, LLC v. U-Haul Int'l, Inc.*, 126 F. Supp. 3d 1263, 1285 (M.D. Fla. 2015) (upholding award of $45 million for corrective advertising).

The idea of punitive damages for trademark infringement seems to deny the possibility of "efficient" trademark infringement. This in turn suggests that trademarks are property and that courts are willing to grant "specific performance" remedies in infringement cases. Does this view make sense?

3. How should damages be measured in cases of reverse confusion? Presumably, a company like Big O Tires might be able to prove that it lost sales (rather than gained them) as a result of Goodyear's use of its "Bigfoot" trademark. But is Big O also entitled to Goodyear's profits from infringement? its "unjust enrichment"? Most courts would say yes, at least where Big O can prove intentional or willful infringement. But doing so can provide a significant windfall to Big O, which would never have made such profits in the absence of infringement.

What unjust profits has Goodyear gained *through infringement*? Must it turn over all its profits from the sale of "Bigfoot" tires, even though it is Goodyear and not Big O that has built a national reputation for the "Bigfoot" name? How about the increase in sales attributable to the use of the name "Bigfoot"? Or are Goodyear's profits from infringement limited to whatever sales it took away from Big O (presumably the same measure as Big O's lost profits)?

PROBLEM

Problem V-23. A small Vermont company named STW (and its predecessors) has used the mark "Thirst-Aid" for soft drinks since 1921. STW has never sold its products widely, however, and in fact its sales are declining. In 1983, Quaker Oats adopted the slogan "Gatorade is Thirst Aid" for its popular Gatorade beverage. STW sued for trademark infringement. At trial, STW proves that Quaker Oats knew of STW's trademark, but its lawyers advised it that the Gatorade slogan made "fair use" of STW's "descriptive" mark. The trial court disagreed, finding that Quaker Oats had infringed STW's mark in bad faith.

During the period that the "Thirst-Aid" campaign ran, pretax profits on the sale of Gatorade came to $247 million on sales of $2.6 billion. Quaker Oats proves that Gatorade had approximately $475 million in sales before the ad campaign. It also demonstrates that STW had previously offered to license the "Thirst-Aid" mark to another company for one-third of 1 percent of sales, and that STW's total goodwill in 1984 was less than $100,000 and declining. What damages should be awarded in this case?

a.   Note on the Trademark Counterfeiting Act of 1984

In 1984, Congress substantially increased the penalties for intentional copying of a trademark (called "counterfeiting").[8] 18 U.S.C. § 2320 makes it a felony to knowingly use a counterfeit mark in connection with the sale of goods or services. It provides for fines and imprisonment of the offenders, and it permits the destruction of goods bearing counterfeit marks (rather than simply the removal of the marks themselves). The Act also added

- Section 34(d) of the Lanham Act, 15 U.S.C. § 1116(d), which provides for the seizure of counterfeit goods and records of sale before trial upon an ex parte application;
- Section 35(b) of the Lanham Act, 15 U.S.C. § 1117(b), which provides for the award of treble damages plus attorney fees and prejudgment interest against counterfeiters unless the court finds "extenuating circumstances";
- Language in § 36 of the Lanham Act, 15 U.S.C. § 1118, concerning the right of the court to destroy counterfeit goods after trial.

An exception to the broad reach of the Act applies to those who are authorized to use a trademark "at the time of the manufacture or production" of the goods. *See United States v. Bohai Trading Co., Inc.*, 45 F.3d 577 (1st Cir. 1995) (upholding the constitutionality of this provision in the face of a challenge on the grounds of vagueness). Although the ex parte nature of the remedies has brought the 1984 Act under constitutional scrutiny, courts have generally upheld the legality of its remedies and procedures. *See, e.g., United States v. McEvoy*, 820 F.2d 1170 (11th Cir. 1987). *But cf. Time Warner Entertainment Co., L.P. v. Does Nos. 1–2*, 876 F. Supp. 407 (E.D.N.Y. 1994) (overturning on Fourth Amendment grounds proposed seizure order drafted by owners of copyrights and trademarks; court cited role of private investigator in conducting seizure and impoundment, failure to provide sufficient particularity for premises to be searched or articles to be seized, inclusion of private residence as site to be searched, and failure to sufficiently describe infringing materials).

---

[8] Section 45 of the Lanham Act, 15 U.S.C. § 1127, defines a "counterfeit" as "a spurious mark which is identical with, or substantially indistinguishable from, a registered mark." While this definition does not contain an explicit intent requirement, courts are generally unwilling to find good faith use of an infringing mark to be "spurious."

COMMENTS AND QUESTIONS

1. The Trademark Counterfeiting Act of 1984 is clearly punitive in nature, providing for both criminal sanctions and treble damages. Is such a punitive approach warranted? If so, why not apply these remedies to all trademark infringements?

2. Are consumers hurt by counterfeiting, or is it only trademark owners who are being protected by the Lanham Act? Where the counterfeit goods are inferior, the problems can extend beyond mere consumer confusion. Counterfeit medicines or auto parts can create a health and safety hazard. But what if the counterfeit goods were not in fact inferior to genuine goods with the same trademark? Have consumers suffered any injury if they mistakenly buy counterfeit goods equal in quality to the trademark owner's goods? Is the mere prospect that goods might be inferior itself a relevant injury.

3. Should it be a defense to a counterfeiting claim that the reasonable consumer was aware that the goods were not genuine (for example, because they were purchased from a street vendor without a certificate of authenticity for approximately 10 percent of the retail price of the genuine goods in stores)? Are consumers likely to be "confused" by such sales?

4. Judge Posner suggests one good reason for multiple damages in counterfeiting cases: deterrence. In holding that treble damages were an appropriate remedy even for innocent infringement, he argued:

> [T]he sale of counterfeit merchandise has become endemic—perhaps pandemic. Most of the infringing sellers are small retailers, such as K-Econo. Obtaining an injunction against each and every one of them would be infeasible. Trademark owners cannot hire investigators to shop every retail store in the nation. And even if they could and did, and obtained injunctions against all present violators, this would not stop the counterfeiting. Other infringers would spring up, and would continue infringing until enjoined. . . . Treble damages are a particularly suitable remedy in cases where surreptitious violations are possible, for in such cases simple damages (or profits) will underdeter; the violator will know that he won't be caught every time, and merely confiscating his profits in the cases in which he is caught will leave him with a net profit from infringement. . . . [T]he smaller the violator, the less likely he is to be caught, and the more needful, therefore, is a heavy punishment if he is caught.

Louis Vuitton S.A. v. Lee, 875 F.2d 584 (7th Cir. 1989). Is this rationale persuasive?

G. INTERNATIONAL ISSUES

National borders are less of a barrier to economic exchange now than at almost any time in history. As economic activity continues its relentless drive toward world-wide scope, trademarks become even more important. Just as the growth of the national economy in the United States set the stage for trademark law of national scope, the growth of the worldwide economy shows the importance of some sort of international trademark system.

1.   U.S. Trademarks Abroad: The New Internationalization

Despite the obvious desirability of international trademark registration, the United States did not join an international convention that goes beyond the rather minimal protections afforded by the Paris Convention until 2002. The Madrid Trademark Agreement (MTA) is the main international trademark convention.[9] The MTA does not itself protect any trademark rights; it simply facilitates trademark prosecution in member states. It is effective in this regard, however: over 290,000 international Madrid registrations are now in force. On average, each international registration is extended to ten countries. Under the MTA, a trademark owner files a single registration with its domestic trademark office. The owner may then extend this "basic registration" by filing, within six months of the original filing, an international application with the domestic trademark office designating other MTA member countries in which protection is sought.

The United States and a number of other countries subscribe to the Madrid Protocol (MP), a corollary to the broader MTA. The MP considerably softens some of the harsher impacts of the MTA, especially on the United States.[10] Specifically, the MP (1) allows for filing in English or French, in the U.S. PTO or any other member country trademark office; (2) allows the filing of an international application based not only on a "basic" (or home country) registration but also on a basic *application*—a substantial advantage given the relatively stringent prosecution standards in the United States, which can lead to long gaps between applications and registrations, and especially now in light of intent-to-use registrations under the Lanham Act; and (3) substantially lessens the impact of a "central attack" provision, under which a trademark invalidated in its home country is invalid everywhere, by allowing an international registrant to convert a successfully attacked registration into a bundle of individual national registrations if the attack occurs during the first five years of the international registration.

Although some problems remain,[11] the MP is a substantial step towards international harmonization. Indeed, some degree of harmonization would seem to be necessary, if only to keep up with trading partners. In Europe, for example, 1995 saw the

---

[9] Madrid Agreement Concerning the International Registration of Marks, Apr. 14, 1891, 175 Consol. T.S. 57. This is an agreement under the Paris Convention for the Protection of Industrial Property, Stockholm Revision, done July 14, 1967, art. 2(1), 21 U.S.T. 1629, 1631, 828 U.N.T.S. 305, 313. There are 56 members, including China and most of the European nations. Various other international agreements exist, but for the most part they only cover relations between pairs of countries. *See, e.g.*, 3 J. THOMAS MCCARTHY, TRADEMARKS AND UNFAIR COMPETITION § 29.10[2] (describing bilateral treaties signed by the U.S.).

[10] Technically, members of the MP join the Madrid Union without signing the MTA. *See* MTA art. 1, 828 U.N.T.S. at 391 (states adhering to the Madrid Agreement "constitute a Special Union for the international registration of marks," known as the "Madrid Union"); Madrid Agreement Protocol, art. 1, at 9 (states adhering to the Madrid Agreement Protocol are also members of the Madrid Union). There are 97 countries in the Madrid Protocol, including all members of the Madrid Agreement.

[11] *See, e.g., Allan Zelnick, The Madrid Protocol—Some Reflections*, 82 TRADEMARK REP. 651 (1992). Zelnick argues that U.S. companies might still prefer to pursue foreign trademark rights by filing individual foreign applications because of the liberality of most foreign trademark systems regarding the classes of goods that can be identified with the mark in the application. (In many countries, a trademark application

advent of the Community Trademark Convention, a treaty providing for a single Community Trade Mark (CTM) based on a single European trademark registration.[12] If further proof were needed, the CTC shows convincingly that the logic of trademark harmonization is compelling in this era of global trade and instantaneous communication.

2. Foreign Trademarks in the United States: Limited Internationalization

Even before U.S. adherence to an international trademark treaty, certain provisions of U.S. law made some slight concessions to the need for foreign trademark owners to register their marks in the United States. Section 44 of the Lanham Act allows foreign trademark owners to register their marks in the United States. Lanham Act § 44, 15 U.S.C. § 1126.

Although § 44(d)(2) requires a statement of bona fide intent to use, no subsequent proof of actual use in commerce in the United States is required to obtain an initial registration. This allows foreign trademark owners to register their marks in the United States on terms somewhat more favorable than those extended to domestic applicants under the Lanham Act.

One court has held that the Lanham Act incorporates the substantive provisions of the Paris Convention governing trademarks and unfair competition, providing a cause

---

can specify *all* classes of goods—giving applicants substantially broader rights than under U.S. law.) According to Zelnick,

> [I]t seems likely that on the whole, most American trademark owners who file abroad today are unlikely to make use of the Madrid Protocol. The reason for this conclusion is that under our practice the specification of goods or services that will appear in domestic application, on which the international application will be based, must be narrowly drawn to the specific goods or services in respect of which the mark shall have been used in interstate or foreign commerce of the United States (in the case of applications based on use) or restricted to the particular items or services identified by their common trade names in respect of which the applicant shall have a bona fide intention to use the mark. Since the international application under the Madrid Protocol will have the same specification of goods or services as the United States application upon which it is based, we will have, in effect, transferred our domestic practice in this regard to United States trademark owners' international filings.

Id. at 652.

[12] Council Regulation (EC) no. 40/94 of 20 December 1993 on the Community Trademark, OJ L 11/1. The CTM Regulation built on a 1980 Directive that substantially harmonized the national trademark laws of the EC member states. Primary features of the recently added CTM are:

- Trademarks with renewable ten-year term, to be registered in the new European rademark Office in Alicante, Spain.
- Marks valid in all member states but invalid everywhere if revoked.
- Substantive requirements for registration and grounds for opposition that would largely be familiar to American trademark practitioners, e.g., registration of nondistinctive marks upon proof of secondary meaning, and for a limited class of goods or services.
- The working languages are German, English, Spanish, French, and Italian. Applications can be filed in any Community language and are translated for free; opposition proceedings, however, are conducted in only one of the official languages, which must be selected at the time of filing.

See Eric P. Raciti, *The Harmonization of Trademarks in the European Community: The Harmonization Directive and the Community Trademark*, 78 J. PAT. & TRADEMARK OFF. SOC'Y 51 (1996).

of action for violation of those provisions. *General Motors Corp. v. Lopez*, 948 F. Supp. 684 (E.D. Mich. 1996).

3. Note on the "Gray Market"

Importation of counterfeit products is illegal. 19 U.S.C. § 1526. But what if the defendant imports products actually made or licensed by the trademark owner abroad? This so-called gray market or "parallel imports" problem is a troubling one for courts and commentators alike. The Supreme Court has described the problem as follows:

> The gray market arises in any of three general contexts. The prototypical gray-market victim (case 1) is a domestic firm that purchases from an independent foreign firm the rights to register and use the latter's trademark as a United States trademark and to sell its foreign-manufactured products here. Especially where the foreign firm has already registered the trademark in the United States or where the product has already earned a reputation for quality, the right to use that trademark can be very valuable. If the foreign manufacturer could import the trademarked goods and distribute them here, despite having sold the trademark to a domestic firm, the domestic firm would be forced into sharp intrabrand competition involving the very trademark it purchased. Similar intrabrand competition could arise if the foreign manufacturer markets its wares outside the United States, as is often the case, and a third party who purchases them abroad could legally import them. In either event, the parallel importation, if permitted to proceed, would create a gray market that could jeopardize the trademark holder's investment.

> The second context (case 2) is a situation in which a domestic firm registers the United States trademark for goods that are manufactured abroad by an affiliated manufacturer. In its most common variation (case 2a), a foreign firm wishes to control distribution of its wares in this country by incorporating a subsidiary here. The subsidiary then registers under its own name (or the manufacturer assigns to the subsidiary's name) a United States trademark that is identical to its parent's foreign trademark. The parallel importation by a third party who buys the goods abroad (or conceivably even by the affiliated foreign manufacturer itself) creates a gray market. Two other variations on this theme occur when an American-based firm establishes abroad a manufacturing subsidiary corporation (case 2b) or its own unincorporated manufacturing division (case 2c) to produce its United States trademarked goods, and then imports them for domestic distribution. If the trademark holder or its foreign subsidiary sells the trademarked goods abroad, the parallel importation of the goods competes on the gray market with the holder's domestic sales.

> In the third context (case 3), the domestic holder of a United States trademark authorizes an independent foreign manufacturer to use it. Usually the holder sells to the foreign manufacturer an exclusive right to use the trademark

in a particular foreign location, but conditions the right on the foreign manufacturer's promise not to import its trademarked goods into the United States. Once again, if the foreign manufacturer or a third party imports into the United States, the foreign-manufactured goods will compete on the gray market with the holder's domestic goods.

K-Mart Corp. v. Cartier, Inc., 486 U.S. 281, 286–87 (1988).

What is wrong with importing gray market goods? Unlike typical trademark disputes, there is no question that the goods are genuine and are being sold as precisely what they are. Further, there is no question that they originated with the trademark owner (at least at some point). If a gray market transaction occurred entirely within the United States, would it constitute trademark infringement? If not, is there any reason to treat importation differently?

One obvious rationale for prohibiting gray market imports is that the United States trademark owner is losing the benefit of what it thought was an "exclusive" right to sell the trademarked goods in the United States. But does it really have such an exclusive right? Certainly, the right to use the Ford trademark on cars in the United States does not prevent bona fide purchasers of Ford cars from identifying them as such upon resale. And even if the United States trademark owner did obtain the exclusive rights to the first sale of goods in the United States from the manufacturer, isn't the problem here really one of breach of contract?

Another justification for prohibiting gray market goods is if they may be different than the goods normally sold in the United States. For example, Coca-Cola sold in Mexico is made with cane sugar, whereas the U.S. version is made with corn syrup. If so, consumers may be confused. Significantly, courts have held that gray market importation is legal unless the imported goods differ in some relevant way from the goods the trademark owner sold in the United States. *See American Circuit Breaker Corp. v. Oregon Breakers Inc.*, 406 F.3d 577 (9th Cir. 2005) (circuit breakers that differed only in color from those sold in the United States could legally be imported after first sale abroad); SKF USA v. *International Trade Comm'n*, 423 F.3d 1307 (Fed. Cir. 2005) (variation in goods could include variation in technical support provided, but in this case plaintiff did not uniformly provide support for its U.S. sales, and so could not complain of gray market imports without technical support); *but cf. Beltronics USA v. Midwest Inventory Distrib. LLC*, 562 F.3d 1067 (10th Cir. 2009) (first sale doctrine does not protect resellers who don't provide the same warranty as the original manufacturer).

Section 1526 of 19 U.S.C., which regulates gray market goods, may violate Article 2 of the Paris Convention because it treats United States trademark holders differently from foreign trademark holders, and United States infringers differently from foreign infringers. *See* Raimund Steiner & Robert Sabath, *Intellectual Property and Trade Law Approaches to Gray Market Importation, and the Restructuring of Transnational Entities to Permit Blockage of Gray Goods in the United States*, 15 WM. MITCHELL L. REV. 433, 441 (1989) (after *K-Mart,* to obtain benefits of Section 526 of the Tariff Act of 1930 and the Lanham Act, companies must separate ownership of foreign and domestic trademarks); *see generally* Note, *The Use of Copyright Law to Block the Importation of Gray-Market Goods: The Black and White of It All*, 23 LOY. L.A. L. REV. 645 (1990).

There is a debate in the economics literature about the wisdom of permitting gray market imports. The argument generally runs along these lines: those favoring restrictions on the gray market cite the importance of encouraging investments in brand quality by retailers, coupled with differing international product quality standards. In essence, the argument is that retailers will not engage in optimal expenditures to promote the product (advertising, clean showrooms, knowledgeable sales staff, etc.) if gray market imports will undercut the retailers' prices. On the opposite side, those who support the gray market say it undercuts blatant price discrimination. *See* Robert J. Staaf, *International Price Discrimination and the Gray Market*, 4 INTELL. PROP. J. 301 (1989) (gray market presents an opportunity for arbitrage, allowing competitors to circumvent attempted price discrimination and therefore benefiting consumers).

4.   Worldwide Famous Marks

Worldwide trademark protection is based on proof of either registration or use in each country in which protection is sought. In theory, this creates a significant burden for companies with marks that are famous worldwide: they must register their mark in every country in the world or risk losing rights to that mark to a competing registrant. In fact, a number of opportunistic individuals have registered famous marks such as "Coke" in countries where Coca-Cola does not yet do business.

This doctrine is recognized in the Paris Convention and TRIPs Agreement. *See* Paris Convention art. 6*bis*; TRIPs, art. 16(3). Courts in many nations have recognized goodwill in a world-famous mark even if the mark is not actually used in the country. *See, e.g.*, *Kmart Corp. v. Kay Mart Ltd.*, Suit No. C.L. 1993, K066 (recognition of K-Mart trademark by Jamaican court); Charles E. Webster, *The McDonald's Case: South Africa Joins the Global Village*, 86 TRADEMARK REP. 576 (1996) (protecting McDonald's mark in South Africa). U.S. courts have generally declined to recognize the "well known mark" doctrine. *See ITC Ltd. v. Punchgini, Inc.*, 482 F.3d 135 (2d Cir. 2007); *Buti v. Impressa Perosa S.R.L.*, 139 F.3d 98 (2d Cir. 1998); *Person's Co. v. Christman*, 900 F.2d 1565 (Fed. Cir. 1990); *but cf. Grupo Gigante S.A. v. Dallo & Co.*, 391 F.3d 1088 (9th Cir. 2004) (making a limited exception where the well-known foreign mark had achieved significant notoriety in the United States even though it was not offered for sale here); *Trader Joe's Co. v. Hallatt*, 835 F.3d 960 (9th Cir. 2016) (applying U.S. trademark law against a Canadian infringer where effects were felt in the U.S.).

CHAPTER VI:
STATE IP PROTECTIONS

A. Federal Preemption   1174
    1. Patent Preemption   1174
    2. Copyright Preemption   1184
        i.   Express Preemption (and Limitations)   1184
        ii. Contract   1190
    3. Trademark Preemption   1201
B. Misappropriation   1204
C. Idea Submissions   1220
D. Right of Publicity   1241

As we saw in Chapter II, state protection of intellectual property—whether rooted in statute or in the common law—has long been a feature of the legal landscape. But state intellectual property law extends far beyond trade secrets. Especially in recent years, state law has reached out to an ever-widening range of issues: from court decisions and legislation on publicity rights to state "anti-dilution" statutes (discussed in Chapter V), "shrinkwrap" and "clickwrap" contracts purporting to protect data, and trespass concepts being used to limit access to websites. States have become a major force in the evolution of intellectual property law in the new technological age. As one commentator has observed:

> [T]echnology in this century has continually outpaced statutory law and litigants have repeatedly turned to judge-made law to protect important rights and large investments in the collection or creation of time-sensitive information and other commercially valuable content. It stands to reason that the faster a technology develops, the more rapidly it will surpass preexisting law, and the more prominent common law theories may become. It is not surprising, therefore, that as the Internet geometrically expands its speed, accessibility, and versatility—thereby vastly increasing the opportunities for economic free-riders to take, copy, and repackage information and information systems for profit— intellectual property owners again must consider the common law as a source of protection at the end of this century, much as it was at the beginning.

Bruce P. Keller, *Condemned to Repeat the Past: The Reemergence of Misappropriation and Other Common Law Theories of Protection for Intellectual Property*, 11 HARV. J.L. & TECH. 401, 428 (1998).

This chapter surveys the most significant ways in which state law protects intellectual property (beyond trade secret and trademark law): misappropriation doctrine, idea submissions (implied contract), and the right of publicity. Before we can delve into these state law protections, it is necessary to address the interplay of federal and state law. Just as different federal intellectual property regimes may conflict—such as, expressive useful articles (patent-copyright) and distinctive product configurations (patent-trademark), tensions that we addressed in Chapters IV and V—state intellectual property law may also clash with the federal intellectual property regime. Thus, we begin by exploring the general contours of federal preemption of state law doctrines. We then build upon these general principles and contours in examining misappropriation, idea submission, and right of publicity law.

A. FEDERAL PREEMPTION

As we have seen throughout this book, the term "preemption" arises in two distinct contexts in intellectual property law. One context derives from economic analysis. Economists use the term to refer to the extent to which the exclusive rights associated with intellectual property bar or "preempt" others, in the absence of a license, from pursuing research or entering a field governed by such rights. The higher upstream or broad the intellectual property protection, the greater the preemptive effect.

The U.S. Constitution speaks to a different form of preemption. The Supremacy Clause of the U.S. Constitution provides that

> This Constitution, and the Laws of the United States which shall be made in Pursuance thereof; and all Treaties made, or which shall be made, under the Authority of the United States, shall be the supreme Law of the Land; and the Judges in every State shall be bound thereby, any Thing [sic] in the Constitution or Laws of any State to the Contrary notwithstanding

U.S. CONST., ART. VI, CL. 2. Thus, the Supremacy Clause nullifies state law attempts to duplicate or interfere with federal intellectual property protection. More difficult cases involve state laws that do not directly conflict with federal authority but instead address interstitial gaps within the federal regime. Courts must grapple with whether Congress intended to leave such gaps unfilled, thereby precluding state protection, or simply allowed state law to fill these voids. This logical structure—which involves a search for the intent behind uncovered cases, sometimes in cases where technology has outpaced legislative foresight—makes preemption particularly challenging. The doctrinal distinctions are subtle and elusive.

This section considers the general contours of federal preemption. Each of the IP laws we have discussed has been concerned with balance, giving enough protection to encourage innovation but not so much protection that the creative work of subsequent developers is stifled. Here, we confront the question whether those individual balances reach more broadly, to preempt state statutes that strike a different balance.

1. Patent Preemption

Kewanee Oil Co. v. Bicron Corp.
Supreme Court of the United States
416 U.S. 470 (1974)

Mr. Chief Justice BURGER delivered the opinion of the Court.

We granted certiorari to resolve a question on which there is a conflict in the courts of appeals: whether state trade secret protection is pre-empted by operation of the federal patent law. In the instant case the Court of Appeals for the Sixth Circuit held that there was preemption. The Courts of Appeals for the Second, Fourth, Fifth, and Ninth Circuits have reached the opposite conclusion. . . .

Petitioner brought this diversity action in United States District Court for the Northern District of Ohio seeking injunctive relief and damages for the misappropriation of trade secrets. The district Court, applying Ohio trade secret law, granted a permanent injunction against the disclosure or use by respondents of 20 of the 40 claimed trade secrets until such time as the trade secrets had been released to the public, had otherwise generally become available to the public, or had been obtained by respondents from sources having the legal right to convey the information.

The Court of Appeals for the Sixth Circuit held that the findings of fact by the District Court were not clearly erroneous, and that it was evident from the record that the individual respondents appropriated to the benefit of Bicron secret information on processes obtained while they were employees at Harshaw. Further, the Court of Appeals held that the District Court properly applied Ohio law relating to trade secrets. Nevertheless, the Court of Appeals reversed the District Court, finding Ohio's trade secret law to be in conflict with the patent laws of the United States. The Court of Appeals reasoned that Ohio could not grant monopoly protection to processes and manufacturing techniques that were appropriate subjects for consideration under 35 U.S.C. § 101 for a federal patent but which had been in commercial use for over one year and so were no longer eligible for patent protection under 35 U.S.C. § 102(b).

We hold that Ohio's law of trade secrets is not preempted by the patent laws of the United States, and accordingly, we reverse. . . .

III.

The first issue we deal with is whether the States are forbidden to act at all in the area of protection of the kinds of intellectual property which may make up the subject matter of trade secrets.

Article I, § 8, cl. 8, of the Constitution grants to the Congress the power

> [t]o promote the Progress of Science and useful Arts, by securing for limited Times to Authors and Inventors the exclusive Right to their respective Writings and Discoveries. . . .

In the 1972 Term, in *Goldstein v. California*, 412 U.S. 546 (1973), we held that the cl. 8 grant of power to Congress was not exclusive and that, at least in the case of writings, the States were not prohibited from encouraging and protecting the efforts of those within their borders by appropriate legislation. The States could, therefore, protect against the unauthorized rerecording for sale of performances fixed on records or tapes, even though those performances qualified as "writings" in the constitutional sense and Congress was empowered to legislate regarding such performances and could pre-empt the area if it chose to do so. This determination was premised on the great diversity of interests in our Nation—the essentially nonuniform character of the appreciation of intellectual achievements in the various States. Evidence for this came from patents granted by the States in the 18th century. 412 U.S., at 557.

Just as the States may exercise regulatory power over writings so may the States regulate with respect to discoveries. States may hold diverse viewpoints in protecting intellectual property relating to invention as they do in protecting the intellectual property relating to the subject matter of copyright. The only limitation on the States is that in regulating the area of patents and copyrights they do not conflict with the operation of the laws in this area passed by Congress, and it is to that more difficult question we now turn.

IV.

The question of whether the trade secret law of Ohio is void under the Supremacy Clause involves a consideration of whether that law "stands as an obstacle to the accomplishment and execution of the full purposes and objectives of Congress." *Hines v. Davidowitz*, 312 U.S. 52, 67 (1941). *See Florida Avocado Growers v. Paul*, 373 U.S. 132, 141 (1963). We stated in *Sears, Roebuck & Co. v. Stiffel Co.*, 376 U.S. 225, 229 (1964), that when state law touches upon the area of federal statutes enacted pursuant to constitutional authority, "it is 'familiar doctrine' that the federal policy 'may not be set at naught, or its benefits denied' by the state law. *Sola Elec. Co v. Jefferson Elec. Co.*, 317 U.S. 173, 176 (1942). This is true, of course, even if the state law is enacted in the exercise of otherwise undoubted state power." . . .

The stated objective of the Constitution in granting the power to Congress to legislate in the area of intellectual property is to "promote the Progress of Science and useful Arts." The patent laws promote this progress by offering a right of exclusion for a limited period as an incentive to inventors to risk the often enormous costs in terms of time, research, and development. . . .

The maintenance of standards of commercial ethics and the encouragement of invention are the broadly stated policies behind trade secret law. "The necessity of good faith and honest, fair dealing, is the very life and spirit of the commercial world.". . .

As we noted earlier, trade secret law protects items which would not be proper subjects for consideration for patent protection under 35 U.S.C. § 101. As in the case of the recordings in *Goldstein v. California*, Congress, with respect to nonpatentable subject matter, "has drawn no balance; rather, it has left the area unattended, and no reason exists why the State should not be free to act." *Goldstein v. California, supra*, at 570 (footnote omitted).

Since no patent is available for a discovery, however useful, novel, and nonobvious, unless it falls within one of the express categories of patentable subject matter of 35 U.S.C. § 101, the holder of such a discovery would have no reason to apply for a patent whether trade secret protection existed or not. Abolition of trade secret protection would, therefore, not result in increased disclosure to the public of discoveries in the area of nonpatentable subject matter. . . .

Congress has spoken in the area of those discoveries which fall within one of the categories of patentable subject matter of 35 U.S.C. § 101 and which are, therefore, of a nature that would be subject to consideration for a patent. Processes, machines, manufactures, compositions of matter, and improvements thereof, which meet the tests of utility, novelty, and nonobviousness are entitled to be patented, but those which do not, are not. The question remains whether those items which are proper subjects for consideration for a patent may also have available the alternative protection accorded by trade secret law.

Certainly the patent policy of encouraging invention is not disturbed by the existence of another form of incentive to invention. In this respect the two systems are not and never would be in conflict. Similarly, the policy that matter once in the public domain must remain in the public domain is not incompatible with the existence of trade secret protection. By definition a trade secret has not been placed in the public domain. . . .

. . . Trade secret law will encourage invention in areas where patent law does not reach, and will prompt the independent innovator to proceed with the discovery and exploitation of his invention. Competition is fostered and the public is not deprived of the use of valuable, if not quite patentable, invention. . . .

The final category of patentable subject matter to deal with is the clearly patentable invention, i.e., that invention which the owner believes to meet the standards of patentability. It is here that the federal interest in disclosure is at its peak. . . .

Trade secret law provides far weaker protection in many respects than the patent law. While trade secret law does not forbid the discovery of the trade secret by fair and honest means, e.g., independent creation or reverse engineering, patent law operates "against the world," forbidding any use of the invention for whatever purpose for a significant length of time. The holder of a trade secret also takes a substantial risk that the secret will be passed on to his competitors, by theft or by breach of a confidential relationship, in a manner not easily susceptible of discovery or proof. *Painton & Co. v. Bourns, Inc.*, 442 F.2d, at 224. Where patent law acts as a barrier, trade secret law functions relatively as a sieve. The possibility that an inventor who believes his invention meets the standards of patentability will sit back, rely on trade secret law, and after one year of use forfeit any right to patent protection, 35 U.S.C. § 102(b), is remote indeed.

Nor does society face much risk that scientific or technological progress will be impeded by the rare inventor with a patentable invention who chooses trade secret protection over patent protection. The ripeness-of-time concept of invention, developed from the study of the many independent multiple discoveries in history, predicts that if a particular individual had not made a particular discovery others would have, and in probably a relatively short period of time. If something is to be discovered at all very likely it will be discovered by more than one person. . . .

. . . Trade secret law and patent law have co-existed in this country for over one hundred years. Each has its particular role to play, and the operation of one does not take away from the need for the other. . . . Congress, by its silence over these many years, has seen the wisdom of allowing the States to enforce trade secret protection. Until Congress takes affirmative action to the contrary, States should be free to grant protection to trade secrets. . . .

Mr. Justice DOUGLAS, with whom Mr. Justice BRENNAN concurs, dissenting.

Today's decision is at war with the philosophy of *Sears, Roebuck & Co. v. Stiffel Co.*, 376 U.S. 225, and *Compco Corp. v. Day-Brite Lighting, Inc.*, 376 U.S. 234. Those cases involved patents—one of a pole lamp and one of fluorescent lighting fixtures—each of which was declared invalid. The lower courts held, however, that though the patents were invalid the sale of identical or confusingly similar products to the products of the patentees violated state unfair competition laws. We held that when an article is unprotected by a patent, state law may not forbid others to copy it, because every article not covered by a valid patent is in the public domain. Congress in the patent laws decided that where no patent existed, free competition should prevail; that where a patent is rightfully issued, the right to exclude others should obtain for no longer than 17 years, and that the States may not "under some other law, such as that forbidding unfair competition, give protection of a kind that clashes with the objectives of the federal patent laws," 376 U.S., at 231 . . .

The conflict with the patent laws is obvious. The decision of Congress to adopt a patent system was based on the idea that there will be much more innovation if discoveries are disclosed and patented than there will be when everyone works in secret. Society thus fosters a free exchange of technological information at the cost of a limited 17-year monopoly. . . .

A suit to redress theft of a trade secret is grounded in tort damages for breach of a contract—a historic remedy, *Cataphote Corp. v. Hudson*, 422 F.2d 1290. Damages for breach of a confidential relation are not pre-empted by this patent law, but an injunction against use is pre-empted because the patent law states the only monopoly over trade secrets that is enforceable by specific performance; and that monopoly exacts as a price full disclosure. A trade secret can be protected only by being kept secret. Damages for breach of a contract are one thing; an injunction barring disclosure does service for the protection accorded valid patents and is therefore pre-empted. . . .

COMMENTS AND QUESTIONS

1. The rule set forth by *Sears, Roebuck & Co v. Stiffel Co.*, 376 U.S. 225 (1964), was fairly clear: patent law reflects a compromise between the goal of promoting innovation and the danger of condoning monopoly. Supplementing the scope of patent law may upset that balance, and is therefore prohibited. Supplementing *enforcement* of the federal intellectual property laws was condoned in dictum at the end of *Compco Corp. v. Day-Brite Lighting, Inc.*, 376 U.S. 234 (1964), a companion case, and in Justice Harlan's concurrence in both cases. After these cases, state law served a very limited function in the scheme of intellectual property protection. States could work to further the goals of federal protection, but they had to work within the parameters set down by federal law. As a result, both *Sears* and *Compco* struck down state statutes providing design protection to unpatentable utilitarian articles.

The *Kewanee* opinion takes a remarkably different tack. Chief Justice Burger's opinion for the Court emphasizes only one of the two policies shaping the patent laws: the goal of promoting innovation. The opinion does not discuss the dangers intellectual property protection poses for free competition. As a result, the *Kewanee* Court finds no problem with trade secret protection that extends beyond the scope of the patent laws. Note that the Court seems to approve not only state laws that protect nonpatentable subject matter (an area in which it could be argued that the federal government has no interest),[1] but also the protection of inventions not patentable for some other reason (i.e., suppression, misuse, lack of novelty, or obviousness).

Is *Kewanee* reconcilable with *Sears*? The *Kewanee* court did not overrule *Sears* or *Compco*; indeed, it cited them in support of its holding. Thus state laws preventing copying were treated differently from trade secret laws after *Kewanee*. The latter, although broader in scope (they prevented far more than just outright copying of products), were permissible; the former were not. *See* Paul Goldstein, Kewanee Oil Co. v. Bicron Corp.*: Notes on a Closing Circle*, 1974 SUP. CT. REV. 81 (1974) (arguing that *Kewanee* "closed the circle" on the open-ended preemption analysis of *Sears* and *Compco*); Camilla A. Hrdy, *State Patents As a Solution to Underinvestment in Innovation*, 62 U. KAN. L. REV. 487 (2013) (arguing that state patents, which preceded the adoption of the Constitution in 1789, are still possible and in some cases desirable despite federal nature of patent law).

2. Is preemption a good idea? That depends on what you think of the balance the federal laws have struck. If you are more concerned about injury to competition by conferring monopoly rights on patentees, you are likely to favor the result in *Sears*. If, on the other hand, you think that innovation is underrewarded, it is reasonable to oppose federal preemption. One way to reconcile these cases may be to read *Sears* and *Compco* as expressing a federal policy in favor of reverse engineering of products in the public domain. If that is the overarching federal goal, it is logical to strike down the laws in *Sears* and *Compco* but not *Kewanee,* since trade secrets statutes (unlike the unfair competition laws we have discussed) generally allow reverse engineering. This result is also consistent with the reading of trade secret laws as merely an application of tort and contract principles.

Bonito Boats, Inc. v. Thunder Craft Boats, Inc.
Supreme Court of the United States
489 U.S. 141 (1989)

Justice O'CONNOR delivered the opinion of the Court. . . .

I.

In September 1976, petitioner Bonito Boats, Inc., a Florida corporation, developed a hull design for a fiberglass recreational boat which it marketed under the trade name Bonito Boat Model 5VBR. Designing the boat hull required substantial effort on the part of Bonito. A set of engineering drawings was prepared, from which a hardwood

---

[1] Even in this area, though, a federal interest may be discerned. If Congress has declared some subject matter unpatentable, that could reflect a federal determination that that matter is unworthy of protection, a determination that state law should not be allowed to upset.

model was created. The hardwood model was then sprayed with fiberglass to create a mold, which then served to produce the finished fiberglass boats for sale. The 5VBR was placed on the market sometime in September 1976. There is no indication in the record that a patent application was ever filed for protection of the utilitarian or design aspects of the hull, or for the process by which the hull was manufactured. The 5VBR was favorably received by the boating public, and "a broad interstate market" developed for its sale.

In May 1983, after the Bonito 5VBR had been available to the public for over six years, the Florida Legislature enacted Fla. Stat. § 559.94 (1987). The statute makes "it . . . unlawful for any person to use the direct molding process to duplicate for the purpose of sale any manufactured vessel hull or component part of a vessel made by another without the written permission of that other person." § 559.94(2). The statute also makes it unlawful for a person to "knowingly sell a vessel hull or component part of a vessel duplicated in violation of subsection (2)." § 559.94(3). Damages, injunctive relief, and attorney's fees are made available to "any person who suffers injury or damage as the result of a violation" of the statute. § 559.94(4). The statute was made applicable to vessel hulls or component parts duplicated through the use of direct molding after July 1, 1983. § 559.94(5).

On December 21, 1984, Bonito filed this action in the Circuit Court of Orange County, Florida. The complaint alleged that respondent here, Thunder Craft Boats, Inc., a Tennessee corporation, had violated the Florida statute by using the direct molding process to duplicate the Bonito 5VBR fiberglass hull, and had knowingly sold such duplicates in violation of the Florida statute. . . .

III.

We believe that the Florida statute at issue in this case so substantially impedes the public use of the otherwise unprotected design and utilitarian ideas embodied in unpatented boat hulls as to run afoul of the teaching of our decisions in *Sears* and *Compco*. It is readily apparent that the Florida statute does not operate to prohibit "unfair competition" in the usual sense that the term is understood. The law of unfair competition has its roots in the common-law tort of deceit: its general concern is with protecting *consumers* from confusion as to source. . . .

In contrast to the operation of unfair competition law, the Florida statute is aimed directly at preventing the exploitation of the design and utilitarian conceptions embodied in the product itself. The sparse legislative history surrounding its enactment indicates that it was intended to create an inducement for the improvement of boat hull designs. *See* Tr. of Meeting of Transportation Committee, Florida House of Representatives, May 3, 1983 ("There is no inducement for [a] quality boat manufacturer to improve these designs and secondly, if he does, it is immediately copied. This would prevent that and allow him recourse in circuit court"). To accomplish this goal, the Florida statute endows the original boat hull manufacturer with rights against the world, similar in scope and operation to the rights accorded a federal patentee. Like the patentee, the beneficiary of the Florida statute may prevent a competitor from "making" the product in what is evidently the most efficient manner available and from "selling" the product when it is produced in that fashion. Compare 35 U.S.C. § 154. The Florida scheme offers this protection for an unlimited number of years to all boat hulls and their component parts, without regard to their ornamental or technological merit. Protection is available for subject matter for which patent protection has been denied or has expired, as well as for designs which have been freely revealed to the consuming public by their creators. That the Florida statute does not remove all means of reproduction and sale does not eliminate the conflict with the federal scheme. *See Kellogg*, 305 U.S., at 122. In essence, the Florida law prohibits the entire public from engaging in a form of reverse engineering of a product in the public domain. This is clearly one of the rights vested in the federal patent holder, but has never been a part of state protection under the law of unfair competition or trade secrets. . . .

Moreover, as we noted in *Kewanee*, the competitive reality of reverse engineering may act as a spur to the inventor, creating an incentive to develop inventions that meet the rigorous requirements of patentability. 416 U.S., at 489–490. The Florida statute substantially reduces this competitive incentive, thus eroding the general rule of free competition upon which the attractiveness of the federal patent bargain depends. . . . The Florida statute is aimed directly at the promotion of intellectual creation by substantially restricting the public's ability to exploit ideas that the patent system mandates shall be free for all to use. Like the interpretation of Illinois unfair competition law in *Sears* and *Compco*, the Florida statute represents a break with the tradition of peaceful coexistence between state market regulation and federal patent policy. The Florida law substantially restricts the public's ability to exploit an unpatented design in general circulation, raising the specter of state-created monopolies in a host of useful shapes and processes for which patent protection has been denied or is otherwise unobtainable. It thus enters a field of regulation which the patent laws have reserved to Congress. The patent statute's careful balance between public right and private monopoly to promote certain creative activity is a "scheme of federal regulation. . . so pervasive as to make reasonable the inference that Congress left no room for the States to supplement it." *Rice v. Santa Fe Elevator Corp.*, 331 U.S. 218, 230 (1947). . . .

COMMENTS AND QUESTIONS

1. Does this result make sense? Is it consistent with *Kewanee*? *Bonito Boats* can be reconciled with trade secrets statutes if one accepts the reverse engineering rationale described above. Whatever one thinks of the *Bonito* result, the last sentence remains troubling. Characterizing patent law as "pervasive federal regulation" suggests that it might preempt the field, automatically striking down all state laws that attempt to regulate intellectual property. If taken seriously, that approach would leave no room at all for state protection of inventions.

2. Note the similarity between the statutes struck down in *Sears* and *Bonito Boats*. In both cases, what was prohibited was the direct copying of a competitor's design. The *Bonito Boats* statute is more limited than that in *Sears*, since it prohibits only one particular method of copying. Nonetheless, the Court struck it down. Why should the

courts be concerned about these comparatively narrow statutes when they allowed the far broader statute in *Kewanee* to pass muster?

3. The *Bonito Boats* decision has been criticized. *See* John S. Wiley, Jr., *Bonito Boats: Uninformed but Mandatory Federal Innovation Policy*, 1989 SUP. CT. REV. 283. *Cf.* Symposium, *Product Simulation: A Right or a Wrong?*, 64 COLUM. L. REV. 1178 (1964) (articles criticizing the analogous decisions in *Sears* and *Compco*). Does this criticism make sense? Or is *Bonito Boats* a needed barrier to the creation of state laws that would undo the balance struck by Congress?

As part of the Digital Millennium Copyright Act, Congress created a new federal intellectual property right protecting "original" boat hull designs. 17 U.S.C. §§ 1301 et seq., discussed in Chapter IV. Can Congress lawfully accomplish here what the states cannot? Does *Bonito Boats* suggest some sort of constitutional limitation on any form of protection (state or federal) in this area?

4. Some lawyers have tried to apply *Bonito Boats* in contexts beyond the patent-like legislation actually considered in the case. This has not met with much success, however; like other broad preemption decisions before it, *Bonito Boats* has been hemmed in by subsequent qualifications. In *Waits v. Frito-Lay, Inc.*, 978 F.2d 1093 (9th Cir. 1992), a right of publicity case based on an advertising campaign imitating Tom Waits' distinctive vocal qualities, the Ninth Circuit had the following to say about *Bonito Boats:*

> *Bonito Boats* involved a Florida statute giving perpetual patent-like protection to boat hull designs already on the market, a class of manufactured articles expressly excluded from federal patent protection. The Court ruled that the Florida statute was preempted by federal patent law because it directly conflicted with the comprehensive federal patent scheme. In reaching this conclusion, the Court cited its earlier decisions in *Sears Roebuck & Co. v. Stiffel Co.*, 376 U.S. 225 (1964), and *Compco Corp. v. Day-Brite Lighting*, 376 U.S. 234 (1964), for the proposition that "publicly known design and utilitarian ideas which were unprotected by patent occupied much the same position as the subject matter of an expired patent," i.e., they are expressly unprotected. *Bonito Boats*, 489 U.S. at 152.
>
> The defendants seize upon this citation to *Sears* and *Compco* as a reaffirmation of the sweeping preemption principles for which these cases were once read to stand. They argue that *Midler* [*v. Ford Motor Co.*, 849 F.2d 460 (9th Cir. 1988) (another sound-alike right of publicity case that is reproduced in Chapter VI(D)] was wrongly decided because it ignores these two decisions, an omission that the defendants say indicates an erroneous assumption that *Sears* and *Compco* have been "relegated to the constitutional junkyard." Thus, the defendants go on to reason, earlier cases that rejected entertainers' challenges to imitations of their performances based on federal copyright preemption, were correctly decided because they relied on *Sears* and *Compco*. *See Sinatra v. Goodyear Tire & Rubber Co.*, 435 F.2d 711, 716–18 (9th Cir. 1970), *cert. denied*, 402 U.S. 906 (1971); *Booth v. Colgate-Palmolive Co.*, 362 F. Supp.

343, 348 (S.D.N.Y. 1973); *Davis v. Trans World Airlines*, 297 F. Supp. 1145, 1147 (C.D. Cal. 1969). This reasoning suffers from a number of flaws.

Bonito Boats itself cautions against reading *Sears* and *Compco* for a "broad pre-emptive principle" and cites subsequent Supreme Court decisions retreating from such a sweeping interpretation. "[T]he Patent and Copyright Clauses do not, by their own force or by negative implication, deprive the States of the power to adopt rules for the promotion of intellectual creation." *Bonito Boats*, 489 U.S. at 165 (citing, inter alia, *Goldstein v. California*, 412 U.S. 546, 552–61 (1973) and *Kewanee Oil Co. v. Bicron Corp.*, 416 U.S. 470, 478–79 (1974)). Instead, the Court reaffirmed the right of states to "place limited regulations on the use of unpatented designs in order to prevent consumer confusion as to source." *Id. Bonito Boats* thus cannot be read as endorsing or resurrecting the broad reading of *Compco* and *Sears* urged by the defendants, under which Waits' state tort claim arguably would be preempted.

Moreover, the Court itself recognized the authority of states to protect entertainers' "right of publicity" in *Zacchini v. Scripps-Howard Broadcasting Co.*, 433 U.S. 562 (1977). In *Zacchini*, the Court endorsed a state right-of-publicity law as in harmony with federal patent and copyright law, holding that an unconsented-to television news broadcast of a commercial entertainer's performance was not protected by the First Amendment. *Id.* at 573, 576–78. The cases *Frito* asserts were "rightly decided" all predate *Zacchini* and other Supreme Court precedent narrowing *Sears'* and *Compco*'s sweeping preemption principles. In sum, our holding in *Midler*, upon which Waits' voice misappropriation claim rests, has not been eroded by subsequent authority.

Waits v. Frito-Lay, Inc., 978 F.2d 1099–1100.

The Federal Circuit has allowed state claims that tread on patent law, particularly where the claims are made against patent owners rather than in an effort to create a new form of intellectual property protection. *See, e.g., Dow Chemical v. Exxon Corp.*, 139 F.3d 1470 (Fed. Cir. 1998) (unfair competition claims by accused infringer based on alleged inequitable conduct not preempted); *Univ. of Colorado Found. v. American Cyanamid, Inc.*, 196 F.3d 1366 (Fed. Cir. 1999) (state claims of fraud and unjust enrichment against patentee who stole invention from plaintiff not preempted). The court has, however, required that state claims that touch on areas of federal patent interest be judged by federal, not state, standards, so that they do not upset the balance struck by patent law. *See Univ. of Colorado, supra; Midwest Industries v. Karavan Trailers*, 175 F.3d 1356 (Fed. Cir. 1999). Is this a reasonable compromise?

5. In a number of cases, restrictions on the content of licensing contracts are said to raise preemption issues. One might question whether contracts are equivalent to state statutes for preemption purposes. On at least one occasion, the Supreme Court has suggested that protection of unpatentable goods (which would be prohibited under state misappropriation statutes) is permissible under contract law. *See, e.g., Aronson v. Quick Point Pencil*, 440 U.S. 257 (1979). On the other hand, there are a variety of circumstances in which federal patent policy precludes the parties from contracting to

the contrary. *See, e.g., Brulotte v. Thys Co.,* 379 U.S. 29 (1964) (holding unenforceable patent licensed in agreement that extends beyond patent term); *Kimble v. Marvel Entertainment, LLC,* 135 S.Ct. 2401 (2015) (upholding *Brulotte*); *Lear, Inc. v. Adkins,* 395 U.S. 653 (1969) (contracts estopping licensee from challenging the validity of a patent are void); *Everex Systems Inc. v. Cadtrak Corp.,* 89 F.3d 673 (9th Cir. 1996) (federal policy precluding assignment of nonexclusive patent licenses prevailed over state doctrine permitting such assignments). Note that in some of these cases, such as *Everex*, federal preemption actually works to the benefit of the intellectual property owner.

Regardless of the particular limitations federal law imposes on licensing agreements, patent licensing in general is a question of state (not federal) law. *See Gjerlov v. Schuyler Labs. Inc.,* 131 F.3d 1016 (Fed. Cir. 1997).

6. A recent development has raised new preemption concerns: State laws providing a remedy when patentees send threatening "demand letters" without adequate research. The laws operate under fair trade or consumer protection statutes in various states. But they obviously have the potential to affect the enforcement powers of federal patentees. *See, e.g.,* Robin Feldman, *Federalism, First Amendment & Patents: The Fraud Fallacy,* 17 COLUM. SCI. & TECH. L. REV. 30, 32 (2015); Paul R. Gugliuzza, *Patent Trolls and Preemption,* 101 VA. L. REV. 1579, 1580 (2015).

2. Copyright Preemption

As we saw in Chapter IV, federal copyright law operated in tandem with state copyright protection for unpublished works for nearly two centuries. With the 1976 Act, however, Congress extinguished such state and common law protection for unpublished works. Nonetheless, Congress carved out several areas in which state law could continue to operate. We begin this section by presenting § 301 and noting some of its complexities. We then examine the particular effect of federal copyright law protection on contract law and licensing.

i. *Express Preemption (and Limitations)*

17 U.S.C. § 301—Preemption with respect to other laws

(a) On and after January 1, 1978, all legal or equitable rights that are equivalent to any of the exclusive rights within the general scope of copyright as specified by section 106 in works of authorship that are fixed in a tangible medium of expression and come within the subject matter of copyright as specified by sections 102 and 103, whether created before or after that date and whether published or unpublished, are governed exclusively by this title. Thereafter, no person is entitled to any such right or equivalent right in any such work under the common law or statutes of any State.

(b) Nothing in this title annuls or limits any rights or remedies under the common law or statutes of any State with respect to—

(1) subject matter that does not come within the subject matter of copyright as specified by sections 102 and 103, including works of authorship not fixed in any tangible medium of expression; or

(2) any cause of action arising from undertakings commenced before January 1, 1978;

(3) activities violating legal or equitable rights that are not equivalent to any of the exclusive rights within the general scope of copyright as specified by section 106; or

(4) State and local landmarks, historic preservation, zoning, or building codes, relating to architectural works protected under section 102(a)(8).

(c) With respect to sound recordings fixed before February 15, 1972, any rights or remedies under the common law or statutes of any State shall not be annulled or limited by this title until February 15, 2067. The preemptive provisions of subsection (a) shall apply to any such rights and remedies pertaining to any cause of action arising from undertakings commenced on and after February 15, 2067. Notwithstanding the provisions of section 303, no sound recording fixed before February 15, 1972, shall be subject to copyright under this title before, on, or after February 15, 2067.

(d) Nothing in this title annuls or limits any rights or remedies under any other Federal statute.

(e) The scope of Federal preemption under this section is not affected by the adherence of the United States to the Berne Convention or the satisfaction of obligations of the United States thereunder.

(f)

(1) On or after the effective date set forth in section 610(a) of the Visual Artists Rights Act of 1990, all legal or equitable rights that are equivalent to any of the rights conferred by section 106A with respect to works of visual art to which the rights conferred by section 106A apply are governed exclusively by section 106A and section 113(d) and the provisions of this title relating to such sections. Thereafter, no person is entitled to any such right or equivalent right in any work of visual art under the common law or statutes of any State.

(2) Nothing in paragraph (1) annuls or limits any rights or remedies under the common law or statutes of any State with respect to—

(A) any cause of action from undertakings commenced before the effective date set forth in section 610(a) of the Visual Artists Rights Act of 1990;

(B) activities violating legal or equitable rights that are not equivalent to any of the rights conferred by section 106A with respect to works of visual art; or

(C) activities violating legal or equitable rights which extend beyond the life of the author.

COPYRIGHT LAW REVISION
Report No. 94-1476 (1976), pages 129–33
Committee on the Judiciary
House of Representatives

SECTION 301. FEDERAL PREEMPTION OF RIGHTS EQUIVALENT TO COPYRIGHT

Single Federal System

Section 301, one of the bedrock provisions of the bill, would accomplish a fundamental and significant change in the present law. Instead of a dual system of "common law copyright" for unpublished works and statutory copyright for published works, which has been the system in effect in the United States since the first copyright statute in 1790, the bill adopts a single system of Federal statutory copyright from creation. Under section 301 a work would obtain statutory protection as soon as it is "created" or, as that term is defined in section 101, when it is "fixed in in a copy or phonorecord for the first time." Common law copyright protection for works coming within the scope of the statute would be abrogated, and the concept of publication would lose its all-embracing importance as a dividing line between common law and statutory protection and between both of these forms of legal protection and the public domain.

By substituting a single Federal system for the present anachronistic, uncertain, impractical, and highly complicated dual system, the bill would greatly improve the operation of the copyright law and would be much more effective in carrying out the basic constitutional aims of uniformity and the promotion of writing and scholarship. The main arguments in favor of a single Federal system can be summarized as follows:

1. One of the fundamental purposes behind the copyright clause of the Constitution, as shown in Madison's comments in THE FEDERALIST, was to promote national uniformity and to avoid the practical difficulties of determining and enforcing an author's rights under the differing laws and in the separate courts of the various States. Today, when the methods for dissemination of an author's work are incomparably broader Sind faster than they were in 1789, national uniformity in copyright protection is even more essential than it was then to carry out the constitutional intent.

2. "Publication," perhaps the most important single concept under the present law, also represents its most serious defect. Although at one time, when works were disseminated almost exclusively through printed copies, "publication" could serve as a practical dividing line between common law and statutory protection, this is no longer true. With the development of the 20th-century communications revolution, the concept of publication has become increasingly artificial and obscure. To cope with the legal consequences or an established concept that has lost much of its meaning and justification, the courts have given "publication" a number of diverse interpretations, some of them radically different. Not unexpectedly, the results in individual cases have

become unpredictable and often unfair. A single Federal system would help to clear up this chaotic situation.

3. Enactment of section 301 would also implement the "limited times" provision of the Constitution, which has become distorted under the traditional concept of "publication." Common law protection in "unpublished" works is now perpetual, no matter how widely they may be disseminated by means other than "publication"; the bill would place a time limit on the duration of exclusive rights in them. The provision would also aid scholarship and the dissemination of historical materials by making unpublished, undisseminated manuscripts available for publication after a reasonable period.

4. Adoption of a uniform national copyright system would greatly improve international dealings in copyrighted material. No other country has anything like our present dual system. In an era when copyrighted works can be disseminated instantaneously to every country on the globe, the need for effective international copyright relations, and the concomitant need for national uniformity, assume ever greater importance.

Under section 301, the statute would apply to all works created after its effective date, whether or not they are ever published or disseminated. . . .

Preemption of State Law

The intention of § 301 is to preempt and abolish any rights under the common law or statutes of a State that are equivalent to copyright and that extend to works coming within the scope of the Federal copyright law. The declaration of this principle in § 301 is intended to be stated in the clearest and most unequivocal language possible, so as to foreclose any conceivable misinterpretation of its unqualified intention that Congress shall act preemptively, and to avoid the development of any vague borderline areas between State and Federal protection.

Under § 301(a) all "legal or equitable rights that are equivalent to any of the exclusive rights within the general scope of copyright as specified by section 106["] are governed exclusively by the Federal copyright statute if the works involved are "works of authorship that are fixed in a tangible medium of expression and come within the subject matter of copyright as specified by §§ 102 and 103." All corresponding State laws, whether common law or statutory, are preempted and abrogated. Regardless of when the work was created and whether it is published or unpublished, disseminated or undisseminated, in the public domain or copyrighted under the Federal statute, the States cannot offer it protection equivalent to copyright. Section 1338 of title 28, United States Code, also makes clear that any action involving rights under the Federal copyright law would come within the exclusive jurisdiction of the Federal courts. . . .

As long as a work fits within one of the general subject matter categories of §§ 102 and 103, the bill prevents the States from protecting it even if it fails to achieve Federal statutory copyright because it is too minimal or lacking in originality to qualify, or because it has fallen into the public domain. On the other hand, § 301(b) explicitly preserves common law copyright protection for one important class of works: works that have not been "fixed in any tangible medium of expression." Examples would include choreography that has never been filmed or notated, an extemporaneous speech, "original works of authorship" communicated solely through conversations or live broadcasts, and a dramatic sketch or musical composition improvised or developed from memory and without being recorded or written down. As mentioned above in connection with § 102, unfixed works are not included in the specified "subject matter of copyright." They are therefore not affected by the preemption of section 301, and would continue to be subject to protection under State statute or common law until fixed in tangible form.

The preemption of rights under State law is complete with respect to any work coming within the scope of the bill, even though the scope of exclusive rights given the work under the bill is narrower than the scope of common law rights in the work might have been. . . .

In a general way subsection (b) of § 301 represents the obverse of subsection (a). It sets out, in broad terms and without necessarily being exhaustive, some of the principal areas of protection that preemption would not prevent the States from protecting. Its purpose is to make clear, consistent with the 1964 Supreme Court decisions in *Sears, Roebuck & Co. v. Stiffel Co.*, 376 U.S. 225, and *Compco Corp. v. Day-Brite Lighting, Inc.*, 376 U.S. 234, that preemption does not extend to causes of action, or subject matter outside the scope of the revised Federal copyright statute.

The numbered clauses of subsection (b) list three general areas left unaffected by the preemption: (1) subject matter that does not come within the subject matter of copyright; (2) causes of action arising under State law before the effective date of the statute; and (3) violations of rights that are not equivalent to any of the exclusive rights under copyright.

The examples in clause (3), while not exhaustive, are intended to illustrate rights and remedies that are different in nature from the rights comprised in a copyright and that may continue to be protected under State common law or statute. The evolving common law rights of "privacy," "publicity," and trade secrets, and the general laws of defamation and fraud, would remain unaffected as long as the causes of action contain elements, such as an invasion of personal rights or a breach of trust or confidentiality, that are different in kind from copyright infringement. Nothing in the bill derogates from the rights of parties to contract with each other and to sue for breaches of contract; however, to the extent that the unfair competition concept known as "interference with contract relations" is merely the equivalent of copyright protection, it would be preempted.

The last example listed in clause (3)—"deceptive trade practices such as passing off and false representation"—represents an effort to distinguish between those causes of action known as "unfair competition" that the copyright statute is not intended to preempt and those that it is. Section 301 is not intended to preempt common law protection in cases involving activities such as false labeling, fraudulent representation, and passing off even where the subject matter involved comes within the scope of the copyright statute,

"Misappropriation" is not necessarily synonymous with copyright infringement, and thus a cause of action labeled as "misappropriation" is not preempted if it is in fact based neither on a right within the general scope of copyright as specified by section 106 nor on a right equivalent thereto. For example, state law should have the flexibility to afford a remedy (under traditional principles of equity) against a consistent pattern of unauthorized appropriation by a competitor of the facts (i.e., not the literary expression) constituting "hot" news, whether in the traditional mold of *International News Service v. Associated Press*, 248 U.S. 215 (1918), or in the newer form of data updates from scientific, business, or financial data bases. Likewise, a person having no trust or other relationship with the proprietor of a computerized data base should not be immunized from sanctions against electronically or cryptographically breaching the proprietor's security arrangements and accessing the proprietor's data. The unauthorized data access which should be remediable might also be achieved by the intentional interception of data transmissions by wire, microwave or laser transmissions, or by the common unintentional means of "crossed" telephone lines occasioned by errors in switching.

The proprietor of data displayed on the cathode ray tube of a computer terminal should be afforded protection against unauthorized printouts by third parties (with or without improper access), even if the data are not copyrightable. For example, the data may not be copyrighted because they are not fixed in a tangible medium of expression (i.e., the data are not displayed for a period or not more than transitory duration).

Nothing contained in section 301 precludes the owner of a material embodiment of a copy or a phonorecord from enforcing a claim of conversion against one who takes possession of the copy or phonorecord without consent.

A unique and difficult problem is presented with respect to the status of sound recordings fixed before February 12, 1972, the effective date of the amendment bringing recordings fixed after that date under Federal copyright protection. In its testimony during the 1975 hearings, the Department of Justice pointed out that, under section 301 as then written:

> This language could be read as abrogating the anti-piracy laws now existing in 29 states relating to pre-February 15, 1972, sound recordings on the grounds that these statutes proscribe activities violating rights equivalent to * * * the exclusive rights within the general scope of copyright. * * * "Certainly such a result cannot have been intended for it would likely effect the immediate resurgence of piracy of pre-February 15, 1972, sound recordings.

The Department recommended that section 301(b) be amended to exclude sound recordings fixed prior to February 15, 1972 from the effect of the preemption.

The Senate adopted this suggestion when it passed S. 22. The result of the Senate amendment would be to leave pre-1972 sound recordings as entitled to perpetual protection under State law, while post-1972 recordings would eventually fall into the public domain as provided in the bill.

The Committee recognizes that, under recent court decisions, pre-1972 recordings are protected by State statute or common law, and that should not all be thrown into the public domain instantly upon the coming into effect of the new law. However, it cannot agree that they should in effect be accorded perpetual protection, as under the Senate amendment, and it has therefore revised clause (4) to establish a future date for the pre-emption to take effect. The date chosen is February 15, 2047, which is 15 years from the effective date of the statute extending Federal protection to recordings.

Subsection (c) makes clear that nothing contained in Title 17 annuls or limits any rights or remedies under any other Federal statute.

COMMENTS AND QUESTIONS

1. *Pre-1972 Sound Recordings.* We discussed state law protection of sound recordings fixed in a tangible object prior to February 15, 1972. *See* Chapter IV(E)(5)(ii).

2. Do you find the language of § 301(b), preserving state law protections that "do not come within the subject matter of copyright" or "are not equivalent to any of the exclusive rights under copyright" to be clear? We explore state protections for misappropriation, idea submissions, and right of publicity, each of which hovers near the federal copyright boundary, later in this chapter.

ii.   Contract

Inventors and creators frequently use contract law, such as license agreements, to achieve some of the goals they might otherwise use intellectual property rights to obtain. They also attempt use contracts to bargain around legal default rules, such as the first sale doctrine and fair use. Thus, contracts are fundamentally intertwined with intellectual property.

ProCD, Inc. v. Zeidenberg
United States Court of Appeals for the Seventh Circuit
86 F.3d 1447 (7th Cir. 1996)

EASTERBROOK, Circuit Judge.

Must buyers of computer software obey the terms of shrinkwrap licenses? The district court held not, for two reasons: first, they are not contracts because the licenses are inside the box rather than printed on the outside; second, federal law forbids enforcement even if the licenses are contracts. 908 F. Supp. 640 (W.D. Wis. 1996). The parties and numerous amici curiae have briefed many other issues, but these are the only two that matter—and we disagree with the district judge's conclusion on each. Shrinkwrap licenses are enforceable unless their terms are objectionable on grounds applicable to contracts in general (for example, if they violate a rule of positive law, or if they are unconscionable). Because no one argues that the terms of the license at issue here are troublesome, we remand with instructions to enter judgment for the plaintiff.

I.

ProCD, the plaintiff, has compiled information from more than 3,000 telephone directories into a computer database. We may assume that this database cannot be copyrighted, although it is more complex, contains more information (nine-digit zip codes and census industrial codes), is organized differently, and therefore is more original than the single alphabetical directory at issue in *Feist Publications, Inc. v. Rural Telephone Service Co.*, 499 U.S. 340 (1991). *See* Paul J. Heald, *The Vices of Originality*, 1991 SUP. CT. REV. 143, 160–68. ProCD sells a version of the database, called SelectPhone (trademark), on CD-ROM discs. (CD-ROM means "compact disc—read only memory." The "shrinkwrap license" gets its name from the fact that retail software packages are covered in plastic or cellophane "shrinkwrap," and some vendors, though not ProCD, have written licenses that become effective as soon as the customer tears the wrapping from the package. Vendors prefer "end user license," but we use the more common term.) A proprietary method of compressing the data serves as effective encryption too. Customers decrypt and use the data with the aid of an application program that ProCD has written. This program, which is copyrighted, searches the database in response to users' criteria (such as "find all people named Tatum in Tennessee, plus all firms with 'Door Systems' in the corporate name"). The resulting lists (or, as ProCD prefers, "listings") can be read and manipulated by other software, such as word processing programs.

The database in SelectPhone (trademark) cost more than $10 million to compile and is expensive to keep current. It is much more valuable to some users than to others. The combination of names, addresses, and SIC codes enables manufacturers to compile lists of potential customers. Manufacturers and retailers pay high prices to specialized information intermediaries for such mailing lists; ProCD offers a potentially cheaper alternative. People with nothing to sell could use the database as a substitute for calling long distance information, or as a way to look up old friends who have moved to unknown towns, or just as an electronic substitute for the local phone book. ProCD decided to engage in price discrimination, selling its database to the general public for personal use at a low price (approximately $150 for the set of five discs) while selling information to the trade for a higher price. It has adopted some intermediate strategies too: access to the SelectPhone (trademark) database is available via the America Online service for the price America Online charges to its clients (approximately $3 per hour), but this service has been tailored to be useful only to the general public.

If ProCD had to recover all of its costs and make a profit by charging a single price—that is, if it could not charge more to commercial users than to the general public—it would have to raise the price substantially over $150. The ensuing reduction in sales would harm consumers who value the information at, say, $200. They get consumer surplus of $50 under the current arrangement but would cease to buy if the price rose substantially. If because of high elasticity of demand in the consumer segment of the market the only way to make a profit turned out to be a price attractive to commercial users alone, then all consumers would lose out—and so would the commercial clients, who would have to pay more for the listings because ProCD could not obtain any contribution toward costs from the consumer market.

To make price discrimination work, however, the seller must be able to control arbitrage. An air carrier sells tickets for less to vacationers than to business travelers, using advance purchase and Saturday-night-stay requirements to distinguish the categories. A producer of movies segments the market by time, releasing first to theaters, then to pay-per-view services, next to the videotape and laserdisc market, and finally to cable and commercial TV. Vendors of computer software have a harder task. Anyone can walk into a retail store and buy a box. Customers do not wear tags saying "commercial user" or "consumer user." Anyway, even a commercial-user-detector at the door would not work, because a consumer could buy the software and resell to a commercial user. That arbitrage would break down the price discrimination and drive up the minimum price at which ProCD would sell to anyone.

Instead of tinkering with the product and letting users sort themselves—for example, furnishing current data at a high price that would be attractive only to commercial customers, and two-year-old data at a low price—ProCD turned to the institution of contract. Every box containing its consumer product declares that the software comes with restrictions stated in an enclosed license. This license, which is encoded on the CD-ROM disks as well as printed in the manual, and which appears on a user's screen every time the software runs, limits use of the application program and listings to non-commercial purposes.

Matthew Zeidenberg bought a consumer package of SelectPhone (trademark) in 1994 from a retail outlet in Madison, Wisconsin, but decided to ignore the license. He formed Silken Mountain Web Services, Inc., to resell the information in the Select-Phone (trademark) database. The corporation makes the database available on the Internet to anyone willing to pay its price—which, needless to say, is less than ProCD charges its commercial customers. Zeidenberg has purchased two additional SelectPhone (trademark) packages, each with an updated version of the database, and made the latest information available over the World Wide Web, for a price, through his corporation. ProCD filed this suit seeking an injunction against further dissemination that exceeds the rights specified in the licenses (identical in each of the three packages Zeidenberg purchased). The district court held the licenses ineffectual because their terms do not appear on the outside of the packages. The court added that the second and third licenses stand no different from the first, even though they are identical, because they might have been different, and a purchaser does not agree to—and cannot be bound by—terms that were secret at the time of purchase. 908 F. Supp. at 654. . . .

III.

The district court held that, even if Wisconsin treats shrinkwrap licenses as contracts, § 301(a) of the Copyright Act, 17 U.S.C. § 301(a), prevents their enforcement. 908 F. Supp. at 656–59. The relevant part of § 301(a) preempts any "legal or equitable rights [under state law] that are equivalent to any of the exclusive rights within the general scope of copyright as specified by section 106 in works of authorship that are fixed in a tangible medium of expression and come within the subject matter of copyright as specified by sections 102 and 103." ProCD's software and data are "fixed in a tangible medium of expression," and the district judge held that they are "within the subject matter of copyright." The latter conclusion is plainly right for the copyrighted application program, and the judge thought that the data likewise are "within the subject matter of copyright" even if, after *Feist*, they are not sufficiently original to be copyrighted. 908 F. Supp. at 656–57. *Baltimore Orioles, Inc. v. Major League Baseball Players Ass'n*, 805 F.2d 663, 676 (7th Cir. 1986), supports that conclusion, with which commentators agree. *E.g.*, PAUL GOLDSTEIN, III COPYRIGHT § 15.2.3 (2d ed. 1996); MELVILLE B. NIMMER & DAVID NIMMER, NIMMER ON COPYRIGHT § 101[B] (1995); WILLIAM F. PATRY, II COPYRIGHT LAW AND PRACTICE 1108–09 (1994). One function of § 301(a) is to prevent states from giving special protection to works of authorship that Congress has decided should be in the public domain, which it can accomplish only if "subject matter of copyright" includes all works of a type covered by sections 102 and 103, even if federal law does not afford protection to them. *Cf. Bonito Boats, Inc. v. Thunder Craft Boats, Inc.*, 489 U.S. 141 (1989) (same principle under patent laws).

But are rights created by contract "equivalent to any of the exclusive rights within the general scope of copyright"? Three courts of appeals have answered "no." *National Car Rental Systems, Inc. v. Computer Associates International, Inc.*, 991 F.2d 426, 433 (8th Cir. 1993); *Taquino v. Teledyne Monarch Rubber*, 893 F.2d 1488, 1501 (5th Cir. 1990); *Acorn Structures, Inc. v. Swantz*, 846 F.2d 923, 926 (4th Cir. 1988). The district court disagreed with these decisions, 908 F. Supp. at 658, but we think them sound. Rights "equivalent to any of the exclusive rights within the general scope of copyright" are rights established by law—rights that restrict the options of persons who are strangers to the author. Copyright law forbids duplication, public performance, and so on, unless the person wishing to copy or perform the work gets permission; silence means a ban on copying. A copyright is a right against the world. Contracts, by contrast, generally affect only their parties; strangers may do as they please, so contracts do not create "exclusive rights." Someone who found a copy of SelectPhone (trademark) on the street would not be affected by the shrinkwrap license—though the federal copyright laws of their own force would limit the finder's ability to copy or transmit the application program.

Think for a moment about trade secrets. One common trade secret is a customer list. After *Feist*, a simple alphabetical list of a firm's customers, with address and telephone numbers, could not be protected by copyright. Yet *Kewanee Oil Co. v. Bicron Corp.*, 416 U.S. 470 (1974), holds that contracts about trade secrets may be enforced—precisely because they do not affect strangers' ability to discover and use the information independently. If the amendment of § 301(a) in 1976 overruled *Kewanee* and abolished consensual protection of those trade secrets that cannot be copyrighted, no one has noticed—though abolition is a logical consequence of the district court's approach. Think, too, about everyday transactions in intellectual property. A customer visits a video store and rents a copy of Night of the Lepus. The customer's contract with the store limits use of the tape to home viewing and requires its return in two days. May the customer keep the tape, on the ground that § 301(a) makes the promise unenforceable?

A law student uses the LEXIS database, containing public-domain documents, under a contract limiting the results to educational endeavors; may the student resell his access to this database to a law firm from which LEXIS seeks to collect a much higher hourly rate? Suppose ProCD hires a firm to scour the nation for telephone directories, promising to pay $100 for each that ProCD does not already have. The firm locates 100 new directories, which it sends to ProCD with an invoice for $10,000. ProCD incorporates the directories into its database; does it have to pay the bill? Surely yes; *Aronson v. Quick Point Pencil Co.*, 440 U.S. 257 (1979), holds that promises to pay for intellectual property may be enforced even though federal law (in *Aronson*, the patent law) offers no protection against third-party uses of that property. *See also Kennedy v. Wright*, 851 F.2d 963 (7th Cir. 1988). But these illustrations are what our case is about. ProCD offers software and data for two prices: one for personal use, a higher price for commercial use. Zeidenberg wants to use the data without paying the seller's price; if the law student and Quick Point Pencil Co. could not do that, neither can Zeidenberg.

Although Congress possesses power to preempt even the enforcement of contracts about intellectual property—or railroads, on which *see Norfolk & Western Ry. v. Train Dispatchers*, 499 U.S. 117 (1991)—courts usually read preemption clauses to leave private contracts unaffected. *American Airlines, Inc. v. Wolens*, 115 S.Ct. 817 (1995), provides a nice illustration. A federal statute preempts any state "law, rule, regulation, standard, or other provision . . . relating to rates, routes, or services of any air carrier." 49 U.S.C. App. § 1305(a)(1). Does such a law preempt the law of contracts—so that, for example, an air carrier need not honor a quoted price (or a contract to reduce the price by the value of frequent flyer miles)? The Court allowed that it is possible to read the statute that broadly but thought such an interpretation would make little sense. Terms and conditions offered by contract reflect private ordering, essential to the efficient functioning of markets. 115 S.Ct. at 824–25. Although some principles that carry the name of contract law are designed to defeat rather than implement consensual transactions, *id.* at 826 n.8, the rules that respect private choice are not preempted by a clause such as § 1305(a)(1). Section 301(a) plays a role similar to § 1301(a)(1): it prevents states from substituting their own regulatory systems for those of the national government. Just as § 301(a) does not itself interfere with private transactions in intellectual property, so it does not prevent states from respecting those transactions. Like the Supreme Court in *Wolens*, we think it prudent to refrain from adopting a rule that anything with the label "contract" is necessarily outside the preemption clause: the variations and possibilities are too numerous to foresee. National Car Rental likewise recognizes the possibility that some applications of the law of contract could interfere with the attainment of national objectives and therefore come within the domain of § 301(a). But general enforcement of shrinkwrap licenses of the kind before us does not create such interference.

Aronson emphasized that enforcement of the contract between Aronson and Quick Point Pencil Company would not withdraw any information from the public domain. That is equally true of the contract between ProCD and Zeidenberg. Everyone remains free to copy and disseminate all 3,000 telephone books that have been incorporated into

ProCD's database. Anyone can add SIC codes and zip codes. ProCD's rivals have done so. Enforcement of the shrinkwrap license may even make information more readily available, by reducing the price ProCD charges to consumer buyers. To the extent licenses facilitate distribution of object code while concealing the source code (the point of a clause forbidding disassembly), they serve the same procompetitive functions as does the law of trade secrets. *Rockwell Graphic Systems, Inc. v. DEV Industries, Inc.*, 925 F.2d 174, 180 (7th Cir. 1991). Licenses may have other benefits for consumers: many licenses permit users to make extra copies, to use the software on multiple computers, even to incorporate the software into the user's products. But whether a particular license is generous or restrictive, a simple two-party contract is not "equivalent to any of the exclusive rights within the general scope of copyright" and therefore may be enforced.

Reversed and remanded.

COMMENTS AND QUESTIONS

1. Section 301 is designed to prevent states from passing or enforcing laws "equivalent" to copyright. Whether a particular law is equivalent to copyright can be difficult to determine, however. Courts generally do not ask whether a body of law as a whole (contract or trade secrets, say) is equivalent to copyright. Rather, the question is whether the application of a state law to a particular factual circumstance would create a state-law right equivalent to copyright. Even *ProCD*, which takes a fairly categorical approach to § 301 preemption, is careful to note that it is not holding that § 301 will never preempt contract terms.

Nonetheless, Judge Easterbrook sees a categorical difference between enforcement of contract law and enforcement of other state laws. The court reasoned:

> Rights "equivalent to any of the exclusive rights within the general scope of copyright" are rights established *by law*—rights that restrict the options of persons who are strangers to the author. Copyright law forbids duplication, public performance, and so on, unless the person wishing to copy or perform the work gets permission; silence means a ban on copying. A copyright is a right against the world. Contracts, by contrast, generally affect only their parties; strangers may do as they please, so contracts do not create "exclusive rights." Someone who found a copy of [the plaintiff's software product] on the street would not be affected by the shrinkwrap license. . . .

Is this distinction between judicial enforcement of contracts and other state laws persuasive? Commentators have been skeptical. Professors Peggy Radin and Polk Wagner point out that the Legal Realist movement in the last century exploded the myth that contracts are purely "private" creatures; they depend on the legal system for their enforcement. *See* Margaret Jane Radin & R. Polk Wagner, *The Myth of Private Ordering: Rediscovering Legal Realism in Cyberspace*, 73 CHI.-KENT L. REV. 1295 (1998). And Professor Mark Lemley observes that "even truly 'private' contracts affect third parties who haven't agreed to the contract terms. Many contracts have significant negative externalities." Mark A. Lemley, *Beyond Preemption: The Law and Policy of Intellectual Property Licensing*, 87 CAL. L. REV. 111 (1999).

Whatever the validity of the general distinction, the court in *ProCD* applied it to validate a "shrinkwrap license," a peculiar form of contract that is drafted by the creator of the product and that purports to bind to its terms anyone who uses the product. While it is technically true in such a case that only "parties" to the contract are bound by it, anyone who has access to the product will automatically become such a party. Scholars argue that shrinkwrap licenses accordingly look less like contracts in the pure sense, and more like examples of private legislation:

> [T]he viability of the distinction between private contracts and public legislation is diminishing day by day. One of the main changes [*ProCD* and its progeny] would make in current law would be to render enforceable contract "terms" to which the parties did not agree in the classic sense, and indeed of which one party may be entirely unaware. [They] would also enable the enforcement of such contract terms "downstream"—that is, against whomever later acquires the software—despite the fact that a first sale under both patent and copyright law would free the purchaser from upstream contractual restrictions. Technology facilitates this change by allowing a vendor to interpose contract terms even in a downstream transaction that would not ordinarily be thought to demonstrate privity between the "contracting" parties.

Lemley, *supra*. On the general issue of standard form contracts and their legal status, *see* MARGARET JANE RADIN, BOILERPLATE: THE FINE PRINT, VANISHING RIGHTS, AND THE RULE OF LAW (2014).

2. Does copyright preemption of state contract law depend on the remedy asserted for breach of contract? Should federal law be more concerned if a party seeks by contract to bring the weapons of copyright law to bear? Note that the legislative history to the Copyright Act states that the first sale doctrine (§ 109(a)) "does not mean that conditions on future disposition of copies or phonorecords, imposed by a contract between their buyer and seller, would be unenforceable between the parties as a breach of contract, but it does mean that they could not be enforced by an action for infringement of copyright." COMMITTEE ON THE JUDICIARY, HOUSE OF REPRESENTATIVES, REPORT NO. 94-1476, p.79 (1976). Contract remedies are ordinarily limited to expectation damages, rather than the consequential damages, statutory damages, attorney fees, and injunctions available under the copyright law. But suppose a license agreement provided that *resale* of a copyrighted work—permissible under copyright law—voids the entire license, rendering the reseller liable for copyright infringement. Should such a contract be preempted by copyright law? If not, is there anything left in practice of the first sale doctrine? Recall that the books at issue in *Kirtsaeng v. John Wiley & Sons, Inc.*, 133 S.Ct. 1351 (2013), covered in Chapter IV(E)(4)(ii), "likely contain[ed] language making clear that the copy is to be sold only in a particular country or geographical region outside the United States." Should we treat that unilateral statement as an enforceable contract that avoids copyright preemption? The Comments and Questions after the case touch on the license/copyright interplay.

3. After *ProCD*, is there any set of circumstances in which § 301 will preempt a contract? Suppose that a contract provided that the buyer of a book could not make fair use of the book. Should such a contract term be enforced? Would § 301 stand in the way? Should the context of the contract (whether it was a shrinkwrap, whether the product was widely sold, whether the buyer was a consumer) matter?

4. After *ProCD* was decided, many worried that its approach would encourage the greater use of contractual mechanisms to control information and thereby undermine the balance underlying copyright. Since *ProCD*, a majority of circuit courts of appeal have adopted t Judge Easterbrook's approach. It remains unclear whether those concerns have been borne out in the marketplace. *See* Guy A. Rub, *Copyright Survives: Rethinking the Copyright-Contract Conflict*, 103 VA. L. REV. 1141 (2017) (contending that *ProCD* has not done significant harm to copyright law and the marketplace for information); *contra* Mark A. Lemley, *Terms of Use*, 91 Minn. L. Rev. 459 (2006) (arguing that the expansion of *ProCD* to browsewrap contracts online is problematic).

5. While we have so far discussed copyright preemption of contract claims, copyright preemption also applies to a variety of state statutes and common law causes of action. Indeed, in *ProCD* itself, the district court held state tort claims for unfair competition, misappropriation, and violation of the Wisconsin Computer Crimes Act to be preempted, because all three claims were based on Zeidenberg's copying of uncopyrightable data. *ProCD, Inc. v. Zeidenberg*, 908 F. Supp. 640 (W.D. Wis. 1996). The Seventh Circuit let these findings stand on appeal. The Eleventh Circuit has held claims for unfair competition and deceptive trade practices preempted where those claims were made in an effort to protect uncopyrightable databases. *Lipscher v. LRP Publications*, 266 F.3d 1305 (11th Cir. 2001). On copyright preemption of trade secret claims, *see Computer Associates Int'l v. Altai, Inc.*, 982 F.2d 693, 715–17 (2d Cir. 1992) (copyright and trade secret claims could co-exist regarding the use of the same computer program, as long as misappropriation of trade secrets is based on a defendant's breach of a duty of trust or confidence). *See also Automated Drawing Systems v. Integrated Network Services*, 447 S.E.2d 109 (Ga. Ct. App. 1994) (copyright law did not preempt Georgia Computer Systems Protection Act, which prohibited the "misappropriation" of source code and provided tort damages).

6. *The "Additional Element" Test for Preemption under § 301.* Courts attempting to determine whether a right was "equivalent" to copyright have introduced a seemingly straightforward test for federal preemption of state laws in the general domain of copyright: the so-called extra element test. Under this test, if state law provides a cause of action that requires proof of at least one element in addition to those required for a copyright infringement claim, the state law survives. The test tries to state simply, in terms of required pleadings for an effective cause of action, the basic idea that a state can proscribe activities in the general domain of intellectual property as long as those activities are qualitatively different from the ones that are the subject of federal protection. Claims for breach of implied contract in the context of idea submissions (as we will see in *Desny v. Wilder*) survive federal preemption as they turn "not upon the existence of a [copyright] . . . but upon the implied promise to pay the reasonable value

of the material disclosed." *Grosso v. Miramax Film Corp.*, 383 F.3d 965, 968 (9th Cir. 2004) (quoting *Landsberg v. Scrabble Crossword Game Players, Inc.*, 802 F.2d 1193, 1196 (9th Cir. 1986)).

As applied, the "additional element" test has an elastic quality. In *National Car Rental System v. Computer Associates*, 991 F.2d 426 (8th Cir. 1993), for example, the court held that a claim for breach of a license to use a computer program was not preempted under § 301 because the claim involved "use" of the program, and "use" of a computer program was not one of the rights conferred by the Copyright Act. If read broadly, so that an allegation of use *in addition to* copying of a copyrighted work survives preemption, *National Car Rental* doesn't leave much of § 301 preemption. Other examples of courts reaching to find an extra element include *Taco Bell Corp. v. Wrench LLC,* 256 F.3d 446 (6th Cir. 2001) (holding that the requirement of an "expectation of compensation" in a claim for implied-in-fact contract saved the claim from preemption).

7. *Supremacy Clause Preemption.* Section 301 is not the only basis for copyright preemption. Congress enacted § 301 because it intended to "preempt the field" of copyright law, precluding states from passing laws that mimicked the federal statute. But even where Congress has not preempted the field, state statutes will still be preempted if they conflict with the specific mandate of federal law, or if they stand as an obstacle to the purposes of a federal statute. In copyright law, such "conflicts" or "Supremacy Clause" preemption obviously occurs when a state law prevents the enforcement of a federal copyright. For example, if the state of California were to pass a law stating that the Copyright Act did not apply to citizens of California, the law would arguably survive § 301 preemption, since it contains an "extra element" (citizenship) and does not create a right equivalent to copyright. But it would surely be struck down by the courts as an interference with the federal scheme.

Not all interferences are so straightforward. In *ASCAP v. Pataki*, 930 F. Supp. 873 (S.D.N.Y. 1996), the court invalidated a state statute regulating the activities of performing rights societies such as ASCAP and BMI. The state statute required, among other things, that such groups provide owners of establishments performing music with written notice of an investigation within 72 hours after it is initiated, thus making it difficult for ASCAP and others to conduct "undercover" investigations for violations of the copyright laws. The court's opinion addressed only the issue of "conflict preemption, which occurs either where compliance with both federal and state regulations is a physical impossibility, or where state law stands as an obstacle to the accomplishment and execution of the full purposes and objectives of Congress." *Id.* The court found that the state statutory provisions "hinder the realization of the federal copyright scheme" for several reasons: the statute made it more difficult for copyright owners to enforce their rights; it effectively established a "statute of limitations" on copyright investigations that was shorter than the federal statute; and it gave copyright defendants a counterclaim that they could use to offset copyright damages. *See also College Entrance Examination Board v. Pataki,* 889 F. Supp. 554 (N.D.N.Y. 1995) (state law requiring disclosure of standardized test questions and answers preempted by

Copyright Act because it conflicted with the rights of copyright owners to restrict distribution of copyrighted material).

Because the Copyright Act is an attempt by Congress to balance the interests of creators and users of intellectual property, state laws that give *too much* protection to copyrighted works may also interfere with the objectives of Congress. *See, e.g., United States ex rel. Berge v. Trustees of the University of Alabama*, 104 F.3d 1453 (4th Cir. 1997) ("The shadow actually cast by the Act's preemption is notably broader than the wing of its protection."). As the Supreme Court explained in *Goldstein v. California*, 412 U.S. 546 (1973), the question is whether Congress intended to place a particular work or use in the public domain:

> At any time Congress determines that a particular category of "writing" is worthy of national protection and the incidental expenses of federal administration, federal copyright protection may be authorized. Where the need for free and unrestricted distribution of a writing is thought to be required by the national interest, the Copyright Clause and the Commerce Clause would allow Congress to eschew all protection. In such cases, a conflict would develop if a State attempted to protect that which Congress intended to be free from restraint or to free that which Congress had protected. However, where Congress determines that neither federal protection nor freedom from restraint is required by the national interest, it is at liberty to stay its hand entirely. Since state protection would not then conflict with federal action, total relinquishment of the States' power to grant copyright protection cannot be inferred.

Although *Goldstein* was decided before the enactment of § 301, that section does not displace preemption based on a conflict between state and federal law. Several cases have gone beyond § 301 to a general preemption analysis along the lines of *Bonito Boats*. In *Associated Film Distribution Corp. v. Thornburgh*, 520 F. Supp. 971 (E.D. Pa. 1981), *rev'd and remanded on other grounds*, 683 F.2d 808, 817 (3d Cir. 1982), the court held preempted a state statute regulating the procedure by which film exhibitors licensed major motion pictures from film distribution arms of the major movie companies. The court went beyond § 301, stating that the "more general question of conflict between the two statutory schemes under the supremacy clause is decisive." 520 F. Supp. at 993. *See also Orson, Inc. v. Miramax Film Corp.*, 189 F.3d 377 (3d Cir. 1999) (en banc) (a Pennsylvania statute that prohibited an exclusive license of a first-run film for longer than six weeks was preempted by the Copyright Act); *but see Allied Artists Pictures Corp. v. Rhodes*, 496 F. Supp. 408 (S.D. Ohio 1980), *aff'd and remanded in part*, 679 F.2d 656, 665 (6th Cir. 1982) (reaching the opposite conclusion). And in *Estate of Robert Graham v. Sotheby's*, 178 F. Supp. 3d 974 (C.D. Cal. Apr. 11, 2016), the court held that the Copyright Act preempted California's Resale Royalty Act, which provided that owners of original works of art who resold them had to pay a percentage of their proceeds to the artist. The court held that the statute was preempted "because the CRRA disrupts Congress's efforts to balance the interests of copyright owners and downstream consumers" under the fair use doctrine.

A number of cases have in fact preempted contract terms that conflict with federal patent and copyright policy. For example, contract terms that purport to extend a patent or copyright beyond its expiration have repeatedly been held unenforceable. On the distinction between "conflict preemption" and copyright field preemption in the contract area, *see* David Nimmer, Elliot Brown, & Gary N. Frischling, *The Metamorphosis of Contract into Expand*, 87 CAL. L. REV. 17 (1999).

8. Is *ProCD* in fact a case of conflict between copyright and contract? The stage for such a conflict is set by the Supreme Court decision in *Feist*, which held that the telephone white pages at issue in *ProCD* were constitutionally ineligible for copyright protection. This mode of analysis parallels the Dormant Commerce Clause doctrine, which holds that a grant of power (protection for original works of authorship) can imply a negative converse—that Congress intended unoriginal works to be unprotectable. Such a policy could well be seen to promote progress by enabling others to build on and develop databases. Does the fact that ProCD's shrinkwrap license gives, if anything, even greater protection than copyright would suggest there is a conflict here? In *ProCD v. Zeidenberg*, 908 F. Supp. 640 (W.D. Wis. 1996), the district court reasoned in dictum that state contract law could not be used to prevent the copying of telephone white pages, which the Supreme Court had determined in *Feist* were uncopyrightable. The district court applied a constitutional copyright preemption analysis similar to the patent analysis undertaken in *Bonito Boats*. The Seventh Circuit reversed the district court's decision, concluding that under § 301 of the Copyright Act state contract law could not be preempted in this case. *ProCD v. Zeidenberg*, 86 F.3d 1447 (7th Cir. 1996). Judge Easterbrook's opinion did not mention Supremacy Clause preemption at all, even though the issue was briefed and was necessary to the decision, leaving the issue in some doubt.

Courts that have considered the question of whether shrinkwrap licenses can be preempted when they conflict with federal policy have split. One court concluded that a state statute permitting enforcement of shrinkwrap licenses was invalid under the Supremacy Clause where the shrinkwrap license at issue forbade reverse engineering that was permissible under the Copyright Act. *Vault Inc. v. Quaid Corp.*, 847 F.2d 255 (5th Cir. 1988). *See also Bowers v. Baystate Technologies*, 320 F.3d 1317, 1337 (Fed. Cir. 2003) (Dyk, J., dissenting) (endorsing this result). On the other hand, two later decisions have found no distinction between shrinkwrap licenses and negotiated contracts, and permitted copyright owners to block reverse engineering using a shrinkwrap provision. *Davidson & Assocs. v. Jung*, 422 F.3d 630 (8th Cir. 2005); *Bowers v. Baystate Technologies*, 320 F.3d 1317 (Fed. Cir. 2003).

If the federal copyright scheme intends unoriginal works like the telephone white pages to be in the public domain, is there any way to prevent the sort of use Zeidenberg made of this data? States presumably would lack the power to do so. There is some question whether Congress could avoid the constitutional limitation of originality in the Copyright Clause by enacting protection for databases under the Commerce Clause. *See United States v. Martignon*, 492 F.3d 140 (2d Cir. 2007) (upholding anti-bootlegging statute which protects unfixed works under the Commerce Clause because it perceived no conflict between the statute in question and the policies of copyright law); *United States v. Moghadam*, 175 F.3d 1269 (11th Cir. 1999). But a Congressional effort to overrule *Feist* might be more problematic. *See* Paul J. Heald & Suzanna Sherry, *Implied Limits on the Legislative Power: The Intellectual Property Clause as an Absolute Constraint on Congress*, 2000 U. ILL. L. REV. 1119.

PROBLEM

Problem VI-1. Presco is in the business of printing and selling academic journals to university libraries. When Presco receives a subscription request, it sends a form contract to the requestor. The requesting library is required to sign the contract before Presco will start the subscription. Presco's form contract provides in part that "Independent of and in addition to any provisions of state or federal law, the parties agree that Subscriber will not make, cause to be made, or allow to be made any copies of any Presco journals without the prior express written consent of Presco." Is the contract provision preempted? Does it matter whether the subscriber's copying would constitute fair use under the copyright laws?

---

3. Trademark Preemption

There has been surprisingly little litigation over the preemptive effect of the Lanham Act. Because the Lanham Act was passed under the aegis of the Commerce Clause of the Constitution, rather than the Patents and Copyrights Clause, other IP preemption cases are not directly relevant to the problem of trademark preemption. Instead, courts turn to Commerce Clause cases, which focus on whether Congress intended to "preempt the field" of trademark law and on whether there is an actual or potential conflict between the state and federal statutes.

Two early cases held that the Lanham Act preempted all state trademark laws. *See Sargen & Co. v. Welco Feed Mfg.*, 195 F.2d 929 (8th Cir. 1952); *Time, Inc. v. T.I.M.E. Inc.*, 123 F. Supp. 446 (S.D. Cal. 1954). But commentators are skeptical of these broad preemptive holdings, largely because Congress clearly intended in passing the Lanham Act to allow it to coexist with some state trademark laws. *See* 15 U.S.C. §§ 1065, 1115(b)(5) (both referring to the continued effect of state law). *See* Richard A. De Sevo, *Antidilution Laws: The Unresolved Dilemma of Preemption under the Lanham Act*, 84 TRADEMARK REP. 300, 301–04 (1994). However, at least some courts continue to hold that state statutes which are directed at the same types of conduct as the Lanham Act are preempted. *See Three Blind Mice Designs Co. v. Cyrk Inc.*, 892 F. Supp. 303 (D. Mass. 1995) (state anti-dilution statute "wholly preempted" to the extent that it seeks to regulate directly competitive goods).

A more difficult question is presented where state trademark statutes may conflict with the general federal rule. Sometimes such conflicts are clear. For example, state laws that attempt to grant priority to a party other than the earliest federal registrant are surely preempted under 15 U.S.C. § 1127, since the laws "interfere" with the rights granted federal registrants under the Act.

Preemption will also occur if the state law is at odds with the "purpose of Congress" in passing the Lanham Act. Depending on the purpose identified, state anti-dilution laws might fail this test, since they do not require a likelihood of consumer confusion. *See* De Sevo, *supra*, at 312–20. Courts and commentators have split on this issue. *See* David S. Welkowitz, *Preemption, Extraterritoriality and the Problem of State Antidilution Laws*, 67 TUL. L. REV. 1, 4 (1992) (arguing that "injunctions like the one issued in *Mead Data Central, Inc. v. Toyota Motor Sales, U.S.A.*, 702 F. Supp. 1031 (S.D.N.Y. 1988), *rev'd on other grounds*, 875 F.2d 1026 (2d Cir. 1989), exceed [constitutional] limits" under the Commerce Clause, though state anti-dilution statutes are not wholly preempted and in many cases injunctions based on state intellectual property law are enforceable under the Full Faith and Credit Clause). *Cf.* Milton W. Handler, *Are the State Antidilution Laws Compatible with the National Protection of Trademarks?*, 75 TRADEMARK REP. 269 (1985); Joseph P. Bauer, *A Federal Law of Unfair Competition: What Should Be the Reach of Section 43(a) of the Lanham Act?*, 31 UCLA L. REV. 671 (1984); Charles Bunn, *The National Law of Unfair Competition*, 62 HARV. L. REV. 987 (1949); Paul Heald, Comment, *Unfair Competition and Federal Law: Constitutional Restraints on the Scope of State Law*, 54 U. CHI. L. REV. 1411 (1987).

The creation of a federal anti-dilution law changes the preemption analysis, of course. Many people expected that such a law would preempt state anti-dilution statutes, replacing the patchwork of inconsistent protections with uniform national protection. Instead, § 43(c)(3) of the Lanham Act charts a narrow course around state anti-dilution laws by allowing them to continue in force but granting owners of federally registered marks immunity from suit under such state laws. Unregistered marks, as well as those registered under state law, receive no such immunity. The legislative history explains:

> Under section 3 of the bill, a new Section 43(c)(3) of the Lanham Act would provide that ownership of a valid federal trademark registration is a complete bar to an action brought against the registrant under state dilution law. This section provides a further incentive for the federal registration of marks and recognizes that to permit a state to regulate the use of federally registered marks is inconsistent with the intent of the Lanham Act "to protect registered marks used in such commerce from interference by state, or territorial legislation." It is important to note that *the proposed federal dilution statute would not preempt state dilution laws*. Unlike patent and copyright laws, federal trademark law coexists with state trademark law, and it is to be expected that the federal dilution statute should similarly coexist with state dilution statutes.

Federal Trademark Dilution Act of 1995, House Report 104-374 (accompanying H.R. 1295), November 30, 1995 (emphasis added).

The situation after the 2006 TDRA is even more complicated. Because of a (likely inadvertent) change to the numbering of statutory sections, Lanham Act § 43(c)(6)(B) can now be read to preempt any trademark-like claim to the extent it is asserted against a federally registered mark.

Thus, parallel state anti-dilution claims will not wither away completely. Indeed, depending on whether state law affords more attractive remedies (note the "injunction only" rule for most cases under the federal dilution provision, § 43(c)(2)), parties may well continue to bring at least some anti-dilution cases under state law. Note that for the most part, however, nationwide injunctions are more difficult to acquire under state anti-dilution statutes, making federal claims more likely if such an injunction is the trademark owner's major goal.

COMMENTS AND QUESTIONS

1. Is the lack of preemption troubling? Consider the following possibilities:

• A federal anti-dilution claim fails because the use is found to be a "fair" one (say, for news reporting purposes). A parallel action is brought under a state statute that contains no such limitation, and the court grants a nationwide injunction against dilution on the basis of the state statute.

• A nationally famous but unregistered product configuration is found to dilute a locally known product configuration under a state statute.

2. Do the state statutes at issue in these cases interfere with federal trademark policy?

B. MISAPPROPRIATION

International News Service v. Associated Press
Supreme Court of the United States
248 U.S. 215 (1918)

Justice PITNEY delivered the opinion of the court.

The parties are competitors in the gathering and distribution of news and its publication for profit in newspapers throughout the United States. The Associated Press, which was complainant in the District Court, is a cooperative organization, incorporated under the Membership Corporations Law of the State of New York, its members being individuals who are either proprietors or representatives of about 950 daily newspapers published in all parts of the United States. . . . Complainant gathers in all parts of the world, by means of various instrumentalities of its own, by exchange with its members, and by other appropriate means, news and intelligence of current and recent events of interest to newspaper readers and distributes it daily to its members for publication in their newspapers. The cost of the service, amounting approximately to $3,500,000 per annum, is assessed upon the members and becomes a part of their costs of operation, to be recouped, presumably with profit, through the publication of their several newspapers. Under complainant's by-laws each member agrees upon assuming membership that news received through complainant's service is received exclusively for publication in a particular newspaper, language, and place specified in the certificate of membership, that no other use of it shall be permitted, and that no member shall furnish or permit anyone in his employ or connected with his newspaper to furnish any of complainant's news in advance of publication to any person not a member. And each member is required to gather the local news of his district and supply it to the Associated Press and to no one else.

Defendant is a corporation organized under the laws of the State of New Jersey, whose business is the gathering and selling of news to its customers and clients, consisting of newspapers published throughout the United States, under contracts by which they pay certain amounts at stated times for defendant's service. It has widespread news-gathering agencies; the cost of its operations amounts, it is said, to more than $2,000,000 per annum; and it serves about 400 newspapers located in the various cities of the United States and abroad, a few of which are represented, also, in the membership of the Associated Press.

The parties are in the keenest competition between themselves in the distribution of news throughout the United States; and so, as a rule, are the newspapers that they serve, in their several districts.

Complainant in its bill, defendant in its answer, have set forth in almost identical terms the rather obvious circumstances and conditions under which their business is conducted. The value of the service, and of the news furnished, depends upon the promptness of transmission, as well as upon the accuracy and impartiality of the news; it being essential that the news be transmitted to members or subscribers as early or earlier than similar information can be furnished to competing newspapers by other news services, and that the news furnished by each agency shall not be furnished to newspapers which do not contribute to the expense of gathering it. And further, to quote from the answer:

> Prompt knowledge and publication of world-wide news is essential to the conduct of a modern newspaper, and by reason of the enormous expense incident to the gathering and distribution of such news, the only practical way in which a proprietor of a newspaper can obtain the same is, either through cooperation with a considerable number of other newspaper proprietors in the work of collecting and distributing such news, and the equitable division with them of the expenses thereof, or by the purchase of such news from some existing agency engaged in that business

The bill was filed to restrain the pirating of complainant's news by defendant in three ways: First, by bribing employees of newspapers published by complainant's members to furnish Associated Press news to defendant before publication, for transmission by telegraph and telephone to defendant's clients for publication by them; Second, by inducing Associated Press members to violate its by-laws and permit defendant to obtain news before publication; and Third, by copying news from bulletin boards and from early editions of complainant's newspapers and selling this, either bodily or after rewriting it, to defendant's customers.

...

The only matter that has been argued before us is whether defendant may lawfully be restrained from appropriating news taken from bulletins issued by complainant or any of its members, or from newspapers published by them, for the purpose of selling it to defendant's clients. Complainant asserts that defendant's admitted course of conduct in this regard both violates complainant's property right in the news and constitutes unfair competition in business. And notwithstanding the case has proceeded only to the stage of a preliminary injunction, we have deemed it proper to consider the underlying questions, since they go to the very merits of the action and are presented upon facts that are not in dispute. As presented in argument, these questions are: 1. Whether there is any property in news; 2. Whether, if there be property in news collected for the purpose of being published, it survives the instant of its publication in the first newspaper to which it is communicated by the news-gatherer; and 3. Whether defendant's admitted course of conduct in appropriating for commercial use matter taken from bulletins or early editions of Associated Press publications constitutes unfair competition in trade.

The federal jurisdiction was invoked because of diversity of citizenship, not upon the ground that the suit arose under the copyright or other laws of the United States. Complainant's news matter is not copyrighted. It is said that it could not, in practice, be copyrighted, because of the large number of dispatches that are sent daily; and, according to complainant's contention, news is not within the operation of the copyright act. Defendant, while apparently conceding this, nevertheless invokes the analogies of the law of literary property and copyright, insisting as its principal contention that, assuming complainant has a right of property in its news, it can be maintained (unless the copyright act be complied with) only by being kept secret and confidential, and that upon the publication with complainant's consent of uncopyrighted news by any of complainant's members in a newspaper or upon a bulletin board, the right of property is lost, and the subsequent use of the news by the public or by defendant for any purpose whatever becomes lawful. . . .

In considering the general question of property in news matter, it is necessary to recognize its dual character, distinguishing between the substance of the information and the particular form or collocation of words in which the writer has communicated it.

No doubt news articles often possess a literary quality, and are the subject of literary property at the common law; nor do we question that such an article, as a literary production, is the subject of copyright by the terms of the act as it now stands. In an early case at the circuit Mr. Justice Thompson held in effect that a newspaper was not within the protection of the copyright acts of 1790 and 1802 (*Clayton v. Stone*, 2 Paine, 382; 5 Fed. Cas. No. 2872). But the present act is broader; it provides that the works for which copyright may be secured shall include "all the writings of an author," and specifically mentions "periodicals, including newspapers." Act of March 4, 1909, c. 320, §§ 4 and 5, 35 Stat. 1075, 1076. Evidently this admits to copyright a contribution to a newspaper, notwithstanding it also may convey news; and such is the practice of the copyright office, as the newspapers of the day bear witness. *See* Copyright Office Bulletin No. 15 (1917), pp. 7, 14, 16–17.

But the news element—the information respecting current events contained in the literary production—is not the creation of the writer, but is a report of matters that ordinarily are publici juris [of public right]; it is the history of the day. It is not to be supposed that the framers of the Constitution, when they empowered Congress "to promote the progress of science and useful arts, by securing for limited times to authors and inventors the exclusive right to their respective writings and discoveries" (CONST., Art I, § 8, [cl.] 8), intended to confer upon one who might happen to be the first to report a historic event the exclusive right for any period to spread the knowledge of it.

We need spend no time, however, upon the general question of property in news matter at common law, or the application of the copyright act, since it seems to us the case must turn upon the question of unfair competition in business. And, in our opinion, this does not depend upon any general right of property analogous to the common-law right of the proprietor of an unpublished work to prevent its publication without his consent; nor is it foreclosed by showing that the benefits of the copyright act have been waived. We are dealing here not with restrictions upon publication but with the very facilities and processes of publication. The peculiar value of news is in the spreading of it while it is fresh; and it is evident that a valuable property interest in the news, as news, cannot be maintained by keeping it secret. Besides, except for matters improperly disclosed, or published in breach of trust or confidence, or in violation of law, none of which is involved in this branch of the case, the news of current events may be regarded as common property. What we are concerned with is the business of making it known to the world, in which both parties to the present suit are engaged. That business consists in maintaining a prompt, sure, steady, and reliable service designed to place the daily events of the world at the breakfast table of the millions at a price that, while of trifling moment to each reader, is sufficient in the aggregate to afford compensation for the cost of gathering and distributing it, with the added profit so necessary as an incentive to effective action in the commercial world. The service thus performed for newspaper readers is not only innocent but extremely useful in itself, and indubitably constitutes a legitimate business. The parties are competitors in this field; and, on fundamental principles, applicable here as elsewhere, when the rights or privileges of the one are liable to conflict with those of the other, each party is under a duty so to conduct its own business as not unnecessarily or unfairly to injure that of the other. *Hitchman Coal & Coke Co. v. Mitchell*, 245 U.S. 229, 254.

Obviously, the question of what is unfair competition in business must be determined with particular reference to the character and circumstances of the business. The question here is not so much the rights of either party as against the public but their rights as between themselves. *See Morison v. Moat*, 9 Hare, 241, 258. And although we may and do assume that neither party has any remaining property interest as against the public in uncopyrighted news matter after the moment of its first publication, it by no means follows that there is no remaining property interest in it as between themselves. For, to both of them alike, news matter, however little susceptible of ownership or dominion in the absolute sense, is stock in trade, to be gathered at the cost of enterprise, organization, skill, labor, and money, and to be distributed and sold to those who will pay money for it, as for any other merchandise. Regarding the news, therefore, as but the material out of which both parties are seeking to make profits at the same time and in the same field, we hardly can fail to recognize that for this purpose, and as between them, it must be regarded as quasi property, irrespective of the rights of either as against the public.

In order to sustain the jurisdiction of equity over the controversy, we need not affirm any general and absolute property in the news as such. The rule that a court of equity concerns itself only in the protection of property rights treats any civil right of a pecuniary nature as a property right (*In re Sawyer*, 124 U.S. 200, 210; *In re Debs*, 158 U.S. 564, 593); and the right to acquire property by honest labor or the conduct of a lawful business is as much entitled to protection as the right to guard property already acquired. *Truax v. Raich*, 239 U.S. 33, 37–38; *Brennan v. United Hatters*, 73 N.J.L. 729, 742; *Barr v. Essex Trades Council*, 53 N.J. Eq. 101. It is this right that furnishes the basis of the jurisdiction in the ordinary case of unfair competition. . . .

Not only do the acquisition and transmission of news require elaborate organization and a large expenditure of money, skill, and effort; not only has it an exchange value to the gatherer, dependent chiefly upon its novelty and freshness, the regularity of the service, its reputed reliability and thoroughness, and its adaptability to the public needs; but also, as is evident, the news has an exchange value to one who can misappropriate it.

The peculiar features of the case arise from the fact that, while novelty and freshness form so important an element in the success of the business, the very processes of distribution and publication necessarily occupy a good deal of time. Complainant's service, as well as defendant's, is a daily service to daily newspapers; most of the foreign news reaches this country at the Atlantic seaboard, principally at the City of New York, and because of this, and of time differentials due to the earth's rotation, the distribution of news matter throughout the country is principally from east to west; and, since in speed the telegraph and telephone easily outstrip the rotation of the earth, it is a simple matter for defendant to take complainant's news from bulletins or early editions of complainant's members in the eastern cities and at the mere cost of telegraphic transmission cause it to be published in western papers issued at least as early as those served by complainant. Besides this, and irrespective of time differentials, irregularities in telegraphic transmission on different lines, and the normal consumption of time in printing and distributing the newspaper, result in permitting pirated news to be placed in the hands of defendant's readers sometimes simultaneously with the service of competing Associated Press papers, occasionally even earlier.

Defendant insists that when, with the sanction and approval of complainant, and as the result of the use of its news for the very purpose for which it is distributed, a portion of complainant's members communicate it to the general public by posting it upon bulletin boards so that all may read, or by issuing it to newspapers and distributing it indiscriminately, complainant no longer has the right to control the use to be made of it; that when it thus reaches the light of day it becomes the common possession of all to whom it is accessible; and that any purchaser of a newspaper has the right to communicate the intelligence which it contains to anybody and for any purpose, even for the purpose of selling it for profit to newspapers published for profit in competition with complainant's members.

The fault in the reasoning lies in applying as a test the right of the complainant as against the public, instead of considering the rights of complainant and defendant, competitors in business, as between themselves. The right of the purchaser of a single newspaper to spread knowledge of its contents gratuitously, for any legitimate purpose not unreasonably interfering with complainant's right to make merchandise of it, may be admitted; but to transmit that news for commercial use, in competition with complainant—which is what defendant has done and seeks to justify—is a very different matter. In doing this defendant, by its very act, admits that it is taking material that has been acquired by complainant as the result of organization and the expenditure of labor, skill, and money, and which is salable by complainant for money, and that defendant in appropriating it and selling it as its own is endeavoring to reap where it has not sown, and by disposing of it to newspapers that are competitors of complainant's members is appropriating to itself the harvest of those who have sown. Stripped of all disguises, the process amounts to an unauthorized interference with the normal operation of complainant's legitimate business precisely at the point where the profit is to be reaped, in order to divert a material portion of the profit from those who have earned it to those who have not; with special advantage to defendant in the competition because of the fact that it is not burdened with any part of the expense of gathering the news. The transaction speaks for itself, and a court of equity ought not to hesitate long in characterizing it as unfair competition in business.

The underlying principle is much the same as that which lies at the base of the equitable theory of consideration in the law of trusts—that he who has fairly paid the price should have the beneficial use of the property. POM. EQ. JUR., § 981. It is no answer to say that complainant spends its money for that which is too fugitive or evanescent to be the subject of property. That might, and for the purposes of the discussion we are assuming that it would, furnish an answer in a common-law controversy. But in a court of equity, where the question is one of unfair competition, if that which complainant has acquired fairly at substantial cost may be sold fairly at substantial profit, a competitor who is misappropriating it for the purpose of disposing of it to his own profit and to the disadvantage of complainant cannot be heard to say that it is too fugitive or evanescent to be regarded as property. It has all the attributes of property necessary for determining that a misappropriation of it by a competitor is unfair competition because contrary to good conscience.

The contention that the news is abandoned to the public for all purposes when published in the first newspaper is untenable. Abandonment is a question of intent, and the entire organization of the Associated Press negatives such a purpose. The cost of the service would be prohibitive if the reward were to be so limited. No single newspaper, no small group of newspapers, could sustain the expenditure. Indeed, it is one of the most obvious results of defendant's theory that, by permitting indiscriminate publication by anybody and everybody for purposes of profit in competition with the news-gatherer, it would render publication profitless, or so little profitable as in effect to cut off the service by rendering the cost prohibitive in comparison with the return. The practical needs and requirements of the business are reflected in complainant's by-laws which have been referred to. Their effect is that publication by each member must be deemed not by any means an abandonment of the news to the world for any and all purposes, but a publication for limited purposes; for the benefit of the readers of the bulletin or the newspaper as such; not for the purpose of making merchandise of it as news, with the result of depriving complainant's other members of their reasonable opportunity to obtain just returns for their expenditures.

It is to be observed that the view we adopt does not result in giving to complainant the right to monopolize either the gathering or the distribution of the news, or, without complying with the copyright act, to prevent the reproduction of its news articles; but only postpones participation by complainant's competitor in the processes of distribution and reproduction of news that it has not gathered, and only to the extent necessary to prevent that competitor from reaping the fruits of complainant's efforts and expenditure, to the partial exclusion of complainant, and in violation of the principle that underlies the maxim sic utere tuo [so use your own as not to injure another's property], etc.

It is said that the elements of unfair competition are lacking because there is no attempt by defendant to palm off its goods as those of the complainant, characteristic of the most familiar, if not the most typical, cases of unfair competition. *Howe Scale Co.*

v. Wyckoff, Seamans & Benedict, 198 U.S. 118, 140. But we cannot concede that the right to equitable relief is confined to that class of cases. In the present case the fraud upon complainant's rights is more direct and obvious. Regarding news matter as the mere material from which these two competing parties are endeavoring to make money, and treating it, therefore, as quasi property for the purposes of their business because they are both selling it as such, defendant's conduct differs from the ordinary case of unfair competition in trade principally in this that, instead of selling its own goods as those of complainant, it substitutes misappropriation in the place of misrepresentation, and sells complainant's goods as its own.

Besides the misappropriation, there are elements of imitation, of false pretense, in defendant's practices. The device of rewriting complainant's news articles, frequently resorted to, carries its own comment. The habitual failure to give credit to complainant for that which is taken is significant. Indeed, the entire system of appropriating complainant's news and transmitting it as a commercial product to defendant's clients and patrons amounts to a false representation to them and to their newspaper readers that the news transmitted is the result of defendant's own investigation in the field. But these elements, although accentuating the wrong, are not the essence of it. It is something more than the advantage of celebrity of which complainant is being deprived. . . .

The decree of the Circuit Court of Appeals will be Affirmed.

HOLMES, J., concurring:

When an uncopyrighted combination of words is published there is no general right to forbid other people repeating them—in other words there is no property in the combination or in the thoughts or facts that the words express. Property, a creation of law, does not arise from value, although exchangeable—a matter of fact. Many exchangeable values may be destroyed intentionally without compensation. Property depends upon exclusion by law from interference, and a person is not excluded from using any combination of words merely because someone has used it before, even if it took labor and genius to make it. If a given person is to be prohibited from making the use of words that his neighbors are free to make some other ground must be found. One such ground is vaguely expressed in the phrase unfair trade. This means that the words are repeated by a competitor in business in such a way as to convey a misrepresentation that materially injures the person who first used them, by appropriating credit of some kind which the first user has earned. The ordinary case is a representation by device, appearance, or other indirection that the defendant's goods come from the plaintiff. But the only reason why it is actionable to make such a representation is that it tends to give the defendant an advantage in his competition with the plaintiff and that it is thought undesirable that an advantage should be gained in that way. Apart from that the defendant may use such unpatented devices and uncopyrighted combinations of words as he likes. The ordinary case, I say, is palming off the defendant's product as the plaintiff's, but the same evil may follow from the opposite falsehood—from saying, whether in words or by implication, that the plaintiff's product is the defendant's, and that, it seems to me, is what has happened here.

Fresh news is got only by enterprise and expense. To produce such news as it is produced by the defendant represents by implication that it has been acquired by the defendant's enterprise and at its expense. When it comes from one of the great news-collecting agencies like the Associated Press, the source generally is indicated, plainly importing that credit; and that such a representation is implied may be inferred with some confidence from the unwillingness of the defendant to give the credit and tell the truth. If the plaintiff produces the news at the same time that the defendant does, the defendant's presentation impliedly denies to the plaintiff the credit of collecting the facts and assumes that credit to the defendant. If the plaintiff is later in western cities it naturally will be supposed to have obtained its information from the defendant. The falsehood is a little more subtle, the injury a little more indirect, than in ordinary cases of unfair trade, but I think that the principle that condemns the one condemns the other. It is a question of how strong an infusion of fraud is necessary to turn a flavor into a poison. The dose seems to me strong enough here to need a remedy from the law. But as, in my view, the only ground of complaint that can be recognized without legislation is the implied misstatement, it can be corrected by stating the truth; and a suitable acknowledgment of the source is all that the plaintiff can require. I think that within the limits recognized by the decision of the Court the defendant should be enjoined from publishing news obtained from the Associated Press for __ hours after publication by the plaintiff unless it gives express credit to the Associated Press; the number of hours and the form of acknowledgment to be settled by the District Court. . . .

BRANDEIS, J., dissenting:

. . .

News is a report of recent occurrences. The business of the news agency is to gather systematically knowledge of such occurrences of interest and to distribute reports thereof. The Associated Press contended that knowledge so acquired is property, because it costs money and labor to produce and because it has value for which those who have it not are ready to pay; that it remains property and is entitled to protection as long as it has commercial value as news; and that to protect it effectively the defendant must be enjoined from making, or causing to be made, any gainful use of it while it retains such value. An essential element of individual property is the legal right to exclude others from enjoying it. If the property is private, the right of exclusion may be absolute; if the property is affected with a public interest, the right of exclusion is qualified. But the fact that a product of the mind has cost its producer money and labor, and has a value for which others are willing to pay, is not sufficient to ensure to it this legal attribute of property. The general rule of law is, that the noblest of human productions—knowledge, truths ascertained, conceptions, and ideas—become, after voluntary communication to others, free as the air to common use. Upon these incorporeal productions the attribute of property is continued after such communication only in certain classes of cases where public policy has seemed to demand it. These exceptions are confined to productions which, in some degree, involve creation, invention, or discovery. But by no means all such are endowed with this attribute of property. The creations which are recognized as property by the common law are literary, dramatic, musical, and other artistic creations; and these have also protection under the copyright statutes. The inventions and discoveries upon which this attribute of property is conferred only by statute, are the few comprised within the patent law. There are also many other cases in which courts interfere to prevent curtailment of plaintiff's enjoyment of incorporeal productions; and in which the right to relief is often called a property right, but is such only in a special sense. In those cases, the plaintiff has no absolute right to the protection of his production; he has merely the qualified right to be protected as against the defendant's acts, because of the special relation in which the latter stands or the wrongful method or means employed in acquiring the knowledge or the manner in which it is used. Protection of this character is afforded where the suit is based upon breach of contract or of trust or upon unfair competition.

The knowledge for which protection is sought in the case at bar is not of a kind upon which the law has heretofore conferred the attributes of property; nor is the manner of its acquisition or use nor the purpose to which it is applied, such as has heretofore been recognized as entitling a plaintiff to relief. . . .

The means by which the International News Service obtains news gathered by the Associated Press is also clearly unobjectionable. It is taken from papers bought in the open market or from bulletins publicly posted. No breach of contract such as the court considered to exist in *Hitchman Coal & Coke Co. v. Mitchell*, 245 U.S. 229, 254; or of trust such as was present in *Morison v. Moat*, 9 Hare, 241; and neither fraud nor force, is involved. The manner of use is likewise unobjectionable. No reference is made by word or by act to the Associated Press, either in transmitting the news to subscribers or by them in publishing it in their papers. Neither the International News Service nor its subscribers is gaining or seeking to gain in its business a benefit from the reputation of the Associated Press. They are merely using its product without making compensation. *See Bamforth v. Douglass Post Card & Machine Co.*, 158 Fed. Rep. 355; *Tribune Co. of Chicago v. Associated Press*, 116 Fed. Rep. 126. That, they have a legal right to do; because the product is not property, and they do not stand in any relation to the Associated Press, either of contract or of trust, which otherwise precludes such use. The argument is not advanced by characterizing such taking and use a misappropriation.

It is also suggested, that the fact that defendant does not refer to the Associated Press as the source of the news may furnish a basis for the relief. But the defendant and its subscribers, unlike members of the Associated Press, were under no contractual obligation to disclose the source of the news; and there is no rule of law requiring acknowledgment to be made where uncopyrighted matter is reproduced. The International News Service is said to mislead its subscribers into believing that the news transmitted was originally gathered by it and that they in turn mislead their readers. There is, in fact, no representation by either of any kind. Sources of information are sometimes given because required by contract; sometimes because naming the source gives authority to an otherwise incredible statement; and sometimes the source is named because the agency does not wish to take the responsibility itself of giving currency to the news. But no representation can properly be implied from omission to mention the source of information except that the International News Service is transmitting news which it believes to be credible.

. . . The great development of agencies now furnishing country-wide distribution of news, the vastness of our territory, and improvements in the means of transmitting intelligence, have made it possible for a news agency or newspapers to obtain, without paying compensation, the fruit of another's efforts and to use news so obtained gainfully in competition with the original collector. The injustice of such action is obvious. But to give relief against it would involve more than the application of existing rules of law to new facts. It would require the making of a new rule in analogy to existing ones. The unwritten law possesses capacity for growth; and has often satisfied new demands for justice by invoking analogies or by expanding a rule or principle. This process has been in the main wisely applied and should not be discontinued. Where the problem is relatively simple, as it is apt to be when private interests only are involved, it generally proves adequate. But with the increasing complexity of society, the public interest tends to become omnipresent; and the problems presented by new demands for justice cease to be simple. Then the creation or recognition by courts of a new private right may work serious injury to the general public, unless the boundaries of the right are definitely established and wisely guarded. In order to reconcile the new private right with the public interest, it may be necessary to prescribe limitations and rules for its enjoyment; and also to provide administrative machinery for enforcing the rules. It is largely for this reason that, in the effort to meet the many new demands for justice incident to a rapidly changing civilization, resort to legislation has latterly been had with increasing frequency.

The rule for which the plaintiff contends would effect an important extension of property rights and a corresponding curtailment of the free use of knowledge and of ideas; and the facts of this case admonish us of the danger involved in recognizing such a property right in news, without imposing upon news-gatherers corresponding obligations. . . .

Courts are ill-equipped to make the investigations which should precede a determination of the limitations which should be set upon any property right in news or of the circumstances under which news gathered by a private agency should be deemed affected with a public interest. Courts would be powerless to prescribe the detailed regulations essential to full enjoyment of the rights conferred or to introduce the machinery required for enforcement of such regulations. Considerations such as these should lead us to decline to establish a new rule of law in the effort to redress a newly-disclosed wrong, although the propriety of some remedy appears to be clear.

COMMENTS AND QUESTIONS

1. Both the majority and the dissent seem to agree that there is no traditional intellectual property right in published news. Copyright law—the most likely candidate for protecting works of authorship—cannot protect AP's news. *See* Chapter IV. And the majority's reference to "unfair competition" suggests that its theory is grounded in the common law of unjust enrichment. *See* Shyamkrishna Balganesh, *"Hot News": The*

Enduring Myth of Property in News, 111 COLUM. L. REV. 419 (2011) (arguing for a non-property based understanding of the hot news doctrine). The Court's reliance on what it calls a theory of "quasi-property", which entitles its holder to protection only against direct competitors, appears to bear this out.

2. How should courts following *International News* determine whether two companies are direct competitors who are then subject to this quasi-property right? For example, suppose that a single newspaper (not a member of AP) had appropriated information from published AP reports. Does the single paper compete with AP in news gathering? Does it matter whether the paper competes directly with one of AP's members, or has its own city monopoly? Or should the test be whether AP could have expected licensing revenues from the paper, whether or not they are in competition? *Cf. National Football League v. Delaware*, 435 F. Supp. 1372 (D. Del. 1977) (NFL cannot prevent Delaware from implementing a lottery based on NFL games, because the lottery is a "collateral service" rather than one in competition with the NFL).

3. How long does this quasi-property right last? The Court suggests one answer: until AP has appropriated its news value as a return on its news-gathering activities. Justice Holmes's concurrence suggests that this would be a matter of hours. But is that necessarily true? What happens when different news media compete? Should there be different rules for CNN, scheduled television news, daily newspapers, and weekly and monthly news magazines? Is AP entitled to protect its news not only from appropriation by "immediate" news sources, but also from the weeklies and monthlies that seek to use its news reports?

4. What if INS or its newspapers had credited AP with reporting the story? In that case, AP would presumably have received some value for its news—credit for the "scoop." But its member papers would still have faced competition from nonmembers that they would prefer to avoid. Should attribution be enough? Justice Holmes says yes, but neither the majority nor Justice Brandeis' dissent see this as the major issue (although the majority notes that INS's failure to attribute the news to AP "accentuates" the unfairness of its competition). Note that attribution should solve any Lanham Act problem that might otherwise arise, since there is no danger that INS or its member papers will be "passing off" AP stories as their own if the source of the story is clearly identified.

This fact points up a significant difference between the tort of misappropriation and trademark infringement. Trademark law is premised on harm to consumers stemming from a "likelihood of confusion." Absent consumer confusion, trademarks (and trade dress) are generally not protectable. *International News* cuts a much broader swath. If it is not based on consumer protection, what is the rationale for the misappropriation doctrine? Is it incentive theory? If so, what exactly is the Court trying to encourage?

5. The *International News* decision has not fared well in the courts. Early decisions by lower courts attempted to construe the decision narrowly. Indeed, in 1929 Judge Learned Hand went so far as to say: "While it is of course true that the law ordinarily speaks in general terms, there are cases where the occasion is at once the justification for, and the limit of, what is decided. [*International News*] appears to us such an

instance; we think that no more was covered than situations substantially similar to those then at bar." *Cheney Bros. v. Doris Silk Corp.*, 35 F.2d 279 (2d Cir. 1929). Judge Hand went on to characterize the problems with the Court's decision as "insuperable," and to state that it "flagrantly conflict[ed]" with the federal statutory intellectual property laws. Id.

After *Erie R.R. Co. v. Tompkins*, 304 U.S. 64 (1938), abolished federal general common law in diversity cases (the grounds on which *International News* was decided), it seemed to many that the *International News* misappropriation doctrine was dead. *See* James Treece, *Patent Policy and Pre-emption: The* Stiffel *and* Compco *Cases*, 32 U. CHI. L. REV. 80 (1964). But the doctrine has since reappeared in a number of cases. *See United States Golf Ass'n v. St. Andrews Systems*, 749 F.2d 1028 (3d Cir. 1984) (*International News* was based on direct competition between the parties; court refused to apply it absent such direct competition); *Imax Corp. v. Cinema Technologies, Inc.*, 152 F.3d 1161 (9th Cir. 1998) (owner of movie projector equipment could recover on a common law misappropriation theory for the use of information disclosed in confidence, despite the fact that the plaintiff could not prevail on its trade secret claim); *Ettore v. Philco Television Broadcasting Corp.*, 229 F.2d 481 (3d Cir. 1956), *cert. denied,* 351 U.S. 926 (1956) (producer of boxing match could recover damages from television station which broadcast the match without permission).

6. *Misappropriation and Copyright Preemption.* With the passage of the Copyright Act of 1976, courts have had to confront whether state common law misappropriation doctrine survives the preemption "of all legal or equitable rights that are equivalent to any of the exclusive rights within the general scope of copyright as specified by § 106 in works of authorship that are fixed in a tangible medium of expression and come within the subject matter of copyright as specified by sections 102 and 103." 17 U.S.C. § 301. The text of the statute does not create an exception for misappropriation claims. As explored in (A)(2)(i), *infra*, however, the legislative history addressed the continued viability of misappropriation claims as follows:

> "Misappropriation" is not necessarily synonymous with copyright infringement, and thus a cause of action labeled as "misappropriation" is not preempted if it is in fact based neither on a right within the general scope of copyright as specified by section 106 nor on a right equivalent thereto. For example, state law should have the flexibility to afford a remedy (under traditional principles of equity) against a consistent pattern of unauthorized appropriation by a competitor of the facts (i.e., not the literary expression) constituting "hot" news, whether in the traditional mold of *International News Service v. Associated Press*, 248 U.S. 215 (1918), or in the newer form of data updates from scientific, business, or financial data bases. Likewise, a person having no trust or other relationship with the proprietor of a computerized data base should not be immunized from sanctions against electronically or cryptographically breaching the proprietor's security arrangements and accessing the proprietor's data. . . .

Committee on the Judiciary, H. R. REP. NO. 94-1476, p.132 (1976).

In *National Basketball Ass'n v. Motorola, Inc.*, 105 F.3d 841 (2d Cir. 1997), the court held that *International News* survives today only where

(i)   a plaintiff generates or gathers information at a cost;

(ii)   the information is time-sensitive;

(iii)   a defendant's use of the information constitutes free-riding on the plaintiff's efforts;

(iv)   the defendant is in direct competition with a product or service offered by the plaintiffs; and

(v)   the ability of other parties to free-ride on the efforts of the plaintiff or others would so reduce the incentive to produce the product that its existence or quality would be substantially threatened.

The court held that these limitations on the misappropriation doctrine made it qualitatively different from a cause of action for copyright infringement. *Cf. United States Golf Ass'n v. Arroyo Software*, 40 U.S.P.Q.2d 1840 (Cal. Super. Ct. 1996), *aff'd*, 69 Cal. App. 4th 607 (1999) (extending misappropriation doctrine to noncompetitors, finding that protection of USGA handicapping formula is necessary to "protect the basic incentive for the production of the idea or information involved").

The Second Circuit revisited the "hot news" misappropriation doctrine in *Barclays Capital Inc. v. Theflyonthewall.com, Inc.*, 650 F.3d 876 (2d Cir. 2011). The plaintiffs—major brokerage firms that engage in extensive research for purposes of advising their clients—sought to prevent an Internet securities news aggregator from circulating their trading recommendations (rating and price target) until after they had lost their "hot news" value. After the district court found that the plaintiffs had satisfied the five-part *Motorola* test, the appellate court reversed on the ground that such an application of *Motorola* would run afoul of the Copyright Act's preemption of equivalent state law causes of action. Of most significance, the court held that the plaintiffs' claim does not meet *Motorola*'s "free-riding" element:

[Theflyonthewall or Fly] is collecting, collating and disseminating factual information—the *facts* that Firms and others in the securities business have made recommendations with respect to the value of and the wisdom of purchasing or selling securities—and attributing the information to its source. The Firms are making the news . . .

. . . In pressing a "hot news" claim against Fly, the Firms seek only to protect their Recommendations, something they *create* using their expertise and experience rather than *acquire* through efforts akin to reporting.

Moreover, Fly, having obtained news of a Recommendation, is hardly selling the Recommendation "as its own," *INS*, 248 U.S. at 239. It is selling the information with specific attribution to the issuing Firm. Indeed, for Fly to sell, for example, a Morgan Stanley Recommendation "as its own," as INS sold the news it cribbed from AP to INS subscribers, would be of little value to either Fly or its customers. . . .

We do not perceive a meaningful difference between (a) Fly's taking material that a Firm has created (not "acquired") as the result of organization and the expenditure of labor, skill, and money, and which is (presumably) salable by a Firm for money, and selling it by *ascribing the material to its creator Firm* and author (not selling it as Fly's own), and (b) what appears to be unexceptional and easily recognized behavior by members of the traditional news media—to report on, say, winners of Tony Awards or, indeed, scores of NBA games with proper attribution of the material to its creator. *INS* did not purport to address either.

It is also noteworthy, if not determinative, that *INS* referred to INS's tortious behavior as "amount[ing] to an unauthorized interference with the normal operation of complainant's legitimate business *precisely at the point where the profit is to be reaped,* in order to *divert a material portion of the profit* from those who have earned it to those who have not. . . ." *Id.* at 240 (emphases added). As we have seen, the point at which the Firms principally reap their profit is upon the execution of sales or purchases of securities. It is at least arguable that Fly's interference with the "normal operation" of the Firms' business is indeed at a "point" where the Firms' profits are reaped. But it is not at all clear that *that* profit is being in any substantial sense "diverted" to Fly by its publication of Recommendations news. The lost commissions are, we would think, diverted to whatever broker happens to execute a trade placed by the recipient of news of the Recommendation from Fly.

Id. at 903–04 (emphasis in original; footnotes omitted). Does the Second Circuit take an overly narrow interpretation of free-riding and the *INS* holding? The Second Circuit's opinion narrows the scope of the hot news misappropriation doctrine to such an extent that the doctrine remains untenable in all but the narrowest of circumstances. *See* Shyamkrishna Balganesh, *The Uncertain Future of "Hot News" Misappropriation After Barclays Capital v. Theflyonthewall.com*, 112 COLUM. L. REV. SIDEBAR 134 (2012). Is this a desirable result overall?

7. Suppose that the plaintiff in *Feist v. Rural Telephone Service*, 499 U.S. 340 (1991), had brought a claim for misappropriation and unfair competition rather than a copyright claim. Should the plaintiff prevail under *International News*? It certainly would be able to claim that it had invested substantial time and effort in putting together a telephone directory, and that defendant (a direct competitor) had merely copied that information as soon as it became public. Assuming this is enough to show unfair competition under *International News,* what does that fact suggest about the interaction between the copyright laws and the unfair competition doctrine? Does it make sense that the rule in *Feist* should coexist with unfair competition law?

8. One solution to the inconsistency between *Feist* and *International News* would be to create an explicit (presumably statutory) property right in factual compilations. Strong arguments in favor of such protection were made in the copyright context both before and after *Feist*. Further, doesn't the Court have a valid point about the incentive

to invest in a productive activity (collecting news) whose benefits will immediately be dissipated by imitators? Isn't that precisely the justification for the patent system?

On the other hand, what problems do you foresee with such a new federal intellectual property regime? Would it overwhelm patent and copyright as means of protecting intellectual property? What effect would it have on businesses? Would it encourage factual research and compilation, or just encourage monopolization of facts? On this subject, *see* Leo J. Raskind, *The Misappropriation Doctrine as a Competitive Norm of Intellectual Property Law*, 75 MINN. L. REV. 875, 876–77 (1991). Raskind argues that:

> when courts hear patent, copyright, and trademark cases in which statutory protection is inappropriate, but nonetheless the conduct of a party is characterized as "chiseling," "piracy," "unethical," or the like, they should begin their analysis by considering the competitive relationship from which the claim originates. The clear legislative expression of a preference for competition contained in federal antitrust laws warrants this approach. Moreover, courts in these cases should recognize the Supreme Court's continued emphasis on the preemptive effect given federal legislation relating to competition. Ancillary doctrines that impinge on competition, such as misappropriation, should be invoked sparingly. From this perspective, courts should consider allegedly "inappropriate" conduct as an element of behavior in a competitive market context; within that framework, courts should view such conduct as an element of cost that a seller, as a competitor, considers when determining how much of a particular product to offer.

9. To what extent was the Court in *International News* merely enforcing the norms of commercial reasonableness in the newspaper industry? *See* Richard Epstein, International News Service v. Associated Press: *Custom and Law as Sources of Property Rights in News*, 78 VA. L. REV. 85 (1992) (noting the different customary rules in the news trade under which "lifting" stories was wrong, but following up on another paper's "tips" to report the same story was acceptable; and concluding that, partially unwittingly, Justice Pitney ended up affirming these customary rules in his opinion); Douglas G. Baird, *Common Law Intellectual Property and the Legacy of* International News Service v. Associated Press, 50 U. CHI. L. REV. 411 (1983); *but see* Stephen L. Carter, *Custom, Adjudication, and Petrushevsky's Watch: Some Notes from the Intellectual Property Front*, 78 VA. L. REV. 129, 132 (1992) ("Even courts inclined to enforce private orderings might not be very good at anthropology. The judge, after all, is on the outside, looking in. Even assuming—and there is no reason to do so—that the parties tell the whole truth, it will not always be so easy for a court to discern an industry's customs."); Jennifer E. Rothman, *The Questionable Use of Custom in Intellectual Property*, 93 VA. L. REV. 1899, 1906-07 (2007) (arguing that the usual reasons for the use of custom in intellectual property adjudication are not convincing).

10. In a 2003 essay, Judge Posner questioned the need for a separate misappropriation doctrine. *See* Richard A. Posner, *Misappropriation: A Dirge*, 40 HOUS. L. REV. 621 (2003). He did not believe that its core principle—discouraging free

riding—is itself a necessary or sufficient condition for IP protection. *See generally* Mark A. Lemley, *Property, Intellectual Property, and Free Riding*, 83 TEX. L. REV. 1031 (2005); *but see* Wendy J. Gordon, *Of Harms and Benefits: Torts, Restitution, and Intellectual Property*, 34 MCGEORGE L. REV. 541 (2003). Upon reviewing the major reported cases, Judge Posner concluded that unsuccessful claimants were properly rejected and that successful claimants could have prevailed under other doctrines (such as copyright law, contract law, or trespass to chattels). He was "hard pressed to find a case in which a claim of misappropriation should have succeeded." 40 HOUS. L. REV. at 633. The following problem indicates that Judge Posner may have changed his mind about the misappropriation doctrine.

PROBLEM

Problem VI-2. The rise of the Internet has imperiled many traditional news-gathering organizations. Sites like Craigslist have reduced the market for classified advertising. The success of Google's AdSense—its keyword-triggered advertising platform—cut deeply into the revenue that had traditionally flowed into print advertising. And the revenue models for many newspaper websites have been hampered by news aggregator sites, news search engines, and bloggers who repackage news. To some extent, most newspapers created the latter set of problems by not choosing the subscription model path (as, for example, the WALL STREET JOURNAL did). Just as misappropriation law bolstered AP's lead-time nearly a century ago, Judge Richard Posner suggests that a similar approach (through an amendment to copyright law) could improve the quantity and quality of news gathering today:

News, as well the other information found in newspapers, is available online for nothing, including at the websites of the newspapers themselves, who thus are giving away content. The fact that online viewing is rising as print circulation is falling indicates a shift of consumers from the paid to the free medium. . . . [M]any of the people who have switched under economic pressure to the free medium may find themselves as happy or happier. . . . Moreover, while in many industries a reduction in output need not entail any reduction in the quality of the product, in newspaper it does entail a reduction in quality. Most of the costs of a newspaper are fixed costs, that is, costs invariant to output—for they are journalists' salaries. A newspaper with shrinking revenues can shrink its costs only by reducing the number of reporters, columnists, and editors, and when it does that quality falls, and therefore demand, and falling demand means falling revenues and therefore increased pressure to economize—by cutting the journalist staff some more. This vicious cycle, amplified by the economic downturn, may continue until very little of the newspaper industry is left. So what will happen to news and information? Online news is free for two reasons. First, in the case of a newspaper, the marginal cost of providing content online is virtually zero, since it is the same content (or a selection of the content) in a different medium. Second, online providers of news who are not affiliated with a newspaper can provide links to newspaper websites and paraphrase articles in newspapers, in neither case being required to compensate the newspaper.

As newspaper revenues decline, newspaper content becomes thinner and thinner—but by the same token so does the linked or paraphrased newspaper content found in web sites that have no affiliation with a newspaper. If eventually newspapers vanish, online providers will have higher advertising revenues (because newspaper advertising will have disappeared) and may decide to charge for access to their online news, and so the critical question is whether online advertising revenues will defray the costly news-gathering expenses incurred at this time by newspapers. Imagine if the NEW YORK TIMES migrated entirely to the World Wide Web. Could it support, out of advertising and subscriber revenues, as large a news-gathering apparatus as it does today? This seems unlikely, because it is much easier to create a web site and free ride on other sites than to create a print newspaper and free ride on other print newspapers, in part because of the lag in print publication; what is staler than last week's news. Expanding copyright law to bar online access to copyrighted materials without the copyright holder's consent, or to bar linking to or paraphrasing copyrighted materials without the copyright holder's consent, might be necessary to keep free riding on content financed by online newspapers from so impairing the incentive to create costly news-gathering operations that news services like Reuters and the Associated Press would become the only professional, nongovernmental sources of news and opinion.

See R. Posner, *The Future of Newspapers* available at http://www.becker-posner-blog.com/archives/2009/06/the_future_of_n.html. What counterarguments would you offer? Do you agree with Judge Posner's prescription?

C. IDEA SUBMISSIONS

Courts have struggled over the years with whether and under what circumstances a person who supplies a valuable idea to another may obtain legal redress. On the one hand, copyright law expressly disavows protection for ideas, *see* § 102(b), and patent law imposes stringent requirements—examination, novelty, nonobviousness, utility, and disclosure—before affording protection. Therefore, it would seem incongruous for state law to protect ideas. On the other hand, we protect valuable information through state trade secret law. Should there be some role for state law to protect promises to pay for an idea that is not a trade secret? What if the idea is communicated without a formal contract being entered into? Without such protection, people with good ideas might lack the legal and economic security to exchange such information with those in a position to develop products, movies, and other valuable works. But if unpatented, nonsecret ideas are protectable, what is left of the public domain?

Nadel v. Play-by-Play Toys & Novelties, Inc.
United States Court of Appeals for the Second Circuit
208 F.3d 368 (2d Cir. 2000)

SOTOMAYOR, Circuit Judge.

Plaintiff-appellant Craig P. Nadel ("Nadel") brought this action against defendant-appellee Play-By-Play Toys & Novelties, Inc. ("Play-By-Play") for breach of contract, quasi contract, and unfair competition. The thrust of Nadel's complaint was that Play-By-Play took his idea for an upright, sound-emitting, spinning plush toy and that, contrary to industry custom, Play-By-Play used the idea in its "Tornado Taz" product without paying him compensation. . . .

Background

Nadel is a toy idea man. Toy companies regularly do business with independent inventors such as Nadel in order to develop and market new toy concepts as quickly as possible. To facilitate the exchange of ideas, the standard custom and practice in the toy industry calls for companies to treat the submission of an idea as confidential. If the company subsequently uses the disclosed idea, industry custom provides that the company shall compensate the inventor, unless, of course, the disclosed idea was already known to the company.

In 1996, Nadel developed the toy concept at issue in this case. He transplanted the "eccentric mechanism"[1] found in several hanging Halloween toys then on the market-such as "Spooky Skull" and "Shaking Mutant Pumpkin"—and placed the mechanism inside of a plush toy monkey skin to develop the prototype for a new table-top monkey toy. This plush toy figure sat upright, emitted sound, and spun when placed on a flat surface.

In October 1996, Nadel met with Neil Wasserman, an executive at Play-By-Play who was responsible for the development of its plush toy line. According to Nadel, he showed his prototype monkey toy to Wasserman, who expressed interest in adapting the concept to a non-moving, plush Tazmanian Devil toy that Play-By-Play was already producing under license from Warner Bros. Nadel contends that, consistent with industry custom, any ideas that he disclosed to Wasserman during their October 1996 meeting were subject to an agreement by Play-By-Play to keep such ideas confidential and to compensate Nadel in the event of their use.

Nadel claims that he sent his prototype monkey toy to Wasserman as a sample and awaited the "Taz skin" and voice tape, which Wasserman allegedly said he would send, so that Nadel could make a sample spinning/laughing Tazmanian Devil toy for Play-By-Play. Wasserman never provided Nadel with the Taz skin and voice tape, however, and denies ever having received the prototype monkey toy from Nadel.

Notwithstanding Wasserman's denial, his secretary, Melissa Rodriguez, testified that Nadel's prototype monkey toy remained in Wasserman's office for several months. According to Ms. Rodriguez, the monkey toy was usually kept in a glass cabinet behind Wasserman's desk, but she remembered that on one occasion she had seen it on a table in Wasserman's office. Despite Nadel's multiple requests, Wasserman did not return Nadel's prototype monkey toy until February 1997, after Play-by-Play introduced its "Tornado Taz" product at the New York Toy Fair.

---

[1] An eccentric mechanism typically consists of a housing containing a motor with an eccentric weight attached to the motor shaft. When the motor is activated, the motor rotates the weight centrifugally, causing the housing to shake or spin.

The parties do not dispute that "Tornado Taz" has the same general characteristics as Nadel's prototype monkey toy. Like Nadel's toy, Tornado Taz is a plush toy that emits sounds (including "screaming," "laughing," "snarling," and "grunting"), sits upright, and spins by means of an internal eccentric vibration mechanism.

Nadel claims that, in violation of their alleged agreement, Play-By-Play used his idea without paying him compensation. Play-By-Play contends, however, that it independently developed the Tornado Taz product concept and that Nadel is therefore not entitled to any compensation. Specifically, Play-By-Play maintains that, as early as June or July of 1996, two of its officers—Wasserman and Slattery—met in Hong Kong and began discussing ways to create a spinning or vibrating Tazmanian Devil, including the possible use of an eccentric mechanism. Furthermore, Play-By-Play claims that in late September or early October 1996, it commissioned an outside manufacturing agent—Barter Trading of Hong Kong—to begin developing Tornado Taz.

Play-By-Play also argues that, even if it did use Nadel's idea to develop Tornado Taz, Nadel is not entitled to compensation because Nadel's concept was unoriginal and non-novel to the toy industry in October 1996. In support of this argument, Play-By-Play has submitted evidence of various toys, commercially available prior to October 1996, which used eccentric motors and allegedly contained the same characteristics as Nadel's prototype monkey toy. . . .

Discussion

I. *Nadel's Claims*

On January 21, 1999, the district court granted Play-By-Play's motion for summary judgment dismissing Nadel's claims for breach of contract, quasi contract, and unfair competition. Interpreting New York law, the district court stated that "a party is not entitled to recover for theft of an idea unless the idea is novel or original." *Nadel v. Play By Play Toys & Novelties, Inc.*, 34 F. Supp. 2d 180, 184 (S.D.N.Y. 1999). Applying that principle to Nadel's claims, the district court concluded that, even if the spinning toy concept were novel to Play-By-Play at the time Nadel made the disclosure to Wasserman in October 1996, Nadel's claims must nonetheless fail for lack of novelty or originality because "numerous toys containing the characteristics of [Nadel's] monkey were in existence prior to[ ] October 1996." *Id.* at 185. In essence, the district court interpreted New York law to require that, when a plaintiff claims that a defendant has either (1) misappropriated his idea (a "property-based claim") or (2) breached an express or implied-in-fact contract by using such idea (a "contract-based claim"), the idea at issue must be original or novel generally. *See id.* at 184 n. 1. Thus, according to the district court, a finding that an idea was novel as to Play-By-Play—i.e., novel to the buyer—cannot suffice to sustain any of Nadel's claims. *See id.*

On appeal, Nadel challenges the district court's conclusion that a showing of novelty to the buyer—i.e., that Nadel's idea was novel to Play-By-Play at the time of his October 1996 disclosure—cannot suffice to sustain his claims for breach of contract, quasi contract, and unfair competition under New York law. Nadel claims, moreover, that the record contains a genuine issue of material fact concerning whether his toy idea was novel to Play-By-Play at the time of his October 1996 disclosure to Wasserman and that the district court therefore erred in granting Play-By-Play's motion for summary judgment.

Nadel's factual allegations present a familiar submission-of-idea case: (1) the parties enter into a pre-disclosure confidentiality agreement; (2) the idea is subsequently disclosed to the prospective buyer; (3) there is no post-disclosure contract for payment based on use; and (4) plaintiff sues defendant for allegedly using the disclosed idea under either a contract-based or property-based theory. For the reasons that follow, we conclude that a finding of novelty as to Play-By-Play can suffice to provide consideration for Nadel's contract claims against Play-By-Play. Accordingly, because we also find that there exists a genuine issue of material fact as to whether Nadel's idea was novel to Play-By-Play at the time of his October 1996 disclosure, we vacate the district court's grant of summary judgment on Nadel's contract claims. With respect to Nadel's misappropriation claim, we similarly vacate the district court's grant of summary judgment and remand for further proceedings to determine whether Nadel's idea was original or novel generally.

A. Submission-of-Idea Cases Under New York Law

Our analysis begins with the New York Court of Appeals' most recent discussion of the law governing idea submission cases, *Apfel v. Prudential-Bache Securities, Inc.*, 81 N.Y.2d 470, 600 N.Y.S.2d 433, 616 N.E.2d 1095 (1993). In *Apfel*, the Court of Appeals discussed the type of novelty an idea must have in order to sustain a contract-based or property-based claim for its uncompensated use. Specifically, *Apfel* clarified an important distinction between the requirement of "novelty to the buyer" for contract claims, on the one hand, and "originality" (or novelty generally) for misappropriation claims, on the other hand.

Under the facts of *Apfel*, the plaintiff disclosed his idea to the defendant pursuant to a confidentiality agreement and, subsequent to disclosure, entered into another agreement wherein the defendant agreed to pay a stipulated price for the idea's use. *See id.* at 474. The defendant used the idea but refused to pay plaintiff pursuant to the post-disclosure agreement on the asserted ground that "no contract existed between the parties because the sale agreement lacked consideration." *Id.* at 475. The defendant argued that an idea could not constitute legally sufficient consideration unless it was original or novel generally and that, because plaintiff's idea was not original or novel generally (it had been in the public domain at the time of the post-disclosure agreement), the idea provided insufficient consideration to support the parties' post-disclosure contract. *See id.* at 474–75.

In rejecting defendant's argument, the Court of Appeals held that there was sufficient consideration to support plaintiff's contract claim because the idea at issue had value to the defendant at the time the parties concluded their post-disclosure agreement. *See id.* at 476. The *Apfel* court noted that "traditional principles of contract law" provide that parties "are free to make their bargain, even if the consideration exchanged is grossly unequal or of dubious value," *id.* at 475, and that, so long as the "defendant received something of value" under the contract, the contract would not be void for lack of consideration, *id.* at 476. *See also id.* at 478 ("[T]he buyer knows what he or she is buying and has agreed that the idea has value, and the Court will not ordinarily go behind that determination.").

The *Apfel* court explicitly rejected defendant's contention that the court should carve out "an exception to traditional principles of contract law" for submission-of-idea cases by requiring that an idea must also be original or novel generally in order to constitute valid consideration. *Id.* at 477. In essence, the defendant sought to impose a requirement that an idea be novel in absolute terms, as opposed to only the defendant buyer, in order to constitute valid consideration for the bargain. In rejecting this argument, the *Apfel* court clarified the standards for both contract-based and property-based claims in submission-of-idea cases. That analysis guides our decision here.

The *Apfel* court first noted that "novelty as an element of an idea seller's claim" is a distinct element of proof with respect to both (1) "a claim based on a property theory" and (2) "a claim based on a contract theory." *Id.* at 477. The court then proceeded to discuss how the leading submission-of-idea case—*Downey v. General Foods Corp.*, 31 N.Y.2d 56, 334 N.Y.S.2d 874, 286 N.E.2d 257 (1972)—treated novelty with respect to property-based and contract-based claims. First, the *Apfel* court explained that the plaintiff's property-based claims for misappropriation were dismissed in Downey because "the elements of novelty and originality [were] absent," i.e., the ideas were so common as to be unoriginal and known generally. *Apfel*, 81 N.Y.2d at 477 (quoting *Downey*, 31 N.Y.2d at 61) (alteration in original); accord *Downey*, 31 N.Y.2d at 61–62 (holding that the submitted idea—marketing Jell-O to children under the name "Mr. Wiggle"—was "lacking in novelty and originality" because the idea was merely the "use of a word ('wiggley' or 'wiggle') descriptive of the most obvious characteristic of Jell-O, with the prefix 'Mr.' added"). Second, the *Apfel* court explained that the plaintiff's contract claims in Downey had been dismissed on the separate ground that the "defendant possessed plaintiff's ideas prior to plaintiff's disclosure [and thus], the ideas could have no value to defendant and could not supply consideration for any agreement between the parties." *Apfel*, 81 N.Y.2d at 477; accord *Downey*, 31 N.Y.2d at 62 (finding that, where defendant had used the words "wiggles" and "wigglewam" in prior advertising, defendant could "rel[y] on its own previous experience" and "was free to make use of 'Mr. Wiggle' without being obligated to compensate the plaintiff").

By distinguishing between the two types of claims addressed in Downey and the different bases for rejecting each claim, the New York Court of Appeals clarified that the novelty requirement in submission-of-idea cases is different for misappropriation of property and breach of contract claims. . . .

Thus, the *Apfel* court refused to read *Downey* and "similar decisions" as requiring originality or novelty generally in all cases involving disclosure of ideas. *See Apfel*, 81 N.Y.2d at 476–77 ("These decisions do not support [the] contention that novelty [in absolute terms] is required in all cases involving disclosure of ideas."). Rather, the *Apfel* court clarified that the longstanding requirement that an idea have originality or general novelty in order to support a misappropriation claim does not apply to contract claims. *See Oasis Music, Inc. v. 900 U.S.A., Inc.*, 161 Misc. 2d 627, 614 N.Y.S.2d 878, 881

(1994) (noting that "the *Apfel* court did not repudiate the long line of cases requiring novelty in certain situations[,] . . . the *Apfel* court merely clarified that novelty is not required in all cases"). For contract-based claims in submission-of-idea cases, a showing of novelty to the buyer will supply sufficient consideration to support a contract.

Moreover, *Apfel* made clear that the "novelty to the buyer" standard is not limited to cases involving an express post-disclosure contract for payment based on an idea's use. The *Apfel* court explicitly discussed the pre-disclosure contract scenario present in the instant case, where "the buyer and seller contract for disclosure of the idea with payment based on use, but no separate post-disclosure contract for the use of the idea has been made." *Apfel,* 81 N.Y.2d at 477–78. In such a scenario, a seller might, as Nadel did here, bring an action against a buyer who allegedly used his ideas without payment, claiming both misappropriation of property and breach of an express or implied-in-fact contract. Of course, the mere disclosure of an unoriginal idea to a defendant, to whom the idea is novel, will not automatically entitle a plaintiff to compensation upon the defendant's subsequent use of the idea. An implied-in-fact contract "requires such elements as consideration, mutual assent, legal capacity and legal subject matter." *Id.* (internal quotation marks omitted). The existence of novelty to the buyer only addresses the element of consideration necessary for the formation of the contract. . . . With respect to a breach of contract claim, the court noted that it would be inequitable to enforce a contract if "it turns out upon disclosure that the buyer already possessed the idea." *Id.* The court then concluded that, with respect to these cases, "[a] showing of novelty, at least novelty as to the buyer" should address these problems.[6]

We note, moreover, that the "novelty to the buyer" standard comports with traditional principles of contract law. While an idea may be unoriginal or non-novel in a general sense, it may have substantial value to a particular buyer who is unaware of it and therefore willing to enter into contract to acquire and exploit it. *See Apfel,* 81 N.Y.2d at 475–76; Robert Unikel, *Bridging the "Trade Secret" Gap: Protecting "Confidential Information" Not Rising to the Level of Trade Secrets,* 29 LOY. U. CHI. L.J. 841, 877 n. 151 (1998) (noting that, if a valuable idea is already known to an industry but has not yet been acquired by a prospective buyer, one of two circumstances may exist: "(1) the person[] ha[s] not identified the potential value of the easily acquired information; or (2) the person[] ha[s] not identified the means, however easy or proper, for obtaining the valuable information"). As the *Apfel* court emphasized, "the buyer may reap benefits from such a contract in a number of ways—for instance, by not having to expend resources pursuing the idea through other channels or by having a profit-making idea implemented sooner rather than later." *Apfel,* 81 N.Y.2d at 478. . . .

In contrast to contract-based claims, a misappropriation claim can only arise from the taking of an idea that is original or novel in absolute terms, because the law of property does not protect against the misappropriation or theft of that which is free and

---

[6] We note that this particular sentence could be read out of context to suggest that novelty to the buyer will alone support a misappropriation claim under New York law. However, nothing in *Apfel* otherwise suggests that the Court of Appeals meant to supplant the longstanding requirement that originality or novelty generally must be shown to support a misappropriation claim. . . .

available to all. *See Murray v. National Broad. Co.*, 844 F.2d 988, 993 (2d Cir. 1988) ("Since . . . non-novel ideas are not protectible as property, they cannot be stolen."); *cf. Ed Graham Prods., Inc. v. National Broad. Co.*, 75 Misc. 2d 334, 347 N.Y.S.2d 766, 769 (1973) ("Ideas such as those presented by the plaintiff are in the public domain and may freely be used by anyone with impunity."); *Educational Sales Programs, Inc. v. Dreyfus Corp.*, 65 Misc. 2d 412, 317 N.Y.S.2d 840, 843 (1970) ("An idea is impalpable, intangible, incorporeal, yet it may be a stolen gem of great value, or mere dross of no value at all, depending on its novelty and uniqueness.").

Finally, although the legal requirements for contract-based claims and property-based claims are well-defined, we note that the determination of novelty in a given case is not always clear. *Cf. AEB & Assocs. Design Group, Inc. v. Tonka Corp.*, 853 F. Supp. 724, 734 (S.D.N.Y. 1994) ("In establishing an idea's originality, a plaintiff cannot rest on mere assertions, but must demonstrate some basis in fact for its claims."). The determination of whether an idea is original or novel depends upon several factors, including, inter alia, the idea's specificity or generality (is it a generic concept or one of specific application?), its commonality (how many people know of this idea?), its uniqueness (how different is this idea from generally known ideas?), and its commercial availability (how widespread is the idea's use in the industry?). *Cf. Murray*, 844 F.2d at 993 ("In assessing whether an idea is in the public domain, the central issue is the uniqueness of the creation."); *AEB & Assocs.*, 853 F. Supp. at 734 ("[N]ovelty cannot be found where the idea consists of nothing more than a variation on a basic theme."); *Educational Sales Programs*, 317 N.Y.S.2d at 844 (noting that an idea "must show[ ] genuine novelty and invention, and not a merely clever or useful adaptation of existing knowledge" in order to be considered original or novel). Thus, for example, a once original or novel idea may become so widely disseminated over the course of time that it enters the body of common knowledge. When this occurs, the idea ceases to be novel or original. *See, e.g., Murray*, 844 F.2d at 989, 991–92 (affirming district court's finding that plaintiff's idea for a television sitcom about "Black American family life" was not novel or original because it "merely combined two ideas which had been circulating in the industry for a number of years—namely, the family situation comedy, which was a standard formula, and the casting of black actors in non-stereotypical roles," even though "the portrayal of a nonstereotypical black family on television was indeed a breakthrough"). . . .

In sum, we find that New York law in submission-of-idea cases is governed by the following principles: Contract-based claims require only a showing that the disclosed idea was novel to the buyer in order to find consideration. Such claims involve a fact-specific inquiry that focuses on the perspective of the particular buyer. By contrast, misappropriation claims require that the idea at issue be original and novel in absolute terms. This is so because unoriginal, known ideas have no value as property and the law does not protect against the use of that which is free and available to all. Finally, an idea may be so unoriginal or lacking in novelty generally that, as a matter of law, the buyer is deemed to have knowledge of the idea. In such cases, neither a property-based nor a contract-based claim for uncompensated use of the idea may lie.

In light of New York's law governing submission-of-idea cases, we next consider whether Nadel's toy idea was original or novel in absolute terms so as to support his misappropriation claim and whether his idea was novel as to Play-By-Play so as to support his contract claims.

B. Nadel's Misappropriation Claim

. . . In this case, the district court did not decide whether Nadel's idea—a plush toy that sits upright, emits sounds, and spins on a flat surface by means of an internal eccentric motor—was inherently lacking in originality. *See Nadel*, 34 F. Supp. 2d at 185 ("[We] need [not] reach the issue of whether combining elements of two commercially available toys to make another toy may be novel or is, as a matter of law, merely a 'clever adaptation of existing technology,' for Play-By-Play has demonstrated that plaintiff's idea was one which was already in use in the industry at the time that it was submitted"). We therefore remand this issue to the district court to determine whether Nadel's idea exhibited "genuine novelty or invention" or whether it was "a merely clever or useful adaptation of existing knowledge." *Educational Sales Programs*, 317 N.Y.S.2d at 844.

Moreover, insofar as the district court found that Nadel's idea lacked originality and novelty generally because similar toys were commercially available prior to October 1996, we believe that there remains a genuine issue of material fact on this point. While the record contains testimony of Play-By-Play's toy expert—Bert Reiner—in support of the finding that Nadel's product concept was already used in more than a dozen different plush toys prior to October 1996, the district court cited the "Giggle Bunny" toy as the only such example. *See Nadel*, 34 F. Supp. 2d at 185. Nadel disputes Reiner's contention and claims, furthermore, that the district court erroneously relied on an undated video depiction of the Giggle Bunny toy to conclude that upright, sound-emitting, spinning plush toys were commercially available prior to October 1996.

With respect to the Giggle Bunny evidence, we agree with Nadel that the Giggle Bunny model depicted in the undated video exhibit is physically different from the earlier Giggle Bunny model known to be commercially available in 1994. Drawing all factual inferences in Nadel's favor, we cannot conclude as a matter of law that the upright, sound-emitting, spinning plush Giggle Bunny shown in the video exhibit was commercially available prior to October 1996, and we certainly cannot conclude based on this one exhibit that similar toys were in the public domain at that time.

Moreover, although we find highly probative Mr. Reiner's testimony that numerous toys with the same general characteristics of Nadel's toy idea were commercially available prior to October 1996, his testimony and related evidence are too ambiguous and incomplete to support a finding of unoriginality as a matter of law. Mr. Reiner's testimony fails to specify precisely which (if any) of the enumerated plush toys were designed to (1) sit upright, (2) on a flat surface, (3) emit sounds, and (4) spin or rotate (rather than simply vibrate like "Tickle Me Elmo," for example). Without this information, a reasonable finder of fact could discount Mr. Reiner's testimony as vague and inconclusive.

On remand, the district court is free to consider whether further discovery is warranted to determine whether Nadel's product concept was inherently original or whether it was novel to the industry prior to October 1996. A finding of unoriginality or lack of general novelty would, of course, preclude Nadel from bringing a misappropriation claim against Play-By-Play. Moreover, in evaluating the originality or general novelty of Nadel's idea in connection with his misappropriation claim, the district may consider whether the idea is so unoriginal that Play-By-Play should, as a matter of law, be deemed to have already possessed the idea, and dismiss Nadel's contract claims on that ground.

C. Nadel's Contract Claims

Mindful that, under New York law, a finding of novelty as to Play-By-Play will provide sufficient consideration to support Nadel's contract claims, we next consider whether the record exhibits a genuine issue of material fact on this point.

Reading the record in a light most favorable to Nadel, . . . we conclude that there exists a genuine issue of material fact as to whether Nadel's idea was, at the time he disclosed it to Wasserman in early October 1996, novel to Play-By-Play. Notably, the timing of Play-By-Play's development and release of Tornado Taz in relation to Nadel's October 1996 disclosure is, taken alone, highly probative. Moreover, although custom in the toy industry provides that a company shall promptly return all samples if it already possesses (or does not want to use) a disclosed idea, Play-By-Play in this case failed to return Nadel's prototype monkey toy for several months, despite Nadel's multiple requests for its return. According to Wasserman's secretary, Melissa Rodriguez, Nadel's sample was not returned until after the unveiling of "Tornado Taz" at the New York Toy Fair in February 1997. Ms. Rodriguez testified that from October 1996 through February 1997, Nadel's sample was usually kept in a glass cabinet behind Wasserman's desk, and on one occasion, she remembered seeing it on a table in Wasserman's office. These facts give rise to the reasonable inference that Play-By-Play may have used Nadel's prototype as a model for the development of Tornado Taz.

None of the evidence adduced by Play-By-Play compels a finding to the contrary on summary judgment. With regard to the discussions that Play-By-Play purportedly had in June or July of 1996 about possible ways to create a vibrating or spinning Tazmanian Devil toy, those conversations only lasted, according to Mr. Slattery, "a matter of five minutes." Play-By-Play may have "discussed the concept," as Mr. Slattery testified, but the record provides no evidence suggesting that, in June or July of 1996, Play-By-Play understood exactly how it could apply eccentric motor technology to make its Tazmanian Devil toy spin rather than, say, vibrate like Tickle Me Elmo. Similarly, although Play-By-Play asserts that it commissioned an outside manufacturing agent—Barter Trading of Hong Kong—to begin developing Tornado Taz in late September or early October of 1996, Play-By-Play admits that it can only "guess" the exact date. Play-By-Play cannot confirm that its commission of Barter Trading pre-dated Nadel's alleged disclosure to Wasserman on or about October 9, 1996. Nor has Play-By-Play produced any documents, technical or otherwise, relating to its purported business venture with Barter Trading or its independent development of a spinning

Tornado Taz prior to October 1996. Based on this evidence, a jury could reasonably infer that Play-By-Play actually contacted Barter Trading, if at all, after learning of Nadel's product concept, and that Play-By-Play's development of Tornado Taz is attributable to Nadel's disclosure.

We therefore conclude that there exists a genuine issue of material fact as to whether Nadel's idea was, at the time he disclosed it to Wasserman in early October 1996, novel to Play-By-Play. . . .

COMMENTS AND QUESTIONS

1. *Idea Submission Causes of Action.* As the *Nadel* case reflects, idea submission cases must be brought within some property, contract, or tort cause of action. Contract law has proven the most resilient basis for protecting ideas. *Nadel* discusses the availability of express and implied contract rights for the disclosure of an idea. In addition, some courts have protected ideas under the law of confidential relationships (and the related body of trade secret protection). *See, e.g., Ralph Andrews Prods. v. Paramount Pictures,* 222 Cal. App. 3d 676, 271 Cal. Rptr. 797 (1990) (trade secret suit alleging that a former employee stole an idea for a game show and sold it to Paramount Pictures). The misappropriation cause of action derives from property and tort principles. It is narrow. Misappropriation and other property-type claims (e.g., conversion) no longer exist as to ideas for copyrightable works—stories, movies, songs. Some states jettisoned such protection expressly. *See, e.g., Desny v. Wilder,* 46 Cal. 2d 715 (Cal. Sup. Ct. 1956) ("California does not now accord individual property type protection to abstract ideas"), excerpted below. State laws protecting such subject matter as of January 1, 1978, were preempted by the 1976 Copyright Act. *See Nash v. CBS, Inc.,* 704 F. Supp. 823, 833–35 (N.D. Ill. 1989), *aff'd,* 899 F.2d 1537 (7th Cir. 1990) (rejecting claim that CBS had misappropriated ideas from plaintiff's book, *The Dillinger Report,* in an episode of the television drama "Simon and Simon").

2. *Requirements.* Based upon the *Nadel* case, under what circumstances can ideas be protected? What elements must one who submits an idea to another prove in order to recover?

3. *Semantics.* The *Nadel* court uses words familiar from the study of patent and copyright law—originality, novelty, and obviousness. But do these intellectual property words of art have the same meaning in the law of idea submissions? What does the court mean by "original," "novel," and "obvious"? How do these meanings compare to the definitions from copyright and patent law? Does the court suggest that the "novelty" requirement for a misappropriation claim incorporates a broader conception of non-obviousness than patent law?

4. The novelty requirement was central to the Second Circuit's decision rejecting an idea submission claim in *Murray v. National Broadcasting Co.,* 844 F.2d 988 (2d Cir. 1988), *cert. denied,* 488 U.S. 955 (1988). In that case, Murray (an NBC employee) submitted a two-page proposal to NBC for a show entitled "Father's Day" that would "combine humor with serious situations in a manner similar to that of the old Dick Van Dyke Show" but with a "Black perspective" and "a contemporary, urban setting." The

proposal specifically identified Bill Cosby as the lead actor. NBC informed Murray that it was not interested in pursuing his proposal. When "The Cosby Show" aired four years later, starring Bill Cosby as Dr. Cliff Huxtable living in a contemporary urban setting with his lawyer-spouse and their five children, Murray sued. The court rejected Murray's claim for lack of novelty:

> [W]e believe, as a matter of law, that plaintiff's idea embodied in his "Father's Day" proposal was not novel because it merely represented an "adaptation of existing knowledge" and of "known ingredients" and therefore lacked "genuine novelty and invention." *Educational Sales Programs*, 317 N.Y.S.2d at 844.
>
> We recognize of course that even novel and original ideas to a greater or lesser extent combine elements that are themselves not novel. Originality does not exist in a vacuum. Nevertheless, where, as here, an idea consists in essence of nothing more than a variation on a basic theme—in this case, the family situation comedy—novelty cannot be found to exist. . . .
>
> Appellant would have us believe that by interpreting New York law as we do, we are in effect condoning the theft of ideas. On the contrary, ideas that reflect "genuine novelty and invention" are fully protected against unauthorized use. But those ideas that are not novel "are in the public domain and may freely be used by anyone with impunity." Since such non-novel ideas are not protectible as property, they cannot be stolen. *Id.* at 992–93.

How does this use of the term "novelty" compare to the patent law's definition?[1] Wouldn't a new combination of known elements be considered novel under the patent law's standards? Isn't the court really saying that the idea was obvious? How would this determination be made under the patent law's standards? Was there a suggestion or motivation to combine? Don't secondary considerations—especially commercial success—weigh against a finding of obviousness? Would the law of idea submissions be improved by adopting the patent law's framework for judging novelty and non-obviousness?

5. *The Novelty to the User Standard and Diffusion of Ideas.* Idea protection today is based upon an express or implied contract between an idea purveyor and a potential user. Under *Apfel* and *Nadel*, the idea purveyor need only show that the idea was not known *to the defendant* in order to satisfy the novelty element. This element provides the consideration necessary for there to be a valid contract. The court notes, however, that "in some cases an idea may be so unoriginal or lacking in novelty that its obviousness bespeaks widespread and public knowledge of the idea, and such

---

[1] It should be noted that Murray's claim of novelty would have surely failed under a patent law standard. Evidence at the trial revealed that Cosby himself had been quoted in a newspaper article 20 years earlier stating that it was his "dream" to appear in a situation comedy along the lines of "The Dick Van Dyke Show," but featuring an African-American family. *Id.* at 989. The court did not base its decision on this evidence, which would have gone to the question of whether NBC had independently developed the idea for the show.

knowledge is therefore imputed to the buyer." Should protection for ideas turn on the sophistication of the buyer?

One justification for such a doctrine is to reward diffusion of ideas to those best situated to commercialize them. As we discussed in Chapter I, economic historians and theorists find that diffusion of knowledge is a crucial element in the creation of social benefit flowing from innovation. This doctrine rewards not the inventor but those who have the insight and possibly the connections to diffuse (or market) information. Certainly, a true inventor can benefit, because being first ensures that the idea will be novel to others. Should the intellectual property system reward diffusion of ideas in this way?

6. *Concreteness.* Some courts consider whether an idea is sufficiently "concrete" in determining liability based on breach of implied contract and confidential relationship causes of action, although not in express contract claims. In the words of one court, "[i]deas are the most intangible of property rights, and their lineage is uniquely difficult to trace. Paternity can be claimed in the most casual of ways, and once such a claim is lodged, definitive blood tests are notoriously lacking." *Burten v. Milton Bradley Co.,* 592 F. Supp. 1021, 1031 (D.R.I. 1984), *rev'd on other grounds,* 763 F.2d 461 (1st Cir. 1985). In assessing a claim to protect the idea of organizing and sponsoring radio broadcasts of student talent shows, the court in *Hamilton Nat'l Bank v. Belt*, 210 F.2d 706 (D.C. Cir. 1953), noted that "[t]he law shies away from according protection to vagueness, and must do so especially in the realm of ideas with the obvious dangers of a contrary rule." *Id.* at 708. Does this amount to an indefinite claiming doctrine? Or is it more akin to a rejection under § 101 of the Patent Act for claiming only an abstract idea?

7. *Contract Analysis; Comparison to Trade Secret.* How does the contract analysis in *Nadel* compare to that in the trade secret/breach of confidence cases involving contracts, such as *Smith v. Dravo Corp.*, discussed in Chapter II? What (if any) differences are there in the relationship of the parties, the duties of the idea/information recipient, and the nature of the idea or information? In the remedies?

8. *Defenses: Waiver/Release.* Many companies and film production studios require that those who submit ideas sign waivers or releases from liability. The release used in the *Downey* case, 286 N.E.2d 257 (N.Y. Ct. App. 1972), stated: I submit this suggestion with the understanding, which is conclusively evidenced by my use and transmittal to you of this form, that this suggestion is not submitted to you in confidence, that no confidential relationship has been or will be established between us and that the use, if any, to be made of this suggestion by you and the compensation to be paid therefor, if any, if you use it, are matters resting solely in your discretion.

Suppose that the recipient used the idea without paying any compensation. Should such a clause be enforceable? Consider the argument put forth by Professor Lionel Sobel favoring enforcement in the context of script submissions: "If courts were to refuse to enforce releases, it is likely that unrepresented writers would be unable to get their material read at all—a consequence more harmful to aspiring writers than the possibility

that releases will bar some of them from suing for the suspected theft of their ideas."
See Lionel S. Sobel, *The Law of Ideas, Revisited*, 1 UCLA ENT. L. REV. 9, 91 (1994).

9. *Remedies.* What should be the remedy for the misappropriation of an idea or breach of a contract to pay for an idea? Assuming that Nadel prevails on his liability claims (misappropriation and contract) at trial, what should be the measure of damages? Assuming that Murray had carried his burden of proof on the novelty of "The Cosby Show," should he be entitled to all of the profits from the show?

Desny v. Wilder
Supreme Court of California
46 Cal. 2d 715, 299 P.2d 257, 110 U.S.P.Q. 433 (Cal. Sup. Ct. 1956)

SCHAUER, Justice.

Plaintiff appeals from a summary judgment rendered against him in this action to recover the reasonable value of a literary composition, or of an idea for a photoplay, a synopsis of which composition, embodying the idea, he asserts he submitted to defendants for sale, and which synopsis and idea, plaintiff alleges, were accepted and used by defendants in producing a photoplay. . . .

[W]e have concluded, for reasons hereinafter stated, that the summary judgment in favor of defendants was erroneously granted and should be reversed. . . . [I]t appears from the present record that defendant [Billy] Wilder [a famous director] at the times here involved was employed by defendant Paramount Pictures Corporation . . . either as a writer, producer or director, or a combination of the three. In November, 1949, plaintiff telephoned Wilder's office. Wilder's secretary, who was also employed by Paramount, answered, and plaintiff stated that he wished to see Wilder. At the secretary's insistence that plaintiff explain his purpose, plaintiff 'told her about this fantastic unusual story. . . . I told her that it was the life story of Floyd Collins who was trapped and made sensational news for two weeks . . . and I told her the plot.' . . . Two days later plaintiff, after preparing a three or four page outline of the story, telephoned Wilder's office a second time and told the secretary the synopsis was ready. The secretary requested plaintiff to read the synopsis to her over the telephone so that she could take it down in shorthand, and plaintiff did so. . . . Plaintiff on his part told the secretary that defendants could use the story only if they paid him 'the reasonable value of it.' . . . She said that if Billy Wilder of Paramount uses the story, 'naturally we will pay you for it.' . . . Plaintiff's only subsequent contact with the secretary was a telephone call to her in July, 1950, to protest the alleged use of his composition and idea in a photoplay produced and exhibited by defendants. The photoplay, as hereinafter shown in some detail, closely parallels both plaintiff's synopsis and the historical material concerning the life and death of Floyd Collins.

Defendants concede, as they must, that "the act of disclosing an unprotectible idea, if that act is in fact the bargained for exchange for a promise, may be consideration to support the promise." They then add, "But once the idea is disclosed without the protection of a contract, the law says that anyone is free to use it. Therefore, subsequent use of the idea cannot constitute consideration so as to support a promise to pay for such use." And as to the effect of the evidence defendants argue that plaintiff "disclosed his material before . . . (defendants) did or could do anything to indicate their willingness or unwillingness to pay for the disclosure. The act of using the idea, from which appellant attempts to imply a promise to pay, came long after the disclosure." . . .

Generally speaking, ideas are as free as the air. . . . But there can be circumstances when neither air nor ideas may be acquired without cost. The diver who goes deep in the sea, even as the pilot who ascends high in the troposphere, knows full well that for life itself he, or someone on his behalf, must arrange for air. . . . The theatrical producer likewise may be dependent for his business life on the procurement of ideas from other persons as well as the dressing up and portrayal of his self-conceptions; he may not find his own sufficient for survival. As counsel for the Writers Guild aptly say, ideas 'are not freely usable by the entertainment media until the latter are made aware of them.' The producer may think up the idea himself, dress it and portray it; or he may purchase either the conveyance of the idea alone or a manuscript embodying the idea in the author's concept of a literary vehicle giving it form, adaptation and expression. It cannot be doubted that some ideas are of value to a producer.

An idea is usually not regarded as property, because all sentient beings may conceive and evolve ideas throughout the gamut of their powers of cerebration and because our concept of property implies something which may be owned and possessed to the exclusion of all other persons. We quote as an accurate statement of the law in this respect the following language of Mr. Justice Brandeis, dissenting in *International News Service v. Associated Press* (1918), 248 U.S. 215, 250: "An essential element of individual property is the legal right to exclude others from enjoying it. [. . .] But the fact that a product of the mind has cost its producer money and labor, and has a value for which others are willing to pay, is not sufficient to ensure to it this legal attribute of property. The general rule of law is, that the noblest of human productions, knowledge, truths ascertained, conceptions, and ideas become, after voluntary communication to others, free as the air to common use."

The principles above stated do not, however, lead to the conclusion that ideas cannot be a subject of contract. As Mr. Justice Traynor stated in his dissenting opinion in *Stanley v. Columbia Broadcasting System* (1950), 35 Cal. 2d 653, 674, 221 P.2d 73:The policy that precludes protection of an abstract idea by copyright does not prevent its protection by contract. Even though an idea is not property subject to exclusive ownership, its disclosure may be of substantial benefit to the person to whom it is disclosed. That disclosure may therefore be consideration for a promise to pay. . . . Even though the idea disclosed may be "widely known and generally understood" (citation), it may be protected by an express contract providing that it will be paid for regardless of its lack of novelty.

The lawyer or doctor who applies specialized knowledge to a state of facts and gives advice for a fee is selling and conveying an idea. In doing that he is rendering a service. The lawyer and doctor have no property rights in their ideas, as such, but they do not ordinarily convey them without solicitation by client or patient. Usually the parties will expressly contract for the performance of and payment for such services, but, in the absence of an express contract, when the service is requested and rendered the law does not hesitate to infer or imply a promise to compensate for it. In other words the recovery may be based on contract either express or implied. The person who can and does convey a valuable idea to a producer who commercially solicits the service or who voluntarily accepts it knowing that it is tendered for a price should likewise be entitled to recover. In so holding we do not fail to recognize that free-lance writers are not necessarily members of a learned profession and as such bound to the exalted standards to which doctors and lawyers are dedicated. So too we are not oblivious of the hazards with which producers of the class represented here by defendants and their related amici are confronted through the unsolicited submission of numerous scripts on public domain materials in which public materials the producers through their own initiative may well find nuclei for legitimately developing the "stupendous and colossal." The law, however, is dedicated to the proposition that for every wrong there is a remedy. . . . To that end the law of implied contracts assumes particular importance in literary idea and property controversies. . . .

[W]e conclude that conveyance of an idea can constitute valuable consideration and can be bargained for before it is disclosed to the proposed purchaser, but once it is conveyed, i.e., disclosed to him and he has grasped it, it is henceforth his own and he may work with it and use it as he sees fit. In the field of entertainment the producer may properly and validly agree that he will pay for the service of conveying to him ideas which are valuable and which he can put to profitable use. Furthermore, where an idea has been conveyed with the expectation by the purveyor that compensation will be paid if the idea is used, there is no reason why the producer who has been the beneficiary of the conveyance of such an idea, and who finds it valuable and is profiting by it, may not then for the first time, although he is not at that time under any legal obligation so to do, promise to pay a reasonable compensation for that idea, that is, for the past service of furnishing it to him and thus create a valid obligation. . . . But, assuming legality of consideration, the idea purveyor cannot prevail in an action to recover compensation for an abstract idea unless (a) before or after disclosure he has obtained an express promise to pay, or (b) the circumstances preceding and attending disclosure, together with the conduct of the offeree acting with knowledge of the circumstances, show a promise of the type usually referred to as "implied" or "implied-in-fact." . . .

Such inferred or implied promise, if it is to be found at all, must be based on circumstances which were known to the producer at and preceding the time of disclosure of the idea to him and he must voluntarily accept the disclosure, knowing the conditions on which it is tendered. . . . The idea man who blurts out his idea without having first made his bargain has no one but himself to blame for the loss of his bargaining power. . . . So, if the plaintiff here is claiming only for the conveyance of the idea of making a dramatic production out of the life of Floyd Collins he must fail unless in conformity with the above stated rules he can establish a contract to pay.

From plaintiff's testimony, as epitomized above . . . it does not appear that a contract to pay for conveyance of the abstract photoplay idea had been made, or that the basis for inferring such a contract from subsequent related acts of the defendants had been established, at the time plaintiff disclosed his basic idea to the secretary. Defendants, consequently, were at that time and from then on free to use the abstract idea if they saw fit to engage in the necessary research and develop it to the point of a usable script. Whether defendants did that, or whether they actually accepted and used plaintiff's synopsis, is another question.

... Literary property which is protectible may be created out of unprotectible material such as historical events. It has been said (and does not appear to have been successfully challenged) that "There are only thirty-six fundamental dramatic situations, various facets of which form the basis of all human drama." (Georges Polti, "The Thirty-Six Dramatic Situations"; *see also*, Henry Albert Phillips, "The Universal Plot Catalog"; Eric Heath, "Story Plotting Simplified.") It is manifest that authors must work with and from ideas or themes which basically are in the public domain. ... Events from the life of Floyd Collins were avowedly the basic theme of plaintiff's story. ...

[A]ny literary composition, conceivably, may possess value in someone's estimation and be the subject of contract. ... Obviously the defendants here used someone's script in preparing and producing their photoplay. That script must have had value to them. As will be hereinafter shown, it closely resembles plaintiff's synopsis. Ergo, plaintiff's synopsis appears to be a valuable literary composition. Defendants had an unassailable right to have their own employees conduct the research into the Floyd Collins tragedy (an historical event in the public domain) and prepare a story based on those facts and to translate it into a script for the play. But equally unassailable (assuming the verity of the facts which plaintiff asserts) is plaintiff's position that defendants had no right except by purchase on the terms he offered to acquire and use the synopsis prepared by him.

[Affirmed in part, reversed in part, and remanded.]

CARTER, Justice [concurring in result] ...

When we consider the difference in economic and social backgrounds of those offering such merchandise for sale and those purchasing the same, we are met with the inescapable conclusion that it is the seller who stands in the inferior bargaining position. It should be borne in mind that producers are not easy to contact. .. It should also be borne in mind that writers have no way of advertising their wares that, as is most graphically illustrated by the present opinion, no producer, publisher, or purchaser for radio or television, is going to buy a pig in a poke. And, when the writer, in an earnest endeavor to sell what he has written, conveys his idea or his different interpretation of an old idea, to such prospective purchaser, he has lost the result of his labor, definitely and irrevocably. And, in addition, there is no way in which he can protect himself. If he says to whomever he is permitted to see, or, as in this case, talk with over the telephone, "I won't tell you what my idea is until you promise to pay me for it," it takes no Sherlock Holmes to figure out what the answer will be! This case is a beautiful example of the practical difficulties besetting a writer with something to sell. ...

I disagree with the statement in the majority opinion that: "The idea man who blurts out his idea without having first made his bargain has no one but himself to blame for the loss of his bargaining power." It seems to me that in the ordinary situation, when the so-called "idea man" has an opportunity to see, or talk with, the prospective purchaser, or someone in his employ, that it is at that time, without anything being said, known to both parties that the one is there to sell, and the other to buy. This is surely true of a department store when merchandise is displayed on the counter; it is understood by anyone entering the store that the merchandise so displayed is for sale. [I]t is completely unnecessary for the storekeeper, or anyone in his employ, to state to anyone entering the store that all articles there are for sale. I am at a loss to see why any different rules should apply when it is ideas for sale rather than the normal run of merchandise.

COMMENTS AND QUESTIONS

1. The concurring opinion makes an interesting point: "[W]hen the writer, in an earnest endeavor to sell what he has written, conveys his idea or his different interpretation of an old idea, to [a] prospective purchaser, he has lost the result of his labor." This general feature of the "market for information" was noted by Kenneth Arrow, in an article entitled *Economic Welfare and the Allocation of Resources for Invention*, in THE RATE AND DIRECTION OF INVENTIVE ACTIVITY 615 (1962). Indeed, the phenomenon is sometimes called "Arrow's paradox of information." Without a property right, Arrow pointed out, the seller of information is in a pickle: if in trying to strike a deal she discloses the information, she has nothing left to sell, but if she does not disclose anything the buyer has no idea what is for sale. Arrow pointed out that when the information involves an invention, patents protect the seller so she can confidently offer her idea for sale. In other words, patents solve Arrow's Paradox. Does the opinion above prove that property rights are necessary to overcome the information paradox?

One problem with giving property rights to abstract ideas is that it can put the recipients of idea submissions in a bind. They are just as bound by Arrow's information paradox as plaintiffs—if they don't listen to the idea "pitch," they will never know whether the idea was worth paying for. The point of intellectual property protection in this situation is to encourage such idea submissions by making the plaintiff confident in her ability to protect her idea. But suppose that a defendant hears a "pitch" for an idea that is old, that she has already come up with herself, or that someone else has already pitched to her. If intellectual property protection extends to idea submissions, the recipient may be forced to pay for an idea she already has! Arguably, therefore, awarding property rights in idea submissions merely changes the nature of Arrow's paradox, rather than eliminating it entirely.

2. Professor Wendy Gordon has explored the notion that a central problem of intellectual property law is to compensate creators of works who bestow benefits on those who follow, up to some socially justifiable point. In this analysis, the basic structure of intellectual property law is closely akin to the law of restitution, which seeks to determine when someone who bestows unbargained-for benefits deserves compensation. *See, e.g.*, Wendy J. Gordon, *On Owning Information: Intellectual*

Property and the Restitutionary Impulse, 78 VA. L. REV. 149 (1992); Wendy J. Gordon, *Of Harms and Benefits: Torts, Restitution and Intellectual Property*, 21 J. LEGAL STUD. 449 (1992); *see generally* Saul Levmore, *Explaining Restitution*, 71 VA. L. REV. 65 (1985). Does this literature help explain the need for a remand in the *Desny* case? Recall that the purpose of the remand is to determine how much Desny's idea contributed to the profits of Wilder's film.

3. The oral presentation of ideas for movies, TV series, etc., is a well-recognized part of the entertainment industry. The holding in *Desny* has been applied and extended in a number of cases. For instance, in *Blaustein v. Burton*, 88 Cal. Rptr. 319, 9 Cal. App. 3d 161 (Cal. Ct. App. 1970), the plaintiff Blaustein orally "pitched" the idea of using Richard Burton and Elizabeth Taylor in a film version of Shakespeare's "Taming of the Shrew." Although there was little that was novel in the pitch, the court held that there were triable issues of fact concerning the enforceability of an implied contract for the idea. The case is notable in that the "pitch" was protectable even though it was never reduced to writing.

4. *Return to Sender*. Under some cases, habitual rejection and return of unsolicited ideas eliminates the prospect of liability. *See, e.g.*, *Davis v. General Foods Corp.*, 21 F. Supp. 445 (S.D.N.Y. 1937) (plaintiff's unsolicited recipe returned with form letter); *Whitfield v. Lear*, 751 F.2d 90 (2d Cir. 1984) (noting, in decision reversing summary judgment for defendant, plaintiff's evidence that it was customary in the television industry for a studio not desiring outside submissions to say so explicitly and to return scripts so submitted without opening them). Is it desirable for firms to routinely reject submissions, some of which may be worth pursuing, for fear of spurious lawsuits? Is this an example of nuisance lawsuits undermining an otherwise mutually beneficial market? Is it an example of the "market for lemons," where bad idea submissions (i.e., ones that lead to spurious suits) drive out the good ones? Is it enough that studios and production companies can rely on trusted middlepersons such as agents to obtain ideas from proven submitters? *See* Julie Salamon, *Bookshelf: Celluloid Immortals and Literary He-Men*, WALL ST. J., July 29, 1992, at A7:

> Whatever the outcome, the suit has made Hollywood acutely aware of where it gets its ideas. "Producers are going to have to be very careful what submissions they read, and that makes it harder in the way they conduct business," says producer Howard Rosenman, co-president of Sandollar Productions, adding, "I never accept any unsolicited material. Ever."

5. *The Hollywood Script Registry*. The Writer's Guild of America, West, developed a "Script Registry" to lower the risks to both aspiring writers and studios. Writers deposit a copy of a script they are going to submit with the Registry, which date-stamps it and stores it for five years. The Registry also operates an arbitration service for resolving disputes over writing credits.

6. *Copyright Preemption*. The Ninth Circuit reaffirmed that *Desny*-type cases— featuring an express or implied agreement to pay for use of the disclosed ideas—possess the extra element required to survive a copyright preemption challenge. *See Montz v. Pilgrim Films & Television, Inc.*, 649 F.3d 975 (9th Cir. 2011) (en banc). Notably, this

is true even where the work in question is not sufficiently similar to infringe copyright. *See Benay v. Warner Bros. Ent. Inc.*, 607 F.3d 620 (9th Cir. 2010).

The Second Circuit followed *Montz* and a host of other cases in holding that express and implied-in-fact contract claims to pay for use of ideas or material provide the "extra element" needed to survive copyright preemption. Plaintiffs alleged that they developed, and pitched to defendants, an idea for a TV series to be titled "Housecall," based on "a doctor who relocates to Malibu, California after being expelled from the conventional medical community for treating patients who could not pay their medical bills. Once in Malibu, the main character becomes a doctor who makes house calls to the rich and famous residents of Malibu—otherwise known as a 'concierge' doctor." The defendant developed a similar series, set in the Hamptons rather than Malibu, under the title "Royal Pains," which aired beginning in 2009. The Second Circuit held that the alleged contract supplied the "extra element" by "not simply requir[ing] USA Network to honor Forest Park's exclusive rights under the Copyright Act (assuming the material at issue to be copyrightable); it require[d] USA Network to pay for the use of Forest Park's ideas. A claim for breach of a contract including a promise to pay is qualitatively different from a suit to vindicate a right included in the Copyright Act and is not subject to preemption." *Forest Park Pictures v. Universal Television Network, Inc.*, 683 F.3d 424, 432–33 (2d Cir. 2012). The court noted, however, that "preemption cannot be avoided simply by labeling a claim 'breach of contract.' A plaintiff must actually allege the elements of an enforceable contract (whether express or implied-in-fact), including offer, acceptance, and consideration, in addition to adequately alleging the defendant's breach of the contract." *Id.* at 432.

7. *Breach of Implied Contract Claim Not Subject to Anti-SLAPP Suit.* California, as well as about half of the other states, deter lawsuits brought primarily to chill the valid exercise of the constitutional rights of freedom of speech through so-called anti-SLAPP (strategic lawsuit against public participation) statutes. The California statute provides that:

> [a] cause of action against a person arising from any act of that person in furtherance of the person's right of petition or free speech under the United States Constitution or the California Constitution in connection with a public issue shall be subject to a special motion to strike, unless the court determines that the plaintiff has established that there is a probability that the plaintiff will prevail on the claim.

Cal. Civ. Proc. Code § 425.16(b)(1). Such statutes afford those seeking to exercise freedom of expression with a quick process for dismissing meritless lawsuits (as well as recovery of litigation costs). The Ninth Circuit ruled that *Desny*-type claims do not arise from an act in furtherance of the right of free speech because the claim is based on a defendant's claim to payment for the use of an idea in a work, not the creation, production, distribution, or content of the works that are produced. *See Jordan-Benel v. Universal City Studios, Inc.*, 859 F.3d 1184 (9th Cir. 2017).

PROBLEMS

Problem VI-3. The Washington humorist and columnist Art Buchwald submitted an eight-page summary of a film idea entitled "It's a Crude, Crude World" to executives at Paramount. The summary described in some detail the storyline, which involved a third-world prince who came to America for "a state visit." Buchwald gave a two-page overview of the plot to Paramount Pictures. Paramount subsequently entered into a contract with Buchwald whereby Paramount bought the rights to Buchwald's story and concept, with the aim of making a movie, starring Eddie Murphy, to be called "King for a Day." Another person would write the actual script, but "King for a Day" was to be based on "It's a Crude, Crude World." Because of various production difficulties, Paramount abandoned the project in March 1985. In May 1986, Buchwald gave an option on his film idea to the Warner Brothers Studio. In the summer of 1987, Paramount began development of a similar script by Eddie Murphy. In this movie—which became the successful film *Coming to America*—Murphy portrayed an African prince who comes to America in search of a suitable woman to marry.

"In Buchwald's treatment, a rich, educated, arrogant, extravagant, despotic African potentate comes to America for a state visit. After being taken on a grand tour of the United States, the potentate arrives at the White House. A gaff[e] in remarks made by the President infuriates the African leader. His sexual desires are rebuffed by a black woman State Department officer assigned to him. She is requested by the President to continue to serve as the potentate's United States escort. While in the United States, the potentate is deposed, deserted by his entourage and left destitute. He ends up in the Washington ghetto, is stripped of his clothes, and befriended by a black lady. The potentate experiences a number of incidents in the ghetto, and obtains employment as a waiter. In order to avoid extradition, he marries the black lady who befriended him, becomes the emperor of the ghetto and lives happily ever after."

"In Coming to America the pampered prince of a mythical African Kingdom (Zamunda) wakes up on his 21st birthday to find that the day for his prearranged marriage has arrived. Discovering his bride to be very subservient and being unhappy about that fact, he convinces his father to permit him to go to America for the ostensible purpose of sewing [sic] his "royal oats." In fact, the prince intends to go to America to find an independent woman to marry. The prince and his friend go to Queens, New York, where their property is stolen and they begin living in a slum area. The prince discovers his true love, Lisa, whose father—McDowell—operates a fast-food restaurant for whom the prince and his friend begin to work. The prince and Lisa fall in love, but when the King and Queen come to New York and it is disclosed who the prince is, Lisa rejects the prince's marriage invitation. The film ends with Lisa appearing in Zamunda, marrying the prince and apparently living happily ever after."

Because of Coming to America, Warner Brothers decided not to pursue Buchwald's story. Buchwald then sued Paramount. The contract between Buchwald and Paramount provided in pertinent part:

"Work" means the aforementioned Material and includes all prior, present and future versions, adaptations and translations thereof (whether written by Author or by others), its theme, story, plot, characters and their names, its title or titles and subtitles, if any, . . . and each and every part of all thereof. "Work" does not include any material written or prepared by Purchaser or under Purchaser's Authority. . . .

["Contingent consideration":] For the first theatrical motion picture (the "Picture"): If, but only if, a feature length theatrical motion picture shall be produced based upon Author's Work."

How should the court rule?

Problem VI-4. If you were an independent scriptwriter, how would you protect your ideas while trying to market them? Under what circumstances would the career damage from obtaining a reputation for litigiousness be worth it? If you were a film studio or television production company, how could you guard against suits by people like Buchwald, or by people who claim to have submitted ideas that no one in your company ever recalls seeing?

Problem VI-5. Lohr, an eccentric engineer, mails an idea she has had for a new invention to several engineering companies. The idea is mailed in a "double envelope." The outer envelope contains a confidentiality agreement, indicating that the contents of a second, sealed envelope are the property of Lohr and may not be used unless the user pays Lohr 10 percent of any profit that results. If the recipient does not agree to these terms, he is instructed to mail back the sealed, stamped, self-addressed envelope containing the idea. The "agreement" clearly provides that by opening the envelope, the recipient agrees to the terms. Dupco receives the agreement and opens the inner envelope. The next day, Dupco discovers that Lohr has posted the complete text of her idea on the Internet with no confidentiality restriction. Can Dupco use Lohr's idea without compensating her? Does it matter how novel or original the idea was on the day Dupco opened the envelope?

D.   RIGHT OF PUBLICITY

The right of publicity protects an individual's marketable image or persona. Although theoretically available to any individual, the right of publicity rarely arises outside of the celebrity realm. The right of publicity developed in response to the rise of mass advertising and the growing recognition that a celebrity's imprimatur on a product or even association of a product with a celebrity's persona enhances its appeal to consumers. This right affords individuals a property-type interest in the use of their name, likeness, photograph, portrait, voice, and other personal characteristics in connection with the marketing of products and services. Jurisdictions approach publicity rights in a variety of ways. Today, 16 states recognize common law rights of publicity, and another fifteen states have codified the right of publicity in statute. Some states, like California, recognize both statutory and common law sources for this form of protection. New York's statutory privacy and publicity protections are embodied in a single statute.

The modern right of publicity reflects two distinct rationales—one grounded in privacy and the other in economic exploitation. The privacy branch can be traced back to an influential law review article published in the late nineteenth century. *See* Samuel D. Warren & Louis D. Brandeis, *The Right to Privacy*, 4 HARV. L. REV. 193 (1890). Lamenting technological and cultural developments invading the private sphere, Warren and Brandeis advocated a right of privacy to forbid the publication of idle gossip and restore "propriety and dignity" to the press. Legislatures and courts gradually came to recognize this interest. New York led the way with its privacy law, enacted in 1903, banning the unauthorized use of "the name, portrait or picture of any living persons" for "advertising purposes, or for purposes of trade." The privacy right was quite limited in practice. Courts tended to view celebrities as inviting exploitation of their image and were reluctant to find the mere use of their image, even in advertising, to suggest endorsement. Even when liability was found, recovery was limited to the personal injury suffered, as opposed to the economic value to the advertiser.

As a result, celebrities pushed for stronger protection for the economic value of their image. In 1953, the Second Circuit found such a right in New York's common law, which it dubbed the "right of publicity." *See Haelen Laboratories, Inc. v. Topps Chewing Gum*, 202 F.2d 866 (2d Cir. 1953). In that case, Haelan had negotiated exclusive licenses from several Major League Baseball players authorizing the use of their images on baseball cards that it included with packs of gum. Topps sold its own gum with photographs of the same players. Although ruling that New York's statutory privacy law did not extend to such uses, the court ruled that "a man has a right in the publicity value of his photograph, i.e., the right to grant the exclusive privilege of publishing the picture, and that such a grant may validly be made 'in gross,' i.e., without an accompanying transfer of a business or of anything else" under New York's common law.[2] The concept was refined in a subsequent law review article by Melville Nimmer,

---

[2] Ironically, *Stephano v. News Group Publications, Inc.*, 64 N.Y.2d 174 (1984), held that *Haelan* had misinterpreted New York law, and that there was no right of publicity independent of the privacy protections in sections 50 and 51 of the New York Civil Rights Law

The Right of Publicity, 19 LAW & CONTEMP. PROBS. 203 (1954). Beginning in the 1970s, a number of states enacted "publicity" statutes, which continue to evolve today. For a discussion of this history, *see* JENNIFER E. ROTHMAN, THE RIGHT OF PUBLICITY: PRIVACY REIMAGINED FOR A PUBLIC WORLD (2018); BARTON BEEBE, THOMAS F. COTTER, MARK A. LEMLEY, PETER S. MENELL, & ROBERT P. MERGES, TRADEMARKS, UNFAIR COMPETITION, AND BUSINESS TORTS ch. 10 (2d ed. 2016); Stacey L. Dogan & Mark A. Lemley, *What the Right of Publicity Can Learn from Trademark Law*, 58 STAN. L. REV. 1161 (2006).

Should a right of publicity be freely assignable to others? Why or why not?

A critical distinction to make among jurisdictions is the extent to which the right of publicity is recognized separately from the right of privacy. Perhaps the most substantial difference between "publicity" regimes oriented toward privacy and those oriented toward property is that, as a property right, a celebrity's interest is assignable and descendable. However, some jurisdictions place limits on the duration of publicity rights following a celebrity's death, and still others do not recognize the descendability of publicity rights at all.

As the home to a significant portion of the film, television, and sound recording industries, California has played a particularly important role in the development of the right of publicity at both the statutory and jurisprudential levels. The main statutory provision, enacted in 1971, provides:

Cal. Civ. Code § 3344. Unauthorized Commercial Use of Name, Voice, Signature, Photograph or Likeness

(a) Any person who knowingly uses another's name, voice, signature, photograph, or likeness, in any manner, on or in products, merchandise, or goods, or for purposes of advertising or selling, or soliciting purchases of, products, merchandise, goods or services, without such person's prior consent, or, in the case of a minor, the prior consent of his parent or legal guardian, shall be liable for any damages sustained by the person or persons injured as a result thereof. In addition, in any action brought under this section, the person who violated the section shall be liable to the injured party or parties in an amount equal to the greater of seven hundred fifty dollars ($750) or the actual damages suffered by him or her as a result of the unauthorized use, and any profits from the unauthorized use that are attributable to the use and are not taken into account in computing the actual damages. In establishing such profits, the injured party or parties are required to present proof only of the gross revenue attributable to such use, and the person who violated this section is required to prove his or her deductible expenses. Punitive damages may also be awarded to the injured party or parties. The prevailing party in any action under this section shall also be entitled to attorney's fees and costs.

(b) As used in this section, "photograph" means any photograph or photographic reproduction, still or moving, or any videotape or live television transmission, of any person, such that the person is readily identifiable. . . .

(c) Where a photograph or likeness of an employee of the person using the photograph or likeness appearing in the advertisement or other publication prepared by or in behalf of the user is only incidental, and not essential, to the purpose of the publication in which it appears, there shall arise a rebuttable presumption affecting the burden of producing evidence that the failure to obtain the consent of the employee was not a knowing use of the employee's photograph or likeness.

(d) For purposes of this section, a use of a name, voice, signature, photograph, or likeness in connection with any news, public affairs, or sports broadcast or account, or any political campaign, shall not constitute a use for which consent is required under subdivision (a).

(e) The use of a name, voice, signature, photograph, or likeness in a commercial medium shall not constitute a use for which consent is required under subdivision (a) solely because the material containing such use is commercially sponsored or contains paid advertising. Rather it shall be a question of fact whether or not the use of the person's name, voice, signature, photograph, or likeness was so directly connected with the commercial sponsorship or with the paid advertising as to constitute a use for which consent is required under subdivision (a).

(f) Nothing in this section shall apply to the owners or employees of any medium used for advertising, including, but not limited to, newspapers, magazines, radio and television networks and stations, cable television systems, billboards, and transit ads, by whom any advertisement or solicitation in violation of this section is published or disseminated, unless it is established that such owners or employees had knowledge of the unauthorized use of the person's name, voice, signature, photograph, or likeness as prohibited by this section.

(g) The remedies provided for in this section are cumulative and shall be in addition to any others provided for by law.

In 1984, California provided for publicity rights in the persona of deceased celebrities. Those provisions have since been amended and are codified as Civil Code § 3344.1. Like the right of publicity held by a living person, § 3344.1(a) declares broadly that "[a]ny person who uses a deceased personality's name, voice, signature, photograph, or likeness, in any manner, on or in products, merchandise, or goods, or for purposes of advertising or selling, or soliciting purchases of, products, merchandise, goods, or services, without prior consent from the person or persons specified in subdivision (c), shall be liable for any damages sustained by the person or persons injured as a result thereof." The amount recoverable includes the greater of $750 or actual damages and any profits, as well as punitive damages, attorney fees, and costs. The statute provides that the post-mortem publicity right is freely transferable before or after the personality dies, by contract, or by trust or will. § 33414.1(b). Consent to use the deceased personality's name, voice, photograph, etc., must be obtained from such a transferee or, if there is none, from certain described survivors of the personality.

§ 3341(c), (d). Any person claiming to be such a transferee or survivor must register the claim with the Secretary of State before recovering damages. § 3344.1(f). Drawing upon the duration of copyrights, the post-mortem right of publicity expires 70 years after the personality dies. § 3344.1(g). The post-mortem statute includes the same exemption for creative expression found in § 3344(d) for "news, public affairs, or sports broadcast or account, or any political campaign." *See* § 3344.1(j). It also expressly affording leeway for "a play, book, magazine, newspaper, musical composition, audiovisual work, radio or television program, single and original work of art, work of political or newsworthy value, or any advertisement or commercial announcement for any of these works . . . if it is fictional or nonfictional entertainment, or a dramatic, literary, or musical work," § 3344.1(a)(2).

COMMENTS AND QUESTIONS

1. Does allowing descendability and transfer of a publicity right make sense? Or is the right more personal to the person being depicted? Whose interests are served by preventing imitation after a singer's death?

2. What justifies giving celebrities an economic right to control use of their name? In what sense is this an intellectual property right? Are we encouraging celebrity?

Midler v. Ford Motor Co.
United States Court of Appeals for the Ninth Circuit
849 F.2d 460 (9th Cir. 1988)

NOONAN, Circuit Judge:

This case centers on the protectibility of the voice of a celebrated chanteuse from commercial exploitation without her consent. Ford Motor Company and its advertising agency, Young & Rubicam, Inc., in 1985 advertised the Ford Lincoln Mercury with a series of nineteen 30 or 60 second television commercials in what the agency called "The Yuppie Campaign." The aim was to make an emotional connection with Yuppies, bringing back memories of when they were in college. Different popular songs of the seventies were sung on each commercial. The agency tried to get "the original people," that is, the singers who had popularized the songs, to sing them. Failing in that endeavor in ten cases the agency had the songs sung by "sound alikes." Bette Midler, the plaintiff and appellant here, was done by a sound alike.

Midler is a nationally known actress and singer. She won a Grammy as early as 1973 as the Best New Artist of that year. Records made by her since then have gone Platinum and Gold. She was nominated in 1979 for an Academy award for Best Female Actress in The Rose, in which she portrayed a pop singer. NEWSWEEK in its June 30, 1986 issue described her as an "outrageously original singer/comedian." Time hailed her in its March 2, 1987 issue as "a legend" and "the most dynamic and poignant singer-actress of her time."

When Young & Rubicam was preparing the Yuppie Campaign it presented the commercial to its client by playing an edited version of Midler singing "*Do You Want To Dance*," taken from the 1973 Midler album, "*The Divine Miss M*." After the client accepted the idea and form of the commercial, the agency contacted Midler's manager, Jerry Edelstein. The conversation went as follows: "Hello, I am Craig Hazen from Young and Rubicam. I am calling you to find out if Bette Midler would be interested in doing . . . ?" Edelstein: "Is it a commercial?" "Yes." "We are not interested."

Undeterred, Young & Rubicam sought out Ula Hedwig, whom it knew to have been one of "the Harlettes," a backup singer for Midler for ten years. Hedwig was told by Young & Rubicam that "they wanted someone who could sound like Bette Midler's recording of [*Do You Want To Dance*]." She was asked to make a "demo" tape of the song if she was interested. She made an a capella demo and got the job.

At the direction of Young & Rubicam, Hedwig then made a record for the commercial. The Midler record of "*Do You Want To Dance*" was first played to her. She was told to "sound as much as possible like the Bette Midler record," leaving out only a few "aahs" unsuitable for the commercial. Hedwig imitated Midler to the best of her ability.

After the commercial was aired Midler was told by "a number of people" that it "sounded exactly" like her record of "*Do You Want To Dance*." Hedwig was told by "many personal friends" that they thought it was Midler singing the commercial. Ken Fritz, a personal manager in the entertainment business not associated with Midler, declares by affidavit that he heard the commercial on more than one occasion and thought Midler was doing the singing.

Neither the name nor the picture of Midler was used in the commercial; Young & Rubicam had a license from the copyright holder to use the song. At issue in this case is only the protection of Midler's voice. The district court described the defendants' conduct as that "of the average thief." They decided, "If we can't buy it, we'll take it." The court nonetheless believed there was no legal principle preventing imitation of Midler's voice and so gave summary judgment for the defendants. Midler appeals.

The First Amendment protects much of what the media do in the reproduction of likenesses or sounds. A primary value is freedom of speech and press. *Time, Inc. v. Hill*, 385 U.S. 374, 388 (1967). The purpose of the media's use of a person's identity is central. If the purpose is "informative or cultural" the use is immune; "if it serves no such function but merely exploits the individual portrayed, immunity will not be granted." Felcher and Rubin, *Privacy, Publicity and the Portrayal of Real People by the Media*, 88 Yale L.J. 1577, 1596 (1979). Moreover, federal copyright law preempts much of the area. "Mere imitation of a recorded performance would not constitute a copyright infringement even where one performer deliberately sets out to simulate another's performance as exactly as possible." Notes of Committee on the Judiciary, 17 U.S.C.A. § 114(b). It is in the context of these First Amendment and federal copyright distinctions that we address the present appeal.

Nancy Sinatra once sued Goodyear Tire and Rubber Company on the basis of an advertising campaign by Young & Rubicam featuring "These Boots Are Made For Walkin'," a song closely identified with her; the female singers of the commercial were alleged to have imitated her voice and style and to have dressed and looked like her. The basis of Nancy Sinatra's complaint was unfair competition; she claimed that the song and the arrangement had acquired "a secondary meaning" which, under California law, was protectible. This court noted that the defendants "had paid a very substantial sum to the copyright proprietor to obtain the license for the use of the song and all of its arrangements." To give Sinatra damages for their use of the song would clash with federal copyright law. Summary judgment for the defendants was affirmed. *Sinatra v. Goodyear Tire & Rubber Co.*, 435 F.2d 711, 717–718 (9th Cir. 1970). If Midler were claiming a secondary meaning to "Do You Want To Dance" or seeking to prevent the defendants from using that song, she would fail like Sinatra. But that is not this case. Midler does not seek damages for Ford's use of "Do You Want To Dance," and thus her claim is not preempted by federal copyright law. Copyright protects "original works of authorship fixed in any tangible medium of expression." 17 U.S.C. at § 102(a). A voice is not copyrightable. The sounds are not "fixed." What is put forward as protectible here is more personal than any work of authorship.

Bert Lahr once sued Adell Chemical Co. for selling Lestoil by means of a commercial in which an imitation of Lahr's voice accompanied a cartoon of a duck. Lahr alleged that his style of vocal delivery was distinctive in pitch, accent, inflection, and sounds. The First Circuit held that Lahr had stated a cause of action for unfair competition, that it could be found "that defendant's conduct saturated plaintiff's audience, curtailing his market." *Lahr v. Adell Chemical Co.*, 300 F.2d 256, 259 (1st Cir. 1962). That case is more like this one. But we do not find unfair competition here. One-minute commercials of the sort the defendants put on would not have saturated Midler's audience and curtailed her market. Midler did not do television commercials. The defendants were not in competition with her. *See Halicki v. United Artists Communications, Inc.*, 812 F.2d 1213 (9th Cir. 1987).

California Civil Code section 3344 is also of no aid to Midler. The statute affords damages to a person injured by another who uses the person's "name, voice, signature, photograph or likeness, in any manner." The defendants did not use Midler's name or anything else whose use is prohibited by the statute. The voice they used was Hedwig's, not hers. The term "likeness" refers to a visual image not a vocal imitation. The statute, however, does not preclude Midler from pursuing any cause of action she may have at common law; the statute itself implies that such common law causes of action do exist because it says its remedies are merely "cumulative." *Id.* § 3344(g).

The companion statute protecting the use of a deceased person's name, voice, signature, photograph or likeness states that the rights it recognizes are "property rights." *Id.* § 990(b). By analogy the common law rights are also property rights. Appropriation of such common law rights is a tort in California. *Motschenbacher v. R.J. Reynolds Tobacco Co.*, 498 F.2d 821 (9th Cir. 1974). In that case what the defendants used in their television commercial for Winston cigarettes was a photograph of a famous professional racing driver's racing car. The number of the car was changed and a wing-like device known as a "spoiler" was attached to the car; the car's features of white pinpointing, an oval medallion, and solid red coloring were retained. The driver, Lothar Motschenbacher, was in the car but his features were not visible. Some persons, viewing the commercial, correctly inferred that the car was his and that he was in the car and was therefore endorsing the product. The defendants were held to have invaded a "proprietary interest" of Motschenbacher in his own identity. *Id.* at 825.

Midler's case is different from Motschenbacher's. He and his car were physically used by the tobacco company's ad; he made part of his living out of giving commercial endorsements. But, as Judge Koelsch expressed it in *Motschenbacher*, California will recognize an injury from "an appropriation of the attributes of one's identity." *Id.* at 824. It was irrelevant that Motschenbacher could not be identified in the ad. The ad suggested that it was he. The ad did so by emphasizing signs or symbols associated with him. In the same way the defendants here used an imitation to convey the impression that Midler was singing for them.

Why did the defendants ask Midler to sing if her voice was not of value to them? Why did they studiously acquire the services of a sound-alike and instruct her to imitate Midler if Midler's voice was not of value to them? What they sought was an attribute of Midler's identity. Its value was what the market would have paid for Midler to have sung the commercial in person.

A voice is more distinctive and more personal than the automobile accouterments protected in *Motschenbacher*. A voice is as distinctive and personal as a face. The human voice is one of the most palpable ways identity is manifested. We are all aware that a friend is at once known by a few words on the phone. At a philosophical level it has been observed that with the sound of a voice, "the other stands before me." D. IHDE, LISTENING AND VOICE 77 (1976). *A fortiori*, these observations hold true of singing, especially singing by a singer of renown. The singer manifests herself in the song. To impersonate her voice is to pirate her identity. *See* W. KEETON, D. DOBBS, R. KEETON, D. OWEN, PROSSER & KEETON ON TORTS 852 (5th ed. 1984).

We need not and do not go so far as to hold that every imitation of a voice to advertise merchandise is actionable. We hold only that when a distinctive voice of a professional singer is widely known and is deliberately imitated in order to sell a product, the sellers have appropriated what is not theirs and have committed a tort in California. Midler has made a showing, sufficient to defeat summary judgment, that the defendants here for their own profit in selling their product did appropriate part of her identity.

Reversed and remanded for trial.

COMMENTS AND QUESTIONS

1. Young & Rubicam licensed the right to record the song "*Do You Want to Dance*" from the owner of the copyright in the musical composition. Why wasn't that enough? Should Midler have the additional right to prevent imitation of her voice? Note that the

owner of the copyright in sound recordings is often the producer or the studio, rather than the singer who made the original recording. Does it matter whether Young & Rubicam could have purchased the rights to the recording of Midler herself singing "*Do You Want to Dance*" from the studio? If an artist doesn't control the rights to her own recording, why should she be able to prevent imitations of that recording?

A related question is whether the right of publicity is subject to an implicit first sale defense. In *Allison v. Vintage Sports Plaques*, 136 F.3d 1443 (11th Cir. 1998), the Eleventh Circuit held that it was. The defendant had purchased authorized sports trading cards and framed them for resale. The court held that the defendant could lawfully resell the images of celebrities that he had lawfully purchased and that he was not impermissibly using the sports trading cards to sell the associated frames.

2. Midler, the imitator, and independent third parties all provided evidence that people hearing the Ford commercial were confused—they thought that Midler was the one singing. Is likelihood of confusion (the test for trademark infringement) the relevant question here? Could Midler prevail even if the attempt to imitate her was not very good, so that most people could tell the difference? If a disclaimer at the beginning of the ad had indicated that the song was an impersonation, rather than Midler herself? *See* Stacey L. Dogan & Mark A. Lemley, *What the Right of Publicity Can Learn from Trademark Law*, 58 STAN. L. REV. 1161 (2006) (arguing that the real issue in *Midler* is consumer confusion).

3. A related question is whether the right of publicity applies only to celebrities. Historically, the answer has been no. The right of publicity is derived from the "commercial advantage" wing of the tort of invasion of privacy, and can be invoked by anyone whose name or likeness was appropriated by another for commercial advantage. *See* RESTATEMENT (2D) TORTS § 652C. Does this lineage suggest that the "likelihood of confusion" test shouldn't limit the right of publicity?

In practice, the public's recognition of, admiration for, or enjoyment of the voice of a person drive the value of (and litigation over) the right of publicity. Hence, most of the cases are brought on behalf of celebrities. The occasional right of publicity lawsuits brought by non-celebrities typically result from inadvertence, such as failing to clear rights to use a photograph in an advertisement. Some, however, reflect the privacy values that originally underlay the right of publicity. *See, e.g.*, *Bullard v. MRA Holding, LLC*, 740 S.E.2d 622 (Ga. 2013) (holding that producer of *College Girls Gone Wild* video violated Bullard's right of publicity by putting a topless photo of her on the cover of the video).

White v. Samsung Electronics America, Inc.
United States Court of Appeals for the Ninth Circuit
989 F.2d 1512 (9th Cir. 1993)

Before GOODWIN, PREGERSON and ALARCON, Circuit Judges.

[The Ninth Circuit panel held that actress Vanna White from the game show Wheel of Fortune could bring a right of publicity action against Samsung, which ran an ad for its electronics products that implied that they would still be around after Vanna White had been replaced by a robot on Wheel of Fortune. The court held that the robot in a dress and wig appropriated White's likeness].

KOZINSKI, Circuit Judge, with whom Circuit Judges O'SCANNLAIN and KLEINFELD join, dissenting from the order rejecting the suggestion for rehearing en banc.

I.

Saddam Hussein wants to keep advertisers from using his picture in unflattering contexts. Clint Eastwood doesn't want tabloids to write about him. Rudolf Valentino's heirs want to control his film biography. The Girl Scouts don't want their image soiled by association with certain activities. George Lucas wants to keep Strategic Defense Initiative fans from calling it "Star Wars." Pepsico doesn't want singers to use the word "Pepsi" in their songs. Guy Lombardo wants an exclusive property right to ads that show big bands playing on New Year's Eve. Uri Geller thinks he should be paid for ads showing psychics bending metal through telekinesis. Paul Prudhomme, that household name, thinks the same about ads featuring corpulent bearded chefs. And scads of copyright holders see purple when their creations are made fun of.

Something very dangerous is going on here. Private property, including intellectual property, is essential to our way of life. It provides an incentive for investment and innovation; it stimulates the flourishing of our culture; it protects the moral entitlements of people to the fruits of their labors. But reducing too much to private property can be bad medicine. Private land, for instance, is far more useful if separated from other private land by public streets, roads and highways. Public parks, utility rights-of-way and sewers reduce the amount of land in private hands, but vastly enhance the value of the property that remains.

So too it is with intellectual property. Overprotecting intellectual property is as harmful as underprotecting it. Creativity is impossible without a rich public domain. Nothing today, likely nothing since we tamed fire, is genuinely new: Culture, like science and technology, grows by accretion, each new creator building on the works of those who came before. Overprotection stifles the very creative forces it's supposed to nurture.

The panel's opinion is a classic case of overprotection. Concerned about what it sees as a wrong done to Vanna White, the panel majority erects a property right of remarkable and dangerous breadth: Under the majority's opinion, it's now a tort for advertisers to remind the public of a celebrity. Not to use a celebrity's name, voice, signature or likeness; not to imply the celebrity endorses a product; but simply to evoke the celebrity's image in the public's mind. This Orwellian notion withdraws far more from the public domain than prudence and common sense allow. It conflicts with the Copyright Act and the Copyright Clause. It raises serious First Amendment problems. It's bad law, and it deserves a long, hard second look.

II.

Samsung ran an ad campaign promoting its consumer electronics. Each ad depicted a Samsung product and a humorous prediction: One showed a raw steak with the caption "Revealed to be health food. 2010 A.D." Another showed [talk show host] Morton Downey, Jr. in front of an American flag with the caption "Presidential candidate. 2008 A.D." The ads were meant to convey—humorously—that Samsung products would still be in use twenty years from now.

The ad that spawned this litigation starred a robot dressed in a wig, gown and jewelry reminiscent of Vanna White's hair and dress; the robot was posed next to a Wheel-of-Fortune-like game board. The caption read "Longest-running game show. 2012 A.D." The gag here, I take it, was that Samsung would still be around when White had been replaced by a robot.

Perhaps failing to see the humor, White sued, alleging Samsung infringed her right of publicity by "appropriating" her "identity." Under California law, White has the exclusive right to use her name, likeness, signature and voice for commercial purposes. Cal. Civ. Code § 3344(a); *Eastwood v. Superior Court*, 149 Cal. App. 3d 409, 417, 198 Cal. Rptr. 342, 347 (1983). But Samsung didn't use her name, voice or signature, and it certainly didn't use her likeness. The ad just wouldn't have been funny had it depicted White or someone who resembled her—the whole joke was that the game show host(ess) was a robot, not a real person. No one seeing the ad could have thought this was supposed to be White in 2012.

The district judge quite reasonably held that, because Samsung didn't use White's name, likeness, voice or signature, it didn't violate her right of publicity. 971 F.2d at 1396–97. Not so, says the panel majority: The California right of publicity can't possibly be limited to name and likeness. If it were, the majority reasons, a "clever advertising strategist" could avoid using White's name or likeness but nevertheless remind people of her with impunity, "effectively eviscerat[ing]" her rights. To prevent this "evisceration," the panel majority holds that the right of publicity must extend beyond name and likeness, to any "appropriation" of White's "identity"—anything that "evoke[s]" her personality. *Id.* at 1398–99.

Longest-running game show.
2012 A.D.

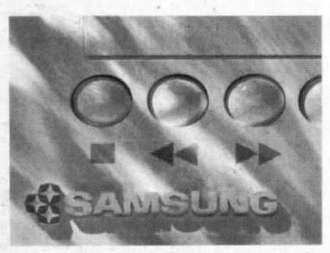

The VCR you'll tape it on.
2012 A.D.
Samsung. The future of electronics.

Samsung's Advertisement

III.

But what does "evisceration" mean in intellectual property law? Intellectual property rights aren't like some constitutional rights, absolute guarantees protected against all kinds of interference, subtle as well as blatant. They cast no penumbras, emit no emanations: The very point of intellectual property laws is that they protect only against certain specific kinds of appropriation. I can't publish unauthorized copies of, say, Presumed Innocent; I can't make a movie out of it. But I'm perfectly free to write a book about an idealistic young prosecutor on trial for a crime he didn't commit. So what if I got the idea from Presumed Innocent? So what if it reminds readers of the original? Have I "eviscerated" Scott Turow's intellectual property rights? Certainly not. All creators draw in part on the work of those who came before, referring to it, building on it, poking fun at it; we call this creativity, not piracy.

The majority isn't, in fact, preventing the "evisceration" of Vanna White's existing rights; it's creating a new and much broader property right, a right unknown in California law.[16] It's replacing the existing balance between the interests of the celebrity and those of the public by a different balance, one substantially more favorable to the celebrity. Instead of having an exclusive right in her name, likeness, signature or voice, every famous person now has an exclusive right to anything that reminds the viewer of her. After all, that's all Samsung did: It used an inanimate object to remind people of White, to "evoke [her identity]." 971 F.2d at 1399.[17]

Consider how sweeping this new right is. What is it about the ad that makes people think of White? It's not the robot's wig, clothes or jewelry; there must be ten million blond women (many of them quasi-famous) who wear dresses and jewelry like White's. It's that the robot is posed near the "Wheel of Fortune" game board. Remove the game board from the ad, and no one would think of Vanna White. But once you include the

---

[16] In fact, in the one California case raising the issue, the three state Supreme Court Justices who discussed this theory expressed serious doubts about it. *Guglielmi v. Spelling-Goldberg Prods.*, 25 Cal. 3d 860, 864 n.5, 160 Cal. Rptr. 352, 355 n.5, 603 P.2d 454, 457 n.5 (1979) (Bird, C. J., concurring) (expressing skepticism about finding a property right to a celebrity's "personality" because it is "difficult to discern any easily applied definition for this amorphous term"). Neither have we previously interpreted California law to cover pure "identity." *Midler v. Ford Motor Co.*, 849 F.2d 460 (9th Cir. 1988), and *Waits v. Frito-Lay, Inc.*, 978 F.2d 1093 (9th Cir. 1992), dealt with appropriation of a celebrity's voice. *See id.* at 1100–01 (imitation of singing style, rather than voice, doesn't violate the right of publicity). *Motschenbacher v. R. J. Reynolds Tobacco Co.*, 498 F.2d 821 (9th Cir. 1974), stressed that, though the plaintiff's likeness wasn't directly recognizable by itself, the surrounding circumstances would have made viewers think the likeness was the plaintiff's. *Id.* at 827; *see also Moore v. Regents of the Univ. of Cal.*, 51 Cal. 3d 120, 138, 271 Cal. Rptr. 146, 157, 793 P.2d 479, 490 (1990) (construing *Motschenbacher* as "hold[ing] that every person has a proprietary interest in his own likeness").

[17] Some viewers might have inferred White was endorsing the product, but that's a different story. The right of publicity isn't aimed at or limited to false endorsements, *Eastwood v. Superior Court*, 149 Cal. App. 3d 409, 419–20, 198 Cal. Rptr. 342, 348 (1983); that's what the Lanham Act is for. Note also that the majority's rule applies even to advertisements that unintentionally remind people of someone. California law is crystal clear that the common-law right of publicity may be violated even by unintentional appropriations. *Id.* at 417 n.6, 198 Cal. Rptr. at 346 n.6; *Fairfield v. American Photocopy Equipment Co.*, 138 Cal. App. 2d 82, 87, 291 P.2d 194 (1955).

game board, anybody standing beside it—a brunette woman, a man wearing women's clothes, a monkey in a wig and gown—would evoke White's image, precisely the way the robot did. It's the "Wheel of Fortune" set, not the robot's face or dress or jewelry that evokes White's image. The panel is giving White an exclusive right not in what she looks like or who she is, but in what she does for a living.[18]

This is entirely the wrong place to strike the balance. Intellectual property rights aren't free: They're imposed at the expense of future creators and of the public at large. Where would we be if Charles Lindbergh had an exclusive right in the concept of a heroic solo aviator? If Arthur Conan Doyle had gotten a copyright in the idea of the detective story, or Albert Einstein had patented the theory of relativity? If every author and celebrity had been given the right to keep people from mocking them or their work? Surely this would have made the world poorer, not richer, culturally as well as economically.

This is why intellectual property law is full of careful balances between what's set aside for the owner and what's left in the public domain for the rest of us: The relatively short life of patents; the longer, but finite, life of copyrights; copyright's idea-expression dichotomy; the fair use doctrine; the prohibition on copyrighting facts; the compulsory license of television broadcasts and musical compositions; federal preemption of overbroad state intellectual property laws; the nominative use doctrine in trademark law; the right to make soundalike recordings. All of these diminish an intellectual property owner's rights. All let the public use something created by someone else. But all are necessary to maintain a free environment in which creative genius can flourish.

The intellectual property right created by the panel here has none of these essential limitations: No fair use exception; no right to parody; no idea-expression dichotomy. It impoverishes the public domain, to the detriment of future creators and the public at large. Instead of well-defined, limited characteristics such as name, likeness or voice, advertisers will now have to cope with vague claims of "appropriation of identity," claims often made by people with a wholly exaggerated sense of their own fame and significance. . . . Future Vanna Whites might not get the chance to create their personae, because their employers may fear some celebrity will claim the persona is too similar to

---

[18] Once the right of publicity is extended beyond specific physical characteristics, this will become a recurring problem: Outside name, likeness and voice, the things that most reliably remind the public of celebrities are the actions or roles they're famous for. A commercial with an astronaut setting foot on the moon would evoke the image of Neil Armstrong. Any masked man on horseback would remind people (over a certain age) of Clayton Moore. And any number of songs—"My Way," "Yellow Submarine," "Like a Virgin," "Beat It," "Michael, Row the Boat Ashore," to name only a few—instantly evoke an image of the person or group who made them famous, regardless of who is singing. *See also* Carlos V. Lozano, *West Loses Lawsuit over Batman TV Commercial*, L.A. TIMES, Jan. 18, 1990, at B3 (Adam West sues over Batman-like character in commercial); *Nurmi v. Peterson*, 10 U.S.P.Q.2d 1775, 1989 WL 407484 (C.D. Cal. 1989) (1950s TV movie hostess "Vampira" sues 1980s TV hostess "Elvira"); text accompanying notes 7–8 (lawsuits brought by Guy Lombardo, claiming big bands playing at New Year's Eve parties remind people of him, and by Uri Geller, claiming psychics who can bend metal remind people of him). *Cf. Motschenbacher*, where the claim was that viewers would think plaintiff was actually in the commercial, and not merely that the commercial reminded people of him.

her own. The public will be robbed of parodies of celebrities, and our culture will be deprived of the valuable safety valve that parody and mockery create.

Moreover, consider the moral dimension, about which the panel majority seems to have gotten so exercised. Saying Samsung "appropriated" something of White's begs the question: Should White have the exclusive right to something as broad and amorphous as her "identity"? Samsung's ad didn't simply copy White's schtick—like all parody, it created something new. True, Samsung did it to make money, but White does whatever she does to make money, too; the majority talks of "the difference between fun and profit," 971 F.2d at 1401, but in the entertainment industry fun is profit. Why is Vanna White's right to exclusive for-profit use of her persona—a persona that might not even be her own creation, but that of a writer, director or producer—superior to Samsung's right to profit by creating its own inventions? Why should she have such absolute rights to control the conduct of others, unlimited by the idea-expression dichotomy or by the fair use doctrine?

To paraphrase only slightly *Feist Publications, Inc. v. Rural Telephone Service Co.*, 499 U.S. 340, 349–50 (1991), it may seem unfair that much of the fruit of a creator's labor may be used by others without compensation. But this is not some unforeseen byproduct of our intellectual property system; it is the system's very essence. Intellectual property law assures authors the right to their original expression, but encourages others to build freely on the ideas that underlie it. This result is neither unfair nor unfortunate: It is the means by which intellectual property law advances the progress of science and art. We give authors certain exclusive rights, but in exchange we get a richer public domain. The majority ignores this wise teaching, and all of us are the poorer for it. . . .

VI.

Finally, I can't see how giving White the power to keep others from evoking her image in the public's mind can be squared with the First Amendment. Where does White get this right to control our thoughts? The majority's creation goes way beyond the protection given a trademark or a copyrighted work, or a person's name or likeness. All those things control one particular way of expressing an idea, one way of referring to an object or a person. But not allowing any means of reminding people of someone? That's a speech restriction unparalleled in First Amendment law.

What's more, I doubt even a name-and-likeness-only right of publicity can stand without a parody exception. The First Amendment isn't just about religion or politics—it's also about protecting the free development of our national culture. Parody, humor, irreverence are all vital components of the marketplace of ideas. The last thing we need, the last thing the First Amendment will tolerate, is a law that lets public figures keep people from mocking them, or from "evok[ing]" their images in the mind of the public. 971 F.2d at 1399.

The majority dismisses the First Amendment issue out of hand because Samsung's ad was commercial speech. *Id.* at 1401 & n.3. So what? Commercial speech may be less protected by the First Amendment than noncommercial speech, but less protected means protected nonetheless. *Central Hudson Gas & Elec. Corp. v. Public Serv. Comm'n*, 447 U.S. 557 (1980). And there are very good reasons for this. Commercial speech has a profound effect on our culture and our attitudes. Neutral-seeming ads influence people's social and political attitudes, and themselves arouse political controversy. . . .

In our pop culture, where salesmanship must be entertaining and entertainment must sell, the line between the commercial and noncommercial has not merely blurred; it has disappeared. Is the Samsung parody any different from a parody on Saturday Night Live or in Spy Magazine? Both are equally profit-motivated. Both use a celebrity's identity to sell things—one to sell VCRs, the other to sell advertising. Both mock their subjects. Both try to make people laugh. Both add something, perhaps something worthwhile and memorable, perhaps not, to our culture. Both are things that the people being portrayed might dearly want to suppress. . . .

VII.

For better or worse, we are the Court of Appeals for the Hollywood Circuit. Millions of people toil in the shadow of the law we make, and much of their livelihood is made possible by the existence of intellectual property rights. But much of their livelihood—and much of the vibrancy of our culture—also depends on the existence of other intangible rights: The right to draw ideas from a rich and varied public domain, and the right to mock, for profit as well as fun, the cultural icons of our time.

In the name of avoiding the "evisceration" of a celebrity's rights in her image, the majority diminishes the rights of copyright holders and the public at large. In the name of fostering creativity, the majority suppresses it. Vanna White and those like her have been given something they never had before, and they've been given it at our expense. I cannot agree.

COMMENTS AND QUESTIONS

1. *More Robots.* The Ninth Circuit partially reaffirmed its *White* decision in *Wendt v. Host Int'l*, 125 F.3d 806 (9th Cir. 1997). That case also involved animatronic robots. These were representative of characters from the television show "Cheers" and were placed in licensed airport *Cheers* bars. The bars had obtained rights from the producers of the television show but not from the actors themselves. The court held that the actors retained publicity rights in their portrayal of the fictional characters under California law and remanded the case for an analysis of the similarities between the plaintiffs and the robots.

Had the actors brought a claim under California law based on the use of their images from the TV show itself, they would have lost. *See Fleet v. CBS*, 50 Cal. App. 4th 1911 (1996) (California publicity law preempted to the extent it imposes controls on the exploitation of name or likeness through distribution of a motion picture in which actor appeared); *Page v. Something Weird Video*, 960 F. Supp. 1438 (C.D. Cal. 1996) (First Amendment allows use of drawing of character in film to promote that film). Should the result be any different where a spin-off product is licensed?

2. Cases other than *White* discuss "celebrity attributes" besides appearance and voice. *See, e.g., McFarland v. Miller*, 14 F.3d 912 (3d Cir. 1994) (granting damages for use of appearance and name of "Our Gang" member Spanky McFarland in restaurant decor). Is there any natural boundary to the right of publicity? If mere "evocation of a celebrity" is required, which of the following could be protected by a right of publicity: (1) a characteristic walk or even running style; (2) a characteristic gesture, such as Clint Eastwood's sneer, or Johnny Carson's musically accompanied golf swing, or Michael Jackson's "moonwalking" dance steps; (3) a "signature" joke, such as Henny Youngman's "take my wife—please," or Joan Rivers' "can we talk?"—notwithstanding that both jokes were well known when they were adopted as "signatures"; (4) a style of chess opening that has become associated with a particular grand master; (5) a shot, move, or technique in sports that is closely identified with a particular athlete—e.g., Tiger Woods' fist pump?

On the other hand, is there any natural limit to Judge Kozinski's reasoning? Or does it suggest that the entire concept of a right of publicity is ill considered? Is there some identifiable reason that Bette Midler's claim seems more plausible than Vanna White's? Should it matter that a consumer might be confused by the Midler imitation, but won't be by the robot?

3. Judge Kozinski emphasizes throughout his opinion that the right of publicity adds extra burdens to the creators of works that draw on celebrity attributes. For example, he states: "We must make sure state law doesn't give the Vanna Whites and Adam Wests of the world a veto over fair use parodies of the shows in which they appear, or over copyright holders' exclusive right to license derivative works of those shows." Judge Kozinski's point is that the right of publicity creates the need for an entirely new "layer" of transactions *on top of* the traditional copyright license. For example, in many of the "voice-alike" cases such as *Midler*, the defendant in the publicity action is a legitimate licensee of the copyright holder in the song that the defendant used. The right of publicity cases thus implicitly hold that the copyright license does not shield the licensee from liability for using the work, at least under some circumstances. It also means that, at least for copyrighted works assigned prior to the rapid growth of the right of publicity, creators of works can use the new right to extract some extra value. *See* Eben Shapiro, *Rising Caution on Using Celebrity Images*, N.Y. TIMES, Nov. 4, 1992, at D20.

4. Does the economic branch of the right of publicity serve utilitarian purposes? In *Zacchini v. Scripps-Howard Broadcasting Co.*, 433 U.S. 562, 575 (1977) (finding that protection of a human cannonball performer's right of publicity against an unauthorized news broadcast of his exhibition did not violate the First Amendment), the Supreme Court commented that "protecting the proprietary interest of the individual in his act" serves in part "to encourage such entertainment," which is "closely analogous to the goals of patent and copyright law." Although it seems unlikely that failure to protect uses of a celebrity's image would discourage the pursuit of fame generally, *see* Diane Leenheer Zimmerman, *Fitting Publicity Rights into Intellectual Property and Free Speech Theory: Sam, You Made the Pants Too Long!*, 10 DEPAUL-LCA J. ART & ENT. L. & POL'Y 283, 306 (2000) (observing that "not a shred of empirical data exists to show

that [celebrities] would invest less energy and talent in becoming famous" without a publicity right), the absence of protection could discourage some performers and interfere with licensing deals that might fund particular creative projects. Is *Zacchini* likely to be such a case? Is *White*? What would such a rationale say about the proper scope of the right of publicity doctrine?

A second utilitarian theory holds that failure to protect a celebrity's image could produce a congestion externality. Under this theory, the value of an image can be inefficiently depleted by oversaturation of the marketplace, which an exclusive right to exploit can prevent. *See* WILLIAM M. LANDES & RICHARD A. POSNER, THE ECONOMIC STRUCTURE OF INTELLECTUAL PROPERTY LAW 222–28 (2003); Mark Grady, *A Positive Economic Theory of the Right of Publicity*, 1 UCLA ENT. L. REV. 97 (1994). Landes and Posner point to the Disney Corporation's self-imposed restraint on commercialization as a response to this problem: "To avoid overkill, Disney manages its character portfolio with care. It has hundreds of characters on its books, many of them just waiting to be called out of retirement. . . . Disney practices good husbandry of its characters and extends the life of its brands by not overexposing them. . . . They avoid debasing the currency." *See* B. Britt, *International Marketing: Disney's Global Goals*, MARKETING 22–26 (May 17, 1990). Landes and Posner suggest that a similar oversaturation can arise with regard to some rights of publicity (use of persona in advertising) and trademarks (justifying protection against dilution by blurring). Do you find this argument persuasive? *See* Stacey L. Dogan & Mark A. Lemley, *What the Right of Publicity Can Learn from Trademark Law*, 58 STAN. L. REV. (2006) (disputing the congestion externality rationale on the grounds that it distorts the market by preventing the dissemination of truthful information); *see also* Dennis S. Karjala, *Congestion Externalities and Extended Copyright Protection*, 94 GEO. L.J. 1065 (2006). If so, how far should it extend in constraining uses of another's image? What about parodies? Satire? Does this theory apply to all celebrity images? If so, how do we account for nearly ubiquitous images, such as Mickey Mouse, Michael Jordan, and the Coca-Cola logo? For images that survive without any protection, such as Uncle Sam or the Statue of Liberty? Is it possible that for at least some images, more exposure means *higher* value? Should the law try to distinguish between such images and those for which overexposure is more clearly a problem—for instance, the Rolls Royce logo? *See* Mark A. Lemley, *Ex Ante Versus Ex Post Justifications for Intellectual Property*, 71 U. CHI. L. REV. 129, 145 (2004) (arguing that the congestion externality may be limited to a narrow subset of images or works that become cultural icons).

Alternatively, is the right of publicity better understood under a Lockean rationale, a Kantian theory of personal autonomy, or a means of preventing of unjust enrichment? *See* Alice Haemmerli, *Whose Who? The Case for a Kantian Right of Publicity*, 49 DUKE L.J. 383 (1999); Michael Madow, *Private Ownership of Public Image: Popular Culture and Publicity Rights,* 81 CAL. L. REV. 127 (1993). What is the basis for this property right? Would a moral right based in personal autonomy justify the transferable property interest celebrities receive under the law today?

5. Consider Judge Kozinski's last argument, that the First Amendment limits the right of publicity. This point has some force. Certainly, newsworthy figures cannot prevent stories from being published about them by invoking the right of publicity. And this is true even though the paper may be using the name or likeness of the newsworthy figure to gain "commercial advantage" in the form of increased sales. In *Montana v. San Jose Mercury News*, 34 Cal. App. 4th 790, 40 Cal. Rptr. 2d 639 (1995), the court held that the San Jose Mercury News had a right to reprint its news story about and picture of football star Joe Montana on promotional posters "for the purpose of showing the quality and content of the newspaper."

For a case holding that there is a constitutionally grounded parody exception to the right of publicity—which might have applied in the *White* case as well—*see Cardtoons v. Major League Baseball Players' Association*, 95 F.3d 959 (10th Cir. 1996). *See also Matthews v. Wozencraft*, 15 F.3d 432 (5th Cir. 1994) (Texas right of publicity does not allow plaintiff to block a fictionalized biographical narrative, even though plaintiff can be identified from the book).

Comedy III Productions, Inc. v. Gary Saderup, Inc.
California Supreme Court
25 Cal. 4th 387, 21 P.3d 797, 106 Cal. Rptr. 2d 126 (2001)

MOSK, J.

A California statute grants the right of publicity to specified successors in interest of deceased celebrities, prohibiting any other person from using a celebrity's name, voice, signature, photograph, or likeness for commercial purposes without the consent of such successors. The United States Constitution prohibits the states from abridging, among other fundamental rights, freedom of speech. (U.S. CONST., 1st and 14th Amends.) In the case at bar we resolve a conflict between these two provisions. The Court of Appeal concluded that the lithographs and silkscreened T-shirts in question here received no First Amendment protection simply because they were reproductions rather than original works of art. As will appear, this was error: reproductions are equally entitled to First Amendment protection. We formulate instead what is essentially a balancing test between the First Amendment and the right of publicity based on whether the work in question adds significant creative elements so as to be transformed into something more than a mere celebrity likeness or imitation. Applying this test to the present case, we conclude that there are no such creative elements here and that the right of publicity prevails. On this basis, we will affirm the judgment of the Court of Appeal. . . .

II. Facts

Plaintiff Comedy III Productions, Inc. (hereafter Comedy III), brought this action against defendants Gary Saderup and Gary Saderup, Inc. (hereafter collectively Saderup), seeking damages and injunctive relief for violation of section 990 [the predecessor to § 3344.1] and related business torts. The parties waived the right to jury trial and the right to put on evidence, and submitted the case for decision on the following stipulated facts: Comedy III is the registered owner of all rights to the former comedy act known as The Three Stooges, who are deceased personalities within the meaning of the statute.

Saderup is an artist with over 25 years' experience in making charcoal drawings of celebrities. These drawings are used to create lithographic and silkscreen masters, which in turn are used to produce multiple reproductions in the form, respectively, of lithographic prints and silkscreened images on T-shirts. Saderup creates the original drawings and is actively involved in the ensuing lithographic and silkscreening processes. Without securing Comedy III's consent, Saderup sold lithographs and T-shirts bearing a likeness of The Three Stooges reproduced from a charcoal drawing he had made. These lithographs and T-shirts did not constitute an advertisement, endorsement, or sponsorship of any product.

The Three Stooges t-shirt image

Saderup's profits from the sale of unlicensed lithographs and T-shirts bearing a likeness of The Three Stooges was $75,000 and Comedy III's reasonable attorney fees were $150,000.

On these stipulated facts the court found for Comedy III and entered judgment against Saderup awarding damages of $75,000 and attorney fees of $150,000 plus costs. The court also issued a permanent injunction restraining Saderup from violating the statute by use of any likeness of The Three Stooges in lithographs, T-shirts, "or any other medium by which the [Saderup's] art work may be sold or marketed." The injunction further prohibited Saderup from "Creating, producing, reproducing, copying, distributing, selling or exhibiting any lithographs, prints, posters, t-shirts, buttons, or other goods, products or merchandise of any kind, bearing the photograph, image, face, symbols, trademarks, likeness, name, voice or signature of The Three Stooges or any of the individual members of The Three Stooges." The sole exception to this broad prohibition was Saderup's original charcoal drawing from which the reproductions at issue were made.

Saderup appealed. The Court of Appeal modified the judgment by striking the injunction. The court reasoned that Comedy III had not proved a likelihood of continued violation of the statute, and that the wording of the injunction was overbroad because it exceeded the terms of the statute and because it "could extend to matters and conduct protected by the First Amendment. . . ."

The Court of Appeal affirmed the judgment as thus modified, however, upholding the award of damages, attorney fees, and costs. In so doing, it rejected Saderup's contentions that his conduct (1) did not violate the terms of the statute, and (2) in any event was protected by the constitutional guaranty of freedom of speech.

We granted review to address these two issues.

III. Discussion

A. *The Statutory Issue*

[The court held that the statute extends to the sale of products featuring a deceased personality's likeness as well as advertisements.]

B. *The Constitutional Issue*

Saderup next contends that enforcement of the judgment against him violates his right of free speech and expression under the First Amendment. He raises a difficult issue, which we address below.

The right of publicity is often invoked in the context of commercial speech when the appropriation of a celebrity likeness creates a false and misleading impression that the celebrity is endorsing a product. (*See Waits v. Frito-Lay, Inc.* (9th Cir. 1992) 978 F.2d 1093; *Midler v. Ford Motor Co.* (9th Cir. 1988) 849 F.2d 460.) Because the First Amendment does not protect false and misleading commercial speech (*Central Hudson Gas & Elec. Corp. v. Public Serv. Com'n* (1980) 447 U.S. 557, 563–564), and because even nonmisleading commercial speech is generally subject to somewhat lesser First Amendment protection (*Central Hudson*, at p. 566), the right of publicity may often trump the right of advertisers to make use of celebrity figures.

But the present case does not concern commercial speech. As the trial court found, Saderup's portraits of The Three Stooges are expressive works and not an advertisement for or endorsement of a product. Although his work was done for financial gain, "[t]he First Amendment is not limited to those who publish without charge. . . . [An expressive activity] does not lose its constitutional protection because it is undertaken for profit." (*Guglielmi v. Spelling-Goldberg Productions* (1979) 25 Cal. 3d 860, 868, 160 Cal. Rptr. 352, 603 P.2d 454 (conc. opn. of Bird, C.J.) (*Guglielmi*).)

The tension between the right of publicity and the First Amendment is highlighted by recalling the two distinct, commonly acknowledged purposes of the latter. First, "'to preserve an uninhibited marketplace of ideas' and to repel efforts to limit the 'uninhibited, robust and wide-open debate on public issues.'" (*Guglielmi, supra,* 25 Cal. 3d at p. 866, 160 Cal. Rptr. 352, 603 P.2d 454.) Second, to foster a "fundamental respect for individual development and self-realization. The right to self-expression is inherent in any political system which respects individual dignity. Each speaker must be free of government restraint regardless of the nature or manner of the views expressed unless there is a compelling reason to the contrary." (*Ibid.,* fn. omitted; *see also* EMERSON, THE SYSTEM OF FREEDOM OF EXPRESSION (1970) pp. 6–7.)

The right of publicity has a potential for frustrating the fulfillment of both these purposes. Because celebrities take on public meaning, the appropriation of their likenesses may have important uses in uninhibited debate on public issues, particularly debates about culture and values. And because celebrities take on personal meanings to many individuals in the society, the creative appropriation of celebrity images can be an important avenue of individual expression. As one commentator has stated: "Entertainment and sports celebrities are the leading players in our Public Drama. We tell tales, both tall and cautionary, about them. We monitor their comings and goings, their missteps and heartbreaks. We copy their mannerisms, their styles, their modes of conversation and of consumption. Whether or not celebrities are 'the chief agents of moral change in the United States,' they certainly are widely used—far more than are institutionally anchored elites—to symbolize individual aspirations, group identities, and cultural values. Their images are thus important expressive and communicative resources: the peculiar, yet familiar idiom in which we conduct a fair portion of our cultural business and everyday conversation." (Madow, *Private Ownership of Public Image: Popular Culture and Publicity Rights* (1993) 81 CAL. L. REV. 125, 128 (Madow, italics and fns. omitted.)

As Madow further points out, the very importance of celebrities in society means that the right of publicity has the potential of censoring significant expression by suppressing alternative versions of celebrity images that are iconoclastic, irreverent, or otherwise attempt to redefine the celebrity's meaning. A majority of this court recognized as much in *Guglielmi:* "The right of publicity derived from public prominence does not confer a shield to ward off caricature, parody and satire. Rather, prominence invites creative comment." (*Guglielmi, supra,* 25 Cal. 3d at p. 869, 160 Cal. Rptr. 352, 603 P.2d 454.)

For similar reasons, speech about public figures is accorded heightened First Amendment protection in defamation law. As the United States Supreme Court held in *Gertz v. Robert Welch, Inc.* (1974) 418 U.S. 323, public figures may prevail in a libel action only if they prove that the defendant's defamatory statements were made with actual malice, i.e., actual knowledge of falsehood or reckless disregard for the truth, whereas private figures need prove only negligence. (*Id.* at pp. 328, 342, 344–45.) The rationale for such differential treatment is, first, that the public figure has greater access to the media and therefore greater opportunity to rebut defamatory statements, and second, that those who have become public figures have done so voluntarily and therefore "invite attention and comment." (*Id.* at pp. 344–345.) Giving broad scope to the right of publicity has the potential of allowing a celebrity to accomplish through the vigorous exercise of that right the censorship of unflattering commentary that cannot be constitutionally accomplished through defamation actions.

Nor do Saderup's creations lose their constitutional protections because they are for purposes of entertaining rather than informing. As Chief Justice Bird stated in *Guglielmi*, invoking the dual purpose of the First Amendment: "Our courts have often observed that entertainment is entitled to the same constitutional protection as the exposition of ideas. That conclusion rests on two propositions. First, '[t]he line between informing and entertaining is too elusive for the protection of the basic right. Everyone is familiar with instances of propaganda through fiction. What is one man's amusement, teaches another doctrine.'" (*Guglielmi, supra,* 25 Cal. 3d at p. 867, 160 Cal. Rptr. 352, 603 P.2d 454, fn. omitted.) "Second, entertainment, as a mode of self-expression, is entitled to constitutional protection irrespective of its contribution to the marketplace of ideas. 'For expression is an integral part of the development of ideas, of mental exploration and of the affirmation of self. The power to realize his potentiality as a human being begins at this point and must extend at least this far if the whole nature of man is not to be thwarted.'" (*Ibid.*)

Nor does the fact that expression takes a form of nonverbal, visual representation remove it from the ambit of First Amendment protection. In *Bery v. City of New York* (2d Cir. 1996) 97 F.3d 689, the court overturned an ordinance requiring visual artists— painters, printers, photographers, sculptors, etc.—to obtain licenses to sell their work in public places, but exempted the vendors of books, newspapers or other written matter. As the court stated: "Both the [district] court and the City demonstrate an unduly restricted view of the First Amendment and of visual art itself. Such myopic vision not only overlooks case law central to First Amendment jurisprudence but fundamentally misperceives the essence of visual communication and artistic expression. Visual art is as wide ranging in its depiction of ideas, concepts and emotions as any book, treatise, pamphlet or other writing, and is similarly entitled to full First Amendment protection. . . . One cannot look at Winslow Homer's paintings on the Civil War without seeing, in his depictions of the boredom and hardship of the individual soldier, expressions of anti-war sentiments, the idea that war is not heroic." (*Id.* at p. 695.)

Moreover, the United States Supreme Court has made it clear that a work of art is protected by the First Amendment even if it conveys no discernible message: "[A] narrow, succinctly articulable message is not a condition of constitutional protection, which if confined to expressions conveying a 'particularized message,' [citation], would never reach the unquestionably shielded painting of Jackson Pollock, music of Arnold Schoenberg, or Jabberwocky verse of Lewis Carroll." (*Hurley v. Irish-American Gay, Lesbian and Bisexual Group of Boston, Inc.* (1995) 515 U.S. 557, 569.)

Nor does the fact that Saderup's art appears in large part on a less conventional avenue of communications, T-shirts, result in reduced First Amendment protection. As Judge Posner stated in the case of a defendant who sold T-shirts advocating the legalization of marijuana, "its T-shirts . . . are to [the seller] what the *New York Times* is to the Sulzbergers and the Ochs—the vehicle of her ideas and opinions." (*Ayres v. City of Chicago* (7th Cir. 1997) 125 F.3d 1010, 1017; *see also Cohen v. California* (1971) 403 U.S. 15, [jacket with words "Fuck the Draft" on the back is protected speech].) First Amendment doctrine does not disfavor nontraditional media of expression.

But having recognized the high degree of First Amendment protection for noncommercial speech about celebrities, we need not conclude that all expression that trenches on the right of publicity receives such protection. The right of publicity, like copyright, protects a form of intellectual property that society deems to have some social utility. "Often considerable money, time and energy are needed to develop one's prominence in a particular field. Years of labor may be required before one's skill, reputation, notoriety or virtues are sufficiently developed to permit an economic return through some medium of commercial promotion. [Citations.] For some, the investment may eventually create considerable commercial value in one's identity." (*Lugosi, supra,* 25 Cal. 3d at pp. 834–835, 160 Cal. Rptr. 323, 603 P.2d 425 (dis. opn. of Bird, C.J.).)

The present case exemplifies this kind of creative labor. Moe and Jerome (Curly) Howard and Larry Fein fashioned personae collectively known as The Three Stooges, first in vaudeville and later in movie shorts, over a period extending from the 1920's to the 1940's. (*See* FLEMING, THE THREE STOOGES: AMALGAMATED MORONS TO AMERICAN ICONS (1999) pp. 10–46.) The three comic characters they created and whose names they shared—Larry, Moe, and Curly—possess a kind of mythic status in our culture. Their journey from ordinary vaudeville performers to the heights (or depths) of slapstick comic celebrity was long and arduous. Their brand of physical humor—the nimble, comically stylized violence, the "nyuk-nyuks" and "whoop-whoop-whoops," eye-pokes, slaps and head conks (*See, e.g., Three Little Pigskins* (Columbia Pictures 1934), *Hoi Polloi* (Columbia Pictures 1935), *A Gem of a Jam* (Columbia Pictures 1943), *Micro Phonies* (Columbia Pictures 1945))—created a distinct comedic trademark. Through their talent and labor, they joined the relatively small group of actors who constructed identifiable, recurrent comic personalities that they brought to the many parts they were scripted to play. "Groucho Marx just being Groucho Marx, with his moustache, cigar, slouch and leer, cannot be exploited by others. Red Skelton's variety of self-devised roles would appear to be protectible, as would the unique personal creations of Abbott and Costello, Laurel and Hardy and others of that genre. . . . '[W]e deal here with actors portraying themselves and developing their own characters.'" (*Lugosi, supra,* 25 Cal. 3d at pp. 825–826, 160 Cal. Rptr. 323, 603 P.2d 425 (conc. opn. of Mosk, J.).)

In sum, society may recognize, as the Legislature has done here, that a celebrity's heirs and assigns have a legitimate protectible interest in exploiting the value to be obtained from merchandising the celebrity's image, whether that interest be conceived as a kind of natural property right or as an incentive for encouraging creative work. (*See* 1 MCCARTHY, THE RIGHTS OF PUBLICITY AND PRIVACY (2d ed. 2000) §§ 2.2–2.7, pp. 2-1 to 2-22 (McCarthy).) Although critics have questioned whether the right of publicity truly serves any social purpose, (*See, e.g.,* Madow, *supra*, 81 CAL. L. REV. at pp. 178–238), there is no question that the Legislature has a rational basis for permitting celebrities and their heirs to control the commercial exploitation of the celebrity's likeness.

Although surprisingly few courts have considered in any depth the means of reconciling the right of publicity and the First Amendment, we follow those that have in concluding that depictions of celebrities amounting to little more than the appropriation of the celebrity's economic value are not protected expression under the First Amendment. We begin with *Zacchini v. Scripps-Howard Broadcasting Co.* (1977) 433 U.S. 562, 576 (*Zacchini*), the only United States Supreme Court case to directly address the right of publicity. Zacchini, the performer of a human cannonball act, sued a television station that had videotaped and broadcast his entire performance without his consent. The court held the First Amendment did not protect the television station against a right of publicity claim under Ohio common law. In explaining why the enforcement of the right of publicity in this case would not violate the First Amendment, the court stated: "'[T]he rationale for [protecting the right of publicity] is the straightforward one of preventing unjust enrichment by the theft of good will. No social purpose is served by having the defendant get free some aspect of the plaintiff that would have market value and for which he would normally pay.'" (*Id.* at p. 576.) The court also rejected the notion that federal copyright or patent law preempted this type of state law protection of intellectual property: "[Copyright and patent] laws perhaps regard the 'reward to the owner [as] a secondary consideration,' [citation], but they were 'intended definitely to grant valuable, enforceable rights' in order to afford greater encouragement to the production of works of benefit to the public. [Citation.] The Constitution does not prevent Ohio from making a similar choice here in deciding to protect the entertainer's incentive in order to encourage the production of this type of work." (*Id.* at p. 577.)

To be sure, *Zacchini* was not an ordinary right of publicity case: the defendant television station had appropriated the plaintiff's entire act, a species of common law copyright violation. Nonetheless, two principles enunciated in *Zacchini* apply to this case: (1) state law may validly safeguard forms of intellectual property not covered under federal copyright and patent law as a means of protecting the fruits of a performing artist's labor; and (2) the state's interest in preventing the outright misappropriation of such intellectual property by others is not automatically trumped by the interest in free expression or dissemination of information; rather, as in the case of defamation, the state law interest and the interest in free expression must be balanced, according to the relative importance of the interests at stake. (*See Gertz v. Robert Welch, Inc., supra,* 418 U.S. at pp. 347–350.)

Guglielmi adopted a similar balancing approach. The purported heir of Rudolph Valentino filed suit against the makers of a fictional film based on the latter's life. *Guglielmi* concluded that the First Amendment protection of entertainment superseded any right of publicity. This was in contrast to the companion *Lugosi* case, in which Chief Justice Bird concluded in her dissenting opinion that there may be an enforceable right of publicity that would prevent the merchandising of Count Dracula using the likeness of Bela Lugosi, with whom that role was identified. (*Lugosi, supra*, 25 Cal. 3d at pp. 848–849, 160 Cal. Rptr. 323, 603 P.2d 425 (dis. opn. of Bird, C.J.).) *Guglielmi* proposed a balancing test to distinguish protected from unprotected appropriation of celebrity likenesses: "an action for infringement of the right of publicity can be maintained only if the proprietary interests at issue clearly outweigh the value of free expression in this context." (*Guglielmi, supra*, 25 Cal. 3d at p. 871, 160 Cal. Rptr. 352, 603 P.2d 454.)

In *Estate of Presley v. Russen* (D.N.J. 1981) 513 F. Supp. 1339 (*Russen*), the court considered a New Jersey common law right of publicity claim by Elvis Presley's heirs against an impersonator who performed The Big El Show. The court implicitly used a balancing test similar to the one proposed in *Guglielmi*. Acknowledging that the First Amendment protects entertainment speech, the court nonetheless rejected that constitutional defense. "[E]ntertainment that is merely a copy or imitation, even if skillfully and accurately carried out, does not really have its own creative component and does not have a significant value as pure entertainment. As one authority has emphasized: 'The public interest in entertainment will support the sporadic, occasional and good-faith imitation of a famous person to achieve humor, to effect criticism or to season a particular episode, but it does not give a privilege to appropriate another's valuable attributes on a continuing basis as one's own without the consent of the other.'" (*Russen, supra*, 513 F. Supp. at pp. 1359–1360.) Acknowledging also that the show had some informational value, preserving a live Elvis Presley act for posterity, the court nonetheless stated: "This recognition that defendant's production has some value does not diminish our conclusion that the primary purpose of defendant's activity is to appropriate the commercial value of the likeness of Elvis Presley." (*Id.* at p. 1360.)

On the other side of the equation, the court recognized that the Elvis impersonation, as in *Zacchini*, represented "'what may be the strongest case for a right of publicity'— involving, not the appropriation of an entertainer's reputation to enhance the attractiveness of a commercial product, but the appropriation of the very activity by which the entertainer acquired his reputation in the first place." (*Russen, supra*, 513 F. Supp. at p. 1361, quoting *Zacchini, supra*, 433 U.S. at p. 576.) Thus, in balancing the considerable right of publicity interests with the minimal expressive or informational value of the speech in question, the *Russen* court concluded that the Presley estate's request for injunctive relief would likely prevail on the merits. (*Russen*, at p. 1361; *see also Factors Etc. Inc. v. Creative Card Co.* (S.D.N.Y. 1977) 444 F. Supp. 279 [poster of Elvis Presley labeled "In Memory . . . 1935–1977" did not possess sufficient newsworthiness to be eligible for First Amendment protection].)

In *Groucho Marx Productions, Inc. v. Day & Night Co.* (S.D.N.Y. 1981) 523 F. Supp. 485, *reversed on other grounds* (2d Cir. 1982) 689 F.2d 317, the court considered a right of publicity challenge to a new play featuring characters resembling the Marx Brothers. The court found in favor of the Marx Brothers' heirs, rejecting a First Amendment defense. In analyzing that defense, the court posed a dichotomy between "works . . . designed primarily to promote the dissemination of thoughts, ideas or information through news or fictionalization," which would receive First Amendment protection, and "use of the celebrity's name or likeness . . . largely for commercial purposes, such as the sale of merchandise," in which the right of publicity would prevail. (523 F. Supp. at p. 492.) In creating this dichotomy, the court did not appear to give due consideration to forms of creative expression protected by the First Amendment that cannot be categorized as ideas or information. Moreover, the court, borrowing from certain copyright cases, seemed to believe that the validity of the First Amendment defense turned on whether the play was a parody, without explaining why other forms of creative appropriation, such as using established characters in new theatrical works to advance various creative objectives, were not protected by the First Amendment. Nonetheless, the case is in line with *Zacchini, Guglielmi* and *Russen* in recognizing that certain forms of commercial exploitation of celebrities that violate the state law right of publicity do not receive First Amendment protection.

It is admittedly not a simple matter to develop a test that will unerringly distinguish between forms of artistic expression protected by the First Amendment and those that must give way to the right of publicity. Certainly, any such test must incorporate the principle that the right of publicity cannot, consistent with the First Amendment, be a right to control the celebrity's image by censoring disagreeable portrayals. Once the celebrity thrusts himself or herself forward into the limelight, the First Amendment dictates that the right to comment on, parody, lampoon, and make other expressive uses of the celebrity image must be given broad scope. The necessary implication of this observation is that the right of publicity is essentially an economic right. What the right of publicity holder possesses is not a right of censorship, but a right to prevent others from misappropriating the economic value generated by the celebrity's fame through the merchandising of the "name, voice, signature, photograph, or likeness" of the celebrity. (§ 990.)

Beyond this precept, how may courts distinguish between protected and unprotected expression? Some commentators have proposed importing the fair use defense from copyright law (17 U.S.C. § 107), which has the advantage of employing an established doctrine developed from a related area of the law. (*See* Barnett, *First Amendment Limits on the Right of Publicity* (1995) 30 TORT & INS. L.J. 635, 650–657; Coyne, *Toward a Modified Fair Use Defense in Right of Publicity Cases* (1988) 29 WM. & MARY L. REV. 781, 812–820.) Others disagree, pointing to the murkiness of the fair use doctrine and arguing that the idea/expression dichotomy, rather than fair use, is the principal means of reconciling copyright protection and First Amendment rights. (2 MCCARTHY, *supra*, § 8.38, pp. 8-358 to 8-360; *see also* Kwall, *The Right of Publicity vs. The First Amendment: A Property and Liability Rule Analysis* (1994) 70 IND. L.J. 47, 58, fn. 54.)

We conclude that a wholesale importation of the fair use doctrine into right of publicity law would not be advisable. At least two of the factors employed in the fair use test, "the nature of the copyrighted work" and "the amount and substantiality of the portion used" (17 U.S.C. § 107(2), (3)), seem particularly designed to be applied to the partial copying of works of authorship "fixed in [a] tangible medium of expression" (17 U.S.C. § 102); it is difficult to understand why these factors would be especially useful for determining whether the depiction of a celebrity likeness is protected by the First Amendment.

Nonetheless, the first fair use factor—"the purpose and character of the use" (17 U.S.C. § 107(1))—does seem particularly pertinent to the task of reconciling the rights of free expression and publicity. As the Supreme Court has stated, the central purpose of the inquiry into this fair use factor "is to see, in Justice Story's words, whether the new work merely 'supersede[s] the objects' of the original creation [citations], or instead adds something new, with a further purpose or different character, altering the first with new expression, meaning, or message; it asks, in other words, whether and to what extent the new work is 'transformative.' Although such transformative use is not absolutely necessary for a finding of fair use, the goal of copyright, to promote science and the arts, is generally furthered by the creation of transformative works." (*Campbell v. Acuff-Rose Music, Inc.* (1994) 510 U.S. 569, 579, fn. omitted.)

This inquiry into whether a work is "transformative" appears to us to be necessarily at the heart of any judicial attempt to square the right of publicity with the First Amendment. As the above quotation suggests, both the First Amendment and copyright law have a common goal of encouragement of free expression and creativity, the former by protecting such expression from government interference, the latter by protecting the creative fruits of intellectual and artistic labor. (*See* 1 NIMMER ON COPYRIGHT (2000 ed.) § 1.10, pp. 1-66.43 to 1-66.44 (Nimmer).) The right of publicity, at least theoretically, shares this goal with copyright law. (1 McCarthy, *supra*, § 2.6, pp. 2-14 to 2-19.) When artistic expression takes the form of a literal depiction or imitation of a celebrity for commercial gain,[9] directly trespassing on the right of publicity without adding significant expression beyond that trespass, the state law interest in protecting the fruits of artistic labor outweighs the expressive interests of the imitative artist. (*See Zacchini, supra,* 433 U.S. at pp. 575–576.)

On the other hand, when a work contains significant transformative elements, it is not only especially worthy of First Amendment protection, but it is also less likely to interfere with the economic interest protected by the right of publicity. As has been observed, works of parody or other distortions of the celebrity figure are not, from the celebrity fan's viewpoint, good substitutes for conventional depictions of the celebrity and therefore do not generally threaten markets for celebrity memorabilia that the right of publicity is designed to protect. (*See Cardtoons, L.C. v. Major League Baseball Players Association* (10th Cir. 1996) 95 F.3d 959, 974 (*Cardtoons*).) Accordingly, First Amendment protection of such works outweighs whatever interest the state may have in enforcing the right of publicity. The right-of-publicity holder continues to enforce the right to monopolize the production of conventional, more or less fungible, images of the

---

[9] Inquiry into the "purpose and character" of the work in copyright law also includes "whether such use is of a commercial nature or is for nonprofit educational purposes." (17 U.S.C. § 107(1).) It could be argued that reproduction of a celebrity likeness for noncommercial use—e.g., T-shirts of a recently deceased rock musician produced by a fan as a not-for-profit tribute-is a form of personal expression and therefore more worthy of First Amendment protection. This is an issue, however, that we need not decide in this case. It is undisputed that Saderup sold his reproductions for financial gain.

celebrity.[10] *Cardtoons, supra*, 95 F.3d 959, cited by *Saderup*, is consistent with this "transformative" test. There, the court held that the First Amendment protected a company that produced trading cards caricaturing and parodying well-known major league baseball players against a claim brought under the Oklahoma right of publicity statute. The court concluded that "[t]he cards provide social commentary on public figures, major league baseball players, who are involved in a significant commercial enterprise, major league baseball," and that "[t]he cards are no less protected because they provide humorous rather than serious commentary." (*Cardtoons*, at p. 969.) The *Cardtoons* court weighed these First Amendment rights against what it concluded was the less-than-compelling interests advanced by the right of publicity outside the advertising context—especially in light of the reality that parody would not likely substantially impact the economic interests of celebrities—and found the cards to be a form of protected expression. (*Cardtoons*, at pp. 973–976.) While *Cardtoons* contained dicta calling into question the social value of the right of publicity, its conclusion that works parodying and caricaturing celebrities are protected by the First Amendment appears unassailable in light of the test articulated above.

We emphasize that the transformative elements or creative contributions that require First Amendment protection are not confined to parody and can take many forms, from factual reporting (*See, e.g., Rosemont Enterprises, Inc. v. Random House, Inc.* (N.Y. Sup. Ct. 1968) 58 Misc. 2d 1, 294 N.Y.S.2d 122, 129, affd. mem. (1969) 32 A.D.2d 892, 301 N.Y.S.2d 948) to fictionalized portrayal (*Guglielmi, supra*, 25 Cal. 3d at pp. 871–872, 160 Cal. Rptr. 352, 603 P.2d 454; *see also Parks v. LaFace Records* (E.D. Mich. 1999) 76 F. Supp. 2d 775, 779–782 [use of civil rights figure Rosa Parks in song title is protected expression][4]), from heavy-handed lampooning (*see Hustler Magazine v. Falwell* (1988) 485 U.S. 46) to subtle social criticism (*see* COPLANS ET AL., ANDY WARHOL (1970) pp. 50–52 [explaining Warhol's celebrity portraits as a critique of the celebrity phenomenon]).

Another way of stating the inquiry is whether the celebrity likeness is one of the "raw materials" from which an original work is synthesized, or whether the depiction or imitation of the celebrity is the very sum and substance of the work in question. We ask, in other words, whether a product containing a celebrity's likeness is so transformed

---

[10] There is a fourth factor in the fair use test not yet mentioned, "the effect of the use upon the potential market for or value of the copyrighted work" (17 U.S.C. § 107(4)), that bears directly on this question. We do not believe, however, that consideration of this factor would usefully supplement the test articulated here. If it is determined that a work is worthy of First Amendment protection because added creative elements significantly transform the celebrity depiction, then independent inquiry into whether or not that work is cutting into the market for the celebrity's images—something that might be particularly difficult to ascertain in the right of publicity context (*see* Madow, *supra*, 81 CAL. L. REV. at pp. 221–222)—appears to be irrelevant. Moreover, this "potential market" test has been criticized for circularity: it could be argued that if a defendant has capitalized in any way on a celebrity's image, he or she has found a potential market and therefore could be liable for such work. (*See* 4 NIMMER, *supra*, § 13.05[A][4] at pp. 13-183 to 13-184.) The "transformative" test elaborated in this opinion will, we conclude, protect the right-of-publicity holder's core interest in monopolizing the merchandising of celebrity images without unnecessarily impinging on the artists' right of free expression.

[4] [The *Parks* case was reversed. *See Parks v. LaFace Records*, 329 F.3d 437 (6th Cir. 2003).—EDS.]

that it has become primarily the defendant's own expression rather than the celebrity's likeness. And when we use the word "expression," we mean expression of something other than the likeness of the celebrity.

We further emphasize that in determining whether the work is transformative, courts are not to be concerned with the quality of the artistic contribution—vulgar forms of expression fully qualify for First Amendment protection. (*See, e.g., Hustler Magazine v. Falwell, supra,* 485 U.S. 46; *see also Campbell v. Acuff-Rose Music, Inc., supra,* 510 U.S. at p. 582.) On the other hand, a literal depiction of a celebrity, even if accomplished with great skill, may still be subject to a right of publicity challenge. The inquiry is in a sense more quantitative than qualitative, asking whether the literal and imitative or the creative elements predominate in the work.

Furthermore, in determining whether a work is sufficiently transformative, courts may find useful a subsidiary inquiry, particularly in close cases: does the marketability and economic value of the challenged work derive primarily from the fame of the celebrity depicted? If this question is answered in the negative, then there would generally be no actionable right of publicity. When the value of the work comes principally from some source other than the fame of the celebrity—from the creativity, skill, and reputation of the artist—it may be presumed that sufficient transformative elements are present to warrant First Amendment protection. If the question is answered in the affirmative, however, it does not necessarily follow that the work is without First Amendment protection—it may still be a transformative work.

In sum, when an artist is faced with a right of publicity challenge to his or her work, he or she may raise as affirmative defense that the work is protected by the First Amendment inasmuch as it contains significant transformative elements or that the value of the work does not derive primarily from the celebrity's fame.

Turning to the present case, we note that the trial court, in ruling against Saderup, stated that "the commercial enterprise conducted by [Saderup] involves the sale of lithographs and T-shirts which are not original single works of art, and which are not protected by the First Amendment; the enterprise conducted by the [Saderup] was a commercial enterprise designed to generate profits solely from the use of the likeness of The Three Stooges which is the right of publicity ... protected by section 990." Although not entirely clear, the trial court seemed to be holding that *reproductions* of celebrity images are categorically outside First Amendment protection. The Court of Appeal was more explicit in adopting this rationale: "Simply put, although the First Amendment protects speech that is sold, reproductions of an image, made to be sold for profit do not per se constitute speech." But this position has no basis in logic or authority. No one would claim that a published book, because it is one of many copies, receives less First Amendment protection than the original manuscript. It is true that the statute at issue here makes a distinction between a single and original work of fine art and a reproduction. (§ 990, subd. (n)(3).) Because the statute evidently aims at preventing the illicit merchandising of celebrity images, and because single original works of fine art are not forms of merchandising, the state has little if any interest in preventing the exhibition and sale of such works, and the First Amendment rights of the artist should therefore prevail. But the inverse—that a reproduction receives no First Amendment protection—is patently false: a reproduction of a celebrity image that, as explained above, contains significant creative elements is entitled to as much First Amendment protection as an original work of art. The trial court and the Court of Appeal therefore erred in this respect.

Rather, the inquiry is into whether Saderup's work is sufficiently transformative. Correctly anticipating this inquiry, he argues that all portraiture involves creative decisions, that therefore no portrait portrays a mere literal likeness, and that accordingly all portraiture, including reproductions, is protected by the First Amendment. We reject any such categorical position. Without denying that all portraiture involves the making of artistic choices, we find it equally undeniable, under the test formulated above, that when an artist's skill and talent is manifestly subordinated to the overall goal of creating a conventional portrait of a celebrity so as to commercially exploit his or her fame, then the artist's right of free expression is outweighed by the right of publicity. As is the case with fair use in the area of copyright law, an artist depicting a celebrity must contribute something more than a "merely trivial" variation, [but must create] something recognizably "his own" (*L. Batlin & Son, Inc. v. Snyder* (2d Cir. 1976) 536 F.2d 486, 490), in order to qualify for legal protection.

On the other hand, we do not hold that all reproductions of celebrity portraits are unprotected by the First Amendment. The silkscreens of Andy Warhol, for example, have as their subjects the images of such celebrities as Marilyn Monroe, Elizabeth Taylor, and Elvis Presley. Through distortion and the careful manipulation of context, Warhol was able to convey a message that went beyond the commercial exploitation of celebrity images and became a form of ironic social comment on the dehumanization of celebrity itself. (*See* COPLANS ET AL., *supra*, at p. 52.) Such expression may well be entitled to First Amendment protection. Although the distinction between protected and unprotected expression will sometimes be subtle, it is no more so than other distinctions triers of fact are called on to make in First Amendment jurisprudence. (*See, e.g., Miller v. California* (1973) 413 U.S. 15, 24, [requiring determination, in the context of work alleged to be obscene, of "whether the work, taken as a whole, lacks serious literary, artistic, political, or scientific value"].)

Turning to Saderup's work, we can discern no significant transformative or creative contribution. His undeniable skill is manifestly subordinated to the overall goal of creating literal, conventional depictions of The Three Stooges so as to exploit their fame. Indeed, were we to decide that Saderup's depictions were protected by the First Amendment, we cannot perceive how the right of publicity would remain a viable right other than in cases of falsified celebrity endorsements.

Moreover, the marketability and economic value of Saderup's work derives primarily from the fame of the celebrities depicted. While that fact alone does not necessarily mean the work receives no First Amendment protection, we can perceive no transformative elements in Saderup's works that would require such protection.

Saderup argues that it would be incongruous and unjust to protect parodies and other distortions of celebrity figures but not wholesome, reverential portraits of such celebrities. The test we articulate today, however, does not express a value judgment or preference for one type of depiction over another. Rather, it reflects a recognition that the Legislature has granted to the heirs and assigns of celebrities the property right to exploit the celebrities' images, and that certain forms of expressive activity protected by the First Amendment fall outside the boundaries of that right. Stated another way, we are concerned not with whether conventional celebrity images should be produced but with who produces them and, more pertinently, who appropriates the value from their production. Thus, under section 990, if Saderup wishes to continue to depict The Three Stooges as he has done, he may do so only with the consent of the right-of-publicity holder.

IV. Disposition

The judgment of the Court of Appeal is affirmed.

COMMENTS AND QUESTIONS

1. The common law tort of right of publicity requires proof that the defendant used the plaintiff's name or likeness in "commercial advertising or promotion." There is no advertising use at issue in *Saderup*. Rather, *the product itself* is alleged to be illegal. Does the California statute go too far by extending the right of publicity from commercial advertising to reach the making of products?

2. Does the court's test adequately protect the freedom of expression? Is the court saying that art needs to go beyond literal interpretation and not be mass-marketed? Or possibly that the stature of the artist (e.g., Warhol) must be balanced against the popularity of the target? Would it be legal under the court's opinion to make and mass-market a statue of Barack Obama?

3. The California Supreme Court's framework rests upon two relatively subjective pillars: fair use analysis and art criticism. Subsequent cases illustrate the unpredictability of this balancing framework. In a case that comes close to the conventional portrayal and direct commercial exploitation in *Saderup*, the majority of a divided Sixth Circuit panel ruled that a limited edition painting featuring Tiger Woods was immune from a right of publicity claim under Ohio common law on freedom of expression grounds. *See ETW Corp. v. Jireh Pub., Inc.*, 332 F.3d 915 (6th Cir. 2003).

Just two years after its *Saderup* decision, the California Supreme Court revisited the interplay of the right of publicity and the First Amendment. Johnny and Edgar Winter, well-known musicians (their 1973 album "They Only Come Out at Night" featured the #1 hit instrumental "Frankenstein" and the top 15 single "Free Ride") with albino complexions and long white hair, brought a right of publicity action against D.C. Comics for its publication of a comic book featuring the characters "Johnny and Edgar Autumn," half-worm, half-human creatures with pale faces and long white hair. The comic books series portrayed them as "vile, depraved, stupid, cowardly, subhuman individuals who engage in wanton acts of violence, murder and bestiality for pleasure and who should be killed." Applying the *Saderup* balancing framework, the California Supreme Court concluded that the expressive qualities of the work afforded D.C. Comics First Amendment protection from a right of publicity claim. *Winter v. D.C. Comics*, 30 Cal. 4th 881, 134 Cal. Rptr. 2d 634, 69 P.3d 473 (Cal. S.Ct. 2003).

Jonah Hex Comic Book

Depiction of Johnny and Edgar Autumn

By contrast, the Missouri Supreme Court held that same year that another comic book publisher's use of a former professional hockey player's name and image as a metaphorical reference to tough-guy "enforcers" "was predominantly a ploy to sell comic books and related products rather than an artistic or literary expression" and hence "free speech must give way to the right of publicity." *John Doe, a/k/a Tony Twist v. TCI Cablevision*, 110 S.W.3d 363 (Mo. S.Ct. 2003).

Is there any other approach to balancing the tension between the right of publicity and the First Amendment? What about the use of disclaimers to the effect that a work of art was not authorized, sponsored, or endorsed by the target celebrity (or the holders of his or her post-mortem right of publicity)? If the right of publicity is predominantly an economic right, should society be deeply concerned about the economic plight of celebrities? Or is the right based on other interests, such as personal autonomy and identity? Do the facts in the *Winter* case suggest the need for a broader foundation for protection?

Professor Robert Post and Professor Jennifer Rothman suggest that the right of publicity in reality embodies four distinct rights: the right of performance, the right of commercial value, the right of control, and the right of dignity. They further argue that breaking down the tort into these distinct rights allows for a more streamlined First Amendment analysis. *See* Robert C. Post & Jennifer E. Rothman, *The First Amendment and the Right(s) of Publicity*, 130 YALE L.J. (forthcoming 2020). Do you agree?

4. *Artistic Advertising.* In its March 1997 "Fabulous Hollywood Issue!," *Los Angeles Magazine* featured an article entitled "Grand Illusions," which used digitally altered film stills to make it appear that the actors were wearing Spring 1997 fashions. The 16 familiar scenes included movies and actors such as *Rear Window* (Grace Kelly and Jimmy Stewart), *The Seven Year Itch* (Marilyn Monroe), and *Thelma and Louise* (Susan Sarandon and Geena Davis). The feature also included an image from the film *Tootsie* in which Dustin Hoffman's head was digitally superimposed atop a picture of another model. The caption read "Dustin Hoffman isn't a drag in a butter-colored silk gown by Richard Tyler and Ralph Lauren heels." Hoffman sued, claiming violation of his right of publicity as well as Lanham Act and other state law claims. The Ninth Circuit reversed an award in excess of $3 million on the ground that *L.A. Magazine*'s appropriation of Hoffman's identity was "communicative" rather than "commercial" and hence was entitled to the highest level of protection under the First Amendment. *See Hoffman v. Capital Cities/ABC, Inc., and L.A. Magazine, Inc.*, 255 F.3d 1180 (9th Cir. 2001); *but see Jordan v. Jewel Food Stores, Inc.*, 743 F.3d 509 (7th Cir. 2014) (holding that an ad for a grocery store chain featuring Michael Jordan's Air Jordan shoes with his iconic #23, ostensibly celebrating his induction into the NBA Hall of Fame, was commercial speech unprotected by the First Amendment despite its communicative message). Can you square the result in *Hoffman* with the California Supreme Court's analytical framework in *Saderup*? Can freedom of expression and marketing be treated separately or are they inextricably intertwined? Will future Dustin Hoffmans abandon careers in acting (or otherwise alter their creative and commercial choices) as a result

of this case? If not, doesn't this case suggest that we need not be so solicitous of right of publicity claimants? What other justifications might support celebrities in such cases?

5. *Artistic Relevance.* How relevant must a creative work be to a person before the author can use their name in the title? In *Rogers v. Grimaldi*, 875 F.2d 994 (2d Cir. 1989), the court held that the maker of a movie about two cabaret dancers who imitated Fred Astaire and Ginger Rogers in their act could title the movie "Ginger and Fred" over Ginger Rogers' trademark and right of publicity. As regards the trademark cause of action, the court construed the Lanham Act narrowly to avoid intrusion on First Amendment values, holding that:

> In the context of allegedly misleading titles using a celebrity's name, that balance will normally not support application of the [Lanham] Act unless [1] the title has no artistic relevance to the underlying work whatsoever, or, [2] if it has some artistic relevance, unless the title explicitly misleads as to the source
>
> or the content of the work.

Id. at 999 (footnote omitted). The court similarly interpreted the right of publicity to allow use of a celebrity's name "in a title so long as the item was a literary work and not 'simply a disguised commercial advertisement for the sale of goods or services.'" *Id.* at 1004 (citation omitted).

An analogous issue arose when the rap group OutKast titled a song "Rosa Parks," after the woman who helped trigger the civil rights movement by refusing to sit in the back of the bus. The only reference to Parks in the song is the line "Ah-ha, hush that fuss. Everybody move to the back of the bus." Parks sued alleging false advertising and violation of the right of publicity. After the appellate court overturned a grant of summary judgment for the defendants on the ground that a reasonable jury could find violations of the Lanham Act and the common law right of publicity, *see Parks v. LaFace Records*, 329 F.3d 437 (6th Cir. 2003), the parties settled with OutKast and its record label paying an undisclosed sum and agreeing to "enlighten today's youth about the significant role Rosa Parks played in making America a better place for all races" by working with Parks and the Rosa and Raymond Parks Institute for Self-Development to promote Parks' legacy. (The record labels and OutKast admitted no wrongdoing.) Other songs lack even that tenuous connection. Hear, e.g., Gorillaz, "Clint Eastwood." Can the title alone ever give political content to a song not otherwise obviously about a famous person?

Ironically, although the Ginger Rogers and Rosa Parks lawsuits focused on name appropriation, the Ninth Circuit has declined to extend the *Rogers* test, which it applies to trademark cases, to right of publicity claims.. *See Keller v. Electronic Arts*, 724 F.3d 1268, 1279-82 (9th Cir. 2013).

6. *Newsworthiness Exception.* Reflecting freedom of speech and First Amendment protections, right of publicity statutes as well as common law rulings recognize a newsworthiness exception. *See, e.g.*, Cal. Civ. Code § 3344(d) (exempting "use of a name, voice, signature, photograph, or likeness in connection with any news, public affairs, or sports broadcast or account, or any political campaign"). The scope of this

exception can be difficult to gauge. Following the murder of a female professional wrestler by her husband, a well-known professional wrestler who committed suicide following the crime, HUSTLER MAGAZINE advertised on the cover of its issue: "WRESTLER CHRIS BENOIT'S MURDERED WIFE NUDE." The table of contents listed "NANCY BENOIT Exclusive Nude Pics of Wrestler's Doomed Wife." Neither the cover nor the table of contents made any reference to the accompanying article entitled "NANCY BENOIT Au Naturel: The long-lost images of wrestler Chris Benoit's doomed wife." The title and page frame, which read "EXCLUSIVE PICS! EXCLUSIVE PICS!," comprise about one-third of the first page. A second third of the page was devoted to two nude photographs of Benoit. The final third of the page discussed Benoit's murder and her nude photo shoot, twice referencing her brief desire to be a model. The second page of the article was entirely devoted to photographs, displaying eight additional photographs of Benoit. After the victim's mother and administrator of the estate sued for violation of her daughter's right of publicity, the lower court determined that this use fell squarely within the newsworthiness exception. On appeal, the 11th Circuit, applying Georgia law, reversed, holding that the publication "of private, nude photographs were not incident to a newsworthy article; rather, the brief biography was incident to the photographs. Additionally, these photographs were neither related in time nor concept to the current incident of public interest." As a result, publication of these photographs fell outside of the newsworthiness exception to the right of publicity. *Toffoloni v. LFP Publ'g Group, LLC*, 572 F.3d 1201 (11th Cir. 2009).

By contrast, noncommercial speech about an individual is generally afforded wide berth. The Ninth Circuit in *Sarver v. Chartier*, 813 F.3d 891 (9th Cir. 2016), affirmed dismissal of a right of publicity complaint filed by a former soldier whose experiences disarming bombs in Iraq allegedly formed the basis for the Academy Award-winning film *The Hurt Locker*. The district court found that the creative and transformative elements added to the story by the scriptwriters qualified the film for First Amendment protection against a right of publicity claim. On appeal, the Ninth Circuit held that the First Amendment "safeguards the storytellers and artists who take the raw materials of life—including the stories of real individuals, ordinary or extraordinary—and transform them into art, be it articles, books, movies, or plays" from right of publicity claims. *Id.* at 905. *See also Rosa & Raymond Parks Institute for Self-Development v. Target Corp.*, 812 F.3d 824 (11th Cir. 2016) (holding that Target was free to sell non-fiction books about civil rights activist Rosa Parks and a plaque that commemorated her work without violating her right of publicity).

7. *Docudramas*. A docudrama is a dramatized retelling of history. Such works are based on actual events, but entail some creative license.

Olivia de Havilland was one of Hollywood's leading actresses during the Golden Age. She was nominated for the Academy Award for Best Actress in a Supporting Role for her performance in *Gone with the Wind* (1939). She went on to win two Academy Awards for Best Actress in a Leading Role (*To Each His Own* (1946) and *The Heiress* (1949)). She was romantically involved with the industrialist Howard Hughes and the actor Jimmy Stewart. Her younger sister, Joan Fontaine, was also a leading actress who won an Academy Award (Best Actress for *Suspicion* (1941)).

In March 2018, FX Networks began airing *Feud: Bette and Joan*, an eight-part docudrama portraying the rivalry between actresses Joan Crawford and Bette Davis, two other leading actresses of Hollywood's Golden Age. The central theme of the miniseries is that powerful men in Hollywood pressured and manipulated women in the industry into very public feuds with one another to advance the economic interests of those men and the institutions they headed.

Academy-Award-winning actress Catherine Zeta-Jones portrays de Havilland in the FX miniseries. The de Havilland role comprises fewer than 17 minutes of the 392-minute miniseries. The role consists of two parts: (1) a fictitious interview in which Zeta-Jones—often accompanied by Academy-Award-winning actress Kathy Bates playing actress Joan Blondell—talks to an interviewer about Hollywood, its treatment of women, and the Crawford/Davis rivalry; and (2) scenes in which Zeta-Jones interacts with Academy-Award-winning actress Susan Sarandon playing Bette Davis. These scenes portray the close friendship between Davis and de Havilland. As played by Zeta-Jones, the de Havilland character is beautiful, glamorous, self-assured, and considerably ahead of her time in her views on the importance of equality and respect for women in Hollywood.

Olivia de Havilland objected to her portrayal in the miniseries and brought suit against FX alleging violation of the California statutory right of publicity, as well as several privacy torts and defamation. In particular, de Havilland alleged that the miniseries falsely indicated that she gave an interview at the 1978 Academy Awards and referred to Joan Fontaine as her "bitch sister,"[2] among other alleged inaccuracies. On FX's motion to strike under California's Anti-SLAPP (strategic lawsuit against public participation) statute, the trial court ruled that FX's portrayal of de Havilland was not protected by the First Amendment because, following *Saderup*, FX wanted to present de Havilland "as real as possible" and hence the work was not transformative. "Moreover, even if [FX] imagined conversations for the sake of being creative, such does not make the show transformative."

On appeal, Judge Edgerton ruled that the First Amendment protects FX's portrayal of de Havilland and dismissed the action. *See de Havilland v. FX Networks*, 21 Cal. App. 5th 845, 230 Cal. Rptr. 3d 625 (Cal. Ct. App. 2018). The court noted that although the *Saderup* transformative test makes sense when applied to products and merchandise, its application to expressive works—such as films, plays, and television programs—is

---

[2] Whether de Havilland ever referred to Joan Fontaine as her "bitch sister," the rivalry between the two was legendary and well-documented. In a 1978 interview, Fontaine said of the sibling rivalry, "I married first, won the Oscar before Olivia did, and if I die first, she'll undoubtedly be livid because I beat her to it!" *See* Adam Bernstein, *Joan Fontaine, Academy Award-winning actress from the 1940s, dies at 96*, Wash. Post (Dec. 15, 2013) (quoting 1967 Hollywood Reporter interview).

more nuanced. The appellate court disagreed with the trial court's conclusion that *Feud: Bette and Joan* was not transformative:

> The fictitious, 'imagined' interview in which Zeta-Jones talks about Hollywood's treatment of women and the Crawford/Davis rivalry is a far cry from T-shirts depicting a representational, pedestrian, uncreative drawing of The Three Stooges. The de Havilland role, performed by Zeta-Jones, constitutes about 4.2 percent of *Feud*. The docudrama tells the story, in nearly eight hours, of the competition between Hollywood's leading ladies of the day, Bette Davis and Joan Crawford, for film roles, attention, awards, and acclaim. The miniseries tells many stories within the story as well: Jack Warner's demeaning and dismissive treatment of director Robert Aldrich; Crawford's and Davis's struggles with their personal relationships: husbands, partners, and children; the obstacles faced by capable women like Aldrich's assistant Pauline Jameson who want to direct motion pictures; and the refusal of powerful men in the entertainment business to take women seriously, even when their movies make money.
>
> In the words of the *Comedy III* Court, Zeta-Jones's 'celebrity likeness [of de Havilland] is one of the "raw materials" from which [the] original work [*Feud*] is synthesized.' (*Comedy III*, 25 Cal.4th at p. 406.) Applying *Comedy III*'s 'useful subsidiary inquiry' here, we conclude as a matter of law that *Feud*'s 'marketability and economic value' does not 'derive primarily from [de Havilland's] fame' but rather 'comes principally from . . . the creativity, skill, and reputation' of *Feud*'s creators and actors. . . . In short, *Feud* constitutes 'significant expression'—a story of two Hollywood legends—of which the de Havilland character is but a small part. . . .

Id. at 863–64. The court concluded that:

> The trial court's ruling leaves authors, filmmakers, playwrights, and television producers in a Catch-22. If they portray a real person in an expressive work accurately and realistically without paying that person, they face a right of publicity lawsuit. If they portray a real person in an expressive work in a fanciful, imaginative—even fictitious and therefore 'false'—way, they face a false light lawsuit if the person portrayed does not like the portrayal. '[T]he right of publicity cannot, consistent with the First Amendment, be a right to control the celebrity's image by censoring disagreeable portrayals.' (*Comedy III*, 25 Cal. 4th at p. 403.) FX's evidence here—especially the docudrama itself—establishes as a matter of law that de Havilland cannot prevail.

Id. at 870–71 (footnotes and some citations omitted).

8. *Video Games Featuring College Athlete Avatars.* Video games have fared less well than movies when they report information about real people. In *Keller v. Electronic Arts Inc.*, 724 F.3d 1268 (9th Cir. 2013), the court rejected a free speech defense offered by a video game maker that included the likeness and biographical information of college athletes in its sports games, allowing players to build "fantasy" football teams.

The court concluded that the use was not transformative under *Saderup* and did not constitute news reporting protected under the public interest exception. The Third Circuit reached the same result in *Hart v. Electronic Arts, Inc.*, 717 F.3d 141 (3d Cir. 2013).

Similarly, the California Court of Appeals held that the video game Band Hero, in which users can perform duly licensed versions of hit songs through avatars based on band members, violates the members' right of publicity. *See No Doubt v. Activision Publishing, Inc.*, 192 Cal. App. 4th 1018, 122 Cal. Rptr. 3d 397 (Cal. Ct. App. 2011). Applying the transformative use test, the court rules that the fact "[t]hat the avatars can be manipulated to perform at fanciful venues including outer space or to sing songs the real band would object to singing, or that the avatars appear in the context of a videogame that contains many other creative elements, does not transform the avatars into anything other than the exact depictions of No Doubt's members doing exactly what they do as celebrities." *Id.* at 411. Activision's use of highly realistic digital depictions of No Doubt was motivated by a desire to capitalize on the band's fan-base, "because it encourages [fans] to purchase the game so as to perform as, or alongside, the members of No Doubt." *Id.*

Does this approach comport with *Saderup*? With the First Amendment? Judge Ambro, dissenting in *Hart*, argued that the video games as a whole were transformative even if the depictions of individual players in those games were realistic:

> To determine whether an individual's identity has been "transformed" for purposes of the Transformative Use Test, I believe it is necessary to review the likeness in the context of the work in its entirety, rather than focusing only on the individual's likeness. . . .

> To me, a narrow focus on an individual's likeness, rather than how that likeness is incorporated into and transformed by the work as a whole, is a flawed formulation of the transformative inquiry. The whole-the aggregate of many parts (including, here, many individuals)-is the better baseline for that inquiry. . . .

> My colleagues' understanding of the Transformative Use Test underplays the creative elements of NCAA Football by equating its inclusion of realistic player likenesses to increase profits with the wrongful appropriation of Hart's commercial value. This approach is at odds with the First Amendment protection afforded to expressive works incorporating real-life figures. That protection does not depend on whether the characters are depicted realistically or whether their inclusion increases profits. *See Guglielmi* [*v. Spelling-Goldberg Prods.*], 603 P.2d 454, at 460–62 (1979) (Bird, C.J., concurring) (concluding that acceptance of this argument would chill free expression and mean "the creation of historical novels and other works inspired by actual events and people would be off limits to the fictional author").

> In sum, applying the Transformative Use Test in the manner done by my colleagues creates a medium-specific metric that provides less protection to

video games than other expressive works. Because the Supreme Court's decision in *Brown* [*v. Entm't Merchs. Ass'n*, 131 S Ct. 2729 (2011)] forecloses just such a distinction, *see* 131 S.Ct. at 2740, my colleagues' treatment of realism and profitability in their transformative use analysis puts us on a different course. . . .

With this understanding of the Transformative Use Test, I conclude EA's use of avatars resembling actual players is entitled to First Amendment protection. NCAA Football transforms Hart's mere likeness into an avatar that, along with the rest of a digitally created college football team, users can direct and manipulate in fictional football games. With the many other creative features incorporated throughout the games, sufficient expressive transformation takes place to merit First Amendment protection. . . .

By limiting their inquiry to the realistic rendering of Hart's individual image, my colleagues misapply the Transformative Use Test. Contrary to their assertion that the other creative elements of NCAA Football are "[w]holly unrelated", those elements are, in fact, related to its use of Hart's likeness. If and when a user decides to select the virtual 2005 Rutgers' football team as a competitor in a game, and to the extent that user does not alter the characteristics of the avatar based on Hart's likeness, the numerous creative elements of the video games discussed above are part of every fictional play a user calls. Any attempt to separate these elements from the use of Hart's likeness disregards NCAA Football's many expressive features beyond an avatar having characteristics similar to Hart. His likeness is transformed by the artistry necessary to create a digitally rendered avatar within the imaginative and interactive world EA has placed that avatar. . . .

The Transformative Use Test I support would prevent commercial exploitation of an individual's likeness where the work at issue lacks creative contribution that transforms that likeness in a meaningful way. I sympathize with the position of Hart and other similarly situated college football players, and understand why they feel it is fair to share in the significant profits produced by including their avatar likenesses into EA's commercially successful video game franchise. I nonetheless remain convinced that the creative components of NCAA Football contain sufficient expressive transformation to merit First Amendment protection. Thus I respectfully dissent, and would affirm the District Court's grant of summary judgment in favor of EA.

Hart v. Electronic Arts, Inc., 717 F.3d 141 (3d Cir. 2013) (Ambro, J., dissenting).

9. *Fantasy Sports Statistics*. The Eighth Circuit held in *C.B.C. Distrib. & Mktg. Inc. v. Major League Baseball Advanced Media LP*, 505 F.3d 818 (8th Cir. 2007) that the use of professional athletes' game statistics by fantasy sports enterprises did not violate the players' right of publicity.

10. *Copyright Preemption*. In *Zacchini v. Scripps-Howard Broadcasting Co.*, 433 U.S. 562 (1977), the Supreme Court rejected the argument that the Copyright Clause

preempts state law publicity rights, holding that state law could protect the unauthorized news broadcast of the plaintiff's entire (15 second) human cannonball. Many applications of the right of publicity—such as the unauthorized use of a celebrity's name to endorse a product—easily survive federal preemption by the Copyright Act because enforcement of the right in such circumstances does not implicate a copyrighted work. Several contexts, however, strain the tests for federal preemption. Consider, for example, the implications of Bette Midler's publicity rights in her rendition of "Do You Want to Dance" for the owner of the underlying musical composition. Midler's right of publicity in her vocal rendition trumps other performers from imitating her version, yet § 114(b) of the Copyright Act expressly authorizes cover recordings that "imitate or simulate those in the copyrighted sound recording." While recognizing this implication, the Ninth Circuit in *Midler v. Ford* breezily concluded that Midler's assertion of the right of publicity was not preempted because "a voice is not copyrightable." 849 F.2d 462. Does such treatment adequately address the apparent conflict with federal copyright law?

By contrast, the Seventh Circuit found that federal copyright law preempted baseball players' assertions of state publicity rights in their images and game performances. *See Baltimore Orioles, Inc. v. Major League Baseball Players Ass'n*, 805 F.2d 663 (7th Cir. 1986). Because each game was embodied in a copyrighted telecast and players uniformly assign their copyrights to their teams, the court reasoned that the game performances could not be the subject of independent state publicity rights. The Seventh Circuit has since construed *Baltimore Orioles* narrowly, *see Toney v. L'Oreal USA, Inc.*, 406 F.3d 905 (7th Cir. 2005) (holding that a model whose photograph was used in connection with packaging and promotion of a hair care product could recover under the right of publicity), and commentators question its logic, *see* NIMMER ON COPYRIGHT, § 1.01 (criticizing the court's premise that a baseball game is a protected "work of authorship" under the Copyright Act); Jennifer E. Rothman, *Copyright Preemption and the Right of Publicity*, 36 U.C. DAVIS L. REV. 199 (2002) (arguing for a broad application of preemption doctrine); *Dryer v. National Football League*, 814 F.3d 938 (8th Cir. 2016) (holding that NFL's use of video footage of players in theme-based audio-visual productions were expressive, rather than commercial, such that the Copyright Act preempted the player's right of publicity claim); *Ray v. ESPN, Inc.*, 783 F.3d 1140 (8th Cir. 2015) (same).

A less controversial application of the preemption doctrine occurred in *Fleet v. CBS, Inc.*, 50 Cal. App. 4th 1911, 58 Cal. Rptr. 2d 645 (1996), where actors in a copyrighted film alleged that the very use of the copyrighted work infringed their state right of publicity. As the court recognized, "a party who does not hold the copyright in a performance captured on film cannot prevent the one who does from exploiting it by resort to state law." *Id.* at 1923. *See also Ahn v. Midway Mfg. Co.*, 965 F. Supp. 1134 (N.D. Ill. 1997) (dismissing right of publicity claims brought by a ballerina and karate black belt who consented to having their movements digitally captured for use in developing characters for the copyrighted computer game "Mortal Kombat").

Copyright preemption does not bar right of publicity actions where a person's image or likeness is used to advertise a product. *See Downing v. Abercrombie & Fitch*, 265 F.3d 994 (9th Cir. 2001) (defendant-retailer published a photograph of the surfer-plaintiffs without their permission in the defendant's catalog to promote the defendant's products as part of its surf-themed advertising campaign, and sold t-shirts like those worn by the plaintiffs in the photograph); *Brown v. Ames*, 201 F.3d 654 (5th Cir. 2000). A court allowed rock star Bret Michaels and actress Pamela Anderson Lee to block the unauthorized distribution over the Internet of a videotape showing them engaged in sex as a violation of their right of publicity. The basis of the right of publicity claim was the use of their names, likenesses, and identities to advertise imminent distribution of the video, and not the distribution of the copyrighted tape itself. *See Michaels v. Internet Entm't Grp., Inc.*, 5 F. Supp. 2d 823, 837 (C.D. Cal. 1998).

PROBLEMS

Problem VI-6. In the late 1980s, the New Kids on the Block were an enormously successful pop music group, especially among the younger teen market. Capitalizing on this success, the New Kids sold over 500 products or services bearing their trademarked name. Among those services were "900 numbers" that fans could call to learn more about the New Kids, or to talk to the New Kids themselves.

During the height of the New Kids craze, the newspaper USA Today conducted a telephone poll that allowed readers to "vote" for their favorite New Kid (or for "none of the above" if they did not like the band at all) by calling a USA Today 900 number. As a part of the poll, the paper included captioned pictures of each of the band members. Suppose that the New Kids on the Block sued USA Today for infringement of their right of publicity. Do they have a claim under California law?

Problem VI-7. Facebook targets advertising to its users based on what it knows about them. As part of this targeting effort, Facebook sometimes shows a user an ad for a product that indicates (truthfully) that the user's friends have "liked" that product on Facebook. Those ads show the name and a thumbnail image of the Facebook friend who liked the advertised product.

Assume Facebook did not get permission from the friend before running the ad. Does the ad violate the right of publicity?

Problem VI-8. Don Henley is a well-known musician and the lead singer of The Eagles. Duluth Trading Company, a clothier, makes a variety of shirts, including the shirt style known as a "Henley."

A Henley shirt is a collarless pullover, characterized by a placket beneath the round neckline with several buttons. It resembles a collarless polo shirt. It is so-named because this particular style of shirt was the traditional uniform of rowers in the English town of Henley-on-Thames.

Duluth runs an advertisement recommending buyers to "Don a Henley" and "Take it easy," the title of an iconic Eagles' song. Henley sues for violation of the right of publicity. What result?